Religion

This volume has emerged from a collaboration among:

The NWO Research Council for the Humanities (GW),
The NWO Research Council for Social Sciences (MaGW), and
The Netherlands Foundation for the Advancement of Tropical Research (WOTRO).

Netherlands Organisation for Scientific Research

THE FUTURE OF THE RELIGIOUS PAST

Hent de Vries, General Editor

In what sense are the legacies of religion—its powers, words, things, and gestures—disarticulating and reconstellating themselves as the elementary forms of life in the twenty-first century? This sequence of five volumes publishes work drawn from an international research project that seeks to answer this question.

Religion

BEYOND A CONCEPT

Edited by HENT de VRIES

FORDHAM UNIVERSITY PRESS   NEW YORK   2008

Library of Congress Cataloging-in-Publication Data is available

Printed in the United States of America
10 09 08   5 4 3 2

Contents

PART II: RELIGION AND PHILOSOPHY

PART III: METHODS OF INSTRUCTION AND COMPARISON

Illustrations

Preface

What do we talk about when we talk about "religion"? Is it an array of empirical facts about historical human civilizations? Or is religion what is in essence unpredictable—perhaps the very emergence of the new, for good and for ill? In what ways are the legacies of religion—its words and things, powers and gestures, but also sounds and silences, shapes and colors, affects and effects—reconfiguring themselves as the elementary forms of life in the twenty-first century? And what role do modern technological media, in addition to economic markets and political conjunctures, with their inevitable upheavals, contribute to their articulation and increasing proliferation, which is a diffusion—hence a disarticulation—as well?

Given the Latin roots of the word *religion* and its historical Christian uses, what sense, if any, does it make to talk about "religion" in other traditions? Where might we look for common elements that would enable us to do so? And which singular features of cultural practices, sensibilities, and imaginations would forbid such generalization? Has religion as an overarching concept lost all its currency, or does it ineluctably return—sometimes in unexpected ways—the moment we attempt to do without it?

This volume explores the difficulties and double binds that arise when we ask "What is religion?" and thus risk turning this notion into an anthropological constant, a historical invariable, a cultural given. Offering a diverse array of perspectives, the book begins the task of rethinking "religion" and "religious studies" in a contemporary world whose institutions and publics are increasingly "post-secular" in their outlook, suspended—at least in the West—between, on the one hand, an Enlightenment project and a democratic republicanism and liberalism originally premised upon rationalization, differentiation, and privatization, and, on the other, a less explicit process of reenchantment, if not outright remythologization.

In this volume, opening essays on the question "What is religion?" are followed by clusters that explore the relationships among religion, theology, and philosophy, and the links between religion, politics, and law. Pedagogy is the focus of the following section. Religion is then examined in particular contexts, from classical times to the present Pentecostal revival. An especially rich set of essays on religion, materiality, and mediatization follows. The final section grapples with the ever-changing forms that "religion" is taking, such as spirituality movements and responses to the ecological crisis.

Featuring the work of scholars from a wide array of disciplines, traditions, and cultures, *Religion: Beyond a Concept* seeks to outline an agenda for religious studies, including the philosophy, anthropology, and cultural analysis of religion, for years to come. It is the first of five volumes in a collection entitled *The Future of the Religious Past: Elements and Forms for the Twenty-first Century*, the fruit of a major international research initiative generously funded by the Netherlands Organization for Scientific Research (NWO).

I would like to thank the members of the Dutch program committee, the distinguished members of our international advisory board, and the program officers at NWO, Dr. Marc Linssen and Danielle Vermeer, for their scholarly and logistical support in making this venture, with its fifteen research projects and yearly international conferences during the funding period from May 2004 through May 2012, a source of great intellectual pleasure. I would also like to express my immense gratitude to my colleague Neil Hertz, who once again kindly accepted our invitation to contribute his wonderful photographs for the book's cover and display pages, and will do so for the following volumes as well. Special thanks to Helen Tartar, Editorial Director at Fordham University Press, for having wisely guided this first volume, like so many previous ones I have had the privilege to publish with her, through all the perilous stages of its composition, editing, and production. She has made this voluminous and complex collection a much better one than it otherwise would have been. May this volume be a worthy opening of this planned mini-series of five, whose general introduction I present below and for whose distinct themes, centering on words, things, gestures, and powers, my colleagues and co-editors will take responsibility.

Hent de Vries, Baltimore-Amsterdam-Paris, Summer 2007

Religion

Introduction

Why Still "Religion"?

Hent de Vries

"Religion" may—or may not—be here to stay. As a "concept" (but which or whose, exactly?), from one perspective it might seem to be losing its received reference (the transcendent, the world beyond, and the life hereafter) and its shared relevance (a unified view of the cosmos and all beings in it; a doctrine of the origin, purpose, and end of all things; an alert, enlightened, or redeemed sense of self; a practice and way of life), if it has not done so already. Yet from another perspective, it continues to claim a prominent role in attempts to understand the past, to grapple with the present, and to anticipate, if not to prophesy, the future. Nothing indicates that it will be easy to tell which of these alternatives—"religion's" eventual fading away or its ongoing and possibly increased influence—is more likely to emerge from a sustained study of the profundity and dust of historical archives, from the acuity and abstractness of contemporary philosophical analysis, from the thickness and everydayness that populate ethnographic description, from the computerized statistics of demographic indicators or the fluctuations of economic markets, or from the soundbites and noise of global media, as well as the uses and abuses to which they are subjected. Nothing allows us to determine in advance, let alone on the basis of some philosophically or transcendentally construed a priori, what, precisely, "religion"—in its very "concept"—may still (or yet again) make possible or necessary, visible and readable, audible and palpable. We do not even know whether these two possibilities—religion's eventual demise or its continuing, or perhaps increased, import—constitute poles between which we must ultimately choose. A different rhythm may well punctuate the phenomena in question, as if "religion" could not but zoom in and out of focus, coming and going with a temporality that is neither linear nor cyclical but momentous, instantaneous, almost aleatory, subject to the least—and quite often unrelated—provocation.

1

Is it too late in the game, then, still to attempt to distill the necessary and sufficient conditions or essential features of this phenomenon or, rather, set(s) of phenomena called "religion," while paying minute attention to (without being buried under) the wealth of historical, empirical, and anthropological data that have been gathered over the centuries, and especially in the modern academic study of this "field"? The question imposes itself with renewed urgency, since the results of genealogical, comparative, and cultural approaches to "religion" are not "givens" of experience, based on immediate sensation or intuition, on observation or introspection. They do not compose themselves out of the conceptless stuff of sense data or psychological impressions, needing only to be enumerated, categorized, and catalogued to result in an understanding—some would say, an explanation—of the phenomenon or set(s) of phenomena at issue. On the contrary, understanding, let alone explanation, does not come from a procedure that Walter Benjamin, in his critique of historicism, scorned for being merely "additive." Rather, it requires a constructive principle, however tentative and hypothetical, fallible and falsifiable. It is no accident, therefore, that *some* reference to *some* generic concept—here, "religion"—is (and must be) kept in place for at least some time to come in even the most radical attempts to de-transcendentalize and naturalize its meaning and use. In short, we cannot just be nominalist about the semantics, let alone the pragmatics of this concept (and even less about what, if anything, might, one fine day, point "beyond" it, rendering "religion" and all "godtalk" superfluous until some urgency propels it back into existence or circulation).

This much is certain: no simple linear narrative or causal explanation, least of all a logic of progressive demythologization, disenchantment, and secularization is capable of assigning a clear, univocal designation to any "concept" of religion. A different logic of attribution and acknowledgment can be found at work in the redistribution of its meaning, uses, and abuses, at least now, at the outset of the twenty-first century. At this moment, a certain philosophical and theoretical convergence concerning the nature of this *seemingly universal yet simultaneously singular term* can roughly be delineated. Or so it seems.

I will identify this convergence with a present need (which may not always have been the case, nor need it always remain so) to be resolutely strategic, selective, and inventive in our dealings with "religion." *Deep pragmatism* is the name I will give to this approach, partly in homage to William E. Connolly's term "deep pluralism." It has been prepared, if I am not mistaken, in the writings of philosophers and critics from different theoretical backgrounds, some of them contributors to this volume.

A preliminary question imposes itself, however. Has the term *religion* ever merely named, then designated, and, finally, conceptualized something remotely specific? Did it somehow, somewhere, and for some demarcate a subject, a theme, a terrain, or a field whose referent, contours, and contents were clear or largely unchallenged? Nothing in the history of traditional doctrinal or confessional theology, let alone in the nineteenth-century invention of the science and history of religion and its twentieth-century successors (the anthropology and cultural study of religions), suggests that this was ever the case.

Or was the primary object of "religion" some "Thing" (*das Ding*, in Heidegger's terms, or *la Chose*, in Lacan's), rather than merely some "things," some "somethings"? Following the demise of *metaphysica specialis* and *theologia naturalis*, supposedly based on common notions of reason, which allowed proofs of God's existence and demonstrations of his essence, does "religion" hibernate in a more abstract or mystical longing for some essential or hyper-essential "Being," whose nature must of necessity remain elusive, to be approached via negative predication alone?

Or does the concept of "religion" call for something more than roughly staking out the circumference of its domain, in a "map," as Jonathan Z. Smith has suggested, that is not the "territory" itself? Has the term *religion* ever pointed to a phenomenon or set(s) of phenomena in a way that could be called deictic or even stipulative? Or is it the result of an observed or assumed "family resemblance," whose traits depend upon as much as they express certain "language games," "forms of life," or a "natural history"—that is to say, the horizontal and vertical axes—of humankind, of the species that "we" are? These characterizations form central motifs in Wittgenstein's *Philosophical Investigations*, explored by Stanley Cavell. Insights from both these thinkers will be essential to determining what a "deep pragmatist" account of "religion" may amount to.

By contrast, has the concept of "religion" ever acquired more specific meaning and sense in precisely spatialized locations, in the eyes of identifiable, countable, and accountable subjects, groups, and collectives, whose testimonies, scriptures, traditions, or direct introspective reportings we can access from a variety of angles? Where and how, in whose name, for what purpose, and with what consequence, is this concept of "religion," if it is one, still invoked, advocated, abrogated, or derogated?

If the question "What, if anything, came before 'religion'?" is perhaps long overdue, what sense might there be in asking what could lie or point *beyond* it? What lies "beyond a concept" with which we seem to have labeled a phenomenon, a notional and experiential complex and structure, whose simultaneous abstractness and concreteness eludes empirical and rational attempts to come to grips with its criteria and governing rules or laws, that is to say, with its "truth," let alone its "moral"? What makes up the halo of interlaced ideas—but also words and things, perceptions and affects, sounds and silences, shapes and colors, gestures and powers, that give "religion" its undeniable, if not always distinctive profile, resonance, and often fateful impact? How is it that this impact ranges from the salutary or even sublime to devastating and horrific effects, to the point that some perceive a *horror religiosus*, an unmistakable violence beyond the reach of moral obligation and ethical life, to be its dominant mood, as does Kierkegaard in *Fear and Trembling*?

Between the New Materialism and the Old Metaphysics

The title of this volume, *Religion: Beyond a Concept*, must imply, first of all, a sense of "religion" pointing to (and beyond) many concepts, in any event, the ones we have come to associate with it too quickly, influenced by a Western and especially Protestant idiom. This identified the phenomenon or set(s) of phenomena of the religious with a process of increasing interiorization, stripping it of its empirical, public, embodied, performative, ritual, and rhetorical expressions, as well as its visual imaginings.[1] Against this identification of "religion" with personally held "beliefs," a whole current of contemporary reflections on the study of religion has stressed the need to explore the hermeneutic corrective of a "new materialism." We must keep in mind a crucial distinction between this important corrective and the perspectives, or perspectivisms, that the present project presents. The new materialism, like the earlier naturalism (or historicism, culturalism, etc.), may not hold all the keys to unlocking the phenomenon or set(s) of phenomena whose enigma and often uncanny appeal we seek to explore here, no more than the seemingly exhausted metaphysics and natural theology of old. Indeed, in a different reading, that metaphysics and natural theology remain alive and kicking, a continued source of reexamination that we have only barely begun to exploit.[2]

Our title also recalls a standing question, to which the religious may still offer the greatest challenge. "Beyond" also hints at the "non-," "pre-," "para-," and "not simply" conceptual. Reference to the "beyond" of any given (or, perhaps, any possible or future) concept of "religion" must gesture toward the "not (i.e., not yet or no longer) quite conceptual." But would this allow us to determine any answer to the questions *what, how, where, when, whence* toward which we—but who, "we"?—are hinting or being directed (compelled, invited, solicited, seduced)?

Here, all answers, as well as the very questions that trigger them, necessarily expose themselves to a loss of meaning and sense. Still, in pondering "Religion: Beyond a Concept," we should be adventurous enough to go there (but where and with what purpose, exactly?) and dare to face the uncanny regions of a *horror religiosus* (Kierkegaard), a *mysterium tremendum* (Rudolf Otto), indeed, of a *surplus of nonsense over sense* (Emmanuel Levinas), with all the delights, terrors, chances, perils, hopes, and despairs they may yet hold in store. Needless to say, the risks of doing so—and going there (but "where"?)— should be gauged. But can they? And, if they can't, would we be well advised not even to try, avoiding temptation and perdition alike? Or would that, precisely, mean missing out on "life"—perhaps, the very "life of the mind"—such as it is?

There is a third way of understanding the "beyond" of a concept, as it figures in our title. Instead of suggesting that we move beyond an established and a largely dogmatic concept (which delivers at best "a" concept of "religion," among many possible and necessary other ones), in addition to venturing into the abyssal and exhilarating dimensions of the nonconceptual, we might also remind ourselves of a critical and perspectival device that Theodor W. Adorno proposed in his earliest programmatic writing (such as his 1930 inaugural address, "The Actuality of Philosophy") and developed in full detail in his mature works (notably *Negative Dialectics*). In this reading, the concept is neither superseded nor subsumed, let alone discarded. Rather, particulars (including concepts as particulars among them) are invited to enter into a "constellation" with others that might allow us to unravel the "riddle" of the real, or make it "readable," at least. The concept, in this view, has the limited yet insurpassable value of a critical corrective. It is neither the beginning, the end, nor the center of our thoughts, nor is it what genuine thought must leave behind. At once stepping-stones and stumbling blocks, in such "constellations" concepts offer thought and experience a vehicle for expressing what no single concept and no mere conceptless (as Kant would have said, "intellectual") intuition could hope to grasp on its own—immediately or nondialectically—but nonetheless hold out a promise of somehow, sometime, somewhere revealing truth and/or justice, beauty and/ or the sublime, the absolute and everything for which the Divine Name ever stood.[3]

So much is clear: beyond the modern definition of the concept, which has so often, and all too hastily, identified "religion" with a "set of beliefs"—in any case, with a mental state or series of states of consciousness, whose content and mode could be described by propositions that map ideas onto the world (albeit an ideal or mythically past and future one)—an altogether different sense or set of senses of the term ought to be envisioned. Only by being willing to move beyond the concept as we (think we) know it can we open ourselves up to a phenomenon or set(s) of phenomena whose simultaneous density ("thickness") and elusiveness (or "thinness") belong to the "heart" of its "matter" and constitute its references in their very "essence," that is to say, their logic and grammar. As we will see, a "deeply pragmatic" approach and a more than simply linguistic phenomenology of "religion" should envision a wide range of particulars, singular terms, signs, and marks (such as words and things, gestures and powers, sounds and silences, perceptions and affects, causes and effects), so as fully to appreciate and critically to evaluate the "total social fact" of its appearances, that is to say, of its modes and moods, its motifs and motivations.

Such sense or senses should begin by resisting ready-made concepts. This is not to say that suspected "sense and sensibilia" (J. L. Austin), the basic particulars, of "religion" elude any possible concept per se. Nor does it imply that "religion" represents an "I know not what" as the principally indeterminate or unmediatizable "stuff" of—fundamentally uninterpreted—experience. Speaking of "Religion: Beyond a Concept" might simply mean that a concept or set of concepts is not yet available for its phenomenon, for its set(s) of phenomena, and hence stands in need of being invented or reinvented, created or revived, coined or rearticulated. Any of these operations constitutes a *philosophical* task par excellence, regardless of the theoretical or intellectual enterprise (whether science, anthropology, phenomenology, or the cultural and comparative study of religion) that would take it upon itself to give the nameless dots a name or to connect them discursively, inferentially, in novel, more experimental and experientially grounded ways. The materialist turn in recent religious studies goes only halfway along that necessary methodological (and, I would add, metaphysical) trajectory.

Making the religious phenomenon or the set(s) of its phenomena explicit, in terms of organizing concepts or critical terms, and articulating their given, possible, or unexpected rationale, affect, and effect is, perhaps, the task of the study of "religion" *always still to come*. Such an endeavor must venture beyond the established antagonism of confessional and dogmatic (biblical, systematic, and practical) theology, practiced in the study of "Divinity," on the one hand, and the more historicist, empiricist, and culturalist approaches of the "science of religion," on the other, each of which *bisect* a more promising and emphatic prospect of the rational criticism of their objects of study, namely, God (without quotation marks) and "god" or "gods" (as cultural significations and markers). The challenge will be to avoid the alternatives of proposing either a "science" of God(s) or a science of "God(s)," either by loosening standards of methodological rigor and sound reasoning or by resigning ourselves to studying "religion" in a merely reductive and naturalist fashion, that is to say, as an "object" (categorized in advance as one) among others.[4]

But there is more. "Religion," it would seem, simultaneously requires—and yields— more and less than the study of *any* (physical, historical, cultural, literary, visual, media, etc.) object can offer. The study of "religion" is an indelibly *normative*, albeit decidedly non- or even antimoralistic, enterprise, whose leading motifs and modalities, motivations and moods, stand in need of constant redescription and rethinking, the redressing of concepts and singular terms, the giving and taking of reasons, and this, as it were, ad infinitum.

In this sense, "religion" could also (still or once again) name a practice or set of practices, a source or set of sources of selfhood and contestation, inspiration and projection, which may—or may not—continue to fascinate or trepidate scholars and the general public, politicians and military planners, activists and artists, not to mention believers, practitioners, agnostics, and seekers, all of whom may or may not learn to identify and locate, shun or adopt—or find yet a different use for—what all along seems to have retained the qualities of a moving target: a now under-, then overdetermined reality (or construct?) that eludes and frustrates inquiry in many ways.

In addition, may we suppose that the task of criticism in religious studies, no less than "secular criticism" in literary and cultural history, is to work through "religion's" concepts, words, things, gestures, powers, and so on, in order to, finally, *dispel* its—now fatal, then merely distracting—spell over us? Would not the question of why and how *still* religion, in this reading, acquire a provocative dual meaning with important *therapeutic*, rather than quietistic or even critical import? It would come to mean, first, to distill "religion's" essential features, to consider it still relevant to us, here and now, in all its elements and forms; second, to still our thirst for it, to silence and soothe its violent, devastating, indeed, demoralizing and nihilistic passions. The question of to why, in the present day and age, we *still* continue to speak about "religion" would, in this reading, find itself in the roughly same predicament as the subject (theme and voice) of Samuel Beckett's last prose piece, "Stirrings Still." No *religio perennis*, no more than any *theologia naturalis*, can permanently hold our attention, but "religion" is a task of infinite proportions, following an infinity of potentially infinite dimensions, with endless repercussions for thought. action, judgment, and sensibility, whose at once specific ("minimal") and global relevance will be with us for some time to come.

The present volume results from a collective, interdisciplinary, and international endeavor to chart new territory and eventually to redraw outdated maps, to find surprising new directions and unexpected signposts, for a phenomenon or set(s) of phenomena whose elements and forms in—and for—the twenty-first century seem, paradoxically, both more prominent and less identifiable, let alone totalizable, than ever before. In recent years, "religion" has attracted increasing attention and acquired unceasingly political weight in modern Western and non-Western democracies, thereby falsifying assumptions concerning its retreat and impending demise. Yet it is less and less apparent *what*, exactly, "religion" is about, just as it is far from clear *what* makes it tick, *how* it operates, *where* it is headed, and *who* (at least rhetorically) endorses or (also financially) sponsors it, for *whatever* reasons, and with *which* (unintended) consequences for all directly and indirectly affected.

Despite the fact that, in historical legacy or contemporary God-talk, ongoing reference to identitarian causes or imagined communal practices, geopolitical presence or mediatized kitsch, "religion" abounds and seems to be on the move, it may have become the one variable—or the very name of or most able figure for virtually any variable—that defies census and censorship, planning and strategy, markets and media, governmental control and political spin, as well as overconfident distinctions between privacy and publicness, individual empowerment and collective rapture, orthodoxy and heterodoxy, free speech and blasphemy, decency and perversion, promise and threat, life and death, immanence and transcendence.

Political theologies are just one of the many supposedly manifest forms "religion" takes to express, impose, and radiate its uncanny appeal, working its way through words, things, gestures, and powers.[5] In fact, many other "elementary forms of religious life," innumerable "varieties of religious experience," to recall the classic titles of Émile Durkheim and William James, should be discerned and analyzed in order to gain a more comprehensive and compelling perspective on the phenomenon or set(s) of phenomena—indeed, the peculiar *phenomenality*—that interests us. The present collection and its planned successor volumes seek to contribute to this program in a modest and preliminary way.

Quid: What Is "Religion"?

"Religion," in its very "concept"—and what may (still?) lie "beyond" it—is clearly one of the most demanding and frustrating objects for research in the humanities and the social sciences, and, increasingly, in the natural sciences, just as it has become a challenge for journalists and government-oriented think tanks. A semantic black hole whose "absence-presence" lets no single light escape, whether from its inner regions or from its surface (as if it were somehow suspended between the two, or nowhere long enough to catch the eye), "religion" has resisted all enlightenment. Attempts to pin down its historical origins, scriptural sources, and ritual practices have not yielded adequate means for grasping its current dimensions, directions, projections, extensions, formal equivalents, nonsynonymous substitutions, structural analogues, and the like. It is hard to tell what is copy, echo, resonance, effect, and what, on the contrary (supposing there is any opposition here), comes first (chronologically, logically, and, indeed, ontologically). It is as if "religion" assumes its roles in a house of mirrors, eluding all mimesis, all representation. Hence, it mirrors no "nature," whether first or second, cosmic or divine, human and/or social.

Yet a different metaphor seems equally appropriate. Often, "religion" manifests—indeed, is said to reveal—itself as a glaring, blinding blaze, straight in our faces, leaving us nowhere to hide, visible from all sides, like a Cubist painting. In consequence of this sensory overload, it becomes almost unnoticeable, invisible, untouchable precisely because all too tangible, a "saturated phenomenon," to borrow Jean-Luc Marion's felicitous expression. "Religion's" presence and essence and everything it stands for—including everything that comes to stand (in) for it—in this second reading turns out to be that of an "icon" to be subtracted (or always already abstracted) from every material and conceptual "idol," in ways that are discursively intractable but can all the more be sensed. It is difficult to tell which is which, when and where: "religion's" darkness and hence invisibility or, on the contrary, its brightness and, yet again, invisibility.

What makes us see one aspect rather than the other is not governed by criteria or rules but depends upon how we are willing to take—or "call"—the phenomenon or configuration of phenomena in question. Much space opens here for confusion and contestation, polemics and inquisition, as well as, conversely, for conversation and translation, syncretism and ecumenics, tolerance and hospitableness. The ontological—even metaphysical, if not always empirical or historical—condition for either one of these possibilities is, strictly speaking, the same. There is a *minimal theological* and, as it were, *globally religious* dimension, a historical, normative, and existential "weight" no less than a potentially liberatory "lightness" to even the most ordinary and everyday elements and forms of contemporary life.

Even as it produces an ever-richer variety of elementary forms at the beginning of the twenty-first century, "religion," along with everything it may still come to signal or be signaled by, seems to absolve itself from any established standards and methods for determining knowledge. "Religion" remains, in this view, the "ab-solute" (from the Latin verb *absolvere*) par excellence. In other words, it remains—or becomes once again, perhaps more poignantly than ever before—a referent or requisite for experience and experimentation. Only a tireless proliferation of conceptual, practical, visual, and even visceral perspectives—call it an intellectual and imaginative *perspectivism for the sake of the "absolute"*—could track the infinite modalities and moods, motifs and motivations, by which "religion" is expressed in "the world," in its words, things, gestures, and powers, as well as the fascination (if not always love) they may still or yet come to inspire.

In most intellectual efforts to define it, "religion" seems to retreat, indeed, to "die the death of a thousand qualifications," as Anthony Flew suggestively remarked.[6] Paradoxically, the more pressure one applies to "religion," to its concept(s), referent(s), and requisite(s), the more resilient these categories tend to become. Even where it is universally repudiated, "religion" might thus still exert conceptual, but also imaginative, rhetorical, and affective force, behind our backs, as it were—subliminally, unconsciously, sublimely, that is to say, metaphysically. Yet where it aspires to reign in the open, "religion" may crumble to kitsch, to the mediatized iteration of emptied words, reified things, voided gestures, naked power. No one can tell with certainty whether the "religious" utterance is—or performs—what it claims. There are simply no publicly ascertainable criteria to separate the genuine from the false. And while the analytical distinction between, say, theology and divine speech, on the one hand, and idolatry and blasphemy, on the other, may be necessary, there is no epistemic or other procedure to establish with any shared certainty which is which. In that sense, there can be no "true religion," just as there can be no "false" religion, no real superstition (sectarianism, or, again, idolatry, blasphemy). In consequence, there can be no strict—theoretically determinable—distinction between, say, the church and the community of believers,[7] or, for that matter, between "culture" and "cult."

The alternation of "religion's" now celebrated then decried ends and revivals, its sacralization and profanation, purification and commodification, mimicry and mockery, seems thus quasi-permanent, with no hope of resolution in sight. Though the variety of its forms need not necessarily (or for always) delimit, let alone exhaust, the range of the possible (thinkable, sayable, doable, sensible, livable), the increasingly complex and mediatized dynamics of these forms leads us to the heart of the matter, revealing the very structure of "the religious." It is *performative* and can attach itself to (and express itself as) virtually any content that it finds pragmatically useful. Yet in inhabiting these relatively new spaces—the "space of flows," as Manuel Castells has called them—"religion" also puts itself (or at least its image as serenity and intactness) at risk. Exposing itself to theatricality and tyranny, to a culture of copy and counterfeit, it invites and increases the occurrence of violence and the worst, whose possibility, in turn, is the very condition of possibility of both peace and the best, as if potential perversion—"pervertibility," in Derrida's term—were a necessary supposition of perfection and perfectibility.

Or, as Emmanuel Levinas puts it, the dimension of the divine is "transcendent to the point of absence," exposing (itself to) a "surplus of nonsense over sense." Like the theoretical skepticism that shadows philosophy, this risk and exposure is that of a spectral coming and going, a *revenant*,[8] an unavoidable danger conjured up at each seemingly secure step along the way. Expressed in a myriad incalculable (hence, unprogrammable and ungovernable) instances, punctuating the rhythm of everyday life, "religion" is nothing more—and nothing less—than the "curvature of social space," in Levinas's phrase. "Religion" provides the name and idiom that—*for the moment*—best captures a pervasive structure and aleatory dynamic of modern life, of its elements and forms for the twenty-first century.

That is to say, in public "religion" continues to draw audiences, haunt headlines, dictate campaigns, initiate and ruin (or, as Richard Rorty says, "stop"[9]) conversation, just as in private it inspires or frustrates thought and experience, action and judgment. It may go on—or, rather, finally start—bringing people together, if only by immediately tearing them apart: from their own former selves no less than from others, turning "religion" into the quintessential *discriminatory act*.

Now that we can no longer dismiss "religion," assuming its pending demise, as thinkers have sought to do since the eighteenth century, how are we to devise genuinely critical, respectful, promising, and salutary—in short, tactful as well as tactical—ways to study it? Several important interventions over the past few years can point the way: Talal Asad's groundbreaking *Genealogies of Religion* and *Formations of the Secular*, Mark C. Taylor's edited volume *Critical Terms for Religious Studies*, Jonathan Z. Smith's *Relating Religion*, Nancy K. Frankenberry's symposium *Radical Interpretation in Religion*, Michael Lambek's *A Reader in the Anthropology of Religion*, Fenella Cannell's collection *The Anthropology of Christianity*.[10] Taken together, they argue for an integrated account of the concept of "religion," but also of what precedes, surrounds, involves, implies, exceeds, and, hence, lies beyond it.

The study of "religion" and whatever may yet come to take its place depends upon a rigorous alternation between the "universal" and "essential" (to be defined) and the "singular" or exemplary "instant," "instance," and "instantiation." Without ignoring or disparaging the invocation of "universals," which responds to a deep-seated need that Wittgenstein ties to the "essence" of language and our "form of life," such inquiry must methodically, or at least strategically, start out from the singular, that is, the particular: namely, words, things, sounds, silences, smells, sensations, gestures, powers, affects, and effects. No ontological primacy can be implied here. Indeed, the very choice of a constitutive pole of analysis is a matter, not just of "cultural politics," as Rorty has suggested, but of a sensibility to changing situations, which vary the weight—and usefulness—of any one category over another. The present emphasis on the singular over the universal may be only a counterpoint. In fact, for reasons we will spell out in a moment, the pendulum may already be swinging back.

Such a strategy is faithful to the "new materialism," of which David Chidester, in a review of Taylor's *Critical Terms for Religious Studies*, has spoken, suggesting that such critical terms are increasingly dislodged from an emphasis on "faith and belief." This reflects a transition to views claiming that "the very notion of belief is methodically suspect," or, more modestly, that "our efforts to understand religious activity are seldom aided by insight into the agent's doctrinal commitment."[11] Some thinkers have located this emphasis on "belief" and its systematization in the age of the Reformation, as it turned away from ritual and the practice of sacraments, but Daniel Boyarin convincingly traces its origin to the fourth century of our common era. Tomoko Masuzawa has demonstrated its consolidation in the nineteenth century, which saw the foundation of an academic discipline of "religion" and its corollary, "world religions," based on an interiorized—and supposedly universal—concept of mental representation.

But is it "useful," as Terry Godlove has suggested, "to view the contemporary offensive against belief as continuous with older attempts to take back the ground lost to the Protestant Reformation"?[12] For one thing, we can hardly suspect the new materialists in the study of religion of wanting to recatholize religion. Rather, a more subtle theoretical, disciplinary, and ultimately philosophical reason for their proposed shift in focus—echoed by our shift toward the "foci" of words, things, gestures, and powers as the elements and forms of "religion"—lies at the source of the materialist impulse, propelled by what, in contemporary debates on the philosophy of mind, has been called "eliminative materialism."[13] This shift has no reductionist naturalist implications for its subject.

Indeed, our willingness to be near the facts, the contexts, as well as the relational features that make certain basic particulars, individual properties, or singular terms (words, things, gestures, powers, etc.) stand out—but always temporarily and pragmatically, for some actors but not for others—does not mean that theory and idealization must be suspended. We are after a different, perhaps less abstract theorizing—or rather, a different kind of abstraction, with different generalities and universals (albeit universals of "the other"). To detranscendentalize reason, including the "reasons that reason knows nothing about" (Pascal), requires one neither to naturalize it nor to abdicate from it, but to retranscendentalize in a different way. The concrete is not the alternative to the formal, but its filled and, as it were, incarnate form. "Religion," like everything else, is nothing outside or independent of the series of its metamorphoses, its metastases. But "it" (but "what," exactly?) cannot fully be analyzed in terms of any single one—or even the sum total—of these instantiations, either.

This brings me to a further thought. It is the suspicion—or happy realization—that the *dual aspect* or "two sources of religion" (to quote Derrida, following Bergson's *The Two Sources of Morality and Religion*)—in other words, the analytical distinction between a general or generic concept or notion ("religion") and its singular instances and instanti-ations (words, things, gestures, powers, etc.) might well reproduce itself in material mo-tifs, as if the turn to and temptation of the transcendental somehow announces itself at the heart of what seems most basic, common, and down to earth. How is that so? To give an example: "things" (like words, gestures, powers, or any other singular term from which we might choose to start out) could be taken to be a general and generic category for all instances and instantiations that we differentiate. After all, words, gestures, powers, and even "religion," insofar as it is a single term, concept, word, or notion, are "things" in the world, which are used and selected by the "beings" that we happen to be in our attempts to cope with the circumstances we encounter and create.

More significantly, in speaking about "things"—for example, the materiality and spa-tiality of the divine, the sacred, or the magical—it would seem that, in our very movement toward the concrete, we must reinstate an indelible reference to, say, the "thing of things," or the "thingness" of things, the thing in itself or the thing as such. By the same token, speaking about "words," "gestures," "powers," and their nonequivalent substitutes con-jures up the wording of words, the gesturing of gestures, and the empowering or disem-powering of powers. This extrapolation is no obscurantist relapse into the transcendental metaphysics and natural theology or onto-theology of old, but a structural necessity in-herent to all theorizing. This (re)transcendentalizing movement is expressive of the im-plicit philosophical moment in all interpretation, given that we not only collect and describe, but also select and arrange or evaluate such materials. This is what "adding up" things and "connecting the dots" or "establishing links" means.

To this insight I would add the hypothesis that the immense archive of reflections on "religion," "religions," and the "theological" offers the greatest resource for understand-ing and redescribing the movement of "transcendence" out of the givens of inquiry.

One might, of course, object that the formalizing and generalizing thrust of this movement of transcendence, when properly understood, is in fact one of immersion or absorption, not in some "beyond," but in immanence, in the everyday or the ordinary, the common and the low, as Stanley Cavell has suggested. But, for reasons that I cannot develop here, this objection, along with the attitude and ways of life for which it stands, may in truth not constitute an alternative (and, in my reading, never intended to be one).

Thus "things" may not be in a better position than words, gestures, powers, or even the most abstract concept of "religion" to keep us firmly grounded. In the end, *we can start from any point of entry*, and each individually and singularly gives access to a different complexity of the same "total social fact," whose nature, logic, or grammar it is strategi-cally necessary to reconceive from the bottom up, starting from "things," from some other element or form, or even, as we do here, from the philosophical consideration of how these might all constitute or call forth each other in a variety of revealing ways.

Our proposed line of approach remains tributary to the new materialism because it moves *beyond the concept* of "religion," just as it steers clear of all confessional theologies. In so doing, this approach seeks to venture into the domains of what we might tentatively call a *negative metaphysics*—more precisely, a *minimal theology*—whose contours and contents are less residues of metaphysics, with its natural or onto-theology, than an exploration of the unprecedented, the encounter, and the new, as it takes shape here and now.

Such an approach, for all its insistence on what are still deemed to be "religious" particularities and identities, faithfully traces the emerging features of an abstract and virtual "global religion," whose emptied center progressively draws us in, again, like a black hole, letting nothing, not the dimmest light, least of all the natural light of reason, escape. Yet this perspective does not present itself to us *directly*, as if the phenomenon of "religion" were experientially or intuitively available, without—or beyond—the endless detour through singular particulars, which, in a sense, are the only "materials" that offer themselves for interpretation, as so many violent encounters for which no concepts, perhaps least of all the traditional and modern concept of "religion," are readily available. Only a radical reinterpretation of this concept, including the philosophical concept of the concept that it presupposes, will enable us to rearticulate the terms of discussion and thereby open new, as well as reopen forgotten, avenues of thought, lines of inquiry, the sensibilities and ways of life they imply, as well as the institutional forms they involve.

Quod: The Mere Fact, Like It or Not, That There Is (Something Called) "Religion"

That "religion" abounds, *that there is* (still, again, or ever more?) religion, seems evident. But *what* or *whose* "religion" is it—alternatively, *which* religion was or will it be? *Where* and in *what numbers* was (and is) religion found, and by which terminological, conceptual, or discursive means or images has it been, does it continue to be, or will it one day be *defined*, but hence also contained or relegated to other supposedly nonreligious and more fundamental domains, whose reference is believed to be more firmly established and more widely shared? Further, are references to these domains, in their attempt to naturalize "religion," any less dependent on normative, not to mention metaphysical, assumptions and claims than were revealed, historical, or positive theologies, which, in their turn, were grafted upon earlier ones (like the Thomistic dictum that *gratia non tollit sed perficit naturam*; "grace does not destroy nature, but makes it more perfect")?

Some scholars have taken the difficulty, unclarity, and sometimes outright confusion in matters concerning religion as an alibi to dispense with the question of the "existence" and "essence"—the *quod* and *quid*[14]—of "religion" altogether. Neither conceptually nor empirically, theoretically nor practically, they believe, does "religion" still constitute an object worthy of interest, warranting an independent field of study in the academy. "Religion" and its cults, so this argument goes, is part of a general culture in which codes and jurisprudence based upon the constitution, upon civil and international law, provide—or should provide—for all in equal ways. Juridical and governmental "neutrality" with regard to matters of faith, ecclesial denomination, religious and theological education, the care for life, marriage, and death, is a *conditio sine qua non* for the flourishing of modern democracies and political liberalism. Even if "political theologies" may have informed the beginnings of modern statehood and its monarchical or republican conceptions of sovereignty, these skeptics reason, they have since lost their legitimacy and practical necessity. Yet modern states are increasingly confronted with a predicament that they can neither embrace nor eschew—that is to say, neutralize—religion. They can at best mobilize the best of religion's motifs and motivations to counteract the worst of its impulses. A third way beyond these extremes—albeit in the name of freedom, democracy, liberalism, and progressive emancipation—is no longer available, if it ever was. The only alternative is a "cultural politics" in which the advocates of secular republican values must be willing to engage, in full consciousness of having to wet their feet, to dirty their hands, to compromise.

Some scholars have chastized the interdisciplinary conglomerate called "comparative religion," in all its culturalist varieties, for entering into an unsavory ideological alliance with the hegemony and growth of Western markets and their opportunistically favored political systems.[15] Whatever the kernel of truth in these indictments, the present collection asks a series of more modest questions, bracketing the modern yearning for semantic clarity, totalizing views, and methodological purity, just as it abstains from grand political diagnoses and the concomitant moralism or victimization. It is not devoted to the seemingly simple—but arguably most difficult and, in the end, unanswerable—question "What *is* 'religion'?" Instead, the following essays and subsequent volumes prepare the ground for a more preliminary and hypothetical approach to the subject by asking what are the concrete and singular *vectors* from which the abstract question of "religion" and its concept emerge. In other words, what are the novel directions into which "religion's" idioms, signs, and marks—words, things, gestures, powers, sounds, silences, smells, sensations, shapes, colors, affects, and effects—lead us? Hence the volume's orientation toward all those quotidian yet extraordinary instances, instants, and instantiations that point beyond an established concept—"religion."

At stake in the dual perspective on religion's two sources or aspects is the co-implication and interplay of its singular terms *and* its general, universal, and global import. Both remain analytically distinct while structurally and rhythmically pushed and pulled toward each other. Small wonder that "religion" is, as we have said, a moving target, good vibrations to some, giving others the jitters.

This dual perspective also reveals religion's inevitable idolatry *and* iconicity, that is to say, the at once simple and tantalizing fact that there is no more—and no less—than an insurpassable idea of the ab-solute, absolving itself from all definition and contextual delimitation. This restrains us from taking any given idol as ultimate, as if anything could be its own icon—an immediacy undisturbed by mediation; a signified without signifier, beyond the differential and non-natural play of the marks and tissue in which all signifiers are irrevocably caught; an event without consequent fidelity and, hence, potential infidelity to it.

A generalized idolatry—like a generalized fetishism—would no longer be thinkable, sayable, practicable, livable. We wouldn't be able to differentiate one image, one picture, from the next, let alone take an image *as* image (or a picture *as* picture). And the absolute, this most formal and formidable aspect of "religion," is therefore not merely another image (or picture). We *cannot*, yet *cannot but*, distinguish it—at least analytically and, however provisionally, hypothetically, falsifiably—from the very aspects (words, things, gestures, powers, etc.) beyond whose singular instances no absolute shows its face without being caught and frozen in a mask, caricature, statue, portrait, photographic image, or cinematic "still." That the absolute thus betrays itself, giving while withholding, retreating by showing "itself," might well be the condition, call it the transcendental grounding and uprooting, of all images and every picture. One would thus need more than one image or picture to "get," "have," "keep," or "lose" one's "religion."

The abstractive approach, absolving itself of all designation (deictic and other) and bordering upon the negative and the void(ed), cannot stand on its own, either. "Religion" reveals itself as what Jean-Luc Marion has termed a "saturated phenomenon." Like this volume's colorful cover, drawn from a photo taken by Neil Hertz in the Indian quarter of Paris in honor of the anthropologist Jim Siegel, a "saturated phenomenon" manifests itself to excess, to the point of rendering itself nearly invisible. It *almost* produces a blur, not for lack of but because of an excess of detail. On the book's cover this is intensified and doubled by the mirroring window's reflection. It not only lets us see through to a host of deities and idols, but also projects the modern everydayness of a Paris street, lined by parked automobiles, a reminder of the possibilities and threats of our modern comings and goings. The occasional, hurried, solitary *passante* strolls out of the picture, a distracted passerby. In front of the showcase that "religion" has become, like her we are beholders on the move, in haste, and mostly looking the other way. It is as if the idols were separated from us by the thinnest and most transparent of membranes, a window sealing us off from what turn out to be *authentic commodities*, of sorts, since for all their opulent display they form part and parcel of a lively ethnic and religious community in the heart of the city that is the mother of all *Lumières*, the capital of modern life.

The picture shows us all and nothing, all at once and individual things in their most singular features, depending on the perspective—or distance—one is willing and able to take as a spectator, perhaps as the *passante* who hurries by, seemingly uninvolved or otherwise and elsewhere absorbed, in a mystic gesture of disengagement that alone allows one to engage for an instant.

Like the Cubist paintings to which Marion refers in *Idol and Distance*, this window withholds nothing. And yet, by giving too much information all at once, it risks offering us nothing, all the same. To fill the space, we must cut out a segment of the general picture, project it alongside the foil of dazzling details, which we cannot take in at once. The separated detail then becomes the backdrop against which other details emerge, in accord with whatever our reasons might be, whether sentimental or deeply pragmatic.

Qua "Religion": Studying a Phenomenon or Set(s) of Phenomena

The intellectual and institutional agenda behind the research program The Future of the Religious Past: Elements and Forms for the Twenty-first Century, stands out for its ambitious—broadly conceived, yet at the same time specific, that is to say, semantically, materially, performatively, and politically articulated—scope and internal organization. It attempts to cut through academic boundaries and to lift the study of religion and its current manifestations out of its traditional scholarly contexts. The program also has wider cultural, political, and juridical, not to mention "global" ramifications. While coming from different disciplinary, methodological, historical, systematic, confessional, and humanistic-secular backgrounds, all contributors to this volume share an interest in the following fundamental question: "*In what sense are the legacies of religion—its powers, words, things, and gestures—disarticulating and reconstellating themselves as the elementary forms of life in the twenty-first century?*" In other words, what would it mean—intellectually and strategically, in the context of the university and in larger institutional terms—to analyze a total social fact (a *fait social total*, to use the terminology introduced by Maurice Leenhardt and Marcel Mauss) by distilling a necessarily limited set of (in principle innumerable) categories, elements, and forms that, together, propel "religion" into existence, give it its weight, and channel its effects? And if analysis, in all of its conceptual, cultural, even chemical associations (one is reminded of Nietzsche's "chemistry of concepts" no less than of recent scientific proposals to determine the physical or biological basis of religious dispositions), *takes* a phenomenon, quite literally, *apart* into the components that make up its past, present, and, perhaps, future, how, then, do we constructively, perhaps deconstructively, put these elementary forms back together again so as to better imagine (in any case, to engage and prepare ourselves for) the many varieties of religious experience that are in the process of emerging or reemerging all around us?

The dual approach of analysis and constructivism intends to historicize, naturalize, and contextualize religion, formalizing its phenomenon or set(s) of phenomena while respecting its variable modes of appearance as it comes into the world—as it makes, promises, and destroys *worlds*, whether a lifeworld, to use the terminology of the later Husserl; worlds characterized by the contrast between imagined "tribes" with their "primitive" languages as opposed to "our" language games and forms of life, as the later Wittgenstein added; or lifeworlds marked by modern public spheres, their "structural transformation," and their contemporary alternatives, as has been proposed in the writings of Jürgen Habermas, Craig Calhoun, and Michael Warner; worlds of entrepreneurship and economic pragmatism, as in the "Islam of the market" evoked by Patrice Haenni; or virtual worlds, as in the constitution of a "virtual Umma" described by Olivier Roy in his *Globalized Islam*. And other possibilities are legion.

Our proposal aspires to lay bare the structure and logic (the "essence" or "grammar," as Wittgenstein says) of "religions" and their "worlds," that is to say, their language games and forms of life, in their "vertical" no less than "horizontal" dimensions. We should do so by simultaneously paying attention both to their larger, intrinsic "natural history" *and* to their singular everydayness and ordinariness, in short, to everything that expresses not just their materiality but also what Emerson and Thoreau call the "low" and the "common."

The double aspect of analyzing existing pictures or images, on the one hand, and their (re)construction, on the other, will require us to maintain two levels of description and exploration at once. Not unlike the infinitely small and infinitely large spaces inside and beyond us on which Pascal muses in his *Pensées*, we face a dizzying task of minutely rendering the most singular of particulars (such as words, things, gestures, and powers), while simultaneously wagering a larger reach toward the general and the generic. Combining the two perspectives responsibly and critically—in a minimal, some would say, negative metaphysics, theology, or even anthropology, of sorts—would mean grafting the two movements onto each other, so as to keep them (and to help them keep each other) *in and off balance*, disallowing any hegemony of either pole.

Starting out from "religion's" words, things, gestures, powers, sounds, silences, smells, sensations, shapes, colors, affects, and effects (again, in the attempt to capture irreducible constituents of "religion" this list need not be complete, indeed, must remain open in principle)—might enable us to chart new vistas and unexpected connections, in a healthy, expansive mode, while nonetheless discouraging the tendency to study religion in view of what, in the most ambitious paradigms of natural science (in its attempt to combine the insights of cosmology and quantum physics) has been called a unified "theory of everything."

In fact, there may be no access to understanding, let alone explaining, "religion" as such or in toto, in a single stroke. *Religion: Beyond a Concept* may well mean to *think*—and eventually, perhaps, to experience, express, organize, legislate, tolerate, and, if need be, combat, in any case, work through—religion in its most concrete, singular, and singularly appealing or terrifying elements and forms, while taking heed of the given and possible connections and relations, that is to say, causalities, implications, inferences, resonances, resistances, attunements, hopes, and deceptions that are at best the sum of our calling—and claiming—things to be so. All depends on our willingness and ability, our attentiveness and perceptiveness, to see things (words, gestures, powers, and the like) in this or that light, as it were, *sub specie religionis*, or not.

Quo: or, Divine Places and the Onto-Theo-Topology of "Religion"

The question What is "religion"?—captured by Latin *quid*—requires less that one find the genus and *differentia specifica* of the phenomenon than that one catalogue or narrate historically and culturally different, often opposing, contrasting, or complementary, definitions of it, without ever pretending to have exhaustively reconstructed the whole past, present, and future renderings of its central features. Moreover, since we have suggested that reference to some "universal" remains unavoidable (as is the seeking out of particulars)—the Wittgensteinian notion of "family resemblance" may not be quite emphatic and expansive enough for our needs. Given the absoluteness of its virtuality, religion allows one to absolve and liberate oneself from—and hence to relativize—the other, which is religion in its positivity, that is, in the multifarious multiplicity and particulars of its instantiations, its instances and instants.

In addition to the question "What?" the contributions to this volume explore possible answers to the question "Where?"—*quo*—religion can (still) be found. From the political and ecclesial principle of *cuius regio eius religio* ("in whose region, whose religion"), introduced during the Reformation in Western Europe to suppress the worst outbreaks of violence and war—but by no means restricted to the sixteenth and seventeenth centuries or to internal Christian feuds between Protestantism and Catholicism—via the many imperialisms, colonialisms, and postcolonialisms, the question concerns *the location, dislocation, and relocation of the divine*. Here, the question of onto-theology reverts into the onto-topo-theology or onto-theo-politology of what Jean-Luc Nancy has aptly called "divine places."[16] I will not further elaborate this question here.

Quantus: On Numbers and Sets

The aspect of space and extension might seem to overlap with that of religion and number, that is to say, with the *quantity* or *quorum* of believers and practitioners, whether in terms of their membership in institutions, the size of their communities and factions, the spread of sectarian groups, and the existence of loners, of outcasts, dropouts, or inner emigrants. Although the question of number has an ontological thrust similar to that of topology in that it measures phenomena or sets of phenomena to determine their strength or impact, just as ontotheotopologies chart their situatedness and locus, the two methods are directed toward altogether different aspects of the problem.

Much in the debates concerning "religion" and "secularization" has revolved around matters of counting and census, of statistics and probability (as in the predictions of demographic and denominational evolution and trends). Yet the relationship between "how many" and "how much," that is, between sheer numbers and factual power, is not necessarily proportionate. Minuscule "splinter" groups can wreak massive havoc, whereas when masses are converted, the very force and core of the message that converted them may thin out or become compromised. While the relationship between the infinitely great and the infinitely small has long been a central trope in religious thinking, well before Pascal's *Pensées* turned it into a haunting theme, their reciprocal relationship and mutual implication has acquired new relevance. Especially in the world of new technological media, there is no longer (any need for) a direct correspondence or correlation between cause and effect, number and influence. This may be one of the reasons why the appeal, integrity, and legitimation of democracy and political liberalisms are coming under increasing pressure.

We can give the question of number and religion a different twist by asking: Is there a mathematics or, more precisely, a set theory of "religion"? What would it mean to study religion, not *more geometrico* (as was, in a sense, Spinoza's aim in the *Ethics*), but *more arithmetico*, with numbers, classes, and sets (and not points, lines, and planes) in mind? Interestingly, "religion" seems to have been an important cultural horizon and, perhaps, intellectual inspiration in the first formulations of the set-theoretical paradigm. But what is a "set" in the context of "religious" matters?

Gottlob Frege, in his *Grundlagen der Arithmethik* (*The Foundations of Arithmetic*), published in 1884, defines cardinal numbers (1, 2, 3, . . . *n*) in terms of classes and sets. As one commentator notes, a number *n* is "the *class* or *set* of all collections with *n* members: '7,' for example would be defined as the set of all collections with *seven* members, everything from the Seven Dwarfs to the Seven Hills of Rome to the seven letters in the word 'letters.'" According to this definition, "a particular number," as Bertrand Russell explains, is "not identical with any collection of terms having that number."[17] As a class or set, any *n* could count several collections or aggregates (of, say, persons, words, things, gestures, powers, etc.) among its members. Categorically distinct from the collections that have it in common (such as Seven Seals, Seven Deadly Sins, Seven Days in Tibet, etc.), any number *n* or *n* + 1 characterizes any given collection whose class or set it is. A set, Frege claimed, is the "extension of a concept": "there can be no sets . . . for which there is no concept: every existing set corresponds to a concept. Or, whenever one has a defined concept, one can directly deduce the existence of a corresponding multiple."[18]

Well before Frege, in 1874 Georg Cantor laid the groundwork for arithmetical trans- or supra-finite set theory, a mathematical science of the infinite based on the intellectual grasp of an *actual infinity*—rather than the potential infinity that the tradition, ever since Aristotle, had reserved for mathematical reasoning. (The realization, in thought, of the actual infinite was left to the divine Being alone.) Aristotle observes in the *Physics* (207b8) that we can always think of larger numbers and that any magnitude can be divided ad infinitum. Both operations leave the infinite merely potential, since, for any given number, the number of parts that can further be added or bisected can always be surpassed.

Cantor's general theory of manifolds (*Mengenlehre* or *théorie des ensembles*) created a revolution by claiming that *actual* infinite sets of numbers can be demonstrated, although often beyond our ability to count them, and can differ in size. On philosophical grounds, Cantor claimed objective existence for such *transfinite* sets, both in the mind of God, the "Absolute," and in created nature. As one commentator, quoting Cantor, observes, he was convinced that "'immanent' and 'transient' existence always occur together, in the sense that an admissible, consistent concept 'always also possesses in certain, and even infinitely many ways a transient reality.'"[19]

Cantor defined the notion of set as follows: "By set what is understood is the grouping into a totality of quite distinct objects of our intuition or our thought."[20] He devised a method for determining an infinitely large number and for analyzing the properties of infinitely large general collections of objects, such as the sets of all natural, rational, or real numbers. In so doing, he was not merely attempting to revolutionize our formal and technical mathematical understanding of the infinite (which had been taken to be merely a way of speaking, an indication of limits, as Carl Friedrich Gauss put it[21]) but also contributing to the ways in which philosophy and theology could come to terms with absolute and actual infinity at the heart of religion. (The idea of an actual infinity had been anathema throughout most of the tradition, notably in Thomism and Neo-Thomism.[22]) Defying fears that the attempt to formalize the actual infinite might unsettle the venerated disciplines of mathematics and theology, Cantor claimed that the paradoxes of the infinite, known since Zeno, could be avoided and the very idea of the actual infinite shown to be an implicit assumption of the potential infinite. A "free" rather than "pure" mathematics, Cantor argued, one that insists on internal consistency alone, might introduce or, indeed, create new distinct numbers—in his case "transfinite" numbers, now added in analogy to earlier inventions of rational, irrational, transcendental, and complex numbers—for which real mathematical existence would then also need to be assumed. Far from limiting the infinite to the "indefinitely growing," Cantor assumed that mathematical sets could be postulated for the infinitely vaster expanse of "the so-called geometric continuum (the 'set of all points on a line')," beyond the reach of natural and rational numbers.[23] His discovery or free invention of transfinite numbers, together with his insistence on the implications of this "continuum hypothesis," opened a whole new "paradise" (as David Hilbert has called it) from which mathematics would no longer let itself be expelled.

Such newly defined entities in the ever-expanding corpus of mathematical knowledge could serve another purpose, which Cantor's biographers and historians of the field have unearthed in his correspondence.[24] Such transfinite numbers "exist at the highest level as eternal ideas in the Divine Intellect (*Intellectu Divino*)."[25] Or, as Cantor put it in a thesis at the end of his *Habilitationsschrift*, echoing an insight of Saint Augustine in the *City of God* (bk. 12, chap. 19): "Integer numbers constitute a *unity* composed of laws and relations *in a manner similar to those of celestial bodies*."[26]

A Platonic and a theological motif thus come together in Cantor's fundamental insight: "the transfinite species are just as much at the disposal of the intentions of the Creator and His absolute boundless will as are the finite numbers."[27] Cantor's most distinguished biographer, Joseph Warren Dauben, suggests that "the efficacy of Cantor's theory was ultimately referred to the Divine Intellect where the Transfinitum, all the transfinite numbers, existed as eternal ideas. This was a strong form of Platonism, but one to which Cantor repeatedly turned for support. The religious connections were as significant to him as the mathematical ones, and in the final analysis, Cantor could only be sure of the propriety of his abstractions because they found their ideal representation in the mind of God."[28] Cantor held that insistence on the actual infinity of real numbers and sets, together with the mathematical freedom it expressed, would contribute to countering the materialism and determinism of the age, without lapsing into pantheism.

In the wake of Pope Leo XIII's encyclical *Aeterni Patris* and the rise of Neo-Thomism, Catholic theologians sought to use Cantor's mathematical infinities to shore up doctrines of Catholic faith, although they had to struggle with "the challenge of mathematical infinity to the unique, absolute infinity of God's existence."[29] Cantor, for his part, claimed that "instead of diminishing the extent of God's nature and dominion, the transfinite numbers actually made it all the greater."[30] In other words, the actuality of the infinite, whether of God's existence and essence, His infinite intellect and eternity, or the reality of transfinite numbers, was taken to be grounded in the Platonic insight in which the theological and the mathematical reinforce and mutually found each other (although the first was held to be the basis for the second, even in Cantor's own account). Understandably, the Church disputed Cantor's claim that the "Transfinitum" exists concretely—as part of the *natura naturata*, as distinguished from the *natura naturans*, to use the terminology of Spinoza, whom Cantor had closely studied as a student—since that risks the "error of Pantheism," formally condemned in 1861 in an encyclical of Pius IX. As Dauben writes, "Any attempt to correlate God's infinity with a concrete, temporal infinity suggested Pantheism. Thus both infinite space and infinite duration, in both of which the infinite was predicated of objects in the natural world, were held to be inadmissible on theological grounds."[31]

Cantor, who refused both the pantheist and the materialist readings of Spinoza, retorted by adding a further differentiation. In a letter of January 1886 to Cardinal Johannes Franzelin, he distinguished between the "eternal, uncreated Infinite or the Absolute [*Infinitum aeternum increatum sive Absolutum*]," which belongs to God and His attributes alone, and the "the created Infinite or the Transfinite [*Infinitum creatum sive Transfinitum*]," represented by the actuality of infinite numbers and objects in the universe. His interlocutor accepted this admission, taking it to indicate a conceptual distinction between a "*properly infinite*" notion of the "Absolute-Infinite," reserved for God alone, and an "improperly and equivocally infinite" notion of the "Actual-Infinite," or the "Transfinitum" of the created order.[32] in this view, the realm of the transfinite would thus be only partly modeled on the theological infinite, without acquiring the same ontological or onto-theological standing. More precisely, the "Transfinitum" lies between the finite order of things and the infinite order of the divine Absolute, since it was created like the first yet is eternal like the second.[33]

Starting from a (strictly?) materialist approach to the epistemology of mathematics, Alain Badiou draws what seems to be a radically different conclusion from Cantor's revolution.[34] Set theory, as one of Badiou's most lucid commentators explains, is based on the assumption that we have

> "the ability to regard any collection of objects as a single entity (i.e., a set)." The precise number of elements involved in any such collection is strictly irrelevant to the definition. . . . The elements thus collected are always themselves sets, however far we go down the scale toward the infinitely small. The sole limit or stopping point of such regression is what is defined as a purely memberless term (or "*Urelement*"). In the strictly ontological, set-theoretic, situation, the only such term is the void or empty set. . . . That the void is alone foundational means that there is no elementary mathematical particle, no indivisible or "smallest possible number": the empty set is never reached by a process of division.[35]

Such reasoning led Cantor to proclaim the nondenumerability (i.e., the noncountability) of the continuum of real numbers, which are more numerous than natural numbers and constitute an infinity of infinities.

Badiou takes this to imply that mathematics, in its set-theoretical articulation, is the privileged discourse for spelling out the elements and formal contours of a materialist, Lucretian ontology. This mathematical ontology finds its prime axiom in the postulated notion of inconsistent, nonunified, impure multiplicity, whose proper name is the "void [*le vide*]," rather than "nothing." It forms the foil against which ordered, structured, and consistent multiplicity—the "multiple of multiples" that makes up "situations"—can take place. It is as if the assumption of the *Urelement* of the empty set, which is "Being" as the "void," were the nondeterminable, infra- or supranumerary point of departure (indeed, the very "basis") for the counting, the "counting-as-one," that makes up the universe as it is presented—"composable according to the one, or the particular (pigs, stars, gods)."[36] Mathematical ontology, in other words, derives from and formally maps out the "effects" (and, all too often, the "one-effect") that the order of presentation (of "normalcy" and the "State") requires, just as it retroactively invites us to point back to the "void" from which this order emerges and proactively, militantly gestures toward its echo, the "event," whose "illegality" is the central characteristic of any "truth" worthy of its name. Put in more technical terms:

> Ontology . . . seizes the in-itself of the multiple by forming into consistency all inconsistency and forming into inconsistency all consistency. It thereby deconstructs any

one-effect. It is faithful to the non-being of the one, so as to unfold, without any nomination, the regulated game of the multiple, such that it is none other than the absolute form of presentation, thus the mode in which being proposes itself to any access.[37]

Might "religion" name (the very postulation of) this void, preceding and exceeding all number, all counting and accountability, just as it—or some of its central concepts or figures, such as the "miracle," as Badiou suggests in his meditation on Pascal—might name the supranumerical quality of the "event"? We can certainly wager this thought, though we can also understand why some thinkers, not least Derrida, prefer to invoke an atheological trope—for example, the Platonic *khōra*—to indicate such a matrix of all matrices. We might also examine why Badiou takes the "something," the "there is," the "phantom" and "remainder" of the "real" that lies at the source of every presentation and all counting and accounting as an "errant cause" (thus citing, like Derrida, another motif from Plato's *Timaeus*, so as to mark his own departure from the materialism of ancient Greek atomism).[38]

Further, could we formalize the infinite series of presentable phenomena that are as many instances, instants, or instantiations—that is, materializations—of this mathematic-ontological axiom as a succession of failed nominations of this postulated "void"? Whatever—again, axiomatically—follows upon it (without being causally derivable from it) is a set (or class) whose number n or $n + 1$ gathers all individual phenomena covered by it in all possible sorts of configurations. Indeed, those "elements" (as they are technically called in set theory)—for which we have here substituted words, things, gestures, powers, and so on—can be formalized and are made up of sets, in turn: "There is no one: every multiple is a multiple of multiples."[39] Indeed, it is a central insight of set theory that the elements of sets constitute sets themselves, just as there can be no ultimate set of all sets—let alone a set of all "objects"—since, paradoxically, such a set would have to include itself.[40]

Would that mean that using *religion* as the "mark" or "proper name" of the imagined one manifold (or set) of all elements (themselves sets) is already *impossible on formal grounds alone* (regardless of any further historical cautions about the use of this term)? And, if so, should that hold us back from using it at all? Is paradox, not to mention contradiction, allowed in some regions and not in others?

As for collapsing elements into sets and sets into elements of new sets, would this not hold true for all words, things, gestures, powers, and so on, from which we have (axiomatically, if not somewhat arbitrarily) decided to take our lead for strategic reasons? Nowhere is it written in stone that these particulars are more fundamental or central—more elementary or encompassing—than anything else. Moreover, if "religion" extends beyond the numerical, just as it comes before it, naming the void that any numeric division presupposes but never attains—further, if the very terms of the set(s) and subsets of its phenomena (words, things, etc.) are infinitely divisible as so many multiples of multiples—does not all that once seemed solid melt into air? Ought the study of religion not concern more than infinitely substitutable variables?[41] Or is such abstraction—or de-objectivation, here in a subtractive mode—religion's most consistent theme, not just in the West or from the nineteenth century onward?

What descriptive, heuristic, or normative value might such an arithmetic or set-theoretical approach have for the phenomenon or set(s) of phenomena called "religion," whose nature is, we tend to believe, the incalculable and, as Badiou says, supranumerical par excellence? Does set theory confirm this point and invite us to read "religion" as (perhaps, all too concretely) naming the actuality of an infinite set of infinite subsets with their respective infinities—in other words, an infinity of infinite sets, rather than merely conjuring up what was traditionally and dogmatically deemed to exceed the finite order of finite things and their formal equivalents (words, gestures, etc.), namely, the "One"?

Badiou uses the set-theoretical conception precisely to forestall any philosophical appeal to a positive or substantial infinite in terms of "presence," as invoked by traditional metaphysics and natural theology, just as it is taken to undermine every gesture of poetic approximation to an "infinite in the intensity or plenitude of our tangible experience, in our perception of reality, or in our appreciation of nature,"[42] as in Romanticism or the mysticisms of negative theologies.

Refusing both religious transcendence and the aesthetic sublime, the set-theoretical notion of the actual infinite—in Cantor's terminology, of the "trans-" and "supra-finite"—is "subtractive" and hence absolves itself from any empirical or metaphysical given, from presentation or representation, without therefore acquiring any mystic or mysterious aura.[43] "That we are subtractively infinite simply means that what we do as subjects, without any reference to an object, has infinity as its dimension. We are infinite because we think infinitely."[44] We can thus imagine—indeed, Badiou claims, mathematically demonstrate—that there are an infinite number of directions in which we might venture, if we so decide (or from which we could refrain or hold back), at each step along the way and at every corner we turn. On each count—and eluding any "count-as-one" or accountability—taking any such direction would be our call, just as its subjective militancy would require a tenacious, though not rigid, "fidelity" to its proclaimed "event."

Is not our attempt to pluralize and materialize "religion" (which in and by or for itself must remain and name a void) and, moreover, to do so by invoking an open-ended series of words, things, gestures, powers, and so on—each of them sets and classes, and substitutable, in turn—a concrete rendering of the subtractive modus operandi, that is to say, of "thinking infinitely"? Does not our reference to "religion" or the "religious" exemplify how such infinite thought is infused with and inflected by historical and contemporary legacies and contexts, which is not the same as being determined or caused by them? Put differently, could speaking of "religion" and the set(s) of phenomena that gravitate around it—in fact, disseminate from it—*deformalize* set-theoretical insights? But should such deformalization not also be formalized, in turn, time and again, so as to keep options—situations, decisions, events, and the discourses based upon them—open in principle, as they must (and should) be?

Set theory and its postulation of actual infinities allows us to formalize series of substitutions, just as the introduction of the absolute, pure, general, and virtual past, inspired by Henri Bergson and Gilles Deleuze, allows us to intuit the passing present, together with its actualization of recollection. Moreover, set theory enables us to conceive the infinite, not as the one-and-all that is the prerogative of a divine mind or transcendent metaphysics, but as the very logic of the prevalence of the multiple over the one. It allows us to imagine "different *sizes* of infinity," by "demonstrating the existence of different numbers of infinity."[45]

This innovation, Badiou suggests, leads to a conceptual revolution and a "laicization" of the infinite. As Peter Hallward notes, this puts "a consequent end to the Romantic or Heideggerian investment of finitude. In the wake of Cantor's invention, it is the finite that must be defined as a derivative limitation of the infinite, and not the other way around."[46] Such "laicization" implies a clear "decision that opts for the multiple over the one," a decision that is "the condition for a truly modern (or 'post-theological') ontology, an ontology pursued in the absence of any One beyond being."[47] In other words, the affirmation that "all situations are infinite" is for Badiou an "axiom" or an "axiomatic" and a decidedly "modern conviction," which is "impossible to deduce."[48] As he claims, it is simply

> better to think that all situations are infinite. Because we come after a long period in which the theme of finitude and the conviction that all situations are finite was dominant. . . . The ethics of thinking today is to say that it is better to think that all situations are infinite, that it is very difficult to reduce a situation to finite parameters. . . . It constitutes a rupture to say that situations are infinite and that human life is infinite and that we are infinite. . . . It is more interesting and more attuned to the necessity of the times than declaring that we are finite and that all is finite, we are mortal being, being for death and so on. We are being-for-the-infinite.[49]

To declare this means countering a long tradition "marked by theological thinking" and substituting for it "the only rational thinking of infinity," which is mathematics, in a "faithfulness to Cantor" that is "not yet accomplished."[50] To opt for the thought of infinity, for "infinite thought," means axiomatically, categorically, *deciding* to do so—indeed, as our, more precisely, my *call*—and requires a fidelity to what it is better for us to believe, on all counts, yet exceeds all calculation. Everything here hinges on the "pure act of nomination," the "pure utterance of the arbitrariness of a proper name," the "*excendentary choice of a proper name*," which is operative in all opting for infinity, as well as in our declaring being, the pure multiple, a void (which, in Badiou's account, is strangely—enigmatically—unique, which is to say, not a nothing and even less so the One, to which traditional ontologies of presence have given so much prominence).[51]

One could draw an analogy between numbers, classes, and sets—which designate a certain commonality while remaining categorically distinct from what they gather—and the Wittgensteinian sense of "family resemblance," as if the former were the formal write-up of the latter. (Wittgenstein would not have accepted this surmise, and Badiou vehemently refuses it.[52])

Badiou, moreover, would enable us to theorize and formalize that "the consistency of a multiple does not depend upon the particular multiples whose multiple it is."[53] Put differently: "The making-up-a-multiple (the 'holding-together' as Cantor used to say), ultimate structured figure of presentation, maintains itself as such, even if everything from which it is composed is replaced."[54] Set theory is an insistence on the "operational permanence" of this "bond—multiple in itself, devoid of any specification of what it binds together."[55] In this view, only the very idea of the "bond"—not the worst translation of *religio*—would be "incorruptible."[56] Or at least insofar as the order of natural things and, more broadly, situations, is concerned, all of which, in their very possibility and existence, are "numbered" in Badiou's ontology.

We are reminded also of Derrida's repeated invocation of numbers, especially of the formula $n + 1$, as well as that of *plus d'un*, the "more or no more than one," which implies a similar structure.

All these thinkers, with their different backgrounds and overall aims, draw our attention to the importance of numbers and to the logic governing their relation or combination—in the study of "religion" in its phenomenality.[57] Many among them argue that numbers reveal something about the structure of the real—of "being" and "events"—and hence have ontological pertinence. Yet few would go so far as Badiou in equating ontology and mathematics.[58]

In his more cautious moments, Badiou writes that his "thesis" does "not in any way declare that being is mathematical, which is to say composed of mathematical objectivities. It is not a thesis about the world but about discourse. It affirms that mathematics, throughout the entirety of its historical becoming, pronounces what is expressible of being qua being."[59] In other words, Badiou's "metaontological thesis" is that mathematics is "the historicity of the discourse of being qua being."[60] With much less reticence, however, Badiou goes on to explain that this interpretation of both ontology and mathesis, in their intrinsic relationship, is decidedly Greek in origin and should not be confused with just any linguistic expression to be found there.[61]

But is an inferential model of reasoning—and a fortiori a mathematically deductive one (even or especially in its post-Cantorian infinitist variety), based on "the most rigid of all conceivable laws, the law of demonstrative and formalizable inference"[62]—the sole option we have to capture what is sayable, discursively or otherwise? Moreover, can "religion" be a subset of ontology as Badiou understands it? Does it constitute a separate and parallel domain of equal importance next to science and politics, art and love?[63] Or could it be claimed with equal right that "religion"—or, in any case, some of its central tropes, such as the "miracle" and "Christ-event"—captures the very structure and movement of the ontological, of being and the event? If this is so, then "religion" is no worse off than, say, "philosophy."[64] Like mathematics, "religion" might be, historically speaking, one of the *"symptoms"* or vectors with whose strategic and always provisional help one might broach the "meta-ontological" question (which, we now know, neither "philosophy" nor even "ontology" can resolve on its own).[65]

In sum, then, not merely the number of members, believers, and practitioners is crucial to the mathematics of "religion." It continues to circle around numbers: the one god among, versus, or substituting for the many, the commandments boiling down to ten, then one, the dogma of the Trinity complicating the already daunting theologoumenon of the two natures of Christ (the *homoousios*), the "Where two or three gather in my name, I am there among them" (Matt. 18:20), the Jewish *minyan*, the number of pages in the Talmud, the mysticism of numbers in the Kabbalah.

In all these domains, the question of number is one of calculation, in more than one sense, expressing how many differentiations a doctrine, practice, or life must minimally and/or maximally contain so as to be worthy of the name. Hovering between *philia* and *filiation*, religion obeys a logic like that Derrida traces in *Politics of Friendship*: its community (like its lists of commandments, doctrines, practices, rites, sacraments, sacred places, relics, etc.) must compose itself of *more* than one ($n + 1$), while limiting its number at the same time. Just as one can presumably not be friends with everyone, neither simultaneously nor consecutively, one has difficulty imagining "religion" as being ultimately as all-inclusive as it often presents itself. Even in its radically universalistic, teleological, and eschatological scenarios of the redemption of all by the One, it operates necessarily with a "holy rest" and does not shy away from excluding or banning many from its midst, making countless victims along the way.

Quomodo: What Modes and Modalities Does "Religion" Adopt; or, How Is One to Go About It Methodically?

Theorizing offers an invitation to realize the semantic, axiological, figurative, rhetorical, and pragmatic complexity of the "religious" phenomenon, the fact that it is made up of incalculable sets of phenomena, each characterized by different senses, sensibilities, affects, and effects, expressed in varying idioms, imageries, and dispositions, together with their irreducible materiality, their ever-more mediatized performances, and their now troubling then promising shades of authority and sovereignty, of powers and emypowerments.

An at once micrological and integral approach to "religion" in its recent manifestations requires not only interdisciplinary collaboration among specialists but the negotiation of their scholarly findings with insights and concerns of the wider political culture in which it plays itself out. The phenomenon "religion" remains palpable underneath (and well beyond) the exponential growth and rise in intensity of the multiple set(s) of phenomena that we associate with it. It is today's "purloined letter," invisible because in plain view, caught up in a dialectic of minimal differences with maximal impacts, as well as of maximal differences with minimal effects.

How and when was "religion" as a distinctive yet multifaceted category first brought to bear upon modern experience, shaping its hopes and fears and projecting a normative aspiration and normalizing self-image well beyond its original context? How and when was "religion" emancipated from its Latin etymologies (*religio, religare*), with their rural and cultic associations, to become an all-encompassing epistemic regime, with expansive force—not to mention imperialist, colonial, and orientalist ambitions—whose political and cultural consequences continue to haunt us? What gave this concept its coherence and sheer force? Why did "faith" and "belief," their interiorization and systematization, succeed in turning a historically contingent representationalist and mentalist regime into the *pars pro toto* for all (past, present, and future) "religion" worthy of the name?

As Tomoko Masuzawa has forcefully demonstrated, in her seminal *The Invention of World Religions*, there are good reasons to question the integrity or even definitional intelligibility of the term *religion* as it was deployed—and effectively invented—in nineteenth-century European academic discourse. The concept of "world religions," she argues, paradoxically enabled a notion of European universalism to be "preserved in the language of pluralism," as if dealing with an ultimately unified field of meaning, an ontological, existential, and social constant, regardless of the de facto diversity of cultural manifestations whose identity with "religion" was taken for granted. This was, she writes:

> a rather monumental assumption that is as pervasive as it is unexamined, namely, that religion is a universal, or at least ubiquitous, phenomenon . . . albeit it in a wide variety of forms and with different degrees of prevalence and importance. . . . It is presumed, moreover, that religion is one of the most significant—possibly the most significant—factors characterizing each individual society, and this is particularly true in "premodern" or otherwise non-Western societies. Broadly speaking, the more "traditional" the society, the greater the role religion plays within it.[66]

Masuzawa sets out to scrutinize the disciplinary—and disciplining—"discursive formation" to which the modern invention of the concept of "world religions" and, fundamentally, of "religion" has led. She interrogates how it has come "to acquire the kind of overwhelming sense of objective reality, concrete facticity, and utter self-evidence that now holds us in its sway." With a wealth of historical detail, she substantiates her claim that the study of "religion" (as a concept and theme, object and field) must be situated against a larger background of imperial no less than missionary interests and hegemonies.

I would speculate, however, that an additional, deeper-seated human need must be assumed to explain the historical, indeed, ontological weight and persistence of the conventions, vocabularies, and habits of thought that first invented, then established "religion" or "world religions." Indeed, focusing on such conventions and vocabularies may restrict, if not obstruct, our comprehension of an evolving subject of massive proportions.

Indeed, before we aspire to dismantle and discard these historical suppositions, layer after layer, a certain proviso is in order. Masuzawa ends her study by urging precisely such caution:

> Today, self-consciously secularist scientists of religion tend to identify the persistence of Christian ideology as the foremost problem in the field of religious studies: not enough cleansing of the past legacy, and too much fresh infusion of religiously motivated interests. . . . If we are serious in our critical intention, the exorcism of an undead Christian absolutism would not suffice. Instead, criticism calls for something far more laborious, tedious, and difficult: a rigorous historical investigation that does not surreptitiously yield to the comforting belief in the liberating power of "historical consciousness."[67]

In the end, then, perhaps the work of historical scholarship and interpretation cannot sufficiently guard against its own inevitable self-deception. But, then, what does? While Masuzawa's book delivers many of the analytical tools for rethinking the inception, conception, and consolidation of "religion" as a field of study, an open question remains: parodying Heideggerian parlance, could we say that "religion" (rather than "Being") remains the "unthought"—the doxa and dogma—of the modern?

With these warnings in mind, should we ask whether the conventions and vocabularies of old, with their presumed comparabilities, can be put in a broader and more unsettling genealogical perspective and counternarrative—call it a virtual history or *a history of virtuality*—that can assign them a crucial, fateful, but also temporally and spatially limited role and thus "provincialize"[68] their European universalist pretense?[69] Could one successfully turn the tables on this modern doxa, which supposes not only the coherence of certain doctrines (notably, theism) but also the assuredness of what are in fact contingent historical outcomes? Should one not challenge the very concept of "religion" or "world religions" by claiming that the more "modern" (rationalized, differentiated, privatized, even secularized) societies become, the greater the *possible* and *virtual* role of "religion" and its successor forms, its "varieties," will be? Well beyond its Protestant coinage as a set of interiorized, systematized propositional attitudes or beliefs, religion may have entered a phase of "deprivatization," as José Casanova has argued. Indeed, our age, without having exited from "religion," may turn out to be characterized by "post-theism," as H. J. Adriaanse has suggestively claimed.

Ironically, the invention of "religion" might tell us less about non-Western, "traditional" societies than about the "future" of a religious "past," whose features were misidentified or misconstrued through a *backwardly directed projection* by European scholars, both Christian and secular, who in part created, in part interiorized, the Protestant doxa of "religion qua faith" (or of "theology qua belief system") and merely flipped its epistemic claims, asserting its falsity or unverifiability, rather than its truth. In this reading, these scholars could be seen as having written and anticipated the history of *a putative future*, rather than as having documented a historical past. They may have both proactively and retroactively construed an object of study on the basis of what was first a misapprehended present. Unfortunately, such lack of perceptiveness and general awareness, more than ill will, have abounded in more than one specialization, as has now been shown by recent scholarship on the tenacious Western and often Romantic preconceptions in the study of Islam, Buddhism, Hinduism, and New Age religion.[70]

Yet, when all is said and done, the question is still open as to *whether, how, and why—to what effect, in whose interests, and with what perils and chances*—"religion," as a concept or beyond a given concept, is (or could have been or has once again become) meaningful. This applies not just culturally and existentially, but also legally, politically, ethically, aesthetically, economically, and globally speaking. "Religion" (and everything that comes to substitute for it) affects the ways in which people conceive of "life," of its "way of life" no less than its life world or form of life, its aspirations toward a fuller or fully human life, or, for that matter, to the true life or life hereafter.

Qui: Who Speaks and Is Answerable to "Religion" and in What Ways? or, How Does Someone or Something Matter in Matters "Religious"?

In *The Claim of Reason*, Stanley Cavell puts his finger on the whole difficulty of the linguistic nomination and predication of concepts, terms, or ideas, notably, the "disappointment of criteria" or lack of "rules" by which they are characterized. Above all, he focuses on the (in his view, deeply problematic) distinction between "knowing *what* a thing is (by means of criteria) and knowing *that* it is."[71]

Knowing *what* a thing is involves identifying an object of knowledge and recognizing it via "marks," "features," or "capacities."[72] Knowing *that* it is regards its existence (its "position" or being "posited," as Kant said; its "positivity," as Hegel added). The distinction is that between the *quid* and *quod* aspects of a phenomenon, which determines—but hardly exhausts—the general difficulty involved in *any* attribution of names and concepts. That this extrapolation is far from arbitrary has been argued by Avishai Margalit and

Moshe Halbertal, who in *Idolatry* establish a close connection between, on the one hand, the biblical prohibition of images, blasphemy, and Maimonides' insistence on negative theological argument and, on the other, the seemingly atheological discussions of logic and semantics in Wittgenstein and Saul Kripke.[73] The structure of knowledge and acknowledgment, the logic of question and answer, address and redress, the giving and taking of reasons, all stand under the aegis of a paradigm of thought, action, judgment, and affect that we tend to baptize "religion," for lack of a better name.

But, as Cavell shows, "religion" is nothing (worth mentioning or worthwhile) in and of itself. It is, as Levinas reminds us in his talmudic lectures, the proverbial chunk of coal that flames up only when we blow upon it—pressing our very spirit up against it. We or, rather, I—and nothing or nobody else—give it the inspiration that, in a second breath, I take from it again, following a rhythm of exhalation and inhalation that, as Levinas knew, punctuates the very life of the mind, of spirituality, just as it characterizes the life of the body, in its very materiality.

"Religion," in Cavell's view, is what we are willing and able to take it to be. Its features and actual existence (for us) will depend on the stakes we are willing and able to grant them. Its import and "importance" can be found only in how we let it matter to us, in the ways we think and act, judge and feel, eat and drink, work and relax, engage and disengage, live and let live, grow up and die. "Religion"—like any other "thing," but also like any "being" in its very "existence" and "essence"—is *our call*, that is to say, nothing but (or beyond) what we claim, proclaim, or acclaim as its name and concept, its uses and abuses, its meaning and end.

What can be gleaned from Cavell's discussion of criteria in our acquisition and application of concepts—especially from his "excursus" on what he calls the Wittgensteinian "vision of language"—is the further circumstance that there is no easily determinable (let alone given or prima facie) limit to the uses to which we may put any number of names or concepts (e.g., "religion"), just as there is no given range of locutions (whether propositions or, say, promises) in which such terms can appear. Not that anything goes, for different contexts will "invite," "tolerate," or "allow" certain uses of language and forbid others. But no strict criterion, no formalizable rule, prejudges such possibilities *in advance* or *once and for all*. The felicity of expressions will depend on our "mutual attunements," on what both Wittgenstein and Heidegger call an *Übereinstimmung*, that is to say, on a certain "acceptance"[74] of the world with its "things" and the "acknowledgment" of others (that is to say, "other minds" or human "beings") in it:

> If words and phrases *must* recur (which means . . . that they must be projected into new contexts, which means that new contexts must tolerate or invite that projection); and if there are no rules or universals which *insure* appropriate projection, but only our confirmed capacity to speak to one another; then a new projection, though not

at first obviously appropriate, may be made appropriate by giving relevant explanations of how it is to be taken, *how* the new context *is* an instance of the old concept. If we are to communicate, we mustn't leap too far; but how far is too far?[75]

Now, in talking about "religion" as I have proposed to do in the preceding pages, have I projected and leapt too far or not far enough? Have I strayed from its path, pushed things too far, been too nominalistic, too lax, too playful, too serious? In short, have I been failing to address what "religion"—the word and concept—means (historically, semantically) or should mean (normatively, stipulatively, ostentatiously, pragmatically), changing the subject along the way? Have I wagered a quid pro quo—a false substitution and metaphorization or allegorization—that leaves us empty-handed and dumbfounded? But is that not, precisely, what "religion" tends to do?

The truth—indeed, the "truth and moral" of modern "skepticism," as Cavell says—is that there is no (a priori, firm, and final) answer to that question, that any invocation of "criteria" will always disappoint us, and that we must take responsibility for the meaning(s) we assign or take for granted, accept or acknowledge. This being so, what can—or do—we do?

As in moral argument, when prompted or challenged to provide a maxim of conduct in performing, condoning, or condemning an act, what may be called for are "elaboratives" (stories and allegories), which explain or justify the position taken and hence the ways we have ourselves become (or have made ourselves) effectively known in acknowledging, avoiding, or annihilating others. Yet there are contingent limits to such elaborations of where we stand, in claiming or reclaiming—in each case, projecting—a meaning for what we say, leaping from one acceptance of words (things, gestures, powers) to, we hope, the next. Whether we succeed depends entirely on us. Again, in Cavell's words: "We have freedom, but we are also subject to the same requirement of all projection, that its appropriateness be made out in terms of the invitation to projection by the context."[76] How do we "know" that this is so? The response Cavell gives is twofold: strictly speaking, we don't, since the question allows no answer in simple epistemic or broadly criteriological terms. But there is another sense in which we just do "know" how to go on, in an acceptance of the world—ultimately, for love of the world—and in acknowledgment of others, neither of which is, again, based upon criteria (especially not upon criteria of an epistemic nature).

How, then, are we to understand the "elaborative" conversation of those whose (mutual?) acknowledgment succeeds in forming a common moral world, however provisionally? What are moral reasons? Do religious arguments—say, having words, including friendly disputes, dogmatic apologetics, benign or aggressive proselytizing, ecumenism or syncretism, even alleged or deliberate idolatries and blasphemies—form part of the articulation of such reasons? Or do they make up a category on their own, governed by their own proper procedures, codes, or canons?

What "hope"—albeit a "hope against hope"—can we still hold out for such reasons' less than foundational, and less than teleological, constitutive or regulative role, under the conditions of modernity, in upholding the promise of all rational argumentation to reach agreement (as Cavell seems at times to suggest they must and can do, though not necessarily through the "force of the better argument," as Habermas would have it)? *The Claim of Reason* proposes several answers.

One motif in this book relates the modern philosophical obsession with skeptical worries concerning "the problem of the other"—now taken more generally to mean either "things," that is to say, material objects; or "beings," that is to say, other minds of a human nature—to be a "spiritual" aspiration, indeed, a "hope against hope." Despite our finite condition, expressed by the inevitable disappointment with criteria, such aspiration is seen as culminating in a "love of the world," which expresses our nonepistemic, noncriteriological way of knowing "How to be surprised *that* there is a world,"[77] as well as our way of receiving that world, its others (whether of matter or mind), with its society and soul, birth and rebirth, initiation and education, confession and conversion, and to do so in a mode and mood of acceptance and acknowledgment that remains alien to quietism, shunning therapeutic no less than critical affectations.

What Cavell writes of the "problem of the other," more precisely, of "other minds," holds true for "religion" as well. While at moments he suggests that religion can be seen, as it is in part by Kant, as "the most famous field of the irrational," characterized by "a particular distortion of human reason," namely, "fanaticism, superstition, delusion, and sorcery,"[78] in *The Claim of Reason* he mentions, in passing, another tendency. Just as science may revert to magic, a certain dialectic of Enlightenment allows "religion" to switch from the sidelines back to center stage. This tendency parallels an eventual upsurge of another source of "religion," this time from the depths of a virtual, absolute, or pure past, which allows it to emerge as a force to be reckoned with in the present and in the novelties that a future may unfold. In consequence, "religion" is the undetermined—and undeterminable. It can adopt different masks in different ways, and one can never be sure that its role has been definitively played out or is the one that the educated public had hoped to reserve for it. As Cavell observes: "Nowadays it is good form to behave as though all prophets and messiahs *must* be false (while at the same time it can hardly ever have been truer that no one giving himself or herself out as a prophet is without a following)."[79]

Cavell further invokes "religion" to characterize a theoretical impasse that he seeks to avoid or, rather, to restate. He notes that "passive skepticism," that is, the circumstance "that I cannot perfectly make myself known," in a certain sense "repeats the condition of prophecy—the singular knowledge of an unquestionable truth which others are fated not to believe."[80] A religious motif, tied in modernity to a certain "esotericism," thus inserts itself at the very heart of the skeptical "recitals" tied to the problem of "the other," including the other that I can be or become to myself, whose origin and referent is as dauntingly (sublimely and terrifyingly) unknown "as God."

Cavell concludes that the two varieties of modern skepticism—skepticism concerning external objects or the external world, and skepticism concerning other minds—entertain radically different concerns with the "spiritual":

> What is the worst that befalls me should it be the case that material objects do not exist? I suffer a generalized *trompe l'oeil*, and of course *trompe l'oreille* as well, and so on; my senses (and what they sense?) cheat me . . . into taking it that there are things when there are only interpreted sensings. . . . But if there are no other human beings, then what befalls me is a generalized and massive *trompe l'âme*; my soul (and what it wishes?) cheats me . . . into taking it that it has company.[81]

It is nothing short of a "biological demand," Cavell asserts, that we cannot live the first skepticism without going insane. Yet it is a "spiritual demand"[82] that, in our dealings with others, we always allow for the possibility—if not strictly speaking, the reality or actuality—of the second. Others remain—indeed, they *must* as well as *ought* to remain—"separate" and, to that extent, unavailable in principle. This is a necessity no less than a command.[83]

Cavell takes "religion" to hinge on the most intimate aspirations and intimations—call them the hopes and horrors—surrounding our nonepistemic awareness of our own finite natures:

> When the development of reason started producing explanations for the occurrence of religion, say as motivated by fear, then it was comparatively easy to imagine that the human race would one day overcome this fear, as if it were a product of the childishness of the race. But suppose that what motivates religion is (also) horror, a response not to the powers and uncertainties of nature but to the powers and uncertainties of others not wholly unlike oneself, so that the promise of religion is not the maintenance of one's existence but the survival of one's intactness.[84]

The worry here lies in the realization of the possibility that we ourselves are (for others as well as for ourselves). The infinities with which "religions" deal are but dots on the *i* of finitude, the highlighting and silver lining—or, on the contrary, the bracketing and obfuscation—of the ordinary and the everyday. "Religion's" genuine mood is that of "horror" (a *horror religiosus*, as Kierkegaard has it), a sensibility that signals confrontation with the permanent possibility of our human nature's being "abrogated,"[85] that is to say, cut short or, while still living, becoming frozen, petrified, buried. "Religion" teaches us what this means—and, perhaps, how to avoid it (or how, when the unavoidable happens, to deal with its consequences, that is to say, with untruth, guilt, alienation, false consciousness, inauthenticity, bad faith, and hypocrisy, which may be another way of saying, with Saint Paul, living the "life of the flesh" and standing "under the law").

But what, exactly, does this mean? What is human? What, in essence, is horror? Cavell defines the latter on two occasions, tying its experience to our sense of being—or being possibly no longer—human:

> If only humans feel horror (if the capacity to feel horror is a development of the specifically human biological inheritance), then maybe it is a response specifically to being human. To what, specifically, about being human? Horror is the title I am giving to the perception of the precariousness of human identity, to the perception that it may be lost or invaded, that we may be, or may become, something other than we are, or take ourselves for; that our origins as human beings need accounting for, and are unaccountable.[86]

A little further he writes, borrowing from the idiom of religion: "The lower limit upon humanity is marked by the passage into inhumanity. Its signal is horror. The opposite of terror is the calm of safety; the opposite of horror would be the bliss of salvation. *Is* there this opposite? Is there an upper limit on humanity? If there is, how would I know I had reached it?"[87]

There is no a priori, firm, or final answer to these questions. I might have to live—"I live my skepticism,"[88] as Cavell says so often—without ever knowing for sure whether others (or I myself) have transgressed an undeterminable limit toward "pure spiritualization" or "pure corporealization, or rather animalization."[89] Moreover, I might never be certain whether the "beings" I encounter are not in fact—or, rather, ontologically speaking—mere "mutations," "perfected automatons," "zombies," "androids," "angels," "aliens of another kidney," "humanish somethings," "non-human beings," or "human non-beings," that is to say, "things," which are neither animated nor embodied, but have become completely materialized, *"wholly* a body."[90] I may never be able to determine with any satisfaction—whether intuitively, immediately, or with epistemic criteria and procedural rules—whether I have not myself become one (or, perhaps, was one all along).

The ground for such concerns stems not from abstract theoretical reflection, undertaken by philosophers meditating in their studies, in isolation from the world and from others: "it is not a skeptical worry, not something beyond the field of everyday life."[91] But the demarcation between the two domains—philosophy and the ordinary—may not be so strict, even in Cavell's own account. In the Cartesian scene, we find the philosopher sitting "in his dressing gown, seated before his fire, in which he is alone and in which, as befits the influence of a private fire, he is already in semi-reverie."[92] He abstracts from an everyday life shared with others, in an introspective monologue that strips him of all that is learned from parents and tradition, through the senses, in short, all attunement and agreement, all commerce and conversation, acknowledgment and avoidance. The philosophical problem must therefore be reformulated by asking: "where does the assumption come from according to which I must have correctly identified you as a human being?

From some such fact as that my identification of you as a human being is not merely an identification *of* you but *with* you. This is something more than *seeing* you. Call it emphatic projection."[93]

Should we approach "religion," or at least its singular mental states, propositional attitudes, performative acts, and cultural practices—that is, its words, things, sounds, silences, smells, touches, shapes, colors, gestures, powers, affects, and effects—any differently? Of course, one can go wrong in all "projection," including an "emphatic" one. It is, Cavell surmises, "not irrational"[94] to assume that some putative others—or "humanish somethings"—do not warrant full attribution of the predicate "humanity." The objection that even to entertain such a thought is irrational, "positively medieval," comparable to the belief that inspired "witch trials,"[95] misses the point. The relevant question is: "how it is that we have recovered from such outbreaks of irrationality, which dot the religious history, i.e., the history of the Judeo-Christian world."[96]

Ultimately, according to Cavell, there is no proof, no epistemic certainty, no criteriological knowledge, no scientific paradigm, in short, no method or rule, that can help us settle the matter as to where "religion" begins and where, if ever, it stops. Roughly situated between myth and science fiction, philosophy and literature, tragedy and comedy, drama and cinematography, the ordinary and the extraordinary, "religion" makes incursions—or is invaded—on all sides. Indeed, "religion" might be the very name for the transgression of domains—discourses or disciplines—a horizontal or lateral transcendence, of sorts, a now centrifugal, then centripetal movement in which each constellation or configuration of elements and forms (of words, things, gestures, powers, etc.) circles at an equal remove from an imagined center (whether a mystic absence, a saturated phenomenon, or a black hole).

Quando: "What Do We Assume When . . ."; or, The Explicit Implicitness of Religion, Radically Interpreted

Cavell's conception parallels—but, in my view, corrects and refines—relevant insights of the "radical interpretation of religion" in analytic or postanalytic philosophy. Here—as in Cavell's interpretation of Wittgenstein's "vision of language" and the everyday, enriched by Austin's "linguistic phenomenology" of the ordinary life of performative and (Cavell adds) "passionate" utterances—"religion," like any other "claim" that can be advanced, is seen primarily as "a form of linguistic behaviour."[97]

As Nancy Frankenberry points out, the concept of "radical interpretation," taking its inspiration from the writings of Donald Davidson, but also from the later Wittgenstein and from the tradition of pragmatism (from C. S. Peirce, William James, and John Dewey, through Richard Rorty, up to Robert Brandom), offers interesting clues to how best to approach the complex phenomenon or, rather, set(s) of phenomena called "religion."

This school of thought, she suggests, helps us explain why "religion," being a simultaneously under- and overdetermined concept, covers a multidimensional field, in which the most diverse intensities, intentionalities, and intentionless natural causes—mental states, processes, attitudes, beliefs, desires, volitions, actions, performances, expressions—reverberate and vie for meaning. In particular, "radical interpretation" helps us understand how it is that such beliefs, actions, and expressions—rather than, say, the perceptual experience of basic particulars, rendered by propositional statements—are the locus and vehicles of the words, things, gestures, powers, sounds, silences, smells, touches, shapes, colors, affects, and effects around which "religion" revolves.

These elements and forms do not correspond to reality in a *representational* way (as had been claimed starting with the emergence of modern epistemology in seventeenth- and eighteenth-century rationalism and empiricism, and had become the dominant "dogma," to use W. V. O. Quine's term, for twentieth-century analytical, positivist, cognitivist, and computational views). Nor do they establish some truth and objectivity by *cohering* among themselves (as seems, at times, to have been advocated by Davidson or especially by Rorty). They neither *mirror* the world as it is, nor do they designate "what is better for us to believe," without any further reason given. Their claims upon us—and our claiming, proclaiming, and acclaiming them—allow and invite (indeed, require) additional things to be said and believed or assumed: things whose nature is mostly implicit, which is not to suggest that they cannot in principle be made explicit or expressed.

Where does this leave the study of "religion"? In Frankenberry's words:

> To many investigators, the phenomenon of religion resembles a petri dish brimming with exotic specimens and puzzling data. Viewed under the microscope, it teems with strange cultures. Even to a trained eye, the study of religion—its structure, persistence, and meaning—poses acute interpretative challenges. Until recently, students of religion usually regarded their work as a matter of uncovering beliefs and worldviews that issue in religious behavior. Interpretation followed representationalist models, of one kind or another, that presumed realist correspondences between language and reality. Currently, however, both the category of "belief" and the act of "interpretation" are receiving critical attention by scholars in such areas as anthropology of religion, ritual studies, cognitive psychology, semantics, post-analytic philosophy, history of religions, and philosophy of religion.[98]

Joining forces, these methodologically diverse approaches have raised "doubts about the utility of 'belief' as an ethnological or analytic category."[99] What emerges are the contours of a "radical interpretation" in which the very "concept" of "religion" dispenses with the centrality of all its traditional and modern ideational, notional, concept-based, psychologistic, idealist, in short, representationalist associations.

Instead, the newly advocated approach stresses "religion's" broadly pragmatic, idiomatic, rhetorical, material, and corporeal features (embodied, again, in words, things, gestures, powers, etc.), whose elements inhabit forms of life and social practices, even down to motor responses. All of these, so the argument continues, are carried by a *web of suppositions*, few of which can be laid out in axioms, principles, and propositions and for which neither (formal) logic nor (physical) science can offer appropriate tools, that is to say, the right—call them "radical"—interpretative keys. What is at issue, then, is a widely shared sense that we must "move away from older models of representation and symbolic expression to holistic ways of thinking about the interrelation of language, meaning, beliefs, desires, and action."[100]

Proponents of radical interpretation assume no metaphysical or ontological privilege or *proprium* for "the religious" but instead inscribe its meaning and function within general patterns of overall human behavior: "Far from treating religion as a *sui generis* phenomenon, they assume that whatever explains how language and minds work generally explains how religious language and religious minds work."[101] This avoidance of the supernatural might make them seem "naturalistic."

Brandom, whose philosophical project rests upon similar claims, refuses this epithet of "naturalism," however, and everything it stands for (mechanicism, materialism, scientism, in short, reductionism). He replaces it with a strictly "normative" (a "conceptual" or "rationalist") pragmatics.[102] I would like to spell out this approach in a few broad strokes, not least because, like Cavell's philosophical project, it seems especially promising in offering ingredients for a theory of "religion" that can keep the disputed term and concept, as well as its historical reference and object(s), in play while redirecting our gaze to the most tangible elements (words, things, gestures, powers, etc.), including the most reasonable forms—claims, assertions, attitudes, and beliefs—in which they are expressed. It is here that they become "posited" and "positive," acquire a "second nature" (to use a Hegelian idiom, adopted by both Brandom and his colleague John McDowell), or form part and parcel of a *dispositif* (to cite Foucault, as read by Giorgio Agamben).

Both Rorty and Jeffrey Stout have provided elements for elaborating a "holist" and "inferentialist" approach, which can help us make a case for such a "radical interpretation of religion."[103] Drawing on Brandom's *Making It Explicit*, they claim that the study of "religion" should be reconceived in a pragmatist perspective that would depart once and for all from the understanding of "beliefs" and "belief systems" in terms of their perceptual and propositional content, representing a potentially supra-natural world of objects and rooted in a theologically structured ontology (or, as Heidegger would say, onto-theology) of our own making.

Rorty highlights how the background of *Making It Explicit* includes Willard Sellars's preparation, in *Empiricism and the Philosophy of Mind*, of a "post-positivistic" analytic philosophy that could be said to venture "'beyond' empiricism and rationalism" by ushering academic philosophy "out of its Humean and into its Kantian" or, more exactly,

"Hegelian stage."[104] In tune with Peter Strawson's characterization of Wittgenstein's *Philosophical Investigations* via its relentless "hostility to immediacy"—and announcing a strikingly dialectical and more broadly German Idealist note—Sellars's essay is guided by a single "fundamental thought": Kant's central insight, in the *Critique of Pure Reason*, that "intuitions without concepts are blind."[105] In Sellars's own idiom: "*all* awareness of *sorts, resemblances, facts*, etc., in short all awareness of abstract entities—indeed, all awareness even of particulars—is a linguistic affair."[106] Sellars calls this conception, somewhat confusingly, "*psychological nominalism*" to distinguish it from the "phenomenalism" of modern and early-twentieth-century empiricism (from Hume to A. J. Ayer),[107] though it strikes a chord with certain aspects of Husserl's and Heidegger's view of phenomenology as well as with Austin's conception of a "linguistic phenomenology."

"Psychological nominalism" names a conception of knowledge that is radically opposed to the psychologism of classical modern epistemology, as well as the philosophy of logic, language, and mind that governed the positivistic phase of analytic philosophy, from the early reception of Vienna Circle logical empiricism in the 1930s until popularized the 1950s by Ayer, in *Language, Truth, and Logic*. The metaphysics and semantics implied in these views can be characterized as *representationalism*.[108] In what sense does Sellars believe that this conception distorts our view of experience, language, and the role of concepts?

Rorty cites and comments upon Sellars's central claim:

"The essential point is that in characterizing an episode or a state as that of *knowing*, we are not giving an empirical description of that episode or state; we are placing it in the logical space of reasons, of justifying and being able to justify what one says." . . . In other words, knowledge is inseparable from a social practice—the practice of justifying one's assertions to one's fellow-humans. It is not presupposed by this practice, but comes into being along with it.

So we cannot do what some logical positivists hoped to do: analyze epistemic facts without remainder "into non-epistemic facts, whether phenomenal or behavorial, public or private." . . . In particular, we cannot perform such an analysis by discovering the "foundation" of empirical knowledge in the objects of "direct acquaintance," objects which are "immediately before the mind." . . . "Empiricism and the Philosophy of Mind" helped destroy the empiricist form of foundationalism by attacking the distinction between what is "given to the mind" and what is "added by the mind."[109]

For Sellars, Rorty notes, there is no "archē beyond discourse."[110] In his self-described "*Méditations Hegeliènnes*," Sellars seeks to combine the Kantian insight that "intuitions without concepts are blind" with those of "that great foe of immediacy," Hegel, so as to liberate philosophy from the central assumption that the British empiricists had naïvely accepted from Descartes: namely, "the habit of asking whether mind ever succeeds in making unmediated contact with world, and remaining skeptical about the status of knowledge-claims until such contact can be shown to exist."[111] This mentalist and representationalist position, codified and systematized by Descartes, Locke, and Hume—and implicitly adopted by most of their twentieth-century heirs in logical empiricism and phenomenalism and, more recently, in certain computational models in the philosophy of mind and cognitive science—should be contrasted with what Brandom, following an alternative tradition running from Leibniz and Kant through Frege to Sellars, works out as an *inferentialist* and *normative pragmatist* program. In Rorty's summary: "The former take concepts to be representations (or putative representations) of reality rather than, as Kant did, rules which specify how something is to be done. Kant's fundamental insight, Brandom says, 'is that judgments and actions are to be understood to begin with in terms of the special way in which we are *responsible* for them.'"[112] Our "answerability to the world," more than any concern with a "mirroring," "picturing," and "representing" of—or "correspondence" with—the nature of reality as it is in itself is at stake in any endeavor to know, whether we realize and acknowledge this or not. No such "answerability" or "acknowledging" can "emerge" in an isolated subject. "Inferentialism," like Davidson's "radical interpretation," with its insistence on "triangulation," thus requires a break with solipsism, together with its epistemic analogon in representationalism. "Answerability" requires interaction and responsiveness between at least two subjects over something in the world.

Such responsibility culminates in what Rorty calls "prope-Hegelianism" and what Brandom himself baptizes more prosaically as "social self-consciousness," in other words, as "the complete and explicit interpretive equilibrium exhibited by a community whose members adopt the explicit discursive stance toward each other."[113] Such a view, Rorty goes on to explain, inaugurates a new appreciation of some of the central tenets of German Idealism—implying nothing short of a world-historical vision, reminiscent not only of Kant's "Project for a Universal History with Cosmopolitan Intent" but also Hegel's *Phenomenology of Spirit*.[114]

Here we are in close company with some of the main sources of Jürgen Habermas's work, which, in complementary ways, ushered German Idealism and Critical Theory into its "analytic" and then "post-analytic" (more precisely, formal-pragmatic) phases, also giving voice to a ubiquitous late-twentieth-century linguistic, postlinguistic, and communicative turn. This turn, albeit not without difficulties of its own, sought to articulate reasons that might motivate a discursive "give and take," edging toward a putative—and always hypothetical, fallible, mutable, in short, provisional—resolution. It attempted to envision a genuine ontological pluralism, together with its institutional (e.g., juridico-political and radically democratic) analogues within the perspective of a nonhegemonic and nonidentitarian inclusion of all by all. In Brandom's words:

The most cosmopolitan approach begins with a pluralistic insight. When we ask, Who are we? or What sort of thing are we? the answers can vary without competing. Each one defines a different way of saying "we"; each kind of "we"-saying defines a different community, and we find ourselves in many communities. This thought suggests that we think of ourselves in the broadest sense as the ones who say "we." It points to the one great Community comprising members of all particular communities—the Community of those who say "we" with and to someone, whether the members of those particular communities recognize each other or not.[115]

Could "religion"—a "religion of the world," say, a "religion of humanity"—name, include, or express such "Community"? Could it do so, perhaps, without ever revealing itself as such, in its own name, but figuring merely as metaphor, metonymy, allegory, or as the spiritual meaning of this "Community's" letter (that is to say, its foundational documents, its written laws, the growing body of its jurisprudence)? Put differently, would "cosmopolitanism" require—rather than merely tolerate—a *political theology* at its center or periphery? This term features in the work of none of these thinkers, but if my speculation has any validity, the difference between center and periphery would matter little, since even minimal reference to any community's (and eventually some ultimate "Community's") transcending movement—and, alternatively, to whatever "t/Thing" or "b/Being" transcends it, albeit marginally—would already suffice to make the point.

Stout emphasizes Brandom's adoption of the later Wittgenstein's understanding of "language games" as an important way to characterize "the ways in which we keep track of the beliefs and intentions we undertake when conversing with other people." Indeed, in *Making It Explicit*, keeping score becomes an important metaphor for the normative dealings we have with one another: "A game, as Wittgenstein realized, is a relatively perspicuous example of a social practice—a relatively simple species of the genus to which ethical discourse belongs."[116] Not just ethical discourse but also political and cultural debate in the broadest possible sense follow this pattern. And, we would have to assume, so does "religion." Or does it?

According to Stout, the way in which *Making It Explicit* elaborates the "analogy" between discursive practices and (language) games enables Brandom to show "how pragmatism can best resist degenerating into something like conventionalism, according to which the tyranny of the majority determines what obligation and excellence are."[117] In his reading, Brandom's "analogy" of "practice" and "game" seeks to bring out the "objective dimension of ethics as a social practice,"[118] which Rorty tends to downplay, if not outright ignore. Between a "solidarity" whose inclusiveness has ethnocentric limitations of scope and political will and a "Community" whose horizons expand to near objective-Idealist proportions (those of a humanized Spirit), a world of difference remains. Mutatis mutandis, Stout suggests, a similar discrepancy opens up between the two conceptions of "religion" that result from Rorty's and Brandom's projects.

Unlike Wittgenstein, whose philosophy, Stout writes, is "an ascetic therapy of desire intended to return himself and others to a form of life that neither is, nor takes itself to be, dependent on an essentially explanatory approach to topics like truth and meaning," Brandom's overall project is no longer "preoccupied" by the supposed "*spiritual* consequences of representationalism."[119] Where Wittgenstein's later work could seen as espousing a specific "form of pragmatism," Stout goes on to explain, "in part because it recommends seeing a life of sound understanding prior to philosophy," Brandom seeks instead to develop "a full-scale theoretical alternative to representationalism," albeit one that is pragmatist in that it considers "reasoning" first of all as a "social practice."[120] Such a program breaks with a long tradition of idealist rationalism, stretching from Plato to Descartes and beyond, and opts for a completely different understanding of the categories of our reasoning: "Pragmatic theories of norms are distinguished from platonist theories, in treating as fundamental norms *implicit* in *practices* rather than norms *explicit* in *principles.*"[121]

Stout summarizes Brandom's "inferentialism" as follows:

> Like representationalism it accepts the burden of explicating the concepts it takes as basic and then accounting for other concepts successfully in terms of those, but here the primitive concepts are normative ones that are implicit in the *activities* performed within our discursive practices. Those practices are understood as belonging to language games that essentially involve . . . self-committing behavior and social interactions. . . . The essential role of inference in such practices is what justifies using the label "inferentialist" as a name for this explanatory strategy. For it is in terms of *social practices that essentially involve inference* that Brandom proposes to work out the most important details of his theoretical structure.[122]

Two observations are in order. First, if all "primitive" concepts are "normative," then there are, in a strict sense, no "primitive" concepts to begin with (or return to and end up with), nor can any concept, whether implicit or explicit in practice, count as more "basic" than others. Further, if all emphasis is put on the discursive web in which things are called by their name, repudiating (in Hegelian terms, undialectical) "immediacy" in favor of a "holism" whose horizon is in principle open-ended, then the prevalence of one concept over another is neither real nor even theoretically possible (in the sense of, say, being enabled or envisioned, let alone given or assured, in advance). Any weight such a concept acquires is thus provisional, reversible, and nonnatural, the result of a normative stance, of seeing, calling, and making things so. Brandom thus confirms Cavell's insight that "what a thing is called" is based on our—in Cavell's view, ultimately *my*—claiming, proclaiming, acclaiming, that is to say, calling it so.

Second, Stout signals a danger in Brandom's labeling of his central pragmatist insight "inferentialism" in that many of the practices invoked "also essentially involve activities that are not strictly speaking inferential, such as observing and acting."[123] These are "non-inferential moves" in the language game, which Brandom designates in technical terms as "discursive entry and discursive departure moves," and which, in the case of observations and acts, entail "physical, causal interaction with physical objects."[124] Brandom assumes that such "moves," which are not characterized by inferences, nonetheless presuppose inferences in more or less indirect or implicit ways: "they are not moves that anyone unskilled in making inferential moves could make."[125] Or again: "Non-inferential moves are not themselves inferences, but they have the significance they have because they are moves in a game that essentially includes inferential moves with which they share terms and to which they are related inferentially. So they are not disconnected from inferential capacities in the way that empiricist references to the immediacy of perception implied."[126] Brandom invokes Sellars's *Empiricism and the Philosophy of Mind* and Hegel's *Phenomenology of Spirit*, especially the chapter on "sense-certainty," to demonstrate that noninferential reports must be inferentially articulated and thus, indirectly or in a second moment, enter the space of reasons given and taken.[127] A basic pragmatist insight is the "normative character of the 'order and connection of ideas,'" together with an insistence on the fact that this normativity and the "justificatory" considerations it allows can only be spelled out "*within* a vocabulary (that is, between different applications of a vocabulary)."[128]

All this implies that any invocation of singular terms—including each of the particulars (words, things, gestures, states, attitudes, events, processes, etc.) for which they stand—is tied to at least one (other) concept, more precisely, to the competent *use* of such a concept and, thereby, *ipso facto*, is also implicated in and, in principle, explicable by endless others. As Davidson, approvingly cited by Rorty and Brandom, has it: "nothing can count as a reason for holding a belief except another belief."[129] Noninferential reports, therefore—including the ones from which we proposed to set out by focusing on words, things, gestures, powers, sounds, silences, smells, touches, affects, and effects—cannot rely only on one inferentially articulated concept. Rather, no such concept can stand on its own or hold sway over all possible others on necessary (natural, a priori, or other than normative) grounds.

The argument that "religion" is, for all our emphasis on singular terms and particulars, *the* concept that underlies, structures, and orients the research program of which this volume is a first fruit is thus *strategic*, based upon a *normative* decision. It might seem, in Rorty's terms, a matter of "cultural politics," for which, in the end, no criteria or rules are readily available. But is this all there is to say? Where norms, criteria, principles, and rules fail us, is there no further ground, no unspecified or unspecifiable "reason," no other pull from the depths of our nature and language, historicity and finitude, corporeality and sociality, that might, if not explain, then at least render more intelligible or acceptable the fact that we *still* talk about "religion"? In what sense could and should we be *deeply pragmatic* about these matters? Are they merely terminological, dictated by preference for

43

a certain idiom and vocabulary that stand in as a figure for historical, social, and cultural facts that could be analyzed in thoroughly empirical and, hence, altogether different normative terms? Would this provide any firmer basis? Strictly speaking, it would not. Brandom's theory, Stout explains, gives us good reasons why this must be so: "Brandom's approach is pragmatic in the sense that he takes the normative know-how of unreflective language-users to be more basic than the reflective expression of norms in rules. This is what Brandom dubs 'a *pragmatist* conception of norms—a notion of primitive correctnesses of performance *implicit* in *practice* that precede and are presupposed by their *explicit* formulation in *rules* and *principles*.'"[130]

We can surmise that in all of this *there is (and remains and will always be) more implicit than what reaches the level of explicitness, of concepts and discourse, of reasons given and taken*. What Wittgenstein calls the "essence" and "grammar" of our language games and forms of life and what Brandom analyzes in strictly normative terms, such as "proprieties" and "entitlements," "commitments" and "claims," does not—and, perhaps, cannot—always and everywhere reach the articulation of propositional, that is to say, statable content, of a substance captured by the categories of semantics, principles, and rules. Here, for necessary reasons, criteria "disappoint" us, as Cavell saw.

To entertain this suspicion is not to give in to the "myth of the given," namely, "the idea, most broadly, that some *thing*, a mere occurrence, or process, could in itself have normative (specifically, epistemic) significance, bind us, oblige us, or entitle us to do something,"[131] let alone to precritical, dogmatic metaphysics. Whatever is "given" or "gives" here hands us, from the depths of our existence, not a signification (which could be criteriologically identified), but some *signifyingness*—call it a metaphysical weight and urgency, a lightness and patience, horror and sublimity—that, by definition, eludes all given concepts, categories, and ideas, hence all ontology and epistemology, semantics and pragmatics. Yet, by the same necessity, such *signifiance* (as Levinas said) may impose itself, time and again, on us and open, widen, or deepen the space into which reasons may enter. "Metaphysical" and "spiritual experience," to use Adorno's terminology, knows something about this.

According to Stout, Brandom's pragmatist conception of inferentialism (to be distinguished from earlier historical examples of this approach in Leibniz, Kant, and Frege), is "ideally suited for application in religious studies."[132] Although "religion" is not Brandom's express concern (even less is it Sellars's), Stout argues that:

When we take religious and ethical discourse as our subject matter, what we are examining in the course of our work, it seems to me, is precisely what Brandom's Sellarsian theory directs us to: the inferences being made by the people we are studying, the transition they make into discourse when they perceive something, and the discursive exits they execute by acting intentionally in the world. These are the sorts of moves we are trying to interpret when we engage in our variety of normative scorekeeping.[133]

One might quibble about the trust put here in "inference" and "intentionality," the holistic interpretation of "perception" and "action," the overall role of "discursiveness," as well as about the metaphor of "scorekeeping," which could attract the kind of skeptical queries that have been leveled at game-theoretical models of understanding language and thought (notably by Cavell, in his discussions of John Rawls, to which we will turn below). Are these adequate notions and metaphors when dealing with the "precinct of the humanities,"[134] and the social sciences or even natural sciences, of which the study of "religion" forms an integral—and, we have maintained, increasingly central—part, if not an organizing, then at least a challenging one?

Does it not make more sense to say that I keep my own "normative score" by acknowledging an irreducible and incalculable asymmetry in my relations to others and otherness? Furthermore, is the world—and others and everything else "in" it—not ultimately "my call," based on my sense that present reasons, given and taken, suffice (that "enough is enough," as Austin exclaimed), rather than on my having to await the final result, agreement, or consensus of deliberation by whatever postulated "we"? Is it not something I alone can claim, acclaim, and proclaim, when all is said and done, and criteria and rules fail me in shoring up my stance, my knowledge, self-knowledge, and acknowledgment of how things are, both in the external world of material objects and in the realm of the "spiritual," that is to say, in the living world populated by other minds, from whose company I can always try to depart in my most interior self?

Clearly, Brandom would not go *that* far and propound, as Cavell does, that the "I" is the "scandal of skepticism," the sole, if not necessarily solitary, instance at which, so to speak, the buck stops. Stout cites a telling passage that illustrates the point:

> What must not be lost is an appreciation of the way in which our discursive practice is empirically and practically *constrained*. It is not up to us which claims are true (that is, what the facts are). It is in a sense up to us which noises and marks express which claims, and hence, in a more attenuated sense, which express true claims. But empirical and practical constraint on our arbitrary whim is a pervasive feature of our discursive practice.[135]

But then, how should we theorize "discursive entry and exit transitions" without falling into the "perils of idealism,"[136] which Brandom's inferentialist semantics seeks expressly to avoid? Does the inferentialist network not stretch the whole way, shedding light on the pre-, para-, post-, trans-, or nondiscursive elements and forms of (linguistic?) utterance—which, with Levinas, we could term the "Saying" preceding and exceeding the "Said"—but also of every perception and each action? Are all implicit commitments really capable of being made explicit? Is, in Spinoza's idiom, every power, affect, and effect *expressive, expressed*, or *expressible* through and through? And if not, are the hopes we have put in the expressive force of singular terms and particulars such as words, things, gestures, powers, sounds, silences, smells, and touches not false or at least naïve? What "reasons" can words, things, gestures, powers, and so on, if not merely inspire, then also implicitly form or explicitly articulate, and, in both cases, involve and express?

Brandom, who in this comes close to the aspirations of Habermas,[137] adopts a broad conception of reason and of "contentfulness," both propositional and conceptual. Although he holds that only "propositions . . . can serve as premises and conclusions of inferences, that is, can serve as and stand in need of *reasons*," he immediately adds that "expressions such as singular terms and predicates, which cannot directly play the inferential role of premise or conclusion in an argument, nonetheless can play an *in*directly inferential role in virtue of their systematic contributions to the directly inferential roles of sentences in which they occur."[138] Specifically, Brandom argues that "even unrepeatable expressions such as demonstrative tokenings play substitution-inferential roles and hence express conceptual content."[139] Yet there remains, in his view, an important semantic-pragmatic distinction between "directly inferential commitments, which relate sentential (that is, claimable or believable) contents," on the one hand, and "indirectly inferential . . . commitments, which relate the subsentential contents of expressions of other grammatical categories,"[140] on the other. Although Brandom takes pains to show how an "inferential approach" to linguistically oriented (and driven?) communication and agency can "generalize beyond sentences," thus allowing *Making It Explicit* to aspire to be "a unified vision of language and the mind,"[141] the distinction between the noninferential and the inferential nonetheless suggests a peculiar hierarchy. But does it necessarily require one?

The asymmetry between two levels of meaning and sense finds its justification in the theory's concept of "expression" as a linguistic affair:

> To express something is to make it *explicit*. What is explicit in the fundamental sense has a *propositional* content—the content of a claim, judgment, or belief (claimable, judgeable, believable contents). That is, making something explicit is *saying* it: putting it into a form in which it can be given as a reason, and reasons demanded for it. Putting something forward in the explicit form of a claim is the basic move in the game of giving and asking for reasons.[142]

But is this an adequate rendering of all the utterances and expressions that we attribute to "religion"? Does not "religion" still subtract and absolve itself from this overall picture, premised on a potential "linguistification" of all experience, or at least of all thought? In other words, is Brandom's "space of reasons" big enough to contain "religion," or are there ways—perhaps as yet unimagined or by now largely forgotten—to exit, enter, or reenter this "space," at least in principle or virtually? Would this condemn "religion" to being "beyond the limits of reason alone," venturing in yet another sense "beyond a concept," as it were? Is "religion" thus rendered speechless, condemned to the ineffable, to unpronounceable divine names and to apophatic theologies, which prepare for, but never witness, their advent? Or may it yet squarely enter the space of reasons, allowing its noninferential moves to become "claims" in the narrowly discursive sense Brandom gives to this term? Can it do so without distorting itself? Things are far from clear at this point. Is "religion" a "Saying" or a "Said," a "gesture" or a "word," a "power" or a "thing," the "space" or the "object," the "foundation" or the "founded," the "archive" or the "document"? And, if "religion" has, indeed, "two sources," as we claim (following Bergson and Derrida)—if it consists in the *claiming* of a claimant, studied by pragmatics, on the one hand, and its/his/her material claim or *content*, studied by semantics, on the other—would *both* constitute a (necessary or sufficient) "reason" in themselves? Or are "reason" and "reasons" to be sought in the very *relation* and link (as in the Latin *religio*) that we discern or enable between the two?

Let's leave aside the question, raised by Stout, as to whether Brandom's theory can account for our ability to address counterfactuals and virtual (no less than actual) histories—including and especially a "virtual past" that, for all its counterfactuality, can count as permanently present, as I will claim.[143] What is important is to be sure that the pragmatic conception of inferentialism does not confine us to what commonly counts as the doxa of our age, that is to say, to an understanding in which the meaning of things is their merely conventional and ultimately ethnocentric usage, based on the normative and normalizing convictions of whatever happens to be our tribe or group. In other words, it must not limit discussion to the views and practices that matter only to those who are talking and present at hand. Not only past and future generations but also those who are geographically, socially, psychologically, or culturally distant and distinct from "us" (like the strangers and neighbors, or the widow, the orphan, the poor, and the mad, outcasts and pariahs whose fate has concerned all religions), no less than the other that, at times, we may become to ourselves, must be seen as part of the horizon of implicitness. To express this and make it explicit may be the most challenging task for philosophy today.

Let me recapitulate. Brandom's pragmatics—by which he means "a theory of the use of language"—is "normative" and "conceptual" in that it proposes "an explication of explicitly normative conceptual contents in terms of implicitly normative practices, rather than a reduction of normative terms to nonnormative ones."[144] It is also "rationalist" in the sense of its claim that normative implicitness can be rendered explicit, if not fully, then at least to a large degree. There is nothing that, he claims, cannot—in principle, if not always de facto or at any time—enter the "space" of reasons given and taken. In his scheme, conceptuality and hence also inference—and, more indirectly (or derivatively), reference—*reach all the way through*, finding no insurpassable intrinsic limits and boundaries to language and expression.

True enough, Brandom argues that there were "no true claimings before there were vocabularies, because there were no claimings at all. But it does not follow that there were no true claimables."[145] We could say that "there were truths about photons before there were people to formulate them. Taking the latter course is entirely compatible with acknowledging that the notion of a fact (true claimable) is only intelligible relative to that of a vocabulary. . . . If we had never existed, there would not have been any true claimings, but there would have been facts (truths) going unexpressed."[146]

Anticipating an argument about memory and the so-called absolute ("pure," "virtual," "general" or "a priori") past to which we will turn below, let me surmise that Brandom's invocation of somehow existing yet nonobserved and nonactual "facts," however defensible it may or may not be,[147] reminds us that any present historical, empirical, anthropological, or, for that matter, theological claim ought to *assume* a pastness to which it has not—and, perhaps, could not have been—witness: a "truth," "fact," or "claimable," of sorts that preexists truths, facts, and claimings as we commonly understand them. This is true of our planetary and biological natural history, to be sure, but it also extends to our cultural and material histories, presents, and futures. But should we say that the latter come with a difference, to the extent that we could imagine things in this domain to have run an alternative course? We would be reminding ourselves, with Adorno, that world history, for all its determinism, should be thought of as "metaphysically contingent," something we would find, perhaps, more hazardous to claim when speaking about natural history broadly conceived. Or is there ultimately no difference—there being de facto no such *natural* history without "us"?

It is as if a deep-seated need compelled us to postulate such metaphysical thoughts about "facts" before the very concept, in a universalizing stretch and transcendental overreach. Nothing else, albeit with the aid of criteria and rules, seems capable of giving our claims and commitments an *answerability to the world*. Such preexisting, prehuman truths or claimables might be conceived in both an implausible ("maniacal") and a more modest systematic metaphysical register, such as Brandom distinguishes. In both cases of this "genre of creative nonfiction writing," we seem to espouse the "imperialistic, even totalitarian, discursive ambition" of crafting "by artifice a vocabulary in which everything can be said."[148] The first, however, seeks to delimit the range of what it possible and thinkable, sayable and doable, in (or with) "all possible vocabularies." By contrast, the second, which is the position of genuinely "historicist pragmatism," holds that we can give "no definite meaning" to the phrase and scope of "all possible vocabularies,"[149] because each new vocabulary expands and changes the makeup of the world as it is, though there are conditions and limitations—though no mythical given—to which our thoughts and acts must correspond or by which they are made possible to begin with: "Every new vocabulary brings with it new purposes for vocabularies to serve. These purposes are not . . . formulable in the antecedently available vocabularies. They are . . . genuinely *created* by our new ways of speaking. As such, there is no way to throw our semantic net over them *in advance* of developing the languages in which they can be expressed."[150]

Brandom returns a decidedly Hegelian insight to the task of philosophy in what we might call a reconstructive or constructive, rather than a merely descriptive, metaphysics. He writes:

> The modest metaphysician aims only to codify the admittedly contingent constellation of vocabularies with which her time (and those that led up to it) happens to present her—to capture her time in thought. She sees her task as that of constructing a vocabulary that will be useful for the purposes of the contemporary intellectual: the one who by definition is concerned with seeing the culture whole, trying to make the vocabularies it now seems useful to employ to get various sorts of practical grips on how things hang together.[151]

The "modest" metaphysician—the philosopher as "intellectual," as it were—in this respect differs from other kinds of scholars and researchers, who tend to "work within definite matrices, pushing back the frontiers of their particular portion of the culture, without in general needing to be concerned with how their area relates to the rest."[152] As paradoxical *specialists of the general*, though not necessarily the universal (the distinction between the qualifiers "everything" and "all" is crucial here), modest metaphysicians would foster a "useful discursive tool among others for getting a grip on our multifarious culture."[153] Such an activity would work in two directions at once: by *sorting* vocabularies, showing which "smoothly fit into the regimented form and those that fit less well"[154]— which is another way of saying that things have "natures" and "histories."[155]

But which of these two metaphysical gestures—each of them as "pervasive" as the history of presuppositions and "dogmatic images" (Deleuze) that governs philosophy in its continued struggle with "representation" and "expression"—represents the ultimate religious-theological move: the "maniacal" or the "modest"? Brandom, in tune with Rorty, thinks the first, "maniacal" metaphysics is what qualifies as "the pursuit of theology with other means."[156] But if what I have been suggesting is not entirely wrong, we should respond that it all depends on how we're willing to take—and find a use for—the designations "religious" and "theological."

"Religion" as "Ontology" or as "Cultural Politics"?

In Rorty's view, the overall implications of Brandom's project—and, more broadly, of the tradition of pragmatism as a whole—suggest that "cultural politics" should be substituted for "ontology" in probing the question of "religion." He insists that to adopt the pragmatist attitude implies that "talk about God should be dropped because it impedes the search for human happiness."[157] Combining Hegel's "historicism" with the later Wittgenstein's insistence on "social practice" in constituting the uses of meaning, while supplementing these authors' basic insights with what he calls a "more carefully worked out" conceptual and argumentative elaboration of semantics and pragmatics in the writings of Sellars, Davidson, and Brandom, Rorty sees new opportunities for restating and reinforcing pragmatism's original ambition. By this he means Dewey's claim that philosophy "is not in any sense whatever a form of knowledge" but instead "a social hope reduced to a working program of action, a prophecy of the future."[158] Indeed, Rorty maintains, James may have been right when he introduced a daring "analogy" and confidently "compared pragmatism's potential for producing radical cultural change to that of the Protestant Reformation."[159]

Is there any room for an analogous formulation—that is, for some form of "social hope," "prophecy," and "Reformation"—under late-twentieth- and early-twenty-first-century intellectual, cultural, and especially political conditions? What, if anything, would "religion"—which not accidentally echoes through all three of these tropes—have to do with it? Is it a resource for or obstacle to the social ideals that Rorty associates with them? Or both? Is it neither one nor the other? Was it always in (or on) the way to progress, and has it only recently become indifferent in ways whose—now comforting, then disconcerting—effects we do not quite fully understand or have not come to appreciate? In short, what does substituting "cultural politics" for "ontology" entail?

For one thing, it would mean, in Brandom's characterization of Rorty's pragmatism:

> seeing norms for belief, no less than for action, as our doing and or responsibility, as not needing to reflect the authority of an alien, nonhuman Reality, which comes to seem as mythical, dispensable, and ultimately juvenile a conception as Old Nobodaddy came to seem to the *érudits*. Richard Rorty, inspired by Dewey and James . . . argues that the move from thinking of moral norms in terms of divine commandments to thinking of them in terms of social compacts should be followed by a move from thinking of the truth of belief in terms of correspondence with reality to thinking of it in terms of agreement with our fellows.[160]

Rorty starts out from Brandom's reinterpretation, well before the publication of *Making It Explicit*, of Heidegger's categories in *Being and Time* to explain how the pragmatic turn in understanding language and agency strips them of mentalist, representationalist, empiricist, and intentionalist misunderstandings. In a fundamental essay, now reprinted in his *Tales of the Mighty Dead*, Brandom reads the first division of Heidegger's work in such a pragmatist vein, suggesting that "all matters of authority, in particular *epistemic* authority, are matters of social practice, and not objective matters of fact."[161] This interpretation, Rorty summarizes, has a startling consequence, since it enables us to free ourselves from metaphysical and ontological constraints upon our intellectual and cultural practices:

is there an authority beyond that of society which society should acknowledge—an authority such as God, or Truth, or Reality? Brandom's account of assertions as assumptions of social responsibilities leaves no room for such an authority. . . . The authority traditionally attributed to the non-human can be explained sociologically, and such a sociological account has no need to invoke the rather mysterious beings that theological or philosophical treatments of authority require. (Such entities include "the divine will," "the intrinsic nature of reality, as it is in itself, apart from human needs and interests," and "the immediately given character of experience.")[162]

A further consequence of this "ontological primacy of the social" (which, paradoxically, amounts to an end of the ontological per se) would be, Rorty says, that one should steer clear of any assumption that our religious vocabularies, or any others, accurately represent reality or nature. Given the pragmatist insistence on the primacy of the "social," one must assume that "the question of the existence of God is a question of the advantages and disadvantages of using God-talk over against alternative ways of talking."[163]

The theoretical basis here is neither that of an a priori, analytically deducible or intuitive truth nor that of an inductively corroborated given. Thus, strictly speaking, it lacks any *fundamentum in re*. Is the pragmatist stance then an axiom, a matter of decision, as Badiou challenges? Or is it the proclaimed or acclaimed statement, acceptance, or acknowledgment of things being "our call," as Cavell suggests?

If any theoretical alternative to these positions can be formulated, it cannot be grounded in a greater adequacy for mirroring or picturing reality but must show its primacy by its greater usefulness for *our* present and more or less immediate purposes. This, Rorty writes, is what Brandom must mean in his account of our discursive scorekeeping of reasons given and taken, which make up our world and, in more complex and derivative ways, are made in response to claims by the world upon us. But to say this can only be part of a stance taken, not a matter of revelation. Rorty baptizes such a stance a specimen or intervention of "cultural politics": "All attempts to name an authority which is superior to that of society are disguised moves in the game of cultural politics. That is what they *must* be, because it is the only game in town."[164] Thus defined, the pragmatist account, while far from being relativistic or skeptical, undermines the notion of "authority" in consequential ways. No theological escape hatch, no metaphysical attempt to ontologically—or onto-theologically—shore up one claim rather than others, can absolve human conversation and interaction of its responsibility in epistemic or normative matters, whether in science or law, art or politics, life or love.[165]

Moving beyond his reference to James's bold assertion that pragmatism inaugurates a spiritual revolution that echoes the Protestant Reformation, Rorty suggests that Brandom's pragmatist inferentialism likewise advocates a historical transition. In his view, it heralds a radical paradigm shift away from modern epistemology that parallels the epochal change from obsolete theism to a genuinely post-theistic viewpoint:

In recent centuries, instead of asking whether God exists, people have started asking whether it is a good idea for us to continue talking about Him, and which human purposes might be served by doing so—asking, in short, what use the concept of God might be to human beings. Brandom is suggesting that philosophers, instead of asking whether we really are in touch with objects "outside the mind"—objects that are as they are regardless of what we think about them—should ask what human purposes are served by conceiving of such objects.[166]

Yet not the least original aspect of *Making It Explicit* is that it gives a transcendental justification, of sorts, for our *deep-seated need for objects and object-talk*.[167] We cannot and should not explain all *credenda* in terms of mere *agenda*, and to have done so is a—reparable—flaw in the earlier pragmatist program.

Brandom's semantics is less residual (a leftover from the representational paradigm) than radically *derivative*, remaining premised on the very pragmatics that—despite all indications to the contrary ("instrumentalism" being the most important)—gives rise to its task. Rorty cites Brandom to underscore the point: "objectivity is a structural aspect of the social-perspectival form of conceptual contents. The permanent distinction between how things are and how they are taken to be by some interlocutor is built into the social-inferential articulation of concepts."[168] To be sure, there can be no claim without a claimant, no thing—no quiddity of existence, no "what-" or "thatness"—without *our* or *my* calling it so. But any claim can be disclaimed, our criteria may disappoint us, and experience (in the processual-holistic sense of *Erfahrung* rather than the instantaneous and supposedly atomistic *Erlebnis*) can always prove us wrong.

It is important to note the difference from Kant here. For Brandom, Rorty explains:

space, time, substance, and causality are what they are because human beings need to talk in certain ways to get things done. In the place of Kant's inexplicable transcendental constitution of the mind, Brandom substitutes practices which helped a certain biological species flourish. So the question about the existence of God-talk is: "can we get as good an argument for the utility of God-talk as we can for the utility of talk about time, space, substance, and causality?" For Brandom, the answer to this question is "no."[169]

For Rorty, there is no further use for "singular terms"—and "God," supposedly, would be such a term, wherever it is used as more than an appellation, a name—*beyond* the practical necessity to talk about "reidentifiable spatio-temporal particulars."[170] Yet things are more complicated. After reviewing Brandom's reinterpretation of the nature and ascription of "existence," Rorty maintains that its central argument does not necessarily *exclude* the affirmation of ideal or intelligible entities—and hence the use of their "singular terms" (or nominations)—per se. In fact, for Brandom, our *knowledge* of existence is not at all co-extensive with (let alone represented by) the "objective" knowledge of material things propounded by the natural sciences. Here lies an important disagreement with Kant, who relegated ideality and ideas—indeed, the very notion of the "thing in itself"—to the realm of the noumenal. The matter of existence is decided *neither* scientifically *nor* ontologically (even though Brandom, in *Tales of the Mighty Dead*, offers an alternative "metaphysics" that covers semantics, pragmatics, and the question of "existence"). From this, Rorty draws a simple conclusion:

> Kant was right to think that there is no reason why existence has to be physical . . . , but he was wrong in thinking that knowledge of existence is limited to knowledge of physical existence.
>
> This is because the question of whether or not to talk about the existence of immaterial and infinite beings is not one for transcendental philosophy but rather one to be turned over to cultural politics. . . . for an inferentialist, what counts as an object is determined by what a culture has definite descriptions of, and argument about what exists is determined by what canonical designators are in place. Yet any culture may be surpassed by another, since the human imagination may dream up many more definite descriptions and equally many lists of canonical designators.[171]

The consequence of such a pragmatist—and ultimately, evolutionary, functionalist, and historicist view, Rorty goes on to suggest, is that there is room for any idealizing claim that is worth its salt, that is to say, that contributes to solidarity and social hopes:

> When a culture wants to erect a logical space that includes, say, the gods and goddesses of the Olympian pantheon, nothing stands in its way. . . . But to ask, after such a culture has become entrenched, "are there *really* gods and goddesses?" is like asking "are there *really* numbers?" or "are there *really* physical objects?" The person asking such a question has to have a good reason for raising it. "Intellectual curiosity" is not such a reason. If one is going to challenge an ongoing cultural practice, one must both explain what practice might be put in its place, and how this substitute will tie in with surrounding practices. That is why to turn a question over to cultural politics is not to turn it over to "unreason."[172]

Rorty further implies that, in tune with what James believed to be pragmatism's elective affinity with basic tenets of the Reformation, Brandom seems to reinforce the arguments of Christian theologians who combated the neo-Thomist or mainstream Protestant varieties of natural and philosophical theology. Rorty refers to the early Heidegger and to Paul Tillich,[173] but other examples could be added (Rudolf Bultmann, Karl Barth, but also Hans Urs von Balthasar and, now, Jean-Luc Marion). In particular, Brandom allows us to see that, if God is not "a being among other beings" (nor "Being-as-such" as Rorty suggests), then "the attempt to characterize him—or, in Brandomian language, the attempt to identify him with the help of an already available list of canonical designators—is hopeless."[174] As in Cavell's discussion of Austin's criteria for empirical knowledge, the important distinction would be, once again, that between "identification" and "existence":

> The fact that "does God exist?" is a bad question suggests that a better question would be: "do we want to weave one or more of the various religious traditions (with their accompanying pantheons) together with our deliberation over moral dilemmas, our deepest hopes, and our need to be rescued from despair? Alternatively: "does one or more of these religious traditions provide language we wish to use when putting together our self-image, determining what is most important to us?" If none of them do, we shall treat such traditions, and their pantheons, as offering mere "mythologies."[175]

Two things should be noted here. First, Rorty observes, such "mythologies" are not "merely" myths, since they still have internal truths and falsities, which can be discussed and appreciated as contributing to our knowledge in some way or another: "It will be true, for example, that there exists a child of Zeus and Semele but false that there is a child of Uranus and Aphrodite, true that there is a Third Person of the Godhead but false that there is a Thirteenth."[176] But this said, no single truth of either one of these narrative elements of the myth in relation to its internal coherence and structure, by its own account, adds up to establishing something like "Truth." The latter value is merely added in view of so-called "cautionary" emphases and uses of such elements of the narrative, *for us, here and now*. To speak of "Truth" here is to put an exclamation mark after the narrative element in question, to proclaim or acclaim its claim (not to add "existence" to it).

Second, and more importantly, Rorty reiterates the point that Cavell has stressed in his discussion of Austinian criteria. Expanding on the distinction between "identity" and "existence," and bringing in our available standards for rationality and irrationality, Rorty writes that, in the final analysis:

> there are no criteria for when it is rational and when irrational to switch from adhesion to a tradition to a skeptical "mere myth" view of it. Decisions about what language games to play, what to talk about and what not to talk about, and for what purposes, are not made on the basis of agreed-upon criteria. Cultural politics is the least norm-governed human activity. It is the site of generational revolt, and thus the growing point of culture—the place where traditions and norms are up for grabs at once.[177]

Rorty explicitly states that cultural politics is not a struggle for compelling truths within the order of things that Paul Tillich calls "symbolical." He takes his distance from Tillich's proposal to learn how to appreciate alternative versions of "an adequate symbol of ultimate concern" that—unlike "purely secular" substitutes for the symbols of old—would give modern subjects a certain renewable "courage to be," more than, say, epistemic, conceptual, and propositional contents. Such a proposal, with its apparent modesty of finally handing genuine, or in any case "literal," truth (i.e., myth) over to the sciences and "common-sense beliefs," while freeing the whole existential domain for the "symbolic," makes a fateful philosophical (mis)calculation: "it relies upon a distinction between the symbolic and the literal that is a relic of representationalist philosophy."[178] It is, Rorty concludes, precisely such a distinction between accuracy (or "literalness") and inaccuracy (or "symbolism") with regard to a supposedly given reality that a radically interpreted pragmatics, in its Brandomian variety, forbids once and for all:

> A Brandomian inferentialist . . . has no use for the literal vs. symbolic distinction. The only relevant distinction she can countenance is one between logical spaces constructed for certain purposes (e.g., those of physical science, of *mathematics*, or of chess) and other logical spaces constructed for other purposes (e.g., those provided by the Platonic dialogues, the Jataka, the Holmes stories, the New Testament, etc.).
>
> Debate about the utility of such logical spaces and about the desirability or undesirability of uniting them with, or disjoining them from, one another is the substance of cultural politics.[179]

Aside from that, we have no criteria, rules, or norms, in short, no reason(s) to decide whether a certain idiom or vocabulary—for example, God-talk—is appropriate, that is to say, either pertinent or harmful. The question to ask, therefore, is: To whom is such talk relevant, when and where or how and for what reasons should it be put—or kept—in circulation? What is the web of sustaining or surrounding concepts involved, and what assumptions have been made? What would it take to render some of these implications explicit so as to readjust the perspectival view of ourselves, of others and the world, where and when needed?

To ask this, Rorty maintains, requires no metaphysical hypothesis, according to which certain things or entities belong to altogether different ontological realms and hence can only be talked about in fundamentally incommensurable ways. Nor do we need to accept the narrowly reductionistic, naturalist view that "discourse about physical objects is the paradigm case for making truth claims, and that all other areas of discourse must be thought of as 'non-cognitive'" (a claim made by mechanicism, physicalism, phenomenalism, behaviorism, computationalism, etc.):

> For Brandom, there is no such thing as a certain kind of object demanding to be spoken of in a certain kind of language. To say that God requires to be talked about

in a certain way is no more illuminating than to say that transfinite cardinal numbers, or neutrinos, demand to be talked about in a certain way. Since we would not know what any of these entities were if we did not know that they were the entities talked about in these ways, the idea that they "demand" this treatment is unhelpful.[180]

This underscores once more that the—meaningful or good—sense of X-talk comes with our ability to give it one (such sense), nothing more, nothing less. There is nothing intrinsic to things, to Xs, that either proscribes or forbids our capacity or propensity to talk about them in certain ways rather than others. Whether we talk about them at all, or whether we actually refer to things seemingly represented or invoked by our words— which are consistently projected as being independent of these words—is an altogether different matter. This seemingly simple insight has enormous consequences. If the philosophical antiessentialism and antistructuralism, in sum, antirepresentationalism, of the twentieth century has taught us anything, it is the need for a certain "insouciance" concerning the age-old "warfare between science and theology."[181] Rorty explains on what grounds such a relaxation of previous opposition might be justified, even though it should not be taken as a license to indulge in obscurantism. Needless to say, there are no guarantees that it will not, for, as no one has demonstrated better than Derrida, *the perfectibility and pervertibility of our discourses go hand in hand*. But, Rorty claims, such perversions have their content and existence—or interest and importance—only as options for "us":

> The language game played by theologians with the transcendental terms, or with Heideggerese, and the one played by philosophers of mind who talk about the independence of qualia from behavior and environment, is as coherent as that played with numbers or physical objects. *But the coherence of talk about X does not guarantee the discussability of the existence of X. . . .* This is . . . because of sociological facts about the unavailability of norms to regulate discussion.[182]

To say this, Rorty concludes, is to espouse an eminently Hegelian view concerning the life of concepts. It is to propose, with Sellars and Brandom, that such a life—and what else can "philosophy" be but the bringing to life of concepts?—cannot "rise above the social practices of its time and judge their desirability by reference to something that is not itself an alternative social practice (past or future, real or imagined)."[183] It is further to maintain that we should avoid postulating:

> a difference between ourselves and the discursive practices in which we are engaged, and that we should not think that those practices are a means to some end; nor that they are a medium of representation used to get something right. A fortiori, we should not think that there is a goal of inquiry which is what it is apart from those practices, and fore-knowledge of which can help us decide which practices to have.[184]

Is "religion," in its systematic, reflective-discursive mode, that is to say, whenever and wherever it becomes theology, an attempt to designate the overall logical space into which reasons for this or that discursive practice must enter? Are its central concepts so many "canonical designators" that demarcate the limits of what is possible and permissible (to think, to do, to feel, to love, to live)? Or does the religious archive hold different concepts—albeit concepts *beyond a concept*—in store, which would allow us to think, imagine, dream, and project the provisionality and fallibility, indeed, the perfectibility, pervertibility, and mutability of our discourses and practices by putting them to a different test?

Such a test, an *experimentum crucis* or spiritual exercise, would not consist in placing such discourses and practices "within a larger context," conceived as a mega- or metadiscourse (and practice) or in drawing up pregiven sets of criteria that would function as "designators" at once "canonical" and "neutral." On the contrary, it would appeal to what can only be called a *no-place*—a "mystical postulate"—as well as to *virtual* terms, neither given nor possible at all times, whose selection is far from "neutral" but always determined by current interests and expressed by the always singular stances of our claims, proclamations, and acclamations. Is this what the historical "repository" of what Rorty calls "vocabularies" is all about?[185] Moreover, what are the political implications of the fact that people are, more than anything else, "incarnated vocabularies"?[186]

"Religion" Reenters the Public Square

Are religious believers and practitioners among those who, at least under the conditions of modernity and liberal democracy, must "opt out" of what Brandom calls "the game of giving and asking for reasons"? Should they consequently settle for "privacy," in its social and juridical, if not necessarily Wittgensteinian, sense? Rorty does not suggest that they always fail to make assertions or that their assertions lack all coherence (although this may, of course, happen here and there); he claims, rather, that they "disconnect their assertions from the network of socially acceptable inferences that provide justifications for making these assertions and draw practical consequences from having them."[187] But what does that mean? Surely the implied claims made by—and "consequences" drawn from—assertions made by religious believers and practitioners are more than merely "practical." Do they not have a cognitive ambition or intention as well, albeit it one that is unrealizable, unfulfillable (hence without proper reference or semantic, propositional content)?

As we found earlier, neither religious nor nonreligious claims or expressions, whether premised on cognitive assertions or otherwise "caught up" in the "game of giving and asking for reasons," can do more than establish the criteria for *identifying* referents, and can never give any credence to the actual *existence* of such referents. Such claims and expressions may more or less successfully enter into and maintain themselves within the "epistemic arena" or "public square." But doing so does not secure them any more stable *ontological* basis. Their ontological weight is at most their being able to position and maintain themselves in the "cultural politics" that, in Rorty's view, substitutes for the very concept and discipline of "ontology." In other words, when it comes to existence, the invocations of religious objects and references are no worse off than nonreligious ones in bridging the gap between "what-ness" and "that- or there-ness."

If "religion" shares certain epistemic conditions with its supposed antipodes, governed by the same "principle of charity" that Davidson ascribes to all beliefs, why assume that it must inevitably create more havoc than other cultural expressions when it emerges in public, where it must, after all, operate under the same communicational (technological, informational, digital, etc.) conditions and restraints as all other beliefs and practices, whether those of science, popular culture, politics, law, or love and sex? Must this be assumed, as Rorty seems to think, because religion did so in a not too distant past, punctuated by inquisitions, excommunications, religious bans, pogroms, exorcisms, fatwas, and ritual sacrifices? Or do we fear this havoc because it continues to work in what are by now not so distant regions of the world, in no longer unfamiliar social strata, and in ways that are all the more palpable—or at least ever more publicized, televised, You-tubed, and so on—to the extent that these regions enter "our" world, which is to say, progressively and virtually everywhere?

This much is clear: "anti-clericalism"—a term Rorty prefers over the classical modern stance of "atheism" (a term whose epistemological and ontological implications, he admits, have become problematic)—can be *de rigueur* and a moral imperative of the day, but it does not necessarily follow from the premises of the pragmatist's overall argument. Its basis is empirical and historical. As Rorty writes: "we secular humanists . . . grant that ecclesiastical organizations have sometimes been on the right side, but we think that the occasional Octavio Guttierez or Martin Luther King does not compensate for the ubiquitous Joseph Ratzingers and Jerry Falwells. History suggests to us that such organizations will always, on balance, do more harm than good."[188]

Consequently, "anti-clericalism's" philosophical and normative case—as well as its "cultural political" relevance—is as weak (or as strong) as that of "atheism" and can thus hardly be a useful substitute for it. It can at best *signal* a standing awareness that we should at all times remain on our guard against the irresponsible uses of authority, whether past, present, or future, against abuses that all too easily slip into forms of hate speech as well as into the violences they propagate, invite, or tolerate. There is simply no criterion that would guarantee a responsible use of religious citations in public debate, so askesis in these matters seems the sole remedy. As Rorty writes:

> it would be nice if I could appeal to a principle which differentiated between citing Psalm 72 in favor of government-financed health insurance and citing Leviticus 18:22

in opposition to changes in the law that would make life in the U.S. more bearable for gays and lesbians. But I do not have one. I wholeheartedly believe that religious people should trim their utterances to suit my utilitarian views, and in that in citing Leviticus they are, whether they know it or not, finding a vent for their own sadistic impulses. But I do not know how to make either of these propositions plausible to them.[189]

What one could do at most with homophobic bigots is not so much appeal to established constitutional laws or juridical custom—indeed, the First Amendment allows people to appeal to whatever canonical texts or spiritual authorities they like—but to "shame" and "socially ostracize" them, since they continue to make certain "moves" that do not befit the arena of modern liberal political debate.[190]

Is "religion" a "conversation-stopper" in the context of cultural political debates, as Rorty claims? Stout, in his *Democracy and Tradition*, draws on some of Brandom's distinctions to show why this is not necessarily so. He makes a seemingly simple distinction between two sorts of religious claims, namely, those based on "faith" and those grounded in "beliefs," which are not necessarily tied to (an act of) "faith." Against Rorty, he maintains that the obvious "pragmatic line should be that religion is not *essentially* anything, that the conventional utility of employing religious premises in political argument depends on the situation."[191] This being said, he singles out one particular religious claim and expression that may prove especially contentious in contemporary cultural political contexts:

> There is one sort of religious premise that does have the tendency to stop a conversation, at least momentarily—namely, faith-claims. We can understand why faith-claims have this tendency if we describe them in the way Brandom does. A faith-claim, according to Brandom, avows a cognitive commitment without claiming entitlement to that commitment. In the context of discursive exchange, if I make a faith-claim, I am authorizing others to attribute the commitment to me and perhaps giving them a better understanding of why I have undertaken certain other cognitive or practical commitments. . . . But I am not accepting the responsibility of demonstrating my entitlement to it. If pressed for such a demonstration, I might say simply that it is a matter of faith. In other words, "Don't ask me for reasons. I don't have any."[192]

Does this seal the fate of *all* "religious" faith-claims, at least those made in the public square, where the give and take of reasons is the rule of the game? Not so, Stout continues, giving two further arguments why "religion" should be more broadly conceived and, in its multifarious expressions, still shares certain conditions of intelligibility with other modes of discourse that make up social practices in the widest possible sense.

In the first place, not all "religions" are faith-claims. Not only may religious people ("people of faith") be willing—and quite able—to defend their claims discursively, Stout suggests, they can also make, respond to, or live by claims whose assertive or meditative nature is not at all that of a propositional content held to be true and representative of a pregiven reality, as its mirror or picture image, of sorts. Taking religion to be a "way of life" would reveal the variety and resilience—even proper rationality—of alternative claims, whose mode of expression is *representative*, but this time in the sense of *exemplary*, or *expressive* in the sense of *performative*. Their *modus loquendi* and *modus agendi* (to cite Michel de Certeau's terminological twist, in *The Mystic Fable*, of Austin's insights into how one can "do" still other "things with words") can be differently articulated and not intent on being informative—or, on the contrary, secretive and esoteric (by withholding information or normative reasons)—at all.

Stout further recalls Brandom's caution that faith and faith-claims in the sense of unwarranted, undefended, or unarticulated beliefs are not the prerogative of religious belief alone. On the contrary, "Everyone holds some beliefs on nonreligious topics without claiming to know that they are true. . . . In fact, the phenomenon of nonreligious faith-claims is quite common in political discourse, because policy making often requires us to take some stand when we cannot honestly claim to know that our stand is correct. That is just the way politics is."[193] Political claims would thus seem—and have increasingly come—to occupy the same space, albeit not one of "reasons" in the strict sense, to which religious beliefs have been relegated by inferentialist theory, as reconstructed by Stout, due to their supposed sublimity, their self-imposed or forced exile, their privatization, and now, we might add, their peculiar mediatization. Each of these inflicts on its "discourse" a certain untranslatable idiom, even a certain indelible madness, however much it tries to (or succeeds in) entering the public domain. Yet, none of this—in the pragmatist account—makes the recurrent emergence of such discourses incomprehensible and incommunicable per se. Brandom's presentation of the matter, which addresses the religious case almost in passing, makes this subtle difference strikingly clear:

> There *is* a certain sort of cognitive irresponsibility involved in those who do not take themselves to be reliable reporters of a certain sort of phenomenon nonetheless coming to believe the reports they find themselves inclined to make. But I do not think that is a decisive reason to deny that it is intelligible to acquire beliefs in that way. Cognitively irresponsible beliefs can genuinely be beliefs. And in these very special cases, such irresponsible beliefs can qualify as knowledge. . . . In fact, there is nothing unintelligible about having beliefs for which we cannot give reasons. Faith—understood broadly as undertaking commitments without claiming corresponding entitlements—is surely not an incoherent concept. (Nor is it by any means the exclusive province of religion.) And should the convictions of the faithful turn out not only to be true but also (unbeknownst to them) to result from reliable belief-forming

processes, I do not see why they should not be taken to constitute knowledge. . . .
Knowledge based on reliability without the subject's having reasons for it is possible
as a local phenomenon, but not as a global one.[194]

The *relative* unintelligibility of certain beliefs (or faith-claims), that is to say, their *ultimate*
inexplicability to others, is supported by the global, if not total, intelligibility of most
other beliefs, whose necessary supposition Davidson has baptized the "principle of charity." There is much more that we do than we do not share in terms of reasons given and
received. Each of our individual concepts and categories is sustained by a web of suppositions whose implicit normativity enables the explicitness of norms, criteria, rules, and
laws to emerge when and where needed. And *wherever "religion" forms an exception to
such a holistic background, it is, well, nothing exceptional.* Every singular claim—and not
just a religious faith-claim—is subject to the same pragmatic logic, to the same semantic
principle, which allows that *some* but not all (or most) claims can take exception to a
rule, a norm, a practice, whose largely implicit presuppositions regulate most moves in
the language game. The fact is simply that, in the social contexts that are ours, not every
exception has the same explaining to do. In Stout's terms: "If the reason for excluding
the expression of religious commitments is that they create this type of discursive impasse,
then the only fair way to proceed is to exclude the expression of many nonreligious
commitments, as well. But if we go in this direction, Rorty's view will require silence on
many of the most important issues on the political agenda."[195]

Stout's arguments are among the considerations that led Rorty to amend his characterization of "religion as a conversation stopper." He concedes "that it is false that religion
is 'essentially' a conversation-stopper, because it is not 'essentially' anything."[196] And yet,
he maintains, certain religious modes of expression (namely those that appeal to the
unquestionable authority of faith or ecclesial authority) *do*, indeed, stop all further conversation. But then, Rorty goes on to acknowledge, the appeal to some leap of faith or
final authority, where no additional reasons seem readily available—or where, as Wittgenstein's *Philosophical Investigations* claims, we merely appeal to whatever it is that we
just happen to do—represents a "kind of reply" that is far from "confined" to the domain
of religious speech: "I should have simply said that citizens of a democracy should try to
put off invoking conversation-stoppers as long as possible. We should do our best to keep
the conversation going without citing unarguable first principles, either philosophical or
religious. If we are sometimes driven to such citation, we should see ourselves as having
failed, not as having triumphed."[197]

"Religion," in this reading, is not the only form of utterance that is tempted to cite
unwarranted—indeed, unwarrantable—claims. Perhaps it is not even the most pernicious
one. Indeed, the role of religion in the public square would seem to flag a general difficulty
that belongs to the heart of social interaction, solidarity, and hope—as well as their opposites—as such: the fact that its "unarguable" differences may—but must not—become

obstacles ("stoppers") to conversations that we cannot but continue to have if we want to avoid conflict as much as we can. "Religion's" conflicts epitomize the elements and forms of "cultural politics"—and, of liberal democracy and all that threatens it today—rather than representing what, in modernity, they have (or should have) moved away from.

"The Matrix Cannot Tell You Who You Are"

Could one grant Rorty's overall point and still withhold one last, minimal—call it *minimally theological* or *globally religious*—reservation? Moreover, could one do so without relapsing into the old ways of thought, by dreaming up a positively stated rather than negatively circumscribed metaphysical nature, avoiding all *theologia naturalis* and all claims based on supposed revelation or unquestioned tradition?

Two observations are in order here. First, Rorty may be right that the very discussability of some thing's criteria of "sense"—that is to say, of identification rather than existence—is fundamentally a matter of social and political controversy and conversation, a question of "cultural politics." This insight has important ramifications for modern problems of knowledge, since it effectively cuts off their supposedly self-evidentiary basis. Indeed, there is no denying that "Philosophy cannot answer: is our vocabulary in accord with the way the world is? It can only answer the question: can we perspicuously relate the various vocabularies we use to one another, and thereby dissolve the philosophical problems that seem to arise at the places where we switch over from over one vocabulary to another?"[198]

Second, Rorty is surely right that some thing's having existence—in addition to the criteria and habitual perceptions that identify its nature and qualities from the outset or over time—cannot be decided by criteria or rules but requires, as Cavell argues, only the singular procedure or performative gesture of our calling or claiming and, hence, proclaiming or acclaiming it so. We might question the responsibility of this procedure or gesture, or ask after its responsible agency: Is it "I" or some "we" who calls the shots here?

Might the first of these two observations be the full answer to the question from which have taken our lead—Why still "religion"? Can it explain why "religion" (or, for that matter, any of its functional equivalents) might still interest anyone? What, in fact or in principle, vouches for Rorty's resorting to "cultural politics" to sort this all out and for his claiming that it is, if not the most adequate or appropriate, then at least the most plausible and useful—and resolutely postmetaphysical—response to the matters at hand? Can a relentless "linguistification of the sacred" or an "inferentialist" perspective convince us when "religion"—at once reduced and inflated, *minimal* and *global*—keeps beating its drum and, far from retreating into mystical silence or private interiority, keeps setting the tone for so many urgent public debates? What makes "religion" resurge and rebound, time and again? And why are its theological and metaphysical concepts and categories still relevant, indeed, unavoidable in our day and age?

Wittgenstein may offer a plausible answer when he appeals to "grammar" and "essence" as a more than merely historical, let alone sociological, societal, or cultural-political, deep-seated need. Rather than providing a strict metaphysical or ontological basis for overarching claims, this need allows certain themes and obsessions to recur incessantly. Might this not account for the fact that some emphatic concepts and categories, such as "religion," remain indefinitely in circulation and, as it were, continue to call out for discussion, whether they are discussable and decidable or not?

It is as if not only our "horizontal" or lateral language games and forms of life but also the "vertical" depths of our "natural history"—the very lineage and embodiment of our conventions—predisposes us to entertain some questions rather than others: problems that impose themselves *with virtual necessity*, but for which we can never hope to determine the answer on purely rational, criteriological, and hence discursive or normative grounds.

Michael Fried recalls a remarkable passage in which Wittgenstein, speaking of the undeniable force and conviction produced by mathematical proofs, imagines the following dialogue between two voices:

> It is as if this expressed the essence of form.—I say, however: if you talk about *essence*—, you are merely noting a convention. But here one would like to retort: there is no greater difference than that between a proposition about the depth of the essence and one about—a mere convention. But what if I reply: to the *depth* that we see in the essence there corresponds the *deep* need for the convention.
>
> Thus if I say: "It's as if this proposition expressed the *essence* of form"—I mean: it is as if this proposition expressed a property of the entity *form*!—and one can say: the entity of which it asserts a property, and which I here call the entity "form," is the picture which I cannot help having when I hear the word "form."[199]

The passage resonates with certain reflections in Cavell's *The Claim of Reason* regarding the meaning of *natural* and *conventional*, just as it reminds us at a greater distance of some of McDowell's discussion of "second nature" in *Mind and Word*.[200] More indirectly, it reminds us of a central concern in Gilles Deleuze's struggle, in *Difference and Repetition*, against what he calls a "dogmatic image of thought": an "image" that, like the metaphysical "pictures" that concern Wittgenstein in the *Philosophical Investigations*, especially in its historically pervasive representationalist articulation, stands in the way of a more "authentic" (the term is Deleuze's) understanding of language and philosophy. Deleuze, especially in his later writings, leaves no doubt that there are other counterexamples and traditions whose alternative "images" merit our attention, just as Wittgenstein does not dismiss "pictures" per se. They diagnose and critique the *conceptual idolatry* of which Jean-Luc Marion speaks in a different register, without postulating a simple outside and neutral stance that could fully escape the web of metaphysical implications or, for that matter, allow one to invoke a pure and normative *archē* or anchor beyond its inevitable distortions (but of "what" or "who," exactly?).

What this motif, strangely common although differently motivated and articulated in each of these thinkers, means, I think, is that one cannot be merely *nominalist* about the subject of "religion." We cannot assume that nothing "real" (nothing of "the Real") is conveyed, invoked, or referenced by its concept, image, or picture; nor, of course, can we assume that *realistic*—general and universal, formal and essential—properties express its nature and essence (its "in and for itself," to use the Kantian-Hegelian vocabulary) per se. Propositional attitudes based on either *de dictu* or *de re* distinctions no longer do justice to the complexity of the matter of "religion," if ever they did (say, during the medieval struggle between nominalists and realists over "universals").

What remains is a simple, if minimal truth: namely, the *more than strictly historical or empirical "fact"* that "something" must have compelled us to see other things (other "somethings," etc.) in a different, special, elevated, and eminent light. This must have been one of the reasons why appeals to "transcendence" and its mirror image, "immanence," have been alternatively venerated and feared throughout so many centuries, well before the arrival of modernity and modernism. Something (some "Thing") in these signifiers kept pushing and pulling toward some signified that could never be had—thought, practiced, perceived, or judged—as such, and whose incommunicable meaning, strictly speaking, made no "sense." Materialism and secularism, no less than "religion," find their origins in this excess of nonsense over sense that ushers itself into the heart and interstices of our vocabularies, imaginaries, practices, and moods.

Some deep-seated need must have propelled to the fore what is otherwise just "a particular way of conceptualizing the world" or, indeed, "an idiosyncratic system of de-marcating certain supposed contents of the world."[201] It must have done so less with good, let alone sufficient, reason than in an "encounter" (Deleuze) with a certain "natural history" (Wittgenstein), a peculiar "naturalness" (Cavell) that makes up our finitude.

To affirm this does not mean proposing a straightforward, down-to-earth, naturalistic genealogy of humankind, of its fits of inspiration and habituations. What is at stake in such indelible pressure, with its irrefutable invitations and irrefusable encounters, is the theme of the *minimalist metaphysical* inquiry that, in our day and age, *minimal theologies* should dare to undertake, without apology, but also without apologetics.

Rorty seems to hint at the legitimacy of such an inquiry when, in response to Gianni Vattimo, he allows for the possibility that love, or *agapē*, in its Christian and Heideggerian sense, could, for us, come to indicate the mode and mood in which we enter, rather than stop, conversations in "cultural politics." Referring to Wittgenstein's term *language-game*, which he deems "unfortunate" because it suggests rule-governed patterns where there are none, rather than teasing out the elements and forms that the *Philosophical Investigations*, in their best moments, consider to be "practices, traditions, the kind of things people pick up without learning any rules but just by 'know-how,'" Rorty supplements this characterization with a remarkable insight. In response to the New Testament conception of love in 1 Corinthians 13, he explicitly states that one might "think of charity as the willingness to pick up other people's practices, to gain other people's 'know-how.'"[202]

The acknowledgment not only resonates with the late Heidegger's musings about the meaning of "possibility" and "possibilization" (*Möglichkeit* and *Ermöglichung*), which should be seen as enabled by a certain "liking" or "love" (as in the German verb *mögen*), it opens up a whole avenue of possibilities—and loves—for *post*-postmetaphysical thinking and a turn to the religious archive, as well.

But can "love" carry all this ontological weight? Can it lead us to the very heart of the *Denken des Seins* (the "thought of Being," in the subjective and objective genitive)? Furthermore, what would it mean, not only historically and culturally, but politically, to ascribe to "love" this pivotal function of inspiring and enabling "willingness to pick up other people's practices, to gain other people's 'know-how'"? Conversely, would "love" play its—however subliminal (sublimed or sublimated)—role on *any* occasion where conversations, practices, or know-hows (albeit the most trivial) are engaged, that is to say, willed or gained, even in the most banal of ways?

Are the religious understandings of "love" less risky (or more useful) when conceived of as metaphors, motifs, and modalities of our points of entry into discursive practices—or, perhaps, as what perpetually sustains such practices—rather than as their utopian "other," as the imagined situation in which all (need for) discussion supposedly ends? Does "love" *need* talk? Or does one no longer need to talk where, precisely, one "loves" or is "loved"? And, as to all talk, whether small-talk or God-talk, could one not ask with equally good reason: "What's love got to do with it?" But were we to abandon this notion, what different conception could fulfill its role? What "image" or "picture" would we want to put in its place of historical, even present privilege? Against what background or foil do we substitute one conceptual tool for another, when its more than merely historical-empirical weight fades and a new constellation of good (or bad) luck allows (or forces) us to change the subject?

That we can ask these types of questions—and that "religion" provides us with the most extensive, most profound resources to theorize their depth and pervasiveness—must mean, in terms of popular culture, that "the Matrix cannot tell you who you are" (even though we may very well—continue to—"live" as if it does). In other words, we may and ought (but must not) keep intact or inviolable a certain distance—however infinitesimally small, yet therefore uncrossable and, hence, at any given moment, of maximal depth, width, and perspectival or performative effect—between our own sense of "ourselves" (more precisely, "me") and all the projections, projects, prolepses, lapses, and even stases we're engaged in, whether voluntarily or against our will.

Let me recapitulate. Words, things, gestures, and powers—like sounds, silences, smells, touches, shapes, colors, affects, and effects—might be seen as instances and instantiations of the "everyday," of the "extraordinariness of the ordinary," of the "ordinariness of the extraordinary," of "the common," "the low," of which Cavell, following Austin, Wittgenstein, Emerson, and Thoreau, makes so much. They are the visible and tangible, the living and enabling conditions of "the religious," just as they typify its supposed counterpart, "the secular," including all the varieties of modern experience in between.

Yet reference to and invocation of generic terms such as *religion*, *the secular*, and their substitutes is solicited and required by the material terms whose study forms the primary object—indeed, a necessary detour—for any inquiry interested in the question "Why still religion?" The broader generic concepts and categories of "religion," the "secular," and their analogues constitute and inflect our understanding of the singular material terms, in turn. They give them their experiential intensity—their transcending, near ab-solute quality—without which, for all their presentness and immanence, they would not *matter in our world.*

The "new materialism" in the study of religion remains thus, paradoxically, premised upon a no less important minimal, some would say negative metaphysics (or, indeed, theology), whose center and content has been continuously split and increasingly vacated so as to become the mere "placeholder" (Habermas) of reason's intelligibility, of its non-bisected rationality, that is to say, of the principal openness for what might still be different (e.g., a further reason), or still and forever "to come" (Derrida).

Every word, thing, gesture, power, sound, silence, touch, scent, affect, and effect can come to this, that is to say, turn into something—some Thing—significant and then revert to insignificance again. In other words, it can switch on and off, change its aspect, alter the face of the earth (for us). This is, precisely, what the different appreciations and evaluations of the everyday and the ordinary—as something to be sought (out) in its sublimity or, on the contrary, to be avoided in its fallenness—have signaled in nineteenth- and twentieth-century philosophy, from Emerson, Thoreau, Kierkegaard, and Heidegger to Wittgenstein, Austin, Cavell, and Fried. Authenticity and inauthenticity, meaning and its destitution, absorption and theatricality form two different—indeed, fundamentally opposed—sides of one and the same coin, tossed up in the air by our natural histories, that is to say, by spatiotemporal necessities, contingencies, or encounters, which defy prediction as much as they elude control, and which signal promises as much as risks and threats.

The Archive; or, Deep Pragmatism and the Site for Philosophical Fieldwork

In the view we have been propounding, one could characterize "religion" as a phenomenon or an ensemble of sets of phenomena that does not just express but is, perhaps, the most telling vehicle of a "cultural memory" (as Jan Assmann calls it) or "chain of memory" (as Danièlle Hervieu-Légier says). To do so does not yet give us an understanding of how it is that "religion's" words, things, gestures, powers, sounds, silences, smells, touches, shapes, colors, affects, and effects are produced and distributed, that is to say, propelled or projected and welcomed, invited, or allowed into the most various—and even most resistant—social and cultural contexts, and now spill into global markets and informational networks, into the new media of digital communication, mobile phones, and bloggospheres.

Only an understanding of the mechanisms that operate on these material instances (instants and instantiations) of the "religious"—or of the process by which such mechanisms, their automatisms and technicities, are operated—would allow us to analyze, interpret, perhaps explain, or make explicit its global phenomenon. By this is meant the very phenomenality of its set(s) of singular terms and events—their grammar and essence, as it were—but also the breaking up and reconstituting of all its constitutive parts, in a host of surprising but often strangely effective new functional relations.

Without merely theoretically assessing and normatively judging "religion" in abstraction, from a bird's- or God's-eye point of view or in toto, such a strategy undertakes a detour through material instances. The method of what I would call a *perspectivism or perspectivalism for the sake of the "ab-solute"* might offer the sole approach available to deal with "religion's" past, presence, and possible futures. It would force us to proceed piecemeal and patiently, sideways instead of frontally, following a rhythm dictated by specific—if not necessarily ad hoc or merely local—concerns.

Furthermore, such an approach would not permit us to macro- or micro-manage "religion," but rather would force us to *work through it* infinitely, with no end or resolution in sight, concentrating on "finite little changes" and, perhaps, replacing "the grandeur of something all-encompassing, something that provides the largest possible framework of discourse and sets the bounds for all thoughts" with what Rorty, following Isaiah Berlin, calls "romantic profundity": in other words, "dropping the notion of something high and vast and remote and replacing it with the notion of something deep within."[203]

But does such a notion not also require that one step beyond Brandom's "synthesis of pragmatism and idealism," with its larger theoretical-philosophical stance that "combines Hegel without eschatology and Heidegger without ontology," that is to say, with its ambition to substitute "conversation" for *Geist*, and the "coherence of beliefs" for the "correspondence to an object"?[204] Put differently, does it suffice to state what seems by now a fairly uncontroversial insight, namely, that different value spheres overlap and resonate, needing no external principle, indeed, no set of internal rules or fixed criteria that would supposedly regulate and distribute (let alone cause, orient, and terminate) them from without or within? Rorty suggests as much: "All these spheres of culture continually interpenetrate and interact. There is no need for an organizational chart that specifies, once and for all, when they are permitted to do so. Nor is there any need to attempt to reach an ahistorical, God's-eye overview of the relations between all human practices. We can settle for the more limited task Hegel called 'holding our time in thought.'"[205]

But the comparison goes only this far, for the proposed *working through* of the material instances that we rightly or wrongly associate with "religion" and that we pursue in lieu—but in view—of their "ab-solute" does not tend toward an eventual overcoming, that is, a conceptual mediation and resolution of the phenomenon (or sets of phenomena) in question. Nor are these an avoidable projection (say, of false consciousness, infantile neuroses, bad faith, hypocrisy, or some earlier evolutionary and biological stage or regression) to whose demise we could—or ought to—aspire. It is more realistic to assume that in matters "religious" we may not even hope to work the phenomena through to the very end. To the extent that any dialectic is at work here, it will be open-ended and, as Adorno taught us, consistently negative (to the point of having to question the very concepts and values of "negation" and "mediation"—and, by implication, of "working through"—themselves).

Against this background, then, we ought not to exclude that "religion," in its present vocabularies, imaginaries, sensibilities, practices, and institutions, signals as many material traces, residues, and sedimentations of an immensely extended, diversified, and deep-seated *archive of the past*—which is, in principle, an actualizable and thus potential *future* as well—whose resources we have barely begun to fathom, to realize, let alone to exhaust. If there was any need for breaking away from "religion" in modernity, in the wake of the Enlightenment critiques of its epistemic bases, moral significance, and political or cultural merit, there may be just as many reasons to *break back through to it again*, at a historical juncture whose violent encounters, predicaments, promises, and threats require that we explore all available sources of the inspirational moods, imaginative motifs, intellectual modalities, and practical motivations that past generations have bequeathed to us.

This admonition to break back through again to the "religious" archive is implied in a proposal made by Job Cohen, the social-democratic mayor of the city of Amsterdam, whose formulation *omgekeerde doorbraak* ("reverse break through") varies and parodies an expression originally introduced by one of the founding fathers of the Dutch postwar Labor Party (PvdA), Willem Banning, when he proposed a new consensus by way of a breakthrough (*doorbraak*) of the ideological, cultural, and institutional barriers between the pillorized social groups of former Marxists, social-democrats, religious socialists, Christian-democrats, personalists, radicals, and progressive liberals. It needs no further explanation that new—similar but different—coalitions and novel constellations in the political arena, based on more than merely tactical compromises, are much needed in contemporary European democracies as they face even more challenging transformations of their public spheres. But the concept "reverse breakthrough" might well contain a further kernel of truth and invite us to think beyond the concepts—to begin with, "religion"—into which we have boxed ourselves in the last few centuries, despite the best of intentions.

What would it mean to break through, away from a present supposedly determined by modern imperatives of secularism, republicanism, cultural liberalism, and the ideals of parliamentary or even radical forms of democracy, *back* to "religion's" past, marred by authoritarianism, communitarian hierarchy, dogmatism, exclusion, and discrimination? What, in other words, would it take to give "religion" a future (again)? How, indeed, could we avoid either progressive or regressive assumptions of a teleological and linear kind, which pretend that either the past finds its extrapolation in the future via the present, or that the future brings past and present (back) into their own? Must all effects follow causes? And do all causes have effects in time? What alternative temporalities—other than circular conceptions—do we already have available to steer clear of such foundational models, which portray the past as the condition or anticipation—that is to say, the *possibility*—of present and future possibilities?[206] Could we think or imagine the past as somehow *virtually present* or *always still to come*? Could the past be thought along lateral and futural lines, which escape and defy genealogy, the logic of historicism, culturalism, the old and new materialism?

As we have said, several strong attempts have been made to analyze "religion" in terms of "cultural memory" or a "chain of memory." In what sense is the conception of "religion" dependent on an understanding of "memory," on an "archive"? In other words, what is the place of the "past"—as in our locution "The Future of the Religious *Past*"—ontologically, heuristically, or strategically? What practical and institutional forms can such a "past" take? Finally, how could such a "past" be fruitfully studied, and scanned or mobilized in search of "elements and forms for the twenty-first century"?

Do we take "religion's" past to be historically accessible, largely known and surpassed, with merely documentary value? Or is this past, in a sense, not so much (or not yet) *behind*, but rather *around*, or *before* us, that is to say, not yet determined, perhaps indeterminable—ab-solute and pure—being constantly revisited in altogether different ways in everything we think and do, gesture and suffer, that is to say, in all that affects us and that we affect and put into effect, in turn? Is "religion's" past a *virtual* shadow that looms over every single instance (instant and instantiation) that punctuates our individual and collective lives, dooming it in advance to transience, contingency, fallibility? Or is such a past an enabling horizon that makes life and its moments possible and meaningful, for example, by elevating it to a level of sublimity (or normalcy) of which we no longer believed our everydayness to be capable? And is this, perhaps, the very basis of our "acceptance" of the external world of material things, of our "attunement" and "agreement" with other minds, including the other that we may, at times, become to ourselves, as our former selves are bracketed, turned around, and converted or lose faith and belief—or "love of the world"—altogether?

Two compelling scholarly works have convinced me of the need to relate an understanding of "religion" as memory and archive (in all the semantic, figurative, argumentative, rhetorical, visual, visceral, affective, and effective dimensions I alluded to earlier) to a more complex and thought-provoking idea of the "absolute"—"pure," "virtual," "a priori," or "general"—"past," as elaborated by Bergson and Deleuze. In these authors' accounts, the "absolute past" is somehow operative and actualized in our present perceptions and the recollections on which they draw for orientation when confronted with practical problems.

Paola Marrati, in her lucid exposition and interpretation of the philosophy of cinema of Gilles Deleuze, deeply influenced by Bergson's *Matter and Memory*, and Alex Lefebvre, in his remarkable study of what he, adopting an expression from Deleuze's *Difference and Repetition*, calls "the image of law," have both convincingly argued that for any plausible contemporary philosophical understanding of the conditions of cinematic invention and of judgment and jurisprudence, respectively, we must, following Bergson and Deleuze, assume that the past is not "past," in the sense of chronologically behind us, as a faded psychological impression or diminished perception of a former present. Rather, it is somehow in its totality *contemporaneous and co-extensive with the present*.[207]

For all of their insistence on the irreversibility and nonlinearity of time, of the non-spatiality and noninstantaneous character of duration, novelty, and encounters, Bergson and, in his footsteps, Deleuze explore a "past in general," a "pure" or "virtual" past whose "absoluteness" consists less in being active in the present, which is characterized by practical needs and sensorimotor agency, or in being a direct repository for a future that is as yet absent, but rather in being a multidimensional realm that is external to our conscious memory, even though it must become actualized at every given instant, for example, in habit memories or wherever present perceptions have a need, desire, or use for it. It is thus that it comes to inform—and also somehow forms itself in—our thoughts and imaginings as a function of our present needs to act (that is to say, to select from the universe of images that envelops us). If memories from the past were just diminished perceptions with less density and intensity, it would be hard to understand why present perceptions have any use for recollections and "attract" them at all. This, in a nutshell, is Bergson's critique of the theories of psychological associationism.[208]

Moreover, if the past were not "pure," "general," "a priori," or "virtual," in other words, if its archive coincided with whatever is somehow on the books or documented, that is to say, in an actual, historical, and empirical archive (of words, things, gestures, powers, etc.), then we could never understand why it is that anything—and a fortiori "religion"—could continue to capture and renew our attention. Only by being irreducible to a given myth or whatever set of data could "religion" invite and tolerate—indeed, force—new interpretations, affects, and effects, or, conversely, fall into oblivion and insignificance. "Religion," as the doctrine or practice revolving around some "absolute," absolves itself from any given meaning, from any historical or empirical given, and hence retains a certain freedom with regard to its proper subject. It hovers between fixity and positivity, reification and fetishization, on the one hand, and the aleatory and nonsensical—just a word, mere *flatus vocis*—on the other; and this for good and for ill, since this oscillation is its perpetual promise and risk at any point in time (which is something we are more aware of nowadays than ever before).

Even where all that counts and punctuates (or punctures) our experience is novelty, nothing can ever be over and done with once and for all. Every difference is repetition, provided we understand the strict implications of these terms: namely, that any repetition is iteration, or that reiteration inscribes change into the very heart of its operation and, as we said, actualizes the internal difference of the "absolute," "general," "pure," or "virtual" past that is contemporaneous and co-extensive with the present (as it will be with what we could call future presents). The future of the "religious" past would thus be, first of all, that of a "virtual" past. This past is neither chronological nor psychological in any strict sense of these terms. Psychologically "unconscious," it has dimensions and proportions that are irreducible to any mental state or process, whether individual or collective. The memory in question is, precisely, not "cultural." And could it be said to form part of a "chain"?

This profound and complex insight—and nothing else could give pragmatism (for which both Bergson and Deleuze declared sympathies) its deeper perspectival dimensions—finds a certain resonance in Derrida's repeated insistence on the importance of the motif of the "archive" as well as in the Levinasian trope (borrowed in turn from Paul Valéry) of a *profond jadis*, a "past that was never present,"[209] in which one could be tempted to find a source of inspiration in addressing an at once observed and strategically—however provisionally—advocated "turn to religion."[210]

One might now add that the Bergsonian and Deleuzian understanding of an "absolute" past, as Marrati and Lefebvre bring it to fruition, holds true for "religion"—in particular, for "the future of the religious past"—as well. Linking up our pragmatist understanding of the "archive" with this decidedly metaphysical (Bergson) and ontological (Deleuze) view would prevent or at least discourage us from thinking about its potentially or virtually infinite resource in merely instrumentalist or voluntaristic ways. Moreover, it would amend the pragmatist, holistic, discursive, and conversationalist view articulated by Rorty and Brandom with a perspective of virtual rather than vertical depth, that is to say, of lateral and horizontal, contemporaneous and co-extensive dimensions that are less empirically given or ready at hand than in need of being chosen and actualized selectively, that is to say, attentively and prudently—in a word, pragmatically—in view of a "greater or lesser advantage" or interest for the action needed to survive situations.[211] Let us call this *deep or virtual pragmatism*.[212]

A further dimension of perspectival depth—namely, that of the "absolute," "pure," "general," "a priori," or "virtual" past—is thus added to the "transcendental field" of *actual* images, in Bergson's view, or the "plane of immanence," according to Deleuze, both made up of material images in movement, constituting a near-Spinozistic universe, "the infinite movement of a substance that continually propagates itself."[213] All of this operates as the open dimension or horizon within which undelimitable variation and combination become possible, according to natural laws, and in which living organisms (conscious subjects) need not just select and choose, isolate and set aside—in short, *subtract*—what to store or restore, give or receive, but may, indeed, must also hesitate and delay, delimit and deliberate, as well. Nothing would happen (or could have happened) without the assumption of this open, multidimensional, de- or a-centered, and unconscious milieu made up of present and especially past (but not future?) images, which condition our consciousness (or, for that matter, conscience and conscientiousness), rather than the other way around (as modern philosophy, especially Kant and Husserl, believed). To perceive and act according to the demands of a pragmatically defined situation, we must assume (in the sense of postulate and take upon us) this "transcendent field" of the "plane of immanence," which will reveal certain images—or reflect and mirror certain aspects—as relevant, leaving most, indeed almost all others implicit, in the dark, or invisible.

Such selection of a particular region, level, or stratum of specificity within the general past takes place as we focus our attention, like a "camera" on its object, zooming in on what need, want, and desire choose to highlight and subtracting everything else. It is thus that certain elements come to the fore "like a condensing cloud" and that the virtual "passes into" the actual.[214] Furthermore, what tends to form itself along these lines are "some dominant recollections, veritable shining points around which the others form a vague nebulosity."[215]

Here also perception proves far from instantaneous, but subtracts and contracts multiplicities of matter and moments—"an enormous multiplicity of [molecular] vibrations which appear to us all at once, although they are successive"—into "one relatively simple intuition."[216] Perception, then, is neither strictly instantaneous nor immediate—in the sense of without means or medium—but needs recollections and acts of memory, which coalesce around its minimal "core,"[217] so as to make it effective in the present. Indeed, the present contracts in itself a multiplicity, an infinity of infinitesimally different (and differential) temporal moments, operations, and registers, whose subtraction produces not only the present as more than merely a succession of nows or instants but also the fact that the past somehow exists alongside it, as our reality's shadow, as it were.

In this reading, the present—or future present—of the religious past can never be fully "religious," as it contracts within itself (within the actual present, that is) an infinity of infinitesimally distinct and qualitatively other particular moments, regions, levels, or strata, which together make up the general past, and all of which affect and act upon it.

All of the non- or areligious past that is part and parcel of the "pure" or "virtual" past co-exists with *all* of the religious past. By the same token, this religious past could be said to be virtually present (if not actual, in any case contemporaneous and co-extensive) in toto with every present or future present, including those presents that are prompted and propelled, contracted and enveloped, in qualitatively different—supposedly nonreligious —ways.

But then, "religion" was *not* always part of the past. The pure past exists and subsists eternally and contains much that preceded the advent or rumor of the revelation of "religion." Ever since it emerged, however, "religion" will forever remain an integral part of that past, although *in or as part of that past* it has no separate or special status. It may, one fine (or terrifying?) day, no longer be of any practical use. In consequence, its recollection would no longer be activated, materialized, or lived. There would thus be no contradiction between the hypothesis of an abiding, eternally subsisting past and the empirical or historical fact that we might, at any given time, somehow lose (out on), if not the past *in its totality*, then at least a particular element of that past. We might, for example, lose (out on) our own past, but also one that, in light of our practical needs, wants, and desires, has not solicited or attracted us so far (and, indeed, may never do so).

But until and even after this has happened, each supposedly "nonreligious" (e.g., "secular," "atheist," "humanist," "materialist") present or future present (whether perception or action, epoch or context) will be shadowed and enveloped in *its* pure or virtual past by just as much "religion" as would have been contemporaneous and co-existent with another actual present or future present that we might feel compelled to designate instead as "religious" through and through.

This is not to say that "religion" will or should attain the same level of explicitness or articulation at any moment in time. Nor could we maintain that it has a determinable distinctness as an infinite or open set of particular memories in the pure or virtual past as such. To make matters more difficult, nothing from the virtual halo surrounding our actual or future present contemporaneously and co-extensively may ever be selected and hence actualize or materialize, that is to say, coalesce around something we need or want. Nor could we suggest that—so far, in what we might be tempted to call past, in the sense of no longer actual, presents—it has *ever* reached a sufficiently recognizable and pragmatically useful level of explication for us. All or most of its (pure, virtual) past might very well have been missed or gone unnoticed in all the presents we have encountered up until now and, in this sense, still lie ahead of us in some future present, assuming that it could—one fine or fatal day—be actualized and (once again?) active or useful, wanted and desired, in any given present at all. More generally, there might always remain more to its implicitness than any explication could—or should—hope to unfold. And, whatever its level of explicitness (actualization or presentness), it could actually, presently disappear in an apocalyptic heartbeat or dissipate without a whisper, or, on the contrary, resurface "like a thief in the night," like a deus ex machina.

"Religion's" pure or virtual past is its "unconscious," its "a priori," posited and presupposed as what is outside and alongside present experience: it is the "already there"[218]—albeit far from "given" and never experienced as such, in its integrity, let alone totality—on which present perception and recollection, in its very actuality and activity, incessantly draws and from whose element it extricates elements whenever it needs them, that is to say, wherever new encounters, situations, and problems invite, allow, or force it to go (or whenever so-called habit memories are actualized in the most mechanical or automatic of our behaviors).

Lefebvre reminds us of Proust's formulation, cited again and again by Deleuze, that the past is "real without being present, ideal without being abstract."[219] Yet in its ideal reality (and empirical nonactuality) it is withdrawn from any psychologistic—or, more broadly, reductionist-naturalistic—explanation and the mentalism and representationalism that comes with it. To the extent that we could call this past a "transcendental" condition of all psychic, social, and cultural phenomena and representations, this ground cannot be located in—or fixed and delimited by—any subject, whether individual or collective, nor could it be simply instrumentally used and abused at will. We are dealing, therefore, with a genuinely ontological, more precisely, metaphysical or transcendental motif, which serves as the dimension or element—a perspective of depth—in which a pragmatic response to situations seeks to act and orient itself as best as it can by soliciting and extricating elements from the past and inserting them into the present. That this cannot be done voluntaristically, as we have said, seems clear: for no present—even though it is followed and enveloped in its very instant by the totality of the pure and virtual past—actively welcomes everything (or all at once). Given the determination of any situation, the overdetermination of any problem, it can have neither interest in nor use for all of the virtual element(s) that—contemporaneously, co-extensively—co-exist(s) with it.

Two remarks are in order here. First, it is as if the elemental realm of the universe of images (*l'élémental*, as Levinas said, "second nature," as some of the neo-Hegelian analytic philosophers, such as McDowell and Brandom now add[220]) prefigures any subsequent configuration and reconfiguration of our perception and action. But would this mean that there always remains a surplus of the implicit or unconscious—even, as Levinas says, of "nonsense"—over all sense we can make of ourselves, the world, and everything in it? Or does it, on the contrary, mean that all there is (or was and will be) is potentially meaningful—perceptible, usable, even conceptual—through and through? Finally, should we treat these two broadly ontological—and deeply metaphysical—views as radical alternatives between which we must choose (or between which we will always already have chosen, depending on how we act or merely react)?

One might, second, wonder to what extent the central motif and modality of the absolute, pure, and virtual past—together with the distinctive philosophical mood and motivation to which it testifies—is adequately captured by other attempts to theorize the ways in which a certain pastness operates as a force (rather than playing) field of agency and passion, practices and powers: as the "curvature," as Levinas says, of its "social space." Can we discern or develop other notions that, while similar in structure to that of the "absolute past," are, perhaps, not as deeply metaphysically or ontologically invested as in Bergson's and Deleuze's proposals? What alternative ways are there to explain how "past" ideas and idioms, perceptions and habitualizations—and "religion," its words, things, gestures, and powers, would be as good a candidate as any other—continue to inflect and propel, if not to organize and orient, current possibilities of seeing or doing things? I can think of at least two proposals, each with its respective strengths and weaknesses, which would be relevant to our project: Foucault's "genealogy" of the discursive and more than simply discursive formation and exertion of power, and Austin's "linguistic phenomenology" of the cultural depository of the ordinary.

First, let us examine Foucault's rediscovery of the *dispositif*, which Giorgio Agamben, in a recent essay, relates back to a theological trope of *dispositio*,[221] more precisely, to the sense of "positivity" that Hegel uses in his early theological writings to designate "the historical element, with all the weight of rules, rites, and institutions that have imposed themselves on individuals due to an external force, but which also finds itself, as it were, interiorized in the system of beliefs and sentiments."[222] In short, Agamben explains, the *dispositif* comes to replace the abstract "universals" (of state, law, sovereignty, and power) as part of a series of different "operative concepts with general import." It captures an articulated *ensemble* of "practices and mechanisms," which are both "discursive and non-discursive, juridical, technical, and military."[223] Interestingly, Agamben leads the import of this type of inquiry back to what he calls "a theological genealogy of economy and government."[224] The complex details of and theological reasons for this "divine economy" or *oikonomia*, which dates back to the time of the Fathers of the Church, need not occupy us here.[225] Theologically, it involves the justification of the Trinity, of divine providence, and of Christ's incarnation. Suffice it to note that the Greek *oikonomia* was rendered by the Latin Fathers as *dispositio* and that, for Agamben, it inaugurates a distinction—indeed, nothing short of "schizophrenia"—between God's "being" in and for himself (his "nature" or "essence"), on the one hand, and his "action" in the world (his "operation," "governance," and "administration" of creaturely affairs), on the other, and hence between "ontology" and "praxis." This split has haunted Western culture ever since.[226] The dual perspective or dual aspect theory of reality is here diagnosed in expressive clinical, not to mention pathological, terms.

Of course, one might ask why this must be so, if the onto-theological basis of such divine economy is, indeed, some analogical continuity and, ultimately, unity of essence between the three registers of Trinitarian logic. What Agamben offers seems merely a somewhat Manichaean reading of the Father, on the one hand, and the Son and Spirit, on the other. Indeed, Agamben proposes "simply a general and massive partition of being in two grand ensembles and classes," that is to say, between "living beings (or substances), on the one hand, and the *dispositifs* within which they are ceaselessly captured, on the other," or again, between an "ontology of creatures" and the "*oikonomia* of the *dispositifs* that try to govern them and to lead toward the good."[227] But let's leave that aside.

It is important to note that Foucault's notion of *dispositif*, as interpreted by Agamben, may serve not only as a reminder that the religious archive—in its very "positivity," which, we have seen, is a virtuality as much as it is a *dispositio*—consists in more than theorems, theologemes, dogmas, and concepts. To weigh its full import, we need to be sensitive to its pervasiveness in all domains of psychic life and society (which, Agamben points out, extend to the late Heidegger's musings about the technological *Gestell*, as yet another disposition or *ponere*, that is to say, *Stellen* or positing[228]). Yet at the heart of the theological origin of the term—which, in Agamben's reading, continues to cast its long shadow on Foucault's use of its derivative—lies a more fundamental worry: the fact, namely, that the term "names that in which—and that by which—a pure activity of governing comes about without the least foundation in being. This is why the *dispositifs* must always imply a process of subjectivation. They must produce their subject."[229]

Two types of *subtraction* are at work here. Whereas Agamben takes "religion" to mean the setting apart and separating, in a "sacred sphere" owned by the gods, of "things, places, animals, or persons," thus subtracting them from free circulation or commerce, he introduces the ancient Roman term *profanation* to designate the contrary movement, namely, the "restitution" of their original common use, restoring their original owner-ship.[230] "Profanation"—the "counter-*dispositif*," the undoing of "separation"—is the op-posite of "sacrifice," which is the "transition from the profane to the sacred, from the sphere of men to that of the gods, via a series of rituals that Hubert and Mauss have inventoried."[231]

One need not share Agamben's insistence on the "caesura"[232] between these two spheres nor accept his bleak diagnosis of the acceleration of processes of desubjectivation under the onslaughts of the "machine of government" in modern capitalism, whose right- and left-wing policies—not to mention well-intentioned pleas to use technology responsi-bly—have become nearly indistinguishable and make no real difference. Worse things have happened, one is tempted to object, than the proliferation of cell phones and the omnipresence of televisual or digital media. Their potential to promote docility, disem-bodiment, or inauthenticity is at least matched by their potential for emancipation in almost every respect.

What remains is the suggestive reference to a "theological genealogy" of the *dispos-itifs*, based on a "Christian paradigm of *oikonomia*," and operative even in the most advanced technological societies.[233] The reference is all the more remarkable since the whole "caesura" it names did not have to wait for the emergence of Trinitarian logic to come about. On the contrary, the conceptual distinction that Agamben has in mind has its roots in the early process of "hominization" as such and is characteristic of the evolution of *homo sapiens*.[234] Why, then, is the theological trope so effective in bringing out its historical and contemporary signification?

What the theological-genealogical reading makes possible is the observation of a remarkable paradox:

> The more [the *dispositifs*] are all-encompassing and disseminate their power in every domain of our lives, the more the government finds itself face to face with an ungraspable element that seems to slip from its grip more than docilely subject itself. That does not mean that this represents a revolutionary element, nor that it can bring to a halt or even merely threaten the governmental machine. Instead of the end of history, which is incessantly announced, we are witnessing pointless grand tours of the governmental machine, which, in a sort of implausible parody of the theological *oikonomia*, has taken upon itself the heritage of a providential government of the world. But instead of saving the world, it remains faithful to the original eschatological vocation of providence and leads it to catastrophe.[235]

Whereas "religion" and sacralization separate and set apart, profanation—as reverse sacrifice, as it were—undoes this separation, thus opening a view of the "Ungovernable," at once "the point of origin and the point of exit for everything political."[236]

The second alternative way of theorizing "pastness" and its future is Austin's sense of methodological propriety in turning his "linguistic phenomenology" back to the archive of "*what we should say when.*"[237] Austin gestures in the direction of a "general"—if perhaps not "absolute" or "virtual"—past from which actual perceptions draw different recollections so as to shore up and orient their pragmatic responses to the encounters that confront them. It would seem that, for Austin, the past, being somehow contemporaneous and co-existent with both the present and the future present, could, if not guide us, then at least provide our utterances or speech acts with the necessary imagery to either generalize or specify our speech acts where needed, giving them the proper perspective, as it were. The sedimented depository of ordinary ways of speaking, far from being trivial, is a genuine storehouse for our present thoughts and actions. In Austin's words: "there is gold in them thar hills."[238] Or again: "our common stock of words embodies all the distinctions men have found worth drawing, and the connections they have found worth marking, in the lifetimes of many generations: these surely are likely to be more numerous, more sound, since they have stood up to the long test of the survival of the fittest, and more subtle, at least in all ordinary and reasonably practical matters, than any that you or I are likely to think up in our arm-chairs of an afternoon."[239] But this should not lead us to assume a privilege for philology per se: on the contrary, what Austin has in mind is a "linguistic phenomenology" ("only that is rather a mouthful," he immediately adds): "When we examine what we should say when, what words we should use in what situations, we are looking again not *merely* at words (or "meanings," whatever they may be) but also at the realities we use the words to talk about: we are using a sharpened awareness of words to sharpen our perception of, though not as the final arbiter of, the phenomena."[240] Austin's turn to ordinary language is, therefore, above all "a good site for *field work* in philosophy," for which he, despite all ambiguity, has the greatest hopes: "Here at last we should be able to unfreeze, to loosen up and get going on agreeing about discoveries, however small, and on agreeing about how to reach agreement."[241] The ambivalence of such "fields" reveals itself, however, a little earlier in the text when Austin cautions that "we should prefer a field which is not too trodden into bogs or tracks by traditional philosophy, for in that case even 'ordinary' language will often have become infected with the jargon of extinct theories, and our own prejudices too, as the upholders or imbibers of theoretical views, will be too readily and often insensibly, engaged."[242]

In sum, the different conceptions of what I have called the "archive" have radically different metaphysical and ontological presuppositions (or seem to steer clear of such suppositions) and articulate their respective senses of, say, "immanence" (Bergson, Deleuze), the "curvature of social space" (Levinas), "power" (Foucault), and the "ordinary" (Austin), in nearly incomparable ways. But they all indicate a direction of inquiry that problematizes the flatness of certain naturalist accounts, whose reductive explanations of the phenomena—not least those called "religious"—are at odds with our intuitions about the pervasiveness and more than merely historical weight of certain notions, figures, and affects, which seem to be neither determined nor arbitrary. Up to a point, I have argued, this past on which our present and future may or may not draw has been captured by the philosophical traditions of pragmatism and moral perfectionism. But, as we have just established, the hunch it registers is not absent from other philosophical methods and inquiries. It will be up to further investigation to analyze and evaluate their parallels and differences, their respective merits and flaws. Here, again, "religion" might be a lens through which matters can better come into focus.

The Essence and Phenomenology of "Religion" Revisited

Reviewing some of the current debates in philosophy and attempting to sound out their relevance for our question, we have suggested a familiar trajectory. From mentalist representationalism (whether in metaphysical onto-theology, rationalist innatism, or empiricist psychologism), we have seen the study of religion move via pragmatist semanticism, inferentialism, and historicism (Davidson, Rorty, Brandom) to moral perfectionism and proclamatory presentism (Cavell), supplemented by a Bergsonian-Deleuzian twist to the "archive." "Religion," we concluded, with its peculiar density and intensity, tenacity and longevity, abstractness and concreteness, ab-solution and virtuality, *makes up* worlds. In an age of new media and global networks, this logic—indeed, this mechanism and automatism—is enhanced, and it may well prepare for something altogether novel—and, who knows, monstrous—as well. Indeed, adopting a formulation proposed by Manuel Castells, we may assume that the "culture of make-believe" is one of "belief in the making."[243]

We have thus indirectly traced a plausible way of reconceiving the emergence of the historical and contemporary conceptualizations of "religion" and the methodical discursive ways in which its "object" or "subject" could be approached. Neither cultural studies, cultural analysis, nor historicism is at issue here. While the "new materialism" should be given all its due, the alternative proposed here is a calculated concern with the singular instances of material and spiritual culture in conjunction with a no less resolute—we might say renewed—metaphysical concern with "essences" and "ideas." The latter echo the Wittgensteinian understanding of "logic" and "grammar," just as they suggest a certain "transcendental historicity" (Derrida) and "historical a priori" (Foucault). Wittgenstein seems to prefigure all of this by introducing the term *natural history*, implying a certain "verticality" of forms of life, in addition to the "horizontality" and laterality that characterizes their succession, their overlap, their conflict.

Such a reorientation of traditional and modern preoccupations enables us to breathe new life into nearly forgotten titles by authors such as Ludwig Feuerbach, Adolph von Harnack, Leo Baeck, Rudolf Otto, Gerardus van der Leeuw, and Heiko Miskotte, whose writings sought for an "essence of religion," "essence of Christianity," "essence of Judaism," or, for that matter, an "Idea of the Holy." Moreover, it puts us in a position to revive—and redefine—a certain understanding and definition of religion's "phenomenology" without resorting to assumptions and methods that have proven either methodologically and epistemologically vulnerable or ethically and politically suspect.

Specifically, we could take words, things, gestures, powers, sounds, silences, smells, touches, shapes, colors, affects, and effects to be so many particulars whose features encapsulate "truths"—if not the "Truth"—to be explicated about "religion," the richness of its pasts, the promise or threats of its presence, and the future of its illusions. But we might venture a step further, beyond the apparent nominalism, historicism, empiricism, psychologism, and culturalism that such an approach might seem to imply, and ask whether such singular truths do not condense and express something of the universal as well. To make them explicit would require a principle of *recollection and projection, reconstruction and construction*, all of which revolve around an involuntary memory, a *reconstitution and explication of a past that as such—in this singular configuration—was never present before*, but whose elements and forms, for all their virtual nature, still cast their shadow or shed their light on the possibilities and challenges that are our own.

Instead of adopting a historicist principle to determine how it was (von Ranke) or espousing a merely "additive" (Benjamin) principle of accumulating facts and figures, the proposed alternative would be *perspectival in lieu and in view of the ab-solute*—and pragmatist, but with a decidedly (negative) metaphysical, minimally theological, and, hence, *deep pragmatist*—twist.

Re-collecting the singular instances that make up the phenomenon and total social fact of "religion" will rely on an at once intellectual, scholarly, and affective—in other words, existential—process, now deliberately voluntary, then involuntary. One cannot necessarily privilege the latter over the former, as Proust insists throughout his *Recherche*. Such re-collection will also accomplish itself in a paradoxical act of passive synthesis, in which *ultimate respect for what was, is, and will be* is paralleled, equaled, and subsequently overtaken by a no less *imaginative production and variation* of knowledge, including self-knowledge, that creates as much as it receives. Paradoxically, in its endless search for further determination—ad infinitum—of its putative "object," such a method might well end up overcoming or getting over "religion" as well, and succeed in doing so to the very measure that it inherits (from) it, each step along the way.

In this sense, what "religion" means (meant or will mean) may be forever relegated to a futurity that only retroactively, through backward projection—reverse implication—constitutes an "object" whose nature (essence, idea, subject, or truth) thus reveals itself only *after the fact* (*nachträglich, après coup*), when all is said and done, as "a past that was never present." This and nothing else is the challenge for which the locution "The Future of the Religious Past" offers an economical formula.

Religion's elements and forms for the twenty-first century might very well deliver the "meaning and end of religion" (Cantwell Smith) after all, so long as we are willing to think of "religion's" essence and idea in radically novel and innovative—material and materialist no less than spiritual, negative metaphysical, and minimally theological—terms. What the thing called "religion" is (was, or will be) would, in this view, basically be our call, that is, for us to say, claim, proclaim, and acclaim, in other words, to argue, strive, and, if need be, fight for. There would be no significance—no affect-effect—of its historical facts, its contemporary events, and its future legacy independent of our willingness and ability to name and explicate and act upon its phenomena, letting its very "essence" and "idea," as Hegel said in his *Phenomenology*, "appear."

Resuscitating, reactivating, remobilizing the archive—what Bergson and Deleuze call the pure or absolute past, the virtual—would mean bringing it into its own, letting it emerge for the first time, giving minimal differences their maximal impact, or, again, letting it condense in the singularity of words, things, gestures, and powers. There would be no *pre-*, *para-*, or *post-*figuration of a single—eternal/historical, material/spiritual, collective/subjective—Truth, but rather the emergence of an infinite, yet incomplete, set of instantiations of truths.

This cautionary rather than inflationary use of the epithet *religion* and its "truths" would allow us to single out and name individual cases and hold them up as examples worthy of contemplation and emulation, inviting new words, things, gestures, powers, and so on to be projected or "repeated" as nonsynonymous substitutions destined to no less virtual infinities of unanticipated contexts.

Sellars and Brandom can be seen as having pointed the way toward a historicizing and pragmatist conception of this revelation-manifestation of all cultural utterance and performance, including that of "religion," beyond the subjectivist and psychologist parameters with which the "phenomenalism" of modern empiricism and logical positivism sought to frame phenomena.

Mutatis mutandis, Davidson's principle of charity and the insight that most beliefs are veridical adds the surmise that, in the end, most of "religion"—including whatever belief or set(s) of beliefs anticipated, surrounded, overcame, or substituted for it—must count as *somehow* necessarily "true." This may sound like a stretch (too good to be true, even too absurd to consider), but the point should be taken as, in fact, a modest one—namely, as the suggestion that any type of inquiry or knowledge accepts and acknowledges more than it can question in good faith (or, indeed, care to know).

This is nowhere more true than where the study of "religion," in all of its facets, is at stake. To the extent that such an enterprise—such a "science" of "religion," with all necessary scare quotes—has a presence or future at all, it should perhaps be seen as paralleling, mimicking, or echoing what Sellars attributes to "empirical knowledge," which, as he says, "like its sophisticated extension, science, is rational, not because it has a *foundation* but because it is a self-correcting enterprise which can put *any* claim in jeopardy, though not *all* at once."[244]

But even where this advice is heeded, not all elements and forms that such "science" produces can be modeled after the inferentialist frame of giving and taking reasons. In the remainder of this all too long introduction, I will once more consider why any serious study of "religion" must aim at no less than a "spiritual" transformation of its subject. Such conversion or turning is the theme and practice of "moral perfectionism." This is Cavell's term, and so we return once more to his writings.

Inferentialism or Moral Perfectionism?

Cavell's views differ in significant ways from pragmatist views, whether in ironist-Romantic (Rortian) or rationalist-inferentialist (Brandomian) orientations. To begin with, for Cavell, moral discourse is neither deductive, inductive, discursive, nor inferentialist through and through. The same holds true for religion and its political, cultural, and aesthetic analogues. Yet it cannot claim a sui generis logic, semantics, or some other type of giving reasons of its own. This said, it does share certain elementary grammatical features of claim making with all human discourse. This basis in *what we ordinarily say, do, mean, or imply* enables us somehow to make sense and to construct and inhabit, as well as destroy, common worlds.[245]

Although *The Claim of Reason* antedates Brandom's *Making It Explicit* and adopts the term in a broader sense, Cavell leaves no doubt that he thinks of moral argument as fundamentally independent of—even resistant to—"inferentialism."[246] "Ethical arguments," all invocations of "ought," "must," "have to," and "supposed to"—which Cavell calls "modal imperatives"—are, as he says, "modes of presenting the very reasons you would offer to support them, and without which they would lack meaning altogether; or they specifically set aside reasons. ('I can do no other.') What makes their use rational is their relevance to the person confronted, and the legitimacy of your position gives you to confront him or her in the mode you take responsibility for."[247]

The difference, for Cavell, between "the moralist" and "the moralizer" would be that the former is "the human being who best grasps the human position, teaches us what our human position is, better than we know, in ways we cannot escape but through distraction and muddle," whereas the latter, in the words of the poet Auden, is exemplified by "the preacher's loose, immodest tone," in other words, by "one speaking in the name of a position one does not occupy, confronting others in positions of which one will not imagine the acknowledgment."[248] The "moralizer," unlike the "moralist"—or, as Cavell will come to say, "moral perfectionist"—endlessly seeks to avoid bearing the consequences of words that, in his mouth, are merely recited, of gestures that, in his demeanor, are simply mimicked, and of powers that, in his force, are merely imposed by authority and not owned, that is to say, merited or lived up to.

In addition to demarcating moral talk from moralizing preaching, the proper rationality of ethical language consists in the willingness and ability to provide reasons, in the capacity and stamina for "giving an account of oneself."[249] Such rationality, Cavell writes, is characterized by our coming to master "the defenses we learn in learning to defend *any* of our conduct which comes to grief: those excuses, explanations, justifications . . . which make up the bulk of moral defense."[250] As we saw, Cavell calls these reasons, which can take the form of narratives (words), attitudes (gestures), consistency (powers), or perhaps even the identification or naming of objects (things), "*elaboratives*."[251]

The "outcome" of moral debate would "affect whether the parties concerned are to continue to live in the same moral world," just as it will influence "whether they will, in the future, accept promises from one another."[252] The latter reference is far from fortuitous, given the centrality of promising in entering into (as well as maintaining) every form of social contract and practice, up to constitutional law and jurisprudence, which make up an important part of the ethical life of any (modern) community, based as they are on patterns of expectation, however implicit and tacit. And if societies' institutions are imagined to be premised on principles and rules, then the many "reasons" that inspire and modulate our initiation in—and commitment to—them are never manifestly or transparently, publicly or explicitly, let alone definitively, characterized.

Rather, when speaking of the promises that underlie and make up the ordinary life and language of shared moral universes, "there is no special procedure to entering it (e.g., no oaths!), no established routes for being selected or training yourself for it, etc."[253] The promise in question is a peculiar performative, absolving itself from any given (context, practice, rule) and, in this sense—as Derrida, following de Certeau, sensed—a "mystical postulate,"[254] which works its way only subliminally through a variety ways of speaking and acting, by way of a *modus loquendi* and *modus agendi*, as de Certeau says in *The Mystic Fable*. It is that upon which "the very existence of human society, and the coherence of one's own conduct,"[255] depend. And yet it is not "*an* institution, but the precondition of any institution among persons at all."[256]

But this "general condition" is, Cavell writes, "not something that promising, whether as action or as a practice, can secure," at least not in any "*general*" or regulatory way, such as the rule-bound account of promising and judging, more Kantian than Wittgensteinian, put forward by John Rawls.

Further, the explicit promise may as such not be as central—or special—as it is often presented in modern theory, in Hume and Nietzsche no less than in Austin and Derrida. The specific words *I promise*, Cavell stresses, do not necessarily form "a sort of ritual of high solemnity." On the contrary:

> there are any number of ways, other than promising, for committing yourself to a course of action: the expression or declaration of an intention, the giving of an impression, not correcting someone's misapprehension, beginning a course of conduct on the basis of which someone else has taken action, and so on. . . . There is nothing sacred about the act of promising which is not sacred about expressing an intention, or any other way of committing oneself. If it is *important to be explicit* then you may engage . . . in . . . the ritual of saying "I promise." It is *this* importance which makes explicit promises important. But to take them more seriously than that, as the golden path to commitment, is to take our ordinary, non-explicit commitments too lightly.[257]

We could even go one step beyond this, Cavell says, by noting that the promise, in addition to being "explicit," is only *special* to the extent that it is *specific* and singles out or selects a certain something (word, thing, gesture, power, sound, silence, affect, or effect) in view of its perceived "importance": "promising is just a specialized form of giving one's word. Rather than being looked upon as an extension of my commitments, the act of promising is better looked at as a restriction of them: take my word only for *this*."[258]

How, then, would the act of promising thus defined reflect (upon) the many performative acts and "passionate utterances" (as Cavell calls them) that, rightly or wrongly, we have come to designate as "religious"? For one thing, we could say that there is nothing "special" or "sacred" about the concept, term, or name of "religion"; in any case, nothing that could not find itself expressed otherwise, in different words and different worlds, expressing other things, gestures, powers, passions, affects, effects, sounds, and silences, and so on. To fail to see this would mean to take "religion" too absolutely, too literally and abstractly, too dogmatically and rigidly, indeed, too solemnly; worse, it would mean to take (its?) ordinary instances, instants, and instantiations not seriously enough. Strictly speaking, "religion" could not matter or weigh in *without, before,* or *beyond* these particular expressions, these singulars, and the whole virtually infinite series of elements and forms they constitute.

To invoke "religion" (the concept, the term) could only serve to *make explicit*—and this means also to *separate out* or *absolve*—the significance (the specialness or, if one wishes, sacredness) of each single one of these moments and momentums. "Religion" would be the name for *the maximal import of the most minimal differences.* Put differently, it could be (and, throughout its history, might very well always have been) a designator that—again, with a merely minimally, barely visible, audible, or sensible variation— renders explicit whatever matters to most, most of the time, and in maximal ways: the ordinary, the everyday, the banal, the profane, life and its world, here and now, and as such. Far from being a "conversation stopper" or, precisely, in bringing to a halt all endless and often unnecessary discourse and deliberation, it would serve as an exclamation mark, of sorts, and thus offer a silver lining to all phenomena so designated and singled out. It would express—and not necessarily verbally (though it could)—what to select for its "importance." Nothing more, nothing less.

Theoreticians of all stripes have forgotten or repressed why this must be so. They insist that the name and rule of the game—"religion"—must encompass or regulate more, whether doctrinally, theoretically, practically, or aesthetically: in short, that the "importance" of "*this*" (as in "take my word for *this*") could not be it, not be important enough. Indeed, it has often been felt that, to deserve its name, "religion" would have to convey—or, if one likes, *consecrate*—a sense of *ultimate* concern, *absolute* obligation, *supreme* value, *eternal* peace, without which nothing in individual and public life, in death and its hereafter, would acquire meaning and sense, semantic density or reference, social cohesion and legitimation, existential worth and beauty. But why, on what grounds, assume that *this* matters more, or in the end?

"Religion" could with equal right be seen as marking and demarcating claims in their "normativity," adorning them with a certain non-naturalist "naturalness" and "conventionality," which distinguish humans, their societies, and "institutions" (just as, Cavell says, "kinship" and "law" do), from biological phenomena such as "hives" or cosmological facts such as "galaxies."[259] In other words, "religion" would capture "general dimensions in terms of which any community can be described," just as much as it might indicate "a *specific* institution"—not unlike "monogamy" or "monotheism," Cavell writes—"in terms of which one society is distinguished from another society, or from the same society at an earlier stage."[260]

Calling such distinctions "religious" would be *neither necessary nor arbitrary.* As Wittgenstein exemplifies throughout the *Philosophical Investigations,* our tendency to overlook the "grammar" of our concepts, of our "criteria" and their inevitable "disappointment," requires that we constantly evaluate our "willingness and the refusal to exchange one word or expression for another, as well as the usefulness or futility in doing so."[261] No a priori principles or axioms, no conventional maxims or norms, could ever relieve us of that responsibility—"commitment"—to the language and singular terms we use. We do not know with certainty or in advance and, indeed, have no available criteria to determine which words, things, gestures, powers, and all their nonsynonymous substitutes may come to matter most, strike us as "important," or not. What holds true for promising and for moral judgment governs *all* actions and passions, events and encounters. And all those we call "religious" form no exception:

> The appeal [to rules] is an attempt to explain why such an action as promising is *binding* upon us. But if you *need* an explanation for that, if there is a sense that something more than personal commitment is necessary, then the appeal to rules comes too late. For rules are themselves binding only subject to our commitment. Why one may think that rules could explain the bindingness of commitment is a question obviously too far for us to reach now.[262]

Its answer, in any scenario, would have to refer less to "knowledge" (unless we could redefine that term in fundamentally nonepistemic ways, drawing on a sense of self-knowledge and knowledge or, rather, acknowledgment of others, including the other we can become to ourselves), than to the "initiation into an entire form of life."[263] Such an answer entails a grasp of the logic or grammar of any such form of life, not so much at its point of entry, but once we have adopted it or been adopted into it. We could start from—or deem "important"—virtually any thing (that is, any word, each gesture, all powers, and the like), but once we have done so certain consequences and limitations will impose themselves, unleashing alternative series in which, however, no single step seems completely given—or dictated—before it is actually made: "Every move changes the situation in which the following move is to be made. Not to know this is not merely to be without the knowledge of a particular practice . . . ; it is to be incapable of engaging in any practice at all; to be unready for responsible (competent) action."[264] In this, there is an analogy with the idea of the contract supposedly underlying social and democratic institutions. As Cavell writes:

> The rules, offices, defenses, actions, etc., "defining the institution," define it by *limiting, specifying*, etc., what counts as an enforceable contract. They do not, however, "define" the form of life generally; one could not understand the particular limitations if one did not already understand the nature of the general form of life; and the Law of Contract itself could only develop in a society in which that form of life already existed.[265]

In other words, my acceptance and acknowledgment of laws and contracts, of the very "Law of Contract itself"—while preventing no disappointment, disengagement, or opting out, if need be—are a priori, that is, come first and are more important. They neither require nor permit any specification or determination in terms of criteria and rules.

Cavell's view, I suggest, comes close to Levinas's and Derrida's conception of obligation and testimony, which likewise imagines a "total" responsibility beyond limit (whether rules and institutions, practices and games, norms and codes).[266] As for them, for Cavell this is a responsibility in which nothing is settled upfront, is nothing clear or simple, with the result that "we are often lost":[267]

> What alternatives we can and must take are not fixed, but chosen; and thereby they fix us. What is better than what else is not given, but must be created in what we care about. Whether we have done what we have undertaken is a matter of how far we can see our responsibilities, and see them through. . . . What we are responsible for doing, is, ineluctably, *what in fact happens.*[268]

And, "*that,*" Cavell concludes, "will be described in as many ways as our actions themselves."[269] Cavell's invocation of "conversation"—as in "*the conversation of justice,*" a locution introduced in *Conditions Handsome and Unhandsome* and in *Cities of Words,* again, in discussion with Rawls—should therefore be taken broadly, since it means not only "talk" but also "a way of life together."[270] Cavell contrasts, rather than opposes, such "conversation" with the concept of "cooperation" and of "games" (if not necessarily language games, as Wittgenstein sees them) each of which has its rules and principles, as they serve as models for deliberation and judgment in Rawls's "Two Concepts of Rules" and *A Theory of Justice*:

> "Cooperation," as general state of social interaction, suggests the idea of society as a whole either as having a project or, at the other extreme, as being a neutral field in which each can pursue his or her own projects. Intuitively, these extremes are analogous to aspects of the interesting institution of competitive games. . . . The idea of "conversation," in contrast, emphasizes neither a given social project nor a field of fairness for individual projects. (Nor . . . does it deny the importance of these ideas.) What it emphasizes is, I might say, the opacity, or non-transparence, of the present state of our interactions, cooperative or antagonistic—the present seen as the outcome of our history of the realization of attempts to reform ourselves in the direction of compliance with the principles of justice. The virtues most in request here are those of listening, the responsiveness to difference, the willingness for change. The issue is not whether there is a choice between the virtues of cooperation and of conversation. God forbid. The issue is what their relation is, whether one of them discourages the other.[271]

Cavell's basic "quarrel" with Rawls is therefore the extent to which games and their rules " 'illustrate' the moral life."[272] For Cavell, in a word, "there is in the moral life nothing that plays the role of a defining rule in games."[273] Furthermore, the stakes are quite different: "It is no cause for intellectual or moral alarm if someone doesn't know the rules of baseball, doesn't know the game of baseball. . . . But it is reason for intellectual and moral alarm if I am to conclude that a mature person doesn't know what a promise (or pact) is."[274]

Moreover, there is a level of remaining *implicitness* or *inexactness* in the moral life that allows for no strict delineation of the beginnings and limits of responsibilities. I may have promised without knowing or wanting to; I may have fulfilled a promise without knowing or wanting it. And, more generally speaking: "No rule tells me when I may end the conversation unilaterally; it is my judgment, not a rule, that lets me conclude that I did what I could."[275] Protesting the "analogy" between games and morality thus comes down to a simple observation that requires the invocation, not of "two types of rules," as Rawls believes, but of two altogether different finalities:

In the moral life the equivalent finality is carried not by a rule but only by a *judgment* of moral finality, one that may be competently opposed, whose content may then enter into a moral argument, one whose resolution is not to be settled by appeal to a rule defining an institution; a judgment, hence, that carries consequences unforeseen or forsworn in games. . . . No judge or rule knows better than we, and we have no rules that will decide the issue or that will rule one of us out as incompetent to decide. This is why there is a moral argument between us, why it has its forms. No explicit promise would have been more sacred than our understanding, or, given our supposed mutual trust, even appropriate.[276]

The matter is important, since it stipulates the degree in which in the moral life we may have incurred debts or made commitments, *beyond our intention*, *unknowingly* and *unwillingly*, which is not to say randomly or mechanically, irresponsibly or uncompromisingly. In "questioning the idea that promising is a practice defined by rules," Cavell confronts Rawls's conception of the rule-governed practice (or institution) of promising with an alternative view: "No office is required, or comprehensible, for my entitlement to make or to accept a promise, any more than to speak responsibly, and none I occupy in general dictates for me the limits of my promise, nor shields me from the consequences of precipitousness in making a promise (or, for that matter, in expressing an intention) or of laxness in breaking or interpreting it."[277] Ultimately—but, paradoxically, always provisionally— the moral life (and everything for which it stands, including my "consent" to "democracy" and my society's related "openness to reform") comes down to an adaptation of Wittgenstein's exclamation, in *Philosophical Investigations* (par. 217), of a certain "Here I stand and cannot do otherwise (for now)": "If I have exhausted the justifications I have reached bedrock and my spade is turned. Then I am inclined to say: This is simply what I do." Cavell takes this to refer to Wittgenstein's insurpassable insight into the "critical impasse in the mutuality of our concepts."[278] But then, as Cavell hastens to add, Wittgenstein's invocation of hitting rock bottom is "meant as *weak*, temporary, open to continuation."[279]

This leads us to the heart of what Cavell terms "moral perfectionism." This is not a thick, substantial conception of the good life that smothers the formal features and structural conditions of the very hypotheticals—the "original position," the "veil of ignorance," "justice as fairness," and the like—that, Rawls argues, form the constitutive and regulative ideas that make up morality or even the moral *life*. "Moral perfectionism" has an equally formal, structural, and tentative thrust of argument and action, passion and suffering. Its perfectionism is premised upon its *perfectibility*, which, as Derrida knew, stands or falls with its ineliminable *pervertibility*. In Cavell's words: "Perfectionism, as I find it defensible, is concerned not to dictate a specialized economy of pursuits, any more than to urge a maximization of certain pursuits throughout society. Its intervention in human life is justified only by the perplexities of human life itself."[280]

All in all, consent to sociality, society, democracy, and justice, while a central presupposition of contractarian theories of natural law and rights, including Rawls's reformulation of the Kantian position in *A Theory of Justice*, cannot merely mean "consent to the principles of justice."[281] Cavell's conjuring up of different modalities, indeed moods, such as "political guilt" and "civil intimacy," "conviction," the "imaginary," "liberality of thought," "imagination or adventure," "joyousness and wonder in the differences of others,"[282] together with many other affects, are indications that a different vocabulary feeds into *our willingness and ability to make the transition from hypotheticals to actuality*, regardless of the fact that such a move will, of necessity, be temporal, tailored to the dictates of the situation, and vulnerable to the threat of skepticism—to the world and others, including ourselves. As Cavell writes, "the sense of society as a voluntary scheme, in which 'its members are autonomous and the obligations they recognize self-imposed' does not do something the classical theorists wanted from the sense of a social contract, namely to *remove* me from a state of nature, make a political being of me, create a polis to which I *belong*."[283] They lack conviction because they lack insight into the logic and force of "conversion" and "aversion," in short, to the "drama of consent," "a theatrical dimension," "the problematic of sympathy (say the evaluation of the other),"[284] and everything that it requires or effects—which is, well, almost everything that pertains to human needs, desires, and cares. These, moreover, are not simply existential, individual, or personal dimensions of justice, each with its own "grammar," nor are they merely a "side effect" of structured practices and "social institutions."

For one thing, Cavell notes, these affects and effects prepare the very establishment of such a thing as "the original position," the mental operation of "the veil of ignorance," and the like. Cavell points out that Rawls, unlike the classical theorists of the social contract, depicts the "state of nature" not as "a scene of violence" but as the very locus for inaugurating "constitutional democracy" as nothing less than "Utopia"; and a "full Utopia," Cavell urges, "must give a place to Perfectionism in a way Rawls seems not to leave open."[285] Rawls thus does not give sufficient attention to the ambivalences of "moral psychology" that explain our "identification" or "bond":

> To clarify what constitutes "identification" here, Freud would have to play a larger role than Rawls allows for him. Specifically, Rawls's principles of moral psychology build up from the law that we love what, in justice, loves us. . . . In Freud's vision we also hate what loves us because, in justice, it also threatens and constrains us. The contract must pose a threat violent enough to overcome the violence of nature.[286]

For another, Cavell perceives moral perfectionism as something of eminent "public importance."[287] Far from being "private," let alone idiosyncratic, it informs the texture of the social fabric and blows "spirit" into the otherwise dead letter of its given words and rules of law. In fact, this is precisely what such conversions and conversational modes and moods, moves and motivations share with Rawls's concept of structured "practices," namely, the fact that they are governed by what Wittgenstein calls "customs [*Gepflogenheiten*]" and "uses," which are partly a matter of mastering a "technique" and of inhabiting (founding, maintaining) "institutions."[288] The "*ways* of doing all of these things," Cavell clarifies, are marked and recognizable by the fact that "they have a grammar, and in that sense are conventional, and in that sense social."[289]

But this does not mean, for Wittgenstein, "that they are conventional or social in the way institutions which characterize particular societies are conventional."[290] The grammar in question is situated at a *deeper* level,[291] which remains largely implicit, even though it is far from ineffable, mysterious, or mystical (or is it?) and can be *made explicit* or at least alluded to in moral argument or, as Cavell says, "moral defense," in short, by means of "*elaboratives*."[292]

But, then, why and how is it that "elaboratives" so often get short-circuited and collapse into what we could only call "explicatives," not just of the inarticulate genre of %*#@!—the not so silent outcry of a suffering nature—but also of the order of either unintentional or deliberate insults, which can be perceived as either outright blasphemous and idolatrous or merely as profane and uncivil? At each stage, it seems, the moral perfection of human nature and existence to which "religion" aspires—in fact, the very idea of perfectibility on which it thrives—can become derouted, revert into its opposite. It is a problem Cavell observes, with reference to Hegel, in striking terms: "What happens to individuals if they tire of history, can take no further mediation, become lost or captivated on the path of self-realization and intersubjectivity—if they become "reified" rather than "concretized"? If we speak of perversions of human existence, this will encompass disturbances of satisfaction no more sexual than epistemological, and no more these than political."[293] Perversion and, Derrida writes, pervertibility—whether perceived as idolatry, blasphemy, scandal, or violence, whether symbolic or "real"—belong to the very heart, to the very essence, of the phenomenon or set(s) of phenomena that make up (or are made up by) "religion" and everything that may or may not take its place.

With further reference to Hegel, Cavell suggests that to analyze and evaluate these matters—in short, the fate of skepticism as a problem, with "an origin and a progress," in modernity, in philosophy, in art, and in our personal and collective lives—requires a "mode of thought" that draws upon a "history . . . regarded as the anthropology of our pasts, of the presents of the distant tribes whose present we are."[294] The diagnosis in question is not merely an abstract theoretical, let alone speculative thesis. On the contrary, to observe this requires us to reassert the "problem of human history (the problem of modern human history; the modern problem of human history)," and this implies the undeniable fact that "the problem is lived, and that this life has an origin and a progress. The idea is that the problem of the other is discovered through telling its history. Then how could this history be recounted; what would it be a recounting of?"[295] The conclusion to be drawn from Cavell's overall account is that no simple answer to this question seems readily available. Yet the name, if not the concept, of "religion"—mentioned so often in passing throughout his writings—may well remain the best designator for this condition, which is the predicament of our disappointment with criteria, but also the sure sign of our freedom, that is to say, responsibility.

Cults, Cultures, Cultivation, Curriculum

A final question remains to be addressed. What do these considerations mean for the study of "religion," "religions," and "the religious" in the academy, within our disciplines, and *beyond*? A renewed theoretical and philosophical diagnosis of the entanglements of "religion," of its very *concept* and what lies *beyond* it, whatever its overall therapeutic value may be, "leaves," as Wittgenstein says, "everything as it is." No direct or immediate normative, let alone institutional or curricular consequences would seem to follow from any formal, structural, semantic, and pragmatic—or "grammatical"—analysis, however much it draws on historical and empirical data, or whatever its success in laying bare the "criteria," "essence," and "logic" of a given "language game," "form of life," or natural history" (to stick to the terminology of Wittgenstein's *Philosophical Investigations*).

Any "formal indication," as Heidegger knew, remains, in its very approximation of the phenomenon of factical life-experience—and hence, in its irreducible generality—a stumbling block no less than a stepping stone, unable to render the phenomenon, its flux and concretion, not to mention the host of its implicit horizons, fully visible, let alone explicit.[296] It may prepare an understanding of "revelation" (*Offenbarung*) by delineating the "revealability" (*Offenbarkeit*) it presupposes, but the two perspectives are not equal in their ontological meaning, even though both have ontic effects. The first conditions the second as much as the other way around, thus compromising the integrity and formality of any theoretical—ontological—discourse, which, for all its abstraction and explication of what makes phenomena possible in the first place nonetheless partakes in the flux of factical life, remaining shot through with an ontic conditionality, in turn.

Would it be possible philosophically to unpack or resolve such complications in order to find sound methodological procedures for disciplinary or interdisciplinary inquiry, while circumnavigating the vague existential, hermeneutic, or fideistic theologies that, rightly or wrongly, take Heidegger or Wittgenstein as their source? Could the preliminary conceptual analysis proposed here yield more than some—similarly vague—insights of a *philosophy* of "the religious"? Can we hope to differentiate the latter from the long tradition of securing philosophical, dogmatic, and natural theologies?

The research program of which this book provides a first documentation is, for all its comprehensiveness, built around a more modest ambition: namely, to foster serious and innovative forms of the study of "religion" in all of its aspects *beyond* the conceptual limitations that historically obvious institutional locations, such as divinity schools, theological faculties, or centers for the study of religion must, of necessity, impose on their subject. To constitute "religion" as a subject, whether sui generis or as a subcategory of the natural or biological make-up of human sociality and culture, to be studied in standard scientific terms, is to underestimate the challenges posed by (and *beyond*) the concept at hand.[297] It would be to assume that "religion" is a given, that its concept refers to a preexisting, largely intelligible and knowable reality, whose "total social fact" is commensurate with the potential grasp of scholarly procedures as they "mirror" or "represent" human nature.

Yet if "religion" always also eludes and absolves itself from any such categorization and explanation—and does so ab-solutely, with an infinitizing movement that perturbs and infinitely modalizes our very finitude, changing its guiding motifs, moods, and motivations—it is not necessarily the impenetrable, ineffable, or, for that matter, untouchable per se. Religion is not necessarily available or intelligible as the diffuse *mysterium tremendum* (Otto), the oceanic feeling (Romain Rolland, Freud), or cosmic consciousness (Hadot). On the contrary, it might well be the case that, in modernity and beyond, the fate of "religion," that is, of the very phenomenon or set(s) of phenomena for which this name, term, or concept still stands, condenses, magnifies, foregrounds, and highlights the most down-to-earth—the broadly epistemic, practical, and existential—difficulties in coming to terms with virtually *any* culturally mediated and mediatized "given." No old or new "myth of the—religiously—given" will allow us to control the at times minimized, then again maximized modes of its manifestation, the in principle undelimitable—hence infinite—modalizations and motifs, moods, and motivations that drive its appearance, to which we are *infinitely answerable*.

Thus the scholarly stakes in methodically discussing "religion" are no mere disinterested intellectual matter. Even methodological atheism and asceticism cannot suppress the passions the subject provokes. An example of the growing need to recognize "religion" in the broadest sense and in all sectors of society is the request Jack Lang, then minister of national education in France, addressed to Régis Debray, the author of a study entitled *God, an Itinerary*,[298] as well as other relevant writings on the material—and, as he calls it, "mediological"—aspect of culture as it grounds all aspirations toward transcendence. Débray was asked to assess how teachers in the Fifth Republic, confronted with the complex demands of a multicultural, multiethnic society and troubled by the controversy over *laïcité* and the prohibition of headscarfs in public schools, could teach "religion" in more engaged, comprehensive, yet intellectually acceptable ways.

Debray's report, "Teaching Religious Facts in Secular Schools" (*L'enseignement du fait religieux dans l'école laïcque*) proposes relegating responsibility for training teachers in this domain to the fifth section of the École Pratique des Hautes Études (EPHE), founded in 1886 and responsible for "Sciences religieuses." In this section such luminaries as Marcel Mauss, Étienne Gilson, Alexandre Koyré, Alexandre Kojève, Lucien Febvre, Louis Massignon, Henry Corbin, Georges Dumézil, and Claude Lévi-Strauss had earlier taught and researched.[299]

Debray's principal justification for his proposal of a new curriculum under the EPHE's auspices is what he puts forward as an insurmountable analytical distinction between two categories that have accompanied and structured "religion" throughout the course of its history: namely, that between "cult" and "culture." Preoccupation with the first, he argues, should, under proper pedagogical guidance, eventually give way to the second.[300] A "cult" is a "religious fact," but also a fact of "civilization," and one that "structures human history." At times it can be a factor of "peace and modernity"; at others, it becomes a source of "discord, murderous conflicts, and regression."[301] Culture, by contrast, displays no such ambiguity and volatility. Teaching "cults" as an integral part of the study of "culture," according to Debray, must be premised on the axiom that "the teaching of *the* religious *is not* a religious teaching." Only thus could the integrity of republicanism as promulgated by the institutions of secondary and higher learning be maintained and the "demons of communitarianism" (feared by secularists) and the "Trojan horse" of "syncretism [*confusionisme*]" and "relativism" (scorned by clerics) be contained.

All would depend on our ability and willingness to avoid blurring the categorical distinction between "catechism" and "information," between "testimony" and "report," that is to say, between a "sacramental relation to memory" and an "analytic" attitude toward "knowledge." Without allowing any confession a necessarily exclusionary claim to authority, let alone a "monopoly of meaning," the Republic, Debray argues, should abstain from putting itself in the position of an "arbiter" and instead offer a merely "descriptive, factual, and notional" approach to the religious phenomenon in its midst. To let "religion" circulate outside accepted institutional channels for the publicly controlled and rational transmission of knowledge would de facto mean relegating it to the terrain of a "pathology." For it to be held in check requires a didactic approach that "stipulates the bracketing of personal convictions," steers clear of the fruitless alternatives of "devitalizing" and "mystifying" tradition, and opts, instead, for informed interpretation of religious, that is to say, sociohistorical, literary, and cultural facts.[302]

We need not investigate here whether the deployment of this (or, for that matter, any other) conceptual alternative creates more clarity, allows for more resourcefulness, in assessing and addressing the phenomenon or set(s) of phenomena whose name or concept we may, indeed, have to change one day. Debray himself has since been critical of the term *religion* per se, favoring what he terms "mediology."[303] Indeed, his more recent *Human Communions: On Being Done with Religion* (*Les communions humaines: Pour en finir avec "la religion"*) explicitly calls for retiring the concept and substituting the more sober notion of "communion."[304] In any event, it remains doubtful that successive functional equivalents for "religion" will escape the long shadow cast by its set(s) of traditions, whose common denominator and supposed commonality, community, indeed "communion" was admittedly always something of a stretch, nothing less than a violent imposition (as any concept would be). Nothing, strictly speaking, *falls under* a concept, albeit the most pertinent and appropriate yet found or coined. In the end, there is nothing but the at once *minimally different* and *infinitely multiple* "beyond" of a concept (e.g., of "religion," but also of "God," "the Other," "communion," even the "beyond" itself) that could interest, captivate, or inspire us. And when and wherever it does, this happens in barely visible (audible, tangible, etc.) yet at the same time radically, globally transformative ways.

Jacques Derrida, who was asked by Jacques Lang to evaluate and respond to Debray's proposals, made an important observation on them during a conference in 2002.[305] The distinction between the "cult" and "culture" of religion or between religious teaching (or teaching religiously) and teaching religion, he argued, is both useful, even necessary, *and* unhappy, indeed, questionable and deconstructable. He approved of Debray's distinction between culture and cult, between teaching religion and religious teaching, but he wanted to try something else, to try to go a little further. Before asking what it would mean "to go further," let us see what promise and difficulty the proposed distinction entails.

The division of labor and interests it implies is at once of pragmatic value and steeped in a deep metaphysical as well as psychological and societal need to separate contrasting, perhaps contradictory, ethical and cognitive domains or "value-spheres." But its inevitable suggestion of dichotomy and methodological or definitional purity is, ultimately, misleading and has no *fundamentum in re.* Derrida did not propose moving "beyond" a concept—"religion" and, we may safely assume, also "cult" or "culture"—but instead asked what would have to come *before* any such guiding concepts, though not in a logical or chronological sense. He hinted at a "space" or "spacing" that is required for any concept—"religion" or each of "religion's" central notions, such as "revelation"—to appear at all. "Revelation" requires some "revealability," less in terms of the latter's logical, chronological, or ontological precedence or prevalence than as a condition or incondition that is, in turn, equally conditioned by what it makes possible. This undercuts every traditional and modern assumption of foundationalism, transcendentalism, possibilism, and the like. As the quasi-condition of any possibility, it would "be" the impossible par excellence and, as such, irreducible to any theologico-religious or theologico–political strategeme.

To indicate this space, spacing, or interval, Derrida invoked Plato's term *khōra* ("place, location"), from the *Timaeus*. We can see it as standing in for the impossible possibility (rather than a possible impossibility, as Heidegger would have phrased it) of, precisely, a *beyond* of any concept. It is unthinkable that we should not attempt to think it, Derrida seemed to say; yet also unthinkable that we find it readily—or, indeed, ever at all—*anywhere present*. One might compare this to what Adorno calls the "unthinkability [*Unausdenkbarkeit*] of despair," while acknowledging (again, like Adorno) that this difficulty can hardly be the source of much hope.

Everything comes down, then, to relating or negotiating two different endeavors, irreducible to each other, but also unthinkable without each other. On the one hand, there would be our talking about "religion," in all our efforts to maintain the term, for lack of better substitutes, while venturing into territories, dimensions, possibilities, and virtualities that exceed its past and present conceptual grasp. On the other hand, there is the need to study the incomplete set(s) of phenomena of apparent historical and systematic relevance for the eventual understanding of "religion's" phenomena and phenomenality (studying words, things, gestures, powers, sounds, silences, smells, touches, shapes, colors, affects, effects, etc.).

Having distinguished these two broadly systematic and roughly empirical approaches to one and the same object, subject, name, or concept, a simple but far-reaching hypothesis imposes itself. What is at stake in these endeavors is less metaphysical dualism between the here and the hereafter (the *Hinterwelt* before, around, beyond, under, or above the world we know) than an at once ontological and methodological duality of perspective: a "dual-aspect theory of reality," to cite Stuart Hampshire's characterization of Spinoza's *deus sive natura* ("God or Nature"), a two-way seeing of "aspects" of which Wittgenstein speaks in *Philosophical Investigations* (invoking the duck-rabbit picture), a differentiation between *langue* and *parole*, as Saussure proposes in his *Course on General Linguistics*, a *double séance* and *double science*, as Derrida proposes in his study of Mallarmé.[306] And the list of exemplifications is far from complete.

"Religion" as a "Way of Life"

A reconsideration of "religion" and its concept need not take an institutional, let alone academic or intellectual, form. Methodic study, when religion is taken to be a "way of life" (Pierre Hadot), may approach the phenomenon from yet another angle, engaging and practicing, dramatizing, and ritualizing it as a "spiritual exercise," instead. Let me conclude by briefly alluding to two examples of such an approach, which should be seen less as alternatives to the dual perspective I have sketched above than as its—subjective, existential, affective—supplement: that is to say, as a singular expression of a general, perhaps universal, "Truth" and "Essence" that enables and instantiates each of our earlier perspectives and aspects, as much as it is carried by them.

From another pragmatist background, in his recent writings Hilary Putnam has stressed the perfectionist theme, conceiving "religion" less as a "theory" or theology than as a mode of living one's life. Trained as a philosopher of mathematical logic and science, and an adamant nonreductionist naturalist, Putnam had earlier noted, on the opening page of his *Renewing Philosophy*, that he knew to "philosophize about" the so-called "religious dimension" only by "indirection,"[307] not just by commenting on Wittgenstein and Kierkegaard but also by effectively deferring the matter at hand. In his recent *Jewish Philosophy as a Guide to Life*, however, varying Hadot's expression "philosophy as a way of life," Putnam starts out from an insight that echoes Cavell's views, even though it charts different territory. Specifically, he takes his lead from the insight that Wittgenstein "never accepted the facile idea that *religion* is essentially a conceptual confusion or collection of confusions":

> To be sure, there are confusions to which religious people are subject, ranging from superstition to a temptation on which Wittgenstein remarks more than once in the *Nachlass*, the temptation to make religion into a *theory* rather than (what he thought it should be) a deep-going way of life. . . . to see religion as *essentially* "prescientific thinking," as something that must be simply rejected as nonsense after "the Enlightenment," is itself an example of a conceptual confusion for Wittgenstein, an example of being in the grip of a picture. This is the reason that Wittgenstein attacked the way in which anthropologists were viewing primitive religion decades before it became "politically correct" to do, and the notes that we have of his fascinating "lectures on religious belief" show that he was largely concerned to *defamiliarize* religious belief, to get us to see how unique a way of living and way of conceptualizing it is.[308]

Wittgenstein, like the great Jewish thinkers of the twentieth century, Martin Buber, Franz Rosenzweig, and Levinas, Putnam explains, shares a sense of the "religious" as an "ethics without ontology,"[309] shunning all onto-theological speculation. Wittgenstein no less than these thinkers refuses to resort to "standard things about religious language," such as claims that it "expresses false pre-scientific theories, but also assuming that it is noncognitive, or that it is emotive, or that it is incommensurable" with ordinary descriptive language.[310] Instead, Wittgenstein, most poignantly in his lectures on aesthetics, ethics, and religious belief, "tried to get his students to see how, for homo religiosus, the meaning of his or her words is not exhausted by criteria in a public language, but is deeply interwoven with the sort of person the particular religious individual has chosen to be and with pictures that are the foundation of that individual's life."[311]

Religious talk, in other words, has its proper spirituality, while dispensing with ontotheology and with all undue theorization, which either reduces its meaning to what it is not or subsumes it under an unhelpful picture, image, or representation. Where religious people express beliefs, as in miracles and the afterlife, Putnam reminds us, such beliefs are, for Wittgenstein, not crypto-theories: "'words only have their meaning in the stream of life'; and the role that such beliefs play in the life of the believer is wholly different from the role that empirical beliefs play. The idea that religion can either be criticized or defended by appeals to scientific fact seemed to him a mistake."[312] What remains, then, is an attempt to reorient our thinking, sensing, and acting in an altogether different direction.

What especially Rosenzweig, for Putnam, adds to the Wittgensteinian or Cavellian insight into the "truth" and "moral" of skepticism with respect to the world and others (including ourselves) in it is that our relationship to them is not only nonepistemic, based on acceptance, attunement, and acknowledgment, but dependent upon a triadic structure and equilibrium or correlation in which God, man, and the world play equally important roles. This does not require a theoretical attitude toward the world or man (adding a divine Being to the list of beings, as it were, as if theism were the point), but what Rosenzweig, in a famous 1925 essay, calls a "new thinking," a "speaking thinking," which translates theological issues into human ones and vice versa. This "new thinking" differs from the old theoretical and metaphysical philosophy as "grammatical" thinking differs from "logical," Rosenzweig says, using a distinction that, as Putnam reminds us, offers a striking resemblance to Wittgenstein's own in *Philosophical Investigations* (par. 108 and 122). Moreover, it revolves around an existential and "simple resolve," that is to say, a "readiness" to be distinguished from any ontological or practical "plan" or "organization." It consists, instead, in (an attitude toward) a way of life: here, the frame of reference of Jewish life, its rituals, commandments, calendar, and holidays.[313]

For Wittgenstein, Putnam goes on to say, a religious belief "could only be something like a passionate commitment to a system of reference. Hence, although it's a belief, it is really a way of living, or a way of assessing. Instruction in a religious life, there, would have to take the form of a portrayal, a description, of that system of reference, while at the same time being an appeal to conscience [*ein ins-Gewissen-reden*]."[314] Such an attitude or disposition, Putnam suggests, is what Rosenzweig called the "capacity to wonder," which, though cultivated by philosophy since its earliest origins, is not its primary activity, let alone privilege.

Eric L. Santner makes a similar observation in a series of remarkable studies. He likewise suggests that if there is any minimal relevance of the religious and the theological in modernity, it is that of a way of life or, in his terms, a "psychotheology of everyday life," whose therapeutics is not that of theoretical quietism, dispensing with skeptical problems in epistemology altogether, but a patient, resolute, and minute interpretation and reorientation of "creaturely life."[315]

The accounts of Putnam and Santner do not constitute alternatives to Cavell's approach (they refer to his writings with admiration), but offer supplements whose subjective stance joins with the moral perfectionist's reservations about and revolt against the argument that moral discourse is governed by games, rules, or criteria on a supposedly inferentialist base.

Both Putnam and Santner stress the importance that Rosenzweig and Wittgenstein give to our sense of "wonder." Wittgenstein, in his 1929 "Lecture on Ethics," presented to the Heretics Society in Cambridge and then again to members of the Vienna Circle, notes: "we all know what in ordinary life would be called a miracle. It obviously is simply an event the like of which we have never yet seen."[316] But he leaves no doubt that what interests him is a different—not relative, but absolute—sense of the term *miracle*. The wonder or "miracle" is not an extraordinary, new, unexpected, and unpredictable fact, the exception to a rule if not the suspending or modification of a law of nature. Rather, it is the "*wonder*" I have at the very "*existence of the world*," at the "extraordinary" circumstance "that anything should exist"[317] at all (what Stanley Cavell, in his discussion of Wittgenstein's "criteria," calls his "being surprised by the fact that there is such a thing as the world"[318]). And this might well be "religion's" most elementary form, bearing its words, things, gestures, and powers.

Conclusion

"Religion," in its very "concept" and "beyond," whether defined and redefined by the state (by constitutional law and jurisprudence) or by a discipline (by expert communities of scholars whose ideological sensibilities may vary from avowed or unavowed confessionalism to unabashed or unacknowledged naturalism and reductionism, methodological atheism, or agnosticism), still eludes classificatory regimes. They are fallible, necessarily incomplete systems of control and intellectual hegemony, ways of world making, coping with finitude, and whistling in the dark.

Yet the appeal to alternative interpretations and practices of "religion"—for example, to the laisser-faire "religion" of the free market of ideas and popular culture, a *bricolage* spirituality, or to a "mundanity" that escapes the contours of (the all too religious, indeed, Christian concept of) "the secular"[319]—all this may still not offer the semantic resistance that would be needed if we were to put things (words, gestures, powers, and the like) in motion again. Indeed, no shift in definitional, methodological, or institutional demarcations might by itself suffice to *undo* and *recast* our investment—historically, systematically, and practically—in the most rigid, dogmatic, or reified fixations of the concept, let alone *distance* and eventually *free* us from our fateful complicity in the most violent among its cultic and/or cultural expressions.

What are we to do, then? Leave things as they are, no doubt, by trusting the self-imposed limits and eventual self-effacement of whatever "concept"—here, that of "religion" and its "beyond"—rather than exposing it to the self-aggrandizing claims of critiques, explanations, geneaologies, and demystifications. Many such offer solutions and supposed "overcomings" whose societal, cultural, and existential effects are worse than the problem they seek to redress. One could thus gloss Adorno: just as attempts philosophically, politically, or aesthetically to overcome "nihilism" were often more dangerous than "nihilism" itself, so also the heroic, stoic, or bitter efforts to rid the world of "religion," of its conceptual unclarities, moral hypocrisy, and kitsch, leave us merely with false hopes and newly raised idols, that is to say, with yet another dialectic of Enlightenment, of reason reverting into its opposite, obscurantism—indeed, mythology, as in the "myth of the given" or the ultimate transparencies promised by "demytholization." In any event, such vain overcomings leave us with fewer semantic, figural, rhetorical, affective, pragmatic, and existential resources and resistances than we may need, not just in the immediate future but for some time to come.

The study and teaching of "religion" as a part of "culture"—while sometimes in tune, then in adamant discord with the religious teaching of "cults," that is, with being, living, and acting "religiously"—means cultivating a sensibility to seemingly ungraspable distinctions and commonalities, which must sometimes be affirmed, sometimes denied, in rhythms whose control escapes us and for which no criteria, no rules, can (so far?) be found. What counts are minimal differences that nonetheless make maximal differences in the world, as if a certain invisibility, imperceptibility, inaudibility, even ineffectiveness could have all the greater impact. *Pianissimo*, as it were.

Such minimal "religion," thinned out as it has become in many regions of modern life, paradoxically takes on the appearance of an increasingly *vague* and *void* "global religion." "Transcendent to the point of absence," it welds the retreat of its signification to a virtually immanent force field to be reckoned with, a "curvature of social space" (to draw once more on Levinas). Moreover, it does so nowhere more poignantly than where it seems to have no assignable discursive or institutional place. To study "religion beyond a concept," then, would require a knowledge, judgment, and sensibility not governed by criteria or rules, in matters whose sense and potential non-sense may elude us at any moment, yet whose reverberations, for this very reason, carry all the more weight.

PART I

"What Is Religion?"

Public Religions Revisited

José Casanova

It has now been over a decade since the publication of *Public Religions in the Modern World*, and it can be asserted with some confidence that the thesis first presented there—that we were witnessing a process of "deprivatization" of religion as a relatively global trend—has been amply confirmed.[1] The most important contribution of the book, in my view, however, was not the relatively prescient empirical observation of such a new global trend but the analytical-theoretical and normative challenge to the liberal theory of privatization, namely, the claim that the thesis of the privatization of religion in the modern world was no longer defensible either empirically or normatively. In a certain sense, the best confirmation of the validity of the deprivatization of religion can be found in the heartland of secularization, that is, in Western European societies.

To be sure, there is very little evidence of any kind of religious revival among the European populations, if one excludes the significant influx of new immigrant religions.[2] But religion has certainly returned as a contentious issue to the public sphere of European societies. It may be premature to speak of a post-secular Europe, but certainly one can sense a significant shift in the European Zeitgeist. At first the thesis of the deprivatization of religion as a new global trend did not find much resonance in Europe. The privatization of religion was simply too much taken for granted, both as a normal empirical fact and as the norm for modern European societies. The concept of modern public religion was still too dissonant, and religious revivals elsewhere could simply be explained—or rather, explained away—as the rise of fundamentalism in societies that were not yet modern. But in the last three to four years, at least, there has been a noticeable change in attitude and attention throughout Europe. Every second week one learns of a new major conference on religion being planned somewhere in Europe, or of the establishment of some newly funded research center or research project on "religion and politics," on "immigration and religion," on "religion and violence," or on "interreligious dialogue." Most tellingly, very few voices in Europe today simply restate the old thesis of privatization unrevised and unadorned. Even the self-assured French *laïcité* is on the defensive and ready to make some concessions.

The terrorist attacks of September 11 and the resonance of the discourse of the "clash of civilizations" have certainly played an important role in focusing European attention on issues of religion. But it would be a big mistake to attribute this new attention solely or even mainly to the rise of so-called Islamic fundamentalism and the threats and challenges that it poses to the West and particularly to Europe. Internal European transformations also contribute to the new public interest in religion. General processes of globalization, the global growth of transnational migration, and the very process of European integration, particularly the possibility of Turkey joining the European Union, are presenting crucial challenges not only to the European model of the national welfare state but also to the different kinds of religious-secular and church-state settlements that the various European countries had achieved in post–World War II Europe.[3]

The purpose of revisiting *Public Religions* is not simply self-congratulatory. Rather, it is a critical attempt to point out what I see as the main shortcomings or limitations of the argument I developed there. The main shortcomings of my argument can be grouped into three categories: (1) its Western-centrism; (2) the attempt to restrict, at least normatively, modern public religions to the public sphere of civil society; (3) the empirical framing of the study as church–state–nation–civil society relations from a comparative national perspective, neglecting the transnational global dimensions.

In many respects those shortcomings were consciously imposed self-limitations for good methodological, substantive, and strategic reasons. I already acknowledged then in the Introduction that the book was a "Western-centered study, both in terms of the particular cases chosen for investigation and in terms of the normative perspective guiding the investigation."[4] The self-limitation of the study to Western Christendom was fully justified in terms of: (1) the genealogical reconstruction of particular historical processes of secularization within Latin Christendom (rather than viewing secularization as a general universal process of human and societal development); (2) the restriction of the study, by and large, to Catholicism and Protestantism as particular forms of religion; and (3) restriction to Western (European and postcolonial) societies. At the time, I pleaded "limited time, knowledge, and resources, as well as a postmodern enhanced awareness of the dangers of excessive homogenization," as well, one could add, of the dangers of "orientalism."

Strategically, I was convinced that it was necessary first to challenge the theory of secularization immanently, empirically, and normatively, from within Western societies and Western discourse, as it were, before one could undertake the even more daunting yet necessary task of going beyond Western Christendom and adopting a global comparative perspective. As I indicated then, "such an immense task would have required a modification and expansion of my typology of public religions, of the theory of religious and political differentiation, and of the general analytical framework employed."[5] To a certain extent, my work since the publication of the book has been an attempt to address and transcend these three shortcomings. I've been impelled in this direction partly by the poignant critique of Talal Asad, partly by my own research on transnational migration and transnational religion, and above all by the inevitability of confronting processes of globalization and their effects on all religions.

Let me now sketch very briefly the way in which I've been trying to address those shortcomings on three levels:

1. Rethinking secularization beyond the West: toward a global comparative perspective;[6]
2. Public religions beyond ecclesiastical disestablishment and civil society: the dual clause and the "twin tolerations";
3. Transnational religions, transnational imagined communities, and globalization.

Rethinking Secularization Beyond the West: A Global Comparative Perspective

While the two minor subtheses of the theory of secularization—"the decline of religion" and "the privatization of religion"—have undergone numerous critiques and revisions in the last fifteen years, the core of the thesis, namely, the understanding of secularization as a single process of functional differentiation of the various institutional spheres or subsystems of modern societies, remains relatively uncontested in the social sciences, particularly within European sociology. Yet one should ask whether it is appropriate to subsume the multiple and very diverse historical patterns of differentiation and fusion of the various institutional spheres (that is, church and state, state and economy, economy and science) that one finds throughout the history of modern Western societies into a single, teleological process of modern functional differentiation.[7]

Talal Asad was the first to call our attention to the fact that "the historical process of secularization effects a remarkable ideological inversion. . . . For at one time 'the secular' was a part of a theological discourse (*saeculum*)," while later "the religious" is constituted by secular political and scientific discourses, so that "religion" itself as a historical category and as a universal globalized concept emerges as a construction of Western secular modernity.[8]

But, as I pointed out in my response to Asad's poignant critique, contemporary genealogies of secularism fail to recognize the extent to which the formation of the secular is itself inextricably linked with the internal transformations of European Christianity, from the so-called Papal Revolution to the Protestant Reformation, and from the ascetic and pietistic sects of the seventeenth and eighteenth centuries to the emergence of evangelical, denominational Protestantism in nineteenth-century America.[9] Should one define these transformations as a process of internal secularization of Western Christianity, or as the cunning of secular reason, or both? A proper rethinking of secularization will require a critical examination of the diverse patterns of differentiation and fusion of the religious and the secular and their mutual constitution across all the religions of the world, and especially across the so-called "world religions," even though we are aware, thanks to Tomoko Masuzawa, how much the "world religions" are also constructs of Western secular Christian modernity.[10]

The contextualization of our categories, such as "religion," "the secular," "the theologico-political," and so on, should begin with recognition of the particular Christian historicity of Western European developments, as well as of the multiple and diverse historical patterns of secularization and differentiation within European and Western societies. Such recognition should allow a less Eurocentric comparative analysis of patterns of differentiation and secularization in other civilizations and world religions, and, more importantly, the further recognition that, with the world-historical process of globalization initiated by the European colonial expansion, all these processes everywhere are dynamically interrelated and mutually constituted.

There are multiple and diverse secularizations in the West and multiple and diverse Western modernities, and they are still mostly associated with fundamental historical differences between Catholic, Protestant, and Byzantine Christianity, and between Lutheran and Calvinist Protestantism. As David Martin has shown, in the Latin-Catholic cultural area, and to some extent throughout Continental Europe, there was a collision between religion and the differentiated secular spheres—that is, between Catholic Christianity and modern science, modern capitalism, and the modern state.[11] As a result of this protracted clash, the Enlightenment critique of religion found ample resonance here; the secularist genealogy of modernity was constructed as a triumphant emancipation of reason, freedom, and worldly pursuits from the constraints of religion; and practically every "progressive" European social movement from the time of the French Revolution to the present has been informed by secularism. The self-narratives that have informed functionalist theories of differentiation and secularization have envisioned this process as the emancipation and expansion of the secular spheres at the expense of a much-diminished and confined, though also newly differentiated, religious sphere. The boundaries are well kept, but they are relocated, pushing religion into the margins and into the private sphere.

In the Anglo-Protestant and Calvinist cultural areas, by contrast, and particularly in the United States, there was "collusion" between religion and the secular differentiated spheres. There is little historical evidence of any tension between American Protestantism and capitalism and very little manifest tension between science and religion in America prior to the Darwinian crisis at the end of the nineteenth century. The American Enlightenment had hardly any antireligious component. Even "the separation of church and state" that was constitutionally codified in the dual clause of the First Amendment was promoted by religious sects and had as much the purpose of protecting "the free exercise" of religion from state interference and from ecclesiastical establishments as that of protecting the federal secular state from any religious entanglement. It is rare, at least until very recently, to find any "progressive" social movement in America appealing to "secularist" values; appeals to the Gospel and to "Christian" values are certainly much more common throughout the history of American social movements, as well as in the discourse of American presidents.

The purpose of this comparison is not to reiterate the well-known fact that American society is more "religious" and therefore less "secular" than European societies. While the first may be true, the second proposition does not follow. On the contrary, the United States has always been the paradigmatic form of a modern secular, differentiated society. Yet the triumph of "the secular" came aided by religion rather than at its expense, and the boundaries themselves became so diffused that, at least by European ecclesiastical standards, it is not clear where religion begins and the secular ends. Yet it would be ludicrous to argue that the United States is a less functionally differentiated society, and therefore less modern and less secular, than France or Sweden. On the contrary, one could argue that there is less functional differentiation of state, economy, science, and so on in *étatiste-laïciste* France than in the United States, but this does not make France either less modern or less secular than the United States.

If the European concept of secularization is not a particularly relevant category for the "Christian" United States, much less may it be directly applicable to other axial civilizations with very different modes of structuration of the religious and the secular. As an analytical conceptualization of a historical process, secularization is a category that makes sense within the context of the particular internal and external dynamics of the transformation of Western European Christianity from the Middle Ages to the present. But the category becomes problematic once it is generalized as a universal process of societal development and once it is transferred to other world religions and other civilizational areas with very different dynamics of structuration of the relations and tensions between religion and world, or between cosmological transcendence and worldly immanence.

The category of secularization could hardly be applicable, for instance, to such "religions" as Confucianism or Daoism, insofar as they are not characterized by high tension with "the world," insofar as their model of transcendence can hardly be called "religious," and insofar as they have no ecclesiastical organization. In a sense, religions that have always been "worldly" and "lay" do not need to undergo a process of secularization. To secularize—that is, "to make worldly" or "to transfer from ecclesiastical to civil use"—is a process that does not make much sense in such a civilizational context. In this respect, China and the Confucian civilizational area have been "secular" avant la lettre. It is the postulated intrinsic correlation between modernization and secularization that is highly problematic. There can be modern societies like the United States, which are secular while deeply religious, and there can be premodern societies like China, which, from our Eurocentric religious perspective, look deeply secular and irreligious.

The concept of multiple modernities, first developed by S. N. Eisenstadt, is a more adequate conceptualization and pragmatic vision of modern global trends than either secular cosmopolitanism or the clash of civilizations. In a certain sense, it shares elements of both. Like cosmopolitanism, the concept of multiple modernities maintains that there are some common elements or traits shared by all "modern" societies, which help to distinguish them from their "traditional" or premodern forms. But these modern traits or principles attain multiple forms and diverse institutionalizations. Moreover, many of these institutionalizations are continuous or congruent with the traditional historical civilizations. Thus, there is both a civilization of modernity and a continuous transformation of premodern historical civilizations under modern conditions, which helps to shape the multiple modernities.

The multiple-modernities position rejects both the notion of a modern radical break with traditions and the notion of an essential modern continuity with tradition. All traditions and civilizations are radically transformed in the processes of modernization, but they also have the possibility of shaping in particular ways the institutionalization of modern "religious" and "secular" traits. Traditions are forced to respond and adjust to modern conditions, but in the process of reformulating their traditions for modern contexts, they also help to shape the particular forms of "religious" and "secular" modernity.

Public Religions Beyond Ecclesiastical Disestablishment and Civil Society: The Dual Clause and the "Twin Tolerations"

My own analysis of the deprivatization of religion tried to contain, at least normatively, public religions within the public sphere of civil society, without allowing them to spill over into political society or the democratic state. Today I must recognize my own modern Western secular prejudices and the particular hermeneutic Catholic and "ecclesiastical" perspective on religion that I adopted in my comparative analysis of the relations between church, state, nation, and civil society in Western Catholic and Protestant societies. The moment one adopts a global comparative perspective, one must admit that the deprivatization of religion is unlikely to be contained within the public sphere of civil society, within the territorial boundaries of the nation-state, and within the constitutional premises of ecclesiastical disestablishment and juridical separation of church and state. We need to go beyond the secularist discourse of separation and beyond the public sphere of civil society to address the real issues of democratic politics around the world. Alfred Stepan's model of "twin tolerations" offers, in my view, a more fruitful approach.[12]

By my hermeneutic Catholic perspective I mean the fact that my theory of "modern public religion" was very much informed by the experience of the official Catholic *aggiornamento* of the 1960s. Of all the world religions, none had seemed as threatened at its core by the emergence of the modern world system of sovereign territorial states as the Roman church. The Protestant Reformation and the ensuing dissolution of Western Christendom undermined the role of the papacy as the spiritual head of a universal Christian monarchy represented by the Holy Roman Empire. The papacy not only lost spiritual supremacy over Protestant territories and peoples, but it lost control as well of the emerging national Catholic churches to caesaro-papist Catholic monarchs.[13] At the Congress of Westphalia in 1648, the concerted effort of Catholic and Protestant princes successfully shut out the papacy from European international and internal national affairs. One by one, from the sixteenth to the nineteenth centuries most of the transnational dimensions of medieval Catholicism receded or disappeared altogether. It is not surprising, therefore, that the Catholic Church remained for centuries adamantly antimodern and developed a negative philosophy of history, which conceptualized modern processes as so many heretical deviations from the Catholic ideal of medieval Christendom. But the lifeworld of Catholicism did not remain frozen in the past of medieval Christendom, nor were the Catholic reactions to modern developments (the Counter Reformation, Counter Enlightenment, Counter Revolution, etc.) simply reactionary regressions to an unchanging tradition. Rather, they were reactive attempts, often awkward ones, to fashion their own, Catholic versions of modernity. Only a teleological, normative version of a single, progressive, and unilinear Western modernity can construct such historical responses as fundamentalist reactions.

The Catholic *aggiornamento* to secular modernity culminated in the Second Vatican Council and is expressed in the two most important documents of the Council, the Declaration on Religious Freedom (*Dignitatis Humanae*) and the Pastoral Constitution on the Church in the Modern World (*Gaudium et Spes*). The official recognition of the inalienable right of every individual to religious freedom, based on the sacred dignity of the human person, meant that the Church abandoned its traditional compulsory character and accepted the modern principle of disestablishment and the separation of church and state. *Gaudium et Spes* represented, in turn, the acceptance of the religious legitimacy of the modern secular age and of the modern secular world, putting an end to the negative philosophy of history that had characterized the official Catholic position since the Counter-Reformation.

The *aggiornamento* led to a fundamental relocation of the Catholic Church from a state-oriented to a civil society–oriented institution. Moreover, the official adoption of the modern discourse of human rights allowed the Catholic Church to play a crucial role in opposition to authoritarian regimes and in processes of democratizaton throughout the Catholic world. Yet the Catholic Church's embrace of voluntary disestablishment meant not the privatization of Catholicism but rather its relocation from the state to the public sphere of civil society. This is the hermeneutic context within which I developed the analytical framework of modern public religions and the theory of deprivatization.

But obviously there are many other forms of modern public religion and other forms of deprivatization.

The transformation of Catholicism is particularly instructive because the modern discourse of secularism was often constructed in relation to Catholicism. There was always some justification, based on the official position of the Catholic Church, for modern secular anti-Catholic discourse. The Church, after all, had resisted or judged negatively most modern historical developments—the Protestant Reformation, the modern secular state, the modern scientific revolution, the Enlightenment, the French Revolution, and the 1848 democratic revolutions—and had officially condemned as "modern errors" or heresies the discourse of human rights, liberalism, Americanism, and modernism. Yet, to a certain extent, Catholicism was also a construct and an effect of anti-Catholic discourse, a discourse that can be traced back to the Protestant critique of Catholicism, through the Enlightenment critique of religion, through liberalism and secularism as critiques of the ancien régime and all the alliances of "throne and altar." Catholicism always constructed itself discursively in dialectical relation with the anti-Catholic discourse of the time. But the varieties of practices and mentalities within the lifeworld of Catholicism always surpassed the homogeneous discursive construct.

Irrespective of how one judges the old anti-Catholic prejudices, the swift and radical transformation of the political culture of Catholic countries as a result of the official reformulation of the religious teachings of the Catholic Church in Vatican II puts into question the notion of the unchanging essence of even a world religion as dogmatically structured as Catholicism. The premise of an unchanging core essence should be even less valid for other "world religions" like Islam, which have a less dogmatically structured doctrinal core or a more pluralistic and contested system of authoritative interpretation of the religious tradition. Islam today has in fact replaced Catholicism as the other of Western secular modernity.

The contemporary global discourse on Islam as a fundamentalist, antimodern, and undemocratic religion shows striking similarities with the old discourse on Catholicism that predominated in Anglo-Protestant societies, particularly in the United States, from the mid nineteenth century to the mid twentieth century.[14] Both discourses have been built upon three similar premises or principles: (1) a theologico-political distinction between "civilized" and "barbaric" religions, that is, between religions that are compatible with Enlightenment principles and liberal democratic politics and religions that are grounded in traditions that resist the progressive claims of the Enlightenment philosophy of history, liberalism, and secularism; (2) a nativist, anti-immigrant posture that postulated the unassimilability of foreign immigrants because of their illiberal and uncivilized social customs and habits, supposedly grounded in their traditional religion; and (3) transnational attachments and loyalties to either a foreign religious authority (i.e., the papacy) or to a transnational religious community (i.e., the *umma*) that appears incompatible with republican citizen principles and the exclusive claims of modern nationalism.

Any of these three principles may have been more or less salient at any particular time and place. It is their superimposition, however, that has given the anti-Catholic and anti-Muslim discourses their compelling effect.

As with Catholicism, the internal and external debates over the compatibility between Islam and democracy and modern individual freedoms is taking place at three separate yet interrelated levels: (1) in debates over "Islamism," the transnational structure of the world of Islam and the alleged clash of civilizations between Islam and the West at the geopolitical level, with clear parallels with earlier debates on the clash between "Republicanism" and "Romanism"; (2) in debates over political Islam and over the democratic legitimacy of Muslim political parties in Turkey and elsewhere, which, like their at first equally suspect Catholic counterparts, may establish new forms of Muslim democracy, akin to Christian democracy; and (3) in debates over the proper articulation of a Muslim *ummah* in immigrant diasporic contexts outside of *Dar el Islam*.

Both discourses, the anti-Catholic as well as the anti-Muslim, have been grounded in the same logic of modern secularism. The "secular" nature of the modern European state and the "secular" character of European democracy serve as one of the foundational myths of contemporary European identity. A frequently heard secular European narrative, usually offered as a genealogical explanation and as a normative justification for the secular character of European democracy, has the following schematic structure. Once upon a time, in medieval Europe there was, as is typical of premodern societies, a fusion of religion and politics. But this fusion, under the new conditions of religious diversity, extreme sectarianism, and conflict created by the Protestant Reformation, led to the nasty, brutish, and long-lasting religious wars of the early modern era, which left European societies in ruin. The secularization of the state was a felicitous response to this catastrophic experience, which apparently has indelibly marked the collective memory of European societies. The Enlightenment did the rest. Modern Europeans learned to separate religion, politics, and science. Most importantly, they learned to tame religious passions and to dissipate obscurantist fanaticism by banishing religion to a protected private sphere, while establishing an open, liberal, secular public sphere, where freedom of expression and public reason dominate. These are the favorable secular foundations upon which democracy grows and thrives. As the tragic stories of contemporary violent religious conflicts around the world show, the unfortunate deprivatization of religion and its return to the public sphere will need to be managed carefully if one is to avoid undermining those fragile foundations.

Until very recently, moreover, the story of secularization was embedded within an even broader narrative of general teleological processes of social modernization and progressive human development. The West simply showed the future to the rest of the world. Today, there is an increasing recognition that we may be entering a global "post-secular" age and that, as Mark Lilla pointed out in a cover story of *The New York Times Magazine*, "the great separation" of religion and politics may be a rather unique and exceptional historical achievement, the more to be cherished and protected.[15]

It should be obvious that such a historical narrative, grounded in the self-understanding of the Enlightenment critique of religion, is indeed a historical myth. The religious wars of early modern Europe, particularly the Thirty Years' War (1618–1648) did not ensue, at least not immediately, in the secular state but rather in the confessional one. The principle *cuius regio eius religio* ("in whose region, whose religion"), established first at the Peace of Augsburg and reiterated at the Treaty of Westphalia, is not the formative principle of the modern secular democratic state, but rather that of the modern confessional territorial absolutist state. Nowhere in Europe did religious conflict lead to the secularization of state and politics, but rather to the confessionalization of the state and to the territorialization of religions and peoples. Moreover, this early modern dual pattern of confessionalization and territorialization was already well established before the religious wars and even before the Protestant Reformation. The Spanish Catholic state under the Catholic Kings serves as the first paradigmatic model of state confessionalization and religious territorialization. The expulsion of Spanish Jews and Muslims who refused to convert to Catholicism is the logical consequence of such a dynamic of state formation. Ethno-religious cleansing, in this respect, stands at the very origin of the early modern European state. Religious minorities caught in the wrong confessional territory were offered not secular toleration, much less freedom of religion, but the "freedom" to emigrate. The Polish-Lithuanian Commonwealth, with its multiconfessional Catholic, Protestant-Lutheran, and Orthodox ruling aristocracies, offers the exception of a major early modern European state that resisted the general European dynamic of territorial confessionalization and offered refuge to religious minorities and radical sects from all over Europe, well before North America and other overseas colonies offered a more safe haven. For the next three hundred years, European societies continued exporting all their religious minorities overseas, while the confessional territorial boundaries between Catholic and Protestant and between Lutheran and Calvinist remained basically frozen until the drastic secularization of post–World War II European societies made those confessional boundaries seemingly irrelevant.

In fact, without taking into account this long historical pattern of confessionalization of states, peoples, and territories, it is not possible to understand the difficulties that every continental European state has, irrespective of whether it has maintained formal establishment or is constitutionally secular, and the difficulties that every European society has, the most secular as well as the most religious, in accommodating religious diversity, and particularly in incorporating immigrant religions.[16] It is true that in the last two hundred years all European states have undergone some process of secularization, and today all of them are formally and/or substantively secular. But the pattern of caesaro-papist regulation and control of religion established by the early modern confessional absolutist state—by Catholic, Anglican, Lutheran, Calvinist, and Orthodox alike—has been maintained, basically unchallenged, until the present.

The particular historical arrangements of separation and church-state relations in Europe tend to oscillate between three patterns: (1) that of formal church establishment with relative "free exercise" of religion in society (England, Scotland, the Nordic Lutheran countries, and Greece are examples of this pattern); (2) that of the formal disestablishment of the church and constitutional separation of the secular state, with strict regulation and control of religion by the state (France and the former communist states follow such a model); and (3) that of the formal separation of church and state, with informal single or multichurch quasi-establishment, along with various corporatist-consociational arrangements and church-state entanglements (bi-confessional countries such as Germany, the Netherlands, Switzerland, the remaining Catholic countries and all post-Communist states follow some version of this model). All of them, with the exception of the United Kingdom, share, moreover, a pattern of limited religious pluralism. In terms of religious majority/minority relations, the model throughout Europe has remained either that of one single national church that claims to be coextensive with the nation or that of two (usually Catholic and Protestant) competing but territorially based national churches, along with an indefinite but limited number of religious minorities, which have assumed the structural position of sects vis-à-vis the national churches.

Indeed, despite all the normative discourse and the often-repeated trope of the modern secular democratic state and the privatization of religion, it is legitimate to question how "secular" the European states really are. How tall and solid are the "walls of separation" between national state and national church and between religion and politics across Europe? To what extent should one attribute the indisputable success of post–World War II Western European democracies to the secularization of society and the privatization of religion, as is so frequently done? If one looks at the reality of "really existing" European democracies rather than at the official secularist discourse, it becomes obvious that most European states are by no means strictly secular, nor do they tend to live up to the myth of secular neutrality.[17]

France is the only Western European state that is officially and proudly "secular," that is, that defines itself and its democracy as regulated by the principles of laïcité. *The disestablishment of the Catholic Church and the hostile separation of church and state had the function of freeing the laic state from ecclesiastical control, but not that of freeing religion from state control. As a secularist republican etatist* ideology, laïcité functions as a civil religion in competition with ecclesiastical religion. It requires the strict privatization of religion and the radical separation of any private religious or ethnic (communitarian) identity from the common public identity of all citizens. The state protects the freedom of religion of all its citizens, Catholic, Protestant, Jew, and Muslim alike, so long as religion remains private. But the French state is far from being neutral to or distant from religious institutions. It frequently regulates religious affairs, establishes institutional relations with the Catholic Church through concordats, and has tried at different times to organize the other religious communities, Protestant, Jewish, and Muslim alike, into churchlike ecclesiastical institutions, which the state can use as interlocutor and institutional partner. As an illustration of the kind of entanglement between national church and state, approximately 20 percent of French pupils attend religious Catholic schools, which cover approximately 80 percent of their finances with state funds. Muslim schools are far from receiving equal state support. Indeed, many Muslim girls attend Catholic schools in order to circumvent the ban on veiling in public schools.

By contrast, several European countries with long-standing democracies have maintained established churches. They include England and Scotland within the United Kingdom and all the Scandinavian Lutheran countries: Denmark, Norway, Iceland, Finland, and, until the year 2000, Sweden. Of the new democracies, Greece has also maintained the establishment of the Greek Orthodox Church. This means that, with the exception of the Catholic Church, which has eschewed establishment in every recent (post-1974) transition to democracy in Southern Europe (Portugal, Spain) and in Eastern Europe (Poland, Hungary, the Czech Republic, Slovakia, Slovenia, Croatia), every other major branch of Christianity (Anglican, Presbyterian, Lutheran, Orthodox) is officially established somewhere in Europe, without apparently jeopardizing democracy in those countries. Since there are many historical examples of European states that have been secular and nondemocratic, the Soviet-type Communist regimes being the most obvious, one can therefore safely conclude that the strict secular separation of church and state is neither a sufficient nor a necessary condition for democracy.

Within this group of European countries with established churches, moreover, there are significant variations in the levels of religious pluralism, from England, one of the most religiously pluralistic countries of Western Europe, to Denmark, one of the least religiously pluralistic countries. One can safely assume that the more religiously pluralistic the country, the easier it will be to accommodate additional religious diversity. More important, however, than the absolute number of minority religions may be the willingness of the established church to tolerate dissenting sectarian movements within its own sphere, such as Methodism and other evangelical movements within Anglicanism, or the evangelical sectarian movement within Lutheranism in Norway. The level of secularization does not seem to be a relevant factor here.

Denmark is undoubtedly one of the most secular countries of Europe, or at least one of the countries with the lowest level of regular church attendance (less than 5 percent, a figure comparable to that of East Germany), with one of the highest levels of religious affiliation (close to 90 percent of the population declare their affiliation with the Danish Lutheran Church, a figure comparable to that of much more religious Catholic countries, such as Ireland or Portugal), and one of the lowest levels of religious diversity (only 2 percent of Danes declare other religious affiliation).

One could, of course, retort that European societies are de facto so secularized and, in consequence, what remains of religion has become so temperate that both constitutional establishment and the various institutional church-state entanglements are innocuous, if not completely irrelevant. This may be so for the national majorities, whether they maintain implicit (i.e., vicarious) or explicit religious affiliation with their national churches. But it can hardly be so for most religious minorities, least of all for new immigrant religious minorities. What is clear is that no European state can be said to meet the criteria of a secular neutral state, which is supposed to offer equal access, equal distance, equal respect, or equal support to all the religions within its territory. In a certain sense, the principle *cuius regio eius religio* has remained a constant in most European societies, even after the transference of sovereignty from the monarch to the people or the nation, and after drastic secularization. Neither democratization nor secularization has radically altered the general continental European pattern of very limited religious pluralism. It is not surprising, therefore, that European societies encounter difficulties in accommodating the religious diversity brought by new immigrants.

Alfred Stepan has pointed out how the most important empirical analytical theories of democracy, from Robert Dahl to Juan Linz, do not include secularism or strict separation as one of the institutional requirements for democracy, as prominent normative liberal theories, such as those of John Rawls or Bruce Ackerman, tend to do. As an alternative to secularist principles or norms, Stepan has proposed the model of the "twin tolerations," which he describes as "the minimal boundaries of freedom of action that must somehow be crafted for political institutions *vis-à-vis* religious authorities, and for religious individuals and groups *vis-à-vis* political institutions." Religious authorities must "tolerate" the autonomy of democratically elected governments without claiming constitutionally privileged prerogatives to mandate or to veto public policy. Democratic political institutions, in turn, must "tolerate" the autonomy of religious individuals and groups not only in complete freedom to worship privately, but also to advance publicly their values in civil society and to sponsor organizations and movements in political society, so long as they do not violate democratic rules and adhere to the rule of law. Within this framework of mutual autonomy, Stepan concludes, "there can be an extraordinarily broad range of concrete patterns of religion-state relations in political systems that would meet our minimal definition of democracy."[18]

Transnational Religions, Transnational Imagined Communities, and Globalization

The empirical case studies in *Public Religions* were framed as national case studies under the premises of the kind of methodological nationalism that has framed so much of the comparative work in the social sciences, whether comparative historical sociology, comparative politics, or comparative economic development. Personally, I was well aware of the transnational dimensions of Catholicism. But for me, the truly revealing lesson of the kind of comparative Catholicism that I undertook was the extent to which the transnational dimensions of Catholicism, which had been characteristic of medieval Christendom, from the transnational papacy to transnational religious orders, to ecumenical councils, to transnational universities and centers of Catholic learning, to transnational pilgrimages, had all substantially diminished, if not disappeared altogether, between the emergence of the Westphalian system of territorial nation-states in the sixteenth century and the early twentieth century. Since the end of the nineteenth century, one can witness the reemergence and reconstruction of all the transnational dimensions of Catholicism on a new, global basis. Catholicism has been reconstituted as a new transnational and deterritorialized global religious regime.[19]

The trajectory and fate of the Jesuits from their foundation to the present offer a perfect illustration of the ebbs and flows of national and transnational Catholic dynamics. They were established at the University of Paris in the mid sixteenth century by a group of Spanish students at a time when both the faculty and the student body of every major European university were still transnational. Soon they became the paradigmatic transnational order, organized militantly to defend the universal, that is, transnational, claims of the papacy against the Protestant Reformation and against the emerging absolutist *raison d'état*. They also spearheaded the early modern phase of Catholic colonial globalization from East Asia to Brazil. But with the emergence of the modern system of nation states, the papacy not only lost control of the Catholic national churches, but the Catholic monarchs themselves attained veto power over the process of papal nomination. In the mid eighteenth century, one Catholic monarch after another expelled the Jesuits from their Catholic domains and then conspired through their "crown cardinals" to elect Lorenzo Ganganelli, who, as Pope Clement XIV, decreed the suppression of the Society of Jesus in 1773. Amazingly, the Jesuits survived by finding refuge in non-Catholic territories in Orthodox Russia and in postcolonial Protestant America.

With the nationalization and democratization of sovereignty in the nineteenth century, we find again the frequent expulsion of the Jesuits from Catholic territories after every liberal revolution. Secularizing laws of education led to their expulsion from France, and they were expelled from Germany during the Kulturkampf. Yet during World War I, at a time when Pope Benedict XIV proved to be one of the few sane voices in Europe, condemning the senseless slaughter of European youth, the order paid more heed to nationalist calls to arms, and both French and German Jesuits returned to serve their nations and die for their fatherlands. It would be unthinkable today for the Jesuits or any other Catholic transnational order to join a nationalist war.

From 1870 to the present, one can witness the reconstitution of all the transnational dimensions of Catholicism that had nearly disappeared with the emergence of the Westphalian system of sovereign territorial states: uncontested papal supremacy, ecumenical councils, transnational religious orders, transnational cadres, a transnational Curia, transnational centers of Catholic learning, transnational pilgrimages, and transnational Catholic movements.

If the transformation of contemporary Catholicism illustrates the opportunities that the process of globalization offers to a transnational religious regime with a highly centralized structure and an imposing transnational network of human, institutional, and material resources, which feels, therefore, confident in its ability to thrive in a relatively open global system of religious regimes, contemporary Pentecostalism may serve to illustrate the equally favorable opportunities that globalization offers to a highly decentralized religion, with no historical links to tradition and no territorial roots or identity, which therefore can make itself at home anywhere in the globe where the Spirit moves.[20] We may take Brazil as a paradigmatic example. The transnational character of Brazilian Pentecostalism is inscribed in its very beginnings. It arrived from the United States in 1910, just a few years after the Azusa Street revival, brought by European immigrants—an Italian and two Swedish missionaries who had encountered Pentecostalism in Chicago. Yet almost immediately Pentecostalism assumed an indigenous Brazilian form. In this sense, Brazilian Pentecostalism represents a dual process of deterritorialization: North American Christianity is deterritorialized by taking indigenous roots in Brazil, a Catholic territory, which therefore leads to the deterritorialization of Catholicism from Brazil. This is the most important consequence of the explosive growth of Pentecostalism throughout Latin America. Latin America has ceased being Catholic territory, even if Catholicism continues to be, for the foreseeable future, the majority religion of all Latin American countries. It is estimated that currently two-thirds of all Latin American Protestants are Pentecostals-charismatics. Latin America, particularly Brazil, has become in a very short time a world center of Pentecostal Christianity, from which it has now begun to radiate in all directions, including back into the United States.

The growth of Pentecostal Christianity in sub-Saharan Africa (Ghana, Nigeria, Zimbabwe, South Africa) is no less explosive. Moreover, African Pentecostalism is as local, indigenous, and autonomous as its Latin American counterpart. The same could be said about Pentecostalism in Korea or in China. Korean missionaries, for instance, are becoming ubiquitous in evangelical missions throughout Asia. Indeed, Pentecostalism's expansion must be seen as a multisource diffusion of parallel developments around the globe. Pentecostalism is not a religion with a particular territorial center like the Mormon church, which is rapidly gaining worldwide diffusion. Nor is it a transnational religious regime like Catholicism, with global reach. As Paul Freston has pointed out, "new churches are local expressions of a global culture, characterized by parallel invention, complex diffusion and international networks with multilateral flows."[21] Pentecostalism may be said to be the first truly global religion. Moreover, Pentecostalism is simultaneously global and local. In this respect, it is historically unique and unprecedented. It is historically the first and paradigmatic case of a decentered and deterritorialized global culture.

Similar illustrations could be offered from other branches of Christianity and from other world religions. The dynamic core of Anglicanism no longer resides in post-Christian England. Today, immigrants from all over the British postcolonial world are reviving Anglicanism in secular England. Think of the transnational politics of the global Anglican Communion over the ordination of homosexual or female bishops, played out between England, Africa, North America, and the Caribbean. The Patriarch of Constantinople is reemerging, at least symbolically, as a deterritorialized global center of Eastern Christianity, in competition with the Moscow Patriarchate and with the other territorial autocephalous national Orthodox churches.

For the "world religions," globalization offers the opportunity to become for the first time truly world religions, that is, global. But it also threatens them with deterritorialization. The opportunities are greatest for religions like Islam and Buddhism, which always had a transnational structure. The threat is greatest for those embedded in civilizational territories, such as, again, Islam and Hinduism. But through worldwide migrations they are also becoming global and deterritorialized. Indeed, their diasporas are becoming dynamic centers for global transformation that affect their civilizational homes.

Trans-societal migrations and the world religions, at times separately but often in conjunction with each other, have always served as important carriers of processes of globalization. In a certain sense, one could argue that the successive waves of migration of *homo sapiens* out of Africa some fifty thousand years ago and subsequent settlements throughout the globe constitute the point of departure of the process of globalization. But these migrations had no subjective dimension of reflexive consciousness and can only now be reconstructed objectively thanks to advances in DNA and other scientific technologies. By contrast, the subjective dimension of imagining a single humanity sharing the same global space and the same global time was first anticipated in all universalistic world religions. Yet these imaginary anticipations, while serving as a precondition for the civilizational expansion of the world religions, lacked a structural, that is, objective and material, global base.

Until very recently, the civilizational *oikoumenē* of all world religions had very clear territorial limits, set by the regimes in which those religions were civilizationally and thus territorially embedded and by the geographically circumscribed limitations of the existing means of communication. The Bishop of Rome may have always claimed to speak *urbi et orbi*, to the city and to the world. But in fact this first became a reality in the twentieth century. What constitutes the truly novel aspect of the present global condition is that all world religions can, for the first time, be reconstituted truly as deterritorialized global imagined communities, detached from the civilizational settings in which they have been traditionally embedded. Paraphrasing Arjun Appadurai's image of "modernity at large," one could say that the world religions, through the linking of electronic mass media and mass migration, are being reconstituted as deterritorialized global religions "at large" or as global *ummahs*.[22]

For that very reason, Samuel Huntington's thesis of the impending clash of civilizations both illuminates the present global condition and is profoundly misleading.[23] It is illuminating insofar as his was one of the first prominent voices to call attention to the increasing relevance of civilizations and civilizational identities in the emerging global order and in global conflicts. But his thesis is profoundly misleading insofar as it still conceives of civilizations as territorial geopolitical units, akin to superpowers, having some world religion as a cultural core.

This process of dissociation of territory, religion, and civilizational culture is by no means uniform or homogeneous across world religions and civilizations, and, indeed, it encounters much resistance by states that still aspire not only to monopolize the means of violence but also to regulate religious groups and cultural identities in their territories, as well by "churches," in the broad Weberian sense of the term, as religious institutions or as religious imagined communities that claim or aspire to religious monopoly over their civilizational or national territories.

There is a fundamental tension in the modern world between two well-recognized principles. On the one hand, there is the principle of the inalienable right of the individual person to freedom of conscience and therefore to freedom of religion, including freedom of conversion. In all modern democratic societies, this principle has assumed the form of an unquestioned, universal human right. Nobody should be coerced or forced to believe or not to believe any particular religious doctrine. Consequently, everybody also has the right to believe or not to believe any particular religious doctrine, including the right of conversion to any particular religion. On the other hand, there is also an increasing recognition of the collective rights of peoples to protect and preserve their traditions and their cultures from colonial, imperialist, and predatory practices. Such recognition is primarily enshrined in United Nations documents concerning the rights of indigenous people. But it could easily be turned into a general principle of the reciprocal rights and duties of all peoples of the world to respect each other's traditions and cultures, constituting the basis of what could be called an emerging global denominationalim.

Actually, one finds almost everywhere similar tensions between the protectionist impulse to claim religious monopoly over national or civilizational territories and the ecumenical impulse to present one's own particular religion as a response to the universal needs of global humanity. Transnational migrations and the emergence of diasporas of all world religions beyond their civilizational territories make this tension visible everywhere. Of course, neither transnational migrations nor the resulting diasporas are a novel phenomenon per se. It is the general, almost universal character of the phenomenon under novel global conditions that makes it particularly relevant for all world religions.

When it comes to Islam, or to an imagined transnational community of Muslims, we in the West are naturally obsessed with state Islamism and *khilafist jihādism* as the two dominant contemporary forms of globalized Islam. But I would like to argue that the majoritarian currents of transnational Islam today, the ones likely to have the greatest impact on the future transformation of Islam, are transnational networks and movements of Muslim renewal, equally disaffected with state Islamism and transnational *jihādism*. They constitute the networks of a loosely organized and pluralistic transnational *ummah*, or global Muslim civil society: from the "evangelical" Tablighi Jama'at, a faith movement highly active throughout the Muslim world and in Muslim diasporas, whose annual conferences in India represent the second largest world gathering of Muslims after the *hajj*, and other transnational *dawa* networks, to the neo-Sufist Fethullah Gülen's educational network, active throughout Turkey, Turkish diasporas, and the Turkic republics of Central Asia, and other Sufi brotherhoods, such as the Mourids of West Africa, who have also expanded their transnational networks into the Muslim diasporas of Europe and North America.

One could make a similar analysis of the formation of a global Hindu *ummah* linking the civilizational home, "Mother India," with old diasporic colonial Hindu communities across the former British Empire, from Southeast Asia to South Africa to the Caribbean, and with new immigrant Hindu communities throughout the West, from the British Isles to North America and Australia. The purification of separate Muslim and Hindu identities in the diasporas of the subcontinent, from South Africa to Guyana, among peoples who have lived together either as colored under apartheid or as Indo-Caribbean in contrast to Afro-Caribbean is one of the most telling manifestation of this global phenomenon.

It is this proliferation of deterritorialized transnational global imagined communities, encompassing the so-called old world religions as well as many new forms of hybrid globalized religions, such as Bahais, Moonies, Hare Krishnas, Afro-American religions, Falun Gong, and so on, that I call the emerging global denominationalism. Of course, they compete with many other forms of secular imagined communities or *ummahs*. But all those transnational imagined religious communities present fundamental challenges both to international-relations theories, which function within the premises of a Westphalian international system, and to secular cosmopolitan theories of globalization.

I use *cosmopolitanism* here in the broad sense of any worldview that envisions the future global order as a single, relatively homogeneous and unified global economic, political, and cultural system or as a single human "universal civilization." To a certain extent, most theories of globalization share similar cosmopolitan assumptions insofar as they assume that economic and technological globalization will determine the shape of global society and of global culture.

Cosmopolitanism builds upon developmental theories of modernization that envision social change as a global expansion of Western modernity, which is understood not as the hegemonic expansion of a particular social formation but as a universal process of human development. In most cosmopolitan accounts, religion either does not exist or it is "invisible," in Thomas Luckmann's sense of being an individualized and privatized form of salvation or quest for meaning that is irrelevant to the functioning of the primary institutions of modern society. In its collective dimension, religion is reduced to just another form of cultural group identity. If and when religion emerges in the public sphere and has to be taken seriously, it is usually branded either as antimodern fundamentalism resisting processes of secularization, or as a form of traditionalist collective identity reacting to the threat of globalization. In other words, religion, in the eyes of cosmopolitan elites, is either irrelevant or reactive. Indeed, when it comes to religion, all forms of cosmopolitanism at least implicitly share the basic tenets of the theory of secularization, which the social sciences and modern liberal political ideologies have inherited from the Enlightenment critique of religion. Cosmopolitanism remains a faithful child of the European Enlightenment.

It is time to revise our teleological conceptions of a global cosmopolitan secular modernity, against which we can characterize the religious "other" as "fundamentalist." It is time to make room for more complex, nuanced, and reflexive categories that will help us to understand better the already-emerging global system of multiple modernities. So long as we maintain the concept of a single, cosmopolitan modernity as a general process of secular differentiation, indeed, as a normative global project, we will be compelled to characterize all forms of religion we cannot accept as our own as threatening "fundamentalism." We thus become ourselves unwittingly partisans in a supposedly worldwide secular-religious conflict and may even help turn the so-called "clash of civilizations" into a self-fulfilling prophecy. What is at stake, ultimately, is recognition of the irremediable plurality of universalisms and the multiplicity of modernities, namely, that every universalism and every modernity is particularistic. One could say that we are moving from a condition of competing particularist universalisms to a new condition of global denominational contextualism.

Under conditions of globalization, moreover, all the world religions draw not only upon their own traditions but also increasingly upon one another. Intercivilizational encounters, cultural imitations and borrowings, diasporic diffusions, hybridity, creolization, and transcultural hyphenations are as much part and parcel of the global present as Western hegemony, cosmopolitan homogenization, religious fundamentalism, or the clash of civilizations.

Provincializing God?

Provocations from an Anthropology of Religion

Michael Lambek

My title exhibits great hubris: in the literal sense, first of all; then toward theologians and members of established religions; then also perhaps toward the many nonanthropologists in this interdisciplinary audience. But more immediately, it exhibits hubris toward Dipesh Chakrabarty, the title of whose magnificent work *Provincializing Europe*, I have appropriated and transformed.[1] Here are some of the objects intended by the "provincializing" of my title: first, the conceptualization of God as singular, unitary, and supreme, and, even though we can never know His mystery, as someone on the order of a human person, most likely a senior male, a patriarch; second, the certainty of many of the followers of such a God that they have exclusive access to the truth and thus can easily dismiss both explicit alternatives and the sort of heterogeneity that arises from preanalytic thought or nonrationalized practice; third, the implicit assumption by many Western scholars that these attributes are general features of religion, that the Abrahamic religions are tokens of a universal or natural type in which distinct religions are bounded entities constituted by belief in God or gods.

Whereas some scholars have argued, as I do here, that such features are locally specific, and hence not the features best suited for defining the type, they have been adamant that religion, defined in other terms, *is* universal, that every society has something comparable to the Abrahamic religions, that there is such a type or at least a universal field of investigation. They have done so in part because such is the power of the Abrahamic religions and the secular models of religion they generate that to have stated otherwise would have been to consign those outside the sphere of religion to heathen darkness and amorality. But this also means that we can describe practices as "religious" only in relation to the Abrahamic type. Therefore one could raise the question of whether this strategy has been misguided, so that the very concept of "religion" should be reserved for phenomena in the Abrahamic tradition. Phrased as either/or, this question is somewhat mischievous. Among other things, answering in the affirmative would play into the politics of the continuing expansion of the Abrahamic religions. Hence my response can only be: both/and.

What attracts me to Chakrabarty is the great seriousness and integrity with which he grapples with the both/and problem of situating European social theory. His exemplar is Marx and, along with Marx, European meta-narratives of social evolution, progress, and political modernity. For my purposes we can add the generation of ideal types like "religion," as well as the discursive projects in which they are embedded or which they make possible, projects such as the development of general theories of religion, programs of research dedicated to understanding such things as "the future of the religious past," or anthologies that claim to cover and reflect a field like "the anthropology of religion."[2] Chakrabarty admits the attraction of European, now cosmopolitan, traditions of thought in such matters, and, at the same time, their radical insufficiency, attempting to show "how the categories and strategies we have learned from European thought . . . are both indispensable and inadequate."[3] As he notes, "If historical or anthropological consciousness is seen as the work of a rational outlook, it can only 'objectify'—and thus deny—the *lived* relations the observing subject already has."[4] He says, "the differences between religions are by definition incapable of bringing the master category 'culture' or 'religion' into any kind of crisis. We know that these categories are problematic, that not all people have what is called 'culture' or 'religion' in the English senses of these words, but we have to operate as though this limitation were not of any great moment."[5]

Chakrabarty sets together two streams of Western thought as represented by Marx and Heidegger, respectively. They can stand for, among other things, the complex relations between "science" and "religion," words that I place in scare quotes, although, in the very dialectic they set up, these scare quotes must be *sous rature*, there and not there, spoken and unspoken, inscribed and scratched out. Chakrabarty's task is, further, to put Europe in perspective, to think through and with European thought, but at the same time to be able to find some purchase outside it, from within another cultural world. To provincialize God is to draw on European thought and yet at the same time to try to step outside the Abrahamic tradition, to recognize how it has influenced secular thought about religion (it doesn't matter here whether the scholars concerned are themselves religious or secular in orientation, or even refuse the relevance of such labels for themselves) and to try to imagine how something like "religion"—here I need those scare quotes—might look outside the Christian and Islamic spheres. To follow Talal Asad,[6] if religion and secularism emerge together, disembedding from some larger whole and mutually defining each other, then to provincialize religion is *not* to examine it from a specifically secular position but rather to provincialize secularism as well, that is, to provincialize the very divide between the secular and the religious. But at the same time, to revert to Chakrabarty, that needs to go along with taking some kind of meta-narrative stance comprehending the "great transformation" that produces the divide in the first place.

Although writing directly about history, Chakrabarty gets straight to the heart of some of my discipline's central dilemmas. If postcolonial thought has offered a stringent and necessary critique of classical anthropology, it has also, in my opinion, opened up the significance of anthropology, showing that the dilemmas and debates central to the field have much broader significance across the academy. Albeit from a different standpoint, postcolonial theory has, in effect, diffused anthropological insight across a multitude of disciplines. It is no wonder that I find Chakrabarty's position intellectually congenial when he says, "the idea is to write into the history of modernity the ambivalences, contradictions, the use of force, and the tragedies and ironies that attend it."[7] I would, however, be prepared to expand these attributions beyond modernity to the human condition writ large. All these features, especially irony and including heterogeneity, are underplayed both in the Abrahamic religions as commonly practiced (excepting perhaps Jewish irony) and in the practice of positivist social science, which is one of its secular offshoots.

It is my understanding that, whatever the personal profession of individual anthropologists, anthropology has been itself intrinsically a secular discipline, constituted out of the very same processes of disembedding as "religion." Thus, the challenge that postcolonial thinkers like Asad and Chakrabarty offer anthropology is how the study of religion can draw on both European thought and history and on thought and history external to Europe (and yet, as we now know, extensively related to it), how it can and must be simultaneously both secular and external to the very conceptualization of the secular. Palimpsests and erasures, phenomenological bracketing and positionality, objectifications and embodiments, identities and dialectics, romanticizations and reductions: you see the great difficulty of the subject—but also its great attraction. The questions are not only can the subaltern speak or whether the intellectual should speak sometimes for or about the subaltern, but whether both intellectuals and subalterns can speak for themselves with a vocabulary that both is and is not theirs, about a subject and about experience that both is and is not theirs.

You could retort that my problem is one of being a secular anthropologist. If I were a theologian, I would not suffer the vertigo of unstable positionality or the dizziness that accompanies bifocal lenses. But I would then, indeed, have another problem, at least equally intractable. The scandal for theology is the heterogeneity of religion. For a theologian of the Abrahamic faiths, the scandal is one of other gods and other worshippers, even of people without an ostensibly single god or exclusive practices of worship. No amount of intellectual rationalizing will solve this problem of who is right and who is wrong in a context in which it is understood that there are absolute divisions between right and wrong. As Monsignor Greg Smith put it in an interview on Canadian radio the day the current pope was elected, there "are fundamental truths that don't change, that will not change." He added that there are no degrees of orthodoxy; either you follow the rules or you don't, either you are orthodox or you are not.[8]

When theologians have taken comparative religion seriously, they have generally done so in a way that does not challenge their own faith. Thus they hypostatize ostensibly universal phenomena like "the sacred" or "mystical experience" instead of problematizing them. Of course, I must add the converse—there are many aspects of Christianity that do aid in discerning the nuances of other systems of thought and practice. Most anthropologists, myself at the forefront, are doubtless incredibly naïve about the nature of Christianity and provincial with respect to the depth and riches of Abrahamic-based theory for the analysis of religious phenomena more broadly no less than for philosophy. I need point here only to the sort of sophisticated conversations continued by Hent de Vries.[9]

Let me try to simplify. Chakrabarty argues for a kind of both/and accommodation of universalizing thought and diverse local or regional traditions. He suggests that we cannot subscribe exclusively to European meta-narratives or the analytic stances they presuppose or generate, but we cannot do without them either. What I want to provincialize is not all aspects of the Abrahamic religious traditions but rather their dedication precisely not to such a pluralist logic of both/and but rather to a binary logic of either/or. Indeed, it is this binary logic of mutual exclusion that also poses the alternative of secularism: either belief in, and invocation of, religion—or not. In a cultural universe characterized by both/and, skepticism and rationalism are simply part of a larger repertoire of attitudes and positions, invoked according to shifting practical considerations, rather than a matter for strict adjudication.

I have been alternating between the words *West* and *Europe* and *Abrahamic religions* rather carelessly. As we know, the placement of boundaries between itself and its others is part of the logic by which the West operates and a matter of some arbitrariness and considerable politics. I hope that my invocation of the Abrahamic religions, a category I borrow from religious studies (and that is doubtless contested therein), serves to trouble rather than affirm such distinctions. In any case, it comprehends not only millions of non-European adherents but, along with Christianity, two of Christian Europe's most "intimate others" and longest-standing perceived opponents. I intend to overlook the very great differences among the Abrahamic traditions and within each of them and present an over-simplified and somewhat stereotyped portrait of certain features they have in common. Whatever the flaws in such a strategy, it cannot be worse than reproducing the oppositions so prevalent in contemporary politics and media.

One of these common features is, of course, God.

Abrahamic religions have a patriarchal God, even if patriarchy is modulated in Christianity by the Son and the Mother. God is gendered—Indo-European and Semitic languages make this virtually inevitable—and parental. Some recent theological interventions and certain long-standing minority positions aside, He is omnipotent and omniscient, but also discriminating, vigilant, and punitive. Appearances often to the contrary, He is also just, compassionate, and merciful, bearing no moral flaws. He is both like a human person and idealized so as to be absolutely not human.

The Abrahamic religions are commonly described as monotheistic. Originally, God is simply jealous; officially, He is single (even if Christianity confuses the point). He also quickly becomes unique; *There is no God but Allah*, begins the Muslim profession. Thus this God not only demands exclusive loyalty of His followers but He says that anyone who prefers an alternative is misguided.[10] Hence the universalist pretensions of Christianity and Islam and their missionary zeal.

God is a sacred word—I still write it with a capital—and remarkably powerful and pervasive. In the West, even self-professed non-Christians have often been deists, believing in a supreme being whose designs are evident in nature. One can have God without advocating religion, as was the case of the founding fathers of the United States,[11] but can one have religion without God? To disregard or question God seems somehow even more dangerous than dismissing religion, which, after all, is merely human and not divine.

In fact, there is no little irony in attempting to provincialize the God of the Abrahamic traditions at the very moment when His influence is expanding faster and further than ever among the world's populations. It is often overlooked that one of the most striking things about this expansion is not the competition between Christianity and Islam, or between Pentecostalism and other forms of Christianity, but the assumption held by an increasing number of people that without belief in God, ethical order would collapse. The assumption is that to be an ethical person one must submit to one of these Abrahamic forms; that admitting to disbelief in God is but one step from happily committing theft, murder, incest, or sorcery. In other words, social and interpersonal trust and good will are predicated on religion; religion is equated with, or reduced to, belief; and religious belief means, or is now restricted to, belief in God. Hence to disavow God, no matter whether He is Christian, Muslim, or Jewish, is to render oneself outside the pale of moral responsibility and virtually of society itself. I should add that I understand this to be a different issue from accepting secularism as a civil or political program.

What appears to be happening in some parts of Africa is a shift from accepting Christianity or Islam within an inclusive both/and universe to accepting them by means of an exclusive either/or paradigm.[12] This outcome is facilitated by the fact that the Abrahamic religions are characterized by having "outsides." What is outside can be conceptualized as radically different and clearly separated from what is inside. Thus, when people are introduced to the Abrahamic religions, the model is not one of adding to a preexisting repertoire but of conversion. "Conversion" is not a neutral, abstract concept from the toolkit of an anthropology of religion. Conversion *to* implies simultaneous conversion *from*.[13] It is a matter of either/or, not both/and. The idea that belief in God requires rejecting alternatives has been characteristic of the Abrahamic tradition and has become part of what Western scholars understand by "a" religion.[14]

The point about having an outside is equally relevant for conceptualizing secularism. The secular is by definition a perspective that imagines it can look at religion from the outside. If Abrahamic religion has often denigrated the practices it locates outside its borders, secularism turns that partly around in order to claim that the external space offers a privileged vantage point from which to view what lies within. Without a sense of clearly bounded entities, it would be hard to conceive of secularism.

In addressing the question of God, I have sidestepped the closely related and mutually reinforcing concept of "belief." This is deliberate, both because this is an area in which the Abrahamic religions diverge from one another and because the Christian biases inherent in a "belief"-based model of religion have been well discussed by others.[15] To these arguments I would only add that the anthropology of religion has largely adhered to what Alasdair MacIntyre has referred to as "the metaphysical realism of Jewish and Christian theism."[16]

The logic of mutual exclusion has struck me because my ethnographic experience has been so different. Among Malagasy speakers in Mayotte and in northwest Madagascar, religion during the last quarter of the twentieth century has been inclusive.[17] People regularly observed that God was the same everywhere and hence it mattered little which avenue one used to approach Him. A devout Malagasy Muslim told me that when he served as a rural policeman in a region without mosques, he simply took part in Christian observances. In some families one child was assigned to ancestral tradition, another to Christianity, a third to Islam. The Antankaraña king was named Isa Alexandre Tsimanamboholahy, each term indexing a different affiliation. This fits with the logic of bilateral descent that is characteristic of the region. Bilateral kin groups are noted for being overlapping and not mutually exclusive. Sakalava can describe themselves as belonging to at least eight descent groups by calculating back to their great grandparents on either side and some would double that. This affords an ironic as opposed to a literal appreciation of identity and affiliation.[18] Instead of absolute and final choice between discrete and ostensibly commensurable alternatives, there is continuous judgment among incommensurables.[19] In such a setting radical acceptance and rejection are not necessary correlates of plurality. Plurality is not a product of juxtaposed discrete fragments but a manifestation of the whole.

Let me turn, then, to some ethnographic material, not to illustrate religious pluralism but to contextualize the Abrahamic deity. However, in order to introduce Sakalava ancestral narrative from Mahajanga, Madagascar, I begin with a story with whose screenplay you are quite familiar.

The Gender of Sacrifice

Scene 1. A stark rocky desert landscape, 1950s MGM-style. The orb of the sun burns pitilessly from a cloudless sky. Father and son, encumbered in orientalist garb, toil up the mountain. The old man has unruly gray hair, a long tangled beard, and a tragic, determined, almost mad look in his eye. The young son is a picture of pubertal innocence. His hair is long, too, but much neater than his father's; it looks freshly washed. He has a gentle face and wide eyes. He looks, frankly, far less Semitic, if you will pardon the expression, than his father, evoking for Christian viewers a distant descendant of whom the boy can know nothing. The son gamely leads an ass bearing a pile of firewood. "But where," he asks with that simplicity, so innocent it makes your heart stop, "Where is the sacrificial offering?"

"God will supply it," gruffly intones the father, his voice disappearing in the wind that suddenly whips up, as if across the centuries.

The boy is puzzled. Why would God provide his own gift?

They reach the summit. Father motions Son to approach. He lays him across the flat rock, exposing a creamy, pulsing neck. He raises the knife.

Suddenly, the script changes. Instead of a ram, a beautiful woman dressed in shiny silk appears, seemingly out of nowhere. She has followed them up this long road, darting from boulder to boulder, staying out of sight. Quickly she approaches and pulls the boy aside. "Mother!" cries the boy. The woman is determined. She lies in her son's place and commands her husband, "Kill me instead so that my son shall live and our descendants after him!" The Father hesitates. The Mother takes the glistening knife and wields it on herself. In this version, there is no God to intervene.

In one stroke, the woman has seized history and overturned patriarchy, or at least inserted herself into it, irretrievably and unforgettably.

Scene 2. Quick cut to Copenhagen, 1843. Johannes de Silentio, a.k.a. Søren Kierkegaard, is at work on *Fear and Trembling*, running his fingers through his locks and saying in passionate despair: How can I avoid simply placing these ideas on "clearance sale"? In the old days, he writes, "faith was a task for a whole lifetime, because it was assumed that dexterity in faith is not acquired in a few days or weeks."[20]

How can I present Sakalava myth without cheapening its power or undermining its allusive and elusive qualities? It is not only that we are so jaded by myth but that the difficulty of expressing Sakalava narratives is part of their message. They are *raha sarotro*—heavy, difficult, valuable, and dangerous things. Sakalava myths are not stories *about* power, but powerful in themselves. They are more powerful unspoken than spoken, yet speaking them can have powerful consequences, especially when proper precautions and permissions are not taken.

I wonder how de Silentio would have represented the Sakalava myth of sacrifice, a foundational event whose power lies in its own pregnant silence, its own unrepresentability? I myself must compromise. I have begun with Abraham in order not only to distinguish the Sakalava story but to try to evoke its urgency and the poignancy and potency of the wife and mother who steps in and offers herself, who is simultaneously sacrificer and sacrificed, who has the insight to know what is required and the determination to carry it out. Her name, in Malagasy, is Ndramandikavavy, Noble Lady Who Surpasses All Women.

Scene 3. Mahajanga, Madagascar. The shrine of the four men.

Dense green mango trees shade a neatly swept plaza of red earth. People move slowly and gracefully within the tropical space. They wear brightly patterned wrappers and the women have their hair hanging in multiple long braids. Gaiety and color, calm and dignity, which could not be more different from the fraught atmosphere of the bleak mountainside. Along the east of the plaza is a long fence of tall spiked poles, behind which can barely be glimpsed the temple building that houses, so the manager of the shrine explains to the anthropologist's tape recorder, four reliquaries, each containing bodily fragments from a royal ancestor, as well as a number of artifacts, notably a sword or knife, the *viarara*. Inside the temple women and men, barefoot and wrapped in colorful Malagasy cloths, having removed vestiges of sewn European clothing, approach respectfully and receptively, crouching low before a tall white curtain behind which the relics reside.

Every year there is a festival to bathe the ancestral relics, a festival of blessing and renewal, a Sakalava New Year, and said to grow from year to year, like a living creature, a tree perhaps, like the ancient mangos, as people come to pay their respects. The festival is the largest in the region, well known throughout Madagascar, and drawing pilgrims from far and wide.

The ancestors whose relics lie within the temple are all men; indeed, they are known as the "four men" (*efadahy*). They include the Father, who conquered the region of Boina around 1700, and the Son, his successor and ancestor of all subsequent rulers. The third relic is known sometimes as the Grandfather, sometimes as the Brother-in-law. The fourth relic is that of this family's own ancestor or diviner, the socially and humanly ambiguous political philosopher-genius who established the structure of the kingdom. It is as though the fourth man, Ndramisara, to whose name the shrine is regularly attributed, were Lévi-Strauss, contemplating this quadripartite structure of male succession and exchange to which he is both inside and outside.

The festival begins officially on the Saturday of a full moon in June/July, when large crowds witness the arrival of prestations from various parts of the kingdom and as far as La Réunion and metropolitan France. These are accepted by the shrine manager on behalf of the living descendants and reigning monarch present. The climax occurs on Monday, as the relics are removed from their sleeping quarters and, with much fanfare, bathed, anointed, and briefly paraded on the backs of their subjects once around the temple building before being restored to their concealed resting places for another year.

Do not be deceived by the public display. Sakalava say, "Full bottles don't rattle" (*feno tsy mikobaña*). Here, what is visible, speaking for or spoken of, and in motion is less powerful, less full, than what is invisible, silent, unmoving. The ancestral relics are concealed, still, and silent relative to their descendants, to commoners, and to the living. And they are revered. But behind them lies the power of the woman. Ndramandikavavy is wife to one, mother to another, possibly sister to a third, and certainly grandmother to all subsequent generations. Before the public prestations that ostensibly open the ceremony, she must be acknowledged, her permission for the service sought and granted. Only once Ndramandikavavy gives her assent and "opens the gate" can the service unfold, the new year begin, the polity renew itself.

Present in her marked absence from the shrine, a place that figures her own death—a place whose very existence is built upon it—she haunts the scene, more authoritative, more fearsome, and more sacred than the eponymous four men, but equally more hidden, more set apart. Her presence is represented—or displaced—by the bloody sword of which she is proprietor. It is bathed each year along with the human relics of the four men and carried in the place of honor at the head of their procession. It is used to kill the cattle that are sacrificed within the temple enclosure. It is the knife that killed her. Like other royal ancestors, the Queen must avoid anything that effected her own death or that could serve as a reminder of it.[21] Hence she cannot rise in spirit possession at the shrine. She is doubly displaced by her own death—and doubly potent for it.

Ndramandikavavy is the wife who sacrificed herself, the mother and grandmother of all subsequent monarchs, whose terrible power and pathos I can only begin to conjure by comparing her to the myth that resonates so powerfully in technicolor to a Western audience and that lies at the foundation of Judaism, Christianity, and Islam, the myth of the displacement of fathers by sons that initiates and legitimates the moral order and social continuity, that passes the Lacanian phallus like a baton in a relay race and establishes the order of the Symbolic, that seals the faith of men in God, the Father (or meta-father) and seals the fate of women as their subjects, and that may serve to demarcate human ethics from the existential absurdity and obligations of religion.

Sakalava sacrifice is different, and it produces a different symbolic order. What would be the position of Jewish, Christian, or Muslim women if Sarah had not tarried by the tent door, wondering what her crazed husband was up to with their beloved, belatedly begotten son? How different would gender have been had the original narrators given the woman an active role, portrayed her as a noble, knowing, heroic victim and agent, as Sakalava have done, or perhaps as simply setting to with a broom and putting a stop to the whole questionable business?

But let us also bear in mind the similarity of the Sakalava to the biblical myth. It too begins with a blood sacrifice carried out within the family. It too demands death for life. It too exhibits the *horror religiosus*.[22]

A week before the annual service publicly begins, a cow is offered in Ndramandikavavy's name. Like all sacrificial animals, this one must assent to its slaughter, must not bellow when it is pushed to the ground onto which its blood will flow. The skin is then dried and applied to the sacred drum, whose annually renewed pulsating beat supplies the energy to the ceremony that transpires.

Whence comes this beast of Ndramandikavavy? It is her own descendants who offer it on her behalf.[23] As if the burden of sacrifice has been displaced onto them, and as if the weight of a human victim has been lightened by a bovine replacement. But it is also as if Ndramandikavavy's original sacrifice is enacted each year, with her very knife, as if it is her vitality that is transmuted to the vibrating drum that sounds and heightens the events that follow, her determination and submission that infuse the actions of her subjects, royal and commoner, living and ancestral spirit (*tromba*) alike.

Ndramandikavavy's sacrifice is not strictly part of the Great Service, but it is a necessary preface, an iconic rehearsal of the beginning of the monarchy, whose success and vitality depend upon on it. It is as if the beginning of the Sakalava kingdom must form the beginning of each Sakalava year. It is as if the determination of the Mother infuses her descendants, as if the voluntary death of a woman is transformed into an act of birth.

Although I have presented neither an explicit account of Ndramandikavavy's story nor an account of her practice, as manifest in spirit mediums, I trust that I have said enough to indicate her deep significance for Sakalava. Elsewhere I have described the complex set of narrative, performative, and practical registers in which she plays a key part as the Sakalava poiesis of history.[24] It would not be a stretch to apply the word *sacred* or to understand what I have just presented as the preliminary sketch of something we might recognize as Sakalava "religion." There are a few differences from religion on the Abrahamic model, however. First, Sakalava are not bound by the law of the father, in either its Abrahamic or its Greek provincial guises. Second, Sakalava mythopraxis was deeply embedded in its own particular political system. Today it is popular beyond the narrowing confines of the traditional political order, but its spread across Madagascar and beyond could hardly be described as conversion. Indeed, for adepts its onset is understood through an idiom of illness, as though, to draw upon a kind of biblical language, one were smitten by the ancestral spirits. Moreover, it elaborates a complex and ironized coexistence with Islam and Christianity, and also weaves those two religions together. Imagine, for example, a Muslim medium possessed by the spirit of a Christian monarch.

Third, and most critical here, while her myth is comparable in its seriousness, sanctity, and foundational quality to the story of Abraham, Ndramandikavavy's sacrifice is neither solicited by a superior, transcendent being nor offered to one, nor does such a being intercede in the process. Technically, it has the form of what Malcolm Ruel calls "non-sacrificial killing in which it is not the life *of* the offering but the life *in* the offering that is at stake."[25] In biblical tradition, Abraham acquiesces, but God intervenes in the sacrifice and thus in history, and everyone is accountable to Him. In Sakalava tradition, Ndramandikavavy acquiesces. But in doing so she is the one to intervene and to insert herself in history, and it is to her that people are subsequently accountable. It is the ancestral heroes who are fierce and who are approached in fear and trembling, but also with affection and intimacy. It is their own acts of sacrifice and violence that render them fearful.

And so it is not to a transcendent God that subsequent generations of Sakalava look, but to a series of ancestors, one of whom is an exigent and somewhat vain but very determined queen who never lets them forget their obligation. Ndramandikavavy is an exceptional person, but she is not a deity. She is perhaps the most powerful and revered among the royal ancestors, but as an ancestor she retains all too human traits. When they appear together by means of spirit possession, she dotes on her son and rudely dismisses her husband, but she is also jealous of women who look his way. Sakalava operate by means of a kind of ethical realism that faces human ambivalence. It is not my purpose to match Sakalava mythopraxis against Kierkegaardian or other criteria of religious commitment. My point is simply a negative one—the absence of God.[26]

And yet the Sakalava word *Ndrañahary*, which has been translated as "God" and refers primarily to the God of Christianity and Islam, is sometimes used to refer to Ndramandikavavy and her ancestral companions. It also identifies the sky spirits (*Ndrañahary añabo*), whose intense possession of their hosts evokes something of the majesty of Hölderlin's poet submitting bareheaded to God's thunderstorms.

Since Malagasy nouns do not automatically distinguish singular and plural and since neither nouns nor pronouns indicate gender, Sakalava are not forced by their grammar to be specific about Ndrañahary's person. But perhaps the grammatical question reaches beyond matters of gender and number. In order to shed some light on this, I turn to a classic site of African ethnography, geographically, culturally, and linguistically very distant from Sakalava, namely, E. E. Evans-Pritchard's account of Nuer in the southern Sudan during the 1930s.

Nuer Social Deixis

In *The Nuer*, Evans-Pritchard describes a system in which the kind of person one is is relative to the social context in which one finds oneself.[27] Identities are not absolute, and—contrary to journalistic wisdom about African "tribes"—they are not primordial. They are deep and significant, but they are also governed by a logic of segmentation such that one identifies oneself by one name or with one group in one context and by a more or less inclusive one in another context, as I might selectively identify myself as Torontonian or Canadian. Segmentary logic is thus not exactly foreign to us, but it is distinct from the formulation of objectified kinds of person making described by Michel Foucault or Ian Hacking. It is distinctive not because of segmentation per se but because it is pervasive in Nuer society, pre-empts abstract or absolute categories, and forms the very basis of the social kinds of which it speaks.

The great insight of *The Nuer* is that social categories, ascriptions, and relations are contextual, relative to the immediate situation of speech, work, or conflict, yet also relative to each other, within the segmentary structure that enables particular kinds of conversation, action, or opposition to be construed as such. In Western ideology identity is often understood either as something essential or—in reaction—as protean. Louis Menand paraphrases C. S. Peirce's ironic insight that "the price of having an identity is an inability fundamentally to transform it."[28] But Evans-Pritchard grasped that for Nuer social identity is contextually established and constrained, always in relation to the intentionality of other parties present, to the time and place of speech, and to the locus of reference. If it is not fixed, continuous, and essential, however, neither is it open, optional, fragmented, or insubstantial, because contexts themselves are generated with respect to structure.

If in *Witchcraft, Oracles, and Magic among the Azande* Evans-Pritchard argues that consistency can only be discovered in practice,[29] in *The Nuer* he implicitly describes himself relearning this lesson. He begins by attempting to elicit and order information as if fixed answers were available. Asking people the ostensibly simple question who they are, he gets annoyed at the confusion of answers he receives, attributing this to Nuer intransigence (a point taken up by later readers, who want to emphasize the colonial and military context). But all this is merely a rhetorical device; he spends the book showing that Nuer answers to such questions can only be contextual and therefore *must* be variable (but, by the same token, never random or unpredictable). In presenting him with different answers to his questions, individual Nuer may have been trying to figure out the nature of the novel context entailed by his asking them. The tension comes in trying to establish within the context of a single kind of speech situation outside ordinary Nuer discourse the logic of a discursive system that depends on a range of relative social contexts. In sum, Evans-Pritchard's problem was that in looking for "sentence meaning" he was receiving "utterance meaning." The very idea of sentence meaning in the abstract, distinct from specific utterances, is a product of modern linguistic analysis, another example of the abstracting gaze of modernity.

Nuer had names for social ascription at multiple levels of segmentation, and certain names were used simultaneously for territories, political units, and descent.[30] They did not appear to have words for these levels in the abstract, however, thus no common nouns indicating what he distinguishes as maximal, major, minor, and minimal lineages or primary, secondary, and tertiary tribal sections as distinct entities. The point is that Nuer concepts of time, polity, lineage, and, as I will argue shortly, deity were not objectifications. If collective identity is always established vis-à-vis a specific location in social space, it is a practical activity, sustained by means of continuous and situated judgment (with respect to an implicit classificatory scheme). As Mary Douglas notes, "This is part of the extraordinary attraction of [the Nuer]: whatever political principles exist are maintained entirely in their minds."[31] The extraordinary attraction of the book is Evans-Pritchard's achievement in, first, discovering social relativity and, second, abstracting the segmentary structure that could comprehend (or generate) specific Nuer statements of identity.

Insofar as the names used for lineal and territorial identities vary with respect to matters of relative inclusiveness and distance specified by the immediate communicative context, Nuer attributions of social identity function in the manner linguists refer to as shifters, referential indexes,[32] or deictics. That is, they combine a referential function with an indexical one. *Index*, a term from Peirce, refers to a sign in which the vehicle "bears a connection of understood spatiotemporal contiguity to the occurrence of the entity signaled. That is, the presence of some entity is perceived to be signaled in the context of communication."[33] Just as the English utterance "here" can vary in reference depending on the location of the speaker and in scope from "right here" to "here in Canada," so too the Nuer word *cieng* ("home") shifts its reference,[34] and so too does political and genealogical ascription. In essence, what Evans-Pritchard observes as the semantic distinction encoded in Nuer shifters is the relative social distance (and hence inclusiveness or opposition) of the speakers or subjects concerned. The level of genealogical or political/territorial distance and difference is at issue in virtually every Nuer communicational context, much as pronominal distinctions of persons are at issue in every English speech context.

Let us look more closely at what anthropological linguists have had to say. "Deixis" writes Jack Sidnell, "is the term used to refer generally to those linguistic elements which make interpretable reference only by virtue of an indexical connection to some aspect of the speech event."[35] Yet, as all linguistic expressions may depend on aspects of context for interpretation, it is usually restricted to "the more or less closed functional categories of [grammatical] person, space, time, [and so on]."[36] Sidnell acknowledges that this typology may reflect grammatical categories of Indo-European languages and he calls for more work on "deictics in interaction. . . . the relation between interaction, lived space and linguistic form,"[37] which, I believe, is prefigured in *The Nuer*.

In his comprehensive analysis, William Hanks distinguishes deixis as "a special variety of reference" from other, nonreferential indexicals, such as accent, indicating the origins of a speaker, and prosody, indicating the mood. Deictics are morphemic and "in most languages make up closed paradigmatic sets," such as pronouns, demonstratives, spatial and temporal adverbs. "Their basic communicative function is to individuate or single out objects of reference or address in terms of their relation to the current interactive context in which the utterance occurs."[38]

Hanks says, "each deictic category encodes a relation between the referent and the indexical framework in which the act of reference takes place. Thus, a single deictic word stands for minimally two objects: the referent is the thing, individual, event, spatial or temporal location denoted; and the indexical framework is the origo ('pivot' or zero-point) relative to which the referent is identified (the speech event in which the act of reference is performed, or some part of this event)."[39] He illustrates by means of different uses of *this*, *that*, *here*, and *now* in English.

Nuer words for descent and territorial segments are partially deictic in this sense. Their application at least implies the (indexical) relationship between interlocutors (or others) pertaining within the particular speech event and in relation to the referent. The referents are not stable, bounded social groups with fixed membership. Evans-Pritchard can remark, "a man can be a member of a group and yet not a member of it. . . . a man is a member of his tribe in relation to other tribes, but he is not a member of his tribe in the relation of his segment of it to other segments of the same kind."[40] Outsiders err if they apply a misplaced concreteness.

Nuer terms for lineal and territorial groups do not have all the functions that linguists ascribe to deictics. They presuppose rather than specifically encode a relationship between the referent and the indexical context. Moreover, the names for Nuer sections and segments are referentially more specific or restricted than the prototypic deictics.[41] There are some people who will always be excluded from them on logical or empirical grounds. Reference is never wholly independent of the context of use, but neither is it wholly dependent on it. "Home" is not always as fully present as "here." Nevertheless, I retain the word *deixis* to indicate words or utterances that conjoin the referential and the indexical.

Hanks remarks that "whereas speakers must choose between . . . proper vs. common nouns, they do not choose between an indexical and a referential object. Rather, they identify the referential in relation to the indexical."[42] This is precisely the crux of the matter. Just as the notion of absolute reference provides a faulty picture of speech or thought insofar as it omits indexicality, so, conversely, does a notion of pure indexicality. Yet the category of deixis implies that the ratio of significance varies. Therefore, it may be useful to examine the relative weighting of indexical and referential functions, or indexical and logical presuppositions, in a range of words and usages. Thus, instead of a clear categorical distinction between deictic and nondeictic words or usages, words may be located along a continuum of referential autonomy and, conversely, their need ultimately to be interpreted with respect to the specific speech acts in which they are embedded.[43]

It is worth remarking that Nuer words for lineal and territorial segments are ostensibly nouns. I say "ostensibly" both because I have not carried out or consulted an analysis of the Nuer language such that I could say what constitutes such a grammatical category in Nuer and because I am not certain whether "proper nouns" ought to be considered nouns at all.[44] On surface appearance, however, the Nuer material suggests that we pay more attention to the indexical aspect of nouns and especially to nouns of social ascription. While English speakers can readily appreciate pronominal or adverbial deictics, we have a harder time with nominal ones.[45] The most common deictic noun in English I can think of is *home*. But note how the nominal quality in a phrase like "I am going home" or "at home" is compromised.[46]

"Deixis," remarks Stephen Levinson, "reminds us natural languages have evolved for primary use in face-to-face interaction, and are designed in important ways to exploit that circumstance."[47] This raises a basic linguistic question about whether there are modes of communication that are organized more or less deictically, especially in reference to the complex distinction between speech and writing.

Hanks points out, "In general, because indexical frameworks change more or less constantly in talk, the deictic forms that make for proper reference to objects change as well. . . . the indexical framework of interaction is in constant flux. This may be due to a variety of factors, including the adjustments in bodily orientation of the participants, any motion they may be engaged in, the arrival of new participants on the scene, as well as background frames that may be activated."[48] This flux of indexical frameworks can only be represented secondarily in written language. Prose is judged "poor" when it is unintentionally ambiguous precisely because the writer fails to imagine the limited indexical context of the reader or to produce a common indexical framework. Whereas the referential range of certain social categories can be relatively open in oral speech, where the interactional context enables supple and subtle shifts in interpretation that do not have to be specified morphemically, writing must operate by means of words whose referential objects are more fixed.[49] Nuer apparently had few abstract (i.e., logically rather than indexically presupposed) terms for time, space, or social units. Hence my rather wild hypothesis that the very nature of social categories may change when writing becomes the authoritative mode of knowledge.[50]

The ideal typical contrast I am drawing between speech and writing is analogous to that between tribal and state political forms in Evans-Pritchard's scheme, between ordered anarchy and institutionalized bureaucracy, between flux and fixity. The significant contrast is *not* between segmentary and nonsegmentary modes of organization per se but whether the relationship between different levels and branches of segmentation is indexically supposed. I certainly do not imply a lack of structure nor do I equate indexicality with open choice. In the absence of fixed ascriptions, shared competence in the underlying structure may be all the more important.

One of the central aspects of deictic analysis, suggests Hanks, is whether or to what degree participants share a common orientation.[51] If deixis raises the question of mutual understanding, then, finally, and quite profoundly, it also reopens the problem of translation.

Deixis and Deity

"The Nuer word we translate 'God' is *kwoth*, Spirit." So, forthrightly, does Evans-Pritchard begin *Nuer Religion*.[52] The rest of the book shows just how ambiguous this careful statement is.

If, as Evans-Pritchard suggests, cultural translation is central to the anthropological enterprise, deixis presents a particular problem, especially where the words to be grasped do not have a parallel deictic usage in both languages. We have seen that many of the words and concepts Evans-Pritchard works so hard to unpack in *The Nuer* are deictic in a broad sense. Indeed, what he describes as "structural relativity" is a socially indexical universe where even seasonality plays a role in shaping the context of predication.[53] Evans-Pritchard brilliantly unravels the complex conjunction of indexical and referential aspects of the terms of sociopolitical ascription. He demonstrates that translating these into the fixed, objectified groups—"tribes" and "lineages"—these words have implied in English would be a major translation error.

In *Nuer Religion*, Evans-Pritchard extends his argument about structural relativity to *kwoth*. Yet here he refuses to go the final step. Thus he speaks about "refractions" of *kwoth* as if there were an underlying unitary God—representable in the final instance by a stable noun—who gets refracted. The alternative would be to see the most general, abstract, or inclusive usage as but another refraction, or—as I would prefer—deictic usage. Perhaps Evans-Pritchard is suggesting this when he gives the additional translation "Spirit."

Where "deity" is a deictic form of speech, we have something radically difficult to translate. That is because, as Hanks notes, "At the heart of deixis is the unique relational structure whereby the referent is identified through its relation to the indexical origo." As he explains, "The origo consists of the social relation between participants, and symmetry is a way of describing the degree to which their respective orientations overlap."[54] It is unlikely that the orientations of most English speakers overlap closely with those of most Nuer, and besides, the point about the indexical origo is that it is always in flux.

The shortcut around the translation problem is, of course, not to recognize the deictic aspect in the first place but to give the word a fixed, nominal gloss. Thus I venture that missionaries throughout Africa, and presumably elsewhere, transformed indexically presupposed concepts into stable, objectified referents.[55] Whether they did so intentionally or in error, the result was that they provided Africans with two incommensurable ways to speak about something possibly translatable as "God," "deity," "spirit," "sanctity," or "power." As Levinson has remarked, in what begins to appear an understatement, "It would seem that indexical or deictic expressions cannot easily be reduced by translation into nonindexical language."[56]

The translation issue, as well as the related misleading question of whether *kwoth* is single or multiple, and hence, whether Nuer were "monotheist" or "polytheist," can be recognized by analogy with the English word *home*. When we speak of "home," is it one or many—or is the very distinction irrelevant to the concept? My home is Canada, or a particular house, or wherever I feel "at home." If you were an anthropologist questioning me and trying to pin down the meaning of the word *home*, my varying answers might induce "Nuerosis."[57] But this would not be the result of my deliberately trying to confuse you, nor of any inherent contradiction in my thought. The difficulty would lie in your misreading my deictic utterances for nondeictic ones. Furthermore, you would be mistaken if you were to assume that all my usages of *home* were "refractions" of some purer, higher, or more abstract (Platonic?) concept of "home."[58]

Evans-Pritchard's analysis of *kwoth* is exemplary for its originality and finely attuned attention to Nuer speech. Yet there is a tension in *Nuer Religion* between understanding *kwoth*, on the one hand, grammatically, with respect to discourse, and implicitly as a product of discourse, by systematically noting the situational quality of invocation, the range of usage, and the problems of translation; and, on the other hand, by means of the assumption that *kwoth* is a symbol directing us toward a real and unitary being. There is thus a pull between demonstrating the openness of the denotatum and personifying, abstracting, or objectifying *kwoth* as "God."[59]

This involves a kind of tension between what I would call Platonic and Aristotelian strains in Evans-Pritchard's thought—between an idealized dualism and a practical inquiry,[60] perhaps between metaphysics and ordinary language. I have emphasized the Aristotelian concern with practical reason, but the fact remains that the Platonic vision may be truer to religion as its adherents understand it. Perhaps the same tension was found among Nuer themselves. Thus, if Evans-Pritchard tends to personify *kwoth* this may be because many Nuer tend in this direction as well.[61] As Evans-Pritchard argues, abstractions and immaterial subjects come to be grasped in the concrete materiality of symbolic forms. But the fact that Nuer do sometimes see divinity in objects or on the analogy of persons does not mean that this is how they understand its essence or—more to the point—that they grasp it as a kind of *thing* or person or even a Platonic form that *has* or *is* a unitary essence. The logic of African religion, and here I am indebted to Malcolm Ruel, is much more an existential than an essentializing one.[62]

In sum, I have argued (1) that deixis adds a level of complexity to the translation puzzle; and (2) that deictic predication of human groupings or collective identities and even of religious constructs may be more prevalent than English speakers can easily imagine. The issue in translating is not only whether we make denotations out of utterances that do quite other things, but whether we interpret the objects of those references as fixed, concrete, or essential rather than structurally generated and context dependent. One of the lessons of Evans-Pritchard's Nuer work is that mistaking indexically supposed words in foreign languages for purely referential nouns in ours is a major pitfall of cultural translation.

I trust I have shown why Evans-Pritchard's initial statement in chapter 1 of *Nuer Religion* is problematic. He translates *kwoth* as "God," but that is to transpose what may be a relatively deictic word into a relatively nondeictic one. If I am correct, then deictic deity is not a person—or at least is a very different kind of person than we are used to conceptualizing, one far more removed from the concept of Western persons than the specific Malagasy ancestral spirits. It may be that such a deity is less transcendent than immanent, and that immanence is another way to talk about deixis.

To consider the possibility of deictic deity is to move far from the field of religion that an Abrahamic model proposes. The question of monotheism—or its polytheist alternative—becomes incoherent. Moreover, a deictic world is one that is open and inclusive, characterized by a both/and rather than an either/or logic. Finally, attention to deixis implies putting practice ahead of belief; it thus supports a turn away from "neo-Tylorean" perspectives in religion, which emphasize explanation and rationality, toward Foucauldian accounts of discipline and neo-Aristotelian cultivation of the virtues.[63]

Conclusion

An underlying question has been whether and how the definitional problems of religion remain influenced by Christianity. Important anthropological attempts to address this question have begun with the issue of "belief," but it is then all too easy to ignore the predicate or to proceed as though verb and predicate were not mutually reinforcing.

The predicate of belief is noumenal beings modeled on human persons, single, discrete, and continuous. This is the Abrahamic view of the God who intervenes in history, who exacts promises, who remembers, keeps His contracts, and demands or expects the same of His worshippers. This forensic quality underlies the boundedness and exclusivity explicit in the Abrahamic religions and implicit in many secular models of religion. I contend that this conceptualization of the subjects and objects of religious concern is not universal. I have intimated that Sakalava achieve deep insight of a kind that has parallels with Abrahamic religion but without recourse to Abrahamic deity. Moreover, if we accept a notion of deictic deity, the question of singular personhood becomes problematic and unstable. God is as substantial and as insubstantial, as specific and as nonspecific, as "home."

Deixis provincializes God quite literally. It locates deity in local, particular, contextually dependent manifestations rather than in grand, reified, and personalized abstractions, in utterance meaning rather than in sentence meaning. The same lesson, perhaps, should hold for theory.

You might think, then, that my argument has led me to abandon the search for a general model or theory of religion. That is only half the case.[64] I want less to dispense with such a perspective than to provincialize it—by setting it alongside other ways of looking at things. Recall Chakrabarty's both/and, which invites attention to both local alternatives and general theorizing. Ndramandikavavy may await her Kierkegaard. Elsewhere I have proposed her story as an instance of the syllogism that sacrifice is an exemplary form of beginning, much as beginning is a kind of sacrifice.[65] I would also note that the nonspecific referentiality of deixis fits rather neatly with Rappaport's depiction of the referential emptiness of what he calls ultimate sacred postulates.[66] While I do not agree with Rappaport's model of religion in its entirety, I think that his arguments concerning the sacred as a property of discourse, the ethical import of ritual performatives, and the problem of over-sanctification are good places both to begin to formulate a general definition or model of religion, should that be wanted, and to understand the present and future of the religious past.

Much as the universalizing ambitions of Islam and the particularizing practices of spirit possession have served to contextualize each other in a place like Mayotte,[67] so too may generalizing theory and historical particularism offset or provincialize each other.[68] From the *Three Rival Versions of Moral Enquiry* put forward by Alasdair Macintyre,[69] this is to take neither the positive, right-hand path of the Enlightenment encyclopedist nor the negative, left-hand path of the Nietzschean genealogist but the middle path of the Aristotelian, who contributes to forging a specific tradition of inquiry. In the case of anthropology this entails close ethnographic inspection and hermeneutics, but anthropology is also a tradition that subverts Macintyre's model of rival alternatives by judiciously drawing upon elements from both the encyclopedist and the genealogical sides. And rather than simply mediating opposing vices into steady virtues, anthropological thought moves dialectically among these modes of apprehension or keeps them in a state of ironic suspension, a state in which I now propose to leave you.

Translating Gods

Religion as a Factor of Cultural (Un)Translatability

Jan Assmann

Translation

The Babylonians were the first to equate two gods by defining their common functional definition or cosmic manifestation.[1] We may call this method "theological onomasiology." By "onomasiology" is meant a method that starts from the referent and asks for the word, in opposition to semasiology, which starts from the word and asks for its meaning. Onomasiology is by definition cross-cultural and interlingual. Its aim is to find out how a given unit of meaning is expressed in different languages.

The Babylonians very naturally developed their "theological onomasiology" in the context of their general diglossia. Their constant concern for correlating Sumerian and Akkadian words brought them to extend this method into fields outside that of lexicography proper. But as long as this search for theological equations and equivalents was confined to the two languages, Sumerian and Akkadian, one could argue that it remained within the frame of a common religious culture. The translation here operates translingually but not transculturally. In the late Bronze Age, however, in the Cassite period, the lists are extended to include languages spoken by foreign peoples. There is an "explanatory list of gods" that gives divine names in Amoritic, Hurritic, Elamic, and Cassitic, as well as Sumerian and Akkadian.[2] There are even lists translating theophorous proper names of persons.[3]

Among the lists from the private archives of Ugarit, a city-state on the northern Syrian coast, are quadrilingual vocabularies that contain Sumerian, Akkadian, Hurritic (an Indo-European language), and Ugaritic (a west Semitic language). Here, the translation concerns three fundamentally different religious cultures and consequently meets with serious difficulties.[4] Sumero-Babylonian *Anum* (the god of heaven) is no problem: it is rendered in Ugaritic by *shamuma* (heaven). But for *Antum*, his wife, there is no linguistic equivalent in Ugaritic. It is obviously impossible to invent a feminine form of *shamuma*. Therefore a theological equivalent is found in the form of *Tamatum* (sea), which in Ugaritic mythology may act as a feminine partner of heaven. The sun god, *utu* in Sumerian, *Shamash* in Akkadian, *Shimigi* in Hurritic, is masculine; his feminine counterpart is called *Aia* in Sumerian and *Ejan* in Hurritic. But the Ugaritic *Shapshu*, notwithstanding its etymological identity with Akkadian *shamshu*, is a feminine deity, for whom there has to be found a masculine counterpart. Again, this problem requires a *theological* solution. Thus, the god Kothar, the god of craftsmen and artisans, appears as a translation of the goddess Aia!

In these cases, there can be no doubt that the practice of translating divine names was applied to very different cultures and religions. The conviction that these foreign peoples worshiped the same gods is far from trivial and self-evident. On the contrary, this insight must be reckoned among the major cultural achievements of the ancient world. One of the main incentives for tolerance toward foreign religions can be identified in the field of international law and the practice of forming treaties with other states and peoples. This, too, seems a specialty of Mesopotamian culture. The first treaties were formed between the Sumerian city-states of the third millennium B.C.E. With the rise of Ebla in northern Syria and with the Sargonid conquests, this practice soon extended far into the west, involving states outside the cultural horizon of Mesopotamia. The Hittites, in the middle of the second millennium, inherited this legal culture from the Babylonians and developed new and much more elaborate forms of international contract.[5] The treaties they formed with their vassals had to be sealed by solemn oaths invoking gods of both parties. The list of these gods conventionally closes the treaty. They had necessarily to be equivalent in function and, in particular, in rank. Intercultural theology thus became a concern of international law. It seems to me probable that the interest in translations and equations for gods of different religions arose in the context of foreign policy. We are here dealing with the incipient stages of "imperial translation" destined to reach all the politically dependent states, tribes, and nations. Later, in the age of the great empires, official multilingualism becomes a typical phenomenon.[6] The book of Esther tells us how in the Persian empire royal commandments were sent to every province in its own script and to every people in its own language. A similar practice seems already to be attested for the Assyrian empire. In this context belong the many bi- and trilingual royal decrees from Persia, Anatolia, and Egypt. Even the Buddhist king Asoka—roughly a contemporary of the Egyptian Manetho, the Babylonian Berossos, and the translators of the Hebrew Bible known as the Septuagint—published his edicts in Sanskrit, Aramaic, and Greek.[7]

During the last three millennia B.C.E., religion appears to have been a promoter of intercultural translatability. The argument for this function runs as follows. Peoples, cultures, and political systems may be sharply different. But so long as they have a religion and worship some definite and identifiable gods, they are comparable and contactable because these gods must necessarily be the same as those worshiped by other peoples under different names. The names, iconographies, and rites—in short, the cultures—differ, but the gods are the same. In the realm of culture, religion appears as a principle counteracting the effects of what Erik H. Erikson called "pseudo-speciation." Erikson coined this term to describe the formation of artificial subgroups within the same biological species.[8] In the human world, pseudo-speciation is the effect of cultural differentiation. The formation of cultural specificity and identity necessarily produces difference and otherness vis-à-vis other groups. This can result in the elaboration of absolute strangeness, isolation, avoidance, and even abomination. Among the Papuas in the highlands of New Guinea, where communication is geographically difficult, this process has led, over some fifty thousand years, to the formation of more than seven hundred different languages.[9] Here, under laboratory conditions, the forces of pseudo-speciation could operate relatively undisturbed. Normally they are checked by other factors promoting communication and translation. The most important among them seems to be commerce, that is, cross-tribal, cross-national, and cross-cultural economy. If we look for regions in which these factors were most operative in prehistory and antiquity we must think of the Near Eastern commercial networks, which already in the fourth millennium B.C.E. extended east to the Indus valley and west to Egypt and Anatolia. Along the lines and on the backbone, so to speak, of these early commercial contacts, political and cultural entities crystallized in the third and second millennia, very much according to the principles of pseudo-speciation, which, however, were always counterbalanced by cultures of translation.

The profession of interpreter is attested in Sumerian texts from Abu Salabih as early as the middle of the third millenium B.C.E.[10] The term *eme-bal*, meaning something like "speech changer," designates a man able to change from one language into another. The Babylonian and Assyrian equivalent of the Sumerian *eme-bal* is *targumannum* ("interpreter"), a word that survives not only in the Aramaic *targum* (translation), but also in the Turkish *dragoman*, *turguman*, and so on, which by metathesis eventually led to the German form *dolmetsch* ("interpreter").[11] In Egypt, too, interpreters appear as early as the Old Kingdom. The monarchs of Elephantine, the southernmost province of Egypt, acting as caravan leaders for the African trade, bore the title "chief of interpreters." Contacts with neighboring and even more remote tribes were always supported by at least an attempt at verbal communication.[12]

The practice of translating foreign panthea has to be seen in the context of this general emergence of a common world with integrated networks of commercial, political, and cultural communication. This common world extended from Egypt to the Near and Middle East and westward to the shores of the Atlantic.[13] I am not arguing that this process of intensified interrelation and unification was a particularly peaceful one—quite the contrary. What might have begun as occasional raids and feuds developed into larger forms of organized warfare. We are not speaking here of peaceful coexistence. But even war has—in this particular context—to be reckoned among the factors of geopolitical unification promoting the idea of an *oikoumene* where all peoples are interconnected in a common history, an idea already expressed by the Greek historian Polybius.[14] And the idea of universal peace reigning in that *oikoumene* developed along with this process, leading to the efforts at imperialistic pacification known as *pax ramessidica* and *pax salomonica* and ultimately culminating in the *pax romana*.

First the conviction of the ultimate identity of the culturally diversified gods, then the belief in a supreme being beyond or above all ethnic deities formed the spiritual complement to this process of geopolitical unification. Polytheistic religion[15] functioned as a paradigm of how living in a common world was conceivable and communicable. The complete translatability of gods founded a consciousness of dealing with basically the same species in spite of all other kinds of cultural alterity.

Conversion

Energeia: *Language in Its Magical Function*

This interpretation of religion as a principle counteracting the factors of cultural pseudo-speciation seems rather paradoxical, for religion is generally held to be the most forceful promoter and expression of cultural identity, unity, and specificity. This needs no further elaboration.[16] Assimilation, the giving up of a traditional cultural identity in favor of a dominating culture, is necessarily accompanied by religious conversion, and religion is universally recognized as the strongest bastion against assimilation. Movements of resistance against political and cultural domination, oppression, and exploitation universally assume the form of *religious* movements.[17] Jewish history provides the model for these movements of liberation, and the Exodus story has been shown to be more or less universally adopted wherever people have revolted against an oppressive system.[18]

This is true, but it applies to specific political and cultural conditions that might be subsumed under the general term "minority conditions." Minority conditions arise where a hegemonic culture dominates and threatens to swallow up a culturally and ethnically distinct group. Here we are dealing with what may be interpreted as an "immune reaction" of the cultural system, a tendency to build up a deliberate "counter-identity" against the dominating system.[19] The cultural system is intensified in terms of counterdistinctivity.[20] We can call this mechanism "second-degree pseudo-speciation," to distinguish it from normal pseudo-speciation, which occurs always and everywhere. Second-degree or counterdistinctive pseudo-speciation occurs mostly under minority conditions.[21] Identity then turns normative, based on "normative self-definition."[22] It is typically under these conditions of resistance to political and cultural domination that religions of a new type emerge. I would like to call these "second-degree" or "secondary" religions. These religions defy translatability. They are entered via conversion and left via apostasy.[23]

I shall not recapitulate Jewish history here. It is a sequence of typical minority situations, starting with Abraham in Ur and Moses in Egypt and continuing via less mythical events, such as the Babylonian exile, the situation of Judaea under the Persians, the Ptolemies, the Seleucids, and the Romans, through the various diaspora places from Alexandria to Cernovic (the historical exception, of course, being the modern state of Israel).[24] The Jewish paradigm is the most ancient and the most typical; perhaps it is also the model and origin of all or most other cases. Egypt is a far less conspicuous case, but also far less known. I shall therefore concentrate on the Egyptian example in showing how religion can work in the direction of promoting untranslatability.

Egypt entered into minority conditions only after the Macedonian conquest. The Libyan and Ethiopian conquerors had adopted Egyptian culture rather than imposing their own. Even the Persians did not really impose their culture on the Egyptians because there were too few immigrants from Persia to form an upper class with an elite culture as the Greeks did later.[25] Under Macedonian rule, Egyptians found themselves in much the same situation as the Jews, but without a stabilized tradition. While the Israelite tradition achieved its final state in the Hebrew canon, the Egyptian tradition had to undergo profound transformations. Some features developed under minority conditions are strikingly similar. The extreme stress laid on purity, laws, life form, and diet in many ways parallel the emergence of *halakha* in Israel. We also find belief in the untranslatability of the Egyptian language.

Hellenized Egyptians were as active in producing Greek texts as hellenized Jews. Quite a few of these texts present themselves as translations from the Egyptian. Translation and interpretation were central among the cultural activities of Greco-Egyptian and Greco-Jewish intellectuals in the literate milieus of Alexandria and Memphis.[26] The question of translation and translatability itself became a major topic in this literature.[27] But there is also a theory of untranslatability that rejects even the principle and practice of translating gods. In Iamblichus (*De mysteriis* 2:4–5) we read, for example, that names of gods should never be translated.[28] In dealing with divine names one has to exclude all questions of meaning and reference. The name is to be regarded as a mystical symbol. It cannot be understood and for this very reason it cannot be translated. Knowledge of the names preserves the "mystical image of the deity" in the soul. For this reason we prefer to call the sun god not Helios but Baal, Semesilam (Shamash?), or Re, and the god of wisdom not Hermes but rather Thoth. The gods declared the languages of holy peoples like the Assyrians and the Egyptians holy, and communication with the gods can only take place in these languages. The Egyptians and other barbarians "always kept to the same formulas because they are conservative and so are the gods. Their formulas are welcome to the gods. To alter them is not permitted to anybody under any circumstances." The *Lautgestalt* here becomes a taboo, the phonetic form of language functioning not as a *signifiant* which stands for some *signifié* but as a mystical symbol, a kind of verbal image full of mysterious beauty and divine presence.

In opposing Celsus's view on the arbitrariness of divine names, the Christian church father Origen uses exactly the same arguments as the pagan magician and philosopher Iamblichus.[29] Both agree that there is a natural link (*sympatheia*, "sympathy") between name and deity and that the magical and "presentifying" power of language rests in the sound and not in the meaning and is therefore untranslatable. A less-well-known treatment of the same topos can be found in the opening chapters of treatise 16 from the *Corpus Hermeticum*. It is presented as the introduction to a translation and thus deals with both translating and untranslatability.

> He said that those who read my books [Hermes Trismegistos speaks] will think that they are very clearly and simply written, when in fact, quite the contrary, they are unclear and hide the meaning of the words and will become completely obscure when later on the Greeks will want to translate our language into their own, which will bring about a complete distortion and obfuscation of the text. Expressed in the original language, the discourse conveys its meaning clearly, for the very quality of the sounds and the [intonation] of the Egyptian words contain in [themselves] the force of the things said.
>
> Preserve this discourse untranslated, in order that such mysteries may be kept from the Greeks, and that their insolent, insipid and meretricious manner of speech may not reduce to impotence the dignity and strength [of our language] and the cogent force of the words. For all the Greeks have is empty speech, good for showing off; and the philosophy of the Greeks is just noisy talk. For our part, we use not words, but sounds full of energy.[30]

The energetic theory of language is magical. The magical force of spells resides in their sound. It is the sound, the sensual quality of speech, that has the power to reach the divine sphere. The *energetic* dimension of language is untranslatable.

Conversion: Revelation Versus Evidence

One of the surest signs that we are dealing with a secondary religion is the phenomenon of conversion.[31] As long as there is the possibility of translation, there is no need of conversion. If all religions basically worship the same gods, there is no need to give up one religion and to enter another one. This possibility only occurs if there is one religion claiming knowledge of a superior truth. It is precisely this claim that excludes translatability. If one religion is wrong and the other is right, there can be no question of translating the gods of the one into those of the other. Obviously they are about different gods.

A very interesting borderline case is provided by the opening scene of the eleventh book in the *Metamorphoses* by Apuleius, in which Lucius prays to the rising moon and sees in a dream the goddess herself. The speech of the goddess first displays the well-known topos of the relativity of names. One people calls her by this name, the other by that name, all adoring her in their specific tongues and cultural forms. But beyond all her conventional ethnic names there is a *verum nomen*, her true name, and this one is known only to the Egyptians and the Ethiopians. Up till now it made little difference whether you worshiped Venus in the way of the Paphians, Minerva Cecropeia in the way of the Athenians, Diana in the way of the Ephesians, or Proserpina in the way of the Sicilians. But now it turns out to be of utmost importance to follow Isis in the way of the Egyptians because only they know the true name and rites. If you are really serious about it, there is no alternative: you must convert to the Isis religion and enter into the group of the initiated.[32]

But still, Isis is a cosmotheistic deity. She belongs to the class of supreme beings who embody the universe in its totality. Her particular power and attraction lie in her double role of cosmic deity and personal rescuer; she is mistress of the stars and of luck and fate. Being a cosmotheistic deity, her name has a rich *signifié*. Presenting herself, she may point to every divine role possible as a manifestation of her power. "I am this, and that, and that, . . . in short: everything," she says to her believers. The god of Israel is the exact opposite. He does not say "I am everything" but "I am who I am," negating by this expression every referent, every *tertium comparationis*, and every translatability.[33] He is not only above but displaces all the other gods. Here, the cosmotheistic link between god and world, and god and gods, is categorically broken.

This is what the enlightened and cultured among the pagans were unable to understand. It was not a problem that the Jews were monotheists: monotheism had long been established as the leading philosophical attitude toward the divine. Every cultivated person agreed that there is but one god and it little mattered whether his name was Adonai or Zeus or Ammon or whether he was just called *Hypsistos* (Supreme). This is the point Celsus made in his *Alethes Logos*. The name is *Schall und Rauch*, as Goethe, another cosmotheist, put it. Varro (116–27 B.C.E.), who knew about the Jews from Poseidonios, was unwilling to make any difference between Jove and Jahve: "nihil interesse censens quo nomine nuncupetur, dum eadem res intelligatur."[34] But the Jews and the Christians insisted on the very name. For them, the name mattered. To translate *Adonai* into *Zeus* would have meant apostasy.

The translatability of gods depended on their natural evidence. They are accessible either to experience or to reason or to both in the form of indubitable, intersubjective, and intercultural data to which one can point in searching for a name in another language. What this form of natural evidence excludes is "belief": where all is "given" there is nothing to believe in. The worship of gods is a matter of knowledge and obedience but not of belief. In his book *Belief, Language and Experience*, the philosopher and indologist Rodney Needham has shown that most languages lack a word for what in the Greek of the New Testament is called *pistis* and what other languages translate as *fides, Glaube, foi,* and so on; in English *pistis* is rendered by two words: *faith* and *belief*. Christian missionaries had great trouble finding words for *pistis* in the languages of the people they wanted to address.[35] In most cases they had to invent a word. Translatability rests upon experience and reason, untranslatability on belief, which in itself proves to be an untranslatable concept. Paul already made the difference quite clear by stating "we are walking not by the sight [*opsis*] but by the faith [*pistis*]" (2 Cor. 5:7). People walking "by the sight" could point to the visible world in telling which gods they worshiped. People walking by faith had to tell a story the truth of which rests on matters outside the visible world. They could translate the story but not the god.

Syncretism: Translation into a Third Language

G. W. Bowersock has proposed that Hellenism was a medium rather than a message. Hellenism provided a common language for local traditions and religions to express themselves in a voice much more eloquent, flexible, and articulate than their own. "Greek," Bowersock writes, "was the language and culture of transmission and communication. It served, in other words, as a vehicle."[36] Hellenism did not mean hellenization. It did not cover the variegated world of different peoples and cultures, religions and traditions, with a unified varnish of Greek culture. Hellenism, instead, provided them with "a flexible medium of both cultural and religious expressions." Bowersock is perhaps somewhat underrating the strong anti-Greek feelings prevailing among the native elites, especially in Judaea and Egypt,[37] and the frequent clashes and tensions between indigenous traditions and the world of the gymnasium. But he is certainly right in pointing out that the culture of late antiquity owed at least as much to indigenous influences as to the Greek heritage and that the Greek universe of language, thought, mythology, and imagery became less an alternative or even antithesis to local traditions than a new way of giving voice to them. This explains why from the Jewish and Christian points of view the differences between Greek, Roman, Egyptian, Syrian, Babylonian, and other religions disappeared. "Hellenism" became a synonym for "paganism," because it served in late antiquity as a common semiotic system and practice for all these religions. As the different traditions were translated into the common semiotic system of Hellenism, the borders between them tended to become much more permeable than they had been within the original language barriers. A process of interpenetration took place, which not only for Jews and Christians but also for the "pagans" themselves made the differences between them much less evident than what they had in common. Hellenism, in other words, not only provided a common language but helped to discover a common world and a "cosmopolitan" consciousness.

Nineteenth-century scholars used to refer to this process of cultural and religious interpenetration as "syncretism."[38] The Greek term *synkretismōs* occurs only once: in Plutarch, where it refers to an archaic custom of the Cretan people to overcome local feuds and to form a sacred alliance to withstand foreign aggression. By way of an erroneous association with *kerannymi* (to merge), which would yield *synkrasía*, the expression came to denote the idea of a merging of gods (*theokrasia*) and then of cultures in a more general sense. But syncretism, as opposed to "fusion," is not simply merging. It describes a kind of merging that coexists with the original distinct entities. The local identities are not altogether abolished; they are only made transparent, as it were. They retain their native semiotic practices and preserve their original meaning. When translated into the third language of Hellenism, however, they assume a new kind of transparency, which smoothes down idiosyncratic differences, allows for interpenetration, and opens up a common background of "cosmotheism." Syncretism requires or offers double membership: one in a native culture and one in a general culture. It does not mean one at the expense of the other. The general culture depends (or even "feeds") on the local cultures.

We can distinguish three types of cultural translation: "syncretistic translation," or translation into a third language/culture; "assimilatory translation," or translation into a dominating language/culture; and "mutual translation" within a network of (economic/ cultural) exchanges.

Syncretistic translation is exemplified by what may be called "cosmotheistic monotheism." The different divinities are not just "translated" into each other but into a third and overarching one, which forms something like a common background. Syncretistic translation renders the common background visible. It presupposes a fundamental unity beyond all cultural diversities. As far as theology is concerned, this unity is guaranteed by the oneness of the world. The world or cosmos serves as the ultimate referent for the diverse divinities. We may compare the unity of syncretism, which is founded on the cosmos, with the unity of anthropology, which is founded on "human nature" ("die Einheit des Menschengeistes," as Thomas Mann called it).

Assimilatory or *competitive translation* is exemplified by the early instances of *interpretatio Graeca*, when Herodotus visited Egypt and formed the opinion that "almost all the names of the gods came from Egypt to Greece." This, he adds, is what the Egyptians say themselves. What Herodotus heard in conversing with Egyptian priests must have been the Greek names. They spoke to him in Greek using the hellenized names of the gods, speaking not of Re, Amun, Thoth, and Ptah, but of Helios, Zeus, Hermes, and Hephaestus.[39] For them, it did not matter whether these gods were called Re or Helios, Amun or Zeus, Thoth or Hermes, as long as the same gods were recognized and addressed by these names. They claimed to have been the first to recognize these gods, to find out their nature by establishing their mythology and theology, and to establish a permanent contact with them: *gnosis theon*, as this particular cultural activity is called.[40] The *interpretatio Graeca* of the Egyptian gods thus turns out to be not a Greek but an Egyptian achievement. We have always assumed this translation to be a manifestation of the Greek spirit and its interpretive openness toward foreign civilizations. But it seems now much more probable that the translation of their national panthea into Greek suited in the first place the interest of the "barbarians." Morton Smith and others have shown that Greek language and learning tended already to be recognized and experienced as an elite or superior culture by oriental peoples under the Persian empire and long before the Macedonian conquest.[41] All the stories about early Greek encounters with Egyptian priests, from Solon and Hekataios down to Herodotus and Platon, show the same Egyptian tendency to impress the Greek visitors with their superior cultural antiquity.[42] What you call culture—the argument runs—and what you are so proud of has been familiar to us for thousands of years, and it is from us that your ancestors borrowed it. This is a very familiar motif in "nativistic" movements of our days. Where Western culture is met by primitive cultures, this is a typical reaction.[43] Greek functions in this context as the other, not as a third language. Translatability into Greek is a question of cultural competitiveness.

Mutual translation seems to apply to the Babylonian material. This type of mutual translation is based on and develops within networks of international law and commerce. The history of these networks leads us back to the very roots both of translation and of mutuality or reciprocity, namely, to the exchange of gifts as the primal form of intergroup communication. Marcel Mauss, in his classic study of the gift,[44] was the first to point out the communicative functions of what Marshall Sahlins later called "Stone Age economics."[45] The basic function of exchange is not the fulfillment of economic needs but the establishment of community by communication, mutuality, and reciprocity. It is therefore anything but a surprise that mutual translation turns out to be the earliest type and something like the "primal scene" of cultural translatability. Translate! is the categorical imperative of early cultures. It is the overcoming of autistic seclusion, the prohibition of incest, the constraint to form alliances outside the narrow circles of house, village, and clan, and to enter into larger networks of communication.

It is revealing to translate these three types into our time. To start with the last one, *mutual translation*: today, when these networks have finally become global, they have lost something of their primary charm. The modern situation is characterized by a strange kind of reciprocity: on the one hand, Western civilization is expanding all over the world; there is hardly any place left untouched by Coca-Cola. On the other hand, cultural fragments from all places and periods are brought into the *musée imaginaire* of Western culture, which is rapidly growing into a supermarket or Disneyland of postmodern curiosity. In pre- and early historical times, reciprocity and mutuality meant a process of growth and enrichment for all cultures involved; today it means loss and impoverishment. Western culture is reduced to Coca-Cola and pidgin English; native cultures are reduced to airport art. The cultural imperative, today, points in the opposite direction: to regionalism, the preservation (or invention) of dying languages and traditions, and the emphasis on otherness. This is also why assimilatory translation or competitive otherness is no longer a valid option. Mutual acknowledgment is suppressed as one culture is used as the negative foil of the other.

There remains the first type to be considered, *syncretism* as defined in terms of *double membership* and a *third language*. Such a language is something not actually given but virtually envisaged and kept up in order to provide a framework in which individual cultures can become transparent without losing their identities.

Hellenism, seen not as a message but as a medium, not as a homogenizing cover but as a flexible and eloquent language giving understandable voice to vastly different messages, preserving difference while providing transparency, might serve as a model. Hellenistic culture became a medium equally removed from classical Greek culture as from all the other oriental and African cultures that adopted it as a form of cultural self-expression. In the same way, a transcultural medium that will not amount to Westernization or Americanization could provide visibility and transparency in a world of preserved traditions and cultural otherness.

The Christian Invention of Judaism

The Theodosian Empire and the Rabbinic Refusal of Religion

Daniel Boyarin

It seems highly significant that there is no word in premodern Jewish parlance that means "Judaism." When the term *Ioudaismos* appears in non-Christian Jewish writing, to my knowledge only in II Maccabees, it doesn't mean Judaism, the religion, but the entire complex of loyalties and practices that mark off the people of Israel; after that, it is used as the name of the Jewish religion only by writers who do not identify themselves with and by that name at all, until, it would seem, well into the nineteenth century.[1] It might seem, then, that Judaism has not, until some time in modernity, existed at all, that whatever moderns might be tempted to abstract out, to disembed from the culture of Jews and call their religion, was not so disembedded or ascribed particular status by Jews until very recently.

Until our present moment, it could be defensibly argued, Judaism both is and is not a "religion." On the one hand, for many purposes it, like Hinduism, operates as a religion within multi-religious societies. Jews claim for their religion a semantic, cultural status parallel to that of Christianity in the West. We study Judaism in programs of religious studies, claim religious freedom, have sections on Judaism at the American Academy of Religion—even one on comparative Judaism and Hinduism—and, in general, function as members of a "faith" or system of ultimate meaning, or whatever, among other faiths. On the other hand, there are many ways that we continue to be uncomfortable and express our discomfort with this very definition. For both Zionists and many non-Zionist Jews (including me), versions of description or practice with respect to Judaism that treat it as a faith that can be separated from ethnicity, nationality, language, and shared history have felt false. Precisely that position of Judaism at the American Academy of Religion has sometimes been experienced by us as in itself a form of ambivalently capitulating behavior (which is not, I hasten to add, altogether unpleasurable). Something about the difference between Judaism and Christianity is captured by insisting on the ways that Judaism is not a religion.[2] This ambivalence has deep historical roots.

My argument is that the cause of this ambivalence has to be disclosed diachronically, that, at the first stage of its existence, at the time of the initial formulation of rabbinic Judaism, the Rabbis, at least, did seriously attempt to construct Judaism (the term, however, is an anachronism) as an orthodoxy, and thus as a "religion," the product of a disembedding of certain realms of practice, speech and other, and identifying them as of particular circumstance. If you do not believe such and such, practice so and so, you are not a Jew, imply the texts of the period.[3] At a later stage, however, according to my hypothesis—that is, at the stage of the "definitive" formulation of rabbinic Judaism in the Babylonian Talmud—the Rabbis rejected this option, proposing instead the distinct ecclesiological principle: "An Israelite, even if he sins, remains an Israelite [one remains a part of a Jewish or Israelite people whether or not one adheres to the Torah, subscribes to its major precepts, or affiliates with the community]." Whatever its original meaning, this sentence was understood throughout classical rabbinic Judaism as indicating that one cannot cease to be a Jew even via apostasy.[4] The historical layering of these two ideologies and even self-definitions by the Rabbis themselves of what it is that constitutes an Israel and an Israelite provide for the creative ambivalence in the status of Judaism today. Christianity, it would seem—or rather, the church—needed "Judaism" to be a religious "other," and maintained and reified this term as the name of a religion.

At the end of the fourth century and in the first quarter of the fifth century, we can find several texts attesting to how Christianity's new notion of self-definition via "religious" alliance was gradually replacing self-definition via kinship and land.[5] These texts, belonging to very different genres, indeed, to entirely different spheres of discourse—heresiology, historiography, and law—can nevertheless be read as symptoms of an epistemic shift of great importance. As Andrew Jacobs describes the discourse of the late fourth and early fifth centuries, "Certainly this universe of discourses engendered different means of establishing normativity: the disciplinary practices of Roman law, for instance, operated in a manner quite distinct from the intellectual inculcation of historiography or the ritualized enactment of orthodoxy. Nevertheless, the common goal of this discursive universe was the reorganization of significant aspects of life under a single, totalized, imperial Christian rubric."[6]

This construction of "Christianness" primarily involved the invention of *Christianity* as a religion, disembedded, in Seth Schwartz's words, from other cultural practices and identifying markers.[7] Susanna Elm shows that late-fourth-century Christians were already committed to the idea of religions and even understood quite well the difference between religious definition and other modes of identity formation. She finds evidence for this claim as early as Julian "the Apostate," who formed his religion, Hellenism, in the 360s on the model of Christianity, but, as we shall see, there is evidence going back at least as far as Eusebius in the first half of the century.[8] He insists that only one who believes in "Hellenism" can understand it and teach it, as justification for his denial of the right to teach philosophy to Christian teachers.[9] Vasiliki Limberis emphasizes how, for all Julian's hatred of Christianity, his religiosity was deeply structured by the model of Christianity.[10] As Limberis puts it: "Christians had never been barred from letters. Not only was this an effective political tool to stymie Christians, it had the remarkable effect of inventing a new religion and religious identity for people in the Roman empire."[11] I would slightly modify Limberis's formulation by noting that Julian did not so much invent a new religion as participate in the invention of a new notion of religion as a category and as a regime of power/knowledge. She writes: "In particular, Julian echoes Christianity's *modus operandi* by turning pagan practices into a formal institution that one must join."[12] The great fourth-century Cappadocian theologian Gregory Nazianzen retorted to Julian: "But I am obliged to speak again about the word . . . Hellenism to what does the word apply, what does one mean by it? . . . Do you want to pretend that Hellenism means a religion, or, and the evidence seems to point that way, does it mean a people, and the language invented by this nation. . . . If Hellenism is a religion, show us from which place and what priests it has received its rules. . . . Because the fact that the same people use the Greek language who also profess Greek religion does not mean that the words belong therefore to the religion, and that we therefore are naturally excluded from using them. This is not a logical conclusion, and does not agree with your own logicians. Simply because two realities encounter each other does not mean that they are confluent, i.e. identical."[13] Gregory clearly has some sort of definition of the object "religion" in mind here, distinct from and in binary semiotic opposition to *ethnos*, contra the commonplace that such definitions are an early modern product.[14]

Gregory knew precisely "what kinds of affirmation, of meaning, must be identified with practice in order for it to qualify as religion":[15] it must have received its rules from some place (i.e., some book? Gregory surely doesn't mean geographical locations, for then he would be playing into Julian's hands) and some priests. While Gregory's definition of *religion* is, of course, quite different from the Enlightenment one (a difference oddly homologous to the difference between Catholicism and Protestantism), he nevertheless clearly has a notion of religion as an idea that can be abstracted from any particular manifestation of it; for Gregory, different peoples have different religions (some right and some wrong), and some folks have none.

Whichever way the "evidence pointed" for Nazianzen, it is clear, as Elm demonstrates, that for Julian "Hellenism" was indeed *a* religion. Gregory affords a definition of religion as clear as that of later comparatists (although quite different from them). A religion is something that has priests, rites, rules, and sacrifices. It is absolutely clear, moreover, from Gregory's discourse that, for this Christian, "the emergence of religion as a discrete category of human experience—religion's *disembedding*," in Schwartz's terms,[16] has taken place fully and finally, as he explicitly separates religion from ethnicity/language.

As Schwartz explicitly writes, "religion" is *not* a dependent variable of *ethnos*; indeed, almost the opposite is the case.[17] A corollary of this is that language itself shifted its function as identity marker. As Claudine Dauphin has argued, by the fifth century linguistic identity was tied to religious affiliation and identity, and not to geographic or genealogical identification.[18]

Gregory, in the course of arguing that Hellenism is not a religion, at the same time exposes the conditions that would enable some entity other than Christianity to lay claim to that name. Before Julian, other fourth-century Christian writers had no problem naming "Hellenism" a religion, thus, I expect, providing Julian with the model that he would later turn against the Christians. Eusebius of Caesarea, the first church historian and an important theologian in his own right,[19] could write "I have already said before in the *Preparation*[20] how Christianity is something that is neither Hellenism nor Judaism, but which has its own particular characteristic piety,"[21] the implication being that both Hellenism and Judaism have, as well, their own characteristic forms of piety (however, to be sure, wrong-headed ones). He also writes:

> This compels us to conceive some other ideal of religion, by which they [the ancient Patriarchs] must have guided their lives. Would not this be exactly that third form of religion midway between Judaism and Hellenism, which I have already deduced as the most ancient and venerable of all religions, and which has been preached of late to all nations through our Saviour. . . . The convert from Hellenism to Christianity does not land in Judaism, nor does one who rejects the Jewish worship become ipso facto a Greek.[22]

Here we find in Eusebius a clear articulation of Judaism, Hellenism, and Christianity as "religions." There is something called "religion," which takes different "forms." This represents a significant conceptual shift from the earlier uses of the term *religion* in antique sources, in which a *religio* is an appropriate single act of worship, not a conceptual or even practical system separate from culture and politics, and in which there is, therefore, not something called "religion" at all, no substance that we could discover and look at in its different forms.

The fullest expression of this conceptual shift may be located in the heresiology of Epiphanius (fl. early 5th c.), although his terminology is not entirely clear. For him, not only "Hellenism" and "Judaism" but also "Scythianism" and even "Barbarianism" are no longer the names of ethnic entities[23] but of "heresies," that is, religions other than orthodox Christianity.[24] Although Epiphanius's use of the term is confusing and perhaps confused,[25] apparently what he means by "heresies" is often what other writers of his time call "religions": "<Hellenism originated with Egyptians, Babylonians and Phrygians>, and it now confused <men's> ways."[26] It is important to see that Epiphanius's comment is a transformation of a verse from the Pauline literature, as he himself informs us.[27] In

Colossians 3:11 we find "Here there cannot be Greek and Jew, circumcised and uncircumcised, barbarian, Scythian, slave, free man, but Christ is all, and in all."[28] This is a lovely index of the semantic shift. For pseudo-Paul, these designations are obviously not the names of religious formations but of various ethnic and cultural groupings,[29] whereas for Epiphanius they are the names of "heresies," by which he means groups divided and constituted by religious differences fully disembedded from ethnicities. How, otherwise, could the religion called "Hellenism" have originated with the Egyptians?[30] Astonishingly, Epiphanius's "Hellenism" seems to have nothing to do with the Greeks; it is Epiphanius's name for what other writers would call "paganism." Epiphanius, not surprisingly, defines "the topic of the Jews' religion" as "the subject of their beliefs."[31] For Epiphanius, as for Gregory, a major category (if not the only one) for dividing human beings into groups is "the subject of their beliefs," hence the power/knowledge regime of "religion." The system of identities had been completely transformed during the period extending from the first to the fifth centuries. The systemic change resulting in religious difference as a modality of identity that began, I would suggest, with the heresiological work of Christians such as Justin Martyr works itself out through the fourth century and is closely intertwined with the triumph of orthodoxy. Orthodoxy is thus not only a discourse for the production of difference within, but functions as a category to make and mark the border between Christianity and its proximate other religions, particularly a Judaism that it is, in part, inventing.

There is a new moment in fifth-century Christian heresiological discourse. Where in previous times the general move was to name Christian heretics "Jews" (a motif that continues alongside the "new" one), only at this time (notably in Epiphanius and Jerome) is distinguishing Judaizing heretics from orthodox Jews central to the Christian discursive project.[32] As one piece of evidence for this claim, I would adduce an explosion of heresiological interest in the "Jewish-Christian heresies" of the Nazarenes and the Ebionites at this time. At the beginning of the nineteenth century, J. K. L. Gieseler already recognized that "the brightest moment in the history of these two groups doubtless falls about the year 400 A.C., at which time we have the best accounts concerning them."[33] Given that, in fact, it seems unlikely that these sects truly flourished at this particular time,[34] we need to discover other ways of understanding this striking literary flowering. The Ebionites and Nazoreans, in my reading, function much as the mythical "trickster" figures of many religions, in that precisely by transgressing borders that the culture establishes, they reify those boundaries.[35] The discourse of the "Judaizing heretics" thus performs this function of reinforcing the binaries.

The purpose of Epiphanius's discourse on the Ebionites and Nazarenes is to participate in the imperial project of control of (in this case) Palestine by "identifying and reifying the . . . religions." Epiphanius explicitly indicates that this is his purpose by writing of Ebion, the heresiarch-founder of the sect: "But since he is practically midway between all the sects, he is nothing. The words of scripture, 'I was almost in all evil, in the midst of the church and synagogue' [Proverbs 5:14], are fulfilled in him. For he is Samaritan, but rejects the name with disgust. And while professing to be a Jew, he is the opposite of Jews—though he does agree with them in part."[36] In a rare moment of mid-rashic wit (one hesitates to attribute it to Epiphanius himself), the verse of Proverbs is read to mean that I was in all evil, because I was in the midst [between] the church and the synagogue. Epiphanius's declaration that the Ebionites "are nothing," especially when put next to Jerome's famous declaration that the Nazarenes think that they are Christians and Jews, but in reality are neither, strongly recalls for me the insistence in the modern period that the people of southern Africa have no religion, not because they are not Christians, but because they are not pagans.[37] Suddenly it seems important to these two writers to assert a difference between Judaizing heretics and Jews. The ascription of exis-tence to the "hybrids" assumes (and thus assures) the existence of nonhybrid, "pure" religions. Heresiology is not only, as it is usually figured, the insistence on some (or another) right doctrine but on a discourse of the pure as opposed to the hybrid, a dis-course that then requires the hybrid as its opposite term. The discourse of race as analyzed by Homi Bhabha proves helpful: "The exertions of the 'official knowledges' of colonial-ism—pseudo-scientific, typological, legal-administrative, eugenicist—are imbricated at the point of their production of meaning and power with the fantasy that dramatizes the impossible desire for a pure, undifferentiated origin."[38] We need only substitute "heresio-logical" for "eugenicist" in this sentence to arrive at a major thesis of this essay. Thus, if on one level, as I have tried to express, orthodox Judaism is produced as the abject of Christian heresiology, and orthodox Christianity as the abject of Jewish heresiology, on another level, the "heretics" and the *minim* are the same folks, perhaps literally so, but certainly discursively so: they constitute the impossible desire of which Bhabha speaks.

Jerome, Epiphanius's younger contemporary, is the other most prolific writer about "Jewish-Christians" in antiquity.[39] Andrew Jacobs reads Jerome's Hebrew knowledge as an important part of the "colonialist" project of the Theodosian age.[40] I want to focus here on only one aspect of Jerome's discourse about Jews, his discussions of the "Jewish-Christians." Hillel Newman has recently argued that Jerome's discourse about the Judaiz-ers and Nazarenes is more or less constructed out of whole cloth.[41] It thus sharply raises the question of motivation, for, as historian Marc Bloch notes, "to establish the fact of forgery is not enough. It is further necessary to discover its motivations. . . . Above all, a fraud is, in its way, a piece of evidence."[42] I would suggest that Jerome, in general a much clearer thinker than Epiphanius, moves in the same direction but with greater lucidity. For him, it is absolutely unambiguous that rabbinic Judaism is *not* a Christian heresy but a separate religion. The *Mischlinge* thus explicitly mark out the space of illegitimacy, of no religion:

> In our own day there exists a sect among the Jews throughout all the synagogues of the East, which is called the sect of the Minei, and is even now condemned by the

Pharisees. The adherents to this sect are known commonly as Nazarenes; they believe in Christ the Son of God, born of the Virgin Mary; and they say that He who suffered under Pontius Pilate and rose again, is the same as the one in whom we believe. But while they desire to be both Jews and Christians, they are neither the one nor the other.[43]

This proclamation by Jerome comes in the context of his discussion with Augustine about Galatians 2, in which Augustine, disallowing the notion that the apostles dissimulated when they kept Jewish practices, suggests that their "Jewish-Christianity" was legitimate. Jerome responds vigorously, understanding the "danger" of such notions to totalizing imperial orthodoxy.[44] What is new here is not, obviously, the condemnation of the "Jewish-Christian" heretics but that the Christian author condemns them, in addition, for not being Jews, thus at least implicitly marking the existence and legitimacy of a "true" Jewish religion alongside Christianity, as opposed to the falsities of the *Mischlinge*. This move parallels, then, Epiphanius's insistence that the Ebionites are "nothing." Pushing Jacobs's interpretation a bit further, I would suggest that Jerome's insistence on translating from the Hebrew is both an instance of control of the Jew (Jacobs's point) and also the very marking out of the Jews as "absolute other" to Christianity. I think that it is not going too far to see here a reflection of a social and political process like that David Chidester remarks in an entirely different historical moment, "The discovery of an indigenous religious system on southern African frontiers depended upon colonial conquest and domination. Once contained under colonial control, an indigenous population was found to have its own religious system."[45] Following out the logic of this statement suggests that there may have been a similar nexus between the containment of the Jews under the colonial eye of the Christian Empire that enabled the discovery/invention of Judaism as a religion. Looked at from the other direction, the assertion of the existence of a fully separate-from-Christianity "orthodox" Judaism functioned for Christian orthodoxy as a guarantee of the Christian's own bounded and coherent identity and thus furthered the project of imperial control, as marked out by Jacobs. The discursive processes in the situation of Christian Empire are very different from the projects of mutual self-definition that I have elsewhere explored.[46]

Hegemonic Christian discourse also produced Judaism (and Paganism, e.g., that of Julian) as other religions precisely in order to cordon off Christianity, in a purification and crystallization of its essence as a bounded entity. Julian cleverly reverses this procedure and turns it against Christianity. In at least one reading of Julian's "Against the Galileans," the point of that work is to *reinstate* a binary opposition between Greek and Jew, Hellenism and Judaism, by inscribing Christianity as a hybrid. Eusebius's claim that the one who leaves Hellenism does not land in Judaism and the reverse now constitutes an argument that Christianity is a monstrous hybrid, a mooncalf: "For if any man should wish to examine into the truth concerning you, he will find that your impiety is compounded of the rashness of the Jews and the indifference and vulgarity of the Gentiles, for from both sides you have drawn what is by no means their best but their inferior teaching, and so have made for yourselves a border of wickedness."[47] Julian further writes: "It is worth while . . . to compare what is said about the divine among the Hellenes and Hebrews; and finally to enquire of those who are neither Hellenes nor Jews, but belong to the sect of the Galileans."[48] Julian, as dedicated as any Christian orthodox writer to policing borderlines, bitterly reproaches the "Galileans" for contending that they are Israelites and argues that they are no such thing, neither Jews nor Greeks but impure hybrids.[49] Here Julian sounds very much like Jerome when the latter declares that those who think they are both Jews and Christians are neither, or Epiphanius when he refers to the Ebionites as "nothing." This would make Julian's project structurally identical to the projects of the Christian heresiologists who, at about the same time, were rendering Christianity and Judaism in their "orthodox" forms the pure terms of a binary opposition with the "Judaizing" Christians, the hybrids who must be excluded from the semiotic system, being "monsters." I suggest, then, a deeper explanation of Julian's insistence that you cannot mix Hellenism with Christianity. It is not only that Hellenism and Christianity are separate religions that, by definition, cannot be mixed with each other, but even more that Christianity is always already (if you will) an admixture, a syncretism. Julian wants to reinstate the binary of Jew and Greek. He provides, therefore, another instance of the discursive form that I am arguing for in the Christian texts of his time, a horror of supposed hybrids. To recapitulate, in Julian's very formation of *Hellenism* (or should I say *Hellenicity*?[50]), as a religious difference, he mirrors the efforts of the orthodox churchmen. This is another instanciation of the point made above by Limberis.[51] While he was protecting the borders between *Hellenism* and *Judaism* by excluding *Christianity* as a hybrid, Julian, it seems, was, unbeknownst to himself, smuggling some Christian ideas into his very attempt to outlaw Christianity.

This interpretation adds something to that of Jacobs, who writes that "among the deviant figures of Christian discourse we often find the Jew, the 'proximate other' used to produce the hierarchical space between the Christian and the non-Christian."[52] I am suggesting that the heretic can also be read as a proximate other, producing a hierarchical space between the Christian and the Jew. This point is at least partially anticipated by Jacobs himself when he writes that "Jews exist as the paradigmatic 'to-be-known' in the overwhelming project of conceptualizing the 'all in all' of orthodoxy. This comes out most clearly in in the [Epiphanian] accounts of 'Jewish-Christian' heresies."[53] One way of spinning this would be to see heresiology as central to the production of Judaism as the "pure other" of Christian orthodoxy, while the other way of interpreting it would be to see Judaism as essential to the production of orthodoxy over against heresy. My point is that both of these moments in an oscillating analysis are equally important and valid. Seen in this light, orthodoxy itself, orthodoxy as an idea, as a regime (as opposed to any particular orthodox position) is crucial in the formation of Christianity as the universal and imperial religion of the late Roman Empire and, later on, of European Christendom.

In a not inconsiderable sense, Epiphanius's *Panarion* (*Medicine Chest*),[54] a classification of all the many varieties of heresy, can be seen as performing a function for the disciplining of religion that Krafft-Ebing's similar work on the perversions played in the disciplining of sexuality at the end of the nineteenth century.[55]

The Conversion of Count Joseph

A puzzling moment in Epiphanius's text, the narrative of the conversion of Count Joseph of Tiberias, supports the suggestion that the exporting of hybridity from within to without in the form of heresiology is complicit in the production of Christianity and Judaism as separate, unequal orthodoxies.[56] Count Joseph was a Jew and a high official in the court of the Patriarch—and thus, certifiably orthodox—who at some time, as reported by Epiphanius, became converted to orthodox Christianity.

After citing the heretical christological doctrines of the Ebionites and related "heresies," Epiphanius remarks that they use only the Gospel of Matthew, called "According to the Hebrews."[57] There follows a strange remark that some will object that the Jews secretly hold in their "treasuries" copies of the Gospel of John and the Acts of the Apostles translated into Greek. "So the Jews who have been converted to Christ by reading it have told me." The text already inscribes, therefore, two differing spaces, a "heretical" one in which the Gospel according to the Hebrews is the Gospel and an "orthodox" Jewish space in which other texts are kept, enabling (inadvertently?) Jews to convert to orthodox Christianity. In other words, the relevant opposition being inscribed is that between orthodoxy and heresy and not between Judaism and Christianity. Orthodox Judaism and orthodox Christianity, as in Jerome's letter, are lined up on one side of a semantic opposition, with the heretics, who do not respect properly the difference between being Jew or being Christian and think to combine them, positioned on the other side. The Joseph story follows immediately upon these declarations and, in my reading, is powerfully contextualized by them. From the beginning to the end of the narrative, Epiphanius emphasizes over and over the "orthodoxy" of Joseph's Christianity. He has as a houseguest Bishop Eusebius of Vercelli, "since Constantius had banished him for his orthodox faith," and, at the very beginning and as a sort of headline to the conversion narrative itself, "Josephus was not only privileged to become a faithful Christian, but a despiser of Arians as well. In that city, Scythopolis, he was the only orthodox Christian—they were all Arian. . . . But there was another, younger man in town too, an orthodox believer of Jewish parentage."[58] The intimate connection between Jewishness and orthodoxy within the Epiphanian discourse is thus doubled in this conversion narrative.

The first step toward Joseph's conversion is his observation (through a keyhole) of the deathbed baptism of no lesser a person than the Patriarch, "Ellel." Thus at the very heart and head of the orthodox Jewish power structure they understand that salvation is only through conversion to Christianity. Joseph is understandably "troubled over the subject of baptism."[59] Upon the death of this Ellel, Joseph and another one of the Patriarch's "apostles" are made regents over his minor son, the Infante Patriarch, one "Judas" by name. This is indeed a name common in the patriarchal family, but Epiphanius twice marks that he does not know that that is his name—"I suppose that he was called that"[60]—suggesting to this reader, at any rate, that the name is being marked as emblematic. This young man is a libertine. While Joseph watches, a beautiful young Christian woman is saved from his magical charms by the cross that she carries, once more raising thoughts in Joseph's mind, "but at this point he was by no means convinced that he should become a Christian."[61] During this time, as well, Joseph reads the Gospels, an Ebionite Matthew (originally in Hebrew), canonical John (translated into Hebrew) and canonical Acts (also translated), which are kept in the secret treasury of the Patriarchs. Upon becoming deathly ill, Joseph is informed by the Elders, who whisper in his ear, that if he believes in the Christian creed he will be healed; Epiphanius has, moreover, heard such a story from another Jew as well. Still Joseph's heart is hard. After the young Patriarch, Judas, grows up, he makes our Joseph tax gatherer for the province of Cilicia, where Joseph lodges next to the church, befriends the bishop, borrows the Gospels, and reads them again. The Jews, full of resentment for his offensive against their corruption, upon discovering that he is reading the Gospels, fall upon Joseph, take him to the synagogue, "and whip . . . him as the Law prescribes."[62] At this point, Joseph accepts baptism, goes to Constantine's court, and is offered very high rank in the imperial realm by the "good emperor—a true servant of Christ, and after David, Hezekiah and Josiah, the king with the most godly zeal."[63] After being permitted to build churches in the Jewish towns of the Galilee, Joseph sets up furnaces to burn the lime for them. The "natural-born Jews" perform sorcery to make these fires deviate from their own nature and be ineffective. When Joseph hears of this, he cries out in the name of Jesus and sprinkles water on the furnaces. The spell is thereby broken, the fire blazes up, "and the crowds of [all Jewish] spectators cried, 'there is (only) one God, the help of the Christians.'" All of the formerly orthodox Jews have now become orthodox Christians, a conversion portrayed as without remainder. The Ebionites, with their heretical Gospel "According to the Hebrews," are safely marked as the true locus of hybridity. The discursive entities orthodox Judaism and orthodox Christianity work very like the discourse of race as Robert Young puts it: "The idea of racial purity [orthodoxy] here shows itself to be profoundly dialectical: it only works when defined against potential intermixture, which also threatens to undo its calculations altogether."[64]

After relating the tale, Epiphanius returns to his main point. He argues, "So much for my account and description of these events, which I recalled here because of the translation of the books, the rendering from Greek to Hebrew of the Gospel of John and the Acts of the Apostles. But I resume—because of the Gospel according to Matthew—the progress of the discussion obliged me to give the sequel of the knowledge which had come my way. Now in what they call a Gospel according to Matthew, though it is not entirely complete, but is corrupt and mutilated—and they call this thing 'Hebrew'!—the following passage occurs."[65] I would argue that this true Gospel and Acts, found in the hands of the true Jews, are being dramatized in opposition to that fake Gospel, neither Christian nor Jewish: "and they [the Ebionites] call this thing 'Hebrew'!"

Most scholars believe that this story has been interpolated into the midst of Epiphanius's account of the Ebionites because of the metonymical link between the books that Joseph found and the Ebionite "Jewish Christians."[66] I think that it plays a more central role in Epiphanius's text. Stephen Goranson sends us in the right direction: "The story of Joseph of Tiberias is of a conversion from one orthodoxy to another, skipping over middle groups, more numerous at the time in Galilee."[67] I submit that the story of Joseph further underlines Epiphanius's distinction between those who are "something"—Jews or Christians or pagans—and those who are nothing, the *Mischlinge*. The function of the story is hardly to use the somethingness of the "religions" in order to establish the "nothingness" of the Ebionites and their associates, but can more plausibly read in the opposite manner, namely, using their nothingness to establish the somethingness of the absolutely distinguished "real" religions.

Thus a narrative that inscribes the binary opposition between a "pure," orthodox Judaism and a "pure," orthodox Christianity, as well as the ambiguous tricksters, the Jewish/Christian hybrids, can be seen to be participating in the same process of the production of absolute boundaries, of "individual and communal stability." I thus read a narrative interposed by Epiphanius, seemingly almost by accident,[68] as a hermeneutic key for understanding at least one of the crucial motives of his text. It is not just, as Goranson puts it, "that the church has in the interim, from the first to the fourth centuries, decided that Ebionites and Nazarenes are heretical," but rather that the discursive project of imperial Christian self-definition requires an absolute separation from Judaism. In order to help produce that, Epiphanius (aka the church) needs to make space for an orthodox Judaism that is completely other to Christianity. Now we can see the fifth-century explicit notices of curses of "Nazarenes" in synagogues as participating in the same project.[69] The Jews who curse the middle groups are discursively necessary for the orthodox project, performing the same function as orthodox Jews, like Count Joseph, who absolutely convert to orthodox Christianity, thus guaranteeing the latter's legitimacy. Joseph was the only "orthodox Christian" in all of Scythopolis. It was his initial complete separation from Christianity as an "orthodox" Jew that enabled his transformation into a purely orthodox Christian. In other words, a Jewish orthodoxy is produced by the Christian legend, in order to help guarantee a Christian orthodoxy, over and against hybrids. The hybrids, however, also produce the no-man's-land, the mestizo territory, that guarantees the purity of the orthodox formations.

Orthodox Judaism as State-Sanctioned (but False) Religion in the Theodosian Code

In support of this interpretation of Epiphanius and Jerome, I would adduce a further bit of contemporaneous evidence of a very different sort, the law code. The relevant code for this particular investigation is the empire-wide Code of Theodosius of 438.[70]

In order to appreciate more fully the import of that code, we must focus on the semantic shift in the terms *religio* and *superstitio*.[71] In Latin, as has been well documented, in its earliest appearances *superstitio* was not in binary opposition to *religio*. Indeed, too much *religio* could be *superstitio*. It was not the index of worship of the right gods, but of the right or wrong worship of the gods.[72] Maurice Sachot concurs that, in the Latin of the early empire, *superstitio* was itself not so much the opposite of *religio* as a type of *religio*, simply a dangerous and illegitimate excess of *religio* itself.[73] As Peter Brown puts it, "Outside Epicurean circles, superstition was not treated as a cognitive aberration—an 'irrational' belief in nonexistent or misperceived beings. Superstition was a social *gaffe* committed in the presence of the gods. It betrayed a lack of the ease and candour that were supposed to characterise a free man's relations with any persons, human or divine. Excessive observance was strictly analogous to flattery and ostentation; and magic was a form of graft and manipulation."[74] Mary Beard, John A. North, and S. R. F. Price write: "[*Superstitio*] was ambiguous between two meanings: excessive forms of behavior, that is 'irregular' religious practices ('not following the custom of the state') and excessive commitment, an excessive commitment to the gods."

In later Christian Latin, *religio* is not defined as the practices that are useful and appropriate for maintaining Roman solidarity and social order, but as the belief in that which is true, that is, as sanctioned by an authoritatively and ultimately legally produced ecumenical orthodoxy. Beard, North, and Price support this point:

> "*Religio* is worship of the true god, *superstitio* of a false,"[75] as the Christian Lactantius remarked in the early fourth century A.D., so asserting that alien practices and gods were not merely inferior to his own, but actually bogus. The traditional Roman distinction seems to have made no such assumption about truth and falsehood: when Romans in the early empire debated the nature of *religio* and *superstitio* they were discussing instead different *forms* of human relations with the gods. This is captured in Seneca's formulation that "*religio* honors the gods, *superstitio* wrongs them."[76]

A somewhat different way of naming this shift is to point out that in the earlier usage *religiones* and *superstitiones* are the names of acts—including speech acts—and the results of such acts. If Judaism (sometimes) and Christianity (always) are referred to as *superstitiones* in non-Christian literature, that is a judgment on all of the acts that members of those communities perform, but not a name for the community itself. After the shift, *religio* and *superstitio* are the names of institutions and communities. Before, one performs a *religio* or a *superstitio*; now one belongs to one.

This helps explain why the Epiphanian narrative of conversion is so crucial in establishing the new sense of *religio*, for the possibility of conversion itself converts Christianity into an institution, rather than only a set of practices, an institution that we might name "the Church." Now it becomes possible for Christianity to be a true *religio*, whereas Judaism and paganism are false *religiones*, another name for which is *superstitiones* in its new sense. This will be clearest if we remember that in earlier antiquity the term *religiones* in the plural never names institutions (much less mutually exclusive ones). After the invention of sexuality in the nineteenth century, everyone has a sexuality; after the invention of religion in the fourth, the same thing happens. Greek, we might say, also rises to the occasion of this semantic and social shift, with the once very rare word *threskeia* stepping into the new semantic slot now occupied by *religio* in its post-Christian sense in Latin. This semantic development is paralleled in Hebrew *dat*, which in biblical and early rabbinic usage means something like *religio* in the old Latin sense and comes to mean "religion" only in the Middle Ages.

A paradox in the representation of Judaism within the Theodosian Code illustrates these points. Throughout the code, Judaism is sometimes nominated *religio* and sometimes *superstitio*, but, as legal historian Amnon Linder observes, after 416 only *superstitio* is used. In the older Roman usage this shift to exclusive designation as *superstitio* ought to mark an absolute delegitimation of Judaism, entirely unlike its prior status as *religio licita*, in Tertullian's famous, if pleonastic, phrase. However, Linder also describes a complex and increasing legislative *legitimation* of Judaism through the fourth and fifth centuries. Both Stemberger and Levine have pointed to the paradox engendered by the fact that the Palestinian patriachate achieved its heyday in the fourth and early fifth centuries,[77] that is, precisely as the Jewish position was otherwise deteriorating drastically.[78]

Moreover, as Seth Schwartz has recently put it, "The legislation incorporated in the Theodosian Code book 16 titles 8 and 9 (and scattered through other books of the Code) constitutes the first more or less systematic exposition in a Roman imperial context of the view that local Jewish communities are fully licit and partly autonomous, and that their leaders are to enjoy the privileges of clergy and the right to rule their constituents in partial accordance with Jewish law."[79] Here, then, is the paradox. How can it be that Judaism definitively became a *superstitio* precisely when "the Christian Empire—to a far greater extent than the pagan Empire—accepted Judaism as a religion rather than as a nation or a people?"[80] The answer I will develop is that *superstitio* itself has shifted in meaning; indeed, the whole semantic field has shifted. First, however, let me sharpen the apparent paradox. The legitimation of Judaism went so far as to comprehend recognition of the Jewish Sabbath and festivals, including Purim [16.8.18][81] (provided the Jews didn't mock the crucifixion on that occasion,[82] an exemplary instance, perhaps, of mimicry turned mockery), the Jewish priesthood,[83] and the synagogue. The following has a particularly "modern" ring: buildings "which are known to be used by Jews for their meetings, and which are described as synagogues, let no one dare to desecrate or occupy; for all shall keep their own with rights undisturbed, without attacks on religion or worship" (16.8.20) of July 26, 412, Honorius).[84] Particularly dramatic is the continued, even enhanced, right of the *primates* of the Jews (including probably Rabbis) to excommunicate (16.8.8).[85] This power continued well after 416, and during that time Jewish religious autonomy was enhanced by other laws as well.[86] Indeed, "in a law of Justinian from 553 (No. 66), the lawful observance of the Jewish religion and its cult was taken for granted."[87] Furthermore, through the fourth century the Jewish religion received greater and greater legitimacy in the recognition of the Jewish Patriarch as the virtual Metropolitan of the Jews.[88] As Schwartz writes: "In the late fourth century the patriarchs reached the peak of their power. The Palestinian church father Epiphanius and the Codex Theodosianius both indicate that the *apostole*, or *aurum coronarium* [the Jewish head tax, exacted by the Patriarchs from the Diaspora], was now collected as if it were a conventional tax." In 397 Arcadius and Honorius affirm that "We shall imitate the ancients by whose sanctions it was determined that those privileges which are conferred upon the first clerics of the venerable Christian religion shall continue, by the consent of Our Imperial Divinity, for those persons who are subject to the power of the Illustrious Patriarchs, for the rulers of the synagogues, the patriarchs, and the priests, and for all the rest who are occupied in the ceremonial of that religion" (16.8.13).[89] This law was reaffirmed in 404.[90] Despite the explicit rhetoric of the law of 397, Schwartz makes the important point that "the laws about the Jews in the Theodosian Code are not at all conservative. By their very existence they constitute a significant innovation, because they imply that by the late fourth century the Roman state consistently regarded the Jews as a discrete category of humanity. I would suggest that the state had not done so, at least not consistently, between the first and the fourth centuries."[91] In my reading of the archives, more even than providing evidence of the growing importance of the Patriarch (which I am not, to be sure, denying), these materials suggest the high importance of the *representation*, perhaps a sort of colonial trompe-l'oeil, in Bhabha's terms,[92] of a powerful and prestigious Jewish Patriarch in the discourse of the orthodox Christian empire.[93]

With the shift in designation Linder dates to 416, Judaism, paradoxically, in effect became a *superstitio licita* (an oxymoron, of course),[94] a genuine, though wrong religion from which conversion was possible, leaving a remainder that guaranteed the existence of the Christian herself.[95] In a law variously dated to 412, 418, and 420,[96] we read, "Let no one, as long as he is innocent, be disparaged and subject to attacks because he is a Jew, *by whatever religion*" (16.8.21, my emphasis).[97] "By whatever religion" must comprehend more than just Christianity, or this sentence would make no sense whatsoever. The licit status of the *superstitio* Judaism, as opposed to "heresy," and consequently the crucial conversion of Judaism from heresy to *superstitio*, or alternative but wrong religion, is beautifully indicated in the following edict of Honorius and Theodosius:

> We punish with proscription of their goods and exile, Manichaeans and those persons who are called Pepyzites [= Montanists]. Likewise those persons who are worse than all other heretics in this one belief, namely, that they disagree with all others as to the venerable day of Easter, shall be punished with the same penalty if they persist in the aforesaid madness.
>
> But we especially command those persons who are truly Christians . . . that they shall not abuse the authority of religion and dare to lay violent hands on Jews and pagans who are living quietly and attempting nothing disorderly or contrary to law. (16.10.24)[98]

If they do so, continues the edict, "they shall also be compelled to restore triple or quadruple that amount which they robbed." As Caroline Humfress remarks on this law of 423, "This vision of peaceful, law-abiding, fifth-century 'pagans' and Jews legally pursuing hard-line Christians through the courts of the Roman empire, for the four-fold restitution of their robbed property, is diametrically opposed to the more usual fifth-century rhetoric of Christian triumphalism. And it provides stimulus and justification for an account of the *evolution* of late paganism as an alternative to a repetition of the traditional historiographical story of its demise."[99] Hal Drake has commented on explicit fourth-century discourse that indicates the co-existence of Christians and "pagans," with "heretics" marked off as the genuine enemy.[100] If that is so for "late paganism," then it is even more so for "early Judaism." Judaism was evolving within the context of the world that Christianity, Christendom, and the Christian Empire had made for it. As Neusner has perspicaciously noted, the success of rabbinic Judaism itself, its final triumph as Judaism *tout court*, was, at least in large part, a product of its effectiveness in providing an answer to Christian challenges, challenges to the relevance of Jewish peoplehood, genealogy, and the physical practice of the Torah. As Neusner writes, "in context Christianity (and later on, Islam) made rabbinic Judaism permanently relevant to the situation in which Jews found themselves." Although I would dissent in some measure from the specific time frame of this argument, its major notional base appeals to me. Rabbinic Judaism was successful as Judaism for two reasons: (1) Christianity "needed" a Jewish orthodoxy with which to think itself, and (2) rabbinic Judaism provided a winning set of responses to Christian questions. "The rabbinic Sages produced responses to the Christian challenge in their enduring doctrines of the meaning of history, of the conditions in which the Messiah will come to Israel, and of the definition of Israel. Rabbinic Judaism's symbolic system, with its stress on Torah, the eschatological teleology of that system, with stress on the messiah-sage coming to obedient Israel, the insistence on the equivalence of Israel and Rome, Jacob and Esau, with Esau penultimate and Israel at the end of time, these constituted in Israel powerful responses to the Christian question."[101]

Christianity needed a Jewish orthodoxy. Everything about Title 8 of Book 16 suggests that Judaism is to be legitimated, while vigorously protecting Christians and Christianity from any temptations to cross the border. The indictment of the Quartodecimans as worse than Manichaeans in the passage just read makes this point eloquently.[102] The trenchant condemnation of the "Caelicolists," by all signs a combination of Christianity and Judaism, in this Title (8.19) immediately preceding a law (8.20) enjoining the absolute protection of synagogue and Sabbath for Jews, also argues for this interpretation.[103] It is hybridity that is at once the threat and the guarantor of the "purity" of Christianity and Judaism, the whole system necessary for the discursive production of an orthodoxy that was "one of the primary discursive formations around which ancient Christian strategies of self-definition coalesced."[104]

Converting Judaism: The Letter of Severus of Minorca

The texts read hitherto and the ways that they suggest an epistemic shift early in the fifth century may provide background for a historicist reading of yet another narrative extensively treated in recent scholarship, the story of the conversion of the Jews of Minorca in the *Epistula Severi*.[105] Epiphanius's story of Count Joseph suggests to us that we can find the traces of this regime of Christian imperial power and knowledge about Jews not only in the texts of heresiologists but also in other narratives about the conversion of the Jews, as well. I wish to suggest a reading in which the *Epistula Severi* is not primarily about an instance of the forced conversion of Jews or in support of forced conversions but an aspect of the invention of "the conversion of the Jew" through which the "Christian only exists," that is, part of a process of the making of a new status for Judaism, one that takes into account the "remainder," the necessity that the Jew paradoxically remain in order for the Christian to find both himself and an Other.

A text from the margins of the Christian discourse of empire will help to articulate this important point. In February of the year 418 after Christ, according to the Encyclical Letter of Bishop Severus of Minorca, there took place "on that lowly thing of the world" events that the author of the epistle thought so significant that he addressed his epistle "to the most Holy and Blessed Lord Bishops, Presbyters, Deacons and to the Universal Brotherhood of the whole world."[106] I will begin with a summary of the plot.

Soon after Severus assumed the episcopate, "a certain holy priest," who as it turns out from other sources was none other than Orosius, the historian and disciple of Augustine, arrived on Minorca, carrying with him the relics of St. Stephen, the protomartyr, "which recently had come to light." He placed these relics in the church of Magona, one of the two cities on the island, "doubtless at the inspiration of the martyr himself."[107] The frenzy that the martyr kindled continued to work, for the bishop and his congregation became filled with holy zeal, evidently leading the congregation of Christians to break off relations with the Jews immediately. Oddly, Severus describes these relations as both an "obligation" and as a "sinful phenomenon" within the same sentence. Indeed, upon the "translation" of St. Stephen's relics to the Christian congregations of Minorca, "even the obligation of greeting one another was suddenly broken off, and not only was our old habit of easy acquaintance disrupted, but the sinful phenomenon of our longstanding affection was translated into temporary hatred."[108] Upon the return of Theodorus, the leader of the Jews and *patronus* of the island, from business on Majorca, the Christians of the entire island declared "war" (*bellum*) on the Jews, preparing dialectical "weapons," which in the end they would not be obliged to use, while the Jews, in turn, prepared themselves for both dialectic and martyrdom, weapons that in the end they would not be privileged to use.

After dreams and miracles, cowardice and bravery, flight and misprision, burning of the synagogue and spoliation of its silver fittings and Torah scrolls, and the forced rebuilding by the Jews of their former synagogue into a church, miraculously all 540 Jews of the island are converted to Christianity in eight short days. At the same time, social relations are restored to what they were. Everyone greets each other again. The former Jew Theodorus is reinstated to his position as *patronus* of Minorca, but obviously now he and all of his former flock are under the still greater patronage of St. Stephen, not only protomartyr but also protoconvert, as well as "first to wage the Lord's wars [*dominica bella*] against the Jews."[109] In the words of Peter Brown: "Within a few weeks, Theodorus and his relatives and congregants had made their peace with the bishop. Through becoming Christians, they maintained their full social status within their own community, though now subject to the higher *patrocinium* of St. Stephen, and seated beside the Christian bishop as Christian *patroni*."[110] It is interesting here to compare Epiphanius's emphasis on the fact that Joseph had held highest rank among the Jews and now held high rank in the Christian empire.[111]

Within the dossier in which the *Epistula* circulated are other documents that are almost certainly of fifth-century provenance, as well. One of them is an account of the miraculous unearthing of the relics of St. Stephen after a dream of the monk Lucianus in Jerusalem in 415, in which their whereabouts were revealed to him by a converted Rabban Gamaliel the Great of the first century.[112] The other is a *Passio* of St. Stephen, "discovered" just before that disinterment, predicting this very apparition. This documentary context will prove fruitful in reading the epistle.

While the *Epistula* may seem to provide evidence of a developing practice of forced conversion at that time,[113] there are other manners of reading and establishing a context for it than attending to its manifest content, interpretations, moreover, that are rendered stronger if the text is a fraud—as it seems to be (although they are possible even if it isn't).[114] Rather than reading the text in the context of events of forced conversion for which it is, in fact, the only evidence, I would read it not so much (or not only) as referring to the conversion of the Jews of Minorca but rather as itself a shard in an early-fifth-century assemblage of relics that points to a conversion of Judaism itself in the discourse of the hegemonic Christians in the first quarter of the fifth century. That is, whatever the truth value of the report of the events themselves—and I submit that we simply cannot know that—its writing and dissemination, together with its associated relics and other hagiographical narratives, suggest to me a moment of epistemic shift, the invention of a new form of "truth," "religion," here manifested by the production of a certain narrative about conversion from Judaism to Christianity.

In *The Cult of the Saints*,[115] Peter Brown has provided a reading of the *Epistula Severi* that turns our attention away from forced conversions and focuses it on a very well-attested contemporary discourse, the developing cult of the saints. Not disagreeing with Brown so much as adding to his words, I would suggest that the letter is an integral part as well in a developing discourse of Judaism and Christianity as separate, if not quite equal, religions. As Brown has shown, this cult had much to do with locations in space, "translations—the movement of relics to people" that "hold the center of the stage in late-antique piety,"[116] as practices for the invention of communities. In his study of the cult of the saints, Brown has illuminated how the festivals that attended the anniversaries of the appearance of relics in particular shrines functioned socially: "The festival of the saint was conceived of as a moment of ideal consensus on a deeper level. It made plain God's acceptance of the community as a whole: his mercy embraced all its disparate members, and could reintegrate all who had stood outside in the previous year,"[117] that is, monks, Frankish counts, and even "striking blonde princesses" from Gaul.[118] As Brown suggests, the "translation" of relics, the resettlement from place to place, permanently transformed the "spiritual landscape of the Christian Mediterranean" by diasporizing (my term) the sacred, converting a system of local saints' shrines[119] into a "dependence of communities scattered all over Italy, Gaul, Spain, and Africa" and even "far beyond the ancient frontiers of the Roman world."[120] One function of a text like the letter of Severus is to accompany the message implied by the translation of the relics with another message meant to spread its influence and, like the body of St. Stephen itself in Augustine's account, "bring light to all lands."[121] The argument that the point of the letter is a "worldwide" communique and its participation in an empire-wide epistemic shift is supported by the address of the epistle "to the Universal Brotherhood of the whole world": Christianity becoming Christendom, an imagined community whose citizens are "naturally" Christians, a quite common device indeed.

Seen in this way, the cult of the saints was an instance of empire-wide communication in a new discursive regime, which Brown's reading in part explains. I would suggest, however, by way of addition to the general interpretation that Brown has afforded, a specific one attendant on the particular rhetorical or historical contexts of Severus's letter. Looking at the forest that Brown has charted, I would hope now to be able to perceive more precisely the specificities and anomalies of this particular Minorcan tree. Bradbury has helped us to do so by locating the *Epistula Severi* at "the confluence of two broad currents in the religious life of late antiquity: the rise of the cult of saints and the increasing intolerance of Catholic Christians against the unorthodox: pagans, heretics, and Jews," especially as attested, in his view, in the Theodosian Code promulgated within a decade of Severus's letter. It is no accident, I warrant, that at that confluence the body of St. Stephen reveals itself miraculously "in waking visions to a certain Lucian, priest of the church on an estate called Kefar Gamala in 415 north of Jerusalem,"[122] no accident that it was 415 (or thereabouts) when this revelation took place, and no accident that his relics were connected with conversions. Something impelled St. Stephen's corpse to rise from the ground at just that time,[123] something having to do with Jews, Palestine, and locativity.

Throughout the third and fourth centuries and into the fifth (as we have seen above), various Christian writers try to make any ambiguities in Jewish-Christian identity impossible. The most famous of these are Chrysostom's sermons against the Jews, which have been decisively interpreted as triggered by Christian attraction to Jewish rites and sites.[124] Another example is Cyril of Jerusalem's mid-century sermons for catechumens.[125] A fully separate category for Jews, "Judaism," the religion, was necessary in order to produce the full identity of the church. The only subject who can be converted to Christianity with that necessary "remainder" of "Otherness" is *not* the ambiguously differentiated Judeo-Christian of earlier centuries, but someone who to begin with has a fully separate identity (someone like Count Joseph or the Jews of Minorca). In the *Epistula*, with its ostensibly totalizing account of the conversion of all of the Jews of Minorca, I find reproduced a discourse of conversion, and therefore of convertibility—of the convertible subject, the Jew. A scholar working in a different tradition (in both senses) has analogously and usefully articulated the point: "The remarkable persistence of ethnic groups is not maintained by permanent exclusion nor by preventing boundary crossing. One might even suggest that it is in the act of crossing boundaries that such demarcations are reaffirmed."[126]

Closer reading of certain passages in the *Epistula* will expose the ambivalence about Judaism that is encoded and enacted in the text. The first is the moment of common hymn singing, taken by Brown to be an illustration of the concord that allegedly obtained between Jews and Christians on the island before the arrival of St. Stephen. As described by Brown, "Theodore and his relatives stood at the head of a community where Jews and Christians had learned to coexist, sharing, for instance, in the same haunting beauty of their chanted psalms."[127] Bradbury, like Brown, interprets this haunting beauty as if it related the halcyon situation of the Jews and Christians on the island before the distressing new events.[128] The passage, however, lends itself to a reading considerably more sinister than Brown's paraphrase implies. At the time of the haunting hymnody, according to the account, Severus is already in the process of zealously attempting the forced conversion of the Jews by coercing them to go to the synagogue in order to reveal that the weapons that they have gathered there for their defense were intended for offensive violence against the Christians and the government: "Then we [Severus and virtually the whole island] set out for the synagogue, and along the way we began to sing a hymn to Christ in our abundance of joy. Moreover, the psalm was 'Their memory has perished with a crash and the Lord endures forever' [Ps. 9:7–8], and the throng of Jews also began to sing it with a wondrous sweetness."[129] Given that the particular verse that is being sung is effectively a prophecy of the doom of the Jews, a fact marked, moreover, by Severus's own "moreover," an ironically bitter reading of this "wondrous sweetness" emerges. Not, in fact, participating in a concord of common worship, the Jews, in a moment of dramatic irony, are unwittingly prophesying the disaster that is about to befall them. That is, in the Christian discourse.[130] As Chava Boyarin has remarked to me, if these events took place in actuality and there were real Jews (under a tree outside Delhi, as it were), they might very well have had a very different intent, prophesying or praying for the downfall of their Christian oppressors through the recitation of these words, an exemplary moment of colonial mimicry, in Bhabha's terms. As ever (or from Justin Martyr on, at any rate), the Jewish text is made to portray the downfall of the Jews and the end of their memory—in both senses. It is in the very next sentence, not surprisingly, that the violence begins. The ambivalence of this moment, with its representation of harmony but implication of coercion, is exemplary of the ambivalence that has been productive of much, if not all, of Christian violence against Jews, with Christianity using the very texts of the Jews to predict the discordant crashing of Jewish memory.

Thus, rather than reading this as a moment of concord and harmony, I would propose reading it as a singular moment of violence in the text. The shared hymn singing, in this reading, is symptomatic of the pervasive ambivalence that drives the narrative. It is the fact that Jews and Christians share the same Scripture and in part the same liturgy that produces the anxiety about borders that our text is so avid to dispel by firming up those very borders. Indeed, the irony that Bradbury refers to, the Easter octave during which the Jews were converted as being itself "from Jewish precedents," is another symptom of the type of religion trouble that mobilizes such textual productions.

The *Epistula Severi* manifests this ambivalence at its very heart. Even as it narrates the conversion of the Jews of the island without remainder, as it were, I would suggest it participates at the same time in the creation of a new status for Judaism, no longer categorized as a heresy of Christianity, as it was in much of the Christian writing of the third and fourth centuries, but as a separate (if wrong) religion. Thus it is the continued existence of "Judaism" and its redefinition as an object on the same semiotic level as Christianity, not the extinction of Judaism, that guarantees Christian orthodox existence. We can observe this shift from heresy to religion taking place within the narrative of the text. At the very beginning of the narrative, after reporting miraculous events that prevent Jews from living in the village of Jamona, the author goes on:

What is even more marvellous is that vipers and scorpions are indeed very plentiful, but have lost all ability to do violent harm. Although none of the Jews, who are rightly compared with wolves and foxes for fierceness and villainy, dares to approach Jamona, not even for the right of hospitality, Magona seethed with so great a multitude of Jews, as if with vipers and scorpions, that Christ's church was being wounded by them daily. But that ancient, earthly favour was recently renewed for us in a spiritual sense, so that, as it is written, that generation of vipers [Luke 3:7], which used to attack with venomous stings, suddenly under the compulsion of divine power has cast aside the lethal poison of unbelief.[131]

These "venomous stings" are plausibly read as a reference to the attraction that the synagogue had for Christians of Minorca, whether actually to abandon the Church, or, more likely, to participate in the preaching and rituals of the Jews and their holidays, much like Chrysostom's Antiochene congregation.

Since the language of "vipers and scorpions" with which the text initially describes the Jews is a topos in contemporaneous depictions of heresy,[132] "Judaism" is at this moment in the beginning of the text being read as a Christian heresy and, therefore, as supremely dangerous for Christians. The original "generation of vipers" were, after all, "children of Abraham" who came to be baptized (but not converted), thus also blurring the boundaries between the old and the new. "Severus" has informed us that on Minorca, while there are snakes and scorpions, they have no venom. Likewise, now, on the spiritual level, a similar miracle has happened, that is, the Jews have lost their power to harm. The implication, however, is that Jews they remain—at least for the purposes of discourse, hence once more that ambivalent slippage on which Christian identity is built, the remains of the Jew.

Through the narrative, however, and thus in part via the agency of the text, Judaism itself will be converted from a heresy, a disease of Christianity, into both a *superstitio* and a *religio*, which are, for the discourse of this time, two sides of the same coin, no longer understood as inappropriate and appropriate worship of the gods, respectively, as they had been in the ancient world, but as false and true modes of belief. It is this conversion— and the shift in semantic fields that lies behind it, a shift brought about in part by the discourse of Christian orthodoxy—that enables the text to represent the Jews of Minorca as having converted. Heretics do not convert to orthodoxy; they repent, while converts move between religions, abandoning the false one for the true. It is, therefore, the representation of the conversion of the Jews of Minorca in the text that interpellates Judaism as a religion, signaling the more radical conversion of Judaism. Christianity herein produces both Judaism and itself as equivalent but opposite entities, each as a separate religion. It is thus that the Minorcan Jews can be seen as converting to Christianity "with a remainder," the remainder that is the Jewish religion. Precisely this narrative of a conversion from Judaism to Christianity produces Judaism as a semiotic object in the same paradigm as Christianity, making it finally impossible to be both, since one is the negation of the other.

The first of the Jews who decides to convert "delighted the hearts of all with a most holy cry, begging that he be released from the chains of the Jewish *superstitio* [*absolvi se a vinculis Iudaicae superstionis deprecabatur*]."[133] When Jews who have not (yet) resolved to convert speak, however, they refer to the act of Theodorus, the converted leader of their congregation, as "apostasizing," and to their own Judaism as "our *religio*."[134] Again, when two "fathers of the Jews" do resolve out of fear to convert, they say, "But even if His great power does not draw you to Christ, my brother, Florianus and I, while we cannot use force against you in your rejection of such great salvation, none the less we, with our entire households, will abandon the mockery of this *religio*, which we lack the strength to defend [*nostra religionis huius, quam astruere non valemus, ludibria deserentes*], and we will join in alliance with the faithful ranks of the Christians."[135] This passage is richly ambiguous, as our two Jewish fathers and brothers seem to be converting out of conviction, but then reveal that it is only because they lack the "strength to defend" their *religio*—a *religio*, however, that they are impelled by the narrator to designate as a "mockery." But a mockery of a religion, that is, an object of the class "religion" that nevertheless is "not white, not quite," in Bhabha's catchy catch-phrase. The ambivalence of this sentence is then the ambivalence of mimicry/mockery itself in the discourse of imperial domination.[136] The "colonial" authority desires the Jewish religion to be not quite a religion, a mimicry of religion, analogous—but not identical—to the British, who set up mock parliaments in their colonies but were very surprised when the colonials "misunderstood," either understanding that they had indeed been authorized to govern, or, alternatively, turning those mimic parliaments into a form of mockery of colonial pretension: "It is out of season to question at this time of day, the original policy of conferring on every colony of the British Empire a mimic representation of the British Constitution. But if the creature so endowed has sometimes forgotten its real significance and under the fancied importance of speakers and maces, and all the paraphernalia and ceremonies of the imperial legislature, has dared to defy the mother country. . . . To give to a colony the forms of independence is a mockery; she would not be a colony for a single hour if she could maintain an independent station."[137] Somewhere in this territory, if not precisely defined by it, lies the status of Judaism, that "mockery of a religion," within that earlier Christian Empire of the fifth century. This phrase is rendered more salient and poignant in the context of the legal authorization (in the Theodosian Code) of the Jewish "mimic church."

One of the Christian leaders, addressing the unconverted Jews, also refers to Judaism as a *religio*: "The Christian throng bore witness and I heard it with my own ears, that your brother, Theodorus, who is greater than you in learning, honour and years, converted to faith in Christ," and then, "Isn't it likely that you too, constrained by the example of your own blood brother, will desert the Jewish religion?"[138] Conversion, then, is the deserting of a *religio*. It makes sense that at the very moment Jews begin converting to Christianity in the narrative, Judaism, even of the unconverted, is no longer represented as a heresy but as a *superstitio* from the point of vew of Christians—that is, a false religion—and as a *religio* from the point of view of unconverted Jews: that is, a true religion. A false religion is that from which one *can* convert. The discourse of "conversion" is what brings into being, in a sense, the episteme of "religions." The text thus dramatizes the social situation of the episteme of "conversion" that it itself is engaged in producing, one in which *superstitio* is merely the dark *Doppelgänger* of *religio*, mimicry/mockery of *religio*, and in which it is the very nomination of Judaism as *superstitio* (as opposed to heresy) that empowers (unconverted) Jews to see it as a *religio*, similar, once again, to the way that projecting the colonized as almost, but not quite, white produced a space of possible resistance for those colonial subjects.

Whether or not some "kernel of truth" is contained in this text concerning the events narrated for its "tiny island," its dissemination with the relics and the miracle tales as a highly stylized, fictionalized hagiographical document for the "universal brotherhood of the whole world" was, I reckon, part and parcel of a well-attested process of the promulgation of a new status for the Jews of Christendom at the beginning of the fifth century, a status as a legitimated but despised "wrong" religion, and not a Christian heresy. True history or no, the text is part of the production of a new form of "truth." In other words, the rhetoric here of "forced conversion" is about the making of the discourse of conversion itself, and therefore of religion. At the same time, then, that the *Epistula* is, at least symbolically, depriving that small island's Jews of any place in the world at all, it can, on one reading at least, be perceived as opening up a space for "Judaism" in the larger world to which it is addressed.

The text, I would hazard, doesn't only "remainder" the Jew but actually opens up a space for a new Jewish subjectivity, a space for the Jews to have and claim a *religio* of their own, paralleling in the story's terms of the individual subject and her speech[139] the explicit "permission" afforded by legal discourse, for, as Seth Schwartz has written, "The law codes demonstrate that the Christian state had an interest, which the pagan Roman state had lacked, in regarding the Jews as constituting a separate and discrete religious community. This is one reason, though not the only one, for the revival of Judaism in late antiquity to which archaeology and an explosion of literary production testify."[140]

The Kingdom Turns to *Minut*: The Rabbis Reject Religion

There is a small but suggestive body of evidence that Christianity takes on a different role in the self-understanding of rabbinic Judaism in this period, as well. As I have noted elsewhere, already in later Palestinian texts—the midrashim—we frequently find the expression "Nations of the World" as a reference to Christianity.[141] In a precise mirror of the contemporary Christian move in which ethnic difference is made religious, for the latter Rabbis religious difference has been ethnicized. Christians are no longer seen as a threatening other within but as an entity fully other, as separate as the Gentiles had been for the Jews of Temple times. It is not that the *referent* of the term *minut* has shifted from "Jewish Christianity" to Gentile Christianity, but that, with the historical developments of the centuries, its significance has changed. Since Christianity itself is no longer a threatening blurring within but a clearly defined without, *minut* comes now simply to mean the religious practices of the Gentiles, the Christian Romans. For the Jews of the fourth century, the Gentiles are now the Christians. Whatever the Mishna (Souṭah 9:15) meant in predicting that when the Messiah comes, "The Kingdom will turn to *minut*," for the Talmuds (TP Soṭah 23b, TB Soṭah 49b), I would warrant: "The Kingdom has turned to *minut*" refers to the Christianization of the empire, but it also means, of course, that *minut* has turned (in)to the empire. The Christians are now the Gentiles.

In the Talmud, *minut* clearly no longer means what it had meant in the Mishna and the Tosefta. As Richard Kalmin observes: the "notion of the powerful attraction that *minut* ('heresy') and Christianity exerted on rabbis and their families is found almost exclusively in tannaitic collections such as the Tosefta, but also in tannaitic sources in the Babylonian Talmud that have toseftan parallels. Statements attributed to later Palestinian and Babylonian amoraim in both Talmuds, in contrast, reveal no hint of this notion."[142] This argument can be further substantiated by observing that the Babylonian Talmud almost systematically "forgets" what the meaning of the term *min* is. Indeed, according to that Talmud, *minut* becomes simply a name for the "other" religion, Christianity to the Jews, Judaism to the Christians. As I have said, it is no longer the name for a Jewish heresy but simply refers to false religious practices, functionally equivalent to *idolatry* in biblical usage and consequently of no particular attraction to Jews, any more than *idolatry* had been in Second Temple times.[143] And they imagine that this is the term under which they might, in turn, be persecuted by the Christian empire. We see, therefore, a real asymmetry. Whereas the Christian discourse in this time develops a three-term paradigm—Christians, Jews, and heretics—rabbinic discourse only imagines two terms: we and the Gentiles. Religious difference has been, it seems, fully re-ethnicized.

Two moments in the Babylonian Talmud support this proposition. The first comes from the continuation of the Talmud's version of the narrative about the arrest of Rabbi Eli'ezer that I have discussed at length in previous work.[144] In one early (mid-third-century) Palestinian story, Rabbi Eli'ezer is arrested by the Romans on suspicion of being a Christian, referred to as *minut* in the story. This is the excerpt:

> It happened to Rabbi Eli'ezer that he was arrested for sectarianism (*minut* = Christianity),[145] and they took him up to the platform to be judged.
>   The ruler said to him: "A sage such as you having truck with these matters!?"
>   He said to him: "I have trust in the judge."

The ruler thought that he was speaking of him, but he meant his Father in Heaven. He said to him: "Since you trust me, I also have said: Is it possible that these gray hairs would err in such matters? *Dimus [= Dimissus]!* Behold, you are dismissed." (Tosefta Ḥullin, 2:24)[146]

Having tricked the Roman, he then confesses to his fellows that he has, indeed, had improper friendly religious conversation with a disciple of Jesus; indeed, on my reading, that he had been "arrested by *minut*," that is, found heresy arresting, and not only arrested for *minut*—the Hebrew phrase allows for both meanings. The fact that this alleged James, the disciple of Jesus, cites midrashic interpretations of his Master makes even more palpable both the Jewishness of *minut* and, as well, that the issue of this story is the attraction of the Christian *minut* for even the most prominent of Rabbis. So far, in this text, which has its origins in Palestine, *minut* means what we would expect it to mean, a Jewish heresy, which we might call Christianity.

In the earlier Tosefta and the Palestinian midrash, this text appears without a sequel, but in the Babylonian Talmud we find the following continuation:

Our Rabbis have taught: When Rabbi Elʿazar the son of Perata and Rabbi Ḥanina the son of Teradyon were arrested for sectarianism [*minut*], Rabbi Elʿazar the son of Perata said to Rabbi Ḥanina the son of Teradyon: "Happy art thou, who have been arrested for only one thing. Woe unto me, who have been arrested for five things." Rabbi Ḥanina the son of Teradyon said to him: "Happy art thou, who have been arrested for five things and will be rescued. Woe unto me, who have been arrested for one thing and will not be saved, for you busied yourself with Torah and with good deeds, while I only busied myself with Torah." This is in accord with the view of Rav Huna, who said that anyone who busies himself with Torah alone is as if he had no God.

In contrast to Rabbi Eliʿezer, where the *minut* involved is explicitly Christianity, these two Rabbis clearly are under no suspicion whatever of Christianity. Their fictive arrest clearly happens during the Hadrianic persecutions of the early second century (not under Trajan in the second half of the first) and has to do with the public teaching of Torah, forbidden by Hadrian for political reasons. In other words, they are arrested for practicing Judaism, not as Christians. And yet the Talmud refers to it as an arrest for *minut*. The term *minut* has clearly shifted meaning for the Babylonian Talmud. It no longer refers to Jewish heresy, but to the binary opposition between Jewish and Gentile religion. Judaism is *minut* for the Romans; Roman religion and Christianity are *minut* for Jews. This semantic shift changes the interpretation of Rabbi Eliʿezer's arrest in the talmudic context via what is in effect a misreading.[147] It is unthinkable to this Talmud that Rabbi Eliʿezer had been under suspicion, much less somewhat justifiable suspicion, for association with *minim*, and therefore the text has to make it a code name for arrest for being Jewish, for teaching Torah—that is, *minut,* heresy, as seen from the viewpoint of the Roman order, not from the viewpoint of Judaism. In my view, we have evidence, then, that by the time of the editing of the Babylonian Talmud, and perhaps at that geographical distance from the center of contact, Palestine, Jewish Christianity (not in its heresiological sense but in the sense of the Christianity of Jews who remained Jews) had receded into the distance for rabbinic Judaism; Christianity was sufficiently definable as a separate "religion" that it no longer posed a threat to the borders of the Jewish community.

We now have an explanation for the well-known fact that in the Babylonian Talmud the term *min* no longer refers to a difference within Judaism, an excluded heretical other, but has come to mean Gentiles and especially Gentile Christians. Once more, as in the period of the Second Temple (up until 70 A.C.) and before, the excluded other of Judaism is the Gentile and not the heretic within.

The second piece of evidence comes from another story, which historians have hitherto read quite differently:

> Rabbi Abbahu used to praise Rav Safra [a Babylonian immigrant to Caesarea Maritima] to the *minim* that he was a great man [i.e., a great scholar]. They released him from excise taxes for thirteen years.
>
> One day they met him. They said to him: "It is written: Only you have I known from all of the families of the earth; therefore I will tax you with all of your sins" [Amos 3:2]. One who is enraged,[148] does he punish his lover?
>
> He was silent, and didn't say anything to them. They threw a scarf on him and were mocking him.
>
> Rabbi Abbahu came and found them.
>
> He said to them: "Why are you mocking him?"
>
> They said to him: "Didn't you say that he is a great man, and he could not even tell us the interpretation of this verse!"
>
> He said to them: "That which I said to you has to do with Mishna, but with respect to the Scripture, I didn't say anything."
>
> They said to him: "What is it different with respect to you that you know [Scripture also]?"
>
> He said to them: "We who are located in your midst, take it upon ourselves and we study, but they do not study." (TB Avoda Zara 4a)

Following the principle set out by Saul Lieberman—that talmudic legend may be read as useful information for the history of the time and place of its production and not the time and place of which it speaks[149]—there is no way that this story, only attested in the Babylonian Talmud, should be taken to represent Palestinian reality. Its existence only there demonstrates that it does not, because the genre of encounters between Rabbis and *minim* is very rare in Palestinian sources, but very common in Babylonian texts, as Kalmin has recently shown.[150] Almost always these Babylonian narratives relate the confrontation between a Palestinian sage and a *min*, of whatever variety. A story such as this may tell us something, therefore, about Babylonian reality in the fourth and fifth centuries.[151] In that time and space, this text explicitly testifies, Christians were no longer an internal threat to the integrity of the religious life-world of the Rabbis: "They [the Babylonians] do not study Bible, because you [the *minim*] are not found in their midst." Although this text is frequently read as indicating that there weren't Christians or Christianity in the Sassanian environs of the Babylonnian Rabbis, this is not, I think, the only—or even the right—way to read it. Christianity may not have been the state religion, but it was certainly present, active, and in open dispute with the Jews there.[152] I would suggest, rather, seeing here an indication of separation of the two "religions." This is not to be taken as a sign that Christianity did not have powerful effects on the historical development of Judaism in Babylonia (and the reverse),[153] but only that, with the borders clearly established, Christianity was no longer considered a subversive danger for believing Jews. It is thus perhaps not surprising that it is in the Babylonian Talmud that early Palestinian Judaism comes to be re-presented as a "a society based on the doctrine that conflicting disputants may each be advancing the words of the living God."[154] With the borders of unanimity secured, there are no more internal others (at least in theory).

In the imagination of the Rabbis, Judaism has been reconfigured as a grand coalition of differing theological and even halakhic views *within the clear and now uncontested borders of rabbinic Judaism*. It is this reconfigured *imaginaire* of a Jewish polity with no heresies and no heresiologies that Gerald Bruns has described: "From a transcendental standpoint, this [rabbinic] theory of authority is paradoxical because it is seen to hang on the heteroglossia of dialogue, on speaking with many voices, rather than on the logical principle of univocity, or speaking with one mind. Instead, the idea of speaking with one mind . . . is explicitly rejected; single-mindedness produces factionalism."[155] The Rabbis, in the end, reject and refuse the Christian definition of a religion, understood as a system of beliefs and practices to which one adheres voluntarily and defalcation from which results in one's becoming a heretic. At this moment, then, we first find the principle that has been ever since the touchstone of Jewish ecclesiology: "an Israelite, even though he sin, remains an Israelite," which we find only once in all of classical rabbinic literature, in the Babylonian Talmud and then in the name of a late amora (Sanhedrin 44a). This same watchword becomes nearly ubiquitous and foundational for later forms of rabbinic Judaism. There is now virtually no way that a Jew can stop being a Jew, since the very notion of heresy was finally rejected and Judaism (even the word is anachronistic) refused to be, in the end, a *religion*. For the Church, Judaism is a religion, but for the Jews only occasionally, ambivalently, and strategically is it so. To add one more piquant bit to the material already adduced above, let me just mention that, when Jews teach Judaism in a department of religious studies, they are as likely to be teaching Yiddish literature or the history of the Nazi genocide as anything that might be said (in Christian terms) to be part of a Jewish religion!

Jonathan Boyarin writes, "The question of the imbalance between a totalizing categorical usage of the term 'diaspora' and the discourses within various diasporic formations that may not recognize that category leads us to the necessary recognition that whatever the criterion for judging our own discourse may be, it cannot rest on a simplistic notion of pluralist (different but in the same ways) tolerance."[156] Empowered by the Christian interpellation of Judaism as a religion, the Jews, nevertheless, significantly resisted the (ambiguous) tolerance enacted by the Theodosian Empire's emplacement of a "a frontier all the more mysterious . . . because it is abstract, legal, ideal."[157] Refusing to be different in quite the same ways, not a religion, not quite, Judaism (including the bizarrely named Jewish orthodoxy of modernity) remained something else, neither quite here nor quite there. Among the various emblems of this different difference remains the fact that there are Christians who are Jews, or perhaps better put, Jews who are Christians, even up to this very day.

The Future of the Religious Past

Charles Taylor

As I start to write this essay, I have great misgivings. Predicting the future is an extremely foolish enterprise. Historians and social scientists know this well, and refrain from it entirely. And although philosophers haven't got much of a reputation for accuracy to lose, it still seems somewhat foolhardy.

But I still my fears by telling myself that what I'm actually going to do is give an account of the vectors of religious development up to the present (itself a high-risk, accident-prone enterprise), from which some very tentative guesses might be made about their continuation or alteration in the future. In short, I'm going to lay out some pieces of my "grand narrative." I do not share the postmodern aversion to grand narratives; this is because I think that we all operate with our own (perhaps confused) version and that the best way to deal with this is to be as clear as we can about the one we're relying on, while being as open as possible to objections to and criticisms of it.

I'm going to rely on my narrative to suggest a set of categories of religious life—belief, devotion, ritual, community, and so on—whose present and future condition, developments, transformations we can then assess.

Before I start, let me make one more disclaimer. My narrative is for the most part about only one civilization: the "West," aka Europe and its extensions, earlier known as "Latin Christendom." There will be some reference to a wider frame in order to set the developments in this civilization in context. And then I will make some tentative remarks about possible parallels with / differences from other parts of the world. But the main story line I will be leaning on is the "Western" one.

I

One of the main vectors over the last six or seven centuries in this civilization has been a steadily increasing emphasis on a religion of personal commitment and devotion, over against forms centered on collective ritual. We can see this in the growth of a more Christocentric religion in the High Middle Ages. It is further evident both in devotional movements and associations, like the Brethren of the Common Life in the fifteenth century, and in the demands made by Church hierarchies and leaders on their members. An early example of the latter is the decision of the Lateran Council in 1215 to require all the faithful to confess to a priest and be shriven, so as to receive communion at least once a year.

From that point on, the pressure to adopt a more personal, committed, inward form of religion continues, through the preaching of the mendicant friars and others, through the devotional movements mentioned above, reaching a new stage with the Reformation. The point of declaring that salvation comes through faith was radically to devalue ritual and external practice in favor of inward adherence to Christ as Savior. It was not just that external ritual was of no effect, but relying on it was tantamount to a presumption that we could control God. The Reformation also tended to delegitimate the distinction between fully committed believers and other, less devoted ones. As against a view of the church in which people operating at many different "speeds" coexisted with religious "virtuosi," to use Max Weber's term, on one end, and ordinary intermittent practitioners on the other, all Christians were expected to be fully committed.

This movement toward the personal, committed, and inward didn't exist only in the Protestant churches. There is a parallel development in the Counter-Reformation, with the spread of different devotional movements and attempts to regulate the lives of the laity according to more and more stringent models of practice. The clergy were reformed; their training was upgraded; they were expected to reach out and demand a higher level of personal practice from their flocks. A striking figure illustrates this whole movement: in the history of Catholic France, the moment at which the level of practice, as measured by baptisms and Easter Communions, reaches its highest has been estimated to fall around 1870.[1] This is well after the anticlericalism of the Revolution and its attempts at dechristianization, after a definite movement toward unbelief has set in among the educated classes. In spite of this incipient loss, the apogee of practice comes this late because it stands at the end of a long process in which ordinary believers have been preached at, organized, sometimes bullied into patterns of practice that reflect more personal commitment.

They have been pressed, we might be tempted to say, into "taking their religion seriously." To take my religion seriously is to take it personally, more devotionally, inwardly, more committedly. Just taking part in external rituals, those which don't require the kind of personal engagement that, for example, auricular confession, with its self-examination and promises of amendment, entails is devalued in this understanding. This isn't what religion is "really about."

Now, a striking feature of the Western march toward secularity is that it has been interwoven from the start with this drive toward personal religion, as has frequently been remarked.[2] The connections are multiple. It is not just that the falling off of religious belief and practice has forced a greater degree of reflection and commitment on those who remain. This has perhaps been evident in more recent times. It is much more that the drive to personal religion has itself been part of the impetus toward different facets of secularization. It was this drive, for instance, that powerfully contributed to the disenchantment of the world of spirits and higher forces in which our ancestors lived. The Reformation and Counter-Reformation repressed first magical practices and then those facets of traditional Christian sacramental ritual that they began to deem magical: for Calvinists, this even included the Mass. Later, at the time of the early American republic, a separation of church and state was brought about, mainly to give space for, and avoid the contamination of, personal religion, which itself had been given a further impetus through the Great Awakening.

We might identify two closely connected vectors here: toward personal commitment and toward the repression of what came to be understood as "magical" elements in religion: practices that suppose and draw upon various intra-cosmic spirits, good or bad, and higher powers inhering in things (e.g., relics). I want to use the word *disenchantment* for this movement of repression. This is a narrower sense than the word often bears, for it is frequently synonymous with the sidelining of religion as such, but it has some warrant in the original Weberian term, *Entzauberung*.

I want now to place this double vector (commitment-disenchantment) in an even deeper and broader historical context, the rise and forward march of what Jaspers called "axial" religions and spiritualities. The whole sweep, as it continues up to and into Western modernity, can be seen as a great disembedding of the merely human, and even of the human individual. The full scale of this millennial change becomes clearer if we focus first on some features of the religious life of earlier, smaller-scale societies, insofar as we can trace this. There must have been a phase in which all humans lived in such small-scale societies, even though much of the life of this epoch can only be guessed at.

If we focus on what I will call "early religion" (which covers partly what Robert Bellah, e.g., calls "archaic religion"[3]), we note how profoundly these forms of life "embed" the agent. They do so in three crucial ways.

First, socially: in paleolithic, and even certain neolithic, tribal societies, religious life is inseparably linked with social life. The primary agency of important religious action—invoking, praying to, sacrificing to, or propitiating Gods or spirits, coming close to these powers, getting healing or protection from them, divining under their guidance, and so on—involved the social group as a whole, or some more specialized agency recognized as acting for the group. In early religion, we primarily relate to God as a society.

We see both aspects of this in, for example, ritual sacrifices among the Dinka, as they were described a half century ago by Godfrey Lienhardt. On the one hand, the major agents of the sacrifice, the "masters of the fishing spear," are in a sense "functionaries," acting for the whole society, while on the other, the whole community becomes involved, repeats the invocations of the masters, until everyone's attention is focused and concentrated on the single ritual action. It is at the climax "that those attending the ceremony are most palpably members of a single undifferentiated body." This participation often takes the form of possession by the divinity being invoked.[4]

Nor is this just the way things happen to be in a certain community. This collective action is essential for the efficacy of the ritual. You can't mount a powerful invocation of the divinities like this on your own in the Dinka world. This "importance of corporate action by a community of which the individual is really and traditionally a member is the reason for the fear which individual Dinka feel when they suffer misfortune away from home and kin."[5]

This kind of collective ritual action, where the principal agents are acting on behalf of a community, which also in its own way becomes involved in the action, seems to figure virtually everywhere in early religion and continues in some ways up till our day. Certainly it goes on occupying an important place as long as people live in an "enchanted" world—a world of spirits and forces, prior to what I am calling "disenchantment." The medieval ceremony of "beating the bounds" of the agricultural village, for instance, involved the whole parish and could only be effective as a collective act of this whole.

This embedding in social ritual usually carries with it another feature. Just because the most important religious action was that of the collective, and because it often required that certain functionaries—priests, shamans, medicine men, diviners, chiefs, and so on—fill crucial roles in the action, the social order in which these roles were defined tended to be sacrosanct. This is, of course, the aspect of religious life that was most centrally identified and pilloried by the radical Enlightenment. The crime laid bare here was the entrenchment of forms of inequality, domination, and exploitation through their identification with the untouchable, sacred structure of things. Hence the longing to see the day "when the last king had been strangled in the entrails of the last priest." But this identification is in fact very old and goes back to a time when many of the later, more egregious and vicious forms of inequality had not yet been developed, before there were kings and hierarchies of priests.[6]

Behind the issue of inequality and justice lies something deeper, which touches what we would call today the "identity" of the human beings in those earlier societies. Just because their most important actions were the doings of whole groups (tribe, clan, subtribe, lineage), articulated in a certain way (the actions were led by chiefs, shamans, masters of the fishing spear), they couldn't conceive themselves as potentially disconnected from this social matrix. It would probably never even occur to them to try.

What I'm calling "social embeddedness" is thus partly an identity thing. From the standpoint of the individual's sense of self, it means the inability to imagine oneself outside a certain matrix. But it also can be understood as a social reality, and here it refers to the way we together imagine our social existence, for instance, that our most important actions are those of the whole society, which must be structured in a certain way to carry them out. And we can see that it is growing up in a world where this kind of social imaginary reign sets the limits to our sense of self.

Embedding in society also brings with it an embedding in the cosmos. In early religion, the spirits and forces with whom we are dealing are in numerous ways intricated in the world. We can see examples of this aplenty if we refer back to the enchanted world of our medieval ancestors: although the God they worshipped transcended the world, they nevertheless also had to do with intra-cosmic spirits, and they dealt with causal powers that were embedded in things: relics, sacred places, and the like. In early religion, even the high gods are often identified with certain features of the world, and where the phenomenon that has come to be called "totemism" exists, we can even say that some feature of the world, an animal or plant species, for instance, is central to the identity of a group.[7] It may even be that a particular geographical terrain is essential to our religious life. Certain places are sacred. Or the layout of the land speaks to us of the original disposition of things in sacred time. We relate to the ancestors and to this higher time through this landscape.[8]

This is something that we, products of the vector toward the personal, the committed, the inward, have trouble understanding. In Latin Christendom, movement along this vector tended more and more to privilege belief, as against unthinking practice. "Secular" people have inherited this emphasis and often propound an "ethics of belief,"[9] where it can be seen as a sin against science or epistemic decency to believe in God. So we tend to think of our differences from our remote forbears in terms of different *beliefs*, whereas there is something much more puzzling involved. It is clear that for our forbears, and for many people in the world today who live in a similar religious world, the presence of spirits and of different forms of possession is no more a matter of (optional, voluntarily embraced) belief than is for me the presence of this computer and its keyboard at the tips of my fingers. Like my ancestors, I confront a great deal in the inner workings of this computer that I don't understand (almost everything, in fact) and about which I could be induced by experts to accept various theories. But the encounter with a computer is not a matter of "belief." It's a basic feature of my experience.

So it must have been for Celestine, interviewed by Birgit Meyer,[10] who "walked home from Aventile with her mother, accompanied by a stranger dressed in a white northern gown." When asked afterward, her mother denied having seen the man. He turned out to be the Akan spirit Sowlui, and Celestine was pressed into his service. In Celestine's world, perhaps the identification of the man with this spirit might be called a "belief," in that it came after the experience in an attempt to explain what it was all about. But the man accompanying her was just something that happened to her, a fact of her world.

We have great trouble getting our minds around this, and we rapidly reach for intra-psychic explanations, in terms of delusions, projections, and the like. But one thing that seems clear is that the whole situation of the self in experience is subtly but importantly different in these worlds and in ours. We make a sharp distinction between inner and outer, what is in the "mind" and what is out there in the world. Whatever has to do with thought, purpose, human meaning, has to be in the mind, rather than in the world. Some chemical can cause hormonal change and thus alter the psyche. There can be an aphrodisiac, but not a love potion, that is, a chemical that determines the human/moral meaning of the experience it enables. A phial of liquid can cure a specific disease, but there can't be phials like those brought back from pilgrimage at Canterbury, which contained a miniscule drop of the blood of Thomas à Beckett, which could cure anything and which could even make us better people—that is, the liquid was the locus not of certain specific chemical properties but of a generalized beneficence.

Modern Westerners have a clear boundary between mind and world, even mind and body. Moral and other meanings are "in the mind." They cannot reside outside, and thus the boundary is firm. But formerly it was not so. Let us take a well-known example of influence inhering in an inanimate substance, as this was understood in earlier times. Consider melancholy: black bile was not the cause of melancholy, it embodied, it *was* melancholy. The emotional life was porous here; it didn't simply exist in an inner, mental space. Our vulnerability to the evil, the inwardly destructive, extended to more than just spirits that are malevolent. It went beyond them to things that have no wills but are nevertheless redolent with evil meanings.

See the contrast. A modern is feeling depressed, melancholy. He is told: it's just your body chemistry, you're hungry, or there is a hormone malfunction, or whatever. Straightway, he feels relieved. He can take a distance from this feeling, which is ipso facto declared not justified. Things don't really have this meaning; it just feels this way, which is the result of a causal action utterly unrelated to the meanings of things. This step of disengagement depends on our modern mind/body distinction, and the relegation of the physical to being "just" a contingent cause of the psychic.

A premodern may not be helped by learning that his mood comes from black bile, because this doesn't permit a distancing. Black bile *is* melancholy. Now he just knows that he's in the grips of the real thing.

Here is the contrast between the modern, bounded self—I want to say the "buffered" self—and the "porous" self of the earlier, enchanted world. What difference does this make?

It is a very different existential condition. The last example about melancholy and its causes illustrates this well. For the modern, buffered self, it is possible to take a distance from, to disengage from, everything outside the mind. My ultimate purposes arise within me, the crucial meanings of things are defined in my responses to them. These purposes and meanings may be vulnerable to manipulation in various ways, including the use of chemicals; but this can in principle be met with a counter-manipulation: I avoid distressing or tempting experiences, I don't shoot up the wrong substances, and so on.

This is not to say that the buffered understanding necessitates taking this stance. It is just that it allows it as a possibility, whereas the porous one does not. By definition, for the porous self, the sources of its most powerful and important emotions are outside the "mind"; better put, the very notion that there is a clear boundary, allowing us to define an inner base area, grounded in which we can disengage from the rest, has no sense.

As a bounded self I can see the boundary as a buffer, such that the things beyond don't need to "get to me," to use the contemporary expression. That's the sense in my use of the term *buffered* here. This self can see itself as invulnerable, as master of the meanings of things for it.

These two descriptions get at, respectively, the two important facets of this contrast. First, the porous self is vulnerable: to spirits, demons, cosmic forces. And along with this go certain fears, which can grip it in certain circumstances. The buffered self has been taken out of the world of this kind of fear: for instance, the kind of thing vividly portrayed in some of the paintings of Bosch.

True, something analogous can take its place. These images can also be seen as coded manifestations of inner depths, repressed thoughts and feelings. But the point is that, in this quite transformed understanding of self and world, we define these as inner, and naturally, we deal with them very differently. And, indeed, an important part of the treatment is designed to make disengagement possible.

Perhaps the clearest sign of the transformation in our world is that today many people look back to the world of the porous self with nostalgia, as though the creation of a thick emotional boundary between us and the cosmos were now lived as a loss. The aim is to try to recover some measure of this lost feeling. So people go to movies about the uncanny in order to experience a frisson. Our peasant ancestors would have thought us insane. You can't get a frisson from what is really in fact terrifying you.

The second facet is that the buffered self can form the ambition of disengaging from whatever is beyond the boundary and of giving its own autonomous order to its life. The absence of fear can be not just enjoyed but seen as an opportunity for self-control or self-direction.

The boundary between agents and forces is fuzzy in the enchanted world, and the boundary between mind and world is porous, as we see in the way that charged objects can influence us. I have just been speaking about the moral influence of substances, like black bile. But a similar point can be made about the relation to spirits. The porousness of the boundary emerges here in the various kinds of "possession," all the way from a full takeover of a person, as with a medium, to various kinds of domination by, or partial fusion with a spirit or God.[11] Here again, the boundary between self and other is fuzzy, porous. And this has to be seen as a fact of *experience*, not a matter of "theory" or "belief."

Besides this relation to society and the cosmos, we can see in early religion a third form of embedding in existing reality. This is what makes the most striking contrast with what we tend to think of as the "higher" religions. What people ask for when they invoke or placate divinities and powers is prosperity, health, long life, fertility; what they ask to be preserved from is disease, dearth, sterility, premature death. There is a certain understanding of human flourishing here that we can immediately understand and that, however much we might want to add to it, seems to us quite "natural." What there isn't, and what seems central to the later, "higher" religions, is the idea that we have to question radically this ordinary understanding, that we are called in some way to go beyond it.

This is not to say that human flourishing is the end sought by all things. The divine may also have other purposes, some of which have a harmful impact. There is a sense in which, for early religions, the divine is never simply well disposed toward us. The gods (or some of them) may also be in certain ways indifferent; or there may also be hostility, or jealousy, or anger, which we must deflect. Although benevolence, in principle, may have the upper hand, this process may have to be helped along by propitiation or even by the action of "trickster" figures. But through all this, what remains true is that divinity's benign purposes are defined in terms of ordinary human flourishing. Again, there may be capacities that some people can attain, that go way beyond the ordinary human ones, which, say, prophets or shamans have. But these in the end subserve well-being as ordinarily understood.

By contrast, with Christianity or Buddhism, for instance, there is a notion of our good that goes beyond human flourishing, that we may gain even while failing utterly on the scales of human flourishing, even *through* such a failing (like dying young on a cross), or that involves leaving the field of flourishing altogether (ending the cycle of rebirth). The paradox of Christianity, in relation to early religion, is that it seems to assert the unconditional benevolence of God toward humans—there is none of the ambivalence of early divinity in this respect—and yet it redefines our ends so as to take us beyond flourishing.

In this respect, early religion has something in common with modern exclusive humanism, and this has been felt and expressed in the sympathy of many modern, post-Enlightenment people for "paganism." "Pagan self-assertion," thought John Stuart Mill, was as valid as "Christian self-denial," if not more so.[12] (This is related to, but not quite the same as, the sympathy felt for "polytheism.") What makes modern humanism unprecedented, of course, is the idea that this flourishing involves no relation to anything higher.

Now, as earlier mentions suggest, I have been speaking of "early religion" to contrast what many people have called "postaxial" religions.[13] The reference is to what Karl Jaspers called the "axial age,"[14] the extraordinary period in the last millennium B.C.E. when various "higher" forms of religion appeared seemingly independently in different civilizations, marked by such founding figures as Confucius, Gautama, Socrates, and the Hebrew prophets.

The surprising feature of the axial religions, compared with what went before, what would in other words have made them hard to predict beforehand, is that they initiate a break in all three dimensions of embeddedness: social order, cosmos, human good. Not in all cases and all at once. Perhaps in some ways Buddhism is the most far-reaching, because it radically undercuts the second dimension: the order of the world itself is called into question, because the wheel of rebirth means suffering. In Christianity, there is something analogous: our world is disordered and must be made anew. But some postaxial outlooks keep the sense of relation to an ordered cosmos, as we see in very different ways with Confucius and Plato. They mark a distinction, however, between this and the actual, highly imperfect social order, so that the close link to the cosmos through collective religious life is made problematic.

Perhaps most fundamental of all is the revisionary stance toward the human good in axial religions. More or less radically, they all call into question the received, seemingly unquestionable understandings of human flourishing, and hence inevitably also the structures of society and the features of the cosmos through which this flourishing was supposedly achieved.

We might try to put the contrast in this way: unlike postaxial religion, early religion involved an acceptance of the order of things, in the three dimensions I have been discussing. In a remarkable series of articles on Australian aboriginal religion, W. E. H. Stanner speaks of "the mood of assent" that is central to this spirituality. Aboriginals have not set up the "kind of quarrel with life" that springs from the various postaxial religious initiatives.[15] The contrast is in some ways easy to miss, because aboriginal mythology, in relating the way in which the order of things came to be in the Dream Time—the original time out of time, which is also "everywhen"—contains a number of stories of catastrophe, brought on by trickery, deceit, and violence, from which human life recouped and re-emerged, but in an impaired and divided fashion, so that there remains the intrinsic connection between life and suffering, and unity is inseparable from division. Now this may seem reminiscent of other stories of a Fall, including that related in Genesis. But in contrast to what Christianity has made of this, for the Aboriginals the imperative to "follow up" the Dreaming, to recover through ritual and insight their contact with the order of the original time, relates to this riven and impaired dispensation, in which good and evil are interwoven. There is no question of reparation of the original rift, or of a compensation, or making good the original loss. What is more, ritual and the wisdom that goes with it can even bring them to accept the inexorable and "celebrate joyously what could not be changed."[16] The original catastrophe doesn't separate or alienate us from the sacred or Higher, as in the Genesis story; rather, it contributes to shaping the sacred order we are trying to "follow up."[17]

Now, axial religion didn't do away with early religious life. In many ways, features of this continued in modified form to define majority religious life for centuries. Modifications arose, of course, not just from the axial formulations but also from the growth of large-scale, more differentiated, often urban-centered societies, with more hierarchical organization and embryonic state structures. Indeed, it has been argued that these, too, played a part in the process of disembedding, because the very existence of state power entails some attempt to control and shape religious life and the social structures it requires, and hence undercuts the sense of intangibility surrounding this life and these structures.[18] I think there is a lot to this thesis, and, indeed, I invoke something like it later on. But for the moment I want to focus on the significance of the axial period.

This doesn't at once totally change the religious life of whole societies. But it does open new possibilities of disembedded religion: seeking a relation to the divine or the Higher, which severely revises notions of flourishing or even exceeds them, and can be carried through by individuals on their own, and/or in new kinds of sociality, uncoupled from the established sacred order. So monks, bhikhus, sanyassi, devotees of some avatar or God, strike out on their own, and from this spring unprecedented modes of sociality: initiation groups, sects of devotees, the sangha, monastic orders, and so on.

In all these cases, there is some kind of hiatus, difference, or even break in relation to the religious life of the larger society. This may itself be to some extent differentiated, with different strata or castes or classes, and a new religious outlook may lodge in one of them. But very often a new devotion may cut across all of these, particularly where there is a break in the third dimension, with a "higher" idea of the human good.

There is inevitably a tension here, but there often is also an attempt to secure the unity of the whole, to recover some sense of complementarity between different religious forms. So those who are fully dedicated to the "higher" forms, while on the one hand they can be seen as a standing reproach to those who remain in the earlier forms, supplicating the powers for human flourishing, nevertheless can also be seen as in a relationship of mutual help with them. The laity feed the monks, and by this they earn "merit," which can be understood as taking them a little farther along the "higher" road, but also serves to protect them from the dangers of life and to increase their health, prosperity, and fertility.

So strong is the pull toward complementarity that even in those cases where a "higher" religion took over the whole society, as we see with Buddhism, Christianity, and Islam—so that there is supposedly nothing left to contrast with—the difference between dedicated minorities of religious "virtuosi" (to use Max Weber's term) and the mass religion of the social sacred, still largely oriented to flourishing, survived or reconstituted itself, with the same combination of strain, on the one hand, and hierarchical complementarity, on the other.

From our modern perspective, with twenty/twenty hindsight, it appears as though the axial spiritualities were prevented from producing their full disembedding effect because they were, so to speak, hemmed in by the force of the majority religious life, which remained firmly in the old mold. They did bring about a certain form of religious individualism, but this was what Louis Dumont calls the charter for "the individual outside the world": that is, it was the way of life of elite minorities, and it was in some ways marginal to, or in some tension with, the "world," meaning not just the cosmos, which is ordered in relation to the Higher or the Sacred, but also society, which is ordered in relation to both cosmos and sacred.[19] This "world" was still a matrix of embeddedness, and it still provided the inescapable framework for social life, including that of the individuals who tried to turn their backs on it, insofar as they remained in some sense within its reach.

What had yet to happen was for this matrix to be itself transformed, to be made over according to some of the principles of axial spirituality, so that the "world" itself would come to be seen as constituted by individuals. This would be the charter for "the individual in the world," in Dumont's terms, the agent who in his ordinary "worldly" life sees himself as primordially an individual, that is, the human agent of Western modernity.

Now, I believe this project of transformation has been carried out in Latin Christendom. The vectors of commitment and disenchantment came about through a series of attempts at reform. The goal was to make over the lives of Christians, and also their social order, in a thoroughgoing way so as to make them conform to the demands of the Gospel. I am talking not of a particular, revolutionary moment but of a long, ascending series of attempts to establish a Christian order, in which the Reformation is a key phase. These attempts show a progressive impatience with older modes of postaxial religion, in which certain collective, ritualistic forms of earlier religions existed in uneasy coexistence with the demands of individual devotion and ethical reform, which came from the "higher" revelations. In Latin Christendom, the attempt was to recover and impose on everyone a more individually committed and Christocentric religion of devotion and action, and to repress or even abolish older, supposedly "magical" or "superstitious" forms of collective ritual practice. Social life was to be purged of its connection to an enchanted cosmos, and all vestiges removed of the old complementarities, between spiritual and temporal, between life devoted to God and life in the "world," between order and the chaos on which it draws.

This project was thoroughly disembedding just by virtue of its form or mode of operation: the disciplined remaking of behavior and social forms through objectification and an instrumental stance. But its ends were also intrinsically concerned to disembed. This is clear with the drive to disenchantment, which destroys the second dimension of embeddedness, but we can also see it in the Christian context. In one way, Christianity here operates like any axial spirituality; indeed, it operates in conjunction with another such, namely, Stoicism. But there also were specifically Christian modes. The New Testament is full of calls to leave or relativize solidarities of family, clan, society, and be part of the Kingdom. We see this seriously reflected in the way of operating of certain Protestant churches, where one was not simply a member by virtue of birth but had to join by answering a personal call. This in turn helped give force to a conception of society as founded on a covenant, and hence as ultimately constituted by the decision of free individuals.

This is a relatively obvious filiation. But my thesis is that the effect of the Christian, or Christian-Stoic, attempt to remake society in bringing about the modern "individual in the world" was much more pervasive, and multitracked. It helped to nudge first the moral, then the social imaginary in the direction of modern individualism. I believe that this is what we see emerging in the new conception of moral order of seventeenth-century natural law theory. This was heavily indebted to Stoicism, and its originators were arguably the Netherlands neo-Stoics, Justus Lipsius and Hugo Grotius. But this was a Christianized Stoicism, and a modern one, in the sense that it gave a crucial place to a willed remaking of human society.

We could say that both buffered identity and the project of reform contributed to disembedding. Embeddedness, as I said above, is both a matter of identity—the contextual limits to the imagination of the self—and of the social imaginary: the ways we are able to think or imagine the whole of society. But the new buffered identity, with its insistence on personal devotion and discipline, increased distance from, disidentification with, even hostility to the older forms of collective ritual and belonging, while the drive to reform came to envisage their abolition. Both in their sense of self and in their project for society, the disciplined elites moved toward a conception of the social world as constituted by individuals.

So to the two linked vectors of personal commitment and disenchantment we can add two more, also closely related, those of the movement to reform and of disembedding, or the rise of modern individualism. These are connected to a fifth, which I think is one of the basic features of modern secularity, if not the basic one.

What do we mean when we speak of Western modernity as "secular"? There are all sorts of ways of describing it: separation of religion from public life, decline of religious belief and practice. While one cannot avoid touching on these, my main interest here lies in another facet of our age: belief in God or in the transcendent in any form is contested; it is an option among many; it is therefore fragile, for some people in some milieus very difficult, even "weird." Five hundred years ago in our civilization, it wasn't so. Unbelief was off the map for most people, close to inconceivable. But that description also applies to the whole of human history outside the modern West.

What had to happen for this kind of secular climate to come about? First, there had to develop a culture that marks a clear division between the "natural" and the "supernatural," and second, it had to come to seem possible to live entirely within the natural. The first was something to strive for, but the second came about at first quite inadvertently.

Very briefly, I believe that it came about as the byproduct of the series of actions in the vector I have called reform. The attempt was to make individuals and their society over so as to conform to the demands of the Gospel. Allied with a neo-Stoic outlook, this became the charter for a series of attempts to establish new forms of social order, drawing on new disciplines (Foucault enters the story here), which helped to reduce violence and disorder, and to create populations of relatively pacific and productive artisans and peasants, who were more and more induced/forced into the new forms of devotional practice and moral behavior, be this in Protestant England, Holland, the American colonies, Counter-Reformation France, or the Germany of the *Polizeistaat* ("police state").

My hypothesis is that this new creation of a civilized, "polite" order succeeded beyond what its first originators could have hoped for, and that this in turn led to a new reading of what a Christian order might be, one that was seen more and more in "immanent" terms (polite, civilized order *is* Christian order). This version of Christianity was shorn of much of its "transcendent" content, and was thus open to a new departure, in which the understanding of good order (what I call the "modern moral order") could be embraced outside of the original theological, providential framework, and in certain cases even against it (as with Voltaire, Gibbon, and, in another way, Hume).

Disbelief in God arises in close symbiosis with this belief in a moral order of rights-bearing individuals, who are destined (by God or Nature) to act for mutual benefit, an order that thus rejects the earlier honor ethic, which exalted the warrior, as it also tends to occlude any transcendent horizon. (We see one good formulation of this notion of order in Locke's *Second Treatise*). This understanding of order has profoundly shaped the forms of social imaginary that dominate in the modern West: the market economy, the public sphere, the sovereign "people."[20]

In other words, the crucial change here could be described as the possibility of living within a purely immanent order; that is, the possibility of really conceiving/imagining ourselves within such an order, one that could be accounted for on its own terms, and thus that leaves belief in the transcendent as a kind of "optional extra"—something it had never been before in any human society. This presupposed the clear separation between natural and supernatural as a necessary condition, but it needed more than that. A social order sustained by a social imaginary having that purely immanent character had to develop; we see it arising, for instance, in the modern forms of the public sphere, the market economy, and the citizen state.

I want to continue a little further laying out features of the narrative I propose, because they are necessary to the categories I want to put forward for understanding our present and future. It is all too easy to see the modern citizen state as in its very nature an implicit rejection of transcendence. This is easier if we focus too exclusively on the great, climactic event of the French Revolution. Sovereignty comes from the people, not from the king; but the king's sovereignty comes from above, from God; so democracy is already an implicit rejection of God. This, of course, can easily fit into a rival master narrative that I want to reject, one in which secularity, defined as the falling off of belief and practice, is generated in a linear way by the conditions of modern life.

On the contrary, what strikes me is the way these conditions steadily destabilize earlier forms, which in turn leads to a "recomposition" of religious life, to use Danièle Hervieu-Léger's expression.[21] The form of divine presence in the French monarchy, which was deeply interwoven with the enchanted world (e.g., the king's two bodies, the power to cure scrofula, etc.), was indeed a casualty of the French Revolution. When Charles X in 1825 tried to have the full, original liturgy of Coronation at Rheims Cathedral, it all fell terribly flat. This was perhaps the final gasp of Bourbon nostalgia.

But with advancing disenchantment, especially in Protestant societies, another model of divine presence took shape, with relation to both the cosmos and the polity. In this the notion of design was crucial. To take the cosmos, there was a shift from the enchanted world to a cosmos conceived in conformity with post-Newtonian science, in which there is absolutely no question of higher meanings being *expressed* in the universe around us. But there is still, with someone like Newton himself, for instance, a strong sense that the universe declares the glory of God. This is evident in its design, its beauty, its regularity, but also in its having evidently been shaped in a way conducive to the welfare of His creatures, particularly of ourselves, the superior creatures who cap it all off. Now the presence of God no longer lies in the sacred, because this category fades in a disenchanted world. But He can be thought to be no less powerfully present through His design.

This presence of God in the cosmos is matched by another idea: His presence in the polity. Here an analogous change takes place. The divine isn't there in a king who straddles the planes. But it can be present to the extent that we build a society that plainly follows God's design. This can be filled in with an idea of moral order seen as established by God, in the way invoked, for instance, in the American Declaration of Independence: men have been created equal and have been endowed by their creator with certain inalienable rights.

The idea of moral order that is expressed in this declaration and that has since become dominant in our world is what I have been calling the modern moral order. It is quite different from the orders that preceded it because it starts from individuals and doesn't see these as set a priori within a hierarchical order, outside of which they wouldn't be fully human agents. Its members are not agents who are essentially embedded in a society that reflects and connects with the cosmos, but rather disembedded individuals who come to associate together. The design underlying the association is that each, in pursuing his or her own purposes in life, acts to benefit others mutually. It calls for a society structured for mutual benefit, in which each respects the rights of others, and offers them mutual help of certain kinds. The most influential early articulator of this formula is John Locke, but the basic conception of such an order of mutual service has come down to us through a series of variants, including more radical ones, such as those presented by Rousseau and Marx.

In the earlier days, when the plan was understood as providential and the order seen as natural law, which is the same as the law of God, building a society that fulfils these requirements was seen as fulfilling the design of God. To live in such a society was to live in one where God was present, not at all in the way that belonged to the enchanted world, through the sacred, but because we were following His design. God is present as the designer of the way we live. We see ourselves, to quote a famous phrase, as "one people under God."

In thus taking the United States as a paradigm case of this new idea of order, I am following Robert Bellah's tremendously fertile idea of an American "civil religion." Of course, the concept is understandably and rightly contested today, because some of the conditions of this religion are now being challenged, but there is no doubt that Bellah has captured something essential about American society, both at its inception and for about two centuries thereafter.

The fundamental idea, that America had a vocation to carry out God's purposes, which alone makes sense of the passages Bellah quotes, for instance, from Kennedy's inaugural address, and even more from Lincoln's second inaugural, and which can seem strange and threatening to many unbelievers in America today, has to be understood in relation to this conception of an order of free, rights-bearing individuals. This was what was invoked in the Declaration of Independence, which appealed to "the Laws of Nature and of Nature's God." The rightness of these laws, for both deists and theists, was grounded in their being part of the providential design. What the activism of the American Revolutionaries added to this was a view of history as the theater in which this design was to be progressively realized and of their own society as the place where this realization was to be consummated—what Lincoln would later refer to as "the last best hope on earth." It was this notion of themselves as fulfilling divine purposes that, along with the biblical culture of Protestant America, facilitated the analogy with ancient Israel that often recurs in American official rhetoric of the early days.[22]

The confusion today arises from the fact that there is both continuity and discontinuity. What continues is the importance of some form of the modern idea of moral order. This gives the sense that Americans are still operating on the same principles as the Founders. The rift comes from the fact that what makes this order the right one is, for many though not by any means for all, no longer God's Providence; the order is grounded in nature alone, or in some concept of civilization, or even in supposedly unchallengeable a priori principles, often inspired by Kant. Thus some Americans want to rescue the Constitution from God, whereas others see this as doing violence to it. Hence the contemporary American Kulturkampf.

The young American republic is one paradigm of this new kind of relation of polity to God (not *the* paradigm, as many Americans are tempted to believe). This is the relation that I have called "neo-Durkheimian."[23] We can discern here a pattern that is central to what we might call the age of mobilization. The modern citizen social imaginary contrasts various premodern forms in that these reflect an "embedded" understanding of human life. In an ancien régime kingdom, we would have been seen as already, since time out of mind, defined as subjects of the king and, indeed, placed more exactly, as serfs of this lord, who holds from a duke, who holds from the king; or as bourgeois of this city, who holds from, and so on; or members of this cathedral chapter, which is under this bishop, who relates to both pope and king; and so on. Our relation to the whole would be mediated. The modern citizen imaginary, by contrast, sees us all as coming together to form a political entity, to which we all relate in the same way, as equal members. This entity has to be (or had to be, if it's already up and running) constructed. However much various modern ideologies, like nationalism, may convince us that we were always, since time out of mind, members of the *X* people (even though our ancestors didn't fully realize it, even were forced/induced to speak the *Y*'s language), and however much this gives us the vocation to construct our own state, *X*-land, nevertheless, this state has (had) to be constructed. People need(ed) to be convinced that they were really *X*es, and not *Y*s (Ukrainians and not Poles).

Two related features are crucial to this self-understanding. The first is that realizing who we really are (*X*es) requires (required) mobilization. We had to be brought to act together to erect our state: rebel against the *Y*s, appeal to the League of Nations, or whatever. The second is that this mobilization is inseparable from a (re)definition of identity: we have to define ourselves, saliently, even sometimes primarily, as *X*es, and not as a host of other things that we also are or could be (Poles, or Catholic-Uniates, or just members of this village, or just peasants, etc.).

These new entities—citizen states or other products of mobilization—are ordered around certain common poles of identity, let's call them "political identities." This doesn't have to be a linguistically defined nation, of course (though it often has been in the West). It can be a religious confession; it can be certain principles of government (Revolutionary France and the United States); it can be historical links; and so on.

This allows us to see the U.S. case as one example of a widespread feature of the modern world in the age of mobilization. Political identities can be woven around religious or confessional definitions. Thus, in the course of modern history, confessional allegiances have come to be woven into the sense of identity of certain ethnic, national, class, or regional groups. Britain and the United States are powerful, independent nations. But this kind of identification often happens with marginal or oppressed populations. Polish and Irish Catholic identities are well-known cases in point. The erstwhile French-Canadian one is another.

The link here between group and confession is not of the "ancien régime" type that we saw in counter-Revolutionary France, even though the same Catholic Church is involved. Throne and altar can't be allied, because the throne is alien, not just when it is Lutheran, Anglican, or Orthodox, but even where it is Catholic (Vienna). Resentment of elites becomes marginal to the extent that these elites lose power and privilege. But the sense of national domination and oppression, the sense of virtue in suffering and struggle, is deeply interwoven with religious belief and allegiance—even to the point of such rhetorical excesses as the depiction of Poland as "Christ crucified among the nations." The result is what I'm calling a "neo-Durkheimian" effect, where the senses of belonging to group and confession are fused, and the moral issues of the group's history tend to be coded in religious categories. (The rival language for oppressed people was always that of the French Revolution. This had its moments in each of the subaltern nations mentioned here: the United Irish, Papineau's rebellion in 1837, Dabrowski's legion; but in each case, the Catholic coding later took the upper hand.)

My "neo-Durkheimian" category can even be expanded to include a founding of political identity on an antireligious philosophical stance, as we saw with the long-standing "republican" French identity. The long-standing *guerre franco-française*, the long-running battle between republicans and Catholic monarchists, was in this sense fought between two neo-Durkheimian identities. These then contrast with other kinds of political identities, those founded on a supposed linguistic-historical nation, for instance, or on a certain constitutional order.

This last, French case shows that neo-Durkheimian identity mobilization extends well beyond established nations, or even wannabe nations, like Poland or Ireland. There are also cases of confessional mobilization that aim to have political impact, even where this is purely defensive and can't hope to issue in independent nationhood, as with Catholics in Germany during the Kulturkampf, and Dutch pillarization.

Now this phenomenon, religiously defined political identity mobilization, obviously has a tremendous present and (I fear) future in our world. We are almost at a point where my narratively based categorization should tip over into a discussion of the contemporary world. I certainly want to undertake this, but I crave the reader's patience, because I want to draw some other categories from our history, including those that arise from the decay of the neo-Durkheimian forms.

Before discussing these, I want to turn to another feature of the age of mobilization, the intrication of religion and morality, or religion and civilization. As a lead-in to this, we should look at the way in which mobilization began to alter the structure of churches.

David Martin, in a number of insightful works,[24] has developed an interesting account of the "Protestant," more particularly "Anglophone," path of historical development. This comes about in societies in which the reigning forms of social imaginary center more and more on the order of mutual benefit, and the ancien régime order is seen as distant and somewhat abhorrent, in short, "Papist."

In keeping with this outlook, it seems more and more evident in these cultures that valid religious adherence can only be voluntary. Forcing it has less and less legitimacy. And so popular alienation from elite-dominated religion can take the form of new voluntary associations, rather different from the earlier churches. The prototype of these is Wesleyan Methodists. But the real explosion in such free churches occurred in the United States at the end of the eighteenth century, and it transformed the face of American religion.

With the Methodists, we have something new, neither a church nor a sect but a proto-form of what we now call a "denomination." A "church" in this Troeltschian sense claims to gather within it all members of society; like the Catholic church, it sees its vocation as being the church for everyone. Some of the main Reformation churches had the same aspiration and often managed to take with them into dissidence whole societies, for instance, in Germany, Scandinavia, and initially England as well.

The denomination clearly belongs to the age of mobilization. It is not a divinely established body (though in another sense the broader "church" may be seen as such), but something that we must create—not just at our whim, but to fulfil the plan of God. In this, it resembles the new republic as providentially conceived in its civil religion. There is an affinity between the two, and each strengthened the other. That is, the voluntaristic dimension of the Great Awakening in the mid eighteenth century obviously prepared the way for the revolutionary break of 1776, and in turn, the ethos of self-governing "independence" in the new republic meant that the second Awakening in the early nineteenth century involved an even greater profusion of denominational initiatives than before.[25]

Now, it is clear that this kind of spontaneously created affinity group offered unique advantages when migration, social change, or class conflict rendered older, more inclusive churches in one way or another alien and forbidding for nonelites. Methodism was certainly not devised in order to accommodate class division; Wesley himself clove to the most unshakeable Tory convictions about social order and even condemned the American Revolution, in which so many of his transatlantic followers enthusiastically participated. Later, the main Methodist connections in England tried to damp worker militancy against employers (although they were ready to mobilize both sides of industry against Tory landowners).

Nevertheless, whatever the original idea of the founders, the form was there, ready to give shape and expression to the religious aspirations and insights of some group, whether defined by class, by locality (such as mining villages in Northern England), by region (like Wales), by region plus ideological affinity (e.g., the splits between northern and southern Methodists and Baptists in the United States), or even by race (again, the U.S. case). Whereas in societies where the model of one big, society-wide church, in continuity with the original divine foundation, dominated the imagination (i.e., Catholic societies, but also some Lutheran ones, and even, to a lesser degree, some Calvinist ones, such as Scotland, finding a creative solution to nonelite alienation within the compass of Christian faith was extremely difficult (but not impossible, as we shall see in certain examples below), where the voluntarist culture of mobilization was already part of religious self-understanding, new faith initiatives could more easily arise. The denominational imaginary made possible a flexibility unknown in most Continental societies.[26]

A number of different initiatives in fact took place, but the most impressive class was made up of what are loosely called "evangelical" modes of revival, which were widespread in Britain and America from the end of the eighteenth century on.[27] At their most intense, these centered on certain central doctrines of the Reformation: our sinful condition and the need for conversion, for a turning to God in faith, which would open us to His grace. The stress was often on this conversion as a personal act, undertaken for oneself, rather than as a disposition inhering in the group; and it was often taken, dramatically, under the press of powerful emotions, and in public.

Here was a powerful transformational perspective, defined on one side by a deep, potentially overpowering sense of sin and imperfection, and on the other by an overwhelming feeling of the love of God and its power to heal—in a word, of "amazing grace." As in the earlier Reformation, this new empowerment was meant to yield fruit in an ordered life. And order and disorder were conceived in terms which were very understandable in the existing predicament of the popular strata of the time, where people often struggled to find their bearings in a more and more market-driven economy, in which survival often depended upon adaptation to new conditions, migration, or adopting new work disciplines outside of traditional social forms. The danger was that of sinking into modes of behavior that were idle, irresponsible, undisciplined, and wasteful. And behind these lay the lure of traditional forms of recreation and conviviality, which could immure you in dysfunctional modes—in the first place, drink and the tavern. That is why temperance was one of the central goals of evangelical cultures, in a way that sounds totally excessive to many contemporary ears. We are perhaps sobered (if that's the word), however, when we learn how much of a curse drink could be; for instance, that in the United States in the 1820s, liquor consumption per capita was four times what it is today.[28]

Along with drink, aiding and abetting it, were other favored activities: cruel sports, gambling, and sexual promiscuity. This understanding of disorder targeted certain long-standing male forms of conviviality outside the family. The new understanding of order was family-centered and often involved identifying the male as the source of potential disruption and the female as victim and as guardian of this ordered domestic space. Callum Brown even speaks of a "demonization" of male qualities and a "feminization of piety."[29] Order required the male to be a family man and a good provider, and this required that he become educated, disciplined, and a hard worker. Sobriety, industry, and discipline were the principal virtues. Education and self-help were highly valued qualities. By attaining these, the man acquired a certain dignity, that of a free, self-governing agent. The goal could be captured in two terms: on the one hand, the "respectability" that went with an ordered life has been much stressed; but along with this, we should place free agency, the dignity of the citizen. Evangelicalism was basically an antihierarchical force, part of the drive for democracy.

This connection of salvation and sanctity with a certain moral order in our lives reminds us of the first Reformation, of which evangelicalism is in a sense a reprise, in different circumstances and with an even more central emphasis on personal commitment. We can also look in the other direction and note how this movement carries on in our day, not so much in its home terrain in Britain and the United States (though it is still very strong in the latter), as nowadays in Latin America, Africa, and Asia.[30] And we can note the same connection between accepting salvation and putting a certain kind of order in one's life, so that men in Latin America become more family-centered, deserting certain kinds of male conviviality that stress machismo, becoming sober and good providers. Indeed, we might even extend the comparison to include non-Christian movements like the Nation of Islam in the United States.[31]

We can see that these movements have a powerful effect in "secular" history, that of enabling certain populations to become capable of functioning as productive, ordered agents in a new, nontraditional environment, be it nineteenth-century Manchester, twentieth-century Sao Paolo, or twenty-first-century Lagos. This gives rise to two reflections. First, will this tight identification of faith and a certain morality or order end up undercutting faith, as I have already argued it did among elites in the seventeenth and eighteenth centuries, and as it seems to have done in Britain in the twentieth? It does indeed seem that a faith that was originally connected with a sense of one's own powerlessness to bring order to one's life unaided, contrasted with the efficacy of grace to do this, will lose some of its relevance and convincing power if/when the required disciplines become second nature and, instead of feeling powerless, one feels in control of one's life. But however this may seem borne out by the long-term fate of earlier waves, we would be very foolish to predict what will happen to current waves of Pentecostalism in the Third World, not only because they have features of their own, unmatched by their predecessors, but because they are happening in a quite different social context, and our past experience concerns only the West.

Once again, I am running ahead of my argument. I have still further categories to bring out. The next flows directly from the above discussion of evangelical denominationalism. This was linked to powerful movements of moral reform, on the one hand, and it could be integrated into a neo-Durkheimian political identity, on the other, as in the United States. But these two links could themselves be inwardly connected. Political identity could itself be partly defined by high moral standards.

Over a long period, for many of the English, Christianity of a certain Protestant variety was identified with certain moral standards, often summed up in the word *decency*,[32] and England was thought to be the pre-eminent carrier of this on the world scene. This was what we could call the "established synthesis." For many, English patriotism was built around this complex of beliefs and norms. Many Protestant Americans, and later some Catholic ones, have thought that the United States has a providential mission to spread liberal democracy among the rest of humankind.

In this neo-Durkheimian form, religious belonging is central to political identity. But the religious dimension also figures in what we might call "civilizational" identity, the sense people have of the basic order by which they live, even imperfectly, as good, and (usually) as superior to the ways of life of outsiders, be they "barbarians," "savages," or (in the more polite contemporary language) "less developed" peoples.

In fact, most of the time we relate to the order established in our "civilization" the way people have always related to their most fundamental sense of order; we have both a sense of security in believing that it is really in effect in our world and also a sense of our own superiority and goodness deriving from the confidence that we participate in it and uphold it. This means that we can react with great insecurity when we see that it can be breached from the outside, as at the World Trade Center, but also that we are even more shaken when we feel that it might be undermined from within, or that we might be betraying it. There not only our security is threatened, but also our sense of our own integrity and goodness. To see this questioned is profoundly unsettling, ultimately threatening our ability to act.

That is why, in earlier times, we see people lashing out at such moments of threat, scapegoating violence against "the enemy within," meeting the threat to our security by finessing that to our integrity, deflecting it onto the scapegoats. In earlier periods of Latin Christendom, Jews and witches were cast in this unenviable role. The evidence that we are still tempted to have recourse to similar mechanisms in our "enlightened" age is unsettling. But it would not be the first such paradox in history if a doctrine of peaceful universalism were invoked to mobilize scapegoating violence.[33]

The point I want to make about British and later American patriotism, based as it was at first on the sense of fulfilling God's design, is that national identity was based on a self-ascribed pre-eminence in realizing a certain civilizational superiority. The superiority may have ultimately been understood as that of "Christendom" over infidel religions, but within Christendom, Britain/America stood at the cutting edge.

This sense of superiority, originally religious in essence, can and does undergo a "secularization" as the sense of civilizational superiority becomes detached from Providence and attributed to race, or Enlightenment, or even some combination of the two. But the point of identifying this sense of order is that it provides another niche, as it were, in which God can be present in our lives, or in our social imaginary—the author not just of the design that defines our political identity but also of the design that defines civilizational order.

But why distinguish the two when they so obviously go together, as in the paradigm case of the United States? Because they don't always fit together in this way, but can operate separately. It is absolutely crucial to much Christian apologetics from the French Revolution onward that the Christian faith is essential to the maintenance of civilizational order, whether this is defined in terms of the modern moral order or in terms of the earlier hierarchical complementarity. This is the very staple of counter-Revolutionary thought, as it flows from the pen, for instance, of Joseph de Maistre. But one can hear something similar today, in a quite neo-Durkheimian context, from some parts of the religious Right in the United States. The doctrine is that our order is not stable unless based on an explicit recognition that we are following God's plan. So much for the belief involved.

But this can issue in a social imaginary: that our order is now stable, because we are following God's plan; or that our order is threatened, because we are deviating from the plan. This sense of the presence or the threatened absence of God in our world, as the designer/guarantor of the civilizational order, can be very present, even where it is not linked with a sense that our nation singles itself out by its pre-eminence in realizing His order. It may be relatively unhooked from our political identity.

Think of the Catholic recovery in France after the Restoration, and of Catholic reactions in Germany to the Kulturkampf. These were, of course, phenomena of mobilization. They had to be; there was no other way to achieve their ends. And in some cases, they were animated by their own definition of national identity, as with Royalism in France. But even in this case, and frequently where there was no such over-all proposal for the nation, as in Germany, they showed an acute sense of the church as essential to civilizational order. This was even the basis of the strange alliance, in so many ways against nature, between the positivist Maurras and right-wing Catholics in France, up to the papal condemnation of Action Française in 1926. And a great many of the conversions to Catholicism in the nineteenth and early twentieth centuries were inspired by, or at least interwoven with, this sense that the Church was a bulwark of order in a world threatened with moral and social disintegration.[34]

There were, in the end, strong analogies between evangelicalism and reconstituted post-Revolutionary Catholicism, for all the differences. We should mention, first of all, new or renewed forms of spirituality, with a strong emotional appeal: conversion to a loving God on one side, and devotions such as the Sacred Heart and that mobilized around the life and example of Thérèse de Lisieux, on the other. It would be a mistake to focus, as perhaps our sociological sensibility invites us to do, simply on the "functional" features of these faith forms, their providing people with the skills and disciplines they needed to operate in their changed circumstances. All may share a certain liturgy and ethos. But various people will feel the need for some special, stronger, more focused, concentrated, and/or disciplined form of devotion, prayer, meditation, or dedication. It may be that they confront a crisis or a tough period in their lives, and they need to concentrate their spiritual resources to meet it. It may be that they feel their lives are too shallow or unfocussed, or all over the place; they need a stronger center, a point of concentration. It may be just that they feel the need to give some expression, some vent, to powerful feelings of gratitude, to acknowledge and rejoice in the gifts of God.

These forms of spirituality on both the Protestant and the Catholic sides were combined with attempts to inculcate the new ethos and disciplines necessary to function in a changed economy and society. The battle against drunkenness was also waged by priests in Irish parishes, at the same time as Nonconformity was campaigning for temperance.[35] On both sides, attempts to set up the necessary organs of economic survival, such as friendly societies and credit unions, were often linked with churches.

The various successful forms of faith in the age of mobilization combine these two strands; not only ethical/disciplinary, in which all (or most) partake, but also a series of special devotions, services, modes of prayer, and so on, for those who from time to time feel the need for some special form of dedication. These arise from individual choices, though they often are carried out in groups. They can be indefinitely varied and allow new forms to be created. A principal site of these on the Protestant side is, of course, the revival. On the Catholic side, we have novenas, retreats, special devotions (as to the Sacred Heart), pilgrimages, the steps of the Oratoire St-Joseph, and forms of service to priests, parish, and the like. St. Thérèse de Lisieux was an important trail-blazer in this kind of devotion.

These special forms were often gendered: Sacred Heart for the women, whereas the men would either opt out altogether from this dimension or else do something "active," like running Catholic trade unions.

I have been identifying three forms of religious life arising in the age of mobilization.

1. There are movements that weave together spiritual and devotional aspirations with personal and often collective empowerment, as in evangelical revivals and various movements of Catholic action, as well as Catholic prayer and devotion. Let's call these modes of empowering devotion.
2. Then there are interweavings of religious or confessional belonging with political identities—the neo-Durkheimian phenomenon.
3. Then there are the various ways in which religious or confessional faith becomes connected to our sense of civilizational order and the sense of security and/or superiority that connects to this. Let's call this the civilizational connection.

These can be happily intertwined, as in Anglophone Protestantism over many centuries; or they can exist quite separately from each other, as with various evangelical or Catholic movements in the non(majority) Christian South, which are modes of (1) unconnected to (2) or (3), or in Catholic or Polish nationalism, where (2) exists without (1) or (3). And (3) notoriously can exist alone among beleaguered elites, who sense that their society is going to the dogs. Or (2) and (3) can be alloyed without (1), as in the nineteenth-century German *Kulturprotestantismus*.

But the major points of tension in the contemporary West come from a further stage of our story, the dramatic collapse in large parts of Western society in the last third of the twentieth century of (2) and (3), in societies where they had been strongly established.

Let's call this the age of authenticity. It appears that something has happened in the last half-century, perhaps even less, which has profoundly altered the conditions of belief in our societies.

I believe, along with many others, that our North Atlantic civilization has been undergoing a cultural revolution in recent decades. The sixties perhaps provide the hinge moment, at least symbolically. It is, on the one hand, an individuating revolution, which may sound strange, because our modern age was already based on a certain individualism. But this has shifted onto a new axis, without deserting the others. As well as moral/

spiritual and instrumental individualisms, we now have a widespread "expressive" individualism. This is, of course, not totally new. Expressivism was an invention of the Romantic period in the late eighteenth century. Intellectual and artistic elites searched for an authentic way of living or expressing themselves throughout the nineteenth century. What is new is that this kind of self-orientation seems to have become a mass phenomenon.

Its most obvious external manifestation has perhaps been the consumer revolution. With postwar affluence and the diffusion of what many had considered luxuries before came a new concentration on private space and the means to fill it, which began distending the relations of previously close-knit working-class or peasant communities, even of extended families.[36] Modes of mutual help dropped off, perhaps partly because of the receding of dire necessity. People concentrated more on their own lives and those of their nuclear families. They moved to new towns or suburbs, lived more on their own, tried to make a life out of the ever-growing gamut of new goods and services on offer, from washing machines to packaged holidays, and the freer individual life-styles they facilitated. The "pursuit of happiness" took on new, more immediate meaning, with a growing range of easily available means. And in this newly individuated space, the customer was encouraged more and more to express her taste, to furnish her space according to her own needs and affinities, as only the rich had been able to do in previous eras.

Of course, the "pursuit of (individual) happiness" has been integral to liberalism since the American Revolution, which enshrined it as one of a trinity of basic rights. But in the first century of the American republic, it was inscribed within certain taken-for-granted boundaries. First, there was the citizen ethic, centered on the good of self-rule, which Americans were meant to live up to. Beyond this, there were certain basic demands of sexual morality, of what later would be called "family values," as well as the values of hard work and productivity, which gave a framework to the pursuit of individual good. To move outside of these was not so much to seek one's happiness as to head toward perdition. There seemed, therefore, nothing contrary to the three basic rights enshrined by the Declaration of Independence in society's striving to inculcate, even in certain cases (e.g., sexual morality) to enforce these norms. European societies were perhaps less keen than the Americans to enforce various modes of social conformity, but their code was, if anything, even more restrictive.

The erosion of these limits on individual fulfillment has been in some cases gradual, with oscillations forward and backward, but with an unmistakable general tendency over the long run. Michael Sandel has noted how the concern for the citizen ethic was much more prominent in the first century of American history. Brandeis could argue the antitrust case at the beginning of the century partly on the ground that large combines erode "the moral and civic capacities that equip workers to think like citizens."[37] But as the twentieth century advanced, such considerations increasingly took a back seat. Courts became more concerned to defend the "privacy" of the individual.

It is really in the period after the Second World War that the limits on the pursuit of individual happiness have been most clearly set aside, particularly in sexual matters, but also in other domains as well. The U.S. Supreme Court decisions invoking privacy, and thereby restricting the range of the criminal law, provide a clear example. Something similar happens with the revisions of the Canadian Criminal Code under Trudeau, which expressed his principle that "the State has no business in the bedrooms of the nation." Michel Winock notes the change in *mentalités* in France during the seventies. "The lifting of censorship, the 'liberalization of mores' . . . became law" with the legalization of abortion, divorce reform, the authorization of pornographic films, and so on.[38] This evolution takes place in virtually all Atlantic societies.

The heart of this revolution lies in sexual mores. This was a long time a-building, as the previous paragraph indicates, but the development took place earlier among cultural elites. In the 1960s, it was generalized to all classes. This is obviously a profound shift. The relativization of chastity and monogamy, the affirmation of homosexuality as a legitimate option, all these have a tremendous impact on churches, whose stance in recent centuries has laid so much stress on these issues and where piety has often been identified with a very stringent sexual code. I shall return to this shortly.

Here I want to concentrate on what is relevant to our purposes, which we could describe as the imagined place of the sacred, in the widest sense. Drawing an ideal type of this new social imaginary of expressive individualism, we could say that it is quite non-Durkheimian.

Under the ancien regime or "paleo-Durkheimian" dispensation, my connection to the sacred entailed my belonging to a church, in principle co-extensive with society, although in fact there were perhaps tolerated outsiders and as yet undisciplined heretics. The neo-Durkheimian dispensation saw me enter the denomination of my choice, but that in turn connected me to a broader, more elusive "church" and, more importantly, to a political entity with a providential role to play. In both these cases, there was a link between adhering to God and belonging to the state—hence my epithet *Durkheimian*.

The neo-Durkheimian mode could involve an important step toward the individual and the right of choice. In societies with the appropriate kind of religious structures, one joined a denomination because it seemed right to do so. Indeed, it now comes to seem that there is no way of being in the "church" except through such a choice. Where under paleo-Durkheimian rules one could—and did—demand that people be forcibly integrated, be rightly connected with God against their will, this now often makes no sense. Coercion comes to seem not only wrong, but absurd and thus obscene. We saw an important watershed in the development of this consciousness in the reaction of educated Europe to the Revocation of the Edict of Nantes. Even the Pope thought it was a mistake.

The expressivist outlook takes this a stage farther. The religious life or practice that I become part of must not only be my choice, but it must speak to me, it must make sense in terms of my spiritual development as I understand this. This takes us farther. The choice of denomination was understood to take place within a fixed cadre, say, that of the apostles' creed, the faith of the broader "church." Within this framework of belief, I choose the church in which I feel most comfortable. But if the focus is now going to be on my spiritual path, thus on what insights come to me in the subtler languages that I find meaningful, then maintaining this or any other framework becomes increasingly difficult.

But this means that my place in the broader "church" may not be that relevant for me, and along with this, my place in a "people under God" or other such political agency with a providential role. In the new expressivist dispensation, there is no necessary embedding of our link to the sacred in any particular broader framework, whether "church" or state.

This is why the developments of recent decades in France have been so destabilizing for both sides of the old *guerre franco-française.* Not only did the church see a sharp drop in adherence, but young people began to drop out of the rival Jacobin and/or communist worldviews as well. In keeping with the dynamic of baroque, paleo-Durkheimian clericalism, the struggle threw up a kind of humanism that aspired in its own way to be a kind of national "church," that of the Republic and its principles, the framework within which people would hold their different metaphysical and (if they insisted) religious views. The Republic played a kind of neo-Durkheimian dispensation against the paleo-Durkheimianism of the clerical monarchists. This tradition even took over the term *sacred* for itself. (Think of *l'union sacrée*, of *la main sacrilège*, which killed Marat, etc. This usage obviously facilitated Durkheim's theoretical use of the term to over-arch both ancien régime and Republic.) It is not surprising that both Catholicism and this brand of republicanism undergo defections in the new, post-Durkheimian dispensation of expressive individualism.

This changes utterly the ways in which ideals of order used to be interwoven with the polemic between belief and unbelief. What has changed to make this much less the case is not only that we have achieved a broad consensus on our ideal of moral order. It is also that, in our post-Durkheimian dispensation, the "sacred," either religious or *laïque*, has become uncoupled from our political allegiance. It was the rivalry between two such kinds of global allegiance that animated the *guerre franco-française.* It was also this older dispensation that could send masses of men into the trenches to fight for their country in 1914 and keep them there, with few desertions and rare instances of mutiny, for over four years.[39]

I speak of this in the past tense, because in many of the countries that were the prime belligerents in this war the new dispensation has probably made this kind of thing impossible. But it is also clear that the geographic area for which this holds true is limited. Down in the Balkans, not that much has changed since the wars that broke out in 1911. And we should not be too sanguine in believing that the change is irreversible even in the core North Atlantic societies.

But for the moment, Western societies seem to have passed a crucial watershed. While in the original paleo-Durkheimian dispensation people could easily feel that they had to obey the command to abandon their own religious instincts, because these, being at variance with orthodoxy, must be heretical or at least inferior; while those inhabiting a neo-Durkheimian world felt that their choice had to conform to the overall framework of the "church" or favored nation, so that even Unitarians and ethical societies presented themselves as denominations with services and sermons on Sunday; in the post-Durkheimian age many people are uncomprehending in face of the demand to conform. Just as in the neo-Durkheimian world joining a church you don't believe in seems not just wrong, but absurd, contradictory, so in the post-Durkheimian age seems the idea of adhering to a spirituality that doesn't present itself as your path, the one that moves and inspires you. For many people today, to set aside their own path in order to conform to some external authority just doesn't seem comprehensible as a form of spiritual life.[40] The injunction is, in the words of a speaker at a New Age festival: "Only accept what rings true to your own inner Self."[41]

Paleo-, *neo-*, and *post-Durkheimian* describe ideal types. My claim is not that any of these provides a total description, but that our Western history has moved through these dispensations, and that the last has come to color our age more and more.

That the new dispensation doesn't provide the whole story is readily evident from struggles in contemporary society. In a sense, part of what drove the Moral Majority and motivates the Christian Right in the United States is an aspiration to re-establish something of the fractured neo-Durkheimian understanding that used to define the nation, where being American would once more have a connection with theism, with being "one people under God," or at least with the ethic that was interwoven with this. Similarly, much of the leadership of the Catholic Church, led by the Vatican, is trying to resist the challenge to monolithic authority implicit in the new expressivist understanding of spirituality. And the Catholic Church in the United States frequently lines up with the Christian Right in attempts to reestablish earlier versions of the moral consensus that enjoyed neo-Durkheimian religious grounding.[42] For all these groups, the idea remains strong that there is a link between Christian faith and civilizational order. But the embattled nature of these attempts shows how we have slid out of the old dispensation. This shift goes a long way to explain the conditions of belief in our day.

The last paragraph takes us into a new terrain. The expressive revolution has undermined not only neo-Durkheimian identities but also the link between Christian faith and civilizational order. A leading feature of many of the religious forms of the age of mobilization described above was their strong sense of an ordered life, along with their attempts to aid, persuade, or pressure their members into realizing this. As I indicated above, it was perhaps inevitable, as the new disciplines became internalized, that this disciplining function would be less valued, that some of the rigid measures earlier seen as essential, such as absolute temperance or total Sabbath observance, would appear irksome to the descendants of those who had put them in place. There was always a certain resistance to evangelicals, on the alleged grounds that they were puritans, spoil sports, sowers of division. Fictional characters like Dickens's Melchisedech Howler and Jabez Fireworks, as well as George Eliot's Bulstrode, express some of this hostility, and there were sometimes criticisms of Methodists, with their insistence on temperance and banning village sports, as disrupting convivial community culture and setting people against each other.[43] A more general reaction set in toward the end of the nineteenth century against evangelical morality as dessicating, repressing freedom and self-development, imposing uniformity, denying beauty, and the like. Writers like Shaw, Ibsen, and Nietzsche articulated this very powerfully, and something of this is expressed in J. S. Mill's famous "pagan self-assertion is better than Christian self-denial."[44] For his part, Arnold bemoaned the lack of cultivation of the Nonconformist middle class. And the culture of Bloomsbury can be seen as formed partly in reaction to this whole religious climate.

All this was intensified by the cultural revolution of the 1960s, not only in that more people were swept into a stance in opposition to much of the religious ethic but also in that the new sexual mores were even more strongly at odds with it. A tripartite connection had in the past seemed to many absolutely unquestionable: between Christian faith and an ethic of discipline and self-control, even of abnegation, on the one hand; and between this ethic and civilizational order, on the other. But, as I described above, the second link has come to seem less and less credible to more and more people. The pursuit of happiness has come to seem not only not to need a restrictive sexual ethic and the disciplines of deferred gratification but actually to demand their transgression in the name of self-fulfillment. The people who feel this most strongly are, of course, precisely those for whom many of these disciplines have become second nature, not needing a strong ethical/ spiritual backing to maintain themselves. To the surprise of many Weberian sociologists of my generation, the children of the 1960s and 1970s managed to relax many of the traditional disciplines in their personal lives while keeping them in their work life. This is not necessarily easy to manage; some people can't make it. There are, moreover, whole milieus where the disciplines are still too new and distant from their way of life for this kind of picking and choosing to be possible. As David Martin puts it, in describing the advance of Pentecostalism in the global South:

> In the developed world the permissions and releases can be pursued by quite large numbers of people while ignoring the economic disciplines, at least for a quite extended period of licence, but in the developing world the economic disciplines cannot be evaded. Though in the developed world you can accept the disciplines in your working life and ignore them elsewhere, in the developing world your disciplines must govern your whole life, or you fall by the wayside—or fall into crime.[45]

This feat of selective assumption of disciplines, which supposes a long, often multi-generational interiorization, is a crucial facilitating condition of the new stance, even though the expressive revolution provided the reason to transgress the old boundaries. At other times and places, such principled transgression seems insane, almost suicidal.

Where the link between disciplines and civilizational order is broken, but that between Christian faith and the disciplines remains unchallenged, expressivism and the conjoined sexual revolution have alienated many people from the churches, on two counts. First, those who have gone along with the current changes find themselves profoundly at odds with the sexual ethic that churches have been propounding. Second, their sense of following their own path is offended by what they experience as the "authoritarian" approach of churches, laying down the law without waiting for a reply.

Churches find it hard to talk to people in this mindset. Talking to them is not a matter of simply agreeing with what they say. There has been too much hype, utopian illusion, and reacting to old taboos in the sexual revolution for this to make sense. And indeed, forty years on, this is more and more evident to lots of young people. (Which is not to say that churches don't also have something to learn from this whole transition.[46])

But just as, in the face of any responsible agent, those who claim to possess some wisdom have an obligation to explain it persuasively, starting from where their interlocutor is, so it is here. The attachment to a rigid code, as well as the sense of being an embattled band of the faithful, that developed through the defensive postures of the last two centuries makes it almost impossible to find language here.

The break has been profound. As Callum Brown has shown for the evangelical case, the ethical stance was predicated on an idea of women as wanting a stable family life, which was constantly endangered by male temptation—to drinking, gambling, infidelity. We see similar ideas propounded on the Catholic side. This way of defining the issues was not without basis in the past, when women feared the consequences for themselves and their children of male irresponsibility and even violence, and it is not without basis in many milieus in the present, especially in the global South, as David Martin has pointed out.[47]

We connect up here with a profound development, evident across the confessional divide over the last two or three centuries, which has been called the "feminization" of Christianity, about which Callum Brown speaks in his interesting recent book.[48] It obviously has something to do with the close symbiosis established between Christian faith and the ethic of "family values" and disciplined work, which has downgraded if not been directed against military and combative modes of life, as well as forms of male sociability: drinking, gambling, sport, which took men outside the arenas of both work and home. This has not just been an issue for churches; we can see the conflict—and the ambivalence—reflected in the whole society, with the development of the ideal of "polite" society, based on commerce in the eighteenth century. Even some of the intellectual figures who defined and welcomed this new development, such as Adam Smith or Adam Ferguson, expressed their misgivings about it. It might lead to an atrophy of the martial virtues necessary to the self-governing citizen. Others feared an "effeminization" of the male.[49] Feminization of the culture went parallel to feminization of the faith

In the Christian context, this was reflected, as well as further entrenched, by a relative drop in male practice as against female. "The men are leaving" is the unanimous lament of priests in the Ain Department in the nineteenth century, particularly in the latter half.[50] This absence often reflects a sense of male pride and dignity, which is seen as incompatible with a too unbridled devotion; there is something "womanish" about this kind of dedication. This sense was connected to, fed, and was fed by a certain mistrust of clerical power: on the one hand, the priest (whose habit resembled that of a woman) had perhaps too much power over wives and daughters; but on the other hand, that was no bad thing, because he taught them chastity and fidelity, and offered security to the male head of the household. At the same time, however good for women, this acceptance of clerical leadership was incompatible with the independence that was a crucial part of male dignity. Obviously, this attitude could give a point of purchase for the philosophical anticlericalism of the Republican.[51]

The present sexual revolution in the West has challenged the whole picture of male and female on which this understanding of civilizational order reposed.[52] It has brought with it a gamut of feminist positions, and in some of these women demand for themselves the right to sexual exploration and unfettered fulfillment that was previously thought central to male desire. This totally undercuts the conceptual base of the hitherto dominant ethic. In a line from a 1970 Church of Scotland report on the issue: "It is the promiscuous girl who is the real problem here."[53]

Of course, not everybody agrees with this account of female desire. But it shows a new uncertainty about the forms of women's identity—matched by corresponding uncertainty among men. It is not possible to address the question of sexual ethics without engaging with these issues.

II

At last I come to our present situation and those elements of it that we might expect to continue into our future. I want to take this in two stages: first, the situation in the "West," and then later some speculations about possible analogies to phenomena elsewhere in the world.

Clearly, the three phenomena I mentioned above are prominent parts of our present/ future: (1) modes of empowering devotion; (2) the neo-Durkheimian phenomenon; and (3) religion as the basis for moral/civilizational order. But a salient feature of the West today is the tension, even conflict, between one or more of these, and the slide toward expressive individualism and an ethic of authenticity. I want to look at several features of our Western situation; let's first take up this tension.

The generations formed by the cultural revolution of the 1960s are in some respects deeply alienated from a strong traditional model of Christian faith in the West. We have already seen how they are refractory to the sexual disciplines that were part of the good Christian life as understood, for instance, in the nineteenth-century evangelical revivals in English-speaking countries. Indeed, the contemporary swing goes beyond just repudiating these very high standards. Even the limitations that were generally accepted among traditional peasant communities, which clerical minorities thought were terribly lax and which they were always trying to get to shape up, have been set aside by large numbers of people in our society today. The clergy used to frown on premarital sex, for instance, and were concerned when couples who came to be married were already expecting a child. But the same peasant communities, although they thought it quite normal to try things out beforehand, particularly to be sure that they could have children, accepted that it was mandatory to confirm their union by a ceremony. Those who tried to step outside these limits were brought back into line by strong social pressure, charivaris, or "rough music."[54]

But we have clearly stepped way beyond these limits today. Not only do people experiment widely before settling down in a stable couple, but they also form couples without ever marrying; in addition, they form, then break, then re-form these relationships. Our peasant ancestors also engaged in a kind of "serial monogamy," but in their cases the earlier unions were always broken by death, while in ours it is divorce (or in the case of unmarried partners, just moving out) that ends them.[55]

There is something deeply at odds here with all forms of sexual ethic—be it folk tradition or Christian doctrine—that saw the stability of marriage as essential to social order. But there is more than this. Christians did see their faith as essential to civilizational order, but this was not the only source of the sexual ethic that has dominated modern Western Christianity. There were also strong images of spirituality that enshrined particular images of sexual purity. We can see these developing in the early modern period. John Bossy has argued that, in the medieval understanding of the seven deadly sins, the sins of the spirit (pride, envy, anger) were seen as more grievous than those of the flesh (gluttony, lechery, sloth; avarice could be put in either column). But during the Catholic Reformation concupiscence as the crucial obstacle to sanctity came to be emphasized more and more.[56]

What was perhaps ancient was to see sexual ethics through a prism of pollution and purity. "Hence the ban on marriage during Lent and at other seasons, the doctrine that sexual acts between the married were always venially sinful, the purification of women after childbirth, the peculiar preoccupation with sexuality among priests."[57] The modern age seems to have spiritualized the underlying notion of purity and made it the principal gateway (or its opposite, the principal obstacle) in our approach to God.

In the terms I have been using in this study, we can think of the Catholic Reformation, especially in France, as an attempt to inculcate a deep, personal devotion to God (through Christ or Mary) in (potentially) everyone, an attempt, moreover, that was to be carried out mainly through the agency of the clergy, who would preach, persuade, cajole, or push their charges toward this new, higher orientation and away from the traditional, community, preaxial forms of the sacred. If we posit this as the goal, we can think of various ways in which one might try to encompass it. A heavy emphasis might be put on certain examples of sanctity, in the hope of awakening a desire to follow them. Or the major thrust might be to frighten people into shaping up, at least minimally. Of course, both of these paths were tried, but the overwhelming weight fell on the negative one. This was, indeed, part of the whole process of reform starting in the High Middle Ages. Jean Delumeau has spoken of "the pastoralia of fear."[58]

Perhaps we might just take this as a given, particularly as the tradition goes so far back before the modern period. But we can perhaps also see it as inseparable from the reforming enterprise itself. If the aim is not just to make certain forms of spirituality shine forth and draw as many people as possible to them but really to make everybody over (or everybody who is not heading for damnation), then perhaps the only way you can ever hope to produce this kind of mass movement is by leaning heavily on threat and fear. This is certainly the pattern set up very early on in the process of reform, in the preaching mission of wandering friars starting in the thirteenth century.

The irony is that, where clerical leadership really managed to transform a community, it was through the personal holiness of the incumbent and not through his parading the horrors of Hell. A particularly striking case is that of the saintly life and persevering ministry of the Curé d'Ars. But you can't expect a Jean Vianney in every parish. If the goal is to move everyone, even through spiritually unimpressive agents, then fear is your best bet.

To quote a mission preacher at the time of the Restoration in France:

> Soon the hour of your death will sound; continue the web of your disorders; sink yourselves deeper in the mire of your shameful passions; insult by the impiety of your heart Him who judges even the just. Soon you will fall under the pitiless blows of death, and the measure of your iniquities will be that of the fearful torments which will then be inflicted upon you.[59]

Once one goes this route, something else follows. The threat has to attach to very clearly defined failures. Do this, or else (damnation will follow). The "this" also has to be clearly definable. Of course, there were periods, particularly in the Calvinist theological context, in which it had to remain ultimately uncertain whether anyone had really been chosen by God. But as Weber pointed out, this is an unlivable predicament, and very soon certain signs of election crystallize, whatever the lack of theological warrant. In the context of the Catholic Reformation, the relevant standards are not signs of election but minimal conformity to the demands of God: the avoidance of mortal sin, or at least doing whatever is necessary to have these sins remitted.

What emerges from all this is what we might call "moralism," that is, the crucial importance given to a certain code in our spiritual lives. We should all come closer to God, but a crucial stage on this road has to be the minimal conformity to the code. Without this, you aren't even at the starting line, as it were, of this crucial journey. You are not in the game at all. This is perhaps not an outlook that squares easily with a reading of the New Testament, but it nevertheless achieved a kind of hegemony across broad reaches of the Christian church in the modern era.

This outlook ends up putting all the emphasis on what we should do, and/or what we should believe, to the detriment of spiritual growth. Sister Elisabeth Germain, analyzing a representative catechism in wide use in the nineteenth century, concludes that "Morality takes precedence over everything, and religion becomes its servant. Faith and the sacraments are no longer understood as the basis of the moral life, but as duties to be carried out, as truths that we must believe, and as means to help us fulfill these moral obligations."[60]

Now one can have clerically driven Reform, powered by fear of damnation, and hence moralism, and the code around which this crystallizes can nevertheless take different forms. The central issues could be questions of charity versus aggression, anger, and vengeance; or a central vector could be the issue of sexual purity. Again, both are present, but with a surprisingly strong emphasis on the sexual. We saw above that, in a sense, the emphasis shifted in this direction with the Catholic Reformation. It is not that sins of aggression, violence, or injustice were neglected. On the contrary. It is just that the code, the definition of what it is to get to the starting line, was extremely rigid about sexual matters. There were mortal sins in the other dimensions as well—for instance, murder— and there were many in the domain of church rules (e.g., skipping mass); but you could go quite far in being unjust and hard-hearted in your dealings with subordinates and others without incurring the automatic exclusion you would incur through sexual license. Sexual deviation and not listening to the church seemed to be the major domains where automatic excluders lurked. Sexual purity, along with obedience, was therefore given extraordinary salience.

Hence the tremendously (as it seems to us) disproportionate fuss that clergy made in nineteenth-century France about banning dancing, cleaning up folk festivals, and the like. (There are analogues, of course, among evangelicals in Protestant countries.) Young people were refused communion or absolution unless they gave these up altogether. The concern with this issue appears at certain moments obsessive.

I can't pretend to be able to explain this; but perhaps a couple of considerations can put it in context. The first is the pacification of modern society that was one of the chief fruits of reform, the fact that the level of everyday violence not related to wars, that caused by brigands, feuds, rebellions, clan rivalries, and the like, declined between the fifteenth and the nineteenth centuries. As violence and anger became less overwhelming realities of life, attention could shift toward purity. The second is the obvious remark that sexual abstinence was a central fact of life for a celibate clergy. It is perhaps not surprising that they made a lot of it.

But there is certainly more to it than these two factors can account for. We have to explain the growing concentration on sexual purity over many centuries and its perhaps dialectical relation with the increasing focus in modernity on sexual relations as a domain of personal fulfillment—all that Foucault was getting at when he spoke, provocatively and paradoxically, of "sexuality" as a modern invention. We have to take into account, for instance, the nineteenth-century obsession with onanism, the concern for sexual "perversion," in the Catholic context with "disorderly" or "unnatural" practices,[61] which led in some countries to legislation against homosexuality.

In any case, it was clearly fated that this combination of clerical reform from the top, moralism, and repression of sexual life would come into conflict with the developing modernity that I have been describing. Emphasis on individual responsibility and freedom would eventually run athwart the claims of clerical control. And the post-Romantic reactions against the disciplines of modernity, the attempts to rehabilitate the body and the life of feeling, would eventually fuel a reaction against sexual repression.

These tensions were already evident before the mid twentieth century. I mentioned above the decline in male practice, in relation to female, starting in the late eighteenth century. One common explanation I mentioned there invokes images of male pride and dignity. But we might also come at the same phenomenon from another direction, stressing that this more rigid sexual code frontally attacked certain male practices, particularly the rowdy life-style of young men. Perhaps more profoundly, it seems that the combination of sexual repression and clerical control, as it was felt in the practice of confession, drove men away. Clerical control went against their sense of independence, and this became doubly intolerable when the control took the form of opening up the most reserved and intimate facet of their lives. Hence the immense resistance to confession, in just about any period, and the attempt to confess, if one had to, not to one's own curé, but to a visiting priest on mission to whom one was unknown. As Delumeau put it, "the main reason for voluntary silence in the confessional was shame about admitting to sexual sins." Eventually, this tension drove men out of the confessional; as Gibson describes the sequel in the nineteenth century, "unable to take communion, and angry at the prying of the clergy, they increasingly abandoned the Church."[62]

The repellent effect of this complex is clearly at its maximum in the age of authenticity, in a widespread popular culture in which individual self-realization and sexual fulfillment are interwoven. The irony is that this alienation took place just when so many of the features of the reform-clerical complex were called into question at Vatican II. Unquestionably, clericalism, moralism, and the primacy of fear were largely repudiated. Other elements of the complex were less clearly addressed. It's not clear that the full negative consequences of the drive to reform itself, with its constant attempt to purge popular religion of its "unchristian" elements, were properly understood. Certain attempts at reform in Latin America, post–Vatican II and in its spirit, like those around "liberation theology," seem to have repeated the old pattern of "clerical dechristianization," depreciating and banning popular cults, and alienating many of the faithful, some of whom—ironically—have turned to Protestant churches in the region, who have a greater place for the miraculous and the festive than the progressive "liberators" had.[63] A strange turn of events, which would surprise Calvin, were he to return! As for the issue of sexual morality, attempts to review this, in the question of birth control, were abandoned in a fit of clerical nerves about the "authority" of the Church.

In fact, the present position of the Vatican seems to want to retain the most rigid moralism in the sexual field, relaxing nothing of the rules, with the result that people with "irregular" sexual lives are (supposed to be) automatically denied the sacraments, while as-yet-unconvicted mafiosi, not to speak of unrepentant latifundistas in the Third World and Roman aristocrats with enough clout to wangle an "annulment" find no bar.

But however incomplete and hesitantly followed the turnings taken at Vatican II, the present position of the Vatican has clearly relativized the old reform-clerical complex. It has opened a field in which you don't have to be deeply read in the history of the Church to see that the dominant spiritual fashion of recent centuries is no longer unquestionably normative. Which is not to say that this whole spirituality, aspiring to a full devotion to God and fueled by abnegation and a strong image of sexual purity, is to be condemned in turn. This would be a clerical-reform way of dealing with the reform-clerical complex! It is clear that there have been and are today celibate vocations that are spiritually fertile, and many of these turn centrally on aspirations to sexual abstinence and purity. It would just repeat the mistake of the Protestant reformers to turn around and depreciate these. The fateful feature of reform-clericalism, which erects such a barrier between the Church and contemporary society, is not its animating spirituality; our world is, if anything, drowned in exalted images of sexual fulfillment and needs to hear about paths of renunciation. The deviation was to make this take on sexuality mandatory for everyone, through a moralistic code that made a certain kind of purity a base condition for relating to God through the sacraments. What Vatican rule-makers and secularist ideologies unite in not being able to see is that there are more ways of being a Catholic Christian than either have yet imagined. And yet this shouldn't be so hard to grasp. Even during those centuries when the reform-clerical outlook dominated pastoral policy, there were always other paths present, represented sometimes by the most prominent figures, including (to remain with the French Catholic Reformation) St. François de Sales and Fénelon, not to speak of Pascal, who, though he gave comfort to the fearmongers, offered an incomparably deeper vision.

But as long as this monolithic image dominates the scene, the Christian message as the Catholic Church attempts to make it its vehicle will not be easy to hear in wide zones of the age of authenticity. But then these are not very hospitable to a narrow secularism, either.

Of course, this tension is not specific to the Catholic Church. We see it in the Anglican communion and in some Protestant churches in the virtual civil war over homosexual marriage and the acceptance of homosexual clergy, and it plays its role in the "culture wars" that bedevil politics in the United States.

So the dominant religious forms of the age of mobilization have been destabilized by the current cultural revolution, even as those of the ancien régime were by the onset of the age of mobilization. The forms of the last two centuries have taken a double whammy: on one side, an undermining of churches connected to strong national or minority identities; on the other, an estrangement from much of the ethic and style of authority of these same churches.

What are the consequences? First, one that everybody will welcome: a breaking down of barriers between different religious groups, a deconstruction of ghetto walls where such existed, as Michael Hornsby-Smith reports for the English Catholic Church after Vatican II.[64] And, of course, the effects of this are even more palpable in what were previously denominationally partitioned societies, like Holland.

But the flip side of this is a decline. The measurable, external results are as we might expect: first, in many countries, including Britain, France, the United States, and Australia, a rise in the number of those who state themselves to be atheists, to be agnostics, or to have no religion.[65] Beyond this, the gamut of intermediate positions greatly widens: many people drop out of active practice while still declaring that they belong to some confession, or believe in God. In another dimension, the gamut of beliefs in something beyond widens, with fewer declaring belief in a personal God while more hold to something like an impersonal force.[66] In other words, a wider range of people express religious beliefs that move outside Christian orthodoxy. Following in this line is the growth of non-Christian religions, particularly those originating in the Orient, and the proliferation of New Age modes of practice, of views that bridge the humanist/spiritual boundary, of practices that link spirituality and therapy. On top of this, more and more people adopt what would earlier have been seen as untenable positions: for example, they consider themselves Catholic while not accepting many crucial dogmas, or they combine Christianity with Buddhism, or they pray while not being certain they believe. This is not to say that people didn't occupy positions like this in the past, just that now it seems to be easier to be upfront about it. In reaction to all this, Christian faith is in the process of redefining and recomposing itself in various ways, from Vatican II to the charismatic movements. All this represents the consequence of expressivist culture as it affects our world. It has created a quite new predicament.[67]

Danièle Hervieu-Léger speaks of a "decoupling of belief and practice," of a "disembedding of belief, belonging, and identitary reference." Grace Davie speaks of "believing without belonging." The tight normative link between a certain religious identity, the belief in certain theological propositions, and a standard practice no longer holds for great numbers of people. Many of these are engaged in assembling their own personal outlook, through a kind of "bricolage," but there are also some widespread patterns that run athwart the traditional constellations: not only declaring some faith in God and identifying with a church without actually attending its services ("believing without belonging"), but also a Scandinavian pattern of identifying with the national church, which one attends only for crucial rites of passage, while professing widespread skepticism about its theology. The tight connection between national identity, a certain ecclesial tradition, strong common beliefs, and a sense of civilizational order, which was standard for the age of mobilization, has given way, weakening crucially the hold of theology. But whereas in other countries this has also meant a decline in identification with the church, that connection seems strong in Scandinavian countries, though deprived of its original theological connotations. The churches are seen, one might say, as a crucial element in historical-cultural identity. This pattern can also be found in other European countries, but in the Nordic nations it seems dominant.[68]

What lies behind these figures and trends? We cannot understand our present situation through a single ideal type, but if we understand ourselves to be moving away from an age of mobilization and more into an age of authenticity, then we can see this whole move as in a sense a retreat of Christendom. I mean by "Christendom" a civilization where society and culture are profoundly informed by Christian faith. This retreat is a shattering development, if we think of the way, until quite recently, Christian churches conceived their task. If we take just the Catholic Church (and there were analogues with the interdenominational "church" in pluralist Protestant societies), its goal was to provide a common religious home for the whole society. We can think in the French case of the seventeenth-century Catholic Reformation, trying to win back ground lost to the Reformed Church, as well as to penetrate segments of rural society that had never been properly Christianized; then, in the nineteenth century, the Church tried again to make up the ravages of the Revolution; the goal of Action Catholique in the early twentieth century was to missionize the milieus that had slipped away. But it is clear today that this ambition cannot be realized.

Our societies in the West will forever remain historically informed by Christianity. I will return below to some of the significance of this. What I mean by "the retreat of Christendom" is that it will be less and less common for people to be drawn into or kept within a faith by some strong political or group identity, or by the sense that they are sustaining a socially essential ethic. There will obviously still be lots of both of these things: at the very least, group identity may be important for immigrants, particularly of recent provenance—and even more among non-Christians, say, Muslims or Hindus, who feel their difference from the established majority religion. And there will certainly remain a core of people who are both members and regular attenders of churches, larger or smaller from country to country (vast in the United States, miniscule in Sweden).

There is another reason that assures the continuing importance of neo-Durkheimian identities. In some societies these are in a quasi-agonistic relation to the post-Durkheimian climate. Think, for instance, of the United States and certain demands of the Christian Right, for example, for school prayer. But these identities are perhaps even more in evidence among groups that feel suppressed or threatened (perhaps this is also the case with the Christian Right?), and often people of a certain ethnic or historical identity will look to gather around some religious marker. I mentioned the Poles and Irish above. These were peoples cast into the modern political form because they were mobilized to attain their independence or establish their integrity, in the context of being ruled from outside, sometimes with heavy oppression. They therefore took on the modern language and the modern conceptions of a political entity; they became in a modern sense peoples. And modern peoples, that is, collectivities that strive to be agents in history, need some understanding of what they're about, what I'm calling "political identity." In the two cases mentioned, being Catholic was an important part of that identity.

This phenomenon remains important in the modern world. From a faith perspective one might be ambivalent about it, however, because there are a gamut of cases, from a deeply felt religious allegiance all the way to situations in which the religious marker is cynically manipulated in order to mobilize people. Think of Milošević or the Bharatiya Janata Party (BJP). But whatever one's ethical judgments, this is a powerful reality in today's world, and one that is not about to disappear. But in general, we can say that in modern societies not riven by ethnic-confessional differences (e.g., we're not talking about Northern Ireland), the recently dominant forms of the age of mobilization will not tend to hold their members.

If we don't accept the view that the human aspiration to religion will flag, and I do not, then where will access to the practice of and deeper engagement with religion lie? The answer is the various forms of spiritual practice to which each person is drawn in his or her own spiritual life. These may involve meditation, or some charitable work, or a study group, or a pilgrimage, or some special form of prayer, or a host of such things.

A range of such forms has always existed, of course, as optional extras, as it were, for those who are already and primarily embedded in ordinary church practice. But now it is frequently the reverse. First people are drawn to a pilgrimage, or a World Youth Day, or a meditation group, or a prayer circle; and then later, if they move along in the appropriate direction, they will find themselves embedded in ordinary practice. And there will be much movement between such forms of practice, and between the associated faiths.

It is often said of the contemporary search for the spiritual, very often through a kind of individualized bricolage, that it is excessively focused on self-fulfillment, on finding one's own path. This is often said in a tone of reproach or deprecation, in a negative comparison with earlier, mainstream forms of religious life. It would be absurd to deny that even the most caricatural portraits are often lived down to, as it were. But these hostile depictions miss something essential. Where a return to religion is not actuated by a strong group or political identity or by a felt need to defend or recover a civilizational order against threatened dissolution, what is the main motivation? In many cases today, it is a profound dissatisfaction with a life encased entirely in the immanent order. The sense is that this life is empty, flat, devoid of higher purpose.

This, of course, has been a widespread response to the world created by Western modernity over at least the last two centuries. We might borrow as its slogan the title of a song by the American singer Peggy Lee, "Is that all there is?" There has to be more to life than our current definitions of social and individual success define for us. This was always a factor in previous returns to religion, like the conversions to Catholicism in nineteenth- and early-twentieth-century France I mentioned above. But there it was interwoven with a neo-Durkheimian identity, and even more, with a project for restoring civilizational order. When these fall away, the search occurs for its own sake. It is a personal search, and can easily be coded in the language of authenticity: I am trying to find my path, or find myself. But this doesn't mean that it has to be self-enclosed, that it can't end up with a strong sense of the transcendent, or of devotion to something beyond the self.

This shows the error of confusing the post-Durkheimian dispensation with a trivialized and utterly privatized spirituality. Of course, there will exist lots of both. These are the dangers that attend our present predicament. A post-Durkheimian world means, as I said above, that our relation to the spiritual is being more and more unhooked from our relation to our political societies. But that by itself doesn't say anything about whether or how our relation to the sacred will be mediated by collective connections. A thoroughly post-Durkheimian society will be one in which our religious belonging would be unconnected from our national identity. It will almost certainly be one in which the gamut of such religious allegiances will be wide and varied. It will also almost certainly have lots of people who are following a religious life centered on personal experience in the sense that William James made famous.[69] But it doesn't follow that everyone, or even most people, will be doing this. Many people will find their spiritual home in churches, for instance, including the Catholic Church. In a post-Durkheimian world, this allegiance will be unhooked from that to a sacralized society (paleo-style) or some national identity (neo-style) or from the (now arrogant-sounding) claim to provide the indispensable matrix for the common civilizational order. If I am right above, the mode of access will be different; but it will still be a collective connection.

These connections, sacramental or through a common practice, are obviously still powerful in the modern world. We must avoid an easy error here: that of confusing the new place of religion in our personal and social lives, the framework of understanding that we should be following in our own spiritual sense, with the issue of what paths we will follow. The new framework has a strongly individualist component, but this will not necessarily mean that the content will be individuating. Many people will find themselves joining extremely powerful religious communities, because that's where many people's sense of the spiritual will lead them.

Of course, they won't necessarily sit as easily in these communities as their forbears did. In particular, a post-Durkheimian age may mean a much lower rate of intergenerational continuity of religious allegiance. But the strongly collective options will not lose adherents. Perhaps even the contrary trend might declare itself.

One reason to take this idea seriously is the continuing importance of what we might call the "festive." I have been talking about the future of the relatively recent past, in the case of the culture of authenticity, only decades old. But here we are speaking of a more remote past, one that was repressed in the whole movement of reform. One byproduct of the culture of authenticity might be a partial return of the repressed.

We saw that reform tended to suppress or downplay the elements of collective ritual and of magic, in favor of personal commitment, devotion, and moral discipline. This was more severe in Protestant than in Catholic countries, but the trend was general across the board. The Counter-Reformation in France, for instance, constantly attempted to change and reform the elements of popular religion the Church did not approve of, and disapproval was particularly strong among the Jansenist clergy.

This was even true of the post-Restoration French Catholic Church. The nineteenth-century clergy were, of course, much more cautious. They saw how excess of reforming zeal could alienate whole populations from Catholicism, and they had felt on their own backs what this could mean in the Revolutionary period. They were much more tolerant of folk religion than their predecessors, but nevertheless, they couldn't resist interfering.[70]

One of their most important targets was the "festive Christianism" of their flocks. It wasn't just that many of the festivals were around some dubious focus, for instance, a pilgrimage to a site of healing, where the rite seemed to have little to do with orthodox Christianity. It wasn't only that the state, using the powers of the Napoleonic Concordat, wanted to cut down on the number of feast days, in the name of greater productivity (in this, following a path already trodden by Protestant countries centuries earlier). What often troubled the clergy was the culture of the feast itself, which mixed some sacred ritual with a lot of very earthy eating, drinking, and dancing, often with unmentionable consequences for the sexual morality of young and old alike. They wanted to clean the feasts up, disengage their properly religious significance from the rather riotous community celebrations, and tone down the latter as much as possible. We connect up here with a long-standing vector of the centuries-long process of reform: visible, for instance, on both Catholic and Protestant sides in the suppression of the "excesses" of Carnival; visible also in the attempts to suppress rowdiness and drinking at the statute fairs and village feasts that Jim Obelkevich describes in nineteenth-century Lincolnshire.[71]

Moreover, the very attempt of the clergy to make people over and raise their level of practice and morality meant that they were constantly pushing, reprimanding, demanding that some cabaret or dance hall be closed, that money be spent on a new church. Conflicts inevitably arose between priests and communities. At first these revolts were quite independent of any philosophical foundation. But through them a new outlook, denouncing clerical power and exalting the moral independence of the laity, could enter. As Maurice Agulhon puts it: "In order for the influence of free thinking to come fully into play, it was necessary first that the influence of the Church be weakened by reasons from within . . . in the foremost rank of these was the birth of conflicts between the people and the clergy."[72] Of course, once the division had set in, the Church could defend itself only by mobilizing its own partisans. So its response to the crisis itself augmented the break, and helped to push along the dissolution of the earlier parish consensus. Religion is now not a community *mentalité*, but a partisan stance.[73]

With hindsight, the pathos of this self-defeating action shows that the Catholic Church was engaged in a mission impossible. This is of wider significance than just the contradictions of Pius IX and the ultramontane Church in the nineteenth century. In a way, it shows up the tensions in the whole project of reform. The strength of the rural parish was its collective ritual and its strong consensual notion of "human respect." But the whole drive of the reform movement, from the high Middle Ages through Reformation and Counter-Reformation right up through evangelical renewal and the post-Restoration Church, was to make Christians with a strong personal and devotional commitment to God and the faith. But strong personal faith and all-powerful community consensus ultimately cannot exist together. If the aim is to encourage Christians in their strong devotional lives to come to frequent communion, then this must, in the end, mean that they break out of the restraining force of "human respect." In theory, any one of these conflicts on the ground could be resolved by a reversal of the local consensus, but in the long run it is impossible that it should always be this way. There can't be a Jean Vianney in every parish (and even he took decades to turn the village of Ars around).

But the nineteenth-century Catholic Church, much to the disgust of certain educated Catholic elites, didn't only take a negative stance toward popular religion. In an age of mobilization, it needed to canalize it. The new building of a mass movement around ultramontane Catholicism didn't just repress or sideline the old festive Christianity that had been so important in the *religions du terroir* of the parish community. It re-created its own versions. Already on the parish level, priests tried not so much to suppress popular feasts and pilgrimages as to gain control of them, redirect them, clean them up, as I described above. One common attempt was to shift the focus from local traditional sites to important regional centers of pilgrimage. As Ralph Gibson puts it, "the clergy tried to redirect the characteristic localism of popular religion in a more universalist direction."[74] In the course of the nineteenth century, there developed in France important national sites, tied to recent apparitions of the Virgin—at, for instance, La Salette, Lourdes, and

Paray le Monial. By the end of the century, people were going to Lourdes every year in the hundreds of thousands, traveling in organized groups, mostly by train.

This was, on one level, a triumph of mobilization. It appears to be the ultimate success of the clergy's attempt to supplant local cults, jealously controlled by the parish community, with trans-local ones, blessed by the hierarchy. But like all the other forms of Catholic mobilization, this one too was ambiguous. In fact, the apparitions of the Virgin start locally; she appears to peasants, shepherds. The hierarchy are at first wary, and anyway, they have to put these new claims to the test. The great trans-local sites of Marian pilgrimage of the last two centuries, from Guadalupe to Medjugorje, all started as new departures in popular religion, and they took off because they spoke to masses of ordinary believers. The clergy can sometimes kill these movements, but they don't create them.[75]

The notion of the "festive" I'm invoking here has to be understood in a broad sense. It includes feasts and pilgrimages. It involves large numbers of people coming together outside of quotidian routine, whether the "outside" is geographic, as in the case of pilgrimage, or resides in the ritual of the feast, which breaks with the everyday order of things. We can recognize as another species of this genus the Carnivals of yore, which still survive in some form in Brazil, for instance. Moreover, this assembly is felt to put them in touch with the sacred, or at least some greater power. This may manifest itself in the form of healing, as at Lourdes. But even where it does not, the sense of tapping into something deeper or higher is present. That's why it is not stretching things to include Carnival in this category. If we follow Victor Turner's account,[76] this world "turned upside down" connects us again to the "communitas" dimension of our society, where beyond the hierarchical divisions of the established order, we are together as equal human beings.

I raise this because I believe that the festive, in this sense, is an important, continuing form of religious and quasi-religious life in our own day. It must be part of any description of the place of the spiritual in our society. We might think that these nineteenth-century Catholic forms didn't have any analogue on the Protestant side. But on a second look, this can be challenged. The revival meeting presents obvious analogues. And when we think of the explosion of Pentecostalism during the last century, now spreading to many parts of the world, we have all the more reason to see the festive as a crucial dimension of contemporary religious life.

People still seek those moments of fusion, which wrench us out of the everyday and put us in contact with something beyond ourselves. We see this in pilgrimages, in mass assemblies like World Youth Days, in one-off gatherings of people moved by some highly resonating event, like the funeral of Princess Diana, as well as in rock concerts, raves, and the like. What has all this got to do with religion? The relationship is complex. On the one hand, some of these events are unquestionably "religious," in the sense in which most people use this term, that is, oriented to something putatively transcendent (a pilgrimage to Medjugorje, or a World Youth Day). What has perhaps not sufficiently been remarked is the way in which this dimension of religion, which goes back to its earliest forms, well before the axial age, is still alive and well today, in spite of all attempts by reforming elites over many centuries to render our religious and/or moral lives more personal and inward, to disenchant the universe and downplay the collective.

In some respects, these forms are well adapted to the contemporary predicament. Hervieu-Léger points out how the traditional figure of the pilgrim can be given a new sense today, as young people travel in search of faith or meaning in their lives. The pilgrimage is also a quest. The example of Taizé is striking in this regard. An interconfessional Christian center in Burgundy, with at its core a community of monks, gathered around Roger Schütz, it draws thousands of young people from a great range of countries in the summer months, and tens of thousands to its international gatherings. The drawing power lies partly in the fact that they are received as searchers, that they can express themselves, without being "confronted with a normative system [*dispositif*] of belief, nor with a discourse of preconstituted meaning." Yet at the same time, the center is clearly rooted in Christianity, and in values of international understanding and reconciliation, whose religious roots are explored through Bible study and liturgy. This whole combination is what attracts young people, who want to meet their counterparts from other lands and explore Christian faith without any preconditions as to the outcome. As one visitor put it, "At Taizé, you are not given the answer before you have posed the question, and, moreover, it is up to each person to search for his or her answer."

Of course, the Taizé experience is not simply and totally in the category of the festive. There certainly is the departure from the everyday, and the contact with something greater, a sense of universal brotherhood, even if not always having its source in the fatherhood of God. But the sense of fusion is not always prominent. It is not, however, totally absent; a central part of the Taizé experience is singing together, chants especially designed by the community, each in his/her own language, a model and foretaste of the reconciliation sought between peoples and cultures. It is not surprising that Taizé should provide the template from which World Youth Days were developed, a form of Christian pilgrimage/assembly for the age of authenticity.[77]

But how about rock concerts and raves? In terms of our criterion, they are plainly "nonreligious," and yet they also sit uneasily in the secular, disenchanted world. Fusions in common action/feeling, which take us out of the everyday, they often generate the powerful phenomenological sense that we are in contact with something greater, however we ultimately want to explain or understand this. A disenchanted view of the world needs a theory to explain the continuing power of this kind of experience. Of course, such theories can be devised; some already have been: for example, Durkheim, Freud, Bataille. But it remains true that the state of mind of the participant is far removed from the disengaged, objectifying stance from which the alleged truth of the immanent, naturalistic worldview is supposed to be convincingly evident. It is not obvious a priori that the sense of something beyond, inherent in these fusions, can be ultimately explained (away) in naturalistic categories. The festive remains a niche in our world, where the (putatively) transcendent can erupt into our lives, however well we have organized them around immanent understandings of order.

If the retreat from Christendom offers one key to our situation in the West, if the connections between faith and national/group political identities and ways of life steadily weaken, this still leaves much that is enigmatic and difficult to understand. Many people have taken a distance from their ancestral churches without altogether breaking off. They retain some of the beliefs of Christianity, for instance, and/or they retain some nominal tie with the church, still identify in some way with it: they will reply, say, to a poll by saying that they are Anglican, or Catholic. Sociologists are forced to invent new terms, such as *believing without belonging*, or *diffusive Christianity*, to come to grips with this.[78]

Now something like this has always existed. That is, churches have always had a penumbra around the core of orthodox, fully practicing believers, whose beliefs shade off into heterodoxy and/or whose practice is partial or fragmentary. We saw examples of this above in the "folk religion" of populations still living partly or largely within ancien régime forms. In fact, the term *diffusive Christianity* was coined for the unofficial popular religion of a more modern, but still not contemporary period, the late nineteenth and early twentieth centuries in the United Kingdom. John Wolffe, following Cox, tries to give a sense of one version of this outlook. It was:

> a vague non-doctrinal kind of belief: God exists; Christ was a good man and an example to be followed; people should lead decent lives on charitable terms with their neighbors, and those who do so will go to Heaven when they die. Those who suffer in this world will receive compensation in the next. The churches were regarded with apathy rather than hostility: their social activities made some contribution to the community. Sunday School was felt to provide a necessary part of the upbringing of children, and the rites of passage required formal religious sanction. Association was maintained by attendance at certain annual and seasonal festivals, but weekly participation in worship was felt to be unnecessary and excessive. Women and children were more likely than men to be regularly involved, but this did not imply that adult males were hostile; merely—it can be surmised—that they tended to see themselves as the main breadwinners, and felt that women should therefore represent the family's interests in the religious arena. The emphasis was on the practical and the communal rather than on the theological and the individual.[79]

Perhaps this kind of penumbra was bigger in 1900, and the core it surrounded somewhat smaller, than at the high tide of the evangelical wave, around 1850. But there has always been such a hinterland, surrounding the central zones of belief and practice in any large-membership church. Only small, committed minorities, battling with their surroundings, have been able to maintain 100 percent commitment by 100 percent of members. In earlier times, the hinterland of lesser orthodoxy lay more in the dimension of folk religion, semi-magical beliefs and practices surrounding the liturgy and festivals of the church. Some of this survived even into the early twentieth century, as the work of Sarah Williams attests, though the "diffusive Christianity" of 1900 was in its essentials different from the religious penumbra of earlier times. But penumbra it was, nonetheless. When one compares these different stages of British Christianity, there is "some foundation for the judgment," Wolffe opines, "that around 1900 the British people were, albeit in a diffuse and passive sense, closer to Christian orthodoxy than they had ever been in their history."[80]

What, then, has happened since 1960? Well, clearly some of the penumbra has been lost; people now stand clearly outside Christian belief, no longer identifying with any church, who were in the hinterland before (or their parents were). Some of these people have consciously adopted some quite different outlook—materialist, for instance—or have adopted a non-Christian religion. Some of this shift is reflected in the rise in numbers of those who declare themselves to have no religion. But that still doesn't account for the substantial number of those who declare themselves still to believe in God, and/or to identify with some church, even though they stand at a much greater distance from it than the "diffused" Christians of a century ago. Their views are more heterodox, for instance (God is often conceived more like a life force), and they no longer participate in many of the rites of passage, for example, baptism and marriage. (In Britain, unlike Germany, religious funerals hold up better than the other rites.)

In other words, the falling off or alienation from the Church and from some aspects of orthodox Christianity has taken the form of what Grace Davie calls "Christian nominalism." Committed secularism "remains the creed of a relatively small minority. . . . In terms of belief, nominalism rather than secularism is the residual category."[81]

How to understand this is as yet unclear. A great deal of ambivalence, of different kinds, inhabits this distancing stance, which Davie calls "believing without belonging." Is it merely a transitional phenomenon, as secularists hold? For some people, undoubtedly. But for all?

In some ways, this phenomenon can perhaps best be described in terms of past forms of Christian collective life. It stands at a distance from "diffusive Christianity," which itself stood at a certain distance from the models of totally committed practice. It is orbiting farther out from a star that is still a key reference point. In this way, the forms of the age of mobilization remain still alive at the margins of contemporary life. This becomes evident at certain moments, for instance, when people feel a desire to be connected to their past: to take the British case, at moments of royal ceremonial, such as the Jubilee and the funeral of the Queen Mum. Here it is as though the full force of the old neo-Durkheimian identity, linking Britishness to a certain form of Protestant Christianity, where oddly, the Anglican Church is allowed to perform ceremonies for everyone (even Catholics!), lives again for a day. Our excentric orbit, which normally carries us far into outer space, passes close to the original sun on those occasions. This is part of the significance, which I mentioned earlier, of the fact that our past is irrevocably within Christendom. A similar moment occurred in France recently, in the celebrations of the one-thousand-five-hundredth anniversary of the baptism of Clovis. Various *laïque* figures grumbled, but the ceremonies went on regardless. History is hard to deny.

The other kind of occasion arises when disaster strikes, such as September 11, 2001, in the United States or the Hillsborough football tragedy in England in April 1989, where ninety-four people died, mostly Liverpool supporters. Grace Davie describes the ceremonies that followed in Liverpool.[82] A recent German case is the school massacre that occurred at Erfurt in April 2002. Here, in the former East Germany, where the level of practice has fallen lower than anywhere else in the world, there was a rush to churches, which are normally deserted.

And, of course, there are events that combine both of the above, such as the mourning and funeral for Princess Di in 1997.

So it appears that the religious or spiritual identity of masses of people still remains defined by religious forms from which they normally keep themselves at a good distance. We still need some attempt to articulate this stance, to describe it from the inside, as it were, as Wolffe attempted for diffusive Christianity in the passage quoted above. There is perhaps also one other clue we can use here. It is, after all, a quite well-known stance to be holding oneself at some distance from a spiritual demand that one nevertheless acknowledges. The famous Augustinian "Lord, make me chaste, but not yet" encapsulates some of this. But it is normally less dramatic; we all have important things to get on with in our lives, and we feel we can't give our full attention and effort to spiritual or moral demands that we hold in some sense valid, that we may admire others for giving themselves to more fully.

Our attachment to these comes in our not wanting to lose sight of them, our resistance to denying them or seeing them denigrated by others. This may be part of what lies behind people answering a survey by saying that they believe in God (or angels, or an afterlife), even though they don't, say, baptize their children or marry in a church, or perhaps do anything else that clearly reflects this belief. It would also explain why the same people may be very moved by actions of others that do manifest their relation to that spiritual source. People may retain an attachment to a perspective of transformation that they are not presently acting on; they may even find themselves losing sight of it from time to time. The reception, as it were, fades in and out, like a city FM station in the countryside. When they see or hear of people's lives that seem really to have been touched by these sources of transformation, they can be strongly moved. The broadcast is now loud and clear. They are moved, and curiously grateful. I remember the response to the life, and particularly the death, of Pope John XXIII. Something similar has happened with some of the actions of John Paul II. These reactions often went well beyond the borders of the Catholic Church. We are dealing with a phenomenon that is not confined to religion. A figure like Nelson Mandela has awakened the same kind of response of confirmation and gratitude.

Perhaps what we need here is a new concept that could capture the inner dynamic underlying this phenomenon. Grace Davie and Danièle Hervieu-Léger seem to have been working toward this in their writings. We might borrow from Davie the term *vicarious religion*.[83] What she is trying to capture is the relationship of people to a church from which they stand at a certain distance but which they nevertheless in some sense cherish, which they want to be there, partly as a holder of ancestral memory, partly as a resource against some future need (e.g., their need for a rite of passage, especially a funeral; or as a source of comfort and orientation in the face of some collective disaster).

In this case, we shouldn't perhaps speak simply of the loss of a neo-Durkheimian identity or connection to religion through our allegiance to civilizational order, but rather of a kind of mutation. The religious reference in our national identity (and/or sense of civilizational order) doesn't so much disappear as change, retreat to a certain distance. It remains powerful in memory, but also as a kind of reserve fund of spiritual force or consolation. It mutates from a "hot" to a "cold" form (with apologies to Marshall McLuhan). The hot form demands a strong, participating identity, and/or an acute sense of Christianity as the bulwark of moral order. The colder form allows a certain ambivalence about historical identity, as well as a certain degree of dissidence from the church's official morality (which these days will be strongest in the domain of sexual ethics).[84]

To take Britain as an example, the original hot form of the synthesis between being British, decent, and Christian was damaged in a number of ways in the twentieth century, perhaps most of all by the experience of the First World War. On the European scene in general, hot, militant nationalism has suffered a great loss of credit through both world wars. But these identities, both national and civilizational, have not just vanished. And the new, fledgling European identity, where it exists, unites these two dimensions; Europe is a supra-national community, which is to be defined by certain "values." But the older identities take a new form, involving distance, passivity, and above all a certain queasiness in face of the assertions of their erstwhile "hot" variants.

Indeed, educated, cultivated Europeans are extremely uncomfortable with any overt manifestations of either strong nationalism or religious sentiment. The contrast with the United States in this regard has often been remarked. And it might help to take up here one of the most debated issues in the field of secularization theory, that of the "American exception"—or, if one likes, seen from a broader perspective, the "European exception." Put either way, we are faced with a strong even if not uniform pattern of decline in European societies, and virtually nothing of the sort in the United States. How can this difference be explained?

Various attempts have been made: for instance, Steve Bruce attributes the strength of religion in America partly to the immigrant context. Immigrants needed to group together with those of similar origins in order to ease their transition into American society. The rallying point was often a shared religion, and the main agency a church.[85]

As to possible other factors, one might be that constitutional-moral patriotism, what I called above the reigning synthesis between nation, morality, and religion, which was very similar in Britain and the United States, was nevertheless much less strong in Britain—indeed, it was much more strongly contested. This was particularly so in the aftermath of the First World War, which was much more traumatic for British than for American society. The challenge to civilization in Britain that this cataclysm represented was certainly lived by many as a challenge to their faith. The strong sense generated by a neo-Durkheimian effect, that everyone shares a certain moral or spiritual coding, that this is how you understand our strong collective moral experience, thus faded more rapidly in Britain, and weakened the code, whereas in the United States many people felt and have gone on feeling that you can show your Americanness by joining a church. In this respect, following the above argument, other European societies are similar to Britain, having gone through the same historical experiences, with similar results.[86]

Another important factor may have been the hierarchical nature of British society. British elites and particularly intelligentsia have been living in a fractured culture since the eighteenth century; the saliency of unbelief may have been lower in certain periods of strong piety, but it was always there. Now, something similar may also have been true of the American intelligentsia, but the position this occupied in its own society was very different. In deferential British society, the pattern of elite life has a prestige that it largely lacks in the United States. This means that elite unbelief can both more effectively resist conforming and also more readily provide models for people at other levels. Again, there are parallels with other European societies, which all in this respect contrast with the United States.[87]

But perhaps the most important factors explaining the transatlantic difference can be formulated in the terms I have been developing here. From this point of view, there are three facets to the American "exception." I have been speaking of the undermining of social matrices that have hitherto kept large numbers of people within the churches, or at least the faith. But what has been suffering the undermining has been different in the two cases. The heart of the American exception is that this society is the only one that from the beginning (if we leave aside the countries of the "old" British Commonwealth) was entirely within the neo-Durkheimian mold. All European societies had some element of the "ancien régime" or the paleo-Durkheimian, perhaps more vestigial than real, like the ritual surrounding even constitutional monarchies, but often important enough—such as the presence of (at least would be) state churches, or of rural communities with their *religion du terroir*. The proportions of paleo- and neo- are very different as we move from

Spain to Britain or Sweden, but all European states contain some mix of the two, whereas American religious life was entirely in the age of mobilization.

This means that in varying degrees some of the dynamic arising from ancien régime structures takes place in all Old World societies. One of these is the reaction against a state church in the context of an inegalitarian society, where the temptation to align established religion with power and privilege is almost irresistible. This cannot fail to produce anticlerical reactions, which can easily turn, given the availability of exclusively humanist options since the eighteenth century, into militant unbelief, which is then available to canalize the full force of popular discontent with established clergy. We see this dynamic played out in France and Spain, even to some extent in Prussia. In Britain, by contrast, much popular anticlericalism found expression in Nonconformity. But even here an alternative stream existed from the beginning, in figures like Tom Paine and Godwin, whereas ideas of this sort didn't have the same impact in the early history of the United States. The imprint of an impressive array of Deists among the founders, most notably Jefferson, seems to have been largely effaced by the second Great Awakening.

The other dynamic that is important in these cases is that the perturbing effect on religious belief of a shakeout that affects both ancien régime and mobilization forms at once is obviously greater than a challenge addressed to neo-Durkheimian structures alone. If peasants being turned into Frenchmen can only be rescued from unbelief by modes of neo-Durkheimian mobilization, then the undermining of the latter has a more profoundly destabilizing effect on belief, or at least practice. In a society, on the other hand, where the move to the age of mobilization has been completed without any significant falloff in belief, the effect of undermining the previously dominant modes of this mobilization will obviously be much less.

This is one facet of the American exception. A second is perhaps this: the actual undermining of neo-Durkheimian modes has been far less severe in America than it has elsewhere. Lots of Americans still feel quite at home with the idea of the United States as "one people under God." Those whom this identity makes uncomfortable are vocal and dominant in universities and (some) media, but are not all that numerous. It is this standoff that makes possible the present American Kulturkampf. The "culture wars" are one offshoot of this, but are misleading about its religious significance, since the polls on abortion or homosexuality are more evenly divided, or show a slight "liberal" majority. But the number of people who can make their peace with "one people under God" is much greater than the "conservative" numbers on such polls; it includes lots of "liberals." This is the more so in that groups of non-Christian and non-Jewish immigrants, who might be thought natural allies of those who want to resist a biblical coding of American identity, are themselves anxious to be co-opted into a suitably widened variation of it. Imams are now alongside priests and rabbis at public prayers, and this pan-religious unity surfaces especially at moments of crisis or disaster, as after 9/11.

Now, this is partly the result of the sheer difference in numbers of people who adhere to some religion in the United States, as opposed to Europe. But it also has to do with the respective attitudes toward national identity. Europe in the second half of the twentieth century has been full of reticences about its erstwhile senses of nationhood, and the events of the first half of that century explain why. The European Union is built on the attempt to go beyond earlier forms, in the full consciousness of how destructive they have been. The full-throated assertion of the older, self-exalting nationalisms is now reserved for the radical right, which is felt by everyone else to represent a pestilence, a possibly deadly disease, and which in turn is anti-European. War, even "righteous" war, as an expression of the superiority of the national project makes most Europeans profoundly uneasy.

Attitudes in the United States seem quite different. This may partly be because Americans have fewer skeletons in the family closet to confront than their European cousins. But I think the answer is simpler. It is easier to be unreservedly confident in your own rightness when you are the hegemonic power. The skeletons are there, but they can be resolutely ignored, in spite of the efforts of a gallant band of scholars, who are engaged in the "history wars." Most Germans have to cringe when they are reminded of the First World War slogan "Gott mit uns" (about the Second World War, the less said the better). But most Americans have few doubts about whose side God is on. In this context, the traditional neo-Durkheimian definition is far easier to live with.

So in terms of my discussion a few paragraphs back, the traditional American synthesis of "civil religion," a strong neo-Durkheimian identity, originally around a nondenominational Christianity, with a strong connection to civilizational order, is still in a "hot" phase, unlike its British counterpart. This goes some way to explaining the American culture wars. The original civil religion gradually moved wider than its Protestant base, but it has now come to a stage where, while the link to civilizational order remains strong, the connection to religion is now challenged by a broad range of secularists and liberal believers. Issues like the banning of school prayer, abortion, and, more recently, homosexual marriage become highly charged. I spoke above of a "Kulturkampf," but another analogy might be *la guerre franco-française*, two strong opposed ideological codings of the same nation's identity, in a context where nationalism (not to say great-power chauvinism) remains powerful. This is a recipe for bitter struggles.[88]

Perhaps a "control case" can be found in the societies of the old British Commonwealth: Canada, Australia, New Zealand. Like the United States, and (almost) from the beginning, they have been in the age of mobilization. But their faith-related neo-Durkheimian definitions haven't fared as well. Either they lived a "British" identity, which has since decayed in the "mother country" as well as the ex-colony, or (as in the case of Quebec), they have undergone a turnover that more resembles the European model. But above all, they are not hegemonic powers, and in one case are constantly reminded of this fact by their proximity to the nation that is. So it is not surprising to find the figures for religious belief/practice in these countries somewhere between European and U.S. ones. It is also not surprising that the issue of gay marriage, while it has been upsetting for conservatives in Canada as well, has not awakened the same degree of heat and indignation in Canada as in our neighbor to the south.

There is a third way of stating the American exception, which overlaps in some respects with the two points above. The United States since the early nineteenth century has been home to religious freedom, expressed in a very American way: that is, it has been a country of religious choice. People move, form new denominations, join ones that they weren't brought up in, break away from existing ones, and so on. Their whole religious culture in some ways prepared for the age of authenticity, even before this became a facet of mass culture in the latter part of the twentieth century. This whole shift was therefore much less destabilizing. We have just to think of the contrast with Germany and France, where the new "cults" deeply disturb people. Even French atheists are a trifle horrified when religion doesn't take the standard Catholic form that they love to hate. It is harder to see the discontinuity in America, and indeed, it was in a sense less, since before the 1960s the culture of authenticity was everywhere present among cultured elites, and the educated were a much larger proportion of the U.S. population even before the postwar expansion of universities.

III

I want now to make a few hesitant comments about developments outside the West, or on a global scale. A problem that has been awaiting us here, and that we must acknowledge, is: What is the West, after all? What are its limits? I have tried to define it by its descent from Latin Christendom. But what about Latin America? Does Mexico belong to the West? And how about the Balkans? And the world of Greek/Russian Orthodoxy in Eastern Europe?

I don't think there is any way to resolve these issues. The boundaries are inherently fuzzy. But what these questions already make evident is that the future of the religious past may present itself quite differently in other civilizations. Japan, in other ways China, went through the axial revolution in a very different way from the civilizations dominated by monotheism, let alone the West. Indeed, it has been claimed that Japanese culture has remained in some ways preaxial.[89] Neither China nor the West comes even close to resembling Indian civilization, where postaxial reforms have taken a very different shape. Hinduism can indeed be related to, even considered as, a civilization, but not because this "religion" defines the shape of a moral-civilizational order, which it sustains and of which it is the bulwark, something that has often been claimed for both Christianity and Islam. In spite of certain nineteenth- and twentieth-century reform movements, influenced by European models, like the Brahmo Samaj, popular piety, replete with preaxial elements, has not been seriously repressed and overhauled—despite the banning of certain practices such as sati or the exclusion of Dalits from temples. Hinduism can indeed be seen as the basis of a civilization, but as its central inspiration, rather than as a moralistic bulwark against chaos and dissolution.

I can't even begin to cope with the immense diversity that a truly world perspective would open up. Here I will attempt only some comments on certain Western forms, which seem in some way to have become "globalized." I shall be looking at variants of the modes of empowering devotion, the neo-Durkheimian phenomenon, and religion as the basis for moral/civilizational order that I have been discussing.

Not all features of Western individualism have "traveled," as it were, into other religious traditions. The stress on inwardness, for instance, may not have straddled the gap. And clearly, the conception of society as made up of rights-bearing individuals has not been everywhere accepted. But the importance of personal commitment and responsibility does seem to have been become an important part of some contemporary ways of being Islamic.

Some of these are characterized by their own adherents, or outsiders, as "Islamist." But there are also those who shun the label, wanting to stress that their interest lies not in politics or state power, but in the recovery of a genuine Islamic piety. This is true, for instance, of the currents within the Islamic revival in Egypt, of which Saba Mahmood has written.[90] It is true of the young preachers of the Tabligh in France. When Moussa Kömeçoglu contrasts their "enlightened and puritanical Islam" to the "routinized and traditionalist Islam" of their parents, he is pointing, I believe, to a similiar shift to individual responsibility.[91] A study of contemporary Islamic coffeehouses in Turkey makes the point that they no longer rely on dress codes and spatial separation, but now have to appeal to inner conviction and self-formation. The "Cartesian dichotomy" of which its author speaks is close to this idea of personal responsibility, which can separate itself from all external forms.[92] This kind of individuation can sometimes have the effect of devaluing certain traditional forms of ritual or devotion as "un-Islamic"; Islamic reformers have frequently in our day not only wanted to return to the full rigors of the *shari'a*, but also looked askance at various forms of devotion, which have sometimes gone under the general descriptive term *Sufi*, and sometimes been targeted because they smack to much of an "enchanted" worldview, which the reformers want to put behind them.

But the shift can also have the effect of breaking people loose from network identities of various kinds—families, clans, villages—precisely the loci in which a "routinized and traditionalist Islam" is often practiced. The break with network identity means the ascendancy of a categorical identity, as Muslims, or real Muslims, and/or Muslims of a certain strict form of practice.[93] Of course, this identity was also in some sense theirs beforehand. The difference is that in many milieus Islam was something one belonged to *through* the collective practice of one's clan or village, whereas now one may be living one's religion against the grain of all this.

Now, this assumption of a categorical identity through one's own responsible commitment pitches one out into a kind of public space of a modern kind. By that I mean a space that is not defined by some pre-existing action-transcendent structure, like a divinely established kingdom or Caliphate, or a tribal law since time out of mind, or a sacred "theater state," or whatever; modern public space is, rather, self-consciously founded by the common action of those who appear in it. An association is formed by people becoming mobilized, or mobilizing themselves, coming together for certain purposes and interacting with a larger space, which may easily be indifferent or hostile to this common purpose. Indeed, if it is not to be indifferent or hostile, this space must itself be produced by mobilization and collective action, as with the rebellion that overturned the Shah and the creation of an Islamic Republic in Iran.

So we have a religious identity that fits clearly within a modern-type public space and presupposes a space of this kind. It requires individual commitment and thus often mobilization into associations, which is a standard feature of modern polities. It thus often proceeds through and makes heavy use of mass media of various kinds to sustain itself and grow. D. Eikelman has noted how much contemporary Islamic movements rely on the printed word, on their members acquiring conviction and commitment through reading, often becoming in this way inducted into polemics with what are defined as hostile ideas: for instance, those of Western secularism.[94] Some of the intellectual leaders of the Iranian Revolution defined their thought partly in relation to various French philosophers, whose thought is also widely read in the West. And everyone is aware of how much Ayatollah Khomeini's revolution depended on cassette recordings of his sermons.

Note that God can figure in public space, and very obtrusively, but this has a different meaning from many premodern forms. These were based on the sacred in a strong, localizable sense; what I have called the paleo-Durkheimian dispensation; like the divinely endorsed kingship of, say, ancien régime France. But there is also the neo-Durkheimian model, best illustrated in the West by the new American republic. God was present here, because the republic was seen as based on a providential design. There are analogies between this and today's Islamic republic, despite all the differences.

People often claim to see a paradox here, in that some of the movements that operate in modern public space themselves claim to be returning to a purer, early form of religion, the movements that tend to be called "fundamentalist" in the West. Of course, there is a paradox only if we accept some overly simple definitions of "modernity" and "religion" as frozen constellations based on opposing premises. Even the paradigm case of "fundamentalism" for Westerners, Protestant biblical literalism, not only makes use of the latest and most sophisticated media, but in many ways only makes sense within modern assumptions, such as a clear and exhaustive distinction of literal versus figurative, which would have been difficult to grasp in earlier Christian centuries.

But although there is no paradox, there can be strains. To be mobilized through an appeal to individual commitment, in what is often an indifferent or even hostile public space, requires a degree of responsibility that may clash with certain features of the code of conduct that reflects the new commitment. This is perhaps clearest in the case of women in Islamic movements, as much of the research of Nilüfer Göle and others has shown. Responsible commitment, in a movement based on mobilization, may require, for instance, one to take leadership positions, act as spokesperson, and the like. And this may conflict with the recessive role the code ascribes to women, who are meant to be anonymous or invisible in public space. The new identity is thus liable to strains, which are an important source of conflict and evolution.[95]

There are clearly certain analogues here with Western forms in the age of mobilization. But more precisely, we can see the development, not just in Islam, of what I called above neo-Durkheimian identities. Indeed, a host of factors, which we often gesture at with such portmanteau terms as *globalization* or *development*, are pushing more and more people into an age of mobilization.

The move of modern history has been toward a wider and wider and wider recruitment of people into what I called above "categorical" identities, from out of earlier, more local identifications, focusing often on kinship systems, clans, or tribes. These early identities are often defined by "networks," where people stand in a dense web of relations, linked to many people but in a different fashion to each one; as in a kinship system, where I am related to one person as father, another as son, another as cross cousin, and so on. By contrast, modern political identities are "categorical," they bind people together in virtue of their falling together under a category, like Serb, or American, or Hindu, where we all relate in a uniform way to a whole.[96]

This movement seems to be accelerating. Many factors are drawing people away from the earlier network identities: not only the efforts of elites to mobilize them but also migration or the effects of globalization, either through the spread of media or by undermining older ways in which we make our living. Migration can mean being mixed with unfamiliar others, not knowing how they will react, being unable to reconstitute the older way of life. Loss of the older forms of making a living can undermine our dignity, our identity, induce a sense of loss and helplessness. The decay of the old often brings disorientation, or feelings of humiliation and lowered self-worth.

In these circumstances, a new categorical identity can offer people something very precious: not only a direction, an orientation, but also a sense of (collective) agency. We are no longer just to suffer a sense of helplessness before dimly understood global forces, but we are to be mobilized against named and identified ills.

The fact that mobilization is often against something brings us to the aspect of these new developments that most strikes us in the West today: the way in which new identities can be turned to foster violence. And indeed, it is often noted that many of the most violent, or at least conflictual, have a religious basis.

This has led to a lot of loose talk about religion as a source for violence, which needs to be examined a lot more closely, precisely with an eye to the different kinds of religious involvements with political identities and civilizational norms that I have been analyzing in the preceding pages.

According to a view of things that has been widespread since the Enlightenment, the sources of hate, conflict, and persecution seem to lie deep in our religious heritage. Indeed, this penchant toward conflict and repression has been seen as particularly strong in the religions that issued from Jewish monotheism. Enlightenment thinkers, with the terrible history of the Crusades and the Inquisition in mind, saw Christianity as particularly culpable, although they often also saw Islam as equally bad if not worse. In many ways this outlook lingers on in liberal, secular circles in the West, in that there is deep suspicion of militant Christianity, and practically a demonization of Islam.

Blaming monotheism is not just a matter of prejudice. It is remarkable how, in the ancient world, Jews and later Christians were condemned by their neighbors as *atheioi* because they broke with the usual mores of mutual recognition of each other's divinities, fading into cross-worship and syncretism. They denied the very existence of other gods, or identified them with demons, and they strictly forbade their adherents to worship them. They set up a clear boundary, and guarded it zealously.

Christianity and Islam inherited this boundary from Judaism, but then added to it a vocation to proselytize, to extend their faith to the whole of mankind. This was the source of religious wars of conquest, often of forced conversions, particularly in Christian history, while the boundary was also defended internally against deviancy and apostasy was sternly punished.

We can build up a picture of a certain kind of religion as the source of group conflict, war, persecution, and enforced conformity. To this was often contrasted the more tolerant attitude of enlightened paganism (Gibbon), or the wisdom of Chinese civilization (an important Enlightenment topos), or, in recent centuries, the loose boundaries of Hinduism and the pacifism of Buddhism.

There is some truth in all this historically, but it's certainly not the whole truth about religion and hate in the twentieth century. Hinduism, in some sense, seems to be the rallying point of a super-chauvinist political movement that has won partial power in India. Terrible violence has been committed in Sri Lanka in the name of Buddhism. Many people have seen in these events a betrayal of the religious traditions concerned,[97] but the implication of religion in violence seems undeniable. Is the persecutory virus of monotheism contagious?

I want to argue that things are not quite as they appear. In one sense, it is not exactly religion that is at the root of violence in many twentieth-century cases. Or, to put it differently, it gets involved through a quite different mechanism, which itself is not intrinsically tied to religion. Already certain notorious cases should alert us to this. They point to a different relation between devotion and violence.

In the bad old days of the Inquisition, for instance, allowing for the usual quota of time-servers and opportunists, the persecutors were often among the most devout and dedicated; they were fired by a holy zeal for the faith. But if one looks at Ulster these days, this is not the pattern one observes. The men of violence are more and more distinct from the really devout Catholics and Protestants, who are more frequently heard as brave voices for peace. The Reverend Ian Paisley, an extremist who is a man of the cloth, seems more and more an anachronistic survival. The killers are certainly full of some kind of zeal, to them no doubt holy, but not for the service of God.

Another striking case is that of the BJP, and its parent organization, the Rashtriya Swayamsevak Sangh (RSS). In what sense, if at all, is this body defined by religious as opposed to secular goals? The assassins of Gandhi didn't reproach him for his devotion to God or the Dharma (how could they?) but for returning its share of the gold stock of the old, undivided India to Pakistan and for opposing militarism. Their successors have now realized one of their long-standing ambitions and made India into a full-dress nuclear power. These are the goals of a certain kind of nationalism everywhere. What do they have to do with religion, and specifically Hinduism?

It is true that the BJP has, in recent years, singled itself out by a campaign to destroy a mosque in the birthplace of Rama and erect a temple on the site. Mobilization to this end has probably helped, on balance, its recent rise to power (although the destruction of the Babri Masjid also frightened a lot of Indians, and the party has played down this part of its program since). So the reality is complex. But when one looks at the goals of the core organization, the RSS, what strikes one is, rather, the exploitation, by an organization whose goals lie in the domain of secular power, of currents of popular devotion. In any case, it is clear here, as in Northern Ireland, that the most active in stirring this agitation are not necessarily among the most devout.

So what is happening here? I want to argue that much of the implication of religion in violence in our century is to be understood as the working out of what can be called identity struggles. These crystallize around definitions of one's own and the other's identities. But these definitions are not necessarily religious. On the contrary, they frequently turn on perceived nationality, language, tribe, or whatever. What drives these struggles is frequently very similar across the different modes of definition. That religion figures in the definition—as against language, say—often changes very little (not always, of course, as I will discuss below). In cases like Northern Ireland or the former Yugoslavia, one is tempted to say that originally religious differences have now hardened into an enmity between "nations," felt and lived as such. Atheists like Milošević will combat the Bosnians or Kosovo Albanians as a "Serb." God and the devotional life of the Orthodox Church don't figure in this conflict. What matters is the historical identity of the people, and here some monasteries and traditional sites of devotion are important markers of territory, but little more.

In other words, even when religion is a major source of definition in modern identity struggles, it tends to figure under a description (e.g., the historical tradition that defines "our" people) that displaces the center of attention from what has always been seen as the main point of religious devotion and practice: God, *moksha*, Nirvana. Which is what raises the legitimate question: Is the struggle "about" religion any more?

These struggles are occurring in a new, modern, structural context. The democratic age poses new obstacles to coexistence, because it opens a new set of issues that can deeply divide people, those concerning the political identity of the state. In many parts of the Indian subcontinent, for instance, Hindus and Muslims coexisted in conditions of civility, even with a certain degree of syncretism, where later they would fight bitterly. What happened? The explanations given often include the British attempt to divide and rule, or even the British mania for census figures, which first made an issue of who was a majority where.

These factors may have their importance, but clearly what makes them vital is the surrounding situation, in which political identity becomes an issue. As the movement grows to throw off the alien, multi-national empire and to set up a democratic state, the question of its political identity arises. Will it simply be that of the majority? Are we heading for Hindu Raj? Muslims ask for reassurance. Gandhi's and Nehru's proposals for a pan-Indian identity don't satisfy Jinnah. Suspicion grows, as do demands for guarantees, ultimately separation.

Each side is mobilized to see the other as a threat to political identity. This fear can then sometimes be transposed, through mechanisms we have yet to understand, into a threat to life; to which the response is savagery and counter-savagery, and we descend a spiral that has become terribly familiar. Census figures can then be charged with ominous significance, but only because in the age of democracy being in the majority has decisive importance.

Democracy thus underlies identity struggles, because the age of popular sovereignty opens a new kind of question, which I've been calling that of the political identity of the state. What/whom is the state for? And for any given answer, the question can arise for me/us, can I/we "identify with" this state? Do we see ourselves as reflected there? Can we see ourselves as part of the people this state is meant to reflect/promote?

These questions can be deeply felt, strongly contested, because they arise at the juncture between political identity and personal identity, meaning by the latter the reference points by which individuals and component groups define what is important in their lives. If it is important to me that I belong to a French-speaking community, then a state defined by its official language as English will hardly reflect me; if I am more than a pro forma Muslim, then a state defined by "Hindutva" cannot fully be mine; and so on. We are in the very heartland of modern nationalism.

But these "nationalist" issues are the more deeply fraught because the personal and group identities that vie for reflection are often themselves in the course of redefinition.

This redefinition is often forced by circumstances, and at the same time can be extremely conflictual and unsettling. We can see the forces surrounding this process if we follow the serial rise of nationalisms in the modern world.

If we try to identify the source of the modern nationalist turn, the refusal—at first among elites—of incorporation by the metropolitan culture, we can see that it often takes the form of the need for difference. This is felt existentially as a challenge, not just as a matter of a valuable common good to be created but also viscerally as a matter of dignity, in which one's self-worth is engaged. This is what gives nationalism its emotive power. This is what places it so frequently in the register of pride and humiliation.

So nationalism can be said to be modern, because it's a response to a modern predicament. But the link is also more intimate. It has often been remarked that nationalism usually arises among "modernizing" elites. The link can be understood as more than accidental. One facet of nationalism, I have been arguing, is a response to a threat to dignity. But modernity has also transformed the conditions of dignity.

These could not but change in the move from hierarchical, "mediated" societies to "horizontal," direct-access ones. The concept of honor, which was in place in the earlier forms, was intrinsically hierarchical. It supposed "preferences," in Montesquieu's terms.[98] For me to have honor, I must have a status that not everyone shares, as is still the case with an "honors list" of awards today. Equal direct-access societies have developed the modern notion of "dignity." This is based on the opposite supposition, that all humans enjoy this equally. The term as used by Kant, for instance, designates what is supposed to be the appanage of all rational agents.[99] Philosophically, we may want to attribute this status to all, but politically the sense of equal dignity is really shared by people who belong to a functioning direct-access society together.[100] In this typically modern predicament, their dignity passes through their common categorical identity. My sense of my own worth can no longer be based mainly on my lineage, my clan. A goodly part of it will usually be invested in some other categorical identity.

But categorical identities can also be threatened, even humiliated. The more we are inducted into modern society, the more this is the form in which the question of dignity will pose itself for us. Nationalism is modern, because it is a typically modern way of responding to the threat represented by the advancing wave of modernization. Elites have always been susceptible to experiencing a dramatic loss of dignity in the face of conquering power. One way of responding is to fight back or come to terms with the conquerors out of the same traditional identity and sense of honor. Another is to forge a new categorical identity to be the bearer of the sought-for dignity. It is (a subspecies of) this second reaction that we call nationalist. But it is essentially modern. The 1857 Rebellion in India was in part an attempt to expunge this perennially possible loss of dignity in a premodern context. In this sense, it was not a nationalist movement, as the later Congress was.

The modern context of nationalism also turns its search for dignity outward. No human identity is purely inwardly formed. The other always plays some role. But it can be just as a foil, a contrast, a way of defining what we're not, for better or for worse. So the aboriginals of the newly "discovered" world figured for post-Columbian Europeans. The "savage," the other of civilization, a way Europeans defined themselves, both favorably (applying "civilized" to themselves in self-congratulation), and sometimes unfavorably (Europeans as corrupted in contrast to the "noble savage"). This kind of other reference requires no interaction. Indeed, the less interaction the better, or else the stereotype may be unable to resist.

But the other can also play a role directly, where I need his/her recognition to be confident of my identity. This has been standard for our relation to our intimates, but it wasn't that important in relation to outsiders in the premodern period. Identities were defined by reference to the other, but not out of the other's reactions. Where the latter becomes so the way we interact is crucial. Perhaps we should correct: the way the interaction is seen by the parties, because of the big part played by illusion here. But the point is that the interaction is understood to be crucial by the identity bearers themselves.

I would like to argue that identities in the modern world are more and more formed in this direct relation to others, in a space of recognition. I can't argue the general case here,[101] but I hope that this is evident for modern nationalism. Modern nationalist politics is a species of identity politics. Indeed, the original species, that is, national struggles, are the site from which the model comes to be applied to feminism, to the struggles of cultural minorities, to the gay movement, and so on. The work of someone like Frantz Fanon,[102] which was written in the context of the anticolonial struggle but whose themes have been recuperated in other contexts, illustrates the connections. Strong national sentiment among elites usually arises in the first phase because an identity is threatened in its worth.

This identity is vulnerable to nonrecognition, at first by members of the dominant societies. Later, there has developed a world public scene, on which peoples see themselves as standing, on which they see themselves as rated, which rating matters to them. This world scene is dominated by a vocabulary of relative advance, even to the point of having to discover periodic neologisms in order to euphemize the distinctions. Hence what used to be called "backward" societies began to be called "underdeveloped" after the war. Then even this came to be seen as indelicate, and so we have the present partition: developed/developing. The backdrop of modern nationalism, that there is something to be caught up with, each society in its own way, is inscribed in this common language, which in turn animates the world public sphere.

Modern nationalism thus taps into something perennial. Conquest, or the threat of conquest, has never been good for one's sense of worth. But the whole context in which this nationalism arises, that of successive waves of (institutional) modernization, and the resultant challenge to difference, that of the growth of categorical identities, as well as the creation of a world public sphere as a space of recognition—this is quintessentially modern. We are very far from atavistic reactions and primal identities.

I have been attempting to give some of the background of modern identity struggles. These have a locus, which is frequently inescapable, in the modern state, which poses the question of political identity—What/whom is this polity for?—and the derivative question: Do I/we have a place here? These issues can be particularly charged, because they are the point at which the necessary redefinition of a traditional way of life can be carried out. Indeed, the very staking of a claim for "us" as a people demanding our own state, or calling for reflection in an existing state whose definition excludes us, this very move to peoplehood in the modern sense will often involve a redefinition of what "we" are. Thus the erstwhile dominant, conservative and clerical, definition of *la nation canadienne-française* was not meant to realize itself primarily in political institutions but rather in the conservation of a way of life in which the Church played the major role. The political strategy was to hold North American anglophone-Protestant society at bay, both in its concentration on economic growth and in its tendency to enlarge the state's role in the management of certain social affairs, especially education and health matters. This required the jealous guarding of provincial autonomy, but also the self-denial of the provincial government, which refrained from itself entering the domains from which it was excluding the federal government. Quite a different self-definition underlies the present identity as "Québécois," which for some people at any rate motivates the demand for separate statehood.

Of course, this move involved a shift away from a religious self-definition. The last fifty years have seen a rapid laicization of Quebec society. But the earlier variant of nationalism also involved a controversial stance on what it meant to be a Catholic community in majority Protestant Canada and North America, as the long and bitter quarrel with Irish clergy testifies.

The point is that the resolution of issues of political identity—What kind of state will one settle for? Do we have a real choice? Can we strike out on our own? Should we accept to assimilate?—goes along with the settling of the major issues of personal or group identity: Who are we really? What really matters to us? How does this relate to how we used to define what matters? What is the important continuity with our past that makes us = us? (E.g., Is it just speaking French in this territory for four centuries, or is it also being Catholic?)

These reassertions or redefinitions are particularly fraught, not just because they are anguishing, the point at which people may feel that there has been a loss of identity or a betrayal, but also because they are often lived in the register of dignity: the issue of whether the identity we end up with somehow will brand us as inferior, not up to the rest, as a group destined to be dominated, cast in the shade by others. This may indeed be how we are seen by powerful others, but the issue is how much this gets to us, how much we feel that only by changing ourselves in some direction ("modernizing" our economy, reforming some of our social practices, attaining statehood or autonomy) could we really refute this disparaging judgment and hold our heads high among the nations.

And our plight is not made easier by the fact that one person's essential reform, by which dignity is recovered, is another person's utter betrayal.

Now, religion gets caught up in this process of struggle through redefinition. Sometimes the result is negative: the old faith is extruded or marginalized, as, for instance, in Jacobin-nationalist or leftist identities. But sometimes it seems to be revalorized. "Reformed" versions of an old religious tradition come forward as the way to embrace what is good in modernity, even rediscover these good things in a neglected part of our tradition (Brahmo Samaj, for instance). Or against these, the counter-claim is made that these reformed versions have abandoned what is essential, and new, more rigorous returns to the origins are proposed. But these latter efforts take place in a modern context, and very often while attempting to meet the demands of power, statehood, and economic and military viability, with full use of communications technology, which belong to this age. And so they are frequently less of a pure return to origins than they claim on the surface to be. The pathos of "fundamentalisms" is always a certain hybridity. Present-day Protestant biblical "fundamentalism" would have been unthinkable in the symbolic universe of medieval Catholicism, where everything was a sign; it presupposes the literal-mindedness of the modern scientific age. Earlier Christian centuries lived in a world in which secular time was interwoven with various orders of higher time, various dimensions of eternity. From within this time sense, it may be hard to explain just what is at stake in the issue of whether "day" in Genesis means "literally" the twenty-four hours between sunset and sunset, let alone see why people should be concerned about it. Or, to take another example, the Iranian revolution and subsequent régime have been deeply marked by modern communications, modes of mass mobilization, and forms of state (a sort of attempt at a parliamentary theocracy).

Now, looked at from a certain angle, these movements can be seen as attempts to live the traditional faith to the full in contemporary conditions. The ultimate goal in each case is something that would be recognized as such across the history of the tradition in question—for instance, in the Muslim case, living the life of submission to God in the light of Qu'ran and hadith—even if some of the forms might seem strange and new. But to the extent that the struggle for reassertion/redefinition becomes entangled in identity struggles, a displacement comes about. Two other goals or issues begin to impinge, which may draw the enterprise out of the orbit of the religious tradition. These are the twin goals/issues of the power and the dignity of a certain "people." These may impose objectives that are more or less alien to the faith, not only as lived historically, but even in terms of what can be justified today.

Constituting a dominant people, especially one with the power to impose its will through weapons of mass destruction, has never been seen as a demand of Hindu piety. A case to the diametrically opposite effect would be easier to make, as Gandhi showed, and as his brutal elimination by the spiritual ancestors of the government in Delhi emphasizes. Nor has genocide been seen as a goal of Orthodox Christianity, even allowing for the worst modes of perversion of the faith historically.

In many of its most flagrant cases, contemporary violence that seems "religious" in origin is quite alien to religion. We might want to protest that it is powered by something quite different. But this would also be too simple. It arises in certain basically modern forms where identity struggles that are constituted by and help constitute "peoples," groups struggling to define themselves and to attain political identity, incorporate religion as a historical marker. Sometimes where this is the case, the demands of piety have utterly disappeared or atrophied: the "Serb" militants, the IRA and Orange killers, much of the leadership of the BJP. A less clear case is the BJP movement as a whole, in which undeniably powerful popular devotion is harnessed to a campaign for political domination, as with the agitation around the Rama temple in Ayodhya.

Even more mixed are various of the militant Muslim movements of our day. Many of these are undoubtedly powered by deeply felt conceptions of piety. But this doesn't mean that their form and course may not be deeply influenced by the context of identity struggle. It would be absurd to reduce Islamic integrism to a single mode of explanation; we are dealing with a complex, many-sided, over-determined reality. I nevertheless would like to argue that its various manifestations have some features of the profile I have been outlining above. The sense of operating on a world scene, in the register of threatened dignity, is very much present, as is the over-vehement rejection of the West (or its quintessence, America, the "great Satan"), and the tremendous sensitivity to criticism from this quarter, for all the protestations of hostility and indifference. Islamic societies are perhaps if anything more vulnerable to a threat to their self-esteem from the impact of superior power in that Islam's self-image was of the definitive revelation, destined to spread outward without check. The Islamic sense of providence, if I may use this Christian expression, can cope with the status of conquerors, but tends to be bewildered by the experience of powerlessness and conquest.

Again, for all their protestations of faithfulness to the origins, this integrism is in some respects very modern, as I argued above. It mobilizes people in a modern fashion, in horizontal, direct-access movements; it thus has no problem using the "modern" institutional apparatus of elected legislatures, bureaucratic states, armies. While it would reject the doctrine of popular sovereignty in favor of a species of theocracy, it has also delegitimated all the traditional ruling strata. The Iranian revolution was carried out against the Shah. Those enjoying special authority are exclusively those who "rationally" merit this, granted the nature and goals of the state, namely, the experts in God's law. Not to mention the Ayatollah Khomeini's media-oriented abuse of Islamic judicial forms in issuing his fatwa against Salman Rushdie. And to what extent was the heinousness of Rushdie's "crime" greatly increased by the fact that he published his "blasphemies" in English and for a Western audience?

Again, we do not understand as fully as we might the tremendous emphasis laid on the dress and comportment of women in contemporary Islamic reform movements. Very often the demands seem to spin out of all relation to Qu'ran and tradition, as with the Taliban in Afghanistan. But we can trace the way in which women have become the "markers" for "modernism" and integrism. Atatürk insisted that women dress in Western fashion, that they walk in the streets and attend social functions, even dance with men. The traditional modes were stigmatized as "backward." Perhaps this has something to do with the extraordinary stress on rigorism in dress and contact imposed on women in many places today. These matters have become internationally recognized symbols of where one stands, ways of making a statement, of declaring one's rejection of Western modernity. The struggle in international public space may be dictating what happens here more than the weight of the shariat, or hallowed modes of piety.[103]

Perhaps the most striking case has come to world prominence with the attack on the World Trade Center of September 11, 2001. The network known as al-Qaeda, headed by Osama bin Laden, has pushed even farther a development already evident in certain Islamist "terrorist" movements; this involves using the concept of jihad and the status of shahid to legitimate a form of action that seems to lie outside traditionally permitted limits. This is so in two respects: first, in its disregard for the distinction between combatants and uninvolved civilians; second, in its recourse to suicide attacks. Either of these alone is problematic, but the combination seems to violate clear precepts of Islam. And some mullahs have made clear that someone who kills himself with the aim of taking with him not even enemy soldiers but defenseless civilians cannot claim the title of shahid.

But the striking fact is how little impact these rulings have had in many Muslim societies. Not only are they totally ignored in the street, as it were, where young Palestinians still refer to suicide bombers, whose only victims may be teen-agers at a disco, as "martyrs," but many of the religious authorities in these "hot" societies go along with their publics rather than endorsing the best jurisprudence. What is happening here? May it not be that "Islamic" action is being driven by the sense that "we" are being despised and mishandled by "them," quite like nationalist reactions that have become very familiar to us? To take an example from Christendom: the clergy of all the combatants in the First World War, with very few honorable exceptions, bestowed God's blessing on their nation's armies. From a certain distance, the betrayal of their Christian commitment is only too painfully obvious.

Moreover, seeing nationalism, proletarian internationalism, and religious fundamentalisms in the same register may help us to understand their interaction, that they are often, in fact, fighting for the same space. Arab nationalism gives way to Islamic integrism,[104] just as the demise of Soviet Marxism opens the way for virulent nationalisms. The search for a categorical identity, to answer the call for difference and become the bearer of a sought-after dignity, can take many forms. It is understandable that the discrediting of some must strengthen the appeal of others.

This discussion yields a rather mixed picture. It cautions us against taking "religion" to be a clearly identifiable phenomenon, once and for all, responding to a single inner dynamic. It ought to be clear that there is more than one dynamic going on today in connection with religion. We must be particularly aware of this if we want to do something to overcome the violence that is often associated with religious differences.

But perhaps we can understand the multiple dynamic with the aid of the tripartite scheme roughly elaborated above. In line with the second term, religion can be a (would be) political identity, of a state, or an alliance of states; this marker can provide the sense of dignity and also the collective efficacy that many people feel are lacking in their world as older forms break down. In the terms of the discussion earlier, religion can be the basis of a "neo-Durkheimian" identity, and this can bring with it hostility or opposition to other groups in the way that national identities often do.

In line with the third term, religion can be felt to be the bulwark of a moral-civilizational order. This can be felt with special acuity in cases where "globalization," migration, and economic development are eroding a traditional way of life.

But there remains the first term: religious belief and piety can also be actuated by other motives, a felt need for anchoring, a desire to come closer to God or whatever is seen as the source of spiritual strength, a sense of emptiness in one's present life, and so on.

Now, these sources can operate together. The second and third are often linked, for instance. Some Islamist identities that focus on attaining political power do so with the idea that Islamic law and civilization is the highest or only true one and see themselves as fighting back the corruption and immorality of Western culture. But this kind of linkage is less evident in the mobilizations undertaken by the RSS and the BJP, which are more purely of the second, political type.

What makes the proclivity to violence of these forms, of the second, and perhaps especially of the second allied with the third? This is a deep question, which needs much more study. But I believe that much would be gained by studying the roots of the perennial attraction of scapegoating. This seems to have something to do with the way we can establish our own sense of purity, goodness, and integrity through the violent separation or expulsion of a contrast case, taken as the embodiment of impurity, evil, and chaos. Reactions of this kind can be discovered in the earliest societies. What is astonishing is that they have somehow survived the progress of "civilization" and "Enlightenment," and even the utter rejection of all religion, as the twentieth-century histories of Russia, China, Cambodia, and so on, can attest. In the light of what are millennial histories of scapegoating and holy wars, it is not surprising that our ills are often attributed to a source in an Enemy who wants to destroy us and whom we must combat. We should measure how overwhelming the temptation can be to go along with this kind of (often murderous) mobilization, where it comes across as the only way to recover orientation, dignity, or agency.[105]

Now, plainly religion as political identity and as the bulwark of a moral-civilizational identity can also be commingled with other, more "spiritual" motives; it can be part of my search for personal piety. But it is also not surprising that this search often finds itself in opposition to the use of religion to forge political identity. People may sense that the search for identity and "our" religion may contradict the demands of a genuine deepening of piety. This seems to be the case with the women's mosque movement in Egypt, studied by Saba Mahmood.[106] These women want to resist the "folklorization" of Islamic practice. They are not into pride in the symbols of Islam but are trying to discover the full, transformative meaning of its practices.

The same unease leads the Iranian dissident 'Abdolkarim Soroush to distinguish Islam as an identity from Islam as truth. Only the latter is really valid in his eyes.[107] A similar logic leads many pious Hindus, some following Gandhi, vigorously to oppose the BJP.

I have argued that there is a particularly modern dynamic that can issue in "religious" hatred and violence, but that is in some ways rather alien to religion in its devotional thrust. There are clear cases in which this alien nature stands out, but there are also very mixed cases, in which religious movements are traversed by a number of different demands—of fidelity to the past, of piety, of recovering social discipline and order, as well as of the power and dignity of "peoples." In these cases, there is no single dynamic at work.

This may be hard to sort out in practice, but it has important policy consequences. Where the dynamic of identity struggles has an important role to play, there is no point in seeking the source in theology. What may be needed is the classic kit for coping with extreme identity strife: trying to give more space to complex, or "hybrid," identities that can diffuse and buffer the standoff. Thus one of the big threats to the BJP's mobilization behind "Hindutva" comes from the scheduled castes and Other Backward Classes (OBCs) in India, for whom this kind of pan-caste solidarity is, understandably, very dubious. From this, it is to be hoped, new kinds of alliances can be made that will blunt the drive to exclusion.

Another set of interesting reflections is inspired by reading Birgit Meyer's interesting study *Translating the Devil*. She relates how a form of North German Pietist Protestantism is transformed in the African context, particularly in that a much greater role is attributed to the devil and his minions, and much greater efforts are made to separate the faithful from these and to exorcise them. Here we have a new mode of the presence (and probably future) of a past. But the past is that of this Nordic Protestantism, and of Christianity in general. Something substantially similar to what these African churches are now doing was already undertaken in the early Christian church, and also has analogies to the post-Reformation period in Europe.

What happened in each of these cases is that the spirits and gods recognized in the earlier "pagan" setting, instead of being simply declared nonexistent, as most modern Western Christians (not to speak of atheists) would say, are understood to be very real, but to be evil, enemies of God and of Christ. We can readily surmise that this reflects a world in which the old religion is still very much alive, in which even converts find it hard to separate themselves from it, and in which therefore both "pagans" and converts live in an enchanted world as porous selves. Just declaring the old gods nonexistent is not only hard to believe but doesn't do justice to the struggle in which converts are still engaged.

There is a parallel to the Reformation period, when a great disenchantment was undertaken by elites and imposed—with only partial success—on the population. The latter lived in a thoroughly enchanted world, inhabited by spirits and the site of magic. The attack on this world couldn't credibly take the form of simple denial, and so it involved a radical change of sign. Magic was formerly both white and black, benign and malign. The new dispensation wanted to deny white magic altogether; all forms of it were declared malign.[108]

This was accompanied by an intensification of concern with witches and witchcraft throughout the whole period of the Reformation. This runs counter to the Whig scenario, which sees Protestantism as more "enlightened" than Catholicism, and then Deism as more enlightened than Protestantism, and so on. A kink appears in the sequencing of this master narrative when we find that Thomas Aquinas seems to have had a more "enlightened" view of witchcraft than, say, Bodin.

What is remarkable about Meyer's account is that, although the practices of exorcism among African converts have some parallels with German peasants in the nineteenth century, this whole aspect of the home religion had not been communicated by the missionaries. It was re-created in situ.

So we might think of the intense concern with the devil and with witchcraft as a transition phenomenon, while the old context is still there and has to be fought. Meyer describes the cures from devil possession as bringing about an individuation, loosening ties with the extended kin within which the old religion operates.[109] One could imagine that, over time, individuation would be accompanied, as in the West, by a buffered identity, and the sense of the presence of the spirits would fade.

The interesting issue is whether this expectation is correct. Are all regions of the world fated to head toward the predicament of Western modernity, with a disenchanted world, a strong sense of a self-sufficient immanent order, and a staunchly buffered identity? If one holds that this is the "normal" human situation, only impeded in the past by ignorance, and/or "superstition," then this may sound likely. But one conclusion that one might draw from the narrative I have been sketching is that all the "forward" movements are bought at a price: the axial revolutions with their notions of our higher good; Western reform with its abolition of enchantment and the repression of collective ritual; the creation of the immanent order. All these "advances" are met at various points with enthusiasm, but a profound ambivalence remains. This expresses itself in nostalgia, the sense that something is missing, a hankering after some richer meaning.

How we can extrapolate from a story of unmitigated advance is different from how we might imagine such a history of ambivalence continuing. In particular, this makes a big difference when it comes to predicting what varieties of religious life can show themselves to be viable over the long term in human history. We have been too long mesmerized by one master narrative of the history of one civilization. We don't even have the concepts to state the differences between civilizations or societies with very different religious forms. (Or perhaps I should say, more modestly, that I haven't grasped these myself. But I may not be totally alone in this.) The varieties of religious past that have a future may be much greater than we have been led to suspect.

Religion as Memory

Reference to Tradition and the Constitution of a Heritage of Belief in Modern Societies

Danièle Hervieu-Léger

From the Decline of Religions to the Dissemination of the Religious: The Context of a Theoretical Revision

Until the end of the 1960s, the sociology of religion was governed by one principal objective: namely, that of illuminating and analyzing the structural connection between the rise of modernity and the cultural and social repression of religion. The readings of the founding fathers of the discipline, dominant up to that time, furnished the theoretical underpinnings for this program: Marx, Durkheim, and Weber have certainly developed radically different approaches to the structures and functions of society, but each has, in his own way, contributed to establishing that the process of rationalization characterizing the advance of modernity is identical to the approaching "twilight of the gods." The conquest of autonomy—that of the subject as well as that of society—is, from this perspective, effectuated through an ineluctable disintegration of the entirely religion-based societies of the past. This theoretical position has the advantage (especially welcome in the context of a French *laïcité* marked by a positivist tradition) of radically simplifying the relationship, always difficult to establish, of sociologists to their object: if the scientific enterprise consists, essentially, in measuring the processes of religion's fatal social eviction, the decisive questions concerning the proper makeup of the religious object and the nature of the critical reduction envisioned by sociology can be opportunely dismissed as being of secondary importance. Placing this fundamental epistemological debate in parenthesis could seem all the more justified in that the hypothesis concerning the structural incompatibility between modernity and religion has found ample confirmation in empirical studies of the evolution of the "great religions" in all developed countries. It has, of course, been observed that the declining rate of actual observance of religious practices, the lessening of the political and cultural influence of religious institutions, and the disintegration of belief do not manifest themselves with equal intensity or take the same form in all national contexts. There is clearly sufficient justification, however, for the point of view that religion no longer subsists in "secular societies" except as an option of personal choice. In this case, the question of the transformation of religion in modern societies has tended to be confused with that of the progressive disintegration of the different religious traditions within the societies and cultures that they themselves helped to shape, but in which they can no longer even hope to play any active role whatsoever.

Since the beginning of the 1970s, changes in the historical evolution of religion have profoundly modified this situation by breaking the continuity (postulated up to that time) between the rationalist hypothesis of religion's inescapable decline in modern societies and the empirical observation of a loosening of the hold religious institutions had on society. The long-standing rise of new religious movements, the growth of religious (neo)-fundamentalisms, the multifarious reaffirmations in the West and elsewhere of the importance of the religious factor in public life, have all provoked a vast reexamination of the fundamental hypothesis of the sociology of religion. And this at the price, perhaps, of a new form of obscurantism that eclipses the fundamental problem raised by the construction of the religious object as an object of sociological investigation. The statement "Religion exists, we have seen it manifest itself" is as empty a proposition as that which, twenty or thirty years ago, affirmed (in diverse ways, none of which, of course, as caricatural as the following) that "Religion is an ideological cloud: the proof is its ceaseless dissipation in our modern rational world." Both statements are empty because, in effect, though the religious object is disintegrating, it simultaneously resurfaces, is reborn, circulates, and displaces itself. The intellectual stakes of the present historical situation can be formulated in the following manner: How, from inside the scientific domain constituted by and within the affirmation of the incompatibility of religion and modernity, can one equip oneself with the means of analyzing not only the importance religion conserves outside of the Western Christian world but of analyzing as well the transformations, the displacements, even the revivals it undergoes in this Western world itself?

This question recalls the fundamental debates concerning religion's future that were already present in the works of sociology's founders. The Marxist vision of religion's decline linked the realization of this decline to the total accomplishment of the communist society, and thus, in a way, pushed back its arrival to the end of time. The Durkheimian vision of a "religion of man" capable of furnishing morality with its indispensable transcendent foundation maintains the social necessity of faith over the triumph of science. Both of these perspectives, in two totally different and even antinomical ways, recognize—to a certain point—the impossibility of sociologizing the rationalist hypothesis of the end of religion: the first, indeed, and up to a certain extent, against its own presuppositions; the second explicitly in the logic behind the definition given of religion as the expression of society itself. The Weberian problematic of the disenchanted world separates the analysis of religious spaces in transformation from all prophecy concerning the meaning of history and accentuates the displacements and resurgence of the religiosity characteristic of secular societies governed by a "polytheism of values." This has, in theory, provided the possibility of freeing the empirical study of the decline of religion's hold from the positivist prognosis of the death of the gods in modern societies. This problematic, at the same time, requires that one directly treat the question of the religious productions of modernity itself.

Religions of substitution, religions of replacement, analogical religions, diffuse religions, surrogate religions: these terms express the difficulty of delimiting the obscure constellations that make up these religious productions of modernity. They are, in effect, as exploded, mobile, and dispersed as the modern imagination in which they inscribe themselves: a loose conglomerate of patchwork beliefs, an elusive hodgepodge of reminiscence and dreams that individuals organize in a private and subjective fashion as a response to the concrete situation with which they find themselves confronted.[1] In the domain of Christianity, this atomized state of signifying systems is directly tied to the rupture of a stable link between belief and practice, a rupture that Michel de Certeau places at the heart of his analysis of the explosion of modern Christianity.[2] Modern Christian belief is—he says—less and less anchored to specific groups and behavioral patterns; it determines fewer and fewer associations and specific practices. The dissemination of modern phenomena of believing, on the one hand, and the evaporation of the socioreligious link that once constituted long-term support for the construction of a religious culture encompassing aspects of social life, on the other hand, are the two inseparable sides of the secularization process, whose historical trajectory is intertwined with that of modernity itself. Nevertheless, beyond the obviousness of this disintegration of the religious in modern societies, one is forced to admit that religion still speaks . . . But it doesn't speak in the areas where one might expect it to. One discovers its presence—diffuse, implicit, or invisible—in economics, politics, aesthetics, the scientific, the ethical, and the symbolic. Instead of focusing one's interest on the relationship between the diminishing domain of the religious (that of its institutions and that of the "historical" religions) and other social domains (the political, the therapeutic, the aesthetic, etc.), one is led to an investigation of the diverse surreptitious manifestations of religion in all profane and reputedly nonreligious zones of human activity. But how far should one push this investigation? Should one stop after identifying the discrete but properly religious influences (Christianity, Judaism, Islam, etc.) at work outside of their usual spheres? Or should one investigate the entirety of the believing, ascetic, militant, or ecstatic phenomena that manifest themselves in the areas of economics, politics, arts, and the sciences? Will it be necessary to concentrate one's efforts on "indisputably" religious phenomena, at the risk of being blinded by their very obviousness, given that it is society itself that thus predefines them? Or, rather, will it be necessary to widen one's perspective in order to bring to light modernity's (invisible) religious logic, at the risk of the dissolution of the religious object as such, at the risk as well of giving to the researcher an exorbitant privilege in the selection of the significant facts?

For a sociology of religious modernity, this situation gives true meaning to the operation of "revising" the concept of secularization, an operation that at present preoccupies researchers.[3] This operation no doubt consists in fine-tuning the analysis of those processes whereby religious space shrinks or grows in society. But it implies first of all that one ask why the sociology of secularization, oscillating as it does between the problematic of the "loss" of the religious and that of religion's "dispersion," thus produces these circumstantially variable versions of religion. Without returning to all the overused problematizations of both the "loss" and the "return" of the religious, how can one grasp the movement whereby modernity continuously undermines the structural plausibility of all religious systems while motivating new forms of religious believing? In order to advance in this direction, one cannot possibly limit oneself exclusively to the rationalist perspective, which links contemporary religious "revivals" entirely to the de-modernizing pressures created by global crisis and the collapse of modernist ideologies of progress (the latter in their diverse liberal or Marxist variants). The religious paradox of modernity stems not from the failure of this modernity but from the structural contradictions that modernity's expansion ceaselessly provokes.[4] It is therefore necessary to break with the paradigmatic incompatibility between religion and modernity, and to abandon the corollary idea of the strict opposition between traditional and modern societies. Above all, it is imperative to return to the inescapable question of religion's definition.

Indefinite Religion: New Clothes for an Old Debate

> It is necessary to begin by defining what is meant by religion; for without this, we would run the risk of giving the name to a system of ideas and practices which has nothing at all religious about it, or else of leaving to one side many religious facts, without perceiving their true nature.

This recommendation, with which Durkheim opens his *Elementary Forms of the Religious Life*,[5] may seem all too evident for those who believe that the first and inescapable step in sociological research is to define the object of one's study. And yet for the longest time sociologists of religion were inclined to consider, on the contrary, that methodological prudence required one to avoid all definition of religion as such and to leave "theorizing" to the philosophers. This reticence, justifiable given the impossibility of assigning precise limits to an object coextensive with the human phenomenon,[6] was for them also a means of defense against the phenomenological temptation to grasp an impossible "essence" of religion. The following consensus was reached: the domain of research of the sociologist of religion covered all objects that the society itself designated as "religious." It was admissible, should the need arise, to extend one's investigation to include the most apparent "analogously religious" phenomena: civil and military rituals, revolutionary cults, and so on. But in this case the relationship between "religion" (in the strict sense of the variants of historical religions) and these "analogous" forms remained carefully untreated.

It is the case, however, that in order simultaneously to understand both the modern proliferation of belief and the deregulation of the domain of institutionalized religion it is no longer possible to maintain this prudent position. If one wants to study how religious beliefs are dispersed and distributed beyond the spaces of believing controlled by the great religious systems, one must be able to identify what, in the modern production of belief, stems from religion and what does not. It is necessary, in other words, to be equipped with a "definition" of religion, one that does not allow us to grasp the ultimate essence of religion but that simply allows for the classification of observable phenomena. To this end, two positions have clarified themselves in the last few years:

1. The first, illustrated in the thoughts of Thomas Luckmann on "the invisible religion" of modern societies,[7] has recourse to an extremely extended definition of religion, one that encompasses the entirety of the imaginary constructs whereby society, groups within this society, and individuals within these groups try to give meaning to their everyday experience and to represent to themselves their origin and their future.
2. The other, resolutely restrictive, reserves, on the contrary, the designation of religion for those "productions of meaning" that explicitly call into service the capital of references and symbols belonging to the traditions of the "historical religions."

What is at stake in the act of choosing between these two perspectives is not an issue of abstract selection: this choice directly concerns the practice of research. This made itself particularly clear in the recent American (then European) sociological debate surrounding the rise of what we have come to refer to as "new religious movements." It is well known that this term covers a great variety of phenomena: cults and sects that have recently come to compete with the historical religions (with the "great churches" or longstanding minority groups), syncretic groups with an oriental influence, revival movements within the organized religions, all of them taking part in the construction of a "mystico-esoteric nebulosity" characterized most notably by its ability to assimilate and reemploy all forms of available knowledge (from the "official" state science to the most marginalized traditional and ancient *savoir-faires*) . . . and this to the end of the self-development of the individual adherent, in both the long and the short term.[8] These highly diverse groups and networks may "graft themselves onto the great oriental religions, take the form of a more or less antiquated esoteric syncretism, or of a new psycho-religious syncretism, or they may even gather individuals around the practice of this or that divinatory art (astrology, tarot, or the I-Ching)." These groups maintain ties with journals, publishers, and booksellers; they hold expositions, offer training courses, and arrange conferences. Their followers go from one to the other, taking advantage of this "self-service acculturation, particularly rich in all kinds of offers allowing for a highly personalized composition *a la carte.*"[9] It is around these kinds of phenomena that the question of the boundary of the religious has been most directly raised, where the debate that provokes the growing dissociation between an "intensive" sociology of religious groups and an "extensive" sociology of phenomena of belief is most concentrated. If these movements offer their followers a kind of "interior fulfillment," one that can be interpreted as an individualized and secular (and therefore modern) road to salvation, is it necessary to see therein the figure of a new modem religion? Or, due to a lack of reference to any transcendence whatsoever, and because these movements are customarily lacking in a larger social project, must one deny them all the qualification of "religiousness"? More recently still, this discussion of the "limits of the religious" has been stimulated by research grouped around the "secular" or "metaphorical" religions. This research is enriched by observations concerning the very general development of an "invisible" or "diffuse" religiousness that arises without the mediation of the specialized institutions. But it has gotten no less bogged down in the infinite rehashing of the classical debate that opposes a "substantive" (and restrictive) definition of religion (implying, as it always does, belief in a supernatural power), and a "functional" definition of religion (one that sees "religion" as the entirety of "ultimate" or "fundamental" meanings that individuals or groups are inclined to produce in order to make sense of their lives). That is: on the one hand, religion is defined according to the content of its beliefs (e.g., belief in God) and the type of ritualized activities linked with these beliefs—in which case it becomes impossible to say anything about the potentially religious nature of phenomena in which some see the modern forms of "sacredness" (from packed football stadiums to outdoor rock concerts, which unite these Durkheimian "crowds in fusion," including as well all forms of "secular religiousness"); on the other hand, one stretches the definition of religion to include everything in our societies that touches upon questions of sense and the search for an ultimate meaning of the world in which we live—in which case, religious phenomena are diluted to the point of becoming indefinite nebulosities of "systems of signification."

Nonetheless, beyond this explicit theoretical conflict, it is not certain that the substantivist and functionalist positions are as antinomical as they formally claim to be. For Luckmann, in whom we admittedly have the most extensive conception of religion, it appears in part that the pulverization of individually constructed meanings that characterizes modern consciousness tends to exclude the integration of these meanings into an organized system of beliefs, a system that would provide collective action with a coherent direction, a power of mobilization, and a stock of imaginary resources. Without these elements testifying to the exteriorization and projection of individually constructed mean-ing onto the universe as such, and in the absence of all possible aggregation and systemati-zation of these individual collages of sense, it is difficult to see what remains of the process of "cosmization" that would transform these phenomena of belief into a "sacred modern cosmos."[10] Luckmann himself considers it highly unlikely that the social objectivization of such themes as self-realization or personal fulfillment—themes that have their origin in the private sphere—give rise either to the articulation of a sacred, well-founded, and closed cosmos or to the specialization of new religious institutions. He nonetheless notes that, within this vague cloud of individual expectations and aspirations, representations that he designates as "specifically religious" may perhaps survive. These specifically reli-gious representations arise from historical and religious traditions and make reference to the "great religions." Their survival depends, according to Luckmann, on their ability to "function," that is, to assure the subjective satisfaction of the individual. But the simple act of designating as "specifically religious" those traditional representations that subsist within this sacred modernity shows what little consistency Luckmann himself accords to the invisible "religion," as well as the implicit weight of substantive criteria, which deter-mine that only the historical religions be considered as religion in the full sense of the word.

A similar ambiguity is visible in the work of R. Bellah and other authors in their studies of the communally shared values of a given society, values that constitute the armature of "civil religion."[11] J. Coleman defines this as the "set of beliefs, rites, and symbols which links the role of man as citizen and his place in society, both temporally and historically, to the ultimate meanings of existence."[12] Is it a question here of religion "in the full sense of the word," or is he merely speaking by analogy? For Bellah, this set of "beliefs, rites, and symbols" is "religion" if one admits—as he himself does—that "one of the functions of religion is to furnish a significant set of ultimate values which may serve as the basis for the morality of a society."[13] But he remains uncertain as to the possibility that these values, as such, could constitute the "substantive core" of a religion in the same way that Christian, Judaic, or Islamic values constitute the substantive core of these historical religions. The substantive definition of religion exercises, paradoxically, its permanent attraction in the works of the very authors who would free themselves of the limitations it imposes upon both empirical research and theoretical elaboration.

The distance, finally, between this vision of a sacred modern cosmos (this haze of atomized significations) and the restrictive perspective incarnated by the work of B. Wil-son is, therefore, less than one might suppose. The latter refuses to consider as "religious" groups and personnel, associations and professionals, whose sole function is to promote, on a case-by-case basis, the harmonization and elaboration of collages of meaning to the sole benefit of the individual. Although Luckmann would probably not refuse to designate the same groups and persons as "religious," he suggests that "religion," thus broadened in its definition, has no effect beyond the subjective satisfaction of the individuals concerned. Yet it is equally conceivable that he could refuse, in the manner of Wilson, to designate as "religious" a behavior that consists in the "ritualistic" washing of one's car every Sunday morning.

In both cases, the question raised is that of identifying universes of religious meaning within the modern kaleidoscope of available universes of signification.[14] One can again schematize the terms of this debate according to the archetypal positions of Luckmann and Wilson:

1. For Luckmann, the difficult point is the evanescent continuity between the modern universes of signification and the religion that is introduced therein through ultimate reference to a sacred cosmos.
2. For Wilson, the problematic element is the discontinuity raised by reference to the supernatural and utopic. If one, in effect, admits that religious constructs are a part of the universe of meaning that society creates, one cannot fix a definition for these constructs, once and for all and in a substantive fashion, without reifying the historical (premodern) situation that led to the Western mode of religious believing, based on an appeal to the supernatural and on a utopic "Kingdom of Heaven."

The same objection can be made concerning the definition proposed by Y. Lambert, which seeks to avoid the dissolution of the concept of "religion" in the multitude of responses to "ultimate questions." His definition, which is meant to be strictly functional, is based upon three discriminating features, whose presence is expressly prerequisite—according to him—in order to speak of religion. The first is the "postulated existence of beings, forces, or entities which exceed the objective limits of the human condition, but which remain in contact with humanity"; the second is the existence of "symbolic means of communication with them: prayer, rites, services, sacrifice"; the third is the existence of "communalizing bodies such as a church, or other body." The construction of a formal model of religion is here limited to the isolation of those traits that serve as the lowest common denominator of the historical religions. Within the scope of Y. Lambert's interest in the comparative sociology of historical religions, this definition is perfectly adequate. But it considerably reduces the possibility of exploring, from the point of view of a sociology of religious modernity, the phenomena of recomposition, displacement, and innovation that arise, in part, from the less plausible position that institutionalized religions now occupy in the modern world.[15]

If the functional definitions of religion turn out to be incapable of mastering the unlimited expansion of the phenomena they try to account for and thus become empty of all heuristic pertinence, the substantive definitions of religion, constructed around the gravitational attraction of the historical religions, condemn sociological thought to being the paradoxical guardian of the "authentic religion" that these historical religions intend to incarnate. The former can do little more than attest to the intellectually recalcitrant dispersion of religious symbols in contemporary societies. The latter are caught up in the indefinite reiteration of analyses revolving around the loss of religion in the modern world. Both are partial but radically limited responses to the question of religion's position within modernity. Religion is (tendentiously) nowhere or everywhere, both of which, in the final analysis, mean nothing.

Getting Out of the Circle: Religion as a Modality (Mode) of Belief

In order to escape this circularity, it is first necessary to persuade oneself that the major problem sociologists confront in the analysis of religious modernity is *not* that of finding better criteria for the delimitation of the social space of religion. It is, rather, to equip oneself with the conceptual instruments that, given the impossibility of satisfactorily localizing the contours of the religious "domain," take into account this very delocalization itself.[16] This perspective implies that one resist ontological definitions of religion by turning the act of definition itself toward the properly sociological perspective that necessitates it. What is of interest to sociology? It is not a question of knowing, once and for all, what religion itself is as such. It is a question of understanding the logic behind the transformations of the religious universe, concretely approached through its sociohistorical manifestations. From this perspective, religion's definition is required only as a tool, a practical instrument designed to aid the researcher in his attempt to think socioreligious change, as well as to think the modern mutation of the religious. It is, therefore, necessary to give attention to the process of change itself: religion's definition (if one can still, and without ambiguity, use this term) is a dynamic concept, an ideal-type that does not aim to fix its object but to designate the axes of transformation around which the object reconstructs itself. In order to grasp this process as a global dynamic of the recasting of the religious, one that encompasses, transforms, and reorganizes the historical religions themselves, it is important that all analysis be focused not upon the changing contents of belief but upon *the mutating structures of believing* that these changes in content partially reveal.

Before going further, it is indispensable to define what one means here by "to believe." This term designates the totality of both individual and collective convictions that do not arise from verification, experimentation or, more generally, from isolation and control criteria that characterize scientific knowledge—convictions that have their basis in the fact that they give meaning and coherence to the subjective experience of those who hold them. If one here speaks of the act of "believing" rather than of "belief," it is because the totality of these aforementioned convictions, in addition to the ideal objects of conviction (the beliefs themselves), incorporates the practices, languages, gestures, and spontaneous automatisms in which these beliefs are themselves inscribed. "To believe" is belief in motion, belief as it is lived. It is, according to the definition proposed by de

Certeau, that which the individual or collective speaker *does* with the statement he claims to believe.[17] The notion of believing, thus widened, is able to include the "practical beliefs" characteristic of populations that live within a monistic universe. Here, the notion of belief alone—given the distance it implies between believer and object of belief—seems to make little sense.[18] The act of believing thus understood allows for the presentation of different structural levels of believing: it includes the variety of "bodily states," treated by Pierre Bourdieu, which are inculcated during initial apprenticeship and of which the initiates themselves are so unconscious that they have the feeling of "having been born with them."[19] Everything that seems to arise out of one's "experience with the world as happening all by itself" belongs to the domain of believing. At the other end of the spectrum, one finds all the formalized and rationalized beliefs for which individuals are capable of accounting and which have practical influence upon their lives. In all cases, the actual act of believing, whether it arises from spontaneous evidence or from theoretical conviction, escapes experimental demonstration and verification. At the very most, one can affirm its existence from the point of view of those who believe, from the presence of a network of indices and signs. But from one moment to the next, to believe implies that both individuals and groups submit themselves (consciously or unconsciously) to an exteriorly imposed order, or to a kind of gamble or choice, more or less elaborated, more or less well argued.

To put the act of believing at the center of one's thinking is to preliminarily admit that believing does in fact constitute a major dimension of modernity. This idea is far from evident. It has often been remarked that scientific and technological rationality have reduced the space of believing in modern societies by displacing the demands for meaning (without which no human society is possible) away from the primordial question of *why* toward the practical question of *how*. But if advances in science and technology have in large part eroded the world's mysteries, they have not reduced the human need for *security*, which is at the heart of the quest for intelligibility, a need that in effect constantly remotivates the question of why. All lived uncertainty, for both individuals and collectives, raises the specter par excellence of, for the individual, death; for the society, anomy. P. Berger, following Durkheim, has reminded us that the sacred is nothing else but the edifice of signification that humankind objectivizes as a power radically other than itself and that it projects upon reality in order to escape the anguish of being swallowed up by chaos.[20] Modernity breaks with the sacred to the extent to which humankind itself, with its own capacities, carries out the work of rationalizing the world in which it lives and of mastering, through thought and action, tendencies toward chaos. But the destabilization alone of "sacred cosmizations" (Berger) occasioned by the process of rationalization does not efface the fundamental need to lessen the structural incertitude of the human condition. But neither does this need subsist as the residue of a now obsolete sacred universe. It arises out of modernity itself, redistributing itself throughout the multiplication of demands of sense. These demands are all the more exigent in that it is no longer a question, for the agents of society, of thinking their place in a stable world seen as the reflection of the natural order itself, understood as a creation, but of situating themselves in an open social space in which change and innovation are held up as the norm. At the very moment when modernity deconstructs systems of signification (systems that, for the individual and the society, formerly expressed the ideal ordering of their world), even during the very movement whereby modernity demonstrates the possibility of controlling and manipulating this world, it develops, to an enormous and proportional degree, the social and psychological factors of incertitude. Modernity itself, therefore, motivates a rebound of the question of sense and the diverse expressions of protestation against the non-sense that is its counterpart.[21] The identification of the modern act of believing is carried out through the analysis of these modes of resolving (or, at least, of hiding) incertitude; modes that are refracted in diverse forms of belief. In the mobile, "fluid" universe of the modern act of believing, liberated as it is from the hold of global institutions of believing, all symbols are interchangeable, combinable, and transposable one into the other. All syncretisms are possible, all recycling imaginable. It is from this observation that one can clarify the sociological definition of religion. The search for this definition, as we have already said, has no meaning outside of *a specific point of view*: that which analyses the dynamic of modernity seen not as a thing but as a process, as motion. One must add that this search is justifiable only insofar as it takes into account this specific mobility of the modern act of believing, an act in which the content of belief can no longer be, a priori, understood as religious, political, or otherwise. This double petition imposes a radical "desubstantialization" of the definition of religion. It further imposes that one admit, once and for all, that religious believing does not refer to the objects of a particular set of beliefs, to specific social practices, or even to representations of the origins of the world. Religious believing can be usefully defined—in an ideal-typical manner—as *a particular modality of the organization and function of the act of believing.*

The identification of this modality of belief consists—classically—in accentuating one or several of the traits that distinguish this modality from others. The voluntarist nature of this way of constructing a conceptual tool for the analysis of religious believing must not be dissimulated. But the only truly fundamental issue here is to know if this tool is useful, that is, if it permits one (among other possible usages) to grasp that which justifies, beyond the commonplace and obvious analogies between "historical" and "secular" religions, the simultaneous sociological treatment of their situation and evolution within modernity. The stated objective is not only to determine whether the beliefs and practices of some ecological or political group, the emotional investment among the spectators of a football game, or the collective fervor of adolescents at a rock concert can be said to be "religious." One seeks to know as well whether this or that modern expression of Christianity, Judaism, or some other tradition that society qualifies as "a religion," can be characterized according to our definition as effectively being "religious." Such a perspective rests, therefore, upon the well-reasoned decision to place oneself—beyond the usual hallmarks of religion, that is, the contents or functions proper to belief—within a perspective that permits one simultaneously to grasp these diverse manifestations of belief in order to compare and classify them. The perspective retained here is one that examines the *type of legitimization* that supports the act of believing. At this stage of our research, the hypothesis that we are advancing is as follows: there is no religion without the explicit, semi-explicit, or entirely implicit invocation of *the authority of a tradition*, an invocation that serves as support for the act of believing. Within this perspective, one designates as "religious" all forms of believing that justify themselves, first and foremost, upon the claim of their inscription within *a heritage of belief.*

This proposition must not be taken as the enunciation of a definitive truth suggesting that religion *is,* exclusively and totally, this heritage. It is a *working hypothesis,* a *perspective* that allows for the creation of *one* sociological approach (among others) to the question of religion. This approach is chosen as a function of an intellectual objective: that of accounting for the mutations of religion within modernity. In order to grasp the effective range of this definition, it is necessary to understand thoroughly that this self-legitimization of the act of believing through reference to the authority of a tradition is much more than the simple assertion of a continuity of belief from one generation to the next. The "religious believer" (individual or group) is not content to believe for the simple reason that "it has always been that way": he considers himself, in the words of the Swiss theologian P. Gisel, as being "engendered."[22] It is not the continuity itself that is of value here, but the fact that this continuity acts as the visible expression of a filiation that the individual or collective believer expressly claims and that integrates him or her into a spiritual community assembling past, present, and future believers. The heritage of belief fulfills the role of legitimizing imaginary reference. It functions simultaneously as a principle of social identification, *ad intra* (through integration into a believing community) and *ad extra* (by differentiation from those who are not of the same heritage). From this angle, "religion" can be seen as an ideological, practical, and symbolic framework that constitutes, maintains, develops, and controls the consciousness (individual or collective) of membership to a particular heritage of belief. From the same angle, religious institutions can be ideal-typically defined as "traditional institutions," governed by the "imperative of continuity." This obviously does not mean that religious institutions are immobile and escape change. But it does mean that change imposes itself only to the extent that it is integrated into the collective representation, perpetually renewed, of a continuity that itself always remains intact. Thus it is that the enterprise of religious reform often presents itself as the return to an authentic tradition, which opposes the distortions of tradition apparent in present usage. Or reform takes on the aspect of a deepened understanding of the tradition itself, an understanding that justifies its own innovation or renovation. The prophet, who directly contests the dominant religious order, regularly justifies his mission by declaiming the necessity of accomplishing what the religious institution has either neglected or forgotten. And the personal revelation of which he is the vessel gives rise to a "religion" only to the extent that it is rendered immutable by becoming the starting point for a new heritage of belief. The imperative of continuity, which imposes itself in the religious domain as such, expresses the founding of the social and religious bond.

Transmission: A Central Question for a Sociology of Religious Modernity

One of the principal implications of this definition is that it puts particular emphasis on the specific type of mobilization collective memory undergoes, a mobilization that is characteristic of all religions thus understood. In traditional societies, where the symbolico-religious universe is structured entirely around an original myth, thus taking into account both the origins of the world and the origins of the group, collective memory is generally a given. It is, in fact, entirely manifest in the structures, organization, language, and daily practices of societies governed by tradition. In the case of differentiated societies, in which the prevalence of founded religions gives rise to self-designated communities of faith, collective religious memory becomes the object of constant reevaluation in such a fashion that the historical event of the religion's founding can, at all moments, be grasped as a totality of meaning. To the degree that all present signification is presumably contained, at least potentially, in the founding event, the past is symbolically constituted as an unchangeable whole, situated "out of time," that is, out of history. In constant contact with this past, the religious group defines itself objectively and subjectively as *a chain of memory*, whose continuity transcends history. The existence of this chain is attested to and made manifest by the specifically religious act that consists in the remembrance (anamnesia) of this past, which gives meaning to the present and contains the future. As a result, religious transmission does more than just assure the passage of a given content of beliefs from one generation to another (through the socialization of newcomers within a community whose norms they accept and who share the community's orientations and values). Insofar as transmission is bound up with the processes of elaboration of this chain of memory whereby a group of believers becomes a religious group, transmission is the very movement whereby the religion constitutes itself in time as a religion: it is the continuing foundation of the religious institution itself.

This proposition contains the possibility of a renewed approach to the religious dilemma of modern societies and, more generally, to the problem of "secularization." One can sum up this approach in the following manner: What becomes of the religious problematic of the continuity of belief in modern societies (and how does one assure the socialization of a universe that remains structured by this imperative of continuity) when these societies have as their distinctive trait, as emphasized by Marcel Gauchet, that of being governed by an "imperative to change"?[23] In these societies, where the differentiation of institutions has been accomplished, the different spheres of social activity exist, with their own distinct and relatively autonomous logics. Individuals intervene in these milieus, in which they come to terms with the complex "rules of the house," as demonstrated in the work of F. Dubet, according to their own personal dispositions, memberships, interests, aspirations, and experiences.[24] It is out of the combined diversity of these interests and lived experiences that individuals construct—in a world of perpetual change where memory, for the most part, has lost its organizing power—the meaning they give to their own existence. In the area of religion, as in all other areas of their personal experience, individuals are confronted with the lack of an organizational centrality capable of offering them a preestablished code of meaning. This being the case, individuals are incited *to produce* (if they do so at all) a relationship to a heritage of belief in which they recognize themselves. One can finally ask: How, then, given the pluralization of processes that enter into the construction of religious identities (a construction in which the subjective work individuals carry out in order to make sense of their experience is the principal motor), how can collective representation of the continuity of a heritage (and its realization in society) still be assured? This question, stemming from the definition of religion proposed above, sketches the bottom line for a sociology of religious modernity.

—*Translated by John A. Farhat*

If This Be Magic . . . : Excursions into Contemporary Hindu Lives

Veena Das

In his commentaries on a series of papers on "Indian Religion," the distinguished philosopher of religion and Indologist Alexander Piatigorski theorizes that, despite the widely accepted notion that the emergence of the anthropology of religion as a science was historically connected with a widespread cultural rejection of religious belief, anthropology remains, from the point of view of an external observer, "an epiphenomenon of Christian culture." This is evident, Piatigorski argues, in the way in which concepts such as "religion," "magic," "god," or "myth" are deployed in scholarly texts. He further claims that, despite the assumption of their universal applicability, all these terms carry traces of their Christian origins.[1] A telling example for Piatigorski is the meaning of the term *god* as it operates in anthropological texts, for it differs completely from the notion of god in Hindu traditions. In them, the idea of god, even when used in the singular, refers to a class of beings rather than a single being. At any point of time and in any given space, this class of beings can be made present as a singular deity, an *ishtadevata* (lit., a "chosen deity"), through ritual or devotional techniques.[2] When scholars of religion use the term *god* to translate terms in Sanskrit or the vernacular languages in India, however, they sometimes fail to recognize the adjectival qualities of these terms. In treating them as names of one or another divine being, they manage to unintentionally inflect the discussion with Christian imaginaries.[3]

Let me begin by spelling out some implications of Piatigorski's claims a little further. Anthropologists have described the various ways in which Hindu devotees enter into relationships or transactions with personal or more generic deities presiding over, say, a family, a lineage, or a village. The fact that the deity is treated, through both word and gesture, as embodied and present in an iconic or aniconic form (which could be an image, a word, an idol, or an inanimate or animate being) leads one some-times to endow it with substantial properties. Even when present in a consecrated space such as a temple, however, the deity can flee; the icon becomes a dead shell if not properly propitiated. Thus ritual and meditative techniques are necessary for a desiring devotee or group of devotees to make a deity present or to ensure its continued presence. What from an external perspective is characterized as "polytheism" or "idolatry" is an extremely complex network of relations in which the desire of the person (man or woman), the desire of the deity, the utterance of *mantras* as either semantic or phonetic strings, and the hidden meaning and use of objects can simultaneously actualize and reveal a particu-lar relation to the divine as the devotee comes to comprehend it. Of course, the techniques for making a deity present either in the imagination or within the concrete structures of a temple are varied and dependent upon sectarian allegiances as well as on local traditions.

Ritual, Belief, and Language

As scholars of Hindu texts and practices have demonstrated, the textual traditions within which debates about what makes a ritual practice efficacious were carried out are ex-tremely complex and tied to deep philosophical questions about (among other things) the fundamental nature of language. Importantly, even today these debates echo through the practices of people who are nonliterate or poorly educated (by modern standards), as we shall see later in this essay. Questions of efficacy were not tied only to technical considerations—for example, whether the ritual has been correctly performed—although these considerations were not irrelevant. One might schematize one set of arguments in the following way. What is the relation between language in everyday life and its opera-tions in the realms of the sacred, for example, sacrificial rituals, meditative techniques, and devotional forms? By focusing on one set of questions, namely, the place of the word and what some scholars call "sonic theologies" in the Hindu imagination of what con-nects our everyday world with that of the sacred, I hope to say something about what was at stake in arguments about what makes a ritual efficacious.[4] Later, I hope to connect this with some contemporary concerns in the understanding of Hinduism(s). Let me begin with a brief description of what was at stake in considering the question of what makes an action into a ritual and what makes ritual efficacious.

Let us consider the three major schools of thought that have influenced the question of ritual efficacy. In presenting these issues in such a schematic form, I am deliberately eclipsing the historical development of these ideas as well as the subtle differences within each school of thought. The texts from which I draw my examples were composed over a long period of time. The Purvamimamsa of Jamini, which interpreted Vedic injunctions about performing sacrifice, is usually considered to have been composed in the third century B.C.E., but the arguments of the text have been argued, refined, and modified ever since. It is generally acknowledged that Bhartrihari (perhaps fifth century) saw the analysis of language as a philosophical problem, though reflections on language were an integral part of the commentary on questions of ritual efficacy. The tantra texts, again, have a long and variegated history. The earliest Shaiva texts of the Kashmir tradition are traced to the first millennium c.e.[5] I hope, nevertheless, that the focus on some of the issues abstracted from the more detailed descriptions of the historical evolution of these schools, as well as detailed descriptions of the minutiae of rituals and practices, will help to establish the distance between concepts such as idolatry, polytheism, primitive fusion, and so on through which such practices have been framed in larger discourses on religion.

First, consider the Purvamimamsa, which laid out the rules and interpretations of Vedic sacrifice. For the proponents of the Purvamimamsa, the authority of the rituals derived from the Vedas, but the Vedas themselves did not derive their authority from any deity or person. The Vedas were seen as self-authored.[6] It was the function of gods not to reveal the Vedas but to hold them between one cycle of time and the next. In some ways the gods themselves depended upon the power of mantras, or sacred utterances, to bring them into existence. (A mantra can be understood as a string either of sounds or of meaning-bearing words. There have been considerable discussions about whether a mantra is "meaningful" or not.) When gods were invited to participate in the Vedic sacrifice, and offerings of both words (mantras) and substances were made to them, it was understood that they were created by the names that were uttered. Hence, for the proponents of the Purvamimamsa there was a deep divide between sacred language and ordinary language. Emphasis was on the syllables and sounds of the words uttered, and it was the *act* of offering sacrifice, rather than pleasing the gods, that was of prime importance. I have elsewhere explored how the proponents of the Purvamimamsa dealt with objections from others (the *purvapaksha*) about their general theories of language, as well as objections to specific ritual procedures.[7] To take but one example, offerings to the gods Indra and Varun were different when they were conjoined by the use of a specific word for conjunction (*cha*) than when the words were conjoined through the grammatical rules of *samas* into a compound word. While opponents of the Purvamimamsa school thought this to be illogical thought, its defenders opined that, since the rules by which the words were conjoined were different, the entities themselves became different and hence had to be honored through different kinds of offerings. It was not that the Purvamimamsa school was somehow ignorant of the way that cause and effect are connected in everyday life or that the rules they proposed would not appear "illogical" to others, but they argued that language functioned in an entirely different modality in the sacrificial arena and that it drew from a region of language in which the relation between the word (*shabda*) and meaning (*artha*) was eternal and nonarbitrary.[8]

One more example of the kinds of debates that marked the question of what was a deity might be of interest. Günter-Dietz Sontheimer contends that in discussing the features of the deity, the *purvapakshin*, or those who offer criticisms to the *siddhantins* (the upholders of the principles), are in fact presenting the features of folk deities, such as corporeality, capacity to hold property, the actual imbibing of offerings, and so on, all of which give a substantive personality to the deity. In contrast, for the upholders of the Purvamimamsa, the act of performing the sacrifice was primary, at least for the obligatory sacrifices, those necessary to preserve the order of the world. Only in the secondary, optional sacrifices did the focus shift from the act itself to the person performing the act. Indeed, the practices of devotees have an impact on how the world is made.

The Mimamsaka interpretations of language emphasized the sound as well as the meaning of the sentence through a prior commitment to its meaningfulness even if it violated commonsense, since the connection between a word (including its sound) and the meaning, in their view, was eternally fixed in ritual injunctions that provided the model for thinking about language. The grammarians, led by Bhartrihari, thought that the basic meaning-bearing unit of language was the sentence and not the word.[9] Though the authority of the sacred word was not in question for them, they were not inclined to emphasize the difference between sacred language and ordinary language. Thus rules for the comprehension of language and its relation to the world were the same in both. The key to deciphering the world, for the grammarians, lay in understanding the different levels of language, and the capability to do so came not from ritual specialists but from the intuition regarding the relation between language and the world that inheres in all human beings. Though the grammarians had a great impact upon aesthetic theory, their views did not seem to have had much impact on the understanding of the place of god or other features of religious life. Guy Beck thinks that this was because, by dissolving the boundaries between sacred language and ordinary language, their views were conducive to authorizing religious experience via the intuitions of ordinary persons, and this was not acceptable to the specialists.

Finally, the theistic schools, despite their allegiance to the signifier in language, assumed that the mediation of a personal deity was essential to ritual efficacy. The inner meaning of sacred language, including the use of mantras or gestures, needed the guidance of a personal deity or a *guru* ("spiritual teacher"). Without the support of the deity, human intentions would never be sufficient to perform the rituals or recite the mantras correctly. Though there are common elements in many religions, including Christianity and Islam, that pertain to the idea of a personal relationship between a devotee and a deity or a saint, the notion of an *ishtadevata* in Hinduism is aligned to an overarching, all-powerful God in somewhat different ways. Not only, for instance, could one's *ishtadevata* require one to perform actions that are considered contrary to common morality, but such a deity might also stand in a conflicting relationship to other deities.[10] Similarly, the importance of the guru lies in the personal mantra that he alone can bestow on the devotee. As in the Purvamimamsa, in the theistic schools, too, the sounds and graphic representations of letters and words are of paramount importance. Despite different sectarian colorings, in all theistic versions of Hindu texts and practices we encounter such ideas as the internalization of the alphabet in different parts of the body, the connection between different sounds or graphic forms of the fifty-four letters of the Sanskrit alphabet and the acoustic body of the deity, and meditative or yogic practices through which the sound that lies inert in different parts of the body can be made animate. In fact, in some *tantric* traditions the emergence of the alphabet itself is a result of the coupling in different modes of the primal male (*purusha*) and female (*prakriti*) principles. Thus meditation on sound becomes vital for many *tantric* practices.[11]

The Christian Framing of Hindu Debates

My sketch of some of the debates on conditions for the efficacy of ritual and different regions of language that the three main orientations to ritual assumed, is, of course, nothing more than a sketch. I allude to these debates simply to point out that what was at stake was not a debate on polytheism versus monotheism—such questions are not of much interest in any of the texts that engage with these issues. Yet, when questions about how to understand Hinduism are raised within any discussions on religious pluralism or Christian-Hindu dialogue, it is assumed that the stakes are the same for Christian theologians and for different kinds of Hindus, or at least that they could be made mutually translatable.

In an extraordinary attempt at religious dialogue, the Christian theologian Hans Küng has responded in detail to the descriptions of various facets of Hinduism summarized with astonishing clarity by the German Indologist Heinrich von Stietencron. I will take up just one strand in this discussion. In a section entitled "Monotheism or Polytheism," Küng initiates his reflections in response to Stietencron in the following way.[12]

> If we work from the standpoint of life as it is actually lived, and not so much about the abstract doctrine, we as Christians will be more careful about accusing Hinduism of polytheism, as has so often been done. Or should there be double standards for Christianity and Hinduism—for Christianity only the high ideal, for Hinduism the sobering reality? No doubt as Christians one feels extraordinary impressions on the holy Ganges at Banaras or in the Hindu sanctuaries of Nepal or Bali, but one is scarcely tempted to become a member of such religions. By the same token would the Vishnuite [sic] or Shivaite [sic] Hindu, visiting a Baroque church in Naples or Bavaria or even St. Peter's at Rome discover in Christianity a Monotheistic revolution (J. Ratzinger) overthrowing all the pagan gods?

The terms here rendered *Vishnuite* and *Shivaite* are in Sanskrit *Vaishnav* and *Shaiva*. Both are adjectives rather than nouns, and they refer to the quality of many objects as well as persons imbued with Vishnu or Shiva. That is to say, allegiance to the deity is integrated within a wide range of persons, objects, words, and gestures. Yet in Küng's rendering the terms already signify tendencies to monotheism, since *Vishnuite* and *Shivaite* seem to center the idea of *belief* in god. This reduces the import of the range of meanings and religious colorings implicated in the adjectival meanings of these terms.

These framing sentences lead Küng to locate two parallels between Christianity and Hinduism. The first is that "If we understand 'God' to be the highest and deepest principle of all, the very first and the very last reality of the world, in human beings, and in things, then most of the *Hindus* are monotheists. In this sense, Hindus, too, believe in only *one God*: in the one primordial Brahma, which is identical with Vishnu or Shiva or Shakti, and so simultaneously impersonal and personal ["transpersonal"]."[13]

The second point Küng makes is that, if we think of God as all those beings who are venerated, then Christians too might be seen as polytheists. This particular way of trying to find lines of connection of course takes the question of monotheism versus polytheism, or questions of *belief in god*, to be the central questions for any religion. These assumptions are themselves the problem. Of course, one can find references to the one god, to Brahman, who is without form and without attributes, to the idea that Brahman was one and then the thought-desire to become many (*eko asmi bahu syam*) became the first point at which one cycle of time was initiated, and many other such formulations within this particular complex of thought, especially in the Upanishads. This might incline one to read a "tendency toward" monism or monotheism. Recall, however, that one can also find in the same or similar texts other notions, such as that the world originated in the sacrifice of the first primeval man, or the idea that gods have to be maintained and nourished through regular offerings, or that gods themselves can become corrupt. The point is that one needs to understand the whole complex of ideas rather than use them selectively to argue for or against monotheism.

Some historians of religion have tried to trace these ideas in terms of historical development as well as clashes among different groups and argued for mutual absorptions of ideas across sects and regions over the years. It is well recognized, though, that major texts, both of the different Vedic periods as well as later remain unknown because critical editions have not been compiled, authorship and estimates of dates remain extremely hard to establish, and in most cases the texts have not been translated. My point is that the very process of dialogue and the method deployed by scholars and theologians such as Küng manage to shift the center of gravity in discussions toward Christian concerns. I think the reason why major scholars of Hinduism have hesitated to identify something like an essence of Hinduism is because of the enormous difficulties of establishing how to receive the ideas contained in these texts in modern scholarship. The political attempts by the Hindu right to appropriate the right to define Hinduism and its general ignorance of the vast and complex literature compounds the difficulties of finding ways to inherit these texts.

Between Texts and Lives

Having framed my questions within this larger story of the interpretation of texts and practices broadly identified as Hindu, my aim in this paper is more modest than to present an alternate large story to that of Christianity. My question is this. We know that many of the ideas and practices that we might encounter today as found in lived experiences of Hindus resonate with issues that can be traced to different kinds of Sanskrit or vernacular texts.[14] We also know that the very languages deployed in various kinds of rituals and other forms of devotion absorbed vocabularies, gestures, and other forms from other religions, as also from other experiences that originated in commerce, law, and other domains that we would not easily identify as "religious." How might we think about what it is to be a Hindu, or for that matter a Muslim, in the everyday contexts of Indian society? What does it mean for people to cohabit the world together? My impulse is to track these questions not through large theological debates but through the minutia of everyday life. I will be able to give only a few examples of descriptive labels necessary to avoid sliding the experiences I document into ready-made categories such as "god," "polytheism," "idolatry," and so on. I will first draw upon some wonderful examples of how languages of commerce or law might function as devotional languages or languages of divination in recent literature, then turn to ethnographic examples from my own work among low-income families in Delhi.

First, consider the case of colonial Bengal. In his study of subaltern religiosity in colonial Bengal, Hugh Urban has translated and analyzed the songs of the Kartabhaja sect, founded in the nineteenth century by the Muslim fakir Aulchand, who is considered to have been an incarnation of Sri Chaitanya, the legendary sixteenth-century Vasihnava poet.[15] As Urban explains, practices of various sects, including the Kartabhajas, came under attack in light of the changing moral norms of British rule and the reform of Hinduism initiated by movements associated with the Bengal Renaissance. Within this context of criticism and controversy, the Kartabhajas concealed their teachings in extremely esoteric forms of poetry. In Urban's words, "Perhaps most striking is that not only do these songs employ a wide rage of esoteric mystical imagery, drawn from the Sahajya and other Tantric traditions of medieval Bengal, but they also clothe this Tantric imagery in a huge amount of idiosyncratic economic discourse, the mercantile terminology drawn from the teeming marketplaces of colonial Calcutta."

Here is an example of a song beautifully translated by Urban.

The good Merchant has returned from England;
So when I bring the news, land, sea, and city, all rejoice!
. . . From beginning to end, the merchandise in Calcutta is being accounted;
The Clerks have begun to calculate and record the value.[16]

The key to interpreting texts such as these is that the company is a metaphor for the Gaudiya Vaishnava tradition, and the songs play on the double meaning of Chaitanya's epithet—*gour* or *gora*—which signifies both the fair one and the Englishman. The merchandise refers to the new teachings of the sect and the hope of dislocating all other small traders of *bhakti* ideals in the religious bazaar.[17]

Like the infusion of religious language with economic language, we find incidences in which relations to the deities, as well as to demonic beings, are expressed in legal terms. Humans and spirits appear as plaintiffs or defendants; they submit to judgment or interrogations that will make the evidence speak, and so on. In the widely popular healing cult of Balaji in Rajasthan, where people possessed by troublesome spirits come to get relief, the ritual forms are recognizable Hindu gestures, such as waving lamps, but much of the language of the proceedings seems to incorporate terms borrowed from Persian, Turkish, and Arabic and integrated into the language of the Indian courts. Other terms in Hindi or Sanskrit, such as *bhagat* ("devotee"), *aarti* ("song of praise for a deity"), *preta* ("ghost"), and so on are from the devotional lexicon but acquire special meaning in the ritual.

Graham Dwyer, in his study of the Balaji temple, describes one of the terms, *peshi*.[18] This indigenous term translates the English word *trance*, but it is a legal term, which literally means a *hearing*. It is used in two senses in the context of a healing ceremony: it refers to the statement (*bayan*) that afflicting spirits make during their *appearance* at Balaji's court (*darbar*), and to dissociation, the actual state of trance in which *bhut-pret* ("ghosts or spirits") speak through those whom they have possessed.

The apparent legal sensibility in the rituals taking place within the Balaji temple as well as in the courtyards outside has not received much attention, whereas the dramatic events of possession and exorcism there have often been analyzed for their psychological meanings (e.g., as the event of hysteria), as well as in terms of family-centered forms of cure.[19] Criticisms of psychological approaches, such as those offered by Dwyer, make the opposite assumption: that the social is the ground of all being, so that once a particular collective logic has been demonstrated, then questions of individual subjectivity can simply be dismissed.

I will revisit this question in the concluding part of my essay, where I will express my reservations about typical binary oppositions, such as classical and folk religions, great and little traditions, or priesthood and possession, in which the relation between the Sanskritic traditions and the practices observed in temples such as Balaji's have been formulated. I think this has relevance for understanding how it is that even in low-income neighborhoods and within a context of urban modernity, in a large population of semiliterate people one can find practices that resonate with the kinds of concerns about the authorization of tradition through language, ritual efficacy, and so on that I discussed earlier. Finally, one could ask if the infusion of religious language with economic or legal vocabulary has implications for political theology, so that, instead of drawing from the more familiar concerns about idolatry or primitive fusion typical of critical practices gene-alogically connected with the prohibition of graven images traced to Christianity, we might be able to at least pose the problem of a different way of looking at these issues.[20]

Meeting a Tantrik in an Urban Mohalla in Delhi

While researching the notions of health and well-being in a low-income locality in Delhi, where houses and markets nestle into one another, I would sometimes find billboards announcing various services that one could broadly define as both medical and religio-magical. One billboard , for instance, announced various diagnostic tests in Hindi: "There are provisions for pregnancy test, sugar test, and treatment for various diseases such as piles, arthritis, and weakness. Here we can also treat you for *uppari chakkar*." The category of *uppari chakkar* was ever-present in discussions of illness or misfortune among the families who lived in these neighborhoods.[21] Literally meaning "wheels above," the term captures the idea that one is caught in forces that are beyond one's control because some-one, out of jealousy, envy, or other hostile emotions, has performed some form of sorcery or magic to cause harm.[22] In my experience these hostile emotions are inevitably attrib-uted to ill-feelings on the part of someone close—a relative or a neighbor. Ranendra Das and I have explained elsewhere how categories of biomedicine circulated along with such terms as *uppari chakkar* in providing explanations of disease and misfortune—the two did not rule each other out. We argue that it is not easy to think of any simple explanatory models of illness in which people would use biomedical categories for material causation and categories such as *uppari chakkar* in response to puzzles such as "Why me?" Here I want to concentrate on the figure of the healer to examine how grammatical features of the broad Hindu tradition that I sketched above are actualized in these settings.[23] What do these tell us about questions about what constitutes the authorization of a tradition?

Let me begin with a man I call Saraswati, whom you could call a "doctor" or a *tantrik,* or simply the *bhut pret wale doctor,* depending upon your perspective.[24] Some people in the neighborhood call him a doctor because, as the hoarding on his shop testi-fies, he has a degree in Ayurveda. This is not because he was trained in the tradition with a guru, as described by Francis Zimmerman, but because a proliferation of ayurvedic practices is made possible by both global programming and the state policy in India of training traditional healers in both traditional medicine and a limited amount of biomedi-cine, so that they can serve the poor in resource-constrained settings.[25] Since sometimes Saraswati dispenses biomedicines, ranging from analgesics to antibiotics, some patients refer to him as "doctor sahib." Many, however, come to him to get remedies for *uppari chakkar*, and I have heard some people refer to him as a *tantrik* who has performed severe meditation to please the goddess. A picture of the goddess Kali and a trident, with which he sometimes touches the patient, are material symbols of this aspect of his practice and the embodiments of his power. Finally, in his absence, I have heard neighbors refer to him as the *bhut pret wala doctor*—meaning one who deals with ghosts and spirits, a term that carries a pejorative tone.

In the course of my visits to the neighborhood, I came to know Saraswati's own story about what he described as a quest in response to a longing for the goddess. He told me that as a young man he began to have repeated dreams about a beautiful woman who was beckoning to him, though he could never discern the meaning of the gesture. Someone told him that he should go to the Rishikesh, at the foot of the Himalayas, where he might find a learned person who would be able to tell him what was required of him. After wandering around in the Himalayas, he found a guru, from whom he learned that the beautiful woman of his dreams was the goddess Kali. The guru instructed him to meditate upon the goddess to achieve *siddhi* ("completion, perfection"). Here are snippets of the conversation that depict his rendering of the events.

> SARASWATI: For six months I sat in a *gufa* ["cave"], alone, and I meditated upon the form of the goddess, drinking only liquor and eating only meat—for those are foods dear to the goddess.
>
> VEENA: So did you get what you desired at the end of six months?
>
> SARASWATI: Yes, I got what I wanted.
>
> VEENA: So did the goddess reveal herself to you—could you get *darshan* ["vision"] of the goddess?[26]
>
> SARASWATI: Now how shall I explain to you? *Darshan* happened but is what happened to me the same thing as "seeing"—now, how shall I explain to you?
>
> VEENA: Did Ma [referring to the goddess Kali] give you a mantra? What powers did you get?
>
> SARASWATI: I received a mantra—I received everything—the mother blessed me. But then something else happened. What happened was that the mantra that the goddess blessed me with gave so much power to my ordinary words that anything that I uttered would turn out to be true—if one wants to return to ordinary life, then that is not possible, not possible to carry all that power, that *ghor shakti* ["a dense, even terrifying, power"] in oneself.[27] I might say something carelessly; I might get angry with a child and in that momentary anger mutter some curse, and what if it turned out to be true? So, I decided to pursue a form of worship [*upasana*] that was more imbued with the *sattvik* qualities.[28] I stayed in a cave for another six months, meditating upon the god Hanuman and, as is appropriate for his worship, I subsisted on milk and fruits till Hanuman gave me his blessings and my powers were tampered with some quality [*bhava*] of peace and tranquility.[29]

How does Saraswati use his powers in the local setting in which he lives and works? Throughout the interview, he assumed that some unspoken desire of mine had brought me to him but that I was too timid to ask for it directly. To encourage me to come out with what I truly wanted, he told me that there are many kinds of "work" that he could perform. Many big, important people come to me, he told me. He named a high-ranking police officer who was charged in a corruption case and who had been exonerated because of Saraswati's intervention. "I will not do anything—I will just sit in the court and the magistrate will dismiss the case. I can make legal into illegal and illegal into legal [*hum legal ko illegal aur illegal ko legal bana dete hain*]." Just as the appearance of Sanskritic terms like *sattva, darshan, and mantra* mark his discourse as participating in a certain region of the tradition of Tantric worship,[30] so the English words *legal* and *illegal* mark the particular way in which his religious powers are related to the powers of the modern state. In the case of the person suffering from possession by demonic spirits who was presented in the Balaji temple, terms such as *peshi* and *bayan*, which ordinarily refer to being present in the court and giving evidence, could be seen as traces of court proceedings introduced by "foreign" rulers. These Persian terms signified both the intrusion of foreign vocabularies and undomesticated spirits. The intrusion of English words in the speech of Saraswati and his interpretation of cure or relief as inclusive of relief from demonic spirits, from illnesses, and from the operations of the law mark the experience of the present in the mythic and ritual register.

"If you have such powerful *bhaktas* [literally "devotees," but in much contemporary usage such words carry an ironic edge, since they can allude to political clients as well as to religious devotees], why do you live in this place among the poor rather than in some other place?" He replied that he had pledged to serve the poor—again he interspersed the term *seva* ("service") with the English word *social service*. "I do not ask for anything— some people who seek my services give me thousands of rupees, silk shawls, and whatever they wish—others might just give a few rupees—it is all the same to me." Economic accumulation here is stripped of the intentions of the receiver and becomes an index of the desire of the giver as much as that of the deity who permits such accumulation to take place.

I was curious that for someone who had done such severe penance and meditation it had been necessary to get a degree in Ayurveda. I also noticed that the billboard on his shop listed his son as practicing there along with his father. His son had a degree in Ayurvedic Medicine and Surgery (BAMS) from another university. Over the course of several conversations, I learned that, since Saraswati also treated patients with biomedicines, he thought it would be safer to get a degree in order to avoid harassment by public officials—so he completed a correspondence course in Ayurveda. His son's degree, which was from a regular college, was a legitimate degree under the Government of India's policy mentioned earlier.[31] By putting his son's name on the billboard, even though his practice was elsewhere in the neighborhood, Saraswati was taking out insurance against police harassment for indulging in an illegal act. As with many other practices in low-income neighborhoods, the line between legality and illegality is difficult to determine, not only because people break laws but also because the law is itself unclear on these matters. Thus, on the one hand, the Government of India itself grants degrees in ayurvedic medicine and surgery in which the curriculum includes training in biomedicine, and, on the other hand, there is legislation, such as the Delhi Quackery Act, that forbids those without a proper biomedical degree to treat patients with any biomedical procedures or products. Saraswati's strategy to deflect any possible governmental action against him for treating patients with biomedicine must be understood not simply as a failure of regulation by state institutions but in light of the fact that the law itself is not unitary.

On one occasion, Saraswati invited a research assistant and me to have tea with him while his patients were consulting with him.[32] I did not see any of the famed patients, but a number of neighborhood women came with varied complaints. (Nine patients came that morning between the hours of 10 A.M. and 12 noon.) One woman said that her husband was unduly influenced by his mother, and she wanted a remedy for this situation. Saraswati asked her to get some sugar from the market—he recited some silent mantra over it and then blew over this treated sugar. He also gave her a black thread tied with thirteen knots and said that she was to wear that on her wrist. Every morning she was to feed her husband tea with that sugar, and in thirteen weeks he would be completely under her influence. The use of this class of mantras, known as *vashikaran mantras*, is commonly understood in the popular imagination to exert a force that would make the person to whom it is directed completely under the influence of someone on whose behalf it is executed. Other patients that day came with varied complaints, including sicknesses that Saraswati did not think were due to *uppari chakkar*. To these patients he dispensed some medications, though two of them insisted that they be touched with the trident.

At one point I asked Saraswati how he would deal with someone who wanted him to use his powers to harm another person.[33] That is not possible, he said, because the goddess would not allow such a person to reach him—his steps would stumble—something would happen, and he would find that, despite his best efforts, he could not reach my place. I do not cite him here to say that indeed Saraswati does not ever use his powers to harm but only to point out that, from his point of view, any action involves not only the desire of the person who is seeking him out but also the desire of the goddess that the power she has bestowed on him be used for good purposes. The ambivalence that surrounds people like Saraswati in the neighborhood hinges precisely on the question of whether mystical/magical powers carry a guarantee of goodness with them and how one is to trust that the being who gave a personal mantra to a healer is a benevolent deity rather than a malevolent force. How is one to construct what or who authorizes "tradition" under these conditions? Indeed, with whom does authorship of action lie, and does that have any relevance for the way that categories of "good" or "bad" circulate in these neighborhoods? A second example of possession in the neighborhood addresses the question from a slightly different perspective.

The Powers of the "Untouchable"

While Saraswati is (or claims to be) a Brahmin, he lives and works in a neighborhood marked by a concentration of lower castes. The next case I present is Nathu Ram, who belongs to what was previously known as an "untouchable" caste. Although in the traditional caste system the untouchable was a bearer of pollution and occupied the lowest rung in the caste hierarchy, he paradoxically held ritual power, especially in relation to death and danger. On the social register the untouchable castes were subjected to many restrictions, and members of these castes have lodged important political struggles against upper-caste oppression. The practice of untouchability is banned in India, and members of these castes are referred to as Dalits, a term that expresses their experiences of deprivation rather than the upper-caste characterization of them as "untouchable."

What interests me here is the widespread assumption in the origin myths of many castes belonging to the Dalit category that they were originally either Brahmins or Kshatriyas—the priestly and warrior castes—who were either tricked by unscrupulous gods or ascetics into accepting a lower-caste position or had to give up their upper-caste positions in some situation pertaining to the defense of *dharma*, which in the broader sense refers to the protection of the cosmic order and in the narrower sense to "righteous conduct" as well as *satya*, or "truth" in the sense of that which testifies to being itself.[34] The higher moral stature of the caste was asserted in such customs as the need of all higher castes to receive the cremation fire from the hands of an untouchable caste and their special functions in the propitiation of dangerous deities.

In the urban context, the relation between caste and occupation has become loose—even when members of some of the Dalit castes are employed as janitors or street cleaners, they do not consider themselves to be engaged in polluting occupations. Members of Dalit households I encountered in the Delhi neighborhoods were working in a range of occupations, including government service as gatekeepers, sweepers, clerks, petty trade, household service, schoolteachers, medical practitioners (trained and untrained), and lawyers. The maximum concentration of these groups, as with other groups living in these areas, was in low-paid work, including in the informal economy.

Nathu Ram lives in a low-income neighborhood, along with his wife and children. Adjacent to his house is the house of his brother. Previously both households formed a joint family, but about ten years earlier, after the death of Nathu Ram's father, the joint family had split into two nuclear units. This split is important if we are to understand Nathu Ram's powers of being possessed by a form of Shiva and being able to heal people, on the one hand, and the controversies over the identity of the deity that possesses him, on the other. Every Thursday evening, Nathu Ram sits in the corner of his one-room house, on a mat spread out on the floor, and sees various people who have come with their problems to seek solutions. Unlike in the Balaji temple, these are not clients who already know that they are suffering from possession by demonic spirits (*bhut pret dosh*).

271

Instead they face various misfortunes and are in search of an explanation of these misfortunes. Sometimes they themselves, or their relatives, are subject to violent emotions that are inexplicable to them. Nathu Ram sometimes identifies the cause of the misfortune to be the play of malevolent spirits, but at other times he may ask the person to consult a physician if the problem is identified as having a natural cause amenable to simple treatment with medication. In any case, it is important to remember that not Nathu Ram but the spirit that possesses him offers the diagnosis of the problem and the cure. I have sat in Nathu Ram's house several times and observed the consultations. I am convinced that my presence sometimes acted to inhibit the full range of bodily and expressive movements that Nathu Ram otherwise displays, which his wife and neighbors have described to me.

The problems people bring to him are similar to the ones I observed in the case of Saraswati, except that fewer people with ordinary fevers or coughs seem to consult him and he does not dispense pharmaceuticals. He claims, however, that he does have knowledge of some medicines, since he works as a gardener in a municipal dispensary. There are very interesting differences between the story of how he came to possess these powers and the account given by Saraswati. There are also important differences in the organization of the session itself.

When Nathu Ram was a young boy, he became fatally ill. No one could understand what his illness was. His father, who worked as an unskilled laborer, went to various healers, but to no avail. Then one day, when Nathu Ram was nearly at death's door, a person whom his father knew and who also worked in a government dispensary offered to cure him, on condition that he would apprentice himself to this person and learn the art of healing. Under the ministrations of this person, whom he simply calls Babaji (a generic term for an elderly holy wanderer), Nathu Ram was cured and also learned that the deity that had cured him was Bhairava—a fierce form of Shiva.[35] After that, his body became a vessel for this deity, who began to possess him. Because the deity now resides in him, he has to allow it to find expression in healing every Thursday.

During the healing session, the person seeking a cure presents his problem to Nathu Ram. On hearing this, his body sometimes begins to sway; sometimes he looses consciousness; and at other times he talks quite normally but says that the deity is informing him what remedies to suggest. He cannot accept any money for these cures, but people can make an offering to the deity. I saw that some people would light a cigarette and offer it to him; at other times they would offer him liquor. Most of the complaints he received were a litany of miscellaneous misfortunes. In most cases his diagnosis of the problem was the identification of a close relative or a neighbor who was jealous and had therefore cast an evil spell with the help of another person who was adept in using the power of the occult. The cure was like that of Saraswati—a black thread tied with several knots, over which he would recite some secret mantras and then blow over it. This was to be tied in the house or on the person. It carried the power of the deity, or rather, became the acoustic body of the deity.

Although the words, gestures, and form of the ritual session were well recognized in the area, Nathu Ram's powers were considered to be extremely controversial, and they were tied up with the quarrel and split between the two brothers. According to the version offered by his brother and family, the holy man who had cured Nathu Ram had in fact blessed the entire family and not only Nathu Ram by giving them a tiny mace (*gada*) and loincloth (*langoti*)—the cloth and the weapon that Hanuman carries. This is what had given Nathu Ram the power to heal. But because he had started using it for personal gain, he was losing his powers. That is when he started many quarrels with his brother and appropriated part of his property, according to Nathu Ram's brother's wife. This branch of the family claimed that he had stolen those artifacts, and that is when he started becoming possessed by another deity. His brother's family refuses to name this deity, though they recognized the gestures of offering a smoke and the changes in his bodily deportment to be common in exorcism rituals. Instead, they used the expression *un pe gandi chez aane lagi*—"a bad/dirty thing started coming upon him." This particular stance of not naming that which one fears, since the sound of that name could activate the spirit, draws from the register of language in which sound is primary and acts independently of either meaning or the intention of the speaker. This shows how complex philosophical questions about the nature of sacred language find resonance in everyday life.

There seems to be some indication that Nathu Ram was indeed troubled by the events of the last few years, though he never referred to the earlier relation to Hanuman. He once said, for instance, that he was exhausted by the spirit that possessed him, but he knew that if he stopped the Thursday séance, he would die. Similarly, the gesture of a *bhakta* lighting a cigarette and putting it in the mouth of the person possessed is a typical gesture that marks the presence of Bhairon Dev. I have witnessed this gesture also for placating a troublesome spirit, who "demands" cigarettes and alcohol but has not been named. Furthermore, recently Nathu Ram's brother's son was arrested for having eloped with a girl, whose parents registered a charge of abduction and kidnapping against him. For all his powers, Nathu Ram could do nothing for his nephew. He interpreted this as having offended the spirit in some way. For his brother's family, however, it was evidence that he was using his powers for the purpose of harming others.

The different routes by which possession, passion, healing, and religious language are inflected with the languages of medicine, economics, and law, which we have seen in the cases of both Saraswati and Nathu Ram, bring me back to the questions I raised at the outset, namely: How are traditions authorized, and what is at stake for participants in the way they practice these traditions? One particularly important question that emerges from the ethnographic details of the two cases is how notions of *adharma* ("violation of righteous conduct") are folded into *dharma* ("righteous conduct") not only for humans but also for gods. A second is how belief and doubt are conjoined as twins. I will now turn to these issues.

Ritual, Language, and the Authorization of Tradition

Saraswati's and Nathu Ram's respective stories receive authorization from a tradition that can be translated into everyday life, even if people cannot name all its elements or quote the sources from which their ideas are derived. The authority of these texts is not derived from experts who have mastered a set of texts. Instead, their respective stories are related to recognizable genres of storytelling. Thus Saraswati's story has recognizable motifs—having a dream, going to the Himalayas in search of a guru who could help him interpret the meaning of his dream, offering meditation, and performing penance. In Nathu Ram's case, the theme of sickness and cure becomes the defining event through which some kind of sacred power is acquired. This is again familiar from both texts and ethnographies. Ambivalence regarding the deity or spirit that has possessed one derives from the themes of skepticism regarding the status of a particular deity, especially one that might have been generated through the anger or lust of a god, even a benign god. Sometimes a deity has committed a sin, and though he or she has been redeemed, the memory of that sin is never erased. Thus, for example, the class of beings known as Bhairon Devs were generated by Shiva explicitly to cut off Brahma's fifth head, which had quite autonomously begun to speak against Shiva. Shiva tricked Brahma into believing that this creature (Bhairondev) was his (Brahma's) own creation. Hence he was caught unawares when Bhairon Dev (or one among them) cut off his fifth head. Bhairon Dev had to carry the head around as penance, however, because he had become guilty of Brahmahatya, or the murder of a Brahmin.[36] He was finally released when the head fell in a spot that is regarded as one of the most sacred spots in Kashi for release from sins. Thus Bhairon Dev appears in the places sacred to Shiva and the goddess but is often given a place outside the temple as guardian. Being master of ghosts and spirits, Bhairon Dev certainly plays an important role in stories of possession, but there are other deities, such as Hanuman and Kali, as we saw, who also figure in these rituals and myths. One might say, then, that the structure of the stories that circulate around Saraswati and Nathu Ram authenticate their claims since they can be recognized within the community as plausible stories. The objects in Saraswati's shop—the picture of the goddess, the trident, the black threads hanging at one side—and the people who come to get remedies for *uppari chakkar* all provide visible evidence to the neighborhood that his claims to authoritative knowledge are received by some if not by all. Similarly, Nathu Ram's bodily gestures, such as swaying, or the suppliant's act of putting a cigarette in Nathu's mouth as an offering to the spirit, locate him within a network of meanings and relationships that can be recognized in this and similar localities. Yet doubts about their claims to be benign healers simultaneously circulate in the neighborhood. These are articulated in gossip or other networks of talk, along with beliefs that diseases, misfortunes, or madness can be visited upon one because occult powers have been mobilized and that ritual experts such as Saraswati or Nathu Ram have the powers to deal with the afflictions caused by *uppari chakkar*. Doubts about a particular healer can be weakly expressed, as when one thinks that someone is just not powerful enough to be a good healer. Or, by contrast, they can be life-threatening doubts, as when one comes under the sway of a healer whose body has become the abode of an extremely evil being. Belief and doubt appear here as twins. It is not that first one has belief and then doubt, but rather that they stand in a hyphenated relation to each other. I would suggest that both can be articulated within the notion of tradition. Let me explicate this by reflecting first on the nature of authority within the specific traditions to which Saraswati is laying claims and second, on the conditions of urban life within which belief and doubt can be joined in this manner.

Concluding Observations

A major aspect of the anxiety that haunts the devotional and healing practices of both Saraswati and Nathu Ram, not only in the community but in their own understandings, is that in the process of meditation, penance, or even in fulfilling a promise made in return for a boon, the body of the subject might become open to a class of dangerous beings who are seeking embodiment. One might thus become an instrument of their will. There is a specific way in which doubt is staged in this scene of possession and dispossession. One puzzle is whether the textual traditions of Hinduism lack centralized authority, hence are themselves formulated in a manner that is conducive to the staging of doubt, or whether it is the new conditions created by urban modernity that have led to a pluralization of authority and hence to the kind of skepticism we encountered in the urban neighborhoods. Let me respond to the pressure of these questions by considering the possibility of two different frameworks of analysis.

First, let us take the general question: What authorizes a tradition? Here I will refer to anthropological works on the nature of ritual and belief in general and ask if these explanations help us to answer our questions. Second, I will put forward some explanations internal to the debates in Hinduism on the nature of language: for instance, are gods, goddesses, and spirits that find it necessary to express themselves by possessing other bodies evidence of a "folk" or "popular" religiosity that continues to defy Brahmanical orthodoxy and its prerogative of defining *dharma*? Or could it be that Indic notions of the relation between selves and bodies, *dharma* and *adharma*, offer the key to understanding why gods become *adharmic*? Why are exorcism rituals performed as if in an Islamic court of law? Why do "doctors" of the occult feel in need of certification by the government to be healers? Are these seen to be the appropriate spaces for dealing with undomesticated deities and with wild emotions?

Anthropologists have argued that the key advance of the 1970s in the study of ritual was the idea of ritual as communication, which not only relies on an analogy between ritual and language but also emphasizes the enunciative aspects of ritual language and the idea of ritual as a "dialogue between man and god."[37] This model was criticized for emphasizing the semantic content of language and for ignoring the importance of performance. The Austinian theory of the performative force of utterances seemed to hold much promise as scholars began to see that the efficacy of a ritual lay in its proper performance (including recitation of ritual formulas); the rationality of ritual performances was to be understood in terms of the analogies that ritual forms established, and meaning could be established by understanding the extensive use of metaphor in ritual.

As an example of the application of this general theory of ritual, John Bowen gives the example of the Islamic prayer *salat* (a form of collective prayer), in which the crucial question is whether the ritual has been carried out properly. Thus the question is not only that of the meaning of ritual but of its efficacy and its significance for establishing the piety of the person performing the ritual. In the Islamic case, the correct form of prayer is established by imitating acts performed by the Prophet Muhammad that were intended to serve as guides for the Muslim community in the performance of prayer as well as other matters. Bowen summarizes this ritual commitment as follows:

> Therefore, in matters of worship one should do precisely what Muhammad did—all of it and no more. That one's own actions are in fact replications of those of the Prophet Muhammad is guaranteed by a verified chain of transmission, a genealogy of knowledge certified by experts in the science of transmission, who inspect all claims to direct communication between one transmitter and the next, as well as the piety and reliability of said transmitters.

This explanation of what authorizes a certain tradition of ritual actions is persuasive. One might ask, however, if this form is specific to Islam, with its strong commitment to authorizing ritual conduct by establishing proper authority for its practices and its fear of contamination by "pagan" practices. Or does this example point to a more general issue in the anthropology of religion? As Bowen points out, despite the clarity of the principle, there can be considerable controversy regarding the piety of the person who is performing the prayer. In fact, there is a whole literature on *shako-shubah* ("doubt"), and many have sought resolution of intriguing questions relating to the correct performance of the *namaz* and on the appropriateness of reading *duas* (a more individual form of prayer that does not have a fixed form) for certain kinds of persons, such as the political leader of a non-Islamic nation. These issues are discussed in collections of *fatawa*, issued from Islamic seminaries or given by respected muftis. Thus, despite clearly laid out rules, what constitutes correct performance in prayer in Islam is subject to different interpretations. While recognized religious authorities and citational practices can help resolve this problem, even in Islam not everything is resolved by reference to an external authority with a recognizable line of transmission. Here is an example of a "rain prayer" that Steven Caton recently came across in Yemen, being recited in mosques to deal with a persistent drought.[38] As Caton notes, the rain prayer is not authorized by either the Qur'an or the *hadith*, yet it has the feel of an Islamic prayer. Thus, for example, the important fragment from the declaration of faith "there is no God but God" is repeated at the end of each segment, interspersed with words imploring God to forgive the community's sins and to release the rain.

Caton argues that the phrase "there is no God but God" is the central tenet of Islam and is taken directly from the Qur'an in the form of "reported speech." For Caton, it is this citational practice that legitimates the prayer. As he says, "Thus the invocation cites Qur'anic discourse in order, metapragmatically, to authorize its own performance or instance of speaking, and it does so in order to call forth a response from God that is material in the form of rain but also spiritual as a sign of forgiveness. It is a dialogical act, or attempts to be one, between man and God." Thus, for Caton, though the citational practice depends upon the authority of the Qur'an, it creates legitimacy through its very utterance. Caton's formulation allows one to see how improvisation in prayer might be authorized but, by putting the entire weight on the linguistic context, he brackets the question of the nonlinguistic, embodied, and sensory character of how one experiences oneself in the act of prayer. In my own fieldwork, I have encountered the problem of improvisation among Muslims as being fraught with the risk that they might be guilty of the sin of *shirk*—or associating another being with Allah. Thus, from my own experience, interspersing an improvised prayer with the statement "there is no God but God" is more a testimony to one's being a good Muslim, especially in the kind of context in which many ordinary Muslims have been criticized by more orthodox or fundamentalist groups for allowing their faith to be diluted by Hindu cultural and religious sensibilities.

To the extent that Austin's ideas about the performative force of utterances may be useful in anthropological discussions of ritual efficacy, it would seem that one would have to consider a whole complex of ideas and practices, including those embedded in the discourse of particular religions, as well as the nonlinguistic context within which questions of faith and doubt come to be articulated and which cannot simply be inferred from an analysis of texts alone. Thus, unlike the examples of illocutionary force in which words could be counted upon to "do things" because the context was in place, questions of context, convention, and what counts as efficacy are much more fraught with danger in the case of ritual than in the kind of examples of legal or political authority on which Austin relies.

Might it be better to be more modest and ask what guidance we might get from the specificities of the Hindu tradition(s) in understanding the futures of the religious past? Sanskrit and vernacular texts contain many references to possession. Thus there are stories of gods, goddesses, kings, and heroes who become possessed by different forces; there are rules for preparing the body or some other object so that it can become a proper habitat for a deity; stories of causing one's own soul to depart from one's body so that it can inhabit another body to experience the other person's life; and also the experience of being seized by a hostile spirit. In his monumental review of the literature on possession in Indic traditions, Fredrick Smith distinguishes between self-motivated possession, which is friendly and benign, and possession from the outside, which generally (but not invariably) carries a malefic sense.[39] The impressive textual evidence he has marshaled shows that the lexicon for possession expanded historically to incorporate various kinds of experiences, although sometimes scholars (and practitioners) tend to collapse any kind of mystical and ecstatic experience into the category of possession.

Many accounts of Hinduism assume that there was a clear distinction between classical and folk religion and that only those gods who had some correspondence to non-Aryan religions tended to possess people. Smith's work, by contrast, shows that myths and rituals in both Sanskritic and so called "folk" renditions contain stories of possession. In view of the long history of intertextual negotiations, imitations, and reinterpretations between classical texts and their regional and local evolutions (or the other way round), it is hard to maintain a strict boundary between the classical and the folk. Moreover, there are also intertextual negotiations between Vedic, Buddhist, Pauranic, Jain, Islamic, Sikh, and Christian traditions, and between religious, medical, economic, and legal vocabularies. All of this makes the question of how tradition is authorized extremely fraught, both for the people involved and for the analyst.

Instead, we can say that a certain tendency toward pluralizing bodies, personhoods, gods, and demons seems to be widely acknowledged. Not only are the boundaries between bodies, persons, and gods permeable, but the boundaries between *dharma* and *adharma* are also constantly being negotiated. On the one hand, religious and legal texts are constantly telling us how boundaries are to be made. Milk-exuding trees, shrines to mother goddesses who have sprung from the earth, invisible lines that commemorate a sacred event from mythic memory—all these are constantly being planted, maintained, and remembered to draw boundaries in space. Lighting the lamp, blowing conch shells, isolating, naming, and placating the inauspicious moments of the day—all these and numerous other activities mark boundaries in time. Simultaneously, though, there are constant attempts at boundary crossing, so that a famous Indologist has been led to observe that India's most powerful and sacred figures engaged in highly touted *adharmic* conduct of an erotic or nonerotic nature.[40] Indian myths and their storytellers are fascinated by the idea of getting to the other side of the boundary without being invited to do so. It is as if the seeds of *adharma* are sown within *dharma* itself. The medicalization of possession that I noted in my fieldwork is to be found in the ayurvedic and Tantric texts, so that many kinds of afflictions might be traced to the fact that one's body is revealed not to be one's body at all or that the center of one's existence is in some other body.

Interesting questions arise when we try to think how general theories of religion are to be brought into conversation with the specific insights we gain from Indian philosophical and literary texts, as well as the practices of ordinary people. The anxiety around one's relation to a divine or demonic other is not the anxiety stemming from a jealous god (though gods do all kinds of *adharmic* things out of jealousy) or from the fear of primitive fusion with another—elements that are often associated with idolatry in Christian imagination. Instead, one expects to encounter beings that are considered dangerous or demonic but then turn out to have been created out of the anger or lust of a god. There are alien deities or spirits who have to be placated and expelled (but never fully destroyed), or those in the wilderness who are domesticated but may get restless and leave. There is thus a sense of oneself as being already a hostage to the other. Within such a grammar of relatedness, it is not the sovereignty of the individual but his or her capacity to sustain the "foreign" within himself or herself that seems to count. Within such a framework, questions of sovereignty, authority, censorship, and criticism lead different kinds of lives. I am not saying that modern concepts of nationhood, law, and sovereignty have not influenced the lives of people, but I am not convinced that, for all the efforts of the Hindu right in India, theirs are the only concepts on offer. I must confess, though, that had I not spent the last few years hanging around these neighborhoods and seen how, despite a certain antagonism maintained between Hindus and Muslims, they inhabit each other's lives in both "joys and sorrows," as they would say, I might not have understood the importance of the Sanskrit and vernacular texts I studied.[41] To take one final example—a Muslim friend from one of the low-income neighborhoods often tries to explain the concepts of Islam to me by using various kinds of analogies from Hinduism. Once he was speaking of the importance of the Qur'an when he said "just as *ishwara* revealed the Vedas . . ." I interrupted him to say, "Well, *bhagwan* did not reveal the Vedas." At which point he interrupted me to say, "I said *ishwara*—not *bhagwan*." I was stunned that he made such a subtle distinction: though both terms could be roughly translated as God, one of the meanings of the term *ishwara* indicates the one who has not been seduced by nature, while *bhagwan* refers to the fact of God's lordship over the universe. Our discussion was long and somewhat acrimonious because I insisted that the Vedas were not the creation of gods or God and he thought that was not possible. But after some days he came up with the information that wise and learned men (*alims*) had been asked at one time in Islamic history to declare the Qur'an too to be self-created but had rejected this request, even though it came from a king. I will have to leave the description of this and other such discussions, with their combination of intimacy, admiration, and subtle recriminations, for another occasion. Perhaps the intense interest in such matters displayed by some of my friends in these neighborhoods bestowed on me some capacity to engage with questions of religion after the long years I spent thinking and writing about violence—violence that left me unable to handle issues relating to the religious aesthetic of life, for all this seemed then to be simply a flight from the enormous harm that could be inflicted in the name of religion.

PART II

Religion and Philosophy

Metaphysics and Phenomenology

A Relief for Theology

Jean-Luc Marion

> My immediate intention is not theology but phenome-
> nology, although one may well say much for the other.
>
> —Husserl, *Ideas* I, §51

1

The question of God certainly does not begin with metaphysics. But it seems—or at least it managed to appear—that, since metaphysics was coming to an end, being completed, and disappearing, the question of God was also coming to a close. Throughout the past century, every-thing happened as if the question of God would have to make common cause, whether positively or negatively, with the destiny of metaphysics. Everything also happened as if, in order to keep the question of God open so as to permit a "rational worship" of him (Rom. 12:1), it was absolutely necessary to stick to the strictly metaphysical meaning of all philosophy.

But could one not, and thus should one not, also pose an entirely different and opposing preliminary question? Is philosophy really equivalent to metaphysics? In order to remain rational, must the ques-tion concerning God necessarily and exclusively take the paths that lead to the "God of the philosophers and the scholars" just because those paths issue necessarily from the decision of metaphysics?[1] On the one hand, this reversal of the question might surprise and even disturb, or, on the other hand, it might appear to dodge the radicality of the past century's philosophical situation. Nevertheless, it seems to me inevita-ble, since only such a reversal still truly leaves open the possibility of taking into proper account at least three questions. I will evoke them here without claiming to answer them explicitly. (1) At least as regards its historical destiny, did metaphysics not reach its end positively with Hegel and negatively with Nietzsche? (2) Was philosophy not devoted throughout an entire century to overcoming that end by assuming nonmetaphysical forms, of which the most powerful (I am not saying the only) remains phenomenology? (3) Does Christian speculative theology, understood in its exemplary figures (and here I am obviously thinking first of Saint Thomas Aquinas), belong to metaphysics in the strict sense, or has it responded to the peculiar conceptual demands of the revelation that prompted it?

In succession, then, we will examine the metaphysical figure of philosophy and the thought of God that it actualizes, then the phenomenological figure of philosophy and the possibility it keeps in store for God.

2

The mere evocation of the concept of an "end of metaphysics" gives rise to controversy. That controversy could undoubtedly be avoided if care were taken to agree first on a precise and verifiable concept of "metaphysics" itself. This is even truer insofar as that concept can be defined historically in an almost univocal manner. In fact, it appears relatively late, but with a clear definition. One of the first to accept it (which does not imply that he made it his own, since he hardly uses it except in commentary on Aristotle and elsewhere with caution), Aquinas establishes its theoretical field precisely: "*Metaphysics* simultaneously determines [how things stand] concerning being in general and concerning the first being, which is separated from matter."[2] Despite some decisive modifications concerning, among other things, the meaning of being in general as an objective concept of being, this dual definition was sanctioned by Francisco Suárez as early as the opening of his *Disputatione Metaphysicae*, a work that itself definitely imposes the concept and the word *metaphysics* on modern philosophy: "This science abstracts from sensible and from material things . . . , and it contemplates, on the one hand, the things that are divine and separated from matter and, on the other hand, the common reason of being, which [both] can exist without matter."[3] This duality of one and the same science that treats simultaneously beings par excellence and being in general will lead, with the "scholastic metaphysics" (*Schulmetaphysik*) of the seventeenth and eighteenth centuries, to the canonical schema of "metaphysics" as divided into "general metaphysics," or *metaphysica generalis (sive ontologia),* and "special metaphysics," or *metaphysica specialis (theologia rationalis, psychologia rationalis, cosmologia rationalis).*[4] Kant's critique stands entirely within this arrangement, since, as is often forgotten, the threefold refutation of special metaphysics in the "Transcendental Dialectic" of the *Critique of Pure Reason* rests on the rejection of the "proud name of . . . ontology" in the "Analytic of Principles."[5] Thus, by a simple survey of a history of concepts, *metaphysics* is defined as follows: the system of philosophy from Suárez to Kant as a single science bearing at one and the same time on the universal common being and on being (or beings) par excellence. This textual fact seems hard to contest.

But the fact remains to be interpreted. The historically narrow sense of *metaphysics* follows from its strict definition, but can this notion be confirmed conceptually? Can one read in it anything more than a mere scholastic or even pedagogical nomenclature that is without any authentically speculative scope and that, in any case, would be incapable of bringing us to the heart of the question of metaphysics? This suspicion would be a serious threat if we did not have at our disposal a conceptual elaboration of this common notion of "metaphysics"—namely, the elaboration furnished by Heidegger in the section of *Identity and Difference* entitled "The Onto-theological Constitution of Metaphysics." We will focus here on only one thesis from that decisive text. Indeed, the principal difficulty of metaphysical science stems from the problematic character of its unity. How can one and the same (*una et eadem*) science treat at the same time (*simul*) common being (and therefore no being in particular) and the being par excellence (and therefore a supremely particular being)? To be sure, in both cases it is a question of an abstraction, but taken in two opposite senses: in one case, an abstraction in regard to all real being and thus an abstraction only of reason; in the other case, an abstraction with a view to being that is all the more concrete insofar as no materiality affects it, and thus a real abstraction. Now Heidegger goes beyond this superficial but traditional opposition by proposing to read the relation between the two functions of the same "metaphysics" as the relation of two intersecting and reciprocal foundations:

> Being [*das Sein*] shows itself in the unconcealing overcoming as that which allows whatever arrives to lie before us, as the grounding [*Gründen*] in the manifold ways in which beings are brought about before us. Beings [*das Seiende*] as such, [namely, as] the arrival that keeps itself concealed in unconcealedness, is the grounded [*Gegründete*], which, as grounded and thus effected [*Erwirktes*], grounds in its way, namely, effects, and therefore causes [*gründet, nämlich wirkt, d.h. verursacht*]. The conciliation of the grounding and the grounded [*von Gründendem und Gegründetem*] as such does not hold them one outside of the other, but one for the other.[6]

The inner unity of "metaphysics," which allows it not to fall apart into two unconnected sciences, stems from the fact that, between the science of being in general and the science of the being par excellence, the single institution of the ground is at work, in modes that are intrinsically conciliated. Common Being grounds beings, even beings par excellence; in return, the being par excellence, in the mode of causality, grounds common Being: "Being grounds being, and being, as what is most of all, causes Being [*gründet Sein das Seiende, begründet das Seiende als das Seiendste das Sein*]."[7] In and beyond the scholastic notion of metaphysics, the onto-theo-logical constitution thus brings out the ultimate concept of "metaphysics" by recognizing its unity in the intersecting conciliation of the ground (by beings as such) with the ground in the mode of causality (by the supreme being). I suggest that we have no other rigorous determination of "metaphysics" at our disposal, that is, no other determination that is historically confirmed and conceptually operative. Because the determination remains precise, it renders thinkable both the possibility and the impossibility of "metaphysics." And for this reason, too, the determination maybe renders intelligible the relief that goes beyond metaphysics and takes it up again in a higher figure.

3

The definition that renders "metaphysics" intelligible also makes possible the thought that it might become impossible. The demarcation of the possible necessarily implies both these postulations, with equal right. In my view, the reciprocal foundation of onto-theology offers the most powerful working hypothesis for the historian of philosophy. It also allows us to understand how it was possible to speak of an "end of metaphysics." Nietzsche's critique of philosophy as a Platonism to be inverted and subverted is in fact perfectly in line with the Heideggerian hypothesis, for that critique amounts above all to a critique of the concept of being in general, reduced to the undistinguished level of one of the " 'highest concepts,' which means the most general, the emptiest concepts, the last smoke of evaporating reality."[8] Nietzsche here contests the legitimacy of a general abstraction from matter and from the sensible, and thus the traditional condition of possibility for a science of being in general (*metaphysica generalis*). Reciprocally, Nietzsche denies that any being par excellence might exercise the function of foundation over common being from some invisible netherworld (his problematic of "vengeance" is added to this). No concept of *causa sui* is admissible, whether as logical principle, as universal cause, or as "moral God." Why would beings as such, that is, as sensible, necessitate that another being overdetermine them as their ground? Why would what *is* have to be given a further ground, instead of answering for itself by itself alone? The original function of the science of the being par excellence (*metaphysica specialis*) is thus called into question. This double disqualification is finally unified in the single identification between becoming (common being, *metaphysica generalis*) and Being (the being par excellence, *metaphysica specialis*): "To impose the seal of Being on becoming . . . —the height of speculation!"[9] Nothing can become ground since nothing calls for or necessitates a ground. Metaphysics no longer has grounds for being, nor Being a metaphysical ground. Nietzsche therefore confirms negatively the Heideggerian definition of *metaphysics* as an onto-theo-logical system of reciprocal foundation between the being par excellence and common being.

What must be concluded from this? First, something obvious: the definition of *metaphysics* that is historically and conceptually the most pertinent also allows one to challenge it. The thought of the ground, precisely because it can account for beings as a whole, can also be denied as ground. If the ground imposes itself metaphysically through its universal capacity to respond to the question "Why a being rather than nothing?" it exposes itself to the nihilistic refutation that asks "Why a reason rather than nothing?" The ground ensures the legitimacy of metaphysics but not of itself. Now, the self-evidence of the question "Why?" can (and undoubtedly must) always become blurred when faced with the violence of the question that asks "Why ask 'why'?" And if metaphysics is indeed defined as thought about a universal ground, it will founder when the self-evidence of the obligation to found being is called into question. This limitation of "metaphysics" is even stronger, first, insofar as it results directly from its definition, which is maintained but turned back against itself, and, second, insofar as a mere suspicion ("why ask 'why'?") and not even a demonstration is enough for metaphysics to be invalidated in point of fact. The "end of metaphysics" is thus in no way an optional opinion; it is a fact of reason. Whether one accepts it or not, it inevitably holds sway over us as an event that has arisen. The very fact that one can deny it and that, in order to do this, one must argue against it and therefore acknowledge it, confirms it sufficiently.[10] It is a question of a fact, and of a fact that is in some way neutral, admitting and affecting all theoretical options equally. Moreover, to refuse the fact of the "end of metaphysics" seems even less defensible insofar as it is a matter of a transitive concept. Its transitivity is formulated as follows: just as the onto-theo-logical definition of *metaphysics* directly implies at least the possibility of the "end of metaphysics," so the "end of metaphysics" directly implies the possibility of the "end of the end of metaphysics."[11] There is no paradox in this: as soon as "metaphysics" admits of a concept that is precise, historically verifiable, and theoretically operative, it follows that this concept can undergo a critique proportionate to its limits, but, thanks to those very limits, it can also offer the possible horizon of its overcoming. In contrast, so long as a concept of metaphysics is lacking, the question concerning the philosophy to come, and thus present philosophy, also remains closed, even beyond its crisis. The "end" [*Ende*], Heidegger suggested, remains fundamentally a "place" [*Ort*]. If the concept of "metaphysics" fixes its limits and thus sets its end, that end remains fertile, with a purpose for philosophy still intact. The transitivity of "metaphysics" leads not only to its "end" but also to its own overcoming—more than a metaphysics at its limit, a meta-metaphysics.

At present the "end of metaphysics" affects most visibly at one privileged point, the being par excellence. Indeed, if the figure of the ground no longer allows us to legitimate the concept of "metaphysics" in general, it follows that the assimilation of God to the function of ultimate ground in particular becomes (or can become) illegitimate. This identification runs through the entire course of philosophy and its metaphysical figure. It always interprets this ground on the basis of effectivity or actuality: "active being by essence," according to Aristotle; "no pure act without any potentiality" for Aquinas; "self-caused cause [*causa sui*]" following Descartes; "sufficient Reason for the universe," with Leibniz.[12] By "God," metaphysics therefore means the being par excellence that operates

287

as and through efficiency such that it can ensure a ground for every common being through the *metaphysica specialis*. The "end of metaphysics" provokes the "death" of *this* "God." Yet one must measure its true scope against the aggressive or resigned platitudes that seize upon this theoretical event. At issue is not denying any greatness to this determination of the divine by the efficiency of the ground, nor is it a matter of underestimating its theoretical fecundity. It is simply a matter of honestly posing this question: Does the effectivity of the ground really allow us to think the way in which God is God, even in philosophy? Even for the "God of the philosophers and the scholars," do *causa sui*, "sufficient Reason," *purus actus*, or *energeia* offer a sufficiently divine name to make God appear? At the very least, it is impossible today not to admit at least the possibility of such a suspicion. Now, this simple possibility suffices for recognizing the "death of God" in the "end of metaphysics," for it should not be possible for the divinity of God to be lacking. If it *is* lacking, if only imperceptibly, then God is already no longer at issue—but rather "God," who is stigmatized as an idol by these quotation marks.

4

If the "death of God" in philosophy belongs essentially to the "end of metaphysics" and if the latter follows essentially from the concept of "metaphysics," then the overcoming of onto-theo-logy becomes the condition for surpassing the naming of "God" in philosophy as efficient ground.

The question of whether philosophy itself can escape its metaphysical figure and thus its metaphysical destiny remains open. To be sure, Heidegger postulated a strict equivalence between "metaphysics" and "philosophy," to the advantage of "thought." But besides the fact that in certain decisive periods even after 1927 he himself claimed that "thought" would have to be introduced into "metaphysics," *Being and Time*, his first step back out of "metaphysics," remains strictly philosophical. How can that be so? By presupposing phenomenology as the method for ontology (understood in a sense radically renewed by ontological difference). In this way, he was content with simply repeating Husserl's gesture, who posited the equivalence between phenomenology and phenomenological philosophy in the *Ideas* of 1913. Despite the hesitations of the two greatest phenomenologists, one should therefore not speak of an ambiguous or undecided relation between phenomenology and metaphysics. One can simply grant that the radical innovation that phenomenology accomplishes in (and for) philosophy has perhaps not yet been measured fully in its most decisive meaning. We must therefore sketch it out, if only in broad strokes.

Phenomenology begins with a tautological principle, the "principle of nonpresupposition," which is formulated as early as 1900 in the opening of the second volume of the

Logical Investigations: "strict exclusion of all statements not permitting of a comprehensive phenomenological realization."[13] The tautology is real but nevertheless meaningful. There is phenomenology when and only when a statement gives a phenomenon to be seen; what does not appear in one fashion or another does not enter into consideration. To understand is ultimately to see. To speak is to speak in order to render visible, thus to speak in order to see. Otherwise, to speak means nothing. But how are we to see? How does the statement make itself seen, taking on the status of a phenomenon? Husserl will respond more explicitly to this second question in the opening of the *Ideas* of 1913, where he posits the "principle of principles," which states "*that every originarily giving intuition is a source of right for cognition*, that everything that offers itself [*sich darbietet*] to us in originary 'intuition' (so to speak, in its fleshly actuality) must be received exactly as it gives itself out to be [*als was es sich (da) gibt*]."[14] To be realized as a phenomenon means to be given in an actuality without reserve, a "fleshly [*leibhaft*] actuality." For a statement to appear phenomenally amounts to its assuming flesh; the phenomenon shows the flesh of the discourse. How does a statement obtain this phenomenal flesh? Through intuition (*Anschauung* or *Intuition*, equally). One intuition of whatever kind is sufficient for the phenomenon, the flesh of the discourse, to occur. Indeed, intuition operates an absolutely indisputable hold and an ultimate cognition, since only another intuition can contradict a first intuition, so that in the final instance an intuition always remains. Intuition accomplishes the most fleshly acts of cognition. The flesh of the discourse appears to the flesh of the mind—the phenomenon to intuition. Phenomenology calls this encounter a givenness [*donation*]: intuition gives the phenomenon, the phenomenon gives itself through intuition. To be sure, this givenness can always be examined, can always be authenticated or not, can always admit limits—but it can never be questioned or denied, except by the authority of another intuitive givenness. The universal validity of the "principle of principles" confirms this.

One could not meditate too much on the scope of this principle, although it is often underestimated. (1) Setting intuition to work as the ultimate instance of givenness, the "principle of principles" gives rise to the extension of intuition beyond the Kantian prohibition. The intuition of essences and categorical intuition are added to sensible intuition. (2) Since intuition gives in the flesh, the Kantian caesura between the (solely sensible) phenomenon and the thing-in-itself must disappear. This is accomplished through intentionality. (3) Since intuition alone gives, the *I* (even the transcendental and constituting *I*) must remain held *by* and hence *in* an intuition. The "originary impression" temporally precedes consciousness precisely insofar as the latter remains pure. It imposes a facticity on consciousness that is not at all derivative, but originary. (4) As determinative as they may be (and none of the later phenomenologists called them into question), these doctrinal decisions must not divert our attention from their source. The "principle of principles" posits that in the beginning[15] (of philosophy and, first, of experience), there is only intuition. Yet insofar as it gives every phenomenon and initiates phenomenality in general, intuition is at work prior to any a priori as an originary a posteriori. An essential paradox emerges: the sole legitimate a priori in phenomenology becomes the a posteriori itself. The formula "principle of all principles" must not lead us astray. The principle here is that there is no principle at all, at least if by principle we mean what precedes, "that starting from which."[16] Or, in other words, what takes the place of a principle—namely, intuition as givenness—always precedes the consciousness of it, which we receive as if after the fact. The reduplication of "principle" in the "principle of principles" therefore must not be understood as the statement of another principle (after those of identity or of sufficient reason) that would be more essentially a priori than the preceding ones. Instead one must think of it in the manner of a superlative, as the (non)principle that surpasses all the previous principles insofar as it states that in the beginning there is no (transcendental) a priori principle but indeed an intuitive a posteriori: givenness precedes everything and always. Hence phenomenology goes unambiguously beyond metaphysics in the strict sense that it gets rid of any a priori principle in order to admit givenness, which is originary precisely insofar as it is a posteriori for the one who receives it. Phenomenology goes beyond metaphysics insofar as it gives up the transcendental project in order to allow the development of a finally radical empiricism[17]—finally radical because it is no longer limited to sensible intuition but admits all originarily giving intuition.

This reversal of the a priori principle in favor of the a posteriori immediately entails two determinative theses concerning *ontologia* and ground, respectively. The first follows directly from givenness: the appearance of phenomena is operative without having recourse to Being (at least necessarily and in the first instance). Indeed, here it is a matter of any "intuition" whatsoever, of the fact of its "giving itself," and of "fleshly presence." These three terms suffice to define the perfect phenomenality of the phenomenon without having recourse in any way to Being, to being, and even less to an "objective concept of being." One might legitimately ask whether every phenomenon, inasmuch as it appears, does not at least initially dispense with Being—a phenomenon without Being. Consequently, phenomenology could free itself absolutely not only from all *metaphysica generalis (ontologia)*,[18] but also from the question of Being (*Seinsfrage*).[19] Phenomenology's relief of the metaphysical and ontological concepts is marked by clearly identifiable transpositions. Let us cite the principal ones.

(1) Henceforth, actuality is replaced by possibility, in the sense that Heidegger ("Higher than actuality stands possibility") reverses Aristotle's fundamental thesis that "the act (*energeia*) is thus prior to potentiality (*dynamis*) according to genesis and time," as well as according to *ousia*."[20] (2) Evidence replaces certainty as the privileged mode of truth. The fact of the givenness of the phenomenon in itself replaces what the ego defines according to the limits of what it sees (*certus, cernere*), according to the phenomenon's own requirements. (3) *Ousia*, as the privileged meaning of being, which is thus the owner of its own goods (according to the primary—landowning—sense of the Greek term), is

replaced by the given of Being, which straightaway defines every being as a being-given.[21] The being-given designates being such that its Being does not first amount to possessing its own funds (*ousia*) but to receiving itself in Being, to receiving Being or, rather, to receiving the opportunity to be. In all of these cases, one would have to extend the status of a beyond of beingness (*epekeina teis ousias*) to every being-given, something Plato reserved solely for the "idea of the good [*idea tou agathou*]."[22] General metaphysics, as *ontologia*, thus would have to yield to a general phenomenology of the givenness of any being-given, of which the *Seinsfrage* possibly would constitute only a simple region or a particular case. The relief of metaphysics (here, of general metaphysics) by phenomenology goes all the way to this radical point.

5

Thus I come to the second thesis that follows from the "principle of principles." This one concerns the *metaphysica specialis* in its more specifically theological function. Following Heidegger but also the facts of the history of philosophy, we admitted that in metaphysics "God" has, in essence, the function of ultimate ground, of "highest Reason," of *causa sui*. It is not a matter here of arguing whether this interpretation of the divine function is suitable or even whether the concept of ground offers a sufficiently divine figure of God according to a renewed problematic of the divine names. At issue is simply whether the connections between "God" and all other beings, or—what amounts to the same thing— with being in general, can be understood and realized as a ground, or even according to an efficient causality. One must ask this since the "principle of all principles" has overdetermined the fact and the effect of being by the most original intuitive givenness, such that being in effect (and thus calling for a grounding cause) is replaced by the being-given (being inasmuch as given). If intuition of itself and by itself alone offers not only the fact of being-given but above all its "source of right," why would this phenomenon still seek the rights of its occurrence in a cause, which would interpret it as an effect? Moreover, would givenness have to be thought starting from the effect or, on the contrary, would the effect have to be received as an impoverished figure of givenness? Precisely inasmuch as it is being-given, the phenomenon itself does not have any "Why?" and therefore does not call for any. In phenomenology, the ground is not so much criticized or refuted (as is essentially still the case in Nietzsche, who undoubtedly never truly reaches his "third metamorphosis"),[23] as it is stricken with theoretical uselessness. "God" cannot be thought as the ground of being as soon as originary givenness delivers (sends, gives) being as a being-given and therefore delivers (frees) it of any requirement of a ground. Consequently, no longer capable of being thought *ad extra* under the figure of the ground, "God" can also no longer be thought *ad intra* under the figure of the *causa sui*. Thus the relief of the *metaphysica generalis* of being as grounded effect by the phenomenological givenness of being-given inevitably entails the relief of the *metaphysica specialis* of the foundation by the phenomenological "source of right" recognized in being-given.

The denunciation—more virulent than argued—of a supposed transposition of special metaphysics into phenomenology or even of a theological highjacking of phenomenology betrays, above all, a deviation that is rather too positivistic in its approach to the phenomenological method. But it conveys, without thematizing it, a fundamental error concerning phenomenology. To stigmatize a return of special metaphysics into phenomenology presupposes that such a return is phenomenologically *possible*. Yet by definition it proves to be impossible, since the requirement of the ground is in principle no longer operative. One might respond, perhaps, that this transposition has in fact taken place, thus proving that certain supposed phenomenologists no longer merit the title—which is precisely what one wanted to show. But this reasoning, in turn, is open to several objections. First, it implies that an essential and often distinguished part of what has always been recognized as belonging to the domain of phenomenological method has in fact ceaselessly betrayed it. This remains to be demonstrated conceptually and in detail—an immense and delicate task. Yet such an undertaking would quickly become dogmatic, since it would presuppose not only that there is a phenomenological method that is unique and that precedes all doctrines but, further, that this method has not evolved since Husserl's idealist and constitutive moment between 1913 and 1929. None of these points is self-evident, especially insofar as it belongs essentially to phenomenology that the a posteriori render it possible and therefore that no a priori prohibition predetermine it. If there is a philosophy that works with an open method and bare thought, it is indeed phenomenology. Against metaphysics, it won the right to make use of the "Return to the things themselves!" which one might gloss "Prohibiting is prohibited!"[24] The sole criterion in phenomenology issues from the facts: from the phenomena that an analysis manages to display, from what the analysis renders visible. What shows itself justifies itself by that very fact.

But if a reestablishment of the *metaphysica specialis* in phenomenology appears to be a pure methodological contradiction, this nevertheless does not imply that phenomenology remains unfamiliar with what the *metaphysica specialis* treated at the metaphysical level. Could not the already-established relief of the *metaphysica generalis* by phenomenology also be repeated with respect to what the *metaphysica specialis* treated in the onto-theo-logical mode? This question does not aim at any restoration—I have just highlighted the absurdity of this—but a relief: to return to the things themselves, and possibly to the same things, in order to let them appear no longer according to the figure of ground but according to that of givenness, in this case no longer according to efficiency (being effect, *causa sui*) but according to the being-given. The three beings that were privileged by the *metaphysica specialis*, namely, the world (*cosmologia rationalis*), the finite mind (*psychologia rationalis*), and "God" (*theologia rationalis*) demand, in the capacity of "thing itself," that we test the possibility (or impossibility) of their phenomenal apparition and therefore of the intuition that could (or not) inscribe them in the being-given. For none of the cases can this requirement be challenged, since it results directly from the phenomenological reduction, namely, to suspend all transcendence precisely in order to measure what is thus given in immanence. Moreover, the phenomenological relief of what was treated by the *metaphysica specialis* already has a long history, going back to Husserl.

A few results can be assumed today as established facts. First, concerning the world: the early Husserl relieves the classical metaphysical aporia (Descartes, Kant) of the necessity, indeed, of the impossibility, of demonstrating the existence of the external "world." Intentionality (and then Heidegger's *In-der-Welt-sein*) directly sets consciousness ecstatically into the world without the screen of representation. It finds the world always already given because it is originarily given to the world more essentially. The relation of constitution between consciousness and its objects will exploit intentionality so far as to put it in danger, but the late Husserl will bring the noetico-noematic relation back under the firm control of the "principle of correlation." The question of the world hence definitely quits the horizon of objectivation for that of the being-given, as *the being-given as a whole*. Next, concerning the finite mind: obsession with the Cartesian ego still keeps Husserl and even Heidegger from giving up on interpreting it. This is, if not still theoretical, at least still constitutive, if only through "anticipatory resoluteness." From this followed the disappearance of ethics or its subordination to theory. It is to the decisive credit of Emmanuel Levinas to have established, in a Copernican revolution, that ontology, even fundamental ontology, cannot reach the ground because that ground belongs to the domain not of theoretical philosophy but of ethics. Not only does ethics thus become first philosophy (*philosophia prima*), which by itself would still remain an arrangement of metaphysics, but it decenters the ego toward the always already open, offered, and abandoned face of the other [*d'autrui*] and thus toward the being-given of the other. The ego no longer ensures any foundation by representing (itself); it finds itself always already preceded by the being-given of the other, whose unobjectifiable counter-intentionality it suffers. Along this line, the passage from the ego to what I call the "interlocuted" [*interloqué*] presents no difficulty: one must simply generalize the reversed intentionality to other being-givens.[25] According to the rule of givenness, the ego thus attains a secondariness[26] that is, nevertheless, more phenomenal than any representational primacy. Put in second place, the ego discovers the other as *the closest being-given*.

The question of "God" remains, which for obvious reasons has remained the question least approached by phenomenology. These obvious reasons spring from different but convergent reservations on the part of Husserl and Heidegger. Husserl clearly indicated (although without returning to the matter, even in his final texts) that the assumption of any "God" whatsoever fell under the blow of the reduction and that "God," transcendent in every sense, therefore did not appear.[27] When Heidegger marks God with the seal of the *causa sui*,[28] he is always and explicitly dealing with the "God" of metaphysics. Can phenomenology go no further than these denials or these warnings?[29] Some would like to leave a choice only between philosophical silence and faith without reason. Such an alternative often clearly has the sole intention of dwelling serenely in silence while banishing reason. Yet outside of revealed theology there is no reason to prohibit reason—here, philosophy in its phenomenological bearing—from pushing reason to its end, that is, to itself, without admitting any other limits than those of phenomenality. The question then becomes: What (if any) phenomenal face can the "God of the philosophers and the scholars" assume? More precisely, what phenomenon could claim to offer a luminous shadow of this "God" so as to correspond to the being-given's relief of being? Does one not, perhaps inevitably, have to answer the being-given with a giver, indeed a being-giver [*étant-donateur*]? And in that case, how could one distinguish that being-giver from a founding being or *causa sui*,[30] and how could one not stigmatize in this long operation a simple restoration of the most metaphysical *theologia rationalis*?

However lucid it may appear to be, this objection remains convincing only if one ignores two arguments. (1) On the hypothesis in which a giver would indeed correspond to the being-given, the giver would be equivalent to a (metaphysical) ground only by maintaining the status of a being and only if the givenness of the being-given given by the giver were still comprehended within the horizon of causality understood as efficiency. Yet neither of these assumptions is self-evident. On the contrary, it could be that givenness can arise only once causality has been radically surpassed, in a mode whose own rationality causality does not even suspect. It could be that givenness obeys requirements that are infinitely more complex and powerful than the resources of efficient causality. Moreover, even in the history of metaphysics, the sudden appearance of efficient causality in the field of "God" marks more the *decline* than the consecration of *theologia rationalis*; Leibniz was the equally lucid and powerless witness to this. The objection thus betrays that it depends on metaphysics much more than does the thesis that it contests, since it cannot prevent itself from understanding that thesis hastily and from the outset in a metaphysical fashion. (2) A second argument, however, renders these precautions useless. The answer to the being-given does not assume the figure of the giver but that of the being-given par excellence. If the world can be defined as what appears as the being-given as a whole, if "I/me" can be designated as what appears as the closest being-given, then "God" would be determined as the being-given par excellence. That excellence indicates neither sufficiency, nor efficiency, nor principality, but it attests to the fact that "God" is given and allows to be given more than any other being-given. In short, with "God" it is a question of the *being-abandoned* [*l'étant-abandonné*].[31]

The phenomenological figure of "God" as the being-given par excellence, hence as the abandoned, can be outlined by following the guiding thread of givenness itself. As the given par excellence, "God" is given without restriction, without reserve, without restraint. "God" is given not at all partially, following this or that outline, like a constituted object that nevertheless offers to the intentional gaze only a specific side of its sensible visibility, leaving to appresentation the duty of giving further what does not give itself. Instead "God" is given absolutely, without the least reserve of any outline, with every side open, in the manner of the objects whose dimensions cubist painting caused to explode, in order that all aspects might be juxtaposed, despite the constraints of perspective. "God" is found given without reserve or restraint. This evidence displays itself in the atonal tonality of bedazzlement. It follows that God diffuses—what God diffuses remains God-self: the Good diffuses itself and therefore what it diffuses still remains itself, perhaps in the way that the modes in which the Spinozist *substantia* expresses itself still remain that *substantia* itself. The givenness par excellence implies an ecstasy outside of self where the ecstatic self remains all the more itself. While the *causa sui* can only fold efficiency back upon itself, the givenness that "God" accomplishes can remain equal to itself (givenness as gift). If the "God" of metaphysics, according to Malebranche, acts only for itself, then the "God" of phenomenology, exactly to the contrary, acts only for what does not remain (in) "God."

This givenness par excellence entails another consequence: the absolute mode of presence that follows from it saturates any horizon, all horizons, with a dazzling evidence. Now, such a presence without limit (without horizon), which alone suits givenness without reserve, cannot present itself as a necessarily limited object. Consequently, it occupies no space, fixes no attention, attracts no gaze. In this very bedazzlement, "God" shines by absence. *Evidence evoids*[32]—it voids the saturated horizons of any definable, visible thing. The absence or unknowability of "God" does not contradict givenness but on the contrary attests to the excellence of that givenness. "God" becomes invisible not in spite of givenness but by virtue of that givenness. One needs a rather weak estimation of transcendence, or even an already militant refusal, to be scandalized by its invisibility. If we saw it, then it would not be "God."

Givenness par excellence can thus turn immediately into givenness by *abandon*. The being-given that is absolutely without restraint exerts a phenomenology such that, due to its intrinsic invisibility, its status as phenomenon might never be acknowledged. The phenomenon par excellence on account of that very excellence lays itself open to not appearing—to remaining in a state of abandon. Indeed, most other phenomena become available to the gaze that sees them, delimits them, and manipulates them. Here, on the contrary, a radical unavailability exposes "God" to the risk of being denied the right to phenomenality precisely because most of the time and at first glance our gaze only desires and only wants to see objects. Givenness par excellence thus turns toward abandon. And this is confirmed every time that one fails to acknowledge givenness under the pretext that, given without return or retreat, it is abandoned to the point of disappearing as an object one could possess, handle, encircle. Givenness par excellence actually lays itself open to seeming to disappear (by defect) precisely because it gives itself without reserve (by excess). A strange but inevitable paradox.

6

Of course, although decidedly opposed to the metaphysical figure of a *causa sui*, "God," the figure of "God" in phenomenology that we have just outlined, nevertheless still concerns the "God of the philosophers and the scholars," and in no way the "God of Abraham, of Isaac, and of Jacob."[33] One could also say that the figure of "God" in phenomenology is hardly distinguishable from this latter. The being-given par excellence in fact bears the characteristics of a very precise type of manifestation, namely, that of the saturated phenomenon, or, more precisely, that of the saturated phenomenon typical of revelation.[34] Would one not again have to fear a confusion between phenomenology and revealed theology here?

It seems to me that such a confusion can be avoided through two clear distinctions. (1) On its own, phenomenology can identify the saturated phenomenon of the being-given par excellence only as a possibility: not only a possibility as opposed to actuality but, above all, as a possibility of givenness itself. The characteristics of the being-given imply that it gives itself without prediction, without measure, without analogy, without repetition; in short, it remains unavailable. Its phenomenological analysis therefore bears only on its re-presentation, its "essence," and not directly on its being-given in fact. More than phenomenological analysis, the intuitive realization of that being-given requires the real experience of its givenness, which falls to revealed theology. Between phenomenology and theology, the border passes between revelation as possible and revelation as historicity. There can be no danger of confusion between these domains.[35] (2) To be sure, phenomenology can describe and construct the being-given and even the being-given par excellence, but it certainly does not fall to phenomenology to approach the givenness that is identified with and in a face. Or rather, even if it can make the face one of its privileged themes in a strict sense, it cannot and must not understand that face as a face of charity. When the being-given turns to charity (the loved or loving being, the lover in the strict sense), phenomenology yields to revealed theology exactly as the second order, according to Pascal, yields to the third. Here again, no confusion could creep in.

Quite obviously, these theses cannot be adequately developed here. They nevertheless will suffice to indicate what new path phenomenology shows to philosophy, beyond the metaphysics that it relieves—and without returning to *metaphysica specialis*. And on that path, the rational thought of God, which philosophy cannot forget without losing its own dignity or even its mere possibility, finds at least a certain coherence.

—Translated by Thomas A. Carlson, with Christina M. Gschwandtner

What No One Else Can Do in My Place

A Conversation with Emmanuel Levinas

Emmanuel Levinas and France Guwy

FRANCE GUWY: Mr. Levinas, to begin with a rather foolish question: Is one born a philosopher, or does one become one?

EMMANUEL LEVINAS: Well, you don't claim the name *philosopher* the way you do a profession. To hear someone say "I'm a philosopher" or "I'm a poet" always shocks me. It's not my style. In the word *philosophy* there is already the impossibility of possessing wisdom; it already implies taking a step back before the word of the wise man. The philosopher is a person who loves wisdom. It is the beginning of an interest in certain questions, certain books.

FG: And what were those books for you?

EL: I've always been responsive to the basic works of world literature, such as those of Shakespeare and Cervantes, for example. And of course the great classics of Russian literature: Tolstoy, Dostoyevsky, Pushkin, Turgenev, Gogol. These texts are constantly questioning what the human being is, and the meaning of life. Their questioning is very close to the essential problems philosophy raises. And it is the same questions that are found in the literary work par excellence—the book of books, the Bible.

The Critique of Western Philosophy

FG: Do you see a contradiction between the Bible and philosophy?

EL: I don't think so. I have never experienced them as contradictory. In both cases it is a matter of meaning, of the appearance of the meaningful—whether in the form of what the Greeks called reason or in that of the relationship to one's neighbor in the Bible. What they have in common is mainly that in both cases it is a matter of the quest for meaning, for the meaningful.

FG: Western thought is rooted in the Bible and Greek philosophy; two sources of thought that are at the center of your philosophy. Does this mean that in your view we should not pursue the search for wisdom beyond the borders of Europe?

EL: I would say that for me these two European forms of the human, which have completed one another in our civilization, are absolutely essential. That does not exclude the possibility of finding significant texts outside Europe. But I am not afraid, for my part, to speak of a certain centrality—of the great importance—of European thought. And I say this without overlooking all the abuses and all the horrors Europe has known.

FG: Are you referring to the horrors of the Nazi regime?

EL: Let me say, Madam, that the most fundamental thing in my life and thought is that, alongside the greatness of European science and intelligence, in that same Europe, the extermination took place—the Shoah, which is the very prototype of the extermination of man by the other. The premonition and the memory of those years are indelible. But we will not find an answer to that drama by seeking a way out in other civilizations. I think that within our civilization itself we must give a central place to certain elements we have underestimated. I don't expect much from my research in the way of changing the course of things, but in any case I work on what I consider to be a disequilibrium, within this civilization, between the fundamental themes of knowledge and the fundamental forms of the relation to the other.

FG: Is that the basis of your critique of Western philosophy?

EL: You know, people allow themselves to use excessive expressions. Talking about the critique of Western philosophy is like denying that the Himalayas are high. That philosophy is so important, essential, and demanding that you have to master it first, before critiquing it.

FG: Yet you wrote: "The history of Western philosophy has been the destruction of transcendence."

EL: I mean that in a very precise sense. The ideal of European philosophy consisted in believing in the possibility of human thought encompassing all that seems to stand in its way, thus interiorizing what is exterior, transcendent. Western philosophy no longer wanted to conceive of divine transcendence or anything going beyond the embraceable, the graspable order: as if the spirit consisted in grasping all things.

FG: You describe it as a philosophy in which the I reigns supreme and knowledge consists more in taking than in understanding.

EL: Yes, a philosophy in which the I, through knowledge, recognizes as the same, as always the same, as reducible to the same, that which appears as other—and I am thinking, of course, first and foremost of the encounter with the other.

FG: It is especially on that point that you criticize Heidegger.

EL: Heidegger reaches one of the highest summits of those Himalayas I mentioned to you, one of the summits of the phenomenological method. That is what I learned in his works. What I reproach him for is that to him the encounter with the other is only a moment in the understanding of the world. Whereas for me the encounter with the other *is* the understanding of the world, the understanding of the bosom of being that is manifested through the world. The other is for me the philosophical term par excellence, the source of intelligibility. There is, in my modest labors, an attempt to place the relation to the other at the center—the other as a human being stripped of social positions, social passions—as being the moment through which the word of God reaches, touches us.

The Priority of Justice

FG: So, if I understand you correctly, the search for truth in itself preoccupies you less than being qua being for the other? In other words: the question of justice before the question of truth?

EL: Of course, I don't want to philosophize about things that are false. In the development of civilization, knowledge and truth are extremely important. But I give a certain priority to the relation to the other, to being for the other, to the social dimension. Truth is based on the necessity of justice, and therefore on a social dimension.

FG: From that priority of the social and of justice it follows that man must draw the consequences on the political level. Would you say, as Jean-Paul Sartre does, that we must take a political stand?

EL: That is not an issue on which I would disagree with Sartre. With him it's common-sense thinking. Even if personally I have no political calling, I would say that in the relation to the other we are immediately faced with his uniqueness, his face, his otherness par excellence, and it is through this face of the other that God calls us. And that immediately implies an obligation. But it goes further, because it is at the same time a matter of obligations toward a plurality of persons, which I call the third party. There is also the fourth, the fifth, and so on, and they, too, are my neighbors. And that introduces the necessity of justice, that is, the consideration of the other, not only through his face, in which he is unique. We must also consider the other in objectivity, and we must therefore compare beings who are incomparable. Thus politics is inevitable. Since we have to do with a number of people in human relations and each one of them is my neighbor, we must establish a rule, a law, in order for my actions and my relations with that plurality to be just. In being good to one, you see, we might put the other at a disadvantage. And so we need rules and laws in order for there to be justice, and an institution to defend that justice with authority. Thus we need the authority of a political state. The fact of living in a society requires justice as a first obligation.

Ethics Precedes Philosophy

FG: How should what you call face be interpreted? For you, ethics precedes philosophy and that ethics is expressed in the epiphany of the face.

EL: That's the main theme of my thought. The other man, who at first is part of the world as a whole, somehow pierces through that world by his appearance as face. And that face is not simply a plastic form but immediately represents a commitment for me, a calling out to me, an order for me to be at the service of that face. This means to serve the other man, who in that face appears to me at once in his nakedness, in his indigence, with nothing protecting him—therefore, in that sense, in his destitution. And at the same time this face is the place that commands me, and that is what I call the word of God in the face.

FG: And this command is "Thou shalt not kill."

EL: The face is what lends itself to murder and what resists murder. "Thou shalt not kill" is a whole program: it means "Thou shalt make me live." There are a thousand and one ways to kill the other, not just with a revolver. We kill the other in being indifferent toward him, in not paying attention to him, in abandoning him. Consequently "Thou shalt not kill" is the main thing: it is the order in which the other man is recognized as that which imposes itself on me.

FG: But that face of the other calls out to my responsibility and in that responsibility you go very far. You even go so far as to say that we must atone for the other, suffer for the other . . .

EL: The word *responsible* is but another way of expressing what I call being for the other. I am responsible for the other, I am answerable for the other, and in sum I am answerable before having done anything. The paradox is that it is a responsibility that is not the result of some act that I have committed, but rather it is as if I were responsible before having committed an act. It is as if it were a priori and consequently as if I were not free to divest myself of that responsibility, as if I were responsible before having done anything wrong, that is, as if I were atoning, behaving as a hostage.

Elective Freedom

FG: But what meaning does freedom and the autonomy of the human being have when, prior to all knowledge and all freedom, it is the other person who puts my freedom in question and requires my responsibility?

EL: So it is that I ask the question: How should we define freedom? Obviously when there is constraint, there is no freedom. But when there is no constraint, is there necessarily freedom? Should freedom be defined in a purely negative way, as the absence of constraint? Or, on the contrary, does freedom mean the possibility of a person's responding to the call addressed to him, and doing something no one else can do in his or her place? In what I call the goodness prior to any choice that is my responsibility, I am, as it were, elected, as if noninterchangeable; I am the only one able to do what I do with respect to the other.

FG: So you agree with Sartre, who says we are condemned to freedom?

EL: That depends. When one is dedicated to something or someone and it is not simply blind necessity, but there is a call to me as the only one who can accomplish what I accomplish—then ethical responsibility is always there. The meaning of my ethical responsibility is that no one other than myself can do what I do. It is as if I were chosen, and it is this idea of elective freedom that I put in place of that purely negative freedom. What shocks us about nonfreedom is that we are just anybody in the responsibility for the other. Whereas I am always called upon as if I were the only one who could do it. Having yourself replaced for a moral act is tantamount to relinquishing the moral act. Sartre thinks in a negative way, while I think in a positive way. What is important to me is that behind each individual, who is just anyone within their genus, I am the only one who can do it. All the rest is commentary. The freedom of free choice is not, in my view, the first human event. If you are asking me what our freedom or our autonomy still mean in this situation in which we are hostage to the call the other addresses to us, my response is that this has nothing to do with constraint or nonfreedom, but that it corresponds to my deepest vocation.

FG: Can you identify with Kant's expression a propos of the Enlightenment: "The Enlightenment is having the courage to follow one's own understanding"?

EL: What I am saying is the clue to what is deepest in me; it is rigorously personal. It is not the same thing as Kant's universal principle. Here freedom means doing something that no one else can do in my place. That is what fundamental freedom is. I would say that it is the freedom of goodness.

FG: And that goodness . . . cannot be commanded?

EL: I will even say, and it is a perilous statement: goodness is not a voluntary act. What I mean by that is that there is not, in the movement of freedom, any particular act of a will that intervenes and decides to be good. One does not decide to be good; one is good before any decision. In my thought there is the affirmation of an initial goodness. When I say that no one is good voluntarily, that is also a response to the Greeks, who used to say that no one is voluntarily bad. I do not say that man is bad, but he is tenacious, and by nature oriented to the perseverance of his being.

A Break with the Order of Nature

FG: And does your thought go against that nature?

EL: My thought breaks with the order of nature. In that order of nature in which everything is bent on remaining itself—the human in that regular order of nature thinks of itself and persists in its being. That is what the great philosopher Spinoza (Jewish, Dutch, but also European) called the supreme act of God: that is, that each being persists in its being.

With what I call the responsibility for the other, that order is broken; it can be broken, it is not always broken. I absolutely do not say that is what always triumphs, but with the human, the possibility of breaking that order is opened. Man has the possibility of thinking, of taking on a commitment, of being concerned with the other man before pursuing perseverance in his own being.

FG: You say: "One cannot remain indifferent to the call of the other." But then how is evil to be explained?

EL: What I mean is that with the human there is that possibility. I don't say it works every day, but with the human there is in a certain sense the possibility of a break with that implacable necessity. And I will add that, of course, this assumes there have been saints and righteous men in human history. What does the holy land mean in the Bible? It is the land that does not allow sin to take root in it, that does not sustain societal misconduct, that does not sustain social injustice. On this subject the most important text says that it is a land that gets sick and vomits out its inhabitants who do not live according to the law, the ethics of justice. That is the only possible enrootedness.

FG: So does your ethics require saintliness?

EL: I do not in the least claim that man is a saint, but man is a being who cannot dispute the value of saintliness.

FG: You mean it is his vocation?

EL: It is his vocation, and I take vocation in the strong sense of the term: there is someone calling. Not someone who is facing me and calling me; but that "someone" who is in the face of the other calls out to me. To call means to obligate without the use of force. There is such a thing as obligation without force, without violence. But alas, after Auschwitz, that is an idea that can no longer be preached. You can say to yourself that God commands without violence, but you don't have the right to preach it, because then you sound like you are justifying Auschwitz. And perhaps we cannot think that all is lost, even if God has kept silent. God after Auschwitz no longer has any justification. If there is still a faith, it is one without theodicy, without our being able to justify God. I do not say it easily, but it is an ethics without hope, which is not made to be preached. Of the three theological virtues—faith, hope, and love—I wonder whether hope does not compromise faith. Hope is too involved in reward. Jewish messianism, too, is involved in that hope.

Our Accounts Are Never Settled

FG: In one of your works, you write: "everyone is the Messiah; I am the Messiah."

EL: To be the Messiah means two things: first, that he atones for the other; and second, you have resurrection in Christianity and the triumphant Messiah in Judaism. I have said, upon occasion, that the Resurrection is not Christianity's strongest point. Those who followed Christ after his death and before the discovery of his empty tomb are in my view much more convincing. And even the discovery of the empty tomb did not satisfy them; they wanted to meet him first. The fundamental point of messianism is that you, as a unique person, must commit yourself in favor of the other. Therein lies the asymmetry of the interpersonal relation. But you cannot preach that, either; you cannot require it from the other for yourself. You can only say it to yourself. And it is in this sense that I might be the Messiah. I am not saying that I am.

FG: Does that have anything to do with a certain grace?

EL: Absolutely not. On the contrary. The subject is not the one who takes possession, but the one who is responsible. And it is that universal responsibility that is incumbent on me. It is my existence, and as subject I myself am responsible. I am called, I am hostage, I am elected to respond to the call of the other man. And therein I am unique. That is, if you like, what I call being the Messiah: I have come to save the world. And of course I forget that; we are all Messiahs who forget it. But it is out of that subjectivity, which I do not conceive of as a power but as an initial and disinterested goodness, that this responsibility arises.

FG: You say: "I incur responsibility as soon as the other looks at me." While Sartre says that the other who looks at me reduces me to the state of an object, that the other means alienation, that the fact that the other looks at me is violence, for you the aggressor is not the other; it is me.

EL: I think that in saying this, I am not inventing a fundamental possibility of man. I say to you: when we are not purely and simply in the state of being, but have understood the otherness of the other, we are never done understanding it. Your accounts are never closed with respect to the other, and it bespeaks a completely bourgeois morality to say at a given moment: I can close the door.

The other regards[1] me, not in the Sartrean sense, in condemning me, but in the sense in which one says in French: your business regards me, your business doesn't regard me, your business always regards me.

FG: It concerns me?

EL: No, it regards me; that is much more brutal. That is the Messianic moment in the human experience. I am not saying the Messiah triumphs; he won't come, you understand. But it is through that vocation that he is unique. Therein lies his individuality.

Responsibility and Asymmetry

FG: In this context you often cite Dostoyevsky: "We are all guilty of everything and to everyone, and I more than the others."

EL: It is clear that one doesn't live that way every day, isn't it? But what I want to express by that is that you should never understand that relation to the other as reciprocal. If you say: I am responsible for him but he is responsible for me, you have already transformed your initial responsibility into commerce, exchange, equality. And you have already misunderstood that sentence from Dostoyevsky, which is a fundamental experience of the human.

FG: And which illustrates what you mean by asymmetry?

EL: Yes, it is a fact that my relation to the other is not immediately a relation between two equal beings as if he were my equal. No, I am above all the one who is obligated, and he is primarily the one toward whom I am obligated. That is the essential modality in the relation to the other, if you like. When I said a moment ago that I cannot preach religion to the other, even if I accept certain principles for myself—to propose them to others would be facile theological prattle. I can accept a theology for myself that I have no right to propose to others. That's what I mean by asymmetry.

FG: But in the social context of the meeting with several others, must not that asymmetry be corrected?

EL: Once I encounter the third, who is also my neighbor, and to whom I also owe everything, I must compare the incomparable, and at that point I return to the domain of justice, I return to the city, to political life, which is inevitable. But even for the citizen who accepts the laws of the city, a kind of wisdom can supervene. A wisdom that is not a law, not a doctrine or set principle, but in which there are possibilities proper to each individual in his or her uniqueness. It is outside logic that the person as such can, while applying justice, further add, in his or her own way, a mercy that is a kind of wisdom. Mercy that is not at all a rule but based on the fact that I am unique and, qua unique, can do something no one else can do in my place, and that is not foreseen in law or justice. Politics is important and necessary, but can never make us forget the uniqueness of the other. In the social context, it is justice that determines the limit of goodness, but goodness can soften the rigor of justice.

To respect social justice prevents no one in his or her unique way from considering the other with a certain charity, with goodness. That goodness is not a law; it is a certain wisdom based on my uniqueness.

FG: How do you interpret the verse: "Love thy neighbor as thyself"?

EL: I was asked that question at the University of Leiden also, and you know what I answered: one must not read this verse as if I were the model of what one loves. "Love thy neighbor as thyself means: Love your neighbor, that *is* yourself, that is your yourself; subjectivity is made of that love of your neighbor."

FG: Yes, but do you accept that it takes a certain self-love in order to be able to carry that out?

EL: Don't misunderstand me. I am not at all saying that you have to torture yourself, but I would like to remind you of what we were saying about the fact of having settled one's accounts with the other. We feel we have done so before we really have—myself included. That's what I mean: that condition of being hostage is not in the least a form of self-deprecation, but is to be interpreted as election. I try to conceive of the individuation of man not at all in terms of time and space but in terms of that election. Do you see? As if the egotism of the I were not at all that of a powerful subject, but like someone who is called to give.

A Masochistic Morality?

FG: Monsieur Levinas, for you the primordial question is not "What is the meaning of life?" but "Do I have the right to be?" How can we live with that counter-natural question?

EL: But everything I have been trying to present is a counter-natural humanity—one that goes against the order of nature. It is a break with the regular order of being, which is concerned with its own subsistence, persevering in being, and even thinking that everything, when it is a matter of its being, is permitted and that in the face of that perseverance in being all the other questions must give way. My thought constitutes a break with that order, and I believe that with the human, that break is possible.

FG: To go against the laws of nature, to give priority to the other, to feel guilty and to atone for the other: Isn't that an almost masochistic morality?

EL: What we call masochism characterizes the illness of a healthy being. I don't think the human being is healthy in the banal sense of the word. I want to part ways with the facile wellness that consists in being chiefly concerned about my own health. It is a solicitude. Not all illnesses are to be treated, you see. Masochistic? I am not afraid of that word.

FG: What you call that facile and banal health has been condensed in Hobbes's proverb: "Homo homini lupus."

EL: History shows that not only is man a wolf toward the other man, but that he thinks he has a right to be a wolf toward the other. That is what we see in totalitarian regimes, in which the idea of the preservation of all by the state is scoffed at. Those regimes are a form of degeneration of what a state should be. In Hobbes's *Leviathan* the state arises from the fact that the wolf realizes that it is in its own interest to enter into an association, and thus that by protecting others it protects itself.

Against Enrootedness

FG: In your book *Difficult Freedom* you author an article titled "Heidegger, Gagarin, and Us." Contrary to Heidegger, you approach the problem of technology and modern science much more positively, in the sense that they lead us beyond enrootedness. But aren't you afraid Heidegger's view of technology as an element of alienation and as the embodiment of death is becoming increasingly current in the anguish caused by the threat of nuclear war?

EL: Yes, I am opposed to the ideal of enrootedness that is frequent in Heidegger: the importance of the site, the little bridge, the stream. The texts Heidegger wrote about central Europe, about Germany, are texts that must be taken literally—they are not metaphorical, you see. Those texts breathe an atmosphere of the idealization and idolatry of nature. In that ambiance, man is a plant, and that's what I wanted to contest. For me, man is a human being. I don't say there is no animal element in man, but I say that man signifies the break with animal or vegetable nature, and therein lies his liberation.

I fully recognize the dangers of technology, the overwhelming enthusiasm for technology, to the point where technology will master man and man become the slave of technology. I can see all that, but if technology is well channeled, it offers enormous possibilities for the resolution of the problems of world hunger, the liberation of man from the servitude of work, and so on . . .

But I definitely don't believe that technology is the alienation of man par excellence. I fear that man's hatred of the other man is a much greater source of alienation. To exalt a certain landscape, to take root in a place that you will subsequently idealize, losing sight of the rest of the world—this is none other than to divide humanity between indigenous and foreign. Judaism has always proved to be reserved with respect to place.

FG: But then what is your position on Israel?

EL: Israel's true vocation is to be sought in ethics. That is her vocation. It is not in the occupation of a land. Even for the country of Israel I don't like the songs that are content with praising the countryside, and that speak of enrootedness. What is certain is that many Jews would stone me for having said that.

Eroticism and Sexuality

FG: With Bataille and Sartre, you refuse to equate eroticism and sexuality, but you differ from them in that you understand eros as a mode of access to the other and not as a form of warfare between two individuals. Do you think real communication is possible in the erotic relationship?

EL: That is a problem that has interested me a lot, but quite independently of Sartre and Bataille, whom I hold in high esteem. But it is not on this point that I have learned anything from them.

For me, the relation to the other is not a contingent one, and it is certainly not to be interpreted as the downgrading of a sort of unity, although that is what constitutes the common theme in erotic literature and in literature in general. In literature, the fact that one person is not at one with another is frequently lamented, or, if you will, the intimate relationship is viewed as deficient unity. In that situation, the relation between human beings is seen as a failure. Sometimes I am prompted to say on this score that you can share your life with someone, but not your existence. Sociality is "better" (in quotation marks, i.e., without value judgment) than unity. Sociality has more meaning than a self-satisfied unity. The lamented ideal of fusion is the disappearance of that excellence: sociality. What is important to me is human relations in which the other is not the result of a contingency, and in which we are not seeking a fusion that ends up in a union closed to others and content with itself.

If by eroticism you mean concupiscence (in Pascal's sense), it is too focused on the possession of the other. I seek in sexuality yet another dimension. A dimension that does not exclude the other person. Where there is sexuality, there is the face, and the relation with the face is a rigorously ethical one, for there is already the concern not to let the other die alone. That is what I call love without concupiscence. For concupiscence is still of the order of grasping, of the order of possession, of concurrence. I seek in sexuality itself the appearance of the child, which is once again a relation with the other that requires responsibility.

The Undesirable par Excellence

FG: You have also called the other "the undesirable par excellence." In this do you agree somewhat, perhaps, with what Sartre expressed when he said "Hell is other people"?

EL: What is the human? For that humanity that is of the order of nature, for that vegetal humanity, that humanity in which all is oriented according to the perseverance in being, the other is the undesirable par excellence. For the other is the nuisance, the one who limits me, for nothing can limit me more than another person. And it is against him—and it is toward him—that you are turned by what I call God in the face of man. It is dramatic. It is a term that comes from my article "God and Philosophy," in which I have tried to show that God's response does not consist in responding to you but in sending you toward the other. God's response is: Go toward that undesirable par excellence.

FG: So the relation to God, to the infinite, is the relationship to the human?

EL: You know, Madame, I am not a Christian, but I find in the Gospel many things that are very close to me, and that seem to me to be, at base, entirely biblical. What I admire most in the Gospels is the twenty-fifth chapter of Matthew. It is the chapter on the Last Judgment, where God says, "You have driven me out, you have persecuted me."—"When did we drive you out, when did we persecute you?"—"When you drove out the poor." And this must not be taken the least bit in a metaphorical sense, but in a Eucharistic one. It is in the poor that the presence of God was.

FG: In the concrete sense?

EL: In the concrete sense. This is more important than the bread and the wine of the Eucharist. That is also how I have always read paragraph 58 of Isaiah, in which the people who seek God are told, "You will find me, but free the slaves, clothe the naked, nourish those who are hungry and let the homeless in"—and that's difficult, because they soil your rugs.

Freeing Man from God

FG: You turn away, you say, from philosophical and theological theories that want results and answers. That, you say, leads toward a nonreligious God. In your work *Totality and Infinity*, I read the sentence: "The soul is naturally atheistic; it is a great glory for the creator to have succeeded in producing a being capable of atheism, because atheism is the condition for a true relation with a true God."[2] Do you want to free man from God?

EL: It is mainly in my book *Of God Who Comes to Mind* that my analysis consists in finding out in what circumstance the word *God* itself begins to have meaning. God cannot be blamed for all that befalls man. That sort of dogma does not interest me. What seems to me essential is that man can move toward God starting out from his goodness, instead of moving toward goodness starting out from God. The fact that without pronouncing the word *God* I am in goodness is more important than a goodness that simply comes to take its place among the recommendations of a dogmatics.

FG: And in that sense you want to free man from God?

EL: Yes, free in that sense. And so what is extremely important is that way of starting out from goodness, not from the creation of the world. The creation of the world must take on its meaning starting out from goodness. And since you are hardly a stranger to religious matters, you know that it is an old belief, that is supposed to be taken from the Bible, that the world is maintained, that the world was created, by ethics, by the Torah, and that the famous word *Bereshit*—that is, "In the beginning" God created—that this word means ethics, or if you will, the Torah. And therefore ethics, the Torah, precedes the world. Obviously all that is said in a mythological way.

Thinking being qua being is preceded by, and takes its meaning from, being for the other. The first meaning is therefore an ethical one.

FG: Ethics is then more important than religion. Speaking of religion, moreover, you say: The only humanity that is worthy of the consolation of religion and of messianic promises is a humanity that can do without them.

EL: By that I don't mean it [religion] is false, and perhaps the spirituality that is attained by ethics is not complete. It is possible that man needs religion to help him go even further. But it seems to me that religion is not the path that leads to spirit in the defining sense of spirit.

FG: You illustrate that somewhere in your writings by the Roman who asks the rabbi: Why is your god the god of the poor? Doesn't he feed the poor? And the rabbi answers: To save humanity from damnation.

EL: That is what the mortal sin is, that is what is scandalous: that men do not help men. If it were God who took responsibility for it, he would have no choice but to leave men to their sins.

FG: But then the churches should be criticized for always having preached a God who rewarded and punished.

EL: I don't condemn the churches. They have a lot to do . . . They have many problems to solve. There are so many important books that the church disseminates and comments on. But perhaps it is what was in the books before that organization existed that is important. For me, spirituality does not begin with the church.

Opening Oneself to the Other

FG: One last question, Monsieur Levinas. When you speak of dialogue, you immediately introduce the ethical dimension, but in the reality of human history, both on the private and the political plane, men have always had a tendency to maneuver from a position of strength with respect to their partner. So I would like to ask you, does not that reality discourage you? Aren't you afraid you are addressing extraterrestrials with your philosophy, in which you give all the rights to the other man?

EL: As far as dialogue is concerned, I know there are abuses, but the very fact of speaking, of continuing the dialogue, is already a relation to the other. Whatever the abuses, dialogue is always useful. In one's attentiveness to the face of the other, there is always a goodness that precedes all wickedness: that is already meaningful.

Addressing your overall point, concerning all the abuses of the relation to the face, I have no philosophy of history that can provide consolation. All that I try to say with my philosophy is that in opening oneself to the other one can penetrate the heaviness of being that is occupied with itself. That this opens the possibility of taking the other into account, of concerning oneself with the other, of having a little goodness for the other and being preoccupied with his or her death prior to one's own.

And I would also say, if you will allow me, that there is no consolation for the discouragement to which you refer. But I often think that in analyses the emphasis must be placed on disinterestedness in interhuman relations. On the disinterestedness of speech that one has with the other and that it is not impossible—but that is beyond philosophy—that those who don't count on any reward are worthy of a reward.

—Translated by Michael B. Smith

Abraham, the Other

Jacques Derrida

"I could think of another Abraham for myself."

. . .

This is a citation. "I could think of another Abraham for myself." One could translate it slightly differently. For the word *think*, one could substitute "imagine" or "conceive": "Ich könnte mir einen anderen Abraham denken"; "I could, for myself, aside within myself [*à part en moi*], as for myself, imagine, conceive the fiction of another Abraham."

The sentence comes to us from a brief parable, two short pages, by Kafka.[1] It bears as a title only a name: "Abraham," precisely. "Ich könnte mir einen anderen Abraham denken." And further: "Aber ein anderer Abraham"; "But yet another Abraham."

Perhaps, perhaps then, there would be more than one Abraham. And this is what would have to be *thought (denken)*. *Perhaps*.

A few weeks ago, in New York, the largest Jewish city in the world, sometimes said to be inhabited by more Jews than Israel itself, Avital Ronell, an American friend and colleague, herself of European and Israeli origins, drew my attention to this apologue or fable of Kafka, which I am about to interpret in my own fashion, still otherwise, and obliquely, elliptically. As brief as it may be, this fiction stages not only another Abraham (*einen anderen Abraham*) but more than one other Abraham, at least two others. It is as if the serial multiplicity of the "more than one [*plus d'un*]" inscribed itself upon the very name of Abraham.[2] The narrator first says: "I could think of another Abraham for myself," and goes on to evoke a first other, a first second Abraham, in order to say: "I do not see the leap" he would have had to make in order to show himself ready to obey God on Mount Moriah—the word *leap* here confirming what is otherwise well known, namely, that Kafka

311

had read Kierkegaard. The narrator then adds: "But there would be another Abraham [*aber ein anderer Abraham*]." This other other Abraham was ready to respond and answer the call, or to answer to the test of the election, but he was not sure of having been called, not sure that it was he himself and not another. He was not sure that it was he, in fact, who was the elected, and not another. He was afraid of being ridiculous, like someone who, hard of hearing, would come to answer "yes," "here I am," without having been called himself, without having been designated; or who would rush to answer the call addressed to another, like a bad student, for example, who from the back of the class, Kafka says, would think that he heard his own name, whereas the teacher had honored another, having meant to reward only the very best student of the class. True, the end of the parable leaves open another possibility: perhaps the teacher intended to stage a confusing test between the two names, or between the two chosen ones, in order to punish the bad student.

Let us leave here, as an exergue, these other Abrahams. Later on I will sketch one of the interpretations that tempt me most. Yet everything that I will risk here could be understood as an indirect response to Kafka's madness, and a post-script to another reading I have offered elsewhere, in *Donner la mort* (*Given Death*),[3] of Isaac's binding and, already, of more than one Abraham: multiple and sometimes fictitious Abrahams, from Kierkegaard to Levinas.

I must begin now to expose myself without sheltering myself behind these fictions.

Is this possible?

I do not believe, in any case, that it would be possible or justifiable for me, within me, and in the final analysis, to distinguish today between two stories. I say specifically "in the final analysis," two stories in the final analysis, there where the analytic account would be difficult, and perhaps interminable.

What stories? How to count them and give account of them, or better yet, how to be accountable for them? How, and by what right, can one distinguish, for example, between that which, in my experience, touches *in part* my "being jew [*être juif*]" at its most intimate, its most obscure, its most illegible (however one takes this "being-jew," and later I will in fact complicate the stakes of this expression—one cannot do everything at once) and *in part* that which, let us say, seems to belong in a more legible fashion to my work, the public work of a good or a bad student, which does not necessarily, nor always, bear visible traces of my "being-jew," whether it concerns itself with writing, teaching, ethics, law or politics, or civic behavior, or whether it concerns itself with philosophy or with literature.

And yet tonight I will act for awhile as if these two orders were distinct, to seek to determine later on, here or elsewhere, at least as a disputable hypothesis, the rule of what passes [*ce qui passe*] from one to the other, the rule of what occurs [*ce qui se passe*] between the two, and for which I would have, in sum, to respond.

Yes, it is a matter, once again, of responding. And *yes*, of responding "yes."

Without even naming Abraham, prior to daring to issue a summons toward the immense figure of the patriarch presumed to respond to the calling of his name, "yes, here I am," "I am here," "I am ready," one must know (and this is the first Abrahamic teaching, prior to any other) that if everything begins for us with the response, if everything begins with the "yes" implied in all responses ("yes, I respond," "yes, here I am," even if the response is "no"), then any response, even the most modest, the most mundane, of responses, remains an acquiescence given to some self-presentation. Even if, during the response, in the determined content of a reply, I were to say "no"; even if I were to declare "no, no, and no. I am not here, I will not come, I am leaving, I withdraw, I desert, I'm going to the desert, I am not one of your own nor am I facing you," or "no, I deny, abjure, refuse, disavow, and so on," well then, this "no" will have said "yes," "yes, I am here to speak to you, I am addressing you in order to answer 'no,' here I am to deny, disavow, or refuse."

One can draw quite a few consequences from this paradox and from this prevalence of an originary "yes"; from this precedence that makes the "yes" an undeniable vigilance [*veille*], the inheritance of a place [*lieu*] that cannot be uprooted; from this "yes" that comes up through every "no" on this earth and survives through all the negative modalities of disavowal (but what does it mean, to "disavow"? this will perhaps be my ultimate question), through all the negativities of questioning, doubt, skepticism, critique, and, sometimes, of a particular and hasty interpretation of deconstruction. One can draw consequences, and I have done so more than once, on many occasions and in many places. I will have to reaffirm this, no doubt, during the next few days.

It would thus be, once again, a matter of responding, of answering oneself, in one's name, or for one's name. Of answering-*to* [*de répondre*-à] (to whom? to someone, always, to a few, to everybody [*à tous et à toutes*], to you), of answering-*before,* therefore, and of answering-for (for one's acts and words, for oneself, for one's name; for example, for one's being-jew or not, etc.). In short, it would be a matter of taking responsibility, a responsibility that we know, in advance, exceeds all measure. How to respond? And first of all, how to respond to questions: for example, to these "questions" that have been announced, and addressed to me, on the issues that Joseph Cohen and Raphaël Zagury-Orly have so prudently, so daringly, called "judeities [*judéités*]," in the plural? Judeities that would remain, above all, in question.

Early on, and for a long time I have trembled, I still tremble, before the title of this conference (questions addressed to me! and concerning judeities!) and never has the privilege of a conference apparently addressed to me intimidated, worried, or flustered me this much, to the point of leaving me with the feeling that a grave misunderstanding threatened to make me forget how much I feel, and will always feel, out of place in speaking of it; out of place, misplaced, de-centered, very far from what could resemble the thing itself or the center of said questions, the multiple questions oriented toward plural judeities and whatever could be implied by this word, *judeities,* in the plural, to which I shall return. Is it really to me, at the back of the class, in the last row, that such questions must be addressed or destined? On the matter of judeity or judaism, the insufficiency, the inadequacy, the failure (all mine, and of which I have not finished speaking) are graver and, I fear, more significant than a simple incompetence, an incompetence and a lack of culture, to which, by the way, I at the same time also confess. But I will have to explain myself, and so I must at least respond, precisely, I must answer for all these faults and failures. I must do so, and I owe it to you [*je le dois, je vous le dois*]; I must answer for them to you, before you, all of you who are here, before those who remarkably honor me by partaking in this experience, assuming its meaning with courage and generosity, while alone I would never have even imagined its possibility. Respond I must, in truth, and I owe this first to my hosts in this place, particularly to Mr. Elalouf and Mr. Marciano;[4] and then to express my anxious gratitude to Joseph Cohen and Raphaël Zagury-Orly, who have done so much, who have succeeded in overcoming my doubts and my skepticism, in order to give to this encounter all its opportunities, that is to say, all its risks. I will no doubt speak of risks more than of opportunities, even if I do not believe it possible to separate the two, risk taken and opportunity given [*le risque couru et la chance donnée*], no more here than anywhere else. One can no more dissociate opportunity from risk in the case, for example, of peace negotiations—if, that is, one truly wants peace. For example, in Israel and Palestine.

Here, however, it is about more than one dissociation that I would like to begin by saying a few words. The dissociations I am thinking of are not necessarily threats to the social or communal bond, since a certain rupture, a certain departure, a certain separation, an interruption of the bond, a radical un-binding remains also, I believe, the condition of the social bond as such. I mean that of love. Of living love and of lifelong love of life [*de l'amour à vie de la vie*], the lively and exposed affirmation of life [*de l'affirmation à vif de la vie*]. So it is that evil, risk, as well as opportunity, have to do neither with dissociation nor with its opposite, but with the experience of a dissociation that is at once possible, necessary, *and* impossible. An alternative at once promised and denied.

A few figures of this alternative, of this necessary but impossible dissociation, already present themselves. Three, at least.

First, a dissociation between *persons,* the grammatical marks of the person, and what they indicate of what was still being called until fairly recently the subject—a word I would prefer to restrict to its purely grammatical meaning. I designate in this way the dissociation between the first, second, and third persons, singular and plural, male and female (I, you, he/she, we, you, they [*ils/elles*]): I am jewish, you are jewish, he/she is jewish [*juif(ve)*], you are jewish [*juif(ve)s*], we are Jewish, they are Jewish, and so on. How do these persons translate into each other and is it possible? Can one authorize oneself to move from "you are Jewish" [*tu es juif ou juive*] to a "therefore I am" [*donc je le suis*]?

Second, the dissociation, and therefore the alternative, between *authenticity* and *inauthenticity* (I do not say truth and un-truth): authentic Jew/inauthentic Jew. Can one trust in this distinction, of which, as I will recall, Sartre made a famous and troubled use right after the war?

Third, the dissociation between *judeity* [jewishness] (the word invoked, in the plural, in the title of this conference: *judeities*) and *judaism.* Can one trust in the alternative (e.g., jewishness/judaism),[5] of which I will recall the letters of nobility conferred on it by Yosef Yerushalmi in his book on Freud's Moses?[6]

But before defending with arguments my doubts regarding the trustworthiness [*fiabilité*] of these *three* distinctions (I/you, I/we, we/you, I-we/they [*ils-elles*], etc.; authentic/inauthentic; jewishness/judaism), allow me to whisper the following, with the tone of a more or less innocent confidence. I hardly dare here—I hardly dared even yesterday—to take the floor, as one says. And no doubt I will only do so to confide in you that which in me, for a long time now, feels—in a place such as this, in a place defined in this way, before a topic so formulated, before the "jewish" thing [*devant la chose "juive"*], at once, precisely, *entrusted,* and *condemned,* to silence [*confié—et* condamné *au mutisme*]. Yes, entrusted as much as condemned. Both entrusted to silence, in the sense that one says entrusted for safekeeping, entrusted to a silence that keeps and guards so long as one keeps and guards it. It is a bit as if a certain way of keeping quiet, of silencing oneself [*une certaine façon de taire ou de se taire*], as if a certain secret had always represented, regarding judaism, regarding jewishness, regarding the condition or the situation of being *jew,* regarding this appellation that I hardly dare, precisely, to call mine—it is as if such silence, a determined silence and not just any silence (for I have never, absolutely never, hidden my jewish descent, and I have always been honored to claim it), as if nonetheless such obstinate reserve had represented a kind of guard, a kind of care-taking, of safekeeping: a silence that one protects and that protects, a secret that perhaps keeps *from* judaism [*garde* du *judaïsme*], but keeps as well a certain jewishness in oneself—here in me.[7] One knows the profound link—it is not only an etymological one—that can be found between keeping guard and truth [*la garde et la vérité*]. As if—a paradox that I will not stop unfolding and that summarizes all the torment of my life—I had to keep myself from judaism [*me garder du judaïsme*] in order to retain within myself something that I provisionally call jewishness. The phrase, the contradictory injunction, that would thus have ordered my life seemed to say to me, in French: "garde-toi du judaïsme—ou même de la judéité." Keep yourself from it in order to keep some of it, keep yourself from it, guard yourself from being jewish in order to keep yourself jewish or to keep and guard the Jew in you. Guard yourself from and take care of the Jew in you [*prends garde au Juif en toi*]. Watch and watch out [*re-garde*], be vigilant, be watchful, and do not be Jewish at any price. Even if you are alone and the last to be jewish at this price, look twice before claiming a communal, even national or especially state-national, solidarity and before speaking, before taking sides and taking a stand *as a Jew*.

Is all of this authentic? I will return to the abyssal ground of this word *authentic*, which is anything but innocent.

To guard the silence that guards me, such would be the *order*—which I understand almost in the religious sense of a community, or rather a non-community, of a solitude of withdrawal from the world—the order to which I would have been entrusted forever, almost forever, a bit the way one entrusts or commits an orphan, a pupil of I don't know what nation anymore, even less what nation-state, a lost child—but who perhaps still gives way to the obscure weakness of feeling as if a bit chosen for this being in perdition [*cet être en perdition*]. Called, at the risk of a terrifying misunderstanding about the proper name.

This watch [*garde*] over the secret to which I seem to have been entrusted, or this watch over the confided secret, a secret so much larger and so much graver than I—it is as if I had received a mission to be faithful to it, so long as a proper word about it were not given or dictated [*donnée ou ordonnée*] to me, a speech that I would have to invent as much as discover, encounter within myself outside myself [*rencontrer en moi hors de moi*]—and defend at all cost. I do not believe, I am not sure, far from it, that the time has come. And I know that were it to come one day, the decision would not be mine, and the certainty would never be secure. A call worthy of that name, a call of the name worthy of the name, must give room to no certainty on the side of the addressee. Failing that, it is not a call.

I was speaking of silence and of mutism, the stubborn silence to which—entrusted to it as I was—I was, so I surmised, condemned. By whom, by what, where and how? Those are my questions. For if trust, if the confidence of having-been-entrusted, through a kind of secret election, though in its essence uncertain, always ready for an apocalyptic or a derisive misunderstanding, an election that above all would not be the election of a people—a counter-election, therefore, the counter-example of election—if, then, I have always, almost always, felt that what has destined, dedicated, and devoted me [*ce qui m'a voué, dévoué, adonné*] to the law of such a silence was the promised chance of a salvation without salvation that came from I don't know where, well then, it is nonetheless the case that I have felt simultaneously, in-dissociably, under house arrest, even denounced, condemned, damned by the same obscure consciousness of election, of fatal choice by which a power, transcendent and without face, was driving me to silence, striking me with muteness as one inflicts an infirmity, a wound or a plague, since birth or *almost* since birth. The silence of which I speak was, then, and still is, both chosen and not chosen, undecidably decided by me without me, by the other in me. At the endless risk of a tragic or laughable misunderstanding.

To be condemned or damned [*condamné ou damné*] is to have to serve a sentence, to repay a damage (*damnum*), a lesion, a fault, a wrong that was committed, or a wrong for which one is a priori indicted, accused ("charged," as one says in English). What fault, what damage, what lesion, what wound? This is perhaps the open question, the question that no more closes than does a scar, and that has always, almost always, haunted my mutism, cutting off my speech, pushing, pushing away, and holding fast to my words on the edge of all language. And here as well, on the edge of what I am tempted to say, I will let myself be guided by a question regarding that question: Why the big enigma, the quasi-universal and ontological thematic of an a priori guilt or responsibility, of an originary debt, a congenital wrong (which one finds everywhere, notably among so-called Christian, anti-Christian, or atheist thinkers, like Kierkegaard or Heidegger)? Why has the universal argument[8] of this singular indictment come for me always, *almost* always, obscurely, as if stuck to the question of my belonging without belonging to jewishness or to judaism? (Again, I leave for later my questions regarding this distinction.)

Tonight, I feel that I will have to avow or disavow this "je ne sais quoi" that has almost always devoted me, entrusted and condemned me, to a "keeping quiet [*se taire*]." I would, at least, have to pretend to break the silence, if only to state one more time—and I will never say it enough—my anxious gratitude to those who have taken the initiative of inventing such a dangerous encounter, one that for me remains still a bit unimaginable. I would be lying, of course, if I claimed that today is the first time that I speak in public of my being—or my *quasi*-being—jew, or of my unbelievable belonging to judaism. I have often ventured this, most of all in the past decade, in numerous places that I will not enumerate. And yet, every time I have done so, I have only *appeared* to do so [*j'ai seulement* paru le faire]. In truth, by the detour of more or less calculated ruses, of generally deliberate ellipses, which were intended to be learned [*et qui se voulaient savantes*], by way of a phenomenological play of suspension, quotation marks, and parentheses, I avoided doing fully what I was then doing: un-signing what I was signing [*de dé-signer ce que je signais*]. Is there a category for thinking and formalizing this gesture, which consists in avoiding without avoiding, in disavowing the very avowal? I do not know. Will it be called denial, inauthenticity (I will return to this word in a moment), a double game? My feeling is that none of these words is adequate to master the "jewish" example or case of which I speak. But that this problematic must be rethought starting from that case, or from the abyss into which it carries everything, including the value of exemplarity.

During the time that preceded this encounter, and even yesterday, I have asked myself whether I should speak of these questions in a scholarly, philosophical, exegetical, or "deconstructive" manner. Without renouncing doing so later on, for example, during the discussions, and since I have done so elsewhere, it seems preferable to expose myself more crudely, for example, by asking myself, by trying to remind myself, by recalling myself *tout court*, and for that by recalling *myself*, to myself, how the word *jew* (before "judaism" and, most of all, before "jewishness") arrived, how it reached me like an arrival [*comme un arrivant*] or a first arrival, in the language of my childhood, landing in the French language of the Algeria of my first sentences. I will not reach, tonight—the occasion does not lend itself to it—such anamnesis regarding the arrival of "jew" in my language, of this word that remains incredible [*inouï*] to me, deeper and more profound in me than my own name, more elementary and more indelible than any other in the world, than the "yes" from which I started and from which I have said that it is impossible to part or depart, from which everything, in truth, proceeds, closer to my body than an article of clothing, than my body itself.

But we know that with the interrogation of a word, of the history of a word, of our relation to a vocabulary, to the vocation or the convocation of a word [*vocable*], the temptation, the impossible desire, is to identify a *first time,* the occurrence without precedent of an appellation so new and then so unique that it resembles the appearance of a proper name. What was, for me, such an epiphany of the word *jew* in my Algerian childhood?

Answering this kind of question is easier, if not always possible, when dealing with actual proper names identified with persons. In that case, we are guided by a reference, we know *who* is called by the appellation, and misunderstandings concerning that person are improbable. We always believe we know when such and such a name or surname of a person appeared for the first time—most often along with its referent. It is much more difficult, for me truly impossible, when dealing with words—names or not—that are, as one says, *common*: adjectives or common nouns.

Now, there are two appellations about which I have never managed to know, to know anything at all, and most of all to know how they came to me or whether they constituted names, common nouns or proper names. These are, so far as I know, the only two words about which I have relentlessly sought to find out, in the darkness of my memory, where, when, and how their epiphany came to light for me, gave birth for me—as far as I am concerned.

These two appellations, these two words that are neither common nor proper, are not "Daddy" and "Mommy," but *God*—and *Jew*. In "Circumfession," I have alluded at least once to the anxious amnesia that surrounds the first epiphany of the word *Dieu* (in French, for it is in French, of a French word that I always speak). I will therefore not return to it directly, nor will I revisit what I have risked writing, in a less autobiographical mode, regarding the name *God* in numerous texts. But as for the word *jew,* I do not believe I heard it first in my family, nor ever as a neutral designation meant to classify, even less to identify a belonging to a social, ethnic, or religious community. I believe I heard it at school in El Biar, already charged with what, in Latin, one could call an insult [*injure*], *injuria,* in English, *injury,* both an insult, a wound, and an injustice, a denial of right rather than the right to belong to a legitimate group. Before understanding any of it, I received this word like a blow, a denunciation, a de-legitimation prior to any right, prior to any legality. A blow struck [*un coup porté*] against me, but a blow that I would henceforth have to carry and incorporate [*porter, comporter*] forever in the very essence of my most singularly signed and assigned behavior [*comportement*]. It is as if I had to countersign the blow thus struck prior even to any possible memory. This word, this performative address ("Jew," that is, almost inevitably, as if it were readily understood as "dirty Jew!"), this apostrophe was, remains, and carries, older than the claim [*constat*], more archaic than any constative, the figure of a wounding arrow, of a weapon or a projectile that has sunk into your body, once and for all and without the possibility of ever uprooting it. It adheres to your body and pulls it toward itself from within, as would a fishing hook or a harpoon lodged inside you, by way of the cutting and wet edge, the body of each of its letters, *j.e.w.* One can, afterward, assume this word, treat it in a thousand different ways, think it honorable to subscribe to it, to sign and countersign it. But, for me at least, it guards and keeps the mark of this assignation, of this unveiling that denounces, even of this originary accusation, this guilt or responsibility, *granted* dissymmetrically prior to any fault or act. And to speak honorably of this word, *jew*—and by honorably, I mean measuring oneself by way of what is worthy of that name or of that adjective in the audible and visible forms of its syllables, in the turbulent life of each of its letters, in the tumultuous movement of its oral pronunciation and of its graphic destiny—the *j* and the *oui* [yes] of *juif*, between the *suis* [am] of *je suis* [I am], *je suis juif* [I am jew], the *juste* [barely, only, just, *or:* righteous, just] of "je suis juste en tant que Juif [as a Jew, I am just *or:* I am only to the extent that I am Jew]," or "je suis juste un Juif [I am just a Jew, no more than a Jew]," or *juste un juste* [only a just person], "rien que juste un Juif juste [nothing but just a just Jew]," "oui, juste un Juif qui jouit à être juste et plus juste que la justice ou que le droit, oui, je suis juste un Juif par ouï-dire qui s'entend à être juste un Juif juste, plus juste que la justice, et qui doit exiger pour le Juif d'être plus juste que la justice, qu'on soit avec lui et qu'il soit pour les autres plus juste, oui que le droit et la justice, etc. [yes, just a Jew who enjoys being just and more just than justice or law, yes, I am barely a Jew by hear-say who has heard of, who understands himself as being, no more than a just Jew, more just than justice, and who must demand for the Jew that he be more just than justice; that one be with him and that he be for the others more just, yes, than law and justice, etc.]." One would have to appeal to a force of poetic invention *and* memory, to a power of invention *like* the boldness of anamnesis. One would need art, or the genius of an archaeologist of the phantasm, the courage of childhood, too, of which I do not feel capable tonight—and which, I fear, neither the setting, the time, nor the space are available to us in such a conference and according to the laws of its genre.

Two brief remarks here, where interminable speeches would be required.

1. *On the one hand,* every time I have had to address seriously, if in a different mode, within the history of philosophy and of onto-theology, for example, in Nietzsche, Heidegger, or Levinas, and in many others as well, this theme of an originary guilt or incrimination, a guilt or a responsibility (*Schuldigsein,* as the Germans can luckily say in one word),

the theme of a debt, an indebtedness, a being-indebted, all originary, prior to any contract, prior to contracting anything; well then, every time I have addressed this great philosophical problematic, I would see returning, from the bottomless ground of memory, this experience of dissymmetric assignation of being-jew, coupled immediately with what has become, for me, the immense and the most suspect, the most problematical, resource, one before which anyone, and therefore the Jew among others (I dare not say the Jew par excellence), must remain watchful, on guard, precisely: the cunning resource of *exemplarism*—of which I will no doubt speak again. Here, exemplarism would consist in acknowledging, or claiming to identify, in what one calls the Jew the exemplary figure of a universal structure of the living human, to wit, this being originarily indebted, responsible, guilty. As if election or counter-election consisted in having been chosen as guardian of a truth, a law, an essence, in truth here, of a universal responsibility. The more jewish the Jew [*plus le Juif est juif*], the more he would represent the universality of human responsibility for man, and the more he would have to respond to it, to answer for it. Such exemplarism is a formidable temptation—to which many have surrendered, even Celan. It operates in every modern nationalism, nationalism never having been the claim to particularity or to an irreducible difference but rather a vocation for universal exemplarity, and therefore for a responsibility without limits, for every one and in front of every one, living and dead, a responsibility that is historically incarnated in this difference (one could give a thousand examples; I will not do so, keeping this question, for now, together with that of a thought of election, that of a people or of an individual, there where it communicates with the immense, grave, painful, and terrible question of the state of Israel—yesterday, today, and tomorrow—a question that I intend neither to run from nor precipitously to broach here. I will return to this, then, and no doubt we will discuss it tomorrow night with Claude Lanzmann, and yet again on the following day).

Under the heading of exemplarity, and above all of what I have repeatedly called the counter-example, when I play without playing, in a notebook from 1976 quoted in "Circumfession," at calling myself "the last and the least of the Jews [*le dernier des Juifs*],"[9] I introduce myself both as the least Jewish, the most unworthy Jew, the last to deserve the title of authentic Jew, and at the same time, because of all this, by reason of a force of rupture that uproots and universalizes the place [*lieu*], the local, the familial, the communal, the national, and so on, he who plays at playing the role of the most Jewish of all, the last and therefore the only survivor fated to assume the legacy of generations, to save the response or responsibility before the assignation, or before the election, always at risk of taking himself for another, something that belongs to the essence of an experience of election; as if the least could do the most, but also as if (you will have noted, no doubt, that I often have recourse to the "as if," and I do so intentionally, without playing, without being facile, because I believe that a certain *perhaps* of the *as if*, the poetical or the literary, in sum, lies at the heart of what I want to entrust to you)—*as if* the one who disavowed the most, and who appeared to betray the dogmas of belonging, be it a belonging to the community, the religion, even to the people, the nation and the state, and so on—*as if* this individual alone represented the last demand, the hyperbolic request of the very thing he appears to betray by perjuring himself. Hence this law that comes upon me, a law that, appearing antinomian, dictated to me, in a precocious and obscure fashion, in a kind of light whose rays are unbending, the hyper-formalized formula of a destiny devoted to the secret—and that is why I play seriously, more and more, with the figure of the marrano: the less you show yourself as jewish, the more and better jew you will be. The more radically you break with a certain dogmatism of the place or of the bond [*du lieu ou du lien*] (communal, national, religious, of the state), the more you will be faithful to the hyperbolic, excessive [*démesurée*] demand, to the *hubris*, perhaps, of a universal and disproportionate responsibility toward the singularity of every other ("every other is wholly other [*tout autre est tout autre*]" is what I responded to Levinas one day, and I will perhaps say later what the hardly controllable stakes of this expression are, an expression that can barely be translated and is perhaps perverse). I speak to myself, then, I address to myself an apostrophe that seems to come to me from the site of a responsibility without limits, that is to say, hyper-ethical, hyper-political, hyper-philosophical, a responsibility the ferment of which—"you understood this immediately," I said to myself—burns at the most irredentist core of what calls itself "jew." Henceforth, one had to grant the terrifying consequence of this superlative antinomy: the least is the most, the least is the paradoxical condition of the most, a certain experience of perjury is the painful and originary enduring of faithfulness. (I have explained this better in *Adieu to Emmanuel Levinas* and elsewhere, as the theme of perjury is among those to which I have stayed the most faithful, and here I would have to speak—as I did one day, by thus entitling a common meditation with Arab and Muslim friends in Rabat—of a "fidélité à plus d'un [faithfulness to more than one, *or*: collective faithfulness]," faithfulness to more than one remaining this impossible and necessary chance that one would have to be "worthy of inheriting [*mériter d'hériter*].") This experience is even more cruel, for I asked myself, and I ask myself still, whether I should not free myself from an unpleasant narcissistic complacency and from this remainder of exemplarism, which would let me believe in some law of hyperbole, in this inversion of hyperbole that, in the end, for the last, makes "the least" into "the most," in this hubris of the law that would still be exemplarily Jewish and would pass through the body, even the circumcised body, of the Jewish man, through the memory of old Abraham, still another, when the covenant named him anew in order to make him the father of nations. From this narcissistic and exemplarist temptation, from this subtle, twisted and difficult [*retorse*], and ego-centered interpretation of election—which can lead, one knows that too, to state nationalism in its most violent forms, even militaristic and colonialist—one also had to free and emancipate oneself through deracination; one even had to oppose this temptation, precisely in the name of the same demand for a universal and hyperbolic justice, a justice that traverses but also exceeds law.

Tomorrow, in a more narrative mode, and no doubt the day after tomorrow, beyond narrative, I shall perhaps try to describe the paradoxical effects of such experiences from my Algerian childhood. I have already spoken of them elsewhere: the constant, general, and virulent anti-Semitism of colonial Algeria, its aggravation, its own overbidding during the war, which preceded and went beyond the politics of Vichy, the loss of French citizenship, the status of indigenous Jew, the exclusion of all Jewish children and teachers from educational institutions without a whisper of protest on the part of the other teachers—at least on the side of the French, since native Algerians sometimes showed more solidarity with the Jews in this ordeal, and so on. In spite of the painful gravity of it, all this was in no way comparable to the tragedy of European Jews or even French Jews, a monstrous tragedy of which we knew nothing and about which later, for this very reason, my compassion and my horrified indignation were and remain such as must move a universal conscience rather than that of a Jew affected in his own kin [*plutôt que celle d'un Juif touché dans les siens*]. Ultimately, the paradoxical effect I wanted to describe schematically is that my suffering as a persecuted young Jew (common enough, after all, and not comparable to those endured in Europe—something that adds to all the reserve and decency that prevent me from speaking of it), this suffering has no doubt killed in me an elementary confidence in any community, in any fusional gregariousness, whatever its nature, and beginning of course with any anti-Semitic herding that alleges ethnic, religious, or national roots and of which my trained vigilance knows how to recognize the signs and decipher the symptoms with a promptness that I would dare call terrifying (I sometimes wonder whether the deciphering of the anti-Semitic symptom, as well as of the entire system of connotations that indissociably accompanies it, was not the first corpus I learned to interpret, as if I only knew how to read—others would say, how to "deconstruct"—because of having first learned to read, to deconstruct even, anti-Semitism). But the same suffering, and the same compulsion to decipher the symptom have also, paradoxically and simultaneously, cautioned me against community and communitarianism in general, beginning with reactive solidarity, as fusional and sometimes not less gregarious than what constituted my Jewish environment. As early as the age of ten (the expulsion from school and the highpoint of official and authorized anti-Semitism in Algeria), an obscure feeling took shape in me, at first uncultivated, then more and more reasoned, of interrupted belonging, a relation vexed *from both sides*: from the side of the declared enemy, of course, the anti-Semite, but also from the side of "my own [*du côté des miens*]," if I may say so. I will speak later of what the consequences were for me and for a kind of political philosophy that began to develop wildly in me, and continues to do so, toward all community, toward all Jewish culture, be it Sephardi or above all Ashkenazi; toward the family, the people, and the communal sentiment, whether it be national or state-national. Of course, this anxious vigilance of a stranger within, this insomniac distrust, has not failed to come up in respect to the still exemplary phenomenon that is the state of Israel, and all the kinds of violence that have marked its young history, the very principle and the conditions of its founding as the politics that, in a more or less continuous fashion, have governed its destiny—and still do so. The childhood and adolescence I am evoking here have coincided in time with the beginnings and then the creation of this state, both so singular and so similar to all others, while the Zionist call was resonating loudly in Algeria after the war. Rightly or wrongly, I have never felt the obligation, the ability, or the wisdom to respond to this call, but I will try to say later, in as just, complex, and prudent, as well as honest, a way as possible, the reasons that I have given myself, that I still give myself in my concerned and noncomplacent judgments about the state of Israel. Yesterday, the day before yesterday, and today. Concerned judgments, certainly, numbed by anxiety and compassion, but judgments that refuse complacency and that address themselves *both* to the justice I believe is owed to Israel and its survival, as a matter of course, *and* to the justice that one expects from Israel, and that a Jew, more and better than any other, even before any other, would have the right to hope for from Israel. The day before yesterday and tomorrow.

All that I would like to emphasize for now is the retreat and retrenchment [*retranchement*] of which I speak, a retreat, a caesura that appeared to decide itself, to carve itself within the very wound, within the wound that will not heal [*la blessure non cicatrisable*], that anti-Semitism has left in me, and a retreat outside of all community, including the one that was called my own, a merciless withdrawal that I felt already, and that I still feel, *at once, at the same time*, as less jewish *and* more jewish than the Jew, as scarcely Jewish and as superlatively Jewish as possible, more than Jew [*plus que Juif*], exemplarily Jew, but also hyperbolically Jew, when I was honing its cultivation to the point of mistrusting even the *exemplarist* temptation—not to mention the even more difficult and problematical language of *election*. This overbidding of an excess that never stops, that pursues and persecutes itself, the most becoming incomparably the least, or the other, a superlative more than a comparative—I have found it everywhere; it has found me everywhere; and one could locate a thousand signs in writings and teachings, in arguments that I did not direct—neither in appearance, nor in reality—toward the theme of any jewish question. I will perhaps give some examples in the discussions that will follow.

2. *On the other hand*, something in me was already living the wound and the retreat of which I just spoke—the first event of which I located in the experience of anti-Semitic violence in the French Algeria of the 1940s—already living these as a trauma at once decisive, determining, inaugural, and already secondary, I mean to say already second, already consecutive and assigned by a law, that is to say, by an nonmemorable and immemorial repetition. I will say nothing of it here, mainly for lack of time, but were I to do so, I would speak of what this retreat would have to do—or not—with the memory without memory of circumcision. The texts I have published, since the 1960s, and not

only those that mention it explicitly, such as *Glas*, *The Post Card*, "Shibboleth," or "Circumfession," all consign an indefinitely insomniac vigil over the event called "circumcision," *my* circumcision, the one that took place only once but of which I have attempted to demonstrate that it inscribed repetition from its first act onward. (A friend asked me whether I thought, as I had told her earlier, that this conference risked being a second circumcision for me. I answered her as firmly as imprudently, "no"—a "no" that I leave to your interpretation. Does it mean that a circumcision worthy of that name must take place and cannot but take place once and only once? Or that I have decided to make sure that it does not happen again? Or that circumcision takes place more than once the moment it first takes place [*plus d'une fois dès la première fois*]?)

To remain with the skeletal logic of this destiny or this *destinerrance*, as I sometimes put it, I will only remark that the dissociation, the retreat, and the hyperbole of this overbidding (the more than = the less and other than), this axiomatics of "I am the last and the least of the Jews," far from reassuring me within distinctions and oppositions, has done nothing but render impossible and illegitimate all distinctions and oppositions. On the contrary, this experience has sharpened my reasoned mistrust of borders and oppositional distinctions (whether conceptual or not), and thus has pushed me to elaborate a deconstruction as well as an ethics of decision, an ethics of responsibility, exposed to the endurance of the undecidable, to the law of *my* decision as *decision of the other* in me, dedicated and devoted [*vouée, dévouée*] to aporia, to a not-being-able-to or not-being-obligated-to [*au ne-pas-pouvoir ou au ne-pas-devoir*] trust in an oppositional border between two, for example, between two concepts that are apparently dissociable. The first paradox or the principial aporia has to do with the fact that the experience of dissociation or of a disseminal heterogeneity is the very thing that forbids dissociation from anchoring itself or being lulled into an oppositional distinction, into a decidable border or a reassuring difference.

I come therefore, and finally, to the *three distinctions or alternatives* announced earlier (Jew/jew, authentic/inauthentic, jewishness/judaism), which you can already feel I hold to be untenable.

1. *First.* Before I even come close to the word *jewishness* [*judéité*], to the plural form, and to the differences that announce themselves in it, I will not have been the only one to recall that there is jew and Jew. "Jew"—is that an adjective? Is it a noun? Can one *convert*, that is to say, translate, without remainder, a sentence such as *je suis juif*, a proposition in which the adjective *juif* is an attribute thus *attributed* (but attributed by whom, in the first place? and who, here, says "I"?), can one innocently convert such a *je suis juif* into this wholly other sentence, "je suis un Juif," the attributed attribute becoming an assumed name, and demanding of French this time to be capitalized? I note in passing that these questions, in their grammatical form, are most troubling in French where the adjective and the name *juif* are homophones, if not homonyms. This is not true in English or in

German. We will have to return to this question of the "French Jew." Not to mention that the attribute thus attributed, *juif*, whether adjective or noun, can designate what one calls, in Cartesian and post-Cartesian philosophy, an essential or principal attribute on the one hand, and a secondary attribute or mode, on the other.

Before any other kind of conversion—of this type or any other—there is one, also grammatical in appearance, that I—and I have every reason to assume that any other Jew will have, like me—found *problematical,* even impossible. This is the conversion that would symmetrically turn the proposition *tu es J/juif, vous êtes J/juifs,* or *J/juive(s)* [you are (a) Jew, jewish] (noun or adjective, singular or plural, male or female) into the apparently reciprocal proposition: "donc je suis J/juif, donc nous sommes J/juifs—ou J/juive(s) [therefore I am (a) Jew or Jewish, therefore we are Jews or Jewish (male or female)]."

I have so far spoken only of the first and second persons, but the third persons have no doubt *already* insinuated themselves into the scene or into the waiting room. Let us enjoy this grace period, for who knows what will befall us next.

This reciprocating conversion of the *you* [*du* tu *ou du* vous] into an "I" or a "we" is problematical, even impossible. It is not sufficient that I be told or that I be assigned a "you are (a) jew," in order for me to subscribe and say "yes, then, since you say so, I am (a) jew, *ergo Judaeus sum*—or *judea sum,* and [I am indeed] the Jew or the Jewess that you say or believe that I am." Saying this is not necessarily, it is above all not, to follow, in spite of the temptation, Sartre's *Reflections on the Jewish Question* [translated as *Anti-Semite and Jew*], a book that mattered very much to me, in the 1950s, as we know it continued to matter for the young French Jews of the next generation. It is a book that is, as always, both so intelligent and so naïve, a well-intentioned and generous book, which one must read, even if this is done less now than before, which one must re-read in its "situation" at that time. It is also a book the logic of which—one that Sartre also called, precisely, the "situation"—turns rapidly around this proposition: "The Jew is a man whom other men consider a Jew: that is the simple truth from which we must start."[10] A truth that is a bit simple, indeed. As if it sufficed for the other to tell me "you are jew or a Jew" for me to be born to my alleged identity as a Jew, to what Sartre calls therefore my *situation* as Jew: "Thus the Jew is in the situation of a Jew because he lives in the midst of a society that takes him for a Jew [*pour Juif*]" (72/88). Or yet again:

> What is it, then, that serves to keep a semblance of unity in the jewish community? To reply to this question, we must come back to the idea of *situation.* It is neither their past, their religion, nor their soil that unites the sons of Israel. If they have a common bond, if all of them deserve the name of Jew [*tous les noms de Juif*], it is because they have in common the situation of a Jew, that is, they live in a community which takes them for Jews. (67/81)

And a bit further: "In this sense the democrat is right as against the anti-Semite for it is the anti-Semite who *makes* the Jew"(69/84). It is not that Sartre's axiom holds no truth at all regarding what is called the "situation" (and like others, at the first reading of this book, as a teenager, I believed that I recognized [*reconnaître*] here, gratefully [*avec reconnaissance*], precisely my experience of said situation, while asking myself already why—a question of good sense—it was these particular individuals and not others that society arbitrarily made into Jews), but before speaking a little more about what I find a bit simple, in fact, in an analysis so necessary after all, I will raise what concerns the third person. Sartre always speaks of the Jews in the third person, and he evokes, as we will hear, the emergence of the third person for the jewish child himself.

Yet what will have infinitely complicated the course of my reading of this very French book, from the beginning of the 1950s, is not only the recourse to a distinction then so confident, which came from Heidegger, between authenticity and inauthenticity (authentic jew and inauthentic jew). And I thus approach the second border I had mentioned, the alleged alternative between the authentic and the inauthentic.

2. *Second.* What worried and, in truth, discouraged my confident reading of these *Reflections on the Jewish Question* is first of all the fact that Sartre determines and confidently limits his discourse by asserting that he will restrict his analysis to the Jews of France, even to the French Jew. This limitation logically proceeds from the concept of "situation," which is the guiding thread and the organizing concept of this entire discourse. Sartre writes: "If I wish to know *who* the Jew is, I must first inquire into the situation surrounding him, since he is a being in a situation. I should say that I shall limit my description to the Jews in France for it is the problem of the French Jew that is *our* problem" (60/73).[11] (Some of the pages of this book are dated October 1944 [71/86], prior to the discovery of Auschwitz, and there would be much to say about Sartre's perception then of what had just occurred in Europe—but let us leave that aside). Here, then, one finds excluded from the analysis not only all non-French Jews—following, in sum, a methodological and situational border quite clearly decidable, but terribly and so artificially, conventionally restrictive, unjustifiable, in truth, in such a singular case—but also, and equally out of range [*hors champ*], if I may say so, are all these strange, nonforeign Jews [*tous ces étranges Juifs non-étrangers*] who, like me, if I dare say so, like the Jews of Algeria of my generation, were in a thousand ways, undecidably, neither French nor non-French. And this indecision of the border had to do not only with citizenship, or with the fact that "we" had lost and then found again, between 1940 and 1944, a young citizenship that was granted less than a century earlier by the Crémieux Decree of 1870. This turbulence regarding French citizenship was complicated, in an abyssal manner, for those who were called, during the war and for a large part of my adolescence, "indigenous Jews" of Algeria (I have made this somewhat clear in *The Monolingualism of the Other* and in "Circumfession"), regarding religion, language, culture, the very singular sequence of a colonial history whose kind, as I have tried to demonstrate, was unique in the world. I am one of those who feel both French, very French, French through and through (without being certain, I have

explained that elsewhere as well, that I could say, like Hannah Arendt about the German language, "French is my only fatherland," even though language, French, in the irredentism of its most untranslatable idiom, is at bottom the passional body of all my passions, even if this body often devotes itself to silence), French through and through, then, but at the same time one must accommodate this, one must address this dissociation, radically eradicated, cultivating the uprootedness, if I may say so, but without any desire to grow roots elsewhere, in some community or identifiable nation-state. I hope to say this better later, but it is certain that without this experience I would not have had the same access, nor perhaps any access at all, to the ethico-political motifs that have occupied me since long ago around what I have called a "new International," beyond even cosmopolitanism (that is to say, a citizenship of the world, against which I have nothing, of course, on the contrary, only that it still implies, as citizenship, the rootedness of the political and of democracy in a territory and state), or around what I have named the desert in the desert, *khōra*, messianicity without messianism, or the im-possible as the only possible event, for example, in the un-conditionality of the gift, of forgiveness, of testimony, of hospitality, and so on. All these motifs are, I hope, coherent, and in any case, they bear affinity with the experience that remains singularly mine, and with a destiny that was sealed from childhood of a little French Jew doubled with a little indigenous Jew of Algeria, an Algeria badly named or over-named [*mal-nommée ou sur-nommée*] French Algeria, being less and less so, and which this child barely knew, in sum, except in time of war, from one war to another, of one war, the other.

I was readying myself to clarify, then, how Sartre, himself speaking of Jews in the third person, was also describing the emergence of the third person in the little French Jew himself, at the origin of the consciousness of the French Jewish child. I will not yet hurry toward the great universal question of the third, which later became for me an essential site of reading, of interpretation and of debate with Levinas, the thought and memory of whom I do not want to delay saluting here, for a thousand all too obvious reasons. Without insisting upon what Sartre's thought may recall for me, as for many others, of my childhood, it is to argue another question, namely, that of the distinction between authentic Jew and inauthentic Jew, that I will cite a passage from *Reflections on the Jewish Question.* Sartre writes here, in italics, the expression "special name." The name *Jew* is a "special name." For my part, I will emphasize, without further commentary, *together* the third person *and* the trans-generational or genealogical logic *and* the "strange and uncanny [*louche et inquiétant*]"[12] or "murky [*troubles*]" words, which beckon toward what Freud or Heidegger regularly thematize under the name of *Unheimlichkeit* (the uncanny [*familière étrangeté*] of what is *at once* at home and not at home, intimate and strange, domestic and foreign, as if *unheimlich* meant, in sum, "jew"—both for the anti-Semites and for the philo-Semites, and, above all or finally, for the so-called Jews themselves: but what is a *so-called Jew* [*un* soi-distant Juif]? here, finally, is perhaps my only question). I will finally underscore what Sartre evokes lightly, as if in passing, as if it concerned a pedagogical figure, destined to help better understand, to wit, the allusion to the sexual violence of a primal scene, when the child, or rather, a boy, a "little Jew" rather than a little Jewess, sees his parents making love. It is from this precocious experience, which Sartre successively calls "truth," "discovery," and "revelation," that jewish children feel themselves—here again are Sartre's more or less calculated words—"separated," "cut off [*retranchés*]." Here, then, is a kind of primal scene during which the revelation of a truth cuts and cuts off [*tranche et retranche*], leaving nothing but traces of trouble in identity, the distinction between inside and outside, the at-home and the not-at-home: "someday they [Jewish children] must learn the *truth*: sometimes from the smiles of those who surround them, sometimes from rumor or insult" (75/91). (If I could allow myself to interrupt this citation for a brief remark, I would clarify that, in my case, which I believe to be very common to many jewish children, it was first of all "through insults," through wounding apostrophes that led me to understand that shame can precede the fault and remain foreign to any possible avowal or disavowal. The insult or injury, prior to qualified injustice but like an elementary injustice, the inflicted wound, "injury," was indissociable from the word *jew*, uttered in French or in Arabic, the same word, name or adjective, the same attribute then incomprehensible and keeping, perhaps forever, some kernel of unintelligible darkness [*quelque noyau de nuit inintelligible*], between "jew" and "just," anti-jew and injustice, the same word, *jew*, constituting, as I said, in the cutting and excising experience [*l'expérience tranchante et retranchante*] of the same cruelty, at once the weapon and the wound, the blade of the knife and the wound forever open.)

> The later the *discovery*, the more violent the shock. Suddenly they perceive that others know something about them that they don't know; that people apply to them this *strange and uncanny* term that is not used in their own family. They feel themselves separated, *cut off* from the society of the normal children who run and play tranquilly and securely around them—those lucky children who have no *special name.* And they return home, they look at their father, they think: "Is he a Jew too?" and their respect for him is poisoned.[13] How can they fail to keep the marks of this first *revelation* all their life? There have been hundreds of descriptions of the *disturbances* [troubles] which occur in a child when he suddenly *discovers* that his parents have sexual relations. But what must happen to the little Jew when he steals a glance at his parents and thinks: "They are Jews." (75–76/92; Sartre emphasizes only the phrase "special name.")

In what Sartre analyzes as a sociologist or a historian of a particular situation, that of the so-called or alleged, the said Jews, one could easily recognize—I will not do so here—the exemplary weave of a universal structure. I will also neglect, for lack of time, the lexicon of the cutting off [*retranchement*] ("They feel themselves separated, *cut off* from the society of the normal children") and the pedagogy of an Oedipal scenario—Oedipus being here the one who responds to the name of man, as always, but, Sartre would say, here he is a man, the condition of a man without human nature: "a child when he suddenly discovers that his parents have sexual relations." This remark will later be followed by a strange reference to Oedipus' daughter, Sophocles' Antigone, and to the advice given to her by Greek wisdom: "modesty," "silence," "patience" in misfortune, all virtues that, Sartre explains, could lead the inauthentic Jew toward anti-Semitism and masochism (109/132). I will only note the constitutive dissymmetry imposed by the law of what announces to the Jew his own identity or his rapport with himself. The "here I am," the "I am jewish," resonate first of all as the accusative of a heteronomous response to the order or the injunction of the other to whom the "I" of the "I am jewish" is first of all the hostage. "I" is not the first to know that "I am jewish." The path is clear now to go on and conclude that I am always the last [le dernier], the last to know. But you will no doubt have recognized in this heteronomous dissymmetry of the hostage that I am [de l'otage que je suis], the very traits, the *universal* features that Levinas gives to ethics in general, as metaphysics or first philosophy—and against ontology. There again is posed the great question of an *exemplarist* temptation, and we could be tempted to analyze here a configuration, which is quite French—and generational—a configuration of discourses that are, indeed, different, but all analogous in the attention they direct toward heteronomy and the subjection of the subject to the law of the other. Including Sartre's discourse (and *Reflections on the Jewish Question* is largely dependent on the universal phenomenological ontology, deployed in *Being and Nothingness*, of the gaze of the other upon me), those of Levinas and of Lacan, the genealogy of this configuration would produce a great rhizome rather than a tree. Alongside the jewish question, one would find Husserl, but also a Freud reinterpreted in light of a very mediated reading of Heidegger and Hegel, by way of a certain Kojève, but let us leave this aside. Were I faithful to the thread of affiliation and of heritage, as to the motif of genealogy, which has always worried rather than reassured me, especially when it takes a hurriedly Oedipal form, I would concede the following: for my part, I belong to the generation of the more or less heretical or bastard grandsons of these French fathers and foreign grandfathers, the first infidelity of the grandson consisting, in this familiar yet *unheimlich* landscape of the extended family, in addressing in a manner altogether different from the said fathers or grandfathers, the woman, the question of the woman, of the mother, of the daughter and the sister, and therefore of the brother—with, and above all without, Antigone.

I will dare to claim—and I would not be the first, even if I wish to do so differently tonight—that the alternative between authentic Jew and inauthentic Jew does not hold up under analysis for a second, even as it appears to play such an essential role in *Reflections on the Jewish Question,* providing the book with something like the vein of an argument or that of a taxonomy, omitting for the moment the considerable if now dimmed resonance of this book in the years that followed its publication. It would require no great

effort to demonstrate that Sartre himself cannot quite believe in it, this distinction between authentic and inauthentic. In good or bad faith, he finds himself compelled to
discredit that alternative with the same gesture that wagers everything on it. One could
sustain this with a luxury of arguments, for which I do not have sufficient time. I am
referring here to the difficulties Sartre encountered at the time of the book's publication.
He admitted one day that some of his jewish friends had asked him to cut the fifty pages
concerning the distinction between authentic and inauthentic Jews. This led him to publish separately and at different times "Portrait of the Anti-Semite" and "The Situation of
the Jews in France."[14]

Sartre himself could not take this alternative between authentic and inauthentic seriously, because it had to appeal to at least one principle of identity, if I may say so, to an
essential being-jew that would be identical to itself, something that seems incompatible
with the concepts of "condition" or of "situation." "Authentic" implies, in Greek as in
French, the assured power, the mastery of speaking and of being oneself, the sovereign
ipseity of one who is sure of oneself and of one's power to be oneself. Authenticity,
according to Sartre, would thus consist in *choosing oneself* [à se choisir, à se choisir soi-
même], freely, *as jew,* while the concept of situation or of condition excludes such autonomous choice that touches upon the being of the "I am."

> Jewish authenticity, Sartre writes, consists in choosing oneself *as jew* [emphasized by
> Sartre, the remark of a phenomenological ontologist that recalls the importance of
> the "as such," which will be emphasized, as well, later on], that is, in realizing one's
> Jewish condition. The authentic Jew abandons the myth of the universal man [a
> proposition that would understandably have shocked many]; he knows himself and
> wills himself [Sartre was just speaking of "choosing oneself," and this voluntarist,
> reflexive consciousness, this confidence in the freedom of a *cogito* and in the "self"
> of "choosing oneself," "knowing oneself," "wanting oneself" has, since then, done
> much, along with existential psychoanalysis and the notion of an originary project,
> to take me away from this sympathetic intelligence] into history as a historic and
> damned creature; he ceases to run away from himself and to be ashamed of his own
> kind. He understands that society is bad; for the naïve monism of the inauthentic
> Jew he substitutes a social pluralism. He knows that he is one who stands *apart,*
> untouchable, scorned, proscribed—and it is *as such* that he asserts his being [*et c'est
> comme tel qu'il se revendique*]. (136–37/166)

Sartre emphasizes again an *as such,* which beckons [*fait signe*], as always, toward the
self-identity of sense, of essence, of oneself, toward an ipseity in general. Toward its autonomy. Like the word *authentic* itself. Yet when he must define this self-identity, this self-
identity of the Jew, Sartre cannot avoid this apophatic form, this rhetoric, some have said,
of "negative theology." Erasing all possible predicates, he transforms the concept of Jew

into a nonconcept, without any attribute that a Jew could attribute to himself, that is to say, that he could assume or claim. This gesture, to make of the Jew a nonconcept, could be interesting, it could lead to a thinking beyond the concept if Sartre did not so much want to convince the Jews authentically to become what they are. Yet following his own reasoning, a Jew, in sum, and an authentic Jew, cannot even speak of himself as a Jew; he cannot define himself, present himself, say "here I am," without misunderstanding. This is because of the following—I quote this passage again:

> What is it, then, that serves to keep a *semblance* of unity [I emphasize *semblance* as I will emphasize, in a moment, the word *quasi*] in the Jewish community? To reply to this question, we must come back to the idea of *situation*. It is neither their past, their religion, nor their soil that unites the sons of Israel. If they have a common bond, if all of them deserve the name of Jew, it is because they have in common the situation of a Jew, that is, they live in a community which takes them for Jews. (67/81)

Since they are not jewish in the truth of their being but only taken as such in a "semblance of unity," one could only escape this absurd circle by determining why the community in the midst of which they live takes these particular individuals, rather than others, to be Jews. Sartre, however, does not offer any answer to this question; he even deprives himself of the principle that would enable such an answer, since all the reasons that would be available to non-Jews for calling anyone jew are unacceptable and justly discredited by Sartre.

A. Indeed, *at times* he makes a strange use of the words *jewish race*—words about which it is difficult to decide whether or not he assumes them for his own account (e.g., in the passage where, speaking in the name of the human and protesting against what would be an inhuman measure, Sartre ends up saying that man does not exist). He evokes a politics of forced assimilation and, while protesting, clarifies that:

> It would be necessary to supplement it with a policy of mixed marriages and a rigorous interdiction against Jewish religious practices—in particular, circumcision. I say quite simply: these measures would be inhumane. . . . No democracy can seek the integration of the Jews at such a cost. Moreover, such a procedure could be advocated only by inauthentic Jews who are prey to a crisis of anti-Semitism; it aims at nothing but [*rien moins que*; I suppose that Sartre wanted to say "nothing less than (*rien de moins que*)"] the liquidation of the Jewish race. It represents an extreme form of the tendency we have noticed in the democrat, a tendency purely and simply to eradicate [*supprimer*] the Jew for the benefit of *man*. But *man* does not exist. There are Jews, Protestants, Catholics; there are Frenchmen, Englishmen, Germans; there are whites, blacks, yellows. (144–45/174–75)

B. *At other times,* on the contrary, and in order to avoid both affirming and denying some essential and proper feature of jewishness or of judaism, Sartre makes a singular appeal to the value of an "as if" or a "quasi," against which I have nothing, and which I have myself cultivated, if differently and for other ends, but of which one can at least say that it ruins the credit that we are asked to grant to authenticity and to the concept of authenticity. How could Sartre himself believe in it, when he twice uses the small and terrible word *quasi*? "The Jewish community is neither national nor international, neither religious, nor ethnic, nor political: it is a *quasi-historical* community. What makes the Jew is his concrete situation; what unites him to other Jews is the identity of their situations. This quasi-historical body should not be considered a foreign element in society" (145/ 176).

Even if, in another logic, which was never Sartre's, one were to take seriously this "quasi" in order to draw numerous consequences (something I have attempted to do elsewhere from another point of view and regarding other examples, which I will not evoke here in order not to deviate from my purpose), well then, this Sartrian description of the Jew and of the jewish community, of its "semblance of unity" and of its "quasi" historicity, remains, I would say euphemistically, light [*légère*]. Even more so on the part of a philosopher who claims to concern himself with history, with situation and condition. The concept of history that orients this book is very vaguely Marxist and revolutionary. It leaves out [*hors jeu*] any other approach to historicity (internal and external) of, let us say in order to remain prudent, jewish memory and law. Sartre appears to have acknowledged, at the end of his life, the ignorance—not to say the *méconnaissance*—of tradition, of jewish traditions, to which his book testifies in the days immediately following the war.

In the same stroke, the Jew who is called upon to become authentic, authentically historical, has no choice but to resolve himself to a *quasi-authenticity*. Besides, the definition, this time, of the inauthentic Jew is enough to make all the Jews of the world—the authentic, the inauthentic, and a few others as well—scream, at the moment when Sartre, in the condescending tone of concession, declares himself ready to accept this inauthentic Jew "as such," in what he calls the "national society":

> We have described objectively, perhaps severely, the traits of the inauthentic Jew. There is not one of them that is opposed to his assimilation *as such* [again, emphasized by Sartre] in the national society. On the contrary [and here is the description of the inauthentic Jew], his rationalism, his critical spirit, his dream of a contractual society and of universal brotherhood, his humanism—all these qualities make him something like [*comme*] an indispensable leaven in that society. (146/176–77)

This figure [*silhouette*] of the inauthentic Jew (rationalism, critical spirit, humanism) in which so many non-Jews and Jews would like to recognize themselves, implies that authentic Jews are, for their part, strangers to rationalism, critical spirit, and humanism. It is understandable that many among them were indignant.

Let us not go further in the direction of edification. My intention here, you understand very well, is not to criticize Sartre. While paying him the homage he deserves, and associating myself with the testimonies of gratitude that many Jews have addressed to him, my concern would rather be to show the essential difficulty that can be found, when facing a certain logic, a powerful logic that is perhaps philosophy itself, in signing (and what one demands of a responsible signature is that it be original and authentic), in underwriting and in countersigning [*à soussigner et à contresigner*] an utterance of the type: "Me, I am jew" (authentic or inauthentic—or quasi-authentic), in knowing and meaning what one appears to be saying. Of this essential difficulty, I want less to indict Sartre's discourse (even if I indeed do find its logic and its rhetoric to be quite fragile) than to testify as well. To say "I am jew," as I do, while knowing and meaning what one says, is very difficult and vertiginous. One can only attempt to think it after having said it, and therefore, in a certain manner, without yet knowing what one does there, the *doing* [*le* faire] preceding the *knowing* [*le* savoir] and remaining, more than ever, heterogeneous to it. What *must not* be done [*ce qu'il* ne faut pas *faire*], and that is the core of my limited reproach to the Sartrian logic, is to pretend to know, to dissemble as if one believed one knew what one said, when one does not know. Here, too, I could deploy these words in another language, and I do so elsewhere, but there is not enough time. If, on the one hand, Sartre implicitly, practically, recognizes that this distinction (authentic/inauthentic) is from the first limited in its pertinence, even untenable, what he does not recognize, on the other hand, is from whence came and toward what the ruin of the distinction is going, wherever it is in use, and in the discourse of the age, first in the Heidegger of *Being and Time*, for whom the question of authenticity was no doubt more originary and more powerful than the question of truth. The ruin of this distinction comes from a bottomless ground [*un fond sans fond*]. And it has incalculable consequences. Some, and I am not one of them, would say that these are disastrous, devastating consequences: affecting the logic of all these discourses, of course; affecting their existential axiomatics, the ethics and the politics they at least seem to call for, but first, affecting the sense of "being-jew," the extent, the very pragmatics of any utterance of self-presentation of the type: "I affirm that I am jewish"; or "here I am, I am a Jew of such and such kind"; or "there is no possible misunderstanding, here is why I call myself, why I am called, me, jew."

What, then, would the undecidable oscillation be, the impossible "either/or" that matters here to me? What is the vacillation that turns the head and produces vertigo, a vertigo one can love or detest, a vertigo through which one can love or hate? It is that the being-jew, the "I am jew [or jewish]," of which one can never decide whether it is or is not authentic, one can either take as a case, an example among others of an originary contamination of the authentic by the inauthentic; or, inversely, one can consider that the experience one calls being-jew, whether it be the so-called or alleged Jew or the other, is exemplarily what deconstructs this distinction, squanders the credit granted to it and with it to so many others—in truth, to all conceptual oppositions. Being-jew would then

be something more, something other than the simple lever—strategic or methodological—of a general deconstruction; it would be its very experience, its chance, its threat, its
destiny, its seism. It would be its hyper-exemplary experience, ultimately, eschatologically,
or perversely exemplary, since it would implicate the credit or, if you prefer, the faith that
we would place in exemplarity itself. Hyper-exemplary, more than exemplary, other than
exemplary, it would threaten, by the same stroke, with all the philosophical and political
consequences you may imagine, its alleged exemplarity itself, its universal responsibility
incarnated in the singularity of one alone or of one people, and with this, everything that
may reassure itself in the sense of the word *jew* and in the eschatological or messian*ist* (I
do not say messian*ic*—we will no doubt come back to this distinction) promises of the
covenant, the election, and, consequently, of the people, the nation, not to speak of the
modern and philosophical figure of the nation-state, armed as it is with all its attributes
from international law, and even well-armed *tout court*. At this point, what I wanted to
confide to you, simply and in my name, if I can still say that, is that I insist on saying "I
am jew" or "I am a Jew," without ever feeling authorized to clarify whether an "inauthentic" Jew, or, above all, an "authentic" Jew—neither in Sartre's limited and very French
sense, nor in the sense that some Jews who are more assured of their belonging, of their
memory, their essence or their election might understand, expect, or demand of me.
Willing or pretending to be neither an inauthentic Jew, nor an authentic Jew, nor a quasi-
authentic Jew, nor an imaginary Jew (although I share much, not everything, of the experience analyzed by Alain Finkielkraut under this title),[15] referring myself to a history that
is not the "quasi-history" of which Sartre speaks, in the name of what and by what right
can I still call myself jew [or jewish]? And why do I hold onto it, even as I am not even
sure of the appellation to which I thus respond, not sure that it is addressed to me, not
sure of what I mean, of what I want to mean here [*de ce que je veux vouloir dire là*], be it
authentic, inauthentic, or quasi-authentic, beyond all identity, all unity, or all community? Well, I know that I do not know that, and I suspect all those who believe they know
of not knowing, even if, in truth, they do know more—I know—much more than I. All I
can say is that, at the limit of my public behavior as a citizen and beyond citizenship, at
the sharpest but also most exposed limit of my work of writing, of thought and of teaching
(of which, as a matter of rule, I have not spoken until now), I could demonstrate that the
logic of this question, of its implications or of its consequences, organizes almost everything. What occurs, what happens to me, what kind of event is it when, responding to
the appellation, I insist on presenting myself as a Jew, on saying and on declaring myself
[*à dire et à me dire*] "I am jew," neither authentic nor inauthentic nor quasi-authentic,
given that I do not know what I mean, that I could criticize, disavow, "deconstruct"
everything that I might mean, and that I suspect so many Jews more authorized than I
am of not knowing any better than I do? What occurs in this case between *doing* and
knowing, between *faith* and *knowledge* [*entre* faire *et* savoir, *entre* foi *et* savoir]? And what
sense can there be in saying, in affirming, in signing, and in maintaining a "here I am,"

me a Jew, beyond sense and meaning [*vouloir-dire*]? In saying "here I am," and insisting, given that I know that perhaps I have not been called, and that perhaps I will never know it is not me who has been called. Not yet. Perhaps in a future to come [*avenir*], but not yet. It belongs, perhaps, to the experience of appellation and of responsible response that any certainty regarding the destination, and therefore the election, remains suspended, threatened by doubt, precarious, exposed to the future of a decision of which I am not the masterful and solitary—authentic—subject [*le sujet maître et solitaire—authentique*]. Whoever is certain—as was not, precisely, the other, the second other Abraham of Kafka—whoever believes he detains the certainty of having been, he and he alone, he first, called as the best of the class, transforms and corrupts the terrible and indecisive experience of responsibility and of election into a dogmatic caricature, with the most fearsome consequences that can be imagined in this century, political consequences in particular.

If there is here an experience of undecidability between the authentic, the inauthentic, and the quasi-authentic, well then—once more and as I have tried elsewhere to formulate it in as formalized a manner as possible regarding decision and responsibility in general—this aporetic experience of undecidability or of the impossible, far from being a suspending and paralyzing neutrality, I hold to be the very condition, in truth, the milieu or the ether within which decision, and any responsibility worthy of the name (and perhaps worthy of the name and of the attribute *jew*) must breathe. At the most acute point, the very limit of this experience, all the problems that have tormented me always, almost always, return in order to insist. Not only is the symmetrical distinction between the "you are jew [or jewish]" and the "I am jew [or jewish]" no more given or certain than that between the authentic and the inauthentic; but I can also not credit the proposed alternative, the third, about which I will only say one word before concluding. It is the one supposed to separate, around an indivisible border, judaism and jewishness. Without being able to go deeper here, as one should no doubt, in a proliferation of proposed gaps between judaism, jewishness, judaicity (Albert Memmi), *Judentum*, *Yiddishkeit*, not to speak of Ashkenazi-ness or Sephardic-ness, I will limit myself, given the title of this conference (Judeities) to the one put to work by my friend Yosef Hayim Yerushalmi in his *Freud's Moses*, an admirable book that I have discussed, from another perspective, in *Archive Fever*. The distinction between judaism and jewishness would illustrate, for example, what Freud, speaking of his judaism *via negationis*, apparently said, either in private or in his preface to the Hebrew edition of *Totem and Taboo*. Acknowledging that he did not know the language of the Holy Scriptures, that he was a stranger to the religion of his fathers and to any national or nationalist ideal, Freud then added more or less the following: If one were to ask this Jew (that is, himself), "'since you have abandoned all these common characteristics of your compatriots, what is left to you that is Jewish?' he would answer: 'A very great deal, and probably its very essence.' He could not now express that essence in words; but some day, no doubt, it will become accessible to the scientific mind."[16] Yerushalmi, too, set his wager on a distinction between *judaism* (culture, religion, a historic, even national or "state national" community, etc.) and *jewishness*, a jewish essence independent of judaism, an essential identity of the being-jew that could interminably survive a judaism that would, for its part, remain finite and terminable (hence the subtitle of Yerushalmi's book: *Judaism Terminable and Interminable*). Yerushalmi thus attributes to minimal jewishness some features about which I have myself asked by what rights they would be reserved in this manner to the Jews (such as, for example, the cult of memory and the openness to hope and to the future [*à l'avenir*]).[17] I imagine the double objection one could address to him from both sides, in order to ruin the very principle of the distinction or at least to limit its relevance, even if one acknowledges it has some such relevance, by pure contextual convenience. Either these minimal features are universal and there is no reason to make them into what is proper to the Jew, save to speculate again on the worrying logic of exemplarity; or, as universal as they are, they will have been announced in a unique and precisely exemplary fashion, by election, in a historical revelation; they would then have to do with writing, with memory or with hope in what one calls judaism. In the logic of both objections, it is no longer possible to separate, in all rigor, these two poles, namely, jewishness and judaism. The memory or the hope that would constitute jewishness seems to be able to emancipate [*affranchir*] itself, indeed, from tradition, from the promise and the election proper to judaism. Yet, whether or not one would have to do so, it will always be possible to re-root the very idea and movement of this emancipation, the desire for this emancipation, in a given of judaism, in the memory of an event that, continuing, as it is, to be threatened by amnesia, would remain a history of the gift of the law and would represent the ultimate guardian of the reference to the jewish phenomenon, to the name or to the attribute "jew," which one continues to inherit in a jewishness that is allegedly without Judaism. This inheritance is uneffaceable, and it endorses even the experience of effacement, of emancipation, of disavowal.

But the oscillation and the undecidability continue, and I would dare say, *must* continue to mark the obscure and uncertain experience of heritage. In any case, I have been unable to put a stop to this experience in me, and it has conditioned the decisions and the responsibilities that have imprinted themselves upon my life. Moreover, it structures the most formalized, the most resistant, the most irreducible logic of all the discourses I believed I had to endorse (I will not impose this demonstration on you tonight), on the subject of writing and the trace, the relations between law, justice, and right, on the subject of what I have called messianicity without messianism, on the subject of the international beyond cosmopolitanism and beyond state or onto-theological sovereignty, on the subject of the democracy to come beyond state-national citizenship, on the subject of spectrality beyond the oppositions life/death or presence/absence, and, most of all, on the subject of *khōra*, as prehistorical place giving (without giving) occasion to any event of anthropo-theological revelation. In all these directions, one could at once and successively accredit two contradictory postulates: on the one hand, it is (from a historical, ethical, political perspective, etc.) the condition that one emancipate oneself from every dogma of revelation and of election; on the other hand, this emancipation can be interpreted as the very content of the revelation or of the election, their very idea. For example, nothing seems more foreign to the God of the Jews and to the history of the law than everything I interpret, even unto its political future to come, under the Greek name of *khōra*, the place, the ahuman and atheological location that opens the place well beyond any negative theology. And yet this manner of interpreting the place can still keep a deep affinity with a certain nomination of the God of the Jews. He is also The Place.

To say that all of this still awaits its interpretation, that this interpretation is not only a hermeneutic or an exegesis, even if such are also necessary, but rather a performative writing and reading, and above all a performative mastery, a hospitality to the event and to the coming occurrence [*arrivance*] of the coming one [*l'arrivant*] (a messianicity without messianism), namely, the to-come [*à-venir*]. The to-come, which is to say, the other, will decide what "jew," "judaism," or "jewishness" will have signified. And although this to-come is not the property of anyone (not the philosophers, the exegetes, the politicians, the military, etc.), it will necessarily depend, as to-come, on an experience of invention that is both prophetic and poetic. The poet-prophets do not always have a name in the Scriptures, and they are not always writers or authors known in the world of religion or in the republic of letters. They can be anyone—and anywhere. They might sometimes be invested, in some situations, with the mission of military generals. There are genius generals, poet-generals, if not prophets, provocative generals, who provoke peace and who sometimes pay for it with their lives. We know one such. On the opposite side of poet-general and just-generals, opposite peace-provoking generals, there are also generals who provoke war. They do, they make others do, or leave for others to do, the worst, without seeing, in their often-shared blindness, that a voluminous appetite for conquistadorlike offensives may dissimulate a death drive and lead, among other crimes, to suicide—theirs and that of their own.

This is why I will always be tempted to think that a Kafka, for example, conjures up more future to come than many others by striking the rock of his fictional writing, and by calling us to this truth (such at least is my interpretation): that anyone responding to the call must continue to doubt, to ask himself whether he has heard right, whether there is no original misunderstanding; whether it was in fact his name that was heard, whether he is the only or the first addressee of the call; whether he is not in the process of substituting himself violently for another; whether the law of substitution, which is also the law of responsibility, does not call for an infinite increase of vigilance and concern. It is possible that I have not been called, me, and it is not even excluded that no one, no One, nobody, ever called any One, any unique one, anybody. The possibility of an originary misunderstanding in destination is not an evil, it is the structure, perhaps the very vocation of any call worthy of that name, of all nomination, of all response and responsibility.

There would be *perhaps* yet another Abraham, not only he who received another name in his old age and, at ninety-nine, at the time of his circumcision, felt, by the blow of a letter, the letter *H* right in the middle of his name; not only he who, later, on Mount Moriah, was called twice by the angel, first "Abraham, Abraham," then, a second time still, from the height of the heavens, as Scripture tells us. There would be perhaps not only Abram, then Abraham, Abraham, twice.

That there should be yet another Abraham: here, then, is the most threatened jewish thought [*la pensée juive la plus menacée*], but also the most vertiginously, the most intimately jewish one that I know to this day.

For you have understood me well: when I say "the most jewish [*la plus juive*]," I also mean "more than jewish [*plus que juive*]." Others would perhaps say: "otherwise jewish [*autrement juive*]," even "other than jewish [*autre que juive*]."

—Translated by Gil Anidjar

From French Algeria to Jerusalem

An Itinerary

Henri Atlan

I grew up in Algeria before and during the Second World War, at a time when Algeria was part of France. Approximately one million French people had been living there for several generations, next to eight to nine million Arab and Berber people, who were treated as second-class citizens. The fifty to one hundred thousand indigenous Jews were granted French citizenship collectively by a special law at the end of the nineteenth century. Thanks to this law, my father and mother were already born French. This was highly appreciated not only because of the rights granted by French citizenship but also because French culture was synonymous with progress, Enlightenment, civilization. My parents spoke Arabic together only when they did not want us to understand what they were saying. Otherwise, French was our mother tongue. In my parents' eyes, French school and studies at the lycée, then at the university, were the biggest asset for us, their children. As in many Jewish families in Algeria—not all, though—Judaism was considered to belong to some kind of primitive past. In other words, I grew up in an assimilated family, ignoring everything about Judaism except for a vague fasting on the day of Kippur and a strange ceremony once a year: ten poor Jews were paid by my father to gather at home and say some prayers in memory of his own father. Otherwise, I never heard at home about the Shabbat or the Seder of Pessah, or things like that. We very much appreciated French food and exotic seafood, and my mother did not have any problem about cooking horse meat for us, especially during the war, when food supplies became scarce. She never stopped cooking traditional Algerian food, however, which she had learned to prepare in her family during her youth.

In other words, I was blessed with a happy childhood in a lower-middle-class French family, where success at school was the highest value, all the more so since my father himself grew up in a very poor family and could not afford to study. Since I managed to learn reading and writing with no particular problems, I was programmed to become a good French boy, a normal student and possibly a physician. The French army medical corps offered stipends that would cover the expense of medical studies, and this was presented to me as a very desirable opportunity when I was a child.

All this did not materialize exactly as planned, however, because of the war and my sudden encounter—at the age of ten—with the fact that I was a Jewish boy. This resulted from the implementation of anti-Semitic laws after France's surrender to Germany and the establishment of a French collaborationist government in Vichy. Of course, this was nothing compared to what happened to the Jews in European countries under the Nazi occupation. Until 1942, the Germans occupied only the northern half of France. They never occupied Algeria, since Allied forces, American and British, prevented them from doing so by invading North Africa.

Nevertheless, before this liberation took place and a free French government was installed in Algiers with De Gaulle, for two years the Jews in Algeria were denied their French citizenship. My parents lost their jobs as government employees, and my father, who had been granted this job as a handicapped veteran of the First World War, had no other choice, to feed his family, than to work as a shoemaker, an occupation for which he had been trained as a child. Last but not least, I was expelled from school, since Jewish children were not allowed to go to school anymore.

Again, this was nothing compared with the horrors of the German occupation, which we discovered after the war. But it was enough, at least for me, to realize that there was a "Jewish problem." At least in the beginning, I was a perfect illustration of Jean-Paul Sartre's thesis that "the anti-Semite is the one who produces the Jew." I was not the only one, and during these years Jewish communities organized themselves in Algeria, especially to confront the problems created for the children, who could not go to public schools. Jewish schools were created in major cities such as Algiers and Oran. In small towns like Blida, where I lived, classes were organized in the houses of improvised teachers. It is worth remembering, in this context, that Albert Camus, who was also born and lived in Algeria, volunteered to teach literature and philosophy at the Jewish school in Oran as a sign of solidarity and opposition to the antisemitic laws. After 1942, these laws were abolished by De Gaulle's government. I went back to school in Oran. After the war, in 1948, I completed my studies in the public high school, the lycée, and I was ready to go to University.

In the meantime, however, I had become more and more active in a Jewish youth movement, the Jewish French Boy Scouts, which was created before the war but expanded in southern France and Algeria during the war. For us, it was a way to get together in response to our new situation in society. In occupied France, very soon this movement became involved in the resistance. At the beginning, it was a passive resistance by way of hiding children in the country with forged identities in order to spare them deportation. At the end of the war, this became active resistance, with participation in armed struggle. Many leaders in this movement were also previously assimilated young Jews who had discovered the "Jewish problem" during the war without having any previous background in Judaism or Jewish history. Several of them were caught and killed, either in combat or by deportation.

The founder of the movement, Robert Gamzon, was the commander of a battalion set up by leaders of the Jewish Boy Scouts that participated in the liberation of France. At the end of the war, he was severely injured. When he recovered, he decided to dedicate his time, for himself and for other survivors, to trying to understand what had happened, and how and why they had been led to do what they did. An engineer by training, he had in mind the model of the École Polytechnique in Paris, which traditionally, since the time of Napoleon, had trained the best scientists, civil servants, and entrepreneurs in France. On this model, he created a school in Orsay, in the outskirts of Paris, where young Jews could be trained in order to be, in principle, future leaders of the community. The idea was that twenty boys and girls, after high school and before or during university, would live together—a small château with a beautiful park was rented for this purpose—and spend a year studying Hebrew, Jewish history, and elements of Talmud, and experiencing the practice of a Jewish life by observing Shabbat and festivals, all in the context of inner seeking and the development of their personalities, by being exposed to various social experiences, political thought, and, of course, participating in the intense cultural life that developed in Paris after the war.

It so happened that I was recruited by Robert Gamzon to participate in this experience during the third year of this school's existence. It was a very special school, which looked like some hippie communes that I encountered twenty years later in California, though with major differences: no drugs and sex voluntarily restricted to flirting, which ended, *sometimes*, in Jewish weddings, with *huppa* and *kiddouchim*. (Some hippies also ended up that way.) In any case, during this year a group of youngsters was offered the opportunity to search for a meaning to their lives after their various war experiences, given that it was clear to them that things could not go on as if after a parenthesis, as if nothing had happened. That is why it was not a yeshiva for *hozerim bitchuva*, as we know them today, where it is accepted from the beginning that one must study Judaism as a religion or as a law after having decided once and for all to be a believer and to accept the authority of the rabbi. We wanted to understand by ourselves that there was something interesting there, maybe worth being studied more deeply, or better, created anew, if necessary—but certainly not something to accept more or less blindly because it was part of our inheritance and tradition. That is why, during the first years this school existed, we, the students, were the ones to decide who should teach us and what and how we should be taught. We were lucky to meet—and attract, I must say—some unconventional teachers, who helped us, little by little, to create a new approach to Jewish studies, somehow between, on the one hand, learning a religion based on belief in articles of faith with plain obedience to the law as the word of God, and, on the other hand, academic studies of the classical science of Judaism, concentrated on pure erudition, as if the object of study were foreign to us, external to our life.

This led us to create what I may call a school of Jewish thought, which Emmanuel Levinas called L'École de Paris, the Paris School. Among other things, we discovered or rediscovered for ourselves authors and texts usually not studied except by specialists, like the Midrash, the Maharal of Prague, the Ramhal Moshe Hayim Luzzato, the *Chnei Luhot Haberit*, by Ishaiah Horowitz, the kabbalist writings of Vilna Gaon's school, the elder Rav Kook, and others. Some of us became particularly interested in Kabbalah, not because of its supposedly mystic nature but on the contrary because we found in these texts that only kabbalist writings really deal with the question of *taamei mitzvot*, the meanings of the commandments. I was introduced to these texts by the late Leon Ashkenazi and Rav Zalman Schneerson, a Habad master in Paris who dissented from the organization when his cousin became the late Rebbe, and later on by the young Rav Mordehai Attia in Jerusalem.

I realized that, if we study these texts not as mere expressions of more or less dogmatic religious beliefs based on articles of faith, then we can find in them a kind of formal rationality associated with their mythical contents. Thus, in the end, these teachings appeared to us, in the light of our twentieth-century critical experience of reason, more rational than most texts of Jewish philosophy and theology, including Maimonidian ones, classically supposed to express the rational path in Judaism, as opposed to so-called Jewish mysticism. One must be careful with these commonly accepted labels, which sometimes are really misleading. Rather than an opposition between rational and irrational trends in Judaism, we are dealing here with an opposition between Jewish Aristotelian theology and other philosophical schools more related to the Stoics and Neoplatonists. (Regarding the Talmud, being a compendium of juridical discussions on how to implement the law, intertwined with legends, it is a kind of rabbinical canonical text, which, like the biblical text, is given to be interpreted in one way or another.)

In parallel, during this period I completed medical and biological studies in Paris and started an academic career of teaching and research in biophysics and cell biology. I spent two years on a U.S. Academy of Sciences Fellowship, working at the NASA Ames Research Center in Moffett Field, California, near San Francisco. I was involved in a research program on the effects of cosmic radiation on living organisms, and I had to take samples of bacteria and fruit flies (*drosophila*) to Berkeley in order to expose them to high-energy radiation produced by the big accelerators at the Lawrence Radiation Laboratory. In the process of this work, I became interested in the mechanisms of aging, and this is how I started my first theoretical works on the logics of biological organization and self-organization. Aging appeared to be related to irreversible *diffuse* errors in the cellular metabolism, due to the accumulation of waste products accompanying oxydation processes, which are themselves part of normal metabolism. In other words, aging is a process of diffuse disorganization produced by the normal functioning of cellular organization. However, in order to describe these processes more precisely, one needed better to understand the nature of biological organization. And in the sixties and seventies biology was dominated by the major discoveries of molecular biology.

The structure of DNA and the role it plays in reproduction were uncovered: how genes are in fact DNA molecules, how they duplicate, and how the information they bear is transmitted to new generations, both within the cells and within the organism itself. At that time, there were two directions in biology. One was the easy and triumphant way, which made use of very loose but powerful metaphors taken from information theory and cybernetics. Since DNA and proteins are information-carrying molecules, the functioning of a living cell or an organism can be compared to an information-processing machine, that is, to a computer. Then, if we push the metaphor further, DNA could be compared to the program of the computer. This is the "genetic program."

We who followed the second path were in the minority. At the time, we knew that the programming analogy was only a metaphor, and a very loose one at that. As a matter of fact, at the beginning this notion of a genetic program written in the linear sequences of the four motives of DNA strings was presented between quotation marks. It was a convenient metaphor for talking about the main findings of molecular biology. But very soon, the quotation marks were dropped, and the metaphor was taken literally as the answer to all questions in biology, as if every property of a cell or an organism could be reduced to the execution of a program instruction written in some gene. Now, when we look at DNA, we don't find any sign of a computer language. It is true that the genetic code was discovered as a *projection* of DNA linear structures onto protein linear structures. Coding must not be confused with programming, however. Therefore we thought that we should not be satisfied with this kind of metaphoric description, and we looked for other alternatives. These turned out to be mechanisms of self-organization.

We could already begin to see self-organization in some models in physics and chemistry. When you have a situation where you put together some chemicals, they react with one another, and, as a result of the reaction, you end up with some structure—such as waves or other spatiotemporal macroscopic structures—then one can understand how self-organization happens. It's not something mysterious, because you understand all the chemicals and all the chemical reactions. Based on that, we tried to design some theories and models about how to conceive the possibility that matter could organize itself without any mysterious mechanism.

My contribution to this work was to show that a necessary condition for self-organization, not sufficient but necessary, was that there should be a way to integrate into the system some degree of randomness. And because I used the formalism of information theory—in information theory, randomness is a source of errors in transmission and this is what is called "noise"—I called this theory of self-organization "complexity from noise."

I must say that this idea was not very attractive to most biologists at the time. Things have changed, however, and now, because of the near completion of the Human Genome Project and other new discoveries in biology over the last few years, these ideas have become very fashionable. But in the eighties, it was supposed that knowing the sequence of almost three billion bases, the four motives that make up human DNA when repeated in a given order, would provide us with something like a program for manufacturing a functional human being. It was supposed to be the "book of man," and deciphering it would uncover the whole of human nature. When the Human Genome Project was launched and needed funding, such statements were written in prestigious scientific journals like *Science* and *Nature*. In a letter from the editor, the chief editor of *Science* stated plainly that deciphering the human genome would not only allow us to cure all diseases—as if all diseases were genetically determined—but also to cure social diseases like crime, violence, and even poverty.

Today, genomes of several animal and vegetal species have been sequenced, and the sequencing of a human one is almost finished. The main result is that we know better what we do not know, as is usual in science. Knowing the structure and location of a gene does not tell us what this gene is doing and how, through which mechanisms. Contrary to what has been written and taught ad nauseum, a gene is not an instruction in a program. As a matter of fact, even the definition of what is a gene has become problematic from the functional point of view. The structure of a piece of DNA participates in the coding of several different proteins, with different functions. And, vice versa, the structure of a given protein is coded by different pieces of DNA, sometimes far apart from one another in the genome and separated by other DNA noncoding sequences. Therefore, one gene—if we define it, for example, as a coding piece of DNA—does not determine the linear structure of one single protein, and it is involved in the synthesis of several different proteins with different functions. In addition, the same protein may have different functions in different cells, sometimes even in the same cell, depending on the other molecules in its surroundings. Moreover, the flow of information that determines the function of a cell or an organism is not unidirectional, from DNA to proteins and functions. Several loops of complex interactions between proteins, RNA, and DNA, on the one hand, and between proteins themselves, on the other hand, regulate different states of the activity of cells and organisms. In summary, when we want to know what a DNA sequence is doing and how, we are faced with networks of interactions among many molecular species (with a formidable complexity), where the structure of the DNA is only part of the story. The functioning of even a single cell, normal or pathological, and the development of an organism depend on many other mechanisms not limited to gene structures and activities, which were known under the name of *epigenesis* for a long time, but were neglected for almost thirty years, when everything was supposed to be produced by a computerlike program written in DNA.

Going back to my first work on biological self-organization, among the few people who were interested in these topics at that time was my former friend and mentor Aharon Katzir, from the Weizmann Institute in Israel, whom I met in Berkeley. He was interested in what I was doing, and he invited me to work with him at the Weizmann Institute. This is what I did for three years. From then on, after his tragic death in the mass killing at Lod Airport in 1972 by Japanese terrorists, I went back to Paris. I started to commute regularly and to share my time between teaching and theoretical research in Paris and running a new Department of Medical Biophysics and Nuclear Medicine, which I was invited to set up and develop in Jerusalem, at the Ein Karem Hadassah Hebrew University Hospital. This is what I have been doing up to now. I have continued to study functional self-organizing properties of biological networks, such as neural networks, in order to understand the emergence of cognitive brain functions. And, for the last fifteen years or so, I have been interested in the applications of these concepts to the study of immunology, because, like the brain, the immune system is made up of complex networks of interacting cells and molecules. As such, it exhibits emergent properties of memory, learning, and adaptation, in self-organizing mechanisms that appear to be relevant to the onset, prevention, and treatment of immune disorders, such as autoimmune diseases. In collaboration with Prof. Irun Cohen, a leading immunologist at the Weizmann Institute, I have been involved, for the last ten years, first in the theoretical work of modeling, then in practical and experimental activity at the Hadassah Hospital, directed toward the study of new cellular therapies for autoimmune diseases and for an autoimmune component of AIDS based on these concepts.

In the seventies and eighties most biologists were not attracted by these theories of self-organization. In other fields, however, such as sociology, economics, physics, computer science, psychology, and artificial intelligence, more and more people became interested in exploring the properties of different models and mechanisms of self-organization. One of the main questions was to what extent those kinds of models, which were inspired by the observation of biological phenomena, were relevant to human organization, that of the psyche and of societies.

Of course, because of my own work, I was involved in this discussion and contributed to it articles and a book, which was a collection of essays. Since I referred from time to time in these writings to Jewish sources, the question was raised about any possible relation between my scientific work and Jewish studies. I had to rule out this possibility because in my work there were no such relations, at least not consciously. Nevertheless, I had experienced that both could be achieved rationally. It was not the case that only science was a matter of rational thinking and Jewish studies a matter of religious belief, based on faith and more or less irrational thinking. Rational critical thinking was used for both activities. Contrary to what the proponents of some New Age ideology had started to say, however, the rationality that is at work in science and in Jewish traditional culture, as well as in Eastern philosophies and mystical traditions, is not the same. It is as if the same person could be playing different games, say, basketball, tennis, and football. Obviously, the rules of the game must be kept different for each. Trying to unify them into the same set of rules would spoil all the games. Similarly, there are different kinds of rationality, making use of reason in different ways, as different tools adapted to different ends. Given that the same person can play different games with different rules at different times, however, the same person can experience these different kinds of rationality at work in scientific reasoning, on the one hand, and in traditional thought of a mythical nature, including that of Midrash and Kabbalah, and of course that of Mishna and Guemara, which constitute the Talmud, on the other.

Undergoing this kind of experience, I realized that some relationship is possible between the two, with no confusion, providing that it is based on analysis of differences between the rules of the games rather than on analogies between them. This kind of relationship is what I have called an intercritique of science and myth, that is, a reciprocal critique whereby scientific reasoning is used as a basis for the critique of mythologies, and, vice versa, the study of myth is used as a basis for the critique of science when science itself tends to become a new mythology.

This dialogue is more important today than before, because of the new ethical problems created by science and technology. The extraordinary development of biological and medical techniques has raised difficult questions about the ethical value of their applications. Biomedical ethics has become a major concern. In 1983, for the first time, a National Advisory Committee for Ethics of Health and Life Sciences was created in France by President Mitterrand, and I was appointed as a member. Bioethics can be defined as follows: it is a set of problems created by biological science and technology that science and technology alone are unable to solve. To give a very simple but striking example: being a mother has always implied two different biological functions, ovarian and uterine. These two functions have previously always been performed by the same woman, the mother being at the same time the provider of the ovocyte and of the uterus for pregnancy. Technology has now made it possible to dissociate these two functions. For the first time in the history of mankind, an embryo can develop in the uterus of a woman different from the one in whom the egg originated. The woman who is pregnant and gives birth can be different from the one who gives the ovocyte with its genetic material. The obvious question is: Who is the mother? This question did not exist before the progress of biotechnology made it possible to separate the two maternal functions. Yet science and technology, which have created the problem, are unable to solve it. Biology alone does not give an answer because both women are biological mothers.

Most of the bioethical problems you hear about in the media—organ transplants, treatment of terminally ill patients, gene therapy, and so on—are of this kind: ethical problems created by biology that biology alone cannot solve. If solutions to these problems created by science and technology cannot come from science and technology alone, where are we going to look for solutions? This is a new way of asking the question of the sources of ethics. Where does ethics come from, if not from the natural sciences?

In answering this question, two sources of ethical judgments are obvious: religion and philosophy, as has always been the case. Yet religion and philosophy, although helpful and even sometimes necessary, are not sufficient to provide universally acceptable solutions to these problems, which are really new, unheard of, because of the extraordinary nature of the techniques that create them.

Many people confronted with difficult problems of biomedical ethics turn to religious teaching for guidelines, even if they do not believe in the articles of faith of this or that religion, and even if traditional views of the world seem obsolete and contradicted by scientific teachings. Restrictive rules enunciated by a church sometimes play the role of *barriers*, even for nonbelievers, to prevent the extreme scientistic attitude that justifies everything in the name of technical progress. As the sole source of ethics for us today, however, religion suffers from several pitfalls. Although it provides believers with meanings and values for our experiences of life and death, it suffers first from a lack of accessibility: the foundations of its teachings, dogmas, and articles of faith are accessible only to a restricted community of believers. Second, in addition to this lack of accessibility, general ideas or articles of faith, such as the image of God, or God's will, or the transcendent and revealed origin of the Law, or even the sacred character of life, serve to justify contradictory attitudes when it comes down to practical applications. God's will, for example, can be used to justify both the desire for procreation at any price and a general prohibition on medically assisted techniques of procreation.

Sometimes religious teachings seem to be consistent with a kind of natural theology, prescribing natural courses of behavior and noninterference with nature—or not playing God, as it is said. This principle does not hold up very long, however, when confronted with practical questions, since plain nature, without intervention, can be responsible for terrible diseases and catastrophes, and plain medicine, even in earlier times, has always been a fight against natural diseases by means of human intervention.

When we turn to philosophy in search of solutions to ethical problems, there is a lot to be learned from the great philosophers of the past and from confrontation with their systems, less at the level of their general principles, as we shall see in a moment, than at the level of their methods, in their use of reason to shuttle between knowledge of nature and subjective experiences of human passion, imagination, and dream associated with reason and language. There is no doubt in my mind, for example, that ancient Stoic philosophy and the *Ethics* of Spinoza, which seek freedom and happiness in a world of absolute determinism, are well adapted to our present-day physico-chemical mechanistic representations of living organisms, including ourselves. Specifically, it would be possible to show that such philosophies are better adapted to the scientific representations of our times than modern Idealist philosophies, Kantian and post-Kantian, based on the idea of a human freedom outside or parallel to the realm of natural laws, as if man were in nature like "an empire within an empire," according to the ironic wording of Spinoza.

Like the great principles derived from theology, however, the great moral philosophical systems fail to provide solutions that everybody could integrate in order to solve ethical problems practically, in real life. Like religious articles of faith, great philosophical principles break down when confronted with complex real situations. If we had more time, I could offer several examples.

In fact, the complexity and the uniqueness of the situations created by new biotechnologies leave us no choice but to resort to casuistry, that is, to case by case analysis. One must avoid arguing about words—such as being pro or con euthanasia in general, or genetic manipulation, or human cloning—and instead look into the details of each technique and application, because related but different techniques may have very different and sometimes opposite ethical implications. Gene therapy, for example, raises very different problems when it is applied to somatic cells (i.e., cells of the body not transmitted to the next generation) or to germ cells, where the modified genes are handed down to offspring. It has taken several years for biologists and physicians to realize that the latter should be forbidden in all circumstances, while the former could be allowed under the usual limits of clinical trials of new treatments. The same holds for so-called human cloning, which raises different problems when it is aimed at producing newborns after pregnancy in the uterus of a woman or at producing embryonic cell lines, in the laboratory, for basic research or for possible medical treatment by cell therapy. Therefore, it is necessary to proceed case by case and to look into the implications for each practical situation. In this kind of approach, there is no doubt that the talmudic and halakhic traditions provide methodological help.

Yet it is important not to remain buried in the techniques and to look at them from different perspectives, such as those of ancient mythologies and literature. Why? Because what is at stake in biomedical ethical problems always has to do with birth, death, sexuality, disease, filiation, and parenthood, all experiences that are the main subjects of ancient myths.

I have served for seventeen years on the National Advisory Ethics Committee in Paris, and I have been kept very busy studying complicated biomedical ethical problems and trying to find appropriate solutions by applying this approach, made up of casuistry associated with inspiration from philosophy and traditional teachings. This led me to publish a recent book called *Les étincelles de hasard* (*The Sparks of Randomness*), in which I try to analyze the relevance of ancient Jewish myths for these problems of today. What comes immediately to mind, of course, are the different stories about the Golem, the building of an artificial man, which are already present in the Talmud. But many other stories are also relevant, like the biblical myth of Adam, Eve, the Serpent, and the Tree of Knowledge, and the lesser-known expansion of this story into the talmudic and kabbalist story of the "sparks of randomness," *nitsoutsot keri* in Hebrew. In sum, this story tells us that after the Fall, Adam and Eve were separated from one another for 130 years. During this long period without sexual intercourse, they lost drops of sperm, which, in the Hebrew of the Mishna, are called drops of *keri*, meaning literally "random events." They are also called *nitsoutsot keri*, that is, "sparks of randomness," because they contain the souls of demons and demonesses that could not be created with normal bodies and that tortured men and women from that time. The whole story of mankind and of the Jewish people is interpreted through the story of these demons. They find ways to become embodied in people, and this creates so-called bad generations, like those of the Flood and the Tower of Babel, and also, later on, the generation of the desert, the people who were liberated from bondage in Egypt. This was supposed to be the end of the story, because these sparks, which were souls of a very high origin at the beginning, had to undergo the process of *tikun*, repair, in order for Adam's sin to be repaired. This repair took place when the Hebrews in the desert received the Torah—and the generation of the desert was then called *dor de'a*, the generation of knowledge. But the fall was repeated after the Golden Calf, then repaired with the building of the First Temple, then repeated and repaired and repeated again with the destruction of the Temple, the building and destruction of the Second Temple. The relationships of knowledge in the biblical sense, that is, sexual intercourse, to science and ethics, and that of randomness to both natural and social laws, and to human freedom and determinism, are the subject of this book, whose first volume has the subtitle *Connaissance spermatique* (*Spermatic Knowledge*), referring to the *Logos Spermatikos* or seminal reason of the Stoics.

At this point, allow me to mention an important encounter, in 1986, with something that is still with me yet was new to me at the time, although I found out that it was familiar and that I knew it beforehand, in some way, without my being aware of that. By this, I mean Spinoza's philosophy. I started to study the *Ethics* of Spinoza after people from different backgrounds told me that they had discovered in my previous works some elements that, to them, sounded like a kind of unconscious Spinozism. After this happened to me on various occasions, I decided that I did not have any choice but to look into the man's work. To my surprise, studying the *Ethics* with precise commentaries that helped me to follow the path of its demonstrations, I found myself in a familiar field, as if I were studying a text of Kabbalah. In consequence, I became more and more Spinozist.

Among other themes in his doctrine, the definition and description of God as an infinite power immanent in Nature, producing every individual being and acting within it, calls to mind several kabbalist descriptions of the relationship between the Ein Sof, the Infinite, and finite individuals in the different worlds. Afterward, I discovered that I was not the first one to discover a proximity between some teachings of Kabbalah and Spinoza's philosophy. Leibniz had already characterized Spinozism as "a monstrous doctrine which had led to the extreme both Cartesianism and the Kabbalah of the Hebrews." This was meant to be a condemnation, but I received it as a correct and positive appreciation. Similarly, Salomon Maimon, the great critic of Kant in the eighteenth century, wrote an apparently paradoxical statement in his autobiography, speaking about his early studies in Kabbalah as an "enlarged Spinozism."

Spinoza himself seems to allude to this proximity. In a letter answering a question about his conception of God and nature, he writes: "I say that all things are in God and move in God, thus agreeing with Paul, and, perhaps, with all the ancient philosophers, though the phraseology may be different; I will even venture to affirm that I agree with all the ancient Hebrews, insofar as one may judge from their traditions, though these are in many ways corrupted." One can show that these ancient Hebrews are most probably to be found in kabbalist writings. I do not have time to elaborate on that here, but I will mention briefly two points relevant to some of the problems that were of interest to me and that appeared earlier in my essay.

One has to do with self-organization: it is clear that Spinoza's idea of God or nature as *causa sui*, that is, cause of itself, operating in everybody and constituting the essence or *conatus* of everybody, may be regarded as a principle of self-organization operating in nature by nature. I know some contemporary Spinozist philosophers, such as Laurent Bove in France, who have elaborated on that point. The second point has to do with the doctrine of absolute determinism, which is one of the most important and difficult teachings of Spinoza. He was accused of being an atheist and his doctrine of immorality, not so much because of his pantheism as because of his denial of free will as a mere illusion due to our ignorance of what makes us decide to do this or that.

The commonly accepted idea is that if everything is determined, including our choices and behavior, then we are not responsible for what we do. No moral judgments are possible anymore because we are responsible only for what we do by free choice. If there is no free will, there is no longer responsibility or ethics. In fact, this widespread belief is a misconception due to the long domination of spiritualist philosophy and theology. The main work of Spinoza is called the *Ethics* because his main concern was precisely to construct an ethics of responsibility and freedom in a world of absolute determinism, where freedom is not to be confused with free will but identified with the joy and happiness that can provide adequate knowledge. In fact, there had always been a minority of philosophers who maintained that a high degree of morality could be attained in a world perceived as completely determined.

It is important to note that this line of thought can also be found in traditional Jewish teaching. This tension between absolute determinism and the experience of human choice is expressed in the paradoxical statement of the *Pirkei Avot*: "Everything is foreseen and the possibility of choice is granted" (3, 15). It is true that most rabbis, including Maimonides, have interpreted this statement by asserting first the reality of free will and free choice. The first part of the sentence, "everything is foreseen," is generally referred to the mystery of God's omniscience. How God knows what we choose freely cannot be grasped by our limited intellect.

There is a trend in Talmudic and rabbinical teachings, however, although it is not the mainstream among modern rabbis, that accentuates the first part of the sentence, the determinism of "everything is foreseen." Then they explain the function of our subjective experience of choice, which plays a role in our salvation, although choices are themselves part of this absolute determinism. Before Spinoza, Hasdai Crescas, Rabbi of Saragossa in Spain in the fourteenth century and a great philosopher and mathematician, developed this line of thought in his master book *Or Hachem*. After Spinoza, one of the great kabbalists at the beginning of the twentieth century, Shlomo Heykhil Eliashoff, expanded these ideas into a tragic form. He built on talmudic and midrashic teachings about a cunning conduct of the world, which seems to play with men, who must believe that they are guilty of their crimes, even though all their doings are the results of an eternal decision from the Infinite:

Everything is essentially decided from above, even when produced by linking of different things with one another and by choice.

It was foreseen that Adam was going to eat from the tree, and die by treachery, and the same for all the terrible things produced on earth from the time that Adam was created until the coming of the Messiah.

For all actions performed on earth there is nothing new under the sun, because they are ready from the world of *tohu* which was before us; everything is being done at its time and moment also in accordance only with the time and moment prepared for it ever since.[1]

The myths of the Midrash and Kabbalah set out by Eliashoff, which might originate in the same traditions of "the ancient Hebrews," describe a world that is also totally determined, but in which determinism that can at least partially be known and understood by men can influence them. This difficult to grasp and long forgotten representation of the world was covered over and hidden by the simpler idea of a responsibility conceivable only out of free will. But it is important to us today to make this difficult Spinozist representation of the world topical again, because it allows us to face the discovery of nature, including human nature, revealed (or made) by biological sciences.

The disparity in understanding between our impersonal science and the commonly accepted ethics of the moral subject endowed with free will is indeed getting greater and greater. Ethics seems increasingly to vanish as we discover new determinations, whether unconscious, biological, psychological, or social, for decisions and deeds that we had believed were freely made choices. The opposition between scientific knowledge, on the one hand, and so-called values, on the other, becomes more and more entrenched. Science reveals more and more mechanisms and reinforces our experience of a determinism of nature extending to all living beings, including human life, whereas moral values are supposed to allow us to exercise freedom and responsibility. The result of this widening gap is a crisis in which more science seems to mean less humanity.

By contrast, Spinozist freedom, as well as the freedom of the *tsadik* and the *hakham*, the righteous and the wise, increases as the science of determinism increases. The relationship between science and freedom is totally inverted. One could almost say that absolute freedom, like God's, would coincide with the infinite knowledge of the absolute determinism of nature.

In order to understand these apparent paradoxes, let us remember a very important point of this deterministic view: nature's laws are timeless and impersonal. Indeed, everything has been reckoned *eternally* and not in the psychological experience of a being existing in time, some super-engineer planning the future. In spite of appearances, this timelessness of determinism is far from mysterious. We experience it each time we know something in a deductive way, as in mathematical knowledge. We can then notice, following Spinoza, that "it is in the nature of reason to perceive things under a certain kind of eternity."[2] Any mathematician or physicist experiences this when he examines a natural law that allows him to predict a temporal phenomenon. The moment the future event is thus predicted, time as we know it no longer exists; rather, it exists eternally in the law describing it. This does not mean, of course, that we cease to exist in time and to perceive events in a different way, depending on their past or future nature.

We must realize that we can experience things in our lives in two different ways: either in time, one after the other, or in a nontemporal way, as when we think about mathematical eternal truths. One finds in Spinoza, as well as in these kabbalist teachings, the same tensions between determinism and apparently free choice, and also between a different aspect of the same problem, namely, that perfection is reality as it is, because the world could not have been different, and yet human existence can become more perfect. There are still differences between a good man and a wicked man for Spinoza, and between a *tsadik*, a just, and a *racha*, a wicked person, for the rabbis.

Can we say, therefore, that this conception of the perfectibility of man by man, notwithstanding the perfection of the world and absolute determinism, is the same in Spinoza's view and in some kabbalists, Crescas and Eliashoff in particular? Probably not, for at least two reasons. First, there is the question of language. Spinoza speaks the language of naturalism and pantheism, while the rabbis speak that of theism. But, as has been observed on many occasions, the theistic language of the kabbalists often hides the pantheistic nature of their thought. Regarding the language of the kabbalists, Scholem once observed that it oscillates between, on the one hand, a mythical representation of a cosmic process, whose mechanical course is intelligible at least in principle if not in all the details of its realization, and, on the other hand, a theistic conception of a personal God acting intentionally.

The second difference between Spinoza and the kabbalist tradition is of greater importance. It lies in the nature of the temporal moral ethic to which we must apply ourselves, after having embarked upon our journey toward salvation and highest perfection, whether we are philosophers, *talmidei hakhamim*, or ignorant fools, *am haaretz*. Both Spinoza and the kabbalists agree that the rational knowledge of good and evil, which enables us to order our passions, is not sufficient, though it is necessary. This rational knowledge has no strength of its own. Inasmuch as it is a purely intellectual, disembodied knowledge, its truth does not enable it to dominate the ideas of good and evil we usually deduce out of our experiences and passions. "True knowledge of good and evil can repress no affect insofar as this knowledge is true, but only as it is considered as an affect,"[3] that is, only inasmuch as it is so internalized and embodied as to acquire the strength of a passion. The use of habit (for educational purposes) for both body and mind is a temporary moral ethic taking into account the strength of passions, on both individual and social grounds. This temporary moral ethic is, in Spinoza's view, justice and generosity, linked to the use of reason, which aims to make us get into the habit of ordering our passions. In the kabbalist rabbis' view, and maybe in Maimonides' too, this temporary moral ethic is the practice of "*torah* and *mitzvoth*," that is, the study of wisdom together with the practice of the commandments and the ensuing experience of joy, the *simhah shel mitzvoth*.

Despite all these differences, Spinoza's words about beatitude at the end of his journey can be applied to the perfectly righteous man, the *tsadik gamur*: "Beatitude is not the reward of virtue, but virtue itself. We do not feel the joy of it because we control our lusts, but on the contrary, it is because we feel joy that we can control our lusts."[4]

Nature as Religious Force in Eriugena and Emerson

Willemien Otten

From its earliest beginnings, Christianity has had trouble finding a proper role for nature. While the ancient concept of *natura* contained strong overtones of a mythological kind, linking natural generation not only with demiurgic guidance, as in Plato's *Timaeus*, but also with sexual desire, as in Plato's *Symposium*, in the later Neoplatonism of Proclus and others such mythological aspects were muted as philosophically stratified forms of organic emanation. The cosmos should above all present traits of rational adornment, it seemed, as the order of nature could only survive by repressing its more animal-like instinctual impulses. On a microcosmic scale, human nature reflected this macrocosmic order. Throughout the early rise of Christianity, it quickly became clear that ancient *natura*, hard-pressed as it was to conform to Neoplatonic structure, would likely rebel against its newly imposed biblical Divine Maker, especially if accepting the cosmic order of Christianity meant that *natura* was forced into a role of passive confinement. Perhaps as an adverse reaction to the former, more active role of *natura*, deliberately and ostentatiously prolonged in Gnostic myth, Christianity sought to tame nature from the beginning by casting it in the role of creation, hence as a material object subjugated to the divine power whence it ultimately originated. Just as it had tamed Babylonian myth before, the creation narrative in Genesis was used to subdue Hellenistic lore and Platonic philosophy. The climax of *natura*'s subjugation came in the idea of *creatio ex nihilo*, with the monotheistic God of Christianity robbing *natura* both of its roots in matter and of its past in pagan myth.

Yet somehow nature's materiality threatened to escape this subordination, either being perceived as resisting the divine imposition of form or as aspiring to rival divine creativity, preferring the realization of its own creative impulses to being a lowly handmaiden to the superior initiative of the divine. It is not surprising, therefore, that the tension between nature and creation, which required constant attention, soon became intertwined with more schematic models of binary opposition: active versus passive, heterodox versus orthodox. As a result of this and other associations, we often encounter the view that the religious intentions of the concept of creation in Christianity can triumph only by violating nature's integrity. In this essay, I will seek to transcend this traditional stalemate, offering an alternative view of nature that will draw on resources within the Christian tradition. In this more theophanic alternative view, nature will emerge not as a rival to creation but as a possible anchor for it. Nature, this essay will argue, can also be seen as a macrocosmic *imago Dei*, with its own integrity and set of desires. Carrying out the important task of co-creating with, rather than being subjugated to, the divine, nature is a worthy object of reverence rather than a mere instrument of human stewardship.

In developing this view of nature, I intend neither to Christianize after the fact what is essentially a pagan concept nor to uncover for *natura* disguised "orthodox" roots in revelation. Instead, I want to emphasize nature's historical role in mediating the divine by delving into its rootedness in temporal existence and contemporaneous cultural circumstance, not escaping from them. I will thereby highlight nature's concrete revelatory character within the Christian tradition, which perhaps relativizes the priority of scriptural revelation that has been stressed in modernity since the Reformation. Furthermore, teasing out the inherent creativity of nature, which received special focus in premodern, especially medieval theology, with its poetic cult of personified *Natura* as semi-goddess,[1] allows us to develop what I have elsewhere called a more "humanist" understanding and appreciation of Christianity. By this I do not refer to the conventional understanding of a rebirth of the classics promoting the awakening of the rational human self and putting Western culture on the road to modernity but appeal to an earlier, more holistic medieval paradigm, in which the right understanding of the dignity of nature is an integral aspect of human (self-)understanding, while serving at the same time as condition for the just worship of the divine.[2] In my opinion, a responsible theology of nature should preferably be developed along such older "humanist" lines. In line with this, its aim should not be to suppress nature's independence in favor of an attitude of obsequiousness and servility, combining a mistaken reading of human stewardship in Genesis with a one-sided interpretation of *creatio ex nihilo*, but rather to engage nature by bringing out the multi-faceted dimensions of its co-creatorship.

To develop such a theology of nature, I will examine two Christian authors from widely different historical periods: John Scottus Eriugena (810–877) and Ralph Waldo Emerson (1803–1882). It is clear that they have not influenced each other, and at first sight they may seem related only insofar as they are not representatives of mainstream Christian thought about creation. Yet on a deeper level their voices have much in common, as they share a profound interest in validating nature's identity as a semi-independent religious force enriching rather than undermining conventional Christian understandings of creation. To combine the sound of these thinkers' voices can be a

355

useful way to pay respect to nature's inherent creativity, making us attentive to an unduly neglected substream in the Christian tradition. I will focus on each of these authors in his own right, but will also bring them into conversation, thereby not only bringing their voices more into unison but making nature's own voice ultimately better heard, as we arrive at a more resilient and dignified sense of the meaning of creation.[3] I will conclude by making a few tentative statements about nature's religious role and about the more "humanist" view of Christianity that can result from taking full account of it.

Eriugena's Nature

By entitling his main work *Periphyseon; or, On the Division of Nature*, the Carolingian polyglot and court intellectual Johannes Scottus Eriugena put himself on the map as a natural philosopher.[4] After a failed stint as arbiter of theological controversies and a successful period as translator of Greek patristic works, in the *Periphyseon* he offers a surprisingly original and highly idiosyncratic synthesis of available Carolingian school knowledge. The work stands out, however, because of its structural focus on nature. Contrary to Carolingian school convention, Eriugena begins with a division, only then to arrive at a definition of nature:

> MASTER: Often as I ponder and investigate, to the best of my ability, with ever greater care the fact that the first and fundamental division of all things that can either be perceived by the mind or transcend its grasp is into things that are and things that are not, a general name for all these things suggests itself which is PHYSIS in Greek or NATURA in Latin. Or do you have another opinion?
> STUDENT: No, I definitely agree. For when entering upon the path of reasoning, I also find that this is so.
> MASTER: Nature, then, is the general name, as we have said, of all the things that are and that are not.
> STUDENT: That is true. For nothing can occur in our thoughts that could fall outside this name.[5]

Dominic O'Meara has traced the impulse to this wide-ranging definition back to Boethius, the sixth-century intellectual whose translations of Plato and Aristotle made him the best-known medieval philosopher prior to the twelfth century.[6] In addition to these translations and to his well-known *Consolation of Philosophy*, Boethius also wrote about the various religious controversies that divided East and West. One of these theological treatises, *Contra Eutychen et Nestorium*, named after the two protagonists whose positions Boethius rejected, dealt with the right understanding of Christ, who united human and divine nature within the identity of a single person. In this work the term *natura* is of obvious importance, as it is linked to the figure of Christ and the possible key to the unity of East and West. Circumspectly, Boethius defines it in three ways, namely, as:

1. that which can only be predicated of bodies;
2. that which can only be predicated of substances, both corporeal and incorporeal;
3. pertaining to those things that, because they are, can somehow be understood by the mind.[7]

While Eriugena may well have used Boethius as a source, given that the relationship between the being of things and their being understood, which dominates his concept of nature, is analogous to Boethius' third predication,[8] their views of nature differ in consequence of the different agendas of their works. Whereas Boethius was engaged in the Christological controversy between East and West, making a nuanced interpretation of terms like *natura* obviously crucial,[9] in Eriugena's early medieval *Periphyseon*, Boethius fades into a distant authority. From the various cosmological labels available to him, Eriugena nevertheless selected *natura*, employing it henceforth as his exclusive organizing principle as he sets out to structure the world around him.

Eriugena may have been attracted to *natura*'s all-encompassing contours because of Boethius's use of it as synonym for *universitas*. In his third predication, Boethius stretched the concept to include even God and matter, although they could be understood only "in a certain way" (*quoquo modo*), and were never to be grasped fully. He made clear, however, that "nothing" (*nihil*) was literally located beyond the pale of his metaphysical project. Holding onto nature's comprehensive function, however tenuous, especially to the inclusion of God,[10] Eriugena was to play out *natura*'s inclusiveness very differently. For him, *natura* covered explicitly also that which cannot be known: not only God but also *nihil*.

This brings us to the central role of negation, in which Eriugena was influenced by another sixth-century authority, the Greek pseudonymous author Dionysius the Areopagite. From him Eriugena adopted the stock phrase "the things that are and the things that are not" to designate the whole of creation. More important than this formulaic expression, however, was Eriugena's importation of the Dionysian practice of negative theology, bringing out God's transcendence through the use of negative epithets. In Eriugena's prudent hands, the *via negativa* proved a helpful tool for human reason to expand its created scope and consider God present inside rather than outside or above *natura*, even if full insight into the divine was not reached. Dionysian use of negation further allowed him to overcome Boethius's qualms about nothingness and nonbeing. Denoting the divine and the created with one concept, Eriugena came to describe *natura* as "that which consists both in the things that can be understood and therefore are, and in the things that cannot be understood and therefore are not." Concurring with O'Meara, I would argue that Eriugena's preference for the precise term *natura* over *universitas* probably reflects his desire to modify Boethius with the help of the Dionysian tradition.[11]

The use of negation had other consequences, as well. By including even that which reason cannot grasp, Eriugena endows *natura* with an inherent dynamism right from the start, since it escapes definition. Consequently, it functions as a concept more of becoming than of being, slipping in a sense of temporality, even if barely noticeable. Eriugena's decision to refrain from ever identifying God with being or *ousia*,[12] for which there was precedent in Augustine's exegesis of Exodus 3:14 (*ego sum qui sum*),[13] should probably be understood in the same way. Rhetorically speaking, the effect of this shift of emphasis from being to becoming is enormous, as that which cannot be understood is now held out as that which was not yet understood, with denial transmogrifying into invitation. *Natura* thus becomes transformed into an increasingly rich and fundamentally open concept, as the *Periphyseon* encourages thinking beyond the received categories of creation, which Eriugena absorbs, incorporates, and transcends at will.

Once *natura* is portrayed dynamically, one begins to see why the concept could be perceived as a threat to traditional notions, even as it incorporated them, for Eriugena is likely to have been familiar with Augustine as well as with Boethius (and through the latter, Porphyry). In particular, Eriugena's dynamic and flexible *natura* appears to violate existing views of creation, which had developed over the centuries as a Christian safeguard against Gnostic and Manichean deprecations of corporeal and material existence. An orthodox alternative to matter's residual recalcitrance, the concept of creation tended to pivot around hard and fast boundaries, fixing and reifying the world as an object rather than a manifestation of divine power. Before Eriugena, the lines in this debate had long been drawn, with God's providence watching over the theater of spatiotemporal creation in which human history was played out. How God was able to do this, having caused the world's initial coming into being through *creatio ex nihilo*, remained a problem throughout the Middle Ages, one that culminated in Aquinas's compromise, namely, that the world's created state is not in contradiction to its eternity.[14] Eriugena's own solution was to change Augustine's seminal reasons (*rationes seminales*)—whose character remains enigmatic, even as they form an interesting middle way between Plato's ideas and Aristotle's forms—into "primordial causes." Reflecting *natura creans et creata*, they form his special connecting link between the oneness of God's uncreated being (*natura creans et non creata*) and the multiplicity of the created material world (*natura non creans et creata*). Though this might seem to solve the problem, the middle position of the primordial causes suggests the imperfection of their created status, even though they are adopted without hierarchy into the fullness of the uncreated Divine Word.[15]

Understanding Eriugena's Nature

Because Eriugena's approach is unique and idiosyncratic, given that he developed his understanding of nature indirectly, through negation and with the help of various mediating instances such as the primordial causes, he has been accused of having a confused grasp of ancient philosophy, to whose legacy heterogeneous scriptural and patristic elements were added. Such a view tends to conflate the experimental nature of Eriugena's approach with his failure to abide by conventional wisdom.[16] An alternative route to understanding the *Periphyseon* is to approach it as an open-ended work, as an invitation to follow the "becoming" of nature in reverse. At first sight, engaging in such a reading might seem deceptive, in much the same way that staring in a mirror is deceptive if what one is really after is self-discovery: the resulting vision inevitably lacks depth. To a certain extent, however, all historical research suffers from this, even more so research that touches on aspects of soul and intellect, as is the case with religious subjects. Rather than adopting fixed categories like creation or emanation in an attempt to continue nature's problematic subjugation, I would like to suggest a more dynamic approach to analyzing the pastness of nature as religious force, one in which nature's innate drive and energy are brought to the fore. While it is obvious that a veil that cannot be lifted, like the tain of a mirror, separates us from the past, it is also true that our own close affinity with past religious themes and figures, the mirror-effect, often makes us overlook the very existence of this veil or become incapable of pinpointing its location.[17] Seeing Eriugena's reflections on nature as primarily a reflection of nature's own coming into being allows us to make full use of this mirror analogy by tracking *natura*'s development alongside Eriugena's investigation of it, with the latter closely resembling our own.

In consequence, our reading can perhaps avoid some of the common pitfalls in interpretations of Eriugena's metaphysics. The first is to see him as a pantheist. This characterized the (Neo)Platonic interpretation current in late-nineteenth-century philosophical speculation, which led to the rediscovery of Eriugena's concept of nature as both monist and pantheist. Hegel's appreciation allowed Eriugena's legacy to be incorporated into the onto-theological tradition, from which the Church had excised it. While appreciating the philosophical genius of Eriugena's thought, this interpretation tends to prefer its heterodox aspects for their very heterodoxy. Beyond his rationalism, taken in a subjectivist and idealist sense, Eriugena's pantheism stood out most.[18] The scriptural overlay of Eriugena's thought, phrased in part as a commentary on Genesis, was seen as an obstacle to its universal accessibility, one that should be eliminated.

The second is to overemphasize his idealist quality. This can be seen in the postmodern interpretation of Dermot Moran, who considers this idealism a corrective to the onto-theological tradition in a Heideggerian sense. Moran sees the division into being and nonbeing as surpassing Dionysian influence, to develop into a full-blown negative ontology or *me-ontology*.[19] In my opinion, this interpretation fails to appreciate the degree to which Eriugena's playful maneuverings with negation reflect his linguistic skillfulness more than a well-defined metaphysical position.[20]

More important, both interpretations suffer from a defensive streak, however mild, since they either see Eriugena as representing a heterodox position (the pantheistic/monist reading), or wish to protect him against such false accusations (the idealist reading). What is overlooked in both cases is not just the mirror but the mirror-effect: to read *natura*'s coming into being as inseparable from the mind's self-discovery. Eriugena emphasizes the reflective character of his investigation of *natura* by opening the *Periphyseon* in Ciceronian terms as a mere thought experiment: "As I frequently ponder [*Saepe mihi cogitanti*]."[21] In other words, nature's genesis is closely linked to the author's own self-awareness.

Seeing Eriugena's reflections on nature as an expression of the coming into being of both nature and self brings us to *natura*'s theophanic aspect, a process that is reflective of how in the *Periphyseon* theophany gradually encroaches on negative theology, replacing it eventually as Eriugena's strategy of choice.[22] From the start of the *Periphyseon*, Eriugena shows an interest in inflating nature to the point of being fully coextensive with divine appearance. Seeing *natura* as theophany may offer us particular advantages, not just with regard to its religious role but also with regard to its proper historical understanding. Through his use of theophany, Eriugena takes with utter seriousness nature's inherent drive to develop toward the divine, while avoiding a standoff between (Christian) creation as opposed to (pagan) nature. Drawing on Augustine's notion of time and temporality, and making special use of his notion that temporal awareness is always tied to the present and hence deprives it of plot—as the past is by definition the present of the past, just as the future is the present of the future and the present the present of the present[23]—we can interpret *natura* as a concept which is both "in flight" and always near at hand. To study the pastness of Eriugena's *natura* under these conditions is to try to rein in something that must inevitably break loose, and therefore requires a constant and reflexive attention to the self. By skillfully playing the roles of eternity and time off against one another, the *Periphyseon* offers us what should in the end be deemed a heuristic investigation, one in which *natura* presents the irreversible ticking of time, even as it seemingly and monolithically lies still under the veil of eternity.

The gravest risk in Eriugena's entire project is the fact that nature's theophanic character can bring the human self dangerously close to divine absorption, thereby eliminating any remaining possibility of human reflection. Here the fact that humanity is made in the image of God proves to be both a help and a hindrance,[24] since Eriugena's central question must inevitably be how to preserve a workable distance between nature's theophanic character, which borders on the status of an acquired macrocosmic image, and the divine image that is humanity. It is, after all, imperative in the *Periphyseon* that the human self be able to conduct an investigation into nature as an investigation that covers all that is and that is not, yet that can still be called its own.

Connecting Eriugena and Emerson

Eriugena is usually localized within various textual traditions such as (Neo)Platonism, the theology of East or West, and negative theology. As a result, he is regarded as standing outside the tradition of mainstream Christianity, a perennial outsider, of sorts. Just as, on creation, he is seen as an unorthodox Christian thinker, so he stands out in the Dionysian tradition because of his Boethian influence; or if he is considered a Neoplatonist, then he is a Christian one. A different way to arrive at an understanding of what he has to say might be to bring him into contact with a thinker from a different historical period. This would imply starting from differences rather than from any overt or hidden similarities, as ninth-century Carolingian thought has little in common with nineteenth-century American Transcendentalism. The advantage here for tracing the development of the idea of nature is that such a proceeding may make us less inclined to frame the thought of our chosen interlocutors in a fixed historical manner; this is especially so if the comparison can be made easier by recognizing a certain affinity of thought. Between Eriugena and Emerson, who is likewise considered an outsider in the tradition of mainstream Christianity, there is definitely an affinity in their engagement with nature as a key concept. What connects Eriugena and Emerson even more in their reflections on nature are its distinct theophanic overtones in their work, while the manifestation of nature in both authors also reveals strong ties to what might be seen as the revelatory genesis of the human self.

Any reexamination of the concept of nature in Emerson obviously carries us into a different world. Encountering a different mindset, we notice that nature yields a rather different set of intellectual problems, even though there is affinity with Eriugena's Platonic outlook. Emerson's succinct definition in the introduction to *Nature* may seem to breathe a dualism that seems hard to reconcile with Eriugena's integrative approach: "Philosophically considered, the universe is composed of Nature and the Soul. Strictly speaking, therefore, all that is separate from us, all which Philosophy distinguishes as the NOT ME, that is both nature and art, all other men and my own body, must be ranked under this name, NATURE."[25]

Upon reflection, however, this dualism foreshadows an incipient dialogue between God and the universe through the (beauty of the) self, which lends itself to further comparison: "The currents of the Universal Being circulate through me; I am part or particle of God. . . . In the tranquil landscape, and especially in the distant line of the horizon, man beholds somewhat as beautiful as his own nature."[26] We are in the fortunate situation, moreover, that not only is there some affinity between their ideas of nature, but some of the problems that I have raised in relation to the *Periphyseon*, such as whether to see Eriugena's investigation of *natura* as a reverse kind of self-investigation, have already been addressed and brought to the surface for Emerson. I refer here especially to the work of Stanley Cavell, whose exquisite musings on Emerson touch directly on the problems surrounding Eriugena as mentioned above.[27] With Cavell as our guide, we can bring Emerson into a more focused dialogue with Eriugena on the idea of nature.

Central to both thinkers is a conviction that nature is a religious force, a more dynamic link and spacing between God and humanity than the traditional unidirectional vector of creation. Since for both the dynamic energy of nature challenges the traditional bounds of creation, the label *pantheism* has been applied to them. Like Eriugena, Emerson has usually been studied outside the orbit of mainstream thought, which is true in religion but no less so in philosophy. The work of Stanley Cavell, regardless of whether Cavell is engaged in reclaiming Emerson's importance, can be of use for reading Eriugena because he shifts the usual terms of philosophical consideration. Cavell uses Emerson primarily as an intellectual lens in order to focus on what he deems to be both philosophy's origin and its true task: namely, conversation.

The notion of philosophy as conversation is of great value as we try to make concrete connections between Emerson and Eriugena. For one thing, it is broad enough to include literary and religious aspects as well as philosophical ones: Emerson's works, in fact, involve all three, as does Eriugena's *Periphyseon*. Of equal importance, the notion allows us to translate or demythologize some of the more medieval features of Eriugena's work, opening it up for dialogical purposes. Rather than stemming from any desire to disqualify him as a medieval thinker, this aim is based on the awareness that good conversation draws in both partners, thereby replacing isolation with company. Since both thinkers can be regarded as outsiders, their peripheral standing is of particular interest, as it may help us to uncover the existence of a different set of historical connections between the conventional ones of mediate or immediate influence as a further way to relativize the received tradition of creation.

What is particularly remarkable about Cavell's position on Emerson, in a view that cannot be so easily extended to Eriugena, is that he appears to consider Emerson's outsider status to be a prophetic office, of sorts. For Cavell, it is as if with Emerson we can finally start anew the conversation that once was coextensive with philosophy. While the assignment of prophetic office is to some extent a Romantic commonplace, Cavell intensifies it in interesting ways by crediting Emerson with using a kind of language that gives serious consideration to the performative aspect of conversation. Cavell does so in part as a strategy to honor the efforts of J. L. Austin and the late Wittgenstein, whose turn to ordinary language philosophy had once and for all done away with any remaining structures of traditional metaphysics.[28] But prophecy always looks forward to the realization of a vision, and the ultimate goal of the conversation as set out by Cavell and mediated through his attention to Emerson lies far beyond philosophical correctness, let alone capitulation to the demands of logical positivism as both opponent to and declared successor of traditional metaphysics. Cavell's visionary view of philosophy reflects a profound desire to restore humanity to its covenantal calling, whose conversational language, comprising both edification and therapy and aiming at the retrieval of "uncorrupted human understanding,"[29] he senses pulsating through the veins of Emersonian thought. In being driven to uphold such a covenant, as brought out by Cavell, and assigning nature a vital part in maintaining it, Emerson seems indeed engaged in what I labeled above, using more medieval terms, the "humanist" interpretation of Christianity: the sense that worship of the divine requires that the dignity of nature be integrated with human (self)-understanding.[30]

Nature and Time in Emerson

If Cavell's aim, brought on by, as well as recognized in, his reading of Emerson, is to conduct philosophy by involving humanity in conversation, then it is clear that what is most problematic in his attempt to recreate philosophy in this way is the problem of skepticism. Not only is overcoming skepticism of key significance if one wants to hold out the possibility of adumbrating truth, but it also serves as an important station on the way to a conversion of the self. Before Eriugena's time, this is brought out especially by Augustine, in the early stages of his own journey toward Christianity, when he struggles with skepticism in his *Contra Academicos*. Augustine's fear was that, if there cannot be any reliable sense of truth, his personal struggle to understand the Christian truth becomes wholly irrelevant. He therefore considered the defeat of skepticism a precondition for his personal acceptance of Christianity and, more importantly, for his self-understanding as a Christian. Articulating the connection between truth and self must inevitably be an important milestone on the road by which Cavell brings philosophy back to its true calling, namely, that of conversation.

The quality and accessibility of the conversation are important elements as well. By contrast to the established European metaphysical tradition, Emerson directs us to sit at the feet of the low and the ordinary as one's gurus.[31] Cavell greatly appreciates this attention to the everyday; moreover, such attentiveness can be turned into a tool for opening us to whoever is speaking. We might even say that Emerson counsels us to put into practice what Brian Stock has called the duty of any good historian, namely, to "listen" for the text.[32]

Sitting at the guru Emerson's feet and listening to his texts, or trying, rather, to make them resonate in the conversation he starts up with readers who let themselves be drawn in, Cavell is fascinated by the mix of reverence and iconoclasm by which Emerson allows his readers to forge the bond between truth and self ever more closely as they perform their own lives, embracing the Whim that they write on the lintel of their own doorpost. As a result, the idea of tradition must make way, must even be violently destroyed, in favor of the here and now. Emerson's idea of, in Cavell's admiring terms, seizing on the ephemeral can perhaps best be seen as the transposition of what he means by "the low and the ordinary" to the category of time, not in the sense of a duration and chronology that aspires to eternity, even if it is the opposite of it, but as profoundly expressive of the fragility of theophanic existence. Some of Emerson's statements about the value of the ordinary seem indeed directly defiant, if not scandalously insulting, of any attempt to cherish a preconceived or closed sense of tradition. Emerson's assertion of a bond between truth and self, his violation of tradition, and his irreverence toward the past are driven by a desire to make room for new impulses, embodied above all in the celebration of a new and universal present, in which theophanic adumbration may blossom into manifest epiphany.

A statement like the following may seem typically American in its concentration on the here and now: "Give me health and a day, and I will make the pomp of emperors ridiculous. The dawn is my Assyria; the sunset and moonrise my Paphos, and unimaginable realms of faerie; broad noon shall be my England of the senses and the understanding; the night shall be my Germany of mystic philosophy and dreams."[33] Yet it also radiates the art of forgetting, which Nietzsche (who was greatly inspired by Emerson) cultivated when he distinguished the antiquarian, the monumental, and the critical approaches to history.[34] In his willingness to encourage history to be at times destructive, to see forgetfulness as an art to be practiced, Emerson is indeed like Nietzsche. One of their crucial points of difference, however, is in the former's explicit appeal to nature as a locus for the self to regain its balance. For Emerson, forgetfulness of the past is deeply rooted in a religious celebration of creation.[35] Either God or his audience is summoned in what is simultaneously a plea and an outcry: "Give me health and a day." The continuum of time may well be shattered, but the pieces that we find lying around are not thereby disembodied. Like seeds of a Stoic *Logos Spermatikos*, they are waiting to bear fruit, for nature deifies us, according to Emerson.[36] He speaks about nature to us in a prophetic-homiletic way rather than in the moral vein of which he can be too easily accused: "All things with which we deal preach to us. What is a farm but a mute gospel?"[37]

More accurately, nature itself is to be considered a divine homily wanting to inspire us. When this inspiration is enforced in strong biblical language, nature can even fall out of its familiar Emersonian theophanic role, as in the following, surprisingly harsh and instrumental quote: "Nature is thoroughly mediate. It is made to serve. It receives the dominion of man as meekly as the ass on which the Saviour rode. It offers all its kingdoms to man as the raw material which he may mould into what is useful."[38] Yet the subtle interplay between the description of nature "receiving the dominion of man" as meekly as the donkey on which Jesus entered Jerusalem, on the one hand, and "offering all its kingdoms" to man, with an oblique hint to live up to the failed promises made by the devil to Christ in the desert, makes clear how nature's mediate role has revelatory and eschatological overtones, reinforced by the Strauss-like suggestion of humanity being identified with Christ.[39] Just as the words that obey the poet ultimately work beyond his prowess, so nature reveals something divine to us beyond its instrumental function. It is as if Emerson's maximizing of nature's servility pushes theophany to become unveiled epiphany.[40]

Two further aspects of Emerson, for which I draw on Cavell's observations, may contribute to a reading of nature that is illuminating for Eriugena as well. The first of these begins from Emerson's moral-homiletic vein. It centers on what Cavell calls the relation between what happens casually and what creates a casualty.[41] Instead of inflating the ordinary—which is always Emerson's base point—to match the cosmic and the tragic, as in many Christian accounts of providence or predestination, whereby time is viewed as stretching directly from God's hand, making creation to some extent a mechanistic affair, Emerson tends to minimize the importance of any grand cosmic scheme, restoring it to its rightful proportions. The result is that he reduces the extravagant to an aspect of the ordinary, as is highlighted by the following journal entry: "The sun shines and warms and lights us and we have no curiosity to know why this is so; but we ask the reason of all evil, of pain, and hunger, and mosquitoes and silly people."[42] Whereas on the one hand we see the same focus on the here and now mentioned above, here the lightness and all-pervasiveness of nature are especially striking, oscillating between questions of theodicy and a daily dosage of sunlight. Nature's mediation could not be more clearly and more "mediately" expressed, so to speak, as in this remarkable quotation spanning the entire register of possible (human and cosmic) dispositions.

At the same time, it is notable how, underneath the ephemeral quality of nature, Emerson subtly inserts a sense of the future into the very idea of nature. For that, we need to invoke a passage from *The American Scholar*, which looks like an earlier appeal to the universal present of the here and now. Once more we hear him talk about the ordinary and the low, as he continues: "I ask not for the great, the remote, the romantic; what is doing in Italy or Arabia; what is Greek art, or Provencal minstrelsy; I embrace the common, I explore and sit at the feet of the familiar, the low. Give me insight into to-day, and you may have the antique and future worlds. What would we really know the meaning of?"[43] In some ways, this might look like the earlier appeal for health and a day. While, on the one hand, it appeals more to the Romantic imagination, on the other, more attention is paid to temporality, or rather, room is made for time's cessation. In a manner comparable to that of Augustine, Emerson here combines the past and the future by collapsing them in the present, in what he deems to be a universal present alongside an introspective one. This present is not conceived as a period of time, however short, but rather as the awakening of the self, of Man Thinking,[44] as a universal present must after all apply to universal man.

The powerful idea of Man Thinking, like the medieval one of the World Soul,[45] exists only by the grace of individual men, who lend each other identity by participating in it through dialogue. While what we have here may seem just another plea, "Give *me* insight into today," it is important to realize that it is phrased in terms of a tradeoff: "and *you* may have the antique and future worlds." This makes the plea part of a conversation that is ongoing precisely because it is carried out in an everlasting present. In this sacrifice of linear temporality, the dialogue that any good conversation essentially is gains in importance proportionate to the degree in which the voices in it, conjoined to a universal present, are transformed into smatterings of the divine, as morsels of incarnation, as in the exclamation from *Nature*: "The currents of the Universal Being circulate through me.

I am part or parcel of God."[46] It is as if the sacrifice of temporality adds to the weight of divine epiphany, canceling out all remains of Platonic dualism in the process.

Underlying the conversation in the present and the possibility of divine epiphany, and giving it substance and depth, lies an interaction with oneself paralleling the interaction with Nature. The two are deeply entwined for Emerson, in a way that will not be unfamiliar for readers of Eriugena. As Emerson puts it earlier, in a passage of *The American Scholar*:

> He shall see that nature is the opposite of the soul, answering to it part for part. One is seal and one is print. Its beauty is the beauty of his own mind. Its laws are the laws of his own mind. Nature then becomes to him the measure of his attainments. So much of nature as he is ignorant of, so much of his own mind does he not yet possess. And, in fine, the ancient precept, "Know thyself," and the modern precept, "Study nature," become at least one maxim.[47]

It appears that the use of nature as "macroscope" for the study of soul is among Emerson's highest goals.

Reading Eriugena Through Emerson: Preliminary Conclusions

In comparing Eriugena and Emerson, I seek to listen carefully to the voice of nature, as it comes to us from their works, lacking the Christianizing overlay of creation. One obvious goal in doing so is to make clear that, through a retrieval of nature's past, read through the lens of the Augustinian *praesens praesentis*, albeit in the form of *Periphyseon*'s relativizing comment *saepe mihi cogitanti* or Emerson's invitation to dialogue "Give me insight into today," the religious role of nature should be recalibrated in a way that is both broader and less static than mere opposition to traditional creation. One way to achieve this is to explore the connection of nature's self-propelling energy as a religious concept, with its historical guise of being ever-present, to the human self, while seeing this condition of being ever-present as a way "to create a future" and initiate development.[48] This means that "timeless" nature must be ready at different moments to break through the veil of eternity by which conventional creation is usually held in place. What deserves serious attention, then, is to what extent and at which turning points nature allows itself to be a medium of revelation by allowing the divine epiphany of incarnation (whether in the guise of theophany, theodicy, or casualty) to become co-extensive with creation.

To what degree might such a reading go against the grain of the Christian creation narrative? In many respects, it does, as we have seen how Eriugena's modification of Boethius's *universitas* and Emerson's sacrifice of the past in favor of the here and now defy standard interpretations of Christian creation. The violence needed to make room for such an alternative reading of nature, however, is not an iconoclastic desire to break out of this tradition in order to correct it, even though such historical reconstructions must also take place, but rather should be seen as germane to the energy springing from nature's own resources, as it demands a place within what has become a lopsided Christian tradition. In such a "violent" yet at the same time introverted reading,[49] as nature reflects self, nature's recalcitrance need no longer be read as an imperative to subdue the material and corporeal order by imposing the straightjacket of creation upon it, but can be seen instead as an open invitation for humanity to embrace its "encampment in nature." As Emerson states in *Nature*: "there is throughout nature something mocking, something that leads us on and on, but arrives nowhere, keeps no faith with us. All promise outruns the performance. We live in a system of approximations. Every end is prospective of some other end, which is also temporary; a round and final success nowhere. We are encamped in nature, not domesticated."[50] Without necessarily reading this as a nineteenth-century comment reminiscent of the semiheterodox Gnostic or medieval *natura* speculation touched on above—and I fully admit that it can be read that way—we can also take this comment as a fair echo of the doubleness that has been endemic in the position of nature in Christianity from its inception. Emerson is right: nature teases and mocks us. But rather than exerting ourselves to become domesticated in nature, relegating its status to that of divine subcontractor in the process, we may choose to embrace its mocking as a valuable way of making actual contact with the divine, a contact that may enable us to turn the passing of time that marks our history into an instance of co-creatorship.

In a more "creative" way than when reducing it to creation, we can perhaps consider nature's recalcitrance a testimony to the fundamental congruity, bordering on indifference, of sacrifice and empowerment of self, in the face of which nature's existence as sheer religious force presents humanity with its own calling, namely, to embrace historical temporality by shattering the mirror of eternity. Reading nature's recalcitrance in this way makes clear to us that in the end, finding the human self is nothing other than being encamped in the world.

Inheriting the Wound

Religion and Philosophy in Stanley Cavell

Asja Szafraniec

Contemporary philosophy has many times disavowed any relationship with religion, yet it remains strangely committed to a distinctly religious vocabulary. Stanley Cavell's work bears traces of such problematic engagement with religion, entwined as it is in the vocabulary of faith, sacrifice, redemption, incarnation, conversion, and confession. While Cavell's engagement with religion is not of a straightforwardly affirmative kind, we can't call it straightforwardly dismissive, either. Rather, we could perhaps speak about a transformation, a "transfiguration" (to use his own vocabulary) of religion taking place in his work.

The question of the function of this commitment is especially urgent, since Cavell, who not without reason made the first steps in his philosophical career with an essay entitled "Must We Mean What We Say?" insists throughout his later work on taking responsibility for every word uttered.[1] A recurring figure in Cavell's work, originally used by Thoreau, is that of writing as hoeing, as removing weeds, hence of a continuous attention to language, an ongoing effort to cultivate, against all odds, not only a responsible but also a "prophetic" language environment, one intended to reshape a community (communities are, after all, "cities of words") or to call into being one that does not yet exist. Meaning what we say is a way of shaping our world, of creating and destroying worlds: "The writer's power of definition, of dividing, will be death to some, to others birth."[2] The surfacing of religious motives in this context of emphatic attention to choice of words calls for examination. I am interested not only in the way those motives can be seen as forming a part of speaking and writing responsibly but also in the way they interact with other parts of Cavell's project.

One of the guiding motives in that project is Cavell's preoccupation with Romanticism, which he conceives as an interpretive filter through which to view the history of our culture in general.³ In Cavell's reading, Romanticism "opens with the discovery of the problem of other minds, or with the discovery that the other is a problem, an opening of philosophy."⁴ Significantly, Cavell also describes Romanticism as an "alternative process of secularization," which faces the "necessity of recovering or replacing religion." (I'd like to emphasize at this point that this is not a process of secularization *tout court*, but one in which religion is to be recovered or replaced.) So understood, Romanticism draws a preoccupation with religion into the center of Cavell's philosophical project: Romanticism not only opens with the discovery of the problem of the other and with understanding that this is the central problem of philosophy, it also reveals the origin and the nature of this problem to be "the trace or scar of the departure of God."⁵

In a certain reading, Cavell's *Claim of Reason* can be said to be about this trace or scar. There Cavell re-reads the Cartesian meditation on the existence of God in order to bring together two fundamental philosophical moments: Descartes' revealing the certainty of our existence to be dependent on the existence of God and Nietzsche's announcement of the death of God: "the idea of God is part of . . . human nature. If that idea dies, the idea of human nature equally dies. . . . So not only the fact . . . of my existence, but the *integrity* of it, depends upon this idea. ⁶ Cavell concludes here that in his effort to demonstrate the existence of God Descartes in fact comes to grasp the nature of his own existence: he arrives at a "self-knowledge." The kind of self-knowledge he gains, as made available to us by Cavell, is the insight that the death of God, hence the disappearance of the ideal, cannot occur without leaving a scar on man—that it must have inflicted a wound on the "integrity" of my "existence."

When investigating religion and violence, it is important not to stop at the level of symptoms: for example, the analysis of violent expressions of religiosity, the investigation of the ways in which religion functions as a political power. One needs to address the genealogy of the problem. By this I mean the violence reported by Nietzsche, the murder of God, and its immediate consequence, the trauma thus inflicted on man, who took God's place. Cavell is among those who have observed that the work of Samuel Beckett can be read as a psychoanalytic recounting of this event, and I shall follow him here. His reading of Beckett's *Endgame* gives us the world after the flood of dogmatic religiosity has receded, the world of which the aftermath of the biblical flood is a figure and a prophecy:

> God shut us in. The result is that the earth is blotted out for man, sealed away by a universal flood of meaning and hope. The price of soaking it up will be no less high, for there is nothing to soak it up with except ourselves. A hope precipitated and concentrated through millennia will not swiftly recede, it comes back in waves. Splash, splash, always on the same spot.⁷

Cavell reads the flood—both ancient and modern—as a token of a departure of God; a departure for good, with no rainbow in sight, making redemption a human task. Just like the biblical flood, in the aftermath of the modern flood man "saw his father naked," that is to say, realized that the authority he took to be absolute (and that he relied upon to justify his own) is finite, imperfect, susceptible to failure. In Cavell's account, *Endgame*'s character Hamm, the survivor of the flood, realizes that if either his or his father's existence "is to be provided with justification, he must be the provider; which presents itself to him as taking his father's place." While there is nothing wrong with the first step of the son's reasoning (that now the burden of justification can no longer rest on paternal authority), the conclusion, Cavell suggests, is somehow twisted: it "presents itself to him as taking his father's place." That it "presents itself" so suggests a deception, or at least a contingency in the son's conclusion. Justifying one's existence by taking the place of God may not be the best option, and certainly is not the only available one. Taking one's father's place, Cavell adds, is "the act that blinds Oedipus," and blindness is a loss of the world.[8] This enigmatic reminder should be put in the context of Cavell's definition of skepticism as "an enforced distance from the things of the world and others in it by the very means of closing that distance, by the work of my senses."[9] Skeptical blindness thus defined is a consequence of an Oedipal attempt to penetrate the world with sight that imitates the sight of God, an attempt to see as God sees, to see even the unfathomable.

The psychoanalytic register to which Cavell has recourse at this point provides us with insight into how he perceives the process of secularization as inflicting a wound and the way our human interactions, our thought, our experience of the world still suffer from this wound. (In his recent *Cities of Words*, Cavell insists that psychoanalysis be seen as a successor to, or transformation of, philosophy.[10] If this is so, it is because Nietzsche's announcement of the death of God is not to be taken as a plain diagnosis of an event that took place once and for all. In his reading of Nietzsche, Gilles Deleuze stresses that, in fact, "Nietzsche mistrusts the death of God"[11]—in the sense that its impact has not been fully understood, accounted for, that it remains a part of the collective unconscious influencing our lives. Cavell shares this opinion: "Positivism said that statements about God are meaningless: Beckett shows us that they mean too damned much."[12]) Aligning itself with Wittgenstein's understanding of philosophy as therapy, psychoanalytic practice as envisaged by Cavell extends this therapy by revealing to us that we tend to project the effects of trauma on our environment. If it is true that the departure of God counts as such a trauma, it is essential to reenact and rethink the topoi of our religious past for the mechanism of compulsively repeated projections to stop or at least to be realized, accounted for.

While religion silently and invisibly pursues its work outside of its own environment—in philosophy, in the everyday—it also continues to work inside it. Philosophy suffers from a wound caused by the departure of God, but it is not the case that religion, still addressing that departed God, is any better off. Cavell addresses this, as well. His understanding of religion bears a certain likeness to Nietzsche's well-known image of religion as a reactive, "base" force. Even though this force is by definition weaker than active forces, it can nonetheless dominate them by stripping them (e.g., the force of destructive, critical, Nietzschean philosophy, but also the force of personal engagement) of their nature, that is, of the way of functioning that is proper to them. In this reading, religion is understood as a set of alibis and excuses.

While Cavell's thinking about religion is indebted to Emerson, Nietzsche's great example, and while this indebtedness sets the tenor of Cavell's critique of Christianity, the critique is not straightforward. In the *Claim of Reason*, Cavell states:

> You may battle against the Christian's self-understanding from within Christianity, as Kierkegaard declares, or from beyond Christianity, as Nietzsche declares. In both cases you are embattled because you find the words of the Christian to be the right words. It is the way he means them that is . . . *enfeebling*. Christianity appears in Nietzsche not so much as the reverse of the truth as the truth in foul disguise.[13]

The words of the Christian are "right," but the way in which they are "meant" is "enfeebling."

Cavell's critique of the "feeble" way in which the Christian "means" his words should not be taken as founded on a supposed lack of sincere intention in the Christian's mind. Cavell's investigation of seriousness and sincerity in *A Pitch of Philosophy* makes clear that to understand the empowerment of words in terms of sincerity (of having a genuine intention, of speaking seriously) is to understand the Christian's words as referring us to an inward act in his mind, hence to understand his words as descriptive, not performative. (Cavell quotes in this context an earlier critique of his teacher Austin: "outward and visible sign . . . of an inward spiritual act."[14]) Besides, the inward spiritual act of sincerity is impossible to fathom; it is open to skepticism (there are no criteria for sincerity), so by holding such a view we would not make the slightest advance in establishing what one means by his words. Seeking to counter such descriptive understandings of what it is to "mean something," Austin takes the words of Hippolytus as his motto: "Our word is our bond." Cavell says of the rigidity of this maxim that, ironically, "meant to free us from metaphysics, it locks us into it." Having exchanged one kind of bondage for another, instead of the "assumption of a spiritual shackle," we are "tethered" to our words. (This is where Austin seems to enter the realm of the tragic; Cavell suggests that a theory of forgiveness could only be formulated in the realm of comedy.) Words functioning as our bond (a petrified bond, like the bond of the Old Testament) lead to tragedies, as in the case of Hippolytus. (Cavell speaks here of a character flaw—narcissism.)

If sincerity is not for Cavell the sense of "meaning something," then what is it? I have noted Cavell's preoccupation with being "serious about philosophy," with the question of how to "speak philosophically and mean every word I said."[15] Cavell does not give in to naïveté here: he is aware that an effort to shape the world (community) by cultivating its language has its reverse side expressed by Austin. Ultimately one is abandoned to one's words. "I read Austin . . . as affirming that I am abandoned to [my words], as to thieves, or conspirators, taking my breath away." That is why "writing as of a testament, in view of one's death, is a description of all serious writing."[16] This is not to say that Cavell would condone the way in which Hippolytus acts. To live is to engage in a movement between controlling one's words and being controlled by them. To act as if these two sides of the movement were the same, as Hippolytus does, is to have, in Cavell's terms, a petrified imagination. To mean every word one says is to assume responsibility for the (criterial) implications of what one says, while in full awareness that those implications may change, that they remain in need of our future interventions, and that they are potentially infinite, so that what we say exceeds our control, so that we will always mean more and less than we do. When discussing, for example, Thoreau's mode of writing, Cavell speaks of being at "war with words, battl[ing] for the very weapons with which you fight"[17]—to prevent them from imprisoning us, suffocating us, from turning into "thieves, or conspirators, taking my breath away." This situation of being abandoned to my words only superficially resembles Cavell's description of the words of a Christian. When Cavell ascribes the enfeebling effect of the words of a Christian to their being pronounced in a context in which "human action is everywhere disguised as human suffering," he sees the Christian as also abandoned to words but not to *his own* words.

Here I'd like to introduce another reason for the attractiveness of Romanticism for Cavell's philosophical project. This is Romanticism's struggle between two competing interpretations of itself concerning whether the Romantic hero is human or divine. (Here again, the grammar to which Cavell appeals encompasses the differences and complementarities between particular Romanticisms.) On the one hand, Romantic literature and philosophy abound with attempts by individuals to control their environment absolutely, to overcome their finitude, their humanity, or to take God's place, all of which Cavell believes leads to skepticism. On the other hand, Romanticism can be shown to explore various forms of attunement to the world (to take on itself "the task of bringing the world back, as to life"[18]) intended to relieve this skepticism. This can be seen as a fundamentally religious attitude (regardless of whether it involves faith in a supernatural being). Cavell attributes this Romantic ambiguity to all writing he calls prophetic: one of the features of such writing resides in "the periodic confusions of their authors' identities with God's."[19] The fact that the Christian's words do not participate in this confusion is in this context a lack, not a merit. This is why, rather than choosing the position of the Christian, Cavell prefers the position of Emerson's ("universally distributed") "genius," in the name of which Emerson is "hectoring . . . his fellows . . . to stop quoting and start saying something, to find their voices, apart from which they do not know they exist."[20] The feeble nature of the Christian's voice is due to its being a quoting voice, as a result of which Christianity has stopped reinventing itself. The Christian accepts the two testaments without realizing that they are only a preparation, an introductory step to a third: his own, individual testament.

This passivity displayed by the Christian might be expressed in terms of psychoanalytic therapy. Cavell understands each of our (serious?) engagements with texts to be a case of submitting ourselves to analysis. Whereas there are commonly acknowledged analogies between interpreting texts and interpreting symptoms, and whereas psychoanalytic theory provides us with a set of themes directly applicable to our readings of texts, Cavell focuses on a perhaps less obvious sense of an analogy between reading and being in therapy. In Cavell's account, to read means first to expose oneself to reading by another: we cannot read without renouncing, at least in part, the full measure of control, without exposing ourselves to the text. In this sense, even before we begin consciously analyzing the text, it reads, analyzes us: it reads our vulnerabilities, it interprets our ability to respond to some parts of it better than to others, to recognize ourselves in parts of it and not in others. It is in this sense that Cavell speaks of finding ourselves understood, known by the text, conducive to our recognizing ourselves in it. When speaking, in "The Avoidance of Love," about the situation of a theatergoer and about theatricality in our own lives, Cavell makes clear that we cannot dispense with this situation of primordial passivity: it gives us time, an opportunity for temporary abdication (one Lear fails to make use of), "of putting oneself aside for long enough, to see through to her and to be seen through."[21] This time of exposure (to the analyst's gaze, to a text, to a theater play) is also a time of abdication: it shelters us from the more fundamental exposure to the world.

It thus bears with it the risk of relinquishing our own voices forever, of becoming hostage to the message of the text. It is as if the character of the Christian appearing in Cavell's *The Claim of Reason* represents the analysand who succumbed to this kind of seduction, whose therapy, far from being complete, stagnated in the phase of identification with the analyst. The envisaged final stage of psychoanalysis is, after all, to overcome, eventually, this initial identification with the person of the analyst. Analogously, reading understood in terms of psychoanalysis (of being analyzed by the text) has as its goal freedom from the person of the author, hence of recovering one's own text.[22]

What is it that is "right," as Cavell puts it, in the Christian's words? If there is something right about them, it must be in the sense in which they are fundamentally Romantic, in their sense of a loss of intimacy and the search to regain it, taking upon themselves the "task of bringing the world back, as to life."[23] The defining words of Christianity—*redemption, incarnation, resurrection*—are expressive of this task and, for Cavell, of our part in it. "If Cordelia resembles Christ, it is by having become fully human, by knowing her separateness, by knowing the deafness of miracles, by accepting the unacceptability of her love, and by nevertheless maintaining her love and the whole knowledge it brings. One can say she 'redeems nature' . . . but this means nothing miraculous."[24] In *Cities of Words*, when analyzing Rohmer's film *A Tale of Winter* Cavell identifies the true discovery of Christianity with Felicie's choice of "a way of life that is not incompatible with Charles' return"—but such an option is perhaps only available in the genre Cavell calls "a comedy of remarriage." Cavell's saying that the words of the Christian are nonetheless the right words may mean that their truth can be recovered from religion while abandoning religion, or it can mean that religion itself could give this truth to itself otherwise. (I imagine the latter to fit into a Spinozist image of reality, in which one cannot but express God in developing one's own individuality).

Yet for the most part this active force is concealed (hence separated from its active nature) by the all-encompassing rhetoric of "human suffering," that is, the rhetoric of passivity: "all appeals to gods are distractions or excuses, because the imagination uses them to wish for complete, for final solutions, when what is needed is at hand, or nowhere."[25] Cavell, in referring to the "enfeebling" way in which the "right" words of religion are meant, exposes (a certain image of) Christianity as a reactive force that is turning on itself, that does not interact with other forces but dominates them by projecting onto them the demand that they renounce their own power. Religion so understood (i.e., as a reactive rather than an active force) demands or at least condones the sacrifice of the autonomy, however finite, of human action, and, Cavell notes, opens in the alibis it produces innumerable ways to cruelty. (Cavell's example of such "radical implication of good in evil" comes from the scene on the heath in *King Lear* in which Gloucester's son, Edgar, prolongs his father's suffering by avoiding recognition, even though he no longer has a reason to hide.[26]) The quest for the unlimited transformation, emancipation, and metamorphosis proper to the human being seems to be difficult to rhyme with the religious requirement of disowning the self.[27]

Religion finds itself in a tension between, on the one hand, its quietist impulse—the requisite sacrifice and renunciation of power,[28] and, on the other, the possibility of resurrection with the force of the religious, the empowerment inherent in "meaning every word one says." Doubtless, this empowerment bears a risk that the religion recovered in this way will perhaps no longer be recognizable as such.

Cavell continues his remark on Emerson's "hectoring his fellows to stop quoting . . . ; to . . . have signatures": "Ghosts have none [i.e., have no signatures]. . . . Moments of adolescence feel so; this is another way of seeing why Emerson's addressee . . . is essentially a youth." Having a signature does not require having new words at one's disposal. Rather, it is a matter of willingness to inherit the old words: "old words brought to a new world,"[29] of recognizing and responding to the disturbing force of having put the new world into old words (analogous to new wine put in old battles). Cavell's project may be read as directed at reactivating those words, returning to those old words their force, which has been alienated by the rhetoric of passivity—the purpose is to recover, hence to re-empower them. The words regain their power by acknowledging the (active) force driving the self that is pronouncing them.

This is Cavell's diagnosis: on the one hand, Christianity is feeble; on the other, philosophy is in need of therapy. In this reading, the wound remains the main motif. In the psychoanalytical register, trauma is a wound that makes the "wax of consciousness" harden[30]—or, in Cavellian terms, turns imagination into stone. This is what threatens my

existence, my integrity, wounded by the departure of God. Receptivity toward new excita-
tions is impaired; the symptoms of the wound keep returning. And the petrified imagination can only repeat, reenact its trauma: it produces petrified images. In Cavell's account
of Othello, this is what is really at stake in this play: Othello does not just figuratively see
Desdemona's body as having the smoothness of alabaster. The figure expresses a hidden
wish that Othello makes come true at the end of the play—to turn his other into stone.
In this Othello reveals himself to be "an idolater." If idolatry is a sign of petrified imagination, then God departed even earlier than Nietzsche thought, in the Old Testament, at
least. Perhaps not only the golden calf but also the stone tablets mark the moment when
religion, in the face of the absence of God, got confused with idolatry.

Othello's act of turning Desdemona to stone, which, according to Cavell, must hide
the fact that he has wounded her (in taking her virginity), hence that she is like him,
implicated in finitude, reenacts the trauma of the biblical Ham (and of Beckett's Hamm),
who cannot bear that he saw his father naked: compulsive reenactment of the event,
repetition of symptoms. So we see in Shakespeare our untreated wound reenact itself in
our world. But Shakespeare's world also reenacts itself in philosophy. When Cavell speaks
of religion as giving us "truth in foul disguise" in the sense that this truth involves a
sacrifice of power, he makes this sacrifice coextensive with the philosophical desire that
the truth be independent of us. We are used to requiring that truth be something that
appears "without my intervention, apart from my agreements." In the end, in philosophy
as in Christianity, "I must disappear in order for the search for myself to be successful."[31]

Now we can sense the way in which Cavell says that, from a certain point on, "the
other bears the weight of God": he bears the weight of God, not his attributes. He bears
God who is so feeble that he has to be carried, the incarnated God. He bears, in other
words, my projecting on him what the departure of God has done to me.

Yet the wound is not only that which must be accounted for, analyzed. More than an
object of therapy, it is for Cavell also that from which we speak. In an as yet unpublished
essay, he identifies a certain wound with what gives authority to prophetic writing: "the
object [of this kind of writing] is not simply to touch but to announce the wound that
has elicited its expression and that gives it authority."[32] It is what we address ourselves to
in speaking, what we silently affirm: like the origin of the law. The wound is not only a
visible sign of a catastrophe from which we are in the process of recovering; it is also a
source of authority.

Cavell hints in this essay at an analogy between Nietzsche's reaction to his discovery
of the death of God and the reaction of one of J. M. Coetzee's characters, Elizabeth
Costello, to her discovery of the suffering humans inflict on animals. In the two lectures
published as *The Lives of Animals*,[33] Costello expresses her horror at the cruelty of the
animal food industry by comparing this cruelty to the Holocaust. Cavell draws an analogy
between Costello and Nietzsche:

One of the moments in Heidegger's *What Is Called Thinking?* that I have been most impressed by is his description of Nietzsche, in trying to reach his contemporaries with his perception of the event of our murder of God. Heidegger writes: "most quiet and shiest of men, . . . [Nietzsche] endured the agony of having to scream." I find it illuminating to think of Elizabeth Costello, in her exhausted way, as screaming.[34]

This might be said to be a wild analogy, at least as wild as Costello's own between the food industry and the Holocaust, which sparks a charge of blasphemy directed at her. But while admitting the lack of proportion, Cavell denies that proportion should be our main concern here. Among other issues, Cavell's essay addresses Costello's touch of madness, symbolized by her self-perception as a wounded animal. Costello's confession, by way of Kafka, of a wound that she conceals under her clothes reveals her horror at slaughtering animals to be grounded in her realization of the fact of the repression of our animal nature, hence her seeing eating animals as a form of cannibalism.

It is again the motif of the wound that interests me here, as indicative of a possible analogy between the departure of God and the repression of our animal nature. Cavell recounts that Costello, in describing herself as a wounded animal, draws another analogy, between herself and the wounded ape in Kafka's tale "Address to an Academy." This analogy immediately points to another one, which is left implicit. "Address to an Academy," one of the stories published during Kafka's lifetime, appeared in the same collection as "Before the Law," Kafka's parable of the human search for the origins of the moral law. I believe this story to be vital to a proper understanding of Elizabeth Costello and what is really at stake in her sense of being a wounded animal. That this is so becomes clear when we remember that the concluding item in Coetzee's "eight lessons" consists in a rereading of "Before the Law." In what follows I would like to point out a number of analogies between these two stories, analogies between what we might see as two kinds of opening: the wound and the gate of the law.

"Address to an Academy" is the story of an emancipated ape. Humanity inflicted a wound on this animal, as is so often the case. But this particular case is exceptional: the wound transformed this animal into a human, not exactly into a human being perhaps but into a hybrid specimen, a humanized ape. In the story, the wound functions as both a means of emancipation and a principle of exclusion. It is as a result of the wound that only with difficulty can the humanized ape endure the company of non- or half-emancipated creatures. "By day I cannot bear to see her; for she has the insane look of the bewildered half-broken animal in her eye; no one else sees it, but I do, and I cannot bear it."[35] The wound heals, leaving merely a scar, an ever diminishing "opening" that links the ape to its past. After a while, only a draft still comes through the door through which the ape walked from its freedom into humanity:

> In revenge, however, my memory of the past has closed the door against me more and more. I could have returned at first . . . through an archway as wide as the span

of heaven over the earth, but as I spurred myself on in my forced career, the opening narrowed and shrank behind me; I felt more comfortable in the world of men and fitted it better; the strong wind that blew after me out of my past began to slacken; today it is only a gentle puff of air that plays around my heels; and the opening in the distance, through which it comes and through which I once came myself, has grown so small that, even if my strength and my willpower sufficed to get me back to it, I should have to scrape the very skin from my body to crawl through.

"I should have to scrape the very skin from my body to crawl through"—which is to say, I should have to reopen the wound.

In Kafka's story "Before the Law," a man who seeks the law chooses to spend his life waiting in front of its gate. The door is shut at the end of his life, with the explanation that this was a unique door meant for him alone. Is the gate traversed by the ape on its way to humanity the same opening before which the man from "Before the Law" is waiting, the ever-deferred source of the law? In both cases, we face in it the threshold of a separation (between man and god, between man and animal). Kafka certainly describes it in the same way. In both cases, the description of the wound/door, whether of the law or of the past, suggests the genital zone, hinting at the origin of the law in sexual repression.[36] The door tends to be remarkably low in both stories, for example—in "Before the Law" the man from the country has to stoop to look through it, suggesting, as Derrida puts it, "a turning away in an upward movement." Those hints at sexual repression in the description of the source of the law are not surprising; we know that Kafka was a reader of Freud. In both stories, the origin of the law seems to have something in common with the Freudian version of morality as "the turning away from impurity."[37] But the "turning away from impurity" is for Cavell only a specific case of a more general "turning away." The motif of sexual repression appears in Cavell's reading of Othello[38]—but there it is just one of the symptoms demonstrating that Othello is not able to bear his finitude, hence his separation, be it from God or from another human being. Othello's and Desdemona's "differences from one another—the one everything the other is not—form an emblem of human separation, which can be accepted, and granted, or not. Like the separation from God; everything we are not."[39] If prophetic writing "announce[s] the wound that has elicited its expression and that gives it authority,"[40] and the wound is a mark of separation (from human, animal and divine)—the very separation that lends authority to prophetic writing. We write out of our separation.

According to Cavell, there is madness in Costello's comparison between death inflicted on humans and death inflicted on animals. Hence there is perhaps madness in a comparison between screaming at the death of God and screaming at killing animals, in view of the realization of the repression of our animal nature. But the madness does not disqualify Costello's words. It reflects the "tickling at the heels" caused by the "gentle puff of air"—the scar of the separation that makes us human.[41]

Kafka's ape notes that the wound has become smaller, yet it has not healed. Which is to say that the gate to the past can no longer be retraversed but nevertheless keeps haunting the animal. The ape is noted to keep displaying the wound in order to prove that it is perfectly healed: "I read an article recently . . . saying: my ape nature is not yet quite under control; the proof being that when visitors come to see me, I have a predilection for taking down my trousers to show them where the shot went in." But the ape also keeps reenacting the wound, projecting its disavowed pain on its environment: "The hand which wrote that should have its fingers shot away one by one." Can we conceive another reaction to the wound, other than reenacting it? It seems to me that, in Cavell's reading, Nietzsche and Coetzee's Costello display their wounds in different ways (Cavell speaks of their bearing the "stigmata of suffering.") He recalls Nietzsche screaming at the departure of God and Costello screaming at the destruction of animals. Theirs "is a voice invoking a religious, not alone a philosophical, register. . . . We could say that the object of the revelation is not simply to touch but to announce the wound that has elicited its expression and that gives its authority."[42] Cavell notes that "Heidegger . . . acknowledges no such wound for him to confess (for him), nor any pain out of which to scream, and it is perhaps in this continence, or absence, that he is cursed."[43] Heidegger, in this reading, appears to have disavowed the constitutive separation from which he speaks, to have hidden it under the appearances of a perfectly healed wound; in other words, he leaves it unacknowledged, projecting its trauma on his world. What does it mean to be cursed in a non-Christian world? What does it mean, on the contrary, to share Costello's desire "to save [her] soul" in the same world? In a non-Christian world in which prophets confuse their identities with that of God, deriving their authority, hence their claim to community, not from the display of a perfectly healed scar but from the confession of their wound, of their separation from God? It is in view of that wound, in front of its gate, that we seek salvation—or are cursed.

Cavell's essay that I have been discussing bears the title "Companionable Thinking." It is a paper about sharing bread: sharing bread as a principle of community (we share it with animals, so we should not kill them); sharing bread as a principle of exclusion (we refuse to share bread with perpetrators of atrocities); sharing bread, hence, as speaking (i.e., sharing a language, our everyday bread). It is an essay on the universal shareability, hence woundedness, of our language. In this reading, our language is an archive of trauma, the archive of the collective unconscious, in which the event of the death of God is recorded. Our language bears witness to wounds in being itself wounded, for example, in the sense that it permits the wildest analogies: between slaughtering Jews and slaughtering cattle; between the death of God and a wounded ape. It is because of its wounds that language requires our constant attention, constant contending with words. My self-knowledge cannot be expressed otherwise than in this wounded language.

The repressed is not something that can be seen as it is. It can be approached from the position of the ape, paradoxically, by departing from it, with the opening that then haunts one from behind one's back, or from the position of the man seeking the law. What is revealed will be different in both cases. What the humanized ape ignores, turns its back on, shows no immediate resemblance to what Kafka's man seeking the law sees in facing it and trying to peek inside. Neither the man nor the ape sees it, each for different reasons. It is from within this knowledge that Cavell inherits Christianity, while traveling, like Coleridge's Ancient Mariner, between the poles of those two points of view: between confessions and denials, departures and returns, just as he moves between owning one's words and being abandoned to them. What one means can only be expressed in a shared language, which presupposes a movement of repeated abdications of and returns to power; a movement between "being silent, stopping and seeing," and then taking charge of things again.

A Deconstruction of Monotheism

Jean-Luc Nancy

Then there is the persisting legacy of monotheism itself, the Abrahamic religions, as Louis Massignon aptly called them. Beginning with Judaism and Christianity, each is a successor haunted by what came before; for Muslims, Islam fulfills and ends the line of prophecy. There is still no decent history or demystification of the many-sided contest among these three followers—not one of them by any means a monolithic, unified camp—of the most jealous of all gods, even though the bloody modern convergence on Palestine furnishes a rich secular instance of what has been so tragically irreconcilable about them.

Not surprisingly, then, Muslims and Christians speak readily of crusades and jihads, both of them eliding the Judaic presence with often sublime insouciance. Such an agenda, says Eqbal Ahmad, is "very reassuring to the men and women who are stranded in the middle of the ford, between the deep waters of tradition and modernity."

But we are all swimming in those waters, Westerners and Muslims and others alike. And since the waters are part of the ocean of history, trying to plow or divide them with barriers is futile.

—Edward Said, "The Clash of Ignorance"[1]

The West can no longer be called the West on the basis of the movement through which it saw extended to the entire world the form of what might have appeared, up until recently, as its specific profile. This form contains both techno-science and the general determinations of democracy and law, as well as a certain type of discourse and modes of argument, accompanied by a certain type of representation—understood in a broad sense of the term (e.g., that of the cinema and the entirety of post-rock and post-pop music). In this way, the West no longer acknowledges itself as holding a vision for the world, or a sense of the world that might accompany this globalization (*its* globalization), with the privileged role it believed it could attach to what it had called its "humanism." Globalization appears, on the contrary, to be reduced, in

380

its essentials, to what Marx had already discerned as the production of the world market, and the sense of this world appears to consist merely in the accumulation and circulation of capital, accompanied by a clear aggravation in the gap between the dominating wealthy and the dominated poor, as well as by an indefinite technical expansion that no longer provides itself—except very modestly, and with disquiet or anguish—the finalities of "progress" and the improvement of the human condition. Humanism opens onto inhumanity: such may well be the brutal summary of the situation. And the West does not understand how it managed to come to this. Nevertheless, the West has indeed come to this: it is the civilization constructed initially around the Mediterranean by the Greeks, the Romans, the Jews, and the Arabs that has borne this fruit. To that degree, then, it cannot suffice to search elsewhere for other forms or values that one might attempt to graft onto this henceforth global body. There is no elsewhere left, or indeed, and in any case, there can no longer be an elsewhere in the old Western sense of the term (like the elsewhere of an Orient refracted through the prism of orientalism or the elsewhere of worlds represented as living in the "primary" immanence of myths and rites).

Our time is thus one in which it is urgent that the West—or what remains of it—analyze its own becoming, turn back to examine its provenance and its trajectory, and question itself concerning the process of decomposition of sense to which it has given rise.

Now, it is striking to note that, inside the West thus described, we quite often interrogate, with a view to reevaluating, the philosophy of the Enlightenment (along the model of a continuous progression of human reason) or the will to power of the triumphant industrial nineteenth century—or again, if differently, the diremptions internal [*déhiscences internes*] to the West (the Slavic and Orthodox world as well as the Arabic and Islamic ones) with their complexities and their lost opportunities—we rarely interrogate the body of thought that, as I see it, organized, first in a gestatory or guiding way, if not the West itself, then at least its condition of possibility: monotheism.

We know—how could we ignore this?—that the threefold monotheism of a threefold "religion of the Book" (with which one could associate ancient Manichaeism, as well) defines a Mediterraneo-European particularity and, from there, diverse forms of global expansion by at least the two junior branches, Christianity and Islam. Yet we consider, perhaps too frequently and too simplistically, that the religious dimension (or what we believe, perhaps wrongly, to be simply "religious") behaves like an accident in relation to the facts and structures of civilization. Or, more precisely, this dimension appears as extrinsic, from the moment that it no longer visibly gives, to the globalized West, its face or profile—even though that globalization is also, as I understand it, in more than one respect a globalization of monotheism in one or another of its forms.

Ultimately, if the capitalist and technological economy constitutes the general form of value or sense today, that is by way of the worldwide reign of a monetary law of exchange (or general equivalency) or the indefinite production of surplus value within the order of this equivalency—a value whose evaluation remains impossible except in terms of equivalency and indeterminate growth. Yet this monovalence of value, or this one-way [*sens unique*] circulation of sense hardly behaves otherwise than as the apparently nonreligious transcription of the monoculture whose monotheistic conception it carried: explicitly, the culture of Rome in its European and modern expansion, from Baghdad and Teheran to London and Los Angeles. The mystery of this history is tied to nothing other than the character—simultaneously absolute and invisible, incalculable, indeterminable, and universal—of the value or unidirectionality [*sens unique*] that is placed now in "God," now in "man," and now in the tautology of "value" itself.

Perhaps it is impossible to take a further step in understanding and transforming our history without extending the interrogation into the heart of this structure of monovalence.

. . .

Since the unfolding of modern rationality and its most recent modalities, all of which were at least implicitly atheist in the sense of being indifferent to the question of "God" (whether it was a matter of knowledge or law, aesthetics or ethics), it might seem useless to refer to monotheism otherwise than in a secondary mode, a mode set in second place, either because it referred to the sphere of "private" convictions, or by virtue of a merely historical perspective.

And yet we know—or ought to know, but with a knowledge that is active, mobilizing, and "deconstructive" in a sense that I will attempt to state—to what degree the most salient features of the modern apprehension of the world, and sometimes its most visibly atheist, atheistic, or atheological traits, can and must be analyzed in their strictly and fundamentally monotheist provenance (thus, to put it rapidly, the universal, law, the individual; but also, in a more subtle manner, the motif of an infinite transcendence surpassing man, and within man). Now, "provenance," here as elsewhere, is never simply a past; it informs the present, produces new effects therein without ceasing to have its own effects. It is therefore, no doubt, important to know how monotheism, while reproducing itself elsewhere or surviving itself (and sometimes radicalizing itself) in religious figures, is the provenance of the West qua a globalization over which something entirely different than a divine providence seems to hover, namely, the somber wing of nihilism.

I will call "deconstruction of monotheism" the operation consisting in disassembling the elements that constitute it, in order to attempt to discern, among these elements and as if behind them, behind and set back from the construction, that which made their assembly possible and which, perhaps, it still remains, paradoxically, for us to discover and to think as the beyond of monotheism, in that it has become globalized and atheized.

. . .

It goes without saying that a program such as this could not be the object of a single talk. So I will immediately narrow the scope of this essay. I will do so in two ways.

First, I will offer a very brief and summary remark on a point that should be developed separately: in speaking of monotheism, I include from the outset the Greco-Roman heritage, understood in its composite character, a heritage both philosophical and state-juridical. Judeo-Christianity would not have been possible if, in the Hellenistic age, a close symbiosis had not come about between Greco-Roman consciousness and the monotheistic disposition. The first of these could be characterized both as consciousness of a logico-techno-juridical universality *and* as the separation between this consciousness and the sphere of some "salvation" (understood as a healing, a delivery from the evil or pain of the world), conceived as a solely internal or private concern. The second—that is, the monotheistic disposition—would be distinguished not by virtue of a single God in the place of many but by the fact that divine unicity is the correlate of a presence that can no longer be given in this world, but rather must be sought beyond it (the presence in this world being that of the "idol," the rejection of which is no doubt the great, generating, and federating motif of the threefold Abrahamic traditions). Between these two providences, the hyphen [between "Judeo" and "Christianity"] represents, in this hypothesis, the very possibility of expressing "god" in the singular, in Plato as much as among the Hebrews, however considerable the differences between those two singulars.

Second, I will limit my analyses here to the form of monotheism that became its most European form—and thus, starting from there, the form that most often accompanied the Westernization of the world, at least up until the middle of the twentieth century—that is, I will limit the analysis to the form that is Christianity. It is also the form of which I am the least incapable of speaking, since it is that of my culture as a Frenchman and a European (which implies, moreover, also a certain distance relative to Orthodox Christianity). But I will do this only on two conditions, which I emphasize as follows:

1. First, we must hold in abeyance, pending the continuation of the work of deconstruction, the other major forms: Judaism and Islam. This is not so much to pass along the same analytic operation from one form to another as to keep in sight the constant interaction in monotheism of its triple determination or of the plural singular that constitutes it. We must therefore also, later on, elsewhere, deconstruct this interaction itself, understand what in the West belongs to the movement by which monotheism has redefined itself at least three times, redefined, taken up, or regrasped and displaced or transformed itself. This too constitutes our provenance: the association and disassociation, the accord and the disaccord [*la mêlée et le démêlé*] of the Jew, the Christian, and the Muslim.

2. Thereafter, in following the red thread of Christianity, we must take care not to leave in the shadows that which in so many ways ties it together with Judaism and Islam—whether these ways are those of correspondence, of contrast, or of conflict: for that too belongs at once to Christianity itself and to that which, along the Christian vector,

shaped the Westernization of monotheism and consequently also its profoundly complex and ambiguous globalization.

. . .

I will thus attempt an initial sketch of a "deconstruction of Christianity." First, let me say that what is important is not the Christian marks, so numerous and so visible, that the West bears, and for which the cross is an abbreviation. What is important is, on the contrary, that Christianity is present even where—and perhaps especially where—it is no longer possible to recognize it. The sign of the cross may well decorate sites or practices wholly drained of their Christianity, and that, as we know, has been going on for a long time. Yet a certain conception of "human rights," as well as a certain determination of the relationship between politics and religion, comes straight out of Christianity.

It is thus important to discern in what sense the West is Christian in its depths; in what sense Christianity is Western as if through destiny or by destination, and in what sense, through this Christian occidentality, an essential dimension of monotheism in its integrality is set into play. It is important to think this, insofar as the Westernized world—or again, the globalized West—is experienced as deprived of sense—of sense or value, if we want to highlight the fact that it has replaced all values with the general equivalence that Marx designated as that of "merchandise." In a certain respect, in effect, and at the price of a brutal simplification that nonetheless touches upon an essential issue, the question takes this form: What connects monotheism and the monovalence of the "general equivalency"? What secret, ambivalent resource lies hidden within the organizing scheme of this *mono-*?

In attempting to respond to this question—but of course to do so we shall have to complicate greatly the rough form I have just given it—we may hope to obtain at least three results:

1. First, to be done once and for all with the unilateral schema of a certain rationalism, according to which the modern West was formed by wresting itself away from Christianity and from its own obscurantism (curiously, Heidegger repeated, in his way, something of this schema), for it is a matter of grasping how monotheism in general and Christianity in particular also engendered the West;

2. But we must also cease all our efforts to "cure" the "ills" of the present-day world (in its privation of sense) by some return to Christianity in particular, or to religion in general, for it is a matter of grasping how we are already outside of the religious;

3. And thus, we must ask ourselves anew what it is that, without denying Christianity but without returning to it, could lead us toward a point—toward a resource—hidden beneath Christianity, beneath monotheism, and beneath the West, which we must henceforth bring to light, for this point would open upon a future for the world that would no

longer be either Christian or anti-Christian, either monotheist or atheist or even polytheist, but that would advance precisely beyond all these categories (after having made all of them possible).

I will call a "deconstruction of monotheism" that inquiry or search consisting in disassembling and analyzing the constitutive elements of monotheism, and more directly of Christianity, thus of the West, in order to go back to (or to advance toward) a resource that could form at once the buried origin and the imperceptible future of the world that calls itself "modern." After all, "modern" signifies a world always awaiting its truth of, and as, world [*sa vérité de monde*], a world whose proper sense is not given, is not available, is, rather, in project or in promise, and perhaps beyond: a sense that consists in not being given, but only in being promised. Now, is this not a characteristic of Christianity and monotheism in general: the contract or the alliance of the promise, the commitment that commits before all else to be committed to it? In Christianity, the promise is at once already realized and yet to come. (But is this not a theme that runs through all the monotheisms?) Is such a paradoxical space not that in which the presence of sense is at once assured, acquired, *and* always withheld, absented in its very presence?

A world whose sense is given in the mode of not being given—not yet, and, in a certain respect, never—is a world in which "sense" itself defies all received and receivable sense. Could this challenge be the one that monotheism has cast us, and that a deconstruction of monotheism would have to take up?

· · ·

In engaging in a "deconstruction of Christianity," in the sense I have specified, we find first this, which must remain at the center of every subsequent analysis and represent the active principle in and for every deconstruction of monotheism: Christianity is by itself and in itself a deconstruction and a self-deconstruction. In this trait, Christianity represents at once the most Westernized form of monotheism—most Westernized and/or most Westernizing, as it were—and a scheme that we shall have to learn to put into play for the entirety of the threefold monotheism. In other words, Christianity indicates, in the most active way—and the most ruinous for itself, the most nihilist in certain regards— how monotheism shelters within itself—better: more intimately within itself than itself, within or without itself—the principle of a world without God.

Today, for this brief talk, I would like only to indicate in summary fashion the principle traces of the self-deconstructive character of Christianity. I will distinguish five traits.

1. The first is a characteristic inscribed in the very principle of monotheism, a characteristic developed most paradoxically within Christianity, yet also exposed in the relations among the three religions of the Book, in their tense and divided proximity. I would state

it thus: monotheism is in truth atheism. In effect, its difference from "polytheisms" is not due to the number of gods. In fact, the plurality of gods corresponds to their effective presence (in nature, in an image, in a mind possessed), and their effective presence corresponds to relations of power, of threat, or of assistance, which religion organizes through the entirety of its myths and its rites. The unicity of god, on the contrary, signifies the withdrawal of this god away from presence and also away from power thus understood. If the God of Israel is an All-Powerful God (a quality he bequeaths to his successors), this is not in the sense of an active power within a differential relation of powers: his "all"-powerfulness signifies that he alone disposes of this power, entirely according to his will, that he can just as well retract it or pull away from it, and that he is, above all, alone in being able to make a covenant with man. Thus, he expects no sacrifices destined to capture the benevolence of his power, but only unconditional faithfulness to his covenant—a faithfulness to none other than the "jealous" election by which he has chosen his people, or his followers, or man as such.

With the figure of Christ comes the renunciation of divine power and presence, such that this renunciation becomes the proper act of God, which makes this act into God's becoming-man. In this sense, the god withdrawn, the god "emptied out," in Paul's words, is not a hidden god at the depths of the withdrawal or the void (a *deus absconditus*): the site to which he has withdrawn has neither depths nor hiding places. He is a god whose absence in itself creates divinity, or a god whose void-of-divinity is the truth, properly speaking. (One might think of Eckhart's phrase: "I pray to God that he make me free of God," or again of Harawi imitating Hallaj: "No one really bears witness to the one God 'that he is one.'"[2]) In its principle, monotheism undoes theism, that is to say, the presence of the power that assembles the world and assures this sense. It thus renders absolutely problematic the name *god*—it renders it nonsignifying—and above all, it withdraws all power of assurance from it. Christian assurance can take place only at the cost of a category completely opposed to that of religious beliefs: the category of "faith," which is faithfulness to an absence and a certainty of this faithfulness in the absence of all assurance. In this sense, the atheist who firmly refuses all consoling or redemptive assurance is paradoxically or strangely closer to faith than the "believer." But that means also that the atheism that henceforth determines the Western structure, which is inherent in its mode of knowing and existing, is itself Christianity realized. (This does not mean that things cannot modulate themselves very differently among the diverse Christianities: for example, that of Latin America is not at all, in this respect, in the same posture as that of North America and that of Europe. But the fundamental stakes are nonetheless the same.)

2. A second self-deconstructive trait flows from the preceding: demythologization. In a trajectory that singularly contrasts those of all the other world religions (we must except Buddhism here, which is not exactly a religion and which, for this very reason, has more than one trait in common with monotheism), the threefold monotheism and in it, more specifically, Christianity has a self-interpretative history in which it understands

itself in a way that is less and less religious in the sense in which religion implies a mythology (a narrative, a representation of divine actions and persons). It translates itself in terms that are no longer those of a foundational and exemplary narrative (Genesis, Moses, Jesus, his Resurrection, etc.), but in terms of a symbolics deciphered within the human condition (human reason, the human being's freedom, dignity, relation to the other . . .). Christianity tends to erase every distinctive religious sign and all sacrality for the benefit of what Kant called a "religion within the limits of reason alone," or again, of what Feuerbach proclaimed in saying that "belief in God *is man's belief in the infinity and the truth of his own essence.*"[3] Henceforth, the democratic ethic of the rights of man and of solidarity—along with the question of the ends to give to that "humanism," or the question of the conquest by man of his own destination or destiny—constitutes, in sum, the durable sediment of Christianity.

3. Christianity presents itself historically and doctrinally as a composition. That is to say, it presents itself not only as a body of narrative and a message (although it does set forth a "good news" proclaimed through an exemplary narrative) but as a complex elaboration, starting with a provenance in and a detachment from Judaism, but also in and from Greek or Greco-Roman philosophy, as much in ontology as in politics. Elsewhere, Christianity also defines itself through a no less complex relationship to Islam, which it rejects while recognizing its co-belonging to and in the Abrahamic faith—and at the same time its role in the history of philosophico-theological thought. In itself, this proclaimed historical complexity—declared, in particular, through various problematics concerning the relationships between "faith" and "knowledge," or between "revelation" and "reason"—already carries the sense of a regime distinct from the regime of a religion *stricto sensu*: as though that regime carried in itself the permanent possibility of dividing or self-interpreting in two distinct registers.

Moreover, the theoretical or dogmatic Christian construction is that of a way of thinking whose center is "the word of God made flesh." Thus, the dogma of incarnation mobilizes the ideas of "nature" or "essence," and of "hypostasis" or "sensuous presentation" in order to establish that the person of Jesus is identically that of a man and that of God in a single manifestation. To be sure, the heart of this dogma is declared "a mystery." But the mystery does not have the characteristics of a myth: it addresses itself to the mind of man; it asks him to consider what (without his being able to understand it) brings light to that mind and about it (that is, once again, concerning an infinite destiny and destination of man). The point of incarnation is obviously the point of an absolute separation from Judaism and Islam. But it is not without value to observe that this point of discord is also that at which, in the first place, the whole question central to monotheism is debated (i.e., What is the covenant or alliance between God and man?), thus the point of the self-ex-plication (i.e., of the unfolding in itself with itself) of monotheism, and the point at which, in the second place, each monotheism can and must find again, in the others, something of itself (e.g., the resurrection, corollary of the incarnation, which be-longs also to Islam, whereas the pardon of sins, another corollary, comes from Judaism, and whereas, in addition, the incarnation does not in fact abolish the indivisible absolute-ness of the Judeo-Islamic god . . .). This divided unity of self, characteristic of monothe-ism most properly, and thus also most paradoxically, makes up the unity of the unique god. We could say, including all possible resonances, that this god divides himself—even atheizes himself—*at the intersection of monotheism and/or the monotheisms . . .*

4. Given these conditions, Christianity is less a body of doctrine than a *subject* in relationship to itself in the midst of a search for self, within a disquietude, an awaiting or a desire for its proper identity (we have only to think of the major theme of the annuncia-tion and the expectation, recurrent in the three monotheisms, unfolded paradoxically within Christianity as hope for the event as advent. This is why, just as Christianity thinks a god in three persons whose divinity consists in the relationship to self, so it divides itself historically into three at least (a division of the community which must at the end be reassembled), and so too it presents the logic of the threefold monotheism as a subject divided in itself (i.e., religion of the Father, religion of the Son, religion of the Holy in the Islamic sense).

The relation to self defines the subject. The structure of the subject appears like the caesura between the ancient world and the Christian occidental world. (We should pause here and consider its Greek provenance, its Augustinian, Avicennian, Cartesian, Hegelian elaborations, and consider the fact that this is the history of all the senses and all the figures of what has called itself "spirit.") This subject is the *self* qua instance of identity, certainty, and responsibility. However, the law of its structure entails that it cannot be given to self before being itself related to self: its relation to self—or "the self" in gen-eral—can only be infinite. Being infinite, it assumes, on the one hand, a temporal dimen-sion (where it sets about having a history, a past and a future as dimensions of sense and presence—though presence is not simply in the present), *and* in the last instance it can only escape itself. This escaping of self defines jointly, in this realm of thought, the life of the creator and the death of the creature. But in this way it is the one and the other, and the one in the other or through the other, who are affected by and with the in-finite in the sense of *finitude.*

5. Christianity (and through this prism, monotheism) has been engaged from its beginning in a perpetual process (i.e., a process *and* a litigation) of self-rectification and self-surpassing, most often in the form of self-retrospection in view of a return to a purer origin—a process that reaches up to Nietzsche and continues today, but that had begun already between the gospels and Paul, between Paul and James, in the origins of monastic orders, and, of course, in the various reforms, and so on. Everything takes place as though Christianity had developed like no other, *at once* a theologico-economico-political affir-mation of power, domination, and exploitation, for which Rome was the weighty symbol

as well as a part of the reality, *and* an inverted affirmation of the destitution and abandonment of self, whose vanishing point is the evaporation of self. The question must thus be
that of the nature and the structure of this evaporation of self: dialectical surpassing,
nihilistic decomposition, the opening of the ancient to the absolutely new . . . In one way
or another, what is in question is: how monotheism engenders itself as humanism, and
how humanism confronts the finitude that entered in this way into history.

. . .

Today I will remain with this briefest of characterizations. I draw no conclusions from it.
It seems to indicate a direction in thinking without which it is impossible to consider
seriously, henceforth, the question of the sense of the world such as the West has given it
to us as heritage—or as escheat.

If we hold ourselves to a schematized, essential observation, then this direction is at
least the following: our task is not to lead toward the fulfillment of a new divine realm,
neither in this world nor in another. Nor is it to rediscover the unity proper and immanent to a world of the myth that has decomposed in the Westernization-monotheization
of the world. Instead, it is to think a "sense-of-world" or a "world-sense" ["*sens-de-
monde*"] in a world divided in its own being-world, in an acosmic and atheological world,
which is still a "world" in some respect, still our world and that of the totality of beings,
thus still a totality of possible senses—it being understood that this possibility is always
also, in and of itself, exposed to the impossible.

Post-Scriptum (February 2002)

The preceding text is that of a talk given in Cairo in February 2001. One year later, that
is to say, one "9–11" later, the talk calls for more than one complement (without speaking
of the fact that in many respects my work on the subject has been displaced, has opened
new paths). If "9–11" made something clear, then it was this: the world is tearing itself
apart around an unbearable division of wealth and power. This division is insufferable
because it rests upon no acceptable hierarchy, neither of power, nor of wealth. A "hierarchy" signifies, etymologically, a sacred character of the principle or the commandment.
Now the world of techno-science, or the world that I have called "ecotechnics"—that is,
a natural environment entirely made up of the human replacement of a "nature" henceforth withdrawn—which is also the world of democracy, the universal rights of a human
being presumed to be universal, the world of secularism and religious tolerance both
aesthetic and moral, not only keeps us from founding in a sacred regime differences of
authority and legitimacy, it makes those disparities or inequalities that overtly violate its
principles of equality and justice seem intolerable.

What we call the scripting or instrumentation of religions, or indeed the deviation, the perversion, or the betrayal of one or another religion (including the national theism of the United States), in no way constitutes a sufficient explication. What is instrumentalized or betrayed gives, in itself, material for instrumentalization or perversion. This material is given, in a paradoxical but evident way, through the motif of the One: it is Unity, Unicity, and Universality that are evoked throughout in the global confrontation, or rather, in the world structured as a confrontation that is in no wise that of a "war of civilizations" (since Islam is also a part of the West, throughout its entire history, and this even if it is not exclusively such).

To the total mobilization (and it is no accident that I use a concept so recently fascist), proclaimed and telecommanded in the name of a single God whose transcendent unicity effectuates an absolute *hierarchization* (God, the paradise of the believers, the dust of all the rest—all the rest being composed also of a lot of dollars, missiles, and petroleum . . .), claims to respond to the total immobilization of the situation (world capital) in the name of a supposed universality for which the Universal is called "man," but who, in his obvious abstraction, immediately hands himself over to another God (*"in God we trust, bless America"*).

The one and the other God are two figures confronted with the identical Unique when its Unicity is grasped as absolute Presence, consistent in itself and with itself, like the punctual and thus invisible summit of a pyramid whose essence it resumes and absorbs. (We could say here, since I am extending remarks made in Cairo: the pyramids of the pharaohs did not draw their value from the null point of their summit, but from the secret of death and life buried deep in their mass. They drew their value from the profound withdrawal into a cryptic obscurity and not from the point of a presence erected as evidence.) And it is certainly permissible to say, without being "anti-American" (a ridiculous category) that this Unifying, Unitary, and Universal model, also Unidimensional, and finally Unilateral (which is its internal contradiction) has made possible the symmetrical and no less nihilistic mobilization of a monotheistic and no less unilateralist model. We tend to be on guard against this model only because it has become the ideological instrument of the "terrorism" we know too well. But "terrorism" is the conjunction of despair and a Unifying will that confronts the other face of the One.

Now, what is thus lost of the very essence of monotheism in all its forms is precisely that the "one" of the "god" is not at all Unicity qua substantial present and united with itself: on the contrary, the unicity and the unity of this "god" (or the divinity of this "one") consists precisely in that the One cannot be posited there, neither presented nor figured as united in itself. Whether it be in exile or in diaspora, whether it be in the becoming-man or in a threefold-being-in-itself, or whether it be in the infinite recoil of the one who has neither equal nor like (thus not even unity in any of its forms), this "god" (and in what sense is it divine? how is it divine? this is what we have to think through) absolutely excludes its own presentation—we would even have to say its own valorization as much as its own presencing.

This the great mystics, the great believers, the great "spiritualists" of all three monotheisms knew, and they knew it in repeated exchanges and confrontations with the philosophers, whom they faced, all the while being strangers to them. Their thoughts, which is to say their acts, their *ethos* or their *praxis*, still await us.

—Translated by Gabriel Malenfant

After Theism

H. J. Adriaanse

> God is a pure nought
> he knows no now or here
> The more you reach for him
> the more he eludes you.
>
> —Angelus Silesius

The Incredibility of Theism: Introduction

The conviction underlying the present essay is that theism in its traditional form has lost its credibility. Convictions, it is sometimes argued,
are the sort of things you have or you don't have. I think this is not
quite right; reasons can be brought forward even for convictions,
though these reasons cannot be considered as the premises from which
the conviction necessarily follows as a conclusion. I shall mention three
of the reasons for abandoning theism.

By theism in its traditional form, I understand something not very
different from what R. Swinburne understands by it in his book *The
Coherence of Theism*.[1] He defines it as the belief in God as "a person
without a body (i.e., a spirit) who is eternal, free, able to do everything,
knows everything, is perfectly good, is the proper object of human worship and obedience, the creator and sustainer of the universe."[2] The
phrasing differs slightly in various contexts in Swinburne's book, but
that is of no great importance to me. Besides, Swinburne suggests that
theism does not involve that each of these properties be ascribed to
God, or that no other properties be ascribed to God.[3] This point does
not matter either. Moreover, although Swinburne offers a very fundamental and detailed explanation of the properties under discussion, it
is not impossible to have a different opinion about the precise meaning
of this or that theistic predicate. Such differences about—as we say in

Dutch—"the decimal places" do not interest me either. What matters is the mode of belief that is characteristic of classical theism. On this point I would like to lay further emphasis on Swinburne's statements or at least to connect them to a piece of argumentation that he develops in quite another place. I have in mind chapter 6 of his book, in which he considers and dismisses the view that credal sentences—sentences that express the existence of a God with such and such properties—do not make claims but only express attitudes or commend ways of life. To him such sentences are or at least imply statements, that is, "claims about how things are."[4] In this chapter he appeals—unusually, if I am not mistaken, for his way of arguing[5]—to "the vast majority of normal users of religious language during the past two millennia" and what they "suppose to be implied by what they say." I am inclined to agree with Swinburne on this point. Theism in its traditional form not only ascribes a certain set of properties to God but in doing so claims also to contribute to human knowledge of "how things are." Doubtlessly theism has practical and affective aspects too, but this "cognitive" or "descriptive" aspect is not absorbed by them. According to Swinburne (if I understand him correctly), it is precisely this cognitive aspect that renders theism philosophically relevant. Here too I agree with him. And I would almost say that by its cognitive aspect theism is rendered scientifically relevant. For science investigates how things are. The age-long conflicts in Christian culture between scientists and the faith of the church indicate that theism has at least the tendency to compete with scientific or objective knowledge. But perhaps this last step goes too far. After all, theism is not prepared to carry out empirical research. In this respect there has been an important difference, at least for the last couple of centuries. But insofar as philosophy is concerned, theism indeed presumes to be directly relevant. By philosophy we must understand here a rational and criticizable discourse that consists mainly in assertions. The kind of belief that is constitutive of theism is a rational one: it is belief claiming to be true in a sense of "true" that makes the difference between true and false capable of being decided and intersubjectively stated. In a theistic sense, "I believe in God, Creator of heaven and earth" is different not qualitatively but only in degree from "I believe it is not going to rain this afternoon." Both utterances express adherence to a phrastic component that is accepted as true or false in the sense indicated above. In believing in God, one is either right or wrong, just as in forecasting future weather conditions. Belief in God is concerned with what is the case, even if the tools of scientific research are insufficient to settle the truth or falsity of what this belief alleges. For that reason, philosophy is the proper tribunal and/or ally.

The philosophical discussion of the credibility of theism can be carried out on various levels. I distinguish three of them: the levels of coherence, probability, and plausibility. My grounds for the conviction expressed at the outset will be spread over these three levels. Decisive in my eyes is judgment according to the criterion of plausibility. That is not to say, however, that the credibility of theism provokes no objections on the other levels. The contrary is the case. I shall argue, first, that the coherence of theism entails at least one more difficulty than Swinburne admits and, next, that the probability of it on inductive evidence is also more open to objections than Swinburne seems to think. I am well aware that, if my argument on the first point is successful, the issue would be settled for many a philosopher. If coherence cannot be stated, they might say, we have a case of incoherence, and whatever is incoherent does not deserve further discussion. Swinburne—again—can teach us that things are not as simple as that. But the middle course he opens up brings a considerable relativization of the importance of the coherence discussion. Questions concerning the credibility of theism can hardly be settled on formal, logical grounds. We are relegated—and this is my thesis—from that level to the long road of experience. But if we really take that road, we cannot leave out the differences in viewpoint and historical situation of various experiencing subjects. Here the distinction between probability and plausibility comes in. The first operates with statistical grounds, whereas the second leaves room for sociological and culture-historical considerations and even for common sense. But now to the point.

Coherence

As I have announced already, in discussing the coherence problem I will concentrate on Swinburne's great and rich book. A coherent statement, he says, is one that it makes sense to suppose true. To meet this criterion, it need not be true; "The moon is made of green cheese" is an example of a false yet coherent statement. An incoherent statement is one with regard to which this supposition does not make sense because "either it or some statement entailed by it is such that we cannot conceive of it being true." One of the examples Swinburne adduces here is "Honesty weighs ten pounds." This statement is incoherent because "honesty is not the sort of thing which it makes sense to suppose weighs ten pounds."[6] If one asks why this does not make sense, the answer obviously has to consist in an appeal to semantic and syntactical rules. These two kinds of rules are a matter of established and acknowledged use, but this use is not fixed once and for all: it is open to modification.

Important for our purpose is the kind of modification made up by the analogical use of words. Whereas the normal use is rooted in a firm albeit sometimes vague relation of a word W to a set of (empirically specifiable) standard examples, analogical use means a loosening of the rules to the effect "that to be W an object has only to resemble the standard objects more than objects which are standard cases of '*not-W*' objects, but need not resemble the former to the extent to which they resemble each other." This is the semantic modification; the concomitant syntactical modification says that the rules governing the relations of W to other words and enabling inferences such as $W \rightarrow Y$, $W \rightarrow Z$ and so on are loosened also, to the effect that "some inferences are no longer valid."[7] Thus, the analogical use of words presupposes their normal use. It should be distinguished carefully from univocal use, even if it involves terms that are applied to God and man alike. Of course, it cannot be denied that, for instance, wisdom as predicated of God amounts to something very different from wisdom as predicated of man, but that is merely a difference of degree. In both cases the same property is denoted; in the first case, too, the predicate "wise" "is being used in a perfectly ordinary sense."[8] With this view Swinburne turns against Thomas Aquinas, for whom all God talk is analogical, that is, neither univocal nor equivocal. According to Swinburne, analogical use is much rarer. Fortunately so, for analogy is used at the cost of informative content. "If theology uses too many words in analogical senses it will convey virtually nothing by what it says."[9]

Swinburne points out with a certain emphasis that his defense of the coherence of the theistic conception of God "has in no way relied on supposing that words are used in analogical senses."[10] Only once, in the final part of the book, concerning the coherence of the claim that the properties discussed previously belong necessarily to God, must he play "the analogical card."[11] Here my doubts begin. First, the analogical use relates here to the term *person* as a noun for a property of God. This term has been used all through the book. It seems very doubtful to me that on all preceding occasions it was completely devoid of analogicity. One could think here of a remark by A. Kenny about disembodied minds: "The minds we know are embodied minds."[12] To begin by calling a being without a body (i.e., a spirit) a person is to use from the outset the word *person* in an analogical sense. Second, the key concept *person* is the core of an entire constellation of terms, such as *animate being, thinks, actions, brings about.* All these other terms are affected by this recourse to analogy. Swinburne himself says, but without attaching any consequence to it: "Thereby we give all these words somewhat analogical senses."[13] In consequence, the corresponding concepts *spirit, free agent, omniscient,* and *creator* come into play, as well. Third, it is doubtful that this network of terms can be contained. Is not the concept of personhood so fundamental for theism that the analogical tincture pervades all discourse about God? If so, then we would have to agree with Aquinas against Swinburne. Now for the decisive point, however. Swinburne remarks, "Once we give analogical senses to words, proofs of coherence or incoherence become very difficult."[14] Here again I wholeheartedly agree with him (perhaps against Aquinas). But if these three doubts are appropriate, then for the domain of theistic theology this remark is even an understatement. In reality, the question of the coherence of theism loses its hold very soon.

Probability

I arrive at the second point, the inductive evidence for the existence of a God conceived of in a theistic way. For the discussion of this point I stick to Swinburne, who rightly establishes a connection between the preceding point and the present one.[15] *Exempli gratia,* I take the cosmological argument, which he develops in his book *The Existence of God.*[16] For the most part, I agree with the criticism of this argument expressed by J. L. Mackie.[17] I will limit myself to the exposition of two of Mackie's objections, which seem to me to be particularly important and to hit the mark.[18] The cosmological argument argues from the existence of the world to God as the rational agent who has intentionally brought it about. God is, Swinburne specifies, the *explanans* of the existence of the world. A "personal explanation" is at stake here, a kind of explanation that is to be distinguished sharply from the scientific or causal one and that owes its relevance to the fact that the world, even if it has an infinite history, still could have gone on otherwise or not at all. Now let *h* be the hypothesis that there is such a God, whose intentional action has brought the world about, and *e* the evidence consisting in the existence of this world, this complex physical universe, and *k* the background knowledge that we take for granted before new evidence turns up. Then it may be true that the probability *P* of *e* in relation to *h* and *k* (in other words: the probability that if there is a God there will be a physical universe) is not very high. Yet according to Swinburne the probability of *e* in relation to *k* is still lower: a physical universe is very unlikely to come about except by God's agency. Consequently, we have

$$P\,(e/h.k) > P\,(e/k).$$

In accordance with generally accepted norms, this counts as a good inductive argument for *h*. To be more precise, a C-inductive argument is concerned here: that is, an argument such that the premises add to the probability of the conclusion (i.e., make the conclusion more probable than it would otherwise be). Such arguments proceed under the condition that the initial probability $P\,(h/k)$ is not 0. This condition gives rise to Mackie's first objection. He asks: "How can we even think about the antecedent probability that there should be a god, given that there was no such universe?" This is hard to say, indeed, for if *e* contains our knowledge of the existing physical universe, then this knowledge has to be withdrawn from *k*. In that case, *k* contains no more than logical and mathematical truths. What likelihood could the god hypothesis have had in relation to these? If a physical universe like ours does not exist, then there is no conceivable way to proceed in order to settle the initial probability of there being a God.

Swinburne, however, seems to have a different idea. In his view there are two rival hypotheses, one contending that there is no further cause or explanation of the complex physical universe, the other claiming that there is an uncaused God who created it, but both taking for granted that this universe exists. The hypothesis of an uncaused God is more probable because it postulates a simpler explanation than its rival, that is, one more likely in relation to our background knowledge—which can now include everything we know about ourselves and the world, though it must exclude any specifically religious beliefs. Here Mackie comes up with his second objection. The rival hypothesis is eliminated too easily. The fact that the universe would, by definition, have no further explanation does not justify Swinburne's claim that it is "strange and puzzling" or "very unlikely." Moreover—and this particularly impresses me—the argument of relative unlikelihood can be turned very well against the preferred hypothesis of divine creation. The question, then, is not only whether it is likely that a God with the traditional attributes and powers would be able and willing to create such a universe as this, but also, and preliminarily, whether it is likely that there is such a God at all. To answer this question, one should ascertain the likelihood of what Swinburne's personal explanation attributes to God as his key power, namely, the power to fulfill his intentions directly, without any physical or causal mediation, without materials or instruments. Then Mackie says: "There is nothing in our background knowledge that makes it comprehensible, let alone likely that anything should have such a power. All our knowledge of intention-fulfillment is of embodied intentions being fulfilled indirectly by way of bodily changes and movements which are causally related to the intended result." To my eyes Mackie is simply right here. I draw a quick general conclusion. Insofar as the explanatory force of theism as an inductive hypothesis about the origin of the universe is concerned, at least on this point Swinburne's argument falls on its own sword: an explanation is meant to diminish the extent of the nonunderstood, but in fact this argument contributes "nothing to support the claim that by adding a god to the world we *reduce* the unexplained element."

Plausibility

As I said, I wish to draw a distinction between probability and plausibility. With the former, the phrastic component of credal sentences is all important; the neustic component is thought to deserve hardly any attention. Why would anybody think or act against his own rational belief? Such a person would be irrational and making the supposition of irrationality means committing philosophical suicide. When we focus on plausibility, even at the risk of such suicide, the neustic component of credal sentences is given much more weight. It is no overstatement to say that, in this view, the entire distinction between phrastic and neustic components of such sentences is put into question; it rejects the idea that there are isolatable belief contents that, as propositions, could be put before the mind, whose judgment would thereupon decide freely between affirming or negating them. In this view, beliefs are always embedded in the concrete biography of an individual, which in turn is a segment of the concrete "biography" of a society. Consequently, it hardly makes sense to deal with the credibility of credal sentences so long as the societal or historico-cultural context is not taken into account. Therefore, one has to admit the relevance of such criteria as cognitive consonance, solidity of plausibility structures, and so on. In my opinion, these new criteria are of the utmost importance for our question. Reckoning with them means a sort of self-relativization of philosophy, but I think that philosophy can no longer claim to be the last court of appeal for truth. If beliefs are sociohistorical realities, philosophy cannot pass judgment on them without acknowledging that she herself is part of the sociohistorical process. This view implies the rehabilitation of empirical evidence and even of common sense as relevant for philosophical reflection.

As for the plausibility of theism, I think that the so-called secularization thesis should be taken very seriously. This thesis—I take here Peter Berger's *The Social Reality of Religion* as my point of reference[19]—starts from "empirically available processes,"[20] which ensures that "sectors of society and culture are removed from the domination of religious institutions and symbols."[21] This complex of processes "affects the totality of cultural life and of ideation, and may be observed in the decline of religious contents in the arts, in philosophy, in literature, and, most important of all, in the rise of science as an autonomous, thoroughly secular perspective of the world."[22] To a certain extent, the secularization process can be seen as "a 'reflection' of concrete infrastructural processes in modern society."[23] Its original locale "was in the economic area, specifically, in those sectors of the economy being formed by the capitalistic and industrial processes."[24] In this milieu arose "something like a 'liberated territory' with respect to religion."[25] In modern industrial society, the area of economy has conquered a central position, with the effect that secularization "has moved 'outwards' from this sector into other areas of society."[26] This central position explains why any attempt to reconquer that liberated territory:

> in the name of religio-political traditionalism endangers the continued functioning of this economy. A modern industrial society requires the presence of large cadres of scientific and technological personnel, whose training and ongoing social organization presupposes a high degree of rationalization, not only on the level of infrastructure but also on that of consciousness. Any attempts at traditionalistic *reconquista* thus threaten to dismantle the rational foundations of modern society. Furthermore, the secularizing potency of capitalistic-industrial rationalization is not only self-perpetuating but self-aggrandizing. As the capitalistic industrial complex expands, so do the social strata dominated by its rationales, and it becomes ever more difficult to establish traditional controls over them.[27]

It is not difficult to see the consequences of this secularization process for theism. From the point of view we are now adopting, theism is to be considered as embedded or incarnated in a religious tradition. It cannot be detached from this tradition. Rather, it constitutes the tradition's heart or organizing principle; it is its "primary determinant of meaning."[28] In a religious tradition, a world is constructed and maintained.[29] The reality of this world "depends upon the presence of social structures within which this reality is taken for granted and within which successive generations of individuals are socialized in such a way that this world will be real to *them*."[30] Religious traditions, in other words, owe their power to "plausibility structures." If these structures lose their integrity or continuity, the world of that particular religion "begins to totter" and becomes in urgent need of legitimation.[31] Now, secularization means precisely the crumbling or even the collapse of the religious plausibility structure. The primary determinant of meaning is inevitably swept along in this fall. The problem is no more this or that detail of the theistic worldview, which could be corrected or substituted for on the basis of an intact whole; the problem is the whole itself, the idea that there should be something like a (theistically conceived) God.

In truth, there is much to object to in the secularization thesis and a fortiori in the present exposition of it. Yet even if it were not 100 percent true, but only 50 percent, it would still be ponderable enough—and, once more, also ponderable philosophically. It implies that there is a dialectical relationship between social structures and religious culture. "The point is that the *same* human activity that produces society also produces religion."[32] It is impossible that a secularization process should take place without having an impact on the religious, or in this case theistic, worldview. Concentrating on philosophy as a practice of knowledge, one could even say: it is impossible that a liberated territory of science should arise without harming the plausibility of theism. In fact, it seems that philosophy has to choose: she cannot both sustain theism and agree with the economy-based, autonomous, thoroughly secular world perspective of science.

Corollary with Regard to Theistic Religions

In my country it is sometimes argued that there is a generic difference between philosophical belief in (a theistically conceived) God and religious, or at least Christian, faith. The collapse of the former would hardly affect the latter. Even more, the collapse of the former would finally liberate the latter from its age-long Babylonian captivity. At last the true, nonphilosophical, nonmetaphysical face of Christian belief in a personal God would come to light, and it would be, so to speak, the grace bestowed on our epoch that we are in a position to see this. To a certain extent, I shall myself adopt this kind of view; in the last section of this essay I shall try to develop it a bit more. Still, I think it is good first to state quite sharply that Christian faith largely coincides with theism and that the possibilities of separating Christianity from metaphysics are very restricted. This is a thesis that concerns not only the historical essence of Christianity but also the nature of faith: one can hardly avoid thinking of faith as having an object, a really existing something or somebody to whom it is referring. Therefore, the contrast Pascal drew between the God of the philosophers and the God of Abraham, Isaac, and Jacob is a very difficult one. It is, in my opinion, certainly untenable if it is posited on the level of conceptual content. Swinburne is right in saying that, in the sense of his definition of theism, Christians, as well as Jews and Muslims, are theists.[33] If Christian theology wants to evade this consequence by retreating to a God-conception whose content differs not only specifically but even generically from that of theism, then it could hardly succeed. In the first place, Christian theology would then have to abandon very central, very fundamental elements of the traditional Christian God-conception, and in the second place—even more importantly—it would *ceteris paribus* do nothing but exchange one metaphysical position for another. Even a "wholly other" God-conception is a God-conception and as such entails certain metaphysical, that is, existential claims. These claims can be made *pianissimo* or cloaked in flowery metaphors, but as such this does not change anything. It merely produces the necessity of rational reconstruction,[34] that is, of a transformation of theological phrasings into corresponding philosophical statements.

Needless to say, the trinitarian God-conception cannot figure as a God-conception that is generically different from theism. Perhaps it is not quite needless to emphasize that Jewish monotheism cannot either. It is sometimes argued that the Christian God-conception has lost the original purity of Jewish monotheism in that it has become amalgamated with Hellenism. In line with this view, a radical rejudaization of the Christian faith is often called for. Now, without a doubt, through its Hellenization the Gospel was brought into contact with metaphysical speculation. But it is an illusion to think that outside the sphere of speculation (which, by the way, has flourished in Jewish mysticism as well) metaphysical implications are nonexistent. Jewish monotheism is theism just as much, and it admits in principle of the rational reconstruction of a metaphysical equivalent, which, then, is just as open to philosophical questioning as the traditional Christian God-conception is.

To sum up: if the argument in the sections preceding this corollary is valid, then it is hard to contradict Wolfgang Stegmüller when, at the end of his long review of Mackie's *Miracle of Theism*, he observes that the author's philosophical position entails the rationally founded statement that the monotheistic religions known to us are based on an existential assumption that is indispensable to them but that is presumably false.[35]

Theism as Heritage: Heritage as Charge and as Benefit

Ideas can be tenacious and survive for centuries beyond the context of their appropriate use. To characterize this postexistence, I choose the metaphor of heritage. This is no recognized philosophical concept; even the very voluminous *Historisches Wörterbuch der Philosophie* (*Historical Dictionary of Philosophy*) offers no entry for it, whereas the thirty-one volumes of the *Archiv für Begriffsgeschichte* (*Archive for Conceptual History*) do not contain any article or even abstract on it, either.[36] Yet it is a juridical concept. For the fun of it, I have looked about in a collection of proverbs and rules of Roman law. I found there quite a few pithy sayings about heirs and legacies. I take the liberty of quoting four of them:[37] (1) "Claims can be made both by and against the heir"; (2) "Legacy cannot be accepted only in part"; (3) "The heir takes over the real [i.e., not the personal] shortcomings of the deceased"; (4) "An inheritance declined passes to the other inheritors, even though they might be unwilling."

Sayings like these seem to me to signify that inheritance is a precarious affair, in need of careful regulation. How easily quarrels can arise here, which then of course affect the most elementary and vital social unit, the family. Moreover, how dangerous and burdensome the position of the heir sometimes is. What is it that he receives? Will it not harm him or involve him in some misadventure? Sometimes it seems best entirely to renounce one's portion. Above all, if one accepts the heritage, what a burden one sometimes takes on. The patrimony is to be carefully kept and administered. According to Roman law, the head of the family had the *heredium* in private property, but it was in practice unavailable to him.[38] Especially this latter aspect provides fertile soil for our metaphor.

It might be objected that this precarious and cumbersome character of heritage is but one side of the matter and that one cannot understand this institution adequately if one does not realize the benefits that are usually attached to it or expected from it. I concede this outright. Heirs enter into the possession of goods without labor. This prospect mostly brightens life to a considerable extent and one's comings and goings are not seldom strongly motivated by the hope of becoming an heir. I would like to instantiate this promising aspect of heritage with a few more sayings. This time I prefer to draw them not from juridical but from evangelical wisdom. I will take the liberty of quoting some significant verses from the New Testament:[39] (1) "And for this cause he is the mediator of the new testament, that by means of death, for the redemption of the transgressions *that were* under the first testament, they which are called might receive the promise of eternal inheritance" (Hebr. 9:15); (2) "And if children, then heirs; heirs of God, and joint-heirs with Christ; if so be that we suffer with *him*, that we may be also glorified together" (Rom. 8:17); (3) "Wherefore thou art no more a servant, but a son; and if a son, then an heir of God through Christ" (Gal. 4:7); (4) "To an inheritance incorruptible, and undefiled, and that fadeth not away, reserved in heaven for you" (1 Petr. 1:4).

If one compares the first set of sayings with the second, one could almost think of the opposition between law and gospel. This impression is, of course, due to my arrangement. Still, I think it is true that the phenomenon of heritage is an ambivalent one and shows up two clearly different aspects. In dealing with the heritage of theism, I want to take this ambivalence as my point of departure. We shall focus first on the encumbering side of it, then on the blessing that it might contain.

The Heritage of Theism as Charge

"One has to be as naive as a freethinker of the Saturday evening market to be happy in the illusion that one frees oneself from Christianity . . . by abjuring the Christian belief in God. For after the great heresy, after we have experienced that 'God is dead,' we stand there with our Christian form as heirs of an age-long Christian discipline . . . , Christians without Christianity, without faith, but nonetheless neither Brahmins nor barbarians."[40] These are the words of the Dutch essayist Menno ter Braak (1902–40), a fiery admirer of

Nietzsche's individualism and therefore a firm adversary of modern collectivisms, whether Communist or Nazi. He was on the blacklist of the new rulers in Germany and was to be arrested immediately after the capitulation of Holland. By killing himself, he was a few hours too quick for his executioners.

As a subject of study, Ter Braak had almost chosen theology. But in his student years he had already taken leave of Christianity; doubt with regard to "higher things" had gained the upper hand. He opted for "the ordinary word"; his 1931 collection of essays *A Farewell to Clergymanland* (a title that became famous in my country) does away with the sermonizing tone, the outward but also the inward sermonizing tone, by which truth is masked. In this book, he also achieved a struggle against himself: "I had to combat the clergyman words of my vocabulary with other words," he wrote in the preface.[41]

My first quotation is drawn from a book he published six years later, under the title *Of Christians Old and New*. The shadow of Nazism was falling over Europe; it was the supremacy of the Cyclops. What could honest people do to survive other than, just like Odysseus and his companions, make a stand together? The book is a plea for democracy. Of course it had to be a democracy without demagogy, without the usual phraseology, and without the sacralization of equality, in short, the democracy of Nobody. Still, a democracy, a collectivity. The resentment of the herd toward the strong individual, from which this political form doubtlessly has its origin, should not only be unmasked but also be accepted. This resentment, then, was aroused and cultivated in Christianity; in consequence, democracy is a result of Christianity and goes back to the Christian principle of the equality of all souls before God. And that is why, face to face with the Cyclops, people should become new Christians.[42]

I would like to highlight two things about this example, one concerning method and the other concerning subject matter. As to method, the heritage of theism asks for an approach different from that appropriate to theism itself. As inheritance, theism has passed into other hands, other forms. It has been divided among many heirs; it is, so to speak, disseminated. Thus it is no longer a topic of philosophical theology *stricto sensu* but a ferment, an essence of certain religious traditions, or more precisely, of the secularized postexistence of such traditions. Accordingly, the object of the philosophy of religion is not of a logical or epistemological kind; rather, it is a factual entity or a plurality of such entities, namely, the comprehensive cultural entities called "religions." Therefore, I think that it is not without reason that the name of our discipline contains the word *religion*. To my knowledge, this name arose at the end of the eighteenth century, simultaneously with a deep crisis in—and on the Continent the almost complete extinction of—rational theology.[43] It is easy to establish a causal connection between these two events and to consider the philosophy of religion to be the transformation, not to say the heir, of *theologia rationalis*. Philosophy of religion thus expresses by its very name a serious rupture in the metaphysical tradition. This name signifies that it is impossible to know God by reason alone; we cannot have knowledge of God other than the knowledge we have of the contingent entities called religions, in other words: the existence and nature of God cannot be brought up[44] except in the forms of human worship. Dealing with the heritage of theism can take place only in the form of a philosophy of culture in which the task of philosophy consists less in analysis or reconstruction than in reflection and recollection. Its concern is to examine the transformations that religious belief in God has undergone and in which it has both gained and lost its identity. The reference to Menno ter Braak is meant to be an application of this different paradigm in the philosophy of religion. A literary text was intentionally selected as point of departure, since not only the arguments of philosophers and theologians are relevant here but also the texts of essayists and other belletrists, whether pious or profane.

As to the relevance of our example for the subject matter under discussion, I would like to make two remarks. First, the example shows the importance or the seriousness of the charge. It relates to nothing less than the condition for decent survival. The foundation of society comes into play. In Ter Braak's view, theism is much more than the maintaining of credal sentences about a metaphysical being: it has shaped a political order, and if it comes to pass away, this order is seriously endangered. In this respect, the book *Of Christians Old and New* seems to me to anticipate the turn to the problem of civil religion, which in American discussions of the last two decades has become a hot issue. Meanwhile, we should realize that in Ter Braak the argument is based not on religion in general but specifically on theistic religion. It is Christian faith that constitutes the charge. The heritage consists in the discipline Christianity brought about by its belief that, in the last resort, in the sight of the Lord, there is no elite, no difference between the strong and the weak, the rich and the poor.

Second, and more importantly, the example selected shows the tenacity, if not the insuperability, of the charge. As a motto for the second part of his book, Ter Braak quotes Ernest Renan: "I feel that my life is governed always by a faith that I no longer have. Faith has the peculiarity that, even when it has disappeared, it still works."[45] The first-person voice of this quotation is, I think, appropriate. In lengthy explanations it is argued to what extent language in Europe has absorbed Christian pretensions and has carried them along far beyond the limits of official, faithful Christianity. "The Christian terminology becomes interesting to us particularly where it is not the terminology of faith any more, where it is used unsuspectingly by freethinkers, Marxists, fascists, and skeptics, for example, *against* faithful Christianity. Language in its modern naïveté is the most delightful masquerade . . . : it outwits the ingenuous, it outwitted the Christians, but as dialectic it even outwitted Karl Marx, the enemy of Stirner!" But we should add—and that is my point—it has outwitted Ter Braak too. Even the values of this Stirnerian individualist are disguises of Christian spirit. There is at least one context in which he admits this quite overtly. He often points to honesty (*honnêteté*) and human dignity as his highest values. In this context he says: "By the notion of 'human dignity' and its equivalents I express nothing but the 'equality of souls before God' . . . without God. I cannot recognize an elite any more: no king, no dictator, and no intellectual either; I only recognize that I am a Christian, an heir, in whom all has become instinct that ancestrally was built up out of compromises between pagan resistance and Christian discipline. . . . Human dignity is a concept that takes its comprehensive and absolute character from its Christian specificity. It is a concept that we cannot go beyond because it sums up our Christian heritage."[46]

Our reaction might be: how very paradoxical all this is! Well, even that is conceded. "Paradox" is indeed a key concept in Ter Braak's thought. On the final page, he suggests that the very form of his book, its open end, "is a symbol of Christian society, which lets its symbols turn into paradoxes. The consistent nonconformist is the consistent proclaimer of nonmetaphysical Christianity . . . because he has understood that Christian harmony comes to an end and that the epoch of Christian paradoxes is emerging."[47] Yet paradox is in Ter Braak not only a "thematic" but also an "operating" concept:[48] that is to say, it is not only in front of him, in his field of consciousness, but also at his back, like a *vis a tergo*. It runs off with him. And this might reveal what his new Christianity is really up to.

To us who stand at a distance of half a century, it is all too evident that in receiving the inheritance of Christian theism this author is ridden by it. Does this mean that we ourselves are free from it? Has one merely to understand this disguise of the charge in order to be rid of it? I am not so sure. I am not fond of mystifications to the effect that whatever has become invisible counts as most real, even more real than it was before, but there is some truth—not only in psychoanalytical respects but also with regard to the history of culture—in the idea of the power of the Unthought (*das Ungedachte*), the forgotten or the displaced. On this point I hesitantly agree with Heidegger and Derrida. So I think that it makes sense to address the question also to ourselves, I mean the question: Under which disguises is theism still exerting its charge after its disappearance?

The Heritage of Theism as Blessing: De re and de dicto

In recent years, the following story has been repeatedly quoted in my country:

> When the Baal Shem had a difficult task before him, he would go to a certain place in the woods, light a fire, and meditate in prayer—and what he had set out to perform was done. When a generation later the "Maggid" of Meseritz was faced with the same task, he would go to the same place in the woods and say: We can no longer light the fire, but we can still speak the prayers—and what he wanted done became reality. Again a generation later Rabbi Moshe Leib of Sassov had to perform this task. And he too went into the woods and said: We can no longer light a fire, nor do we know the secret meditations belonging to the prayer, but we do know the place in the woods to which it all belongs—and that must be sufficient. And sufficient it was. But

when another generation had passed and Rabbi Israel of Rishin was called upon to perform the task, he sat down on his golden chair in his castle and said: we cannot light the fire, we cannot speak the prayers, we do not know the place, but we can tell the story of how it was done. And, the storyteller adds, the story that he told had the same effect as the actions of the other three.

The reason for the popularity of this story might be found in malaise. People recognize in it their own situation, a situation at the end of a process of decay. In a series of generations, a breakdown was accomplished, in steps that can almost exactly be marked: the breakdown first of the infallible authority of Scripture, then of the provident guidance of God in history and one's own life, then of personal immortality or postmortem existence, then of the church-going way of life. And just as in the story, the process passed from thing to word; faith that initially was *de re* ended up being *de dicto*. What more can happen? What else than that even the words will die down?

Of course, malaise is an aspect of the situation, and I do not exclude that in some cases the reference to this story is inspired by it. But the story itself—and perhaps the quotation of it too—has another tenor. We can become aware of this if we put the story into one of its best known contexts, the context of the conclusion of the book *Major Trends in Jewish Mysticism*, by the great Kabbalah expert Gershom Scholem. There we learn that the milieu the story reflects is that of the mystical revival movement of Hasidism in eighteenth-century Eastern Europe. It is not only a story about Hasidism but also, as Scholem makes clear, a story of the Hasidim themselves. And their intention with it was (according to his interpretation) almost the contrary of what malaise is inclined to hear in it. The story about the words and deeds of famous Zaddikim is the greatest creation of Hasidism. Not a few Zaddikim, above all Rabbi Israel of Rishin, the founder of the Eastern Galician Hasidic dynasty, laid down the whole treasure of their ideas in such tales. Their Torah took the form of an inexhaustible fountain of storytelling. Nothing at all has remained theory; everything has become a story. In this sense I understand Scholem's puzzling comment on the story quoted above: "You can say if you will that this profound little anecdote symbolizes the decay of a great movement. You can also say that it reflects the transformation of all its values, a transformation so profound that in the end all that remained of the mystery was the tale. That is the position in which we find ourselves today, or in which Jewish mysticism finds itself. The story is not ended, it has not yet become history, and the secret life it holds can break out tomorrow in you or in me."[49] The comment is puzzling because of its lack of articulation. No "but," no "on the other hand," no "nonetheless." What is opposed to what in this text, what is to be stressed? As I said, I take it that this wonderful sequence of sentences means to embroider on the idea that everything has become a story. It then says that whenever the *dictum* comes to life the *res* itself is there.

The Blessing of Thick Language

This idea is the point of departure for my thoughts about the heritage of theism as bless-ing. Briefly stated, the blessing consists in the availability of a very thick language. The adjective *thick* refers to a context in Gilbert Ryle.[50] What is *The Thinker* doing? Ryle asks. The usual answer, that the thinker is saying things to himself, fails badly. Perhaps he says nothing at all, and at any rate, he is doing a number of other things, which can best be described by saying that "he is trying, by success/failure tests, to find out whether or not the things that he is saying would or would not be utilizable as leads or pointers." Such a description is thick because it is using "constitutionally adverbial verbs—active verbs that are not verbs for separately do-able, lowest-level doings."[51] Examples of such verbs are *to mimic, to do something experimentally* (which differs from just doing it), *to do things as steps toward or stages in some ulterior undertaking*, and—to my taste a particularly fine example—*to undo*. Now, the point that interests me is that in many cases these adverbial verbs are, so to speak, stackable. A good example is "the adverbial verb 'to think'" itself.[52] According to the description I just quoted, thinking is a sort of trying. The thinker is not so much guiding himself anywhere as "trying to find out whether this or that track of his own making would or would not qualify as a guiding . . . track."[53] This kind of exploring is different from piloting others on a track that has already been cleared, and this in turn is different from following a pilot's lead. The difference lies in the levels of sophistication: of these three doings, the first one, according to Ryle, lies on the highest sophistication-level and the last one on the lowest.[54] Elsewhere he speaks in the same sense about "ac-complishment-levels" corresponding to the order in which the lessons of experience must be learned. "Some lessons are intrinsically traders on prior lessons. Such tradings can pyramid indefinitely. There is no top step on the stairway of accomplishment-levels."[55] A thick description encompasses these different levels.

In Ryle *thick* is an adjective modifying *description*, whereas I want to use it as an adjective modifying *language*. That is quite a difference, and I am afraid that Ryle would have deemed this innovation a sign of confusion. With regard to those adverbial verbs (and whatever classes of words), I merely think that it is not a matter of course that, qua bits of language, they are at hand. Without the availability of an appropriate language, the pyramid of accomplishment-levels could not be built up. The possibility of a thick description is dependent on the existence of a thick language.

Three short remarks about what is to be understood by "language" here. In the first place, it is to be seen as a historical entity, susceptible to change. It undergoes expansion as well as reduction. This explains the difference between the phases of one and the same natural language and partly also the difference between one natural language and another: one develops in a tempo different from the other. Thus it may happen that in a given natural language words fail: they are not yet there or they are not there any more. In the second place, language is, although subject to change, relatively stable. Usually the evolution proceeds rather slowly, so that people of different generations can more or less understand each other. Moreover and especially, what is not actively used does not immediately disappear. It is preserved like a fund, from which we can draw at the proper time. That is why speaking a language always has an aspect of making the past present, or, to borrow a beautiful expression from Hegel, the aspect of *Erinnerung* (i.e., both recollection and interiorization). In the third place, there is a connection between language and experience. Language is the reflection of the contact of a cultural community with reality. It is thus a reminder of the lessons learned by this cultural community. Of course, we have to understand this distributively: the cultural community is a collection of communities, which, in part, fight each other. Language has this differentiation too: the experience it embodies is by no means homogeneous. Be that as it may, experience has the property of self-generation. Experience discloses new experience. This is to say that actual experience is prefigured in preceding experience. That feature is reflected in language. The language we speak in order to express our understanding of reality opens up, by itself, new possibilities of articulation.

A thick language, then, encompasses a wide range of accomplishment-levels—of experiences, memories, thoughts, fictions, and feelings telescoped in basic doings. A very thick language encompasses virtually all accomplishment-levels. Theism has made language very thick—I mean, the natural languages of the cultures in which it has lived or is still flourishing, either as philosophical or as religious belief. The reason why this is so can easily be grasped. Both in its philosophical and in its religious form (and in the many, many hybrids), theism has been an exercise in the sophistication of consciousness. The usual word for what, with Ryle, I call here "sophistication" is *transcendence*. Theism has been connected, at least since the beginning of modernity, with a demand to go beyond the world of everyday things. W. Trillhaas has set out his critical account of belief in God under the title "intentional transcendence." I recall some of the relevant contexts of his *Religionsphilosophie*. Transcendence cannot mean an object, a second world "behind" ours; it denotes a movement accomplished by the religious subject. "In its devotion the religious subject itself 'exceeds' the 'reality' that is confined by mere sense-data and which can be controlled experimentally and registered mechanically. It also 'exceeds' mere historical facticity." Using Husserl's terminology, one can speak here of an intentional surplus of meaning (*intentionale Mehrmeinung*). It is as if something is added to normal perception, for instance, a natural phenomenon is apperceived as "creature," or a word addressed to me and touching my conscience is apperceived by me as "Word of God." "In this surplus the horizon of the moment is widened so as to include past and future. In this surplus I leave my narrow shell; my fellow-human is not an object any more; I see myself in his mirror, I meet his expectation for me and experience my responsibility, which, just like love and guilt, exceeds all momentary need. I come to myself, I become a person in that I gain distance from myself. All that, however, is but a beginning. Religion means a fundamental transcendence of experience, which impregnates the substance of mere everyday experience and fulfills it with 'meaning' in a density that perhaps never can be closed once and for all." This ultimate opening is warranted by the religious idea of God. In accordance with the "transcendence postulate," the word *God* means the "ultimate goal of intentional exceeding," that is, "'God' itself cannot be exceeded intentionally. . . . *Deus semper maior.*" Trillhaas explicitly links up the transcending character of religious experience with language. This link is given by the fact that experience is a social event. It is the attempt to make sense of human existence, in which I find myself involved together with other people. The meaning structures resulting in this collective and personal attempt are not demonstrable, but they find their "intersubjective confirmation and interpretation in language. In language the transcendence of experience obtains its particular objectivity."[56] So much for Trillhaas. My conclusion, once more, is that the theistic practice of surpassing everyday experience has helped to develop a virtually infinite stairway of accomplishment-levels or sophistication-levels, in other words, that it has substantially contributed to the birth and the maintenance of a very thick language.

Is this a blessing? We need not hesitate long about that. It can be a blessing, without a doubt. It is a magnificent language to play in. Acting, pretending, simulating, ironizing, imagining, joking, singing, praying all go very well in it. And of course storytelling also. What, for instance, would a novel like *The Name of the Rose* be without the very thick language of theism? Eco manages to show up the traces of this language virtually everywhere. Due to these traces, the movement of intentional transcendence can be triggered at any moment. Thus I think that the heritage of theism guards us from the enthroning of thinness, that is, from a culture that ignores systematically and on a large scale what Ryle makes clear with his example of *The Thinker*, namely, that what *The Thinker* is "thinly" doing—for instance, producing *sotto voce* words, phrases, and sentences—"*must* have a 'thicker' description."[57] Much more could be said about this thinness. If I am not mistaken, philosophical analyses of modern culture converge in the diagnosis of a thinning down, a loss of substance, with its unfathomable depth. I leave all that aside here, but there is one more remark to be made. One could also characterize this tendency of our culture (if it is one), in a far echo of Ernst Cassirer's terminology,[58] as functionalization. Then it is to be stressed that the counterweight that the language of theism provides for this tendency cannot itself be functionalized. Theism, or at least its language, is not the kind of thing that could be appreciated because of its functionality. The point is that this language is a real blessing, that is, a good that is not a means, a good that, in a sublime sense of the word, is useless.[59]

Enjoying the Blessing

But how can the blessing of the heritage of theism be enjoyed without making the metaphysical claims implied in theism? "Legacy cannot be accepted only in part." This is the problem I want to face in concluding this essay. I should like to say two things about it. I do not conceal the fact that there is a huge tension between these two things.

The first of them concerns the *ceteris paribus* proviso I made above under "Corollary with Regard to Theistic Religions." There I said that so long as metaphysical, that is, existential claims are implied, theistic religions remain on a par with theism as rational belief and share the destiny of the latter. But by now the moment might have come to remove this proviso and to focus on the difference that is relevant here.

It is the difference between making a metaphysical claim and echoing it. Making a claim can be done in many different ways: you may whisper it, or wrap it up in curlicues and flourishes, or merely signal it without words. In such cases, it may be necessary to make inquiries. But then the matter will be settled: if the claim is indeed made, it will be affirmed upon inquiry. In this sense the theist, as I defined him, is indeed making metaphysical claims. Willingly and knowingly, he assumes the pretension that his belief in a person without a body, and so on, is rational—that is, on a par with objective (philosophical or even scientific) knowledge—and that it is even true.

Let us take, by contrast, the example of Menno ter Braak. In vindicating the discipline of Christianity, he received the remnants of the language Christianity had developed in order to achieve this discipline, and therewith he consciously took in the metaphysical claims implied in this language. Is this to say that he also made these claims? Clearly not. He plainly rejected them. He opted for a secular way of life and thought, even in his capacity of "new Christian."

Now, the point is that this is possible and that consequently the distinction under discussion is valid. Ter Braak and kindred spirits cannot simply be said to be victims of delusion. Here I would like to express my reservation with regard to a certain use of the idea of an ubiquitous metaphysics. It might be argued that the echoing of a metaphysical claim is not really different from the making of it because the distinction between knowing and willing and not-knowing and not-willing is not tenable. Reference might for instance be made to Derrida's magnificent text "Préjugés: Devant la loi" ("Before the Law"),[60] in which the freedom of judgment necessarily implied in such a distinction is shown to be founded on prejudice. Judgment in all its forms—attitude, operation, statement—is conditioned by a pre-judice that is absolutely heterogeneous to its rules, to the rules, that is, of any possible judgment. The law by virtue of which judgment is performed is not there, is not at our disposal: rather, we are "before" it, just as in Kafka's tale. In this way, the idea of an original and inescapable guilt toward metaphysics can be made very tempting indeed. But this does not take the edge off the distinction. There is quite a large gap between our debt to this (quasi)-transcendental kind of prejudice and our would-be debt to the pretty solid and positive existential claim of theism. Derrida's negative theology does nothing to bridge this gap, quite the contrary.[61]

If, then, the distinction under discussion should not be abandoned too soon, it might be applied to the field of religious belief as well. Why should not whatever holds for the form of life of the completely secularized "new Christian" Ter Braak also hold for a worshipping form of Christianity? As a matter of fact, Christian faith (as well as theist faiths in general) is used to claim the objective truth of the knowledge it embodies. But why should it be incapable of desisting from that claim? Why should it not be in a position to say the prayers, sing the hymns, and tell the tales it has always cherished, just for the joy and the pleasure and the relief and the edification of performing them? It might well be that in faithfulness to the *dictum* the *res* itself is given. And I do not see why, in this nonmetaphysical vein, it would not be possible even to develop some sort of theology. Why should reflective faith, instead of constantly accounting for the rationality of incredible existential claims, not be able to swerve round them? Why could it not step to a higher sophistication-level and start playing with that echo, modulating, counterfeiting, quoting, displacing, interpreting, hiding, and seeking it?

The second thing I want to say about enjoyment of the blessing is this. At least insofar as the apex of the heritage of theism is concerned, there is no escape from metaphysics. This apex consists in the word *God*. I simply do not see how we could use this word or even how it could cross our minds[62] without getting entangled in metaphysics, that is, in the general idea of what there is, which has been debated over the twenty-five centuries of Western philosophy. Here we can learn a lesson from Heidegger. As is well known, Heidegger announced in his earlier writings the program of an *Überwindung* ("surmounting") of metaphysics. But later on he found that this term is too straightforward, and he replaced it by *Verwindung*, which means not only "surmounting" but also "coiling." Metaphysics cannot be undone; the *Schritt zurück* ("step back") cannot mean that we get away from it. Metaphysics is, rather, the background or even the "partner"[63] in the face of which philosophical thought has to go its way. It is hard not to attach this sense also to the new term *postmetaphysical*, even though this interpretation goes against the *mens auctoris*.[64] What comes after metaphysics is indeed metaphysics again.

But perhaps there are examples of honorable entanglement in metaphysics. I would think especially of Theodor W. Adorno and Michael Theunissen.[65] For the sake of brevity, I limit myself to pointing to one idea of the former. In the last chapter of his *Negative Dialektik* (*Negative Dialectics*), entitled "Meditations on Metaphysics," Adorno states that, in order to be truthful, thinking should, at least nowadays—that is, after Auschwitz—also think against itself and match itself with the extreme that retreats from conceptualization. It should, that is, confront itself with what is other than concept, with the nonidentical. In doing so it takes over the task of metaphysics, the knowledge of the Absolute, which in the last couple of centuries has become marginalized. It was expelled from its institutional housing; it was fatally thrust into the realm of the apocryphal; it had to flee from (positive) religion into profanity; at present it is leading a homeless and unsightly existence. It has been overthrown, but the thinking that confronts the nonidentical, Adorno says in the last line of his book, keeps solidarity with it in the moment of its downfall.

I take this word *solidarity* in its strong, original sense, as joint and several liability. The thinking of the nonidentical takes the place of the dethroned. The question then arises in what sense the heritage of theism, which at least at its apex is entangled in metaphysics, can be said to be an enjoyable blessing. Is it not the gravity and mourning of deposition instead of joy that sets the tone here? One part of the answer to this question might be found in the *Historisches Wörterbuch der Philosophie*, in the article "Genuß." There I learned that this word has meanings other than that of cheerful consumerism, which is dominant today. In J. G. Herder, for example, at the end of the eighteenth century, *Genuß* is seen to underlie the whole way in which the subject appropriates his world; it means the original opening up of reality. Thus existence itself is *Genuß*. Likewise, the blessing of the heritage of theism is not the kind of thing we can have in an external manner, keeping ourselves out of it.[66] That this involvement must make us feel jolly is not at all implied. The other part of the answer I find in Adorno. The gravity of despair knows its own strange bliss, and this momentary bliss is *pars pro toto*. I cannot resist quoting the context: "The disturbed and damaged course of the world is, as in Kafka, incommensurable [with the concept] also in the sense of its pure meaninglessness and blindness. It cannot be stringently constructed according to these principles. It contradicts the attempt of the despairing consciousness to posit despair as something absolute. The course of the world is not absolutely closed. . . . All traces of the other in it are fragile; all happiness is distorted due to its revocability. Nonetheless, in the faults that belie identity, beings are pervaded with the constantly broken promises of that other. Each happiness is a fragment of the entire happiness."[67]

By Way of Conclusion

God does not reign over the spirit of all people. Many of them, and among them the most learned, the best, the wisest, reject and deny him as a useless hypothesis, as a sort of crutch that mankind, finally recovered, would no longer need. Yet I have some doubt that this idea of God can ever be torn loose, up to the root, down to the heart, from the restlessness of man. Science, morals, and history can do very well without God. It is humans who cannot. Not so much to understand as to dream. To suffer and to rejoice. To commemorate and to hope.

It is under the aspect of a dream that I write these pages. And when they will be ready this dream will have taken a shape. In the beginning was God. And then, step by step, his own creation will have repressed God. It will have found him oppressive, ridiculous, absurd, entirely useless and superfluous, truly pernicious. It will have reduced him to the humiliating status of one of those child's dreams that we shake off in awakening . . . in order to pass on to serious things: money, power, revolution, science. I have taken up this feeble child's dream. I have not said: "This is God. He has such and such a figure, and a beard. It is him. Listen to him. Tremble. Obey." I say: "The dreams are ideas. And the ideas are real." At the end of this book, God will be an idea, a memory, a hope. In my modest way I shall have re-created God. That is merely just compensation. Because God has created me.

. . . I believe it, I feel it, I know it, I am sure: I have been borne by something. By what? Who will tell me? By time, by history, by the whole of mankind, by the laws of nature. It is all this that I call God. Vocabulary is free and I have a generous mind: I have been created by God.

And I bless him for having created me. For having let me be. For having permitted me to deny him. For permitting me to sing for him and to be, after so many others . . . the herald of his glory and his omnipotence.

. . . I wrote somewhere that I am a skeptic. That is true: I do not believe much, in fact almost nothing. Or perhaps even nothing at all. I do not believe in myself or in others. I believe that the moral values, the societies, the forms of art, the political and intellectual systems, all these human constructions will do nothing but pass away and are not worth a jot. I believe only in time, in history, and in God. Because God is time. He is all the rest too, by the way, because he is all at once. But, at any rate, time. He is the absence of time, and at the same time, time.

We—I mean mankind—fall short of earnestness to a bewildering extent. We are dealing with everything except the whole, I mean God. I do not believe anything. Take it all away: I believe in what remains. Due to a marvelous paradox, which is the key of this book, if you take it all away, what remains is all. The first whole, that is, the details, the anecdotes, the futility of knowledge, the frivolity of power. The second whole is all. It is God. And it is this book about which I am prepared to say anything except that it can be modest. Lord! Bless it! And that thy holy name be blessed.

So here I write, this book, under the regard of God who is nothing other than my dreams. And my dreams are from God. And all that I am is from God. And all that you are is from God. And when you read these lines while I am already elsewhere, you will wonder perhaps where this book has been before it was written. Well, it was in God. . . . And when there is nobody any more to read it, it still will be in God's bosom. And because it is not finished yet, it still is in the bosom of God.

There is, I admit, something fairly comic in seeing that God through me glorifies his holy name. What do you want? That is the way it is. I cannot change it. I shall not speak about myself. I shall only say that God bloweth where he listeth. He blows upon Karl Marx, upon the clochard around the corner, upon Caesar, upon Galileo. . . . He blew upon Lucifer. He blew upon Judas. He may also blow upon me.[68]

PART III

Methods of Instruction and Comparison

Teaching Religious Facts in Secular Schools

Régis Debray

Preface

A truly secular school must give each student access to an understanding of the world. For this reason, it has always been possible to speak of religions in the schools of the Republic, insofar as they are facts of civilization. Contrary to a tenacious prejudice, the content of our schools' curricula attests to this, and has long done so.

While respecting *laïcité*, a principle of harmony, teachers give the knowledge of religions its fair place in the teaching of their disciplines. History, philosophy, literature, the plastic arts, music . . . here we can rightfully call upon the humanities.

Without privileging one or another spiritual option, and deliberately distancing themselves from any *religious instruction*, teachers approach religions as defining and structuring elements in the history of humanity; sometimes agents of peace and modernity, sometimes sowers of discord, murderous conflicts, and regression.

It is thus within the framework of the existing disciplines—and not as part of a hypothetical new school subject—that religious facts must be presented. Carrying this out, however, is difficult for a number of teachers. It appears necessary to better train all teachers to address religious facts calmly.

It was with this in mind that I entrusted Régis Debray, the author of a brilliant recent work, *God, an Itinerary*, with the mission of reflecting on and making concrete proposals for *the teaching of religious facts in secular schools*.

In order to do this, Régis Debray has widely consulted: teachers in elementary schools, middle schools, and high schools; university professors; general inspectors for the National Education system; and associations and unions.

I wish to thank him for the quality and density of his report, as well as for his rapidity in completing the task. Above and beyond the decisions to which he has inspired me, I am certain that we will draw a collective and long-lasting benefit from the reflections contained in his report.

It is for this reason that I want it to have a wide distribution.

Thanks to Odile Jacob for having so promptly and generously brought it to completion.

Jack Lang
Minister of National Education

What Grounds?

There is an apparent consensus. French opinion by and large approves the idea of reinforcing the study of the religious in public schools. This is not only the result of traumatic current events or intellectual trends. Starting in the eighties and culminating in the 1989 report of Rector Joutard, the fundamental reasons for this have been elaborated on many occasions and from many angles—calling, essentially, for a reasoned approach to religions as facts of civilization.

It is a well-known argument. There is the threat, more and more palpable, of a collective escheat, of a rupture in the links of national and European memory, such that the missing link of religious information renders completely incomprehensible, even uninteresting, the tympana of the cathedral of Chartres, Tintoretto's *Crucifixion*, Mozart's *Don Juan*, Victor Hugo's *Booz endormi* (*Boas Asleep*), and Aragon's *La semaine sainte* (*Holy Week*). There is a flattening, a dulling of the everyday environment once Trinity is no more than a Metro station; once holidays, Easter vacation, a year of sabbatical, are coincidences of the calendar. There is anxiety about a communal dismembering of civic solidarities, a dismembering to which our ignorance of the past and the beliefs of the other, full of clichés and prejudices, contributes in no small part. This sparks a search, through the universality of the sacred, with its interdictions and permissions, for a source of federative values that could take over more fundamentally from civic education and temper the shattering of reference points, as well as an unprecedented diversity of religious affiliations in a country that is open, fortunately, to immigration from all over.

Patrimonial, social, moral distress? Increase of opacities, confusions, and intolerances, of ill-ease and wanderings? To the disquiet experienced by many—here is not the place to evaluate its pertinence or impact—let us add a more properly pedagogical reason. The collapse or erosion of the old vectors of transmission constituted by churches, families, customs, and civilities transfers onto public schools the elementary tasks of orienting the young in space and in time, tasks that civil society is no longer capable of fulfilling.

This transfer of the burden, this change in its bearer from the private sphere to the school for all, took place some thirty years ago, at the very moment when the classical humanities and literary studies were being deserted: when the preponderance of the visual, the new demographic makeup of schools, as well as a certain formalist technicity in the educational approach to texts and works, were all more or less marginalizing the old disciplines of meaning (literature, philosophy, history, art). An unfortunate coincidence that didn't make things any easier.

The "religious lack of education" of which one hears so much (in front of a Botticelli Virgin, "Who is that chick?") does not as such constitute a subject. It is a part and an effect, deriving from a more fundamental "non-culture," a loss of codes of recognition that equally affects knowledge, *savoir-vivre*, and discernment, a loss of which the National Education system has long been aware, and for good reason—since it has been on the front lines and has day after day had to fill in the breaches. It is thus not a question of reserving a special status for religious facts, by granting them a superlative privilege, but rather of making available the entire range of tools enabling middle-school and high-school students, otherwise trained for and by the consumption-communication tandem, to remain fully civilized by guaranteeing their right to a free exercise of judgment. The goal is not to put back "God in the school," but to prolong the human journey, with its multiple paths, insofar as *cumulative continuity*, which is also called *culture*, distinguishes our animal species from other, less fortunate ones. Religious traditions and the future of the humanities are in the same boat. One will not reinforce the study of the religious without reinforcing study in general.

It is here that the history of religions can take on its full educational relevance, as a means for linking the short to the long term by recovering successions and engenderings specific to humanity, which the audiovisual sphere—repetitive apotheosis of the instant—tends to efface. What we, no doubt wrongly, call the "lack of culture" of the younger generations is *another* culture, which one may define as a *culture of extension*. This culture gives priority to space over time; to the immediate over duration, taking advantage, for this, of new technological offerings (sampling and zapping, the cult of the live and the immediate, instantaneous montage and superspeed travel). A vertiginous enlargement of horizons and a drastic narrowing of chronologies. A planetary contraction and the pulverization of the calendar. One de-localizes oneself as quickly as one "de-historicizes" oneself. Would not, then, an efficacious remedy to this imbalance between space and time, the two fundamental anchors of any state of civilization, be found by bringing to bear the genealogies and underlying structures of the most recent and pressing current events? How can one understand September 11, 2001, without going back to Wahhabism, to the various Koranic filiations and the avatars of monotheism? How can one understand the conflicts that rent Yugoslavia without going back to the *filioque* schism and to the earlier confessional partitions in the Balkan zone? And how can one understand jazz and the pastor Martin Luther King without mentioning Protestantism and the Bible? The history of religions is not a collection of memories from the infancy of humanity, or a catalogue of amiable or fatal oddities. By attesting that an event (let us say, the Twin Towers) only takes on its depth, its signification, against the backdrop of time, it can help students relativize the conformist fascination exerted by images, the giddiness of publicity, the puffing and panting of information, by giving them additional means for escaping from the prison of the present, in order to *return, but with a deeper understanding, to the world of today.* This has nothing to do with some stitched-together project of "moral rearmament," with some idea for a fixed minimum dosage of spirituality, or with a complacent and exclusively patrimonial nostalgia.

In the first ranks of the effort to be undertaken, and on an equal footing, are: teachers of literature and of languages, since they are the most apt at explaining the different modes and strategies of discourse, the different turns of phrase used by the human being depending on whether he is speaking his faith, describing facts, or emitting hypotheses, which cannot be evaluated according to the same criteria or type of archive; teachers of philosophy, whom the current curriculum as well as their own reflection cannot but incite to make explicit the difference between magical, rational, and religious relationships to the world; artistic teachings, because the study of forms, symbols, and representations is necessarily confronted with religious cultures; teachers of history and of geography, since the contemporary map of the world is unintelligible without reference to the ways in which religion structures cultural regions.

What Resistances?

Remarkable steps forward have been made, particularly since 1996, in the introduction of new and excellent orientations for the history and French programs (sixth, fifth, second, and first grades[1]). It cannot seriously be said today that Islam, for example, is absent from school learning. This has become an untruth. That having been said, once one tries to go deeper into the matter, consensus crumbles. The tensions surrounding the ways and means to a better inclusion of religious questions into an entirely nonreligious teaching are and remain strong. Going from pious promises to practical decisions immediately awakens inveterate suspicions. There are symmetrical distrusts on each side; distrusts that, according to logic, should cancel one another out but that instead, in accordance with psychology, double the inhibition.

The secular side denounces, in more or less veiled words, what is seen as the Trojan horse of a masked clericalism, the ultimate ruse of proselytism (what's more, a soundly defeated proselytism) or the blind instrument of a papist Reconquista of Europe, of antiscience, or of the return of the magicians. The fox in the henhouse. Not to mention the justified fear of awakening, at the heart of the transcommunitarian school, the demons of communitarianism by bringing up questions that anger atheists no less than others. From this stems the understandable reaction: "We're not here to catechize."

The ecclesiastic or believer side denounces a different Trojan horse, that of a denigrating syncretism and a relativism which, by juxtaposing facts rendered inert and faded, would erase the boundaries between the ineffable and the dogmatic, between the "true religion" and "false" ones. How can the examination of facts be separated from the interpretations that give them meaning? Can one reduce an inner, lived engagement to a rhapsody of cold, detached observations? It would be like reducing music to a suite of notes on lined paper, or asking a blind person to speak of colors . . .

These objections have their validity. They are, however, fed in part by certain misunderstandings or mechanically made amalgamations, which it would be prudent to dissipate right away, before putting anything into practice. To address the first of these conflations: the teaching of *the* religious *is not* a religious teaching.

The vigilant defenders of free thought and of the "emancipatory school" are aware of the following distinctions, but what goes without saying is always better said.

1. No one can confuse catechism and information, profession of faith and the offering of knowledge, testimony and report. Nor the epistemology of revelation with that of reason. The sacramental relation to memory aims to increase and refine belief; the analytic relation, to increase and refine knowledge. The first type of teaching, no matter how well argued or dialecticized, presupposes the authority of a revealed word, incomparable to any other; a supernatural givenness ultimately regulated by the institution. The second proceeds by a descriptive, factual, and notional approach to the plurality of religions present from the Far East to the West, without seeking to privilege any one in particular. It is not the role of the Republic to arbitrate between beliefs, and the equality that holds in principle between believers, atheists, and agnostics is valid a fortiori for the various confessions.

2. "The quest for meaning" is indeed a social reality, which the National Education cannot neglect, but one should not, in response to this demand and out of facility, recognize "religions" (an equivocal term, by the way, which appeared rather late and is often inappropriate to the realities it designates) as having any kind of monopoly on meaning. As regards the metaphysical anxieties of human beings, where it is a matter of what binds the individual to time, to the cosmos, and to his fellow men, instituted religions have a priori neither exclusivity nor superiority. Schools of wisdom, philosophies, systems of knowledge, and art itself have for three millennia explored the relations that can be formed between our cardinal points, without necessarily responding to "the call from the other side." These profane answers to the questions posed by death, by the origin and finality of the universe, fully contribute to the creation of meaning. The reminder of this obvious fact does not prevent us from realizing that today, like yesterday and probably like tomorrow (if one admits that the successive ages of the history of mentalities do not

supplant one another but constitute structural stages of the human psyche), people live and kill each other for and in the name of symbols. Just as they tear one another apart, literally, for logos, ads, and images. Cultures, languages, religions, identities, and patrimonies bring millions of protestors to the streets, today even more so than yesterday (and one has seen this in Paris, with the matter of schools, in both ways[2]). And it is in regard to the symbolic universe as such—into which law, morals, the history of art, and myth may also enter, in different capacities—that the school has a duty to promote critical and reflexive thought, especially through the teaching of philosophy. How can the irreversible adventure of civilizations be retraced without taking into account the wake left by the major religions?[3] This task urges itself all the more so today in that the economy, new technologies, and references to business and management are imposed upon or proposed to students—the milieu demands it—as the sole and ultimate horizon of reference.

3. The relegation of the religious fact outside the boundaries of rational transmission and publicly controlled knowledge favors the pathology of this terrain rather than cleansing it. The market of credulousness, the press and the bookstore, swell the wave of esotericism and irrationalism. Is it not the obligation of the Republican school to counterbalance audience ratings, charlatans, and sectarian passions? To abstain from the subject is not the solution. Rodin's *The Thinker*, who, with a negligent kick, sends the Bible flying into the distance (as seen in a caricature) forgets that the holy Book does not then disappear into nature or become lost to everyone. Fundamentalist readings will be provided elsewhere (out of contract), all the more pernicious in that the young indoctrinates will not have received any qualified perspective on this text of reference. It has been proven that, for many young fundamentalists, an objective and contextualized knowledge of holy texts, as well as of their own traditions, leads to shaking the guardianship of fanaticizing authorities, who are sometimes ignorant or incompetent.

The educated representatives of the confessions know this well, but it is useful to repeat clearly some other pieces of evidence in addition to the foregoing, for the sake of believers who may still be hesitant.

4. Just as the scholar and the witness do not invalidate one another, the *objectifying* approach and the *confessing* approach do not enter into competition, provided that the two can exist and prosper simultaneously (which is allowed for by the freedom of conscience, and in particular, by the various schools of theology, certain of which belong to the state, as in Alsace-Moselle). The proof of this lies in the fact that the two can co-exist in certain people. (An exegete can be both critical and ordained.) The point of view of faith and the point of view of knowledge do not constitute a zero-sum game. This latter takes as its premise the presupposed divide between the religious as *object of culture* (falling within the scope of the responsibilities of public instruction, which has as its obligation to examine the contribution of different religions to the symbolic institution of humanity) and the religious as *object of cult* (requiring a voluntary personal investment, within the framework of private associations). The chemistry of colors does not rule out

the history of painting, no more than the formula H_2O undermines the presentation of thermal baths, or disfigures the immemorial resonances of water rituals. *Laïcité* is only concerned with what is common to all; that is to say, the visible and tangible imprints of various collective faiths on the world shared by humans—without, out of prudence and decency, mixing in that which is common only to some, namely, intimate experiences.

5. Teaching deontology, which applies to the presentation of doctrines in philosophy as well as to that of social systems in history, stipulates the bracketing of personal convictions. To make a reality or a doctrine available for knowledge is one thing; to promote a norm or an ideal is another. Teachers are well versed—beyond the simple obligation to keep their reserve—in the art of reducing without flattening, explaining without devaluing, allowing something to be felt without highlighting their own position. The family of so-called literary disciplines has long led them to balance a comprehending proximity with a critical distance, empathy with detachment, whether in relation to texts, to civilizations, or to individuals. A didactic of sciences of religions, which undoubtedly remains to be created or perfected, will be able to take over from there, with the help of pedagogical experimentation. Religions have a history, but they are not only history, and even less so statistics. Certainly. To tell a historical context without the spirituality that animates it is to run the risk of devitalizing it. Inversely, to speak of a form of wisdom without the social context that produced it is to run the risk of mystifying it. The first abstraction is what makes the entomologist—if not the Grévin Wax Museum. The second makes the guru—if not the Sun Temple. Here one must count on a third way, one, however, that represents nothing new for the best of our school tradition for over a century now: to teach facts in order to cultivate their meanings.

6. The lack of religious culture, according to numerous indicators, affects private confessional schools just as much as it does public schools. Several indicators show that ignorance in this area is correlated, on a large scale, with the level of study of students, and not with their religious background or family belonging. Given that religious schools [*boîtes cathos*] are no longer—far from it—the "fortresses of faith" of yesterday, the traditionalist call for "each one in his or her place" seems to lack realism. Apart from the differences created by social selection, which constitute no meager advantage, private and public schools are faced, ultimately, with the same amnesia, the same deficiencies.

What Constraints?

Both secular precaution and the saturation of the educational system lead us to ratify the options already taken: that is, to reject the proposal, sometimes made, for an additional and distinct "subject" of religious studies in primary and secondary education.

The history of religions, just like the history of arts and of sciences and techniques, can, undoubtedly, constitute a specific discipline of higher education and research, as an autonomous branch of preexisting disciplines (history, philosophy, sociology, mediology). But it cannot, any more than its peer disciplines, lay claim to a place of its own in high school and middle school. The responsibility for teaching it is incumbent upon the personnel in place, via the disciplines already recognized. But this means that these teachers must be accompanied and supported in the pursuit of their efforts.

Public schools cannot alone take on responsibility for all the problems unresolved by society. In the crisis of growth they are undergoing—the expansion of high schools, an overload of activities, the cramming of schedules, the piling up of curricula—at a time when one speaks, perhaps too much, of lightening and reducing the load, it would not be reasonable to add a new square to a grid already greatly encumbered, one whose weight and the difficulty of "passing it on" to heterogeneous classes many teachers already regret. To promote the history of religions as a specific discipline in secondary education would be to do the greatest disservice to it, since, in a schedule as full as an egg, it would only be able to occupy a decorative place and a marginal time, like that of music class.[4]

In the longer term there would also be the danger of substituting clerics for lay persons, thus circumventing the regular national examinations for teachers (*licence, agrégation*, or *CAPES* [*Certificat d'Aptitude au Professorat de l'Enseignement Secondaire*]) and the validation of their knowledge by an independent institution (the National Council of Universities). Sooner or later, outside interveners, and not just any ones, might be proposed to replace teachers: graduates of theological schools and established representatives of different confessions, who would be able to assert real qualifications and age-old experience in this regard. Jules Ferry would at that point no longer recognize his peers.[5]

It is therefore fitting to direct efforts to the content of what is taught, by a more reasoned convergence between existing disciplines, especially to direct them to the preparation of teachers. It is they whom we must incite, reassure, and uninhibit, and, to this end, better arm intellectually and professionally in the face of an always sensitive question, one that touches the deepest identity of students and families. A greater competence in a subject judged, not without reason, to be thorny or complicated (and socially much more of a "hot" issue, in fact, than the history of science or of art) should allow for tension and passion to be removed from the subject and even, let us risk the word, for its banalization—without detracting, entirely to the contrary, from its intrinsic dignity.

This teaching of teachers requires bringing together the two blades of a single pair of scissors, as yet too far separated: the school and the university. There has been a disjuncture between specialized research and general teaching, between the internal evolution of knowledge and the ordinary practice of its transmission, between a "high culture" reserved for a social or intellectual elite and a "middle level" exposed, by a kind of wind tunnel effect, to the simplifying currents of the media. This has as one consequence, among others, comical or heartbreaking misunderstandings. Don't certain school manuals, labeled "secular," contain certain formulas worthy of nineteenth-century sacred history ("Abraham, father of the Jewish people," or "Jesus, founder of Christianity")—

oversimplifications from which the specialist in religion would abstain? It is necessary to oppose such a segregation of university and school, a segregation that is hardly democratic and is as harmful to the tasks of the former as to those of the latter.

To organize the national archipelago of "sciences of religion" into a network, to open up the enclave of research so that it can expand outward, and to avail the teaching world of quality professional training: these three instances are but one, since they condition one another.

What *Laïcité*?

The principle of *laïcité* places freedom of conscience (the freedom to have a religion or not) over and above what is called in certain countries "religious freedom" (that of being able to choose a religion, provided one has one). In this sense, *laïcité* is not one spiritual option among others; it is what makes their co-existence possible, for that which is common to all people by right must take precedent over that which separates them in fact. The faculty, inherent to all individuals endowed with reason, for accessing the globality of human experience implies a struggle against religious illiteracy and the study of existing beliefs. Thus, one cannot separate the principle of *laïcité* from the study of the religious (whence the title of the module suggested further on). Moreover, it is important to *begin* with a first lesson on the foundations and requirements of this principle: a principle that is, all in all, hardly banal and that it would be wrong to believe has become custom; a principle whose relevance is constantly being increased by the fury surrounding it. Far from constituting an exception to *laïcité*, a concession to lobbies, or the effect of an inexorable erosion of the principle, to carry out the projects developed here requires, rather, that the public school show itself not one bit less secular, but even more so, by grounding itself from the outset in a clearly proclaimed order of values, no less constraining than those of the religious and occasionally opposable to certain of them. (To each one his credo. We respect yours. Respect ours . . .) The procedure proposed here must openly recognize its own limits from the outset, even as it seeks the best possible understanding of the symbolic and existential sense that rituals and dogmas have for believers. It cannot and must not claim or attempt to reach the beating heart of lived faith or to substitute for those whose vocation this is. Personal adherence is not within its province, no more so than it is within it to refuse such adherence. Within and because of this self-limitation, the spirit of *laïcité* should have nothing to fear here. This is for three reasons.

1. To extend the discourse of reason into the domain of the imaginary and the symbolic, without fleeing difficulty, is to pursue the "combat for science," which frees us from fears and prejudices. A *laïcité* that ducks this task cripples itself. To open young minds to the whole range of comportments and cultures in order to help them discover

the world in which they live, and to what collective heritages they are accountable, must lead to shedding light upon what is obscure. This means overcoming a certain naive scientism, which was the childhood illness of a progressing science, just as a certain shadowy secularism [*laïcisme*] was the childhood illness of the freedom of examination.[6] The repression of the religious as the black hole of reason, outside the realm of what could be divulged at the risk of fueling mysticism, perhaps testified to a *laïcité* that still had the complexes of the conditions of its birth—a "Catho-secularism"—or to a counter-religion of the state marked by the battles it had to lead, at full force, against the Catholicism of the syllabus and of the moral order. Two centuries later, everyone can breathe more easily: the historical landscape is no longer the same.

2. Only a proven secular deontology can prevent the confusion of authorities by the impartiality and neutrality it demands of teachers, by refusing anything resembling the "conflict of two Frances" (the principle of *laïcité*, from its origins on, having been marked by militant antireligiosity). To teach under this banner is to regain the "high period" of secular and republican laws, which led, in fact, to the creation of an autonomous sector of the École Pratique in 1886, for the study of religious phenomena in a nontheological mode.

3. If *laïcité* is inseparable from a veritable democratic aim, then to transcend prejudices, to promote the values of discovery (India, Tibet, America), to loosen the grip of identity, at the heart of a society exposed more than ever before to the parceling out of collective personalities, is to help defuse the various fundamentalisms, which have in common this intellectual deterrent: that one must be of a culture to be able to speak of it. It is precisely in this sense that one may advance the following, without excluding other confessions of faith: *laïcité* is an opportunity for Islam in France, and the Islam of France is an opportunity for *laïcité*.

In this respect, it is not a matter of *aggiornamento*, but of a rejuvenation. Nor is it a matter of a pluralized *laïcité*, open and repentant, but rather a *laïcité* refounded, refreshed, reassured of itself and of its own values. The stability of the philosophical postulates on which it is based does not, fortunately, prevent its implementation from being evolutionary, from being innovative. The stormy and strained conditions surrounding the emergence of the Republic made advisable a deliberate and justified abstention regarding this subject, and that is completely to the honor of those teachers, since this abstention stemmed as much from a respect for intimate beliefs as from an awareness of the divisions they could create among students. This methodical abstention has been interpreted, sometimes wrongly, as a denegation of the object itself. The time seems to have come now for a passage from a *laïcité of incompetence* (the religious, by construction, is none of our business) to a *laïcité of intelligence* (it is our duty to understand the religious). There are neither taboos nor zones forbidden to the eyes of the secular. The calm and methodical examination of religious facts, within the refusal of any confessional alignment—would this not be, in the end, the touchstone and test of truth for this intellectual ascesis?

Inscribed in the Constitution, more demanding than a juridical separation of church and state and more ambitious than a simple "secularization" (which de-confessionalizes religious values in order better to deploy them within civil society), our national approach—a principle of universal right, the application of which is, in France, although imperfect, more advanced than elsewhere—constitutes a singularity in Europe. Mexico and Turkey were or are other such singularities. This fundamental originality is sometimes imputed to us as a wrong, and voices are raised to bring what is considered an anachronism or a defect into line with the European norm, by exhorting the black sheep to align itself with the "communitarian model." This is to forget two things. First, insofar as the teaching of religions is concerned, there is not one single model but as many situations as there are countries. In Ireland, where the Constitution gives homage to the Holy Trinity, and in Greece, where the autocephalous Orthodox Church is the state's, this teaching is confessional and obligatory. In Spain, where religious instruction is a matter of catechism, given by teachers who are chosen, to be sure, by the public administration, but from a list of candidates presented by the diocese, it has become optional. In Portugal, despite the proclaimed principle of neutrality, to this day it is provided in public schools by the Catholic Church. In Denmark, where the Lutheran Church is the national church, there is no catechism but, at each level of the "school of the people," a nonobligatory class on "knowledge of Christianity." In Germany, where education varies according to the *Länder*, Christian religious instruction is part of official curricula, often under the control of the churches, and the grades received in religion class count toward passing to the next grade. In Belgium, the state schools allow a choice between religion class and a nonconfessional ethics class. In sum: there is no European norm on the matter; each collective mentality deals with its historical heritage and relations of symbolic forces as best it can. Second, this "European" teaching is often in crisis, provoking protest from the "unreligious" and desertion by others. Let us note that in Alsace-Moselle, where schools follow the German model and where religious teaching is obligatory and of a confessional nature, requests for exemption now come from four-fifths of the high-school population (one-third in primary schools). It would be wrong to believe that the demand for "religious culture" is a demand for religion, in the institutional sense of the term. To confuse these two systematically, in the world such as it is, would be harmful to the undertaking.

From this point on, it is permissible to think that our European neighbors and friends might regard with interest a more balanced or more distanced approach. Far from being, in this matter, the caboose, our Republican school finds itself, shortly before the centenary of the separation of church and state, the locomotive of the future. The outmoded at the forefront? These things happen.

What Recommendations?

These considerations lead us to submit to the minister twelve concrete propositions, of unequal scope and bearing, but which together can shape the new impetus we envision.

1. Immediately to ask the corps of general inspectors whom this concerns— essentially history-geography and literature—for an *evaluation report* regarding the 1996 modifications to programs, relying for this on the corps of regional inspectors. This initial assessment, at the end of an accelerated procedure, will convey what has been gathered through experience in the field to the *Desco* [*Direction de l'enseignement scolaire*]: difficulties encountered among students, hesitations or discomforts experienced by teachers, choices made within the framework of curricula. In this way, one will be better able to adapt instructions and orientations to real conditions . . .

2. It would be of great benefit to reestablish coherence in the curriculum, especially in the *seconde*[7] history programs, whose six themes lead into one another.[8] Previously, teachers were invited to lighten the program by making certain chapters optional, whereas the ensemble is inscribed within a cultural continuity that loses much of its meaning if divided up. This point applies to more than one discipline. How can one teach sixteenth-century French literature if the history of the Renaissance is not well known? How can one understand the state of nature in Rousseau or the Hegelian odyssey if one has never heard of Adam and Eve?

3. The new orientations in *middle school* (within the central cycle, *cinquième* and *quatrième*[9]) and, in particular, the *paths of discovery* programs should be formatted to allow for the discussion of religious questions in a concrete and personalized form, in relation to the already modified programs of French and history. Of the four proposed domains, "arts and humanities," just like "languages and civilizations," offers favorable entryways to the study of, for example, practices of pilgrimage, rites of purification, or various religious architectures. A new supporting document for pedagogical teams could encourage and clarify this possibility.

4. In high school, in addition to efforts within the disciplines, which remain important, *structured personal exercises* (TPE [*travaux personnels encadrés*]) could favor sensitive, transverse, and interdisciplinary approaches to religious phenomena. It would be worthwhile—taking into consideration the desiderata of students and local resources (museums, churches, mosques, synagogues, religious festivals, etc.)—to have students study, for example, in comparative terms: fasts (Ramadan, Yom Kippur, Lent), the social status of women, the figuration of the divine in monotheism and polytheism, and so on. *Arts teaching* can here, along with history and philosophy, play a key role, approaching these matters through major works of religious patrimony, just as through cinema, photography, dance, musical education, or live spectacles.

5. For future teachers in *initial training*: the creation of a module in the IUFM (Instituts universitaires de formation des maîtres, university institutes for the formation of teachers, which have replaced the old Écoles normales). There are many cultural contributions that can be made to the general formation of teachers in training, and modules have accumulated here and there, sometimes excessively, on various subjects. The theme of "*laïcité* and religions," however, as distinct from the history of art and even the history of sciences, seems directly linked to the founding principle of the teaching profession. Thus, if one were to envisage a national framework for training courses and if certain priorities were recognized within it, this module would certainly have a role to play. The national guidelines for the IUFM would call for an *obligatory module* entitled "philosophy of *laïcité* and the teaching of religious facts, " to be entrusted to the professors of philosophy, literature, and history of each school district, as well as to certain resource personnel; university academics specialized and trained to this end (see below). Co-interventions would be systematized according to local conditions. This module (ten additional hours per year) would not take place until the second year, after the entrance exam, and it would be proposed to future teachers of primary school as well as to those of secondary school (general, technical, and professional schools). Either there should be a formal validation of this module, or these themes should be allowed as subjects of professional theses. The thirty-some IUFM, at the juncture (in virtue of their position, not of their status) of "higher" and "primary/secondary" education, seem perfectly designed to serve as a point of irrigation and contact between research labs and schools. As it has been recognized (Comité national d'evaluation, 2001) that "culture is the poor relation of the IUFM," given that they are more geared to using documents than to problematizing them, the introduction of such a module would contribute to widening this horizon, opening onto the most burning issues and realities of the vast world (including in its most exotic or disorienting forms for us: Buddhism, Hinduism, Shinto).

6. For continuing training: a *national multidisciplinary workshop*, an annual meeting written into the calendar, would bring together for three days, starting next school year, on the one hand, a group of renowned researchers assembled around the fifth section of the EPHE (École pratique des hautes études,) and on the other, a group comprising one regional pedagogical inspector per school district, in history-geography, philosophy, literature, languages, and the arts, accompanied by one teacher-instructor per discipline of his or her choice from each school district.[10]

Why proceed this way, in stages and by relay? Because there are, on the one hand, about forty thousand teachers of history-geography (*certifiés, agrégés, PEGC, PLP2,*[11] etc.), sixty thousand teachers of literature, six thousand of philosophy, without counting the thousands of language and arts teachers, and so on; and, on the other hand, a few hundred potential high-level instructors. These orders of scale, and their dissymmetry, make it necessary, if one wants high school and middle school teachers to have solid references at their disposal, to proceed by stages and increments.

The program for the three days of this seminar of higher study, covering the range of major religions present in France (plus the question of sects), whose elaboration would be entrusted to the Religious Sciences section of the EPHE—a section in which Sylvain Lévi, Marcel Mauss, Étienne Gilson, Alexandre Koyré, Louis Massignon, Alexandre Kojève, Georges Dumézil, Claude Lévi-Strauss, and others distinguished themselves—would be divided between lectures and workshops. The conferences would be recorded, and the cassettes made available to school libraries via the CNDP (Centre national de documentation pédagogique). The CNDP Internet site would take care of any follow-up.

This workshop could be held at the ENS (École normale supérieure), rue d'Ulm, more specifically, in number 29, the former movie theater, the Jules Ferry room. The ENS would provide, at the intellectual level, its own researchers, and, at the material level, administration. This, in the spirit of the mission entrusted to it by its lyric founder, Lakanal: to act as a reservoir for Enlightenment, guaranteeing multiple channels of diffusion.[12]

7. In order to provide truly continual training, the theme *laïcité*/history would be written into the documents of the national management program for rectors' offices, which could include it in their books of specifications and then solicit the participation of the universities. Thus, activities would be planned within the *academic training program*, led by the participants in this national seminar, on an interdisciplinary basis. Summer university courses would then take over the rest, according to demand.

8. The possibility of placing the religious sciences section of the EPHE at the head of a network of the best centers of study existing in France (CNRS research laboratories, universities of Paris and of the regions) would be explored, in order to be able to respond to this ensemble of demands for initial and continuing training. It would perhaps be desirable to have a European Institute of Sciences of Religion, identifiable on the international scene, of which the "Fifth Section" would be the spearhead,[13] a transformation that would put an end to its relative lack of visibility, the scattering of its locales across Paris, and the underutilization of its scientific potential. This federative institute, within the framework of a general renewal of the EPHE, would reinforce its scientific research projects but would also be endowed with the means for offering to the IUFM the same kinds of services it already offers in the history of sciences through the *cité des Sciences et de l'Industrie* [science and industry complex in Paris] (distance education, video conferencing, bibliographies, dossiers, etc.).

The advantage of such a move would consist in making available a recognized organizational center, independent of ecclesiastical or ideological influence, that would guarantee objectivity and be prepared to take on various schools of thought and disciplines, as well as to validate, under certain circumstances, a particular outside contribution. If the centers of scientific excellence do not, in this matter, necessarily respect the private/public or religious/secular division and if, in our humble opinion, it would be wrong to be deprived of the support of such competences (the Biblical and Archeological School of

Jerusalem, the Institute of Training for the Study and Teaching of Religions [IFER, Institut de formation pour l'étude et l'enseignement des religions] of Dijon, faculties of theology, etc.), nevertheless, it is necessary that there be a specifically university decision-making body, capable of evaluating and selecting, on the basis of purely disciplinary and scholarly criteria, these potential contributors to the tasks of communal training. This change of image, scale, and administrative status, which would testify to a clear will, would only make sense by bringing library, administration, and classrooms together at a single address, in order to ensure a singular presence, in keeping with a mission of national interest.

As a prefiguration, an "education/society/religion" research group of professor/researchers, attached directly to the DES (Direction de l'enseignement supérieur) and to the Desco, could be created.

9. The Institute would have as one of its missions to develop adequate pedagogical tools (on paper or CD-ROM) and to contribute to a better evaluation of the existing publications on the educational market. It would be a shame if, in this regard, the report of Dominique Borne on the "school manual" were to remain a dead letter. In order to carry this out, the representatives of religions present in France, as well as those of other families of thought, should have the possibility of being given a hearing, as need be.

10. The minister, for his part, could ask the National Council of Curricula (Conseil national des programmes) to bring together a group of experts belonging to the various disciplines involved (art history, history, literature, philosophy, languages, plastic arts, music) in order to produce a collection of dossiers and pedagogical tools for students. The General Inspection should of course be associated with this. It would be a matter of favoring a head-on approach to religious facts through their artistic and cultural manifestations.

11. It would be appropriate to extend the core program of the aforementioned training to administrative and support personnel and in particular to the heads and directors of schools, who are daily confronted with the test of these topical questions (refusal to take biology or civic education classes, wearing of the veil, co-education), for it is they above all who come into conversation with minority groups invoking supposed religious knowledge in order to obtain modifications of school regulations. "Philosophy of *laïcité* and the teaching of religious facts," based on the study of pertinent cases, is an element to be integrated into the training program for territorial inspectors (at least six hours), and to be put into place under the authority of the DPATE (Direction des personnels administratifs, techniques et d'encadrement; Direction of administrative, technical, and support personnel). The same goes for the Academic Teams of School Life (EAVS; Équipes académiques de la vie scholaire) charged with training the heads of schools.

12. The opinion of the minister's recently established committee for reflection and propositions on *laïcité* in the school could be solicited for developing the new module intended primarily for the IUFM. It would be equally appropriate that the committee be

associated with the preparation of the annual national workshop organized by the European Institute of Sciences of Religions.

Let us recapitulate. These propositions, deliberately pragmatic and modest, are only valid though their reciprocal articulation. Some will judge them to be quite limited. In spite of appearances, upon closer examination, the refusal to advocate a separate school subject can be an intellectual benefit, since the religious traverses more than one field of study and human activity. Inversely, however, this can become a pedagogical danger: the danger of treating the matter in a dispersed or offhand manner. We must thus make our way, in the climate of the times, between too much and too little. The simultaneous execution of these various propositions stems from a measured ambition: to reach, within the school and beyond, a "critical mass."

Postscript, Letter of Invitation

Republic of France
Ministry of National Education
The Minister

Paris, December 3, 2001

Dear Professor Régis Debray:

After years dedicated to the subject, you have recently published a much-noted work on the knowledge of religions, entitled *God, an Itinerary*.

In it, you discuss in passing the question of teaching about religions in school. "The Republic, rightfully, does not *recognize* any religious system. Must it therefore refuse to *know* any?" you emphasize.

This question does indeed present itself in our teaching, notably, in the programs of history and philosophy.

In order to pursue the renewal in public service to which I have engaged myself, it appears to me necessary to reexamine the place accorded to the teaching of religious facts. This, within a secular and Republican framework. That is the mission I hope to entrust to you.

I thus ask you to analyze what exists on the subject and to draw up propositions for me concerning curricula and above all the training of teachers. Considerable steps forward have been made in this direction, since and including the report requested by Lionel Jospin from Rector Joutard in 1989. This effort must now take the next step.

The various branches of the Minister of National Education will be available to facilitate your mission.

You can equally solicit the help of the general inspection of the National Education—in particular of the groups of history and geography, philosophy, literature, and artistic instruction—the school district offices, and university teacher training institutes. Qualified personnel of your choice will be associated with this mission. You could also consult qualified religious and civil authorities.

A first stage of your mission will consist in turning in, on March 15, 2002, the first elements of your reflection.

I am counting on you.

With all my friendship,
J. Lang

—translated by Daniela Ginsburg

Secularization: Notes Toward a Genealogy

Jan N. Bremmer

In his fascinating but not always easy to follow study "What Might an Anthropology of Secularism Look Like?" Talal Asad embarks on an important quest, namely, to determine the nature of the secular. He takes it that the secular is "a concept that brings together certain behaviors, knowledges, and sensibilities in modern life." Moreover, he stresses that "the secular is neither singular in origin nor stable in its historical identity, although it works through a series of particular oppositions." In fact, Asad takes the view "that 'the religious' and the 'secular' are not essentially fixed categories." He also assumes "that there were breaks between Christian and secular life in which words and practices were rearranged, and new discursive grammars replaced previous ones." That is why, in his study, he takes up "fragments of a discourse that is often asserted to be an essential part of 'religion'—or at any rate, to have a close affinity with it—to show how the sacred and the secular depend on each other.'" Asad himself draws his material "almost entirely from West European history because that history has had profound consequences for the ways that the doctrine of secularism has been conceived and implemented in the rest of the modernizing world."[1]

Asad's discussion shows the problems that arise from the use of modern terms with the root *secular*. Eventually, they all derive from the Latin *saecularis*, the adjective of the noun *saeculum*. The etymology of the latter word is unknown, like many words with *–ae-*. Originally, the term denoted a long period of time, and it is perhaps best known in the *Ludi saeculares* of Augustus. Only in Christian times did the meanings of *saeculum* and *saecularis* undergo important changes. Prominent Christian theologians, such as Tertullian and Augustine,[2] developed the notion of *saeculum* as the world in which we live, a world that is characterized by sin and the rejection of God.[3] This notion remained alive during the whole time Latin played an important role in the world of scholars and clergy, and it is therefore not surprising that *saecularis* gave birth to the terms *secular*, *secularism*, and *secularization*.

A thorough exploration of these terms would transcend my present scope. I will therefore limit myself to investigating the term that is perhaps the most influential in discussions of religion in recent decades, namely, *secularization*. Like Asad, I, too, will limit myself to Western Europe, but I am interested in a national differentiation regarding the rise of this concept. In which countries was it coined in its present meaning? Genealogical investigations of terms are always problematic. Who can claim to have read everything, or even the majority of the relevant literature? Certainly not this author, but there is always room for a modest beginning, with perhaps some observations of interest, and that is all I claim for my contribution.

As a noun, *secularization* originated in France.[4] In the second half of the sixteenth century, we already find *sécularisation* and the corresponding verb *séculariser*, meaning "the transfer of goods from the possession of the Church into that of the world."[5] The time of the word's origin cannot be chance. It was in the religious struggles caused by the Reformation that the problem suddenly became acute, as it would remain for a long time.[6] The terms did not immediately gain general acceptance in France, however. In 1611 the Latin term for the same process, *saecularisatio*, was still qualified by *ut dicunt*, "as some people call it." Subsequent dictionaries use the verb only in the meaning *clericum religiosum ad seculares clericos referre* until the middle of the eighteenth century, when the meaning "transfer of goods from the possession of the church into that of the world of the lay people" became gradually accepted. This can be seen in the lemma "Sécularisation" of the famous *Encyclopédie*, although it still has *l'action de render séculier un religieux* ("the action of rendering a religious secular") as its first meaning.[7] It fits this slow development of the French term that *saecularisatio* is not attested in French canonical law before the seventeenth century and becomes normal only in the eighteenth century.[8] Earlier Latin used the expression *profanatio* or *reductio ad saecularitas*, which may have been the basis for the French vocabulary.[9]

The French usage became known in Germany on the afternoon of Tuesday, May 8, 1646. Then Henri II d'Orléans, Duc de Longueville,[10] the leader of the French delegation at the negotiations in Münster to end the Thirty Year War, used the verb *séculariser* for the complicated question of the status of Catholic goods in the Protestant countries. And just as above the expression *ut dicunt* indicated a lack of familiarity with the Latin term in France, so it is only natural that its usage in Germany raised some eyebrows. This appears from the German report of the negotiations, which specifies that, regarding *Geistlicher Güter* ("spiritual goods"), Longueville stated that it was unthinkable that those "that had been taken away from the Catholic Church would be *secularized*, as he said [*wie er redete*], unless with the express consent of the Pope."[11]

Despite its innovative character, the term was an instant success, and the closure of monasteries or the liquidation of goods of the Catholic Church immediately became known as *saecularisatio* and *secularizare* in legal terminology in Germany,[12] as witness the titles of books and pamphlets regarding the subject. Unsurprisingly, these terms are found first in treatises by Protestant authors.[13] Yet it is not until the eighteenth century that we find the German terms *Secularisiren, Secularisirung, Secularisation* accepted in a leading German lexicon, which clearly considers *Secularisirung* and *Secularisation* still to be homonyms.[14] The famous *Reichsdeputationshauptschluss* of 1803, the last important law of the ancient German Empire, which compensated the German emperor with goods from the Church for the loss of the left bank of the Rhine to Napoleon, popularized *Säkularisation* in Germany, and in this meaning the word remains alive in German until the present day.[15]

In the nineteenth century, there are no new semantic developments in this particular field in Germany. Admittedly, we find an extremely differentiated vocabulary for what we nowadays call "secularisation," but the German equivalent of that term was accepted only in the twentieth century. During the whole of the nineteenth century, German thinkers virtually always use the term *Verweltlichung*, even though Marx already uses *Säkularisation* in a context that suggests the possibility of a development toward the modern notion;[16] similarly, the philosophers Paul York von Wartenburg and Wilhelm Dilthey occasionally use the verb *säkularisiren* to indicate development toward a world in which man leads a life independent from the Church.[17]

It is only with the generation, at the turn of the twentieth century, of Werner Sombart, the man who coined the term *capitalism*, Max Weber, and Ernst Troeltsch that a new era in the usage of *Säkularisation* gradually becomes visible.[18] Weber was the first to look at the prominence of clubs and societies in Western society as a consequence of the "secularization process . . . into which in modern times phenomena born of religious conceptions everywhere decline,"[19] but the idea did not become a central concept in his sociology of religion.[20] Nevertheless, the names Sombart, Weber, and Troeltsch indicate that the rise of the term in Germany was a matter of reflection within, or stimulated by, the Protestant tradition, which was more self-critical and more self-reflexive than the contemporary Catholic tradition.[21] At the same time, this reflection was stimulated by the loss of Christian influence in Germany, a loss that perhaps was stronger than in any other European country, making Berlin the least religious capital of its time.[22]

This reflection received a strong stimulus at a conference of the International Missionary Council in Jerusalem in 1928. Here the American Quaker theologian Rufus Jones contributed a preliminary paper entitled "Secular Civilization and the Christian Task." He stated that the greatest rival of Christianity was not any of the great world religions but "a world-wide secular way of life and interpretation of the nature of things."[23] The lecture provoked a tremendous response: the relevant section had to meet twice, and nearly half of all the participants of the conference came to the discussion.[24] Its impact was especially visible in Germany, where the themes of secularism and, in its wake, secularization clearly had struck a nerve.[25] Not only was secularization an important theme of subsequent German missionary conferences in Bremen (1930) and Halle (1931),[26] but the first, if hardly satisfactory, German investigations into the history and meaning of the concept of *Säkularisierung* appeared around 1930.[27] The interest was still so fresh, however, that the lemma "Säkularisation" in the second edition of the leading German Protestant authoritative lexicon, *Die Religion in Geschichte und Gegenwart* (*Religion in History and the Present*) of 1931 did not refer to its "sociological" meaning. Yet the *Grossen Herder* of 1935 carried a lemma "Säkularisierung" in the modern meaning,[28] and from the 1930s on this term gradually became the German equivalent of the English *secularization*, whereas *Säkularisation* became limited to the transfer of church goods into worldly hands.[29]

Unfortunately, the rise to power of the Nazis in 1933 put a lid on further discussions. Only around 1960 did interest flare up again, but the discussion hardly transcended the German-speaking world.[30] The third edition of *Die Religion in Geschichte und Gegenwart* in 1961 still does not contain a lemma "Säkularisation, Säkularisierung" with its "sociological" meaning, and Hermann Zabel's solid dissertation of 1968 on the history of the concept of secularization ends its main text with a discussion of Hans Blumenberg's *Die Legitimität der Neuzeit* (*The Legitimacy of the Modern Era*)—not a word about the recent Anglo-American studies.[31] Even Zabel's impressive lemma in the *Geschichtliche Grundbegriffe* (*Basic Historical Concepts*) of 1984 does not display any familiarity with the Anglo-American developments. Globalization finally also reached Germany, however,[32] and around the year 2000 the four most important German lexica of theology and religious studies all have an entry "Säkularisierung,"[33] though it was still lacking in the "*grosse*" *Duden* of 1994.[34]

In the United States, secularization as a theme has been on the scholarly agenda for longer than in any other Western country. In fact, already in 1912 there appeared a book called *The Secularization of American Education*.[35] As with many American scholars in later years, though, the term is used for just one section of society and thus in a worn-away metaphorical usage of the original meaning. Pitirim Sorokin still used the term in quotation marks in his influential 1937 study *Cultural and Social Dynamics*.[36] The exceptions to this rule were a group of sociologists from the University of Chicago and the Lynds of *Middletown*.

Robert and Helen Lynd introduced the term *secularization* in their famous 1929 study *Middletown* to denote many of the developments that later would be generally accepted in the secularization paradigm, such as the separation of religion from politics, the restriction of religious activities to certain buildings and times, the growth of civil marriage or—an interesting observation—change in the nature of titles of books.[37] In 1928, the Chicago scholar Everett Hughes was the first to use the term in a more theoretical discussion,[38] shortly followed by Howard P. Becker, in a more elaborate study of 1931. Becker connected the process of secularization with the growing mobility and concomitant changes in personality of modern man and referred to the interest in secularization of Tönnies, Durkheim, Malinowski, and Shotwell, in none of whose works the term actually plays a major role. Becker had studied twice in Cologne in the 1920s, however, and there can be no doubt that his interest was fueled by German developments.[39]

It is not so easy to determine when *secularization* became the paradigmatic term in the United States for the changing role of religion in modern society. It seems that the term grew only gradually in importance and content, with an increasing reliance on empirical data from the late 1950s onward.[40] Only about 1963, when two Central Europeans, Peter Berger and Thomas Luckmann, started publishing studies regarding secularization, did the term receive more or less its modern meaning. Their writings proved very influential in England and Germany, but at the time the spread of the term must have been perceived by only a small circle of scholars, since the authoritative *International Encyclopedia of the Social Sciences* (1968) still lacks a lemma "Secularization." In fact, there are virtually no American books or articles with *Secularization* in the title, but there is now a lemma "Secularization" in the new *International Encyclopedia of Social and Behavioral Sciences* of 2001.[41]

Unlike in Germany, secularization became a concept of discussion relatively late in England. Admittedly, Hugh McLeod claims that the Anglo-Irish historian Walter Lecky was, in 1865, the first to use the term in a wider sense.[42] It is true that Lecky refers to a "general secularisation of the European intellect" and a "secularisation of politics,"[43] but in these cases the older meaning of *secularization* is still in the background, and similar expressions had already occurred earlier in France. The rise of the term in the English world is clearly related to the theological debates of the 1960s,[44] when we find the term *secularization* for the first time in the title of an English book, namely, *The Secularisation of Christianity*, by the English theologian Eric Mascall, whose work was a reaction to the then famous 1963 studies *Honest to God*, by John Robinson, and *The Secular Meaning of the Gospel*, by Paul van Buren. These books, helped by Harvey Cox's *The Secular City* (1965), contributed to the sociological discussion of secularization that became so popular in the late 1960s in the works of Bryan Wilson and David Martin, a Methodist in those days, who has since become a rather High Anglican. It is suggestive of the contemporary transformation of *secularization* from a purely descriptive term into a paradigm that already in 1965 Martin felt compelled to publish an article called "Towards Eliminating the Concept of Secularization,"[45] even though his protest proved to be unsuccessful. Yet despite all this attention, the wider meaning of the term was not yet recorded in the second edition of the *Oxford English Dictionary* of 1989.[46]

Let us conclude our *tour de horizon* with the country with which we began, France. Most surveys mention that the pupils of Victor Cousin praised his struggle for "a secular teaching of philosophy" as a "consequence of the secularization of the state" and remembered his statement that "philosophy is secularized,"[47] but these expressions were only metaphors and had no consequence for subsequent discussions; similar expressions can also be found in other French and English studies.[48] In fact, the term *sécularisation* in its modern meaning is still absent from the great *Trésor de la langue française*, the authoritative dictionary of the French language from the Revolution until 1960.[49] In French, the term seems to have been applied first to the modern developments by the Protestant theologian Roger Mehl in a 1950 article,[50] followed by a 1957 translation of an article by Talcott Parsons. Typically, though, the translator put the term within quotation marks, indicating that it was still regarded as a new coinage in France.[51] The term received general prominence in France only in the wake of the theological discussions of the 1960s and Vatican II, as after 1970 we suddenly find a spate of theological books with *sécularisation* in the title.[52] In France one might assume that the modern meaning of the term remains limited to the small circle of theologians and sociologists of religion, since a relevant lemma still does not occur in the most recent standard dictionaries, the *Grand Larousse* (1977) and the *Grand Robert* (2001).

What can we conclude from this survey? It seems clear that the acceptance of the term as a major sociological concept originated in the early 1960s, a process strongly influenced by the fact that Berger and Luckmann belonged to the more hermeneutically oriented sociologists. That orientation must have facilitated their reception by other theologically interested sociologists and sociologically interested theologians. We also note that the major names (Berger, Luckmann, Wilson and Martin) all belong to the same generation, which may have well promoted their interdependency. Moreover, although Olivier Tschannen stresses the Catholic contribution to the rise of the concept of secularization,[53] in this early phase most active users of the concept of secularization were still of Protestant origin. The Catholic influence, as represented by Thomas O'Dea and Karel Dobbelaere, came slightly later, even if it would also prove to be highly influential. The timing of this origin can hardly be separated from the growth of affluence in the final stages of the reconstruction phase after World War II. Even if they did not yet perhaps know it themselves, the scholars who popularized the concept of secularization already saw the shadows of the decline of the Christian West. Finally, *secularization*, as the term to denote a number of developments connected with modernity, was accepted much more slowly than we would perhaps think today. The influence of scholars in society is always less than they like to imagine.

An Alternative View of Christianity

A Troeltschean Perspective

Arie L. Molendijk

"Despite the efforts of doubters, sceptics and adversaries, the most influential general account of religion in modern Europe, and in the modern world, remains the theory of secularisation."[1] Notwithstanding its obvious shortcomings, secularization is still the reigning paradigm when the fate of religion in modernity is discussed. This raises the question of why secularization theory is so persistent. The foremost answer is that it is the master narrative by which many of us have learned to perceive religion in the modern world, the paradigm that shapes our view of religion. Moreover, it fits in all too well with the very real phenomenon of de-Christianization that Western Europe has experienced in the last four decades. The cognitive and moral claims of the old religion are no longer convincing to many Westerners, including scholars and intellectuals. Apart from the fact that the conviction that religion is on the wane is so deeply entrenched, the range of the theory—or better theories—of secularization is very broad indeed. If one merely glances at the entry "Secularization" in dictionaries, one is already impressed by the huge variety of concepts and theories of secularization that it covers.[2] Should one determinable aspect be refuted, there are countless other aspects or elements of the thesis ready quickly to take its place. The enormous range of the theory makes it almost impossible to falsify.

Secularization theories draw on the juxtaposition of religion and modernity (science, rationalization). Most of the time the relationship between the two is described as antagonistic. An influential older handbook of the "scientific" study of religion started with Reinhold Niebuhr's famous question: "Why has religious faith persisted for three centuries after the first triumphs of modern science?"[3] His answer was that religion secured the basic trust we need to survive in a world of contingencies. The question may have been put in a rather crude way, but the functional understanding of religion as the caterer to "ultimate contingencies" (*Kontingenzbewältigungspraxis*), above all death, is still popular.[4] Even if we reject such a general, and sometimes even acultural understanding of religion and opt for a more contextualized, historical approach, we should not overlook the fact that religion and modernity are intricately connected with each other. Strongly put, one might say that "religion" is essentially the problem and, to some extent, even the creation of modernity. The Treaty of Utrecht in 1713 was probably the last major occasion on which public reference was made to the *Republica Christiana*, the "Christian Commonwealth." This understanding was gradually replaced by the notion of Europe,[5] and religion came to be perceived as a domain in its own right.

The perception of religion as a distinct sphere of human culture is related to major developments in the modern Western world. The revolutions of the late eighteenth century eventually led to the separation of church and state in most Western countries. The creation of the modern nation of equal and free citizens became possible only when religious difference no longer played a dominant role in the public sphere. From this point of view, the disappearance of the old status quo, in which religion and political authority were intimately connected, led in time to the autonomization of religion, which consequently could be studied in its own right.[6] Peter van Rooden has argued that the creation of the modern nation state brought about—at least to some extent—a transformation of religion from the visible social and hierarchical order to "the inner selves of the members of the moral community of the nation."[7] This alleged relocation of religion with the breakdown of the confessional state would be the beginning of an alternative master narrative.

In this essay, I will not present an alternative master narrative of my own but will explore what we can learn from Ernst Troeltsch concerning these matters. How did this master of historical narrative plot the history of modern Christianity in general and Protestantism in particular? Troeltsch was one of the pioneers of what we call in retrospect the modern sociology of religion. Scholars such as Emile Durkheim, Max Weber, and Troeltsch considered religion to be an important element of social life, one that influenced other domains, such as politics and economics (and the other way around). Troeltsch was well aware of the metamorphoses of Christian religion in the modern Western world that had such dramatic consequences for the established churches, including the Lutheran church, to which he belonged, but he could not imagine a society without religion. In what follows I will take up, albeit rather freely, some of his basic insights into the history of Western Christianity. Perhaps he did not give a clear-cut master narrative of religious history, but he surely tried to describe and explain the major transformations of Christianity in modernity.

Universal History?

Troeltsch and his friend and colleague Max Weber spoke unrestrainedly about "world history" and the *universalgeschichtliche Probleme*. In the preface to his collected essays on the sociology of religion, Weber put the whole research program within precisely this framework: "A product of modern European civilization, studying any problem of universal history, is bound to ask himself to what combination of circumstances the fact should be attributed that in Western civilization, and in Western civilization only, cultural phenomena have appeared which (as we like to think) lie in a line of development having *universal* significance and value."[8] Weber wanted to use comparative religious studies to contribute to an understanding of developments in the Western world. Whether he thought that the process of rationalization would necessarily lead to the disenchantment of the world and the end of religion is an issue of debate.[9] Recent research shows us a much more nuanced and differentiated Weber, who dissolved universal history into a plurality of various cultural histories.[10]

Troeltsch attributed to Weber a heroic skepticism regarding religion.[11] The famous ending of Weber's "Science as Vocation" would be a fine example of this attitude.[12] Without trying to unravel their personal and intellectual relationship,[13] it is not too bold to claim that Troeltsch had a much higher opinion of the role of (Christian) religion in late modernity than did Weber. Another evident difference is the fact that Troeltsch confined himself mainly to Western—Christian—religious history, whereas Weber claimed an overall perspective, which included "world religions."[14] This was a matter not only of scope of research, but also of principle. The possibility and meaningfulness of universal history *stricto sensu* is denied by Troeltsch. Humanity as such has no unity and therefore no uniform development.[15] To talk about such a nonexistent subject is to tell metaphysical fairy tales. To take European-American history to be the history of the world is a token of colonial and missionary arrogance. Instead, Troeltsch proposes narrowing down universal history to Western history, including the history of North America and Russia, and to accept the possibility that the former colony will outdo the old colonial powers.[16] He coined the concept of "europeanism" (*Europäismus*) and searched for the thriving forces of the Western world ("Hebrew prophetism, classic Greekness, ancient imperialism, and the Western Middle Ages").[17] Important in this context are not Troeltsch's speculations about these forces (which are, paradoxically, all premodern), but the way he tried to mediate between actual historical research and speculative philosophy of history. It is called a second-order or reflective historicism because it accepts the historicity of our thinking and takes into account its own point of view as historically mediated.[18]

Troeltsch's way of dealing with historicism, however, is not the topic here. It is relevant insofar as even this final, grand *tour-de-force* on the "problems of historicism," which aims at a new "cultural synthesis" (*Kultursynthese*), shows a clear awareness of the European context of the whole undertaking. Actually, the voluminous book on historicism contains a lot of methodological and theoretical reflection, and does not present a global history of Western civilization. Although Troeltsch was accused by contemporary professional historians of giving only rough historical outlines based on secondary literature, he did not overlook the various different historical contexts he was discussing. He even invented new instruments to describe religious history and to understand the various Christian religious groups and how these were related to modernity, which he analyzed as a complex of related but highly diverse phenomena.

Christianity and Modernity

Let us see, in general, what types of narrative Troeltsch tells about religion in the modern world.[19] Modernity starts, according to him, with the Enlightenment, which is, intellectually (although it is more than an intellectual movement), the critique of tradition and authority. He complements this line of thought in various ways. Historically, he introduces subsequent modernities, such as German Idealism and the vaguely indicated "nineteenth century," which is characterized by the growing power of a "democratically tinted" imperialism and capitalism.[20] Both forces lead to a stress on earthly life (*Diesseitigkeit*), an emphasis that poses a threat to traditional religion. Eventually, Troeltsch tells a long story about the trajectory—or, better still, trajectories—of religion in the West. This thoroughly historical approach leads him to refine and extend his view of modernity and religion.

There is no simple way to define modernity; essentially, if this word is permitted, it refers to a multifaceted phenomenon that can only be understood via a broad spectrum of analysis. One of the main devices Troeltsch uses is to list characteristics of modernity, which may vary according to the theme that is treated. He mentions, for instance: the growth of mobility, the rise in life expectancy, this-worldliness, the growing influence of technology and the sciences, the dominance of capitalism, the power of the bureaucratic welfare state, individualism, and the ideals of personal self-realization and autonomy.[21] The denial of supernatural authority implies, according to Troeltsch, individualism and this-worldliness, but the idea of autonomy as such, he stresses, is empty and thus compatible with a large range of world views, including a Christian one. It is not helpful to focus on the critique of religion as a distinct mark of the Enlightenment or to describe modernity as the rise of modern paganism. On the contrary, Troeltsch was looking for the contribution of various Christian groups and principles to the rise of the modern world.[22] This does not mean that he perceived the modern world to be the product of Christianity, but it would be wrong, in his opinion, to see it merely as in contradiction to Christianity.

Church, Sect, and Mysticism

Troeltsch defends the view that Christian individualism itself did much to break the power of the old state churches.[23] Individualism is characteristic of Christianity and was reinforced by the Reformation, especially by sectarian groups such as the Anabaptists and so-called free "mystical" or "spiritualist" groups. These emphasized the importance of lay piety, tolerance, and personal religious experience. The trajectory of Christian individualism is evidently connected with the typology of church, sect, and mysticism. This typology has even been read as a periodization of the history of Christianity.[24] That is a bit far-fetched, but one should not overlook the diachronic aspects of the types, which are immediately relevant for Troeltsch's view of modernity and religion.

The types are ultimately rooted in different basic soteriological convictions. The institution (*Anstalt*) is rooted in the notion of grace (the church as guardian of the *depositum fidei* and the sacraments, which mediate salvation); within the association (*Verein*, the sect), salvation is attained by individuals' ethical performances; the loose mystical groups stress personal communion with God.[25] Even if the third type caters to more diffuse and individualistic forms of Christian and even non-Christian religiosity, it is, according to Troeltsch, deeply embedded in the Christian tradition.[26] He himself had a predelection for the mystical type, but he did not see it as the future form of Christianity, which will still need strong but flexible institutions. The culture of compulsion, that characterized the old churches is no longer acceptable, which means that they must be radically transformed. The churches are, thus, "losing their hold on the spiritual life of the nations, and many of their functions are now being exercised by educationalists, writers, administrators, and by voluntary associations."[27]

These functional losses could be described in terms of "secularization." Although Troeltsch did not defend any secularization thesis, he considered the "secularization of the state" (the separation between state and church) to be "the most important fact of the modern world."[28] The modern state is free to pursue its own this-worldly legal, political, military, and economic objectives. The sovereignty of God is replaced by that of the state. This means the end of the medieval *corpus christianum*, the close cooperation of state and church. Consequently, religion turns into a separate domain and the church gradually loses its privileged position. In principle, there is no obstacle to new competitors on the religious market, and a plurality of churches or religious groups can develop. Joining a particular religious community becomes a matter of personal choice.[29]

We must understand Troeltsch's distinction between Old and New Protestantism against this background. The term *New Protestantism* not only designates the free, liberal Protestantism that Troeltsch himself favored, but has a more general meaning: the Protestant churches that function on the basis of the secular state.[30] Old Protestantism—above all, Lutheranism and Calvinism—is almost by definition a premodern phenomenon. Troeltsch evidently did not consider the Reformation the beginning of the modern world. Much to the outrage of contemporary German historians and theologians, he characterized Old Protestantism as "simply a modification of Catholicism."[31] Luther and Calvin inherited from Catholicism the basic idea of the church as "wholly authoritative, purely Divine ordinances [an institution] of salvation."[32] Despite obvious mystical tendencies in

Luther's work, this idea shaped the actual policy of Lutheran church formation, and, in Troeltsch's view, that is what counts.

Typology enables Troeltsch to analyze the fundamental sociological structures of Christian forms of community. The types are ideal types, which implies that one often encounters "mixed" forms, for instance, the church type with some sectarian traits, as is evident in his analysis of Calvin and Calvinism. "Calvin, for his part, approached the notion of sect on its strong, dominating, and social reform side by adopting the idea of holy religious communities and of the enforcement of their sanctity."[33] Troeltsch admired (and overestimated) the Calvinist potential for social reform and economic activity, by contrast to the alleged quietism of Lutheranism.[34] In conclusion, he was primarily interested in religious ideas that had a direct social and ethical impact. His typology selects Christian ideas that determine different principles of Christian organization. Once one has understood the various sociological structures of churches, sects, and groups, the next step is to analyze how these institutions and groups were related to the "world." The two main research goals of his great work *The Social Teachings of the Christian Churches and Groups*, are thus: first, to inquire "into the intrinsic sociological idea of Christianity, and its structure and organization";[35] and second, to research the relation between this sociological organization and the "social," that is, the state, the economic order, and the family.

The Transformation of Christianity

Troeltsch tries to lessen the gap between the Old and the New Protestantism to some extent by pointing, for instance, to spiritualist elements in Luther, which—although in fact suppressed—are seeds of modernity. More often than not, however, he stresses their differences. Referring to the ideas of the Dutch theologian and prime minister Abraham Kuyper, Troeltsch emphasizes the new traits of Neo-Calvinism, contrasting it with the Old Protestantisms.[36] "Neo-Calvinism . . . requires the Christian-Liberal organization of the State and of Society, independence and freedom for the individual, equality of opportunity as well as in the eyes of the law [*Gleichheit des Rechts und der Lebensmöglichkeiten*], the organization of international peace, and the conquest of the struggle for existence by means of self-discipline and active social help through associated effort [*tätige soziale Vereinshilfe*]. . . . The patriarchal conservative elements of the Christian ethic have receded, and the aspects of social reform and love of liberty have come to the front."[37] The role of associations and the principle of free churches make Calvinism and "related" sects, such as Baptists and Methodists, extremely successful.

The success of Pietism—which is one of the major and most complex issues discussed in Troeltsch's *Social Teachings*—is largely explained by its sectarian traits.[38] Pietism is for many believers a good alternative to the high state church because it is more directly adjusted to the spiritual needs of "common" people, who are more directly involved in their own religious groups. It sets free a lot of religious energy and striving: "it displays a great deal of genuine, warm, and self-sacrificing piety, but it also displays that pettiness of religious groups which compensates for their detachment from the world by a still more thorough spiritual pride; affecting to despise worldly influence, they strive to attain it by personal scheming and intrigue, and they give vent to their passions in all kinds of religious bickerings."[39] Troeltsch explains Pietism in typological terms by saying that it represents the sect ideal within the churches. He also noticed, however, that it did not always remain within these confines but led, in fact, to separation, as with Labadism in the Netherlands and Methodism in England.

In his analysis of the contribution of Christianity, especially Protestantism, to modernity, Troeltsch uses a two-fold strategy. On the one hand, he singles out the novelty of modern culture as compared to the world of medieval Catholicism and that of Luther and Calvin, claiming that the foundations of modern society, economy, the arts, the sciences, and so on have developed independently of Christianity. On the other hand, he maintains that "modern" ideas of individualism and personal freedom are also rooted in the Christian tradition. Sectarian and mystical groups, the "step-children of the Reformation" that facilitated the transition of Christian religion to modernity,[40] deserve special mention. In a way, they are the missing link between the Old and the New Protestantisms.[41] The concepts of free religious association, liberty of religious conscience, and basic human rights have their roots in sectarianism and mysticism.[42] It is not easy to determine the precise contribution of each group discussed by Troeltsch to the emergence of these modern principles. In various contexts he refers, among others, to the Anabaptists, the Quakers, mystical spiritualism, "Pietistic Calvinism with a radical bent," and also to old-Calvinist ideas of sovereignty and the right to revolution.[43]

The English Revolution, Troeltsch told the assembled German historians at their 1906 meeting in Stuttgart in his lecture on the meaning of Protestantism for the emergence of the modern world, was the event in which this amalgam gained its enormous historical momentum. The "great ideas" of the separation of state and church, the toleration of various religious groups, the principle of free religious association, and the freedom of conscience and opinion originate in this period. This marks the decline of a culture of state-church compulsion and the beginning of modern, church-free individualist culture.[44] In his later work, especially in *The Social Teachings*, he makes a not unsuccessful attempt to disentangle this amalgam by making a distinction between the sect and the mystical type. Freedom of association, it will turn out, is distinctive of the sect, freedom of conscience of the mystical type. The Anabaptists opted for toleration, but not for freedom of conscience within their own circle.

"Mysticism is a radical individualism, very different from that of the sect. While the sect separates the individuals from the world by its conscious hostility to "worldliness" and by its ethical severity, binding them together in a voluntary fellowship . . . mysticism lays no stress at all upon the relation between individuals, but only upon the relations between the soul and God."[45] It will be evident that the term *mysticism* is not used by Troeltsch in a traditional technical sense. It simply emphasizes the personal relationship with God, which can do, in principle, without the historical, authoritative, and ritual elements in religion. Paramount examples are Sebastian Franck, Sebastian Castellio, Dick Volckertszoon Coornhert, and large parts of modern German philosophy of religion. The presumed sociological character of the mystical type is controversial; it is doubted whether mysticism implies some sort of factual community that sociologists might study.[46] Troeltsch, however, maintains that the mystical type has sociological value: group formation is occurring in these circles, and individualism is an extremely important sociological fact in itself.[47]

The Uses of the Typology

If one asks how Troeltsch uses the typology, the first answer probably is that it is a historiographical tool for highlighting historical diversity and specifying the particular contribution of various religious groups to modern developments. The typology concerns not only principles of organization (e.g., the sectarian principle of voluntary association), but also more general principles, such as the separation of church and state, freedom of conscience, and other liberties. In sum, it enables him to give a structural—a sociohistorical—history of Western Christianity.

Second, an analysis of the historiographical use of the typology reveals Troeltsch's interest in the impact of religious *ideas and institutions* on society. This does not mean that he overlooks the influence of economic, political, and social factors on religion.[48] He aims at an integral cultural history of Christianity, which takes the reciprocal relations between, in Karl Marx's terms, base and superstructure into account. But surely it was of extreme importance to Troeltsch to maintain that the Christian religion was an independent variable that could not be reduced to, let's say, economics. The ideal types of church, sect, and mysticism guaranteed this independence of the Christian religion, which was, apparently, basically a pluriform phenomenon. The types represent fundamental aspects of the Christian religion and the ways it has evolved.

Third, a view of development is implicit in the typology. As I have said, it would be overly simple to say that the three types stand for three phases in history, experiential, individualistic "mysticism" being the last one. In this respect, Troeltsch gave no linear master narrative. He tells several stories about new forms of Christianity, typologized as sect and mysticism, and about the transformation of the old church institutions, which were constructed by "compulsion and relentless insistence upon rigid conformity to a uniform type of doctrine and organization" and at present have to allow for much more tolerance, if they want to survive.[49] The fact that Troeltsch is critical of the old ecclesiastical "culture of compulsion" (*Zwangskultur*) does not imply that we have now entered a splendid new era of religious freedom. A religious market based on free choice easily leads to a chaotic diversity and divisiveness (*chaotische Zerspaltenheit*).[50]

Fourth, the typology is used to formulate the ecclesiastical ideal of the flexible German *Landeskirche* or *Volkskirche*, which integrates a variety of Christians under the same roof. Troeltsch was not blind to the success of American Christianity, which is clearly based on the principle of voluntary association and competition between religious groups,[51] but he strongly favored a churchly institution that is capable of containing a large diversity of Christians. Interestingly enough, Max Weber also denied that sectarianism was a viable option for Germany.[52] Sects do not care much for learned theological scholarship: they stress religious needs and not general cultural values.[53] But, one is tempted to ask, is not this precisely an explanation for the attraction of "sectarian" groups? Has not the voluntary principle in the modern world proved to be stronger than Troeltsch thought? Even the old Western European churches are by many considered to be nothing more than associations. Is not the pursuit of the "unity of the heterogeneous" (*Einheit des Heterogenen*)[54] doomed to fail in a context of radical plurality?

After Troeltsch

In conclusion, I will touch upon the question of what historians can learn from Troeltsch's work. First, however, a few comments on its limitations are due. The history of modern Christianity given by Troeltsch is very much a history of Protestantism. Large parts of Christian religious history—prominent examples being the Anglican Church and Eastern Christianity—are not or are only superficially treated. Furthermore, it is possible and necessary to criticize his view of the various Protestantisms. The sharp contrast he draws between dynamic Calvinism and quietistic Lutheranism has been criticized. Various readjustments have to be made.[55] Yet we can find in Troeltsch's work a variety of perceptive remarks. I am not prepared to give here a balanced appreciation of Troeltsch's contribution to the historiography of Christianity. Instead, I would like to end with a few remarks that will put the strong sides of Troeltsch into perspective.

Without reducing religious history to ideas or mentalities, Troeltsch's cultural history of Christianity takes the importance of religious ideas and their interplay with other factualities into account. The same applies, of course, to Weber's *Protestant Ethic*. Historical change cannot be explained only by reference to economic and political developments, but must also take into account motivational factors. Troeltsch summarized his view of the Middle Ages as follows: "To the extent that medieval social teachings became practical realities and accomplished something significant, they stemmed by no means from religious conceptions alone but from the ancient Greek cultural heritage, the Roman art of government, Germanic law, and new conditions emerging with the times. The really significant contribution, in fact, was the relatively unified correlation of a system of life and thought, which entered the imagination and standards of the masses and created a common psychological sphere."[56] The question in the context of this essay is not whether this is true or false, but that it shows Troeltsch's awareness of the interplay of various factors, including motivational religious ideas.

He was, as we have noticed, primarily interested not in ideas per se, but in ideas that have factual impact. In the phrasing of Charles Taylor, Troeltsch was not primarily interested in sets of ideas, but in modern religious imaginaries, which enable religious practices and make sense of them.[57] The religious imaginary enables the practices of believers, who most of the time don't know the theory involved in a particular imaginary. Like Taylor, Troeltsch stresses the importance and even priority of ideological factors in enabling practices, and he pays special attention to the mediation of ideas. The typology is a good example of mediation, because Troeltsch argues that various soteriological ideas determine the basic pattern of how religious communities function. Not only is the structure of a religious group to be understood on the basis of formative religious ideas, but this very structure predisposes people to certain beliefs and ways of life. The individualistic mystical type, for instance, does not mediate ideas concerning the state or the economy, but "within the sphere of the sex ethic and of the family . . . this type of thought displays features which are peculiar to itself."[58] It can hardly be denied that some sort of revolution in these spheres has taken place in the twentieth century.[59]

It would be wrong to assume that Troeltsch thought that the mystical type represents the only truly modern—individualistic and subjectivized—form of religion. Yet the concept can be used to cater to this development in modern religious history. Various volatile and free-floating forms of religiosity or spirituality can be included and analyzed under this heading. The phenomenon of the privatization of religion can also be related to this type, although, as Troeltsch knew very well, it would be wrong to claim that this is the fate of religion in modernity. The separation between church and state in the Enlightenment period does not forbid a *public* role for religion. As José Casanova has shown, churches can adapt to the new paradigm by evolving from state-oriented into society-oriented institutions.[60] It is evident, however, that not all forms of religion adapt to the new paradigm. "Strong religions,"[61] as they are called nowadays, and fundamentalisms dominate public discourse, and the rise of these forms of religion will probably contribute more to the dissolution of the secularization paradigm than the many intellectual critiques that have been ventured in recent decades.

As Close as a Scholar Can Get

Exploring a One-Field Approach to the Study of Religion

André Droogers

Among all the phenomena that scholars study, religion occupies an exceptional position because as a form of knowledge it is commonly presented as the opposite of science. Religion, as we now use the term, is a relatively recent construct, formed explictitly in contrast to science. When in modernity science came into a dominant position, religion was categorized in accordance with its nonscientific nature, given that the transcendental reality to which it refers is not open to empirical verification. That nonempirical reality could not be accepted as a causal factor in explaining religion. As a consequence, theories of religion refer primarily to nonreligious processes and aspects. Religious experiences, practices, and beliefs are thereby reduced to nonreligious factors of a psychological, social, political, or economic nature. Moreover, because of the contrast, science, being considered a superior form of knowledge, has directly or indirectly contributed to the secularization process.

The delicate relationship between religious studies and its object creates a methodological problem that other disciplines need not face. If the scholar's task is to study empirically a field whose defining part cannot be verified empirically or is even denied reality, special caution is necessary. One must then ask whether the accepted asymmetry between science and religion may not hamper scholarly understanding. Moreover, the secularizing critique of religion on scientific grounds invites reflection on the degrees of objectivity and subjectivity in the study of religion. Objective distance and a critical attitude make human subjects into objects. This may have advantages, but it may also estrange the researcher from the field. In view of the distance that has resulted, it may be worthwhile to consider more empathic ways of studying religion. This essay seeks to explore the potential of a one-field perspective, one that brings science and religion together into a single field instead of treating them as two distinct fields. In fact, when science—including the study of religion—is critical of religion and contributes to the erosion of religion in society, the two already belong to one field. Besides, fieldwork involves personal contact. Moreover, in other respects the distinction is not as neat as has often been thought, for example, when we look at the place of religious studies in academia, often in or near theology schools.

A one-field approach does not maintain distance but moves as close as possible to the object under study. It considers religion without the subjectivity of critical opposition, yet it is aware of possible other subjectivisms. Which possibilities would become available if scholars were to experiment with the boundaries that are usually drawn between the study of religion and the religion being studied? When the scholar engages in the religious field, he or she must to a certain degree be physically present and involved there, participating in this field with body and soul. As an anthropologist of religion, I intend to explore what would change when, if only as an experimental line of thought, one were to adopt a perspective that would assume that scholars—not only anthropologists—and believers are inevitably operating in a single field.

This is not a new proposal. Phenomenologists of a variety of types have experimented with this approach by bracketing presuppositions. Moreover, anthropologists have accumulated expertise in qualitative fieldwork methods, especially participant observation, which demands that the researcher reduce the usual "objective" distance. In a similar vein, the human capacity for play can be put at work, given that play allows simultaneous orientation to two realities.[1]

Room for a one-field approach has also been opened by a change in views of the mission of science. In recent decades, constructivist insights have helped to acknowledge the spectrum of positions that scholars may take with regard to the phenomena studied. If knowledge is constructed through some form of intersubjectivity between scholar and informant, then they are assumed to belong to the same social field. As a consequence, the idea that scholars and believers may form one realm is no longer aberrant. By making room for some form of empathy and closeness, such an approach may at least complement the way studies of religion have been done so far, that is, by maintaining critical distance. A one-field approach may suggest new methods that have never been taken seriously because they were outside the two-field scope that had been adopted.

Once the researcher is viewed as part of the religious field, he or she is as much an object of study and analysis as the believers being studied. This obliges the researcher constantly to be aware of his or her degree of involvement. Any researcher, even when attempting to be objective, is an idiosyncratic representative of a particular cultural and religious—or secular—context and of a specific academic subculture. Since the scholar's representation of religion and religions is inevitably colored by his or her training, by a particular perspective on religion, and by a personal background, explicit reflection on the scholarly habitus is to be recommended. This is, of course, a normal condition in a (neo)positivist setting, where objectivity is a core value of the profession. It becomes even more important when some degree of experimentation with subjectivity is allowed.

In this essay I will first discuss the ambiguous position of religious studies as already having some one-field elements in its history. The methodological consequences of the one-field approach will then be stipulated. Special attention will subsequently be given to the body's role in the study of religion, as a consequence of the researcher's involvement. The general and abstract argument is then illustrated by the study of Pentecostalism, the field in which I happen to be active. In conclusion, I then summarize the relevance of this exercise for the general issues discussed in this volume. I propose there a definition of religion that might match the one-field approach.

Ambiguity in the Study of Religion

In developing its identity, the study of religion had to come to terms with the changing position of religion in society, especially in Western Europe, and with the discipline's position in academia. I will start with the dynamics of religion in society, especially the increasing importance of the dichotomy between the religious and the secular and the secularization process.

After modern science began to influence society in radical ways, the religious came to be defined and positioned in contrast to the secular, and vice versa. Science is the model representation of a secular world, no longer inhabited by the sacred. It is now the dominant frame of reference, just as religion had been before the days of Galileo Galilei. The comparison between the religious and the secular is therefore primarily given form by submitting religion to scientific criteria, not the other way around. Religion is then found lacking.

In this context, science commonly has positivist connotations, with a strong emphasis on the empirical method, taking the natural sciences to be the prototype and the laboratory model to be the prime example. Reality exists when it can be verified empirically. In studying processes, a selected number of variables are controlled and experimentally changed, looking for causality. In principle it does not make a difference whether one looks for the effect of a change in gas pressure or in the frequency of church visits. As a consequence of scientific dominance, the rational and empirical are contrasted with the irrational and nonempirical, as is reflected in definitions of religion that contain these words. J. van Baal and W. E. A. van Beek, for example, define religion as "all explicit and implicit notions and ideas, accepted as true, which relate to a reality which cannot be verified empirically."[2]

When discussing religious dynamics, one cannot avoid the debate about secularization. According to Peter Berger, who was one of the early proponents of the secularization thesis and is now one of its critics, a "thin but very influential stratum of intellectuals—

broadly defined as people with Western-style higher education, especially in the humanities and social sciences" forms one of the few strongholds of secularization.[3] The proper study of religion has contributed to the process of secularization; thus the discipline is in the unusual position of having contributed to the elimination of its own topic. From its patriarchs Marx, Durkheim, Weber, and Freud it inherited a critical view of religion, their interest in religion being in part inspired by the illogic and puzzling resilience of religion and religions. The comparative study of religion has eroded any religion's claims to truth and exclusive uniqueness, making religious truth something dependent upon context and coincidence. The fact that most scholars have now abandoned the idea that secularization will produce the end of religion in the world represents a new challenge to the study of religion.

The secularization thesis stimulated reflection on the definition of religion, leading to the distinction between a substantive and a functional definition. Whereas a substantive definition limits religion to a view concerning the nature of the transcendental—or more precisely, supernatural nonempirical reality—the functional type of definition includes views concerning life and the world that do not refer to divine entities but nevertheless serve the same function as religions in the substantive sense had done. Thus any secular ideology, but also soccer, could be called a religion in the functional sense, despite secularization. This move can be appreciated as a way of showing continuities, notwithstanding the erosion of religion in the substantive sense. At the same time, the notion of religion has been broadened to an extent that some would reject as blurring unacceptably the border between the secular and the religious. The question of definition illustrates what a process occurring in the field under study does to the discipline that studies the phenomenon and its concepts. With regard to the religious and the secular, the definition debate suggests that the boundaries adopted between the secular and the religious have not been made from all eternity.

More recently, nonpositivist views of the task of science have been developed, especially by postmodernism and constructivism.[4] These lines of thought draw attention to the way in which the discipline has, since its patriarchs, constructed its categories by contrasting the religious and the secular. These new views thereby show the relativity of the conceptual framework insofar as it is a construct. Though postmodernism contains a devastating secularizing critique of religion, it has also had the effect that scholars, whether they embrace postmodernism or not, may have become aware of their way of representing the religious field, including the changing boundaries between the religious and the secular.

We need also to look at the discipline's home in academia. Though the academic seems to be synonymous with the secular, the scientific study of religion has not occupied an unambiguous academic position. As a discipline, the science of religion or comparative religion is often accommodated in theology departments, because theologians were the first to turn to the study of religion and religions.[5] In some cases, the study of religion

451

was included in departments of social science, as has happened with the anthropology and sometimes the sociology of religion. Interestingly, theology can be considered an academic discipline that represents an exception to the contrast between religion and science. One of the oldest disciplines, it has succeeded in occupying an intermediate position between science and religion. Theology thus offered some compensation for science's secularizing tendencies, in many cases maintaining itself as an integral part of universities. In return, it appears to serve two mistresses, science and religion. Theology, being the scientific and systematic reflection on the nonempirical sacred, has developed systematic formulations of faith, especially as representative of and directive for the mainline churches. These doctrinal systematizations obey a more or less rational need for logical thinking, despite presupposing sacred entities whose existence cannot be proven empirically.

The position of religious studies in theology departments has influenced the way religion and religions have been studied. The theological example of offering a systematic and historical overview of Christian thought was copied in the study of non-Christian religions. The image of religion in general was influenced by the Christian case. Moreover, the official version that the leadership of a religion—including its theologians—represented was usually reproduced in accounts of non-Christian religions. Church history found its parallel and extension in the history of religions. The ethnocentrism of this approach can be shown if the perspective is inverted and, for example, emic concepts from Buddhism are used to describe Christianity.

Representations of other religions were thus ideal and systematized versions of doctrine and, to a lesser degree, ritual. This approach included a focus on written sources, if available, as codifications of this ideal version. Similarly, the anthropology of religion has mapped so-called symbolic systems. Only later on was the difference between official and popular religion made visible. Yet textbooks on world religions still show this practice of presenting a systematic and consistent overview of official ideas, doctrine, scriptures, and rituals, modeled after Christianity and from the clergy's point of view. Accordingly, popular religion and magic have often been neglected, or they have been defined and described as deviant, second-rank, sectarian, or illegitimate religion. Even the term *religiosity* has this connotation.

Yet scholars from the field of religious studies have also sought to maintain an independent position. They have often had difficulty in defining their own identity in relation to their theological colleagues. The discipline of religious studies has for a long time struggled with this ambiguous position. Differences from theology have therefore been emphasized. In their professional activities, students of religion have not identified primarily with Christianity, whereas their theological colleagues have. Whether they did so privately is another question altogether. By contrast to theologians, students of religion have not taken a stance with regard to religious truth claims but have sought to represent the world's religions, their history and scriptures, in an objective, descriptive way. Students of religion have also applied a comparative method, which led to the phenomenology of religion. This particular subdiscipline showed the relativity of Christian expressions, putting them in the same categories as those of other religions. Of course, these categories had usually been copied from Christianity in the first place. Nevertheless, the comparison redefined phenomena that had been seen as unique to Christianity as common to all religions, those religions being described according to such subdivisions as: scriptures, views concerning human beings and salvation, images of God or gods, ritual, ethics, and degree of institutionalization. At the same time, the problem has been that phenomenological comparison tended to emphasize common traits, thereby making scholars blind to idiosyncrasies and to the unique constellation of elements in a particular religion or religious group. In that respect, anthropologists especially were critical of phenomenologists, the anthropological trademark being a holistic and contextualized approach. Yet as students of religion became specialists, taking one of the world religions as their area, they began to treat it in a holistic manner.

This review of the ambiguous position of religious studies shows that any scientific effort to study religion has had to come to terms, explicitly or implicitly, with the fact that in our society, that is, within a single field, religion is contrasted to science. The definition debate is a more recent example, blurring the usual distinction between the religious and the secular. The history of the discipline shows that the possibility of a one-field approach has been there from its beginnings in theology departments, even though it was later rejected because of Christian bias. The price paid for an independent identity, however, was distance and alienation from the believing subjects who were to be studied.

Methodological Consequences

Anthropological fieldwork has a long tradition of a one-field approach, with the researcher seeking to be as much part of the context under study as is possible. Though the basic method of participant observation contains a paradox—simultaneous participation and observation being logically impossible, at least in positivist scientific terms—this research technique has proved productive.

The peculiar advantages of the method can best be shown by contrasting it to the survey and polling methods used in other social sciences of religion. In surveys, following the laboratory model of positivist origin, the researcher measures the influence of variables and looks for causality. He or she is instructed not to influence the interview situation and to take an objective position, as if he or she were not there or were substitutable, just as a lab researcher would be. The experiment must be repeatable and therefore impersonal. Participant observation, by contrast, uses the researcher's personality as a tool in seeking rapport with the people studied. Positivist-minded scholars often consider the result of such an approach biased and subjective. It sins against the rule of the strict separation of researcher and object of research. Even when participant observation is combined with open, in-depth interviews, the same judgment applies, casting doubt on the validity of data obtained in this way. Yet anthropologists have now for almost a century shown that such fieldwork allows for insight from the inside. Though statistical generalization is not possible, case studies show the plausibility of cultural and social processes. Narratives make up for what statistics cannot show and often tell more than numbers do. Especially in the study of religion, where people's stories about their experiences with the sacred are important, such an internal perspective produces data that cannot be obtained in any other way. To study the idiosyncrasies that generate religious experience, methods of fine-tuning are needed. In short, subjectivity must be considered as a tool.

If scholars in religious studies have come from theology or are believers themselves, their personal experience with religion may be helpful in fieldwork when they seek to understand co-believers. If these scholars do fieldwork in another religion, the advantage of knowing religion through private experience might turn into a disadvantage. The researcher, as we say, may model the other religion after his or her own—for example, Christian—religion, or implicit preferences and prejudices may color the representation. Thus the advantage of being familiar with religion may turn into a handicap. Yet when this risk is explicitly reflected upon and sufficient attention is given to possible religiocentrism, being a religious scholar of religion may have an extra value in research. In that sense, when a one-field approach is adopted, the ambiguous position that students of religion who operate from theology departments may have could give them a head start. For different reasons, those who on purpose maintain their distance from religion and shun the experience that comes with it could also claim an advantage, being free from the subjective risk that a believing scholar runs. Yet in their case bias is not excluded, since not having a religion may come with a—perhaps unconscious—subjective critical position regarding religion and its claims.

In any case, participant methods are a way of entering the one field and immersing oneself in it. Because subjectivity can be both an asset and a risk, there is a need for explicit reflection on the scholar's involvement. Philosophical phenomenology, having contributed to the classical understanding of religion, has been rediscovered for its way of introducing new possibilities for documenting experiences.[6] In anthropology this approach has inspired a new school of phenomenologists.[7] The fieldworker's body becomes a tool for research. Evocation is more important than objective representation. Metaphors are not viewed primarily as cognitive means but as "phenomena of intelligent and intelligible bodies that animate lived experience."[8] The focus is on the lived experience of scholar and believer, both being in the world.

Elsewhere I have proposed a way to overcome the paradoxical distance between observer and participant by referring to the human capacity for serious play.[9] Religion is actually one of the fields in which this capacity—to deal simultaneously with more than one reality—can be observed. Believers play with the possibility of two realities, one natural and one supernatural. Their play can become so engaged that the two realities merge into one or at least position themselves on the same spectrum. The capacity for play and the experience of an extra dimension in reality reinforce one another. The use of tropes, especially metaphors, important in religions, is another form of play with two domains, one in need of clarification, the other offering a clear image. When believers express their experience, they switch from one domain to the other. Thus God has come to be called "Father," or "Mother," linking the religious and kinship domains.

The use of play is not limited to believers. The explicit reference to play also suggests a possible position scholars may choose with regard to their study of believers' religious experiences. It is common to distinguish between three scholarly postures regarding religious claims. Methodological theists (or religionists) accept the possibility of experiencing the manifestation of the sacred. They include some reference to a divine agency in their explanations of religion. Methodological atheists (or naturalists and reductionists) reject precisely that. In between the two, methodological agnostics abstain from an opinion in this matter. They will neither deny nor affirm such a sacred agency. In research practice, methodological atheists and agnostics will describe data that support the religion's claim—for example, when believers refer to corporeal experiences as one of the proofs that the sacred manifests itself. But they will not accept the reality of these experiences as a cause when explaining religion. Instead, scholars with these leanings often appeal to reductionist explanations for these experiences, pointing to nonreligious elements and mechanisms of a variety of kinds.

In contrast to and complementing these three positions, I have proposed methodological ludism, inspired by the anthropological tradition of participant observation and by authors who have written about play.[10] In play, human beings are capable of dealing simultaneously with two or even more realities. This also holds, as we have seen already, for believers who presuppose a sacred reality. But it would also be possible for a researcher who put himself into the believer's view of reality, if only for a moment. By temporarily, but as completely as possible, sharing the concrete bodily experiences of the people being studied, the researcher gains in understanding of the role of these experiences. Though requiring the seriousness of playing a role, methodological ludism is as methodological as the other three options and thereby independent of the researcher's personal conviction with regard to religion. A playful attitude reduces the distance between the student of religion and believers. Moreover, it acknowledges the constructionist insight that knowledge should be construed in the interaction between the scholar and the person who is the object (read: the other subject) of the research.[11] Incidentally, play can also be used in debates on theoretical paradigms, obliging one temporarily to adopt the opponent's point of view.

We may conclude that, once the possibility of a one-field approach is accepted, several methods present themselves. Though never fully eliminating the distance between scholar and believer, they explore the possibilities that become available when a strict separation between the two is no longer required. The consequence of this approach is that we must acknowledge the role of the body as a research tool.

Religion Incorporated

The one-field approach brings the bodily involvement of the researcher with it. Whereas believers use all their senses to register manifestations of the sacred, the people who study them have tended to limit themselves to reading texts, watching behavior, and, with less distance and more bodily involvement, listening to people. That seems to have been a consequence of the need for objectivity and distance, reinforced by the need to differ from theological neighbors in the same department, who by definition were participants in Christianity. It reduced bodily involvement and excluded participation, creating a rather cerebral climate for the study of religion. Accordingly, little room was left for what Birgit Meyer has called "sensational forms," which make the transcendental capable of being sensed: "authorized modes of invoking, and organizing access to the transcendental, thereby creating and sustaining links between religious practitioners in the context of particular religious organizations."[12]

This exclusion of the body copied the perspective of Christian leadership. Whether influenced by Victorian prudery or not, for the past century Christian leaders have had difficulty in formulating a view of the role of the body in believers' lives. This has contributed to a church climate in which attention to religious experiences has been more the exception than the rule. Bodily experiences were associated with sectarian groups. In general, Western culture for quite some time did not facilitate the study of the role of the body, neither in theology nor in the social sciences. As Thomas J. Csordas observed of the last few decades: "the notion of 'experience' virtually dropped out of theorizing about culture."[13] Bodily experience also tends to be a blind spot in social science's religious studies. Religious experiences have been reduced to religious representation, bodily symbols to their meaning, despite the attention that in some other disciplines has been paid to corporeal religious experiences. One may think of the psychology of religion and its individual-centered tradition, which started with William James, or of the philosophy of religion and the tradition that began with Friedrich Schleiermacher and was given form by Rudolf Otto.[14] In the study of religion, corporeal experiences disappeared behind the veils of a systematization of ideas and articles of faith, and also a focus on the social order.

Admittedly, not all religious activities are easily accessible, especially not those that demand specific sensational forms. Believers themselves already have difficulty in expressing their experiences. Religious corporeal experiences are by definition difficult to document. Though anthropologists of religion use participant observation as one of their basic methods, and therefore could have done better than their colleagues from the science of religion, their degree of participation has varied.

Religious experiences could have been a key element in ritual studies, however. Yet—symptomatically so—*ritual* is a contested term, since it is identified as a contaminated Christian term.[15] Moreover, defining the behavior that is proper to ritual is thought to be too difficult. The presupposition that ritual has a meaning outside itself—usually a meaning that corresponds to doctrinal ideas or even myth—has been contested. The focus on meaning, following the Christian theological example, as a way of connecting ritual and doctrine may have led to a neglect of bodily experiences as crucial ingredients of ritual.[16] Evidently, looking for the symbolic meaning of ritual has indirectly facilitated the application of the Christian theological model in the study of other religions.

Behind this contrast between meaning and experience there is an asymmetrical relation between mind and behavior, with the mind occupying a primordial position over the body.[17] Reflecting the contrast between thinking and acting, scholars consider religious corporeal experiences to be on the behavioral and thus on the ritual side. The same contrast between mind and behavior appears in the debate between intellectualists and symbolists—ritual as an epistemology of explanation, prediction, and control that is comparable to science versus ritual as a symbolic behavioral statement about social order.[18] The two competing models have in common that the role of religious bodily experiences is reduced either to knowledge and meaning or to their contribution to the social order.

A comparison of the role of the body in religion and in religious studies points to a surprising parallel. Students of religion and religious leaders may show unexpected common characteristics that cannot be explained only by the use of the Christian model as normative for the description of other religions. The parallel has to do with the focus on order and the uncontrollable place of the body in both the clergy's and—for other reasons—academia's interest.

To begin with religious order, one can refer to the fact that visionary mystics and other persons who emphasized their corporeal experiences as a source of authenticity and authority sometimes were persecuted by religious authorities. Even though there were also mystics who became part of the honorary gallery of religious heroes, and despite the fact that founders of world religions often were driven by similar corporeal experiences, the doctrinal and cerebral side has usually predominated. The way people interpret their experiences can, of course, not be isolated from doctrinal socialization, and the contrast, therefore, should not be exaggerated. The fate of bodily experiences must be understood as a consequence of the manner in which religious control, organization, and power work.[19] The leadership cannot easily control idiosyncratic ecstatic manifestations and so will introduce behavioral codes with set times and places. Priest and prophet do not get along easily—to use a Weberian example from the Christian religion. The first generation of believers will ultimately have to submit to the ritual control and routinization of their spontaneity. The body is domesticated, and the believer incorporates the power structure into his or her body language. One may suspect here also a case of male domestication of female bodies and their experiences—for example, in spirit mediumship and other extrasensory experiences. Doctrinal orthodoxy is an even easier and safer instrument at the leadership's disposal than control of diverse experiences, since it is easier to maintain social structures and boundaries when the ideas that legitimate the identity of the group are clear, predictable, and undisputed. Spontaneity and playfulness form a weak basis for social order.

Moving now to the parallel between religious leaders and students of religion, many social scientists are, consciously or not, as focused on the question of how social order is possible and can be maintained as is the religious leadership. Therefore, the starting point of many explanations of religion and religious success is religion's contribution to social order, and not the obvious center of religious practice: experience. This does not mean that religious corporeal experiences are never mentioned, but often they are submitted to a reductionist treatment. A rediscovery of experiences' role in religion may lead to a rehabilitation of religion as it was before success linked it to the powers that be.

When the role of the body in religion is emphasized, new concepts may need to be developed. One way of bringing and keeping body and mind together is to use the concept of schema, as defined in cognitive anthropology.[20] Schemas are culturally accepted minimal scripts (or scenarios, prototypes, or models) for and of a certain thought, emotion, perception, or act.[21] They contain a limited number of elements, which are common to similar concrete situations. Thus the conversion-experience schema contains a number of characteristics that are normally part of the event, despite personal and contextual differences. Claudia Strauss and Naomi Quinn have defined schemas as "networks of strongly connected cognitive elements that represent the generic concepts stored in memory."[22] Schemas are physically anchored in the body as connections between millions of neurons in the brain.[23] In fact, this view goes beyond the dichotomy of mind and body. Schemas generate religious corporeal experiences, just as experiences inspire the formation or alteration of schemas. One way of mapping what happens in bodily religious experiences is to describe them by discovering the schemas that are at work. Schemas do not stand alone, but form repertoires that characterize a particular field—for example, that of a religion. Believers and scholars both have their own repertoires of schemas to make sense of their fields.[24]

When we wish to understand why bodily religious experiences have until recently been a neglected area in the study of modern religion, we should also refer to the metaphors that inspire its methodology. Thus "text" has been described as "a hungry metaphor" that "gobbled up the body itself."[25] The emphasis in religious studies on sacred texts and on official views reflected this metaphor. Another popular metaphor does refer to the body, but in a one-sided way: there is a strong visual bias and a use of optical metaphors in scholarly vocabulary and method.[26] Scholars commonly speak of a view, a point of view, a vision, a focus, an interview, a worldview, a perspective, the invisible, and so on. Objectivity has visual connotations as well, already in the sense of "objectives" as in lenses, suggesting unbiased observation as through a camera. Moreover, for optical reasons, observation is thought to demand the same distance that—at least in the (neo)-positivist view—scientific research requires. As J. L. Austin and Pierre Bourdieu suggest, science tends to neglect the other senses, represented by nose, tongue, and fingertips, because they require a closeness that sins against the rule of necessary distance. The blind spot (another optical metaphor) of religious corporeal experiences seems for a long time to have escaped scholarly attention because students of religion were "optically" misled.

We may conclude that the one-field approach includes a challenge to employ more senses in fieldwork than the common optical instrument. This is necessary because religious experience goes beyond the rule that what you see is what you get. When we invite the use of other senses, unexplored dimensions of religious practice come into view, and not only that. Moreover, doing so may lead to another view of ritual. Besides, common believers fall within the range of research, complementing the usual focus on religious leadership and on holy texts. More than order, deviations become interesting for research, doing justice to the way in which religions have their beginnings.

The Case of Pentecostalism

The history of the study of Pentecostalism aptly illustrates my arguments in favor of a one-field approach. Pentecostalism seems a particularly relevant example for understanding the study of religion as an academic subculture and its need to update the discipline's praxis in accordance with changes occurring in the religious field. It is a new form of Christianity, which began in a revival on Azusa Street, Los Angeles, in 1906. It is typically modern in its focus on the individual, its world-wide mission, its rapid spread around the globe, its use of modern communications techniques, but most of all in its critical reaction to modernity and its excesses. It emphasizes the influence of the Holy Spirit, given at Pentecost, as narrated in Acts 2. It challenges established views of mainstream Christianity and thereby indirectly the accepted models based on it that are applied to other forms of religion. Pentecostalism welcomes the charismata, such as healing, glossolalia, and prophecy. As a consequence it allows much room for bodily experiences, despite the fact that, following the perspective of mainline churches, it is said to be focused exclusively on the soul, with a concomitant moral depreciation of aspects of the body. Its exceptional expansion over the past century reflects the appeal of a religion that emphasizes the role of the body, especially in relation to the changes brought about by modernization, globalization, migration, consumerism, and individualization. These processes affect the body, and Pentecostal churches offer care for the ills they entail. The Pentecostal movement is also interesting because the majority of Pentecostals live in the Southern Hemisphere, where these processes at present have an especially strong impact. Being a new phenomenon, Pentecostalism demands new methods. In fact, a one-field approach offers surplus value here.

If one takes the broadest possible definition of Pentecostalism, the number of Pente-costal believers in the world is now estimated at half a billion people, a quarter of all Christians.[27] As recently as 1975, the number was estimated at seventy million. Even if one adopts more exclusive definitions, by not including, for example, African indepen-dent churches or excluding so-called charismatic movements in mainline churches, the numerical growth is impressive. Philip Jenkins predicts that Pentecostal believers will form the hard core of a conservative, Southern Hemisphere Christianity that will charac-terize the twenty-first century.[28] The majority of Pentecostals are women, usually being led by men, which makes the movement interesting from the viewpoint of gender.

The study of this phenomenon was slow in starting, as if the mainline church view that Pentecostalism is a sect made it less interesting. For decades, more was known about non-Christian religions than about this new sector of Christianity. Labeled as sects, Pente-costal churches did not obey the church model of established Christianity. But the church/sect typology is itself an expression of the mainline perspective, which sees itself as normal, sects as a deviation. This typology dates almost to the same time as the advent of Pentecos-talism, and it was developed in connection with its emergence.[29] The comparison was influenced by the opposition between systematic doctrinal formulation, on the one hand, and religious experiences involving the body, on the other. The elitist view of sects as places of ecstatic behavior reflected this. Not being part of the establishment, Pentecostal "churches" were depicted as deviant, or even as backward and irrational. In fact, the experiences of the charismata were difficult to combine with the cerebral theological cli-mate. In terms of power, the Pentecostal groups were a threat to the established churches because of the possible exodus of members to these "sects." As a consequence, only in the sixties did Pentecostalism become an established subject for academic research. The theologian and missiologist Walter Hollenweger, who completed a ten-volume thesis be-tween 1965 and 1967 and was personally involved in Pentecostalism, was one of the first to study these churches in a scholarly way.[30] Emílio Willems and Christian Lalive d'Épi-nay, both working on Latin American Pentecostalism, opened the field of Pentecostalism in social science studies.[31]

In attempting to explain Pentecostalism's appeal and expansion, these social scientists referred primarily to nonreligious factors and their supposed interaction with this reli-gion. From a functionalist perspective, the role of Pentecostalism in society was proposed as an explanation of its popularity. External causes of Pentecostal growth received much attention, whereas less attention was given to the identity and attraction of Pentecostalism itself, as a religion with its own doctrine and practice. This might be seen as a symptom of the problem, in social theory, of not knowing how to approach the role of corporeal experiences. As I suggested above, bodily religious experiences had been given a lower status, as a result of an overly rational approach. Although Pentecostalism is unique be-cause of its exclusive focus on the Christian concept of the Holy Spirit and it is often opposed to syncretism and an existing, pre-Christian religiosity, some strands appear to connect the sinful and demonic body of the past to the converted body of the present, despite the contrast. Bodily manifestations of the sacred are well known, often in connection with healing and problem solving, in many cultures and religions, though in very diverse ways. Basic religious experiences are impossible without the body, which is the locus of the Spirit's manifestation. Thus Pentecostal message is not new, even though its interpretation of these basic experiences is.

In the globalizing world, security and insecurity come together in the body. Feelings of well-being as well as affliction are expressed through the body. Material conditions affect a person's corporeal existence. The body is what is deprived in poverty and attacked in violence, but it is also existentially the support for human existence. Especially in the Southern Hemisphere, the need for healing has increased because, though medical conditions have improved with modernization, the concomitant demographic explosion has had the much stronger side effects of conflict over scarce resources, increased pollution, and an unequal distribution of income. These have both exacerbated causes of disease and made medical care inaccessible. Besides, the many life-styles that consumerism and the media encourage raise questions of identity and prosperity—of how one can pay for these attractive life-styles. Where the "gospel of prosperity" is part of the Pentecostal message, suggesting that the faithful will be richly blessed, this offers another reason for the new religion to be welcomed, because it addresses this side of the body.

In view of the role of the body in the Pentecostal experience, the usual models and methods for the study of religion, developed in the context of Christian theological departments, which are often linked to mainline churches, no longer match the changed situation. The dramatic and intense Pentecostal experience cannot be understood from a distance. Pentecostals usually would love to see the researcher become a member of their church, and exert pressure toward that end. Yet the fieldworker may have some difficulty in identifying with the recruiting believer, not least because the corporeal experiences that come with the charismata are not quick or automatic. Nevertheless, better understanding of what drives Pentecostal churches, how they attract people looking for bodily experiences, demands that scholars try to understand what these experiences mean to them. The methods I have proposed may well help in this search for understanding. A one-field approach seems necessary for a fruitful study of this type of Christianity, in view of the central role of the body.

Conclusion

The scholar's current habitus in the study of religion can be characterized as the outcome of tensions between:

1. Science's demand for positivist and empirical objectivity, and a recent constructivist alternative;

2. The optical bias, and a recent call for the deployment of other senses;
3. A limited view caused by the dichotomy of the religious versus the secular and other parallel dichotomies, and new ways of going beyond these distinctions;
4. Disembodied Christian theological practice, which focuses on systematic and rational representation, and a new emphasis on the way people use their bodies in their religious praxis;
5. A reductionist social-scientific emphasis on social order and on religion's function as a way of guaranteeing this order, and an appreciation of the unpredictable dynamics of human behavior.

Within the traditional academic infrastructure, the object of research has been constructed in a specific and limited way. A discourse and a research practice have dominated that, while elaborating the cerebral, systemic, and social sides of religion, have been insufficient to assess the role the body plays in religious experiences. The body as the crossroads where powers of sacred and secular natures meet has not received the attention it deserves. The framework adopted in fact allowed the researcher to ignore the body as a methodological tool—except, perhaps, for the head. A one-field approach forces us to reassess the distance the researcher has kept with regard (note the optical metaphor) to the believer. It draws the researcher and his or her body into the field.

Whither religious studies? A change in emphasis on bodily experience in the globalizing world demands a change in thematic options, theoretical perspectives, and methodological preferences. The division between mind and body, along with the dichotomies that come with it, should be overcome. Trends such as Northern Hemisphere New Age and Southern Hemisphere Pentecostalism have popularized religious corporeal experiences. Indeed, religious bodily experiences are prominent in large parts of current global consumer culture. Advertisers for brands that sell products for the body, especially, use religious vocabulary, suggesting divine, heavenly, magical, ecstatic, or ultimate sensations. Some of these brands enjoy cult status. The long-standing emphasis on the cerebral side of religions as systems of thought needs to be complemented by an appreciation of religions as the locus for experiencing the sacred in and through the body. The mind can thus be reconnected to the rest of the body, and lived religious experiences rehabilitated.

Part of the one-field perspective is a critical way of dealing with dichotomies. An effort must be made to go beyond—or at least become aware of—accepted dichotomies, such as those between body and mind, the secular and the religious. Many of them are the product of religious *and* academic socialization. Except in extreme cases, themselves one-sided interpretations of dichotomies, unilateral emphases must be avoided.

Scholars studying religion may consider exercising some self-reflexivity regarding their own field of expertise, as I have tried to do here for Pentecostalism. As a result, they may develop a certain degree of consciousness of the academic subculture into which they have so far been socialized and by which they have been conditioned. That subculture reflects a past period of modern culture and religion and has been influenced by contextual factors that were not directly part of the field of study itself. These factors are now outdated, at least in their one-sidedness. The current situation demands changes in the professional subculture, a reconsideration of explicit and—more importantly—implicit presuppositions, another way of using dichotomies, a more hybrid and intersubjective position, and possibly another academic home base.

Part of what has thus far been held to be outside the academic scope must be introduced within it, just as part of what seemed indispensable for the profession should perhaps be put between brackets. The inexpressibility of religious corporeal experiences should no longer be taken for granted, but faced as a real challenge. Scholars could make an effort to experience them themselves. They might consider seeing themselves in a hybrid way, as part of the religious field, and immerse themselves in it as much and as long as they can, thanks to or despite their personal views on religion. After having for a long time worked on the basis of a contrast between religion and science, they might now search for commonalities between the two. After having been "mindful" of religion, they might now try to use the rest of the body and "incorporate" the study of religion, including the mind's role in this. This conversion will not take place overnight, as cultures and subcultures usually are resilient. In a reassuring way, the old habits will still eclectically be experienced, protecting against a new one-sidedness. But the effort should be made.

As a consequence of the approach suggested here, the definition of religion can playfully be revised, integrating the researcher into the field in a constructivist manner. Whereas the usual definitions of religion refer only to believers, the one-field approach must necessarily make room for scholars. In that way, the constructed nature of the concept of religion and of the discipline's knowledge can be acknowledged.

The definition I propose reflects the fact that, as human beings, both researched and researchers have to deal with dichotomies, some of these similar, despite their different perspectives. Dichotomies refer, for example, to individuality and belonging, inexpressibility and representation, distance and closeness, diversifying identity and unifying identification, variety and unity. This rapprochement would help the student of religion deal with contrasts between the religious and the secular, religion and science, and distance and involvement, contrasts that have hampered the understanding of religion, especially religious bodily experiences. This common struggle with dichotomies can be reflected in the following rather substantive definition of religion, albeit with some fresh functional undertones:

> Religion is the field of experiencing the sacred in the body—a field in which both believers and scholars act, each category applying the human capacity for play, within the constraints of power mechanisms, to articulate basic human dichotomies, thus adding an extra dimension to their view of reality.[32]

In this hybrid way, viewing scholar and believer as part of a single field, we can develop a new view of religion and its study.

"Religion" in Public Debates

Who Defines, for What Purposes?

Willem B. Drees

A question central to this volume is "What is religion?" In this essay I want to focus on a related question, namely: "Who is to say what religion is?" That is, who defines what is to be considered as fitting the concept "religion"? I also think it useful to consider a related question: "What purposes are served by using the concept in a particular way?" I'll discuss this in two steps. The first section will deal with the question "What is religion?" as an academic question. However, I hope to make clear that the academic question, as a quest for disinterested understanding, is not the main context of the question of what religion might be. Second, I'll consider the question "What is religion?" as a question that arises in a social context, where tactical reasons may be more important than a thirst for knowledge for its own sake. One important example will be the understanding of "religion" in public debates, where advocates of strong religion and advocates of secularism may work with an understanding of religion that excludes large segments of the population.[1]

"What Is Religion?" as a Question for Academics

Is the question "What is religion?" an academic question, concerning the meaning of a concept? Is posing this question just like asking "What is a black hole?" in astrophysics, a purely scientific question? If so, to answer the question would be the business of those who study religions, or more broadly, of those who study human societies. They would need to propose distinctions that might best serve to clarify the phenomena.

To continue the analogy with the natural sciences, three observations may be relevant.

First, the best definitions don't come at the beginning of research, but rather at the end of our explorations. They embody the insights gathered so far, for instance, regarding the best way to classify objects. If one begins with definitions that separate mammals and fish by whether they live on land or in water, the whale is to be classified as a fish. Further study of the organisms, however, gives us good reasons to classify whales with the mammals of the land rather than with the fish of the sea. After studying whales one may have a different, improved understanding, which finds expression in new definitions of fish and of mammals.

We already have a whole history of research on religion, both theologically inspired, in broad terms, and anthropological. One anthropologist who has studied religion is Clifford Geertz. He observes that "sacred symbols function to synthesize a people's ethos—the tone, character, and quality of their life, its moral and aesthetic style and mood—and their world view—the picture they have of the way things in sheer actuality are, their most comprehensive ideas of order."[2] This insight regarding the role of symbols in synthesizing ethos and worldview brought him to an oft-quoted definition: "a religion is (1) a system of symbols which acts to (2) establish powerful, pervasive, and long-lasting moods and motivations in men by (3) formulating conceptions of a general order of existence and (4) clothing these conceptions with such an aura of facticity that (5) the moods and motivations seem uniquely realistic."[3] This definition is, as a definition of the empirical phenomena of religiosity, not perfect. The definition puts too much emphasis on the cognitive role of symbols as contributing to conceptions of the order of existence, thus bypassing ritual, social, and other noncognitive roles of religion. The definition can also be challenged as inadequate with respect to philosophical complexities of representation and truth.[4] Besides, the definition suggests a causal arrow from symbols via conceptions to moods and motivations, whereas the symbols may also *express* moods and motivations—the previously quoted observation about synthesizing ethos and worldview has less of this causal suggestion. Insofar as the definition concerns the cognitive side of a religion, however, what could be called a "theology," it highlights the observation that in religious thought conceptions of the order of existence are intertwined with the appreciation of reality and behavioral norms. To speak of the world as God's creation has both descriptive and prescriptive aspects.

When it comes to religion, such definitions are always highly contested, due to differences in perspective between theological and anthropological understandings, as well as differences within each approach, broadly conceived. Thus, even though some definitions, such as Geertz's, may have substantial support, the issue of defining is not a neutral preliminary to scholarship. Rather, definitions must be argued for on the basis of research.

Second, the role of a definition is to some extent *pragmatic*. Physics handles concepts such as energy and gravity very well, but the question "What is energy?" makes physicists uneasy, as most of them would consider this a question that is not within their domain, or not even properly posed. In his *Lectures on Physics*, Richard Feynman has a section

465

titled "What Is Energy?" He speaks of the conservation of energy as "a strange fact that we can calculate some number and when we finish watching nature go through her tricks and calculate the number again, it is the same." At the end of the section, he writes: "It is important to realize that in physics today, we have no knowledge of what energy *is*."[5] Many are able to work with the concept and the mathematics, but do we know what it is? A metaphysical claim as to what energy is might be beyond our reach.

Third, the boundaries of a concept may be vague, sometimes necessarily so. If one is to develop a theory about the way biological species emerge out of earlier species, even how multiple species may have a single ancestral species, then one may need a concept of species that allows for a transition, where it is not clear whether organisms belong to the earlier or to the later species. That the boundary is not sharp need not count against the usefulness of the concept; the vagueness of the transition from day to night does not make the concepts "day" and "night" meaningless.

Of course, one also needs a provisional grasp of the area to be explored and analyzed. Thus, one may prefer to begin with a few *examples* of what is considered to be religious and suggest studying other phenomena sufficiently similar. However, this strategy of operating on the basis of a few examples has certain risks, as peculiarities of the exemplars chosen may skew the analysis.

This is certainly the case when we study "religion." In the history of the concept "religion," Western Christianity has been the most prominent model, and this brought with it certain expectations. A "Holy Book" seemed characteristic of Christianity, for instance, and also of Islam and Judaism, being the alternatives best known to scholars of religion. Thus, when exploring Asia in the colonial period, Max Müller and his colleagues collected various writings in the series *Sacred Books of the East*—assuming the same type of canonical authority for different books. This is still very much a popular misunderstanding, even in approaching the various "religions of the Book" as if they have books that may differ in content but are similar in kind.

Furthermore, since the Roman empire or even earlier, the acceptable religion has been tied up with the state, and loyalty to the state is supposed to be exclusive. Christianity, with its emphasis on the importance of "true belief," has continued this exclusionary stance. It thus was assumed that one adheres to a single religion, at most. However, this may not do justice to countries such as Japan, where ritual practices from different religious traditions such as Buddhism and Shintoism are part of the life of a single individual, even though in distinct spheres of life.

A third example of the risks of relying too much on one tradition concerns the roles played by religious officers. Assuming that an imam in an Islamic community fulfils the same roles as a Catholic priest or a Protestant minister may thus be mistaken, academically speaking. However, there may be various societal reasons to posit this identity of roles: for instance, it may serve to argue that political arrangements made for the services of priests and ministers in the army and in prisons should be applied also to the work of imams, pandits, and rabbis.

Thus, if we begin with a single exemplary tradition, or at most a few, we may skew understanding via assumptions adequate for the example but not for other traditions. If we begin at the other end, with *general categories* in order to understand religious traditions, we face very serious differences as well. One area where this shows up is in comparative studies of religion. I will consider briefly two methodologically quite different approaches.

At Boston University, Robert Neville has coordinated a substantial project on comparing religious ideas. This project has resulted in three volumes concerning understandings of the human condition, of conceptions of truth, and of ultimate realities—a plural chosen so as not to skew the comparison in favor of monotheistic views. Each of these volumes contains six case studies on particular traditions, framed by essays by Neville and Wesley Wildman on strategies and problems arising in comparative studies. They seek to overcome the methodological difficulties due to differences by acknowledging a variety of levels of analysis, both general (with *"vague concepts,"* as they call them) and more specific.[6] Thus, at the expense of vagueness (and on the basis of a moderately ahistorical and acontextual understanding of religions as systems of beliefs) they seek to develop comparative studies.

In contrast to such a bottom-up approach, one might look at the approach of John Hick (and other religionists in the background, such as Rudolf Otto and Mircea Eliade), who stresses commonalities beyond all the particular differences. As I read Hick's work, especially his *An Interpretation of Religion,*[7] he selects from the various traditions aspects and authors that allow for comparison in moral and soteriological orientation, and then uses this selection to make the case that, deep down, in all religions we have the same aspirations and ideals. In my opinion, the *selection* does most of the work. Despite this argumentative weakness of Hick's approach, many, myself included, find his approach sympathetic. I suspect that this is not just for scholarly purposes, but rather because the resulting view of "the religious" suits particular preferences and agendas. The approach serves the cause of inter-religious cooperation and dialogue, while within the various religious traditions also serving the cause of those who are open to the idea that there might be truth in other traditions as well, who acknowledge the human, historical, and constructed character of religious views rather than ascribing to them absolute authority based in revelation, and who are morally universalist in orientation, extending moral norms that apply to fellow believers beyond the boundaries of one's own religious community. Such work on the understanding of religion and religions may be laudable for the aspirations that drive it. Academically speaking, however, the approach seems inadequate, given the dominance of its universalist orientation in selecting among the world's religious practices and ideas.

If asked by academics, the question "What is religion?" may be an academic matter, but it need not be. Often, even within the academic sphere, the societal and personal dimension is of paramount importance in choosing a particular understanding of the concept, and thereby in assuming the authority to be the one who defines what is to count as religion.

"What Is Religion?" as an Apologetic or Political Question

"What is religion?" thus seems to be, at least partially, a question that is asked in the context of morality or politics. Asking "What is a human?" or "When does life begin?" in the context of a dispute on the rights of human embryos may seem a scientific question, but it is not. It shows itself to be a political issue.

If the nature of the question "What is religion?" is of such a kind, clarification and explanation is not the primary purpose. Rather, the purpose of the question may be to ascribe a certain status to the phenomenon thus classified. Or the purpose may be to dismiss certain challenges as irrelevant. As an example of the latter, one may think of Galileo's letter to Archduchess Christina in 1615. Galileo wrote in order to defend the claim that his astronomical work was not in conflict with Scripture, given that a cardinal had said that the Bible does not intend to teach us how the heavens go, but how to go to heaven. Religion is about redemption, not about scientific facts. By offering a particular understanding of what genuine religion is supposed to be, certain challenges can be dismissed as mistaken, or as applying only to superstition but not to genuine religion. (By the way, academic definitions of superstition are also difficult if not impossible to come by; the point of the label is mostly dismissive.)

That understandings of religion have political significance is typical of the debates over evolution and "intelligent design" both in the United States and elsewhere, including the Netherlands today. Defining religion as belief in the authority of Scripture in all matters, both moral and metaphysical, is more likely to result in opposition to evolution than is emphasizing the message of the Sermon on the Mount as the heart of Christian faith, or stressing a metaphysical distinction between primary and secondary causes or between values and facts, or some other distinction. Thus, even though the dispute seems to be about science, the struggle is to a large extent about the nature of religion. Whether one sees evolution as a challenge to faith or as irrelevant to faith reflects different understandings of the nature of faith.

In 1981, for instance, the legislature of the State of Arkansas passed a law that described its purpose as "An act to require *balanced treatment* of creation-science and evolution-science in public schools; to protect academic freedom by providing student choice; . . . to bar discrimination on the basis of creationist or evolutionist belief." This law was challenged in court by parents and teachers, as well as by bishops of the United

Methodist, Episcopal, Roman Catholic, and African Methodist Episcopal Churches; the principal representative of the Presbyterian Churches in America; United Methodist, Southern Baptist, and Presbyterian clergy; three types of Jewish organizations; and various mainstream religious organizations. Thus, the case was not just one of "science" versus "religion" but at least as much a case of "religion" versus "religion." The judge, William R. Overton, concurred, as he deemed "creation-science" a religious rather than a scientific position. Thus, the law favored a particular religious position over other religious views, namely, over the separation of church and state. Therefore the judge declared the law unconstitutional.[8]

The offence that creationist or intelligent design presentations give to mainstream believers is not just that they disagree about a particular detail of faith, but that the creationists claim to represent genuine faith and thus claim to represent religion as it really should be, thereby relegating the more liberal believers to secondary status if not almost to that of atheists. And vice versa—adherents of the mainline churches (to use this label for simplicity's sake) may well dismiss the other voice as not grasping what religion is about and thus clinging to the wrong issues.

One recurrent pattern in defining religion for tactical reasons can be found when we consider the understandings of religion in public conversations in secular democracies. In this setting, extremes seem to provide a useful service to each other by sharing the answer to the question "What is religion?" even though advocating different policies.

"Religion" and Secular Politics

In his *Democracy and Tradition*, the American scholar of religion Jeffrey Stout discusses the role of religion in public discourse in democratic societies. He discerns two positions that are prominent in public debates. On the one hand, there are authors who prefer to exclude religion from public debate because they consider religion to be private and hence unable to provide generally accepted premises. Religious expressions and arguments may have a role temporarily, but they require us to find a suitable replacement that is couched in terms acceptable to all. An example, for Stout, is the position of the ethicist and political theorist John Rawls; another, that of the philosopher Richard Rorty. It may even be inappropriate to refer to one's religious preferences, because religion serves as a "conversation stopper" (Rorty). Stout holds that these positions rest upon a particular understanding of the neutrality of the state and a dichotomy of reason and faith.[9] On the other hand, in opposition to the secular exclusion of religion from the public sphere, some advocates of religious positions have challenged and rejected secular liberalism, suggesting that secular views fall short in providing substantial values that are essential to a flourishing human society. Stout's examples for this position are John Milbank and other advocates of Radical Orthodoxy, as well as Alisdair MacIntyre and Stanley Hauerwas.

Advocates of religious and secular views co-produce each other, in that they create a polarized field in which there seem to be just two options. Public controversies on religion in the Netherlands seem to have certain characteristics that resemble the American pattern described by Stout, with a mutual exclusion of secularism and religion advocated by certain secular thinkers (e.g., Paul Cliteur, Ayaan Hirsi Ali, Herman Philipse, Rudy Kousbroek), while some religious leaders or religiously inspired politicians, such as our current Prime Minister, Jan-Peter Balkenende, lean toward a communitarian perspective on social values, and thereby oppose the secular character of the state which the others consider essential.

Let me consider briefly an example of the question-begging moves that may be involved. The atheist Paul Cliteur titled a collection of columns, in Dutch, *God Does Not Like Liberal Religion*.[10] How does he know? Not from God, I assume. He knows by asking genuine believers. But who are the genuine believers? Cliteur knows how to pick them. Slightly less selective is Herman Philipse, who, in his *Atheistic Manifesto*,[11] also in Dutch, criticizes some forms of belief as being implausible (thus he concludes in favour of atheism), while dismissing others as being vacuous (which results in semantic atheism, as he calls it). With his dichotomy, he passes by those believers who consider their religious beliefs to be interpretations that are meaningful even though not empirically testable.

The definition of religion shared by secular voices and religious traditionalists results in understanding the situation as a choice between two positions. But is this adequate? Empirical results seem to suggest that the exclusion of the middle excludes a major segment of the population from having a voice in matters that they consider important. In the Netherlands, a poll held in 2004 showed that adherents of the theistic and the secular positions together form just about one-third of the people (20 percent believe in a personal God; 13 percent are atheist), whereas another one-third said they believe in "something," and a final third consider themselves agnostic. In a more recently published survey, slightly over a quarter of the population can be considered, qua lifestyle, to be members of a church, and one in four as more or less humanist or atheist. About one in five is considered neither religious nor humanistic in orientation; this more "nihilistic" orientation goes with distrust in government, society, and groups with a different orientation. One in four considers himself or herself religious or "spiritual," but without belonging. Members of this group, as well as quite a few religious humanists and mainstream church members, are not well served by the strong definition of religion shared by advocates of secularism and religious traditionalists.[12] Numbers may be different, but religious positions that are less explicit by the standards of traditional religion are present also in other Western countries, including the United States.

In response to exclusionary ways of defining religion and democracy that do justice only to a few outspoken theocratic and atheistic thinkers, Stout argues that in the United States we find an "Emersonian piety" alongside an "Augustinian" one. "Emersonian piety" refers to Ralph Waldo Emerson, but Stout uses it as a label for a religious attitude that does not defer to higher powers, to theological truth as a given. Nor is it reverence for authority. Rather, it is characterized as self-reliance, as taking responsibility for one's own thinking. This is not self-reliance as if our achievements were ours in isolation from a tradition shaped by earlier generations, but rather gratitude to earlier generations and above all to the whole of nature, the source of our existence. This gratitude does not show itself in receptivity alone, but in moving on, in further explorations. A similar attitude could be articulated by referring to various thinkers of the Enlightenment, even though Stout finds Kant's approach historically and sociologically inadequate. Following Dewey, Stout emphasizes the piety of this attitude, stressing self-reliance's "dependence on the natural and social circumstances without which it would be nothing."[13]

Stout's description of the religious landscape is not empirical, a conclusion of statistical research. Rather, he argues a systematic thesis, namely, that the polarization between the secular exclusion of religious voices and the religious sentiment against secular culture rests upon a shared assumption regarding the nature of religion and, even more, regarding the nature of secular culture. Thus, democracy needs to be reconceived if one is to escape this polarity. Whereas a highly absolutist, authoritarian understanding of religion makes it hard to incorporate religious voices in a democratic process (thus justifying the secular exclusion, as well as the fear that religious voices are excluded), a more tentative form of religious life is not at all in conflict with democracy, then understood as a process of conversation, of exchanging reasons for one's values and concerns when challenged, rather than as the exclusion of all religious voices.

The empirical observations regarding the Dutch religious landscape and the systematic position defended by Stout suggest a similar point. There are strong forms of religion and outspoken opinions on democracy and Enlightenment values that exclude each other, but do so on the basis of a shared understanding of the concept of religion. Those who are moderate may be more comfortable with Stout's characterizations of religion and of democracy than with the more exclusionary ones. The controversy is to some extent a controversy over the meaning of "genuine religion."

Conclusion

By way of summary, I want to emphasize three theses.

First, a choice concerning what counts as "genuine religion" and thus who is to decide this is a major component in controversies involving positions of authority in religious communities and whether religious contributions are to be allowed in or excluded from the public sphere.

Second, strong forms of secularism and strong forms of religion serve each other well, to the exclusion of moderate religious and secular voices. They so by sharing (broadly speaking) a particular understanding of religion, in which theological truth claims and piety as deference to authority are important characteristics.

Third, such definitions are inadequate in scholarly terms, since they exclude various other options. Rather than serving academic analysis, the images of religion they typically frame serve advocates of strong religion and advocates of strong secularism by focusing the debate on their own positions and their preferred opponents, to the exclusion of moderate alternatives.

Let me add one self-reflective worry as a question for future research. I challenge advocates of the secularization thesis and adherents of strong religion who may deplore secularization but agree with the others on the understanding of religion. But could one not challenge critics of the secularization thesis who claim to witness a "return to religion" or a transformation of religion? Are these interpretations of the developments not useful to some, such as church leaders who need a market and those believers who want their church to be a community open to all who earnestly seek—whether they seek God or their deepest self? And, more self-critical, are observations about the persistence of religion not also suspiciously useful to scholars of religion, including myself, who thereby justify their existence in a way that would not have been possible in the context of the polarized understanding of present developments in terms of strong religion or secularization?

The Field of Religion and Ecology

Addressing the Environmental Crisis and Challenging Faiths

Tony Watling

This essay is concerned with "religion and ecology," or religious environmentalism. It analyzes how religious traditions are used to understand and interact with the environment and environmental issues, suggesting ways of relating to these that are different from and possibly less destructive and ecologically harmful than those of the modern secular worldview. It argues that religious traditions may thereby be gaining new private and public relevance, while perhaps also being changed in the process, becoming more environmentally friendly and ecumenical. The article ethnographically and qualitatively analyzes a "field of religion and ecology" comprising ecologically minded academics and representatives of various religious traditions who promote such ideas, stimulating new eco-spiritualities and theologies, possibly even a new eco-religious movement. It also explores the environmental reinterpretation of several religious traditions within the field, highlighting not only some influential images and views but also any commonalities or convergences that may be arising or being encouraged between them.

I will seek to analyze how religion and religious concepts can be (diverse and dynamic) sources of communities, images, morals, and vocabularies for articulating human identity with and responsibility for nature, particularly in response to a secular identity and secularly defined nature that is resulting in environmental destruction. Religious concepts have been prominent in discourse on environmental responsibility: for example, "caring for creation," "co-creation," "Earth goddess," "Earth theology," "ecological sin," "integrity of creation," "nature as Eden," "stewardship." Such ideas stress that the environment demands a wider sense of identity than the merely human, a sense of an ecological and spiritual whole beyond reductionist and materialist concerns, one that would temper hubristic human self-centeredness and embrace the wider community of life. Environmental concerns and the religious thought and action they provoke may, therefore, be challenging concepts of personal and social identity, including religious identity, forcing reassessment and change. Environmental issues may thus provide a new context in which religious traditions, or individuals and groups within them, may reinterpret their beliefs, challenge dominant views, and regain legitimacy and public relevance through reimagining the environment, providing explanations of and answers to environmental problems.

This essay will analyze ways in which the field of religion and ecology encourages, stimulates, uses, compares, and combines different religious traditions to understand and reinterpret the environment and the human relationship to and role within it, challenging environmentally destructive views and actions and (ideally) contributing to new environmentally responsible ones. In this it seeks to provide a concrete example of the dynamic development and possible role of religion in the modern world. It argues that an ecological consciousness may be arising and coalescing within religious traditions, stimulated by the field, centered on ecologically aware individuals and groups within them. The result may be a field that in effect constitutes a new environmentally based religious movement in which different traditions express diverse and/or common and syncretized environmental views. Exploring this question, I will also analyze a sample (inevitably limited and somewhat simplified) of environmental views stressed in the field by academics and representatives of two Eastern and two Western religious traditions: Buddhism, Chinese traditions, Christianity, and Islam, examining how these different religious ideas of nature may challenge or set boundaries to environmental attitudes and behavior (and thus also challenge and change the traditions). These issues probe the consistency and rigidity versus flexibility and fluidity of religious beliefs in the face of moral urgency and social commitment. They highlight the *process* of religion, ways in which traditions can be and are used, reinterpreted, and reempowered in response to the modern worldview (which is itself a process) in a changing and endangered world.

Religion and the Environmental Discontents of the Modern World

We are currently facing an environmental crisis in which the works of what J. Baird Callicott calls *homo petroleumus* threaten the Earth's ecosystem in a biocide that is coming to be seen as the defining challenge of our age.[1] The necessary response involves more than economic or technological adjustments and extends to moral, social, and spiritual issues. This puts in question a particular cultural view of the world: the modern secular worldview, described as the Enlightenment mentality that has arisen in the last five centuries. Proponents of this worldview initially saw it as a way to liberate individuals from dependence on the natural environment, seen as bound up with superstition and the Christian church, by placing priority on reason, objectivity, and progress. They thereby developed a self-centered desire to dominate and transcend the natural environment, manipulating it to serve humanity's needs, with little thought of the consequences or of the moral issues involved. In this scheme, humanity and environment are separated; the previous, animistic ways of perceiving the environment, which saw nature as a living, sacred cosmos, were replaced with a secular, mechanical one, with nature reduced to material resources without life or spirit. The resultant worldview has become the dominant social form, defining truth and reality, and leading to what has been described as a disenchantment or desacralization of the world.[2] Tu Weiming sees this as the crisis of modernity, an inability to experience nature as the embodiment of spirit, seeing it merely in the light of economic or technological needs. This has resulted in an ecological illiteracy and biophobic destructiveness in which humans, as Mary Evelyn Tucker and John Grim observe, make macro-phase (environmental) changes with micro-phase wisdom.[3]

Such a disenchanted or desacralized way of looking at the world is, of course, socially constructed (as was what it replaced), for what is known as "the environment" or "nature" is a complex, diverse, and malleable concept that is also a social practice.[4] Counterstories and critiques (a politicization of nature) are thus seen as being able to create wider awareness of and diverse access to the construction of reality, possibly paving the way for a change away from a dominant anthropocentric view of nature to more biocentric ones that see nature and humanity as interdependent and mutually beneficial (while remaining aware of modern successes and the dangers of a simplistic romanticizing of nature). Such views, it is hoped, might then also lead to ecologically responsible lifestyles based on changing human beliefs and practices away from ones that devalue and manipulate the environment to thoughts of interconnectedness, revaluation, and care.[5] Because this may demand a radical change in lifestyle, religion has been invoked as a means to achieve it, via a reenchantment or resacralization of the world, involving wisdom and reverence for life.[6]

Religion has been seen as disempowered and in decline in the modern world, its meanings no longer relevant within the dominant secular worldview. Institutional churches have lost control of social life to secular bodies (in processes of secularization and privatization). Religion (and secularization) may not be as static or unified as was previously thought, however. (This may be a consequence of modern Western bias, as, for example, Talal Asad argues,[7] of the [liberal] differentiation of society that separates the religious from the secular, defining the former as unified traditions concerned with private spiritual beliefs rather than practical public issues.) Rather, religion may be more dynamic and volatile, a complex process of individual and social, official and unofficial, private and public actions in particular contexts. It may, therefore, still have a role to play in the world and be a valid way of inspiring, mediating, ordering, or re-creating personal and social environmental beliefs and identities (or, in Grace Davie's terms, "memories"), albeit in more diverse and dynamic forms than had previously been thought. This may particularly be so as the deleterious effects on the environment of modern technology evoke an ethical response from individuals whom modernity has isolated from the moral resources needed to address those effects. New avenues of explicit and implicit awareness, belief, and action may thus result within religious traditions, diverse spiritualities, or new religious movements. ("Spirituality" is often evoked as a concept that might stand alongside or replace "religion."[8]) Linda Woodhead and Paul Heelas, for example, suggest several coexisting or conflicting religious responses to the modern world: "religions of difference," which distinguish between God, humans, and nature (e.g., charismatic, fundamentalist views); "religions of humanity," which balance the divine, humans, and nature (e.g., liberal religion, denominationalism); and "spiritualities of life," which adopt a holistic perspective and assert an identity between the divine, humans, and nature (e.g., New Age, Neo-Pagan views).[9]

All this ferment provides a context in which new religious forms can arise, perhaps involving both secularization and sacralization, old faiths and new movements. An "ethical religion" or "world theology," for example, may coalesce around global ethical issues such as the environmental crisis. It may allow religions to regain moral, political, and social capital, as well as to inspire new attitudes and actions. In this sense, religions may hope to engage the problems created by modern society and create innovative responses, assuming a universal, trans-social role of defining and maintaining the global common good, becoming resources for re-creating private beliefs (e.g., existentially reconnecting individuals to nature) as well as publicly addressing issues such as the environmental crisis. They may thus enter a discursive space of public interaction, questioning modern society and forcing it to reflect on its beliefs, structures, and actions. Religion may thus help us to address crucial global issues and the discontents of the modern world, providing alternatives that ethically unite humanity. Initially this might well still occur in a Western liberal democratic and dialogic format, but religions might even challenge and change this.[10]

Peter Beyer, in particular, sees environmentalism as one possible way to revitalize religion and influence the global system, in an eco-theology that would have eschatological implications for all of humanity. In this scheme, religion would address residual matters of the dominant system (i.e., its ethical, environmental, or social consequences), bridging the gap between private and public, linking religious function (belief) and performance (application, public influence). Here environmental issues provide an arena for religious expression, not only as critical matters of public concern but also as indicators of root causes of the problems, which are seen as moral and spiritual values, with religion being necessary for their resolution. Religious environmentalism may thus become a social movement based on religious resources, giving meaning to and promising the power to overcome the consequences of modern secular values and structures. Assuming a priestly and prophetic role, religion would then present the environmental crisis as a problem of disordered or unjust human relations and provide the ideological and organizational resources to conceptualize these and deal with them.[11]

To do this, however, religions may need greater private and public environmental consciousness. Lynn White, for example, argues that the Judeo-Christian tradition is anti-environmentalist because of its anthropocentric views. Even religious traditions that seem more biocentric and environmentally friendly, such as those in China, have been subsumed in political regimes that are ecologically destructive, for example, the Chinese Marxist system.[12] Nevertheless, ecological awareness has been growing within religious traditions, in the form of a nonanthropocentric reinterpretation of humanity, nature, and the sacred, during a period that Roderick Nash terms the "greening" of religion. This stems from developments in the American National Council of Churches and the World Council of Churches in the 1980s and in the work of such writers as Thomas Berry, Wendell Berry, Fritjof Capra, John Hart, Jurgen Moltmann, Theodore Roszak, and Paul Santmire. It can be traced back further, however. In the 1970s arose John Cobb's "process theology," influenced by Alfred North Whitehead and Teilhard de Chardin. The 1960s saw a growing interest in religious viewpoints outside the Judeo-Christian, especially in Asian and indigenous traditions. Richard Baer and the "Faith-Man-Nature" group of American eco-theologians, influenced by Saint Francis of Assisi and Aldo Leopold's "Land Ethic," flourished at that time. The 1950s witnessed Joseph Sittler's "Theology for the Earth." Indeed, the genealogy stretches back to David Henry Thoreau and John Muir in the nineteenth century and John Ray and Alexander Pope in the seventeenth.[13]

At present, to consolidate and further this religious greening there has developed what two of its leading exponents, Bron Taylor and Mary Evelyn Tucker, have described as a "field" of religion and ecology: an academic, religious, and social arena that seeks to enable the exploration and promotion of eco-religious ideas, a deepening spiritual awareness of nature, and religious ecological activism.[14] Here religion, in diverse ways within multiple traditions, is invoked as a means for engaging the modern secular worldview and environmental issues, addressing private preferences and public consequences. It is viewed as oriented to something other than egoism and materialism, highlighting the order, interdependence, and spirituality of the world, with humanity as only one part rather than as its raison d'être. It is also viewed as offering resources for experiencing creative power, whether that of a deity or of nature; for defining humanity's place in the cosmos, as well as people's obligations to each other and to other life forms; and for reinforcing personal and communal connections to a wider truth. Those active in this field hope that religious traditions may have the moral authority, collective vision, and legitimating narratives to provide existential and social guidance, as well as the critical and prophetic potential—and numbers of adherents—to challenge destructive lifestyles and stimulate change.[15]

The Field of Religion and Ecology

The field of religion and ecology coordinates and encompasses a range of literatures and actions (hovering between the academic and the practical, the why and the how, and aiming for a fluid, self-reflexive approach) involving religious traditions, new religious movements, and environmental movements (including reflections from science, public policy, and ethics). All this is coalescing into a recognized religious and social form. A few recent influences on this field and actions within it include:[16]

1. The 1986 meetings in Assisi, sponsored by the World Wildlife Fund, resulting in the Religious Declarations on Nature, in which religious traditions stressed their concern for the environment and how their faiths lead them to care for it;

2. Global Forums of Spiritual and Parliamentary Leaders, from 1988 to 1993, especially the 1990 meeting Preserving and Cherishing the Earth: An Appeal for Joint Commitment in Science and Religion;

3. The Joint Appeal (for the environment) in Religion and Science, a statement by religious leaders at the 1991 Summit on the Environment;

4. Activities since 1993 by the National Religious Partnership for the Environment in the United States and the Religion and Ecology Group of the American Academy of Religion;

5. Activities since 1995 by the Alliance of Religions and Conservation in conjunction with the World Wildlife Fund and the World Bank, for example, the Sacred Gifts for a Living Planet conference in 2000;

6. Declarations by the Dalai Lama, Pope John Paul II, and Ecumenical Patriarch Bartholomew I in the Religion, Science, and Environment Symposia from 1994 to 2002;

7. The United Nations Environment Programme, Interfaith Partnership for the Environment; for example, the World Peace Summit of Religious and Spiritual Leaders in 2000;

8. Religious input in the UN-stimulated Earth Charter Initiative, a statement of ethical principles aimed at guiding humanity toward a sustainable future.

Perhaps the most in-depth engagement occurred from May 1996 to July 1998 in the Center for the Study of World Religions at Harvard University, when a series of ten conferences were organized under the title Religions of the World and Ecology. These were led by academics Mary Evelyn Tucker and John Grim, stimulated by theologian Thomas Berry, and attended by around seven hundred academics, religious leaders, and environmental specialists. Each conference covered a major religious tradition—Buddhism, Christianity, Confucianism, Daoism, Hinduism, indigenous traditions, Islam, Jainism, Judaism, and Shinto—and explored it for images and views that could be related to ecology. Following these conferences, and arising out of and extending their dialogue, the Forum on Religion and Ecology was initiated in 1998.[17] Its goals include:

1. Identifying ecological attitudes and practices within traditions; highlighting resources within cosmology, ritual, sacrament, and scripture; analyzing commonalities and identifying common ground on which to base discussion and action;

2.   Establishing religion and ecology as an area of academic study; fostering research; organizing conferences and curricular resources; linking religion to wider environmental movements, business, education, and the media; and contributing to a functional environmental ethics grounded in religious traditions;

3.   Providing books, essays, and official statements on and by religious traditions and intersecting areas such as gender, economics, ethics, policy, and science, as well as providing examples of environmental action by religions, in what are called "engaged projects."[18]

The most recent major addition to the field is Bron Taylor and Jeffrey Kaplan's *Encyclopedia of Religion and Nature* (in conjunction with the International Society for the Study of Religion, Nature, and Culture and the *Journal for the Study of Religion, Nature, and Culture*), to which over five hundred thinkers and activists contributed, in over one thousand articles. This aims to explore the relationships between humans, their diverse religions, and the earth, examine religious perceptions of the earth (environmentally friendly or otherwise), and assess if and how religions might be reshaping the ecological, political, and religious landscape.

Such initiatives aim to reclaim and reconstruct religious traditions or stimulate new ones so as to promote flourishing human-earth relations. They see transformative possibilities in religion, viewing it as a legitimate, meaningful, and powerful way of inculcating environmental consciousness, capable of reconceptualizing attitudes to the environment and existentially engaging humanity with it, as well as taking on political and social ecological issues and stimulating ecological concern. No one religious tradition or new movement, no hegemonic worldview acting in isolation, is seen as appropriate, however. There is a perceived need to go beyond static, hegemonic interpretations of religion or nature, to seek a diversity of views, actions, and discourses in self-reflective communication with one another. Truth claims are respected, but are explored as different avenues to truth, on the common ground of the earth itself.[19] Suggested methodologies include:[20]

1.   The historical and textual investigation of cosmological and scriptural ideas, identifying and stressing ethical codes and ritual customs that pertain to ecological issues;

2.   Evaluating the present relevance of tradition and widening religious beliefs to include other worldviews and nonhuman nature;

3.   Suggesting ways of adapting different traditions in a creative modification, ecumenically using or combining elements, either where they are needed or where they interact on specific issues;

4.   Making an amalgam of new ideas, practices, and organizations activating the human imagination toward a celebration of life and dynamizing human energy toward participating in and encouraging its flourishing.

Such an approach is envisaged as moving beyond dogmatism to a shared sense of the common good of the planet, revivifying rituals and symbols in connection with the biological context, combining transcendence and immanence via the presence of the divine in the world, and enlarging ethics to include ecocentric concerns. The aim is not only to stimulate new, ecologically based religious thinking within traditions but also to create shared religious-ecological vocabularies and actions. There is a perceived need for mutually enriching cross-cultural comparisons of religious concepts of nature.[21]

Max Oelschlaeger and Mary Evelyn Tucker advocate religious metaphors as a means to enable understanding and shape thought and action. Such metaphors locate personal and social identities in particular places and practices by re-creating conceptions of the world and the human place in it. They provide ethical rationales for behavior by relating a meaningful, persuasive, cosmological language that suggests, evokes, and inspires by stating paradigmatic truths that define possibilities and limitations, implying or prescribing ethical principles and actions and combining the ought and the is. Oeslchlaeger points out that creation stories legitimate the present by locating it in sacred time, providing a common cognitive legitimacy and meaningfulness, and linking moral orientations and actions to accounts of cosmic origins. Different creation stories may also coalesce around common ground, for example, the interrelation of humanity and nature (e.g., a "caring for creation" metaphor). Rethinking or reappropriating accounts of creation may stimulate a rethinking of ecological behavior. New ecological religious metaphors are thus seen as able to alter conceptual systems and stimulate new perceptions and actions conducive to cultural change. They may thus create a new imaginative language involving cooperation and reverence for life, rerooting humanity in the earth and evoking wider environmental identity and passion.[22]

The field of religion and ecology thus encourages and initiates the reassessment of religious traditions for ecological metaphors and themes, exploring their differing concepts of nature with the aim of challenging modern secular views of the environment and humanity's role in it, as well as challenging the traditions themselves. Questions posed to stimulate such religious and ecological reinterpretation and reimagination include:[23]

1. What cosmological dimensions in traditions help relate humans to nature?
2. How do traditions and sacred texts challenge or support nature as a resource?
3. What core values within traditions might lead to an environmental ethics?
4. Is it possible to identify responsible ecological practices within traditions?

In the final section, therefore, I will concentrate on some influential metaphors and themes stressed in the field's ecological reinterpretations of Buddhism, Chinese traditions (Confucianism and Daoism), Christianity, and Islam and assess any commonalities or convergences between them that might highlight new eco-religious forms. This is an inevitably selective group, dependent on space and chosen for contrast and comparison; Hinduism, indigenous traditions, Jainism, Judaism, or Shinto, all explored in the Harvard conference series, and concepts such as deep ecology, Gaia, or the epic of evolution could also be explored in this way.[24] Such interpretations themselves are, of course, new religious forms: the "Buddhist," "Confucian," "Daoist," "Christian," and "Islamic" views I analyze are recent, ecologically based interpretations of diverse and often context-dependent traditions by environmentally aware individuals or groups, and have not been unchallenged. Moreover, my selection, by focusing on their main points, inevitably simplifies their ideas. The idea of unified "religious traditions" or "world religions" has been questioned, for example, by Tomoko Masuzawa. The notion is especially fraught for assessing Eastern forms.[25] Nevertheless, the ideas expressed show how religion is creatively and dynamically (and, in the field of religion and ecology, reflexively) being readdressed in the contemporary context, how religious individuals and traditions (which are fluid, living traditions) may be reassessing their views, recovering forgotten ecological themes or stimulating new ones, interacting and possibly converging.

Religious Traditions and Ecology: Reimagining the World

Buddhism

"The Six Great Elements are interfused and are in a state of eternal harmony. The Four Mandalas are inseparably related to one another. When the grace of the Three Mysteries is retained [our inborn three mysteries will] quickly be manifested. Infinitely interrelated like the meshes of Indra's Net are those we call existences." Paul Ingram sees these lines from a Shingon Buddhist poem as highlighting a Buddhist organic, holistic view of nature. Here the six elements—earth, water, fire, wind, space, and consciousness—highlight the timeless, nondual harmony of the universe, existing within (inter)dependent co-origination, in which beings co-arise in the interactions of mutual causality, with the aim of existence being to become aware of and experience this. To achieve this, four mandalas (paintings of the Buddha in colors representing the interpenetrating elements) offer visualizations for meditation on harmony, integrating three mysteries—body, speech, and mind. This is correlated with Indra's Net of many-sided jewels, each reflecting the other, highlighting their (and the world's) interdependence: what happens to one thing in the universe affects all other things.[26]

These ideas highlight what Stephanie Kaza and Alan Sponberg call "Green Buddhism," a movement that uses Buddhism as a source for environmentally friendly advice.[27] In this scheme Buddhism is seen as an "ecological religion," with concern for nature integral to its beliefs and practices. Buddha's Four Noble Truths—the universal reality of suffering, desire as the cause of suffering, freedom from desire as freedom from suffering, and freedom as lying in moral discipline and spiritual depth—are especially highlighted for their ecological importance. The basis for any Buddhist environmental ethics, therefore, is arguably the recognition that disharmony and suffering (*dukkha*, alienation from the world) is caused by *trishna*, an illusory, obsessive, selfish attachment to existence and desire for autonomy within an egoistic "I-self." To overcome this and achieve nonself—*anatman*, rejecting autonomy and a separate self—requires moral and spiritual learning to realize the true nature of things (which is the ontological interrelation of the world) and to create oneness with it, abandoning desires and the need to possess and overcoming ignorance in a "we-self" that is equivalent to enlightenment. In this sense, then, nonattachment to self is empathy with and commitment to the whole of nature, a healing process and healthy mind in mental balance, based on an emphatic caring at the core of one's being, a nonheroic self that values nature intrinsically, not for its usefulness.[28]

These ideas are linked to Buddhist teachings concerned with *dharma*, here meaning path to truth and things in nature, highlighting interdependence. All beings are *dharmas* or have *dharma*-nature (a universal essence in life). All have the potentiality to express this and act communally and compassionately, within (leading to) the *sangha*, or community, and to become enlightened, namely, to be liberated from suffering (something that David Landis Barnhill extends to a "Great Earth *Sangha*," where nature is the community). The doctrine of *karma*, or cause and effect, and *samsara*, or rebirth, where all thoughts, words, and deeds shape experiences in the future via reincarnation, link life in an interrelated moral continuum: good and bad actions lead to better or worse rebirths and ultimately to enlightenment.[29] Donald Swearer writes that to achieve such enlightenment involves understanding personal karmic history, then humanity's karmic history, and finally the principle underlying suffering in a vision of interdependence and a model for moral reasoning.[30] Alan Sponberg sees this as a "hierarchy of compassion," in which, unlike Western views, progress is an evolution of consciousness toward the cultivation of interdependence with and responsibility for life.[31] This is a progress away from selfishness and consumerism, a virtue ethic of the "threefold learning" of morality, meditation, and insight, leading to loving kindness and *ahimsa*, or nonviolence. It involves mindful awareness and living, as well as the "middle path," a moderate, restrained lifestyle providing stability and balance, highlighted by traditional precepts such as not creating evil, practicing good, actualizing good for others, and the "eight-fold path" of right understanding, intention, speech, action, livelihood, effort, mindfulness, and concentration. This culminates in the *bodhisattva* ideal and enlightened practice as exemplified by Buddhist monks.[32]

Chinese Traditions: Confucianism and Daoism

For ecological purposes, Chinese traditions are seen as sharing a worldview that is organic, vitalistic, and holistic. They are held to view the universe as a creative, harmonious process, in what is termed *sheng-sheng*, or production and reproduction. In this scheme the universe is self-generating, with heaven and earth, spirit and matter, being interdependent via ongoing processes and relationships. The aim of life is to realize harmony with the natural rhythms of the cosmos in accordance with "the Way (things are)" (*Dao*), the primeval wisdom of reality.[33] This nonduality of traditional Chinese thought is linked to the concept of *qi*, a "vital energy" at once material and spiritual. The *qi* circulates in accordance with certain principles, the most basic being the oscillation between *yin* and *yang* (female and male, negative and positive, or any other polar opposites). Relational change, therefore, is the principal characteristic of the cosmos, and correct human existence is an attempt to align oneself with the principles governing changes so as to flow with rather than resist them. This involves nourishing and channelling the *qi*. Traditional Chinese medicine, *fengshui*, and *taiji* exercises all seek to do so, bringing about relational balance in the landscape or the body and thereby allowing the *qi* to flow.[34]

Mary Evelyn Tucker holds that Confucianism and Daoism interpret and experience a single cosmological worldview in different ways. The former she sees as stressing harmony within human society, the latter, a spontaneous closeness to nature. Confucianism is viewed as stressing social and political commitment, correct relations among people, and correct practice in the form of rites and ritual behavior, so that these will mirror cosmological processes. Daoism, by contrast, is thought to encourage withdrawal from political affairs in order to cultivate a more direct engagement with natural processes. In this scheme, in an ecological sense Confucians might encourage moral education and responsibility, while Daoists might stress the unfolding of natural processes and noninvolvement.[35]

Confucian views have been represented as a cosmic humanism because in traditional Chinese thought human beings form one body with the cosmos. Humans are seen as a triad with heaven and earth, their upright stature linking the two in what has been called an anthropocosmic view. In an ecological sense, humanity may thus have a special role, being charged with enhancing the balance of nature. Humans are situated within the organic processes of nature and exist in concentric circles of relationships, radiating outward from the family, with a mutual reciprocity of obligations and a larger sense of common good, something which Tu Weiming interprets as enjoining them to take part in cosmic transformation.[36] Joseph Adler, Robert Weller, and Peter Bol describe this as a relational resonance in tune with a cosmic resonance, a mutual response to the myriad things. Human thoughts, feelings, and actions thereby respond to movements of *qi*, both within individuals and in the world. Appropriate responses to these movements must accord with *li*, the patterns of the cosmos.[37] Confucian humanity, then, involves continuous self-transcendence, overcoming egoism by practicing *ren*, or humaneness. Its highest exemplar is the sage, who is attuned to the environment (the *Dao*), instantiating the perfection of both natural and social orders in thought and action.[38]

A central concept in Daoism is *wuwei*, roughly translated as "nonaction" or "nonassertive action," involving yielding rather than assertion, softness rather than hardness.

Here, appropriate actions are those that produce the best results with a minimum of effort, avoiding over-doing and letting the desired result come about as if by itself. The aim is to mirror the *Dao* and the "self-so-ness" of its operations, to be like water—soft and yielding, yet able to wear away rock. This is in accord with the *Dao*, which is empty yet full of potentiality, allowing things to develop in their own ways. In this scheme, Daoist ecology would not, then, be an intellectual principle; knowing would involve comprehending existence through relationships attuned to the rhythms of the cosmos, improving them not by manipulation but by perfecting that attunement.[39] Daoism, in this scheme, is seen as trusting natural processes in their operations and seeking to align humanity with these processes in order to achieve harmony. In this sense, nonaction is compassionate, whereas action can cause unintended problems. The practical result of this is asceticism, training the will to follow nature's ways.[40]

Christianity

When seeking resources within Christianity for sound ecological attitudes, those in the field of religion and ecology stress several biblical themes: God created a harmonious world with humans in His image in order to enable a relationship with Him and with creation; humanity sinned against this, seeking self-awareness and thereby becoming alienated from God and creation; God provides the means to overcome this in a new creation, namely, Jesus. Added to these are the commandments to love God and love your neighbor and that the fear of God is the beginning of wisdom. These themes are thought to provide the groundwork for an earth-centered Christianity, one that would value nature, highlighting a balanced, reciprocal mutuality among God, humanity, and creation. Human rebellion against God or lack of respect for creation, in this scheme, harms this mutuality, causing deterioration and alienation. Human respect for God and care for creation do the opposite.[41] Central to such ideas is the "integrity of creation," the idea that the world was (and continually is) created and sustained by a just, loving, and righteous God, being His gift, made to reveal His creativity. Creation, therefore, matters to God (He sees it as good) and worships Him in its being (it reflects His perfect intent, being His "book of works" or, for John Chryssavgis, an "icon" of Him, and thus having intrinsic worth). Therefore, to worship or fear God in a human sense means caring for creation. To abuse it is to abuse God. Creation in this sense will be witness to humanity's care or abuse and an administrator of retributive justice.[42]

Humanity thus has a special role in creation by virtue of the *imago Dei*. This is interpreted not as dominion over the world but as responsibility for it. Humans are seen as God's stewards, in fellowship with other creatures and embedded in the environment, yet given the covenantal task of tending it, being called to be humane neighbors of creation, interacting with it in a empathic, interdependent, "I-Thou" (rather than an instrumental "I-It") way. In this sense, biblical rules and laws concerning the treatment of nature, for example, the "Sabbath" principle of letting the earth rest and recover, imply that creation is to be enjoyed in the fruitfulness of bio-diversity. In a similar way, psalms are seen as encouraging the celebration of nature, while earth elements (bread, earth, oil, water, and wine) in rituals or ideas such as "the salt of the earth" or Jesus as "vine" are seen as highlighting the divine presence in nature.[43] In this sense, the effects of sin are that humanity does not care for creation as God intended because we are fallen, self-centered, alienated from creation, and doing harm to it. To overcome sin, then, is to recover a right, harmonious relationship to God and creation. To this end, God became incarnate in Jesus and embodied (or, for Duncan Reid, "en-fleshed") in nature, demon-strating the need for self-sacrifice. Other authors, for example, Matthew Fox and Sally McFague, extend this theme, referring to a "cosmic Christ" who redeems not only hu-manity but all of creation. McFague sees the world as part of God's body, being a dynamic, relational system evoking and mediating the sacred.[44]

For several authors—for example, Denis Edwards and Mark Wallace—the Holy Spirit, seen as present at creation as a life-giving force and as still dwelling in the world, courtesy of Jesus, provides a useful approach to the environment. It is seen as creatively present in evolving creatures and natural processes, affirming matter in a "deep incarna-tion," giving intrinsic value to life, and providing the "power of becoming": the possibility of redemption and the capability of attaining the perfection of a new creation by guiding humanity to discern an appropriate (caring, harmonious) way of acting.[45] Nature is thus not just the setting for salvation but integral to it. In a similar way, the concept of wisdom (inherent in creation, embodied in Jesus) is also seen—for example, by Celia Deane-Drummond—as providing an environmentally friendly Christianity, where a "wise" (car-ing, harmonious) interaction with the environment follows from discerning the Holy Spirit, with the teleological goal of the redemption and beatification of creation. Given that wisdom is viewed in her ancient guise as Sophia, and thus as female, this strain of thought links with feminist theology (in, say, the "eco-feminism" of Rosemary Radford Reuther) in the struggle to overcome patriarchal transcendence (God as father or king, creating dualism and alienation from and domination of nature) by stressing maternal immanence (God as mother or companion, creating holism and kinship with nature) in an ethic of partnership with nature. Here the exemplar is Saint Francis.[46]

Islam

Islamic ideas about ecology, viewed as possibly addressing environmental issues in a par-ticular, non-Western way, are derived from: the Qur'an, argued to be replete with refer-ences to nature; the words and deeds of Mohammad, which are seen as showing concern for natural resources; and the *fiqh* law, or codified norms, and the *Sharia*, or divine law, which are seen as stressing the importance of nature and animals. These sources are held to be supported by the fact that the term *Islam* is derived from *salam-silm*, meaning peace, security, and wholeness.[47] Unity, therefore, is argued as being the essence and impetus of Islam. *Tawhid,* or the unity of creation, in this sense is part of the oneness of God and is an interlocking pattern of peaceful and just relationships. To be Islamic, therefore, is to establish *tawhid* and to promote peace and justice through moderate behavior. All of creation, in this sense, is an interdependent family of God. If one part suffers, all suffer, in what is termed *ulm-al-nafs,* or self-injury. Such a sense of unity means that the divine and nature are inseparable, with the environment (and all life forms) being a sign or mirror of God, *ayat* or *sunnat Allah,* the "way of God."[48] Ibrahim Ozedmir even views the natural environment as capable of being "Muslim" in that it submits to God's will. S. Nomaul Haq points out that it works according to *amr,* commands, in an ordered pattern of relationships. Similarly, it may be seen as a "mosque," a place of purification where one practices submission to God. To defile the environment, therefore, may be blasphemous and impious. Paradise is seen as a garden, and life on earth as a preparation for it, so making a garden of the earth is pious. For Mawil Izzi Dien and Nomanul Haq, concepts such as *haram,* sacred precincts, and *hima,* common or protected land, provide the promise of environmental protection, of bringing to life (*ihya*) dead wastelands (*mawat*).[49]

In line with such ideas, Islam is seen as promoting a "cosmology of justice," an existential social contract for human action within a world in a just balance, where Muslims are called critically to establish social and environmental justice. Nomanul Haq stresses that this is humanity's *amr,* a covenantal vice-regency or servantship, termed *khalifa,* in which humans are seen as the trustees and guardians of creation, learning and applying the divine signs of the Qur'an and nature in a unified, caring way, to benefit all life. Among the privileges seen as thereby conferred are free will and the faculty of reason, the ability to assess *mizan,* or the due balance of creation, and the ability to behave justly, balancing human needs with those of nature. This is seen as conferring a moral commitment to act with moderation, given that extravagance and waste are against God's design. In this scheme, to be "Muslim," humanity must, like nature, submit to God's will, God's purpose for it. It is God who owns nature, not humanity. While nature submits automatically, however, humanity *ought* to do so, having free will, and to bring this ought and the is of action together is the privilege and risk of being human.[50]

Saadia Chishti relates this human *amr* to *fitra,* or humanity's primordial place in creation. In this scheme, true humanity is connected to nature, not separate from it, and humans must use their talents to care for it, acting, as Nawal Ammar and Daniel MaGuire say, with *haya,* reverence or dignified reserve, the opposite of hubris. Mawil Izzi Dien declares the aim to be encouraging *hisba,* the application of good and the removal of evil. It is exemplified by the *muhtasib,* or volunteer, while the Five Pillars of Islam (almsgiving, fasting, pilgrimage, ritual worship, and testimony) may also be seen in this light. This is the "striving" or greater *jihad,* the inner struggle to purify the self and to behave correctly. In this sense, humanity is the moral telos of creation, and Frederick Denny suggests that what may be needed is a "green *jihad,*" with humanity, as Mohammad Parvaiz writes, being *musleheen* (correctors, rectifiers, or reformers), creating peace, justice, and order in nature, rather than *mufsideen* (corruptors, mischief makers, or spoilers), causing *israf* and *fasad*, wastefulness and disorder, in a true fulfillment of Islam as *din al-fitra*, or "religion true to the primordial nature," that being a unified creation.[51]

Conclusion

This essay has sought to analyze and highlight ways in which religion is being reinterpreted, revitalized, and reempowered to engage an environmental crisis thought to have resulted from modern ways of thinking and doing. Environmental issues provide an arena for religious traditions to address crucial private and public matters, providing communities, rituals, and vocabularies for humans to use in seeking to understand the environment and articulate environmental concern. The process challenges these traditions to adapt or extend their views, to reassess themselves environmentally, and thereby possibly ecumenically, and/or to stimulate new movements. The field of religion and ecology seeks to locate, promote, and encompass such religious environmental engagement, providing common environmental purpose and a shared commitment, encouraging and comparing environmental concern and an understanding among traditions, and then channeling their diverse views into mutually enriching dialogue, ethics, and action. The aim is thus to stimulate a religious reimagining of the environment and of humanity's relationship to it, place within it, and actions toward it, one that ideally would reach beyond "religion" narrowly defined and influence the secular.

My analysis suggests the following shared attitudes that those working in the field have drawn from the four religious traditions that I have examined.[52]

1. The environment is seen as having intrinsic worth, by virtue of being in a state of constant, divine creation. It is envisioned as a balanced, interdependent whole.
2. The world is a reciprocal web of life infused with a flow of energy or spirit. It embodies, mirrors, or worships the divine.
3. Humanity, by virtue of its self-consciousness, has a limited but special role. It is part of the web of life, yet enables creation to achieve a harmonious state.
4. Anthropocentric, egoistic human action upsets the ecological and spiritual balance, being destructive (an unnatural state).
5. Humanity needs to experience the flow of energy, spirit, and wider environmental being and to embrace selflessness (its natural state).
6. The ideal human role is moderate, nonviolent, and relational, with minimal accumulation, consumption, or waste (a life of self-sacrifice).

These shared resources highlight the powerful metaphoric resources and social and cultural avenues available to religious traditions to provide a sense of moral urgency concerning environmental issues, as well as pointing to alternative, ecocentric views and explanations. In the process they may challenge, adapt to, or mold contemporary ideas, re-creating individual conceptions of self-identity and social and ecological practices. One might raise questions about the attempt to reconcile different traditions by overlooking the differences within or between them. Moreover, one might point out that this is a liberal process with overarching ecumenical concerns, showing a possible Western bias about what constitutes religion and nature. One might also question the ability of traditions to challenge the dominant secular system, or worry that religious concepts might be simplified in the process, becoming deprived of their deeper religious relevance. Counter-arguments could of course be made: religious traditions are never static; adherents interpret them in different ways depending on context; and they are always open to reinterpretation. Religion, nature, and secular society are not necessarily separate but rather may be mutually constitutive arenas. The point to recognize is that the field of religion and ecology, like religion itself, is a complex and often self-aware *process*, a variety of beliefs and actions in continuous assessment. Understanding and exploring this may enable greater appreciation of how religion develops and evolves, declines or survives, and can serve as a relevant resource for facing new challenges.

PART IV

Emerging Contexts

The Politics of Love and Its Enemies

David Nirenberg

Theology and the Political, the latest volume in Slavoj Žižek's series SIC, comes with an introduction by the Archbishop of Canterbury, Rowan Williams. Within its brief compass, the archbishop's introduction outlines two views of meaningful action. The first understands meaningful action as assertion, existing only where "a particular will has imprinted its agenda on the 'external' world"; the second insists that "meaningful action is action that is capable of contributing to a system of communication, to symbolic exchange." The first "pervades so much of modernity and . . . postmodernity," including "popular liberal and pluralist thought," and "raises the specter of the purest fascism." The second relates intelligible action to "divine action whose gratuitousness (or love) motivates and activates an unlimited process of representation without simple repetition (and thus posits irreducible human and other diversities)." This second view, Williams concludes, this patterning of human communicative action after divine love, is urgently necessary in the midst of our "late capitalist . . . countdown to social dissolution and the triumph of infinite exchangeability and timeless, atomized desire."[1]

Pope Benedict XVI chose a similar theme for his first encyclical, *Deus caritas est* (*God Is Love*, January 25, 2006), dedicated to the argument that neither justice nor economics but only love, patterned after God's gratuitous love manifest in the Incarnation, can cross the gap that separates us from each other and create a truly human community. Both the pope and the archbishop are professors as well as priests, and their treatments of love represent powerful currents in the academic as well as the clerical world. In its many forms (*eros, philia, agape*, to use just some of the Greek names) and especially in its more religious flavors *love* has once again become a key term in phenomenology, ethics, political philosophy, and critical theory.[2]

With notable exceptions (Derrida's *Politics of Friendship,* for instance), many who invoke love are optimistic about its powers. Writing of Adorno and Levinas, for example, Hent de Vries has observed that they turned to the "domain of the erotic" in order to represent experiences (such as the metaphysical) and relations that they believed could not "be translated in terms of economic exchange or even relationships of possession."[3] The erotic, in other words, provided them with a world of metaphors imagined as free of the sphere of circulation. But the freedom ascribed to love and its servants extended far beyond the creation of a specialized vocabulary of noneconomic representation. Levinas put plainly the sweeping pretensions—political, ethical, and ontological—of the loving relation: "This deposition of sovereignty by the *ego* is the social relationship with the Other, the dis-inter-ested relation. I write it in three words to underline the escape from being it signifies. I distrust the compromised word 'love,' but the responsibility for the Other, being-for-the-other, seemed to me . . . to stop the anonymous and senseless rumbling of being."[4] Similar claims are made today by those who advocate love as an antidote to the logic of economic exchange, to instrumental reason, even to intentionality.[5]

It is easy to understand why, in the face of stark inequalities produced by global regimes of exchange, this antidote seems so attractive. It is also not too surprising that in the present desecularizing age it should so often take theological forms. What is startling is that those who prescribe love and its politics are untroubled by or unaware of its long history of disappointment. That history is almost as old as thought about the mediated nature of communal and communicative life—that is, almost as old as politics itself.

This "almost" is an important qualification. The dry-farming societies of the ancient Mediterranean world that produced some of our earliest written records were all built out of a vast array of reciprocal relations of varying degrees of formalization and asymmetry, ranging at one extreme from master-slave, through patron-client, lord-vassal, and creditor-debtor relations, to relations of hospitality, friendship, kinship, and marriage, on the other. None of these societies had a vocabulary dedicated to such relations; on the contrary, terms of kinship (such as *father* and *son*) and affect (such as *love* and *friendship*) were "promiscuously employed . . . for all manner of social, commercial, and legal relations."[6] This promiscuity meant that the many forms of reciprocity and exchange, ranging from the contractual to the emotional, from the most extremely hierarchical to the explicitly egalitarian, could all be incestuously related to one another and encompassed by the terms we translate into English as *friendship* and *love*.

If today love can seem a liberation from possession and exchange, it is because this ancient incest has been repressed. The pages that follow provide an etiology of this repression and its costs. They focus on a few moments of sharp contraction in the meanings of love. Each of these moments produced a heightened awareness of love's limits, each generated specific figures of exclusion (we might even call them enemies) in order to imagine the overcoming of those limits, and each of these figures in turn constrained the ways in which future loves could be conceived. I will begin this history with Hebrew scripture and Greek philosophy, before moving on to the Christian terms that bound the two together in one of love's most beguiling forms. Throughout, and at its simplest, my claim will be that, far from being an antidote to instrumental reason or to relations of possession and exchange, the fantasy that love can free interaction from interest is itself one of the more dangerous offspring of the marriage of Athens and Jerusalem that we sometimes call the Western tradition.

1

Etymology is not destiny, but it is worth remembering that the most common word for love and friendship in the Hebrew Bible, 'ahabah, is related to the triliteral root y-h-b, associated with gifts and giving.[7] This rooting of biblical love in the language of exchange is entirely in keeping with the ancient Near Eastern context within which these scriptures were produced. The recovery of that context, and the reinterpretation of Scripture in its light, is one of the many achievements of modern biblical scholarship. W. L. Moran, for example, related the word 'ahavta in the injunction to "love the Lord thy God" (Deut. 6:5) to a legal term (root 'hb) borrowed from the Assyrian vocabulary of treaties of subjection or alliance and suggested that the Deuteronomist expressed the reciprocal obligations of God and man in terms of legal love drawn from the ancient Near Eastern lexicon of covenant between polities.[8] Other scholars have compared King David's political loves (of Jonathan, of his allies, and so on) to Homeric relationships of hospitality, alliance, and dependency (philia and xenia).[9] And throughout the Hebrew Bible, from its earliest books to its latest, political relations could be represented through yet other exchanges of love, sexual and uxorious (e.g., Sarai before Pharaoh in Genesis, Esther before Ahasuerus in Esther).

In sum, the Hebrew vocabulary of love was rooted in a fertile semantic field extending across the ancient Near East, which encompassed a broad variety of human relations mediated by exchange. But within the Israelite corner of this common field, the vocabulary of love developed a particular strain, one marked by heightened anxiety about love's power in human relations. This anxiety increased the tension between the various forms of reciprocal relation that coexisted within the term love, and this tension in turn encouraged the cultivation of unusually hierarchical discriminations between various types of love and their associated politics.

It is often remarked that in Deuteronomy, and in the Pentateuch more generally, the command to love is oriented toward God, not man (the sole but important exception being Leviticus 19:18, "Love your neighbor as yourself"). This orientation had important implications for a political economy. In the Israelite "kingdom of priests" (Exod. 19:16), for example, the power that accrued from asymmetrical relations of exchange between people was meant to be credited not to human givers and patrons but to the sovereign God. Man's own capacity to oblige other men through such exchanges, by contrast, was dangerous insofar as it might reorient affection away from God[10]—hence the ideal of the sabbatical year, designed to reestablish equity between men and return the economic order to God's original distribution. Properly oriented toward God, Israel's love would yield the blessing of wealth gained by asymmetrical exchange not within Israel but with those outside it: "you will be creditor to many nations, but debtor to none" (Deut. 28:12). If instead Israel preferred the gifts of man to those of God, she would not only become a debtor nation but suffer terrible curses (Deut. 28:15–28).[11]

Many ancient Near Eastern polities understood their balance of payments as a leading indicator of divine love. What made the Deuteronomic encoding distinctive was its greater emphasis on the rewards brought by direct relations of dependence ("love") between man and God, and its deeper suspicion toward economies and institutions ("loves") that might tend to rival or obscure that dependence. The material condition of Israel became, in that encoding, a diagnostic of the stress at the constitutional foundations of the polity, that is, of the tension between love as the cornerstone of man's relation to God and love as the mortar that binds man to man. In (Christian) retrospect we are too well aware of the potential for aporia in these treatments of things in the world as signs of divine love. But the political institutions envisioned by our prophetic sources sought to span these "abysses for the profound," not leap into them, and it is worth asking how they did so.[12]

Monarchy was one of the most important of these institutions. Deuteronomy allows Israel the privilege of interposing a king between itself and the divine sovereign, but only grudgingly and conditionally: "You shall be free to set a king over yourselves, one chosen by the Lord your God," but "he shall not have many wives, lest his heart go astray" (Deut. 17:15–17). It is not clear to me why too many wives should seem the chief threat to a monarch's affection for the divine. What is clear, given that royal polygamy was a basic tool of political expansion and incorporation in the ancient Near East, is that this restriction of the Israelite sovereign's sexual alliances was both distinctive and meaningful. It became a central theme of political and religious critique in Hebrew Scripture, most famously in the story of how King Solomon's seven hundred wives and three hundred concubines brought him fabulous wealth but estranged him from the love of God and led to the destruction of his kingdom. These stories use carnal error to confront the constant danger of a greater error, the preference for loving created things rather than the Creator God—that is, idolatry. But they also channel the danger of this error into a specific figure, foreign and female.[13]

This strategy is systematically deployed in the only political manual included in the Hebrew Bible, the Book of Proverbs, which introduces itself as advice addressed by a king to his sons. Proverbs belongs to wisdom literature, a genre of advice books rare in Hebrew Scripture but common in the ancient Near East.[14] The authors of Proverbs, like those of the Pentateuch, understood many types of exchange as potentially corrupting (e.g., Prov. 15:27: "The maker of profits destroys his house [*beyto*], but the hater of the gift will live").[15] The governing strategy of Proverbs is to contain that danger by giving it a human form:

> My son, heed my words; and store up my commandments. . . . From the window of my house, through my lattice, I looked out and saw . . . a woman. She lurks at every corner. She lays hold of him and kisses him. . . . She sways him with her eloquence, turns him aside with her smooth talk. Thoughtlessly he follows her, like an ox going to slaughter. . . . Now my sons, listen to me, pay attention to my words; Let your mind not wander down her ways. . . . Her house is a highway . . . leading down to death's inner chambers. (Prov. 7:1–27)

The alien woman whose honeyed lips seem pleasant but lead directly to the grave moves throughout Proverbs as a figure of false love.[16] Set against her is the good woman, sometimes depicted as Wisdom personified, leading her lovers along the path of life. But the good woman of Proverbs (like the foreign woman) is not only a figure of thought. She is also one of flesh and blood. Thus the book ends with marital advice (the *Eyshet Chail*, still repeated every Sabbath by the pious): choose a virtuous woman rather than a rich girl for a wife, for the good management of the former will earn you wealth that is greater and more enduring than what the latter would have brought. This test of wealth returns us to the difficulty: even good love cannot transcend the relations of accumulation and exchange that apparently threaten relations with the divine. Proverbs does not confront this danger. Rather, by projecting it onto foreign flesh, it seeks to contain the terms of its own critique.

2

Similar difficulties—and similar solutions—appear in the Greek-speaking Mediterranean. The history of Greek love is very long and deserves, as Émile Benveniste put it in his essay on the Greek word *phílos* ("friend/lover"), "a full examination." Benveniste began with Homer in order to "expose a long-standing error, which is probably as old as Homeric exegesis," which understands *phílos* as originally a possessive adjective. Instead, he argued, "we must start from uses and contexts which reveal in this term a complex network of associations, some with institutions of hospitality, others with usages of the home, still others with emotional behavior; we must do this in order to understand plainly the meta-phorical applications to which the term lent itself."[17] I am not in a position to say whether Benveniste was right to dissociate the philological origins of *phílos* from possession.[18] I wish only to demonstrate that in a context in which democratic politics had heightened anxiety about the power of "complex networks of association" between citizens to threaten the political community as a whole, some influential Greek thinkers were engaged in a struggle to emancipate political love from certain forms of possession and exchange.

Plato was perhaps the most important of these thinkers on the subjects of mediation, love, and politics, which were as inextricably linked in his thought as they were in that of the Hebrew prophets. Like the prophets (though perhaps more systematically), for example, he thought a great deal about the problems caused by the use of language as the means of human communication.[19] The *Seventh Letter* (342b–d) ascribed to Plato makes clear his awareness that whatever knowledge is attainable to souls in the body comes only through the "inadequate" mediation of names, descriptions, and images, sounds or signs that point to things.[20] Language always has, for Plato, "two forms, true and false." Truth "dwells above, among the gods, whereas falsehood dwells among men below." This gap, which is also the gap between words and the things they represent, cannot be closed without destroying language itself (*Cratylus* 408c, 432b–d). Even the philosopher who ascends from the cave to perception of the intelligible realm in the *Republic* can only apprehend and communicate those truths through analogy with the material (506c–519a). This dependence threatens to make "true" knowledge (if by "true" we mean independent of the material realm), which is also to say philosophy, impossible. But though Plato describes this potential for aporia, he does not dwell in it. On the contrary, he counters it by positing love as a mediating figure capable of bridging all these gaps.

Eros ("desire, love"), says Plato in *Symposium* 202a–e, is the *metaxu*, the "between." Just what kind of a force *eros* is—a goddess? a cosmic binding force? a memory of originary hermaphroditism?—is debated in the *Symposium*. Socrates himself subscribes to the view attributed to Diotima of Mantinea, for whom *eros* is the daimonic principle of mediation between higher and lower, divine and material, immortal and mortal. Neither gods nor humans, daimons "are between the two estates, they weld both sides together and merge them into one great whole" (202e).[21] *Eros* is that daimon who, placed between wisdom and ignorance, beauty and ugliness, is a lover of wisdom and beauty. His longing takes him constantly across the space between particular and universal beauty and finds unity in diversity (210e–12a). It is his ability to carry us through the gap between the sensible and the intelligible that makes the pursuit of knowledge—philosophy—possible. Plato's optimism on this point varies, reaching its apogee in *Phaedrus* 256b–d, where love's power seems almost to guarantee that man's desire for sensible beauty will lead *toward* knowledge and not *away* from it, and where the bonds that *eros* establishes between men on earth are said to persist even in heaven.

Thus far we have seen that love is an important mediator in Plato—indeed, *the* mediator that makes it possible for humans to approach eternal truth despite their dependence on words and things. We have not, however, spoken explicitly about politics. Implicitly, of course, love's political importance is already evident because, for Plato, true politics requires philosophical knowledge, which in turn depends upon love (as we have just seen). Moreover, since in the *Republic* (368d, 434d–35c) the polis is analogous to the human soul, we should expect that the importance Plato ascribes to love in the management of relations between the parts of the soul (as, e.g., in the *Symposium* and the *Phaedrus*) will be matched by an equal importance in the management of human relations in the polity.

Whether or not this expectation is fulfilled has long been a matter of debate. On the one hand, Plato's undeniable tendencies toward dualism underwrite pessimism about the possibility of a politics of love in the city. On the other, Plato's emphasis (especially in the dialogues of the middle period: *Phaedrus, Symposium, Republic*) on the mediating power of love encourages optimism on this score. The difference between Derrida's and Catherine Pickstock's readings of *Lysis*—a dialogue devoted to the description and definition of love/friendship—provides an example of the contrast that is particularly relevant to current debates about the possibility of a politics of love.[22]

Like many Platonic dialogues, *Lysis* proceeds by testing descriptions and definitions—in this case of love and friendship.[23] What is love? Is it the attraction of similarity (of like to like: e.g, of the good to the good) or of difference (of the older to the younger and vice-versa)? What is the purest case of love: mutual love, with its reciprocal exchanges and benefits, or the gratuitous love of a lover whose love is not returned by the beloved? These and many other questions are asked of love and friendship in *Lysis*. To a degree unusual in Plato's dialogues, they yield no answers; every attempt at a conclusion collapses in aporia. One might think, for example, that love should be between people who are alike (both good, e.g., or both wealthy, or both beautiful) because difference would tend to induce calculations of utility that would compromise friendship. But if people are alike they have no need of each other and are unlikely to become friends with each other (218d–e). The opposite position, that love binds the unlike, is equally problematic because it leads to the conclusion that the strongest attraction of love will be to one's enemy (216a–b, 220e–f). Socrates himself proposes a third possibility, that we are attracted to those who are neither like nor unlike us, or, as he puts it, "that which is neither evil nor good becomes friendly with good, on account of evil [in itself]" (216c–d). This proposal brings us close to the "betweenness" of the daimon Eros in the *Symposium*. The proximity is interesting, but proves inconclusive. The dialogue culminates in an impasse: "If neither those who love or are loved, neither the like nor the unlike, nor the good, nor those who belong to us, nor any other of all the suppositions which we passed in review—they are so numerous that I can remember no more—if, I say, not one of them is the object of friendship, I no longer know what I am to say" (222e).

The collapse seems so total that Derrida takes the highly aporetic structure of the dialogue as symptomatic of some of the abysses he sees beneath any attempt to build democracy on love (e.g., does not every choice of friend require the unethical exclusion of the non-friend?); hence it serves as the starting point for his deconstruction of the politics of friendship. Pickstock, by contrast, sees in the dialogue a performance of the link between friendship and philosophy. "For our hearers here," says Socrates at the end of the *Symposium*, "will carry away the report that though we conceive ourselves to be friends with each other—you see, I class myself with you—we have not yet been able to discover what we mean by friend." "One senses," Pickstock writes, "that a link between philosophy or dialectics and friendship has been indirectly revealed; that all the time that these interlocutors were engaged in their debate as to the nature of friendship, they were entering into its estate, even without knowing it." For Pickstock, the lesson of the dialogue is not that political friendship leads to aporia but "that friendship does not admit of a definition. . . . It is, like philosophy, a way of life, rather than a static thing to be examined."[25]

Pickstock's reading seeks to present love in Plato as a political force capable of negotiating all difference (between material and eternal, man and god, self and other). As a leading advocate of a Christian political theology of love, her Platonic project is designed to recuperate Plato for that theology. That project seems to require (judging from her insistence on the point) that Plato's worries about mediation be minimized: "It becomes impossible to sustain any notion that Plato systematically denies mediation, whether inter-personal, mythical, daimonic, linguistic, or even poetic"; or, as she puts it in another essay, "Plato had his own way of valuing and even exalting all such mediations."[26]

There are voices in Plato that do exalt mediation and advocate a love every bit as promiscuous as the ancient Near Eastern ones with which we began, a love that arbitrates every human activity. Of these voices, Diotima's in *Symposium* 205d is the most powerful:

> For "Love, that renowned and all-beguiling power," includes every kind of longing for happiness and for the good. Yet those of us who are subject to this longing in the various fields of business, athletics, philosophy, and so on, are never said to be in love, and are never known as lovers, while the man who devotes himself to what is only one of Love's many activities is given the name that should apply to all the rest as well.

But Diotima's promiscuity should not be confused with Plato's. For although it is true that in his view love makes it possible for some symbolic economies and forms of communicative exchange (such as language) to move toward truth, there are others it cannot redeem. Diotima's "business" is one of these, especially insofar as that business depends on money. In *Laws* 743c–744 Plato formulates his most extreme version of the problem:

> Now the fundamental purpose of our laws was this,—that the citizens should be . . . in the highest degree united in mutual friendship. Friendly the citizens will never be where they have frequent legal actions with one another and frequent illegal acts, but rather where these are fewest and least possible. [Hence] we say that in the State there must be neither gold nor silver, nor must there be much money making by means of

vulgar trading or usury. . . . Wherefore we have asserted . . . that the pursuit of money is to be honoured last of all: of all the three objects which concern every man, the concern for money, rightly directed, comes third and last; that for the body comes second; and that for the soul, first.[27]

For Plato in the *Laws*, relations mediated by money and contract are not even classified among those categories of human relations oriented toward body or soul. They point instead toward a third category, in which man seeks only to "sate himself to repletion, like a beast, with all manner of foods and drinks and wenchings" (831a–e; *L*, 2:135). In order to discourage bestial wenchings and encourage human love, Plato bars the citizens of Magnesia from oath, contract, and trade, placing these forms of unfriendly and inhuman exchange entirely in the hands of aliens and noncitizens.

This move is not occasioned by Plato's economics:

> The natural purpose for which all retail trading comes into existence in a State is not loss, but precisely the opposite; for how can any man be anything but a benefactor if he renders even and symmetrical the distribution of any kind of good which before was unsymmetrical and uneven? And this is, we must say, the effect produced by the power of money, and we must declare that the merchant was ordained for this purpose. (918b; *L*, 2:405)

This seems to suggest that in a "natural" community of friends, exchange, even monetary exchange, would be symmetrical and benevolent.[28] But Plato also seems to think that monetary exchange makes such a community of friends impossible, because monetization tends to turn exchanges of goods into relations of hostility, as in the example of innkeepers and guest: "instead of treating them as comrades and providing friendly gifts . . . he holds them . . . as . . . captive foemen in his hands, demanding very high sums of unjust and unclean ransom money" (919a). Hence the need to banish these corrupting forms of exchange into the hands of "non-friends" and noncitizens if the friendliness of the community is to be maintained.

Plato does not blame the need for symbolic mediation (as in the need for money in order to establish value in the exchange of goods) for this corruption. He blames, rather, "the disposition of the mass of mankind . . . when they desire, they desire without limit, and when they can make moderate gains, they prefer to gain insatiably" (918d). It is Plato's psychology of desire and appetite *(epithumia)* that is pessimistic here, not his economics or his hermeneutics. And, once again, a particular type of love is the problem, not love of idols or alien women as in the Pentateuch but of an even greater enemy of the polity: love of self. "There is an evil, great above all others, which most men have, implanted in their souls. . . . It is the evil indicated in the saying that every man is by nature a lover of self, and that it is right that he should be such" (731e; *L*, 1:339).[29] The dangers self-interest poses to the polity are many, but we have already touched upon one of the most important: its tendency, in a monetized economy, to turn men into creatures whose appetites cannot be sated. It is therefore self-love and its physical accessories of mediation (gold, silver, contracts, and so on) that Plato exiles from the category of love, and from the polity, and assigns to the alien.

This is no trivial exclusion because, for Plato, the exchange of goods is the reason for the foundation of the polis. As Socrates puts it in the *Republic*:

> the origin of the city . . . is to be found in the fact that we do not severally suffice for our own needs, but each of us lacks many things. . . . As a result of this, then, one man calling in another for one service and another for another, we, being in need of many things, gather many into one place of abode as associates and helpers, and to this dwelling together we give the name *city* or *state*. . . . And between one man and another there is an interchange of giving, if it so happens, and taking, because each supposes this to be better for himself. (369b–c)

But though this self-interested exchange is the basis of the political for Plato, it cannot be the basis of justice. (I leave aside here the complex history of the word *dikaiosune* ("justice"), revealingly associated in archaic Greek primarily with the payment of debts.)[30] Thus, after dismissing several "self-interested" definitions of justice in books 1 and 2 of the *Republic* (such as Polemarchus's claim that justice is doing good to one's friends and harm to one's enemies; 311b–c), Socrates enunciates a distributive principle. Justice is achieved when the polis reflects and preserves the distribution of innate abilities among different classes of men, maintaining the natural distributions of goods and divisions of labor in society (370a–372c). The farmer should farm, the plough maker make ploughs, and the cobbler stick to his last, each minding his own business and providing for the proportional needs of the other.[31]

Such a conception of politics and justice seems to require a symbolic economy capable of negotiating the difference between goods (e.g., between ploughs and shoes) and establishing a common value between them. Plato could here have developed—as Aristotle would—a theory of value that embraces monetary mediation. Why should not money too be a daimon if, as Aristotle says, money is the "intermediate" that "measures all things"?[32] Plato, however, says nothing of the sort. Instead, he divorces monetary exchange from love and banishes it from the citizen class, a move that almost amounts to an exile from the polis of the political itself and places a telling limit on Plato's "exaltation of all . . . mediations."

Plato's problem is not far from that of the Pentateuch, and his solutions are in some ways similar, albeit more extreme. Whereas in Leviticus self-love is promoted as the source of political love (remember Lev. 19:18: "you must love your neighbor *as* yourself"), in the *Laws* self-love is downplayed as the enemy of politics. And where the Pentateuch recognizes the necessary mediation of material, contractual, and even explicitly asymmetrical relations of exchange among Israelites, even as it seeks to limit their impact through poor laws and sabbatical years, the more radical surgery of the *Laws* is an attempt to free love and friendship entirely from monetary mediation.[33] Given how impracticably dangerous this amputation is, I find it difficult to be optimistic about the possibilities for a Platonic politics of love in the material world. From a pragmatic point of view, we should perhaps treat the *Laws* more as a provocation than as a prescription, a deliberately extreme formulation designed to bring the constitutional crisis of love into high relief rather than to overcome it.

3

Aristotle's treatment of love in the *Eudemian Ethics* represents one response to that provocation. The problem emerges clearly at the beginning of book 7, "On Friendship."[34] How can one achieve a politics of love or friendship if (1) "it is thought to be the special business of the political art to produce friendship," (2) "those who are unjustly treated by one another cannot be friends to one another," (1234b), and (3) so many of the relations of exchange that traditionally bear the name of love (even the exemplary one between lover and beloved!) are seemingly asymmetrical and therefore unjust? Plato's answer had been to exile such exchanges and their instruments from the category of friend and from the ideal polity. Aristotle opts instead for a more inclusive taxonomy. He does have a sharp hierarchy of friendships, with legal relations of self-interested or material exchange at the bottom and the nonutilitarian loves of more godlike spirits at the top. But every one of these is capable of supporting a politics and a just constitutional order because every one of them produces equality:

> Justice seems to be a sort of equality and friendship also involves equality, if the saying is not wrong that "love is equality." Now constitutions are all of them a particular form of justice; for a constitution is a partnership, and every partnership rests on justice, so that whatever be the number of species of friendship, there are the same of justice and partnership; these all border on one another, and the species of one have differences akin to those of the other. (1241b)

Indeed, precisely the sorts of friendship that Plato banned from his city are those that Aristotle designates "civic": friendships of utility, sometimes "strictly legal," sometimes moral (i.e., without contract), but always governed by an economic calculus. "Civic friendship looks to equality and to the object as sellers and buyers do; hence the proverb 'a fixed wage for a friend'" (1242b).[35]

Though Aristotle restricts his simile of sellers and buyers here to civic friendship, the phrase is far more than a metaphor. In fact, he will apply it to all types of love and friendship because his theory about how love calculates difference and establishes equality between men turns out to be the same as his theory of economic exchange. It is, of course, not difficult either in friendship or in trade to produce equality when exactly similar quantities of exactly similar friendship are exchanged (though Aristotle seems to agree with Plato that there would be little motivation for such exchanges). The problem arises when different quantities or different kinds are in question. How, for example, should the quid pro quo be calculated in asymmetrical relationships of friendship such as those of lover and beloved or teacher and pupil ("for knowledge and money have no common measure")? Aristotle is confident that the value of any friendship can be equated to that of another through a

> measurement by one measure, only here not by a term but by a ratio; we must measure by proportion, just as one measures in an association of citizens. For how is a cobbler to have dealings with a farmer unless one equates the work of the two by proportion? So to all whose exchanges are not of the same for the same, proportion is the measure, e.g., if the one complains that he has given wisdom, and the other that he has given money, we must measure first the ratio of wisdom to wealth, and then what has been given for each. (1243b)

Two things seem to me remarkable about this passage. The first is its stunningly promiscuous conflation of love, politics, and economics. We move from measuring love, to political distributions, to the exchange of shoes and vegetables. The second is Aristotle's confidence in his "measure," that is, in the power of his "proportions" (*analogon, analogian*) to make all seemingly disparate exchange (whether of love or of political or economic goods) commensurable.[36] It is this confidence about the ability to calculate equivalencies that allows Aristotle to classify as "loving" forms of relation that the Pentateuch and Plato had feared, and to integrate exchanges ranging from the most material to the most ideal into one harmonious economy.[37]

We can already see that Aristotle depends on his mediating proportions to do a great deal of work, not only in his theory of friendship but also in those of justice and of exchange. His theory of justice, for example, is often summarized in the aphorism "Treat equals equally, unequals unequally." Justice is, in other words, distribution in accordance with proportional equality.[38] Because so much rides upon the power of Aristotle's proportions, we should ask just how robust they are. The answer, it turns out, depends a great deal on the realms in which they are deployed.[39]

In his discussion of commensurability in book 7 of *Physics,* the criteria are strict. In order for two things to be commensurable—equatable through proportion—there must be a property that both share, even if they have it to differing degrees. There follows a lengthy discussion of what it means for two things to share a property, leading to the conclusion that neither the property of comparison nor the recipients being compared can admit of any "specific difference." The example he gives is that of color. Two things, such as a horse and a dog, may be made commensurable in terms of a specific color (say, white) but not in terms of color in general (249a3–26). Comparison and commensurability, in other words, are possible only within the same species, not across species within a genus.

The same mathematics of proportional commensurability deployed in the *Physics* applies in Aristotle's theories of commensurability in love, justice, and economic exchange, but the stringent condition of species identity for comparison does not. The reasons for this return us to our earlier discussions of love. Consider the basic problem of both love and economic exchange, as Plato and Aristotle imagined it: "We do not have an association [of exchange] between two physicians, but between a physician and a farmer, and in general between different and nonequal; but [in order to have an association between different and unequal people] we must equalize them" (*Eth. Nic.* 1133a16–18).⁴⁰ Economic exchange is, in this sense, generally asymmetrical and incommensurable *(asummetra)*. Aristotle's way around this problem is to discover a "measure" that can equate them, and the one he first proposes is money, the intermediate that "measures all things" (*Eth. Nic.* 1122a19–20). This solution runs into the difficulty that money cannot be said to be a shared property of any of the things it is meant to mediate between (except when the trade is in currency itself).⁴¹ Aristotle quickly moves on to another possibility: "Everything must be measured by some one thing, as we said before. In reality this thing is need [*chreia*], which holds everything together" (*Eth. Nic.* 1133a25–27). But although need (sometimes translated tendentiously as "demand") can render disparate things commensurable (it is, for example, the builder's need for shoes and the cobbler's need for a house that establishes the proper ratio of exchange between them), it is not itself a measure. Currency is therefore necessary to act as a magnitude for measuring need, a "kind of pledge of need by convention" sufficiently stable (one hopes) to create harmony in the polis (*Eth. Nic.* 1133a28–30, 1132b34).

When it comes to exchange, then, we can say that Aristotle's proportions, his "measurements by one measure," are not very robust, for the mediating measure (need) turns out not to be a measure at all and itself requires the mediation of another intermediate (currency), which is, strictly speaking, capable of measuring only itself. There is an aporia here, though Aristotle does not surrender to it. Instead, he uses convention to bind the two intermediates, need and currency, together. If buyers and sellers, citizens and friends, understand that the currency in which they conduct their relations is not a need but only a token of a promise of need—and if they are disposed to honor the promise signified by the token—then Aristotle's theory of proportionality in exchange will work. His theory, in other words, requires what it is meant to produce: the virtue of all parties involved in exchange.

Of course, Aristotle realized that this requirement was far from being met. As he put it in the *Eudemian Ethics,* "most 'political' men are not truly so called; they are not in truth 'political,' for the 'political' man is one who chooses noble acts for their own sake, while most take up the 'political' life for the sake of money and greed" (1216a23–27). Two semiotic errors produce this majority of false political men. The first denies mediation itself: "the bad prefer natural goods to a friend and none of them loves a man so much as things; therefore they are not friends. The proverbial 'community among friends' is not found among them; the friend is made a part of things, not things regarded as part of the friend" (1237b30–34). Such men (to put it in anachronistic but fashionable terms) are not "other-regarding." Since they reduce the other to the objects he possesses, their transactions (can we properly call them exchanges if they are not between two subjects but rather between subject and thing?) presumably cannot establish proportional equalities of need between participants. They therefore produce neither justice, nor friendship, nor political community.[42] The second error, which Aristotle at one point attributes specifically to the "illiberal man," is also a mistaken attitude toward mediation: "the lover of money is a man eager for the actual money, which is a sign of possession taking the place of the accidental use of other possessions" (1231b–32a). Such men forget the conventional role of money as a measure of need. They confuse the signifier with the signified, and live only to accumulate the symbol itself.

If these errors afflict the majority, if only a minority of men have a virtuous attitude toward symbolic economies that a political economy of love requires, then how can Aristotle maintain the possibility of such a political economy? Plato's solution, like that of the Pentateuch, is to limit or forbid the forms of exchange that seem most dangerous. Aristotle, as we have seen, does not do so; indeed, he deploys his theory of a mediating proportionality to make all exchanges potentially loving. He limits instead the category of political man, so that it includes only those who possess the virtues that politics requires. This is a division that cuts as much through the category of man as it does through that of the political. Just before observing that most who call themselves political men are not truly so, Aristotle establishes "a division of the kinds of life" in which those lives "only pursued for the sake of what is necessary, e.g., those concerned with the vulgar arts, or with commercial and servile occupations," as well as those pursued "for the pleasure of eating or that of sex," are not political lives.[43] They are not even fully human, "for it is clear that to the man making this choice there would be no difference between being born a brute and a man; at any rate the ox in Egypt, which they reverence as Apis, in most of such matters has more power than many monarchs" (*Eth. Eud.* 1215b35–39).

Plato makes a tripartite hierarchical distinction between lives and polities oriented toward the needs of money, body, or soul. Aristotle makes a bipartite one, between an existence oriented toward necessity (defined as money as well as physical appetites) and a life that is human and political insofar as it is oriented toward friendship rather than toward things. The first he expels from both the human and the political. The biopolitical vocabulary that Aristotle develops in his ethics to unfold these distinctions enjoys a great deal of attention in critical theory today (think of the work of Giorgio Agamben). Less often noted are the semiotic origins of these distinctions, which are (for Aristotle) fundamentally differences between men in their relation to the mediation of signs. Unlike an animal, the bad man is capable of using symbols, but unlike a fully human and political man, he does not use them correctly. The existence of such creatures prevents symbolic economies from achieving what Aristotle considers their natural and transcendent goal of overcoming difference, maximizing friendship, and achieving "unity, the good in itself" (1218a20). The extrusion of these creatures into some category other than humanity (e.g., bare life) becomes a step toward the realization of a politics of love.

4

Thus far my claims have been that for quite different reasons Israelite prophets and Greek philosophers worried in structurally similar but autonomous ways about the power of reciprocal exchanges that were generally understood in terms of love. In both cases their anxieties resulted in hierarchical distinctions between types of love and exchange, which led to the exclusion of certain forms of desire from the category of love entirely. And, in both cases, these parallel anxieties produced similar ways of containing the contradictions produced by the inescapable importance of material mediations considered dangerous, namely, the extrusion of the danger into specific figures of thought, such as "foreign women," aliens, or inhuman men.[44] After Alexander's conquests brought the relative autonomy of these anxieties to an end, we find a number of attempts to bring them together (e.g., in *The Wisdom of Ben Sira*).[45] But from our point of view, the most important of the marriages of Israelite and Greek thought on these matters is the Christian one.[46]

An early example of the political form these questions took in Christianity is the famous formula of Matthew 5:43–48:

> You have heard how it was said, you will love your neighbor and hate your enemy. But I say this to you, love your enemies [*diligite inimicos vestros / agapate tous echthrous*] . . . and pray for those who persecute you, so that you may be children of your Father in heaven, for he makes the sun rise on the just and the unjust. . . . For if you love those who love you, what reward will you get? Do not even the tax collectors do as much? And if you save your greetings for your brothers, are you doing anything exceptional? Do not even gentiles do as much? You must therefore be perfect, just as your heavenly Father is perfect.[47]

Carl Schmitt, eager to maintain the enemy at the heart of the political, claimed that Jesus meant here only the personal enemy (Lat. *inimicus,* Gk. *echthros*), not the political one (Lat. *hostis,* Gk. *polemios*). The distinction is absent in the Greek of the Gospels and untenable in Matthew's hypothetical Aramaic precursor. It is in any event unnecessary, for Jesus' claim to a more perfect polity of love, like the earlier Israelite and Greek claims we have looked at, was clearly dependent on certain exceptional exclusions. This is evident already in the passage from Matthew, with its sharp distinction between the perfect love advocated by Jesus and the imperfect loves that have come before.[48] Matthew's misquotation of Leviticus (which enjoins love of neighbor but not hatred of enemies) suggests which of these previous politics he was most anxious to appropriate, transform, and supersede: those of the false Israel, that is, the Israel that rejected Jesus' claim to be the fulfillment of God's love. The gospels work, each in its own way, to identify and condemn figures of this false love and its politics: the Pharisees, for example, in Matthew, or the Jewish followers of the princes of this world in John. The product of all this work is Jesus' sovereignty, as he himself proclaims it in the Gospel of Luke: "But as for my enemies, who did not want me to be king over them, bring them here and slay them before me" (19:27).[49]

My goal here is neither to resolve this apparent contradiction within a Christian politics of love nor to wallow in it. My point is only that Christian perfections of love were beset by the same difficulties as Greek and Israelite ones and that the paradoxes generated by these difficulties were sometimes similarly extruded into exceptional figures: in this case, those of the "Pharisee" or the "Jew." The problem extended far beyond the topic of sovereignty, for the mediation of love was crucial to nearly every vital question confronting the followers of Jesus. What is the proper form of relation of the true Israel to the false, of the lover of God to the material world, or of God to flesh? The tensions inherent in each of these questions could easily be driven toward polarity. Consider the Christological debates over the nature of Jesus himself. Did God's love for man require him to take material form in order to redeem the human? And if so, how could perfect love become material without declining from perfection? The many answers produced by the early followers of Jesus ranged from the "Gnostic" claim that the loving God has nothing to do with the material world of flesh and therefore could never have created the world (as the Hebrew Bible has it) or taken human form, to the "Ebionite" position that Jesus was the human Messiah promised by God in the Hebrew Bible but not himself divine. Scholars sometimes call the Christology that eventually triumphed paradoxical. It maintained that Jesus united man and God, and that the Hebrew Bible had promised precisely such a mediator. The fact that advocates of this Christology came to represent all their rivals as "Judaizing" may tell us something about how this victory of paradox was achieved.[50]

I say "may" because to make my claim historically would require me to hack slowly through the tangled underbrush of early Christian and patristic sources and their contexts rather than swinging, as I have done throughout this essay, from one outrageously lofty limb to another.[51] But I must simply swing to another limb, one high enough to give us a good view of the forest's topography if not of its history, and stout enough to propel us into the Middle Ages.

That limb is Saint Augustine. Like many of his colleagues, Augustine was acutely concerned with questions about how words and things mediate between men and God, but being a recovering dualist himself, he was more aware than most about the ease with which solutions to these questions tended to split paradox into polarity. This awareness is especially evident in his approach to the crucial question about how scriptural language works. Advocates of a paradoxical Christology had tended to defend their appropriation of the Hebrew Bible against the attacks of both dualists (who dismissed it as carnal) and Jews (who insisted on the ongoing validity of its laws) by thoroughly spiritualizing its words. They argued that those who read the Hebrew Bible literally, whether in order to reject it—like the dualists—or to take up some of its commandments, were "Jews."[52] Such thoroughgoing spiritualization and de-Judaization of Hebrew Scripture helped Christians claim it for their own, but this widening of the gap between literal meaning and spiritual truth was also dangerous. The more the spiritualists devalued the literal, historical, and carnal meanings of Scripture, the more they themselves risked becoming dualists and thereby "Jewish."[53]

That Augustine felt this risk keenly is evident in his criticism of Saint Jerome and other followers of the allegorizing hermeneutics of Origen of Alexandria.[54] In an extraordinary series of letters (395–404 C.E.) that Augustine exchanged with Jerome, he argued that denial of the literal meaning of God's words, whether in the Old Testament or the New, opens the door to the dualists, "perverse men" who deny the Hebrew Bible and dismiss New Testament passages awkward to their cause as strategic falsehoods rather than literal truths.[55] No passage of Scripture, he insisted, should be denied a literally true meaning, lest "nowhere in the sacred books shall the authority of pure truth stand sure" (*Ep.* 28.4; *Ep.* 40, 3.3). Jerome's response was telling. For nine years he did not reply, judging Augustine's argument "tainted with heresy" (*Ep.* 72, 1.2). When he finally did, it was with the ill-tempered charge that Augustine's stress on the literal meaning of scriptural language was "reintroducing within the Church the pestilential heresy" of Judaizing that "will make us Jews" (*Ep.* 75, 4.13).[56]

Of course, Augustine had no intention of turning Christians into Jews, and he was well aware of the Judaizing danger inherent in Christian hermeneutics. He himself outlined the danger with characteristic clarity in *De doctrina christiana* (3.5.9):

> The ambiguities of metaphorical words . . . demand extraordinary care and diligence. What the Apostle says pertains to this problem. "For the letter killeth, but the spirit quickeneth." That is, when that which is said figuratively is taken as though it were literal, it is understood carnally. Nor can anything more appropriately be called the death of the soul than that condition in which the thing that distinguishes man from beasts, which is the understanding, is subjected to the flesh in pursuit of the letter.

This servitude to the letter is the error of the Jews, says Augustine. Christians could steer clear of this Jewish error and avoid the danger of elevating the literal over the figurative by following a simple rule: whichever reading leads to love of God or neighbor (in that order) is to be preferred; whichever leads to lust for the world is false, for "scripture enjoins nothing but love, and condemns nothing but lust."

This hermeneutics of love, like some of the others we have encountered, depends on a fairly sharp distinction between seductions that lead toward the divine and those that lead toward the material world. Unlike the Gnostics, Augustine does not condemn the latter, but he does, like the Platonists, insist on an ontological difference between the two; hence the famous distinction in *De doctrina christiana* between the "use value" of the material world and the "enjoyment value" of the divine (*uti/frui*). Unlike Aristotle, in other words, Augustine opts for two theories of value rather than trying to unify the field of human relations within one. Nevertheless, like Aristotle, Augustine understands the basic problem to be confusion about how symbolic economies work, and he describes that confusion in terms of biohermeneutic and biopolitical figures, derived now from the scriptural vocabulary of "false Israel," understood as the Jews.

In his *Contra Faustum* (*Against Faustus the Manichee*) of 398, for example, the figure takes the form of Cain. Like Cain, who was a tiller of the earth, the Jews were tillers of text (the Old Testament) who killed the very thing they were meant to cultivate (the promised Messiah). In punishment for this killing they became, like Cain, both hypercarnal and alienated from the world: "you are cursed from the earth . . . for you shall till the earth, and it shall no longer yield unto you its strength." Likewise is their reading of Scripture fruitless: "they continue to till the ground of an earthly circumcision . . . while the hidden strength or virtue of making known Christ, which this tilling contains, is not yielded to the Jews." Hypercarnal as they are, the Jews are even alienated from their own mortal flesh, as Cain had been:

> So Cain . . . said: . . . "I shall be a mourner and an outcast on the earth, and it shall be that everyone who finds me shall slay me." . . . "Not so," [God] says; "but whosoever shall kill Cain, vengeance shall be taken on him sevenfold." That is . . . not by bodily death shall the ungodly race of carnal Jews perish. . . . So to the end of the seven days of time the continued preservation of the Jews will be a proof to believing Christians of the subjection merited by those who . . . put the Lord to death. (12.9–13)[57]

Trembling in this figure of abjection is Augustine's so-called doctrine of Jewish witness. Unlike some of his contemporaries, Augustine did not imagine a world free of God's Jewish enemies.[58] Instead, he transformed them into an enduring monument to the truth of Christian hermeneutics, an eternal admonition to those who would either deny the literal sense of Scripture or fixate upon it. Augustine's concern here was not the fate of the Jews.[59] His goal was the creation of a more durable paradox, one that could resist the attack of spiritualist or literalist without threatening to become either dualist or "Jewish" itself. Nevertheless, his solution was, for the Jews, a fateful one, insofar as it preserved them, as it were, in formaldehyde—inert testimony, like Einstein's brain in a jar, to a revolution in man's understanding of the cosmos.

Augustine's deployment of Jewish flesh helped stabilize certain paradoxes but sharpened others. For our purposes here, the most interesting of these were political. Augustine himself realized the political utility of his figures of Judaism. In his exegesis of Psalm 59 against the "Origenist" Pelagius, for example, he explained, citing Romans 9:22, that God had poured his message into two vessels, one of mercy, the other of wrath, the former perceptible through the latter.[60] "For so God, willing to show wrath, and to manifest His power, has brought in with much patience the vessels of wrath, which have been perfected unto perdition." These vessels of wrath were God's enemies the Jews, destroyed spiritually but preserved in the flesh ("dead men") so that His sovereignty over the earth might be clearly shown. Hence, according to Augustine, the Psalmist sang, "Slay them not, lest sometime they forget your law" (Ps. 59:17–19).

In other words, the continued existence of the Jews as abject biopolitical figures made Christian claims to sovereignty historically legible, just as the their continued existence as biohermeneutic figures demonstrated the historical truth of orthodox Christian scriptural interpretation. Behind this parallel stands a broader confidence in the interlegibility of political history and salvation history. Augustine was far from the first to feel this confidence, which was widespread in the first century of Christian empire, but he was among the first to experience its crisis. Late in his life, with the Visigoths beating down the gates of Rome, history became less legible for Augustine, the relationship between God's polity and man's more opaque, and the union of a scriptural hermeneutics of love with earthly politics more untenable.

This crisis of confidence is nowhere more evident than in *The City of God*, where Augustine abandons the dream of aligning the politics of the earthly city with that of the heavenly one. Within the *saeculum* (by which he means the inseparable interpenetration of the earthly and the spiritual, as well as the demonic and the divine, that constitutes the world until the apocalypse), no amount of hermeneutic good faith, no approach to symbolic economies, no matter how loving, can effectively mediate between earthly and heavenly politics. Unlike others we have seen encounter this aporia, the elderly Augustine seeks neither to leap into it (like the Gnostics) nor to overcome it (as do the advocates of a politics of love). He opts instead to mark it as a permanent feature of the unperfected world.

He does, however, mark it with a specific name and assign to it a specific figure. In *The City of God* the name is Cain's; Cain is the "founder of the earthly city" and the first practitioner of its politics. Like Cain, the founder of every polity is of necessity "a fratricide" (Augustine gives the example of Romulus). Like Cain, who sinned by subjecting his reasoning soul to the desires of his flesh, every earthly city "has its good in this world, and rejoices in the material world with such joy as such things can afford," so that it will at the end of time be "committed to the extreme penalty." Terrestrial politics gives mistaken priority to flesh, "that part which the philosophers call vicious, and which ought not to lead the mind, but which the mind ought to rule and restrain by reason."[61] Plato or Aristotle might have agreed with the distinction, but not with the use to which it is put. Whereas for them the proper analogy for the city and its politics had been the soul, for the elderly Augustine it became the body—the body, moreover, already alienated from itself.

Operating as it does under the curse of Cain, the earthly city begins to look perilously like the alienated figure of Judaism. Augustine does not seek to slay this figure. Instead, he immures her, like the furies under Aeschylus's Athens, as a permanent reminder, exiled but not exorcised, of an aporia at the foundations of the polity. Eventually the living logos will return to smash these foundations and reconcile the two cities. But until then, according to Augustine, no reading of Scripture, no matter how loving, can fully emancipate secular relations from "Judaism" or produce a true politics of love.[62]

5

Of course, the millennium and a half of politics after Augustine did not renounce the ideal of a polity of love or cease to develop theories of mediation and exchange, some neo-Platonic, some neo-Aristotelian, some neither or both, through which to fantasize its realization. Just one example may suffice to make clear the impact of these fantasies on modernity. Like the Archbishop of Canterbury with whom I began, the young Karl Marx sketched two visions of society in the notes he took on James Mill. The first was governed by the idea of private property and led ineluctably to alienation and inhumanity. "Man as a social being must proceed to *exchange*," but in a society with private property "the mediating process between men engaged in exchange is not a social or a human process, not *human relationship*." The result of exchange in such a society must be

> that the *mediating activity* or movement, the *human*, social act by which man's prod-ucts mutually complement one another, is *estranged* from man and becomes the attribute of money, a *material thing* outside man. Since man alienates this mediating activity itself, he is active here only as a man who has lost himself and is dehuman-ized; the *relation* itself between things, man's operation with them, becomes the oper-ation of an entity outside man and above man. Owing to this *alien mediator*—instead of man himself being the mediator for man—man regards his will, his activity, and his relation to other men as a power independent of him and them. . . . It is clear that this *mediator* now becomes a *real God*, for the mediator is the *real power* over what it mediates to me. . . . Hence the objects only have value insofar as they *represent* the mediator, whereas originally it seemed that the mediator had value only insofar as it represented *them*.[63]

In societies with private property, Marx is suggesting, human communication is foiled by the attraction of the mediating sign itself. "The only intelligible language . . . consists of our objects in their relation to each other. We would not understand a human language and it would remain without effect." Even our own production becomes only the "*sensuously perceptible covering*, the *hidden shape*," of another's object (*E*, 227).

Against this society and its symbolic economies, Marx posits another, one without private property, one that "carried out production as human beings," for the sake of relation rather than exchange. The benefits of such production would be many, but among the greatest is that "in my production. . . . I would have been for you the *mediator* between you and the species, and therefore would become recognized and felt by you yourself as a completion of your own essential nature and as a necessary part of yourself, and consequently would know myself to be confirmed both in your thought and in your love." Only within such a society, says Marx, can I realize "my true nature, my *human* nature, my *communal* nature" (*E*, 228).

With these passages I do not mean to promise a careful comparison of Marx's thinking on love and exchange with that of the Israelite prophets, Plato, Aristotle, or Augustine, though such a comparison might be fruitful. I mean only to suggest that the problems Marx is discussing are very much theirs and that the terms in which he does so echo theirs as well. The longing to experience mediation as love, anxiety about the ease with which that mediation becomes alienated idolatry, the biohermeneutic description of the danger, all of these are familiar to us from the long history we have just surveyed. Familiar, too, is the figure into which Marx distills the danger in the essay he writes about the same time that he took his notes on Mill, the figure whose disappearance from the community will proclaim the overcoming of man's alienation from himself—the figure of the Jew in *On the Jewish Question*.

For nearly a century various versions of Marx's communitarian vision provided the dominant alternative to what was imagined as a liberal capitalism in which politics amounted to nothing more than exchange. Today the limits of those alternatives are clearer, as are the extrusions, exclusions, and exterminations that they, like all preceding attempts at the perfection of exchange, tended to generate. But the hunger for a politics that is more than mere exchange has not lessened; indeed fears of globalization and "Americanization" have only sharpened its pangs. It is this hunger, combined with the collapse of alternatives like Marxism, that drives the current search for more perfect political unions once more toward love.

Some of these searches, like the ones with which I began, advocate explicitly Christian political theologies patterned on incarnational mediations. Scholars again debate the differences between erotic and agapeic sovereignty; call for a "revolutionary Constantinianism . . . committed to the Logos as the foundation of all political discourse"; and recommend Thomism as a solution to the metaphysical and epistemological crises of postmodernity.[64] Obviously I cannot critique here all of the Christian politics (much less those of other religions) offered today as prescriptions for an imperfect world. Since past results are not a guarantee of future ones, it is not enough to point out that in their earlier incarnations none of these approaches led to a politics that we today could recognize as loving.[65] But, at the very least, my survey of the foundations of these political theologies has made plausible the suspicion that their promise of universal love depends upon and produces the very exclusions and enmities it claims to be overcoming.

Other contemporary quests for a politics mediated by love are neither Christian nor theological, or at least not explicitly so. Consider, since we have space for only one example, the politics of recognition advocated by Charles Taylor, Axel Honneth, and others as a potential counter to a politics of distribution.[66] For his part, Honneth's vocabulary of love is spare, but insofar as his notion of "recognition" derives from Hegel's it is inescapably rooted in that vocabulary. Hegel called his dialectic of the moral relationship, which he represented in terms of love, the "struggle for recognition." As he put it in his first Jena lecture, "In love the separated entities [*das Getrennte*] still exist, but no longer as separated: as united [*Einiges*]." In his second lecture, love became the "knowing" (*Erkennen*) of the "I" that recognizes itself in the other. (Habermas outlines with characteristic clarity how this loving model of intersubjectivity animated Hegel's theories of communicative and symbolic action, and generated distinct dialectics of representation and of labor.)[67] Marx's distinction between alienating exchange and a loving mediation producing recognition, Habermas's distinction between "work" (purposive-rational action) and "interaction" (communicative action), Honneth's distinction between a politics of distribution and one of recognition: each is in its own way a detheologized descendent of Hegel's Christian love.[68]

Why should we worry about the abiding importance of love in our attempts to imagine more perfect forms of community and communication? There are those (like Carl Schmitt) who believe that the language with which we represent the political is extraneous to the question of determining the essence or concept of the political itself. I have tried to show that the opposite is true. Particular histories of struggle to reconcile the inescapably mediated nature of communal and communicative life with evolving political ideals of love generate specific anxieties and figures of exclusion, figures that shape the ways in which political love can be imagined and eventually lend their form to concepts of the political itself. If this codependence is difficult to concede, it is in part because the vocabulary of love has a most peculiar virtue. Through it we fantasize the overcoming of the very exclusions that the history of its use has generated. Hence this essay has focused on that history's exiles. Their suffering may help to remind us that, whatever love's attraction as an antidote to the inequalities generated by our contemporary systems of exchange, any politics that acts in love's name will have the potential to produce its enemies (to paraphrase Marx on Judaism) "out of its own entrails," as "the alienated essence of man's labor and life."[69]

Religious Indifference

On the Nature of Medieval Christianity

M. B. Pranger

More often than not, we can read as nonreligious written and visual medieval sources that at first sight seem replete with religion, specifically, Christianity. How can this be so? If we want to avoid the anachronistic opposition between religious and nonreligious, we could rephrase this question: Why does the religious element often manifest itself as intrinsically indifferent?[1] Not only does this "indifference" apply to the obvious cases of logic and semantics, and, more generally, to scholastic sources, it also underlies texts that are thoroughly devout. Whether we are dealing with the logics of Abelard, Ockham, or Buridan, or with Thomas à Kempis's *Imitatio Christi*, both types of source material are somehow shot through with what I would like to call "religious indifference." Before trying my hand at explaining what I mean by this concept, let me trace its complicated recent prehistory, which, in my view, at once echoes what in the Middle Ages was, roughly speaking, considered "religion" and at the same time prevents us from grasping its historical shape.

Recent research has emphasized that what we used to call "medieval" often proves to be a nineteenth-century phenomenon. From Romanticism to the Neo-Gothic movement, from *Génie du christianisme* (*The Genius of the Christian Religion*) to *Aeterni Patris*, medieval Christendom was characterized as covering all domains of life. Many studies have now unmasked this universal idea of the Middle Ages as being basically a nineteenth-century concept.[2] I see unmasking anachronisms, although part of the historical trade, as not all there is to it. We should ask whether, even if medieval religion is deprived of its characteristic of universality and reduced to a plurality of historical phenomena, we have the means to reconstruct it, for instance, with the help of anthropology and sociology. Such efforts are, in my view, quite legitimate and there is no reason to fear that religion proper will dissolve into disparate elements such as man, society, and (pagan) rites and practices. Yet the roots of nineteenth-century medievalism itself remain an unsolved problem. This is particularly true of a universal concept of religion, so anachronistically applied to medieval source material. Traces of medieval (and Baroque) religion are in fact present in nineteenth- and twentieth-century discussions of the presence and shape of medieval religion—as, for instance, in French and Belgian anticlericalism and the Catholic defense against it.[3] Academic trends tend to move faster and in a more radical, albeit more isolated, context than society at large. To give one example, the explosive growth of the study of medieval logic and semantics in the second half of the last century was often initiated by scholars with a clerical background, and for some of them the secular study of, for instance, scholasticism, which proved to be capable of banishing or isolating religion proper, was dialectically related to their own religious past. Possible conflicts and tensions between the religious and the secular ceased to be a problem for their students, most of whom appeared to be free, so far as religion was concerned, from (nineteenth-century) historical contagion and, consequently, from any *parti pris* in this matter. If such indifference contributes to academic progress, so much the better. But that should not blind us to developments around us in the "real" world, which is witnessing a return of particularism in religious ideology.[4] Because we Western academics tend to view religion as having a universal and reflective nature, manifestations of particularist religion in a fundamentalist guise (whether Christian, Jewish, or Muslim), which lack reflection of any kind, seem alien to us. Even in their most intolerant past manifestations, we had been accustomed to associate these religions with some degree of reflectivity.

To get a better grip on the various historical strands underlying our present religion, I want to make a few tentative suggestions. The first reason we still tend to think of religion as a universal phenomenon is, in my view, the still pervasive influence of Schleiermacher, who successfully defended religion "against its cultured despisers." Criticizing Kant's reduction of religion to a phenomenon "within the limits of reason alone," Schleiermacher claimed a separate and independent status for religion: the province of feeling, next to theoretical and practical reason. Up to the present day, the respectability of religion—of Christianity, that is—is primarily based on its emotional power, manifest through the ages.[5] This focus on affect and emotion runs from the medieval *Dies irae* and the *Stabat Mater* right through the pietism of the *St. Matthew's Passion*. That Schleiermacher's broadening of pietism into feeling was a stroke of genius becomes evident from its tenacious survival in modern notions of religion. Moreover, it solves two issues that are offensive to the modern mind: the self-identification of the church as an institution with claims to authority over morality, politics, and so on, and the doctrinal claims to truth by separate, confessional denominations and religions. Even though Christianity, especially in its Platonic guise, had long been familiar with tensions between word, image, and an ideal essence, Schleiermacher outdid his predecessors by furnishing the world behind the screen of appearances with a powerful anthropological foundation. Never before had relativizing both the distance and the proximity between the language and the experience of faith so successfully turned out in favor of the latter.

In addition to Schleiermacher's successful proclamation of religion as feeling, another, more controversial mode of religious civilization should be mentioned, which had an enormous radiance both backward and forward: late-nineteenth- and early-twentieth-century Neo-Scholasticism. Admittedly, unlike Schleiermacher's reformulation of religion, this particularly learned form of religion has failed to convince "its cultured despisers."[6] It did, however, succeed in shaping their view of religion beyond its emotional and imaginative aspects. Despite all the efforts at modernization since Vatican II, it still is the image many intellectuals have of Roman Catholicism: a religion that is not only concerned with piety and morality, but is all-pervasively present in each and every domain of human existence, all of which are underpinned by a theoretical foundation and a continuous explication of doctrine. Even though the "cultured" outsider may be indifferent to such a religion, he often fails to realize to what extent his rejection follows the model of an anachronistic, scholastic procedure. If the unbeliever takes any trouble at all to articulate his unbelief, he will very likely do so in terms of a more or less scholastic debate, for instance, by saying that he does not believe the proposition "God exists" to be true. The very fact that such an isolated statement about the existence or nonexistence of God can be made at all derives from the scholastic method and echoes the *utrum deus sit*, as well as its methodological contradiction *videtur quod non*. The rapid decline of the Neo-Scholastic movement in the second half of the twentieth century should not blind us to its historical importance and to the fact that, in more than one respect, some of its elements, like Schleiermacher's religion of feeling, still survive in our general Western discourse on God and religion.[7] This being so, it raises the question to what degree we must, or can, rid ourselves of the preset ideas about religion that shape our vision of the past in order to get a grip on what is characteristic of, and different in, medieval religion. To put things more cautiously, how can we purge our historical gaze so as to distinguish between historical authenticity and anachronism?[8]

One aspect of the problems we have been discussing seems to be undisputed, and that is the civilized nature of Western religion. By this I mean that, without denying its primitive and pagan undercurrents throughout the ages, Christianity, as it has manifested itself in historical documents, has been a highly artificial construct.[9] In that respect, both Schleiermacher and the Neo-Scholastic theologians and philosophers have only confirmed a dimension of Christianity that had been inherent in it from its early origins. If we have a closer look at late-medieval scholasticism and devotion, on the one hand, and the nineteenth century, on the other, we may conclude that, despite all the problems concerning the poor schooling of the clergy, especially in the countryside, it was not only priests and ministers (including the most orthodox ones) that were well educated. From the *Heidelberg Catechism* to François de Sales' *Introduction à la vie dévote* (*Introduction to the*

Devout Life), lay people also participated in this civilizing process. This may have little bearing on the Middle Ages proper, apart from the fact that we are faced here with a historical development that is somehow rooted in the Middle Ages. A little patience may be needed in order to make our detours meaningful and gain proper access to the Middle Ages.

If we cannot ignore the nineteenth century with impunity when trying to coin a historical concept of religion, this obtains even more for the preceding period, that between 1500 and 1800. If we next wonder what, if anything, connects both Schleiermacher and Neo-Scholasticism with that preceding period, it might be the fact that both periods have tended to create an absolute religion and generalize it into the universality of both an affective and an intellectual universe. This seems unproblematic for the religion of feeling, since up to the present day we are accustomed to regarding pietistic devotion having been transformed and modernized by Schleiermacher, as well as regarding late-medieval devotion through the same Schleiermacherian lens. Things would seem to be different for Neo-Scholasticism, since historical scholarship has taught us that religion is not by necessity an intrinsic, or, to put it less radically, a dominant part of this movement. Unlike Neo-Scholasticism—and, it should be added, the theology of the Counter-Reformation, as well as Protestant scholasticism of the seventeenth and eighteenth centuries— its medieval predecessor cannot be characterized as exclusively religious, nor was it expected to produce exclusively religious results. This lack of religious pressure resulted in a more relaxed and varied way of reasoning, which enabled logic and semantics to flourish freely without suffering from affective or religious constraints. Conversely, Neo-Scholasticism has always been shot through with ulterior religious motives in the service of religious homogeneity. Even the great Etienne Gilson felt compelled to reassure his readers that possible disagreements between Thomas Aquinas and Bonaventure were based on their fundamental accord: a harmony, in other words, that automatically ironed out any possible discursive tensions and inequalities that might have existed between the two saintly scholars.[10]

Before turning to the Middle Ages proper, I would like to make one or two preliminary remarks about the period between 1500 and 1800. This period is utterly intriguing, because the nineteenth-century "restoration" of religion as outlined above can be seen both as continuing and as ignoring it. To illustrate this point, I shall give two brief examples, which, although the way we perceive them tends to be fashioned after the Schleiermacherian and Neo-Scholastic image, both show clear signs of nonmedieval characteristics yet can help us bring out quintessentially medieval aspects that shed light on the gap separating us from the Middle Ages.

As my first example, I want to reflect on two famous statements by Pascal: "Jesus will be in agony till the end of time; during that period one should not sleep"; and "A king needs an entire crowd of busybodies for no other reason than to prevent him from having to think about himself."[11] Both statements can be found in the unfinished *Pensées*, which aimed to give an integral defense of the Christian faith. In my view, we are not capable of taking in those two statements at once and appreciating them within one homogeneous framework. Inevitably we read the first statement, about Jesus' agony, through the lens of Schleiermacherian and existential philosophy and theology, and we are struck by its deeply religious tone. In the second statement, about the king, we primarily admire Pascal's literary talent and acknowledge his position in the great tradition of French moralists such as Montaigne, La Rochefoucauld, and De la Bruyère.[12] But who would dare to say that the scene of Jesus' agony has been written with as light and French a touch as the scene of the king's boredom? Yet the former is no less a *bon mot* than the latter. And, before medieval scholars proudly point out that the blend of deep religious feelings and "moralistic" insights into the human condition can be seen as a quintessentially medieval phenomenon and that, furthermore, such religious-secular witticisms could have been produced effortlessly by great medieval authors such as Gregory the Great, Bede, Abelard, the Archpoet, Bernard of Clairvaux, and many others, we should realize that Pascal's Jesus in agony is more "humanistic" and his king more "religious" than any of the medieval precedents would or could have been. The fact, then, that these two statements tell one and the same story deprives the reader of both religious and secular support. The king's desire for entertainment cannot be separated from the agony of Jesus; the one, the entertainment, is in a sense a caricature of the other, the agony, and vice versa. Both are two sides of the same coin. Our inability to grasp the unity of these two scenes can once more be attributed to our modern tendency to associate religion primarily with devotion, while banishing its dimension as entertainment. It is the very special and impalpable integrity of Pascal's "thoughts" that turns him into the fathomless thinker he is and lends his *Pensées* a kind of indifference that reinforces its solitary and inaccessible nature.

My second example is taken from Ignatius of Loyola's *Spiritual Exercises*. Discussing the appropriate moment to take a decision, Ignatius prescribes the following mental attitude:

> It is necessary to keep as my objective the end for which I was created, viz. to praise God Our Lord and save my soul, and at the same time to be in an attitude of indifference, free from any disordered attachment, so that I am not more inclined or attracted to accepting what is put before me than to refusing it. Rather I should be as though at the center of a pair of scales, ready to follow in any direction that I sense to be more to the glory and praise of God Our Lord and the salvation of my soul.[13]

Not surprisingly, the indifference presented in this passage has, rightly or wrongly, led many to believe that it offers a way out of moral dilemmas that seem rather arbitrary. In religious terms, this meant that during his lifetime Ignatius could be suspected of illuminism, associating him with the Alumbrados or even the Protestants.[14] Conversely, his followers can be seen as having toned down possible radical implications of this indifference by surrounding it with a *cordon sanitaire* in the shape of a mix of mysticism, doctrine, and scholasticism, elements, that is, which kept Ignatius's indifference firmly embedded in ecclesiastical structures. What remains, however, is the potential of radical indifference (despite the caveat, added by Ignatius, that the making of a choice can be directed only at things that are either morally indifferent, good in themselves, or not contradictory to church doctrine). This indifference is no less enigmatic than Pascal's religious indeterminacy. *Les extrèmes se touchent.* The Jansenist-Augustinian determination of Pascal reflects, in a sense, the basic indifference of Ignatius. In the guise of Jesus' vigilant agony and the intensity of indifference concerning decision making both Ignatius and Pascal can be said to focus on vigilance. But if we found ourselves incapable of pinning down the religious and Christian, or, for that matter, nonreligious and human, side of Pascal, in Ignatius's case things look even more complicated. Their determinacy notwithstanding, it is ultimately unclear what Ignatius is up to with his *Exercises*, or, to put it differently, exactly what is so Christian or religious about them.

All this suggests that, in looking for ways of access to medieval religion, we face some serious aporias. Without them it would be so easy. How tempting it might be to trace both Ignatius and Pascal back to medieval and early Christian sources, as, for instance, by identifying Jesus' agony as part of the omnipresent Augustinian motif of religious affection and by characterizing the bulk of medieval religious literature, from the early days of monasticism to the flourishing devotion of the Franciscans and the imitation of Christ in the Modern Devotion, as one gigantic spiritual exercise! As for the notion of "exercise," we could link it to the ideas of Pierre Hadot, who, in his *Philosophy as a Way of Life: Spiritual Exercises from Socrates to Foucault*, argues that a major part of ancient philosophy is to be considered a spiritual exercise, starting a line of thought and mentality with a long aftermath in Christianity.[15] In Hadot's view, the heritage of ancient Stoic and Epicurean philosophy exercised a greater influence on Ignatius than late-medieval devotion and mysticism. Regardless of the way in which specialists covering different periods in the field of medieval studies approach their sources, we would have here a common denominator, which could serve as an explanatory model of the technical structure of medieval religiosity, from penance to exegesis, from visual art to meditation. Even scholasticism could in a way be appreciated as part of this general phenomenon of spiritual exercise, starting from the Augustinian *exercitatio mentis* to Abelard's *Sic et non*, right through the methodological doubt that keeps being part of the scholastic *videtur quod non*. But to what degree is all this still to be called specifically religious or Christian?

To find an answer to those questions, the first pitfall we should avoid is, in my opinion, the temptation to reduce philosophical elements as much as possible to the category of pagan influences on Christianity. Such an approach fails to do justice to the precise nature of the integral phenomenon of the Christian religion, as it manifests itself in a great number of medieval sources.

If, for practical purposes, we maintain the link between "Christian" and "religious," it is clear that religion has been an all-pervasive presence in medieval culture. To put it in the words of Louis Drumont:

> medieval religion was a great cloak—I am thinking of the Mantle of Our Lady of Mercy. Once it became an individual affair, it lost its all-embracing capacity and became one among other apparently equal considerations, of which the political was the first born. Each individual may, of course, and perhaps even will, recognize religion (or philosophy), as the same all-embracing consideration as it used to be *socially*. Yet on the level of social consensus or ideology, the same person will switch to a different configuration of values in which autonomous values (religious, political, etc.) are seemingly juxtaposed, much as individuals are juxtaposed in society.[16]

In his *Genealogies of Religion*, Talal Asad perceptively lays bare the flaws and anachronistic presuppositions in this passage:

> According to this view, medieval religion, pervading or encompassing other categories, is nevertheless *analytically* identifiable. It is this fact that makes it possible to say that religion has the same essence today as it had in the Middle Ages, although its social extension and function were different in the two epochs. Yet the insistence that religion has an autonomous essence—not to be confused with the essence of science, or of politics, or of common sense—invites us to define religion (like any essence) as a transhistorical and transcultural phenomenon. It may be a happy accident that this effort of defining religion converges with the liberal demand in our time that it be kept quite separate from politics, law, and science—spaces in which varieties of power and reason articulate our distinctly modern life. This definition is at once part of a strategy (for secular liberals) of the confinement, and (for liberal Christians) of the defense of religion.[17]

Asad's criticism of Dumont stems from his difference of opinion with Clifford Geertz on the issue of the status of religion. While Geertz defines religion as a closed system ("a system of meanings embodied in symbols"), which subsequently, in a separate move, can or cannot be related to "social-structural and psychological processes," Asad considers those two dimensions to be one and the same. For him, the anthropologist and the historian do not find religion pure and simple in their path, but rather a dynamic process consisting of heterogeneous and ever-moving and changing elements:

> For the entire phenomenon is to be seen in large measure in the context of Christian attempts to achieve a coherence in doctrine and practices, rules and regulations, even if that was a state never fully attained. My argument is that there cannot be a universal

definition of religion, not only because its constituent elements and relationships are historically specific, but because that definition is itself the historical product of discursive processes.[18]

Referring to Peter Brown's classic *Augustine*, Asad illustrates his thesis with the example of Augustine's attitude toward the Donatists.[19] Since the conflict between Augustine and the Donatists was mainly concerned with the issue of church discipline and the status of the church's sanctity as either guaranteed by God (Augustine) or by human efforts (the Donatist view), Asad quite rightly brings up the concept of discipline as here comprising religious, political, and anthropological aspects. It would be too simple, Asad argues, to apply Geertz's formula to the Donatist problem in order "to accommodate the force of this [Donatist] religious symbolism . . . ranging all the way from laws (imperial and ecclesiastical) and other sanctions (hellfire, death, salvation, good repute, peace) to the disciplinary activities of social institutions (family, school, city, church) and of human bodies (fasting, prayer, obedience, penance. . . . Even Augustine held that although religious truth was eternal, the means for securing human access to it were not."[20] The use of the words "even Augustine" here does not betray a deep understanding of the Church Father who can be held responsible for providing Pascal with the concept of intrinsic temporality, as evoked in the scenes of Jesus' agony and the king's boredom. In other words, Asad's phrase "even Augustine" seems to presuppose the existence of precisely that which Asad wants to refute, that is, the existence of an identifiable religion. In Augustine's case, that would boil down to his preoccupation with the eternal, with grace and god-given sanctity, in short, with religious metaphysics. It is well known, however, that, despite his monomaniacal emphasis on divine grace, Augustine the bishop could not afford to stay aloof from the practicalities of the Christian life. In that respect, his involvement in the subtle web of politics and religious practice and discipline was no different from that of the Donatists.

If I have a criticism to make of Asad, it will not concern his refusal to consider symbols, rites, and texts to be programs that can automatically be deciphered. One can only agree with Asad's criticism of Geertz. When Asad, in a subtle chapter, "On Discipline and Humility in Medieval Christian Monasticism," establishes a clear link between monastic rites such as the keeping of the Rule as a law and precept and "the formation of a virtuous will," he is right to point out that "reading [the Rule and Scripture] is the product of varying disciplined performers who discourse with one another in historically determinate ways."[21] If Asad is to be criticized, it is because he lends his historicizing vision still too great a measure of eternity, making the "historically determinate ways" a bit too determinate. Paradoxically, this element of overdetermination is not to be found in the text, the rite, or the symbol proper, but rather in the underlying discipline, which is used as a tool to bring out those texts, rites, and symbols as historical phenomena. As we have seen with Ignatius, however, that discipline itself is faceless, indifferent; it contains an indeterminacy that, ultimately, freezes history, as it were.

I shall try to illustrate this paradox, or rather, this enigma of historicity, temporality, and their underlying indifference—mental, linguistic, rhetorical, religious, or otherwise—with the help of the conflict between Bernard and Abelard. I have selected this example because, throughout medieval and early modern Christianity, Bernard has come to embody religion in its most affective and devotional guise. Thus he can, in a sense, be seen—retrospectively, at least—as a prototype of Schleiermacherian religion. For him, religion seems to be all-embracing, leaving no room for moments of indifference. Conversely, Abelard has come to represent, if not indifference, then certainly scientific distance and remoteness with regard to the "object" of religion—the object, that is, of rational scrutiny. Admittedly, Bernard's devout admirers have always appreciated his literary skills as the expression of a mystical fire burning in his soul, yet they have never felt the need to assess Bernard's hard-core rhetoric, which is by definition indifferent insofar as there is no external criterion by which those rhetorical skills, as well as their product, could be exclusively qualified as religious. In that respect, Bernard's *mots* are as much *bons mots* as those of Pascal.

In his famous diatribe against Abelard in his *Epistola* 190, Bernard appeals to the authority of the Fathers and their fixed concept of the form and content of the *catholica fides* against the despicable efforts of the "new theologian who, since his childhood, has been playing with logic and now, having entered upon the study of Holy Scripture, has gone mad and transgressed the old boundaries set by the Fathers. . . . Where all say *sic*, he says *non sic*. . . . I," Bernard says, "listen to the Prophets and the Apostles, I obey the Gospel, not the Gospel according to Peter. Do you reveal to us a new Gospel? The Church has never accepted a fifth Gospel."[22]

The example is famous, and so is the religious conflict it has come to represent: Bernard's love of the affect and orthodoxy of church doctrine versus Abelard's fondness for logic and argumentation. But, apart from the fact the Abelard has been as innovative in the field of affect and devotion as Bernard, we must conclude that the way the two men have been represented over time has become asymmetrical. While it is easy to position Abelard within the culture of the liberal arts, Bernard is often seen as representing not only an antirational but also an anticultural stance.[23] As a result, many an interpreter has overlooked the fact that Bernard, despite his intense use of Scripture and of the Church Fathers, felt as "free" (in the sense used in the "liberal" arts) in his use of rhetoric when reading and commenting on the Bible as Abelard did in his use of logic. In that respect, he can be said to be as much or, for that matter, as little on the side of religion, tradition, and authority as his opponent. In other words, "the boundaries [*termini*] set by the Fathers" prove to be much more fluid and flexible—and, it should be added, much more a product of exercise and imagination—than rhetorically suggested by Bernard and subsequently believed by both his critics and his followers. The fact that, as Asad points out, issues such as power politics, social institutions, and the like have also played their role in this process only complicates the picture, making it more diffuse and, thereby, more historical.

All this is not to say that there was no doctrinal continuity in the Middle Ages, no *depositum fidei*, to which appeals could be made. However, so seemingly fixed a doctrinal body was always of an intrinsically historical nature, and as such subject to reading, exercise, meditation, and recitation. Even if the last and most literal of these terms, (liturgical) recitation, seems to boil down to sheer repetition, which would keep a historical body such as liturgy intact by performing it, as much as possible, always and everywhere in the same manner, to believe this claim to sempiternity would be a distortion of history, or rather, wishful thinking about what history should have looked like. If anything was subject to change in the Middle Ages, it was the "fixed" body of liturgy: How else can transubstantiation and *realis praesentia* be characterized but as a civilized erosion from within?[24]

My conclusion can only be that religion as a generic concept is of little help in interpreting medieval culture. On the one hand, such a concept smells too much of a Schleiermacherian universal religious experience; on the other hand, the influence of Neo-Scholasticism is still too strong, in that experiential concepts of religion go hand in hand with descriptive ones. Precisely the descriptive concept of faith tends to evoke its experience (as, e.g., in pietism), while shutting it out in a semi-detached form.

What does this mean for the status of religion in the Middle Ages? Of course, it would be quite an exaggeration to deny the religious and Christian nature of the Middle Ages altogether, although, in view of the many anachronisms discussed above, we often do not have a clue as to exactly what notions such as "Christian" and "religion" did in fact mean then—and we certainly do not have the analytical tools to establish this.

As I have been trying to point out, the problem lies in the fact that thus far we have not been able to articulate the precise nature of the indifference as well as the outlook toward exercise in medieval religion. This inability is partly due to the overpowering influence of scholasticism, even though it is perhaps in scholasticism that the status of religion is least problematic. The prescholastic period is even harder to characterize in religious terms, since we do not have at our disposal the categories that would furnish prescholastic Christianity with the performative components that would constitute a historical appearance that we could "read" in its totality.[25] Of course, Asad has notions of discipline in a historical context, and, in a wider sense, cultural anthropology has a historical focus, but in my view even those modern disciplines cannot do justice to the wealth of the source material. To put it, once more, in anachronistic terms, seen from the enlarged perspective of the *après*-Middle Ages, we should admit that we do not know how Ignatian indifference (which, in one way or another, is rooted in each and every practice of medieval devotion) can be squared with the intensity of Pascal's Jesus, who, in turn, cannot be detached from the king in search of entertainment.

To cut a long story short, the fact that medieval religion as we know it is first and foremost seen as an expression of civilization considerably hampers our properly understanding it. On the one hand, Christianity as a monotheistic religion of the book can take on any shape any reader lends it. On the other hand, historically speaking, things might in fact have developed along less arbitrary lines. In that case, we would see the question as being how to fill in the "free" space between God and his Book *and* the practicing reader, offering the latter the opportunity to shape him or herself in a process of continuous exercise. Whether that should be called "religion" depends on how broadly or how strictly one wants to define this concept. It is no doubt to be called "Christian," if only because of its subject matter, even though that does not tell us much about the underlying techniques of reading and imagination.

In conclusion, I want to invoke Bernard's rhetorical imagination in order to get some grip on the problems discussed so far. When, in his sermon "In assumptione beatae Mariae,"[26] Bernard brings up one of his favorite themes, the resurrection of Lazarus, he does so in a repetitive, enchanting, exorcising and almost liturgical manner by repeating the *Lazarus, veni foras* (John 11:43). While, with the voice of Jesus, urging dead Lazarus to leave behind his desperate state of bodily decomposition, putrefaction, and stench by coming out, he repeats the call *Lazarus, veni foras*, in a dramatic version: "*Abyssus vocat abyssum* [Psalm 41:8]: the abyss calls upon the abyss, the abyss of light and grace upon the abyss of misery and darkness." Here the ingredients of discipline, rule, and performance converge in the present of ritual preaching: one familiar voice (*Lazarus, veni foras*) mixing with another (*Abyssus vocat abyssum*), the two of them transforming into one, single new voice. Somehow this splendid rhetorical move is reminiscent of the *bons mots* of Pascal.[27] We shall know exactly what is so Christian or religious about this, however, only if we are able to comprehend the indifference underlying the making and performing of those *bons mots*. If there is a utopian aspect to the understanding of medieval religion, it is to be found in this enigmatic blend of focus, intensity, and indifference.

Christ at Large

Iconography and Territoriality in Postwar Ambon

Patricia Spyer

> Not only Christ but the whole universe disappears if neither circumscribability nor image exists.
>
> —Patriarch Nikephoros, *Antirrhetics*

Picture a situation of blindness, invisibility, and uncertainty, where the sense of unseen and faceless danger prevails, where what was once familiar becomes unfamiliar, where everyday appearances hide unknown horrors. This is one way of describing the recent war in Ambon, the capital of the Moluccas in eastern Indonesia. The Malino Peace Agreement in early 2002, following three years of intermittent violence, left a city divided into "Christian" and "Muslim" territories, with up to ten thousand persons killed and close to seven hundred thousand displaced, equaling one-third of a total Moluccan population of 2.1 million, including those fleeing violence on neighboring islands.[1] Elsewhere I have written about the kinds of "anticipatory practices" and "hyper-hermeneutics" ordinary Ambonese developed during the brutal conflict that, from early 1999 to the official peace in 2002, with outbreaks thereafter, pitted Muslims and Christians against each other in vicious, destructive battle.[2] Deploying an exacerbated sensibility, these practices aimed to anticipate the unforeseen by mining sensory signs for what might lie beneath their surface manifestations in order to head off pervasive uncertainty and perceptions of imminent danger. An aesthetics of hidden depth, such anticipatory practices and hyper-hermeneutics comprised a discourse of disguise and revelation following armed confrontation in which enemy corpses and garments were said to yield further signs of pernicious identity and design—an army uniform concealed under a *jihadist's* robe, *ilmu* or black magic amulets hidden on bodies, incendiary pamphlets, and so on. As responses, such practices were both adaptive and productive of the radical transformation of Ambon City—of its social and material arrangements, of common bodily rhythms, of patterns and assumptions underlying interactions as well as appearances—friendship, contact, animosity, avoidance, trust, cohabitation—of tacit understandings of time, space, density, distance, proximity, and of the gradual sedimentation of violence as productive of a context congenial to more violence.

In Ambon today, new anxieties as well as phantasms of the past animate the city; radicalized and invigorated during the war, they insert themselves in novel ways into its contested, territorialized spaces. Thus, one current residue of the aesthetics of hidden depth in the postconflict situation is an increasingly consolidated discourse concerning the face of the other, according to which many Muslims and Christians claim to discern under an ordinary Ambonese face its respective Christian or Muslim contours.[3] Taking the fraught unseeing and a concomitant exacerbation of the sensorium as simply one among several points of departure, I will focus on the postwar proliferation of billboard portraits of Jesus and gigantic murals rising out of war's ruins along the city's main thoroughfares and at Christian neighborhood gateways. These paintings bear witness and give material form to Christian anxieties about invisibility, while aiming to alleviate the condition of being unseen. They also speak, more generally, to the hypervisibility that is part and parcel of the transient production of places as media "hot spots," wounded, traumatized cities, and war zones within current globalized conditions. Although I cannot develop this here, at issue is how the stability of the nation, once assumed, is increasingly shot through, undermined, and eroded by transnational processes—specifically, here, the wider humanitarian apparatus and the national and international media organizations that descend en masse upon a given place, only to move on, frequently following a dynamic internal to themselves—when another "hot spot" flares up. Of interest in this respect are less tired metropolitan reactions to the numbing seriality of such hot spots than the erratic rhythms and effects in places beyond the metropole of such momentary, if intensive, mediations.[4]

W. J. T. Mitchell argues that "visual culture" entails, among other things, a meditation on blindness, the invisible, the unseen, the unseeable, and the overlooked.[5] Against the backdrop of multiple visibilities, blindness, invisibility, and the unseen figure in a number of ways. First, as I have already intimated, the Ambonese sense that they cannot trust appearances, cannot see or foresee what might come. The war radically refigured not simply subjectivity but, more precisely, sensory subjectivity. Second, there is a pervasive sense, among ordinary Ambonese, that they themselves were unseen, that their massive suffering went unnoticed by the Indonesian government, their fellow countrymen, and the larger world. Among minority Christians—who as a result of the official "islamicization" of Indonesia during the late Suharto era,[6] the current heightened public visibility of Islam nationally and transnationally, and the recent war saw their longstanding privileged social, political, and economic position drastically diminished, this sense of being unseen was especially strong. And if Muslims from May 2000 on, or a good year after the conflict began, had their own side reinforced by the influx of *jihad* fighters from around the archipelago,[7] Christians, by contrast, felt abandoned by the United Nations, the European Union, and the Netherlands, on which many had set serious hopes.[8]

For Christians, compelling historical reasons underwrite this dramatic sense of displacement. Thus, historians of the Moluccas conventionally refer to Ambon's Muslim population as the city's "Other Half."[9] They also document the irrelevance of Central Moluccan Muslims to the colonial government in the wake of the Dutch East India Company's imposition of a trade monopoly on spices from the seventeenth century on. Marianne Hulsbosch, for instance, in her dissertation on the history of Moluccan dress, notes how "successful [the Dutch colonial government was] in isolating the Ambonese Muslims from the rest of the Muslim population in Indonesia until well into the twentieth century"—when, by contrast, Christian Ambonese, or the colony's "Black Dutchmen," were well ensconced within the ranks of the colonial army and bureaucracy. With respect to visibility, in particular, Hulsbosch observes how "this virtual isolation from other Muslim communities in the Indonesian archipelago and their insignificance in the eyes of the colonial government is reflected in the amount of visual information available. Few, if any, early-twentieth-century images of Ambonese Muslim women [or, by extension, men] have been captured . . . [while] it is remarkable that [colonial officers] like Riedel (1886) and Sachse (1907)," writing in the late nineteenth and early twentieth centuries, "did not even consider Muslim dress, although both wrote descriptive notes on Christian and native appearances. For them the Muslims were invisible—a sad statement considering at the end of the nineteenth century they made up 28.3 percent of the population. On the main island of Ambon, the Muslim population even topped 38 percent. This ignorance says much about colonial regard for the Muslim [as opposed to Christian] population."[10] From Indonesian independence in 1945 through the early 1990s, the general privileging of Christians, especially locally in the Moluccas, but also nationally under the quasi-secularist, nationalist politics of Presidents Sukarno and Suharto, kept this asymmetry largely in place.

Much more could be said about the complicated, skewed, and in part, but *only in part* bifurcated history of Ambon's peoples. Here, I invoke it merely as one among other factors contributing to the current shock prevalent among Ambon's Christians at finding themselves outside the national spotlight. In everyday discourse, this shock congeals in the statement, uttered by Muslims and Christians alike when commenting on the many twisted outcomes of the recent war, that "Christians are now *becak*—that is, pedicab—drivers." Before the war and their forced evacuation from Ambon during the conflict's very first days, migrant Muslims from South Sulawesi predominated in this menial occupation. As a profession, it stands in sharp contrast to the high social status and privileges of the *pegawai*, or government bureaucrat, in which Ambon's Christians until recently prevailed—and still do, to a considerable extent. The deceptively casual observation about

Christians being *becak* drivers registers the extent to which the fortunes of Ambon's Christians are understood locally to have plummeted. At issue is nothing less than a "sundering" of these subjects from their former place in social, political, economic—indeed, even metaphysical—terms.[11] Both the *longue durée* and the postconflict redeployments of the performative loci of subjectivity inform the widespread perception among Christians of being forgotten and overlooked. And within the general blindness of the war, more radical even than the sense that their suffering went unnoticed by Jakarta and elsewhere or the shock at postwar predicaments is the doubt, implicit in some current practices and discourse, that Christian Ambonese and their desperate circumstances may have been invisible even to God himself.

The Absence of God

A theological impossibility, the absence of God is never explicitly proclaimed. Instead, it compels statements about *other* Christians who "doubted" his omniscience during the war; it also partially explains the rising numbers of Ambonese who convert from the mainstream Moluccan Protestantism of the GPM (*Gereja Protestan Maluku*), or Protestant Church of the Moluccas, to "purer," "born again" forms like Pentecostalism, as well as the occasional iconoclastic outburst. More directly relevant, though, are the insistent, repetitive statements—a kind of protesting too much—that during the war God was *here*, present and truly here, watching over Ambon. This kind of statement cropped up frequently in my discussions with a handful of Christian painters. Popular and largely untrained, during the war and since they have been plastering their city with mega-portraits of Jesus and murals depicting scenes from his life, Christian symbols, martyrdom, and resurrection. Among these painters, no more than a dozen in all, there are considerable individual differences in style, personal conviction, and artistic, religious, and commercial understanding of their work. They also differ in biography, current occupation, and so on. To give a sense of the range, among the painters I worked with most closely there is the former director of Ambon's *Siwalima* museum, devoted to traditional Moluccan culture. He is the only one among the local Christian painters with any formal art-academy training. Another learned to paint and notably airbrush in the streets of Jakarta, near the market area of Blok M, during a brief sojourn in the Indonesian capital. Yet another has some technical training as a draftsman. Employed at Ambon's Telecommunications Office, he maps the city's underground infrastructure of cables and teleconnections. Finally, another is a self-taught, formidable archivist who, through multiple media—paintings, statuary, a music and dance group, historiographic writings, and his own museum— documents Central Moluccan Seramese culture. Such impressive diversity among these Moluccan Christian painters should not, however, obscure their fundamental similarity as pivotal figures in the postconflict reinvention of Christianity and Christian Ambonese subjectivity from the sidelines and often quite literally sidewalks of the city.

That painters—and these are, importantly, people who love to paint, besides being Christians—should insist so much on the presence of God is hardly surprising, since one recurrent way they seem to think and talk about their work is as a kind of presencing of God. Again, this insistence on God's presence registers, I believe, a terrifying and inexpressible doubt—namely, its opposite, the possible absence of God—whose trace is felt only in the vehemence with which this possibility is repeatedly foreclosed, in part by the pictures themselves and their assertive spread across Ambon. Certainly, during the war the production of these paintings, or the more violent portrayals that preceded them, may have entailed an important leap of faith—an act of blind faith, as it were, in circumstances where the faith of many seems to have been pushed to the limit. Whatever its more existential aspects, for the painters I work with in Ambon, this limit assumed concrete forms: one man described painting fearlessly with bombs exploding close by and bullets flying around him (but magically diverted in other directions); another, who lost much of his life's work and almost his life when forced to flee his burning home, now draws on surrealism to translate his own and others' apocalyptic visions; yet another suffered assault by iconoclast Christians, who destroyed some of the cement statues of pagan warriors and headhunter portraits that crowd this eighty-five-year-old former prison director's tiny museum. This man recently resumed painting, following what his son, a Protestant minister, called a "crisis of doubt." Christian themes and scenes of war's devastation now flank the modest miniature—as opposed to former life-size—faces of Seram Island's most renowned ancient "warlords." I use the notion of limit in several ways here—to invoke the uncertainty that hovers at the edge of faith and to characterize the overwhelming impulse to *picture* or *represent* in the midst of crisis.

Yet above all it is the paintings themselves that most clearly describe a limit. In their performative presencing, their channeling of a host of forces and phantasms through God's eye, and their monumentalization of the horizons shaping Christian Ambonese existence, the paintings telescope a theory of community: a theory of how it is made, how it is produced, out of what, in relation to what, against what, in opposition to what, in spite of, and by the grace of what.[12] While their explicit aim is to reproduce the canon of standard Christian iconography—itself tailored, crucially, to a world in place—the paintings assume this reproductive work during war and its aftermath—with, as we will see, important consequences. For the moment, suffice it to say that in their own fashion they might be seen as "captions of an unstable cityscape."[13] But before turning to the pictures and asking ourselves, following Mitchell, what they might *want*, a few orienting remarks are in place.

On the face of it, the Christian topos of God's visual appraisal of his creation, the foundational separation of lightness from dark, the preeminence of vision as "the sovereign sense," and the illumination widely held by Ambonese Christians to enhance their own faces, by contrast to the dark illegibility of the Muslim, undoubtedly shed light on a crucial dimension here. These Christian pictures, however, are shot through with multiple other visualities and thus suggest a much broader thematization of the visual than the purely theological or one or another mode of mystical seeing or being seen. To enumerate, these include: the imperfect human eye; the evidentiary eye of news broadcasts, human rights, and Truth commissions; the legitimizing bureaucratic eye of state seeing;[14] the eye of the international community, felt by many Indonesians to be upon them after Suharto's fall—*di mata internasional,* a common trope, following Strassler, of *Reformasi*[15]—the "spotlight" that singles out and multi-mediates successive "hot spots" around the globe and the reality effects thereof; and the promotional commodification of places as "images" for tourism and other commercial ends. To be sure, as a globalizing religion, Christianity is always already at large. Yet perhaps here such overreach is singularly salient, with Christ standing in for and subsuming a host of powerful forces and authorizing instances realized as an array of visualities.

Condensing so much into so little, the paintings also draw explicitly and implicitly upon different visual genres—most obviously, as suggested, those of Christian iconography. A number of Ambon's painters use standard books featuring color-saturated Christian scenes as models for their murals; others find inspiration from T-shirts, posters sold on the streets and in local stores, the jacket covers of Christian music CDs (*lagu-lagu rohani),* or popular films, such as Mel Gibson's *The Passion of the Christ.*[16] More covertly, the violent murals that, set in local topography, documented the destruction of key sacred sites, such as Ambon's Silo Church, but are now overpainted with "comforting"(*sejuk*) scenes—in one painter's words, like crucifixion—undoubtedly refracted the graphic "martyrdom" of video CDs produced by both Christians and Muslims during the war.[17] Graffiti comprised another relevant genre here, less for their formal qualities than for their performative punch—as the local expression of powerful *emosi* ("passion," commonly suggesting the potential for violence) and for the larger defacement of Muslims contained in the communicative force of a (Christian) *God is/was here.*

I would like to highlight a few things in the accompanying pictures. First is the prevalent reproduction of the Christian canon; pictures are often copied straight from books, so that one sees the same scene reproduced by different painters. Second is the prominence of the face of Jesus, manifest in different ways. The portrait of Jesus is commonly set apart from other pictures: it stands next to or floats on a billboard above the mural it flanks or is offset as a "cameo" within an otherwise chronological series leading from birth through martyrdom to resurrection. Free-standing Jesus billboards rise along the highway leading from the airport into Ambon. Third is the way in which Christ's face is either figured alone or overlooks scenes of suffering, moral decay, apocalyptic destruction, actual warfare, or the demolition of Christian sites. The final aspect I want to point out is the new publicity of these pictures, with the migration of standard Christian iconography from local church interiors and the walls of Christian homes to public urban space.

FIGURE 1
Jesus billboard.
Ambon, 2006.

FIGURE 2
Jesus billboard.
Ambon, 2006.

FIGURE 3   Jesus mural with cameo portrait. Ambon, 2006.

FIGURE 4   Jesus mural with cameo portrait. Ambon, 2003.

FIGURE 5
Jesus billboard.
Ambon, 2003.

FIGURE 6   Painting based on a prophetic vision of Ambon's destruction. Ambon, 2006.

FIGURE 7   Painting of an indigenous Christ. Inscription reads,
"Your suffering is in the hands of Jesus." Seram, 2005.

FIGURE 8   Painting of Jesus overlooking the destruction of Silo Church. Ambon, 2005.

FIGURE 9   Prayer niche in a private home. Note the book that
serves as the model for the mural. Ambon, 2005.

It should come as no surprise that the practice of painting—its location, scale, import, inspiration—was, like so much else in the war, not immune to the radical transformations taking place in the city. Before the war, several of Ambon's present painters
found occasional employment decorating the interiors of the city's newly built churches
or those on neighboring islands, such as Saparua, with Christian scenes and symbols—
angels with trumpets, Christ on clouds, and so on—or embellishing their exteriors with
statues and reliefs. The move of such pictures out of churches and the revisions they have
undergone are part of the wider fissuring of public space during and after the war by
highly visible, publicized, and competing forms of religion. Ambon's Christians took to
the streets during the conflict with Bibles in hand, pictures of Christ floating above the
crowd, ambulatory public prayer sessions, and red headties. Muslims wore white headties,
carried banners with Arabic inscriptions and green and white flags, and met Christian
cries of *halleluyah* with their own *allahu akbar.* The aggressive mutual engagement and
mirroring has left its legacy in the city: for instance, in the Christian convention, dating

from the war, of using *syalom* as a greeting "since the Muslims have *wassalamu alaikum*," or in the current need, when addressing a young Ambonese, to determine quickly whether he is a Muslim *bang* (from *abang*) or a Christian *bung*, or she a Muslim *cece* or Christian *usi*.[18]

Christ at Large

Asking, as Mitchell does, *What [do] these pictures want?* is a good place to start.[19] One indication that they want something is a departure, in *some* of them, from conventional Christian iconography. A canon presumes a delimited, knowable, and, in the Christian case at least, somewhat orderly visible world. When the world is more or less in place, the appearance of things and the actions of one's fellows correspond to common expectations. Subjects and objects moor each other in predictable ways, enabling the canon to unfold its conventional images in a world where family, churches, community, and the like are more or less in place to receive them. When, by contrast, the world falls apart, the canon may succumb to unprecedented pressures. What images want becomes frustrated, since their correspondence to the world no longer applies. As a result, they may burst from their frames, like the mouth in Cronenberg's *Videodrome*, moved by its desire to devour the world around it. In such moments of intensified desire and frustration, pictures come out—becoming assertive and monumental, like the gigantic lips thrusting forward from the TV, they demand new forms to satisfy their needs.

Here I am seeking to expose the inherently delicate, transitory nature of the associations that pertain between any given setting and the image world to which it is provisionally conjoined. The necessity of attending to the particular constellations and transformative possibilities of such provisional life- and image-world affinities follows from this insight.[20] In Ambon, one consequence of the war has been that Christ comes up close. Stepping out of conventional Christian iconography, he witnesses *directly* the devastation of Silo Church, looks down sorrowfully upon the suffering of Seramese Christians in Soahuku, sheds bloody tears on a map of the island, and oversees the city from Karpan, the privileged high place, featured in tourist brochures, that is held to offer the best view of Ambon. In so doing, he confirms the insistent claim of the painters that God is/was *here*, present and truly here, watching over Ambon. He also underwrites the view of some who, wondering why God inflicted the war upon them, see it as a way of "promoting" Ambon (I. *dipromosikan*)[21]—unlike Bali, unknown to most outsiders—for business and other profitable aims.

The exacerbated condition of Christ at large, comprising both Christ's coming up close and the assertive spread of Christian pictures in the city, took place due to a radical unmooring of the urban landscape, along with the conventional modes of apprehending it. Let me recall briefly some of the dramatic dislocations of the war. BBMers—Buginese,

Butonese, and Makassarese migrants—were driven out of Ambon during the conflict's first days. The Ambonese, virtually overnight, were turned into refugees in their own city. An influx of people came in, fleeing outbreaks of violence on neighboring Moluccan islands. *Jihadists* arrived from Java a good year into the conflict. There was the ongoing, largely disruptive presence of National Army troops, Special Forces, police reinforcements, local militias, and youth gangs, and, last but not least, the flood of representatives from diverse religious and humanitarian organizations, NGOs of varying provenance and scale, and media practitioners from a range of national and international electronic and print media institutions. As the war dragged on, many Ambonese fled the city, retreating to villages on the island or surrounding ones, while storeowners and some civil servants fled, if possible, even further afield, occasionally as far as Manado, the predominantly Christian capital of North Sulawesi Province or, in the case of Muslims, to Makassar in South Sulawesi. In Ambon City itself, other signs of the many dislocations affecting the urban landscape included transitory sightings of Christ, apocalyptic apparitions, and violent disturbances inflecting banal objects and locations, such as pineapple jelly coagulating into blood or blood coursing from faucets.[22]

During the war, there came to be a brisk traffic between the apparitional and the more conventionally portrayed, which persists today. Christ's common depiction as a European derives, Ambonese often insist, not only from the pictorial examples provided in church and schools but from his own occasional appearance to them in visions and dreams.[23] Time and again, during the conflict, rumors circulated of Christians having spotted Christ rising as a great white commander with flowing golden hair upon the city's battlefields. One of the few Ambonese with the gift of prophecy even engaged painters to commit his visions to canvas, as in one picture dated carefully just days before the conflict, forecasting Ambon's apocalyptic ruin.

Times Rich in Demons

If Christ is at large, so, too, these "times [are] rich in demons."[24] The import of what Michel de Certeau calls a "diabolical crisis" lies both in its disclosure of the fault lines and imbalances permeating a culture and the way it hastens this culture's transformation. In a situation where uncertainty reigns, the taken-for-granted social arrangements and values of everyday existence are shot through with suspicion and hollowed out, and the world shifts intolerably under one's feet. Deviltries then abound as both symptoms and transitional solutions.[25] Ambon at war was no exception, and religion became a privileged language through which much uncertainty found expression. There are good reasons for this in Ambon, as well as in the larger context of post-Suharto Indonesia, to which I will soon turn. First, however, I will offer a brief sense of the devil at work in Ambon and, relatedly, the enhanced publicity of religion, together with its newfound mobility.

A Protestant minister with whom I spoke on several occasions attributed much of Ambon's turmoil and the long-term ferocity of the conflict to the widespread use of magic or *occultisme* on both sides. The GPM's head of Pastoral Counseling recalled the vast collection of protective cloth cords (I. *tali kain*) that he and others had amassed during extra afternoon prayer sessions, held at 3:00 P.M. for four consecutive years beginning in 1999, at the GPM's head Maranatha Church. In the first four months alone, four large boxes were filled with the talismanic cords, voluntarily surrendered by Ambonese at the conclusion of these daily prayer sessions and subsequently burned. Symptomatic of a much larger problem, the tenacious hold of pagan or tribal religion (I. *agama suku*) at the core of Ambonese existence aggravated and amplified the conflict. For the minister, this presence was exemplified in the deployment of magic by Christians and Muslims alike during the war, whether to protectively "seal" their villages against enemy assaults, call upon the spirits of former warlords from around the Moluccas (A.M. *kapitan-kapitan*), or invoke the martial prowess of ancient times, for which Moluccans are renowned throughout Indonesia. Initially I took him to mean that beneath the successive waves of world religions that had washed over the Moluccas—Islam, Roman Catholicism, Protestantism—and been "received" by the local population, what he called the tribal "nucleus" might actually be understood as unifying Muslims and Christians. Seen in this light, they would be equally Ambonese if, at the same time, equally troubled by a persistent paganism. On another occasion, however, when the minister described for me the diabolical possession and exorcism of a Javanese convert to Protestantism, a woman who had been possessed by the (Muslim) daughter of the Sultan of North Moluccan Ternate, it became clear that no unity could in fact be assumed.

To make a long story short, the possessions began in a Christian prayer group of five persons when the woman in question introduced to its members a small stone that had been given to her by a woman clad solely in black. Strange things began to happen. Whoever held the stone fell ill, while the entire group started to pray as Muslims—with their hands held out flat and open in front of them as if supporting the Qur'an. Possession here appeared to lay bare the fault lines of a highly fraught, religiously mixed urban society—it came via a Muslim convert to Christianity, turned a Christian prayer group into a Muslim *pengajian* (a Qur'anic reading session) and introduced the formerly powerful, ancient North Moluccan sultanate of Ternate into the core of Christian worship.[26] Rather than a pure if problematic tribal core around which successive competing world religions wrapped over the centuries, or even the realities of a city barricaded and blocked off into distinctive Muslim and Christian quarters, possession disclosed and unleashed a devilish mix, where what was once Muslim and once Christian—or where these, respectively, had been held to begin and end—collapsed violently into one another. As René Girard once so aptly put it, "It is not the differences but the loss of them that gives rise to violence."[27] Such, indeed, are the symptoms of a world where numerous entities—here

"religion," or *agama*, foremost among them—are in turmoil and undergo radical mutation. Seen in this light, all the dialectical tension between Muslims and Christians in
Ambon betrays the historically deep-rooted entanglement of the two communities more
than any separation. With the breakdown of important differences and increased porosity
between them, the mutual beholdenness of the two communities has given way to a sense
of threat. The Christians especially feel embattled, even haunted and possessed by the
Muslim other.

Previously, the relations between Muslims and Christians had, by and large, been
kept in place through a variety of factors, including the Suharto regime's policies toward
religion, a colonial and postcolonial history in Ambon of Christian privilege and Muslim
marginality, the intervillage *pela* alliances that conjoin some Ambonese Muslim and
Christian communities,[28] and the tacit understanding that living together meant living
not only with difference but even with occasional violence. Under the Dutch, relations
among the proponents of different faiths had been ordered and their places of residence
commonly segregated, whether by village or in cities by religiously and ethnically defined
quarters. In the Moluccas, for example, not only did a segregated settlement pattern separate Muslims and Christians but to this day Protestants and Catholics tend to reside
separately as well. This has a clear colonial legacy: in the late nineteenth century, when
Catholic missionaries aimed to establish a station in the area, they were instructed to
avoid Ambon, where Protestants had long prevailed, and were offered the southeastern
Moluccas for their proselytizing instead.[29]

More generally, in the immediate postindependence period, Indonesian public life
could be described by the presence of diverse *aliran* or "educational and associational
currents."[30] At the time, these became reconfigured as political parties, which, in turn,
were identified with clusters of nationalist organizations based on shared experiences,
institutional affiliations, and religious or secular persuasions. As scholars of Indonesia
have often remarked, this kind of public ordering recalls the system of *verzuiling*, or
pillarization, prevalent in the Netherlands from the late nineteenth century through the
mid-1960s. Following this form of governmentality, social and political life was organized
around religious difference, with society comprising a series of religiously marked pillars,
each with its own political party, media institutions, and universities—an ordering so
extensive that at the village level bakeries, butchers, greengrocers, and the like were all
informally pillarized as well. The Dutch colloquial expression "two religions on one pil-
low, the Devil lies in between" captures the logic of this sociopolitical arrangement.

As political scientist John Sidel observes of the Moluccas, the pattern of strict spatial
segregation between Muslims and Christians characteristic both of villages scattered
across the region and of urban neighborhoods (I. *kampung*) in Ambon "was reinforced
by government policies [under Suharto] prohibiting interfaith marriages, expanding religious instruction in schools, and promoting a pattern of recruitment into the bureaucracy
through networks based on religious affiliation."[31] In the wake of the 1965–66 massacres

of communists and alleged communists that brought Suharto to power, having—as opposed to "not yet having" (I. *belum beragama)*—one of the five officially recognized religions was one way many Indonesians tried to avoid being cast as communists. Under Indonesia's first president, Sukarno, religion had already been enshrined within the state ideology of Pancasila as a crucial criterion of national membership. There it figures as the first of Pancasila's five principles, namely, the belief in a Supreme Being (I. *Sila Ketuhanan yang Maha Esa).*[32] Much as the public crafting of religion as a privileged tool of government became extended under Suharto—with the equation of "the having of a religion" and citizenship drawn increasingly tight—so, too, did Pancasila itself undergo transformation. In 1985, for instance, it was declared the "sole basis [*azas tunggal]*" of the state—styled a Negara Pancasila or "Pancasila State."[33] For ordinary Indonesians the close link between citizenship and religion was codified on the KTP (I. *Kartu Tanda Penduduk),* or citizen's identity card, which demanded allegiance to one of the alleged monotheistic religions recognized by the state: Islam, Protestantism, Catholicism, Hinduism, Buddhism.[34]

The Indonesian state's partial withdrawal in the wake of Suharto's May 1998 stepdown and the launching in 2000 of a national program of decentralization introduced crisis into this form of governmentality based on the state's strict apportioning and vigilance over the identities of the country's citizens.[35] Religion was foremost among these state-enjoined identities. Following Sidel, "the boundaries of identities and interests in Indonesian society, long determined by a fixed, hierarchical source of recognition firmly anchored in the state and centered in Jakarta, were left in flux. . . . If under a centralized, closed authoritarian regime, claims of representation had been imposed and enforced from above, now under conditions of political openness and competition the boundaries of religious authority have to be affirmed from without and from below."[36] Generally speaking, this situation accounts in part for the outbreak in many parts of Indonesia of what sociologists conventionally call "horizontal" violence. In Ambon, specifically, it forms an important backdrop to the proliferation of Jesus portraits that proclaim the powers of Protestant religion and, with these, the installation, as I argue below, upon the ruins of recent warfare of a source of authorized recognition for the Ambonese Christian community as well.

Often in Ambon and occasionally elsewhere in Indonesia, journalists, NGO activists, or even some religious leaders would object to me that, appearances notwithstanding, religion was not in fact what lay at the heart of the city's conflict. By way of explanation, they commonly sought refuge in conspiracy theories, allusions to military connivings, or to the rotten politics of the state, identified simply as "Jakarta" or *Pusat,* the Center. Take, for instance, Sammy Titaley, the renowned Ambonese minister and GPM Synode head during the first part of the conflict: "I told the President, Gus Dur—I said how is it that you don't have the means to stop this. We met the American Ambassador and he said 'your government has no willing [sic] to stop the conflict in Ambon.'" Invoking a common Ambonese expression for the province's alleged manipulation by Jakarta politicians, he summarized the situation: "Other folk beat drums [in Jakarta], we dance to them [in Ambon] [A.M. *orang lain pukul tifa, kami yang nari*]." He continued:

> Everyone went to Jakarta to ask for help in 2001 during the Megawati era. They went to General this, General that, and they asked them, right? And then these Generals would reply "What, you mean Ambon isn't destroyed yet?" "No way!" Then when the fighting was still going on, a Commander was sent to Ambon who was in charge of all the soldiers from Java who were based in the Moluccas. A Balinese, he was called the Territorial Commander. In Ambon he went to the Maranatha Church, to visit it, right. So we talked there and all kinds of people gathered around, [he said], "Boy, I'm from Java, right, and as far as I knew Ambon had already been leveled." So just imagine how confused this one Commander was. Amazing. This means that as far as they were concerned [in Jakarta] Ambon had already been destroyed. So this means that we can know right away what kind of plot (I. *scenario*) was going on here, right?[37]

During such conversations, especially journalists and NGO activists would, each in their own fashion, often go on to explain how religion had been instrumentalized under Suharto or, in a somewhat different sense, made what anthropologists call "good to think with." In either case, whether following Sidel's argument concerning a nationwide crisis afflicting the constitution of religious authority in Indonesia today or the former New Order regime's codification of religion as a privileged instrument of governmentality amenable to a range of different objectives—including the production of violence—the absolute centrality of religion is underscored.

To designate those forms of societal difference that were banned as either topics of discussion or sources of conflict, the Suharto regime coined the acronym SARA—comprising the first letters of the Indonesian words for tribe-religion-race-class (I. *Suku–Agama–Ras–Antar-golongan*). With the fall of the authoritarian regime, SARA has been lifted and we find, along with violence conducted in the name of religion, a new openness toward and about the subject. Religion is a privileged topic of discussion on television, the radio, and the Internet, as well as in offices, houses, markets, and the streets; it is the recurrent focus of a wide variety of public fora, call-in programs on television and the radio, and interfaith dialogues and initiatives; and it is often at the center of the ubiquitous *semiloka*, or seminars, held all over the country since the New Order's demise. The Suharto state was the arbiter that allotted religious identity and also guaranteed that religion remained in its proper place; with the reconfiguration of the state post-Suharto and its retreat on some fronts, religion appears to be obeying a logic of its own—albeit one that was enabled and energized by the New Order's particular mode of governmentality.

Kept under tight wrap during the long Suharto era, religion is out in the open in Indonesia today, with religions bursting from their allotted places in public search of audiences, bodies, and spaces.

If religion enjoys a newfound openness, it is also very much on the move. The assertive portraits and murals erected by Ambon's Protestant Christians emerge within a highly mobile religious terrain. One clear indication of this mobility is the move out of Christian homes of religious iconography—an iconography that, until recently, was decidedly small-scale and confined to calendars and the like. Another is what for lack of a better term might be called a larger "iconographic turn," of which both the Christian pictures' mobility and their monumentalization are crucial components. The particular Protestant tradition that since the seventeenth century has historically been present in Ambon is, even among Protestants, a radically iconoclastic one, deriving from the Calvinist Dutch Reformed Church, of which Ambon's GPM is a direct descendant.[38]

Besides the other factors previously named, an additional factor probably at work in this "iconographic turn" is the unprecedented rapprochement of Ambon's Protestants and the city's Catholic population, both during and since the war. This rapprochement between what in the Moluccas had always been religious rivals is evident in the use by Protestants, during the war, of Catholic rosaries and pocket-size prayer books produced by nuns as protective amulets.[39] It also informs the practice of "pulpit exchange" (I. *tukar mimbar*), according to which a Protestant minister will lead a service in a Catholic church and vice versa, the ecumenical processions of Protestant and Catholic clergy to protest, for instance, the forced conversions of some Moluccans to Islam, and the postwar participation of Protestants in the Catholic Easter Passion parade performed in Ambon's streets. Last but not least, the rapprochement of the Protestants and the Catholics is evident in the iconography itself—not only the very fact of the turn to the iconographic but also the conscious pilfering by Protestant popular painters of some obvious Catholic imagery, such as the Sacred Heart.[40]

Part of this rapprochement has to do with how initially Ambonese Protestants and then the city's Catholics found a common enemy in Islam. Yet beyond the context of the city's war, many Indonesian Christians are both cognizant of and concerned about the increasing presence of Islam in everyday settings across their country. With respect to Islam's current striking visibility and publicity in Indonesia, scholars speak of a public Islam manifest, for instance, in the many new mosques erected around the country (often in Middle Eastern style) and in the popularity of Qur'anic reading sessions and typical Muslim fashions like *jilbab* for women and *baju koko* for men, of Muslim clothing fashion shows, and of makeup and skin products stamped with the label *halal*, "permissible."[41] Add to this the rise in the number of Indonesian Muslims performing the *hajj*—some on fancy package tours with five-star services—the resurgence of Islamic print media, the development of new forms of *da'wa*, or proselytizing, such as cyber *da'wa* and cellular *da'wa*, and the burgeoning of Islamic economic institutions, such as banks, insurance houses, credit unions, and so on. All of these developments are, not surprisingly, not lost on Indonesia's Christians.

This general religious outreach is also evident in the self-conscious emphasis by both Muslim and Christian practitioners on the most universalizing dimensions of religion. If Muslims can appeal to the *ummah* as the all-encompassing framework from which their religious identity derives its significance, so, too, Christians seem to be driven by ever more ecumenical aspirations toward what one might call a Christian *ummah*, of sorts. Just as Indonesian Muslims should, if they are in physical and financial condition to do so, perform the *hajj*, so, too, do increasing numbers of Catholics perform their own religious pilgrimages to, for instance, Lourdes. By the same token, the popularity of package tours to the Holy Land is on the rise among Indonesian Protestants. If, then, in an immediate sense the rapprochement between Ambon's Protestants and Catholics has its roots in the city's recent war, in a larger sense it can be seen as part of developments that are not specific to Indonesia but evident elsewhere: the more universal dimensions of religion become elaborated in the context of powerful deterritorializing and globalizing forces. Seen in this light, the proliferation and monumentalization of Jesus portraits in Ambon are compelled by conditions that are simultaneously local, somewhat more than local, and somewhat less than global—they are a consequence, in other words, of anxieties afflicting Ambon's Protestant Christians in the immediate wake of the war and the refiguration of their country post-Suharto. At the same time, they partake of more momentous transformations worldwide in the status and public location of religion.

Like and in the Image of God

With the largely unmoored landscape of Ambon City as backdrop, I will hone in now on the face as a privileged feature of the pictures, singled out not only in the revamped Christian iconography but often in conversation with the painters themselves. If asking *what pictures want* is a good place to start, following this with the question *What does this face want?* and *Whose face is it?* adds precision to the specific desires at work by interrogating the forms used to picture and represent. I understand representation, following Louis Marin in his *Portrait of the King*, in essentially two ways: to represent is to make the absent—the dead man, Marin says—come back, as if he were present and living(a kind of second coming, if you like); it is also to intensify presence with the aim of instituting and valorizing it as a subject of representation, like a birth certificate, a national ID card, or a passport flashed at a border.[42]

Yet if in Marin the portrait constitutes the king as absolute subject with implications and consequences that I will not address here, in Ambon the portraits of Christ constitute the people or the community. This, at any rate, is the general idea. And if, in modern times, a community is commonly constituted in reciprocity with the figure of the state through its many representatives, then the withdrawal of important state tokens throws the community into disarray. It is out of such a distressful void that the Christ pictures emerge—both mirroring and summoning an absent yet desired community for each and every Christian Ambonese. In the case of the absolutist king, a belief in both the effectiveness and the operation of his iconic signs was obligatory, since failing this the monarch would be emptied of all substance (through lack of transubstantiation), leaving only simulacrum. More poignantly, Ambon's Christians, faced with their abandonment by authority, themselves generate authority's monumentalized iconic signs. In so doing, they not only give material form to anxieties about invisibility but also emblematize authority as a numinous source of recognition, in the desire that it might protect, valorize, illuminate, and constitute the Christian Ambonese as a particular community, as a "chosen people." Thus, ideally, through this theologizing move the emblems that Christians erect around the city acquire the community-making force that not only makes possible their reproduction as Christian Ambonese but endows such reproduction with its sanctioned, authoritative foundation. At stake, in other words, is representation in Marin's double sense: both de facto, as presencing, and de jure, as the authorization and valorization of such presence.

Conversations with painters allude to both senses of representation—the assertion *God is/was here* is underscored by the depiction of Christ witnessing his creation in crisis up close, by the claim that Christ is a living God in contrast to the gods of other religions, and by the belief of some in an imminent Second Coming. The intensifying, legitimizing dimension of representation, or that which authorizes and valorizes the subject as a subject of representation, manifests itself in different painters' common focus on the face. One painter said he prays fervently before painting the face of God and insists that he portrays Christ as an adult so that people will know what he looked like as a grown man—more precisely, the grown man of thirty-three who was sentenced to death and subsequently martyred by the Roman Imperial authorities. When I remarked upon the carefully traced frayed edges of the Jesus cameos introduced by this painter into his murals, he invoked the worn edges of old parchment. As in the movies, he explained, the Romans presented their legal decrees and pronouncements to the people on pieces of parchment; unrolled in public, these would be read aloud and hung in prominent places for the populace to see. Unlike the sweaty, fringed characters of Roland Barthes' famous essay, these Romans in films are the exemplars of the republican tradition of law and state authority.[43] Thus, Romanly framed, Jesus' giant mug shot circulates, I suggest, among the beleaguered Christian Ambonese as an appropriately oversized, monumentalized, community ID.

But how does this work? In another conversation, this particular painter—let's call him John—supported his statements about the face by quoting from the Bible. We are created, he said, "like and in the image of God (*serupa dan segambar Tuhan*)"—a claim I often heard echoed in the city, whether from church pulpits or citizens' mouths. Anticipating objections, the painter enacted for me an imaginary conversation:

> There are many versions, no? In Europe they say his face looks like this, in America they say it looks like that—maybe different. There are many, many [different] appearances, right? . . . earlier I said that us humans are created like and in the image of God. This means that his nose, his mouth, his eyes are like ours. It doesn't matter then what kind of appearance [it is], maybe it's not like mine, but the important thing is that it is *like and in our image*. This is the essence for me, this in itself is what makes me paint. So sometimes people say, "He, here Jesus has a different face, this Jesus face is different," [but I answer] "No, that's not true, that face is also like your face, right? It also has a nose, it also has a mouth, it also has eyes, the point being: the face of Jesus is like your face.

More than merely creating a glossy surface, the aim here appears to be to install a face that faces and illuminates the Christian beholder, a face that is your face, that is *our* face, the generalized face of the Christian Ambonese community. John often compares his paintings to a Protestant minister's sermon. Whereas the minister relies on words, he produces images to subtly sway people to conduct themselves as better Christians. Indeed, according to John, this is also the best and perhaps only way to proceed with tough Ambonese—through quiet influence rather than direct admonition. John understands his work as dialogic, yet he also clearly doubts whether his imaginary interlocutor is as firmly in place as he would like—hence the imaginary conversation he enacted for me in which he tries to persuade a spectator—who for him is interchangeable with all other Christian Ambonese—of the intimate identity between the spectator's own face and that of Jesus. Uncertainty animates this entire imaginary exchange, as it also fuels the desire to find a face for Christian Ambonese. Recall how John insists that the face of Jesus is like and *in our image*. This for him is "the essence," and it is, he claims, what makes him paint. He paints, in other words, over and over again, a monumentalized face infused with the desire that it will reflect back to us *our image*. By implication, *our face*, as Christian Ambonese, has become obscured; in the city's postwar context, *our image*, its status and very existence, is elusive and up for grabs.

At stake and at risk here are the very conditions for the production of the identity of Ambonese as a uniquely Christian community. This is less the narrow production of *Christians* with a capital *C*—under conditions reducible either to theology or to religion—than the production of *Ambonese* Christians, that is, in terms of a historically sedimented sense of entitlement, first under the Dutch colonizers and subsequently within the Indonesian Republic, with corresponding assumptions of superiority and privilege, then the fears and phantasms unleashed during the war.[44] As in the larger landscape of the city, what authorized, legitimized, and kept Ambon's Christians more or less in place, offering an image to them of who and what they are and locating them within the Indonesian nation-state, no longer applies. Like blood coursing from faucets or uncanny shadows flitting across church walls, these eruptions of strangeness and uncertainties about the sources of identity have violently unsettled the conventional claims and wisdoms of what was once an everyday more or less religiously mixed urban lifeworld.[45]

Before the war, God presumably gazed upon Ambon from afar; looking down upon the city and its inhabitants, he saw that it was good. There was then no strangeness to the Christian images in the city—the innocuous angels, Jesus majestically poised on clouds—none of this was out of the local Christian ordinary; all of it assumed an orderly Christian community devoutly in place. Strikingly, the essential foreignness of this God or the many other forces and phantasms fed through him only became apparent within the desperate, radical dislocations of the war. Only in such circumstances did a gap open between Ambonese and the authorizing foreign gaze—itself refracting, once again, a host of multiply mediated and signifying capacities. Beyond ordinary everyday uncertainties, only then did such a gap intolerably loom. Only then did Ambonese feel abandoned and forlorn, and only then, too, did Christian pictures migrate from church interiors and set themselves up in public as monuments to community. It is this gap that local painters and those who support them aim to bridge and cover over when they depict Christ coming up close.[46] This pictorial form of protesting too much animates the proliferation of Jesus billboards and murals across the city; it also moves the painter John to persuade a score of imaginary others of the perfect fit between their own faces as interchangeable Christians and that of Christ.

This Face Wants YOU

This face wants YOU—this is what the Christian murals say to the pedestrians, motorcycles, cars, and minibuses that pass them by. It is also what they say to the young, often un- or underemployed men who in many Christian neighborhoods hang out on raised platforms facing the mega-pictures—passing their time, chatting, smoking cigarettes, and awaiting the odd motorbike-taxi customer. Grouped into neighborhood associations with their own names and emblems, these young men, by and large, are those who sponsor the pictures, supplying the painters with paint, cigarettes, and snacks while they work, assisting them, offering occasional upkeep when the murals are done, and decorating them with lanterns on the eve of important Christian holidays. They are also those who, in the wake of war, are, with the exception of refugees, in many respects the most adrift, with their past clouded and often violent, their present precarious, and their future up for grabs.[47] Perhaps most interestingly, due to their age and gender they inhabit a place at authority's edge: their creative activities are not sanctioned by the local churches, and they are the object of recurrent state suspicion and surveillance.[48] It is these young men whom the painter John has in mind when he describes his murals as pictorial *khotbah*, or sermons, and he claims some success—sitting across from Christ's face, these men are less inclined to drink and fool around with women, or so John says.

Much like gang emblems, the pictures erected at the gateways of Christian neighborhoods and strategic sites in the city throw up strict boundary markers in an already radically territorialized urban situation. Commonly they stand on the same site or are next to the very same structure as the command and communication posts (*posko*) set up during the war—places where prayers were said and trumpets sounded before battle, the neighborhood watch was based, and multiple other strategic and social needs were addressed as, indeed, they continue to be today. Gigantic glossy surfaces, like the billboard advertisements whose location they often usurp, the Jesus pictures simultaneously "gate" the community and brand it as decidedly Christian. A border phenomenon through and through, the pictures extend an invitation outward—this face wants You, stranger—to look back, authorize, legitimize, and thereby bestow on us, Christian Ambonese, a face. At the same time, the billboard face that is God's face and *your* face also faces inward, isolating Christians among their own "comforting" images and thereby intensifying, in Marin's terms, the subject's representation, something that in this case implicitly stakes out a source of legitimization—tenuous as it may be—that is like, in the image of, yet also different from the seeing of a state.[49]

Comforting as they may seem to Christians, these pictures intimate many risks—marking a blind spot, they reenact the hyper-visibility of Christians against the deep shadow of Muslim invisibility that, more aggressively than elsewhere in the archipelago, distinguishes Ambon's history. Today they do so in circumstances that are radically at odds with those productive of that particular phantasm. Potentially the paintings claim a source of validation for the community beyond the state, even if, or, more likely, because the Jesus portraits refract the Citizen's Identity Card so crucial to the state-seeing legitimacy and the fiction of state protection propagated by Suharto.[50] Implicitly, at least, and without the Ambonese themselves or the Indonesian authorities noticing it, Ambon's sidewalk painters and their young male supporters have hijacked the crucial state prerogative of assigning identity and belonging and have bent it to their own designs. Inhabiting a place at authority's edge, they replicate and reinstate the former patriarchal authority of the New Order state, claiming it for themselves.

A more immediate risk is the inherent violence at the core of these Christian pictures, though this, too, leads potentially in different directions. Born out of conflict and installed as an intimate part of the scene of war, Christ at large is an emblem of violence, in which the difference between self-love and other-directed aggression is hard to discern. Lamenting their situation during the war, Christians frequently claim "Christ was our only weapon" as they go on to describe the flimsy bows and arrows, makeshift rifles, homemade poisons, and occasional black magic (*ilmu*) with which they aimed to protect themselves. One picture of Jesus of the Sacred Heart—a clear instance, as mentioned

FIGURE 10   Motorbike-taxi driver and mural. Ambon, 2006.

FIGURE 11   Mural across from motorbike-taxi stand. Ambon, 2006.

FIGURE 12   Motorbike-taxi stand. Ambon, 2006.

earlier, of Catholic iconography's influence and therein the rapprochement of Ambon's Protestants and Catholics during the war—looks to some like an exploding bomb encased in barbwire. Seen in this light, it vividly intimates the easy collapse between Christ and violence. Bullet holes with bloody skin bent back to frame motorbike-association emblems or pistols in the place of heads on torsos, inscribed with local insignia, are also popular.

Such signs are a common part of a wider masculine Moluccan youth culture. This culture undoubtedly draws energy and identity from both the recent war and religion, but it is also, crucially, based on consumption. The young motorbike-taxi drivers I hung out with in Ambon during the summers of 2005 and 2006, and those I interviewed in April of 2006 in the North Moluccan city of Ternate (where the population is predominantly Muslim), draw inspiration and emblems from loud musical groups like the Sex Pistols, Guns and Roses (both allegedly with DVD covers boasting bullet holes reminiscent of heraldic shields), Limp Biskit, Linkin Park, or the Indonesian *Reformasi* cult singer Iwan Fals. Beyond the consumerism of youth, the Christian billboards often stand on the same kind of location, along the city's main thoroughfares, as commercial advertisements—if, indeed, they have not actually been painted over billboards, as was the first Christ portrait in the city, which overlay a former cigarette advertisement. A study of the stratigraphy of the Christian billboards and murals would reveal other group markers as well, such as those of political parties and soccer teams.

Given all of this, and notwithstanding attempts by the painter John and others to foster a face to face identification between Ambon's Christians and Jesus Christ, the ways in which the paintings have arisen in the orphaned postwar landscape of the city may invite such a focused form of looking less than the more distracted kind commonly identified with the urban passerby. Yet both Christians and Muslims can often recall from memory certain Jesus pictures or details thereof, and at certain times of the year the pictures do invite more specific forms of engagement. On the eve of holidays, for instance, the pictures are repainted and illuminated, and Christians of the neighborhood have their photos taken before them, much as, during the war, young men similarly posed for their portraits holding weapons and framed by Christ's face behind them.[51]

In short, the billboards beg the question of what the limits of the face are: When is the Jesus face a face, of sorts, and for whom—a face that looks back at the observer, that recognizes and legitimizes the Christian community? When is it a brand, an emblem, a boundary marker, or simply another advertisement? And when is it no longer a face but a stereotype instead? All of these possibilities are undoubtedly at work in the Jesus pictures, depending upon who "consumes" them, under what conditions, at what locations, and at what times. To be sure, as I have argued, there is an attempt to install and monumentalize a source of recognition for the Ambonese Christian community. There is also the impulse to reproduce the Christian iconographic canon qua canon or, in other words, to reiterate the familiar and stereotypical. And there is the place of these pictures within both the larger media world and the more immediate media ecology of which they form a part—an Indonesian urban landscape where the portraits and murals stand side by side, compete with, blend and fade into cigarette and cell phone ads, army- and police-sponsored banners mimicking—usually poorly—Ambonese Malay language and calling for anything from postwar reconciliation and peace to proper garbage disposal, and myriad announcements of public events: Islamic fashion shows, calls from universities for student registration, Christian pop music performances, motorbike rallies, and so on.

Given these different possibilities, it is difficult really to gauge the import of the violence entailed in the Christian pictures. As with most things, only circumstances can tell or influence the kinds of inflections these may take. A final risk intimated by Ambon's Christian billboards and murals, perhaps the biggest of all, is that these "comforting" pictures represent—inevitably—no more than a passing consolation for Ambon's Christians, especially for the young men who day after day sit before them, facing or not facing a recent history of violence, the bleak conditions of the present, and a future holding little promise. Staking out territory in so many different ways, these paintings offer little possibility of moving beyond it.

Renewing Time

Charismatic Renewal in a Conservative Reformed Church

Peter Versteeg

Time is an important structure of social life. As an image of life and its phases of growth and decay, it is associated with qualities such as endurance and transformation. As a social construction, time is a narrative through which events and nonevents are ordered in relation to people. Within society, time sets some crucial standards for living. Both individuals and societies try to reproduce themselves and try to keep themselves healthy, sometimes in conflicting ways. They do not always succeed in these efforts, and they sometimes run out of time.

Religions create and inhabit their own time to avoid running out of time. Religious time frames, comprising both narratives and ritualizations, may stress rejuvenation of a small group, securing its survival from one generation to another. On the one hand, religions can impose their calendars on the secular, making the secular "profane," that is, a reality preceding the sacred and awaiting its fulfillment through sacralization.[1] Some religions, on the other hand, stress a golden age that serves as an example to the present. Under certain conditions they will try to force the rebirth of that golden age in the present, sometimes violently. Some religions perceive other time frames as threatening. This is so in societies where cultural and religious pluralization increases, stimulating competition between worldviews and their corresponding time frames. Secularization poses another threat to religion because it dictates its own sense of time, which may carry the message that time has lost its ultimate meaning. A secularized society is unable to mediate time for individuals or to offer a passage through time, since it lacks a "transcendent vantage point."[2] A similar observation can be made about the differentiation of social domains, in which every domain has its own time frame, without being hierarchically integrated into an overarching narrative. Society moves people from temporality to temporality within a highly individualized time frame, which carries its own meaning but lacks a promise of ultimate perfection.

In this essay I will explore how a particular form of Protestant Christianity deals with this aspect of secularization by creating its own time frame, moving beyond its tradition. Specifically, I will examine how a church produces time through practices and experiences in order to survive in relation to secularizing and traditional time frames.[3] The church studied renews time by creating moments in which God's presence and future break through, a strategy typical of many forms of charismatic and Pentecostal Christianity worldwide.[4] This strategy creates a sense of time that is understood as a social and religious revitalization but that is at the same time highly subjectivized.

First, I will situate the Netherlands Reformed Church (NRC) of Houten, the church I have studied, within the Dutch Protestant landscape and describe its nature as a renewed church. Despite the fact that charismatic renewal involves many more aspects of church life, I will, second, focus on the church service. Third, I will discuss how charismatic practices introduce a different time frame in relation to tradition and to the secular. Finally, I will draw some conclusions that will lead to questions about time as an angle in the study of charismatic/Pentecostal religion.

NRC Houten

NRC Houten is part of the Netherlands Reformed Churches, a small conservative Reformed denomination of 31,000 members, which originated in the 1967 schism in the Reformed Churches in the Netherlands *Vrijgemaakt* (RCN-V).[5] Houten is an expanding suburban town near the city of Utrecht, in the center of the Netherlands, with nearly 44,000 inhabitants. NRC Houten is an example of the growing influence, in the last fifteen years, of charismatic/evangelical beliefs and practices in Dutch mainline Protestant churches. Although this influence has been noticed by researchers, its extent and nature have been little documented. Protestant churches have long treated evangelical movements as alien elements that, in the end, are not to be taken too seriously.[6] The relationship between Protestantism and evangelicalism has a long history, however: for example, mainline Protestants have sung evangelical songs and have visited evangelical rallies and campaigns for almost a century. One of the key players in the process of evangelicalization is undoubtedly the Evangelical Broadcasting Company (EO), a conservative Christian media organization founded in 1967. The EO has succeeded in attracting Christians from different denominations, and it has become an important platform for the exchange of ideas within Dutch conservative Christianity. Currently, we may safely assume that charismatic/evangelical influences are widespread among Protestants, ranging from moderately liberal/ecumenical congregations to conservative Calvinism. But the nature of these influences is not always clear. Different evangelical streams inside and outside of the churches carry different agendas, and opponents and adherents in the mainline churches have their own interests in portraying evangelicalism in a certain way.

Within this spectrum NRC Houten represents an interesting case, because it is outspoken about its identity as a Reformed church with a charismatic/evangelical church praxis.[7] The NRC has an organizational structure that leans toward congregationalism, which means that local churches have great freedom in the way they run their congregations. In practice this stimulates a variety of church styles, ranging from traditional Reformed to evangelical. Generally speaking, the NRC has been more open to evangelical influences than other conservative Reformed denominations, such as the RCN-V and the Christian Reformed Churches. In this respect, the NRC is also more liberal about questions of gender and church offices. Women deacons are common, and since 2004 the offices of elder and minister have also been open to women.

NRC Houten started in 1988 as an independent congregation, following an influx of NRC members who had moved from Utrecht to Houten.[8] From its inception, the church has had an open and experimental nature, evident in a variety of church services, an increasing participation of church members in them, a diverse song repertoire, and the attention given to children and youngsters in the services. The small congregation has shown a pioneering spirit, reflecting the situation of Houten as a place for uprooted and young newcomers. As one of the older members says: "They started without tradition but they wanted to be faithful to the Bible." The early pioneers had a clear sense that the idea of what it meant to be a Netherlands Reformed congregation had changed and that they now had the opportunity to do it their own way. Starting with a few families in the 1980s, NRC Houten has now grown to more than one thousand members, with a growth rate of 10 percent per year. NRC Houten has three services every Sunday, each with a different style. Apart from the regular afternoon service, which I will introduce in more detail below, there is a "traditional" morning service and a 1:00 P.M. service, located in the south of Houten, in the vicinity of the newly built neighborhoods of the town. The church has several lay preachers who regularly lead services. NRC Houten does not own a church building but has to rent room for its services. In the near future, the NRC will build its own church, in which different church services will take place. The church has been particularly successful in attracting young families with children—about 40 percent of the congregation is below the age of twenty. Church members have various Christian backgrounds, but most come from one of the Reformed denominations. There has also been some trafficking of believers between the local Protestant congregation and NRC Houten. A small number of members have no Christian background.

In 1993 the church got its own pastor, Westerkamp, a former missionary from Rwanda, who had experienced a personal renewal of his faith in the mission field through his contacts with charismatic Anglicans. This pastor stimulated an outspoken direction and style for NRC Houten within clear theological and practical parameters, emphasizing renewal through the Holy Spirit. Important factors in bringing about this change were the involvement of NRC Houten in the New Wine network and the adoption of the Alpha course, both originating in the Church of England. New Wine is an international charismatic movement that stimulates traditional churches to become open to spiritual renewal through practical Bible teaching, equipping believers through "ministry in the Spirit," and "passionate" worship, terms and practices that echo the impact on charismatic Anglicanism of the late John Wimber and his Vineyard movement.[9] The movement of Vineyard churches started in California in the late 1970s as a spinoff of the so-called Jesus Movement. Vineyard churches are characterized by an informal, laid-back style of belief, accompanied by an affective and sometimes ecstatic form of worship and prayer. A central aspect of this Vineyard-style approach is that ministry is not restricted to gifted religious specialists but every believer can be empowered by the Spirit to pray for healing or prophesy.[10]

In the Netherlands, New Wine is most active in promoting "ministry," a kind of intercessory prayer, through ministry courses and in helping churches start their own programs of church renewal.[11] New Wine also organizes worship and teaching meetings, several yearly national conferences, and a yearly retreat for pastors. In NRC Houten "ministry" has been implemented in the Sunday afternoon church service, and it is used in the prayer pastorate. Many NRC Houten members have received training in "ministry" prayer.

The Alpha course is the other important factor in the charismatic orientation of NRC Houten. Alpha is a low-key evangelistic course aimed at people who are interested in the Christian faith.[12] Although the Alpha course claims to teach Christian "basics," the themes discussed show a clear evangelical emphasis, focusing on the divine inspiration of the Bible, the necessity of being saved through Christ, and the idea of a personal relationship with God. Moreover, Alpha has a distinctly charismatic flavor, emphasizing the work and gifts of the Holy Spirit and culminating in the so-called Holy Spirit weekend. NRC Houten adopted Alpha enthusiastically and with great success: the church claims that many of its new, formerly unchurched converts came straight from the Alpha course.[13] Currently, NRC Houten is greatly involved in the promotion of the Alpha course in churches at the local level as well as in the national organization of Alpha.[14] It is also keen to adopt new products from the Alpha branch, such as the Marriage course, which works with a similar method. Because Alpha is always first introduced to church members, one of its important side effects is internal revitalization. In NRC Houten, for example, the vast majority of the members have done Alpha. The result is that people have the opportunity to reconsider and refresh their beliefs but are also exposed to charismatic teachings and practices, such as the invocation of the Holy Spirit, laying on of hands, and speaking in tongues. In this way, Alpha may shape people toward more charismatic beliefs and expressions.[15]

Effects of renewal are visible in many aspects of church life, creating space for new practices in the fields of prayer, evangelism, the pastorate, and the children's ministry.[16]

Similar developments are visible in the organization of the church, most notably in its move toward a neighborhood-based cell structure, and the church strives to have a staff of paid professional workers. The charismatic-evangelical characteristics of NRC Houten seem to be its main point of attraction for aspiring members, who sometimes live a fair distance from Houten. Indeed, Houten currently is seen as an important hotspot for church renewal in Dutch Protestantism, a fact that became more visible after the conservative Reformed newspaper *Nederlands Dagblad* started writing about the developments in the local NRC. In 2000 a reporter interviewed the pastor and his wife before the first New Wine conference in Houten.[17] Several, sometimes critical, articles from theologians followed. In 2003, Pastor Westerkamp wrote two articles in which he made a plea for more openness to the work of the Holy Spirit in the Reformed churches.[18] The readers' response to these articles was unprecedented for *Nederlands Dagblad*, and it showed that the subject was very controversial in conservative Reformed circles. One reader stated that the knowledge of being saved through grace could become "cold": "I have lived for years with the knowledge of being saved through Jesus. A rational fact that did not affect me. After all, why should it? Grace was enough, now we only had to wait for the Second Coming—no real relationship with God."[19] People who really know what it is to receive grace will become hungry to receive more from God, said this reader, and she testified that her enthusiasm for God started only when she came to know the work of the Holy Spirit. But besides these approving voices there were also doubts and fierce resistance to what was seen by some as a form of spiritual elitism and subjectivism, leading to division within the churches. Longing for "more" became something of a shibboleth: recognized and embraced by some, rejected by others. The media discussion about the work of the Spirit ended in a radio-broadcast debate between Pastor Westerkamp and one of his opponents. Westerkamp kept stating that charismatic renewal was not alien to Reformation theology, and he showed how the two streams could and should benefit from each other. A church in decline needs "more," which means living from the full biblical promise. The church needs the power of the Holy Spirit, who will demonstrate the reality of God's saving grace in the lives of people, believers and nonbelievers alike. This approach to charismatic renewal, which is both church oriented and conservative Reformed, enables the NRC Houten to occupy a specific niche that may appeal to Reformed people who are looking for a more spiritually satisfying way of believing. Within NRC Houten, charismatic renewal is no longer controversial, and the critics have reluctantly accepted that this is the direction their church will take. This does not mean, however, that there is no critique at all. On Pentecost in 2005 one of the lay preachers spoke about the meaning of having received the Holy Spirit. It is wonderful when we speak in tongues and have all kinds of special experiences, said the speaker, but the greatest gift of the Spirit is that we can say "Jesus is Lord!" In a subtle way, this lay preacher proclaimed the importance of faith over charismatic experience, thus affirming a more traditional Reformed discourse about the work of the Holy Spirit.

In and Beyond the Church Service

At first glance, a regular Sunday afternoon service in NRC Houten seems far removed from what one expects to find in a church with a charismatic style. The liturgy looks quite Protestant, focused on the sermon rather than on a dramatic moving by the Holy Spirit, and the people in the congregation are most of the time quite reserved in their expressions. Longstanding members agree: apart from an extended stretch of musical worship, led by a band and a worship leader instead of an organ, and the introduction of "ministry" after the service, liturgical change has not been substantial.

Yet despite the continuity of a Reformed liturgical structure, worship and ministry do represent a change that reflects a wider process of ideological and experiential transformation in this church. In the words of the pastor, this change can be summarized as "expectation," the belief that we may expect God to do more than we can imagine. This "expectation" can be found in the experience of church visitors actually "getting something out of it" because they have a sense that they have the chance to encounter God and be changed in the process. Thus, although musical worship in the Sunday service is rarely as expressive or intimate as in other charismatic or Pentecostal groups, the singing is, for many believers, a very important experience of the relationship between God and the individual or between God and the congregation. As Pastor Westerkamp says, Reformed liturgy is a "hop, skip, and jump" (an expression that means doing something without a clear direction), which does not lead people into the presence of God. The fact that the term *worship* is not translated into Dutch indicates that what is being done is seen as different from traditional congregational singing. Through the use of the term *worship*, NRC music leaders claim an affinity with its charismatic meaning, namely, an event of surrender and spiritual experience. Similarly, the prayers and the sermon conceal a sense that something relevant is happening between God and his children. In his sermons the pastor addresses the reality of God's presence through the working of the gifts of the Spirit, encouraging people to reach for whatever gift God has for them and to use it to serve him. Interestingly, sermons are always concluded with a moment of prayer and silence, in which God's Spirit is invoked to "preach in the heart" of the believers, which is in fact an old Reformed expression. People respond to the blessing at the end of the service by extending their hands in a receiving manner, a gesture that is becoming more common in other Protestant churches. The most visible charismatic expression happens after the service. While the majority of visitors move to the coffee room to get some refreshments and to meet each other, a small group lines up before the stage, waiting their turn to be prayed for. This is called "ministry."

Like *worship*, the term *ministry* is not translated into Dutch. This is primarily done for practical reasons, because in translation the term can have different meanings within the different Christian traditions.[20] *Ministry* is intended here to name a form of individual-directed intercessory prayer, performed by a team of two people. Central to "ministry" is the belief and expectation that the Holy Spirit will enter into the here and now of an individual situation. The attitude of the prayer team and the person being prayed for is one of surrendering to what God wants to do.[21] Deriving straightforwardly from its New Wine origin, "ministry" clearly bears the mark of "ministry time" as it was invented in the Vineyard movement. In Vineyard churches "ministry time" is a moment in the church service when the Holy Spirit is welcomed as a presence within the congregation, where it is believed to reveal certain kinds of needs and problems and to empower believers to "minister" to other people. Strikingly, this kind of prayer can involve every person in the congregation and not just a charismatically gifted religious specialist. This is basically what is happening in "ministry," although the atmosphere is emotionally and physically much more restrained than in Vineyard churches. In practice, every question or need may be addressed through "ministry": for example, asking for strength for a school exam or praying for physical healing. The individual does not pray herself, and the praying team is open to the Spirit, who may respond with encouraging words. Thus there is a sense that God speaks at that moment through the praying team. At the same time, the team looks for a response from the person being prayed for, in order to understand what the Spirit is doing.

Besides the church services, NRC Houten organizes New Wine nights, in which the encounter with God is emphasized much more. Although the worship, teaching, and ministry in these events are similar to the Sunday service, their intensity is much higher. New Wine nights are, indeed, announced as intense events, with "passionate" worship, "inspiring" teaching, and "personal prayer in the power of the Holy Spirit." "Passionate" worship means a longer period of singing, which may include dance, "prophetic" music, and singing in tongues. "Inspiring" teaching means, above all, that there is a close relation between what is being said and how it is put into practice, which happens quite literally in "ministry." People are encouraged to reach for what God has to give to them, and they receive it through the Holy Spirit in a personal time of prayer. "Ministry," the demonstration that God is actually present and involved with everybody personally, is fully integrated into the meeting. New Wine thus offers more room for emotional religious expressions and outspoken charismatic practices, and as such it forms an important part of the charismatic reservoir of the NRC. Contrast to the regular Sunday afternoon service shows that charismatic renewal within a single church is a relative phenomenon, a question of "more" or less, distinguishing different groups within the church. In this respect, New Wine is clearly focused on a specific target group that wants "more," and that focus indicates its bounds within a specific formation of time and space.[22]

Although the Reformed message of salvation through grace is still affirmed as essential, within a strict Reformed framework it is felt to have little relevance for present-day people. The time frame one observes in NRC Houten can be described as a revitalization and regeneration of the historic church in the face of the perils and doubts of the modern world. The Holy Spirit, with its connotation of being the creator of new life and the refiner who will sift out what is dead and impure, is a natural symbol for this.

The Renewal of Time

As context for an interpretation of the time frames in play here and what they mean in relation to secularization, let me first make some broader observations about the way the Christian tradition has dealt with time. The basic Christian time frame is determined by the idea of eternal life, characterized as a time of judgment and final redemption. For the believer, this means that there is a very thin line between life and eternity; he or she must be prepared to stand the test when the end has come. For the church, it means knowing that one day time will end for everyone. So the church must be prepared, as well. Both believer and church therefore have to buy time through redemptive means or by taking care of the redemption of others. Throughout Christian history, anxieties about running out of time have resulted in various strategies. The end as a future event whose timing became less and less evident made a theology of the "meantime" necessary.[23] From a theological perspective, the Eucharist is a perfect example of this, as it belongs to the past, present, and future at the same time. In the Eucharist, eternity arrives within time as the real presence of the dead and risen Christ, a moment when God is present to be consumed by believers. Consumption here means enduring time until time has finally ended. But the church also invented means to buy time after death, such as the concept of Purgatory. With the advent of Protestantism, time became far more individualized. Protestants could no longer cling to the earlier ritualizations of an immediate and sacred time but had to attune their ears to the Word, through which they could hear God speaking in their conscience. Time could no longer be saved in a religious way; rather, salvation had to happen within a secularized, chronological time frame. With the arrival of evangelicalism, other narratives and ritualizations became more important, such as millennialism, which is a way of speeding the end of time. For many evangelicals, the baptism of believers became a central liturgical practice, signifying the break with a sinful past and the transition to God's future.

In the twenty-first-century case of NRC Houten, we witness another way of dealing with time. Charismatic renewal should be seen as an important strategy for survival against the background of rapidly declining Christian churches. It is a social and religious revitalization of a local congregation, which leads to more participation by members, multiplication of church ministries, and the attraction of new believers. Renewal is a particular narrative, which shows a way out of a tradition that many feel has become lifeless. Indeed, many believe that without renewal tradition cannot live very long. Therefore we may call it a revitalization of "Reformed tradition" too, although it is clear that the meaning of Reformed tradition is still a matter of debate. A crisis of tradition seems imminent, however, since many believers see tradition as being unable to bring the past into the present. After all, what is the relevance of someone dying for you if it does not relate to your daily life? Within the time frame of renewal, the charismatic moments of personally encountering God in worship and "ministry" are crucial, because it is there that sacred time breaks through, creating a contrast to the meaningless time of the secularized everyday, as well as revitalizing the dead time of tradition.

If we look more closely at the details of particular liturgical practices in NRC Houten, we see how individual experiences are linked to this renewal time frame. Clearly, religious experience is the most important thing NRC Houten has to offer to its members. This must be viewed against the backdrop of secularization as a force that makes religious meanings relative and private. It is difficult to be a conservative Christian without having some sense of proof that what one believes is indeed true, given that one is daily confronted with a reality that questions this truth. Experiencing the reality of God through the Holy Spirit is a powerful strategy for acknowledging this truth and overcoming doubt. The New Wine nights show that these charismatic moments of experience can be enhanced. Here we see precisely where tradition fails and what the time frame of renewal accomplishes, namely, making God present in the here and now through individual experience.

The personal nature of the experience, being something intimate between the individual and God, also points in another direction, namely, to the fact that this sacred time is itself secularized. Danièle Hervieu-Léger has stated that, as a result of secularization, religious language becomes more and more instrumentalized in order to fit subjective experience. She argues that, whereas in the Christian tradition healing was once a metaphor for salvation, something that would ultimately happen in a reality after this life, in the modern world this relation has become inverted: salvation means healing in the specific sense of finding complete emotional and social fulfillment.[24] Practices such as affective musical worship and "ministry" are thus therapeutic strategies to heal the self of the demands and traumas of the everyday world. From the perspective of the NRC, this subjective turn is only natural, because it is in the private encounter with God that a relationship is restored and people can receive a sense of purpose and meaning in their lives. They believe that this is how God wants to work to reach people, and they would therefore rather speak of an adaptation of language than of instrumentalization. The time of tradition speaks a language of waiting and is therefore unable to address the needs and questions of people living in a secularized culture, whereas in the time of renewal God speaks in many different ways to touch many different people.

In an interview with a critical NRC member, it became clear to me how different the senses of time are in the tradition and renewal. This member commented on charismatic influence in the church by comparing Israel with the New Testament church. Israel, in his view, had no real sense of the heavenly Canaan but instead wanted to inherit the land, whereas the New Testament church knew that its destiny was not in this life but in an eternal place. In the context of the interview, it was clear whom he saw as Israel: the charismatic-evangelical majority in the church, who, from his point of view, were too busy bringing heaven on earth. Although this is the view of someone who does not adhere to the charismatic renewal in his church, it shows clearly that charismatic experience means renewing time by affirming that God can break through secular reality with gifts of love and healing. Where traditional critics see the charismata as something from the past, without any use in the present-day church, the charismatics see them as signs of the future intervening in the present. If the Spirit did not move, the reality of God would indeed belong to a different time, and the church would die.

Conclusion

In this essay, I have attempted to show how a particular religious option creates different time frames that buy time to regenerate the religious system. We have seen how time is molded through affective narrative and ritualization to make possible the immediate experience of a sacred presence. More comparative research should be done on other specific cases to explore how different religious forms produce time frames that reinterpret people's experiences of living in a world of pluralizing and fragmenting structures. Although the relation between religion and time is a theoretical question, it should be dealt with in an empirical, preferrably ethnographic, way. Only then can we begin to see how in the present age religious time frames, in particular those that belong to successful religions, compete with other time frames linked to specific sociocultural contexts. Thus distinguishing specific configurations of time will enhance our understanding of the attraction of certain religions for large numbers of people. In this way, we can begin to develop a more systematic approach to how time is linked up with and created by religious practice and power.

PART V

Religion, Politics, and Law

Neutralizing Religion; or, What Is the Opposite of "Faith-based"?

Winnifred Fallers Sullivan

The Center for Studies in Criminal Justice at the University of Chicago Law School held a two-day conference in May 2001 entitled "Faith-Based Initiatives and Urban Policy."[1] The principal focus of the conference was the then relatively new use of private "faith-based" social service agencies in addressing the needs of the urban poor. Could churches replace or supplement government agencies by delivering social services in a more effective manner? Speakers and participants were largely expert in sociology or criminal justice. None were in religious studies, however loosely defined. From time to time, the question would surface as to exactly what "faith-based" meant and whose faith determined the nature of such initiatives. One participant made the suggestion that in the context of urban church/police partnerships the "faith" element encouraged the attitude that "at-risk" youth were to be thought of as "children of God."[2] Children of God, the argument went, are understood to be capable of personal transformation and therefore would not be treated by law enforcement as part of a permanent underclass. In other words, religion could be useful because it helped the law to be a more effective control mechanism. Faith-based initiatives were to be judged by whether they were useful in reducing street crime.

The last session of the Chicago conference addressed the constitutional issues surrounding state funding of such faith-based initiatives. Michael McConnell, now a judge on the U.S. Court of Appeals for the Tenth Circuit, outlined the last fifty years of constitutional jurisprudence on the establishment of religion. Moving rapidly from *Everson v. Board of Education* to *Employment Division v. Smith* to the White House Office on Faith-Based Initiatives, he observed that provisions in recent welfare legislation guaranteeing "charitable choice" had simply made a long-overdue correction in First Amendment interpretation, one that ended discrimination against religion.[3] Discrimination could be seen in the past use by the Court of the words "pervasively sectarian" to describe religious institutions and activities that could not constitutionally receive state aid. They were, he said, actually code words for "Roman Catholic." Their use had signaled an anti-Catholic bias that underlay and determined the Court's establishment clause jurisprudence over the course of most of the twentieth century. McConnell concluded with the view that "pervasively sectarian" had more recently come to signal a bias on the part of the Court against all religion rather than just against Catholics. Now, with the law mandating charitable choice, he said, that new take on an old bigotry had itself been vanquished.

Scholars of American religion and law would by and large agree that anti-Catholicism has historically been one motivating factor in the development of church-state doctrine in this country at least since wide-scale Catholic immigration began in the 1830s. Moreover, the words "pervasively sectarian" have certainly carried and partially concealed a heavy Protestant bias against Catholics and Catholic institutions.[4] Such a subtext can still be read without much effort even in more recent opinions of the Court.[5] The argument by McConnell and the proreligion lobby today is that this widely acknowledged anti-Catholicism has been insidiously succeeded by a generalized hostility to all religion as the single motivation for keeping the wall of separation high. Patently, the argument then goes, because anti-Catholic bigotry is bad, antireligious bigotry is also bad. Charitable choice is succeeding, on this reading, in ending discrimination against "religion in general" and restoring the First Amendment religion clauses to the "original meaning" intended by the founders, namely, as a protection for, not against, religion.

McConnell's highly compressed and rhetorically skillful account of the history of First Amendment interpretation (and he is not alone in espousing it—it is orthodoxy for the new religionists in the academic legal community[6]) is a breathtaking revision of the history of the Supreme Court's First Amendment jurisprudence. It is certainly of a piece with a much broader effort to rewrite the history of law and religion in the United States, perhaps even the history of American constitutionalism. But let us put aside for a moment whether this is an accurate retelling of this piece of legal history. If you are in the business of worrying about what religion is and what words should be used to talk about it, you should worry about this easy equivalence of anti-Catholic bigotry with what McConnell and others term hostility to all religion.[7] It is fairly easy historically to identify what we mean by anti-Catholicism in the United States, and it is fairly easy to see what is repellant in it. What is meant by "antireligion," and is it also repellant? What does it mean to discriminate against "religion," and is it bad to do so? One might read Justice David Souter's opinion in the Court's most recent religion case to be making the argument that being skeptical about, if not downright hostile to, religion in general has a respectable and very American pedigree, one that was not foreign to the founders.[8] The sleight of hand achieved by McConnell is to use a conventional contemporary squeamishness about nineteenth-century anti-Catholicism as a lever with which to deliver a twenty-first-century evangelical reading of the clauses in question.

What can the academic study of religion learn from or contribute to these debates about the proper uses of the First Amendment religion clauses? This article will have three movements and a conclusion. I will first briefly introduce the First Amendment religion clauses. Then I will discuss the establishment clause, followed by the free exercise clause. Finally, in conclusion, I will place these parts in the context of a larger conversation about law and what it can and should do with respect to religion. I will suggest that religious pluralism and notions of equality, both in the courts and in the academy, have propelled a progressive erasing of difference with respect to the category of religion for U.S. law. (The appendix contains the texts of the First and Fourteenth Amendments to the U.S. Constitution and of a recent Florida statute.)

The First Amendment

The word in First Amendment religion clause jurisprudence today is "neutrality." Both religionists and separationists say that they want the government to be "neutral" toward religion, understood in a broad sense as a mandate neither to promote religion nor to inhibit it. But this seeming unanimity at the most general level conceals profound differences with respect to the actual legal regulation of religion. In this article, I will look closely at two recent cases to see how neutrality plays out, first in an establishment clause case and then in a free exercise clause case. Two models of religion—two theologies, if you will—inhabit the American courts' language about the First Amendment and about neutrality. I will denominate these two, rather crudely for these purposes, the "religion-is-the-same" model and the "religion-is-different" model.[9] If these models are consistently employed, which they rarely are, one model supports a demand for equality for religion, whether you are favoring it or critiquing it, while the other supports a demand for separation for religion, whether to protect it or to protect people from it.

These models have corollaries, of course, in the academic study of religion. The religion-is-the-same position reads religion as continuous with other social and cultural phenomena and argues that the academic study of religion should not, indeed cannot, with any integrity, without theologizing, distinguish religion as a category.[10] The religion-is-different position reads religion as distinctive and capable of being, even demanding to be, studied as such.[11] The Supreme Court, for reasons primarily having to do with larger social and cultural changes in the United States but also for reasons having deep roots in the church history of the last five hundred years, has moved rapidly in the last fifty years or so toward a religion-is-the-same model, a model that has been deeply unsatisfying to both the right and the left among religious and political activists, albeit for different reasons.

The First Amendment to the U.S. Constitution reads, in part, "Congress shall make no law respecting an establishment of religion or prohibiting the free exercise thereof." Two characteristics should be noted about these words. First, this prohibition is addressed to Congress. The First Amendment religion clauses were not applied to the states until the middle of the twentieth century. Second, the words are usually understood to speak two separate commands to Congress (and later, to the states): no law may be made respecting an establishment of religion, and no law may be made prohibiting the free exercise of religion. These two commands are referred to by the Court as "the religion clauses."[12] Although all cases brought under the First Amendment religion clauses arguably have both establishment and free exercise implications, depending on the angle from which they are viewed, cases in the courts are usually designated by lawyers and judges as either "establishment cases" or "free exercise cases." An establishment case is initiated by a party seeking to challenge state action because it is a law "respecting an establishment of religion." A free exercise case originates with an action by the state against a party who then seeks to defend on the ground that he was required by his religion to take the forbidden action. Judicial interpretation of the two clauses is distinct and the histories are often contradictory.[13]

Much could be said about the history of what Thomas Jefferson called "the separation of church and state" in the United States, and much has been said.[14] For the purposes of this article, I am going to restate the thesis of a small but important book on the history of the interpretation of the First Amendment, one that remains one of the best. In *The Garden and the Wilderness: Religion and Government in American Constitutional History*, Mark de Wolfe Howe argued that the Supreme Court's preoccupation in the second half of the twentieth century with neutrality in its implementation of the religion clauses—neutrality as between religion and nonreligion as opposed to neutrality among religions—was a by-product of its preoccupation with achieving racial equality in law.[15] According to Howe, this concern with equality and neutrality was in stark contrast to the preoccupations of the drafters of the clauses. Howe argued that at the time of the writing of the First Amendment, the reigning theory among both religious and political thinkers concerning the relationship of religion and government was what he calls an "evangelical" construction of their proper roles. In other words, what I am calling the religion-is-different model was the dominant model among religious and political thinkers espousing separation.

Howe uses Roger Williams, the Puritan divine who was exiled from the Massachusetts Bay Colony in 1636 and who founded Rhode Island, as the spokesperson for the evangelical argument for separation. Williams wrote:

> The faithful labors of many witnesses of Jesus Christ, extant to the world, abundantly proving that the church of the Jews under the Old Testament in the type, and the

church of the Christians under the New Testament in the antitype were both separate from the world; and that when they have opened a gap in the hedge or wall of separation between the garden of the church and the wilderness of the world, God hath ever broke down the wall itself, removed the candlestick and made His garden a wilderness, as at this day. And that, therefore if He will ever please to restore His garden and paradise again, it must of necessity be walled in peculiarly unto Himself from the World; and that all that shall be saved out of the world are to be transplanted out of the wilderness of the world, and added unto his church or garden.[16]

For Williams, Christians existed, if any could be said to do so after the first century, only in small gathered communities of the faithful. The trappings of legally established and institutionalized religion were not true Christianity. For Williams, religion was different, emphatically so. The wall of separation was necessary to maintain the church's purity. (Although interestingly, this separatist theology did not prevent his espousing a robust civil community without religion.)

On Howe's reading, the First Amendment religion clauses, notwithstanding remnants of colonial establishments existing at the time of their passage, acknowledged only what was widely accepted: religion was different and legal separation was necessary for church and state. Evangelical separation also assumed, however, and Howe makes this clear, that a de facto Protestant cultural establishment of religion was acknowledged and respected as a *social* reality.[17] By the mid twentieth century, and on the eve of the Court's decision in *Brown v. Board of Education*,[18] the religion-is-the-same model was beginning to take the place of the religion-is-different one. The de facto Protestant establishment, for social and legal reasons, had been widely undermined by this point, and neutrality as between religion and nonreligion has increasingly determined the Court's decisions in religion cases, with a very few notable exceptions.[19] What was apparent to Howe in 1965 has only intensified since then, notwithstanding periodic bursts of zeal for treating religion differently. Williams's fierce sectarian and evangelical commitment to church-state separation has become a minority view on the Court, one now represented, ironically, only by those who are seen by many as Jefferson's heirs. The majority, often understood to represent an evangelical worldview, in fact are ready to embrace the religion-is-the-same model.

Establishment Clause Neutrality

The first Supreme Court case to interpret the establishment clause was *Everson v. Board of Education*, decided in 1947.[20] *Everson* concerned a New Jersey state law reimbursing parents for the cost of busing their children to school, whether public or private. By 1947, the legal battle between Catholics and Protestants over public education was well over a century old, but this was the first time the Supreme Court of the United States was presented with the question: Is it constitutional for a state to give aid to parochial schools?[21] In a widely cited opinion for the majority, Justice Hugo Black reviewed the history of one of the First Amendment's predecessors, the Virginia Statute for Religious Freedom.[22] Black lovingly recalled the roles of James Madison and Jefferson in the drafting and sponsorship of that legislation and concluded the following about the establishment clause:

> Neither [the federal nor the state governments] can pass laws which aid one religion, aid all religions, or prefer one religion over another. Neither can force nor influence a person to go to or to remain away from church against his will or force him to profess a belief or disbelief in any religion. No person can be punished for entertaining or professing religious beliefs or disbeliefs, for church attendance or nonattendance. No tax in any amount, large or small, can be levied to support any religious activities or institutions, whatever they may be called, or whatever form they may adopt to teach or practice religion. Neither a state nor the Federal Government can, openly or secretly, participate in the affairs of any religious organization or groups and vice versa. In the words of Jefferson, the clause against establishment of religion by law was intended to erect "a wall of separation between Church and State."[23]

Black's insistence on a high and impregnable wall of separation seems to leave no room for church-state partnership. Notwithstanding this bellicose Jeffersonian reading of the First Amendment, however, the majority in *Everson* held that the New Jersey law, in Black's words, merely "help[ed] parents get their children, regardless of their religion, safely and expeditiously to and from accredited schools."[24] In other words, the law gave aid to children, not to religion. The wall, then newly found to border state, as well as federal, government, was, in fact, already being undermined by the religion-is-the-same model. While speaking of religion as especially in need of separation, Black was also insisting on equality between religion and nonreligion. His words and the result in the case speak of neutrality. Over the following fifty or so years, the Court struggled—in numerous cases brought to strike down laws providing assistance of one kind or another to students at religious schools—to draw the line between permissible aid to children and impermissible aid to what they have indeed called "pervasively sectarian" schools. Clarity has been elusive, in part because of a profound and continuing ambivalence about whether religion is to be treated as the same or as different.

The school cases are a special set within First Amendment establishment cases. The Court has repeatedly noted that children are especially vulnerable to state-sponsored religious indoctrination. What might be considered harmless in another context—government-sponsored prayer in legislatures, for example—has been condemned when it occurred in primary and secondary schools.[25] But the school cases also bring out competing American political visions, a libertarian one that sees schools as a place where all individuals and groups have the right to enact and proselytize their social philosophies and one that sees them, in Justice Felix Frankfurter's words, as "the most powerful agency for promoting cohesion among a heterogeneous democratic people."[26] The first one prizes equality as "liberty," while the older view values an "equality" dependent on assimilation that sees us, in some sense, as the same and made so largely through the beneficial effects of public education.[27] Liberty takes a back seat.[28]

The most recent among the many school cases, *Mitchell v. Helms*, decided in 2000, appeared exactly two hundred volumes of the United States Reports after the decision in *Everson*.[29] The issue before the Court in the *Mitchell* case was the constitutionality of Chapter 2 of the Education and Consolidation Improvement Act of 1981.[30] Chapter 2 directed the federal government to distribute funds to state and local agencies that, in turn, loaned "educational materials," including computers, to elementary and secondary schools, both public and private. In 1985, some taxpayers in Louisiana brought an action challenging distribution of funds to religious schools under Chapter 2, arguing that such distribution violated the establishment clause of the First Amendment. As is commonly the case with religion clause decisions today, the Court was divided. The majority opinion, holding that the statute was not "a law respecting an establishment of religion," was written by Justice Clarence Thomas, joined by Chief Justice William Rehnquist and Justices Antonin Scalia and Anthony Kennedy. Justice Sandra Day O'Connor voted with the majority but wrote a separate concurring opinion. Justice Souter wrote a dissenting opinion, joined by Justices John Paul Stevens and Ruth Bader Ginsberg. The majority's position coincides neatly with the result in *Everson*, agreeing that the law benefits children, not religion, but Thomas's opinion effectively dismisses as bigoted Justice Black's, and others', concern about direct aid to religion.

The U.S. District Court for the Eastern District of Louisiana, the first court to hear *Mitchell*, had held that Chapter 2 was unconstitutional because it resulted in "direct aid" to schools that were "pervasively sectarian."[31] The U.S. Court of Appeals for the Fifth Circuit had concurred; and the Supreme Court had granted certiorari. Echoing Justice Black's evenhandedness as between religion and nonreligion but rejecting his hard line on aid to religion, Justice Thomas, for the majority, argues that "direct aid" is not necessarily unconstitutional and that "neutrality" is the goal: "If the religious, irreligious, and a religious [sic]," he concludes, "are all alike eligible for governmental aid, no one would conclude that any indoctrination that any particular recipient conducts has been done at the behest of the government."[32] Addressing the dissenting opinion of Justice Souter, Thomas says: "The pervasively sectarian recipient has not received any special favor, and it is most bizarre that the Court would, as the dissent seemingly does, reserve *special hostility* for those who *take their religion seriously*, who think that their religion should affect the whole of their lives, or who make the mistake of being effective in transmitting their views to their children."[33] Reviewing the anti-Catholic bias implied by the use of the words "pervasively sectarian," Thomas concludes that "nothing in the Establishment clause requires the exclusion of pervasively sectarian schools from otherwise permissible aid programs. . . . This doctrine, born of bigotry, should be buried now."[34] As with charitable choice, equality means equal participation. Religion is not different. It is the same.

Ironically, perhaps, one could argue that it is the dissent—by seeing religion as different, as something that should be kept separate—that, in Thomas's words, "take[s] their religion seriously." Justice Souter, repeatedly quoting Madison, argues vociferously that neutrality is not the only value underlying the religion clauses. The First Amendment establishment clause, he says, "bars the use of public funds for religious aid," for the sake of religion as well as for the sake of the state.[35] The governing principles in the interpretation of the establishment clause with respect to religious schools, he says, also echoing Justice Black's words in *Everson*, are as follows, according to Souter:

1. Government aid to religion is forbidden, and tax revenue may not be used to support a religious school or religious teaching.
2. Government provision of such paradigms of universally general welfare benefits as police and fire protection does not count as aid to religion.
3. Whether a law's benefit is sufficiently close to universally general welfare paradigms to be classified with them, as distinct from religious aid, is a function of the purpose and effect of the challenged law in all its particularity. . . . Evenhandedness of distribution as between religious and secular beneficiaries is a relevant factor, but not a sufficient test of constitutionality. *There is no rule of religious equal protection* to the effect that any expenditure for the benefit of religious school students is necessarily constitutional so long as public school pupils are favored on ostensibly identical terms.
4. Government must maintain neutrality as to religion, "neutrality" being a conclusory label for the required position of government as neither aiding religion or impeding religious exercise by believers.[36]

Only government benefits that are available to everyone, such as police and fire protection, are prima facie neutral.

A government aid program benefiting only a portion of the population, in Souter's view, triggers an examination of the actual statutory effect on religion. Carefully distinguishing among three different uses of the word "neutrality" by the majority, he emphasizes that nothing less than "universal neutrality" is constitutionally permissible. According to Souter, the majority's use of the word "neutrality" to characterize evenhandedness in the distribution of government benefits justifies that which was specifically prohibited by the First Amendment and is a radical departure for the Court:

Adopting the plurality's rule would permit practically any government aid to religion so long as it could be supplied on terms ostensibly comparable to the terms under which aid was provided to nonreligious recipients. As a principle of constitutional sufficiency, the manipulability of this rule is breathtaking. A legislature would merely need to state a secular objective in order to legalize massive aid to all religions, one religion, or even one sect, to which its largess could be directed through the easy exercise of crafting facially neutral terms under which to offer aid favoring that religious group. Short of formally replacing the Establishment Clause, a more dependable key to the public fisc or a cleaner break with prior law would be difficult to imagine.[37]

Establishment clause jurisprudence was being reduced in the Court's majority opinions to what Souter calls "religious equal protection." Very little remained of earlier concerns about the dangers of direct government funding of religion itself. Establishment clause neutrality, for the majority on the Court, prohibits legislative acknowledgment of any distinctiveness about religion. To regard religion as different is to sneer. Souter, however, passionately insists that religion is different: "At least three concerns have been expressed since the founding and run throughout our First Amendment jurisprudence. First, compelling an individual to support religion violates the fundamental principle of freedom of conscience. . . . Second, government aid corrupts religion. . . . Third, government establishment of religion is inextricably linked with conflict."[38] One hears in Souter's insistent dissent a demand that history be respected. Neutrality as equality flattens out and dismisses as irrelevant the complex, sometimes destructive, but always changing role of actual religious institutions in American public life.

What is also apparent in Thomas's and Souter's opinions are different understandings of what law is. For Souter, fairness is to be found in laws that are universally applicable, that is, supported by universal values. Religion must be kept separate because it creates division and because it exists to be a critic of law. For Thomas, law exists to ensure maximum liberty. Exercising religion is only one way of exercising that liberty. It is not to be regarded as legally different from other ways. *Mitchell,* thus, continues an erosion of difference made apparent by the Court's decision in *Rosenberger v. Rector and Visitors of the University of Virginia.*[39] Ronald Rosenberger and friends had challenged the University of Virginia's decision not to extend university funding to a Christian student magazine entitled *Wide Awake.* In their brief, Rosenberger equated *Wide Awake's* Christian viewpoint with "a gay rights, racialist, or antiwar point of view" in terms of its constitutional significance and demanded equal treatment.

Free Exercise Clause Neutrality

Free exercise clause jurisprudence begins earlier—with *Reynolds v. U.S.*—decided by the Court in 1878.[40] George Reynolds, a Mormon, was prosecuted in federal territorial court under the Morrill Act for bigamy.[41] He defended on the ground that he had acted as a matter of religious duty. His religion required him to practice plural marriage, he said, and he would be damned if he refused. The Court took the opportunity to consider for the first time "what is the religious freedom which has been guaranteed" by the Constitution. Reviewing the history of the Virginia Statute and Jefferson's and Madison's views on the separation of church and state, the Court held that "Congress was deprived of all legislative power over mere opinion, but was left free to reach actions which were in violation of social duties or subversive of good order."[42] Concluding that "polygamy has always been odious among the northern and western nations of Europe," Reynolds's petition was denied.[43]

Reynolds remains good law. After an experiment with religious exemptions in a few cases in the 1960s, the Supreme Court, in 1990, reaffirmed *Reynolds* in *Smith v. Employment Division*.[44] Alfred Smith and Galen Black, Native American employees of an Oregon State drug rehabilitation program, had been fired because they had illegally used peyote in a Native American Church ritual. Smith and Black were later denied unemployment compensation because they had been fired "for work-related misconduct." The two brought an action against the State of Oregon, claiming that they had been unconstitutionally denied unemployment compensation because the illegal activity in which they had been engaged, using peyote, constituted a sacrament, an exercise of their religion protected by the First Amendment. The Court, in an opinion by Justice Scalia, held against Smith and Black, ruling that under *Reynolds* the free exercise clause gives full protection only to religious opinions and not to religious acts, which remain subject to neutral laws of general application. To regard any religious acts as constitutionally protected raises in the minds of judges impossible line-drawing challenges, and it also backs courts into the establishment clause. If it is a violation of the free exercise clause not to permit an exemption, is it a violation of the neutrality required by the establishment clause for religiously motivated persons to be given exemptions from the law not available to secularly motivated violators of the law?

As Howe warned in *The Garden and the Wilderness*—referring to the periodic bills introduced in Congress to declare the United States a Christian nation—each time the Court engages in a "burst of Jeffersonian zeal" in a particularly "separationist" opinion, there has been "a flowering of responsive nonsense" from the other branches.[45] The "responsive nonsense" resulting from Scalia's remarkably severe and uncompromising opinion in *Smith*—an opinion that cleverly realigns the precedent and in which plaintiffs' religious practice is referred to once in half a sentence—continues to flower. The decision in *Smith* raised the consciousness of religious activists across the political and theological spectrum. Together, they sponsored the Religious Freedom Restoration Act of 1993 (RFRA), Congress's attempt to reverse the *Smith* decision.[46] Since the Court's 1997 decision in *Boerne v. Flores* declaring RFRA an unconstitutional usurpation of judicial power, the coalition has sponsored the Religious Land Use and Institutionalized Persons Act, intended to cure the constitutional problems with RFRA, as well as the International Religious Freedom Act of 1998, requiring the president to take action to protect religious freedom around the world.[47] The recent inclusion of charitable choice provisions in the welfare laws and the establishment of the White House Office on Faith-Based Initiatives could also be seen as part of the fallout from Scalia's opinion in *Smith*.

While declared unconstitutional in its federal incarnation by the Supreme Court, RFRA has been resurrected in the states. In response to the *Boerne* decision, activists went to state legislatures to lobby for what are referred to as "mini-RFRAs." The first mini-RFRA was passed in Florida in 1998. The Florida law, like the federal law, provides in sec. 761.03 that "(1) The government shall not substantially burden a person's exercise of religion, even if the burden results from a rule of general applicability, except that government may substantially burden a person's exercise of religion only if it demonstrates that application of the burden to the person (a) is in furtherance of a compelling governmental interest; and (b) is the least restrictive means of furthering that compelling governmental interest" (see appendix for full text).[48] In other words, as with the federal version of RFRA, if you can prove that the government is "substantially burdening" your "exercise of religion" and the government cannot show that its action was "in furtherance of a compelling governmental interest" and that the act that results in the burden is "the least restrictive means of furthering that governmental interest," you are exempt from that law. The Florida statute, in an effort to forestall a more restrictive interpretation that had been dominant in federal judicial interpretation of RFRA, further explicitly provides in the "definitions" section, that the statute protects all exercise of religion, "whether or not the religious exercise is compulsory or central to a larger system of religious belief."[49]

I served as an expert witness in the first RFRA trial in Florida.[50] The trial concerned Boca Raton City Cemetery, a small, modern, and very modest cemetery. A lawsuit had been brought challenging the cemetery regulations restricting grave decorations. For the most part, in the newer section of the cemetery, the graves lack stone markers. They are marked by flat identifying plaques and decorated with flowers (mostly artificial), small statues, and religious symbols. None of it is high art—it is dime-store piety, most of it popular and often kitschy Catholic piety. On my second visit to the cemetery, I was accompanied by John McGuckin, professor of early church history at Union Theological Seminary and a Romanian Orthodox priest. We had both read descriptions of the cemetery and seen snapshots sent to us by the lawyers, but being there was different. John's reaction was immediate and strong. This cemetery displayed, he said, a typical Orthodox and Latin piety. He was particularly struck by a grave with a large, upright cross decorated with silk lilies. We knew that the deceased and her husband were Lebanese immigrants who had become, in their words, "born-again Christians." This grave, John said, was characteristic of Lebanese memorial art. We moved slowly around the cemetery as John commented on the various grave ornaments. John and I were there to give our opinions as to the "religiousness" of the grave decorations. Legally speaking, were these grave decorations "religious"? Did they amount to an "exercise of religion" that triggered the protection of the Florida RFRA? Were they different? Religion must be different to receive special legal protection under RFRA.

The regulations of the Boca Raton cemetery had, since 1982, prohibited any grave decoration except a small flat identifying plaque with a removable flower vase, and indeed many, perhaps half, of the graves had no other decoration. Beginning in the mid-1980s, notwithstanding the regulations, city cemetery managers had permitted families to install a range of nonconforming items—statues, crosses, ground cover, Stars of David, benches, stone vases, and so forth. More recently, however, the city had decided to enforce the regulations and had ordered removal of the items, claiming that they could not otherwise properly and economically maintain the cemetery. Plaintiffs, a class of families owning nonconforming graves in the cemetery and represented by the American Civil Liberties Union, had brought an action under the Florida law (and under the free exercise clause of the First Amendment) seeking an order restraining enforcement of the city's regulations.

Various plaintiffs testified at the trial about the grave decorations. Two sisters, Cuban-American immigrants, testified that the statues on their brother's grave, and their daily prayer at his grave, were necessary for the salvation of his soul, which was in grave danger because of his unforgivable sin of suicide. They further testified that they had chosen this cemetery because they saw religious expression that would not have been permitted in Cuba. A father testified that his son's grave had been carefully fenced, covered, and marked with a stone Star of David to prevent people from walking on it because he had been taught by his parents that that was a necessary practice in Jewish tradition. He further testified that the city's removal of these items without his permission had reminded him of Nazi desecration of Jewish graves. A mother testified that the statues of children on the empty grave adjacent to her child's grave were a witness to her child's continued life after death—a two-year old child who had been swept to sea with his nanny. A husband testified that the large, upright cross on his wife's grave was a symbol of the resurrection.

There was also expert testimony. The Florida court had to decide, as an initial matter, whether plaintiffs' actions constituted an "exercise of religion" under the statute, before proceeding to determine whether that exercise was "substantially burdened." Plaintiffs argued that all religious conduct was protected by the statute and that only in the event that plaintiffs could not prove a substantial burden or that the city could prove that it had "a compelling interest" and that it had used the "least restrictive means" could the city remove the decorations from the graves. Experts for the plaintiffs testified that the grave decorations, although not mandated by the religious traditions in question as defendants insisted they be in order to receive statutory protection, were, for both the Jewish and the Christian plaintiffs, consistent with a long history of burial customs.[51] McGuckin testified concerning the practices of the early church, Michael Broyde outlined a history and geography of Jewish burial practices, and I testified concerning the subjective nature of American religious authority. We all agreed that removal of the decorations could well constitute a substantial burden to plaintiffs' exercise of their religion. One difficulty was that as we extended the definition of religion to include what might be termed, by some, "folk customs," "religion" blended into, and became synonymous with, "culture," and it became less clear whether religion so understood was different enough to be protected.

The city's experts offered two different tests by means of which Judge Kenneth Ryskamp could decide that plaintiffs' activities were not exercises of religion under the statute. They offered arguments that allowed the court to say that while there might indeed be religion that was sufficiently different, these examples were not. Nathan Katz, professor of religion at Florida International University, testified that religion could be usefully divided into "high traditions" and "little traditions":

> By "high tradition" is meant the textual-legal side of religion, usually male-dominated and church or synagogue-centered. By "little tradition" is meant the folkways and home-centered observances, usually orally rather than textually transmitted, often the domain of women in a traditional culture. "Little tradition" customs are nowhere codified; indeed, by their nature they are oral rather than textual, and as such run the risk of being idiosyncratic. . . . If we accept all "little tradition" customs as valid and binding in the same way that "high tradition" laws and doctrines are, then we run the danger of falling into a relativism bordering on anarchy.[52]

The decorations on the graves, Katz opined, were part of little traditions, and the removal of them could not, therefore, be a substantial burden on plaintiffs.

The defendants' second expert, Daniel Pals, professor of religion at the University of Miami, testified that religious traditions can be usefully mapped as a circle with essential practices at the center. As you got toward the edges, he said, you got to less important practices. He further said that for Christians, the center is spiritual, not embodied, and that this had been true from the time of the early church. In his expert report, he announced that "substantial burden" could be determined by deciding whether a particular prohibited practice is "integral or essential to" a religious tradition. He offered four questions to be used in making this determination: "(1) Is it asserted or implied in relatively unambiguous terms by an authoritative sacred text? (2) Is it clearly and consistently affirmed in classic formulations of doctrine and practice? (3) Has it been observed continuously, or nearly so, throughout the history of the tradition? (4) Is it consistently practiced everywhere, or almost such, in the tradition as we meet it in more recent times?"[53] These questions, he said, would allow the delineation of a continuum of practices. The plaintiffs' practices were, in his opinion, neither "essential" nor "integral to" the Jewish and Christian traditions.

Both of the city's religion experts accepted the invitation of the city's lawyers to provide a legal test for Florida courts to follow, a test that would determine what religion was different enough to deserve legal protection. Judge Ryskamp's opinion explaining his decision denying plaintiffs' request for an injunction is revealing. Almost mechanically, he goes through the motions of constructing and adopting a statutory test based on the testimony of Katz and Pals. He seems thereby to endorse the treating of religion as special and different at least in some cases. Katz and Pals described religion as something that could be known through examination of texts, institutions, and doctrines and then legally reified. Judge Ryskamp announced his own definition: "A review of the statute's history, its plain language and the application of ordinary rules of statutory construction reveal that the Florida Legislature intended to limit the statute's coverage to conduct that, while not necessarily compulsory or central to a larger system of religious beliefs, nevertheless *reflects some tenet, practice or custom of a larger system of religious beliefs.* Conduct that amounts to a matter of *purely personal preference* regarding religious exercise does not fall within the ambit of the Florida RFRA."[54] The judge established two categories: legally protected religious exercise, on the one hand, namely, exercise that he believed "reflected some tenet, practice or custom of a larger system of religious beliefs," and unprotected religious exercise, on the other, namely, exercise that was a matter of "purely personal preference." Using the Pals and Katz tests to decide whether the plaintiffs' practices reflected some tenet, practice, or custom of a larger system of religious beliefs, he then determined that plaintiffs' conduct was guided by purely personal preference. There was really no other alternative in his mind. "Plaintiffs' proposed construction of the statute," he concluded, "would lead to cemetery anarchy."[55]

Judge Ryskamp seems by this scheme to be leaving room for the possibility that there might be religious practices that would qualify for RFRA protection. At the very end of his discussion of RFRA, however, Ryskamp drops a very interesting footnote: "Because the Court finds that the plaintiffs have not established a cognizable claim under the Florida RFRA, the Court need not address the statute's constitutionality. The Court does note, however that the statute, which operates to exempt religious but not secular conduct from compliance with neutral laws of general applicability, evidences a preference for religion which arguably runs afoul of the Establishment Clause of the First Amendment."[56] It is not too farfetched to read this footnote as Judge Ryskamp's real opinion. Neutrality demands that religion and nonreligion be treated the same. Anything else would constitute a denial of equal protection of the laws to atheists in violation of the Fourteenth Amendment to the U.S. Constitution (see appendix for text).[57]

Conclusion

For purposes of the establishment clause, neutrality has come to mean that religious institutions and religiously motivated individuals are seen as having a right to equal access to benefits. For purposes of the free exercise clause, religious motivation has no more status than nonreligious motivation when it comes to exemption from neutral laws of general application. As long as laws restrict everyone's behavior, the religiously motivated person must be treated the same as everyone else. Faced with the politics of equality, the U.S. Supreme Court has neutralized the First Amendment by acknowledging and condemning the de facto establishment of a certain brand of American religion on which an evangelical reading of the clauses depended. An evangelical reading of the clauses depended on a model that sees religion at once as different and as culturally embedded—a model indebted to a peculiarly American conjunction of Enlightenment rationality and reformation theology, the evangelical and the Jeffersonian versions of separation. The eclipse of both has led to the neutering of the religion clauses. A religious landscape of many complex and shifting religious identities, a landscape in which religion is the same, will no longer support the political judgment that led to the passage of the clauses. The religious majority is more interested in access to public funds than it is worried about the burdens majoritarian culture places on religious minorities.

A strong argument can surely be made that persons should stand equally before the law whether they self-consciously identify or are identified by others as religious—whether the government is conferring a benefit or restraining a person's action. One can also argue, and people have, that American law has been largely driven by a demand for greater and greater equality of persons.[58] At the end of *The Garden and the Wilderness*, Howe comments that "the legal history of American equality is the story of an accelerating awareness that the government's endorsement of natural and artificial disparities between persons and classes breeds grave injustice."[59] Once people are modified—male people and female people, gay people and straight people, or black people and white people—red flags should go up, and American law requires a very high showing that such classifications should have legal consequences, whether negative or positive. This is a question of justice, but it is also a question of definition. Do these modifiers describe real distinctions, or are they descriptive poles that produce serious distortions when given as permanent legal identities to actual individuals? A particular person may be black and white, gay and straight, even male and female. Given these difficulties when dealing with what sometimes appear biologically determined, it is that much harder when talking about religion. Certainly a person, a school, or a cemetery, like a crèche, can be both religious and nonreligious.[60] And that person, school, or cemetery can be religious one day and not the next.

Can religious classifications ever be constitutional? While Judge Ryskamp might have difficulty defending his definition of religion to scholars of religion, his impulse with respect to the law is mainstream American. As long as everyone is treated the same, it is OK. Once special privileges are handed out on the basis of distinctions among persons, the threshold should be very high—a threshold that historically has been met most convincingly only with respect to remedying the effects of racial discrimination—although that, too, is eroding. So, in one sense, religion is only a special case of a much wider social shift—a shift toward an insistence on greater and greater equality.

The neutralizing of religion is also the result of a specific critique of law and of its relationship to religion. There have been dramatic changes in the academic study of American law in the last twenty-five years. Stung by the devastating ideological deconstruction of legal positivism—of the languages of, and pretensions to, impartiality of law—by the "crits," as critical legal theorists are called, legal scholars have proposed a number of different solutions to fix American law. One diagnosis has seen the problem as secularism. One source of solutions has been religion. Twenty-five years ago there was a more or less fixed consensus among academic lawyers that the wall of separation should be assiduously maintained. Religion knew its place and its place was not in the law. Law schools did not have courses on religion. Courses on the First Amendment were about free speech. That has changed. Law schools are now full of religion—courses on religion and student organizations identified by religious tradition. Law reviews are full of religion and legislatures are full of religion. There are law firms dedicated to shoring up religious freedom. Religion or theology is seen in some circles as the solution for law. Proponents of a reconciliation between law and religion argue that disestablishment was a mistake and that the apparent aridity and amorality of the law is evidence enough. We just need to recover our faith.[61]

Law's critics on the Right and the Left have exposed the limitations and possibilities of law with great energy and precision. There is an important acknowledgment to be made that skepticism and dogmatic secularism can be destructive, that positivist notions of law are deeply flawed, and that the all-encompassing nature of religious claims makes separation very difficult, maybe impossible. But there is a further affirmative claim being made by those seeking to restore religion's place: law ought to have its foundation in religion—in love.[62] Ending discrimination against religion, it is said, will permit this long overdue reformation in the law. In contrast to Jefferson, and Williams, and Justices Black and Souter, what McConnell and Justice Thomas are saying is that religion does not want to be different. Difference leads to inequality and segregation and secularism. Much of the impetus for the current enthusiasm for government assistance for faith-based initiatives results from this demand for equality, not a demand for special treatment. And it speaks the same language as the civil rights movement.

To say that the politics of equality and increased religious pluralism have created a situation in which the Supreme Court has backed away from enforcement of a robust reading of the religion clauses is not, however, to deny the continued force of the impulses that led to their creation in the first place. Separation arguably made possible the universal norms on which liberal politics still bases its claims, including that of equality. The fiction that law is value-free brings real benefits, to the church and to the state.[63] As Williams cautioned, "when they have opened a gap in the hedge or wall of separation between the garden of the church and the wilderness of the world, God hath ever broke down the wall itself . . . and made His garden a wilderness." For liberals the gap threatens the state as well. In establishment clause terms, the threat is that neutrality will have a libertarian flavor that permits devolution of state power to religious institutions. In free exercise terms, the threat is that neutrality will mask discrimination.

Because separation is no longer possible, the dangers of religious establishment have to be addressed through other means. The church can solve its problems by keeping away from government, if it has the will. As far as the state is concerned, state action will have to be scrutinized based on neutral criteria like those of the equal-protection and due-process clauses of the Fourteenth Amendment and the free-speech and free-association clauses of the First Amendment. As for the academic study of religion, surely, in our desire to be helpful, we must be careful about the consequences of legislating either that religion is the same or that it is different.

Appendix

UNITED STATES CONSTITUTION

First Amendment: Congress shall make no law respecting an establishment of religion or prohibiting the free exercise thereof; or abridging the freedom of speech, or of the press; or the right of the people peaceably to assemble, and to petition the Government for a redress of grievances.

Fourteenth Amendment, sec. 1: All persons born or naturalized in the United States, and subject to the jurisdiction thereof, are citizens of the United States and of the State wherein they reside. No State shall make or enforce any law which shall abridge the privileges or immunities of citizens of the United States; nor shall any State deprive any person of life, liberty, or property without due process of law; nor deny to any person within its jurisdiction the equal protection of its laws.

FLORIDA RELIGIOUS FREEDOM RESTORATION ACT

Sec. 761.03(1): The government shall not substantially burden a person's exercise of religion, even if the burden results from a rule of general applicability, except that government may substantially burden a person's exercise of religion only if it demonstrates that application of the burden to the person (a) is in furtherance of a compelling governmental interest; and (b) is the least restrictive means of furthering that compelling governmental interest.

Sec. 761.02(3): "Exercise of religion" means an act or refusal to act that is substantially motivated by a religious belief, whether or not the religious exercise is compulsory or central to a larger system of religious belief.

Reflections on Blasphemy and Secular Criticism

Talal Asad

For many years now there has been much talk in Euro-America about the threat to free speech, particularly whenever its Muslims have raised the issue of blasphemy in response to some public criticism of Islam. The most recent crisis was the scandal of the Danish cartoons. A decade and a half after the Rushdie affair, the old religious denunciation of "blasphemy" had reared its head again among Muslims in Europe and beyond, seeking to undermine hard-won freedoms. Or so we were told. There were angry protests and some violence on one side, many affirmations of principle and expressions of contempt on the other.[1] The affair was discussed largely in the context of the problem of integrating Muslim immigrants into European society and related to the "global menace" of Islamists.[2] Coming after the attack on the World Trade Center and the London bombings, the cartoon scandal was made to fit neatly into a wider discourse: the West's "War on Terror," a conflict that many see as part of an intrinsic hostility between two civilizations, Islam and Europe.[3] Thus the Danish press and many Danish politicians began to criticize Islamic studies scholars for disregarding this fundamental antagonism. It was argued that these scholars had intentionally avoided certain civilizational topics, such as the ways in which Islam is an obstacle to integration and is a potential security threat.[4]

The attitudes displayed in the cartoon affair by Muslims and non-Muslims were quite remarkable. This paper is not, however, an apologia or a critique; it is an attempt to think through the idea of blasphemy in more complicated ways. In what follows I look at blasphemy from various angles and treat it as the crystallization of a number of moral, political, and critical problems in liberal European society. So I will have less to say about traditions of Islamic thought and behavior than about the modern condition we all inhabit. When I do refer to that tradition it will be to try and raise questions about liberal modernity and secularity.

Blasphemy and the Clash of Civilizations

The conflict that many Euro-Americans saw in the Danish cartoons scandal was between the West and Islam, each championing opposing values: democracy, secularism, liberty, and reason on the one side, and on the other the many opposites—tyranny, religion, authority, and unreason. The idea of blasphemy clearly belongs to the latter series and is seen by secularists as a constraint on the freedom of speech guaranteed by Western principles and by the pursuit of reason so central to Western culture. Pope Benedict's Regensburg lecture in 2006 emphasized the idea of a civilizational confrontation between Christianity, which reconciles Greek reason with biblical faith, and Islam, which encourages violent conversion because it has no faith in reason.[5]

Blasphemy has a long history in Christianity, in which it has been described as an insult to God's honor, as a sin that can be committed in many ways. In England, it became a crime in common law only in the seventeenth century, at a time when national courts were taking over from ecclesiastical courts and the modern state was taking shape. Common law did not distinguish between heresy (the holding of views contrary to faith) and blasphemy (the utterance of insults against God or His saints), as medieval canon law had done. So from the seventeenth century on the crime of blasphemy was entangled with the question of political toleration and the formation of "secular modernity"—otherwise known as "Western Civilization." Over the next two centuries differences of legal opinion arose as to whether public statements lacking defamatory intent or expressed in moderate language were liable to criminal prosecution. It was felt that scholarly debate and discussion needed protection, even if they appeared to be "irreligious." This led to increasing legal attention being given to the language (style and context) in which "blasphemy" appeared, regardless of how disruptive of established truth it was.

The tendency to emphasize manner of expression—to see blasphemy in terms of form rather than content—had, however, some interesting legal implications: vulgar working-class speech was less protected than the polite speech of the middle and upper classes. A scholar who has studied blasphemy trials in nineteenth-century England calls them "class crimes of language" on account of the class bias they indicate.[6] That an exceptionally large number of them took place during a period when a modern class system began to appear is itself of some significance. For this reason I am inclined to say that, rather than simply indicating class bias, the identification of blasphemy helped to constitute class difference. But most important, I want to suggest that we see blasphemy in these cases not as instances of the suppression of free speech but as the shape that free speech takes at different times and in different places, because there is no such thing as free speech in the abstract.

Free speech, it is said, is central to democracy. Consistent with the standpoint of Pope Benedict and many of the defenders of the Danish cartoons, it is often claimed that democracy is rooted in Christianity and is therefore alien to Islam. There is a widespread conviction that Christian doctrine has been receptive to democracy because in Christendom (unlike Islam) church and state began as separate entities. But it must not be forgotten that the Byzantine state-church was the space in which central Christian doctrines were formulated and fought over, that even in the Middle Ages and well beyond the separation between religious and political authority was far from complete, and that social inequality was generally regarded as legitimate. This is not to say that all those who sought to maintain inequality were Christian and that their opponents were always non-Christian. The struggle for equal rights was ideologically and socially complicated.

Many Euro-Americans, including most recently Francis Fukuyama, have traced "democracy" through "political equality" to the Christian doctrine of "the universal dignity of man," in order to make the claim that it is a unique value of Western civilization.[7] In medieval Latin, however, *dignitas* was used to refer to the privilege and distinction of high office, not to the equality of all human beings. Christianity does have a notion of universal spiritual worth (as, for that matter, does Islam), but that has been compatible with great social and political inequality. In the nineteenth century some writers (e.g., the very influential George Grote[8]) began to trace the concept and practice of modern democracy not from Christianity but from classical Greece. Pre-Christian Athens certainly had a concept of equal albeit restricted citizenship and rudimentary democratic practices, which included the right to speak freely in the political forum, but it had no notion of "the universal dignity of man." In European Christendom it was only gradually, through continuous conflict, that many inequalities were eliminated and that secular authority replaced one that was ecclesiastical.

There is a story told by writers of whom Marcel Gauchet is a much-cited example:[9] Christianity is the seed that flowers into secular humanism, destroying in the process its own transcendental orientation and making possible the terrestrial autonomy that now lies at the heart of Western democratic society. (This contrasts with Muslim societies, which remain mired in their religion.[10]) Christianity, out of all "religions," gives birth to a plural, democratic world; out of all "religions," it begets unfettered human agency. The elemental *human dispossession* that characterizes all religion is paradoxically overcome by and through a unique religion: Christianity. This story of "Western Christianity" as a parent metamorphosing into its offspring (modernity), as transcendence becoming worldly (secularity), as the particular thinking the universal, is remarkable for the way it mimics the sacred Christian narrative, in which Jesus incarnates the divine principle, dies, and is reborn to take his place at the right hand of the Father, a narrative whose telos is redemption for all humankind. Transcendence thus remains in our redeemed world, our secular "European civilization," although now it has a different content as well as a different place. Santiago Zabala, surveying the postmetaphysical trend in Euro-American philosophy, puts it a little differently. Secularization, he writes, is not merely produced by a Christian past but is also a testament to the enduring presence of Christianity in its post-Christian mode (European civilization).[11]

How, given the present political climate, are we to understand stories that recount the flourishing of a distinctive European civilization, with Christianity as its historical foundation, in conflict with another called "Islamic"? As part of a political discourse, its function is to facilitate hostile action against Muslims under the rubric of "defense," but its logical implication is that the absence of "democratic traditions" in Islamic civilization explains Muslim resort to the coercive notion of blasphemy and their refusal to grasp the supreme importance of freedom. This appears self-evident. But is it?

From a sociological point of view, populations that belong to "European civilization" are highly differentiated by class culture and religious doctrine, by language and region. They have often been riven by internal conflict, in which warring parties have used the same principle of critical public speech to attack each other, and in which alliances have sometimes been made with Muslim princes. There have always been important movements that have sought to censor public communication in the West, to restrain and control democratic tendencies, in the name of freedom or equality or stability. The entire history of European countries in the Americas, Asia, and Africa (with all its denials and repressions of the indigenous populations they ruled over) has been an integral part of "European civilization." Hannah Arendt persuasively argued that the racist policies of European imperialism were essential to the development of racism—in particular, of modern anti-Semitism—in totalitarian Europe. It is not easy, therefore, to understand what exactly is being claimed when "democracy" and "free speech" are said to be intrinsic to "European civilization," and inequality and repression are attributed to "Islamic civilization."

True, democratic institutions are now more firmly established within Western post-Christian states than in Middle Eastern ones,[12] and the legal systems of Muslim-majority countries were not, until they imported Western law, built around the idea of legal equality and *universality*. But instead of regarding the concern with the particular as opposed to the universal as a *lack*, as an absence that leads to political intolerance and to the infliction of social indignities, we might examine more closely the forms in which the universal drive to freedom appears in liberal societies. Thus one form of universalization central to liberal politics and economics is the *substitutability* of individuals: in the arithmetic of electoral politics, each voter counts as one and is the exact equivalent of every other voter—no more, no less, and no different. Each citizen has the same right to take part in the political process, and to be heard politically, as every other. Substitutability is more fundamental for liberal democracy than *electoral consent*, from which Western governments are said to derive their legitimacy, because such consent is dependent on counting substitutable votes.

Substitutability is more than a principle of electoral politics. It is also a social technique essential to bureaucratic control and to market manipulation, both being ways of normalizing (and therefore constraining) the individual. This is why statistical modes of thinking and representation—the construction of political and economic strategies on the basis of proportions, averages, trends, and so on—are so important to liberal democratic societies. The fact that individuals have equal value and so may be substituted for one another is, however, what helps to undermine the liberal notion of personal dignity, because for the individual to count as a substitutable unit, his or her uniqueness must be discounted. Thus, even when we use Western criteria of democratic virtue, "liberal European civilization" emerges as highly contradictory. Contradiction does not in itself signify a pathology, but it does complicate the idea of a conflict between two civilizations, one of which supposedly upholds human dignity and the other doesn't.

A word on my use of the term "liberal" in this paper: I am aware that liberalism is a complex historical tradition, that Locke is not Constant and Constant is not Mill and Mill is not Rawls, that the history of liberalism in North America is not the same as that in Europe—or, for that matter, in parts of the Third World where it can be said to have a substantial purchase. But as a value-space, liberalism today provides its advocates with a common political and moral language in which to identify problems and to dispute. Such ideas as individual autonomy, freedom, national self-determination, limitation of state power, rule of law, and religious toleration belong to that space, not least when they are debated. It is precisely the contradictions and aporias in the language of liberalism that make the public debates among liberals possible, in a space that is vigorously defended against those who would introduce a radically different language.

Democracy and freedom are central to "Western Civilization," and the universal right to free speech is central to democracy. Or is it? How does the idea of cultivating elite sensibilities (quality) implied by "civilization" fit with the idea of mass equality (quantity) implied by "democracy"? This question was raised in nineteenth-century Britain when the extension of the suffrage was debated. Thus Mill argued for a system of plural voting that would give greater weight to the educated ("more civilized") classes to balance the working-class majority.[13] But the problem has remained unresolved. Answers at a philosophical level are plentiful, however, in which mutual trust, amicability, and self-reliance are made essential to democracy. For this reason Zabala, whom I cited earlier, believes that secularity provides the key: "It was Dewey's merit that we achieve full political maturity only at the moment when we succeed in doing without any metaphysical culture, without the culture of belief in non-human powers and forces. Only after the French Revolution did human beings learn to rely increasingly on their own powers; Dewey called the religion that teaches men to rely on themselves a 'religion of love' (the complete opposite of a 'religion of fear') because it is virtually impossible to distinguish it from the condition of the citizen who participates concretely in democracy."[14]

This talk of representative democracy having its ethical roots in secularized Christianity is not uncommon today, but it is not as scrupulously thought through as Max Weber's more famous attempt to link capitalism to Christianity. Careful scholar that Weber was, he preferred to speak of "an elective affinity" rather than a generative relation.

It is worth recalling, incidentally, that the French Revolution was not simply an event introducing solidarity, democracy, and freedom into the modern world. Revolutionary armies themselves sought to promote liberty, equality, and fraternity by conquest. The Revolution inaugurated the age of modern empires, unleashing modern warfare, nationalism, racism, and genocide (of, notably, American Indians, European Jews, and Gypsies) around the world. All of this is certainly part of "Christian" Europe's history. Of course it is not the sum, still less the essence, of Western history, but it is a part. Is it not also part of its inheritance? The distinguished philosopher Richard Rorty has talked about rehabilitating the idea of "the European *mission civilisatrice*" with reference to its democratic values—its unique attachment to equality and freedom.[15] But he does not explain who will decide what really represents "European values," and how they will be maintained. Nor does he address the problem, identified by Hannah Arendt, among others, of the capacity of modern states to eliminate minorities and to wage wars on the basis of decisions arrived at democratically. As perceptive commentators have noted, *actually existing democracy* is as capable as any nondemocracy of legislating repression at home and depriving the liberty of weaker peoples abroad, whether by military means or economic ones. What kind of *mission civilisatrice* should one expect from Europe?

Free Speech and the Concept of the Human

The charge of blasphemy is said to be an archaic religious constraint and free speech a principle essential to modern freedom. But if the West is a civilization with Christianity as its historical foundation, does the concept of blasphemy have any place in it now that it is secularized? Are there any connections between the idea of blasphemy and the prohibitions established by secular law? Do prohibitions—whether "religious" or not— tell us something about the idea of "the human" defined by them? How does blasphemy relate to worldly criticism?

There is nothing new or remarkable in saying that there are emotional dimensions to communication, especially to the giving and taking of provocation. But if one were to go beyond the contrast between formal civilizational principles—freedom on one side, unfreedom on the other—and go beyond the simple notion of emotion as an obstacle to rational communication, one might ask just how affect articulates valued behavior and speech. For affect is not merely contingently related to speech, energizing utterances in defense or attack: it *constitutes* speech and action. How one speaks and behaves when one is in love, for example, or when one is guilty over what one has done or said to another, or how one abstains from some speech out of reverence for the gods (or for certain human beings)—these are not just speech events to which emotion is attached but distinctive ways in which body-mind-emotion articulates value in relation to other persons.

Although this is not a new point, it tends to be forgotten by universalists, who are quick to dismiss some of the reactions of those who objected to the cartoons as merely irrational.

If blasphemy indicates a limit transgressed, does criticism signify liberation? Let's bear in mind that the term *criticism* embraces a multitude of activities. To judge, to censure, to reproach, to find fault, to mock, to evaluate, to construe, to diagnose—each of these critical actions relates persons to one another in a variety of affective ways. Thus to be "criticizable" is to be part of an asymmetrical relation which may or may not reflect unequal power. One should be skeptical, therefore, of the claim that "criticism" is aligned in any simple way with "freedom."

Modern societies *do*, of course, have legal constraints on free communication. Thus there are laws of copyright, patent, and trademark, and laws protecting commercial secrets, all of which prohibit in differing degree the free circulation of expressions and ideas. Are property rights in a work of art infringed if it is publicly reproduced in a distorted form by someone other than the original author with the aim of commenting on it? And if they are infringed, then how does the sense of violation differ from claims about blasphemy? My point here, I stress, is not that there is no difference, but that there are legal conditions that define what may be communicated freely, and how, in liberal democratic societies, and that the flow of public speech consequently has a particular shape by which its "freedom" is determined.

There are other laws that prohibit expression in public and that appear at first sight to have nothing to do with property: for example, indecency laws and laws relating to child pornography, whose circulation is prohibited even in cyberspace. The first set of laws, you might say, has to do with the workings of a market economy and so with property, whereas the second is quite different because it deals with sexual propriety. But although it is the laws relating to the latter whose infringement evokes the greatest passion, both sets of constraint are clues to the liberal secular ideal of the human, the proper subject of all freedoms and rights. Both sets of limits articulate different ways in which property and its protection define the person. In a secular society these laws make it possible to demarcate and defend one's self in terms of what one owns, including, above all, one's body. Thus our conceptions of "trespassing" on another's body and of "exploiting" it are matters of central concern to laws regulating sexual propriety. They also relate to slavery, a nonliberal form of property, for modern law holds that one cannot transfer ownership of one's living body to another person or acquire property rights in another's. Freedom is thus regarded as an inalienable form of property, a capacity that all individual persons possess in a state of nature, in the living body. There are, of course, exceptions to this principle of absolute ownership in one's body, some old and some new: for example, suicide—destroying oneself—is not only forbidden but also regarded by most people in liberal countries with horror, even though the person is said to be the sole owner of the body she inhabits and animates. This exception to self-ownership is often explained by secularists in terms of the humanist principle of "the dignity of human life," a principle that is not seen as conflicting with the brutality of war. Warfare is presented, regretfully, as a mode of killing and dying in the name of one's nation or of universal human redemption ("we may make terrible mistakes but the overall intentions should remain humane").

Apart from this old contradiction there is now a considerable area of legal and moral confusion regarding the ownership of donated human organs and human tissue taken as samples for medical research.[16] This confusion adds to the growing sense that the sacred conception of the self-owning human, the foundation of freedoms in modern society, is under threat.

In theory, the self-owning liberal subject has the ability to choose freely, a freedom that can be publicly demonstrated. The reality is more complicated. Famously, there are two subject positions—one economic and the other political—whose freedom is invested with value in liberal democratic society, both of which are linked to a conception of the freely choosing self and the limits that protect it. Thus, as a citizen the subject has the right to criticize political matters *openly and freely*, and to vote for whichever political candidate she wishes—but she is obliged to do so *in strictest secrecy*. There is a paradox in the fact that the individual choice of candidates must be hidden to be free, while critical speech to be free must be exercised in public; the former takes for granted that the citizen is embedded in particular social relationships; the latter assumes that he is an abstract individual with rights. As an economic individual, the subject is free to work at, spend, and purchase whatever she chooses, and has the right to protect her property legally. Marx was surely right when he pointed out that in modern liberal societies the freedom of the producer is a precondition for the growth of capital—or, as we might put it today, unrestricted consumption is a source of corporate power. What he failed to point out, however, is that *that* power in turn serves to limit the liberty of the citizen.[17] Social constraint (and, as Freud has made us aware, even psychological constraint) lies at the heart of individual choice. It seems probable, therefore, that the intolerable character of blasphemy accusations in this kind of society derives not so much from their attempt to *constrain* as from the theological language in which the constraint is articulated. Theology invokes dependence on a transcendental power, and secularism has rejected such a power by affirming human independence. But that authenticity is secularism's formal claim. In fact, as I have just suggested, following others who have written on this topic, constraint and dependence are massively present in our secular world. The subject is not autonomous. His body, his sentiments, his speech are not entirely his own.

So my main concern is not to make the banal argument that free speech is never totally free. It is to ask what the particular patterns of restriction can tell us about liberal ideas of the *free* human. The self-owning individual is a famous liberal idea, and although there are some limits to what one may do to oneself there is greater latitude in relation to one's material property. The ownership of property doesn't only establish immunity in relation to all those who don't own it. It also secures one's right to do with it what one wishes—so long as no damage is done to the rights of others.[18] The right to choose how to dispose of what one owns (one's body, one's affections, one's speech are all *personal property*) is integral to the liberal subject. It is worth reflecting on the fact that in liberal society rape, the violent subjection of a person's body against his/her wishes for the purpose of sexual enjoyment, is a serious crime, whereas seduction—the mere manipulation of another person's sexual desire through calculated speech—is not. In the latter case no property right is violated. Compare this with ancient Greece, where seduction was a more serious crime than rape because it involved the capture of someone's affection and loyalty away from the man to whom they rightly belonged.[19] What this indicates is not only that the woman's viewpoint did not matter legally in the ancient world, but also that in liberal society seduction is not considered a violation—except where minors are concerned. In liberal society seduction is not merely permitted, it is positively valued as a sign of individual (sexual) freedom.[20] Every adult may dispose of his or her body, affections, and speech at will so long as no harm is done to the property of others. That is why the prohibition of seduction between adults—like the curtailment of speech—is regarded as a constraint on natural liberty itself.

In a detailed account of the legal disputes over the perpetuity of copyright in late-eighteenth-century England, Mark Rose has demonstrated how the idea of incorporeal property (the literary work) emerged through the concept of the author as proprietor: "First, the proponents of perpetual copyright asserted the author's natural right to a property in his creation. Second, the opponents of perpetual copyright replied that ideas could not be treated as property and that copyright could only be regarded as a limited personal right of the same order as a patent. Third, the proponents responded that the property claimed was neither the physical book nor the ideas communicated by it but something else entirely, something consisting of style and sentiment combined. What we here observe, I would suggest, is a twin birth, the simultaneous emergence in the discourse of the law of the proprietory author and the literary work. The two concepts are bound to each other."[21]

This genealogy of modern authorship makes it clear that the law of copyright is not simply a constraint on free communication but a way of defining how, when, and for whom literary communication (one of the most valued forms in secular liberal society) can be regarded as truly free, truly creative. A person's freedom to say whatever he or she wants, how he or she wants, depends on a particular notion of property. It implies a particular kind of property-owning subject whose freedom of speech rests on the truth of what is spoken (created). Historians of literature have begun to trace the strong Romantic roots of the concept of "the literary work."[22] It remains to be investigated to what extent "freedom of speech" in general also has those roots. A genealogy of that right has still to be traced that will show it not as the expression of progressive reason but as the outcome of an imaginative enterprise that was given a Romantic justification. The Romantic movement, it will be remembered, infused the French Revolution—the Rights of Man and

Citizen inscribed liberty; the Revolutionary wars promoted it—and propelled the drive to freedom as autonomy.

The main point I want to make here, however, is that blasphemy (like other forms of verbal transgression) may be seen not simply as a bid for free speech against irrational taboos but as violence done to human relations that are invested with great value, as violence, therefore, to the limits that define a particular kind of free human being. I will take up this point again and at length in my final section.

How Do Muslims Think of Blasphemy?

What *are* Islamic ideas of blasphemy? Obviously not all Muslims think alike, but questions about Islamic ideas of blasphemy are aimed at a moral tradition. But even that tradition contains divergences, tensions, and instabilities, which cannot be equated with an entire "civilizational people." Nevertheless, I will draw on aspects of that tradition in order to explore further some liberal ideas about freedom. One of these is the assumption that the Islamic tradition is rooted in a more restrictive system of ethics, that it does not allow the freedom (especially the freedom of speech) provided and defended by liberal society. Although there is something to this, the simple notion of liberty that is either present or absent seems to me unsatisfactory here.

It is true that Islamic religious regulation restricts the individual's right to behave as he or she wishes through public prohibition, so that the line between *morality* and *manners* (a crucial distinction for the worldly critic) is obscured and the space of free choice narrowed. The worldly critic wants to see and hear everything: nothing is taboo, everything is subject to critical engagement. If speech and behavior are to be constrained, it is because they should conform—willingly—to civility. Good manners take the place of piety; the private and the public are clearly separated. But the situation on the ground is more complicated than the simple binary (the presence or absence of free choice) allows. Consider the following sociolegal situation.

The law in a liberal democracy guarantees the citizen's right to privacy, on which her moral and civic freedom rests. But with the emergence of the liberal welfare state, new tensions arise between the abstract ideal of equality under the law and the particular ways in which the law is applied. The idea that morality is properly a "private" matter and that what is private should not be law's business has, paradoxically, contributed to the passing of legislation intended to deal with "private" trouble cases that force themselves into the legal arena. The legislation has given judges and welfare administrators greater discretion in matters relating to the family (custody, childcare, divorce, maintenance, matrimonial property, and inheritance).The sentiment guiding this move is that a more humane way of dealing with conflicts is called for, in which different personal beliefs, emotions, and circumstances can be taken into account. The individuality of the person must be respected, which means it must be fully identified. So discretion and private hearings are necessary. Displays of sensibility and hysteria (inscriptions of emotion on the body) must be observed and assessed. Justice, consequently, becomes individualized. Thus the intervention by social workers into ("private") family life in cases of suspected incest or child neglect or spousal abuse is a function of "public" law authorizing bureaucratic action in "private" domains. In short, although religious morality (piety) is not allowed to impose norms of proper speech and behavior on the individual (as would be the case in Muslim ethics), these legal developments redraw the boundaries of individual freedom. The subject's right to relate to her own children is circumscribed by the welfare agency's right to inspect and intervene in that relationship. New sensibilities regarding what is decent—and therefore also what is outrageous—are created. The breaching of "private" domains in this way, incidentally, is disallowed in Islamic law, although conformity in "public" behavior may be much stricter. Thus, the limits of freedom are differently articulated in relation to spaces designated "private" and "public," and different kinds of discourse are made socially available to distance what is repugnant, whether transcendent or worldly.

This brings me to the Islamic vocabulary that overlaps in some respects with *blasphemy* (the category applied to an outrageous "religious" transgression) in the Christian tradition.

Although the Arabic word *tajdīf* is usually glossed in English as "blasphemy" and is used by Christian Arabs to identify what in European religious history is called "blasphemy," Arabic speakers, in the case of the Danish cartoons, did not (so far as I am aware) employ it. The theological term *tajdīf* has the particular sense of "scoffing at God's bounty."[23] Of course, there are other words that overlap with the English word *blasphemy* (e.g., *kufr* "unbelief," *ridda* "apostasy," *fisq* "moral depravity," and *ilhād* "heresy, apostasy"), but these were not, to my knowledge, used in response to the Danish cartoons. As accusations against non-Muslim journalists, they would, in any case, be inappropriate. When the World Union of Muslim Scholars made its statement on the Danish cartoons affair, for example, it used the word *isā'ah*, not *tajdīf*. And *isā'ah* has a range of meanings, including "insult, harm, and offense," that are applied in secular contexts.[24] One of the cartoons, it will be recalled, depicts the Prophet Muhammad as a suicide bomber—a figure at once absurd and barbaric. The World Union states that it has waited a long time so that the efforts exerted by numerous Islamic and Arab organizations, and by several states, would elicit an appropriate apology, but to no avail. Therefore "the Union will be obliged to call upon the millions of Muslims in the world to boycott Danish and Norwegian products and activities."[25] The freedom to campaign against particular consumer goods is opposed to the freedom to criticize beliefs publicly: one social weapon faced another, each employing a different aspect of the modern idea of freedom. If physical violence was sometimes used by some of those who advocated a boycott, this should not obscure the fact that a commercial boycott is always a kind of violence, especially if it is infused with anger, because it attacks people's livelihood. The European history of boycotts (the refusal to purchase commodities) and strikes (the withholding of labor), with all their accompanying violence, has been a story of the struggle for modern rights. And yet in the present case European commentators described the two differently: the one as an innocent expression of freedom, the other as a vicious attempt at restricting it, and thus as yet another sign of the conflict between two civilizations having opposed political orientations.

In liberal democratic thinking the principle of free speech cannot be curtailed by the offense its exercise may cause—so long as it is not defamatory. More interesting is the argument that it was even a good thing that pious Muslims felt injured, because being hurt by criticism might provoke people to reexamine their beliefs—something vital both for democratic debate and for ethical decision making. This point, in contrast to the first, valorizes the consequence of free speech rather than the act itself. The criticism of questionable (religious) beliefs is presented as an obligation of free speech, an act carried out in the knowledge and power of truth. Western post-Christian society thus agrees with Christianity that *the truth makes one free* (John 8:32).

That this is not an Islamic formulation emerges from an examination of the widely discussed trial of Nasr Hamid Abu Zayd, a professor in Cairo University, for apostasy (*ridda*) because he had advocated a radically new interpretation of the revealed text of the Qur'an.[26] Of course, both *truth* and *freedom* are greatly valued in the Islamic tradition, but they are not tied up together quite as they are in Christianity. (It may be pointed out in passing that the many cases of apostasy in the contemporary Middle East that have received much publicity in the West are actually relatively recent and closely connected with the formation of the modern state, a modern judiciary, and the rise of modern politics. In this context one may recall the burst of blasphemy trials in nineteenth-century England to which I referred earlier.) A question worth considering, however, is whether these trials should be seen simply in terms of the suppression of freedom: What do they tell us about the liberal idea of the human subject?

In a book that deals with the Abu Zayd case,[27] Islamist lawyer Muhammad Salīm al-'Awwa emphasizes that the shari'a guarantees freedom of belief. "Freedom of belief means the right of every human being to embrace whatever ideas and doctrines he wishes, even if they conflict with those of the group in which he lives or to which he belongs, or conflicts with what the majority of its members regard as true."[28] He goes on to say that no one may exert pressure to get another to reveal his or her religious beliefs—that is to say, the shari'a prohibits the use of inquisitorial methods.[29] The right to think whatever one wishes does not include, however, the right to express one's religious or moral beliefs publicly with the intention of converting people to a false commitment. Such a limitation may seem strange to modern liberals (although not to Kant),[30] for whom the ability to speak publicly about one's beliefs is necessary to freedom. It is, after all, one aspect of "the freedom of religion" that is guaranteed by a secular liberal democracy. Al-'Awwa is aware of this, and he cites two Qur'anic verses that seem to guarantee freedom of religion: *lā ikrāha fi-ddīn*, "There is no compulsion in religion" (2:256), and *faman shā'a falyu'min wa man shā'a falyakfur*, "let him who wills have faith, and him who wills reject it" (18:29). But for the community what matters is the Muslim subject's social practices—including verbal publication—not her internal thoughts, whatever these may be. In contrast, the Christian tradition allows that thoughts can commit the sin of blasphemy and should therefore be subject to discipline: thoughts are subject to confession.[31]

According to al-'Awwa, publishing one's thoughts changes their character, makes them into publicly accessible signs: "To publish something," he quotes an old saying, "is to lay oneself open to the public."[32] It is one thing to think whatever one wishes, he argues, and a different thing to seduce others into accepting commitments that are contrary to the moral order. In a well-known book published in Lebanon in 1970, responding to the accusation of apostasy against the Syrian philosopher Jalal Sadiq al-'Azm for his famous *Naqd al-fikr al-dīnī* (*The Critique of Religious Thought*, 1969), Shaykh 'Uthman Safi makes a similar distinction, but without reference to Islamic religious authorities. His approach instead is to make an explicit distinction between "natural, innate freedom" and freedom as defined and limited by the law. The individual may give free rein to his thought and imagination, accepting or rejecting as he wishes within the limits of his contemplation. "When these possibilities of freedom that the human being enjoys remain within his soul, the law, especially, cannot interfere with them except when the belief is moved from secrecy to broad daylight [*min as-sirr ila al-jahr*]."[33] When, in the Abu Zayd case, the highest court of appeal in Egypt distinguished between the inviolability enjoyed by private belief and the vulnerability of published statements to the charge of *kufr* ("apostasy, blasphemy, infidelity"), the court was saying that the legal *meaning* of the latter was not to be decided by its *origin* in the intention of a particular author but by its *function* in a social relation. The effect of his making them public was therefore his responsibility. This position is close to, but not identical with, a modern liberal view.

The liberal view assumes that the crucial relationship in this matter is between two things: a person, on the one hand, and the written or spoken words he or she asserts and believes to be true (assents to mentally), on the other. These statements are—like all empirical statements—subject to criteria of verification. Belief, however, has an ambiguous status—at once internal and external. It is the internal sense that most modern Westerners have taken as being primary, although it is generally recognized that it is possible to externalize it. Thus, when Kilian Bälz writes that "belief is a spiritual affair which is not readily accessible to investigation in the court room,"[34] he is restating the secular idea of "religious belief" understood as a private spiritual matter. But the view that "religious belief" is not readily accessible in a courtroom should be understood, I suggest, as a claim of immunity (the court has no authority to intrude) rather than of principled skepticism about the court's practical ability to extract the truth. It is quite different, in other words, from the classical shari'a tradition, in which Islamic jurists adopt the principle of episte-mological skepticism, insisting that the judge cannot distinguish with absolute certainty a truthful utterance from a lie when that is unsupported by sensory experience. Although divine revelation, together with the tradition of the Prophet and the consensus of jurists, *do* provide Muslims with "indisputable and certain knowledge" (*'ilm yaqin*), jurists held that this certainty relates to the legal and ethical rules they establish and not to the truth of what claimants say are facts in a given case.[35] A secular state, by contrast, has to deter-mine whether a particular doctrine or practice belongs to a "religion" and therefore quali-fies the believer or practitioner to equal treatment with members of other "religions."[36] Hence belief *must* be externalizable as doctrine ("I hold the following things to be true"), whether voluntarily or by force.

The issue in this case is not the correctness or otherwise of "belief" in this sense, but the legal and social consequences of a Muslim professor's teaching a doctrine that was said to be contrary to Islamic commitment.[37] (The Arabic word commonly used for "be-lief," *i'tiqād*, derives from the root *'aqada*, "to put together." This root gives the word *'aqd*, "contract," and its many cognates, and thus carries a sense of social relationship. Its primary reference in classical Arabic is to the bond in which the believer is committed to his or her God.[38]) In the classic shari'a position, the strength of personal conviction is said to be a matter between the individual and his God (*baynahu wa bayna rabbih*). Disbelief incurs no legal punishment; even the Qur'an stipulates no worldly punishment for disbelief. In the classical law, punishment for apostasy is justified on the grounds of its political and social consequences, not of entertaining false doctrine itself. Put another way, insofar as the law concerns itself with disbelief, that is not as a matter of its proposi-tional untruth but of a social relationship being broken ("being unfaithful"). Legally, apostasy (*ridda, kufr*) can therefore be established only on the basis of the functioning of external signs (including public speech or writing, publicly visible behavior), never on the basis of inferred or forcibly extracted internal belief.[39]

In contemporary Egypt, conviction of a Muslim for apostasy in a court of law has consequences for civil status, because the shari'a (the "religious law") has become the law of personal status there. A legal consequence is the automatic dissolution of an apostate's marriage if it was contracted according to the shari'a. There are also social consequences, among them the concern that an apostate who is responsible for teaching Islamic thought may suppress the truth through the unrestrained publications of spoken and written signs. (This point should not be confused with the judgment of the Court of Appeal in the Abu Zayd case when it declared that an attack on Islam is an attack on the foundations of Egypt as a Muslim state. *That* consequentialist argument—as well as claims that the feel-ings of Muslims are offended—is quite different.)

The crucial distinction made in liberal thought between *seduction* and *forcible subjec-tion* (legally permitting the former and penalizing the latter) is here absent—at least in al-'Awwa's argument. To seduce someone is to connive at rendering them unfaithful, to make them break an existing social commitment. Even in medieval Christendom, the term *infidelitas* could be used not only in relation to personal departures from church doctrine but also, in a secular sense, to breaking a contract.[40] "Unfaithfulness" in this worldly sense now has a quaint ring about it in modern liberal society and relates only to sexual seduction.

But is the concern about seduction entirely absent in secular liberal society? It is, of course, absent in the way Muslims typically express it. Nevertheless, among some secular liberals too there is concern over the impact of published or broadcast material on young listeners (or viewers). That concern, however, is not with protecting them against *false religion* but with ensuring that whatever is published will not distort the correct formation of their subjectivity, and especially of their ability to choose freely, because that is the precondition of moral autonomy. Thus in the recent "Islamic veil" affair in France, French liberals explained that even if Muslim pupils wanted to express themselves by wearing this religious symbol, they shouldn't be allowed to do so in public schools: "An attitude of enquiry, and of open-mindedness to knowledge is incompatible with the peremptory assertion of an identity more fantasized than freely chosen [*une identité plus fantasmée que librement choisie*], especially at an impressionable age. . . . Many of the pupils are minors and it is unrealistic to maintain that they know clearly who they are and what they do."[41] Only when they have learned how to negotiate the endless world of signs *properly*—to distinguish clearly between "reality" and "fantasy"—do they acquire the status of moral adults.[42] And moral maturity is demonstrated by the exercise of free choice.

So how clear is the liberal distinction between seduction and free choice? As a consumer and as a voter the individual is subjected to a variety of allurements through appeals to greed, envy, revenge, vanity, and so on. What in other circumstances are identified and disapproved of as moral failures are here essential to the functioning of a particular kind of economy and polity. Numerous studies have described how television as a medium of communication seeks to shape viewers' choices of commodities and candidates.[43] (In film generally seduction is central, even where no political or commercial message is intended.) To seduce is to incite someone to open up his or her innermost self to images, sounds, and words offered by the seducer and to lead him or her unwittingly to the desired end.

In Islamic theology, seduction is a notion of great concern—and not merely in the sexual sense. The Qur'an contains numerous words that can be glossed as "seducing" and "deluding"—among them the verbal roots *fatana*, *rāwada*, *gharra*. *Fatana* (from which comes the familiar noun *fitna*) always has the sense of "temptation and affliction as a testing," of "persecution,[44] treachery, or social strife." But the temptation referred to by this term in the Qur'an is not sexual. (Even in modern Arabic *fitna* is not used exclusively in a sexual sense; it can also mean enchantment and fascination generally.) It is the word *rāwada* that is used in the Qur'an to refer explicitly to sexual seduction. *Gharra* refers to delusion through attachment to fancies, to the act of deceiving oneself. The nominal form *ighrā'* can be glossed as "excessive attachment, self-love, desire, incitement," but it also connotes "social unrest and instability." Muslim theologians and jurists assumed that seduction in all its forms was necessarily dangerous not only for the individual (because it indicated a loss of self-control) but for the social order too (it could lead to violence and civil discord). They were wrong, of course, because they didn't know about capitalist democracy, a system that thrives on the consumer's loss of self-control and has learned to employ political seduction while maintaining overall political control.

So under what circumstances can one say that one is choosing what one truly believes—and that therefore, in *choosing*, one is expressing one's true beliefs? When can one say that it is in expressing one's beliefs *because one must* that one provides evidence of what one's true beliefs are? According to Susan Mendus,[45] John Locke propounded his theory of political toleration on the basis of the psychological principle that belief can never be determined by the will. This principle rests on a new psychology of the will that was beginning to emerge in seventeenth-century Europe, as well as a new understanding of "belief." In the Middle Ages a contrary doctrine prevailed. Thomas Aquinas, for example, took it for granted that belief (a commitment, a holding dear) could indeed be willed. It was this modern psychology that allowed Locke to insist that the Prince's attempt to coerce religious belief—including belief in the salvational implications of religious practices—was irrational. All that force could secure was an insincere profession of faith. Of course, the Prince might have other reasons for imposing conformity on his subjects than an aim for their salvation—such as upholding law and order—that would not render his coercive efforts necessarily irrational. The presumption that political attempts to coerce belief are irrational because impossible has been the focus of an interesting debate summarized by Mendus. The Muslim position, as expounded by 'Awwa, is different from Locke's. Since, according to the latter, it is impossible to coerce belief, the mind becomes the site of true religious belonging, and physical force as the arm of civil government should therefore confine itself to civil interests—the protection of life, limb, and property—only. According to the former, religious *belonging*, as distinct from religious belief, *can* be forced (or seduced) but it is illegitimate to do so. This accords, incidentally, with the central Islamic tradition about Christians and Jews, whose understanding of divine revelation is considered to be distorted (the Qur'an is perfect)—*but who are not therefore required to abjure their error*. What matters, finally, is belonging to particular ways of life in which the person does not own himself.

Mendus's view is that Locke was right to make the presumption about the impossibility of coercing religious belief, and she defends him against his critics on this point by making what she regards as a critical distinction within the individual's consciousness—a difference between *sincere* and *authentic* belief—which she borrows from Bernard Williams. This allows her to argue that a forcible conversion (brain-washing) may at most obtain a *sincere* belief, not an *authentic* one. But the conditions cited by Mendus—

beginning with the so-called "acceptance" condition—are, I think, questionable. Thus her claim that the alternatives of deliberate reticence (not saying what one really believes) and insincerity (affirming what one doesn't believe) must *always* exist as possibilities in order to determine whether a belief is really authentic or genuine seems to me unconvincing. The alternatives at issue must surely signify something more than abstract possibilities; they must appear to the person concerned as *real* options, within a given sociopsychological situation, from among which he can actually choose. But if that is so, then certain kinds of religious acts are ruled out a priori: "bearing witness" in public where one feels *one has no choice* but to speak the truth—in anger, say, or in compassion—would have to be identified as "inauthentic."[46] Should the impossibility of remaining silent about what one believes to be morally right in such situations be taken to mean that the belief is inauthentic?

It is hard to avoid the conclusion that talk of philosophical criteria determining "authentic belief" is little more than a way of devaluing moral passion, of disregarding the way passion constitutes moral actions so as to render the matter of choice irrelevant. One consequence of that devaluation is that it becomes difficult for the secular liberal to understand the passion that informs those for whom, rightly or wrongly, *it is impossible to remain silent when confronted with blasphemy*, for whom blasphemy is neither "freedom of speech" nor the challenge of a new truth but something that seeks to disrupt a living relationship.

It is important to note that passionate reaction to "blasphemers" is typically directed not at the latter's disbelief but at their violent act. I stress that I make no claim to know the real motives of all those who shout about blasphemy. My argument is that we will not understand "blasphemy" if all we see in it is a threat to freedom, even though historically the charge of "blasphemy" has usually been accompanied by powerful punitive apparatuses.

Blasphemy as Violence

Of course there is no place for blasphemy as a religious crime—as "treason against God"[47]—in a secular liberal society: The crime of treason can only be committed against the sovereign nation-state. But is there a place for blasphemy as a distinctive mode of understanding and addressing our world—a world in which verbal and physical violence are variously constitutive? Is it possible to think worldly matters in theological language, to trace the genealogies of contemporary public discourse in that language, to explore possibilities without belief or disbelief?

Archbishop of Canterbury Rowan Williams is a distinguished theologian whose writings have often proved thought provoking for non-Christians such as myself. Recently something he said helped me to understand the conceptual and emotional structure of blasphemy a little better. A year after the London bombings by young British Muslims in protest against the war in Iraq, Williams delivered a sermon at York about contemporary terrorism. He declared:

> People of faith have had to try and come to terms with the horrible fact that there are those who want to serve their God and their idea of justice by organised slaughter and suicide. They want to display strength; they want to secure their vision by force and *to clothe suicide with the spiritual power of martyrdom.* . . . this represents a condition of spiritual weakness that is both pitiable and terrifying. For the person who resorts to random killing in order to promote the honour of God or the supposed cause of justice, it is clear that God is not to be trusted. God is too weak to look after his own honour and we are the strong ones who must step in to help him. Such is the underlying blasphemy at work.[48]

In Williams's eyes suicide bombers are not simply misguided, they are blasphemers, and they are blasphemers because their action implies they believe that God is dependent upon them. One may note in passing that "promoting the honour of God" is not, to my knowledge, a reason given by Muslim suicide bombers. Unlike the Christian concept of the Godhead (who is a person), Muslims insist that God is *not* a person—and therefore honor and dishonor cannot accrue to him. Justice, however, *is* often given as a reason, and although these young men might have been misguided in believing that their cause was just, and although they certainly used cruel means in promoting it, it is not immediately clear why *that* should make the action "blasphemous." But from Williams's perspective it is blasphemy—a horrific violation of sacred truths. He reasons that if the blasphemer's belief were really true, "it would mean that all we had to hold on to was our own power, the fantasy of being in total control that fuels every kind of pathological violence, domestic or public." The blasphemy here consists in violence based on delusions of absolute control. So perhaps Williams would think of the War on Terror as blasphemy, both because it attempts to secure absolute control through secret surveillance of all citizens and because it involves the use of total violence (including torture) as an instrument for reshaping the world.

The sermon also evokes a more intriguing question: How has violence come to be regarded as a scandal in "religion" but not in "secular" life? Why has critique sought a *justifiable* place for inflicting violence outside of "religion"? Why, in other words, is death-dealing as such not what matters but how it is motivated, played out, justified? What notion of the responsible person and of the act of lethal violence does this imply? What, to be specific, accounts for the fact that when terrorists, invoking a transcendent cause, murder civilians (however few) this appears to us more shocking than when military aircraft bomb whole cities for worldly reasons? Is this because the first case is presented as criminal intent and the second as military strategy? The effect of this difference is that in the first case the killer is situated *within* his action (inviting us to take the question as essentially a moral one) and in the second, *external* to it (where we are induced to regard the issue as primarily technical). It is the latter that allows for unending arguments about how accurate the information at the disposal of the military commander was, and how necessary the killing was to his strategy, and therefore creates an area of moral uncertainty. At any rate, Christian and non-Christian liberals have long entertained an interesting paradox without resolving it: on the one hand, religion and violence "naturally" go together (hence the necessity of a secular state); on the other hand, religious violence is especially shocking becaust it strikes against "true" religion.

Christianity has a long history of reflection on violence,[49] whether intended to be lethal or not,[50] specifically on the theological concepts of "just war" and "proper punishment," which have long been the object of humanist theorizing. One may wonder why Archbishop Williams did not take up this ambiguous aspect of violence as blasphemy—as the breaking of moral limits.

There is, however, something even more interesting in the sermon than this question. The essential shock effect of suicide bombing, he lets us understand, is due not merely to its destruction of innocent human life (that's the stuff of war) or to its being a crime of murder (that is common enough in peace) but to its status as a performative: suicide bombing is blasphemous not because of its violence but because it *says* something about the sacred and what it says is a travesty. It "pretends," as Williams puts it, "to clothe suicide with the spiritual power of martyrdom." A sign, whether verbal or visual, evokes horror when it turns out to be *profoundly* deceptive—when it undermines the basis on which one's moral world, and therefore one's identity, is built. The condemnation that attends the act of blasphemy—including humanist apprehensions of blasphemy—is nurtured by a theology that has its own modes of decipherment, its own disavowals, its own apprehension of how destruction is related to truth.

The French historian Alain Cabantous once noted that when Jesus claimed for himself a divine nature, this was condemned as blasphemy. That blasphemy led to his death, and the death was followed by resurrection. "In this one respect," he writes, "blasphemy *founded* Christianity."[51] Cabantous doesn't say this, but every new tradition, whether it is called religious or worldly, is founded in a discursive rupture—which means, through violence.[52] He might have observed, however, that the blasphemy was not perceived as such by *believers*. From a Christian point of view, that charge of blasphemy was merely an expression of disbelief. And although that disbelief eventually led to Christ's death, the violence done to him must have been part of a divine plan. Did Christ *want* his unbelieving listeners to take what he said as blasphemy because his crucifixion was essential to the project of human redemption? His claim to divinity *was*, after all, outrageous in the context of Jewish religious life, as it would be in that of Muslims. The Passion with which this blasphemy was played out was essential to the narrative that bound his death (and resurrection) to the life and death of all human beings and that inaugurated a *particular* universality. Part of that universality was the guilt and punishment imposed through the centuries on Jews—which became, in a sense, the paradigm of violent justice.

So, strictly speaking, what founded Christianity was not blasphemy itself but a new narrative of sacrifice and redemption—a story of martyrdom (witnessing) that would be, for believers, the door to eternal life. The truth, said Jesus to his followers, will set you free. The unredeemed human condition is lack of freedom; free speech—truthful speech—releases the human subject from his or her servitude. The truth must be spoken publicly, even if those who do not possess the truth regard it as blasphemy. A modern New Testament scholar writes: "In spite of the opposition of those who are unbelievers, of those who criticize the apostle [John], the Christian may speak freely because he knows Him who conquers all opposition, because he knows that wonderful communion with God which transcends everything in the world."[53] Islamic tradition does not speak of freedom in this way.

Why does the Christian today (as well as nonbelievers brought up in a *Christian civilization*) recognize blasphemy in the suicide bomber's act? What makes for the horror it evokes? Here is a tentative answer: unlike later cases of blasphemy, which carried the ultimate punishment, death in this case did not follow accusation but preceded it. And in itself the death did not convey the truth of life eternal, it expressed the banality of profane violence. In Christian—and post-Christian—eyes, I suggest, suicide bombing is seen as a caricature of the crucifixion. The bomber brings death to other human beings by suicide (soldiers kill but hope to live). He does not get others to kill him but kills himself, and he does not promise immortality to believers but to an abstract community (the *umma*). What the internal beliefs of its members are is of no concern to him. His is therefore a gratuitous act of cruelty, whereas the cruelty of the crucifixion story is integral to a redemptive martyrology. For Williams, to call something "blasphemy" is to denounce its factitious claim to martyrdom. But for liberals inhabiting a secular society, acts of self-immolation for a sacred purpose are entirely barbaric, just as the violation of sacred words is merely an absurdity.

The willful destruction of signs—the assault on images and words that are themselves invested with the power to determine what counts as truth—has a long history. Like iconoclasm and blasphemy, secular critique also seeks to create spaces for new truth, and like them it may do so by destroying spaces that were occupied by other signs.

Historical Notes on the Idea of Secular Criticism

Let me elaborate a little on the idea of criticism that is said to be everything that the idea of blasphemy rejects. The language of blasphemy has no place for rational criticism; it provides instead for anathematizing (cursing and expressing loathing). The modern responsible citizen and modern knowledge-producing disciplines (like anthropology) are equally dependent on reasoned critique. Both are secular in their fundamental assumptions about the world, and both find in the claims of blasphemy nothing more than intolerance, closed-mindedness, and irrationality. All of this is familiar enough. But to understand how intolerant, closed-minded, and irrational the idea of blasphemy is one must turn to how secular criticism liberates us for the world.

In an essay entitled "Secular Criticism," Edward Said wrote that "Criticism . . . is always situated, it is skeptical, secular, reflectively open to its own failings."[54] Leaving aside for the moment the important idea of situatedness, I would merely add three things. First, criticism's *secular* character is often based on the assumption that the distinction between the *real* world and a *representational* one is essential, and—like the difference between "maturity" and "childishness"—it can easily be identified. Second, since criticism employs *judgment*, it seeks conviction (in the transitive sense as well as intransitive), especially when confronted with doubt. Finally, secular criticism regards itself as liberatory, although extra-discursive conditions have to be right for the liberation to be achieved. So: *What is critique?*

That, of course, is the title of a well-known late essay by Michel Foucault.[55] In it Foucault seeks to equate critique with the Kantian notion of Enlightenment and thus to present it as the singular characteristic of the modern West:

> it seems that between the lofty Kantian enterprise and the small polemico-professional activities that bear the name "critique," there was in the modern West (dating, roughly, from the fifteenth to the sixteenth century) a certain manner of thinking, of speaking, likewise of acting, and a certain relation to what exists, to what one knows, to what one does, as well as a relation to society, to culture, to others, and all this one might name "the critical attitude."[56]

It is not clear whether Foucault wishes us to understand that "the critical attitude" is specific only to the modern West, or that the critical attitude distinctive of the modern West is quite different from what is found elsewhere (able to think for the first time of "the transcendent"). At any rate, it is clear that in Foucault's view to be enlightened is equivalent to adopting a critical attitude, and to engage in critique, as the West has done for over two centuries, is equivalent to living in Enlightenment. This seems to me somewhat surprising coming from a genealogist, because it sets aside the need to think through the various historical determinants whose effect—in different circumstances—has been a diversity of "critiques." Neither the concept nor the practice of critique has a simple history, and that genealogy has yet to be written. What follows is a set of disparate historical notes in which I focus on criticism as the kind of free speech that lies at the center of the Danish cartoons affair.

The word *criticism* has its origin in the Greek verb *krinō*, meaning "to separate," "to decide," "to judge," "to fight," "to accuse." It seems to have been first used in the juridical sphere, where both the act of accusing and the giving of a verdict were called *krinō*, and thus referred to the ability to differentiate, to ask probing questions, and to judge. In this worldly arena the semantic beginnings of what we now call "critique" did not aspire to conquer universal truth but to resolve particular crises justly and to correct particular virtues within a particular way of life.[57]

Criticism could also take the form of "free and open speech [*parrhesia*]" in the political forum. Critical preaching, especially associated with the Cynic philosophers of the fourth century B.C., was directed at everyone, and its aim was to teach people how to assess critically their own personal mode of life.[58] Christianity drew on this tradition of free and open speech, transforming the word *parrhesia* in the process to its own end. Criticism and the open call to the truth have remained an important part of popular preaching throughout the Christian era.

In the late medieval period, preaching in public places was practiced by the Friars, who censured particular ways of living and advocated others. At an academic level the idea of critique was employed in a number of university disciplines, but not until the theological disputes of the Reformation did it denote the same notion regardless of whether it was applied to classical texts, the Bible, or social life. So to the question "What is critique?" the answer would then have been: "The evaluation and interpretation of the truth of Scripture."

At first criticism aimed only at the production of an authentic text and at its meaning, but eventually, as it began to be concerned with the reality represented in the texts, it became what would be called historical criticism. A major figure that exemplifies this development is Pierre Bayle.[59] For this seventeenth-century skeptic, critique was the activity that separated reason from revelation by the systematic exposure of errors and by the rhetoric of ridicule. In effect, Bayle tried to analyze and dissolve each theory in its own terms and to demonstrate that everything confidently accepted on the grounds of reason could be undone by critical reasoning. The use of critique here turned out to be as much an argument for the necessity of faith as it was an attack on the absolute reliability of reason. This was not the old theological use of reason to underwrite revelation, but a new, secular demonstration that if critique is pushed far enough it collapses. Politically Bayle's extreme skepticism was premised on the notion of an egalitarian "republic of letters," in which one could engage equally with others instead of submitting to authority. In the newly emerging discipline of experimental philosophy, criticism took a prudent middle position between skepticism and credulity. In this seventeenth-century culture of knowledge production, social trust and gentlemanly authority became—as Steven Shapin has shown—the basis of reliable testimony and restrained criticism.[60]

At the end of the eighteenth century, German Idealism was strongly influenced by Immanuel Kant. For Kantians, political revolution appeared to be the alternative to philosophical criticism; freedom for philosophical critique thus became a means of forestalling political revolution. It was Kant who replaced the model of the "republic of letters" with another model: the "court of reason." This followed not only from his direct philosophical concern with *judgment* but also indirectly from his view that truth was guaranteed no longer by freedom from political and ecclesiastical constraint but by the progress of rational science. To the "court of reason" was given the important task of imposing peace on the apparently unending war of doctrines. For Enlightenment philosophers prior to Kant, critique had been rooted in a secularized metaphysics (in the idea of human reason) and directed against ecclesiastical and state pretensions. For Kant critique became the process of epistemological self-correction by strict reference to established rational limits and the fixed boundary between private faith and public reason. But his formula for critique as an inquiry into the preconditions of scientific truths cut it off from politics as well as from faith. In Kant's political philosophy it is *law*, not critique, that ends the chaos of metaphysics and that holds the corrosive effects of skepticism in check. And its concern is no longer with mundane life but with epistemology.

Only when the Romantics returned to problems of aesthetics was the dominance of Kantian discourse challenged. The most prominent figure here is Hegel, who took critique to be immanent in reality: thought and reality should not be separated as transcendental reason and phenomenal object, respectively, as Kant had separated them. They are, Hegel maintained, both dialectically opposed parts of the real—as contradictory parts of a developing self and of the world in process of becoming. The Kantian discipline of epistemology was thus set aside. From this emerged the famous Marxian dictum that critical theory is itself a part of social reality. Marx's Hegelian premise that the existing world is characterized by contradictions led him, however, to the anti-Hegelian conclusion that their removal depends not on new philosophical interpretations but on the practical transformation of reality itself. The reality to be transformed was politico-economic, not moral.[61] In a rapidly industrializing world, critique and revolutionary violence thus no longer appeared as alternatives but as complementary forms of class struggle, and the critical politics this called for was that of organized working-class movements.

In the twentieth century, Neo-Kantians again limited the concept of critique to epistemology, with the intention of opposing Hegelianism and Marxism. Critique or criticism then became a weapon directed at ideological politics and radical intellectuals. Among this group of philosophers, criticism again became the criterion of universal reason, a principle held to be crucial for the natural *and* the human sciences. They defined a scientific *fact* as one that can be criticized—and that can therefore be falsified. Because religious values are immune to rational critique, because they are based on *faith*, they are neither neutral nor objective, and they cannot therefore have the authority of scientific facts.[62] To the extent that a "belief" is presented as a candidate for truth, it must be held provisionally—that is to say, it must not be taken too seriously. Falsificationists like Popper reaffirmed a more direct connection between epistemology (what are the criteria of valid knowledge about the world) and politics (how one can legitimately use power to make or remake the social world).

My final example is of secular critique as modern theology. The example is the Regensburg lecture by Pope Benedict XVI in 2006, whose opening salvo against Islam evoked predictable anger from Muslims across the world. What he believed he was doing in this lecture is not of concern to me here. What *is* interesting is the way he links his discursive attack on Islam to his critique of European reason. According to Benedict, Islamic theology separates the concept of God from reason (making him utterly unpredictable, therefore irrational), whereas Christianity maintains their inseparability in its harmonization of Hellenic rationality with the status of the divine: "In the beginning was the *logos*, and the *logos* is God, says the Evangelist." Thus Benedict. This fusion explains why Christianity seeks to lead the individual to the truth through reasoned persuasion and why Islam, by contrast, uses force to convert non-Muslims and to punish people for holding false beliefs. The inner rapprochement between biblical faith and Greek philosophical inquiry that constituted Christianity "was an event of decisive importance not only from the standpoint of the history of religions, but also from that of world history—it is an event that concerns us even today." Hence his critique of the successive waves of de-Hellenization in European thought—from the Reformation via Kant and liberal theology to scientific positivism—by which, he claims, the inner bond between faith and reason is ruptured. In spite of his polemic against what he takes to be Islamic doctrine (and therefore, arguably, against Muslim immigrants in Europe) and in spite of his assertion that Europe is fundamentally Christian, Benedict's critique is not merely political: it is aimed, in a very modern way, at reaffirming the identification of reason with divinity. His critique of de-Hellenization is aimed at what he regards as a dangerous restriction of reason's scope—and he calls, therefore, for an unrestricted pursuit and enunciation of the truth. The truth must be presented publicly even if those not possessing it regard the offer of truth as blasphemy. This is how Benedict concludes his university lecture: "This attempt . . . at a critique of modern reason from within has nothing to do with putting the clock back to the time before the Enlightenment and rejecting the insights of the modern age. . . . The scientific ethos, moreover, is—as you yourself mentioned, Magnificent Rector—*the will to be obedient to the truth*, and, as such, it embodies an attitude which belongs to the essential decisions of the Christian spirit." Thus, while for Kant critical reason appeals to transcendental law (while paradoxically insisting on the autonomy of the subject), Benedict gestures to a Christian life of obedience that accepts *logos* as at once persuasive *reason* and divine *authority*. The Christian obeys not because she thinks it reasonable to do so but because the authority of received truth compels her to obey. The apparent contradiction between reason and authority in this argument might be resolved if reason ceases to be regarded as a matter of autonomous intellection (the knowing subject confronting "reality") and becomes instead embedded in a relationship, a way of life. In this shift, critique too changes its character. But if *logos* is a dialogue, it is not clear from this lecture who the interlocutors are and how open-ended (and mutually influencing) the dialogue is allowed to be.

In presenting these notes on thoughts about critique, I have tried to underline the very different understandings people have had of it in Western history, which can't be captured by the familiar distinction between secular criticism (freedom) and religious criticism (oppression). Perhaps these notes should be supplemented, however briefly, by some remarks about the practice of critique. After the public freedoms established by the French Revolution, the progress of rational critique emerged as the opposite of physical violence. Historically this opposition has not been easy to maintain because critique has also legitimized violence in several ways. The practice of critique has been entangled with legitimate violence in the policing of society, in the penal system of the state, and in the conduct of war. It is itself a weapon that can violate the sense of self and sociality that people have.

The practice of criticism is now a sign of the modern, of the modern subject's relentless pursuit of truth and freedom, of his or her agency. It has become a *duty*, closely connected to the right to free expression and communication. Particularly in the universities, critique of one kind or another has become essential to useful knowledge production, but that *professional* critique has less to do with the right of free speech than with the reproduction of intellectual disciplines (whence the class dimension of modern blasphemy, to which I referred earlier). Jon Roberts and James Turner have described the emergence of the modern university in the United States, together with its "secular" culture, starting in the last quarter of the nineteenth century. They recount how the marginalization or exclusion of formal "religion" in the American university was accompanied by an emphasis on research, professionalization, and specialization, and how that, in turn, led to a fragmentation of the traditional map of knowledge, which had until then been articulated in a theological language. It was in this situation that the humanities eventually emerged out of the traditions of moral philosophy and philology, and restored a coherence to knowledge while according it a distinctive "religious" aura. One consequence was that a less sectarian, less doctrinal idea of religion became part of a liberal culture and therefore part of its understanding of criticism. "This new edition of liberal education had two key elements," they write. "The first was to acquaint students with beauty, especially as manifest in 'poetry' broadly conceived. . . . A second element thus entered the humanities: a stress on continuities linking the 'poetry' of one era to that of succeeding periods and ultimately our own." Hence there developed a sharper sense of imparting the moral essence of European civilization to students in higher education through the study of great literature and the recognition that *literary criticism* was the disciplined means to that end. The *literary* discipline thus constructed called for the production of public speech that was carefully regulated.[63] This is one aspect of secular criticism. But there is another.

Over the last few centuries, modern powers have encouraged and used the developing sciences to normalize and regulate social life—and therefore have legitimized a particular kind of disciplinary criticism. That is why, perhaps, critique that is integral to the growth of useful knowledge—and therefore of modern power—is part of a process whose major lineaments have not been effectively reduced to doubt, a process that is rarely itself the object of public critique. Thus, while the freedom to criticize is represented as being at once a right and a duty of the modern individual, its truth-producing capacity remains subject to disciplinary criteria, and its material conditions of existence (laboratories, buildings, research funds, publishing houses, personal computers, etc.) are always provided and watched over by corporate and state power to ensure that citizens can be *useful*. In this context, where critical knowledge is produced by disciplinary power, the phrase "truth makes one free" strikes an oddly uncomfortable note.

In short, critique is not *necessarily* aware of its own failings, even when it regards itself as worldly. On the contrary, it is partly sustained by the patterns of trust and authority that prevail among members of scholarly communities, and partly constrained by corporate and state power. In that sense, critique is based partly on faith and partly on accommodation, a state of affairs in which its own failings are suppressed. It is not entirely correct to say, therefore, that criticism is the expression of modern Enlightenment. It is more accurate to say that modern Enlightenment has produced a particular *concept* of critique: an abstract, universalized concept. Every critical discourse has conditions of existence that define what it is, what it recognizes, what it aims at, what it is destroying. There is no such thing as a transhistorical attitude of worldly criticism that is "open to its own failings" or that is distinctive of the last five centuries of secular modernity. It matters greatly whether critique presupposes a republic of letters (where open-ended questions are exchanged) or a court of reason (by which conviction is authoritatively secured); it matters by what criteria "its own failings" are recognized as such, and who sets them. Finally, it matters whether critique is directed against others or against oneself (the confession of sins, auto-critique, speech under analysis). But always, the person who practices critique is a specific kind of subject—a scandal monger, a satirist, a critical philosopher, an experimental scientist, a religious preacher, a literary critic, a psychoanalyst, a pope. His formation, and the form of society in which he can flourish, are essential preconditions of the many ways critique is performed.

Blasphemy as the Breaking of Taboo

What, then, was the impulse that drove the Danish cartoons affair if it was not truth? Muslim immigrants in secular Europe responded, it was said, to a legitimate act of worldly criticism in violent religious terms. They claimed threateningly that the cartoonist had blasphemed. In fact it was simply that a Muslim taboo had been broken. Appeal was made to the court of reason by many secularists, who responded vigorously to Muslim protests. "Your Taboo, Not Mine," declared Andrew Sullivan defiantly in a *Time Magazine* article on the cartoon affair[64]—dismissing the limits Muslims sought to put on the

Enlightenment right to free speech. What are we to understand by the frequent use of the term *taboo* in the conflict over the Danish cartoons?

The category of taboo as applied to the behavior of Muslim immigrants in Europe serves, paradoxically, at once to confirm and to deny *difference*. Angry Muslim responses to the publication of the cartoons are seen by secularists as attempting to reintroduce a judgment that was once a means of oppression in Europe, while they see themselves critiquing, in the name of freedom, the power to suppress human freedom. For the worldly critic, there can be no acceptable taboos. When limits are critiqued, taboos disappear, and freedom is expanded. *This* criticism didn't merely liberate ideas from taboos, however, it also reenforced the existing distinction between the paradigmatically human ("Judeo-Christian" Europeans) and *candidates* for inclusion in humanity (Muslim Europeans), who do not as yet display full ownership of their bodies, emotions, and thoughts. It reenforces, in other words, the ideological status of Muslims as not fully human because they are not morally autonomous and politically disciplined.

An important study that bears on this topic is a book by the anthropologist Franz Steiner published posthumously half a century ago.[65] In it Steiner provides a genealogy of the reception and use of this term, noting that the word *taboo* was first encountered by European mariners in Polynesia in the latter part of the eighteenth century—where it signified limits set by chiefly power—and was subsequently misunderstood by many post-Enlightenment writers as the primitive encounter with the sacred. The *problem* of taboo, Steiner argues, was a Victorian invention and obsession, because the notion of taboo is compounded of quite disparate ideas and practices. He gives two reasons for its extraordinary prominence in nineteenth-century European thought and society: on the one hand, "the secularization of modern religion," and on the other, the multiplication of taboos in Victorian social life.

The increasing application of reason to what had previously belonged to religion still left certain recalcitrant areas (attitudes, behaviors) that appeared irrational. In fact—Steiner claims, this "irrationality" was the product of the wider process that had deprived these attitudes and behaviors of the frame that had originally given them their sense. It was in this context, he suggests, that the category "taboo" acquired an indispensable explanatory function for modern secular subjects: by being represented as the fear of offending an imaginary power (a sacred power), "taboo" could account for the irrational prohibitions of premodern "religion." To critique taboos was thus to attempt to free the human subject from his religiously maintained infancy. Whereas "taboo" had once regulated behavior, it now signified irrational attachment to belief. In this story it is not restraint on speaking freely that is the object of primary attention but the virtue of criticism as liberating speech.

In addition to this conceptual analysis, Steiner advances a historical narrative that he thinks explains the Victorian obsession with taboo. The nineteenth century witnessed a dynamic, industrializing society, in which new groups and classes sought to establish and defend new lines of linguistic and behavioral demarcation and to suppress even the memory of old ways of life. The rapid changes in society continuously generated elaborate tactics of suppression and invention. The changes incited some people to assault the new—but inevitably temporary—demarcations by which attempts were made (more often than not unsuccessfully) to fix, generalize, and protect cultural values.

If Steiner's account has any validity for late-nineteenth-century Europe (and I believe it has), then it must also apply, at the turn of the twentieth century, to Europe undergoing even more rapid change. The *problem* of blasphemy, one might say, adapting Steiner, is a European obsession. For a secular society that doesn't acknowledge the existence of such a thing as blasphemy, it is quite remarkable how much public discourse there is about it—and about those who complain of it or claim to be affronted by it. Quite remarkable, too, is the obsessive need to repeat again and again the words and images that secularists think will be regarded as blasphemy. Who, one might wonder, are these defenders of worldly criticism trying to convince? Alternatively, whose *conviction* (criminalization) do they seek? It is too simple, I think, to claim—as some Danish commentators have done—that the publication of the cartoons merely sought to overcome the crippling fear that Europeans had of criticizing Muslims.[66] But there is certainly something complicated going on beyond the demonstration of political freedom, something that has to do with an attempt at reassuring the limitless self.

Since its auto-destruction through war at mid-century, Europe has undergone enormous transformations. It lost its imperial possessions, imported Asians, Africans, and West Indians (many of whom had fought in Europe's wars) to rebuild its economies, and attempted to construct a supra-national European union. Legally it proscribed discrimination on the basis of race, gender, and sexual orientation. And yet, although public *declarations* of these principles of liberty and equality have been frequent, the attempt to eliminate the unequal conditions in which the principles are applied has not been very effective. Perhaps more important, the principle of democratic freedom has often been given priority over the encouragement of civility and decency.

Nevertheless, Europe remains divided in the way Europeans understand their collective identity, and the entry of the more Christian East European countries to join the more secular West Europeans has aggravated the problem. This was made evident in the responses both to the vote for the European Constitution and to the question of Turkey's entry. Even post-Christians have been trying to rearticulate their "Christian heritage"—and talk of "Judeo-Christian civilization" is one consequence of that. Thus, although Europeans have rejected any formal reference to Christianity in the E.U. Constitution, they have helped to delay indefinitely Turkey's entry—on grounds that are not formally religious but that clearly display an extreme discomfort with "the alien character of Islam." The notion of a Europe defined by a Christian heritage is without doubt very strong, for Christians as well as post-Christians, but what that heritage consists of—what limits it articulates and who controls it—are questions neither generally agreed upon nor widely debated.

When Sullivan speaks of taboo, he is referring to the notion of a civilization whose liberties he considers to be now endangered—not by the increasing control of the media by corporate capitalism or by the new laws put in place by the security state but by the different appearances, sensibilities, and memories of African and Asian immigrants and their offspring. But perhaps more important is this: there seems to be little awareness of how liberty is shaped in and through actively maintained social relationships, of how relationships that are more than simple calculations of individual advantage *must* recognize and maintain limits.

Increasingly, European Muslims are being asked to assimilate as a solution to the perceived problem of "civilizational difference"—not unlike the way European Jews were required to assimilate prior to 1933. Most Europeans feel they relate productively to Islamic traditions, and so assimilation or expulsion are the only alternatives offered European Muslims. Although the majority of European Muslims have now been born in Europe, they show their difference in different forms. One of these (but only one) is a re-appropriation and transformation—by *some* of these Muslims—of the Islamist movements that emerged on the southern shores of the Mediterranean. This European form of "Islamism" aims not at establishing an Islamic state in Europe (recognized as a practical absurdity) but at securing an Islamic heritage in the face of a hostile, non-Muslim majority, at demanding political rights from the states of which they are citizens and at negotiating their identity within the society at large.[67] Apart from those who may be described as Islamists in this sense, there are small groups of *salafists*, doctrinaire traditionalists who seek to minimize their exchange with the surrounding non-Muslim population; they are pious exiles in a heathen land, suspicious and inward looking. And finally, of course, there are even smaller numbers of *jihadists*, ready to use violence in a religious cause regardless of whether their victims are military or civilian, adults or children, Muslims or non-Muslims. There is little contact between the "Islamists" and the other two, but secular Europeans who are used to thinking in term of a clash of civilizations tend to categorize all of them together. Hence the E.U. officially rejects any connection with Islamist NGOs and charitable or humanitarian associations.

The situated character of Muslim demands and complaints adds greatly to the anxiety of many Europeans not so much because of security considerations (this European Islamism is not political in the sense that Middle Eastern Islamist parties are) but because they believe Islam should have no place in European public life. There is place for varieties of belief as well as unbelief in secular Europe—even for different adjustments to the state of self-declared religious institutions—but not for the figure that negatively helps to define "European identity": Islam. Why is Christianity so important for a largely nonbelieving and nonpracticing European population? In the European imaginary, Christianity is the parent of Reason, and Islam is the embodiment of Unreason.

There is a paradox here, for while Europe claims to be entirely oriented to a continuously new future, its "civilization" is presented as an immutable heritage from the past, especially a Christian past. Liberal Europeans have repeatedly said that modernity—their modernity—consists precisely in the continuous re-creation of individual experience and political-economic futures through the exercise of auto-critique, yet in their relationship to European Muslims a limit seems to have been reached, a limit that is insupportable. *Their* conception of criticism is motivated by the dark face of religion, *ours* by secular debate, democratic openness, and joyous satire; their anger undermines freedom, ours informs its defense; they seek to impose limits (in the idea of blasphemy), we overcome them (by secular critique).

Worldly criticism is held by many Europeans to be an unassailable right. But all is not well, for although the rights-bearing subject is assumed to be free (and worldly criticism is part of her freedom) and required to authenticate herself, she is at the same time subjected to the normalizing effects of uncontrollable powers: the security state and the neo-liberal market. When she speaks it is in someone else's words, when she is silent it is someone else's silence. The future holds out promises and also denies them.

As Steiner argues, limits to possible forms of action are articulated by fundamental social values. Perhaps another way of putting it is that all values are necessarily defined by limits. And of course all limits are invested with potential violence, even (especially) the value of limitless self-creation. Certainly the violent language and the riots that greeted the Danish cartoons are evidence of one kind of concern about limits. But so too, in even more terrifying ways, are the modern wars (preemptive and humanitarian) that seek to establish a moral order in the world or to make liberal democracy safe within its own bounded spaces. The real problem of blasphemy in Europe lies, I suggest, not in the resurgence of religious passions into the public sphere or in the threat posed to the principle of free speech by Muslim immigrants and their offspring. It lies in the *repression* of the particular contradictions in which Europeans now live and the anxiety that this generates, in the drive to break all limits while at the same time being obliged to maintain them.

Here is a final thought: What would happen if religious language were to be taken more seriously in Europe and the endorsement of a War on Terror (together with the associated discourse of Islamophobia) were to be denounced as "blasphemy," as the flouting of fundamental moral limits for the sake of unlimited freedom? What if this were to be done without any "religious" belief or disbelief—*and yet done in all seriousness*, as a way of rejecting with passion the aspiration to totalized global control and the hatred of stubborn foreign identities that the war involves? Europe's proscription of theological language in the political domain makes this use of the category "blasphemy" inconceivable, of course. But does this impossibility merely signal a justified reluctance to politicize "religion," or is it the symptom of a moral incapacity?

Is Liberalism a Religion?

Michael Warner

I have no interest in answering the question of my title. For most people the obvious answer would be "no." For Stanley Fish, among others, the answer is "yes." Dissatisfied with the terms on both sides, I wish to analyze the question itself and the conditions under which it has come to seem meaningful. The point is not to single out Fish, since his basic claim is one that has wide currency, especially in conservative legal circles and among Christian critics of secular law, from Michael McConell and Stephen Carter to Stanley Hauerwas. Nor is it to defend liberal secularism. It is to show some flawed assumptions on both sides. Indeed, I think the Fish critique is essentially locked into the same conceptual vocabulary that gave us disestablishment in the late eighteenth century.

Fish is concerned to puncture the confidence of those who "believe that democracy's imperatives—one man one vote, majority rule, freedom of speech, the right to petition, respect for individuals and their opinions—should apply always and everywhere." "The religious," he adds, "of course believe the same thing about God's imperatives."[1] Secular law, in other words, cannot in innocent neutrality govern "the religious" because it is a rival metaphysics, and one that (unlike religion) cannot own up to the contested character of its own commitments.

In a column about the Danish cartoon furor, Fish went further, arguing that religious zeal is preferable to liberal tolerance. He begins by quoting Flemming Rose, the Danish editor who first printed the cartoons, to the effect that he had no intent to provoke or offend; he merely wanted to test the self-censorship of Western journalists: the intention was "to put the issue of self-censorship on the agenda and have a debate about it." Fish then declares: "Mr. Rose may think of himself, as most journalists do, as being neutral with respect to religion—he is not speaking as a Jew or a Christian or an atheist—but in fact he is an adherent of the religion of letting it all hang out, the religion we call liberalism."[2] My point of departure will be this choice of the word *religion* as the damning name for a deep normativity in liberal culture.

This being Stanley Fish, one might be forgiven for thinking that this is a mischievous rhetorical flourish—that he says this in order get the goat of anyone who identifies his or her liberalism with neutrality toward religion, since it is *only* such a person who is likely to be outraged by the idea that liberalism is a religion. Fit the insult to the victim. Just as the point of the cartoonists seemed to be nothing more than breaking taboos for the sake of making nothing taboo, without any serious commitment to the content, so it might be Fish's aim here to say the one thing held to be shocking in the place where nothing is held to be shocking.

An unsympathetic reader might push this point a little farther, to wonder whether there might be a performative contradiction in the accusation. The inflammatory provocation of Fish's essay, in other words, is only another version of letting it all hang out. To read Fish in this way would be to see his piece as an instance of what has become a very common phenomenon in academic criticism: crypto-liberal antiliberalism.[3]

This suspicion gains a little force from the fact that Fish must define liberalism in a manifestly cartoonish way (as it were): "The first tenet of the liberal religion is that everything (at least in the realm of expression and ideas) is to be permitted, but nothing is to be taken seriously." This of course requires a special sense of what it is to take something seriously.

> I would bet that the editors who have run the cartoons do not believe that Muslims are evil infidels who must either be converted or vanquished. They do not publish the offending cartoons in an effort to further some religious or political vision; they do it gratuitously, almost accidentally. This is itself a morality—the morality of a withdrawal from morality in any strong, insistent form. It is certainly different from the morality of those for whom the Danish cartoons are blasphemy and monstrously evil. And the difference, I think, is to the credit of the Muslim protesters and to the discredit of the liberal editors.

Liberals, like Muslims, have a morality. But they have it in a different way: not "in any strong, insistent form." The key opposition here is weak and strong. Liberalism is defined as the weak holding of beliefs, religion as strong belief. Further, to hold belief as a private matter—no matter how much *individual* conviction one might have—is to hold it weakly; beliefs are strong when they are insistent, when one is willing to act coercively. Refusal to do so is a sign of indifference. "This is, increasingly, what happens to strongly held faiths in the liberal state. Such beliefs are equally and indifferently authorized as ideas people are perfectly free to believe, but they are equally and indifferently disallowed as ideas that might serve as a basis for action or public policy."

Now it might be a surprise to be told that strong beliefs are currently disallowed as a basis for action or public policy. This obviously does not describe our world on the face of it and only makes sense if "strong beliefs" is code for religion in some other sense; even then we would be required to forget to what a degree religious beliefs are and always have been a basis for action and policy, at least in America. It also might be a surprise to be told that the purely *personal* or private quality of a conviction renders it weak, since it was of course the soul-saving function of belief that led Protestants such as Locke and Isaac Backus to argue for its immunity. (This is a real contradiction and not a mistake: the trend toward the personalization of belief in the long history of Christian reform is a trend toward intensification and propositionalization simultaneously, and it is the latter that liberalism stems from.) It is similarly odd to imagine the desire to prevail and the willingness to coerce enemies as the distinguishing indices of strong faith. In contemporary religious culture people often deploy most force in connection with issues that are fairly minor from a theological point of view, mere bumper-sticker religion (such as the mobilization against gay marriage and domestic partnership), while many of the strongest religious convictions have to do with the need to disregard the political and one's contemporaries altogether. Religious culture itself gives abundant examples of intense normativities that do not find direct expression in dominance. So to place liberalism and religion on a weak-to-strong gradient of belief—with liberals once again the girlie men among the manly faithful—hardly seems to describe the social facts.

But it does describe something about the ideology of religion. What interests me is how easy it is for the question of religion to be posed as one of attachment to one's beliefs (and by extension to define liberalism as a negation of that attachment). The notion of belief itself has complicated philosophical baggage; yet it is remarkable how often the synonymity of religion and belief can pass as common sense in a post-Wittgensteinian world. Within religious studies, and the emerging realm of secular studies, the definition of religion as a matter of belief and attachment to belief has been very closely analyzed, by Talal Asad, Charles Taylor, Webb Keane, and many others.[4] These people have observed that a great deal of religious practice—ritual observance, dietary regulation, personal law—often has little to do with credal proposition or with personal sincerity. It is also true that "belief" in the sense that is usually meant here makes imperfect sense in relation to many religious cultures, including the more theologized forms of Buddhism, where the object "God" is unavailable as the projected correlate of an intentional mental state, or to some other recognizable forms of religiosity.

That religion can be defined this way, then, turns out to be a mark of liberalism's emergence within Protestant concerns for true religion.[5] Liberal governance makes sense in those contexts where local religious cultures have already come to define themselves in terms of sincere personal attachment to belief. It is often said that liberal secularism is a religion: it is Protestant Christianity. It would be more precise to say it is the metareligious understanding of post-Calvinist Protestantism, generalized as an understanding of religion per se. In the eighteenth-century arguments that led to the supremacy of the tolerant state, the key premise was the saving character of conviction. Thus what is often called the "privatization" of religion was not an across-the-board diminution of religion; on the contrary, the tolerationist compromises of the eighteenth century left a legacy of categorical respect for religion per se, independent of any particular religious conviction, and this generalized deference drew great force from evangelicalism. (Thus it contributed to what Robert Bellah calls "civil religion.")

Fish's essay is symptomatic of this condition, upon which it plays in an especially artful way. Implied in Fish's criticism is the idea that strongly held belief is by definition not susceptible to rational grounding; to subject a belief to examination, criticism, and debate is to hold it weakly. Fish also implies that the desire to subject beliefs to the test of debate is itself a commitment that cannot be subjected to that process. Hence the premise of Fish's argument turns out to be a definitional paradox: liberalism, defined as willingness to subject all beliefs to debate, must necessarily be a religion, defined as belief held to be immune from debate.

(The basic move here is more than formally analogous to the problem of the sovereign exception, or the critique of law as force; in each case rational procedures are said to require a normativity that they cannot supply by their own means. I say that the resemblance among these arguments is more than formal because it seems to me true that in modernity the governmental concern—what can be said publicly or coercively or with violence—conditions what we would like to think of as the ethical concern with our own beliefs and our relation to them. And vice versa. The topic of religion invites slippage between these two levels.)

For Fish, the lesson of the paradox is: liberalism is wrong, kill the liberals. Or maybe: don't we envy the people whose beliefs are so strong that they want to kill the liberals. The last thing I want to do is undertake a theoretical defense of liberalism; I want to call attention to the way Fish's essay exposes the mutual constitution of liberal governance and the category of "religion." The very neatness of his paradox—liberalism strongly requires weak belief, religion is strong requirement of belief, therefore liberalism is religion—performs as a kind of joke what in fact goes on all the time: that in order to manage religious freedom, secular government first regulates what counts as religion. This point can be made in a number of ways, and to different ends.

Many critics, including Kirstie McClure and Partha Chatterjee, have noticed how often the liberal state is required to act as a theological authority, in apparent contradiction to its own legitimating claims. I can illustrate with two contemporary American examples, one from foreign affairs, one domestic. American foreign policy, as Saba Mahmood shows in a new essay, increasingly involves intervention in Muslim theology: "training Islamic preachers, establishing Islamic schools (madrassahs) that counter the

teachings of the now notorious fundamentalist madrassahs, reforming public school cur-
riculums, and media production (which includes establishing radio and satellite television
stations, producing and distributing Islamic talk shows, and generally shaping the content
of public religious debate within the existing media in Muslim countries)."[6] There has
been debate about this policy within the State Department, since it seems manifestly to
violate the liberal understanding of neutrality toward religion. And there are many ironies
here: as Mahmood notes, this secular agenda of governance is itself shot through with the
interests of the Christian Right. What is especially interesting is that the focus of this
growing interventionist effort is not so much on particular theological doctrines—the
proper attitude to bear in prayer, the duty of justice to the poor, the proper way to stone
a homosexual—but rather on the inculcation of a subjectivity in which all such doctrines
would be realigned. (In Fish's terms, they would be held more weakly.)

One study produced by the Rand Corporation lays out the strategy very clearly. The
aim is to intervene in the traditionalist understanding of the nature of doctrinal authority.
This understanding is targeted even though the traditionalists tend not to be the exponents of violence; indeed, they are often the providers of charitable and educational services that supply key social needs in areas with weak or indifferent regimes. The Rand
Report, Mahmood notes, argues that it is not the substantive positions of the traditionalists that are intolerable, so much as their attitudes about their beliefs and modes of reasoning: "Traditionalism is antithetical to the basic requirements of a modern democratic
mind-set: critical thinking, creative problem solving, individual liberty, secularism."[7] Secular governance, Mahmood concludes, does not maintain neutrality toward religions or
adjudicate equally among them; it actively inculcates the subjectivities that it recognizes
as legitimate forms of religiosity.

Now it might seem that Mahmood and Fish are making very similar observations.
But there is a significant difference. Mahmood is centrally concerned with questioning
the mentalist and propositionalist biases in the equation of religion with belief. Appealing
to a Foucauldian understanding of the ethical production of subjectivity in order to understand both the practices of piety *and* the ethical orientation toward freedom in liberal
subjectivity, she is not inclined to contrast these as weak or strong forms of attachment.
Both are problematics of ethical struggle. Thus where Mahmood, like Fish, shows that
liberal governance does not have the kind of difference from religion that it thinks it has,
she argues (1) that it has to produce this difference and (2) it is no more empty of the
ethical than it is neutral toward religion. Her conception of the ethical allows her to see
the self-negating impulse in liberal subjectivity as normatively rich and effortful. Her
analysis also brings to the fore a very sharp contrast between some pious Muslim and
some liberal subjectivities: in the sensorium, the practical realization of faculties, means/
ends relationships in ritual, and so on. So, rather than flattening liberalism and religion
into two forms of religion, unrecognized and recognized, she continues to think of these

as qualitatively different in more fundamental ways. To miss this is to take liberalism at face value as an account of liberal culture.

That is what Fish does: he accepts the terms by which liberalism distinguishes itself from religious belief in order to invert those terms. Strong beliefs, which are explicitly held and violently asserted, trump weak beliefs, which are covertly held and self-delimiting.

There is considerable irony here, as the key tenet of the liberal religion as Fish understands it—"that no idea is worth fighting over to the death"—is the very impulse to which Louis Menand traces the development of American pragmatism.[8] "Liberalism" might be the theory of this attitude in law schools (thanks in large part to the pragmatist Oliver Wendell Holmes, Jr.), but that theory and the evaluative stance it encodes might be quite different. As is so often the case when academics want to put distance between themselves and "liberalism," the basic attitudes and norms identified as liberal also characterize a wide range of nonliberal or even antiliberal movements, ranging from democratic socialism to evangelicalism.

My second example of the liberal production of religion raises a different kind of issue. I have in mind a very interesting study by Winnifred Sullivan, called *The Impossibility of Religious Freedom*.[9] It is a study of a court case involving cemetery regulations in Florida; a municipal authority was sued on first-amendment grounds for having banned funerary monuments. Since people invoked religious conviction as their reason for wanting the monuments, the court was in a position of having to decide which putatively religious beliefs were protected. Sullivan shows that law routinely has to decide which beliefs presented by people as religious are in fact religious in the law's terms.

Many of what Americans regard as their own religious beliefs, of course, do not match orthodox legitimate forms of religiosity. Historians refer to this as "lived religion," meaning that its intensities are at some remove from theological tradition and ecclesiastical legitimacy. Thus grave marking can be seen by people as mandated by their religion, even where the orthodox form of their avowed religion treats it as an optional matter and they have no explicitly theological dissent from the orthodoxy. The problem is that these religiosities present themselves for protection under claims of religious freedom. But they cannot always be recognized in protected terms, because judges and regulatory agencies can require other criteria besides intensity of belief. In the case described by Sullivan, the one set of guidelines proposed was that protected religiosities—real religion—were those (1) asserted in an authoritative sacred text, (2) affirmed in classic doctrine, (3) continuously observed through the history of a tradition, and (4) consistently practiced everywhere in the tradition. As Sullivan observes, no religious center in America meets these criteria.[10]

Sullivan's conclusion is that the ideal of offering legal protection to all religions cannot be realized. She wants American law to face up to its implication in the legitimation of some forms of religiosity at the expense of others—though what this would mean she does not say. Returning to my opening question: she would not be saying that liberalism *is* religion, but she makes in a different way the point that neutral governance is an illusion, and that the form of the category itself is at issue.

Interestingly, Sullivan also shows in her own language the tendency to define religion as the other of liberal subjectivity: "It is the peculiar nature of religion," she writes at one point, "to restrict freedom."[11]

Rather than belabor this point, I would like to conclude by showing how the problem of the construction of religion points to another, less commonly recognized problem: the circulation of macrosociological categories in practice.

The actual religiosities of Americans in fact shade off in all kinds of non–theologically sanctioned directions. And if it is hard for the law to tell which ones are "religion" and which are not, so it is equally hard for us to say which kinds are "lived religion" and which are "lived something else." Where people are using overt symbolizations of recognized religious orthodoxies—a cross, a saint's statue, a picture of Jesus—their practices will tend to be counted as lived religion, even though the theological warrant for the practice in question might be nonexistent. Other ways of registering ethical obligation or devotion—even around the topics that are often definitively associated with religion, such as death—have just as much subjective normative intensity even though they do not meet the criteria of "lived religion."

What this consideration leads us to ponder is the salience of the category of religion itself in the practices and norms we call religious. Since the eighteenth century, when this abstraction took on its modern shape, what we mean by religion has increasingly involved religiosity about religion. Adherents of Christianity frequently see themselves not just as advocates of Christianity in opposition to all other religious traditions but as advocates of religion, in a way that is thought to put them on common footing with non-Christian religions.

The ultimate expression of this attitude might be the remark attributed to Dwight Eisenhower in Robert Bellah's classic "Civil Religion in America": "Our government makes no sense," Eisenhower is reported to have said, "unless it is founded in a deeply felt religious faith—and I don't care what it is."[12] What matters is not ritual observance or cultivated habits; it isn't even *what* people believe, but how deeply they feel their belief.

The point of this analysis has been that "religion" is to be treated not as a real substance, or as a reliable analytic category, but rather as an abstraction immanent to the practices of liberalism and its religiosity alike. To the extent that it can be said to exist, however, it is because it is understood to exist as a general phenomenon whose generality conditions the practice of any particular version. Thus, where it is perceived to be the opposite of rationalism, any strong sense of the mysterious will be regarded as religious— and sometimes cultivated as such. And where it is held to be the opposite of reflexively contingent belief, it can generate a veneration for strongly held belief that, like liberal respect, holds the veneration to be due not just to the content but to its being strongly held. Voicing the same scorn for weak attachment that leads Fish to admire the Muslim protesters over the liberal editors, and understanding the contrast in very similar terms, many people draw the conclusion that religion—precisely as religion, so defined—deserves not only the kind of privatizing respect accorded to it in liberalism but indeed an active embrace. There are folk versions of this scorn for the weak attachments of "secular humanism," as well as relatively sophisticated versions.

Thus Stanley Hauerwas, whose understanding of liberalism as "self-devaluating values" is quite close to Fish's: "The project of modernity was to produce people who believe they should have no story except the story they choose when they have no story. Such a story is called the story of freedom and is assumed to be irreversibly institutionalized economically as market capitalism and politically as democracy. That story and the institutions that embody it is the enemy we must attack through Christian preaching."[13] As I have said, I think this is to take liberalism's account of liberal culture at face value. And to some degree Fish's own position, that liberalism has commitments that are *not* "self-devaluating values," should also work against the reductive story that Hauerwas and other apologists tell.

So, for that matter, should the category of religion itself. The liberal framework for the construction of religion cuts both ways. It treats religion as essentially private, as critics of secularism like to complain; but it also bestows upon religious discourse, practices, and institutions a deference that is precisely commensurate with the category of religion per se, unearned by any approval of those practices or their metaphysical commitments. Critics of liberal secularism like to think that they are opening space for more public significance of religion, that they are bringing religion "into the public square," as the cliché goes (as though it has ever not been there), but any critique that would like to see liberal governance and religion as equivalent versions of metaphysical commitments will also have to undo the categorical privilege around religion. This categorical privilege is institutionalized, as Sullivan shows, in countless legal matters, not least of which is the tax exemption for churches. But it also characterizes the rhetoric of antisecularists themselves. The liberal framework for the construction of religion generates a melancholic desire for strong attachments, no matter what they are. We see this in Hauerwas's rhetoric as well as in Fish's, and we see it everywhere in popular culture.

The category of religion thus performs much of the same work that Fish despises in liberalism. It values strong private attachments with no regard for the particular content of those attachments or the validity of the public expressions they might inspire.

By arguing that liberalism is a religion, Fish clearly intended to devalue liberalism, but the critique fails to notice the degree to which its picture of legitimate religiosity is just the mirror image of that liberalism. We would only have to take Sullivan's analysis a step farther, or to give Fish's argument another turn, to arrive at the opposite, or perhaps complementary, conclusion: religion as strong belief, religion *as religion*, deserves no respect.

Social Democracy and Religion: The Reverse Beakthrough

Job Cohen

Someone who knows the history of this building is likely to think it appropriate that a symposium entitled Religion and Politics is being held here in the Koepelkerk, or "domed church," also known as the Round Lutheran Church. The original church here on the Singel was built in 1671. Since then it has twice been destroyed by fire. The first Lutheran church was built in 1633 at Singel 411, on the corner with the Spui. Most of that building is now used by the University of Amsterdam.

Because that church soon became too small for the growing Lutheran community, in 1667 the Lutherans were given permission to build a second church. The New, or Round Lutheran Church at Singel 11 was built by the architect Adriaan Dortsman between 1668 and 1671. But in the seventeenth century religion was also politics, and the city council would not permit the Lutherans to build a church tower. Only the Dutch Reformed Church was allowed to do that. The Lutherans therefore built a domed church crowned with a lantern—a small structure to let in light or air. On top of the lantern was a swan, a traditional Lutheran symbol. This solution, which served both religion and politics, was typical of the seventeenth century.

Ladies and Gentlemen,

I have been asked to say something about social democracy and religion to round off this symposium Religion and Politics, which has been organized by the Wiardi Beckman Trust and the socialism and ideology working group of the Dutch Labor Party (PvdA).

I accepted this invitation with a degree of hesitation. I've been a social democrat since the age of eighteen, but being a secular Jew, I know virtually nothing about religion. I'm not like Willem Banning, the free-thinking Protestant minister and founding father of the Dutch Labor Party, who in 1946 formulated the "breakthrough" idea on the basis of his life as a Christian and his profound experience of socialism. I'm a pragmatic social-democratic politician who, as mayor of the biggest city in the Netherlands, has come to the conclusion that religion is a significant factor in the politics of the twenty-first century. I discussed this assertion in depth in my lecture entitled "Binden" ("Uniting") in December 2003. It is included in your conference papers. I refer to it, but I will not be expanding on it here today.

In order to play a credible role in politics in the twenty-first century, every political movement—including the Dutch Labor Party—must ask itself how it sees religion as a political factor. Or, to put it another way: if religion is a political factor in twenty-first-century society, social democracy must establish a relationship with religion. This means more than looking beyond current horizons to different religions and their believers: it is also a process of reflection about the moral foundations and objectives of social democracy. What do you want to achieve, and how and with whom do you want to achieve it? What is good, and what is less good or even wrong, and why? In other words, it's a moral assessment.

Let's take a look at how we could develop this new courtship between religion and social democracy. I would prefer to begin with the latter—an assessment of the moral foundations of social democracy. They say that charity begins at home, so let's start off in our own backyard, because we certainly have something to say about it. Although they call us the "left-wing Church" (don't they?), we're not accustomed to talking about other religions—that's not our cup of tea. What I will be saying today is, to a degree, intuitive and exploratory: I don't have any cut and dried answers.

The Moral Foundations of Social Democracy: A Reverse Breakthrough?

When the Dutch Labor Party was founded in 1946, Banning—its founding father—believed that the party had a moral necessity that went further than serving the specific needs of the different factions that found a place under the new party's umbrella. It was not set up in order to represent narrow proletarian class interests. The goal was nothing less than the creation of a just society. It was necessary to broaden the support base of the old Social Democratic Workers' Party in order to achieve this. Thus it was essential to achieve cooperation with progressives in all camps. In a nutshell, this called for collaboration with politically active Christians of various persuasions. In view of the strongly denominational nature of Dutch society at the time, this was a breakthrough. The fine essay by Herman Noordegraaf—"Breakthrough Then and Now: Sixty Years of the Dutch Labor Party"—shows that it was no picnic. A copy of this essay is also among your conference papers. Many Christians were not able to reconcile their religious beliefs with socialist views. But there was also resistance from the other corner. A "socialist" was different from a "Christian" when it came to life in general and politics. Noordegraaf also relates that the breakthrough *inside* the Dutch Labor Party largely succeeded, although that certainly cannot be said about its effect on Dutch society as a whole—that is, until the secularization and individualization of the 1960s, when the whole issue became less important.

In my opinion, since then a whole generation of party members has been involved in a more or less secular way in the party. Until recently, many of us thought that the secular way of life was the way of the future and did not believe that religion would make a comeback. Now that we see it *has* made a comeback in many regards (I've already referred to the fact that I discussed this in "Binden"), many secular people are finding it difficult to determine their stance. They had come to see religion as a relic of a bygone age, an obstacle on the road to "progress" and a progressive society. And if this didn't apply to all religions, it certainly did to Islam! It followed that "progressive" and "religious" do not go together.

Why, then, is there this renewed interest in religion? It also exists inside the Dutch Labor Party; many party members are fascinated by religion. The fact that this subject is alive says something. But what? That is much more difficult to say. As Paul Kalma suggests, it could indicate a lack of morality and meaningfulness within the narrow parameters of today's pragmatic politics, the one-sided economic paradigm, and the dogma of enlightened self-interest. This lack is not being eradicated by our prosperity, which has never been greater than it is now. We seem to take our prosperity for granted, and even appear to look on it as something to which we are entitled.

And yet this affluence does not make people satisfied or happy. At times we act like spoiled children, who consider everything around them to be normal and grumble if there are problems. By complaining like this, we are souring ourselves and society. This overindulgence leads to complacency, which in turn reduces our capacity to fight for the principles we stand for. How can we turn the tide?

Is it possible that there is a moral shortfall that is not being made good on the basis of a renewed assessment of the sources of social democracy—with which only a few people are still familiar? So far as I can see, there is little debate in our party over the question of what weight should be given in this postmodern era to such important social democratic concepts as solidarity, equality, justice, responsibility, and caring about others. A number of these concepts were included in the Dutch Labor Party's manifesto of principles in order to underline their importance to social democracy, but that's about as far as it goes. The manifesto of principles says the following about morality: "We defend a liberal morality in which—against the backdrop of basic rights that apply to everyone—there is scope for different ideologies, lifestyles, and cultures." There is no further explanation of what exactly this "liberal morality" is. Without further clarification or more detailed definitions, we run the risk that these concepts will degenerate into mere words, without much significance.

In my view, pragmatism, economics, and enlightened self-interest cannot give satisfactory answers to the political and social issues that confront us: effectively combating the formation of a colored underclass in our country, supporting the redistribution of wealth, fighting for freedom and against poverty on a national and an international scale, tackling the enormous environmental problems we are facing, helping different groups to live together. We will succeed in doing these things only if we can sort out our moral precepts, if we give morally charged concepts such as justice and solidarity a key position in our political thinking and actions. The same applies to such concepts as (mutual?) dependence and gratitude. Each of these concepts has just as many religious connotations.

It is therefore not so peculiar that people are looking to religion. Over the centuries, religions have fulfilled the need to give human existence a purpose. And even today they have holy books from which people draw inspiration. At the same time, we need to realize that followers of Christianity, Islam, and other persuasions have a moral agenda that in many cases is at odds with a number of more or less accepted practices in our society. Take, for instance, views about alcohol and drugs, divorce, pornography, fraud, and the commercialization of our lives and human relationships. This may give us cause to reflect. It may also appeal to those who want to rise above the existential vacuum of secular society. Regarding this last point, the actual dynamic force of religion can be understood only if we appreciate that religions give their faithful the prospect of a just, or a more just, society. It is obvious that religions will gain ground if societies cannot offer this prospect in some other way.

Are we prepared to examine our own society critically, and are we willing actually to put these vital issues up for discussion? I believe that we should answer these questions, in the best tradition of our movement, by unhesitatingly saying "yes." The quest for a fair society could be the key point on which believers and secularists can join hands. In this context, you could speak of a *reverse* breakthrough.

Just after the war, Christians had to be convinced that they could work together with the Dutch Labor Party across denominational boundaries to create a fair and social society. Now, secularists in the party, who make up the overwhelming majority, could be persuaded that they can also consult these religions regarding moral reevaluation. Such collaboration with believers from the different denominations can be worthwhile in achieving the goals of social democracy and resolving issues about which we all feel the same. And the inspiration that emanates from a faith can be a fountainhead in realizing social democratic aims without the need for one to be or to become a believer. The alternative is decline and the absence of social inclusion.

The Dutch Labor Party: A Party with Room for the Faithful

Let's assume that cooperation with believers is a good thing. That still leaves the question of how we can convince the faithful that our party is the right place for them to be—that they are welcome in our party, as believers and with their faith, and that they will be accepted not just because they can enable us to meet our objectives. After all, a relationship is only a relationship if both sides benefit.

In other words, what would the Dutch Labor Party look like as a party with a place for believers of various persuasions and their faiths? This is what the second half of my talk is about.

To answer this question, we shall once again turn to Willem Banning. Banning formulated a number of principles that are still topical. Let me quote two of them, as listed by Noordegraaf:

1. Ideology and religion are essential to social democracy—which is what I've just been talking about.
2. This implies an explicit formulation of the principles and goals of social democracy, including in moral terms.

This means attempting to redefine the concepts I discussed earlier, such as solidarity, equality, justice, caring about others, and responsibility, which are so important in the social democratic tradition. But as I said earlier, they are crucial concepts not just in social democracy but also in different religious traditions. This means recognizing that religions can be partners in creating a just society. The reverse breakthrough I have been talking about is, moreover, not possible if we do not reevaluate our moral foundations.

We reject the idea of political parties along denominational lines, but we also reject the notion that religion is a purely private matter.

In other words, the party welcomes people who hold widely varying beliefs but who agree with its basic principles. The 2005 manifesto of principles says this in so many words:

> For over a century, social democratic ideals have united and inspired people with very diverse backgrounds and ideologies. The Dutch Labor Party wants to mobilize all these people and offer them a place where they can dedicate themselves to their ideals, both inside and outside politics, but always in accordance with democratic principles. First and foremost, we hold the conviction that politics can make the difference between a marginal and a decent existence, between humiliation and equality of opportunity, between rivalry among nation states and international cooperation, between oppression and freedom: politics matters.

As Banning and the Dutch Labor Party's 1947 basic principles noted, there is a profound link between ideology and political opinions, and the Dutch Labor Party appreciates how this emerges in the course of work for the party. As far as I'm concerned, this is still true today. But, as the Breakthrough movement knew very well, this does not suggest for a minute that there's a direct connection between ideology and a political platform. Here it is necessary, for several reasons, to be aware of the links between religion and politics, but not to confuse religion and politics.

We must explicitly acknowledge the right of churches to speak out regarding political and social life for the sake of the spiritual and moral welfare of the people.

In the twenty-first century, this continues to mean giving churches and other religious groups freedom to manifest themselves in the public domain—including inside the party—and to play an active role in public debate, with all the associated implications. On the one hand, believers are swayed as a result; on the other hand, these views, precisely because they are part of public discourse, can be critically analyzed, as is right and proper in every public debate. This is because giving the churches leeway does not mean simply accepting everything they say. Listening critically to one another and participating in dialogue and discussion are requirements for the optimal use of the scope offered in the public domain. Giving the churches scope to manifest themselves in the public domain is not a charter to demand their views about everything under the sun, or license for them to give such views. Jacques Janssen—who was scheduled to be the first speaker at this symposium, but who unfortunately was hindered—quoted and agreed with Ella Kalsbeek in her 2001 Bazuin Lecture. As a member of parliament, she described the churches' input as "often meager and facile." The contribution from the churches "should be of a high standard and have depth," "be pastorally responsible," "be worthy and leave room" for others.

Janssen himself said that the churches, and certainly not just the Christians, have shown signs of sectarianism since they have been left to fend for themselves in an individualizing society. I would imagine that improvements can be made here—in the interest of the spiritual and moral welfare of the population. Former Amsterdam mayor Schelto Patijn said that the churches need to get their spiritual act together. In a speech to an association of cooperating churches in 2000, Patijn said:

What will happen to you and to us if the traditional religious message is not or is only barely heard, celebrated, and lived by? If you can no longer understand any of the medieval paintings in the Uffizi Gallery in Florence because you know nothing about the Old and New Testaments?

I therefore propose that you should, in addition to your work for your fellow man, put your own house in order.

Emphasize the other "good" message of the Gospels as opposed to the daily, pointed messages from the worlds of management and commerce.

Stress the forming of a community of Christians in a multicultural society.

The priority of the churches should therefore be to think through and discuss once again Christian values and standards in an urban, multicultural society. A caring church in the Netherlands and beyond is, moreover, of vital importance.

What Patijn says here about the Christian churches could of course also be said about other denominations. In my opinion, the contribution of Islam to current social discussions is still too small.

And the final "breakthrough" principle: nonetheless, the state itself is not organized on the basis of any ecclesiastical or religious foundation whatsoever.

This corresponds to my views as expressed on various occasions (see "Binden," for example), namely, that only a secular state creates the freedom to accommodate the great diversity of groups, lifestyles, ideologies, and religions that is characteristic of our modern Western society.

I should like to add the following, however, to the breakthrough principles derived from Banning:

1. Leeway for a *positive* elaboration of the constitutional freedom of religion—as advocated by Thijs Wöltgens. In other words, freedom of religion is not defined only as the right not to be harassed by the government or by others, be they well meaning or malicious, but also as the right for a religion to be active in the public domain.
2. Freedom to be different from one another is a necessity in a pluralistic society. This freedom must be linked to an upbringing that imparts respect for this plurality and teaches children that in our society we must do things together.
3. Leeway to live your life the way you want to live it is one of the great achievements and freedoms of our society. This leeway implies the freedom to go through life as an unbeliever as well as the freedom to be religious. The government must respect both choices and provide the public with protection from one another if necessary.

Ladies and Gentlemen,

I shall conclude with an anecdote about the Protestant clergyman Nico ter Linden. The following took place shortly after the Second World War, when he was in primary school. I quote:

> Times were hard. Teaching aids were few and far between, and so we had to make do with a Dutch Reformed Protestant history book. After William of Orange, most of the pages were devoted to Abraham Kuyper, and there was a special map to show where the good man first saw the light of day. We were also told in great detail about the Dordrecht Synod: the Remonstrants taught this and that, whereas the Counter-Remonstrants taught something or other and so, the Counter-Remonstrants were right. It was with this direct hit that the chapter ended.
> "What did the Remonstrants teach?" asked my mother, to help me review.
> I told her.
> "And the Counter-Remonstrants?"

I duly spouted that, too. "And the Counter-Remonstrants were right," I added as an encore.

I will never forget my mother's dismay at this presumptuous stupidity. "You can never say that," she told me, "because it's a matter of belief."

"But if the teacher asks who was right?"

"Then you must say that you don't know."

"But then I won't pass the test!"

This was how tolerance in religious matters was instilled in the young Nico ter Linden by his mother.

And what applies to religion also applies to politics. Nico ter Linden did not fare badly.

Toward a Politics of Singularity

Protection and Projection

Samuel Weber

1651: England is in the midst of civil war. Cromwell has defeated the Royalists and is preparing to assume the title "Great Protector." Thomas Hobbes begins the concluding paragraph of his treatise *Leviathan, of the Matter, Forme, & Power of a Common-Wealth Ecclesiasticall and Civill* with the following resumé of the work:

> And thus I have brought to an end my Discourse of Civil and Ecclesiastical Government, occasioned by the disorders of the present time, without partiality, without application, and without other design than to set before men's eyes the mutual relation between *protection and obedience*; of which the condition of human nature, and the laws divine, (both natural and positive) require an inviolable observation. And though in the revolution of states, there can be no very good constellation for truths of this nature to be born under, (as having angry aspect from the dissolvers of an old government, and seeing but the backs of them that erect a new;) yet I cannot think it will be condemned at this time, either by the public judge of doctrine, or by any that desire the continuance of public peace.[1]

In thus emphasizing the object of his treatise as being nothing other than setting "before man's eyes the mutual relation between protection and obedience," Hobbes closes the circle of the work that began with the following determination of the Leviathan:

> Nature (the art whereby God hath made and governs the world) is by the *art* of man, as in many other things, so in this also imitated, that it can make an artificial animal. . . . *Art* goes yet further,

imitating that rational and most excellent work of nature, *man.* For by art is created that great LEVIATHAN called a COMMONWEALTH, or STATE, (in Latin, CIVITAS) which is but an artificial man; though of greater stature and strength than the natural, *for whose protection and defence it was intended*; and in which, the *sovereignty* is an artificial *soul,* as giving life and motion to the whole body. (7)

The raison d'être of the state qua Leviathan is thus none other than to provide the "protection and defence" of natural man, whose fallen and sinful body is vulnerable in a way that the body politic of the Leviathan is not. This is, of course, not to say that the body politic is invulnerable: writing at the time of the English Civil Wars, Hobbes could hardly have thought that. Rather, the principle of "protection" informs both the goal of the body politic and its operations: it must protect itself in order to protect its members. And it must afford protection if it is to expect obedience from its members in exchange. The principle of sovereignty thus depends entirely on the ability of the sovereign to protect: itself no less than its constituents.

In what does the protection consist? What is to be protected from what? There are, of course, multiple answers and aspects to this question. But already from the initial sentences of the *Leviathan*, it is clear that what ultimately has to be protected by the Leviathan is life and livelihoods: above all, that of the Leviathan itself, since only as long as it thrives can the lives of its individual members be assured.

Hobbes's conception of the Leviathan as an artificial living body, constructed to complement and palliate the vulnerabilities of actual living bodies, determines its governing principle—that of *sovereignty*. The principle of life, as Hobbes defines it, is that of immanence: "Life is but a motion of limbs, the beginning whereof is in some principal part within," he writes. If it is to be a living body, the body politic must also have its principle of motion "within" itself. Sovereignty is thus determined by Hobbes as "an artificial soul" capable of "giving life and motion to the whole body." The "whole body" here, of course, is that of the body politic, which includes its various elements: human and nonhuman "magistrates, and other officers of judicature and execution," which Hobbes compares to the "joints" of the artificial body; wealth and riches, its strength; *salus populi* (the people's safety), its business; and, finally, "pacts and covenants," said to resemble "that *fiat* by which God let there be light—and created the world" (7).

But the basic "pact and covenant" is that which proposes to assure the *salus populi* in exchange for the obedience of that *populus* to its laws and decrees. It is not insignificant that this covenant is likened to the divine *fiat* "by which God let there be light—and created the world," for the exchange of obedience for protection is a direct result of the Christian interpretation of the fall of man. Hobbes quotes Paul (I Cor. 15:21–22): "For since by man came death, by man came also the resurrection of the dead. For as in Adam all die, even so in Christ shall all be made alive" (298). In the interval between the departure of Christ and the Second Coming, it is the artificial body politic of the Leviathan that must assure the *salus populi* through "its power of life and death" (297). It is this that justifies and maintains the obligation of subjects to obey the sovereign. If the latter fails in its mission to protect, the contract ceases to exist:

> The obligation of subjects to the sovereign, is understood to last as long, and no longer, than the power lasteth, by which he is able to protect them. For the right men have by nature to protect themselves, when none else can protect them, can by no covenant be relinquished. The sovereignty is the soul of the commonwealth; which once departed from the body, the members do no more receive their motions from it. The end of obedience is protection [. . .] And though sovereignty, in the intention of them that make it, be immortal; yet is it in its own nature, not only subject to violent death, by foreign war; but also through the ignorance, and passions of men, it hath in it, from the very institution, many seeds of a natural mortality, by intestine discord. (147)

The pages and pages devoted by Hobbes to combating the confusion of the Kingdom of God, in which there would be eternal life, "with the present Church or multitude of Christian men now living, or that being dead, are to rise again at the last day" (404)—are necessary not simply because of the role of religion in the political conflicts fought out in his time, concerning the status of the Church of England, but because the justification of the sovereign State is informed by a notion of "protection" modeled upon Christian redemption and salvation, even if—and this is the crux—access to that redemption is no longer direct in a world that has been both visited and forsaken by God in the form of his Son, Jesus the Christ. What is left behind is the promise of a salvation that in the meantime takes the form of public safety, whose protection is the task and mission of the state as Leviathan.

Politics, from this perspective, is thus dependent upon a function of protection that is intrinsically paradoxical, if not aporetic, for the state that is entrusted with the protection of its subjects must itself be protected—it must protect itself, qua state, in order to fulfill its function of protecting its subjects. It must safeguard the Christian promise of salvation not directly, through ecclesiastical means, but indirectly, through the assurance of public safety and security, which in turn presupposes its ability to protect itself. Self-protection thus becomes the first and foremost task of the state, and of the politics that is informed by it.

But if the obedience required by the state depends upon its ability to protect those who are to obey, and if the model of such protection is based on the Christian promise of redemption, the question arises of how those who are to obey can decide whether or not the contract is being fulfilled, whether or not they are being afforded the protection they require. Without providing an answer, Hobbes describes the problem as the impossible task of construing infinity:

Whatsoever we imagine is *finite*. Therefore there is no idea, no conception of any-thing we call *infinite*. No man can have in his mind an image of infinite magnitude; nor conceive infinite swiftness, infinite time, or infinite force, or infinite power. When we say any thing is infinite, we signify only, that we are not able to conceive the ends, and bounds of the things named; having no conception of the thing, but of our own inability. And therefore the name of God is used, not to make us conceive him; (for he is incomprehensible; and his greatness, and power are unconceivable;) but that we may honour him. . . . No man can conceive anything, but he must conceive it in some place; and endued with some determinate magnitude; and which may be divided in parts; nor that any thing is all in this place, and all in another place at the same time; nor that two, or more things can be in one, and the same place at once. (19)

Hobbes conceives thinking as the production of images on the basis of what he calls the "senses," in particular, on the basis of what is interpreted as the *visual perception of objects as forms or figures*, which is to say, as located "in some place; and endued with some determinate magnitude" and consequently as excluding the possibility of existing in more than "one, and the same place at once." From this it results that whatever legitimacy can be accorded sovereign states will have to be grounded in an experience or consciousness informed by what I will call *unitary localizability*: a single body in one place at one time.

This suggests how the "self" that must be protected at all costs by the Leviathan has to be conceived: as a single body occupying a single place at one and the same time. The singularity of the body thus localized individualizes the self, makes it this self and not another. Since neither time nor place stands still after Adam's fall and expulsion from the Garden of Eden, however, the self cannot simply rely on its bodily localization to assure its ability to be—which is to say, to *stay*—one and the same. Only as the external but indispensable vessel of the soul can it assure this function. The political correlative of this is the relation between state and territory: the latter must be contiguous in order for its soul, the Leviathan, to have a self to protect. But the stability of that contiguity is deter-mined by what it excludes as well as what it includes—by what it excludes as other states ruling over other territories, and by the terms of the pact or covenant by which its subjects exchange obedience for protection.

But this structural instability, this permanent state of urgency, is in fact a state of emergency in the most literal sense, since it derives from the *emergence* of the Leviathan itself. The Leviathan is constituted through the decision of a multitude of individuals living in a common, contiguous territory, to constitute a state in order better to protect themselves. They give up whatever powers they have and invest them in this new, artificial being, the Leviathan. This creates, however, a fundamental contradiction: the multitude becomes a "people," that is, a political body, only by abandoning its prerogatives qua individuals to the sovereign state. But in thus creating the state that is designed to protect them, they tend to abolish themselves as an independent political entity, as a people. As the French political theorist Gérard Mairet puts it in his introduction to the French translation of *Leviathan*:

> The unity of a people thus created does not have its center in this same people, like the circle in geometry, because the center of gravity of the unity of a people is exterior to itself: it is the sovereign designated by the people. At the very instant when the individuals speak, they cease to be individuals in a multitude, and form a people; but this people in turn, at the moment when the sovereign is instituted, disappears *qua people*. The people finds the center of its being outside of itself (in the sovereign). It exists only as a linguistic fiction, without reality since its corporeality is entirely incarnated in the sovereign.[2]

Although Hobbes does not make explicit the paradox of a people dissolving itself at the moment that it incarnates itself in the Leviathan, the effects of this problematic incarnation emerge in the following passage:

> This done, the multitude so united in one person, is called a COMMONWEALTH, in Latin CIVITAS. This is the generation of that great LEVIATHAN, or rather (to speak more reverently) of that *Mortal God,* to which we owe under the *Immortal God,* our peace and defence. For by this authority, given him by every particular man in the commonwealth, he hath the use of so much power and strength conferred on him, that *by terror thereof,* he is able to conform the wills of them all, to peace at home, and mutual aid against enemies abroad. And in him consisteth the essence of the commonwealth; which (to define it,) is *one person, of whose acts a great multitude, by mutual covenants one with another, have made themselves every one the author, to the end he may use the strength and means of them all, as he shall think expedient, for their peace and common defense.* (114)

Since all the "power and strength" of the assembled individuals have been transferred to the Leviathan, the result of that transfer is the simultaneous institution and dissolution of the very self—that of the "people"—that the Leviathan is created to protect. As a result, the "terror" through which the state is able to "conform the wills of them all, to peace at home, and mutual aid against enemies abroad" becomes a means not only of defending the body politic but also of constantly reconstituting it, or rather, of repeating its auto-constitution, which converges with its auto-dissolution. It is like a pilot light that, in being lit, constantly goes out. It is in the blinking light of terror that the Mortal God pursues its ever-problematic mission of self-protection.

If one compares the early "deconstructive" texts of Derrida with those written in the last fifteen years of his life, one can discover, first, an underlying consistency and, second, within it a significant shift. The consistency can be described as a focus upon the problem of identity and identification, as epitomized in the concepts of the self, the I, and the subject. The shift takes place in the way the deconstruction of these categories is construed. In one of his earliest, ground-breaking texts, *Speech and Phenomenon*, Derrida demonstrates how the Husserl of the *Logical Investigations* seeks to map out a sphere in which thinking, equated with self-consciousness, can constitute itself without getting caught in the "external" and indeterminable relativity of linguistic signification. The crux of Husserl's demonstration reposes on the notion of self-perception: the speaking subject hears and understands itself (*sich vernimmt*) without having to depend essentially upon a system of signification that inevitably introduces distance and indeterminability into its operation. The key term used by Husserl in this context, which Derrida highlights, is *Selbstaffizierung*, "auto-affection":

> The operation of "hearing oneself speak" is an auto-affection of a unique kind. On the one hand, it operates within the medium of universality; what appears as signified therein must be idealities that are *idealiter* indefinitely repeatable or transmissible as the same. On the other hand, the subject can hear or speak to itself and be affected by the signifier it produces, without passing through an external detour, the world, the sphere of what is not "his own." Every other form of auto-affection must either pass through what is outside the sphere of "ownness" or forgo any claim to universality. When I see myself, either because I gaze upon a limited region of my body or because it is reflected in a mirror, what is outside the sphere of "my own" has already entered the field of this auto-affection, with the result that it is no longer pure. In the experience of touching and being touched, the same thing happens. In both cases, the surface of my body, as something external, must begin by being exposed in the world.[3]

The concept of auto-affection is, Derrida argues in this early text, never "pure" in the way Husserl would have it: as "affection" it always involves an opening, an "exposure in the world" and to the outside, to what is alien and unappropriable. Husserlian phenomenology, as a "metaphysics" of "presence," is also "a philosophy of life," which is to say, a philosophy that insists on the immanence and integrity of life, in regard to which "death is recognized as but an empirical and extrinsic signification, a worldly accident" (10).

The Husserlian effort to construct a notion of "auto-affection" that would be "pure"—that is, purified of all constitutive relation to the external and the alien—is thus already, implicitly, interpreted by Derrida as a defensive effort to protect the notion of a "self" that could "express" itself without losing itself in a process of signification that is irreducibly heterogeneous. Derrida's demonstration, which we cannot elaborate here, consists in showing that the very process of repetition Husserl invokes to distinguish "ideality"—that which stays the same over time and space—from empiricity harbors within itself an irreducible dimension of difference as well as sameness, and that these two cannot be radically disassociated from one another. This "primordial structure of repetition that . . . govern[s] all acts of signification"—which Derrida will later designate "iterability"—is here mobilized to reveal that there can be no representation that is simply expressive, in the sense of establishing an uninterrupted continuum between the consciousness of a speaking subject and his speech. As a function of repetition or iteration, all "ideality" is always in advance composed of sameness and difference, and thus is never simply self-identical or "ideal." Or, as Derrida puts it: "Auto-affection is not a modality of experience that characterizes a being that would already be itself (*autos*). It produces sameness as self-relation within self-difference; it produces sameness as the nonidentical" (82). Derridean deconstruction thus has as its initial object the "self," the *autos* of auto-affection, of *Selbstaffizierung*, or "self-presence." *Speech and Phenomenon* concludes with the following words:

> Contrary to what phenomenology—which is always phenomenology of perception—has tried to make us believe, contrary to what our desire cannot fail to be tempted into believing, *the thing itself* always escapes.
>
> Contrary to the assurance that Husserl gives us . . . "the look" cannot "abide." (104; my emphasis)

In the over forty years during which Derrida wrote and published, a primary focus of his attention remained the "self" and its inevitable but futile efforts to "assure" itself of its identity in a self-identical world, a world of "things in themselves." A necessary correlative of this project was that of exploring the various ways in which "our desire cannot fail to be tempted into believing" that such is the case—that we inhabit a world of "things in themselves" in which "the look" might be able to "abide." The mechanism that drew his attention again and again, in demonstrating both why such desire had to be continually reassured, and also could never be satisfied with any assurance, remained the same: the "repetitive structure" of all signification, of all marking and demarcation, of all identification and, hence, of all identity—but which, being irreducibly heterogeneous, inevitably came to mark with a sameness that is never simply identical. The very existence, in English, of the word *selfsame* bears witness to this sameness that is never simply self-identical.

So much, then, for the continuity to which I have referred. The shift with which I am concerned emerges during the last decade of Derrida's writing, beginning (to my knowledge, at least) in 1993 with *Specters of Marx*, elaborated and transformed in works such as *Politics of Friendship* (1994) and "Faith and Knowledge" (1996), and culminating, no doubt, in *Rogues* (2003). It is marked by the introduction of a term that resembles the earlier one I have been discussing sufficiently to make its divergence all the more worth reflecting upon: the term *autoimmunity*. In place of the earlier "affection," the notion of self is now linked to that of "immunity." The context of the two terms explains the shift, at least in part. Here, three points can be noted.

First, the titles of the books mentioned all deal either directly or indirectly, not exclusively or primarily with philosophy, but with politics. (This fact becomes even more evident if we add another text in which Derrida elaborates the notion of autoimmunity, the interview given shortly after September 11, 2001, to the Italian writer Giovanna Boradorri, published some years later in English under the title—surely not from Derrida— *Philosophy in a Time of Terror*). The only partial exception is the essay "Faith and Knowledge," which, as its subtitle indicates, is concerned with "The Two Sources of 'Religion' at the Limits of Reason Alone." But Derrida's discussion of "religion" clearly places it in a context that is political—both geopolitical and, in its own, quite distinctive way, "biopolitical."

Second, this word, *biopolitical*, which Derrida does not use, brings us to the second aspect of the shift I am describing. The term *autoimmune* comes from the life sciences, in particular, from medicine, not philosophy. It thus suggests a shift from the discourse of philosophy to that of the life sciences. To determine just what may be new here in Derrida's work is complex, since, as we have just seen, deconstruction constituted itself in an encounter with what Derrida, in *Speech and Phenomenon*, describes as a "philosophy of life" (10). In this respect, the question of "life" was already at the heart of Derrida's earliest writings. The "metaphysics of presence" thereby appears as a defensive effort to offer "assurances" to a desire all too ready to accept the same no matter what the cost: assurance that life could be construed as pure immanence, as life present to itself, and that death could consequently be seen as its external and extraneous other. Life was thus to be considered as the "norm," and death as the exception. But in his reading of Husserl, Derrida demonstrated that the very arguments that sought to purify "auto-affection" of all constitutive relation to alterity also irrevocably estranged it from the self-identity of an "I," whose ideal "significance" (*Bedeutung*) had to be universally intelligible in the absence of the singular entity uttering it and designated by that utterance. This might thus enable the mark *I* to outlive the presence of its original author or referent, but it did not establish the domain of pure interiority, of pure self-affection, that was required to establish a transcendental, that is, a lasting process of thought. This suggests one aspect of the shift in question, namely, from the singularity of the "I" to the generality of a self whose identity could now be construed as being species-specific rather than tied to individuals. This search for a self-contained and meaningful *norm* thus shifts from the effort to describe the auto-affection of an individuated, albeit also transcendental, consciousness to a discourse centered on the generality of living species, also known as the "life sciences."

At the same time, and this is the third point, in adopting the term *autoimmunity*, Derrida clearly seeks to detach it from the biomedical normality that construes it as an essentially *pathological* process. For Derrida, *autoimmunity* does not designate an illness that more or less accidentally befalls an intrinsically healthy organism, no more than "auto-affection," in its "impure" and differential dimension, could be construed (I repeat here the passage quoted previously) as: "a modality of experience that characterizes a being that would already be itself (*autos*). It produces sameness as self-relation within self-difference; it produces sameness as the nonidentical" (82). Yet this passage also suggests the considerable distance that separates the term *auto-affection* from its successor in Derrida's later work. Whereas auto-affection could be said to "produce sameness as the nonidentical," *autoimmunity* seems more sinister: in seeking to protect the organism, it attacks and destroys it. Or rather, in the singular interpretation given the term by Derrida, it attacks and destroys *itself*: namely, the protective defenses of the system. The mechanisms and processes that seek to protect a living system against threats from without attack its own defenses, thus rendering the organism all the more vulnerable to destruction.

Or—and this complicates the process—rendering it more open to transformation. It is this that enables Michael Naas, in an extremely helpful and comprehensive discussion of the concept, to suggest that the term functions as "the last iteration of what Derrida called for more than forty years *deconstruction*."[4] Autoimmunity is thus both suicidal and self-transformative. Or rather, it *is* suicidal, and it *can be—but is not necessarily—* transformative. This, at least, is what emerges from several—although not all—of its formulations in the writings of Derrida, perhaps most clearly in one of its earliest articulations. In *Specters of Marx*, Derrida uses the term to describe an attitude shared by both Marx and the object of his scathing critique in *The German Ideology*, Max Stirner:

> Both of them love life, which is always the case but never goes without saying for finite beings: they know that life does not go without death, and that death is not beyond, outside of life, unless one inscribes the beyond in the inside, in the essence of the living. They both share, apparently like you and me, an unconditional preference for the living body. But precisely because of that, they wage an endless war against whatever represents it, whatever is not the body but belongs to it, returns to it: prosthesis and delegation, repetition, difference. The living ego is autoimmune, which is what they do not want to know. To protect its life, to constitute itself as unique living ego, to relate, as the same, to itself, it is necessarily led to welcome the other within (so many figures of death: difference of the technical apparatus, iterability, non-uniqueness, prosthesis, synthetic image, simulacrum, all of which begins with language, before language), it must therefore take the immune defenses apparently meant for the non-ego, the enemy, the opposite, the adversary and direct them at once *for itself and against itself*.[5]

In order to protect itself, the "living ego" must not just defend against what it considers to be foreign, it must also "welcome the other within" in the different forms of technical prostheses, substitutes, supplements, and simulacra of all sorts, including language and its antecedents. This dependence on the foreign, the ego-alien, complicates the task of the immune system. If it protects by attacking only those elements that it considers alien to its body, then it runs the risk of impoverishing, weakening, and ultimately destroying that body. And thus it can come to do what for many years medical science considered exclusively as an abnormal and pathological process,[6] namely, attack itself, which is to say, attack its ability to attack antigens. To fulfill its mission of protection, it must turn against the system of protection itself, against itself. Autoimmunity thus emerges as the aporetic norm of the singular living being: it can survive only by protecting against its own protection.

The passage from *Specters of Marx* links autoimmunity to *life in the singular*, which is to say, to the individual body and to the first person singular, the ego or I. But only in "Faith and Knowledge" does the political potential of autoimmunity begin to emerge with clarity:

> Community as com-mon autoimmunity. No community, that would not cultivate its own autoimmunity, a principle of sacrificial self-destruction ruining the principle of self-protection (the preserving of the integrity of the self), and this in view of some sort of invisible and spectral sur-vival. This self-contesting attestation keeps the autoimmune community alive, which is to say, open to something other and more than itself: the other, the future, death, freedom, the coming or the love of the other, the space and time of a spectralizing messianicity beyond all messianism.[7]

"Community," political and otherwise, thus is the product not just of "the principle of self-protection" seeking to preserve "the integrity of the self"—the self as integral and integrating—but also of the protection that protects against protection, in the sense of excluding or neutralizing what is held to be alien and extraneous. The latter includes the "space and time of a spectralizing messianicity," as well as "the future, death, freedom" and "the coming or the love of the other."

In order for a community to survive—and a community that does not have a certain duration is not a community—it must protect not just against its own system of protection, but against the prevailing actualization of that system as a unified self. In short, it must protect against the principle of sovereignty, which, since Bodin and Hobbes, has served as the defining principle of the state and, in the period of liberal individualism, also increasingly of its individual members qua egos.

For Derrida, one of the privileged if infinitely problematic sites from which this link between ego and state can and should be pursued—although this has not yet been developed very far—is psychoanalysis. That this has not happened, despite an auspicious beginning in the work of Freud, is due not simply to external resistances but also to internal ones. In a long interview with Derrida, the French historian of psychoanalysis Elisabeth

Roudinesco asks him if the resistance of universities to Freud and his followers is not the result of "fear of the unconscious."[8] Derrida's reply probably surprised her:

A "subject," no matter of what kind (whether individual, citizen, or state) constitutes and institutes itself only out of such "fear," and therefore it always has the force or *the protective form* of a dam or a barrier [*un barrage*]. It interrupts the force that it then stores and channels. Despite their differences, which are never to be forgotten, our European societies always stand under the aegis of something like *an* ethical, legal, and political "system," *an* idea of the Good, of Right, and of the Common-wealth. . . . What I in abbreviated form here call a "system" and an "idea" must be *protected* against that which might threaten it from psychoanalysis—which nevertheless arose in Europe and in the person of Freud continued to be thoroughly informed by a European model of culture, of civilization, and of progress.

This "system" and this "idea" are designed above all to resist whatever is felt to be a threat. For the "logic of the unconscious"[9] remains incompatible with that which determines the identity of ethics, of the political and of the juridical not only conceptually, but no less in its institutions and consequently in the experiences of human beings. (290)

Psychoanalysis thus challenges, according to Derrida, not simply an established discipline or series of disciplines—psychology, medicine, and so on—but rather an entire "system" of Western culture and civilization, in its "ethical, legal, and political" dimensions. This challenge has not simply been rejected by those institutions, it has also—and this is perhaps more serious—been largely ignored in everyday life, and this not just *outside* of psychoanalytical institutions: "If psychoanalysis were to be taken seriously, really, practically, there would result an earthquake that is difficult to imagine. Something indescribable. Even for psychoanalysts" (290). This unimaginable "earthquake," which is scrupulously ignored by both institutions and individuals, is nevertheless in full swing, but so deeply embedded in everyday experience that it is difficult to discern and easy to overlook:

Meanwhile, this seismic threat plays itself out within ourselves, within each single individual. In our lives, as we know only too well, . . . we generally act as though psychoanalysis had never existed. Even those who, like ourselves, are convinced of the inescapable necessity of the psychoanalytical *revolution*, or at least of its *questions*, still act in their lives, in their ordinary language, in their social experience as though nothing had happened. . . . In an entire realm of our lives we act as though we still believed, at bottom, in the sovereign authority of the I, of consciousness, and so on, and employ the language of this "autonomy." We know, to be sure, that we speak several languages at once. But that makes almost no difference, either in our souls or in our bodies, whether in the body of each individual, the body of society, the body of the nation, or the body of the discursive and juridical-political apparatus. (291)

The questions of psychoanalysis thus cut across and link the realms of what is usually separated as "individual" and "collective," "personal" and "institutional" experience, and its cut goes to the root of the modern notions of subjectivity as autonomous. Instead, the subject, "no matter of what kind: individual, collective or institutional . . . constitutes itself only out of fear," as an instance of protection. Protection therefore, like auto-affection and autoimmunity, is not something that befalls a subject already constituted as self-consciousness. Rather, self-consciousness constitutes itself as identical in, through, and *as* the response to danger that we call *fear*. This, Derrida asserts, is as true on the institutional and political level as it is on that of individual experience.

That is why the notion of sovereignty becomes for Derrida not simply a political notion but more generally one that sustains—and is sustained by—the modern notion of an autonomous self. In a keynote speech delivered in the summer of 2000 before an international meeting of psychoanalysts in Paris, Derrida situates the link between individual, collective, and categorical "sovereignty" by relating it to what he designates as a "metaphysics of sovereignty" in an age of "globalization":

The world, the world-wide process of globalization, with all of its consequences—political, social, economic, legal, technical-scientific, and so on—without a doubt resists psychoanalysis. . . . It mobilizes against it not only a model of positive science, which can be positivist, cognitivist, physicalist, psycho-pharmacological, genetic, but also at times a hermeneutics that becomes spiritualist, religious, or simplistically philosophical; in this mobilization participate institutions, concepts, and archaic ethical, legal, or political practices that are informed by a distinct logic, namely, by a certain metaphysics of *sovereignty* (autonomy and omnipotence of the subject—whether individual or statist—freedom, egological will, conscious intentionality, or, of you prefer, the ego, ideal-ego, super-ego, etc.). The first gesture of psychoanalysis will (have to) be to provide an account of the unavoidability [of this mobilization], although at the same time it will have to aim at deconstructing its genealogy—which also traverses a cruel murder.[10]

The concluding allusion to the "cruel murder" recalls how, in both *Totem and Taboo* and *The Man Moses and Monotheistic Religion*, Freud links the process of civilization to the murder of the founding figure, be it the Primal Father in the speculative Primal Horde or Moses as the Egyptian, that is, the alien, founder of the Jewish people. However skeptical he remains about the historical accuracy of such speculations, Derrida insists on their symbolic significance as reminders of the violence required by all institutionalization, whether individual (of the ego) or collective (of the state or nation). The notion of indivisible sovereignty, with its powers over the life and death of its subjects, is here characterized as a power of *mobilization*, setting into motion for the purpose of affirming the self—and consequently of resisting the aspect of psychoanalysis that calls into question the self and its autonomy. The "metaphysics of sovereignty" defends its system against the challenges of a psychoanalysis that, however, is also part of it, and that therefore acts in a similar manner. The resistance, once again, comes not just from without but, as always, also from within: "For this resistance is also a resistance against itself. There is something wrong [*il y a un mal*], at any rate *an autoimmunizing function* within psychoanalysis as everywhere else, a rejection of itself, a resistance against itself, against its own principle, against its *own principle of protection*."[11] If such an "autoimmunizing function" is as inevitable as it is ubiquitous, the question then becomes that of distinguishing between its different directions and effects. It can either insist on preserving and protecting what cannot simply be protected—the given, actual self-identity of the institution or the individual—or it can offer an opportunity to transform that self-identity by no longer simply protecting it as it was but opening it to a transformation, to the heterogeneity that it has always contained but has also sought to reduce and dissimulate.

This is why Derrida includes the "metapsychological" concepts of psychoanalysis, including the triad of ego, superego, and id, in the list of concepts belonging to the "metaphysics of sovereignty." And why his interest in psychoanalysis has always been situated on its margins: either where Freud disrupts his previous system deliberately, as in *Beyond the Pleasure Principle*, or where he allows himself to be drawn into areas that are difficult to integrate into the existing psychoanalytic conceptuality, as in his famous essay "The Uncanny."

That essay has often been read—perhaps first by Hélène Cixous—as being itself uncanny. Freud claims that he has long since ceased to have any direct experience of the uncanny, and he therefore has to resort to literary examples. Yet, as Ernest Jones, his biographer, long ago noted, he interrupted writing the essay until he reached the age of sixty-three because he was afraid of dying at the same age as his father. In the text, Freud gives as an example of an uncanny belief in numbers the number 62—without, of course, acknowledging the significance it had had for himself and for the writing of the text. But there is a more systemic explanation for Freud's uncanny excursion into the uncanny, a realm he seeks to appropriate for his psychoanalytic system. At the time he writes the essay, he is in the process of rethinking the entire basis of the system, associated with the "pleasure principle." Under the aegis of that system, anxiety—the general class to which the uncanny belongs (but does not exhaust)—was seamlessly integrated as the result or effect of repression, explained as a result of the pleasure principle. A representation comes to be associated with displeasure and is therefore repressed, banished from consciousness, and replaced with a substitute formation, another "idea." When the substitute idea loses its power to keep the repressed, unpleasant representation from becoming conscious, there occurs a "return of the repressed," which—according to this first psychoanalytic theory of anxiety—brings with it the experience of the uncanny, that which had long been familiar but precisely because of its familiarity could not be integrated into the "household" of self-consciousness.

Already in that essay, however, Freud has to acknowledge that this explanation falls short, since not every "return of the repressed" produces anxiety, and not every anxiety can be equated with the uncanny. A few years later, after discarding the pleasure principle due to his discovery of the repetition compulsion and the death drive, Freud also reverses his first theory of anxiety into a second one. According to this theory, most fully elaborated in the 1926 essay *Inhibition, Symptoms and Anxiety*, anxiety is no longer the effect of repression but its cause. This inversion does more than just operate an exchange of places between anxiety and repression. In placing anxiety at the origin of repression, Freud acknowledges, at least implicitly, that his psychoanalytic system is incapable of providing an adequate causal explanation of psychic structure. As he emphasizes in the 1926 text, anxiety presupposes something like an ego or a proto-ego, which therefore must be reckoned with from the beginning, as it were, even before the ego can fully constitute itself. For Freud, the ego is, on the one hand, not given from the start: it has to be developed, and a certain form of repression is required for its development. But at the same time, if anxiety functions as the cause of repression, then the ego has to be somewhere in the wings, inasmuch as anxiety is defined by Freud as the reaction of the ego to danger. "Danger," Freud explains, is a relational concept: it is always a danger *for* or *to* something else. In this case, the danger involved has to be defined in terms of the disruption that it can bring to the psychic instance or agency—the ego—that seeks to establish a certain degree of unity and coordination among the differing components of the psyche, between "id" (or "it") and super-ego. Now the ego, as Freud describes it, is not there from the beginning: it is formed through a gradual process that Freud describes in a late, unfinished essay, his last attempt to provide a synoptical overview of his entire system, "Outline of Psychoanalysis":

> Under the influence of the surrounding real external world, a part of the Id (It) undergoes a particular development. Originally equipped as an exterior surface with organs for the reception of stimuli and with an apparatus for *protection against stimuli* [*mit den Organen zur Reizaufnahme und den Einrichtungen zum Reizschutz*], a particular organization emerges that from now on will mediate between It and external world. This realm of psychic life we assign the name *I* [or ego].[12]

This passage, written in 1939, takes up almost literally an earlier description written some twenty years earlier in *Beyond the Pleasure Principle* (1920), but with a significant shift. The earlier text, which for the first time places the development of a "protective shield" (*Reizschutz*) at the core of psychic formation, describes not the development of the I (ego) but rather that of "consciousness." At first, however, Freud describes the process as though it concerned the development of an organic system per se, not a psychic one:

> This little fragment of living substance is suspended in the middle of an external world charged with the most powerful energies, and it would be killed by the stimulation emanating from these if it were not provided with a protective shield against stimuli. It acquires the shield in this way: its outermost surface ceases to have the structure proper to living matter, becomes to some degree inorganic and thenceforward functions as a special envelope or membrane resistant to stimuli. . . . By its death, the outer layer has saved all the deeper ones from a similar fate—unless, that is to say, stimuli reach it that are so strong that they break through the protective shield. *Protection against* stimuli is an almost more important function for the living organism than *reception of* stimuli.[13]

Even before he arrives at the description of the death-drive, a certain death—that of the surface "membrane"—becomes the condition of survival for the organism and, as we shall see, for the psyche—and ultimately for the ego as well. Only such a death—the transformation of organic into inorganic matter—creates the "protective shield" that is necessary if the organism is to survive. In a certain sense, then, "trauma"—the breaking-through of the protective shield—is the condition against which the organism, consciousness, and the ego must defend and protect themselves: not just at the origin, but constantly thereafter as well. Everything, then, depends on just how this process of protection is to be construed.

In *Beyond the Pleasure Principle*, Freud throws out a number of suggestive speculations, without being able to develop any of them. The first describes the process of defense and protection as a kind of sampling that implies both being able to localize the "direction and nature of the external stimuli" (53) and also then being able to organize it in a way that diminishes its traumatic potential. This involves the development of what might be called "attention," although Freud does not do so—later, in *Inhibitions, Symptoms and Anxiety*, he will, however, call attention to a related defensive process, which he calls "isolation" and which involves separating the potentially dangerous stimulus or representation from its ramifications and connections to other things.[14] Since the danger comes not from individual sources but rather from their cumulative and disintegrative connections, such isolation is as, if not more, effective than repression in the traditional sense. It is, Freud notes, also very difficult to identify—one could also say, to "isolate"—since it overlaps with what is the core of "normal" thought processes, namely, "concentration." When, therefore, in *Beyond the Pleasure Principle* Freud emphasizes both the spatial and the temporal aspects of the "sampling" of potentially threatening stimuli—and he even goes so far as to speculate that the "Kantian theorem that time and space are 'necessary forms of thought'" (Kant, of course, speaks of *Anschauung*, "intuition," literally: "look-ing-at," rather than of "thought" in general)—what he is actually describing is the use of spatiotemporal coordinates to *locate* and thus partially to neutralize the potential threat to consciousness, the ego and indeed to life itself.

To understand wherein lies this threat, this danger against which the ego defends both through its protective shield and through anxiety, as a signal of a potential danger, requires interpretation. Freud himself tends to formulate the threat in terms of an excess of energy, a quantitative amount of energy that cannot be absorbed by the system—organic or psychic—that it threatens. But given that the two systems concerned are, first, consciousness, and, second, the ego, we can reformulate the nature of the threat involved: the quantitative excess that threatens the ego and consciousness is one that cannot be *integrated* into the systems concerned. What is at stake is an irreducible multiplicity or differentiality that as such threatens the *unity of consciousness and of the ego.* Indeed, it is not consciousness as such that is threatened—indeed, consciousness as such is, as Freud recognizes again and again, a far more mysterious and enigmatic entity than is commonly realized—but rather the *unity of a consciousness that therefore must be understood as self-consciousness.* It is the unity of a consciousness that seeks to repeat itself as one and the same, despite the irreducible differences involved in all repetition. Hence, the "demonic" quality of the repetition compulsion, which Freud acknowledges in *Beyond the Pleasure Principle*: it is demonic but also fascinating, precisely insofar as it entails a repetition that does not come full circle, that produces the same but without resolving it into the unity of a self. It is this that makes it demonic, but also automatic: a repetition that produces the same as the nonidentical, to recall the formulation of Derrida. It entails "sameness without self," if by self is understood self-identity.

The protective defense against this danger always involves the effort to reduce multiplicity to unity, difference to identity, sameness to self. Since the danger comes not simply from without but also from within—since the protective shield is required in order to establish the very difference between outside and inside, and therefore continues to im-pinge upon the inside that depends upon it, that is, upon the outside—one, if not the preferred, mechanism for protecting against internal difference is what Freud calls "pro-jection": "the tendency to treat them [stimuli] as though they were acting, not from the inside, but from the outside, so that it may be possible to bring the shield against stimuli into operation as a means of defence against them. This is the origin of *projection*, which is destined to play such a large part in the causation of pathological processes" (56).

Earlier in *Beyond the Pleasure Principle*, Freud introduces a distinction that is by no means specific to the discourse of psychoanalysis but that can be extremely illuminating in the context of this discussion of *protection through projection*: that between "fear," "anxiety," and "fright" or "terror" (*Schreck*):

"Anxiety" describes a particular state of expecting the danger or preparing for it even though it may be an unknown one. "Fear" requires a definite object of which to be afraid. "Fright," [or Terror] however, is the name we give to the state a person gets into when he has run into danger without being prepared for it: it emphasizes the factor of surprise. I do not believe that anxiety can produce a traumatic neurosis. There is something about anxiety that protects its subject against fright and so against fright-neuroses. (30)

If we take this description together with Freud's speculation about how a certain "sampling" can function as a protective measure by determining the direction from which danger comes, we see how time and space can be mobilized and perhaps even constructed as a framework in which such protection can be construed: time and space are "forms" in which a potential danger can be located as an object of *Anschauung*, to recall the Kantian term, in which space and time are defined as forms of outer and inner *Anschauung*, respectively. We see here how misleading the consecrated English translation of *Anschauung* as "intuition" can be, for what is at stake—in this context, at least—is the possibility of literally being "looked *at*," and thereby localized, identified, and potentially, at least, assimilated and brought under control. This in turn presupposes a certain distance *through* which one can look "at" something, envisage or imagine it. What ultimately has to be "protected," then, is the distance that separates the perceiver from the perceived, subject from object—separates but also joins through the supposed homogeneity of the space "in between."

The three interrelated terms *fear, anxiety,* and *terror* (my translation of *Schreck*) are thus all part of a single process: that of responding to and protecting against an unassimilable alterity or difference, which per se cannot be unified or reduced to the selfsame. "Anxiety" thus mediates between the relative stability of fear and the relative instability of terror or fright: it involves, as Freud stresses, a certain "preparedness" (*Angstbereitschaft*), which in turn is directed as much to the future as to the past: to the past, since it cannot imagine or envisage danger without recurring to memory and reproducing analogous situations; to the future, since danger is always yet to come. The child's game of throwing the spool out of the playpen and then hauling it back, accompanied by the sounds "oooo—aaa," which Freud translates as *fort-da*, "gone-there," indicates how certain repetitive gestures can be used to mimic the preparedness that is required to protect the ego from future losses and threats. But qua repetition, what returns as "there" is never simply "here"—it returns as the "same" perhaps, but never simply as the selfsame, never as a simple unity. What returns can therefore be designated as the aftereffect of the "singular," which is a differential and relational notion that can be experienced only in its disappearance, only in its "traces," as the early Derrida might have said. The "singular" in this sense is very different from the "individual," if we take that term literally, for the "singular" is always divided in and of itself, always separated from the selfsame, and it is this that constitutes both its uniqueness and its inaccessibility. We can never experience the singular in and of itself, directly, but only in what remains, what is "there" but never simply "here": the resource of the German *da*, which is not simply *dort* (the equivalent of "there" as opposed to "here"). What is *da* is both here and there, and thus never simply in one place at a time: a body, perhaps, but not in the sense defined by Hobbes—taking up a definition that goes back to Aristotle—as that which can only be in one place at one time and can also never share that place with anything else.

It is this definition of bodies and places, based on a certain notion of identity as isolation, that Benjamin, following Freud (but unaware of his thoughts on isolation) picks up in his study of Baudelaire and relates, as did Freud before him, to memory. Or rather, to different sorts of memory: to that which is presupposed by *Erlebnis*, by a "lived experience" that seeks to protect itself by putting experiences temporally in their proper places, by isolating them, and by *Erfahrung,* which, although Benjamin does not stress this, is constructed on the verb *fahren,* "to travel or traverse," and thus entails movement and alteration:

> Perhaps the special achievement of shock defense is the way it assigns content an exact place in time [*eine exakte Zeitstelle*] in consciousness, at the cost of the integrity of the content. That would be the greatest achievement of reflection. It would make the incident into an *Erlebnis*—a lived experience. If it is omitted, what would ensue is the joyful [*freudige*] or (mostly) unpleasant terror [*Schreck*] that according to Freud sanctions the failure to defend against shock.[15]

It should be noted that Benjamin, via a wordplay on Freud's name (*freudig* = "joyful"), opens up what Freud himself does not easily acknowledge, although he is later obliged to concede that nonintegrated "tensions" can indeed be a source of pleasure and not merely of pain.[16] In short, for Benjamin the unitary perspectives of self-consciousness and of the ego do not constitute the court of last resort. It is significant that his notion of an "experience" that cannot simply be reduced to a notion of "life" based on the unity of self-consciousness—*Erlebnis*—is made in the context of a discussion of poetry, that of Baudelaire, or literature more generally, that of Proust, for instance. The latter provides Benjamin with a model of "awakening," in which the unity of the body and the unity of consciousness are dislocated simultaneously, when Marcel recalls via the experience of individual bodily members, no longer integrated into the body as an organic whole, container of an equally unified self. Instead of the self-contained body, the nonintegrated relations of individual bodily members to singular contexts constitute the "experience" as one of irreducible alterity:

> A man asleep holds in a circle around him the thread of hours, the order of years and of worlds. He consults them instinctively in waking up, and reads there in a second the point of the earth that he occupies, the time that has passed before his wakening; but their ranks can become mixed, break apart. If toward morning, after

a night of insomnia, sleep overtakes him as he is reading, *in a posture too different from that in which he habitually sleeps*, all that is necessary to stop the sun and make it go backward is for him to raise his arm, and, at the first minute of his wakening, he will no longer know the time and will think that he has just gone to bed. And if he falls asleep in a position even more displaced and divergent, for example, after dinner seated in an armchair, the transformation will be complete in worlds out of orbit, the magic armchair causing him to travel at great speed in time and in space, until, at the moment of opening his eyes, he will believe that he fell asleep several months earlier in another country.[17]

Benjamin, who refers to Proust but does not cite this passage, surely had it and others in mind when he made his distinction between *Erlebnis* and *Erfahrung*, between "lived experience" and "experience" that is not simply "lived," if by "lived" is meant, as it usually is, that which is reducible to the specious unity of self-consciousness. Instead, the dislocation of the body into singular members and nonunifiable experiences traversing multiple places at one and the same time dislocates that "one and the same" and opens it to an experience of events that are as singular as they are finite. Or, rather, *indefinite*: the never entirely definable singularity of events that are "one" but never simply the "same."

Thus, the sovereignty of the subject is dislocated by an experience of the indefinite singularity of events, which inevitably entails both pain and pleasure, fright and joy. By a "motion of limbs," which, as we remember, was Hobbes's definition of life. But it is a life that cannot be assimilated or reduced to the unity of a "whole body," the correlative of that wholeness of the body politic without which sovereignty, as indivisible, cannot be conceived.

Benjamin turns to literature and poetry, that of Baudelaire and Proust, to find in-stances of an experience of singularity that is neither simply protective nor projective, that does not turn anxiety into a "signal," as Freud puts it, through which to "prepare" for an assimilation of what is to come. That anxiety, even terror, can be a source of pleasure, if not of joy, is an experience that increasingly informs politics today. But whether that pleasure can be acknowledged without being entirely assimilated—whether, in short, not just a poetics but a politics of singularity can come to replace the politics of the sovereign self—remains an open question.

PART VI

Materiality, Mediatization, Experience

Troubles with Materiality

The Ghost of Fetishism in the Nineteenth Century

Tomoko Masuzawa

> The theological period of humanity could begin no otherwise than by a complete and usually very durable state of pure Fetichism, which allowed free exercise to that tendency of our nature by which Man conceives of all external bodies as animated by a life analogous to his own, with differences of mere intensity.
>
> —Auguste Comte, *Cours* (1830–42)

> The form of wood, for instance, is altered if a table is made out of it. Nevertheless the table continues to be wood, an ordinary, sensuous thing. But as soon as it emerges as a commodity, it changes into a thing which transcends sensuousness. It not only stands with its feet on the ground, but, in relation to all other commodities, it stands on its head, and evolves out of its wooden brain grotesque ideas, far more wonderful than if it were to begin dancing of its own free will.
>
> —Karl Marx, *Capital* (1867)

The Scandal of a Practically Extinct Theory

Upon hearing the standard disciplinary history of the science of religion (*Religionswissenschaft*),[1] one might get the impression that, by the second half of the nineteenth century, talk of fetishism should have been all but dead. By then, "fetishism" as a particular type or form of religious belief and practice was supposedly no longer a viable or respectable category in debating the origin, evolution, or morphology of religion. Thus we read in the Victorian chapter of this history about the rise—and usually also the fall—of various theories concerning the origin of religion, such as Edward B. Tylor's animism theory, Robert Ranulph Marett's preanimism theory, Andrew Lang's or Wilhelm Schmidt's primitive monotheism theory, F. Max Müller's (and others') nature-myth theory, Durkheim's or Freud's totemism theory, and so on—but nobody's "fetishism theory."[2] Even by Victorian standards, we are led to believe, the notion of fetishism was already embarrassingly outmoded, something rather more reminiscent of certain older habits of thought than a critical tool of the emerging scientific discipline. So we see one of the earliest chroniclers of the comparative study of religion, Louis Henry Jordan, making the following pronouncements in 1905: "Fetishism . . . to-day is almost universally admitted to be an inadequate theory when offered in explanation of the origin of Religion. . . . One need not delay to mention a list of the leading writers who have openly espoused and defended this theory; for . . . this branch of the School of Evolutionists in Religion is now practically extinct."[3]

As speculation on the origin and development of religion increasingly foraged through the material made available by ethnography—thereby becoming, if only vicariously, empirical to a degree—it appears that "fetishism" as a classificatory category proved no more serviceable for *Religionswissenschaft* than such flagrantly prejudicial terms as *superstition*, *idolatry*, or *heathenism*. If we look further into the details of this disciplinary history, we will learn, for example, that, in an influential two-part treatise entitled "The Worship of Animals and Plants," published in 1869 and 1870, John F. McLennan offered an entirely new perspective on the subject by suggesting that so-called fetishism was but one aspect of the real elemental form of religion, totemism, which he defined as animal (or sometimes plant) worship plus matrilineal exogamy.[4] Sometime thereafter, his friend and fellow Scotsman W. Robertson Smith carried this idea further and proposed that the ancient sacrificial rites of the Semites—including many that are documented in the Hebrew Bible—could be understood in light of such primitive totemism.[5] Meanwhile, Tylor—who was destined to become the most celebrated Victorian anthropologist—shifted attention away from the fetish object to the supposedly spiritual entity that, he said, the savage falsely assumed to be animating such an object; Tylor thus established the theory of animism as the most rudimentary religion.[6] These and other developments, so the story goes, effectively dashed any hope of a serious scholarly career for "fetishism."

It is all the more surprising, therefore, that talk of fetishism is in fact everywhere in the Victorian literature, in ethnography as well as in history of religions.[7] To be sure, the subject does not usually occupy a conspicuous place, nor does it always seem a particularly welcome topic even to authors, who might obligingly treat the matter as an unavoidable subject, sometimes criticizing it as a regrettably confused notion, which ought to be reclassified under some other category, or which might be better controlled by means of a more stringent definition. Suffice it to say that by the turn of the century fetishism was not much of a theory anymore, but evidently remained a problem nonetheless. The trouble was—and there seems to have been near consensus on this point—that the use of the term *fetishism* tended to be too liberally expansive and uncritically inclusive, so that just about anything could count as an instance of fetishism for the advocate of fetishism theory, just as any piece of rubbish, trifle, or trinket was said to be a potential fetish for the practitioner of fetish religion.

A typical Victorian account of fetishism would rehearse the etymology of the word, in the course of which we would be transported back to the scene of the first encounter between Portuguese sailors and the savages[8] of the Gold Coast. At this point we would be led to examine the Portuguese word *feitiço*, meaning "charm," "amulet," or "talisman," which in turn might lead us back through medieval Christian history to a Latin term *factitius*, meaning, variously, "manufactured," "artificial," "enchanted," or "magically artful." Then the narrative would likely go forward to 1760, when the French Enlightenment thinker and acquaintance of Voltaire, President Charles de Brosses, coined the term *fetishism* in the now-celebrated monograph *Du culte des dieux fétiches* (*On the Cult of Fetishistic Gods*). At the same time, it would be noted how de Brosses himself prepared the way for the future abuse of the term and the erosion of its original definition, such as it was, because he chose to include in the same category not only observances more in line with the etymological sense of the term—that is, customs involving certain portable objects, either naturally found or "manufactured"—but also such divergent and heterogeneous practices as animal worship (zoolatry), star worship (Sabeism), and the veneration of the dead.[9]

In sum, not only was there abundant discussion of the topic of fetishism during the Victorian period, there was also a standard litany for chastising this prolific and unruly discourse. In any event, talk about fetishism they did, even if in a manner that would suggest that this was a vaguely illegitimate bit of business left over from previous generations, an embarrassing remnant of humbler times when the discriminating terminology of scholarship had not been developed. In effect, "fetishism" was an obsolete piece of language that refused to fall away, despite the progressive retooling of scientific discourse.

Indeed, "fetishism" remained a regular nuisance for many decades after the science of religion had soundly denounced it. Thus, as late as 1948 we find, in a popular survey text, the following disclaimer:

> The magic charm takes innumerable forms. . . . One word that has been applied to charms is fetish, and no term has proved more troublesome than this and its companion, fetishism. The derivation is from the Portuguese *feitiço*, "something made," and was used by the early Portuguese to denote the charms and images of African peoples. These terms are mentioned here because they are encountered so often in the literature, as when it is said that "fetishism is the religion of Africa." When used at all, they should be employed in the sense of "charm" and "magic"; but they are far better omitted from any discussion of the means whereby man controls the supernatural.[10]

Here, again, is the familiar mantra of *Religionswissenschaft* dispelling the evil of the confounding fetishism discourse. A somewhat abbreviated formula this may be, but all the essential ingredients are there: the Portuguese etymology, the historical African connection, the subsequent proliferation of the term's indiscriminate use, and finally the blanket statement about its general uselessness. Yet the very repetition of the same mantra, intended to disenchant the powerful discourse, testifies to just how ineffectual such disciplinary pronouncements really were against the rampant circulation of this made-up term. Like bad money, it was going around faster than any theoretical categories from more creditable mints.

F. Max Müller on Fetishism

The problematic status of fetish discourse during the Victorian era is well attested by the inaugural series of the Hibbert Lectures, delivered in 1878 at Westminster Abbey by F. Max Müller.[11] Already anointed as the patriarch of *Religionswissenschaft*, Müller addressed himself in the second of his seven lectures specifically to the topic: "Is Fetishism a Primitive Form of Religion?" In a word, Müller's answer to this question was "no," and there was not much ambiguity about it. To put it in a few more words, Müller's position was the following. Fetishism is not a form of religion, nor a stage of religious development, let alone the original stage, but a mere tendency, a certain inferior disposition or weakness to which anyone at any place or any time is, in principle, susceptible. We humans have a proclivity for developing a fetishistic attachment to what Müller calls "casual objects," clutching whatever is thrown up on our path by happenstance, because flesh is weak, because our intellectual conceptions often require a tangible reminder or a material abode that can provide the intangible idea with solace and safe haven. A fetish is that which even our most sublime spiritual ideas seek, and from time to time find, to lean on: In effect, it's a prop. As such, this secondary object has no essential place in the origin and development of religion. It is always incidental, always dispensable.

This definitive opinion, pronounced from so exalted a position by so eminent a scholar, ultimately did nothing to quiet the talk of fetishism. On the contrary, Müller's high-profile performance immediately elicited a pointedly critical response from Andrew Lang, another Victorian mythologue-folklorist-historian of religion, who was rising in prominence. Lang singled out the fetishism lecture to mount a wholesale attack on Müller's theory of religion, his method, and his authoritative and privileged access to, and reliance on, the *Rig Veda* as a preeminent source of ancient history.[12] This objection and other criticisms led Müller to qualify his position on the issue of original religion versus secondary corruption, and—at least according to Goblet d'Alviella, who himself rose to the podium as the 1891 appointee of the Hibbert Lectures[13]—Müller presented a revised expression of his views at another prestigious lecture series that he inaugurated, the Gifford Lectures of 1888, 1889, 1890, and 1891.[14] Whether or not his stance was modified in any significant way, Müller was to continue to address, if only incidentally and obliquely, the problem of fetishism for another two decades, which is tantamount to saying until he died. What is more, a number of his successors at the Hibbert and the Gifford Lectures, as well as other writers who appropriated "history of religion" as their topic or their book title—Goblet d'Alviella being but one example—kept on referring to fetishism, sometimes dismissing, other times seeking to improve upon, the notion. This explicit discussion of fetishism continued well into the 1920s and 1930s among European and American scholars of utmost respectability.[15]

In marked contrast to this state of affairs, the conventional wisdom perpetrated and reproduced by many of today's disciplinary historians of religious studies holds that the idea of fetishism, though undoubtedly originating in the exploration of primitive religion and thus having provenance in the history of religion, lost much of its efficacy by the middle of the nineteenth century. Supposedly, fetishism gave way to other, newer, and supposedly more exact concepts, or various new "isms"; meanwhile, fetishism's principal arena of operation shifted to other emergent discursive domains—above all, Marxist political economy, the scientific sexology of Alfred Binet, and Freudian psychoanalysis, where it thrives to this day.[16] Yet if we were to observe this history from the vantage point of Müller's lecture in 1878, it would appear that fetishism had been dominating the debate on the origin of religion for a century,[17] and, far from undergoing the quiet death of obsolescence, it was to live on for at least another half century.

The questions I should like to entertain in light of this incongruity are the following. If Müller was right in the first place when he claimed that primitive fetishism had been, and was still, "dominating" the debate on the origin of religion, then what was the mode of this domination? How do we explain the alleged predominance of fetishism theory when relatively few treatises on the origin and development of religion explicitly upheld the position—as had earlier writers from de Brosses to Comte—that fetishism was the original form of religion? Second, how do we account for the easy dismissal of the fetishism discourse by historians of the study of religions (as early as Jordan in 1905), despite the palpable fact that a good many people kept on mentioning fetishism, especially in association with the savage, the primitive, and the "degenerate races"? Combining the two questions, we may arrive at the following formulation: Given that the theory of primitive fetishism reputedly had already lost much of its credibility—or, perhaps more to the point, its respectability—by the 1870s, what was doing the "dominating" in the name of "fetishism"? Why did it continue to be useful or necessary to mention fetishism, and why did fetishism continue to be consistently associated with the rudimentary, the degraded, or the lowest, despite—or possibly because of—the devaluation of the concept itself? Is the general disrepute of "fetishism" among ethnologists and *Religionswissenschaftler* in some way directly related to the facts that, on the one hand, nineteenth-century sexologists found it a suitable name for a certain type of psychosexual disorder and, on the other hand, Marx used it to name an analogously aberrant and pathological object relation endemic to social production under capitalism?

Here, I must not delay in conceding that my aim in the present essay is not nearly as ambitious as to offer definitive answers to this cluster of questions. Rather, my immediate objective is to recover, by means of an efficacious mix of empathy and suspicion, the logic and sentiment that seem to have been sustaining and mobilizing the self-deprecating fetishism discourse of the Victorian era. As we begin to examine the nature of the rampant, imprecise, and disorderly talk of fetishism (which the best scientific minds of the time repeatedly tried and failed to control), our attention is invariably drawn to a broader domain of social and cultural practices well beyond the academic scruples endemic to a particular human science. In short, the subject of fetishism calls for a more general study of the discourse network in which this peculiar word/idea evidently had an especial resonance and potent communicability. The task of such a study is obviously beyond the scope of the present essay. This palpable limitation notwithstanding, in the latter part of the essay I will take the liberty of pointing toward possible answers to these questions. I offer these tentative signals in full awareness that, as they stand, they may amount to no more than an assemblage of suggestive images or a stimulating montage, rather than, say, a clearly defined set of research directives packed with definitive analytic strategies.

As for the more circumscribed field of interest pertinent to the disciplinary history of *Religionswissenschaft*, it may be useful to recall that, just when fetishism bashing was at its height—roughly from the time of Müller's pronouncements to the 1930s—scholars of religion were beginning to speak routinely about "religions of the world." During this period, "religion" was becoming a general category to which belonged all modalities of practice from the lowest to the highest—that is, from fetishism to modern Christianity. It became normal to speak about a common, permanent, and universal essence of religion, or about "the lowest common denominator" of religion present in all its historical manifestations.[18] Moreover, just as scholars began to lend credibility to something like a common universal core of all religions, high and low, a powerfully innocuous-sounding rhetoric of "world religions" was being born. Today, the discourse of "world religions" has become a basic, all-encompassing strategy for understanding the phenomenon of religion. This discourse supposedly replaced—but in fact has revised and retained—the developmental and hierarchical assumptions inherent in the so-called "evolutionary" mapping prevalent in the nineteenth century.[19] It is in the context of this transition from the unilinear evolutionary schema typical of the Victorian era to the pluralist yet deeply universalist world-religions discourse typical of the twentieth century—that is, this transmutation of the universalist history of religion(s)[20] from the evolutionist mode to the world-religions mode—that I situate the lingering problem of the value unaccountably invested in the disreputable concept of fetishism.

Fetishism *au fond*

Whichever side one stood on in the primitive fetishism debate, one thing was certain about the subject: fetishism was low. Whether this debased state, or stage, was presumed to be at the very beginning of human evolution,[21] right next to the absolute zero-point of cultural development, or at some later degenerative period in the imagined chronology, fetishism always marked the nadir of cultural value, the polar opposite of the telos of the civilizing process. Moreover, fetishism as a category is repeatedly and consistently characterized as inchoate, erratic, and unprincipled. In effect, fetishism is said to be no more than an incidental assortment of "the worship of odds and ends of rubbish,"[22] a misguided adoration of objects that are intrinsically worthless, such as "stones, shells, bones, and such like things"—in other words, "casual objects which, for some reason or other, or it may be for no reason at all, were considered endowed with exceptional powers."[23]

Fetishism's lowly character is evidenced above all by a tenacious attachment to the base materiality of the object and, by the same token, to its physical immediacy, its incidental nature, and its radical finitude.[24] The fetish is materiality at its crudest and lowest; it points to no transcendent meaning beyond itself, no abstract, general, or universal essence with respect to which it might be construed as a symbol. It is this special tie to materiality, or rather, this ineradicable essence of the fetish as materiality, and the alleged absence of any symbolic (or supra-material) dimension, that distinguishes fetishism from idolatry, or "polytheism," as idolatry came to be more commonly called in the course of the nineteenth century.[25] As a matter of fact, it may be speculated that the positing of fetishism as a third category in addition to polytheism and monotheism—or "fetish" as a third category in addition to "idol" and "icon/symbol"—helped clarify and justify the often difficult to sustain distinction between the illegitimate and legitimate uses of material objects in religious practice. On the one hand, a mere multiplicity of material representations of spiritual reality amounts to idolatry, or a cult of many (false) gods; on the other hand, the equally multiple iconic/symbolic representations of the truly spiritual God do not seem to threaten the unity of that deity. But how do we tell the difference? By positing the fetish as the opposite extreme in contrast with iconic/symbolic representation, one can render idolatry as something of a transitional stage in the development of religion, a midway point between absolute materiality and true spirituality, between, on the one hand, the total absence of the sense of unity and, on the other, the apotheosis of the idea of unity itself, or the idea of the singular Author of the entire universe, the idea central to so-called ethical monotheism.[26]

The notion of the three-stage development—that is, first fetishism, then polytheism, and finally monotheism—first articulated by de Brosses and later made famous by Comte,[27] John Lubbock,[28] and others, has proven so durable as to be reiterated even by those who ultimately sought to discredit the theory of primitive fetishism. In the 1920s, for example, Schmidt insisted on a stricter definition of "true fetishism, in which the object of worship is not symbolic but is worshipped for itself and not as connected with, or representing, a deity or spirit." To be sure, Schmidt is merely quoting this definition from P. Amaury Talbot, only to press the point that genuine fetishism in this exact sense of the term is not to be found anywhere, in Niger or any other of the usually suspected places in Africa.[29] Likewise, while Alfred Haddon for all intents and purposes denied the existence of any predominantly fetishist society,[30] he upheld the assumption of the hierarchy all the same. Never mind that fetishism as such did not really exist, he went on to assert: "Fetishism is a stage of religious development associated with a low grade of consciousness and of civilization, and it forms a basis from which many other modes of religious thought have developed, so that it is difficult to point out where fetishism ends and nature worship, ancestor worship, totemism, polytheism, and idolatry begin, or to distinguish between a fetish, an idol, and a deity."[31]

As difficult as it may be to make these distinctions *empirically*, the hierarchy of value from the most material to the most spiritual does not seem to be affected by this difficulty, but rather it remains paradigmatic in all these texts. It reflects a general assumption that has never been relinquished, and which has to do with a particular ideology of cognition and, concomitantly, a particular epistemic order. This order of knowledge is predicated on a logic of representation that posits the knowing subject and the object to be known, mind and matter, in a specific, hierarchical relation. In contrast to us moderns, Washburn Hopkins suggested, in 1923, the inability to discern this relation in the proper manner characterizes our primeval ancestors and contemporary savages alike:

What is really found in the lowest mental state is not lack of logic but inability to distinguish between mind and matter. To early man all substance is the same, neither material nor immaterial. The most primitive savages do not regard the two as separate. All matter is sentient and has mentality; all spirits are analogous to the minds of men, that is, encased in body, or rather indissolubly one with the material in which they appear. It is not a distinct spirit in a thing which such savages recognize but, so to speak, a spiritized thing, an object imbued with power.[32]

As far as these writers are concerned, the primitive confounding or indifferentiation of matter and spirit/mind does not result in an alternative ontology—say, a mystical monism as an alternative to Cartesian dualism—any more than magic is an alternative science. Rather, according to their opinion, any system based on a mind-matter confusion is bound to get mired in unreality, even if such an illusion may offer a secondary dividend of psychological comfort.

This general idea, of course, was later elaborated by J. G. Frazer (in connection with "sympathetic magic"), Sigmund Freud ("the omnipotence of thought"), and Lucien Lévy-Bruhl ("primitive mentality"). Early in *The Golden Bough*, Frazer famously characterized magic as "a false science, as well as an abortive art," which is to say, a spurious theory and practice predicated on "misapplications of the association of ideas."[33] Freud, drawing a complicated analogy between obsessive neurotics and savages, theorized this notion more explicitly and proposed that the proclivity to confuse what occurred merely in thought and what actually took place—that is, conflation of a psychical/subjective reality and a material/objective reality—were common to both sorts of people. In effect, according to Freud, magic, taboo, and other such superstitions—that is to say, observances obviously inefficacious yet tenaciously adhered to—owe their compelling power to the infantile tendency for thought-reality confusion, for easy psychic transfer from subjective to objective, from a mental wish to its material fulfillment.[34] It is therefore evident that the primitive undifferentiation of matter and spirit/mind is more or less a direct echo of what Tylor had identified decades earlier: "Among the less civilized races, the separation of subjective and objective impressions, which in this, as in several other matters, makes the most important difference between the educated man and the savage, is much less fully carried out."[35]

The clarity and lucidity of the demarcation between the subject and the object of representation is presumed to be essential to the modern epistemic order, especially to science. As Frazer put it bluntly: "The principles of association [of ideas] are excellent in themselves, and indeed absolutely essential to the working of the human mind. Legitimately applied they yield science; illegitimately applied they yield magic, the bastard sister of science."[36] From the point of view of these mental/spiritual developmentalists, the ability to extricate the subjectivity of the knower from the material contingency of the object and from the physical and corporeal immediacy of the experience of cognition is the hallmark of reason and civilization, and this ability is equated with the power of abstraction, generalization, and universalization. Like its concomitant, "magic," fetishism—whether it is believed to be an empirically extant condition among tribespeople somewhere or merely a virtual point of reference—is consistently marked as the opposite extreme to this ideal of true knowing.

Beyond the invariable baseness of "fetishism," the scholars of the period from the mid-nineteenth century to the early twentieth opined more or less in unison that there was no clearly articulable, logically coherent principle for its definition. Consequently, the concept of fetishism was considered inherently liable to confusion and abuse. Writer after writer would warn the reader that there was something incorrigibly imperfect or incomplete about the concept, that the concept itself was rather "common" and "unscientific," and thus that its very entry into the scholarly vocabulary was somehow "unfortunate."[37] In short, if a fetish was a contemptible little object in the eyes of reason and science, its iniquity seems to have been transferred to the theory of fetishism itself, as this latter was also spoken of as being beneath the dignity of science. Yet somehow science could not make fetishism go away. Tenacious attachment in defiance of common sense and reason appears to be the defining characteristic not only of the fetish, but also of fetishism theory. Already beyond such obsession himself (or so we are led to believe), Müller describes the irony in this way: "It will be difficult indeed to eradicate the idea of a universal primeval fetishism from the text-books of history. That very theory has become a kind of scientific fetish, though, like most fetishes, it seems to owe its existence to ignorance and superstition."[38]

Curiously, the very authors who despised the fetishism concept and denounced the theory of primitive fetishism in one breath seem to have believed that there was a way to restore something like the original meaning of "fetish," that is, the true definition of fetishism, which had eluded even de Brosses, who invented the term. They sought to ascertain this proper, authentic concept of fetishism by means of etymology. It is largely on account of this desire for a correct definition of an inherently flawed concept that we are referred back, again and again, to the Portuguese and the savages of the Gold Coast, their shared superstitions recalcitrantly attached to materiality in its most trivial forms, their uncanny exchange rooted in misrecognition, their shady trade based on bogus values heaped upon rubbish, trinkets, and unfamiliar objects of foreign manufacture.

Fetishism in the Eye of the Beholder

In all these respects, Müller's attitude toward the problem of fetishism is more typical of his time than it is exceptional. What is not so typical, however, is his way of accounting for the conceptual origin of fetishism: that is, his explanation of how the initial erroneous estimation of an insignificant material object could have taken place. There is something slightly eccentric about his account of how such prodigious values and powers came to be ascribed, quite irrationally, of course, to the humble materiality that is the fetish. As we have seen, in nineteenth-century discourse a fetish is a "mere object," taken to be a singular being endowed with supernatural and superlative virtues and efficacy. How could an inanimate, intrinsically valueless object come to be charged with such nonmaterial, almost ghostlike, "spiritual" values? How could this purely material object come alive, as it were, in this way?

In a nutshell, Müller's argument amounts to this: the initial misrecognition of an inert material object as a fetish, as something believed to be animate and powerful *in and of itself,* lies ultimately on the side of the European travelers rather than the savage natives of Africa. To be sure, in Müller's estimation, the Europeans in question were not exactly Christians of the modern, rational, enlightened sort. Indeed, he implies it was their impure Christianity and their own residual savagery that was responsible for the mistaken conception:

> Why did the Portuguese navigators, who were Christians, *but Christians in that metamorphic state which marks the popular Roman Catholicism of the last century* [emphasis added]—why did they recognize at once what they saw among the negroes of the Gold Coast, as *feitiços*? The answer is clear. Because they themselves were perfectly familiar with a *feitiço*, an amulet, or a talisman; and probably all carried with them some beads, or crosses, or images, that had been blessed by their priests before they started for their voyage. They themselves were fetish-worshippers in a certain sense.[39]

As Müller goes on to suggest, this apprehension of sameness—that is, the instantaneous recognition of the identity between the European self and the African other with respect to certain religious observances—is coupled with an equally instantaneous apprehension of difference, or rather, an immediate presumption of radical disparity between the civilized self and the savage other, Although they are ostensibly similar in that they both perform certain acts of veneration toward special little objects, the Portuguese of course "knew" that there was more to their own religion than this particular type of personal practice with *feitiços*. They did recognize, however imperfectly, the invisible reality and the formidable institutional apparatus associated with it—namely, Christianity—which purportedly empowered their precious objects and made them sacred in the first place. By contrast, the Portuguese failed to perceive any comparable system of invisible power in relation to the African practice, and immediately assumed the total absence of any such higher order of reality. Müller thus concludes: "As [those first European visitors to the Gold Coast] discovered no other traces of any religious worship [among the Africans], they concluded very naturally that this outward show of regard for these *feitiços* constituted the whole of the negro's religion."

In sum, the African observances involving small, portable objects were recognized by the Portuguese sailors as *religious* acts (hence belonging to the same genus as their own devotional acts predicated on Christianity). At the same time, the African and European forms of *feitiço* veneration were sorted out into two entirely separate categories and made incommensurate: On the one hand was the primitive worship of purely material objects, eventually to be called "fetishism," and on the other hand, a peripheral manifestation of Christianity still prevalent among the uneducated—that is, superstitious veneration of icons and amulets. Thus it came to pass, according to Müller, that half-civilized Europeans in a transitional state of religious development took the first erring step along the course leading to the illusion that was fetishism, and eventually to the benighted theory of primitive fetishism.[40]

In Müller's opinion, the notion that a purely material object could *in and of itself* generate a nonmaterial power/entity is an illogical—indeed impossible—idea. If one wants to claim that such an irrational, spontaneous generation of the immaterial/spiritual from the material cannot take place in the exterior world of nature, then one must be prepared to recognize that it cannot happen in the interior world of the savage mind either. By ascribing fetishism to the Africans, Müller here seems to say, those theorists fell into the same "superstition" that they attributed to the savages. By disputing the theory of primitive fetishism and thus exonerating the Africans of any such confounding beliefs, Müller restores their rudimentary religiosity to the proper sphere of pure spirit. In his view, all forms of veneration and worship, however humble, always refer to the Infinite (the unitary, invisible, and spiritual), regardless of what particular finite objects or entities may come to stand as a vehicle or as a mediating agent for it. Unilaterally championing unbounded spirit over finite matter, Müller would vanquish the specter of fetishism. Once this is accomplished, at least to his own satisfaction, we hear no more from him about this curious tale of cultural hybridity, the lawless commerce of novel objects, and the spontaneous generation of disproportionate values taking place in the contact zone of Africa meets Europe. Here, what might have been an opening of a new ground for colonial cultural criticism, a crevice we could glimpse in the passage quoted above, was henceforth closed off. Instead, on the basis of this closure and the triumph of the Infinite, Müller was to engender an altogether different kind of discursive tradition: an idealist history of the spiritual—that is, the history of religions as we know it today.

All the same, it is noteworthy that, from his position in the nineteenth century, Müller has reminded us that it was on the volatile ground of disjointed colonial exchange between incommensurable systems that the fetish, at once an idea and an object, was born.

Troubles at Home

> I reduce the systems of philosophy concerning man's soul to two. The first and most ancient is materialism. The second is spiritualism.
>
> Those metaphysicians who suggest that matter might manifest the faculty of thinking have not dishonored reason. Why not? Because they enjoy the advantage (in this case it is one) of expressing themselves poorly. Strictly speaking, to ask if matter sheerly in itself can think is like asking if matter can tell the time. Already we see that we shall avoid this reef, on which Mr. Locke had the misfortune to run aground.
>
> Leibnizians, with their *monad*, have set up an unintelligible hypothesis. They have spiritualized matter rather than materialized the soul. But how can one define a being whose nature is absolutely unknown to us?
>
> Descartes and all the Cartesians . . . made the same mistake. They said man consists of two distinct substances, as though they had seen and counted them.
>
> —Julien Offray de La Mettrie, *L'Homme machine* (1747)[41]

> After days and nights of incredible labour and fatigue, I succeeded in discovering the cause of generation and life; nay, more, I became myself capable of bestowing animation upon lifeless matter.
>
> —Mary Shelley, *Frankenstein* (1818)

If we have learned something from Müller's explanation concerning the hybrid formation of "fetishism," we may now reformulate our earlier question more exactly: If fetishism continued to be a viable topic after its official demise, then what was it in the nature of those nineteenth-century intellectuals that could not help resonating with this seemingly exotic subject and the similarly outlandish theory about it?

As we have seen, the contempt in which both the fetish and fetishism theory were held—hence their easy dismissal—stems from the apparent absurdity of the notion that the pure materiality of "sticks and stones" is inherently and essentially commingled with a supra-material reality of some sort—let us call this "spirituality," for short—or from the even greater absurdity of the notion that materiality in and of itself generates spirituality and, consequently, that spirituality is ultimately nothing but a peculiar mutation of materiality. The more we look into the matter, the more difficult it seems to differentiate clearly and distinctly the superstition of fetishism from the superstition of fetishism theory—that is, on the one hand, the belief that certain material objects are more than "mere matter" but magically spiritual, and, on the other, the belief that a mere material encounter with some physical object of no particular significance can instill in the savage mind the idea of spirituality. In either case, the material object seems to keep generating its own phantom other. Yet this specter does not leave the body behind; rather, it inheres in the very materiality of the body. Conversely, it is as though materiality itself—"dead matter," the cadaver—began to move, even to think and to speak, all on its own.

Materialism

A few years before Müller's lecture on fetishism, on the pages of the journal that was bringing to public attention such works as Herbert Spencer's "The Genesis of Superstitions" and "Idol-Worship and Fetish-Worship,"[42] another scandal of materiality was unfolding. The beginning of the controversy was the presidential address of the British Association, delivered in Belfast on August 19, 1874, by an eminent physical scientist and friend of Spencer, sitting president of the Royal Institution of Great Britain and successor to Michael Faraday in this capacity: John Tyndall. This address—and its expanded printed version—was partly an evocation of the nobly enduring history of scientific materialism, which harkened back to the pre-Socratic atomists, and partly a plea for the right of science to explore all aspects of nature according to its own principles, free from theological sanctions and dogmatic prescriptions.[43] Among the immediate reactions provoked by Tyndall's speech, the most substantial came in the form of another address, delivered in London on October 6 of the same year by a distinguished Unitarian and author of numerous treatises on theological subjects, James Martineau. The full text of Martineau's address was published early in 1875 as *Religion as Affected by Modern Materialism* and was prefaced by an introduction written by a certain Rev. Henry W. Bellows.[44] The opening remarks of this introduction signal much about the controversy that was to ensue:

> Is the mind of man only the last product of the matter and force of our system of Nature, having its origin in the blind or purposeless chance which drifts into order and intelligence under a self-executing mandate or necessity, called the survival of the fittest? . . .

It is certain that a spirit older than matter, an intelligence other than human, a will freer than necessity, does not enter into the causes of things contemplated by the new science. It studies a mindless universe with the sharpened instincts of brutes who have slowly graduated into men—themselves the most intelligent essence in existence. Consciousness, reason, purpose, will, are results of blind, undesigning, unfeeling forces, inherent in matter. (5–6)

If this grievance sounds a trifle hackneyed to our twenty-first-century ears, it is nonetheless noteworthy that, with proper distillation, the Reverend's protest boils down to a case against the atomist theory, which supposedly holds that mere matter—or atoms in random motion—can generate *of its own accord* the entire gamut of ideational phenomena, from the most visceral feelings to the highest form of intelligence, which is manifest (so says the theologian) in the total design of the universe. In effect, one might say that the atomistic materialism of "the new science" is exposed as a kind of fetishism, as a belief in material objects (here, atomic particles) endowed with, or inherently capable of generating, supra-natural powers, insofar as nature is defined and determined exclusively in terms of (inanimate) materiality. If the atom is a kind of fetish, then atomistic materialism would be a form of scientific fetishism. Thus vaguely adumbrating the train of thought that we saw at work in Müller's argument against the primitive fetishism theory, Martineau arrives at this observation: "It is not in the history of Superstition alone that the human mind may be found struggling in the grasp of some mere nightmare of its own creation: a philosophical hypothesis may sit upon the breast with a weight not less oppressive and not more real" (26–27).

Meanwhile, the editor of *Popular Science Monthly* stepped forward as a partisan on the side of the new science. In the "Editor's Table" of the November 1874 issue, he defended Tyndall unequivocally, but in a language that did not necessarily contradict the theologian's accusations: "Prof. Tyndall claims that there is a great deal more, in this mysterious and unfathomable something which we call matter, than has been hitherto allowed; he sees in it 'the promise and potency of every form and quality of life.' Much horror has been expressed at this statement, but the expressions seem to us quite gratuitous."[45] Tyndall's stirring language of material potency and vitality quoted here harks back to the eighteenth-century French materialism of Julien Offray de La Mettrie. As a matter of fact, following the cue of the renegade French physician, Baron d'Holbach expressed the following opinion in 1770, entirely in line with Tyndall's view: "A satisfactory definition of matter has not yet been given. Man, deceived and led astray by his prejudices, formed but vague, superficial, and imperfect notions concerning it. He looked upon it as a unique being, gross and passive, incapable of either moving by itself, of any thing by its own."[46] From the perspective of the nineteenth-century materialists, it appears, this unsatisfactory conception of matter had not changed appreciably in the intervening hundred years.

In any event, there is little room for concession to Christian orthodoxy in this tradition of materialism. We might safely surmise, therefore, that the suspicion of theologians, far from being quelled, was rather ominously compounded by the editor's endorsement of the materialist new sciences. Their "horror" may very well have been already exacerbated by his earlier reference to a sixteenth-century Dominican philosopher and Church-certified heretic, Giordano Bruno, who had evoked, instead of the almighty Father-Creator and cerebral Designer of the Universe, something resembling the Earth Mother. Bruno believed, the editor comments approvingly, that "Matter is not that mere empty capacity which philosophers have pictured her to be, but the universal mother who brings forth all things as the fruit of her own womb."[47]

We shall not follow here the full extent of this debate,[48] which, in variously transmuted forms, continues to this day.[49] Suffice it to say that the initial rift was established on the basis of divergent (and contradictory) conceptions of materiality and over the question of whether or not matter as such was inherently inert, blind, deaf, dumb, and generally unfeeling—in effect, dead. The trouble was—perhaps by irony, perhaps by necessity—that the more "dead" matter was assumed to be, the more haunted the material world seemed to become.

Spiritualism

As far as Victorian intellectuals are concerned, haunting by the spirit may or may not be an ordinary state of affairs in Africa, Polynesia, or other far-flung primordial locations. That is one thing, but it is quite another when something similar is suspected of happening in the world of educated Europeans, especially among the cutting-edge scientists of the time. Yet the controversial atomism that scientists advocated and theologians tried to exorcise was but one instance—and by nature a highly circumscribed one—of this phenomenon. Another, no doubt more sensational spirit manifestation was the sudden vogue of Spiritualism in the latter half of the nineteenth century, which swept across the darkened parlors of some of the most respectable households in Victorian England and North America. Highly fashionable men and women gathered around a person functioning, usually for a fee, as a medium—an often slightly disreputable, exotic character, typically migrating from another continent, another region, or another class—for an evening of mysterious rapping, table-tipping, and other tangible signals from the spirit-world of the dead. Many emerging middle-class intellectuals—anthropologists and historians of religions among them—came into the orbit of this phenomenon. Some of them, such as Alfred Russel Wallace and Andrew Lang, became enthusiasts, while others, like Müller and Tylor, took the position of the recalcitrant skeptic.

The latter's skepticism, however, did not necessarily signify their indifference to the spiritualist phenomenon. On the contrary, especially in the case of Tylor, one might surmise that his unyielding disbelief and high-handed dismissal of the spiritualist phenomenon was in part an expression of his annoyance at the senseless—yet all the more symptomatic—fad raging all around him. As he saw the matter, "Spiritualism" was not only instigating false hopes and fears among the gullible and the weak-minded but also threatening to cause undue confusion of scientific categories. The point of controversy here—which, in fact, mirrors that of the materialist debate—was whether some essentially immaterial power (or disembodied "spirit") could temporarily activate inanimate objects (including such quotidian items as tables and chairs, or even a whole house) or communicate through foreign bodies (spirit mediums). As a way out of the conceptual mire and as a definitive move against this (for him) alarming insurgence of primitive irrationality, Tylor proposed a new theory that at once described the precivilized mode of thought and explained the origin of religion. As it happens, this theory was also a way out of the benighted problem of "fetishism."

Several years before the publication of his most famous work, *Primitive Culture* (1871), Tylor incrementally ushered his signature theory of "animism" into being through a series of articles.[50] A passage in the first of these articles makes evident that the idea of "animism" initially emerged as a way of correcting an earlier misconception that went by the name of "fetishism." Here is what appears to be the inaugural moment in the transformative overcoming of "fetishism":

> Readers familiar with the study of human thought in its lower phases will ere this have missed the familiar name of "fetishism," as denoting this very opinion "by which man conceives of all external bodies as animated by a life analogous to his own, with differences of mere intensity;" but the word is so utterly inappropriate and misleading that I have purposely avoided it. A *fetish* (Portuguese *feitiço*, "charm, sorcery") is an object used in witchcraft; and the mistake of applying the word to religion at all has arisen from the images and other inanimate objects used by sorcerers being confounded with idols, which we thence find commonly, but very wrongly, called fetishes. The theory which endows the phenomena of nature with personal life might perhaps be conveniently called Animism.[51]

Clearly, this emergent discourse on "animism" is a virtual prototype, one might say, for what we referred to earlier as a mantra protecting the rational mind against the disorderly proliferation of fetishism discourse. The language here is typically disdainful and dismissive. Yet this is not all. While the newly coined *animism* was above all meant to disable the unruly currency of "fetishism," this neologism was also designed to eschew, circumscribe, and inoculate us against another term/category—namely, *Spiritualism*.

As Tylor later noted in *Primitive Culture*, insofar as the minimum definition of religion that he settled for was "the belief in spiritual beings," the naturally appropriate term for the most primitive form of religion would have been "spiritualism," had it not been for the fact that "the word Spiritualism . . . has this obvious defect to us, that it has become the designation of a particular modern sect."[52] Needless to say, with his new theory of primordial religion, Tylor did not wish to evoke first and foremost the images of the table-tipping, self-levitating parlor spiritualists regularly observable in his own society. This is not to say, however, that this urban Spiritualism is entirely unrelated to what Tylor has chosen to call "animism." He proposed *animism* in lieu of *spiritualism* not in order to isolate and exclude the latter from consideration but, on the contrary, in order to include and contain it as a subcategory of the former, and an exceptionally ludicrous one at that. In his opinion, the fact that this was very much a modern "sect," emerging in the midst of the most civilized populations, by no means entailed that it should be presumed any less savage or barbarous. As he declares summarily: "The modern spiritualism, as every ethnographer may know, is pure and simple savagery both in its theory and the tricks by which it is supported."[53] And Tylor was most assuredly one of those ethnographers who knew—and knew at first hand.

Like many anthropologists of his time, Tylor's theoretical construction of "animism" was based not on his own experience living among savages in distant places but on books and reports made available to him secondhand. Of course, this condition is typical of the "armchair anthropologists" of his time, and this fact often affords contemporary anthropologists—in whose career formation "fieldwork" is mandatory—an occasion for condescension. As it turns out, however, Tylor—the paragon of Victorian armchair anthropology if there ever was one—was for a time engaged in a certain kind of "field" observation after all, though not too far away from home.

We learn about his firsthand ethnographic adventure thanks largely to George Stocking's 1971 article, "Animism in Theory and Practice: E. B. Tylor's Unpublished 'Notes on "Spiritualism."'"[54] These notes proffer a view—a better view than Tylor's published works would allow—of the background negotiations leading to the ultimate triangulation of the key terms *animism*, *fetishism*, and *spiritualism*.

Beginning in 1867, and especially intensively in 1872, Tylor attended some of the most prominent spiritualist séances in London,[55] out of scientific curiosity, one would assume, or, as he puts it, in order "to look into the alleged manifestations."[56] In effect, these notes, dating from November 4 through 28, 1872, are a rough equivalent to the field notes of "participant observation," in a rather literal sense of the term. To be sure, his mode of participation/observation was significantly at variance with what is meant by that term in contemporary ethnographic methodology. He "went up to London," much as a news reporter might, to see "it" with his own eyes, in order to determine whether it was genuine or a fraud. As a piece of investigative reporting, the result was a rather disappointing one, as his last entry reads:

Nov. 28. Returned home. What I have seen & heard fails to convince me that there is a genuine residue. It all might have been legerdemain, & was so in great measure. . . . My judgment is in abeyance. I admit a prima facie case on evidence, & will not deny that there may be a psychic force causing raps, movements, levitations, etc. But it has not proved itself by evidence of my senses, and I distinctly think the case weaker than written documents led me to think. Seeing has not (to me) been believing. I propose a new text to define faith: "Blessed are they that have seen, and yet have believed." (Quoted in Stocking, 100)

In the last analysis, then, as intrigued as he had been by the spiritualist vogue, and despite empirical evidence seeming to support its authenticity (that is, despite whatever it was that he "saw"), Tylor gained the same skeptical distance from this "modern sect" as from the indigenous animism of distant savage tribes. He regards both as results of the unconscious complicity between the gullibility of the many uncritical minds and the deceitfulness of a cynical few who would manipulate the credulous. Tylor's new scientific ethnography thus stands apart equally from primitive animists and from modern spiritualists, as well as from the previous generation of anthropologists, mired in the "utterly inappropriate and misleading" notion of fetishism. Stocking helpfully summarizes this outcome in this way:

> Intellectually, [Tylor's theory of animism] had its roots . . . in Comte, and more especially in De Brosse's concept of fetishism. Empirically, Tylor seems to have drawn on the observed behaviour of children, as well as on his own extensive ethnographic reading. Nevertheless, it is worth noting that between 1866 and 1871, the concept moved away from its roots in the notion of fetishism, and that it did so in the context of an increased interest in modern spiritualist analogues . . . . Indeed, the essay "On the Survival of Savage Thought" would suggest that the spiritualist movement provided a major source of the empirical data in terms of which that concept was developed. (90–91; my emphasis)

In effect, it appears that Tylor sought to achieve scientific equilibrium by means of his new theory, which objectified—and thereby distanced—not two but three forms of superstition: (1) the fetishism/animism of the primitive savages, which is predicated on a misguided notion of materiality and vitality, as well as on the fundamental inability to distinguish the subjective from the objective; (2) the Spiritualism fashionable among fellow Victorians, which for him was nothing other than an atavistic return of primitive animism and which, no less than the animism of the savages, conflated and confused subjective thought and objective reality by positing certain dubious notions of the material and the spiritual and an improbable idea about their relation; and (3) the fetishism theory, also popular among the Victorians, which failed to resolve this confusion and ultimately compounded it by repeating it.

It's Alive!

For the time being, a certain aspect of our historical interest may rest satisfied by the knowledge that at least two representatives of the Victorian human sciences, Tylor and

Müller, resolutely rejected the vagaries not only of modern Spiritualism but also of the modern theory of primitive fetishism. To be sure, their views do not speak for the whole, nor probably even for the dominant majority of the learned opinions of the time. Indeed, there were many other possible positions to occupy as Victorian men and women of letters alternately struggled and consorted with the problem of materiality, or with whatever was supposedly other than materiality. In order to project a compelling historical picture of the cultural discourse of the time, I must take into account those alternative and dissonant positions. Among the converts to and committed enthusiasts for modern Spiritualism were, for instance, the folklorist and novelist Andrew Lang, who at different times positioned himself as a conspicuous opponent to both Müller and Tylor, and Harriet Martineau, a celebrated translator of Comte, the sister of James Martineau, and, unlike her brother, a noted atheist. These are but two figures, representing altogether different perspectives on the subject of materiality and nonmateriality. Instead of following their leads, since an expedition in this direction would certainly digress from the limited objective of this essay, I will conclude with a sketch of one more figure: Alfred Russel Wallace.

Today mainly remembered as a collaborator and interlocutor of Charles Darwin and an advocate of certain controversial ideas about "race" and evolution, Wallace had seen some faraway regions of the world and, in the course of his turbulent career, had espoused varying positions with regard to the questions of materialism and spiritualism. The product of a socialist experiment in education for the working classes, Wallace was exposed to progressive ideas and scientific skills in his adolescent years, when he was being trained as a land surveyor, amateur geologist, and botanist. By the time he reached adulthood, as he himself testified decades later, he was a thoroughly nonreligious scientific materialist.[57] All in all, he led an eventful life with little insurance, making a precarious, often impecunious living. His first great misfortune was an actual shipwreck in 1852, on his way home from four years of expedition in the Amazon. With nearly all of his entomological and botanical specimens—the fruit of years of labor in the tropics—lying at the bottom of the sea, he could do nothing but write about the whole affair, which he did in *A Narrative of Travels on the Amazon and Rio Negro* (1853).[58] He came to renounce the materialism of his youth and became an ardent believer in Spiritualism during the 1860s. He was convinced that "spiritual facts" were real enough to manifest materially from time to time under certain favorable circumstances, through especially sensitive individuals or instruments, such as mediums and "spirit-photographs." Eager to shed some scientific light on the matter, he persuaded Tyndall and Tylor to attend séances. Ultimately, he could not sway either of them.[59]

Paradoxically—yet perhaps in the last analysis, inevitably—Wallace's spiritualism was an almost perfect mirror image of the brand of materialism, full of mystery and wonder, endorsed by the editor of *Popular Science Monthly*. There is an unmistakable symmetry between these positions: either seemingly dead matter turns out to be intrinsically or potentially animate, or immaterial spirit comes to possess, disrupt, and intervene in the otherwise quiescent (dead) material world. One of Tylor's passing comments in *Primitive Culture* is illuminating here:

> It is extremely difficult to draw a distinct line of separation between the two prevailing sets of ideas relating to spiritual action through what we call inanimate objects. Theoretically we can distinguish the notion of the object acting as it were by the will and force of its own proper soul or spirit, from the notion of some foreign spirit entering its substance or acting on it from without, and so using it as a body or instrument. But in practice these conceptions blend almost inextricably.[60]

Wallace's life course and his changing outlook from materialism to spiritualism may be a fitting emblem for this fundamental difficulty—or impossibility?—of telling apart, once and for all, intrinsic (self-) activation and extrinsic (foreign) possession.

· · ·

As we attempt to take stock of the situation, we are left to wonder why the matter-spirit relation has come to seem so problematic, so permeated with the smell of death. When did matter as such become so dead, and its animation so ghoulish? Has it always been this way?

Of course, there would be a materialist answer and a spiritualist answer to this question. Spiritualists might say that it is the mechanistic, scientistic, technologized ideology of materialism (and the industrialization beholden to this ideology) that has been choking all the living spirit out of the world. Materialists might in turn blame the mystifying theological obscurantism of the spiritualists for cadaverizing the body and matter, for making it impossible to read any pulse and appreciate any sign of life in the material world, the world of "flesh and blood," as Feuerbach once put it. Clearly, these are not propositions to be fairly compared or easily mediated and reconciled. In fact, the contention has gotten considerably more complicated over the years, because neither "theologians" and "scientists," nor "religionists" and "secularists" fall neatly onto opposing sides, but rather cross over the materialism-spiritualism divide in multiple, confusing ways.

There is still a little room for an alternative speculation, a wager, an idea to be thrown into the fray. This speculation has an affinity with what might be described as dialectical materialism, or, before this term was coined in the late nineteenth century, what Engels called "Marxist materialism" (as distinct from the "vulgar materialism" of some of his contemporaries), and what was for Marx simply a "new materialism." In any event, the speculation will be in the spirit of Marx.

If materiality was becoming "dead matter" as modernity progressed, and, as is often said, we humans were becoming increasingly differentiated, abstracted, and alienated from the rest of the world, it was also in the course of these changes, as many historians of modernity have observed, that "we" were becoming solidified and disciplined into subjectivity, individuality, and agency. At the same time, the rest of the world other than "us" was becoming progressively the world of *things*, and, as Marx would point out, under the spell of a capitalist economy certain things never remained *just* things but were destined to enter an altogether new and different system of value and circulation—that is, they became *commodities*. As a commodity, a thing, dead or alive, leads a kind of double life: on the one hand, in its "natural," intrinsic being (use value) and on the other, in its capacity as a measure of equivalency in relation to all other commodified things (exchange value). As commodities, then, material or embodied objects are essentially non-subjective, nonhuman, inert beings that are nevertheless endowed with a seemingly mysterious power to circulate and substitute, either actually or virtually. But this power appears mysterious, Marx would argue, only insofar as its real nature is hidden from our view. According to Marx, the exchange value of commodities is none other than the effect of our material and social relation to the world and to our fellow human beings through the process of labor and social intercourse. It is therefore because of our alienation from our social production under capitalism that material beings qua commodities come to seem at once inert (dead) and animated (possessed).

Having examined several scenes from Victorian science and culture more or less anecdotally, I do not, of course, imagine myself to be in a position to conclude definitively, for example, that it was capitalism that rendered materiality at once dead and possessed, while turning certain material objects into veritable fetishes, even if that seems to be just what Marx *does* suggest when he refers to the fetishism of commodities. Let me instead conclude by observing that there was nothing *merely metaphorical* about Marx's appropriation of the concept of fetishism. For, if the problem of materiality in the nineteenth century turns out to be the problem of *commodified things*, and if the problem of fetish embodies the problem of materiality as such, then we have reason to suspect that the uncanny object first conjured up in the encounter with African primitives was directly, that is, nonfiguratively, relevant to the understanding of the everyday mystery of modern economy.

It is no wonder that the fetish discourse could not be shed, and that it continued to haunt the science of religion for decades.

Salvation by Electricity

Jeremy Stolow

Whether looking at matters of invention and design, of distribution and ownership, or of reception and use, histories of technology are typically framed within one of two metanarratives: the optimistic or the dystopian. In the former, technologies are seen as benign instruments that fulfill the needs, intentions, and desires of their human users. An extreme form of such technophilia can be found in the pages of the American magazine *Wired* and among techno-gurus such as Nicholas Negroponte, who wax poetic about an imminent world populated by therapeutic Barbie dolls, self-cleaning shirts, driverless cars, and a range of devices enabling immediate access to inexhaustible supplies of media and information. This optimism has a considerable progeny, one root of which might be traced back to early modern European conceptions of the mechanical order of nature and its susceptibility to ever-advancing human powers of inspection and rational design. In this tradition, technology is a pliable handmaiden to the forward march of history, taking such forms as the Haussmannized city, the Macadamized countryside, the prosthetically enhanced body, or the digitized archive. By contrast, there is a tradition of thinking about technology, as in the philosophical writings of Martin Heidegger or Jacques Ellul, that is both dystopian and technophobic. Here one is presented with a vision of technology as an autonomous, self-directed realm, indifferent and impervious to our feeble calls for restraint, democratic control, or humane purpose. In this scheme, modern technologies resemble juggernauts running loose in the world, devouring the natural environment and even human bodies, and transforming them into raw materials for their own mechanical processes.

The aim of this essay is not to resolve the ongoing dispute between optimistic and dystopian accounts of technology, nor to offer a "better" theoretical construction of what technology is and how it relates to the making of history.[1] It will be concerned with a somewhat different set of questions, based on the observation that both the optimistic and the dystopian narratives of technological modernization share a common location in a deeper—and thus more insidious—history of secularist thinking about the relationship between humans and things, between the lived body and the realm of imagination, and between the known and the unknown.[2] From a secular perspective, technology refers to the order of things that are "supposed to work," and the failure of any given technology to do so is usually attributed to problems of misapplication or errors of design. Religion, by contrast, is often defined as precisely that which is *not* supposed to work, at least in the sense that actions and perceptions falling under the rubric of religion are assumed not to produce any objectively measurable effects within the order of the real. In the anticlerical tradition of the Enlightened *philosophes*, this distinction further serves as the basis for understanding the "true" origin of religious phenomena, such as miracles or divine retributions, as products of wholly human thoughts and actions. Attempts to define what is religion (and in the same breath to demarcate the realm of the secular) thus end up working to delegitimate and deauthenticate religious practices and modes of discourse by presenting them as infantile delusions, or as tricks of mystification designed to exploit the credulities of the innocent. In these terms, secularist critiques of religion have long been tied to broader political projects to foster new, "reasonable" forms of religious discourse and practice: religions that "know their place" by remaining safely segregated from the performative, epistemological, and instrumental prerogatives of—among other things—modern techno-scientific practice.[3]

The more carefully one looks, however, the more difficult it becomes to determine where, or even how, to draw the line separating "religious" and "technological" dimensions of social life. The action systems of modern technologies (especially advanced, complex systems that require considerable operational expertise and institutional infrastructure) are typically distinguished by their inability to be fully captured by the instrumental intentions of their users. To that extent, they reference a transcendent realm not unlike actions normally associated with "religion," such as prayer or ritual performance. Technologically mediated actions are also often governed by principles of automaticity, reproducibility, and extension through virtual space, making them phenomenologically comparable to "religious" experiences of the numinous, the miraculous, the providential, or the mysterious. Numerous historical and ethnographic studies have likewise shown how the skilled techniques and representational systems of modern techno-scientific practice—in laboratories and workshops, at conferences, and in other public and institutional spaces—resemble systems of magic or religious action: as pragmatic engagements with the world through skilled techniques, disciplined perceptions, and autotelic mechanical devices; or through the institutional organization of "faith" regarding the true workings of an imperceptible natural order.[4] All of this suggests that religion and technology are far more tightly woven together than secularist discourse might have us believe. Denials of this mutual contamination of religion and technology can thus be understood as part of a larger strategy for securing secularist certainties about the division between real and unreal worlds, and the forms of political authority and legitimacy that rest upon their segregation.

This essay contributes to a growing scholarly suspicion about secularism, and in particular secularist conceptions of technology, by considering a parochial but I think quite exemplary story: the story of the Spiritual Telegraph.[5] The term *Spiritual Telegraph* refers to the deep and inextricable relationship between, on the one hand, the circulation of ideas and practices of spirit communication embodied in the nineteenth-century religious movement known as Spiritualism and, on the other hand, the institution and spread of the telegraph: a technology that can be singled out as the first significant industrial application of electricity in the nineteenth century and an important harbinger of the networks of global communication that define our contemporary "digital age." As we shall see, the relationship between Spiritualism and telegraphy is not simply fortuitous. By recounting their conjoined history, I hope not only to demonstrate the importance of both Spiritualism and telegraphy for the constitution of modernity but also to slip out of the secularist grip on the very notions of religion and technology, in order to imagine them differently.

It is not coincidental that the story I have chosen takes place in the nineteenth century, since this was a period of intense technological transformation and also of the dramatic growth of religious movements. Especially during the latter half of the century, the industrializing societies of the North Atlantic witnessed a succession of technological inventions that radically expanded the terms of human contact, labor, knowledge, and imagination along the axes of transmission and recording: new technologies for erasing distance (such as telegraphy, telephony, and radio) and new forms of mechanized inscription and reproduction (such as photography, phonography, radiography, and cinema). These revolutions in mediated communication had deep and globally extensive repercussions, animating such diverse phenomena as the setting of new standards for measuring world time and space, an increasingly bureaucratic mode of capital accumulation, the ideal of "objectivity" in journalism and other professions, the enforcement of new, gendered distinctions between private and public, or the success of new popular cultural forms.[6] At the same time, the nineteenth century set the stage for a dramatic restructuring and flourishing of religious activity, coincident with North Atlantic projects of nation-state formation, the consolidation of powers of colonial domination, and the adoption of new organizational formats designed to exert influence "among the masses." One might even characterize this period as a golden age for the flourishing of religious movements, as evident from the creation of missionary societies, religious publishers, or international congresses devoted to the expansion and deepening of religious sentiments and commitments across an increasingly interconnected global space.[7] The Spiritual Telegraph is emblematic of this global shift in institutional, epistemological, representational, and performative dimensions of both religious and technological spheres of life, whose consequences continue to be felt.

Nineteenth-Century Spiritualism

According to its creation myth, Spiritualism was born in 1848, outside Rochester, New York, with the discovery by sisters Kate and Margaretta Fox of a means of communication with the dead. This discovery launched the young women onto the path of international stardom, while unleashing a new era of learned attention to and popular fascination with the "other world" and its secrets. One thing that makes the story of the Fox sisters so interesting is its location at the fertile intersection of a popular religiosity—more properly stated, a predominantly feminine religiosity—that proliferated across the nineteenth-century Atlantic world and an expanding public culture made possible through new communications media. Here we find, on the one hand, a growing number of spirit mediums attempting to renegotiate existing lines of (cultural, scientific, ecclesiastical, and political) authority and sources of legitimate knowledge, and to link such efforts on a world-wide scale. On the other hand, it is equally striking that such efforts were bound up with the power of the new technology of the telegraph, which provided both the metaphorical language and the material infrastructure for sustaining contact with various worlds lying "beyond" the local everyday life situations of relatively powerless people.

This conjunction of popular religion and new communications technology was present not only in the very idea of contact with the dead (through the medium of intangible wires) but also in the ways such technologies enabled Spiritualists to embrace new organizational forms and techniques within the religious field. Indeed, the spread of Spiritualism did not depend on the establishment of a circle of virtuosi (such as priests or hierocrats) who monopolized religious knowledge, guarded the portals of access to ritual practice, or derived their authority from routinized exchanges of money, gifts, and services with "ordinary" folk. Instead, this was very much a grassroots, "do-it-yourself" movement, consisting in loose networks of like-minded actors who established their own local circles largely on the basis of information acquired from an emergent news industry and a rapidly growing market for popular print (whose dynamism, not coincidentally, was closely connected to the advent of electrical telegraphy). These were the terms with which the nineteenth century bore witness to a startling multiplication of Spiritualist séance circles, periodical publications, national and international conferences, scientific committees of investigation, and no small number of fraudulent opportunists, skeptical critics, and curious onlookers.

In the wake of the Rochester Rappings, as they came to be known, Spiritualism developed into a major international movement and cultural trend, centered on the practice of communication with the dead (typically, through the dramaturgy of possessed bodies, mysterious appearances of disincarnate voices, images, and other sensations), and with the various benefits accrued from such communications, including personal solace, health, prestige, and even the authority to undertake moral or political campaigns. Understood in its broadest sense, the term encompasses a family of movements—Victorian (i.e., American, British, and Canadian) Spiritualism; Theosophy; French, Brazilian, and Cuban Spiritism (i.e., Kardecism); and Christian Science, to name the most obvious—which crystallized in the mid to late nineteenth century and have survived in myriad forms into the present. These groupings spread around the Atlantic and eventually found their way into every region of the world, from Russia to the Philippines, India, and Australia, among other places. As a globally resonant cultural force, Spiritualism provided a canopy for a wide range of adherents, drawing in literally millions of working-class women and men,[8] as well as social elites, including doctors, artists, scientists, politicians, and engineers, who lent an aura of respectability and authority to the cause.[9]

Spiritualism was the product of a multiplicity of overlapping philosophical legacies, having varying degrees of accommodation with established Christian doctrines and drawing upon mystical traditions from both within and outside Europe and the North Atlantic world.[10] As many have also noted, Spiritualism was predominantly a women's movement, not unlike many other forms of popular religious activity in the nineteenth century, such as the multiplying sightings of the Virgin Mary, to cite an obvious example. In fact, Spirit mediums—the indispensable technicians in the control of access to the supernatural world—were overwhelmingly women, and mediumship in general was culturally coded as a "female gift."[11] Especially (but not exclusively) in the context of the antebellum United States, Spiritualism is understood to have provided women with opportunities for social advancement and public legitimacy through their participation in séance practice and, more broadly, in the social networks such associations opened up for them. Making artful use of widespread nineteenth-century tropes of moral purity and assumptions about the sensitive nature of "the weaker sex," Spiritualist women were able to speak out while avoiding the responsibilities of authorship, proclaiming merely to convey the judgments of the world of spirit upon the world of the living. This placed the authority of dead voices in alliance with the desires of Spiritualist women to make themselves heard and, indeed, to remake the world, not least through their involvement in political movements advocating the abolition of slavery, temperance, or women's suffrage.[12]

Because Spiritualists were concerned above all to cultivate a direct union with the world of the dead, spirit mediumship has also been treated as a variant of a much larger family of religious practices concerned with possession, spiritual healing, and supernatural communication, known to societies around the world.[13] Any comparison of Spiritualism with "non-Western" rituals of possession, however, is complicated by the former's intense engagement with a range of Western sciences and para-sciences, from physics to phrenology, and also with the theoretical and practical frameworks of emerging professions, such as electrical engineering and psychology. The seemingly omnivorous character of the movement suggests, in fact, that Spiritualism cannot readily be contained within the tidy binarisms of religious/secular, modern/primitive, erudite/popular, or scientific/magical. Precisely because of this indeterminacy, Spiritualism also provides an instructive vantage point from which to survey the dramatic cultural changes that accompanied broader processes of industrialization, colonial encounter, and the formation of new national and international public spheres over the course of the latter half of the nineteenth century. As we shall see, Spiritualism developed a vocabulary for making sense of the ascendant technologies of nineteenth-century industry and communication, and a repertoire of ritual activities designed specifically to accommodate the performative demands such technologies elicited in various contexts of private and public life. To those extents, the movement casts light not only on evolving conceptions of the world of spirit but also on the deep entanglement of such ideas with the history of technological development, in particular with the world-transforming technologies of communication that made their appearance in the latter half of the nineteenth century, beginning with the telegraph.

Wired Modernity

The telegraph was the most revolutionary media technology of the nineteenth century.[14] This is because, as James Carey proposes in his widely cited work on the topic, with the advent of Samuel Morse's electrical telegraph in 1844, communication was for the first time "freed from the constraints of geography."[15] Thanks to telegraphy, information transmission could now proceed much faster than physical transportation, and on this basis could redefine longstanding spatiotemporal relations of center and periphery, the global and the local, or the proximate and the distant. Of course, no technology is created *ex nihilo*, and in this respect it is important to recall that electrical telegraphy was preceded by a variety of techniques and instruments for what we might call "deterritorialized" communication, such as semaphores and optical telegraph systems,[16] to say nothing of the quite ancient practices of sending signals by smoke or mirrors. But the electric telegraph involved a far more radical separation of signifying systems from the physical movement of objects, engendering entirely new possibilities for social relations based on the "economy of the signal."[17] These were relations predicated on (relative) simultaneity, impersonal contact, and increasingly centralized administrative control, as was quickly made evident in a variety of economic, technical, and social arenas: the coordination of capital investments and strategic transactions in international commodity markets;[18] the standardization of news reportage;[19] shifts in modes of international diplomacy;[20] and even new possibilities for romance, fantasy, or criminal enterprise.[21]

Being the first successful application of electrical energy outside the realms of scientific experiment and medical therapy, telegraphy constituted what we might even be tempted to call the world's first truly globalizing telecommunications infrastructure, not least because of the systemic nature of its technical application. Telegraphic communication was characterized by its capacity for rapid, unidirectional, and asynchronous transmissions of information across potentially limitless distances, thanks to its innovative use of integrated electrical circuitry and its ability to compress complex language through the use of a binary system of signs (Morse code). The electric telegraph was also distinguished by the restrictive interface between the medium and its end-users, materialized in the institutional space of the telegraph office, its bureaucratized labor force, and its hierarchical ordering of communication processes according to criteria of efficient time management and priorities of commercial and governmental interest.[22] In all these respects, this technology represented a significant harbinger of the contemporary global communications environment, with its proliferating networks of computers and satellites, and the institutional architecture governing transnational flows of digital information.[23] Even the legal instruments designed specifically for telegraphy foreshadowed our contemporary era of global media flows. So, for instance, the most important prototype for modern international telecommunications policy and interstate co-ordination emerged with the founding of the International Telegraph Union in 1865.[24] Telegraphy not only demanded new forms of cooperation among states, it also contributed to a dramatic transformation in the exercise of political power within and across state structures, such as drawing peripheral regions of the world into ever more intimate contact with capital cities, especially the great imperial metropoles of Europe and the United States.[25] In short, through the networking of regional, national, and international telegraph systems, the design of the human-machine interface, and the organization of institutional environments for these communicative practices, telegraphy stood at the forefront of a radical revolution in mediated communication, with global consequences.

The story of the telegraph's rapid extension is well known. In 1848, only four years after Morse successfully introduced the technology, there were already 2,000 miles of wire in existence; by the early 1870s, over 650,000 miles of wire linked together a sprawling network of telegraph offices, submarine cables, international connection treaties, ancillary technologies (such as pneumatic tubes), and messenger boys (who hand-delivered messages wherever cables did not exist), in their conjunction servicing over 20,000 towns and villages in a vast area of the world from Europe to America, India, Japan, Australia, and South America.[26] By the dawn of the twentieth century, the technology had enveloped even the most remote hinterlands of the world.[27] This relentless expansion was dominated by British-owned cabling companies, which benefited from British hegemony in related fields, including marine traffic, and control of the trade in copper and in gutta percha (an early form of rubber crucial for submarine cable construction), facilitating the formation of vast international telecommunications concerns.[28] As these networks of telegraph cables encompassed the globe, drawing all regions into their orbit—although, we should concede, with quite uneven levels of access and control—telegraphy contributed decisively to the formation of a new, supraterritorial social space, existing everywhere and nowhere.

This new geography was defined by the logic of "the grid," which did not respect long-standing temporal frontiers of day and night, or work-week and Sabbath, or other ways of marking time locally, and worked instead to impose upon the entire planet a single, temporally homogeneous map of world space, reflected in the development of standardized time zones,[29] or in the drive to produce detailed representations of hitherto unknown (and largely unconsidered) world spaces, such as the ocean floor.[30] Although its potential remained only partially realized, forever plagued by financial and technical impediments, telegraphy thus promised a new alignment of knowledge, representation, and communicative practice, encompassing the entire planet, from the most temporally remote locales of human habitation to the darkest corners of the natural order.

The infrastructural project of telegraphic modernization not only accelerated and expanded communication on a global scale, it radically altered its conditions of possibility. Advances in electrical engineering allowed for new technological capacities not simply for relatively instantaneous but, more specifically, for *disembodied* communication and contact. In other words, beginning with the telegraph, the new media technologies of the nineteenth century occasioned new opportunities, and also new expectations, for sustaining one's presence in an autonomous, ethereal world of electrical currents and flows. This was a universe into which human bodies—covered in flesh, impaired by weak sensory organs, prone to fatigue, and slow to move—could never fully enter. To the extent that electrical media were capable of duplicating and distributing human presences in this ethereal world of information exchange, the very terms of human communication had been forever changed. To interact with others now meant to read the traces of their virtual presence.[31]

At the heart of this nexus of virtual presence stood the enigma of electricity itself. Like all things that flow, seemingly autonomously and autotelically—water, money, or even the stream of poetically inspired thought—electricity provided both the metaphorical and the practical groundwork for the key scientific orthodoxies and technocratic instrumentalities, and much popular thinking, that shaped the industrializing modernity of the Atlantic world in this period, and it was through the medium of electricity that the nineteenth century produced a supra-territorial form of global connection. As a master trope, electricity facilitated the articulation of new modes of industrial and political power with new scenes of scientific inquiry and new regimes of cultural production. The power of electricity thus offered a particularly vivid language for charting the imagined world of disembodied presence that had been brought into being by new communications technologies, beginning with the telegraph. In its terms, new homologies could be forged between the representation of social life, even of the human body itself, and the geography of industrial modernity, whereby, for instance, the electrical flow of a telegraph network could be likened to the arterial architecture of the human nervous system or, for that matter, the nervous twitches and flows of city traffic.[32] The model of the electrical flow thus served both metaphorically to represent and materially to enable "human intelligence" to be extended and duplicated in new ways, such as by passing through the networked circuitry of a telegraph system.

It is, of course, too simple to suggest that the representational power of electricity was a direct product of the invention of the telegraph, since the cultural and scientific contexts in which electrical flow was formed as an object of knowledge have a long history.[33] In the European context, it is possible to trace at least two millennia of competing accounts of the nature of magnetic attraction, electrical excitation, sympathetic vibration, and other forms of action at a distance. At times, these were explained by the Aristotelian notions of a universal ether pervading the universe, or as emanations of an imponderable substance, destitute of weight, or as invisible effluvia that communicated through the percussion of material bodies.[34] By the eighteenth century, these debates about how to represent electrical flow were registered in the study of a wide variety of phenomena, including gravitational attraction, the body's nervous functions, acoustical and optical effects, and, most importantly, electricity. Eighteenth-century natural philosophers were widely convinced that electricity, weather, and life were intimately connected, as Benjamin Franklin's experiments with lightning,[35] or later the work of the Italian anatomist Luigi Galvani, famous for his elaborate theory of animal electricity, seemed to confirm.[36] With the invention of the telegraph, these longstanding conjunctures of scientific knowledge and cosmological speculation were simultaneously confirmed and reworked. Telegraphic applications of electrical energy now enabled diverse commentators to consider anew how the idea of electrical flow related to the mysteries of human intercourse and the natural order, and above all, the possibility of communication with "a world beyond" the spatially and temporally localized situations of everyday life experience.

These, then, are the terms in which telegraphy encompassed important elective affinities with religious movements and with the work of the religious imagination in the nineteenth century, especially with regard to circulating ideas about progress, transcendence, social and ecological harmony, health and vitality, death, and the afterlife. If the actual experience of sending and receiving telegraphic communications was somewhat more arduous (and, for most people in the nineteenth century, prohibitively expensive), the rhetoric of telegraphic entrepreneurs and supporters characterized the technology in terms of an instantaneous disembodiment of human consciousness and the transmutation of information from its physical repositories of voice and ear, paper and ink, into the nebulous world of electricity. Indeed, telegraphic communication was frequently described in the nineteenth century in terms of miracles and sacramental power. Even among ardent secularists, the language of miracle resonated with a technological utopianism that exerted considerable appeal: a popular faith in the progressive powers of technology—and in particular, of electricity—to deliver long-awaited promises of freedom, ecological harmony, and democratic community, all of which James Carey (paraphrasing Leo Marx) has aptly described as "the rhetoric of the electrical sublime."[37] For others, telegraphy was not so much the token of a new utopia as the sign of a pervasive dehuman-ization of social relations, against which images of a prelapsarian pastoral life were pre-sented as a final refuge from the foreboding world of industrial machines.[38] More often than not, at the level of popular culture, such debates concerning the moral implications of electrical technologies such as the telegraph were absorbed into a largely animistic understanding of the universe, where the lines dividing science, spectacle, and magic were exceedingly difficult to draw. It therefore behooves us to attend carefully to the existence of a range of responses to, and accounts of, the sacramental powers inhering in such remarkable, world-transforming instruments as the telegraph. A striking case in point is the Spiritualist involvement with this technology, to which I shall now turn.

Out of the Ether, into the Body

Spiritualist engagements with telegraphy have already been noted by several scholars. Werner Sollors, for instance, has drawn attention to the striking historical and geographic coincidences between the birth of American Spiritualism and the advent of the telegraph, when "the most intensive years of telegraph expansion coincided with the years of the rise and rapid proliferation of its spiritual counterpart."[39] The telegraph thus proved itself, to paraphrase Claude Lévi-Strauss, a productive "thing to think with," not only for the technological literati, whose experience with electrical instruments afforded them sym-bolic power as "experts,"[40] but also for those engaged in the business of occultism. As shown by the Fox sisters, communication with the dead could be achieved by opening and manipulating a channel, not unlike a telegraph circuit. Apparently, the Fox family home served as an ideal site because the dwelling "was charged with the aura requisite to make it a battery for the working of the [spiritual] telegraph."[41] Spiritualists even argued that the very idea of electromagnetic telegraphy was originally an inspiration coming from the spirit world: a gift presented to humankind in order to facilitate communication among the living and the dead. And, just like the terrestrial telegraph, the technology of the Spiritual Telegraph was the object of evolving ideas about application and design. In 1854, the American Universalist minister John Murray Spear was a recipient of detailed plans, provided by the spirit of Benjamin Franklin, for the construction of a "soul-blend-ing telegraph": [42] an intercontinental telepathic transmitter to be powered by a corps of sensitized mediums installed in male/female pairs in high towers, which would compete with the existing telegraph service and would succeed where much-vaunted attempts to lay transatlantic cable had yet to prove their worth.[43]

In the context of an expanding reading public conversant in scientific discovery and the marvels of modern engineering, many Spiritualists seized upon the example of telegra-phy in order to elaborate a grand theory of supernatural presence, grounded in the power of electromagnetism. Andrew Jackson Davis, a leading American Spiritualist, proposed that "the conditions and principles upon which spirits answer to the inquiries of man . . . are no more complicated or wonderful than the principles upon which the magnetic telegraph is daily operating along our great commercial avenues."[44] Allan Kardec (the *nom de plume* of Léon Dénizarth Hippolyte Rivail), the Mesmerist, educational theorist, and chief architect of the Spiritualist movement in France, similarly described spirit mediumship in telegraphic terms. The work of the medium, Kardec reported in his 1861 manual *The Book on Mediums*:

> is that of an electrical machine, which transmits telegraphic despatches from one point of the earth to another far distant. So, when we wish to dictate a communication, we act on the medium as the telegraph operator on his instruments; that is, as the *tac-tac* of the telegraph writes thousands of miles away, on a slip of paper, the reproduced letters of the despatch, the visible from the invisible world, the immaterial from the incarnated world, communicate what we [spirits] wish to teach you [living people] by means of the medianimic instrument.[45]

The invisibility and intangibility of electric current, and its capacity to collapse time and space into a single, continuous plane of reference, provided the perfect analogy for the existence of the human soul beyond the body. After all, if telegraphic technologies could harness electromagnetic forces in order to communicate intentional messages, why should it not also be possible to develop comparable techniques in order to communicate with the dead? From this perspective, Spiritualists proposed merely to enlarge the range of possible interlocutors within the new social environment created by the telegraph, accounting for a semiotic space in which, strictly speaking, communication with the distant and communication with phantasmic traces of the dead are phenomenologically indistinguishable.[46] In other words, what Spiritualists presented was a technically plausible explanation for occult knowledge, aligned with the authority of nineteenth-century science and engineering, and the tantalizing promises that lay beyond as yet unexplored avenues for the mingling of spiritual forces and electrical fluids. As Kardec reasoned:

> A hundred years ago, a person who should have proposed to transmit a despatch five hundred leagues and receive an answer in a few minutes, would have been called a fool: had he done it, it would have been thought that he had the devil under his orders; for at that time the devil alone was capable of travelling so rapidly. Why, then, should not an unknown fluid have the property, under given circumstances, to counterbalance the effect of weight, as hydrogen counterbalances the weight of the balloon?[47]

The analogy of spirit mediumship and telegraphy worked because it referenced a deeper cosmological claim about electricity as a form of "universal fluid," permeating all forms of animate and inanimate being, and enabling their intercourse with one another. For some, such as John Dods, a New England Universalist Church minister, amateur scientist, and prominent trance speaker of the 1850s,[48] electricity was part of a natural theology in which electromagnetic energy was interchangeable with the grace of God and the holy sacrament (or, for that matter, the experience of falling into a trance state) was defined as a mechanism for aligning oneself with God's transcendent energy. "All motion and power originate in the mind," Dods argued, "and just as the human spirit, through an electromagnetic medium, comes into contact with matter, so the infinite Spirit does the same, and through this medium he governs the universe."[49] Not unlike a Christian receiving divine communion, or a cable receiving an electric charge, or a sensation passing through the nervous system of the body, spirit mediumship was a means of receiving and further transmitting fluid energies that emanated from somewhere beyond. In each case, reception requires the host's capacity for proper attunement. For the spirit medium, this meant being endowed with the correct "electro-medianimic machinery," as Kardec called it. In order to receive a spirit, Kardec explains:

> there must exist between the spirit and the medium influenced a certain affinity, a certain analogy, in a word, a certain resemblance, which permits the . . . fluid of the incarnated to be mingled, united, combined with that of the spirit who desires to produce the effect. This fusion should be such that the resulting force becomes, so to say, *one*; as the electric current acting on the coal produces one flame, one single brightness.[50]

Claims about the receptivity of spirit communication were thus inextricably tied to claims about the body of the spirit medium herself, constituted as a complex of nervous pathways and "cerebral batteries" enabling the immaterial and the material to communicate properly.[51] More than simply a metaphor, the Spiritual Telegraph was a *model* for the working of the body, and also a model for the practice of communication itself, worked out through the electrical principles of current and charge, capacity and resistance, circuit and field. As a model, the Spiritual Telegraph provided a context for both representing and animating the body in ways appropriate to the conditions of life routinized through the spread of electrical technologies.

I stress the notion of the Spiritual Telegraph as a model for action if for no other reason than to dispel any lingering assumptions that Spiritualism was just another "religious" response to the electrical industrialization of the Atlantic world of the nineteenth century.[52] The history of Spiritualism must not be reduced to an exotic episode of initial contact with the disorienting effects of modern technologies: an experience, one might further presume, that was eventually displaced by more sober, disenchanted apprehensions of their "true" functions, as revealed in routine practices of labor, business, statecraft, and science. This is a common interpretation of the movement's popular appeal and of its eventual demise (especially with regard to the industrialized North Atlantic world). From that perspective, Spiritualism resembled a "primitive" possession cult, whose performances could be read as symptoms of trauma, or an infantile retreat into a world of fantasy.[53] A complementary interpretation of Spiritualism as nothing more than a palliative practice might emerge from the observation that Spiritualist performances were typically staged in the darkened parlor of the bourgeois home. The parlor, after all, provided a richly auratic environment that contrasted dramatically with the harsh lights and fast movements of the modern city. Surrounded therein by the tactile signs of domesticity and intimacy—of hands linked together and hushed voices—séance clients seemed insulated from the disenchanting and enervating effects of industrial labor and the cold calculus of capitalist exchange. In this reading, Spiritualism was so popular because it offered a return to the maternal womb, a reenactment of the scene of primary narcissism.

But that line of interpretation should not distract us from noting that the feminine-coded interiority of the bourgeois parlor was hardly a static place. On the contrary, its boundaries were continually being renegotiated, as Spiritualist activities extended out from local sites into national and international arenas of public visibility.[54] The séance chamber was often proclaimed to be hermetically sealed from the world of the mundane and open only to the universe of spirit. But in their actual activities, séance practitioners almost invariably opened themselves to the penetrative powers of the capitalist market, the machinery of advertising, and the logics of spectacle, rationalized labor, and scientific induction that by the late nineteenth century were converging to create the new cultural spaces of transatlantic modernity. And were there any agents more capable of effecting such penetrations than emergent technologies of electrically mediated communication?

This question, I think, sheds considerable light on Spiritualism's deep entanglement with the embodied sensations and imaginative powers elicited by new technologies such as the telegraph. Enveloped in promises of bringing together the visible and the invisible, the public and the private, and the global and the local, the telegraph provided more than a convenient analogy for Spiritualist séance practice. It pointed toward a new type of human subject. This agent was now located in a cosmic order that mirrored the developing logic of communication technologies in the nineteenth century and their performative goals of erasing distance, freezing time, or circumventing what seemed otherwise to be an inevitable route toward inertia and decay of bodies and things.

Sensuousness, Credibility, and Faith in the Age of Electrical Automation

Perhaps the most serious challenge to the conception of the séance chamber as a place of "primitive sensation" comes from the ways Spiritualists deployed innovative techniques and technologies for unraveling the mystery of spirit communication. In fact, at séances it was hardly uncommon to find an array of mechanical devices, such as cameras, magnets, metal cables, speaking trumpets, clocks, scales, pressure gauges, radiometers, planchettes, or ouija boards, among other things. Such devices enabled Spiritualists to register, measure, transmit, and reproduce "wondrous signs" emanating from the afterworld, including rappings, mysterious musical sounds, flying objects, or instances of automatic speech and writing. By helping to locate the presence of spirits directly within the natural order, modern technologies also allowed Spiritualists to demonstrate to their competitors and critics their deep commitment to the language of investigation, exhibition, exposure, and evidence. Thus one might treat the introduction of evolving media technologies into the séance chamber as an index of the growing subordination of feminine domestic power to the powers of inspection and protocols of male-dominated science.[55]

In the struggles among Spiritualists and their detractors, the séance chamber was transformed into a sort of laboratory: a stage for investigating the spirit world, for obtaining its secrets, and also for surveilling the body of the spirit medium as a source of certain knowledge or, as the case may be, a site of misinterpreted evidence, indeterminacy, or even duplicity, imposture, and fraud.[56] For their part, Spiritualist testimonials concerning supernatural communication were buttressed by the authorizing presence of a remarkable lineage of scientists and engineers. This is well illustrated in the case of Cromwell Fleetwood Varley, the chief consulting electrician of the Atlantic Telegraph Company and of the Electric and International Company, one of the great engineers of transatlantic telegraphy in the 1860s and also a committed Spiritualist. Varley used his engineering expertise with submarine telegraphy in order to contribute to the establishment of a credible "science of Spiritualism" and also to develop new séance protocols that would incorporate the skills and resources of the telegraph testing room. These included the application of instruments such as a magnetized helix, resistance coils, and a mirror-galvanometer, all of which Varley had originally designed in order to test signal retardation on possible Atlantic cable designs and to teach novice clerks the art of efficient deep-sea cable signaling. In the séance chamber, the same devices were utilized in order to measure "circuit effects" upon the medium's body during moments of spirit communication.[57] In a similar vein, the chemist William Crookes, renowned among other things for the discovery of thallium, applied his knowledge of radiation effects under conditions of high vacuum by bringing a radiometer to the séances he regularly attended during the mid 1870s—including those held by the celebrated mediums Kate Fox, Florence Cook, and Daniel Dunglas Home—where he conducted extended tests to disprove natural explanations for their extraordinary powers.[58]

Figures such as Varley and Crookes were joined by a large number of respected advocates of the Spiritualist cause, including Oliver Joseph Lodge, a pioneer in the development of wireless telegraphy, and the eminent biologist Alfred Russel Wallace, a tireless defender of the plausibility of spirit rapping, table-turning, spirit photography, and related phenomena through his published letters, articles, books, and courtroom testimony, beginning with his first séance experience in 1865.[59] In Victorian Britain, these efforts to establish a credible scientific account of spirit communication culminated in 1882 with the formation of the Society for Psychical Research, having as its first president the distinguished moral philosopher Sir Henry Sidgwick. The society was charged with the mission of investigating the large body of "debatable" phenomena designated by the terms *mesmeric*, *psychical*, and *spiritualistic*, without prejudice or prepossession, and through the application of protocols for scientific research that had been developed in other fields, such as physics and biology.[60]

On the other side of the fence stood a long line of skeptics, such as the physicist Michael Faraday, who conducted widely publicized experiments disproving the supernatural source of table-turning in the 1850s,[61] or William Benjamin Carpenter, the prominent physiologist and president of the British Association for the Advancement of Science. Carpenter penned a series of vitriolic diatribes against Crookes in particular, and more generally against the credibility of all forms of spirit communication, as little more than the work of talented frauds and the wishful thinking of their gullible clients. More precisely, Carpenter identified the true source of the entranced states so commonly found among Spiritual mediums and their audiences in terms of the principles of "ideomotor activity" (involuntary muscular actions produced during mental states of expectant attention and anticipation), and "unconscious cerebration" (a reflex action based on the anatomical relation of the cerebrum to the sensorium, enabling the seemingly spontaneous formation of ideas).[62] In his widely celebrated *Principles of Mental Physiology*, first published in 1874, Carpenter characterized spirit mediums, not as the delicate and finely tuned electrical machines Kardec had described, but rather as hosts of an abnormal nervous system. This aetiology allowed him to bring the "gift" of spirit mediumship into close alignment with "morbid states" he found elsewhere, such as in cases of epilepsy and hysteria.[63]

Critiques of Spiritualism thus relied upon the expert knowledge of physiologists, but also of psychologists and anthropologists, united in their commitment to principles of induction and controlled observation.[64] But in their public life, the accounts of Spiritualism produced by scientific experts were almost invariably jumbled together with a heteroglossia of theological denunciations of "enthusiasm," journalistic sensationalism, gossip, and the exemplary performances of stage magicians.[65] In the latter half of the nineteenth century, these diverse registers of speech and practice gave shape to a pervasive philosophical naturalism that imputed invisible, yet entirely explicable, forces as the source of explanation for observable effects. At the same time, this concern with invisibility was framed by a deeper anxiety about the human sensory faculties—especially the faculty of vision—as sources of knowledge and of normative subjectivity: a growing distrust of the unseen that was being fed by gathering physiological knowledge about the sensory organs, and at the same time by an expanding popular culture of mediated images.[66]

The language of demand for visibility and exposure allows us to compare, on the one hand, the procedures by which a figure like James Braid, the "father" of modern hypnotism, exposed the mysteries of Mesmerism and animal magnetism, having rooted them in the "observable" phenomena of unconscious expectation and involuntary muscular action; and on the other hand, the work of a stage magician like Harry Houdini (*né* Ehrich Weiss), who brazenly offered cash prizes to any medium who could prove to his satisfaction the existence of spiritual forces without the use of trickery.[67] In fact, it is not surprising that the two sorts of experts to whom the credibility of Spiritualist claims were most frequently referred were scientists and stage magicians. Both groups had vested interests in denouncing Spiritualist claims, and both possessed a well-developed discourse and performative repertoire to provide "natural" explanations of the ostensibly supernatural occurrences within séance practice, in particular, to demonstrate the likely techniques of sensory misdirection employed by spirit mediums in their acts of subterfuge. According to the maxim of the philosopher George Henry Lewes, a hardened skeptic of Spiritualism, "nothing is more inexplicable than a good conjuring trick; nothing is more intelligible than when the trick is explained."[68]

Despite the opposing conclusions they reached, both the advocates and the detractors of the Spiritualist enterprise adhered to protocols of precise measurement, controlled observation, and the reproducibility of experimental conditions and results that had been accredited in other scientific domains. For both groups, therefore, questions of faith in spirit communication were properly and legitimately addressed through the discovery of tangible, sensuous evidence. This contributed to a dissolution of the enigmas of the spirit world and the mobilization of new operating principles for dealing with invisible things. Michel de Certeau has described precisely such a set of principles in his account of the "dogma of the real," a modernist narrative that "first arose out of a methodic effort of observation and accuracy that struggled against credulity and based itself on a contract between the seen and the real . . . and [that now] offers to *sight* precisely what must be *believed*."[69] Spiritualism was likewise organized by a dogma about the indisputability of the senses. It presented, in the words of the historian Laurence Moore, "a religious faith which depended upon seeing and touching."[70] Even skeptics such as G. H. Lewes were forced to concede how central was the idea of the "irresistible evidence of the senses" for the constitution of Spiritualist faith.[71] In an apposite description of the process of conversion to the movement, Lewes noted how:

> There is probably not a single convert who does not assure his listeners that he began by being incredulous of the facts narrated by spiritualists. Like other people he thought "the whole thing a transparent humbug." He derided the credulity of believers; but, skeptical though he was, he had enough candour to admit the facts if they could be proved. He went as a scoffer, and returned a convert: facts vanquished him; he could not distrust the evidence of his senses.[72]

Lewes's description of conversion to Spiritualism as a process of acquiring conviction through the senses brings us to the very heart of nineteenth-century struggles to define, defend, or even to denounce séance practice. As I have suggested, the appeal to sensory evidence certainly was at work in competing efforts, on the one hand, to establish a credible science of Spiritualism, and on the other, to demarcate experiences of spirit communication, at best as matters of false inference and pseudo-scientific theorizing, and at worst as the mark of feminine pathology, infantilism, and primitivism. But whatever credence was given to Spiritualist testimonies, the intense focus on and concern with "sensations" also indexed a much deeper (and culturally more pervasive) set of questions about how to construe faithful relationships between the receptive body and the immateriality of messages "from beyond." As we have seen, starting in the mid nineteenth century, this "beyond" was being radically reconfigured through a succession of revolutions in mediated communication, defined by new interfaces of humans and machines. In this rapidly changing context, Spiritualism was not haphazardly constituted as a religious faith of the senses. It would be more precise to say that "faith" emerged here as the product of a continual process of renegotiation between the agency invested in emerging technologies of inscription and transmission, and the agency of the human sensorium as it navigated this strange new world governed by invisible electrical flows. By the same token, the credibility of spirit communication did not rest simply on the observable condition of the spirit medium's body. It also rested upon her talent for translating the invisibility and intangibility of the spirit world into recognizable gestural codes, in other words, for performing the act of possession in ways that would sustain the bonds of trust with her audience. And in the context of the rapid technological shifts that defined the late nineteenth century, one of the most important ways that spirit mediumship could be secured as a trustworthy source of knowledge was through its conformity with what I shall call a "syntax of automatism," which was modeled on (dare one say mimicked?) the work of electrically powered machines.

Lisa Gitelman has offered an insightful account of how advancing media technologies and spirit mediums shared this common syntax. Her analysis focuses on the notion of "automatic writing" and its applicability to a broad range of nineteenth-century practices and technologies of inscription. According to one definition, automatic writing referred to the Spiritualist practice of writing "mediumistically": that is, the enactment of the authorial agency of the dead through the receptacle of a living body and the production during trance states of elaborate texts, memoirs, lists, maps, or even entire works of literature or music.[73] At the same time, in the context of late-nineteenth-century bureaucracy, the term *automatic writing* referred to the work performed by autonomous technologies of inscription and transcription, such as telegraph machines, stock tickers, and the related business machinery of phonographs, mimeographs, telephones, and typewriters.

As Gitelman points out, the impetus for the technical development of these machines was rooted in their capacities for speedier transmission of information (duplex, and later quadruplex telegraph receivers, for instance, could work ten, twenty, or even fifty times faster than human telegraph operators) and thereby the lowering of overhead costs, precipitating a deskilling and simultaneously a marked feminization of office labor.[74] Such inventions also bore the traces of concern about authority and authorship, witnessing and evidence, and the reliability of existing modes of transcription, interpretation, and reportage embodied in such figures as the court stenographer or the office clerk (which until the late nineteenth century, not coincidentally, had been largely the preserve of skilled male workers). What was hailed as the precision and selfless operation of modern machinery, and more generally the "superiority" of electrical automation, thus allowed for a renewed examination of how much intelligence was required for accurate inscription and how reliable were human eyes, ears, and fingers for "effective work" in modern offices and related scenes of labor. With the introduction of so-called automatic-writing machines, the concerted attention that skilled operators needed for controlling instruments, such as the telegraph, was steadily displaced onto the concerted attention that employers and technical experts could now devote to the smooth operating of the communicative apparatuses themselves and the firm management of an increasingly female office workforce.[75] In this context, automaticity referred to the kind of work performed by partially conscious and distracted subjects, whose bodies were increasingly being encased in the prosthetic shell of modern office technologies.[76] Here once again, the trope of feminine passivity dovetailed neatly with the demand for an undistorted mediation of information. The pliability of the female body to the pressures of mechanical equipment was conceived here as a privileged source of "'mechanical objectivity,' a presumed freedom from human subjectivity, and consequently from error."[77]

The performance of the Spiritualist séance and of modern office work thus shared a strikingly common preoccupation with the sensory and an ambivalence about where to locate authoritative agency in the interface between humans and machines. Like a spirit medium and her séance clients locked in the darkness of the séance chamber, modern business workers were consumed by the power of invisible technologies of inscription and the presence of mysterious utterances increasingly divorced from the graphical accoutrements of authorship and the textures and particularities of handwriting.[78] And much like modern office labor, Spiritualist performances exhibited principles of automatization and dematerialization that had been given new impetus by a range of instruments and institutional arrangements, beginning with the space of the telegraph office. The act of being possessed by a spirit was thus phenomenologically comparable with the autotelic labor of telegraphic machinery (telegraphy, of course, serving as a metonym for the range of electrical communications media that came to the fore in the nineteenth century).

These electrical analogies further invite us to describe the work of Spiritualists *within* the séance chamber in terms of the cultivation of forms of psychological attentiveness, motor readiness, and kinesthetic adaptation that were also emerging *outside* the séance chamber, in the broader, media-rich culture of nineteenth-century metropolitan life.

Indeed, spirit possession and its related states of bodily and psychological heteronomy—such as magnetized healing, somnambulism, clairvoyance, or hypnotic trance—provided a model for participation in diverse scenes of action, including the increasingly rationalized and mechanized factory system, the new forms of travel that typified the nineteenth-century cityscape (such as on trains or in subways), or the thrills and distractions of circuses, fairs, arcades, and related industries of leisure and consumption. In all such cases, what was brought into existence was a system for the circulation of sensory perceptions and actions freed from the "normal" conditions of individual human subjectivity, where one is supposed to enjoy mastery over one's conscious intentions and one's own body. In its place, we find a congeries of dissociated perceptions, involuntary reflexes, and absorbed states, operating more or less independently of the synthetic powers attributed to the normative ideal of the unified and sovereign personality.[79] What scientists such as Michael Faraday or W. B. Carpenter had earlier defined as the "true source" of séance practice—involuntary muscular action or improperly attuned powers of attention—can now be counted among the central organizing motifs of the laboring body and the distracted subject in the age of electrical automation.[80]

In these terms, I propose that the history of the Spiritual Telegraph offers crucial insight into a much larger set of cultural, scientific, and technical projects to accommodate human agents to the temporalities and rhythms of transatlantic modernity. By embracing technologies and performative principles that existed both within and beyond the séance chamber, Spiritualism gathered under its penumbra what could only superficially be understood as disconnected activities of religious faith, scientific experimentation, medical intervention, entertainment, or rationalized labor. And the telegraph, for its part, possessed an elective affinity with Spiritualism because, perhaps more than any other technology, it signaled the coming of a new global order of instantaneous virtual presence and a new way of dreaming about the liberation of the soul from the mortal body. There is, of course, much more that can and should be said about the formation of the Spiritual Telegraph and its legacy. Among other things, it should not escape attention that the version of history narrated here has largely been contained within the parochial framework of the North Atlantic world—and especially the metropolitan urban centers of the United States, France, and England—in the late nineteenth century. This should lead to the acknowledgment that technological developments occurred elsewhere at different rates and intensities, and according to varying particularities of cultural reception. Simply put, there exist numerous histories of the Spiritual Telegraph, and many of these have yet to be written. For the time being, suffice it to propose that few (if any) of those stories can feasibly be written from within the dominant secularist narratives about technology with which this paper began. On the contrary, through their intense engagements with modern technologies of communication—beginning with the telegraph, as the emblem of a new age of electrical salvation—Spiritualists challenge us to define religion as something located within, not beyond, the indeterminate spaces of exchange between humans and their machines.

Cybergnosis

Technology, Religion, and the Secular

Stef Aupers, Dick Houtman, and Peter Pels

> Recite to yourself some of the traditional attributes of the word "spiritual":
> mythic, magical, ethereal, incorporeal, intangible, nonmaterial, disembod-
> ied, ideal, platonic. Is that not a definition of the electronic-digital? . . .
> These "spiritual" realms, over centuries imagined, may, perhaps, now be
> realized!
>
> —Timothy Leary, *Chaos and Cyberculture*[1]

Thus spoke Timothy Leary, one of the most prominent spokesmen of
the spiritual counterculture in the 1960s and 1970s, who converted
from "psychedelia" to "cyberdelia" in the 1990s.[2] Together with computer scientist Eric Gullichsen, Leary considered the emerging realm of
cyberspace—first imagined by William Gibson in his 1984 *Neuromancer*
and popularized by the personal computer and the Internet—an "experience" of a "quantum universe" of digital information. Since the world
is held hostage by "white, menopausal men," the young "cyberpunks,"
"electro-shamans," and "modern alchemists" have a duty to turn this
experience into personal transmutation by means of "the ecstasy of the
'ultimate hack'" or the "satori of harmonious human-computer communication" and thus "start [their] own religion"—which is Evolution-
ism.[3] Leary was but the *eminence grise* of a movement that, especially in
the early 1990s, gathered together gurus, hackers, and ravers hoping for
a new technological salvation in the quest for "Cyberia."[4]

Is this religion? Is this science or technology? In this essay, we want
to argue that these questions may fail to do justice to such phenomena.
We suggest that Leary's mode of reasoning epitomizes a discursive phenomenon characterized by epistemological, ontological, and social features that cannot be reduced to religion or technoscience (or faith and
reason) and that is embedded in social relationships that distinguish it

from the relations we commonly expect to typify either science or religion. We call this phenomenon "cybergnosis," a new manifestation of the "modern gnosis" that emerged as a discursive practice together with the discursive practices of "religion" and "science" (as we now understand them) in the nineteenth century. Inspired by Wouter Hanegraaff,[5] we think of modern gnosis as comprising a personal experience of revelation that can be conveyed neither through discourse (which would be "reason") nor through higher authority (which would make it "faith"). This personal revelation demonstrates the existence of a radically other world of salvation and transforms and liberates the knower in, socially speaking, an antinomian and democratic fashion, via knowledge of this other world. Its most well-known manifestations are the movements that, from Theosophy and modern occultism in the nineteenth century to New Age today, dominate the field of "post-traditional religion." Leary's cybergnosis is its most recent manifestation—though one that may already be redefining some of its antinomian characteristics. Since the economic bubble that carried cybergnosis in the 1990s has meanwhile burst, an examination of this "countercultural" refusal of the material world seems timely.

As Leary's hyperbolic language indicates, cybergnosis is characterized by a "fast-forward" recycling of religious and technoscientific repertoires, mostly outside the social circumstances in which scholars traditionally expect to find religion and science. Cybergnosis must, therefore, be understood against the background of the specific discursive and social place of gnosis in modernity. In the following section, we will locate modern gnosis in a world dominated by print capitalism and the institutions it favors. This will raise a number of questions about the theoretical status of "religion" and "science" in modernity, especially since it runs counter to a common view of secularization as the spread of rationality through technology.[6] We will then, therefore, discuss the relative positions of religion, the secular, and technology in modernity, attempting both to criticize the ideological effect of a "modern constitution" that suspends current societies between religion and science (or the secular),[7] and to do justice to the empirical reality of some of the secularization processes that—paradoxically—give religion a new future in our present. Finally, then, this will allow us to set out the manifestations of cybergnosis and draw some conclusions about its possible future enchantments.

Modern Gnosis and Print Capitalism

Modern gnosis is a typical product of the nineteenth century, and it arose together with the concepts of "religion" and "science," at least in the way we understand them now. "Religion" and "science"—as well as the related, more epistemological notions of "reason" and "faith"—attained their meaning simultaneously, as the opposite and mutually exclusive pairs of an indivisible modern dichotomy. The notion of science as the study of "nature"—in which the latter concept was understood to refer to the material world of matter and force regulated by universal laws—"hardened," in Raymond Williams's words, only in the early and mid nineteenth century.[8] The process by which religion was increasingly understood as referring to morality and the supernatural provided the opposite to this conception of science, and although this is by no means the whole story about religion in modernity, it determined most of our understanding of religion and science until recently.

This crystallization of usage partly arose from a process in which, at least from David Hume's work onward, both religion and science became increasingly understood in a *propositional* sense, as making statements about the world and/or nature, and faith came to be understood as assent to the truth of these religious propositions.[9] In this comparison, when religion came to be understood as "an alternative account of the natural world," it increasingly came to be seen as a false one in comparison, for example, to Newton's laws.[10] But it was also seen to produce propositions of a moral or metaphysical kind, whose truth could not be ascertained by recourse to nature or the material world.[11] Hence the rise of the sciences of religion (*Religionswissenschaft*, the history of religion, and the anthropology, sociology, and psychology of religion), whose main office was to demonstrate, by comparing religions from all over the world, their shared superstitious nature or their formulation of universal morality and original (metaphysical) revelation.[12] By assuming this dichotomous understanding of religion and science, modern scholarship often disregarded or dismissed developments of the religious heritage that had little to do with its understanding in propositional terms—religious nationalism, the increasing emphasis on religious feeling, the rise of "spirituality," to name just a few. Modern gnosis was one of these developments.

Modern gnosis did not arise with a similarly recognizable label, even though terms such as *Theosophy* (since the 1780s)[13] and *occultism* (starting around 1880)[14] indicate its presence. It descended from Western esotericism and emerged within movements of Romantic thinkers who, starting in the late eighteenth century, also drew inspiration from non-Christian religions (Jewish Kabbalah, the Egyptian cult of Isis, Hinduism, Buddhism) and from more or less marginal sciences such as Mesmerism, physiognomy, ethnology, and phrenology. Including scholars, activists, and artists such as Richard Payne Knight, Count Volney, Sir William Jones, William Blake, Robert Owen, and Edward Bulwer-Lytton, these movements culminated, most famously, in the Theosophical Society of Madame Blavatsky, founded in 1875.[15]

The concept of gnosis refers back, of course, to the creeds and sects that flourished in the early centuries of the Christian calendar and that—combining elements of Christianity with Platonism and Eastern (especially Manichean) religious inspirations—considered the physical world to be a prison and an illusion, created by a false god (the Demiurg) and guarded by evil demons (the Archons), and aspired to release the "inner man" from these bonds, returning him to his native divine realm.[16] Epistemologically, gnostic knowledge does not arise from a reality "out there": it can neither be found by rationally and systematically scrutinizing the external world, nor revealed by a transcendent God. It instead relies on an "inner source"—on personal experience, imagination, or intuition.[17] Moreover, unlike the propositional knowledge based on faith or reason, gnostic knowledge is of a transformational nature: "being concerned with the secrets of salvation, 'knowledge' is not just theoretical information about things but is itself, as a modification of the human condition, charged with performing a function in the bringing about of salvation."[18] Hence the role of *imaginatio* as "the main instrument for attaining *gnosis*,"[19] for the imagination is creative and therefore changes one's self and the world around one.

Modernized in the Romantic imagination of the creative artist (who himself embodied a secularization and democratization of divine creative power), by the end of the nineteenth century this transformative power became psychologized and was increasingly understood in terms of mental evolution.[20] Thus, modern gnosis counters and aims to overcome the propositional statements of faith and reason with the implicit argument that the scientific conception of evolution boils down, in the end, to the transformative experience of a transcendental "mind" (or will, or consciousness, or intelligence) by one's personal imagination. Gnostic epistemology, in short, presupposes a dualistic ontology by juxtaposing two radically different worlds, one evil and alienating and the other offering salvation from suffering, defining the movement from the former to the latter by means of a transformative experience of a transcendental mind. This is crucial for understanding the holism characteristic of modern occultism and New Age: the primacy of a dualistic ontology for gnostics indicates that their holism is not (yet) realized: it is an ideal, a cure for the disease diagnosed as dualism.

Because gnostics think that the alienation imposed by the world can only be overcome through transformational knowledge based on personal experience, they radically question mainstream institutions, dogmas, and authorities. This emic sociology marginalizes gnostics, who blame the establishment for clinging to power, for its passive inability or active refusal to admit that the world is evil, and for not taking personal experience, as distinct from institutionalized roles and routines, seriously. Nineteenth-century gnostic movements actively opposed the established church and academy, not only because their participants felt alienated from these institutions but also because they were sometimes excluded for reasons of religion or class. Indeed, the modernity of modern gnosis is determined precisely by its antinomian attempt to counter and overcome the propositional knowledge of faith and reason that seemed to dominate established institutions: modern gnosis redefines established churches, universities, laboratories, governments, and big corporations as the Archons of modernity—the guards of the alienating prison that the world has become under their influence.

Antinomian spiritualities typically adhere to a kind of spiritual democracy, which manifested itself during the nineteenth century in feminism, socialism, or anticolonialism but which could also ally itself with virulent forms of racism, especially as the century drew to its imperialist close.[21] Modern gnosis tends toward individualism and anarchism in its organization—a tendency continually displayed by the nineteenth-century proliferation of spiritualistic associations and offshoots of the Theosophical Society,[22] as well as the fissionary tendencies of twentieth-century human potential movements (such as Scientology, est, Landmark, or Essence), wiccan covens, and coteries of high magicians. Few religious movements seem to offer similar scope for individual authority, with perhaps the exception of the Pentecostal forms of Christendom, which feature strongly in the genealogy of modern gnosis.[23] From the start, then, antinomian spiritualities could not be easily grouped under a single label. Outside the domestic sphere, they were rarely permanently institutionalized and took root instead in temporary voluntary associations, in commercial religious spectacle, in the latter's spillover into entertainment, and in the rising publishing industry (including the world of the mystery novel), thus adopting the forms of "selling God" associated with popular Christianity.[24]

The antinomian character of modern gnosis does not, however, necessarily justify the claim that "the traditions based on *gnosis* can be seen as a sort of traditional Western counter-culture."[25] The leading Gnostics of antiquity did, indeed, display "pronounced intellectual individualism," and the personalized nature of gnostic knowledge made nonconformism "almost a principle of the gnostic mind."[26] But modern gnosis is distinct from its ancient predecessor in that its antinomian attitude is embedded in a "Romantic ethic" that is fed by and feeds into consumerism, that is part of a systematic pattern of conflict and symbiosis with the more puritan ethics of modernity, and that is therefore a significant part of the "core" of modern culture.[27] Historians of religion and occultism have generally neglected this paradoxical fusion of antinomian attitudes and mainstream consumerism because they have focused exclusively on religious phenomena per se. Occultism, by contrast, was disseminated by popular, commercial books and thus by the market for books.[28]

Occultism, therefore, resembles nationalism in being a specifically modern cultural form spread by "print capitalism."[29] Benedict Anderson's analysis of ties between nationalism and print culture, however, reproduces modernist ideology by portraying secular nationalism as replacing religion. He fails to consider that print capitalism includes "the simultaneous growth of serialized novels published in periodicals and the enormous expansion in the market for imaginative 'literature.'"[30] Starting in the mid nineteenth century, simultaneously with and parallel to the quiet commodification of the Bible,[31] the market for mystery and imaginative literature became a core institution for spreading modern religious repertoires. While the sales of, for example, *The Celestine Prophecy* justify the assumption that a majority of Euroamerican households possesses a copy of this New Age best seller, the common scholarly failure to recognize these sociocultural carriers of modern religion has resulted in the fact that much of the history of nineteenth- and twentieth-century print capitalism's contribution to the dissemination of modern gnosis still remains to be written. It nevertheless seems clear that one of its central storylines would focus on the emergence of the mystery novel and its crucial role in the rise of the best-seller industry. The early mystery novelist Edward Bulwer Lytton, who was a Rosicrucian and whose narratives were filled with sorcery and magic from Egypt and India, inspired Madame Blavatsky's invention of the Theosophical Masters.[32] Mesmerism, Spiritualism, and various theosophical inspirations found their diverse ways into the work of Edgar Allan Poe, Charles Dickens, Robert Louis Stevenson, Arthur Conan Doyle, H. Rider Haggard, and H. G. Wells, as well as a host of lesser writers.[33] Best-selling anthropologists—experts in the exotic and religious—also spread the occult word, whether they liked it (like Andrew Lang) or not (like James Frazer).[34] The commercial world of mystery was fed by modern gnosis just as much as occult bestsellers fed back into the development and spread of what came to be known as science fiction, fantasy, adventure, and horror—a dialectic between occultism and print capitalism that, from the New Age adoption of J. R. R. Tolkien and Marion Zimmer Bradley in the 1960s to recent blockbusters like *Harry Potter*, is still increasing in importance. This dialectic indicates how modern gnosis was embedded in institutions that work through consumer choice. Mail-order magic, commercial courses at centers for self-realization, occult bookshops, television shows by New Age high priestesses like Oprah Winfrey, and (not least) the Internet institutionalize modern gnosis in public consumerism, public domesticity, and leisure.[35]

This is why we insist on studying modern gnosis as a discursive practice rather than a movement or a collection of cults. "New Age" is, indeed, a *lingua franca* more than a movement.[36] One cannot become a member of a discourse: using a modern gnostic discourse does not immediately make one a member of a modern gnostic movement. One can adopt the use of gnostic discourse just as one chooses to buy a commodity in the marketplace: it may or may not identify you, it may or may not make you a member of an identifiable group, you may use it only to forget it again at some later moment. A modern gnostic, therefore, is not like a member of a church and cannot be counted as such. Whether she is inspired by a gnostic book in her leisure time, adopts a New Age vocabulary in her Christian ritual, or realizes her true self during a management-training course, there is nothing in all those activities that prevents her from identifying herself by means of church attendance when she is counted by the kind of statistical devices developed to measure the latter. This explains why the membership of adherents to "spiritual" movements in Western societies never seems to rise much above 20 percent, while the sales of certain New Age titles such as *The Celestine Prophecy* indicate that tens of millions of people in Western countries must possess a copy. Modern gnosis, even if we (partly) need to study it as religion, does not gain its impact through religious institutional membership.

Religion, the Secular, and Communications Technology

Because "religion" or "faith" and "reason" or "science" have, as mutually exclusive categories, dominated Western intellectual traditions, the importance of modern gnosis for these traditions has been consistently underestimated. This may be because modern gnosis is part of the networks and mediations that are obscured by the purified dichotomies of the "modern constitution,"[37] or because the dichotomy of religion and science imposes a pure system on otherwise chaotic or dangerous experiences.[38] We hesitate, however, to subsume modern gnosis under terms like "hybrid" or "translation,"[39] or to call its experience "inherently untidy."[40] Syncretisms and hybrids of religion and science do, of course, exist: Auguste Comte's nineteenth-century religion of science and twentieth-century creationism are examples that come to mind. The epistemological, ontological, and sociological features of modern gnostic discourse and its modern institutionalizations, however, suggest that we should treat it as a phenomenon sui generis, if only to be able to outline the extent to which cybergnosis differs from its nineteenth- and early-twentieth-century predecessor.

Modern gnosis is neither purely religious or scientific nor simply a combination of the two. As a phenomenon sui generis, it disturbs classical theories of secularization, which were largely predicated on the replacement of religion by science in the most important social realms. As Leary's example suggests, cybergnosis confuses the dichotomy between religion and science, allowing religious and technoscientific contents (such as hacking, evolution, satori, and shamanism) to cohabit in the same discursive realm. But if modern gnosis allows for futures of the religious past outside of religious contexts strictly speaking, we must try to understand such co-existence and intertwining of both secularizing and sacralizing processes in the modern world. It makes little sense to use modern gnosis to support or debunk the secularization thesis unless this leads to better insight into how it deals with the secular.[41] Conversely, one cannot comprehend cybergnosis without understanding how gnosis is related to the sacralization of technology.

To understand modern gnosis, it is crucial to realize that "the secular . . . is neither continuous with the religious that supposedly preceded it (that is, it is not the latest phase of a sacred origin) nor a simple break from it (that is, not the opposite, an essence that excludes the sacred)."[42] This means that the hegemony of secularism in modern states should not be allowed to obscure the large variety of trajectories that combine the secular with the religious. We can roughly trace the genealogy of the secular to three intellectual realms: the Renaissance doctrine of humanism, the Enlightenment concept of nature, and the nineteenth-century conception of history.[43] And we might say of modern gnosis that its specific understanding of the secular replaces man-made history with mental evolution by sacralizing the humanistic self. The Romantic humanism of self-realization through the creative imagination, combined with the comparative and largely secular project of finding the true core in every religion, led to a conception of evolution whose end point lay in the realization of human spiritual powers—the power of mind over matter, of "creating one's own reality."[44] This definition of evolution—and thus of secular "nature"—in mental or spiritual terms determines the extent to which gnostic salvation can be achieved by technological progress and may explain why modern gnosis appears to have a specific relationship with certain *communications* technologies in particular.

Salvation by technology—the liberation of humanity from toil and want in order to indulge in the development of its "higher nature"—has, of course, long been a feature of European thought. David Noble argues that the "religion of technology" of the Western world finds its roots in the monastic environment of the medieval period and its attempts to approximate Eden via human inventiveness, and that, since then, it has been marked by a recurrence of forms of technological millenarianism.[45] Freemasonry and Comteism came close to turning the engineer into a latter-day priest,[46] while especially in North America, the development of a "rhetoric of the technological sublime" in the mid nineteenth century mass-produced images of a secular, mechanistic Eden, a "machine in the garden."[47] Late-nineteenth-century Gnostics (the spiritualists, in particular) seem to have derived a kind of optimistic reassurance about the scientific and secular basis of their mystical visions from electricity, magnetism, the technology of the telegraph and telephone, and photography.[48]

Every communications technology generates its own balance between the real and the imaginary, and thus its own secularity and sacredness. Print, for example, has relied to a large extent on the private imagination of the consumer of books and journals. The telegraph and telephone may have been especially attractive to spiritualists because they work via a bilateral exchange between individual minds (or spirits). Print, telegraph, and telephone all seem, in the imaginative possibilities they support, rather different from the much bleaker and alienated mystical "presence" of the broadcast media that characterized the larger part of the twentieth century. While radio and television give their consumers an impression of connectedness, they also limit consumers' participation to the passive role of listeners and viewers of messages, eventuating in a sense of individual isolation in an ether encompassing global and outer space.[49] This "alien ether" seems less hospitable to some of modern gnosis's core features—especially its antinomian desire for salvation through personal experience—than either print or the "spiritual telegraph," since the "other world" of broadcasting quickly turned into a centralized network, "quite literally a net covering and ensnaring its audience."[50] Jeffrey Sconce argues that it promoted fantasies of extraterrestrial invasion rather than personal salvation.[51] Yet twentieth-century communications technologies could also help to transform the possibilities of salvation: the camera allowed the cinema audience to have virtual experiences of love, adventure, or violence without risking their bodies, by providing a "magical double" on the screen.[52] Thus, the screens of film and television can compress the time and space that separate everyday from imaginary lives and promise an immediate experience of transportation into another world—an experience that may have increasingly come to replace the classical humanist and secular ideal of *Bildung* with a desire for more magical and instant forms of salvation.[53]

We need a much more detailed cultural history of twentieth-century transformations of popular culture to flesh out these relationships between communications technology and modern gnostic movements, including the conceptions of the secularity and salvation they entail. It is evident, however, that our current form of modern gnosis—"New Age"—arose against the background of the "alien ether" of broadcast media, especially through the UFO-craze of the 1950s.[54] New Age has, for the most part, been interpreted in terms of a "return" to (human) nature, in which talk of technology was focused on "small is beautiful" and an "appropriate technology" modeled on the human body.[55] Explicitly or implicitly opposed to the alienating technologies of "materialist" society, the 1960s counterculture and 1970s New Age seemed to interpret technology as "anti-nature,"[56] and in retrospect one can say that this holds true for a large number of manifestations of modern gnosis since the 1870s—one can think of the "bio-dynamic" agriculture of anthroposophy or Jungian "archetypes" of human psychic nature as particularly illustrative examples. Thus, secular nature—understood in terms of the "appropriate technology" of biological growth—became for many New Agers an important source of salvation.

It is far too simple, however, to conclude from the above that New Age discourse is inhospitable to the rhetoric of the technological sublime or the religion of technology. It is more complicated than that: films like the first *Star Wars* trilogy, for example, which is saturated with New Age discourse, are made up of a "struggle between anti-technological narrative and hyper-technological aesthetic."[57] As we shall see, the relationships between New Age, the counterculture, and computer technology, in particular, are much more intimate than the dominant image of New Age as an antitechnological discourse suggests.

This most recent convergence of religion and technology seems to be taking place on the basis of a novel transformation in our conceptions of the secular in terms of "information." Starting in the 1950s, "cybernetics" redefined the conception of material "nature," the humanist concept of the person, and our common understanding of the machine (and thus, of history).[58] Subsequently, the "Information Revolution" seemed to take off in the late 1970s and early 1980s, giving the British Tory government, *Time* magazine, and an assorted crowd of cyber-gurus (among others) opportunity to herald the coming of an "Athens without slaves"—a new version of the religion of technology.[59] This slow emergence of the "digital sublime"[60] from post-1945 information theory crystallized only in the 1980s, in a paradigm that radically separated a universal informational code from its material carriers and that came to be dominated by the notion of virtuality.[61] Imagining the humanistic, secular person in terms of information implies continuing yet radicalizing the liberal humanist tradition of reducing persons to their minds.[62] Imagining nature in terms of information produces "cybernature," viewed as a universal informational code that constitutes the structure of everything that exists, on which technology draws to become "second nature."[63] By juxtaposing the world of mind and information to that of the material body and the Newtonian billiard-ball universe, this conception of virtuality divides the secular against itself, not least by opposing physical space to cyberspace.[64] This complicates the dictionary meaning of *secular*—"worldly"—which implies that there is only *one* world from which we take our measure (and, by implication, it also complicates the classical Weberian distinction between "this-worldly" and "other-worldly" concerns in the sociology and anthropology of religion). Once awe—reserved, in the Enlighten-ment, for sublime nature,[65] then transferred to technology by nineteenth-century Ameri-cans,[66] and regarded as the basic attitude of religion and magic by early-twentieth-century anthropologists[67]—can be attached to nature-as-information, a new fusion of religion and technology in cybergnosis becomes possible.

Cybergnosis

Timothy Leary is just one example of the ways in which, since the 1980s, the emergence of cyberspace has evoked countless religious, mystical, and metaphysical speculations—speculations that have, as we have shown, a long and checkered heritage. Spiritual gurus, cyberpunk writers, virtual reality specialists, and academics began to describe cyberspace and virtual reality in vocabularies derived from religious and metaphysical traditions. Cyberspace became, for instance, "Platonism as a working product,"[68] a "new Jerusa-lem,"[69] "paradise,"[70] or a "technological substitute for the Christian space of Heaven."[71] Others have said it stimulated "another, unheard-of dimension of spirituality."[72] Intellec-tuals such as Leary were joined by others—psychedelic ethnobotanist Terence McKenna, chaos mathematician Ralph Abraham, mathematician and science fiction writer Rudy Rucker, to name a few—who defined the realization of this spiritual realm as a phase of evolution in which digital technology would allow humans finally to become conscious of the "morphogenetic fields," made up of information patterns, that make up the "global brain"—a later incarnation of J. E. Lovelock's Gaia hypothesis, which was prominent in New Age circles.[73] By digitalizing such New Age views, cybergnostics drew inspiration from the "New Age Science" of people like Rupert Sheldrake ("morphogenetic fields"), David Bohm (the "implicate order" of quantum physics), and Lovelock, on the one hand, and the heritage of High Magic and neo-paganism (on a "technoshamanistic" and cyber-netic "astral plane"), on the other.

This awe for Cyberia and belief in its promise of liberation have strong gnostic fea-tures. The transformative experience that marks off modern gnosis from faith and reason resides in the common assumption that surfing the datastream (i.e., hacking, but also simply communicating on the Internet without any expertise whatsoever), taking psyche-delic drugs, dancing to computer-generated house music, or simply using one's digital imagination gives access to, even creates, the hidden reality of the world—the "implicate order" that is the world of information itself and that forms the perennial truth hiding behind every surface appearance of religious or scientific convention.[74] This cybernetic world of salvation is inherently free and unfettered and realizes humanity's "true" evolu-tionary destination, as against the "giants of flesh and steel"[75] or the "white, menopausal, mendacious men now ruling the planet earth"[76] that identify today's Archons—still iden-tified with the powers of materiality and convention that inhibit the unfolding of humani-ty's potential. All this is available to anybody who is willing to seek out that transformative experience, whether through the "consensual hallucination" of cyberspace, the hallucinogens of rave and house culture, or their combination in the "hallucinogenique" of Leary and Gullichsen's "digital polytheism."[77] What some see, however, as the democratic fact that "anyone can now access the datasphere," others see as a "lure" to "create a globally predictable consumer culture."[78]

These speculations about cyberspace—just a handful from the cornucopia available—indicate a remarkable elective affinity between digital technology and modern gnosis.[79] This affinity results to a considerable extent from the fact that our current computer world emerged from countercultural 1970s California—the world of drugs, rock, revolution, and spirituality. We will zoom in on the epistemological, ontological, and social dimensions of modern gnosis to bring out this relationship with digital technology in more detail.

Cyberspace as Transformative Experience

Gnostic epistemology is at the heart of the popular imagination of cyberspace, both among certain computer hackers and in cyberpunk literature, various science fiction movies, and contemporary online computer games. As one hacker (who is also a fan of the Californian rock band the Grateful Dead) said, real hacking is "tapping into the global brain. Information becomes a texture . . . almost an experience. You don't do it to get knowledge. You just ride the data."[80]

This experience was made mythical by William Gibson's cyberpunk science fiction novel *Neuromancer*, which "brought romance" into hacking by celebrating its hero Case's "bodiless exultation of cyberspace," thus providing the hacker community with an exemplar that, to many, slowly seemed to turn from technological fantasy to engineering fact.[81] The transformative experience of cyberspace was dramatically materialized by movies such as *The Lawnmower Man*, *eXistenZ*, and *The Matrix* trilogy.[82] The world of computer games, where players are invited to "follow a personal path," is also characterized by strong "emotional involvement,"[83] a sense of "authenticity,"[84] and the way it encourages a "kind of spiritual development" through the game experience.[85] In the words of one game designer: "Why should we settle for avatars, when we can be angels? . . . Spiritual experiences are, in fact, our business."[86] As Morpheus tells Neo (in *The Matrix 1*), before his rebirth into freedom: "unfortunately, no one can be told what the Matrix is. You have to see it for yourself."[87]

This experience is, indeed, a transformative one: these movies' protagonists usually develop from ordinary humans into posthuman entities with supernatural powers: they walk through walls, bend the laws of gravity, and affirm their omnipotence by saying such things as "I am god here!" (*The Lawnmower Man*). But other cybergnostics and virtual reality specialists also stress that full-fledged "sensory immersion" in virtual reality offers limitless subjective experiences and possibilities of reenchantment.[88] In consequence, the "real" becomes a personal, subjective experience—if one that gives access to a higher truth that remains hidden to the unenlightened body. In the words of Morpheus (*The Matrix 1*): "What is real? If you're talking about what you feel, taste, smell, or see, then real is simply electrical signals interpreted by your brain."[89] In fact, the illuminating experience may not even need the mediation of a computer screen or a virtual reality headset: the DJs and VJs of a rave or house party can turn the experience on the dance floor into a collective manifestation of a "fractal" that transports one into the implicate world of the morphogenetic fields of information.[90]

This transformative experience—which Leary referred to as "the ecstasy of the ultimate hack," manifesting a "satori of harmonious human-computer communication"[91]—is often described in terms of an instant evolution, a moment either that one experiences while surfing the datastream or that may result in a collective mutation—usually put, by the followers of Terence McKenna, as occurring in the year 2012—that will release humanity from its current, materialist paradigm and make it "slip out of history" into a cybernetic Eden of fully realized human potential.[92] Thus, the slow organic evolution of the body is being replaced by a notion of teleological mental evolution,[93] in which the end of human development is being realized "cybernaturally" in a man-made, technological time-compression of biological evolution that can now be cultivated as an "inalienable right."[94]

While companies such as Amazon.com, World Online, World Com, and America Online have, since the end of the 1990s, increasingly colonized and commodified the Internet and cyberspace, this process does not seem to have eroded cyberspace's potential for inducing spiritual experiences. To the contrary: commercial providers of chatgroups, virtual communities and online games have further encouraged it. Writing on the "experience economy," Joseph Pine and James H. Gilmore argue that "cyberspace is a great place for . . . [escapist] experiences" and maintain—very much like Morpheus in *The Matrix*—that "there is no such thing as an artificial experience. Every experience created within the individual is real, whether the stimuli be natural or simulated."[95]

"The new home of the mind"

The emergence of cyberspace has also reinforced and reinvented modern gnosis's dualistic ontology.[96] William Gibson's hero, "console cowboy" Case, craves the experience of cyberspace after his employers punish him for theft of information by feeding him a Russian neurotoxin that bars him from accessing the heavenly space of information: "For Case, who'd lived for the bodiless exultation of cyberspace, it was the Fall. In the bars he'd frequented as a cowboy hotshot, the elite stance involved a certain relaxed contempt for the flesh. The body was meat. Case fell into the prison of his own flesh."[97] As Heim notes, "Gibson evokes the Gnostic-Platonic-Manichean contempt for earthy, earthly existence."[98] This dualistic conception of the body as "meat" and cyberspace as the "new home of the mind" is probably the most central problematic in the academic literature on cyberspace.[99] But where scholars often question the possibility of attaining a computer-driven "escape velocity" to leave the body behind,[100] cybergnostics celebrate the possibility of the "liberation from human nature" achieved by uploading one's mind into a machine,[101] of a happy determination "by individual whim, style and seasonal choice" of whether one will become a "human-as-program" or a "human-in-program,"[102] and often display a profound contempt for the archaism of "wetware"—that is, organic substance. Such contempt of the body, shared by many more than we can discuss here, reached its ultimate realization when the members of the Heaven's Gate sect collectively killed themselves to "upload" their consciousness from their bodies to the extraterrestrial vehicle of a comet in 1997.

Such fantasies of a man-made, immanent "other world" are, in fact, more than fantasies. Margaret Wertheim discusses the different conceptions of space as described by modern physicists and rejects the applicability of any of those to the realm of cyberspace. She argues: "The electronic gates of the silicon chip have become, in a sense, a metaphysical gateway, for our modems transport us out of the reach of physicists' equations into an entirely 'other' realm. When I 'go' into cyberspace I leave behind both Newton's and Einstein's laws. Here, neither mechanistic, or relativistic, or quantum laws apply."[103] Wertheim makes a strong case for considering cyberspace as an alternative world of human construction. We do not need to determine whose laws apply there to see that all speculations on the ontology of cyberspace that identify it as a man-made yet other-worldly realm effectively pluralize our conception of the secular. This destroys the possibility of an unambiguous determination of what is "this world" and what is an "other world": for some, the engineering of cyberspace creates another world that is just as immanent, and just as natural, as the "this world" that used to be defined by the secular, Enlightenment or Newtonian concept of "nature." (Others, of course, would argue that these beliefs deny the material, political, and economic conditions of their production.[104]) At the very least, this means that the dualistic ontology inherited by the cybergnostics is powerfully supported by the realization that there may be another immanent world, realized by technology and irreducible to the "General-Motors concepts" of the bodies, masses, and forces of the Newtonian universe.[105]

Cyberspace is, indeed, easily seen as a realm beyond linear time and geographical space.[106] Gibson already noted that "there is no there there." When surfing on the Internet, people's locations can no longer be fixed in physical space, while, on a more mundane level, geographical barriers become irrelevant. In a sense, then, the Internet does not simply realize a "global village,"[107] a metaphor still based on a geographical notion, but is in fact a place *beyond* geographical places. The Internet also transforms linear time, to produce a "sense of immediacy that conquers time barriers."[108] Hypertexts, linkages, and the recycling of various historical genres on the Internet also disrupt the sense of linear time: "timing becomes synchronous in a flat horizon, with no beginning, no end, no sequence."[109] It becomes "timeless time." In other words, the technology of cyberspace provides an enormously receptive context and breeding ground for the dualistic ontology of modern gnosis.

Social Context: Fom Counterculture to Experience Economy

The countercultural sociology of modern gnosis regained momentum in the 1990s with the engineering of the World Wide Web. In 1996, John Perry Barlow, former writer for the Grateful Dead, wrote his *Declaration of the Independence of Cyberspace* against the "giants of flesh and steel" of the "industrial world," who should not be allowed to bar people's right to access the "new home of the mind."[110] Timothy Leary's cyberdelia resulted in a similar manifesto, declaring the sovereignty of the new young cyberspecies against "all governments controlled by the menopausal" and their "organic duty" to "mutate, to drop out, to initiate a new social structure"[111]—thus conflating natural process and human culture. Together with others who had their roots in the 1960s and 1970s, Leary promoted a "digital remastering of the counterculture."[112] In many ways, the 1990s seemed, in Mark Dery's succinct cyberphrase, "The Counterculture 2.0."[113]

Theodore Roszak has pointed out the real continuities between the militant counterculture of the 1960s and 1970s and the cyberdelia of the 1990s.[114] While his own earlier assessment of the counterculture emphasized its rebellion against a traditional morality based on technocratic thinking and its desire to go "back to nature,"[115] the seeds of a countercultural and gnostic celebration of technology, leading to a movement "from satori to Silicon Valley," were already sown in the 1970s: "it is within this same population of rebels and drop-outs [of the 1970s counterculture] that we can find the inventors and entrepreneurs who helped lay the foundations of the California computer industry."[116]

A technophile counterculture in the form of a "hacker ethic" had, in fact, already formed among the hackers working with the TX-O computer at the MIT artificial intelligence lab in the late 1950s and early 1960s. Its opposition to the "Priesthood" guarding the giant computers of IBM and other large corporations encouraged hackers to acknowledge that "all information should be free," that one should "mistrust authority" and "promote decentralization," and that when hacking would be trusted on its merits and allowed to unfold its own creative art, computers would "change your life for the better."[117] At the Stanford artificial intelligence lab, the hacker ethic found a new home (in rooms named after J. R. R. Tolkien's Middle Earth locations) and quickly spread into other countercultural movements, such as the People's Computer Company—which, just like Ted Nelson's *Computer Lib* (1974), wanted to bring computing to everybody—and the hardware hackers of the Homebrew Computer Club (founded in 1975), the most important breeding ground of the personal computer. Steve Jobs (Apple) and Bill Gates (Microsoft) were acid-heads and "part-time Buddhists" at the time, while the hacker ethic was also well received in the pages of the countercultural *Whole Earth Catalog* and among the psychedelic fan club of the Grateful Dead—which counted among its members many of those who were to set up one of the first bulletin boards (the Whole Earth 'Lectronic Link—WELL) and the Electronic Frontier Foundation.

Here, forms of modern gnosis and digital technology first converged. One of the first personal computers, the IMSAI, was the product of a group of adherents of Werner Erhardt's human potential training.[118] PCs were often described and experienced as "magical"—as places where, in the words of Les Solomon, "every man can be a god."[119] The hacker's expectation that the world would be better if everyone had access to a computer was in itself a fantasy of personal transformation by technology.

It would be wrong, however, to describe this earlier period purely in terms of gnosis: the full blossoming of cybergnosis only became apparent after much of the countercultural movement's political thrust had dissipated in the late 1970s and early 1980s, leading to the "culture of narcissism" of the New Age and to a new trust in technological salvation in the mid 1980s and early 1990s. Popular magazines, such as *Mondo 2000, Wired Magazine,* and others, made the countercultural message available for a mass and mainstream audience. *Wired Magazine*, Jedediah Purdy argues, introduced a "new brand of libertarianism" and "the Wired temperament is contemptuous of all limits—of law, community, morality, place, even embodiment. The magazine's ideal is the unbounded individual."[120] *Mondo 2000* was even more radical in its libertarianism, stating, "We're talking about Total Possibilities. Radical assaults on the limits of biology, gravity and time. . . . Highjacking technology for personal empowerment, fun and games. Flexing those synapses! . . . Becoming the Bionic Angel."[121] The booming industry of computer games epitomized the commercialization of these countercultural ideals and their translation to huge numbers of European and American households.

This incorporation of a countercultural or antinomian temperament into mainstream technophilia is perhaps best represented by Jody Radzik, one of the foremost gatekeepers of Cyberia in the San Francisco house and rave scene in the early 1990s. For Radzik, cyberdisco was the vehicle for disseminating the awakening of the planet's awareness into "a direct experience of the infinite" and an incorporation into the fractal pattern of metaconsciousness by using marketing "as the perfect transformational tool": "The kids now are not going to turn on, tune in, drop out. They're going to drop *in*."[122] The 1990s reinvention of the counterculture of the 1960s—while retaining, in certain sectors, the political critiques and "hacktivism" of the latter—became largely geared to a modern gnostic rather than political antinomian attitude, one that is fully in line with the culture industry's production of an "experience economy" for an audience of mass consumers, and with the commercialization of the Internet.[123] Especially through the massive investment of both producers and consumers of computer games in the increasingly sophisticated simulations made possible by the computer, a kind of gnostic amnesia of the physical and mechanic supports of cyberspace has been made possible, supported by the inventions of the graphics user interface and the Internet. Thus, the cultural connection between a Romantic antinomian ethic and the culture of consumerism, which emerged at least from the late nineteenth century onward, is further reinforced by the commercialization of computer technology.

Conclusion

We do not pretend to be able to predict the future of cybergnosis, nor can we say whether it will overwhelm, or give way to, other forms of cyberspace salvation, of connecting the computer to current utopian thinking, or (most likely) finding salvation in another new technological development. Often cybergnosis seems too disembodied and playful to support a viable "posthuman" future.[124] For us, the interest of this phenomenon lies in a different direction, related to a broader understanding of transformations of religion in modern society. Cybergnosis is an indicator of the current "experience economy," yet it seems to speed up these experiences to such an extent that one wonders whether they still deserve the term. Cybergnosis popularizes a countercultural attitude, but in the sense in which advertising, too, admonishes all people to "be their true selves" and oppose convention by buying certain widely available commodities.[125] Cybergnosis does seem to make a difference to our imagination of the religious and the secular—by pluralizing the secular and highlighting the salvation made possible by the "this-worldly other world" of information—yet the cybergnostic choice of the world of information alone, as against the world of "meat," seems to reduce these possibilities at the same time.

We find it more important to emphasize that computer technology has helped make modern gnosis progressively more at home in modern society. Incorporated into the mainstream from society's countercultural fringe, having lost much of its critical political posture in the process, it has moved to the very center of contemporary culture and society.[126] "Contrary to predictions that New Age would go mainstream, now it's as if the mainstream is going New Age."[127] This phenomenon—and this would go for current Western societies in general—cannot be studied in terms of a kind of "science-plus-religion" sum, since it subsumes the this dichotomy in a new discursive formation. This gnostic formation has a tremendous capacity for recycling the "pasts" of faith and reason—in fact, with the coming of computer technology, this recycling has become even more rapid, eclectic, and perennialist, leaving no holy or evil stone unturned.

Put crudely, whereas classical social science expected the world of religion to be increasingly subverted and marginalized by science and technology, we suggest that religion has had to make way in many sectors of Northern European and North American societies for a modern gnosis that is not just privatized, but made massively present in the consumerist public sphere. This contemporary form of enchantment receives a tremendous boost from science and technology, now especially in the guise of the engineering of the immanent, "this-worldly other world" of cyberspace. While this may seem to testify to a process of modernization, it is not a modernization that can be grasped by opposing science, reason, the secular, and technology to religion and/or faith. Instead, the phenomenon of cybergnosis shows that both the secular and technology have to be dislocated from this binary opposition and relocated in a third term in order to understand how and why modern people use and need *both* the sacred and the secular in order to portray themselves as modern people.

Religious Sensations

Why Media, Aesthetics, and Power Matter in the Study of Contemporary Religion

Birgit Meyer

Whether we like it or not, religion appears to be of the utmost importance in the early twenty-first century. The idea that the public relevance of religion would decline with modernization and development, yielding a disenchanted world, has been contradicted by actual developments, from the manifestation of so-called political Islam to the rise of Pentecostal-charismatic movements propagating the Gospel of Prosperity, from wars that mobilize religious convictions to acts of terror in the name of God, from contests over blasphemous representations and sacrilege on the part of Muslims and Christians to the deep entanglement of religion and entertainment, from accusations of witchcraft to the organization of Wicca fairs, from online wonders to magic in advertisements, from public crusades dedicated to defeating the Devil to high-tech evangelical youth conventions, from Internet religiosity to the upsurge in religious tourism. Religion, in a variety of guises, is found to thrive not only in the so-called non-Western world but also in the supposed strongholds of modernity. It is clear that religion has become a matter of concern and a topic of public debate, even for those who strongly defend a secular social order, a rational outlook, or even, as advocated by Slavoj Žižek in a recent issue of *Lettre International*, reappraise atheism.[1]

Public debates and concerns about what is popularly framed as the "return of religion" are often based on rather simplistic ideas about the relationship between religion and modernity, as if more education would entail the demise of belief in God, or progress and democracy would yield a secular, more rational attitude and above all ensure a clear distinction between religion and politics. The study of contemporary religion requires more sophisticated approaches.[2] By now, many scholars state that the notion of secularization is inappropriate as a theoretical point of departure.[3] The proposition made by Jürgen Habermas in the aftermath of 9/11, that of characterizing our contemporary era as "post-secular," does well to take seriously the relevance of religion as a political and social force.[4] Given the frequent appeal made to secularism in public debates, however, I am hesitant to qualify our contemporary era as post-secular. In order to grasp the relevance of religion, we need what I would like to call a post-secular*ist* approach, post-secularist in the sense that, rather than inscribe into our theoretical frameworks the opposition between secular and religious that has entered our modern social imaginaries, we need to take this opposition as an object of study, as Talal Asad suggests in his *Formations of the Secular*, and investigate the question of religion with open minds.[5] We need to develop alternative theoretical frameworks that do not approach contemporary religion as an anachronism we expect to vanish or to become politically irrelevant with modernization, but instead seek to grasp its appeal, persistence, and power. This essay is meant as a contribution to this larger project.

Given that the substance, role, and place of religion in political and socioeconomic power structures is subject to historical change, I am not in favor of defining religion in universal terms, as if it had an ever-valid essence. Talal Asad has pointed out that the supposedly universal definitions developed since the rise of the study of religion as a scientific discipline in the mid nineteenth century are derived from a specific modern religiosity, which does not necessarily fit in with different cultural contexts and other religious traditions.[6] Rather than working with universal definitions, we need to realize that religion is always situated in history and society. Calling for the study of contemporary religion, then, means situating religious organizations, such as churches, cults, movements, or networks, in relation to the economic, social, and political power structures that shape our contemporary world. In so doing, we need to be alert to both the specificity of *and* the manifest and structural similarities between religious organizations.[7] In this sense, the study of contemporary religion must entail detailed empirical research *and* comparison.[8]

It may appear inconsistent that I reject a universal definition of religion and yet dare to talk about religion. But it is not.[9] I take it that, broadly speaking, religion refers to the ways in which people link up with, or even feel touched by, a meta-empirical sphere that may be glossed as supernatural, sacred, divine, or transcendental.[10] What interests me as an anthropologist is how people's links with this meta-empirical sphere are shaped by, as well as shape, links among them and organize them into particular social forms, thus sustaining particular modes of being and belonging. In the following, this meta-empirical sphere is referred to as "the transcendental," because this term best captures the sense of going beyond the ordinary that is at the core of religious sensations, the central theme of this essay. To avoid misunderstanding, I would like to stress that, being a social scientist, I do not approach the transcendental from a theological perspective.[11] My key concern is to grasp how experiences of the transcendental are invoked in the here and now and underpin individual and collective identities. In this sense, my approach to the transcendental is resolutely down to earth.

Having outlined the vantage point from which I propose to study contemporary religion, I will now call attention to my central theme: the question of "religious sensations." Then I will turn to: (1) modern media and mediation, (2) aesthetics and aisthesis, and (3) power. It is my sincere hope that, after moving through this trajectory, I will have made clear why and how media, aesthetics, and power matter in the study of contemporary religion.

Religious Sensations

In research on modern religion, approaches emphasizing religious sensations have existed in the shadow of narratives stressing what Max Weber called the "disenchantment of the world." According to Weber, we may recall, Protestantism played the role of midwife for the emergence of modern capitalism, but its spirit, once able to overwhelm believers and generate the pious attitude and work ethic necessary for the rise of capitalism, had died out.[12] Modern people were stuck in what he famously called *ein stahlhartes Gehäuse* (imperfectly translated as an "iron cage"): a disenchanted society in which persons had become subject to the forces of capitalism, its rigid time regime, its devastating consumption of natural resources, and the nervousness of urban life. They might long for a "return of the gods," deep spiritual experiences, and new charismatic leaders—something Weber increasingly felt in his own life—but there was no way back, certainly not for an intellectual like Weber, who felt driven mercilessly to deconstruct such attempts as vain chimeras.[13]

Weber's notion of the disenchantment of the world, and the role Protestantism played therein, had a stronger impact on our thinking about religion and modernity than his rather gloomy reflections on the modern condition, which give a glimpse of his personal feelings and the overall mood of the fin de siècle that ended with the First World War. The former fits in easily with an understanding of modernity in terms of increasing rationalization and the demise of religion.[14] For my purposes—contributing to a postsecularist framework—it is useful at least to acknowledge the desperate, somewhat nostalgic longing for spiritual fulfillment that thrives in the shadow of disenchantment (a fulfillment that would eventually rejoin a person with his or her own nature or *Kreatürlichkeit*). Nineteenth-century orientalist searches for an Eastern spirituality and the emergence of movements such as New Age or the Wicca in our time promise to fulfill as much as nurture such a longing.[15] But this longing also has been found to be at the basis of modern consumerism, or modern people's quest for authenticity.[16]

In the study of religion, no one interested in the question of feelings can bypass the seminal work of the American philosopher and psychologist William James. James circumscribed religion as "the feelings, acts, and experiences of individual men in their solitude, so far as they apprehend themselves to stand in relation to whatever they may consider the divine."[17] Although James's attention to religious feelings and experiences is much to the point, it is also problematic for at least two reasons. First, his emphasis on feelings and experiences is predicated upon a strong distinction between the body, as the locus of senses and emotions, and the mind, as the site of intellectual knowledge. This distinction, which has had repercussions in the study of religion up to the present, reaffirms the Cartesian split between body and mind. Paying attention to religious feelings and experiences would then almost by necessity imply a disregard for more intellectual, rational dispositions (as if these would not also generate and sustain particular feelings and experiences). In my view, this is a vain, unproductive opposition, one that I seek to circumvent.[18]

Second, in James's perspective religious feelings and experiences are by definition private, subjective, and primary, whereas religious organizations such as churches and their doctrines and practices are regarded as secondary. Emphasizing the primary experience of God with the pathos typical of his writing and speaking, James did not realize that the disposition of the lonely individual in search of God is part and parcel of a discursive, and hence shared, cultural construction. The fact that he and those working in line with his ideas take the existence of a primary, authentic, and in this sense seemingly unmediated religious experience at face value is misleading. Indeed, as Charles Taylor puts it in his critical discussion of James's approach to religious experience: "Many people are not satisfied with a momentary sense of wow! They want to take it further and they're looking for ways of doing so."[19]

Without the particular social structures, sensory regimes, bodily techniques, doctrines, and practices that make up a religion, the searching individual craving experience of God would not exist. Likewise, religious feelings are not just there, but are made possible and reproducible by certain modes of inducing experiences of the transcendental. While from the insider perspective of religious practitioners religion may seem to originate in initially unmediated, authentic experiences of an entity perceived as transcendental, I propose taking as a starting point of our analysis the religious forms that generate such experiences.

In this context it is important to realize that sensation has a double meaning: feeling[20] *and* the inducement of a particular kind of excitement. This inducement is brought about by what I would like to call *sensational forms*, which make it possible to sense the transcendental. Sensational forms, in my understanding, are relatively fixed, authorized modes of invoking and organizing access to the transcendental, thereby creating and sustaining links between religious practitioners in the context of particular religious organizations. Sensational forms are transmitted and shared; they involve religious practitioners in particular practices of worship and play a central role in forming religious subjects. Collective

rituals are prime examples of sensational forms in that they address and involve participants in a specific manner and induce particular feelings. But the notion of sensational
form can also be applied to the ways in which material religious objects—such as images,
books, or buildings—address and involve beholders. Thus, reciting a holy book such as
the Qur'an, praying in front of an icon, or dancing around the manifestation of a spirit
are also sensational forms through which religious practitioners are made to experience
the presence and power of the transcendental.

The stance I propose has consequences for conceptualizing the transcendental. Religious sensations are about human encounters with phenomena or events that appear as
beyond comprehension: a sublime that induces, as we learn from Kant and Burke, a sense
of simultaneous beauty and terror.[21] Such encounters invoke sensations of awe vis-à-vis a
transcendental entity that by definition resists being fully known and yet makes itself felt
in the here and now, in the immanent. In his *Threshold of Religion*, Robert Ranulph
Marett introduces the notion of awe as part and parcel of his theory of "religion as a
whole," that is, "the organic complex of thought, emotion, and behaviour."[22] What Marett called "the religious sense" is to be sought "in the steadfast groundwork of specific
emotion, whereby man is able to feel the supernatural *precisely at the point at which his
thought breaks down*."[23]

I find his thoughts about "emotions as awe, wonder, and the like" quite stimulating.
By contrast, for instance, to Rudolf Otto, for whom the Numinous (*das Heilige*) exists sui
generis, and hence prior to and independent of the emotions that it arouses in the feeling
subject,[24] Marett places at the center of attention the person facing the limits of understanding. In his view, feelings of awe *yield* objectifications of "the mysterious or 'supernatural' something felt" as something beyond comprehension. Being a social scientist, I am
highly sympathetic to taking as a starting point the feeling subject rather than a transcendental entity. Still, it would be short-sighted to understand objectifications of the transcendental simply in terms of an initial unmediated experience.[25] In the context of
religious traditions and in the praxis of religious organizations, objectifications of the
transcendental are more or less fixed, rendered reapproachable and repeatable across time
(and possibly space), and determined as to be handled in particular ways. Invoking, framing, and rendering accessible the transcendental, such objectifications are what I mean by
sensational forms. Linking up with the transcendental via sensational forms that shape or
even produce the transcendental in a particular manner, religious practitioners are made
to sense a limit of understanding. Indeed, it is the sense of limit that evokes the experience
of something beyond and organizes feelings of "awe, wonder, and the like." It is a limit
that does not simply limit, but above all *enables* the experience of the sublime in the here
and now.[26] In this sense, the sublime features as an, as it were, "impossible representation," which is acknowledged to exceed people's representational capacities and yet can
be rendered accessible via a particular sensational form.[27] Thus, a sense of limit is enshrined in the notion of the sublime. The sense of limit, it needs to be stressed again, is

evoked by the particular sensational forms though which religions organize the link between human beings and the transcendental. A sense of awe, wonder, and other forms of amazement, then, are generated in the context of power structures located in the immanent.[28]

Let me start to clarify how religious sensations, in the sense of experiences and feelings, are organized by sensational forms, and hence are subject to social construction and power structures, by turning to my own research. A red thread in my work on Christianity, popular culture, and modern mass media in Ghana concerns the connection between local Africans' conversion to Protestantism and their concomitant incorporation into a modern state and a global capitalist market.[29] This interest has also pushed me to investigate the current appeal of Pentecostal-charismatic churches.[30] By contrast to mainstream Protestantism, Pentecostal religiosity is far more geared to publicly expressing religious feelings.[31] This expressive, public emotionality has pushed me to think about the question of religious sensations.

These churches, to adopt an expression from Bonno Thoden van Velzen, operate as a kind of "pressure cooker—or even microwave—of the emotions"[32] in that they not only generate but also heat up and intensify religious feelings. Pentecostal services are powerful sensational forms that seek to involve believers in such a way that they sense the presence of God in a seemingly *immediate* manner and are amazed by His power. Still, the Holy Spirit does not arrive out of the blue. I have witnessed many such services, in which the pastor and congregation pray for the Holy Spirit to come. After some time, the prayers become louder and louder, and many start speaking in tongues. This is taken as a sign that the Holy Spirit is manifest. At a certain moment the pastor indicates the end of the prayer session and calls upon the Holy Spirit to heal the sick, protect the vulnerable, and expel demonic spirits. The desire for such a seemingly direct link with the power of God via the Holy Spirit is what made, and still makes, many people migrate to Pentecostal churches and to become born again.[33] Though in principle all born-again believers are able and entitled to *embody* the Holy Spirit, charismatic pastors are prime exponents of divine power. Indeed, this is what their charisma depends upon and what draws people into their churches.

The latest brand of Pentecostal-charismatic churches, which started to thrive in Ghana in the early 1990s, are run in a businesslike fashion by flamboyant pastors. Making skillful use of the modern mass media, which have become deregulated and commercialized in the course of Ghana's turn to a democratic constitution, Pentecostal-charismatic churches have become omnipresent in the public sphere.[34] Like American televangelism, many of them make use of the mass media to produce and broadcast spectacular church services to mass audiences. Recorded during church conventions yet edited carefully so as to ensure utmost credibility, such programs claim to offer eye-witness accounts of the power of God to perform miracles via the charismatic pastor and his Prayer Force.[35]

Featured as an embodiment—indeed an objectification—of divine power, the pastor conveys a sense of amazement and wonder. These programs address anonymous viewers, asking them to participate in the televised event with their prayers so as to feel the presence of God. Some people report that they have been truly touched by God when viewing such programs.[36] What emerges is a new sensational form that makes miracles happen on the television screen and seeks to reach out to a mass audience, which is invited to "feel along" with the televised spectacle witnessed on screen.

I find this incorporation of dramatized, mass-mediated performances of divine power and miracles highly intriguing. This phenomenon is not confined to Pentecostal-charismatic churches but is of broader importance. Modern media have become relevant to religious practice in many settings and shape the sensational forms around which links between human beings and the transcendental evolve. Although I will keep returning to my own research throughout this essay, I hope to be able to show that the question of religious sensations far exceeds that particular ethnographic setting. Though sensed individually, religious sensations are socially produced, and their repetition depends on the existence of formalized practices that not only frame individual religious sensations but also enable them to be reproduced. That is, again, why I talk about sensations in the double sense of persons having particular sensations *and* the inducement of these sensations via sensational forms, forms that encompass the objectifications of "the mysterious or 'supernatural' something felt" addressed by Marett, as well as Pentecostalism's televised spectacles and all kinds of less spectacular devices designed to link people with the transcendental and each other.

Modern Media and Mediation

Thinking about the at times spectacular reports in the daily news about the incorporation of television and the Internet into religious traditions, one might be led to think that the presence of media is a distinct characteristic of contemporary religion. Pentecostals' televised performances of miracles, of which I have seen so many in Ghana and elsewhere, are no doubt highly remarkable events. Still, it is important to realize that media are not foreign or new, but intrinsic to religion. As Hent de Vries has argued, religion may well be considered a practice of mediation.[37] Positing a distance between human beings and the transcendental, religion offers practices of mediation to bridge that distance and make it possible to experience—from a more distanced perspective one could say produce—the transcendental. Take, for example, the Catholic icon: though it is carved from wood, painted, and set up—thus obviously manmade—to the believing beholder (and possibly to its maker) it appears as an embodiment of a sacred presence that can be experienced by a contemplative gaze, a prayer, or a kiss. In this perspective, the transcendental is not a self-revealing entity but, on the contrary, always affected or formed by mediation processes, in that media and practices of mediation invoke the transcendental via particular sensational forms. These sensational forms not only mediate the transcendental but often, and in our time increasingly so, depend on modern media such as print and electronic audio-visual devices. In order to avoid confusion, I would like to stress that, in this understanding of religion as mediation, media feature on two levels. Not only do modern media such as print, photography, TV, film, or the Internet shape sensational forms, the latter are themselves media that mediate, and thus produce, the transcendental and make it available to the senses.

For a staunch Protestant, for example, the Bible is never just a mass-produced book but is sacralized as the medium through which God has revealed himself. For Muslims the Qur'an is a holy book. Popular images of Jesus, as David Morgan has shown, are regarded not simply as mass-produced representations but as able to intimate the presence of Christ.[38] In India, as the work of Christopher Pinney has shown, mass-produced chromolithographs of Hindu gods become sites of worship.[39] Similarly, mass-produced portraits of the early-twentieth-century Thai King Chulalongkorn play a central role in popular Buddhist worship practices.[40] In Pentecostal circles, television is regarded as exceptionally well-suited to screening the born-again message for a mass public.[41]

During my research in Ghana, I encountered many people who referred to televised miracle sessions as being true depictions of the power of God. Television (and video) are seen as modern media that can be used to prove the existence and efficiency of divine power and sustain the belief that "your miracle is on the way," as one popular Pentecostal slogan goes. During my stay in Ghana in 2002, I was told about a Nigerian video that depicted a Pentecostal pastor who brings back to life a dead person, taken to church in his coffin. The idea of making audiovisual technologies reveal the reality and power of God and affirm His superiority over the power of the Devil is popularized by local video-filmmakers, among whom I have conducted research on the intersection of Christianity, media, and entertainment. Surfing along with the popularity of Pentecostal Christianity, many of them frame their movies as divine revelations that visualize the operation of the "powers of darkness" with the help of the camera and computer-produced special effects. Although spectators know quite well how these movies are made, many still insist that the audio-visual technologies mobilized for the sake of revelation show "what is there," yet remains invisible to the naked eye. In discussions about witchcraft, those defending the position that witchcraft is real refer to Ghanaian and Nigerian video-films, thus backing up their claims with audio-visual evidence. In this sense, these movies are viewed as offering a kind of divine super-vision that enables viewers to peep into the dark.

What all these examples have in common is a salient fusion of media technologies and the transcendental, which they are made to mediate via particular sensational forms. At the same time, precisely because media are indispensable to, and interwoven with,

711

religious mediation, religious practitioners may find new media to be entirely inappropri-ate, or at least very difficult to accommodate. This is so with indigenous cults in Ghana, whose priests are adamant that cameras may not be brought into their shrines.[42] Con-versely, processes of religious innovation are often characterized by the adoption of new media, entailing fierce assaults against older media, as in the case of Protestant missionar-ies' dismissal of Catholicism and indigenous cults as "idol worship" that should urgently be replaced by a thorough focus on the true source of God's Word: the Bible as mother tongue. The sensational form evolving around the icon was to be replaced by a new sensational form evolving around the book.

These examples not only suggest that mediation objectifies a spiritual power that is otherwise invisible to the naked eye and difficult to access, thereby making its appearance via a particular sensational form depend upon currently available media and modes of representation, they also highlight that mediation itself tends to be sacralized by religious practitioners. By the same token, the media intrinsic to such mediations are exempted from the sphere of mere technology and authorized to be suitable harbingers of immedi-ate, authentic experiences.[43] Religious sensations of a presumably immediate encounter with God, or of having direct access to his power, do not happen just "out of the blue"—however much those experiencing these sensations may think so. Such sensations, it needs to be stressed, are prefigured by existing mediation practices, which make it possible for believers to be touched by God in the first place.

Although I have emphasized that religious mediation happens in the immanent and hence depends on human activities, I would be wary of anchoring religious mediation in theoretical approaches that affirm a contrast between "real" and "made-up." Certainly in the study of religion, we need to recognize the phenomenological reality of religious expe-rience as grounded in bodily sensations. Since I am a scholar rooted in the social sciences, it is not my professional task to make statements concerning the true or imagined exis-tence of the transcendental, or the ontological status of reality. Above all, as social scien-tists we have to come to terms with the *mediated* nature of experiences that are claimed to be *immediate* and *authentic* by their beholders and are authorized as such by the religious traditions of which they form part.[44] It is neither enough to deconstruct and dismiss these experiences as "made up" and "faked" nor to take their authenticity at face value.[45] I will return to this point in the section on aesthetics.

The adoption of new media does not happen in a vacuum, but is bound up with broader social and cultural processes. By instigating the shift to the new medium of the printed book during the Reformation, for example, Protestantism also associated itself with new, modern techniques of the self and modes of perception, that is, with the emerg-ing print capitalism that has been crucial to the genesis of the modern nation-state.[46] The shift to televangelism, which not only occurs in Christianity but also appeals to members of other religious traditions, can be viewed as an attempt to rearticulate religion in what Walter Benjamin called the "era of technical reproducibility."[47] If only what is shown on

TV truly exists, then the power of God has to appear on TV. As belief becomes thus vested in the image, it becomes hard to distinguish between belief and make-believe, miracles and special effects, or truth and illusion.[48] The accommodation of such new media and the new sensational forms that go along with them ensure the up-to-dateness of Christianity and its public presence. We could even say that television is called upon to authorize religious sensations as true, while the body of the spectator brings televised images to life, as in the Venezuelan María Lionza Cult studied by Rafael Sánchez, who shows that cult members are possessed by the spirits of TV personae and personalities.[49] The entanglement of religion, media, and the forces of commercialization, though allowing for the public presence of religion, erodes the possibility of maintaining a clear distinction between religion and entertainment.[50] In this sense, as Jeremy Stolow puts it, media and mediation always constitute "inherently unstable and ambiguous conditions of possibility for religious signifying practices," and thus challenge the maintenance of religious authority.[51]

While the adoption of modern audiovisual media certainly transforms practices of religious mediation and the sensational forms through which the transcendental is rendered accessible, we must be careful not to overestimate the power of media per se to change the world.[52] The adoption of modern media, as we found in the context of the research program Modern Mass Media, Religion, and the Imagination of Communities, which I directed from 2000 to 2006,[53] always involves complicated negotiations, yielding processes of transformation that cannot be attributed either to media alone or to the persistence of a fixed religious message. The adoption of modern media allows for the reformation and reactivation of religion in our time. As Mattijs van de Port shows in his study of Brazilian Candomblé, cult members' practices of "visualizing the sacred"—which is supposed to remain secret—in soap-opera-style videos reveal an "inextricable entanglement of religious and media imaginaries that should guide studies of religion in contemporary societies."[54]

Precisely because media are intrinsic to religion, in the study of contemporary religion we need to pay utmost attention to attitudes toward modern media and their adoption into established practices of religious mediation. Given the strong visual orientation of such modern media, we are well advised to link up with the recent interdisciplinary field of research on visual culture. Important questions for further research are: How does the availability of modern media change religious mediation, and hence the ways in which the transcendental is expressed via particular sensational forms? Are there significant differences between the ways in which different religious traditions, groups, or movements adopt and appropriate different kinds of modern media? What contradictions and clashes arise from the coexistence of the interdiction on making images of God, as found in Judaism, Islam, and Christianity, and the dynamics of contemporary visual culture, which thrives on visibility? What kind of religious sensations, in the sense of feelings, are generated when religions adopt new sensational forms, such as the spectacle?

Aesthetics and Aisthesis

Understanding religion as a practice of mediation that organizes the relationship between experiencing subjects and the transcendental via particular sensational forms requires that the material and sensory dimension of religious mediation become a focal point of attention. For me, this understanding implies the need to pay attention to aesthetics. My understanding of aesthetics exceeds the narrow sense advocated by Baumgarten and Kant, in which aesthetics refers to the beautiful in the sphere of the arts, more or less confined to the disinterested beholder. Instead, I follow a suggestion made by anthropologists Christopher Pinney and Jojada Verrips, namely, that we link up again with Aristotle's notion of *aisthesis*, understood as organizing "our total sensory experience of the world and our sensitive knowledge of it."[55] To trace such an understanding of aesthetics in terms of aisthesis or sense experience back to Maurice Merleau-Ponty's phenomenology of perception,[56] or to relate it to the phenomenology of religion as developed by Rudolf Otto, Gerardus van der Leeuw, or Mircea Eliade,[57] would be outside my present scope, not to speak of discussing the ins and outs, pros and cons, of phenomenology in general. Let me briefly explain, on the basis of some examples, why I deem it useful to consider the aesthetic dimension of religion.

In order to account for the richness and complexity of religious experience, we need theoretical approaches that can account for its material, bodily, sensational, and sensory[58] dimensions. The problem with, for example, interpretive approaches in the study of religion is that they tend to neglect the experiencing body in order to focus on religious representations that are submitted to a symbolic analysis. While it is of course undeniable that symbols feature in religious mediation, I find a focus on symbolic representations as the key entry point into "the interpretation of religion" quite problematic, for at least two reasons.

First, a symbol is understood, as we have learned from Clifford Geertz and others, to be a "vehicle of meaning" that stands (in the tradition of Saussure's structural linguistics) in an arbitrary relation to its referent in the outside world.[59] Such a view fails to grasp the possible blurring of a representation with what it represents. In other words, it fails to conceptualize the power that a religious artifact—whether an image, a text, or any other objectification—may be perceived to wield over its beholder.[60] During my own research in Ghana, for example, two born-again girls made me understand that a painted image of Mami Water we had bought from a local artist and displayed in our living room was a threatening, demonic presence.[61] They urged me to take away immediately this image of Satan's most seductive demon, who is held to lure even unsuspecting beholders right into her sensual, scandalously immoral consumer paradise at the bottom of the ocean. Their fear that this image might not be just a piece of popular art—and thus not a mere representation—but bring the actual presence of this dangerous spirit right into our lives highlights the point: the visceral power of such images can only be grasped if we do not just read them as, and reduce them to, mere symbols of something else (such as, in the case of Mami Water, the eroticism of wealth), but see them as an embodiment of a spiritual presence.[62]

Second, a focus on the symbolic usually goes hand in hand with textual modes of analysis that regard cultures as texts, as famously elaborated in Geertz's analysis of the Balinese cockfight.[63] Such approaches fail to appreciate religious objects as constitutive elements of the religious life-worlds of their beholders and hence as key to the possibility of "authentic" experience. In his analysis of the Jewish Orthodox Artscroll publishing house, for example, Jeremy Stolow has shown that copies of sacred texts sold via the Internet are made to embody a sense of gravity that seeks to anchor readers in a tactile rather than merely intellectual relationship with the text.[64] The heaviness and tactility of these books is part and parcel of a religious sensory practice in which religion is less about interpreting than about being in the world.

Thus, my plea to acknowledge the aesthetic dimension of religion is grounded in my realization of the shortcomings of more conventional interpretive or symbolic approaches in the study of religion. Sensational forms, though produced and in a sense "made up," appear as situated beyond mediation exactly because they are—literally—incorporated and embodied by their beholders. These forms evoke and perpetuate shared experiences, emotions, and affects that are anchored in a taken-for-granted sense of self and community, indeed, a *common sense* that is rarely subject to questioning exactly because it is grounded in shared perceptions and sensations. Common sense is what gets under the skin, enveloping us in the assurance "this is what really is."

On the level of theory, there are more and more investigations that no longer privilege the symbolic over other modes of experience. Susan Buck-Morss has argued that the aisthetic way of knowing the world, involving all the senses, has been pushed into the background with the rise of what has been called modern ocularcentrism, which brought about a mode of knowing the world through a distant, objectifying gaze.[65] Ocularcentrism means that the sense of sight is understood to dominate people's perception of the world, which appears as a kind of "picture" to be looked at (as Heidegger suggests), rather than to be experienced in full, with all the senses. The exposure of the faults of modern ocularcentrism and the regimes of surveillance it implies have yielded much important work on the anaesthetizing implications of Western visual regimes, for example, in the colonized world.[66] Currently we find ourselves in the midst of what is being called "the pictorial turn," which calls attention to the visceral impact of images on their beholder.[67] Scholars have developed a keen interest in other senses than, and alternative understandings of, vision. Critical of the capacity of "modern representationalism" (and its twin sister, ocularcentrism) to govern modern modes of thinking completely, they seek to reappraise the relevance of the senses and the body.[68]

My ideas about the aesthetic dimension of religion have been particularly stimulated by the work of David Morgan.[69] On the basis of his highly original investigation of the role of mass-produced images in popular American Protestantism, he proposes understanding religious images as artifacts that attribute reality to representations of the divine, making it appear as if the picture possesses "its referent within itself."[70] Such religious images are important examples of what I call sensational forms. Being part and parcel of religious mediation, they can best be understood as a condensation of practices, attitudes, and ideas that structure experiences of the transcendental and hence "ask" to be approached in a particular manner. Far from resembling Kant's disinterested beholder of an aesthetic object, believers (have learned to) expect that images mediate the transcendental in a process that miraculously vests them with divine presence. Believers are led to engage in particular religiously induced "looking acts" so as not only to see the image but to sense the divine power that shines through it. Such "looking acts" are not confined to seeing alone but induce sensations of being touched. In this sense, religious images do not just meet the eye but have a thoroughly carnal dimension.[71] Thus, rather than being persuasive in and of themselves, religious images work in the context of particular grammars and traditions of usage, which evoke religious sensations by teaching particular ways of looking and induce particular dispositions and practices toward them. In other words, such images are part and parcel of a particular religious aesthetic, which governs believers' sensory engagement with the transcendental and with each other.[72]

Morgan's work is not only useful for the study of religious images per se,[73] but can be extended to religious sensational forms in a broader sense, that is, the whole range of religious materials conveying a sense of the sublime, from images to texts, from objects to music. Mediating the transcendental and raising religious sensations, these material sensational forms require our utmost attention. They are the anchor points from which religious aesthetics unfold. At the same time, it is important to realize that significant differences exist between the sets of sensational forms (and the religious aesthetics that go along with these sensational forms) that are at the core of particular religious traditions, groups, or movements at a given time. Different media appeal to the senses in different ways: it makes a big difference whether a religious organization is rich in imagery and foregrounds vision or poor in imagery or even iconoclastic and foregrounds listening.[74]

Of course, the aesthetic that goes along with a particular sensational form does more than just organize vertical encounters of religious subjects with the transcendental. Aesthetics is also key to the making of religious subjects in a broader sense. Religious organizations can be characterized as having distinct sensory regimes. As Talal Asad, Charles Hirschkind and Saba Mahmood have argued, specific bodily and sensory disciplines give rise to particular sensibilities.[75] These sensibilities impart a particular sense of the self and one's being in the world—if you wish, a particular identity.[76] Religious subjects are created (ideally, that is) by a structured process—a religious didactics—in which the senses are called upon and tuned in a way that yields a habitus.[77] This process not only entails a strong emphasis on specific, privileged, sensory and extra-sensory perceptions but also the tuning down or anaesthetization of other senses or sensory perceptions.[78] We are all familiar with the fact that an overabundance of sensory perceptions may impede our—and our children's—concentration and attention;[79] techniques of meditation, for instance, are called upon to overcome such distracting perceptions and concentrate on what "really matters." Charles Hirschkind has argued that Islamic reform movements incorporate the use of mass-produced cassette sermons into an "ethics of listening," which emphasizes the importance of the ear as the key site for raising a pious Muslim subject.[80] In the midst of the soundscape of the city of Cairo, seated in taxis or in noisy environments, young Muslims create their own soundscape by listening to cassettes. In her work on the Catholic charismatic renewal in Brazil, Zé de Abreu has shown that the priest and pop star Marcello Rossi is able to tune tens of thousands of people into "the aerobics of Jesus," which entails distinct breathing techniques to induce an exhilarating, albeit ephemeral, feeling.[81]

My plea to pay more attention to sensational forms and aesthetics is driven by the wish to better understand the genesis and sustenance of religious experiences and feelings. Of course, religious aesthetics do not operate in an, as it were, automatic manner but are transmitted in concrete social situations. Not all people are prepared to open themselves up in the same way, and there are different degrees of participation, ranging from striving to emulate the ideal religious subject to a more casual and diffuse affiliation. Such differences, and the extent to which religious aesthetics do or do not work, need to be investigated in concrete research settings. We also need to realize that the creation of religious subjects in our contemporary world occurs in a broader context, which is characterized, more often than not, by experiences of fragmentation and distraction. The extent to which religious followers are actually prepared fully to adopt the sensory regimes and bodily disciplines that characterize particular religious organizations varies widely. This also depends on the will and capacity of religious authorities to influence and control believers' behavior, either via external structures of authority or internalized modes of self-control. Religions also differ in the degree to which they advocate sensory regimes that are conducive to generating intense religious sensations and the kind of sensations—from joy and bliss to terror and fear—that predominate.

Still, it seems that religious sensory regimes allow many people to make sense of—and regain their senses in—our increasingly fragmented and distracted world. Conversely, given the plethora of sense impressions ventured via the mass media, religious authorities appear to find it increasingly difficult to tune the senses and to shape and link the bodies of their members in an enduring manner.[82] In our contemporary world, many people seem to crave the kind of existential security that is one of the trademarks of religion, a point that also receives attention in the research program Constructing Human Security in a Globalizing World at the Free University of Amsterdam. As I have explained, however, by adopting modern media and new sensational forms, religions themselves become subject to the very forces of fragmentation and distraction that they claim to remedy.

The bodily and sensory disciplines implied in making religious subjects are also key to invoking and affirming links among religious practitioners. In this sense, aesthetics is central to the making of religious communities. Style is a core aspect of religious aesthetics.[83] Inducing as well as expressing shared moods, a shared religious style—materialized in, for example, collective prayer, a shared corpus of songs, images, symbols, and rituals, but also a similar style of clothing and material culture—makes people feel at home. Thriving on repetition and serialization, style induces a mode of participation via techniques of mimesis and emulation that yields a particular habitus. In a world of constant change, style offers some degree of continuity and stability (though style is at the same time subject to change, as styles come and go). In this sense, style is the sine qua non of identity. Sharing a common aesthetic style via a common religious affiliation not only generates feelings of togetherness and speaks to, as well as mirrors, particular moods and sentiments: such experiences of sharing also modulate people into a particular, common appearance, and thus underpin a collective religious identity.

Attention to the aesthetic dimension of religion enables us above all to grasp the perspective—or should I say perceptions—of insiders. This kind of understanding has of old been one of the central concerns in the anthropology of religion.[84] Paying attention to religious aesthetics and sensory regimes in a comparative manner, of course, highlights the relativity of each of these regimes. And yet, as suggested earlier, I would find it short-sighted to circumscribe these regimes and the religious subjects and communities they create as "mere constructions." Such a qualification has an all too derogatory slant, in that it makes it seem as if what is constructed might not really exist. But, as Bruno Latour has pointed out, there is nothing beyond construction, and thus we had better take constructions seriously.[85] The fact is, religious aesthetics and the sensory regimes entailed by it modulate people of flesh and blood, seeking to inscribe religion into their bones. In the context of their religion, believers are not only subject to bodily disciplines and particular sensory regimes, but their bodies may also be authorized as harbingers of ultimate truth and authenticity.[86] Exactly for this reason, believers are able to perceive and by the same token authorize the *mediated* experiences of their encounter with the transcendental as *immediate* and *authentic*.[87] Conversely, the perceived failure to have certain religious experiences—for instance, the feeling of being in touch with God—may yield skepticism and doubt, and ultimately make a person say farewell to his or her religion.

Interestingly, once implanted in a person, religious aesthetics may endure independently of exterior religious regimes or an active religious affiliation. Anyone having decided to step out of a particular religion may be puzzled about the resilience of particular religiously induced bodily disciplines and sensory practices, which it may be impossible to shed entirely.[88] A good many ex-Protestants are still gripped by a diffuse feeling of awe when they hear the sound of a church organ. In Holland there are many post-Calvinists who regard themselves as secular and yet espouse an aesthetics that is deeply rooted in Calvinism. In situations of religious change, people may feel torn between the sensory modalities of the religion they embrace and that of the religion they have left behind.

African converts to Christianity may still feel touched—or even get possessed—by the sound of "pagan" drums.[89]

Conversely, encounters with a new religion often work through the body, making it difficult for researchers to maintain an outsider's position. Many anthropologists have reported how they have been sucked into the sensory modes of the religion they have studied, without even being aware of it—as in the case of Susan Harding, who found her mind being taken over by the voice of the Baptist pastor who had been preaching to her for more than four hours.[90] Such examples stress the importance of aesthetics in underpinning people's sense of belonging and being in the world. But taking into account the aesthetic dimension of religion may also help us realize why it is that religious people may feel offended, or even hurt, when they are confronted with blasphemous images or sacrilegious acts, from Christians' being shocked by desecrating images of Mary or the crucifixion staged by pop singer Madonna in her 2006 performance, to Muslims' distress over illicit representations of the prophet about which we now hear so much in the news.[91] Precisely because religious mediations objectify the transcendental in sensational forms that call upon the body and tune the senses of religious practitioners so as to invest these forms with ultimate truth, emphasis on the aesthetic dimension of religion is indispensable. Indeed, focusing on mass media and religious mediation calls for attention to the senses and the body. Therefore, in our research we need to explore how modern media and the body, the audio-visual and the material, intersect.[92] Important questions for further research are: What kinds of bodily disciplines and sensory regimes are peculiar to particular religious organizations, including both those that belong to major world religions and new modes of spirituality, as in New Age? What are the differences? Which senses do specific sensational forms, from the Bible to virtual sites of worship in cyberspace, from icons to mass-produced posters, address? What impact do religious aesthetics have on the making and appeal of religious identities, and on the dynamics of exclusion and inclusion of which they are part? How do religious aesthetics relate to other identities, and why and how do they survive, even though a person may leave a particular religion?

Power

The last theme I will address concerns the vast issue of power. In a sense, I have been addressing the question of power throughout this essay, trying to show that religious aesthetics deploy, affirm, and sustain particular sensory perceptions, experiences, and thoughts, even granting them the status of "truth," at the expense of other experiences and thoughts. If closing off other possibilities that may not even have been conceived and vesting particular sensory perceptions, experiences, and thoughts with truth is what power achieves, then religion is power *pur sang*.[93]

Rather than focusing on religion from a perspective from "within," as I have done so far, in this section I wish briefly to situate contemporary religion in society, that is, as embedded in political and economic power structures. Let me begin with political power and the question of the nation-state. In the introduction I intimated that what we mistakenly take for a universal definition of religion actually mirrors the (ideal) role and place of religion in modern times. Many scholars have argued that religion as we know it in the West today arose gradually in the aftermath of the Reformation. With the rise of modern nation-states, a new power balance between religion and the political emerged. Increasingly, religion was held to be placed outside of the domain of power, devoted to the task of assigning to believers symbols that help them make sense of the world and orient themselves within it. The idea that modern religion is subject to secularization and hence confined to the private sphere and the inner self expresses an ideology more than a historical reality. But it is still true that religion's place and role in society became subject to the power of the modern nation-state. In the Netherlands, for example, until the 1960s religion offered the grid for the organization of society in pillars, the remains of which are still with us today.

In the course of colonization, the modern state was introduced all over the world. While the notion of the "imagined community of the nation" could not be implemented in entirely different political contexts as if it were a transportable module, the right to exercise control over religion and the supernatural or transcendental in general, claimed by colonial and later postcolonial states, instigated new relationships between religion and politics.[94] Recently, Oscar Salemink, for instance, has pointed out how the Marxist Vietnamese state carefully orchestrates the coexistence of different religious affiliations in public national rituals.[95] While it seems that the state is still more or less in charge, there are indications that it proves increasingly difficult to hold religion in check.

Ironically, religion thrives in the wake of IMF-instigated policies in favor of "democratization" and plays a major role in current politics of belonging. The balance of power between religions and states seems to be changing. In a host of contexts, politicians make sincere attempts to negotiate and even surf along with the appeal of Fundamentalist or Pentecostal Christianity, Islamic reform movements, or Hindu nationalism. How religious identities, formed as they are by distinct bodily disciplines and sensory regimes and vested with the aura of truth, relate to national and other identities is a question that calls for our utmost attention. Are religious identities, as called into being by, for example, Pentecostalism or Islamic reform movements, so compelling because they entail a religious aesthetics that not only forms subjects in a way that goes beneath the skin but also vests them with the power of God? To what extent can secular identities compete with this strong appeal to the sublime? What does it mean for our understanding of politics that politicians such as George W. Bush, in their post 9/11 speeches, tap into religious language all the time?

The relation of transformation between religion and politics cannot be analyzed without taking into account the global spread of capitalism, which institutes new ways of organizing production and consumption, and brings forth, as much as it requires, a new ethics and aesthetics.[96] We need to investigate how all kinds of practices of religious mediation and the sensational forms produced and sustained by these practices are situated in the broader power structures that characterize neo-liberal capitalism.[97] My point here is, of course, not to launch an outdated view of capitalism in terms of a simplistic (so-called vulgar) Marxist economic determinism. It is entirely inappropriate to regard religion as merely an ideology that reflects and sustains a particular mode of production. This, of course, was the key point made by Max Weber in his *The Protestant Ethic and the Spirit of Capitalism*. While Weber stressed the elective affinity between the Protestant work ethic and the rise of capitalism, he neglected the sphere of consumption, as has been pointed out by Collin Campbell.[98] In our time, it is of eminent concern to investigate how religious organizations of all kinds relate to the spheres of both production and consumption.

Let me return to Pentecostalism once again. As David Martin has argued, Pentecostalism, with its emphasis on a "mobile self" and a "portable charismatic identity," is a religion that speaks to experiences of dislocation, fragmentation, and increasing mobility.[99] While one can certainly discern an extraordinary consonance between Pentecostalism and neo-liberal capitalism, the question still is how both are thought to be related. In the study of Pentecostalism, one often comes across the proposition that conversion to this religion helps people cope with the intricacies of modern life. With their emphasis on an individual, born-again religiosity, which severs people from family-based networks of mutual obligations, their strict morality, which rejects alcohol, sexual promiscuity, and other vices, and their overall methodological mode of conduct, Pentecostal churches empower members to improve their socioeconomic position in society. While I would not deny that conversion to Pentecostalism may be of help in solving everyday problems, I still find it problematic to explore the consonance of Pentecostalism and capitalism merely through the prism of coping.

This view of religion as a reactive force fails to consider the extent to which Pentecostalism, or other contemporary religions, may actually be formed by and partake in the culture of neo-liberal capitalism. I have already pointed out that, far from retreating into the sphere of religion, in the sense of a relatively autonomous, semi-private realm, Pentecostals instigate a Christian mass culture that inevitably gets caught up with the forces of entertainment, as well as politics. Pentecostal-charismatic churches are run as global business corporations and feature as icons of ultimate presence and success. Embracing the Gospel of Prosperity, they regard wealth as a divine blessing. All this suggests that Pentecostal-charismatic churches easily adopt and incorporate themselves into the culture of neo-liberal capitalism, so successfully that it becomes impossible to state where religion begins or ends.

I have invoked Pentecostal-charismatic churches because they are part of my own expertise, not because I would like to suggest a specific elective affinity between this religion and neo-liberal capitalism. Examples of the entanglement of other religious organizations with capitalism abound. In the press we read about the seamless articulation of Confucian or Buddhist work ethics into capitalist labor in Southeast Asia.[100] It is of great importance to develop comparative research to investigate how religious groups and movements in different localities not only relate to and help people cope with but are also formed by the culture of neo-liberal capitalism.

But what, then, is capitalism, we may feel pressed to ask? In a fragment that has received attention only quite recently, Walter Benjamin has characterized capitalism as a religion that "essentially serves to satisfy the same worries, anguish and disquiet formerly answered by so-called religion."[101] In his view, capitalist consumer culture has developed into a new kind of undogmatic cult that makes people worship the secret God of debt. This is more an intuition than a conclusion based on sound analysis. Benjamin, indeed, found it difficult to "prove capitalism's religious structure," given that "we cannot draw close the net in which we stand."[102] The fragment remained unfinished. The big question he raises is from which standpoint it might be possible to grasp power—as that which underpins everything that is—in our contemporary world. There may be good reason to agree with Fredric Jameson's idea of capitalism as a sublime power that resists representation, yet all the more requires to be understood.[103] Research on religion, conducted along the lines outlined here, may be of some use in helping us unmask this sublime power, without, however, denying its capacity to capture as much as to puzzle us.

Conclusion

Although I am an anthropologist, in my title I have invoked the study of contemporary religion rather than the anthropology of religion. My point is that anthropology has much to offer but can also gain from interdisciplinary exchanges with scholars not only in the broader social sciences but also in religious studies, visual culture, philosophy, and theology. We need to ground our understanding of contemporary religion in thorough ethnographic studies and broader comparisons. It is my sincere hope that in this essay I have been able to make clear why and how media, aesthetics, and power matter in this endeavor. All three are useful points of entry that allow us to explore the making of contemporary religious experience. I do not use the term *matter* by accident. My plea to pay attention to (1) the modern media that play a role in objectifying the transcendental into material, sensational forms, (2) the particular religious aesthetics that modulate the body and tune the senses in a specific way, and (3) power as bringing into being subjects and communities with distinctive religious identities and styles stresses the importance of approaching religion from a material angle. Clearly this is a materiality that is not opposed to, but rather a condition for, spirituality. Indeed, the fact that religion matters so much in our contemporary world is grounded in the very concrete, material dimension of religion that I have tried to outline here. Inducing sensations through sensational forms, contemporary religion is not just about ideas and interpretations but is relevant to our being and belonging in a more basic sense.

Can Television Mediate Religious Experience?

The Theology of *Joan of Arcadia*

Angela Zito

American prime-time television has recently seen a number of programs that deal with spiritual issues from various perspectives.[1] These
wildly successful primetime dramas have included the much-older
Highway to Heaven and its successor *Touched by an Angel* (both featuring angels on earthly missions among ordinary people), *Buffy, the Vam-
pire Slayer,* popular among young people for its heroine who secretly
fights against evil spirits, and science-fiction shows like *The X-files*,
which had the FBI investigating strange phenomena from alien space-
ships to extrasensory perception.[2] These shows raise interesting questions about "theology and its publics" in the U.S. context. What form
does religious discourse take in public spaces in a country dedicated to
the separation of church and state? Is mass-media entertainment, in
fact, an "open space" for such discourse to appear in a politically non-
conflictual fashion? Can such entertainments be described as "theological" and if so, what sort of theology is it?

In this essay, I will discuss one of these programs, *Joan of Arcadia*,
which aired for two seasons (from fall 2003 to spring 2005) on Friday
nights at 8 P.M. on the CBS network. *Joan of Arcadia* takes off from the
story of St. Joan of Arc, the young heroine who led the armies of medieval France upon divine command. In the TV version, Joan is an ordinary teenager to whom God—the God of Christianity—appears on a
daily basis, giving her tasks to perform that will quietly transform the
everyday life of her family and friends. The show did well enough, but
due to a ratings drop was cancelled in May 2005. Nonetheless, it provides us with much food for thought.

I will first introduce debates about religion in primetime U.S. television, discuss "mediation" in the deep theoretical sense of the term to
understand how it intertwines with religion, and then analyze *Joan of*

Arcadia using excerpts from the pilot episode, interviews with its creators, and the writings of critics, bloggers, and fans.[3] I will propose that we might compare "process theology" and New Age conventions in making sense of the theological implications of the show but conclude that these hermeneutic attentions to the text of the show are, in the end, trumped by the performative action of its cancellation.

Religion on TV

Protestant Christians in the United States were very early users of "televangelism," employing the medium of TV for preaching and fundraising on an ever-increasing scale.[4] If at first this programming was marginal, the past fifteen years have seen a startling growth in what one might almost call a parallel universe of media production by fundamentalist evangelical Christians in America. These productions include: radio; pop, rock, and country music; movies; and entire TV broadcasting networks, which produce programming of every sort, from cartoons to news to talk shows to drama.[5] Though surely it has exerted some influence on taste, that is not the world I am discussing: I am talking about mainstream network broadcasting, a realm of television that, until recently, was known for shying away from any sort of overt religious themes, especially in the evening primetime hours. A realm, in short, known as "secular."[6]

When people argue over religion on *that* sort of television, the terms of the debate seem to follow what I consider the three main areas of intersection between religion and media more generally, as we study it at New York University's Center for Religion and Media:[7] religion *in* the media, religious people's *use of* media, and how media can function in ways similar to religion. A conference at the University of California at Los Angeles in 1995 brought together religious leaders, media makers, and scholars to discuss *Religion in Primetime Television*—the title of the proceedings, published in 1997. The religious leaders were mostly interested in how religion appears on TV: Are its images positive? Are there any at all, or is religion ignored? They argued that religion is too profound a part of human life to be left out of such an important medium. But it must also be noted that, as believers, they felt that they, like anyone else who constitutes a community in the United States, were entitled to see themselves on television.

This interested stance by religious leaders provoked anxiety on the part of the attending scholars, who were not particularly in favor of more religious programming. Michael Suman notes that the most vocal critics of a dearth of TV programming on religion are among the Christian right. It is not that they are simply in favor of "religion in general"; rather, he notes, "What is most important to them is not that people are religious in some way, but that they are religious in a particular way, their way."[8]

The third group of participants in the conference, the media makers, noted that introducing religion into TV programs has the potential of alienating great portions of the possible audience. The networks especially, with their emphasis on wide audience, have historically shied away from the niche marketing left to cable TV. So the mid-nineties answered the question of whether mass-mediated entertainment like TV can or should provide open space for religious discourse very cautiously. Anxiety over content ran high. In ten years, the situation altered radically. As TV critic Gloria Goodale wrote in 2005, "religious-themed programming is here to stay."[9] She notes long- and short-term trends.

First, Hollywood has discovered the evangelical Christian audience, estimated to be 25 to 75 million strong, as a new advertising niche. As the Christian media industry I mentioned above has distributed its novels, music, and films through stores like Wal-Mart, those products become ever more visible. It was the blockbuster success of *The Passion of the Christ* in 2004, however, that really opened producers' eyes.[10] In fact, Jeff Zucker, head of NBC Universal Television Group, said candidly of religion, "We looked at it as something that was underserved in network television."[11] Second, the baby-boomer generation has matured and is searching for values in life. This search may not lead to institutionalized religion, but it does lead to "spirituality."[12] Third, after September 11, the media chose to play up—following the lead of the U.S. government—a religiously inflected picture of the "War on Terror." And finally, the availability of wonderful special effects calls forth plots of the miraculous.[13] These many reasons why religion appears more often on television address the first two aspects of "religion and media": how the media treat religion and how religious people mediate themselves.

Here I am most interested in exploring a third possibility: whether and how media themselves can function religiously, a possibility that rests upon understanding both religion and media as aspects of "mediation" more generally. What aspects of a show induce audience commitment to combine the fervor of personal, ongoing devotional attention with community building as fans? When a show's content is specifically religious, a powerful possibility for theology in public is produced.[14] That being so, what happens when the interior of a theological plot crashes into the encompassing material circumstances of its production?

Of Mediation

What do I mean by "mediation in the deep theoretical sense of the word"? In a dialectical model of the construction of social reality, people are constantly engaged in producing the material world around them, even as they are, in turn, produced by it.[15] Every social practice moves through and is carried upon a material framework or vehicle. One can follow this line of theorization from the Marxist Bakhtin circle in the Soviet Union in the 1920s, especially in the writing of V. N. Vološinov, who noted that "the existence of the sign is nothing but the materialization of (that) communication" to its later bourgeois incarnation in Clifford Geertz's cultural anthropology.[16] The critical theory of the Frankfort School has contributed consistently to viewing culture as that which *"mediates* the interaction between the material and the mental, the economic and the socio-political."[17] This active sense of world making lies at the heart of the antipositivist mission of critical theory and of the turn toward practice in the social sciences in general, especially in the British cultural studies of the Birmingham School and certain strands of American cultural anthropology. It takes strict empirical account of the world as it exists without assuming that this world is forever given as it is, as an unchanging facticity. As both historian and anthropologist, I find it important to station an analytic between embodied actors and the things of the world, grasping their mutual constitution as a process of mediation, always giving sufficient attention to possibilities of agency.[18]

People are aware of these processes of endless mediation to differing degrees. Take language. All humans are meant to speak it, and for most of us it just appears when we open our mouths. But for poets and ad copywriters, every word is precious and carefully wrought, producing a language resistant with a life of its own. We might, in an older idiom, say "reified." That would imply, however, that someday de-reification would come and we could live in an im-mediate reality, when in fact such a sense of "natural" immediacy is itself a mediated effect. The production of social life proceeds so well because most of us do not notice it happening and proceed to devote our energies to the world unhampered by self-reflexivity. It provides us with a ground of "natural" culture, which functions like a bowl of water in which we swim like fish, unaware of the edge or end of our horizon of survival.[19]

Language and the gesturing bodies that speak it may be the most naturalizing media through which human life takes place.[20] At the opposite end of the spectrum are entire industries of media production—print, radio, television, film, video, the Internet—which, in a world of increasing commodification, appear as reified products for consumption.[21] And yet, the complexity of the media industries' productions, which include their own constant publicity, results in many moments of self-conscious disclosure of their processes of signification (e.g., the many "Making of . . ." documentaries, Entertainment News on broadcast and cable TV, tabloid magazines, "Reality TV," etc) Thus the machinations of artifice become more and more obvious to more and more people. People face their mediated representations more forthrightly—noticing that someone might be in charge of them, that they might be experiencing an interruption of the imagined flow of authentic, im-mediate experience. We then see efforts to seize the means of mediated production, a phenomenon increasingly found in indigenous and religious communities worldwide.[22] Just as often, however, people rush in the opposite direction, giving vent to longing for im-mediate, authentic experience, relieved of such burdens of knowledge, sure that if only we could turn off the TV, we would all have a better grasp on the truth of our lives.

The practices often named "religion"—as a subset of the processes of the mediation of social life that I have just described—have much in common with the problems of the

727

media. Religion, like the media and mediations of all sorts, also functions best when no one notices it, when people appropriate it as an always-already present aspect of social life. Yet religious believers also have had prophetic epiphanies and transformations at times of self-reflexive understanding, and certainly the longing for "religious experience" as the definition of "the spiritual," that ever-present default position in modern religious life, reveals a similar wish for im-mediate, unmediated reality.

So, from the point of view of the mediation of social life, "religion" and "media" can be seen to function in surprisingly intimate ways and to form even more potent forms of social practice when deliberately intertwined.[23] They both involve and mobilize epistemological and cosmological matters of the constitution of the real. The stakes could hardly be higher and in their details raise questions of great import for theorizing. As media theorist James Carey notes: "Reality is a scarce resource . . . the fundamental form of power is the power to define, allocate and deploy that resource."[24]

Joan of Arcadia: Casting God?

Joan of Arcadia was the creation of Barbara Hall, an experienced television writer and producer who is now a practicing Catholic. The show first aired on September 29, 2003, was nominated for an Emmy, and received the People's Choice Award for Best New Drama. Despite these successes, it was cancelled in May 2005, to the surprise and dismay of its writers, cast, and fans. The reason given was that its audience had dropped from 10.1 million in the first year to 8 million by the end of the second season. More significant was the demographic of the audience: a mean age of 53.9. CBS, driven by advertising, anxiously pursues the younger audience, aged 18 to 49, and that season replaced a number of successful shows with new ones for the fall. As Les Moonves, president of CBS, said of a new show where a young woman speaks to the dead: "I think talking to ghosts will skew younger than talking to God."[25]

Joan of Arcadia tells the story of a young high-school student to whom God begins to speak in the form of various people she meets in her daily life: first a "cute guy," then a cafeteria worker, a jogger, a little girl playing in a park, a fat construction worker . . . the list is endless, extending during the two seasons to a dog walker, an old woman who manifests as a nurse, a school volunteer, a Goth student, and so on.[26] Neither Joan nor the audience knows when God will pop up. Joan's family has just moved to the town of Arcadia, where her dad has taken over as police chief. Her mother is an artist who has given up painting, and her younger brother is a brilliant young scientist/geek. But it is her older brother who provides a kind of moral engine to the show: he is now paralyzed and in a wheelchair after a car accident—once a powerful athlete bound for college on a scholarship, he is a despairing young man who provides the show's sense of theodical urgency as the family grapples with the question of why such a terrible thing could happen.

The opening of the show's pilot episode cuts back and forth between a crime scene and Joan asleep in bed. It is very dreamy. Is the crime real or Joan's dream? A voice calls her, she wakes, but rejects it by putting on her headphones to listen to music . . . Was that God? The audience wonders . . . Then we meet the family at breakfast, and we realize that the police chief from the crime scene the night before is her father.

Everyone has agreed that the show's innovation lay in introducing God as an actual character. Bob Gale, writer and producer, pointed out how dangerous this can be to dramatic plotting: he fantasized about what would happen if you had a show where people prayed, hoping God would answer—and decided, based on the theological proposition that God can do anything and might indeed answer, that the result would be profoundly boring.[27] Barbara Hall faces this theological dilemma directly by reversing the action: God takes the initiative, appearing to Joan unexpectedly, speaking through random people she encounters, and assigning her mysterious tasks, whose reasons only become clear as the plot unfolds. Neither Joan nor the audience knows what will happen. God has a plan; Joan has doubts. God is like the writer; Joan is the actor who (along with the audience) must make sense of the script. Clearly, the dramatic possibilities rest upon *how God is written as a character*.

Theological issues arise on two levels. First, how is God imagined by humans? And second, should God be imagined and "cast" this way at all? Various traditional, biblically oriented Christian critics objected to the show precisely because they think God should not be represented. Stephen Keels, a youth minister at Good Shepherd Community Church, disliked seeing God portrayed in human form at all. He maintained that "the series creates a God with limitations that he [Keels] cannot accept."[28] He might have objected, as well, that the show's "God" was not declared to be the Christian God per se, but was resolutely nondenominational, thus skirting the ongoing problem of network TV—that of alienating a portion of audience demographic by too narrowly casting the religious message.

By contrast, most commentators embraced the premise of the show: that God is among us and can take human form. They described him as manifesting in the everyday; as being "the one you talk to in turbulence over the Atlantic Ocean" (Joe Mantegna, who plays Joan's father); as "personal" and not "religious" (Amber Tamblyn, who plays Joan); as a "sort of cosmic super shrink"; as working through nonreligious people; yet, despite this closeness to human reality, as ultimately "mysterious."[29]

Let us look at a few manifestations of God to Joan. Eight minutes into the first episode, Joan meets a cute boy on the bus. He follows her to school, starting up a conversation. He explains that he was standing outside her window that morning after she got dressed for school. She gets very angry and says:

JOAN: What are you talking about? What do you want with me? Because I 've got to warn you, my dad's a cop. Not just any cop, he is THE cop . . .

GOD: I know who your father is . . .

J (frightened): Who are you?

G: I've known you since before you were born. I'm God.

J: I'm going to ask you one more time . . .

G: I'm God.

J: You're what?

G: God.

J (long pause): Don't ever talk to me again.

When he tells her he is God, she rejects him as crazy. Joan tries to avoid him, but he finds her again after class. She greets him sarcastically with, "Hey, God, get lost. I mean it!" But he perseveres, telling her things about herself no one could possibly know: "You said you'd study hard, stop talking back, clean your room, and even go to church if I let your brother live."

Joan begins to believe him, and listens as the boy as God says:

"Let me explain something: I don't look like this. I don't look like anything you'd recognize. You can't see me. I don't sound like this. I don't sound like anything you'd recognize. You see, I'm beyond your experience. I take this form because you're comfortable with it. It makes sense to you. Do you get it?" Joan then confesses that she is not religious. He answers—in a key point of the show's theology—"It's not about religion, Joan. It's about fulfilling your nature."

In this conversation Joan is slowly convinced because of God's intimate knowledge of her past, especially her prayers when her brother nearly died. He gives her a first, mysterious, task—to get a job in a bookstore. And we learn that God has no fixed form, that he "appears" solely that Joan may "see."

In the final short scene, God contacts Joan again, because she has not gotten that job in the bookstore—and God has changed! Joan is in line in the school cafeteria, getting her lunch. An elderly black woman serving behind the food counter suddenly asks seriously, "How come you didn't get the job?" Joan is completely startled—just as he warned, this time God looks completely different. She is nervous and annoyed and demands, "Could we possibly talk about this somewhere else?" And the old woman as God answers sharply, "Well, just do what I tell you and we won't have to discuss it. Couldn't be easier. Move on now. You're holding up the line."

The rest of the pilot episode shows Joan getting the job, with the surprising result that her older brother in the wheelchair is shamed by his younger sister's initiative while he is complaining about his life and refusing to go out in the world. He tells her she has inspired him to look for a job and move on with his life. Now that we have met "God" as a cast member, let us turn to the theological arguments about his representation in this show.

Douglas Leblanc, founder of *getreligion.org*, an online religious magazine, writes in a story for *Christianity Today* that the show can be theologically misleading. "*Joan* requires that Christians check their credulity at the door. God's instructions to Joan are often mysterious. . . . These revelations are not specific enough to withstand a testing by Scripture, by any historic creed, or even by messages Joan might hear in church. . . . *Joan of Arcadia* is not a source of systematic theology, even at a popular level."[30] He also notes the objections to God's appearance at all as an affront to the rejection of "graven images" but overall approves of the show's ethical value.

Other Christian critics have objected to the absence of Jesus, since it is a tenet of evangelical Christianity that the way to the Father lies only through salvation in the Son—at least since the New Testament. But Catholic priest and author Andrew Greeley writes very positively about the show, saying: "Producer Barbara Hall asks the really important questions about God—who he is, what's he up to, why he sometimes seems to go away, why he permits bad things to happen. God, in the various forms in which he appears to Joan, provides no easy answers to these questions. Rather He or She is usually content with two claims (1) He knows what he is doing even if we can't figure it out, and (2) He loves all of us."[31]

Greeley finds the show squarely in a theological stream he calls the "Hidden God" tradition, dating back at least to Saint Augustine. In this tradition, God is unpredictable, unfathomable, and "ineffable." Though "most Americans don't think this kind of God is fair," Greeley approves of the mysterious power God displays on the show, even as he appears in human form right next to Joan. This power does not take the form of fancy special-effects miracles but rather appears in the show as a kind of conversational reticence. As Greeley says: "He does not explain or apologize, much less give political advice. Any god who is not mysterious is not God. Any god who is willing to play our game is not God. Any god who whispers answers to important questions in our waiting ears is not God." He describes this Hidden God, in the theological tradition of St. Augustine, Kevin Smith (director of the film *Dogma*), and Barbara Hall, as "a mysterious and unpredictable reality, a God of implacable love and constant surprises."[32]

Barbara Hall—the show's creator and producer, and thus, in this case, the creator of God, as it were—obviously does not accept the theological premise that God is unrepresentable. Recall that one of the first things God explains to Joan is that he must take form, mediate himself, so that she can experience him at all. Hall felt that about ten million viewers did not mind seeing God everywhere. She was hyper-aware, however, of the problems of writing him as a character, thus returning us to the first theological issue above. She honed a quite precise vision of how her show's writers should imagine God—even cleverly putting out what she called her "Ten Commandments":

1. God cannot directly intervene.
2. Good and evil exist.
3. God can never identify one religion as being right.
4. The job of every human being is to fulfill his or her true nature.
5. Everyone is allowed to say no to God, including Joan.
6. God is not bound by time—this is a human concept.
7. God is not a person and does not possess a human personality.
8. God talks to everyone all the time in different ways.
9. God's plan is what is good for us, not what is good for Him.
10. God's purpose for talking to Joan, and to everyone, is to get her (us) to recognize the interconnectedness of all things, i.e. you cannot hurt a person without hurting yourself; all of your actions have consequences; God can be found in the smallest actions; God expects us to learn and grow from all our experiences. However, the exact nature of God is a mystery, and the mystery can never be solved.[33]

Hall's theology is close to Andrew Greeley's vision: a loving yet mysterious God who works through human beings, who makes suggestions, leaving plenty of room for choice, free will, and thus human agency.[34] In the show's stories, direct, im-mediate experience of God is avoided. This is not mysticism; God is experienced by Joan socially, through the medium of other speaking and gesturing bodies. She herself serves as God's medium to do his will in the world—when she gets up the nerve and stops doubting. In this sense, God is grasped by humanity only as an immanent presence. We are in a linguistic epistemology: no language, no God. Seen in this way, Hall's theological vision is profoundly anthropocentric, placing the acting person (in this case, literally the "actors") at the hub of a cosmology.

Many people have commented in the press on how much they appreciate this human-centered notion of God, how very comforting they find Him. Jason Ritter, who plays the crippled Kevin on the show, says: "I think a lot of people are liking the God we are portraying. I've had people come up to me and say 'I believe in that God! Find me a religion that has that God—a loving God that's all-inclusive and without punishment!'"[35] Yet there may be other ways to read this representation of divine presence.

New Age or Christian Theology?

The cosmology of the show likewise poses the interpenetration of good and evil. Following Hall's second writers' commandment: "Good and evil exist," the show has built into it the terrible crimes that Joan's father must solve almost every week. This was done to keep things from becoming too simple and sentimental. As Hall puts it in the producer's voiceover on the DVD version of the pilot episode: "The idea that good and evil exist. . . .

is part of the ten commandments [for writing the show] because I am not interested in talking about God in a benign universe. That's not an interesting entity to deal with. It's trying to deal with God when we have to confront in a world where there are serial killers."

Her production partner, James Hayman, who has directed several episodes, agrees: "Good can't exist without evil . . . without it, we would not be able to explore the good. Those things have to co-exist. They don't have any meaning without each other. If you look at any spiritual path, that's the concept—you have to have one to have the other."

Significantly, Hayman refers to "any spiritual path." In a crucial moment in God's first dialogue with Joan, she says: "I'm not religious, you know." And he replies "It's not about religion, Joan. It's about fulfilling your nature." Indeed, many moments in the show's total of forty-eight episodes reinforce this turn away from organized religious practice toward what Americans call "spirituality." Neither Joan nor her family ever goes to church; the only clergy we meet are a rather ineffectual young Catholic priest, the rabbi father of one of Joan's friends, and a nun who has left her order. Hall said in an interview: "We forget that this is a very spiritual country. . . . People have always been open to questions of spirituality . . . and it's non-denominational. There simply seems to be a large number of people with a spiritual bent."[36]

One online critic of the show named this sort of spirituality "New Age." Elliot B. Gertel not only notes that "the religion it advances is New Age doctrine" but goes on at great length to analyze how this New Ageism leads to anti-Semitic stereotyping of the show's various Jewish characters. Gertel notes that "New Age manifestos depict Jews as unspiritual—earthly, lustful, perpetually insensitive," while "New Age writers" insist that "monotheistic religions like Judaism [or Christianity or Islam] imprison people with ritual and requirements that stifle true spirituality."[37] We should especially note Gertel's point that a number of beliefs associated with New Age religiosity quite deliberately skew a classically monotheistic view of divinity. These ideas include:

1. There are many paths to a single divine source. Thus, all religions are basically versions of one truth, and the truly spiritual can see through their differences to the underlying meaning.
2. There is an emphasis upon personal experience rather than doctrine.
3. The true or deeper self is divine.
4. Our purpose as humans is to cultivate this deep self so as to connect with the divine forces of the cosmos.
5. The universe is in a state of constant becoming, in which we share.[38]

"Spirituality's" emphasis upon the self and its personal creativity has profoundly influenced the arts in the United States.[39] This seems to be to be reflected in Hall's "Ten Commandments," which seize the power to "create God" (as she often has put it) for her writers, celebrating artistic human creativity in a compelling way as encompassing in its agency the creation of its Creator. However, the turn to "spirituality" has also been critiqued as a symptom of radical possessive individualism, a kind of ultimate privatization of religion made famous by Robert Bellah's description of Sheila Larson, the nurse who described her religion as "her own little voice: Sheilaism."[40] Writer Austin Bunn criticizes the show: "Joan's idea of morality is a clueless stumble toward self-actualization. . . . It's a message perfectly tuned for audiences interested in spirituality."[41]

Yet the undoubted presence of peoples' allegiance to this self-description in America does open the door to public discussion of ethics and values. As Hall herself says:

> [The show] came out of my process of studying world religions. After Sept 11, there was a paradigm shift and people were willing to talk about issues of faith. Lots on TV about 9/11 about how it affected people's faith. I was fascinated by that. The character of Will the dad is based on stories of people who did courageous things in 9/11 but they weren't religious, it wasn't about faith, about God, it was just about the right thing to do. And I love the idea of morality, of people who have an innate sense of right and wrong not based on religion but because they're good people.[42]

Rather than dismiss such popular entertainment as silly distraction, or such folk notions of spirituality as merely diluting and degrading real religion from a golden past, it seems to me to be more useful to investigate actual theological genealogies for such discourses. One place we might turn is to "process theology."

Process theology grew out of an engagement with theories of Darwinian evolution and Einsteinian relativity. These provided models of a dynamic, ever-changing cosmos at the turn of the twentieth century. At that time, familiarity with Buddhism was also a factor. William James, John Dewey, Henri Bergson, and especially Pierre Teilhard de Chardin and Alfred North Whitehead drew upon these cosmological shifts in their creation of new social theory and theology. American process theology, especially as formulated by Charles Hartshorne, took from Whitehead a sense of God as dynamically and intimately relating with the world, not separated from it, as in traditions after Aquinas.[43]

Whitehead's God is not the unmoved mover of Aristotle, nor is he the imperial ruler of Roman Christianity, not even "the personification of moral energy" of the Jews.[44] God is the dipolar ground of all opposites and contains the world, which operates in a similar and complementary fashion. As Whitehead says: "It is as true to say that God is one and the World many as it is to say the World is One and God is many."[45] God begins in primordial potentiality and requires the world's primordial actuality to complete him. God does not produce the world *de novo*; he arises with it, as it, of it. "He does not create the world; he saves it [in the sense of cherishing and preserving]; or more accurately he is the poet of the world, with tender patience lending it his vision of truth, beauty, and goodness."[46]

Hall's God comes as close to Whitehead's vision of a summarizing, beneficent force as it does to Greeley's loving benefactor. Her God is not personified in a principle that possesses an ontology of separate presence, but only in the flesh of the actors through whom God speaks. Hall's seventh commandment for writers says baldly: "God is not a person and does not possess a human personality." He thus lacks human-style tendencies, such as the wish to intervene (see commandment number one), or have religious preferences (see number three). Instead, his purpose is to foster what I would call a Whiteheadian understanding of the interconnection of all things (see number ten).

The God who manifests on *Joan of Arcadia* is deliberately imagined as both accessible and mysterious, willing to suggest but not impel, limited in his omnipotence by Joan's human senses. In this very embracing of contradictions, s/he also resembles the dipolar God of process theology. The connection between that theology and New Age spirituality is not direct, but they do share a genealogy. Besides influencing process theologians, who are highly philosophical speculators in the scholarly reaches of religious enclaves, post-Einsteinian physics and its cosmology of constant dynamic change has also deeply influenced important threads in New Age spirituality. From the popular (and still in-print) books in the seventies connecting physics with "Eastern Mysticism,"[47] to the independent movie hit *I Heart Huckabees* (2004), this mode of finding the universe itself sacred and responsive to human desire inverts natural science's objectified positivism, bending it to a human-centered agency and forging newly imagined connections that are labeled "spiritual" rather than utilitarian. Ironically, this impulse yields an idealist version of critical theory's rigorously antipositivist critique of science and technology.

To be fair, Hall finds "God" central to her show's power in a way that might seem to challenge this New Age hypothesis. A Beliefnet interviewer said, at the end of the show's first season in May 2004, "Yet on TV these days God seems more acceptable than ever." She answered: "But none of those shows identify God. If you want to do the supernatural, that's one thing, and I enjoy that genre, but we're trying to dramatize something that, from my vantage point, could be real. It's not some force, or energy, or the hellmouth—it's God." She then fell right into the close connection between God and science we described above as so central to progressive Christian theology in the twentieth century:

One thing I want to do is to debunk the notion that science and spirituality are natural enemies. Joseph Campbell said it's impossible to live without a mythology and it always baffled him how we live without one. But we don't. Our mythology is science—actually it's shifting now to celebrity, but we believe deeply in science. We don't realize that science is a very spiritual concept. There are aspects of it that are completely in line with spirituality. Theoretical physics to me is just the math of God. I didn't make that up—Einstein thought so.[48]

If not New Age, at least worthy of Whitehead.

Conclusion

In conclusion, I would like to return to the question of media, mediation, and their connection to the modern concept of religion. The great Mediterranean monotheisms have had a love/hate relationship with the image. Dealing with it today seems inescapable, however, and therein lies a challenge for theologies, like the one underpinning *Joan of Arcadia*, that would taken into account an electronic public. Scholars have pointed to the ritualizing dimensions of our engagement with television watching: it is repetitive, providing us with a sense of continuity in everyday life, and, most importantly, it helps us to understand ourselves in the context of a larger community.[49] In other words, television is a vehicle (along, now, with video and the Internet) that can deliver the words and *images* that socially mediate religion in powerful ways. Television, film, and video games offer the opportunity to reengage notions of the divine in a current media-saturated context. Taking an optimistic and somewhat utilitarian view of the inevitability of mediation, theologian Richard Woods puts it like this:

> Symbol and myth, the concrete elements of spirituality as the story of our life-journey, are themselves constructions of the human spirit, specifically of our *imagination*—the power to represent the world cognitively and aesthetically, especially through visualization. Image is to spirituality what concept is to theology. As images, symbol and myth are *functions of human creativity, a prime instance of our participation in the divine order itself.*[50]

Woods's collapse of human image making into the divinity of universal order reminds me very much of Barbara Hall's willingness to cast God, and thus to cast herself as the creator, producer, and director of the divine. In making a show of God among us, she illustrates the process of creatively harnessing divinity to human ends. This is presented to us as an intimate art: when God appears to Joan, the first indication of presence is usually some stranger calling her name.[51] She is hailed in that most intimate of ways—God always already knows her. As audience we are always already ready for this display of interpellation as she responds to the hailing. We oscillate between identification with the thrill of Joan's being divinely known and knowing ourselves the truth of the origins of the script: it is just a story, a story made from nothing but the human imagination.

This process of back and forth mimics our engagement with television in a larger sense, as a medium that has increasingly blurred the sense of fiction and fact. Nick Coudry points out that "media claim to connect us with a shared social reality." One needn't even include Reality TV to understand that something about television as a broadcast medium intrinsically accomplishes that sharing:

Live transmission (of anything whether a real event or a fictional narrative) guarantees that someone in the transmitting institution could interrupt it at any time and make an immediate connection to real events. What is special about live transmission is the potential connection it guarantees with real events, rather than an actual portrayal of real events themselves. . . . Liveness guarantees a potential connection to our shared social realities as they are happening. Because of this connection, "liveness" can properly be called a ritual category which contributes to the ritual space of the media.[52]

It is especially television's longstanding claim to bring us our social reality "live" that underlies the power of *Joan of Arcadia*'s representation of the divine and, paradoxically, makes it vulnerable. The show's devotion to the quotidian does double duty: its absolute rejection of special effects to carry divinity to the viewer not only presents a picture of God as available to us daily, our knowingness about Barbara Hall's writerly "theology" embeds the sense of the sacred in everyday *television* reality.

Here we see how television naturalizes itself through its claim to provide "liveness"—returning us to the point made earlier about the relationship between religion and mediation in the deep sense of that term. Mediation that can disappear, allowing the light of the divine to shine through: that is what viewers of *Joan of Arcadia* sought, even as they knew perfectly well the show was brought to them by a team of writers following their own "Ten Commandments." This gratification of the fantasy of im-mediacy was rudely interrupted, however, with the abrupt and surprising cancellation of the show on May 18, 2005.

The cast and production team were stunned; fans were outraged.[53] Ironically, the show had just made the metaphysical leap of including a representative of Satan in the form of the character Ryan Hunter—who also talked to God, he just didn't agree with the divine plan. In boldly casting its plotlines beyond the cozy sense of the divine carefully cultivated in its two successful seasons, the show managed, in an important sense, to refuse to grant immanence the last word. As it did so, this bit of popular culture finally may have had a truly late-modern "religious" moment: after bathing happily in the heart-warming pleasures of an everyday God, its audience and its makers were jolted out of a complacency summed up best by the title of an essay on the Web site failuremag.com addressing the cancellation: "A Plea to the Television Gods: Joan Fans Try to Keep the Faith."[54] These "gods" are, of course, the network executives whose decision processes are as mysterious as those of the Hidden God. At precisely this crossing of religion and popular culture, we can see how they become the "site for the negotiation of critique, remembrance and emancipatory projections."[55] Fans gathered over 23,000 signatures to bring the show back. Their Web sites hummed for over a year. As Eduardo Mendieta notes, in his discussion of critical theory's approach to religion:

> Religion gives words to non-conceptual experiences. . . . In this way religion harbors a lexicon of transcendence and anti-fetishism . . . both inexhaustible, albeit always succumbing to decay and forgetfulness, and renewable via new experiences of the liminal and numinous, albeit gropingly searching for words beyond the quotidian. . . . It is the medium in which that from which it flows is both accessed and hindered from being encountered. The concept becomes the wall between the subject and the non-conceptual . . . thus religion is to be secured by means of the relentless criticism of religion.[56]

In the struggle to make visible and then interpret encounters with the divine in *Joan of Arcadia*, Hall and her audience performed such an effort to immanentize the transcendant and overcome quotidian expectations of institutionalized religion. That they failed because of the demands of the market upon this particular technology only reminds us that the effort was real, "live," and not merely just a "story" after all. That this struggle over the articulation of theological propositions should be adjudicated in the realm of "the market" is precisely why it can occupy public space at all, why its closing off is not understood as involving issues of free speech or politics, since the price of being able to utter "religion" in the space of dramatic primetime television remains silence about the "political."

A "Sense of Possibility"

Robert Musil, Meister Eckhart, and the "Culture of Film"

Niklaus Largier

The—at least slightly—enigmatic title of this essay begs for some pre-liminary explanation. As is well known, Robert Musil plays in the very title of his novel *Der Mann ohne Eigenschaften* (*The Man Without Quali-ties*) on an expression coined by the medieval German mystic and phi-losopher Eckhart von Hochheim. In many of his sermons, Eckhart speaks of man "without qualities [*âne eigenschaften*],"[1] thus fashioning a term and a concept for a religious ideal that embodies specific aspects of detachment, freedom, and salvation. Musil's references to Eckhart in his great, unfinished novel do not end with the allusion in the title, however. In addition, he inserts into his text a series of quotes and excerpts from Meister Eckhart, whom he had read in a number of an-thologies and in the translation published by Hermann Büttner in two volumes between 1903 and 1909.[2]

The so-called Büttner edition of Eckhart's works was remarkably successful and popular during the first decades of the twentieth century. It had been studied by everybody in the intellectual world of the time, including Georg Simmel, Max Weber, Karl Mannheim, and Martin Buber, but also Ernst Bloch, Georg Lukács, and Belá Balázs. In pointing out one of the many reflections of this interest in the "mystical tradi-tion" and in Meister Eckhart, one might mention an intense and heated discussion that erupted after a lecture by Ernst Troeltsch at the First Convention of German Sociologists on the topic of the emergence of modernity.[3] The conversation focused on the relation between mystical traditions and the genesis of the modern world. At another moment, when Karl Mannheim and Georg Lukács met for the first time, they discussed Lukács's plan to write an "essay on mysticism."[4] At this point, Lukács had already translated some of Eckhart's texts, and he wrote shortly thereafter an essay, deeply inspired by his reading of Eckhart, with the title "Über die Armut am Geiste" ("On Spiritual Poverty").[5] Among the readers and translators of Eckhart's writings is Béla Balázs, an author whom we know today mainly through his book on film, *Der sichtbare Mensch, oder die Kultur des Films* (*Visible Man, or the Culture of Film*), published in Vienna in 1924. He plays a role for Musil and his engagement with Eckhart as well, since Musil wrote a review of Balázs's book that evokes—quite surprisingly—a specific relationship between the "culture of film"and its aesthetic, and a convergence of mystical experience and utopian thought.

We might be tempted to discuss this interest in Eckhart and his writings, and more generally the fascination with mystical traditions, in terms of a fashion that took hold in intellectual life shortly after the turn of the century.[6] It is indeed a surprising and intriguing phenomenon of reception that brings rather difficult and sometimes quite esoteric medieval texts into the realm of early-twentieth-century culture, philosophy, and intellectual conversation. My interest does not lie, however, in this fascination, in the nostalgia, the so-called irrationalism, and the esoteric inclinations that motivated this renaissance of mystical literature. I will not focus on the historical aspects of reception and influence, either. Instead, I want to discuss the productive side of how Musil uses some of his often quite fragmented references to Eckhart—references in which he explores the possibilities of how to read Eckhart and how to deploy a specific critical and utopian discourse on the basis of his engagement with Eckhart's texts. We might call this an intersection where we can trace the ways of encounter and engagement with concepts inherited from Eckhart and the ways in which this engagement sustains the formation of something new, namely, an aesthetic and ethic of possibility.

The notion of "possibility [*Möglichkeit*]" emerges in this context as a key term, resonating beyond Musil's text with a short note in Lukács's *Heidelberger Notizen* (*Notes from Heidelberg*), written between 1910 and 1913. There, in the midst of a large body of excerpts, Lukács speaks surprisingly and rather enigmatically of "Eckhart's teaching about possibility." Unfortunately, he does not give us more than this quick note: "Cf. Eckehart's teaching about possibility and his notion of Christ."[7] It will never be known whether Musil and Lukács discussed this or something along those lines when they met in Balázs's apartment in Vienna during the years Balázs spent there, mainly as a film critic.[8] This might have been a nice piece of anecdotal evidence. What we know for sure, though, is that Lukács's later thought turned toward a rather different concept of utopia and a moral rigor that seems diametrically opposed to both Musil's and Balázs's thought. I would like to show how the configuration of this "philosophy of possibility" is a cornerstone of Musil's project that has heretofore not found the attention it merits. It also forms, and this will be the link to Balázs's book on the culture of film, the core of Musil's engagement with this early theory of film when he reviewed the book in 1925 under the title "Ansätze zu neuer Ästhetik: Bemerkungen über eine Dramaturgie des Films" ("Beginnings of a New Aesthetic: Remarks about a Dramaturgy of Film").[9]

Musil Reads Eckhart

At this point, let us return to Musil's text via an extensive quote. In the fourth chapter of *The Man Without Qualities*, still within the first part of the book, which is called "Eine Art Einleitung" ("A Sort of Introduction"), Musil writes: "To pass freely through open doors, it is necessary to respect the fact that they have solid frames. This principle, by which the old professor [i.e., the father of Ulrich, the man without qualities] had always lived, is simply a requisite of the sense of reality. But if there is a sense of reality, and no one will doubt that it has its justification for existing, then there must also be something we call a sense of possibility." Musil continues in the next paragraph:

> Whoever has it does not say, for instance: Here this or that has happened, will happen, must happen; but he invents: Here this or that might, could, or ought to happen. If he is told that something is the way it is, he will think: Well, it could probably just as well be otherwise. So the sense of possibility could be defined outright as the ability to conceive of everything there might be just as well, and to attach no more importance to what is than to what is not. The consequences of so creative a disposition can be remarkable, and may, regrettably, often make what people admire seem wrong, and what is taboo permissible, or, also, make both a matter of indifference. Such possibilists are said to inhabit a more delicate medium, a hazy medium of mist, fantasy, daydreams, and the subjunctive mood. Children who show this tendency are dealt with firmly and warned that such persons are cranks, dreamers, weaklings, know-it-alls, or troublemakers. Such fools are also called idealists by those who wish to praise them. But all this clearly applies only to their weak subspecies, those who cannot comprehend reality or who, in their melancholic condition, avoid it. These are people in whom the lack of reality is a real deficiency. But the possible includes not only the fantasies of people with weak nerves but also the as yet unawakened intentions of God. A possible experience or truth is not the same as an actual experience or truth minus its 'reality value' but has—according to its partisans, at least—something quite divine about it, a fire, a readiness to build and a conscious utopianism that does not shrink from reality but sees it as a project, something yet to be invented. After all, the earth is not that old, and was apparently never so ready as now to give birth to its full potential.[10]

I quote this passage in full because it brings together all the elements that play a role in my reading of Musil—which, in any case, can only be a very partial reading of this essayistic novel and even of this short passage. What appears are not only references to the "unawakened intentions of God," the "divine" character of a "conscious utopianism," the allusion to the image of the "holy fool," and the conjunction of "creativity" and "birth," all of which connects this text with Eckhart's thought, but the very notion of "possibility," as it is introduced by Musil in a chapter of his novel that ends with a discussion of "being without qualities" (*Eigenschaftslosigkeit*). It is this notion of "possibility" and some of its conceptual aspects that Musil quotes from a sermon by Eckhart,[11] reconfiguring its meaning in view of a nonmessianic, ethically refined, and—as Musil calls it—"essayistic . . . utopia of precision." The human being engaged in this "utopia of precision," he writes, "would be full of the paradoxical interplay of exactitude and indefiniteness," and thus the "stable internal conditions guaranteed by a system of morality have little value for a man whose imagination is geared to change."[12] "Ultimately," he goes on, "when the demand for the greatest and most exact fulfillment is transferred from the intellectual realm to that of the passions, it becomes evident . . . that the passions disappear and that in their place arises something like a primordial fire of goodness."[13] Thus, "the pallid resemblance of actions to virtues would disappear from the image of life; in their place we would have these virtues' intoxicating fusion in holiness."

What then, we might ask, is the connection between this image of an absorbing holiness, an ethics beyond morality, a "conscious utopianism," and the notion of possibility? And how does Musil reconfigure Eckhart's thought, which is the source for his concepts of holiness and possibility? Musil's reading of Eckhart is, indeed, not a return to or a recovery of an "irrational mysticism," as one often reads, but an exploration into the territory of rationality and "exactitude," which engages Eckhart's text in substantial ways. In order to explain this, I want to return to Musil's notion of a "utopia of essayism." Utopias, he writes, are "much the same as possibilities." They are results of a *praxis* that disentangles something from its restraints and allows it to develop, quite like what happens "when a scientist observes the change of an element within a compound and draws his conclusions." In other words, the "utopia of essayism" is to be seen as the practice and the result of an "experiment, . . . in which the possible change of an element may be observed, along with the effects of such a change on the compound phenomenon we call life." Thus, it is allowed "to exert its exemplary influence on everything it touches." The "paradoxical interplay of exactitude and indefiniteness" is the consequence of this experiment, the utopian state itself or, if we think in terms of literature, the "essayism" and the essayistic explorations that Musil's own work embodies. The essay is the medium through which, the very space where, thought experiments with itself, exploring its exactitude in and through words and elaborating from within this engagement, time and again, a world of possibilities and new relations among words, things, and concepts. As we will see, this world includes not only thought but also sensation and emotion in the interaction with things, the world, animals, and people.

All this might at a first glance seem quite removed from Eckhart's writings, although many of his sermons can indeed be read, especially in Büttner's translation, as essayistic in style. I want to suggest, however, that Musil not only refers to key elements in Eckhart's theological discourse, picking up some vague ideas of "possibility," of "holiness," and of an ethics beyond bourgeois normativity and morality; rather, he reconfigures the quotes he uses in view of his utopian essayism.

The very notion of "possibility" appears in Eckhart's so-called speculative mysticism as the concept that moves and determines its critical character. He uses this concept to reinterpret the essence of negative theology. The divine "darkness," Eckhart points out, can be "called . . . a possibility or receptivity," and this possibility and receptivity can be traced in the life of our intellect.[14] Where the intellect effaces its own discursive activity, where it becomes silent, it turns into possibility and receptivity. It no longer determines God, the world, and itself but turns into the possibility of "becoming everything." Thus, Eckhart argues not for a radical iconoclasm and a seemingly irrational flight into mystical unity but for an intellectual engagement. This engagement of the intellect involves acknowledging the determining nature of the intellect—its activity and reality—the finite character of this activity, and its ground in "possibility." Using Musil's term, we can call this Eckhart's version of a thought of exactitude and an exactitude of thought, which realizes its own finitude and turns itself into possibility time and again. The very desire that moves reason, the very nature of the intellect, finds expression in its exploration of possibility. Eckhart's text reads: "The soul will never be calm until she will have found fulfillment in the fullness of her reality; in this she is like matter, since matter never stands still until she has unfolded into everything that lies within the realm of her possibilities." He continues: "Our life has its ground in the fact that we become aware of God and all things in the way of pure possibility."[15]

As Eckhart argues, this does not mean that thought and reason have to be left behind. Rather, thought that engages with itself discovers its own discursive character and acknowledges that in its discursive form it imprisons itself in a seemingly stable order of reality. Every word and every sentence is, insofar as it is knowledge of an object and a subject, a structure that deprives this object and subject of their freedom. Thus, reason is limiting, determining. It deprives the world of possibilities and shuts it up in the realm of "quality." By acknowledging this, by perceiving its own finite nature, when it explores itself the intellect discovers itself as the place of transcendence and freedom. It does so exactly insofar as it sees itself in its ground—negatively—as an ever new realm of possibility. In realizing what it is in its ground, in acknowledging its own finitude, reason thus becomes for Eckhart the space of the emergence of the possible.

As I have said, this notion of mysticism entails not an abandonment of reason but an engagement with it that liberates it from its determining and determined shape and opens up the very realm of possibility. Key terms, such as *detachment* (*Gelassenheit, Abgeschiedenheit,* or *Bildlosigkeit*), refer to this intellectual practice, which, as Eckhart would have it, liberates not only thought but also all the things that otherwise get caught up in the order imposed on them by reason. As he states in a passage that is important in view of Musil's reading, a person who could see "a fly," "grass," "a stone," or a "piece of wood" without the order imposed on it—and thus as a sheer event in a realm of possibi-lites—would not need a sermon or even the Scriptures.[16] This person would see it "with-out qualities" and "without a why," not as something, as this or that, but in a moment where intellect and love, reason, sensation, and affect converge, where the human mind would grasp the infinite and the unsayable in and through the irreducible particularity of the "piece of wood"—and of every other thing it sees and encounters.

In the conclusion to the short essay he writes on Balázs's theory of film, Musil calls this moment of encounter "vision [*Schau*]," and he connects it with the experience of film: "In this vision film uncovers . . . the infinite and ineffable character of all beings—as if put under glass, so that we can watch it."[17]

An Ethics of Possibility

My reading of Eckhart, one might tempted to argue, seems to be inflected by Musil already. Indeed, this is what Musil makes us do when we read his text and the quotes he incorporates. He forces or seduces us to follow the path of his essayistic engagement with the material he uses, the conversations that develop around the quotes, and the voices that engage with them throughout his novel. In his reconfiguration of Eckhart's concept of possibility in conjunction with his notion of the "experiment," he thus translates his own readings, fashioning them into a realm of possibility from which the "utopia of essayism" emerges. What he opens up here, however, is not just this. It is a fascinating reading of Eckhart, which takes into account an important element in his thought: namely, the intricate connection between the liberation of reason that emerges when it sees itself as a realm of possibility and attention to the presence of a world of things and images. This can already be found in Eckhart's sermons. What Musil picks up on and inserts into his text is the specific ethical relationship that, once it has turned itself into possibility, reason entertains with images and things. What he cuts out, one might say, is often "God"—while he nevertheless retains the moments of the "infinite [*Unendlich-keit*]," and the "ineffable [*Unausdrückbarkeit*]" that mark both Musil's and Eckhart's texts. In both, this "infinite" takes shape as a realm of possibilities that opens up when things, images, and words are set free through the engagement of reason and can be traced in the ways in which they affect our attentive emotions, senses, and thought.

Later in Musil's novel, Agathe's and Ulrich's adventure, the encounter between the siblings, is characterized in terms that return to this point, emphasizing the moment of attention to the particular by both the reader and the protagonists:

> When she now spoke to Ulrich he had not even noticed how long the interruption had lasted. But whoever has not already picked up the clues to what was going on

between this brother and sister should lay this account aside, for it depicts an adventure of which he will never be able to approve: a journey to the edge of the possible, which led past—and perhaps not always past—the dangers of the impossible and unnatural, even of the repugnant: a "borderline case," as Ulrich later called it, of limited and special validity, reminiscent of the freedom with which mathematics sometimes resorts to the absurd in order to arrive at the truth. He and Agathe happened upon a path that had much in common with the business of the possessed by God, but they walked it without piety, without believing in God or the soul, nor even in the beyond or reincarnation. They had come upon it as people of this world, and pursued it as such—this was remarkable about it.[18]

Again, the denying force of negative theology characterizes this moment: "some tissue of habit tears"; "purposeful, practical connotations" have "suddenly" been "lost"; and "what is left on the pictorial plane might best be called an ocean swell of sensations that rises and falls, breathes and shimmers, as though it filled your whole field of view without a horizon."

Ulrich continues his conversation with Agathe, describing the visual impression of a herd of grazing cattle upon the mind of a contemplative observer: "Of course, there are still countless individual perceptions contained within it: colors, horns, movements, smells, and all the details of reality; but none of them are acknowledged any longer, even if they should still be recognized. Let me put it this way: the details no longer have their egoism, which they use to capture our attention, but they're all linked with each other in a familiar, literally 'inward' way."[19]

Once again, at first glance, this passage seems to be nothing more than a reminiscence of vaguely characterized mystical feelings and a somewhat indistinct sentiment in which things lose their ordinary nature. This, however, would underestimate the analytical sharpness that characterizes the conversation between Agathe and Ulrich as it unfolds. This conversation itself brings out the possibilities of thought and returns us to the role of attention to the particular and an ethics of the particular in this utopian language. If we are dealing with mysticism here—and again, the pages are interspersed with quotes from Eckhart and other medieval mystics—it is a mysticism without salvation and without the imaginary of salvation (or even an absolute presence of a mystical moment). Instead, the "suddenness" is seen in terms of what could be called moments of emergence that subvert the real critically, liberating it from its orderly nature and transforming it into the realm of an ethical encounter, within the realm of the possible, which is full of particularities and has gotten rid of all normative constraints.

Consequently, the conversation between Agathe and Ulrich turns from the aesthetic toward the ethical, fashioning utopian essayism into an exploration of its ethical implications. At this point, again, Musil inserts into the conversation several allusions to Eckhart's sermons. When Agathe says, "One possesses nothing in the world, one holds onto nothing, one is not held by anything," she refers to a state beyond "good and evil," a state where—in the words of Ulrich's response—"one slips away from a life of inessentials" and "everything enters into a new relationship with everything else." Ulrich adds, emphasizing the negative character of the event:

> I would almost go so far as to say into a nonrelationship. For it's an entirely unknown one, of which we have no experience, and all other relationships are blotted out. But despite its obscurity, this one is so distinct that its existence is undeniable. It's strong, but impalpably strong. One might put it this way: ordinarily, we look at something, and our gaze is like a fine wire or taut thread with two supports—one being the eye and the other what it sees, and there's some such great support structure for every second that passes; but at this particular second, on the contrary, it is rather as though something painfully sweet were pulling our eye beams apart.

At this point, Musil adds two other quotes from Eckhart's sermons. First, in Ulrich's voice, referring to the "saints": "they say that nothing can happen in that condition which is not in harmony with it." Then, in Agathe's voice, a little later, after some thoughts about this state of being: "A good person makes everything that touches him good, no matter what others may do to him; the instant it enters his sphere it becomes transformed."[20]

The specific character of the moment that Agathe and Ulrich evoke is part of the conversation. It is part of the two siblings' exploration of the possibilities and impossibilities of their relation to each other. It is at the same time, however, the moment when an ethics of attention (*Aufmerksamkeit*) emerges. Musil inserts the allusions to Eckhart, devoid of their immediate theological background, to articulate the ethics that emerges from the encounter with the particular and the harmony that establishes itself within it. It is an ethics that recognizes the aesthetic impression of the particular as that which guides the attention and undermines the violence imposed on things and the world by the "sense of reality [*Wirklichkeitssinn*]."

The "Culture of Film"

What, you might ask at this point, does all this have to do with film or the culture of film—apart, maybe, from the short and emphatic mention of "vision" that I have quoted above from Musil's review of Balázs's book? For Balázs, who called his book *Visible Man*, silent film gives us something to see that has been obliterated by the hegemonic power of words, the violence imposed on things by words. Film is not just another form of theater or pantomime, as some critics would have it, but something entirely different. Its force lies in what Balázs calls its "physiognomic" character. This is to be found in the way film shows us the visible face not only of humans, but also of animals, landscapes, teacups, bridges, gestures, and everything else that surrounds us. Silent film has the power to move us through these images, selecting them, combining them, reconfiguring them, and thus elaborating ever new possibilities of figuration and effects that lie in things, faces, and gestures. As Balázs points out, this implies not that the images "mean" something new in the modern medium of film but rather that they have a specific effect on our thoughts: "The images should not mean thoughts but form and evoke thoughts—thoughts that emerge as consequences, not as symbols or ideograms, which have already taken shape in the image."[21] Using the term *physiognomy*, which he inherits from Goethe and Lavater, Balázs does not imply a predefined meaning or character of the things we see in a film. Instead, he focuses on the "visible gesture," the specific surface and superficiality that is liberated in the film and that in turn is able to liberate possibilities of thought, emotion, and sensation—possibilities that have been obscured by the predominance of the word in human culture and that are able to recast the world in its very visibility. Even the word itself, Balázs will argue in defense of the presence of sound in film, appears in a new visibility and audibility, together with a "rediscovery of our acoustic environments." "Film," he writes, "is an art of the surface," which embodies "the being of matter." Balázs uses the Middle High German verb from Eckhart's texts here, "das *wesen* der Materie," adding, "a useful old verb!" In its reduction to surface, to the living face of things and faces, film offers a time-affirming phenomenology of possibilities that inhabit the face of things and people and that move us along. Thus, the medium of film inherits the space of possibilities that intimately connects being and intellect in Eckhart and in Musil's reading of his texts.

For Balázs, what happens in film is this opening of a space of possibilities, for example, in the face of Asta Nielsen in a scene from a silent film that Balázs describes in the following words:

There is a film where Asta Nielsen looks through a window, observing somone approaching her house. A deadly fear, a petrified terror appears on her face. Then, slowly, she realizes that she has been wrong and that the person who is approaching doesn't mean something unhappy but the greatest happiness instead. And slowly, moving through the scale of possibilities, her expression changes from terror to a timid doubt, to uncertain hope, finally to careful joy and to an ecstatic happiness. We watch her face for about twenty meters in close-up. We observe each trait of her face, the movements around her eyes and mouth, the change that takes place. What we see during those minutes is an organic *history of the evolution of her feelings* and nothing else. This is the story we see.[22]

Both Musil's and Balázs's emphasis on the surface of things, the face of things and faces, the discovery of the visual, which might undermine the predominance of the word in the modern world, has sometimes been explained in terms of a discourse of "attention" and of discussions about the nature and media of perception in the early twentieth century. This reference does indeed explain key aspects. It does not exhaust the problem, however, nor does it explain Musil's statements about the "mysticism of film" in his review of Balázs's book. Musil speaks of "the face of things and their awakening in the stillness of the image," and he points out: "What is extraordinary is that a book on film reaches this point at all, and touches quite consciously on the border between these two worlds," that is, "the normal condition of our relationship to the world, to people, and to ourselves," as well as a "positive, causal, mechanical way of thinking," on the one hand, and the sensible, affective, and experiential condition, on the other. In the latter "world there is neither measure nor precision, neither purpose nor cause; good and evil simply fall away, without any pretense of superiority, and in place of all these relations enters a secret rising and ebbing of our being with that of things and other people. It is in this condition that the image of each object becomes not a practical goal, but a worldless experience."

The very muteness of things makes them visible, the very muteness of faces transports sensation, affects, and cognition. This leads back to the thought of possibility, or, maybe better, the emergence of possibilites in the realm of visibility that has taken leave of words, which frame and determine the nature of the "real" world. "Visible possibilities" is a title in Balázs's essay, and the "theory of film" itself is for Musil a genre that points toward the possibilities of a new aesthetic and ethic, analogous to his understanding of the work of the essay. It is something he also discovers in Balázs's "style," which he characterizes in the following words: "the ingenious style, which creates an atmosphere that immediately relates each impression to many others, and above all the clear, profound, ordered layering of this atmosphere—these are personal qualities of Balázs the writer." Balázs is the scientist, the "anatomist and biologist" of film who develops "experientially and scientifically" an "unexpected paradigm."[23] The key term in this paradigm is for Musil, as well, the "only-visible," an abstraction that "is just as much a matter of increase in impression as a reduction." Thus, he argues against the "concepts of purposeless beauty or of beautiful illusion," which "have something of a holiday mood about them," in favor of a "negation of real life," which, in turn, can be compared to the "special attitude toward things that [Lucien Lévy-Bruhl, in his "How Natives Think" ("Les fonctions mentales des sociétés inférieures")] calls participation." What we see are not things we know but things that have been experimentally set free in a realm of possibilities, that move us emotionally and intellectually, thus allowing us and forcing us to follow the ways in which they deploy themselves, their realms of meaning, and their relations with each other. "Precisely this," Musil writes, "allows us some hope that film will contribute to a new culture of the senses" and of emotions through the excitement it transports when words are silenced. It brings out something that is there in literature, as well, since "even on a page of prose deserving of the name, one can recognize that a general excitement is communicated *before* the meaning."[24] What film brings to our attention, then, is also there in literature. The silent film, however, moves it to the surface, opening up a space of possibilities that tends to be obliterated by words, evoking not only the particular and its face but also a world of intensities in which each particular event evokes new relations and thus allows for the exploration of new possibilities of relations between things and between things and viewers. As Musil points out, these new relations change both the things and the viewers, liberating them for a moment from a discursive regime and thus opening up a horizon of new aesthetic and ethical relations that he calls "utopian."

Conclusion

Musil's engagement with Eckhart's thought is too manifold to be summarized here. More-over, it follows the law of Musil's essayism, that is, the multiplication of perspectives and the layering of readings he tends to work with. There is one point, however, I would like to emphasize, and that is the transformation of some elements Musil draws from Eckhart into what could be called an "art of attention" and an "essayistic utopianism." Thus, Musil turns Eckhart's mysticism into a figure of reflection about attention and about intellectual, emotional, and sensual engagement with things, people, and the world. He does not discard the theological context of Eckhart's thought absolutely, but he frames its critical potential in view of an intellectual experiment capable of setting free possibilities of interaction, perception, and communication that have not been observed before. The very fact that he values Balázs's theory of film is part of this elaboration of a "conscious utopianism." As Musil emphasizes, Balázs's book is exactly that, a "theory," a movement of the mind, which exposes itself to an object and its possibilities, the silent movie, and traces its own movements, affects, and cognitions in the form of an essay.

In his own review of Balázs's book, Siegfried Kracauer expresses his doubts about the viability of this utopian discourse. Turning against Balázs, he writes critically and dogmatically: "The new visibility of man that is presented to us in film is in fact the contrary of a turn toward true concreteness. Instead, it is the confirmation and conserva-tion of the bad rationality of capitalist thought. Only insight and language can bring radical change."[25]

In his defense of Balázs's emphasis on the "visibility of man," Musil participates in the same discussion about "change [*Umschwung*]." Inspired by Eckhart and Balázs, he offers an intriguing reformulation of "conscious utopianism" as an art of the elaboration of the possible. What Kracauer doesn't *see*, we might say, is the fact that the film does not "represent" or "illustrate [*veranschaulicht*]" the new visibility of man, but that it *is*—analogous to the the practice of Musil's utopian essayism—an experimental form of attention, in which possibilities are explored in correspondence with the ever new and suprising ways in which they are set free.

Intimate Exteriorities

Inventing Religion Through Music

Sander van Maas

> The question of the arts would not merit attention (artists having taken it well in hand) if it did not hide the stakes of a beyond-religion which is now ineluctable—but of a beyond that owes nothing to the (bourgeois, as no one dares to say anymore) cult of Art.
>
> —Jean-Luc Nancy, *The Muses*

It is not a rare phenomenon today to find a concert hall—that bourgeois temple of the cult of Art—filled with religious music. This may not seem surprising, since soon after its invention in the eighteenth century the concert hall became a location for the performance of religious repertoires. The times have changed, however, and the position of religion today can hardly be compared with the one it occupied centuries ago. The presence of religion in classical music performances today is mostly historical in character, such as, for instance, when Handel's oratorios are played, or Mozart's *Requiem*.

Much less frequently, but all the more significantly, one hears new works of religious or "spiritual" music, composed by composers of our own time. On these occasions, there is an important change in the concert situation. Rather than relating ourselves, as listeners, to a historical expression of faith from times when we imagine religious experience to have been less complicated (which, of course, it never was), we now have to face an expression of religion from a contemporary, perhaps even a compatriot. From the Western European perspective from which I am writing, anything seems more attractive than this. As the music critic Elmer Schoenberger once said, we seem more ready to accept the faith of a Russian composer who was born and raised in wholly different circumstances than ours than that of an equal composer from our own cultural time zone.[1]

The credibility of religious expressions in the domain of Western contemporary art music is in a state of crisis. This seems as much related to the collapse of the cult of Art that we are presently witnessing as to the problematic status of religious expressions in the public domain in general. The first of these motives will be my main concern. If composed (i.e., "classical," "literate") music has been based on ideological premises that are losing their dominance, the question arises of how religious music will change accordingly. On the one hand, the retreat of Romantic notions that construed music as a quasi-religious phenomenon seems to give music back to those who have been reluctant to accept art as revelation. On the other hand, however, it appears that the values and artistic norms that guided the development of music in the nineteenth and twentieth centuries have been rediscovered by institutional religion. In his 2003 appraisal of an important papal text about music from the early twentieth century, Pope John Paul II reaffirmed the importance of artistic qualities in the music of the Catholic Church.[2] As I will discuss below, this belated attempt to save church music from some of the effects of the 1960s *aggiornamento* will have to face the significant changes in values such as musical "substance."

In order to understand the present situation of religious "new music for the concert hall," it will be valuable to discuss the conceptual strategies employed by composers who work in this area. I have chosen to focus on a small number of composers whose music gained popularity in the early 1990s, at a time when religious and spiritual themes became more explicit. Since then, the music of these composers, among whom figure most prominently John Tavener, Henryk Górecki, and Arvo Pärt, has become widely accepted by the public. Although there is no personal link between them, their work is collectively referred to as "new spiritual music," or, less neutrally so, "Holy Minimalism" or "New Simplicity."[3] The tone of these critical labels reflects the debate this music has engendered among specialists. In contrast to their popularity with the wider audience (Górecki's Third Symphony even topped the Billboard charts), there has been great critical resistance to the alleged "insubstantiality" of the music. The debate has focused on issues that reflect the difficulties and paradoxes that surround the composition, production, and appraisal of religious art music at the turn of the millennium.[4]

What might seem a confrontation between modernism and its religiously inspired critics in fact reveals structural tensions. The musical "turn to religion" has been more than an empirical-historical trend; it refers to the *possibility* of conceiving and practicing a form of religious art at the present moment. Given the secularized status of art music, this practice often appears as an attempt to leap over its own paradoxes and impossibilities. As I will argue, the key to understanding the situation of contemporary religious music is to understand this music as the production of a *situation*. The first step will be to see how critical evaluation of the "New Simplicity" is guided by the concept of substance. The case of John Tavener suggests that, unless the role of music's technicity is taken into account, strategic options for assessment remain limited to the onto-theological and apophatic. The second step will be to listen carefully to Jean-Luc Nancy's reinterpretation of the notion of *technē* in his engagement with Hegel's religious aesthetics. This will strike the chord for a discussion of the topography of insides and outsides (surface, depth, inwardness, and the figure of musical touch) that determines the criteria for religious music in the Platonic-Christian tradition. After reinterpreting music's quasi-religious inward "touch" in terms of subjective trembling, the final section will deal with the way in which music (Xenakis, this time) may produce, through its excessive production of trembling, a situation of near-transcendence.

Music Without Substance

The reason why the New Simplicity has become such an item for discussion is partly to be found in the proclamations made by its composers. John Tavener is the most talkative representative of this informal group. His readiness to explain the ins and outs of his approach to composition belongs to the modern tradition of *intellectualité musicale* according to which composers not only write music but also produce ample reflections on their own work.[5] This gesture further complicates the structure of the phenomenon of contemporary religious music.

Tavener, who converted to Greek Orthodoxy in 1977 and ever since has made his faith central to his creative work, presents a number of his ideas on a DVD that is mainly devoted to the performance of his *Fall and Resurrection*, a piece from 2000 for four vocal soloists, orchestra, and choir. In an interview entitled "The Eye of the Heart," Tavener responds to the by then habitual criticism that his work lacks something called "musical substance." His response to this criticism is telling, with regard both to Tavener's own viewpoint and to that of his critics. It touches upon one of the most profound issues in the ontology of music. For this reason I shall quote it in full:

> It doesn't surprise me that certain critics say there is no substance in my music, because, well, probably the last thing I want to have in it, is substance. . . . I love the initial ideas of Beethoven perhaps, for instance—is it the barcarolles he wrote for piano all his life?—particularly the last ones, when he was very near death. Not so much the quartets, because he still has this need to develop. Who wants to know what Beethoven thinks of the material that I believe comes . . . maybe the initial idea is a spontaneous idea that comes from, let's say, the Holy Spirit, call it what you will. Or comes from God if you like, or that he picks up in the music of the spheres, or whatever it is. But once he starts developing, I lose him completely, because it becomes what Beethoven thinks about God. And in the *Missa Solemnis*, you have this passage in the *Agnus Dei* where he *rails* against God, and that's the beginning of a

whole load of composers, like Mahler, who does the same thing. It's touching, but it's not much more than that.[6]

Given his religious and theological engagement, Tavener could be expected here to be referring to the onto-theological notion of substance. His apparent indifference to this notion could then point toward apophatic views of God as being beyond essence. This would also be supported by his general critique of the Aristotelian tradition, which, according to Tavener, caused theology to enter into "a ruinous epoch of abstraction and theory."[7] Despite these plausible resonances, however, there is no reason to believe that he is referring here to theology; the discussion takes place on a technical musical level.

That is just where the problems begin. As Tavener suggests in the remarks quoted above, the category of substance is subsumed in the order of technics. It refers to something that is *produced* by developing an original, god-given "material" or "idea." In Tavener's view, therefore, to want more "substance," that is, more technics, is to want less "God"; the touch of human hands can only spoil the material (qua *idea*).[8] Distancing himself, for this very reason, from the problem he refers to as "Beethoven," Tavener equally distances himself from a good number of his musical peers:

> If they [the critics in America and England] are looking for the kind of thing they find in Harrison Birtwistle they won't find it in me. They write the usual sort of things, lack of substance and so on. I take comfort from the fact that they are the kind of people who praise Harrison Birtwistle and do I want to be praised by the kind of people who praise Harrison Birtwistle? But the audience reaction [in San Francisco, to *Lamentations and Praises*] was quite extraordinary, people coming up to me and hanging on my hand, talking to me for maybe five minutes at a time and saying they won't wash their hand for a week.[9]

Tavener is not just a playing around with the notion of substance. Having been an avant-garde composer in his early years, he is well aware that his music lacks something—the "thing" critics tend to find in "Birtwistle" (or, for that matter, "Beethoven"), which he agrees to call "substance." By contrast to these critics, however, he regards it as something to be avoided, as though he were programming some kind of musical—that is, technical-substantial—apophasis.

Now, exactly, what is musical "substance," and why is it considered important by so many critics? According to Josiah Fisk, who has been one of the foremost critics of what he calls the "New Simplicity," the issue is rather serious. "Musical substance," we learn from Fisk, is a notion comprising all that Western music positively stands for. "Like the best examples of any art form, the best works of Western music seem actually to be alive, richly animated with a sentience that responds to a hundred different probings of the ear and the intellect."[10] Fisk relates this "live" aspect to a conservative notion of human subjectivity, based on the expressionist balance between inside and outside, as well as a certain internal structuring of each. He continues, "These works carry meanings within themselves, presenting them to us in all their cross-grained complexity as their stories unfold. They do that most human of things: they approach you, greet you, and proceed to engage you in dialogue." Music's "inner life"—a notion central to Fisk's argument—is said to be produced by the ambiguity of musical structure, by the work's play with the listener's expectations, by the element of dialogue ("between ideas, between form and content, between composer and history") and interplay, by the logic of linearity and narrativity, along with, and supported by, "values" such as "highest respect" for the past, musical skill, and "traditional expertise," the sound morality of hard labor, a preference for density of content, and a stable relation between structure and emotion. All this in view of a music that is "solidly intellectual and at the same time seductively playful, [that] engages the ear and the mind, but always with the purpose of speaking to the heart."[11]

Fisk's implicit emphasis on inward dimensions (the "heart," the "inner life," the content of form, musical ideas, honest intentions) leads him to dismiss the New Simplicity as offering nothing but "surface." "And so we have," he writes in his conclusion, "a music that, for the listener who seeks more than the token of classical music, offers no dialogue, no ambiguity, and no inner life. What we are left with is *a surface that speaks of depth, and a depth that speaks of nothing*."[12] The music of Tavener, like that of Pärt and Górecki, is "a form of substance and depth" that, on close inspection, turns out to be based merely on a "tide of undifferentiated emotionalism." What we are offered here is hardly more than musical "raw materials," which are passed "along to us with only minimal craftsmanship—commodities still partly in their original wrappers."[13] The listener's attention is diverted by the "rich and enveloping sound" of the recordings and the general "aural-emotional experience" it offers as a substitute for compositional structure. Rather than becoming engaged in a play of interpretation, she or he is "sent away empty" and more often than not misguided by the "protective coating of extraneous ideas," which are "sent to do the heavy lifting that the music can't do itself." As far as Fisk is concerned, the New Simplicity drapes itself in the gestures and materials of the Western classical tradition only to underline its infinite distance from this tradition. "The sounds that at first blush tell us this is classical music give way to a center that is classical music's opposite—more completely so than any other type of music. What we gain in this bargain is a way of asserting faith in simplicity. What we give up is faith in music as an art."[14]

Fisk's conclusion is interesting for a number of reasons. First, it suggests a dialectical tension between "substantial" classical music and the specter of classical music that comes to occupy its very center. The New Simplicity does not simply propose an alternative practice, projected elsewhere or elsewhen. Rather, it inscribes itself, as Fisk rightly notes, in the most "classical" of musical gestures, instruments, performance spaces, and so on. As he also underlines, the "emptiness" of this music is heir to John Cage's reductionist approach to the internal structuring of works. In other words, the New Simplicity's apparently most offending feature does not originate from outside the classical tradition, but belongs to the very core of its recent modernist history. There is no easy way to avoid this piece of history; nor is it easy to ignore the questions this movement has posed itself qua tradition.

Second, throughout his discussion Fisk construes the substance that defines music as art in terms of *technics*. The art of music, insofar as it is art, appears to be dependent upon the technical production of its own essence. It does not possess a substance of its own, by force of ontological necessity. Rather, as one may gather from the polemic against the New Simplicity, music is forced to combat its apparent lack of given substance by producing it. This task of producing "inherent" meaning, according to Fisk, is the responsibility of the composer, who "toils" and "labors." Interestingly, this state of affairs points toward a rupture within the concept of musical art. The musical need for self-grounding severs the element of technics from the essence that is to be produced. In order to produce the substantiality that saves it for the category of art, music needs to sacrifice its conceptual unity. This disengagement between substance and technics, that is to say, the conceptualization of substantial music outside of its technicality, which Fisk criticized so fiercely in the New Simplicity, is unavoidable if music is to belong to the concept of art.

Third, since for its substance music cannot count on a given ontology, it operates in a curious ontological space. The substance that lends music its status as art is not given, and in those instances when music's substance appears to be naturalized, it remains subjected to the instabilities of its virtuality. Since it is a product of technics, music's substance remains a promise, a horizon against which it may be projected as an object of faith. Fisk acknowledges the fiduciary character of our relation to the concept of music as art. As we have been aware since the late eighteenth century, music may hold promises of plenitude, revelation, immediacy, and truth. Fisk's portrayal of the "Western tradition" and what it stands for partakes in the specific temporality that supports it as an object of faith. Pitting one faith against the other, his polemic in the name of secular principles becomes itself religious. On either side of the divide, there is virtuality and faith.

And finally, Fisk draws attention to the particular temporalization involved in the project of the New Simplicity. Rather than presenting a new form of religious art available for contemplation here and now, the New Simplicity takes place in a unique temporal space. While intending to answer the contemporary crisis of musical culture by turning toward religious models, that is to say, models based on a metaphysical model of presence, this music slides its listener into a kind of fold. Through the use of historically informed methods of composition and references to Byzantine and medieval sources, this music leads the listener into a space in between the present and a past that—as Fisk is right to point out—is a wholly imaginary one.[15] The temporal mode of the musico-religious requires a twisting of the ear in order to hear a holy music arriving from the space that opens in between the dystopian present and the imaginary past.[16]

Much of this debate echoes the thesis on the end of art. In his study of Hegel's aesthetics, Jean-Luc Nancy summarizes this thesis by noticing that "It is now well established that what has been imputed to Hegel as the declaration of an "end of art" is but the declaration of an end of what he called "aesthetic religion," that is, of art as the place where the divine appears."[17] With regard to religious music, this thesis seems to be multiplied by Hegel's struggle with, and eventual dismissal of, purely instrumental music. If art is no longer the "place" where the divine appears, this will always already have been an impossibility for music, because, according to Hegel, music never actually possessed the capacity to express any definite substance. Music is merely a vehicle for the expression of "pure inwardness," mimicking the tidal movements of the inner life of feeling. Thus, from the Hegelian perspective, the notion of a contemporary religious music runs into a double impossibility. First, qua art it can no longer be expected to express the ideal by force of the historical dialectic of the Spirit; second, qua music, it has never even come close to being a candidate for such expression, because it structurally lacks that specific capacity (for Hegel, classical Greek sculpture fulfills that purpose). With regard to the first point, Nancy shows how the notion of Christian art, which dominates the scene of the New Simplicity, posed a problem for Hegel. In the *Phenomenology*, Christian art is not even mentioned as a possibility, and remarks on that point in the *Phenomenology of Religion* only affirm that, for Hegel, Christian art contradicts itself as a concept because it aspires to overcome the (Greek) art of "beautiful ideality" by absorbing, through death or transfiguration, the moment of exteriority into pure interiority.[18] According to Nancy, this dialectical movement is impossible in a pure sense; any attempt to surpass art's exteriority by means of sublation is doomed.

> The moment of art in religion cannot . . . remain a moment. Irresistibly it autonomizes itself, and it does so, perhaps, because it is precisely the moment of the thorough autonomy of manifestation—of an autonomy that no longer retains anything of interiority or of spirituality as such. Art would thus behave like a sort of "sublation in exteriority" of religion—but since religion has its truth only in the return of the spirit to itself, art is also the definitive alienation of the religious, which also might be expressed thus: the technics of the beautiful, or better still, the beautiful as technics in (the) place of divine presence.[19]

With regard to the second point (i.e., music's structural insufficiency as a medium for religion), these remarks are important. Nancy stresses the exterior aspect of art, which he construes as a remainder that will forever resist the spiraling sublation of art into religion and philosophy. As an alternative to the Hegelian reduction of art's exterior moment to the inward immediacy of the spirit (a movement that both culminates and breaks down in Hegel's analysis of poetry), Nancy proposes a radical autonomization of purely formal exteriority. Art's singularity resides in the presentation as such of "*entirely exposed interiority*, but at the point at which it no longer even refers to itself as to some content or some latent presence, having become on the contrary the *patency of its very latency* and thus irreconcilable with any interiority (with any divinity)."[20]

Criticizing the primacy of interiority that informs and orients the aesthetics of Hegel so profoundly, Nancy seems to traverse the distance between Fisk and the New Simplicity. Fisk criticizes Tavener and his colleagues for presenting the listener a mere "surface" and blames the misleading suggestion of "depth" on the deliberate absence of technically produced "ambiguity," "dialogue," and "inner life." Nancy, on the contrary, affirms the patent, superficial character of art. He does not subscribe, however, to the Tavenerian rejection of technique as an interference with the original divine idea. Rather, Nancy points toward the centrality of technique to all questions concerning grounds, origins, and ends:

> Technique is the obsolescence of the origin and the end: the exposition to a lack of ground and foundation, or that which ends up presenting itself as its only "sufficient reason," experiencing itself as radically insufficient and as a devastation of the ground, the "natural," and the origin. Technique extends a withdrawal of the "ground," and the most visible part of our history consists in this extension. Technique as such, in the common sense of the word, at the same time extends and recovers this *Grundlosigkeit* or *Abgründigkeit*. This is why there is not "technique" but "techniques" and why the plural here bears the "essence" itself. It might be that art, the arts, is nothing other than the second-degree exposition of technique itself, or perhaps the technique *of the ground* itself. How to produce the ground that does not produce itself: that would be the question of art, and that would be its plurality of origin.[21]

This plurality will be the immanence, the pure patency, of "color, nuance, grain, line, timbre, echo, cadence."[22] That is to say: of a quasi-topological surface without reverse side, a Möbius strip of sorts, which will only ever produce immanences and transimmanences.[23] Does this eventually converge with the vacuity of Tavener's music without substance? Yes and no. On the one hand, Tavener's music does indeed avoid the grand gestures of traditional religious art music since the nineteenth century, leaving ample room for disappointment with regard to the image of the sacred he evokes. Those drawn toward his music by a desire to be fulfilled by gestures of plenitude will probably encounter a strange lack of, indeed, *religious* substance.[24] The apparent emptiness of his music unwillingly refers to the exodus of the religion of sublimity typically found from Haydn all the way to Messiaen—an exodus that leaves a vacant space, opening a kind of sonorous desert within sound itself. To the topology of this desert, as well as its technical aspect, we shall return.

Yet Tavener tries hard to restrain the kind of immanence described by Nancy by speculating, in a very traditional gesture of religious music, on a contemplative attitude that would be willing to Platonize the mere "surface" of his music, that is, to understand its vacuity by relating it to a plenitude elsewhere or elsewhen, of which the enigmatic place of the "heart" is, according to Tavener, focus, origin, and destiny. Again, as Burcht Pranger has demonstrated so convincingly, this kind of contemplation too would require a refined use of technics.[25] It would seem, then, that technics is where the question of religious art begins and ends—that is to say, *virtually*:

> The technicity of art dislodges art from its "poetic" assurance, if one understands by that the production of a revelation, or art conceived as a *phusis* unveiled in its truth. Technicity *itself* is also the out-of-workness [*désoeuvrement*] of the work, what puts it outside itself, touching the infinite. Their technical out-of-workness incessantly forces the fine arts, dislodges them endlessly from aestheticizing repose. This is why art is always *coming to its end*. The "end of art" is always the beginning of its plurality. *It could also be the beginning of another sense of and for "technics" in general* [my emphasis].[26]

Touching Music

The bifurcation Nancy discerns between art and religion originates in his reinterpretation of the notion of *technē*. This notion, rather than rendering the substance (i.e., essence) of "Art," refers to "the naked presentation of the singular plural of obviousness."[27] What Nancy foresees *technē* doing is participating in the production of those "*other formations than religion*" that Hegel programmed, as the latter puts it, "ones which must be more satisfying for the human spirit than those that religion offers him."[28] Religion cannot easily be discarded, however. With the intention of showing that, starting from the Hegelian analysis, religion has nothing that is truly proper to it, Nancy notes in passing that "art is the truth of religion from the side of exteriority as nonrevealed exteriority in interiority (and philosophy is the symmetrical truth from the side of interiority)."[29] Hence he contends that religion "tends to be nothing other than the untenable, undecidable line of cleavage between art and philosophy."[30]

Precisely *as* such a line of cleavage, however, religion is neither without importance nor without phenomenology. Religion turns out to be a kind of chiasmic *point de capiton*, a turning point (a point "with no dimension," as Nancy often likes to say) around which philosophy and art revolve, keeping their distance with respect to one another, but also holding onto their alliance. Religion is like the tain of the mirror or the *khōra*, which has no proper place but without which there would be no reciprocal play of outsides and insides, of places and mirrorlike heterotopias, of sensing senses and thought sense. "Religion" is, one might provisionally say, the very fact that art and thinking touch, each highlighting its respective, irreducible *remainders*. It is where the nakedness of art's patency touches on itself *as thinking*, where *technē*—that is, the relation to the "endless ends" of art—gains its other sense. Religion is where the one-sided surface (Massumi) of artistic experience receives the torsion (a technics of sorts) that will turn it into a kind of Möbius strip: the continuous and continual transition between insides and outsides, without ever exiting the logic of pure patency.[31] This view of "religion"—a term that should now be kept in suspension in accordance with the quasi-spectral status of religion after the "end of art"—as a buffer zone, a line of both contact and separation between art and reflection, underlines the close relation between religion and the topos of *touch*. Religion may even be touch as such, the enigma of *ça touche*, which, according to Nancy, remains untouchable.[32]

The topos of touch brushes up against music's most traditional affinity with metaphysics and religion. An ability to touch the soul profoundly and with great force has always been a key figure in metaphysical speculation on music. It also has been central to the acceptance—however equivocal—of music in theology and in religious practice. Music often appears to be the medium of touch par excellence, associated with notions of emotion, penetration, the touching of one's heart, and so on. Music seems to live through the many ways it produces senses of contact—without any form of contact whatsoever. In this sense it intensifies an aspect that seems to belong to the aural in general. As Roland Barthes notes, "The injunction to listen is the total interpellation of one subject by another: it places above everything else the quasi-physical contact of these subjects (by voice and ear): it creates transference: '*listen to me*' means '*touch me, know that I exist.*'"[33] What remains to be understood, however, is the *situation*, even more concretely, the *locality*, of this touching. What does music touch when it appears to be touching? What notion of space does this concept of musical affection presuppose? What does it mean to be penetrated by that into which at the same time—something seemingly impossible—I am drawn?

In music, the spatiality connected with the notion of touching has a particular history. The key figure of touching already appears in classical Greece. According to Plato in the *Timaeus*, music (i.e., "*mousikē* insofar as it uses audible sound") is capable of influencing the soul if it is endowed with a *harmonia* "akin to the revolutions of the Soul within us."[34] Music, he contends, may be used to restore the soul to "order and concord with itself" whenever it has lost its harmony. Since *harmonia* is a gift of the divine Muses, this attunement of the soul by means of music necessarily has a religious aspect.[35] In addition, it may be called metaphysical in that the content of this gift involves the eternal Pythagorean numbers, thought to be constitutive of all being. In other words, attunement offers, musically, a harmonious order that underlies all good and beautiful being. Music's ability to "take strongest hold upon [the soul]," however, to "touch [it] strongly" (*errō-menestata haptetai*), is not primarily based on the qualities of the *harmoniai* as such.[36] Rather, it is based on the "kinship" (*syngeneis echousa*) between musical *harmoniai* and the *harmoniai* of the soul.[37] This "kinship," Plato suggests, produces in the soul both virtuous harmony, understood as the orderly balance between the various parts of the soul (*nous*, *thumos* and *epithumia*), and intellectual delight (*euphrosunē*, literally "good movement") in the recognition of "divine harmony manifested in mortal motions."[38]

In Plato's account, three important factors contribute to the production of a specifically Platonic context for the idea of music's immediate effects. First, in the context of the *Timaeus*, as well as in earlier dialogues, the soul that is touched by music's penetration should be understood as not possessing a comprehensive unity. The soul is threefold and consists in a heterogeneous constellation of functions, powers, and faculties. It is not a subject in the sense of a unifying substrate or in the sense of a constitutive "I." Second, the soul is immaterial. Insofar as it is a harmony, it is not—as is defended by Simmias in the famous passage in *Phaedo*—a Pythagorean harmony of physical components, which is destroyed once these components perish; rather, according to Plato, it is a principle that exists above and beyond the physical, and that may inhere in the physical.[39] Third, the soul does not have a phenomenological locality; although Plato speaks in terms of "penetration" and "inmost soul," a phenomenology of inwardness is not yet involved in this use of topographical imagery. The Platonic soul is like an eye that looks outward, above and beyond the visual world into the world of intelligible Forms, and that is incapable of looking within its own self.[40] These three contextual precautions may indicate that, on the one hand, Plato's account of "touching" cannot be understood in terms of contemporary subjective selfhood; on the other hand, they also indicate that the scene he describes is remarkably close to what many today still experience as the power of music. It should be noted that Plato specifies neither the type nor the types of music that have this ability to penetrate and touch.[41] Nor does he—here or elsewhere in his dialogues—differentiate among them with respect to their "haptonomic" power.

Plato occasionally uses the language of inwardness in order to describe the intelligible world of ideas—"the intelligible place"—as being above and beyond the world of the senses. But not until Plotinus was this world thought of as possessing a proper space within the soul. In order to construct this new space, Plotinus combined two preexisting views of the soul. First, he used the Platonic notion of the soul as "akin to [*syngenes*: of common origin] what is pure and everlasting, immortal and always the same," that is, the eternal Forms. Second, he drew upon the groundbreaking Stoic notions of inwardness, outwardness, and the call to turn to the source of goodness, which they thought to reside "within." Since the Stoics had a materialist view of the soul, they did not need to posit an inwardness as opposed to the material world of the senses. By contrast, Plotinus did experience this need. He combined the idea of an "inward turn" with the notion of the soul being an "intelligible world," ending up with an new space: an inner world within the soul.[42] Turning inward (*epistrophē, conversio*), the contemplating soul immediately looks into the metaphysical realm of the divine. Phillip Cary, synthesizing a number of passages from the *Enneads*, draws the following picture:

> Plotinus' talk of the soul turning "into the inside" belongs to a set of images he uses to give a memorable picture of the relations between the three divine levels of being. He likens the incorporeal universe to a set of concentric circles. At the center is the One, like an infinitesimal point, simple, without internal structure, parts, or boundaries—but like the center of a circle it is the source of all around it. Radiating from it like a sphere of light is the divine Mind, which contains all the Platonic Forms with their mutual distinctions, complex interrelations, and fundamental unity. Revolving around this central sphere is Soul, which can either look outward to the dim world of bodies or turn "into the inside" and behold the divine Mind and the One. When the soul does turn inward, therefore, it gazes not at a private space, but at the one intelligible world that is common to all; and likewise the soul is united to the core and center of its own being, it is united to the one core and center of all things.[43]

Discussing the topic of music, Plotinus mentions the musician among the select group of those involved in the higher dialectics that leads up to this insight. The path leading to "the topmost peak of the Intellectual realm" starts with conversion. Alongside the metaphysician and the lover, the musician starts his journey by performing this conversion, which in his case begins with an outer stimulus. Many Platonic motifs surface in this description. "The musician we may think of as being exceedingly quick to beauty, drawn in a very rapture to it: somewhat slow to stir of his own impulse, he answers at once to the outer stimulus: as the timid are sensitive to noise so he to tones and the beauty they convey; all that offends against unison or harmony in melodies or rhythms repels him; he longs for measure and shapely pattern."[44] Next, the musician "must be led to the Beauty that manifests itself through these forms; he must be shown that *what ravished him was no other than the Harmony of the Intellectual world and the Beauty in that sphere*, not some shape of beauty but the All-Beauty, the Absolute Beauty."[45] This is to say that the ravishing moment of his soul being touched by music must lead the musician toward an "inward turn" through which he may immediately contemplate the source of his state, that is, the realm of the Mind. The general scheme of this event is clearly Platonic, but the topograhy has gained a new dimension—a inner *world* into which music penetrates (a world, however, which, given the singularity of Soul, is in no way a *private* world).

Adding another dimension to this topography of inwardness, Augustine invented the inner self. By contrast to Plotinus, the inner world Augustine conceives is not one with the Divine Mind, but retains a difference with respect to "the unchangeable light" of intelligible Truth. Admonished by "the books of the Platonists," Augustine recounts what he found when he turned inward:

> These books served to remind me *to return to my own self*. Under your guidance *I entered into the depths of my soul*, and this I was able to do because your aid befriended me. I entered, and *with the eye of my soul*, such as it was, I saw the Light that never changes casting its rays *over the same eye of my soul, over my mind*. It was not the common light of day that is seen by the eye of every living thing of flesh and blood, nor was it some more spacious light of the same sort, as if the light of day were to shine far, far brighter than it does and fill all space with vast brilliance. What I saw was something quite, quite different from any light we know on earth. It shone *above my mind*, but not in the way that oil floats above water or the sky hangs over the earth. *It was above me* because it was itself the Light that made me, and I was below because I was made by it. All who know the truth know this Light, and all who know this Light know eternity. It is the Light that charity knows.[46]

Cary renders the movements in this passage from the *Confessions* as follows:

> Augustine's inward turn requires a double movement: first *in* then *up*. In contrast to Plotinus, the inner space of the Augustinian soul is not divine but is beneath God, so that turning into the inside is not all there is to finding God. We must not only turn inward but also look upward, because God is not only within the soul but also above it. In the interval between the turning in and looking up one finds oneself in a new place, never before conceived: an inner space proper to the soul, different from the intelligible world in the Mind of God. The soul becomes, as it were, its own dimension—a whole realm of being waiting to be entered and explored.[47]

In contrast to Plotinus, this inner realm is a *private* space, belonging to a particular individual soul. It results from the soul's estrangement from the divine source of Truth and Wisdom common to all; that is, it results from its sinful turning away from God. In and through this movement the soul loses the plenitude and perfection of its being. "The soul has its own kind of being, distinct from the immutable being of God above and from the spatial being of bodies below it."[48] And while being separated from its divine source, it is also separated from other souls living in the same predicament. According to Augustine, the privacy of the soul is neither natural nor good (as we tend to think today), even though it remains an eschatologically temporary condition.[49]

The concept of "inner space" relates to a variety of notions that further articulate this inwardness in religious terms. In Augustine, these notions—such as the inner eye—often refer to the Pauline *topos* of the "inner man," who is imagined to have subtle versions of bodily sense organs. Another important, and still older, notion is the "heart," which has particular value for understanding Augustine's discussion of musical experience. The heart, as Cary reminds us, is a Hebrew notion referring to the faculty of understanding and thought as well as feeling, and it tends to be connected more with hearing and understanding than with seeing and examination.[50] In the Christian tradition, it is one of the most vital figures for the economy of devotion, repentance, and the return to the inward source of eternal Life. The heart is at once the meeting place with one's mutable self and the meeting place with the immutable divine other, who dwells in this place. According to Augustine, the soul is mutable because it is now wise, now foolish; now willing, now unwilling. It "lives in misery when inclined toward the lowest, in happiness when turned toward the highest." Being mutable "not at all in space, but only in time," the Augustinian notion of the soul suggests a natural kinship with music.[51] In the *Confessions*, Augustine affirms that "all the affections of the soul, by their own diversity, have their proper measure in voice and song, which are stimulated *by I know not what secret correspondence*."[52] Music, he confesses, has always been able to move him deeply, to hold him firmly, and to bring him to tears.[53] Augustine refers to the place where this touching and holding and moving takes place as "my heart," and he adds that the "sweet and skilled voice" that is responsible for all this is hard to assign its proper place in this heart. Sometimes, it seems as though it is granted more respect than is fitting, in particular when the voice takes the lead over the words sung. The Platonic figure of music's touching has by now received a completely different context. The "secret correspondence" between music and the state of the soul, as well as music's power to penetrate its depths and grab it firmly, now occur in (and to) an inner space that, being a private space, has an *owner*. Augustine speaks of *his* heart being touched as an event that happens not to "Soul" (as in Plotinus), but to his own proper self. He is addressed by this experience in a personal way; the "sweet voice" penetrates the solitude of his inner seclusion.

Although his conception is still different from the modern notion of the self, the break with the Platonic view is significant. First, the Augustinian listening self is relatively united. The loose variety of functions, powers, and faculties that could be predicated of the Platonic soul are here kept together within a coherent notion of an inner space belonging to a particular soul.[54] To a certain extent one could speak of a synthesizing phenomenology of the soul. Despite this relative unity, however, Augustine leaves plenty of room for further determination. His use, for instance, of the distinction between, on the one hand, the notion of the soul as *anima* (referring to the living aspect of plants, animals, and human beings, as well as to the soul as the source of sensation and appetition) and, on the other hand, the soul as *animus* (referring to the rational aspect of the human soul only: mind or *mens*), is not very consistent. This leaves room for debate about the question on which of these two levels music acts and how these levels interrelate.[55] Second, Augustine's language of inwardness should not hide the fact that he regards the soul as immaterial. The centeredness of the self is contradicted by the notion that the soul has no physical location—neither somewhere "in there" in the space of inwardness nor somewhere in the body (as the popular notion of the heart suggests). Music may be said to penetrate the soul, but this penetration does not seem to take place in any space other than the space of which *the soul itself* consists. This spaceless space does not necessarily coincide with the spatiality of the body. Augustine even tends to locate the soul outside of the body, when he speaks of the perception of things at a distance, or of the awareness of things absent, or, again, of the remembrance of things past. The Augustinian soul is a location unto itself, a nonspatial dimension that nevertheless serves as the focal point of selfhood. In addition—both anticipating and contradicting the contemporary debate on musical emotion—it serves as the *terminus a quo* for any notion of inner content and (self-)expression.

The recontextualization of music's touching in this Platonic and early Christian tradition shows how the spatiality connected to this key figure transforms according to the changing conceptualizations of human individuality. As Cary argues, this history is not just a progression toward an ever more monadic subjectivity. Rather old conceptual strata remain present under newer ones, and, indeed, it remains a "live option" in modernity to dig beneath the concept of Augustinian inwardness to uncover the ruins of the ancient Plotinian, and perhaps Pythagorean, view of the soul.[56] As has already been noted, this view was often described in musical terms, the soul being likened to a musical harmony or even a musical instrument. The musical aspect of the soul here referred to differences that were primarily conceived in terms of spatial distances, such as distances on the instrument, distances between the sites of tone production or between surfaces and volumes of resonance, or distances within and between the soul's constituent spheres. In contrast to later philosophies of the subject, which tended to adopt a pointilist and inwardized view closely related to the experience of subjectivity as temporality, the individual's individuality was here primarily conceived in terms of spatiality. An archeological excavation that aims to reach underneath the Augustinian concept of inwardness will accordingly need to prepare for a turn toward a "spacious" conception of music's metaphysical-religious touching.[57] The locus of contact will have to be sought in a variety of archeological strata (and, for that matter, a variety of temporalities) rather than somewhere "in there," in the full intimacy and immediacy of a singular musico-emotive presence.

The archeological metaphor, in other words, intensifies the delocalizing movement, the "plasticity," already present in the Augustinian notion of the soul. It suggests a sliding movement from the topography of inwardness toward an outside that knows no inwardness whatsoever but that remains a possible site of contact—that is to say, of "presence"— nevertheless. Now, what does this view of presence as a *situation*, as an intimate exteriority, mean for the theoretical understanding of contemporary religious music?

Here and There

If, according to Fisk, the New Simplicity is the very opposite of classical music, it may well be understood to be the very end of music qua art, marking the extreme limit of where the art of music can go without losing its substance. The impression that this should be the end of music is strengthened by a number of phenomena that, according to Gianni Vattimo, belong to the constellation of the "death of art." Vattimo argues that this death, rather than being a notion "which could be said to correspond (or fail to correspond) to a certain state of things," is instead "an event that constitutes the historical and ontological constellation in which we move."[58] According to Vattimo, the end of art appears under the guise of three figures, each of which seems important for the analysis of the New Simplicity. First, the end of art signifies a general aestheticization of culture, which is inspired and determined by the advent of new technologies, in particular those empowering the mass media. According to Vattimo, this cultural trend leads to the loss of art "as a specific fact," but, one should add, it is also closely related to the becoming-*Kitsch* of the search for authenticity. In Tavener, this double movement surfaces in the seemingly impossible attempt to mediate his critique of (musical) modernity and his aspiration to religious authenticity through the gestures of mass-media communication. An excellent example of these can be found in the finely tuned photographic portraits of Tavener that are disseminated through the covers of CDs, books, and DVDs. These often show him in the posture of a glamorous and self-conscious visionary, with eyes searching invisible horizons, long hair referring to a tradition of male "spiritual" looks, and a suit that seems slightly too mundane for religious occasions.[59] These conscious mediatizations of the turn to religion seem to acknowledge the contemporary inevitability of mass-media engagement for any successful artist, and at same time they seem to demonstrate the paradox inherent in any mediatized construction of religious authenticity. In addition, the double bind that lies at the heart of the credibility crisis from which the New Simplicity continues to suffer is only intensified by the spectacular sales figures of its major composers.[60]

Vattimo contends, second, that the death of art is expressed by the "suicidal gesture of protest" that some contemporary artists make in the face of *Kitsch* and mass-media manipulation: "in a world where consensus is produced by manipulation," he writes, "authentic art speaks only by lapsing into silence." As already discussed, Tavener consciously chooses to silence his art qua art (defined, as he very well realizes, in terms of substance) and intends to open this space—that is to say, the empty space left behind by this particular response to the death of art—to a religiously inspired compositional practice. It remains a question whether this space is newly occupied by some artistic act of, to quote Tavener's tellingly loose phrase, "let's say, the Holy Spirit, call it what you will," or whether, as Fisk seems to argue, it is preserved at the heart of Tavener's "classical" gestures.

Vattimo's third and final point is connected to this question in that he regards the utopianism of Adorno and others to be a temporalizing response to the immediate threat of both *Kitsch* and radical negativity. Tavener's project merely seems to be related to this temporalizing shift by its quasi-historical retrojection of his art's moment of truth. The imaginary "ikon in sound" on which he intends to model his compositional practice not only receives its truth from some eternal archetype, but, as the use of the image of the icon also suggests, it may have had a historical point or scene of origin.[61] As we have noted, one of the key words for this virtual scene is *Byzantium*.

Vattimo's notions of *Kitsch*, silence, and utopia are figures that enable us to picture the deferred mode of presence of contemporary religious music. Their common denominator is the anachronism inherent in this phenomenon. Contemporary religious music cannot exist insofar as this existence is conceived in terms of presence—the *contemporaneity* of the musico-religious is virtualized by "the historical and ontological constellation in which we move." The apparent presence of this music, that is, the empirical fact that it is *still there* despite the "deaths" of both art and God, which should make its very concept tremble, can only be approached through the various notions of the anachronistic that seem to make it obsolete. As I have argued with reference to the allegedly metaphysical-religious power of music to touch, that is, to produce an intense inner sense of actuality, of presence, this temporal displacement can best be understood in terms of space. "Zum Raum wird hier die Zeit," as Nancy reminds us. These words, sung by Parsifal's companion Gurnemanz in the first scene of Wagner's most outspokenly "religious" music drama, accompany the miraculous turning inside out of the stage, representing the transformation of the transfigured forest into the sacred interior of the Grail castle.[62] Similar and no less miraculous movements occur when a musico-religious turning-to-the-inside leads to the experience of an incomparable outside, as was exemplified by the sliding movement from Augustinian inwardness toward the ancient Soul's cosmic exteriority-without-inwardness. How can we account theoretically for the *kind of space* in which these movements take place? I will suggest that one possibility consists in a combination of an analytical engagement with topology, a reinterpretation of musical form, and the heuristic equation of tone and place.

According to Leonard Lawlor, the reading of time as a kind of space belongs to the most proper features of structuralist and poststructuralist theories and philosophies. Its most prominent figure is that of archeology—a figure that, as Lawlor demonstrates, is rooted primarily in Freud.[63] Indeed, the context in which Freud considers the psychoanalytic archive is a discussion about religious feeling, as he calls it, the "'oceanic' feeling." In *Civilization and Its Discontents*, Freud responds to the idea of such a feeling, which, according to his friend Romain Rolland, is expressive of, in Freud's words, "something limitless" and of "an indissoluble bond, of being one with the external world as a whole."[64] Rather than considering it a feeling that reveals the actual entanglement of subject and world through the religious experience of originary unity, Freud construes this "oceanic feeling" as a remnant of some early stage in the subject's psychological development. The feeling is like an old layer in the subject's stratified structure that has not been replaced by more recent stages of development. Succeeded genealogically without being overwritten, it is "there" without being actual, without belonging to the present qua present. Freud suggests understanding this preservation of the past by shifting from a temporal to a spatial mode. The mature subject's "mental life," he contends, is more reminiscent of an age-old city than a mature organism in which early stages have disappeared without a trace. This calls for detailed attention to the distribution and layering of contiguous and overlapping sites, which are heterogeneous in a temporal respect, while simultaneously being "there." Thus, the nonpathological experience of an "indissoluble bond" between ego and world, which to some extent parallels the simultaneously invasive and enveloping power of music, leads Freud to observe that "the boundaries of the ego are not constant" and that they seem to move through an archeological space.[65] Parts of this archeological space, such as "absolute memory," may not even be positively identifiable by the subject as belonging to its proper mental life.[66] In short, as Derrida writes, "Freud's contribution consists in saying that the psyche is structured in such a way that there are many places in which traces are kept, which means that within the psyche there is an inside and an outside."[67]

If we take this methodological shift from genealogy to topology as a lead, the situation or locality of music's touching becomes less a matter of looking for its presence than a search for the topology of its *touchés*, contacts, connections, contiguities, and foldings. Inevitably, this brings the experience of music closer to its cosmological past, that is, to the spatial relationality of its structures and resonances, and to the de-definition and plasticity of the listener's individuality.[68]

This particular spatiality, which has virtually nothing to do with the concrete spaces in which musical events are said to take place, reveals itself only if music is taken in its proper, that is, *formal*, sense. As Samuel Weber notes in his analysis of the concept of form in Kant, form, rather than being some quality belonging to the object, is an unstable, intermediary element, which posits itself in between the aesthetic judgment and what it is judging. "If form can be said to arise when a multiplicity of sensations are 'connected' to one another, thus resulting in a perceptual, but not conceptual, unity, such a *perceptum* cannot be attributed to the object itself but rather only to how that object *appears at a certain time and place*."[69] The formal element of music should not be mistaken for the logical, procedural, or structural aspects of its ontology. Rather, it defines itself, as François Nicolas has amply shown, as the point of diffraction between music's architectural and topological dimensions. On the one hand, viewed as a mereological entity, music can be described as a unity consisting of parts and wholes that intersect on a variety of levels. The totality of a piece of music qua object here results from the completeness of its constitutive parts. Typically, music analysis aims to describe and account for the mereological structure of musical works, focusing on the definition of parts and wholes and their interrelations. On the other hand, there is an aspect of music that eludes this architectural dimension. On only rare occasions, but very significant ones, a piece of music produces, as a kind of excess, a *second coherence* that appears to be independent of its mereological completeness.[70] Nicolas refers to this coherence as "Form" and speaks of a *rupture de plan* between the formal level and the piece's architecture. Introducing a topological distinction, he describes their difference as follows:

> The Form of a given work is what grasps it in its entirety starting from its sonorous unfolding (rather than starting from the score). Thus, one distinguishes the Form from the work's architecture (whether preestablished or not is of little importance) when one understands the work's architecture to be the large-scale structuring of large parts that one discerns by looking at it frontally, that is, from an examinatory distance rather than along the endogenous line of (a) listening [*fil endogène d'une écoute*]. Accordingly, the privileged vehicle for such an architectural structuring is the score, because it lays out [*dispose*] this face-to-face in a sufficiently stable manner.[71]

Seen from the viewpoint of Form, music is no longer a architectural structure imagined to be located at a certain point in geometrical space and open for inspection from a distance, but is itself a kind of space or place.[72] Perhaps this is the more profound reason why Tavener refers to the notion of *temenos*, of sacred place, in conjunction with his music: not just in referring to the concert spaces where his music is performed, which he obviously would like to sacralize, but more particularly in order to indicate the specific spatiality music can itself produce qua place or *temenos*.[73]

To experience music as a place, or as a multiplicity of places, means to be engaged, in a wholly dependent way, in that *situation* called music on the level of participation (*methexis*).[74] Nancy describes the topological structure of this mode of being present (*le présent sonore*) when he analyzes the way in which sound inaugurates a space that simultaneously constitutes the sonorous "object" and the "listener":

> To listen [*écouter*] is to enter that spatiality by which, *at the same time*, I am penetrated, for it opens up in me as well as around me, and from me as well as toward me: it opens inside me as well as outside, and it is through such a double, quadruple, or sextuple opening that a "self" can take place. To be listening [*être à l'écoute*] is to be *at the same time* outside and inside, to be opened *from* without and *from* within, hence from one to other and from one in the other.[75]

In other words, a topological view of music describes it as a *topophony* that articulates the local—that is to say, the inside and outside places involved in the sonorous event ("my inwardness," the "sound object")—with the global, that is to say, the continuous "spatiality" that mediates the torsional relation between those places. It views music as a heterotopia that, on the aural-sensible level of musical Form, actualizes the seemingly impossible of being here *and* there, inside *and* outside, *at the same time*—a thing of which only the gods are said to be capable. "And that is," the composer Iannis Xenakis once noted, "the mystery of space: what does that mean, being here *and* there?"[76]

What is the meaning of being here *and* there at the same time? Of dwelling in a kind of archival space, being on the outside while remaining on the inside, traversing along this axis a temporal distance as well?[77] The question of contemporary religious music eventually leads to questions about the anachronisms and archival topologies involved in the peculiar, and to some extent unforeseen, "presences" that are brought to bear on this phenomenon—in particular, by those who have the strongest faith in this music. Up to this point in my argument, the case of Tavener has only served to explore the historical-theoretical *momentum* in which this kind of music is situated at present, having focused in particular on its relation to the deaths of art and God. A final example, taken from the opposite end of the musical spectrum, that is, from the domain of the high modernism that Tavener has attacked so vehemently, may elucidate the ways in which contemporary music traverses this moment. As we have seen, it does so by sticking to the poietic rule that *tone is place*, creating in sound a desert, a heterotopia, a *temenos*, or, as we shall now see, a *khōra*-effect.

The music of Iannis Xenakis is generally associated with unparalleled forces and intensities. It refers to awesome sonorities that inspire what could be called a situation of trembling, that is, a situation in which sonic vibrations touch with such intensity that a new topological spatiality (a new Form) seems to emerge. As Nancy puts it, in a phrase that seems particularly apt for this Xenakian experience: "Trembling is the act of being-affected—a passive acting that merely makes the body vibrate, that unsettles substance. The self trembles at being touched, awakened, roused; it trembles as much at the feeling of its fragility as in the desire for its freedom."[78] As biographer Nouritza Matossian recalled in an obituary, *freedom* was an important word for Xenakis. "Yes, every discussion, every conversation, ended with the words, 'But you see, Nour, the most important thing in art, and in life, is to be free.' "[79] For Xenakis, this freedom seems to have been a desire to be touched by an ineluctable and violent force, an aural fate, of sorts. The touch of Xenakis's music differs drastically from the touch of musical *Empfindsamkeit*. His is neither a touch in search of the plenitude of emotion nor one in search of tears over some matter of content. It is an affect, a *touché*, which aims at a merely *formal* contact, producing, on a quasi-physical level, a feeling of existence. Again, Nancy's work offers phrases to describe what happens here: " 'I' is a touch."[80] To be, that is, to sense a self *in trembling*, is to be touched—which means, at the same time, to touch. Xenakis's music seems to generalize this interconnection between contact and existence. The torrential force of his music effectively produces a sense of "self," but consistently without reference to subjective selfhood. It produces a new here (or there, which topologically amounts to the same) by means of its force simultaneously to shut and to open. The situation created by Xenakis's music is a like a fold: it folds back the sonorous plane onto itself, creating a new situation—a sense of being irreducible to preexistent subjects and objects.[81]

Xenakis's music exerts a power that, using the words of composer Jonathan Harvey, could be described in terms of the "*near*-transcendent."[82] Its relation to the transcendent (i.e., the divine or metaphysical *archē*) can only be approached in terms of nearness, contiguity, or connection, that is to say, topologically. Although Xenakis is not particularly known for his engagement with religion, his music seems to call for an engagement with the question of religion because of its archaic character. Asked about the religiosity of her father, Mâkhi Xenakis once ironically remarked that he "believed in Zeus."[83] As is well known, Xenakis adored the ancient Greeks, and he is said to have had a special preference for the Mycenean period, "because we know little about it, being for that reason surrounded by mystery."[84] Figuring often in his works for choir, the ancient texts related to this period, such as the *Oresteïa* and *Oedipus in Colonus*, represent a theme that also pertains to the structure of his work in general. As François-Bernard Mâche remarks, there is in his music a singular "alliance between logical speculation and physical violence," which virtually reactualizes the Mycenean clash between, as Xenakis put it, "the archaic law and the new law."[85] For Xenakis, this clash is obsessive; as the titles of his works indicate, there is a continual alternation in his musical thought between "the colours of death and those of life."[86] This *rapprochement* between death and life often seems unmediated, like the beautiful but dead girl painted by John Everett Millais in his *Ophelia*.[87] Yet, I would suggest, there is a space here within which *toucher* takes place. This space is a distinct and singular *tone*, which can be heard in his works from *Metastaseis* onward. Perhaps one could call it the *tone of the archaic*.[88]

Rather than simply reactualizing, in a quasi-theatrical manner, the conflict of *archai*, the tone of the archaic produces a region (*khōra*) in which constitutive touching can take place.[89] Music, according to Xenakis, is the domain of "a truth immediate, rare, enormous, and perfect," "toward" which it draws by means of its "means of expression." To the extent that it succeeds in doing so, music is "beyond music," and can lead, Xenakis contends, "to realms (*régions*) that religion still occupies for some people."[90] Rather than positing realms that exist separately from the act of music, however, I suggest reversing the schema by positing that it is music itself that creates the realms toward which it seems drawn. The nearness to which Xenakis refers is a topological figure, not some position on the map of finite immanence indicating its distance relative to the transcendent and immediate "truth" that lies beyond its edges. His music has the gift of producing the *khōra*-effect, the distinct sense of *temenos*, the holy region, by means of the affinity between *tone* and *place*. Its apparently naked disposition of raw sensibility and raw speculative reason actualizes the remainders of sense, which, as a kind of monument, refer to the outside of their touching. As suggested above, "religion" is linked to the enigma of *ça touche*. Xenakis's music gathers and situates that enigma under the guise of a sonic "here" (which, as indicated, is a "there")—a "presence" that can only be linked, as Mâkhi Xenakis has rightly done, to the figure of the specter. *Laisser venir les fantômes* (*Let the Ghosts Come In*), including myself as a listener. In the electronic work *Bohor* from 1962, the lines of cleavage between life and death take the shape of a manifold spectral hovering. The trembling produced by their "being there" may very well hint at the possibility of a religious music, after the end of art, the death of God, and the "Resurrection of Tedium" as registered by the critics of the New Simplicity.[91]

Death in the Image

The Post-Religious Life of Christian Images

Alena Alexandrova

Is every work of art a fake acheiropoieton?

—Marie-José Mondzain, *Image, Icon, Economy*

Placing Religion and Contemporary Art

A number of group and solo exhibitions offer evidence that both curators and visual artists are increasingly interested in the controversial
issue of religion and its role in the contemporary art scene.[1] Artworks
that deal with or refer to religious themes and motifs constitute a very
heterogeneous group. They have in common the fact that they do not
function in religious contexts and cannot be described as "religious
art." Instead, these artworks are *about* religion and its practices, concepts, ideas, and images in the sense that they thematize its continued
cultural relevance. Curators and artists interested in religious themes
are aware that it is not necessary (and in fact not possible) to erase all
traces of religion in their work in order to posit a rupture with the past
that will secure a safe, external, and perhaps more valid point of view
concerning it.[2]

I will argue that, in general, contemporary artworks *about* religion
resemble images that belong to religious art, or refer in another way to
a religious theme. Precisely the modality of being "about" enables these
artworks to pose critical questions concerning the visual legacy of religious traditions such as Christianity. Yet the word *about* does not seem
to capture the full complexity of the dialogue between contemporary
art and its religious past. Arguably, there is something of religion *in*
contemporary art, an opaque residue that resists explanation in terms

of the distinction between religious art and secular art, and that conceals some of the complexity of their repositioning with regard to each other. This "something" is, I believe, related to how Christian religion developed a complex economy of the image, having at its heart a transcendent and invisible truth.[3] In other words, the relevance of religion for art produced in the present has to do with the complex entanglement between power, truth, and the political, and only to a lesser extent with something particularly sacred or spiritual. The presence of some elements pertaining to religion *in* contemporary artworks does not mean by necessity that they *visually resemble* religious images. Rather, it concerns general aspects of the regimes under which images are produced and circulated. Indeed, many artworks that explicitly engage with religious issues remain (post)modern and secular: for instance, Andy Warhol's *Twelve Crosses* (1981–82) cannot be considered to be religious art, even though it explicitly refers to a religious symbol.

Addressing the issue of the "strange place" of religion in contemporary art, art historian James Elkins argues that contemporary art today is "as far from organized religion as Western art has ever been" and that religion is seldom mentioned in the art world, with the exception of cases when "there has been a scandal: someone has painted a Madonna using elephant dung or put a statuette of Jesus into a jar of urine."[4] The scandalous is certainly a powerful way to attract attention, but that does not mean that the artwork that provokes it is genuinely critical. In this essay I hope to demonstrate that the critical potential of contemporary artworks dealing explicitly with religious themes lies somewhere apart from art's rejection or mocking of religion. The scandalous is a tricky modality, both for those who produce it and for those who condemn it, since it reproduces what it attacks and thus runs the risk of affirming its importance. No matter how the scandal is read and the scandalous issue interpreted by those who scandalize and those who are scandalized, its intention or gesture can easily be turned against itself. Some interpretations of Chris Ofili's *The Holy Virgin Mary* (1996) and Andres Serrano's *Piss Christ* (1987), to which Elkins refers, essentially appropriate them as religious art. The use of elephant dung in Ofili's piece can be interpreted as "linking the Christian message, an important part of the artist's upbringing, with his cultural and ethnic roots in Africa" and *Piss Christ* can be seen as bringing back the shock of the crucifix to the eyes of those who, over the centuries, have become desensitized to it.[5]

In the context of the general skepticism about expressing explicitly religious content in contemporary artworks, several pieces by the Belgian artist Berlinde de Bruyckere offer an interesting case, which cannot neatly be categorized as religious, nonreligious, or antireligious art. *Jelle Luipaard* is a sculpture made out of wax casts of body parts assembled to form a figure that hangs on an iron hook attached to the wall of the exhibition space.[6] A wooden bar is inserted into the flesh of the figure. The separate parts out of which it is assembled do not form a normal human body—there is no head or indication of gender, and only part of an arm is attached to the torso. The technique of casting used by the artist made it possible to render minute details such as the toenails of or the texture of

FIGURE 13 *Jelle Luipaard,* by Berlinde de Bruyckere. Wax, iron, epoxy and wood, 2004.

the flesh in an almost uncannily realistic way. The overall shape of the body parts is distorted: they are elongated and joined, or rather welded, together in such a way that the flesh of the this mutilated body seems to be melting over the supporting structure.

In my discussion of De Bruyckere's piece, I will first analyze the way in which contemporary artworks that explicitly refer to religious imagery position themselves in time. Second, I shall address the conditions under which an image can be considered to be the medium of religious or aesthetic truth, as well as the intricate relationship between representations of death and iconoclasm. Finally, I come to the conclusion that *Jelle Luipaard* articulates a way for artworks to appropriate critically religious motifs without being seen as scandalous (i.e., inherently religious).

Breaking Resemblance

Jelle Luipaard, named after the person who was the model for the sculpture, opens complex questions concerning how an artwork can be religious and nonreligious at once. It does so by evoking, almost involuntarily or as if by mistake, images from the past. The figure is familiar, and yet not quite—the familiarity is interrupted. The work hangs on the wall in a way that reminiscent of a crucifix. Yet the headless body does not represent Christ, and the iron hook is not a cross. Besides the most obvious and general visual reference to the Cross, the position of the figure reminds one of the figurative language of pain developed by late medieval and Renaissance painters to depict the tortured bodies of the two thieves crucified next to Christ.[7] The slim and disfigured body also resonates with the figure of Death, which reached its apogee in the art of the sixteenth-century German painter Hans Baldung Grien.[8] These are just a few examples of the figures associated with death and suffering with which this sculpture resonates. These visual resemblances place *Jelle Luipaard* in dialogue with the tradition of Western religious art. This piece cannot qualify as religious art, however, because it neither treats a religious theme explicitly nor refers to Christian iconography in any straightforward sense. The piece conflates different images, which makes it impossible to read it as a reproduction of a particular religious figure. Could it be that precisely through that *interrupted* resemblance this work of contemporary art acquires the power to address critically not only the role of the representations of violence massively present throughout the history of the Christian image, but a set of deeper questions concerning the functioning of the image as a religious medium?

The familiarity of the figure both invites the viewer to identify the model that the image resembles and makes it impossible to link that resemblance to any single image. One effect is to foreground the problem of resemblance itself. Reformulated in religious terms, this problem relates both to the question of the *imago dei*—of just what resemblance is implied in the claim that man is made in the image of God—and to the prohibition of visual representation of God, thus the suspicion attached to any humanly created image that circulates in a religious context, or any image that involves the work of an artist's hand. By making her hand as an artist strongly present, De Bruyckere redefines that drama of lost resemblance as a drama of resemblance *between images* and not between an image and something that will guarantee its truth, whether that be God or a divine origin. In this way, she engages the image historically as one of the media for *making* religious truth. *Jelle Luipaard* intervenes in the history of images and in the history of making images as an image with a double face (what Walter Benjamin would call a dialectical image), in that it keeps something of religion *in* itself and is *about* religion, simultaneously evoking the past and addressing the present.

Counter-Time

The ambiguous resemblance to religious iconography places *Jelle Luipaard* in what we might call *counter-time*. With this term, I attempt to capture two interrelated aspects of the temporal complexity of this artwork. On the one hand, it is anachronistic to the extent that it is a work of contemporary art that resembles images from the past. On the other hand, it positions itself with considerable self-awareness against them. Art historian Georges Didi-Huberman addresses the issue of the complex positioning of images in time his *Devant le temps* (*Confronting Time*).[9] He argues that visual objects are temporally impure or anachronistic by virtue of the complex interrelation between the image, the artist, and a gaze situated in a later moment of time (that of a historian). The artist is not only a figure at a certain moment in the past but also works *with* time. Fra Angelico, for instance, is both an artist of the historical past and an artist who manipulates memory, "an artist contra his time."[10] The multiple strata of time within images appear though what Didi-Huberman calls "displaced resemblances," or resemblances between images belonging to distant moments in time.[11] Being temporally complex, images resist attempts to inscribe them into linear explanatory narratives of history, which are often implicitly conditioned by what Didi-Huberman calls the metaphysical abstraction of the pure past.[12] To pose the question of anachronism implies interrogating the fundamental plasticity and mixing of different times at work in images.[13]

Jelle Luipaard embodies a fold in time—it is a work of *contemporary* art, a body-object placed in the space of the present-day gallery, but *simultaneously present* on its surface are images that we usually attribute to different moments in time: a crucifix, the figure of Death, but also all the images of suffering we see in the mass media. By borrowing imagery from both the past and the present, De Bruyckere goes contra her time. The temporal complexity that results cannot be explained within a linear model of time. It seems necessary to introduce a second layer of time—counter-time. On the one hand, this refers to the fact that her piece *turns toward the past* and borrows motifs from religious art; on the other, it refers to the *simultaneous presence* of several different images or motifs.

Crucial to this mode of co-presence is the impossibility of entirely disentangling the different motifs. In other words, they are not isolated units, which could be identified or located in separate parts of the piece. The term *counter-time* is used in music to designate the simultaneity of two different tempi, that is, a unity built out of two heterogeneous elements. In *Jelle Luipaard*, we see a crucifix *and* the figure of Death *and* a mutilated body. By this juxtaposition, or rather layering, of different motifs, De Bruyckere places her piece in dialogue with two different regimes of images—religious and aesthetic.[14]

The term *counter-time* helps articulate the critical potential of artworks such as *Jelle Luipaard*. It overlaps to some degree with the term *preposterous history*, coined by Mieke Bal. In *Quoting Caravaggio*, she argues that contemporary art works can both be analyzed within, and open possibilities for, a *preposterous history*, because they "demonstrate a possible way of dealing with the 'past today.' This reversal, which puts what came chronologically first ('pre-') as an aftereffect behind ('post-') its later recycling, . . . is a way of 'doing history' that carries productive uncertainties and illuminating highlights."[15] Being a present-day artwork and an image in counter-time, *Jelle Luipaard does* preposterous history. The displaced resemblances that appear on its surfaces productively disturb our gaze in the present and open possible ways of seeing the past anew.

Faith Displaced

Several authors have indicated that the complexity of the dialogue between religion and contemporary nonreligious art can be understood better if we relax the rigidity of the distinction between religious and secular art. Elkins insists that contemporary art that sets out to convey spiritual values is simply bad art, since it goes against the grain of the history of modernism.[16] He points out, however, that it is no longer possible to ignore some religious inspirations in abstract art (from Kasimir Malevich and Vasily Kandinsky to Barnett Newman). Thierry de Duve, a historian and theorist of modern art, acknowledges the need to address the continued relevance of some religious themes and concepts for contemporary art. In his text for the catalogue of the exhibition *Look! 100 Years of Contemporary Art* (2002), De Duve analyzes the way religious thought and practices have conditioned some aspects of contemporary art and its perception. He points out that one of the key painters in the development of modernism, Édouard Manet:

> had certainly no knowledge of the theological bedrock of his practice, but, like all his colleagues, he was dependent on a long tradition which had assimilated its tenets, secularised them, and forgotten their origins, but in which they remained subterraneanly active. They would stay active throughout the history of modernist painting.[17]

De Duve argues that a key aspect of that subterranean presence of religious meanings in modernist art is the displacement of faith. He writes that "the best modern art has endeavored to redefine the essentially *religious* terms of humanism on *belief*-less bases," in that way retaining something of religious spirituality.[18] In his understanding, by inoculating itself with a small dose of doubt, modern art in fact succeeded in keeping faith alive.[19] An example of such a strategy is Kazimir Malevich's *Black Square on a White Ground* (1913), an artwork that inoculated "the tradition of the Russian icon with a vaccine capable of preserving its human meaning, for a period in which faith in God could no longer keep alive."[20] Discussing Manet's *Dead Christ and the Angels* (1864), De Duve concludes that this painter problematizes the distinction between faith in God and faith in painting. By treating a Christian theme in a way that deviates from a canonical interpretation of a biblical scene, Manet invites his audience to see his painting not only as a religious representation but exclusively as art. His artistic strategy was successful to the extent that it demonstrated that the separation between faith in God, faith in painting, and faith in man was not self-evident for his nineteenth-century audience.[21]

One of De Duve's central points is that religious faith, or the need to have faith, did not die but displaced itself: "Museums have become churches while churches have become museums, as if religiosity, determined not to die, obeyed a strange law of communicating vessels."[22] He demonstrates that the status of images within the space of a communal gaze is dependent upon a complex texture of social pacts that grant to a *thing* the status of an artwork, investing it with the truth of being art with a capital *A*. This mechanism has tautology at its heart, as Marie-José Mondzain points out in her analysis of a visual object that is considered to be one of the few images for the Christian believer that carries within itself profound spiritual truth—the Holy Shroud: "It is not because it is true that it has power. It is because it has power that it becomes true, *that it must be true*."[23] This truth, be it religious or aesthetic, is itself not part of the object in question. It is, strictly speaking, invisible. According to De Duve, the quasi-invisible locations of power in museum space, which embody the power of the social pacts that deem things to be artworks, are the devices that present the objects: frames, stands, pedestals. De Duve argues further that the presentational device is "what lives on of God the Father when God is dead—fascination with Power in its almightiness," or, finally, the authority of the museum to determine which objects will be seen and in what way.[24] With his famous *Fountain* (1917), Marcel Duchamp addressed precisely the mechanism for inventing truth invested in visual objects. At a later stage, however, as De Duve writes, this piece circulated in terms of the very situation that it addressed critically:

> Boy, how we've turned Duchamp into the parodying officiating priest of a cult, which focuses, like the Christian mass, on the consecration! "*Hoc est corpus meum*, this is art," and that's done the trick. All the public has to do is to share, rapturously, in the belief in the Duchampian transubstantiation, at the risk of seeing the museum-temple occupied by that nihilist god, the power of the art institution. When art for art's sake has become power for power's sake, we've reached that stage. It is easier today to *deify* Duchamp's urinal—especially if it's out of derision or desecration—than to

find within it *human* qualities justifying our treating it with the respect due to works of art.[25]

He concludes that objects of contemporary art retain something of "religion," but by insisting on the quotation marks, he points out that they are imposed by a long history that gradually prompted humans to do without gods, then without God, and finally brought them face to face with Absence as such.[26] For art explicitly to take on the task of presenting this Absence required a spectacular secularization of minds. Art's struggle with absence or the desire to *present* it resulted in a permanent crisis in representation, which is "one of the names of a God-less world."[27]

> the greatest artists knew that the function of art was to fit Absence with a void *at the heart of the social* and to display the void to those willing to look. Yet this metaphysical void is not displayable as such. It cannot be put on a stand and presented. Nobody can say that he or she has seen death itself, which is its sign here on earth. It is only negatively displayable, which is an unfathomable paradox, given that, for us, death is only absolute negation.[28]

De Duve concludes that art has an irrepressible desire to show the void at the heart of the social, and this is why it is "doomed" to resurrection. That makes the works it produces into focal points of acts of faith. They are deemed to be alive, are venerated, and are placed in museums. As De Duve puts it: "The artist's task is to turn a thing into a living being so that it can be mortal."[29] Resurrection then becomes a matter of common belief that this or that is a work of art. It amounts to a thing presenting itself: "Here I am." As De Duve points out, it is no more than that, nothing very religious or glorious.[30]

The importance of De Duve's approach is related to the fact that he directs his attention to an aspect of the relationship between contemporary art and religion that has been insufficiently addressed and that opens a way to think about how religious elements are still present *in* artworks that does not explicitly refer to religion. His analysis exceeds the simple analogy between some aspects of modernist art and theological doctrines, and addresses the issue on the plane of the complex interrelation between the political, the aesthetic, and the religious. Thus, it sheds light on the conditioning of some aspects of contemporary art objects and practices by the way religion has managed and used images. An important conclusion emerging from De Duve's analysis is that this presence of "something" of religion in the contemporary art scene is not strictly visual, nor is it necessarily related to visual resemblance to religious art. It is related to the way images function as focal points of social pacts that invest them with a transcendent and therefore invisible truth.

Presentability, Truth, and Power

In her book *Image, Icon, Economy*, Mondzain argues that in order to understand the extraordinary power of contemporary images and media we must consider them in view of the legacy of the theological thinking of the image. She points to the proximity between the modern art object as the ready-made and a type of image that is considered to be especially authentic in the Christian tradition, since it is not created by human hands—the *acheiropoietic* image. According to her, the Holy Shroud demonstrates a surprising similarity to the way visual objects today acquire their status as artworks through procedures of presentation that invent their "truth." She suggests that the Shroud cannot be seen only as an artifact situated in the distant past. It is not only a focal point of religious power but demonstrates proximity to notions belonging to different regimes of modernity:

> the Holy Shroud is manifested under the different regimes of modernity in the discourse it generates: that of the stain without an author, that of the self-portrait, and that of the ready-made. A distinguished image that has the value of a signature; self-designation offered of all gazes, which will answer for its authenticity. Whoever the real author may be, her or his power stems from the power it gives to whomever beholds it.[31]

Following Mondzain, I argue that when discussing images it seems necessary to place the word "truth" in quotation marks. There "truth" stands for the desire for authenticity embodied in the operations of its invention. Mondzain and others have demonstrated that images considered to be "true" function as focal points, an imagined stable and common point of reference for regimes of belief that give meaning to the world we share. She argues that the Shroud: "Incarnates incarnation and expects those who contemplate it to have the open gaze of faith. 'They have eyes and do not see' becomes 'we give ourselves the eyes which construct what we want to see.' An eminently modern art situation such as the cinema, stemming from photography, inaugurated it."[32] That power and the continued relevance of such an image are not related to the miracles it performed or the conversions it has facilitated. The status of the Shroud is exceptional because as an image-imprint it shares with the modern medium of photography the principle of producing images by leaving a trace on a sensitive surface. A photograph and the Shroud make similar claims to truth based on producing an image without the hand of a maker, manipulator, or counterfeiter.

Didi-Huberman likewise points out that in the famous cases of Veronica's Veil and the Holy Shroud, which have the special status of "divine productions," "what strikes one immediately . . . is the triviality, the extreme humility of the objects themselves, which have nothing to show, but the tatters of their material."[33] Thus they do not re-present but *present* the privilege of having been *touched* by a divinity. In other words, their importance lies in their *presentability* to a communal gaze. These images claim to bear direct witness to the event of Incarnation and are deemed to be true precisely because they are not representations and are not result of the work of any artist. To add the hand to them, as sociologist of science Bruno Latour points out, would be to "weaken their force" and "nullify the transcendence of the divinities," thus emptying "the claims of a salvation from above."[34]

Jelle Luipaard is a contemporary artwork that problematizes this key juncture between presentability, truth, and power. It is in that sense, I would suggest, that it retains something of religion in itself. The piece addresses the issue of truth as an aspect of images through the technique of its making. For this work De Bruyckere used direct casts of body parts in colored wax, which resulted in a very realistic rendering. The feet of the figure, with miniature details such as toenails, look so uncannily present that they transform the figure hanging on the wall into a quite confrontational object, which is no longer simply a sculpture but can be perceived as a real corpse. To the extent that casting is based on direct contact between a model and a material that receives the imprint, and thus reduces the role of the hand of a maker, it resonates strongly with the acheiropoietic image, including its claim to authenticity and truth. But *Jelle Luipaard* is not just a hyperrealistic representation of a dead or mutilated body. The distortion and the joining of its separate parts, which make the figure look like an empty skin draped over a pole, are by no means realistic and cannot possibly happen to a real body. By deforming both the normal shape of a human body and the way it would be if it had really been mutilated, De Bruyckere makes the work of her hand as an artist strongly present. In a sense, her hand as an artist mutilates mutilation. With this meta-gesture she foregrounds the very operations of making present in every image. So if an image like the Shroud claims to carry profound truth because it was not touched by an artist's hand, if it is true precisely because it is *not made*, *Jelle Luipaard* foregrounds the making, showing that that there are no true images but that truth is *made* in images.

In that critical sense *Jelle Luipaard* overlaps with some aspects of the ready-made. On the one hand, the creative hand of the artist is downplayed, which is the defining feature of the ready-made. On the other, the sculpture foregrounds presentational procedures that place an object on display, saying "This is art!" and thereby investing it with the truth of being Art. If Duchamp's *Fountain* addresses that power mechanism by placing in the museum space and presenting as art a banal object not made by a human hand, De Bruyckere inserts the presentational device—the metal hook and the wooden bar—*into* the flesh of her sculpture. *Jelle Luipaard* is not framed or presented as an intact object; it is violently cut by its presentational device. By juxtaposing the material of hyperrealistically rendered flesh to the invisible truth of Art associated with the presentational device, De Bruyckere foregrounds the fact that the procedures of putting things on display in the museum space do not always equal veneration, as De Duve argues, but can be inherently violent. They are also procedures of objectification that nail the meaning of the object on display to a reading associated with the regime in which it is shown.

De Bruyckere is aware that a dead body cannot present itself without the help of a presentational device. In many of her pieces, she uses stands and vitrines that simultaneously present and shelter the sculptural figures, faceless bodies hovering between life and death. By placing a dead body without possibility of resurrection on a presentational device, in *Jelle Luipaard* she addresses the "void at the heart of the social" that, according to De Duve, art has an irresistible desire to show because it shows our absolute negation—death. In her work the dead body, or its representation, coincides with its life as an artwork. Thus it is the very mortality of the flesh that is resurrected. In that way, De Bruyckere puts her finger on a neuralgic spot: we must have faith in art to confront a corpse as an artwork; without that faith we confront death. In other words, with this piece the artist addresses the power of art to present death to us.

Critical Embodiment

As a complement to De Duve's analysis of the way modernist art incorporates and retains something of religion, I suggest that it is important to look at the way contemporary artworks both retain something of religion *in* them and acquire critical agencies through being *about* religion. Bruno Latour proposes this modality of "being about" as a point of departure for reevaluating the multifaceted phenomenon of iconoclasm. In his introduction to the exhibition catalogue *Iconoclash*, he delineates the possibility of a critical reevaluation of iconoclastic practices. He points out that the exhibition is not iconoclastic, but *about* iconoclasm. It attempts to suspend the urge to destroy images and instead embeds the destruction of images in the museum space in order to reflect on it and to interrogate the worship of iconoclasm itself. Such a stance implies taking iconoclasm out of its role of overarching meta-language and *thematizing* it as a topic.[35]

By embedding a motif—specifically, one of the central and most recognizable images in the Christian tradition—*Jelle Luipaard* turns religion into a topic in a similar way. Here, unlike in the situation described by Latour, the artwork and not the museum space embeds the motif. Still, this work similarly takes a critical stance without rejecting or destroying the thing it criticizes. It is important to note that my distinction between being "in" and "about" religion does not concern two entirely separable aspects of an artwork. On the contrary, they overlap to a great extent, since they are co-present in the same image. Whereas in *Iconoclash* iconoclasm is turned from resource into topic, allowing its critical reevaluation, in *Jelle Luipaard* religion as a resource and as a topic are co-present. This artwork is not only a "resurrected" object (as De Duve would have it), deemed alive and placed in a museum or a gallery space. It looks at its own resurrection in the sense that it shows that it is aware of the displacement of faith from faith in God to faith in art, since it interrogates the way the status of the object is produced or invented for a certain community of gazes (believers, art connoisseurs). By being *about* religion, or by embedding a visually recognizable motif, *Jelle Luipaard* critically addresses violence as a key aspect of Christian images on at least two planes—as violence against images and as a representation of violence in images.

The analysis by art historian Joseph Leo Koerner of the notion of specifically Christian religious iconoclasm and some of its internal dynamics can shed light on how artworks such as *Jelle Luipaard* position themselves with regard to Christian iconography. In his article "Icon as Iconoclash," he points to the inherently paradoxical situation of the religious iconoclast, who *believes* that the image is everything for someone else and attacks not the artifact itself but the deception he believes to be attached to it.[36] The fact that the iconoclast believes that others blindly believe in images makes him simply "another person with 'a strong commitment to representation,' in this case, that of naïve belief itself."[37] In other words, the act of breaking a religious image paradoxically means recognizing its power.

In the Christian case iconoclasm has great internal complexity because, as Koerner points out, Christian images are inherently iconoclastic: "At the center of the great machinery of Christian images stood the paradox of the cross: what to the rest of the world was the ultimate punishment . . . was for Christians the emblem of their God."[38] This determined the Bible's aesthetics as an aesthetics of the ugly, not of the beautiful. Consequently, its ontology of the image was based as much on dissimilarity as on resemblance. By placing at its center an image of "God's only son, an image not made by a human hand (*acheiropoetos*)" that is already broken and transformed into "the ugliest of things," the Christian image acquired power, since with that it preemptively questioned its subsequent criticisms and rejections.[39] This gesture of letting death insist in the religious image resulted in what Koerner calls infinite regression. It is related to the question: How is it possible to break an image that is already broken?[40] He concludes that, by attacking the crucifix, the iconoclasts "at once negate and repeat the likeness cultivated in their target. Their blows are negations of a negation, 'no's' canceled by an ultimate 'no.' Religious imagery has iconoclasm built into it."[41]

A discussion of the issue of iconoclasm in my analysis of images produced in the present is necessary for two reasons. First, to point out how some appropriations of religious themes and motifs by contemporary artworks are inherently in danger, like the iconoclasts, of affirming the power of that which they try to disempower. Second, to indicate that the artworks I am interested in, which are *about* religion, are smart enough not to be iconoclastic or scandalous because they are aware of the internal iconoclasm already embedded in the way Christianity thought of its images. The modality of being "about" is their way of being critical in nonreligious terms.

The mutilated, fragmented figure of *Jelle Luipaard* is already a broken, self-negating image. This work does not simply *resemble the dissemblance* that Christian images show—

the drama of resemblance between God and man that ends with the breaking of God's true image. The body of *Jelle Luipaard* dissembles itself before or apart from the fact that it resembles a crucifix. In other words, it does not embed a Christian motif in order to break it. The resemblance to a crucifix is ambiguous, and that leaves the image open to other possible readings. Precisely that openness does not allow us to see *Jelle Luipaard* as an iconoclastic work. It frees the body from being an *image of* invisible divinity and demonstrates the power of images without breaking them. This places the piece in the role of an agent performing a deconstruction of "the great machinery of Christian images,"[42] where deconstruction is performed from within and the image is the very medium of a critical gesture that does not lapse into repeating, and thus bringing back, that which it criticizes.

Dying Image

Jelle Luipaard critically addresses the violence in Christian iconography, which placed at its center an image of a body that dies and no longer *resembles* itself. This violent imagery, Didi-Huberman argues, was determined to a large extent by the doctrine of the Incarnation, at whose center stands the communal desire to kill death itself. In his *Confronting Images*, he discusses the crucial place of the Incarnation in Christian art from the perspective of a possible history of art that would be a history of "the limits of representation" and a "history of the representation of those limits."[43] He argues that, although Christian art can be envisaged globally under the authority of mimetic representation inherited from the Greco-Roman world, such notions ignore their own limitations by blocking access to their own crises. Didi-Huberman suggests that, in order to gain access to the internal complexity of Christian art, it is important to consider it within the power of the complex and open word *incarnation*.[44] An important consequence of the incarnation was that to alter the sameness of the transcendent god in order to think the drama of the lost resemblance between God and man as turning around the death of the god-image required by his very incarnation. This ended in rending, wounding, the ideal appearance of his body.[45] A crucial aspect of the role of Christian images, of their anthropological efficacy, then, would be to continue that drama of resemblance in order to allow the communal management of the fear of death: "It is perhaps the fundamental dialectic of incarnational images to carry within themselves this double, contradictory movement . . . *to carry death* within them, to proceed to something like perpetual 'putting to death'—a sacrifice, then—to the end of managing religiously the common desire for the death of death."[46] In order to kill their own death, Christians gave themselves "the central image of God who agrees to die for them," but in order to do that it was necessary to "*let death insist in the image*. To open the image to the symptom of death."[47] Thus the images of Christian art carry the double desire to kill death and to imitate death at once, in order to allow believers to believe that "they have killed their own death, always in the image of their resurrected God."[48] The invention of the incarnational schema can be interpreted as an act with which Christian religion empowered itself, since the coming to visibility of a transcendent and invisible god through a body implies the power to constitute and manage a common gaze or the desire to see together "the death of death." Mondzain also points to the inherently political question that Christian images answered. She points out that the shared show of Christ's passion "became the foundation of the solidarity of a Christian community freed from all anxiety of death."[49]

Jelle Luipaard embodies a double drama of resemblance—it both resembles and differs from a body and a crucifix. By resembling ambiguously, this piece retains something of the incarnational logic and reappropriates it in order to recast critically the sacrificial drama present in Christian images. The absence of a head makes this body anonymous and detaches it from the central figure of Christ, making *Jelle Luipaard* a body that shows only itself and does not represent a sacred figure, which could focus gazes in their desire to kill death. Still, the figure resembles a crucifix and thus criticizes incarnation by being incarnate in a critical sense. It rescues the body from being a degraded copy of any transcendent and invisible truth by confronting its viewer with the presence of its flesh. As a result the figure of *Jelle Luipaard* interrupts the regime of religious representation as a regime that imposes a particular type of gaze. The ambiguity of this body, its modality of resembling, sends back a question to the religious gaze by reclaiming the vulnerability of the body from its appropriation by the religious spectacle of violence that will kill death for those who believe. Its message is that death cannot be killed and that the communal desire to kill it is violent. Thus its powerful address consists in its insistent and *blind* presence. It says: "I accuse you of the violence of seeing!" It is a blind image, but, as De Duve would put it, it "knows that it is being beheld and lets this be known to the beholder."[50]

Image and Power

By resembling in an ambiguous way a central religious image, *Jelle Luipaard* addresses the issue of power and images on several levels. Next to religious power associated with "the shared show of Christ's passion," it addresses the power of images to make us respond. One of the central points made by David Freedberg in *The Power of Images* is that images that disturb us deeply or invoke a powerful response in their beholders tend to be excluded from the museum space. According to him, the most effective images, in other words, images that have power, do not qualify unquestionably as art.[51] He argues that those who want "to install the shocking in the museum" first have to deem it to be art in order to be able to cope with the impossibly upsetting powers of those images. To call them "art" is a way of making them safe, or of taming them, as Roland Barthes would put it, by stripping the image of all reference or by saying that the sign, that is, the image, *is* the signified[52]—in other words, by separating radically the reality of the art object from reality itself. But as Freedberg argues: "However much we strive to do so, we can never entirely extract ourselves from our sense of the signified in the sign; and our responses are irrevocably informed by that."[53]

Jelle Luipaard touches upon the primary power of images to make us respond. The broken, mutilated body with the hyperrealistic rendering of its flesh mirrors our own flesh, thus making us uncomfortably aware of our presence. It is almost impossible to remain at a safe distance from the figure by assuming that it is just an object of art, because it confronts us with the reality of flesh, as if it were before the sign, or before being a representation. Yet in order to deal with this image, to bear its presence, we must suspend the reality of the mutilated body by looking at it as an object of art. This headless figure is an image-body that is blind, vulnerable, and deprived of its primary physical agency—the ability to move. Still, it has enormous power: the material, physical power of the weight of the hanging body, the gravity of flesh as expressed through the way it drapes over the supporting structure.

I see *Jelle Luipaard* as a critical image in a double sense. On the one hand, it criticizes the violence in religious iconography because it displaces a religious image we are used to seeing and repeats its violence in order to confront us with its logic. In that way *Jelle Luipaard* acquires a critical agency without being a scandalous image from a religious viewpoint. That makes it impossible to affirm its religiosity, to appropriate it as a religious image. On the other hand, it addresses critically our "consistent folly," as Freedberg puts it, in making images safe by deeming them to be art. Thus addressing the power of religion or of Art with a capital *A* to tame images and direct gazes, *Jelle Luipaard* stands in front of us as an anxious image, an image that repeats the obsession of the Christian image with the limits of representation and the representation of these limits, and that by perpetually presenting its *body* to us foregrounds the procedures of the invention of God's invisibility in images.

PART VII

Spiritual Exercises, Selves, and Beyonds

Spirituality in Modern Society

Peter van der Veer

In December 1911, Wassily Kandinsky published his *Über das Geistige in der Kunst* (*Concerning the Spiritual in Art*). The book's main purpose was to arouse a capacity to experience the spiritual in material and abstract things, for Kandinsky believed this capacity enables experiences that in the future would be absolutely necessary and unending. Kandinsky emphasizes that he is not creating a rational theory, but that as an artist he is interested in experiences that are partially unconscious. One of the formative experiences he describes in his book *Rückblicke* (*Glances Back*) is his encounter at a French exhibition with Monet's *Haystack*: "And suddenly for the first time I saw an *Image*. That it was a 'haystack' I learned from the catalogue. That I had not recognized it was painful for me. I also thought that the painter had no right to paint so unclearly. I experienced dimly that there was no object in this image. And noticed, astonished and upset, that the image not only catches but imprints itself indelibly in memory and floats in always totally unexpected final detail before one's eyes."[1]

Abstract art is one of the most distinctive signs of European modernity. One can study its development out of the Impressionism of Monet and others, but it is hard to escape a sense of drastic rupture with representational art. Kandinsky, one of the pioneers of abstract art, connects abstraction with the spiritual. This may be somewhat unexpected for those who understand the modern transformation of European life in the nineteenth and early twentieth centuries in Weberian terms, as a process of demystification. In one of the most pregnant expressions of modernity, namely, in modern art, the spiritual stages a comeback as the return of the repressed.

But what is the "spiritual"? It is a term scholars like me would like to avoid as much as possible because of its vagueness. Treating it as a marginal term, used only at the fringes of intellectual life—in our period, for instance, with reference to the New Age movement—easily accomplishes this. I want to suggest that, on the contrary, spirituality is a term central to understanding modern society. This is why I am currently writing a book on the construction of spirituality in modern India and modern China from a comparative perspective.[2] At the same time, it is necessary to reflect on the nature of this kind of concept. Certainly, it conjures up all the conceptual difficulties one encounters with terms like *religion, belief,* and *the secular.* Perhaps even more so. Nevertheless, it is used quite loosely, even by leading contemporary philosophers such as Charles Taylor.[3] Obviously, its conceptual unclarity and undefinability make it useful to those who employ it. It suggests more than it defines. Like the term *religion,* it can be used as a cross-cultural, global concept that captures a great variety of traditions and practices. This universalizing of the concept of religion has its roots in the notions of natural religion and rational religion, which arose in the aftermath of the religious wars in Europe and in conjunction with European expansion into other regions of the world. By the nineteenth century, however, the concept of "religion" also becomes part of the narrative of decline or displacement that has been systematized in the sociological theory of secularization. The gradual transformation of a transcendent hierarchical order into a modern egalitarian immanent order has displaced institutional religion, while freeing a space for spirituality. Spirituality escapes the confines of organized, institutionalized forms of religion and thus the Christian model of churches and sects, which cannot be applied in most non-Christian environments. It is, correspondingly, cross-culturally more variable and more flexible, and thus cannot easily be fitted into sociological models.

Like *religion,* the term *spirituality* has a kind of global bridging function, connecting several conceptual universes that are increasingly in contact starting in the second half of the nineteenth century. Connecting is different from translating, in the sense that translation always strives for correctness. There is no term equivalent to "spirituality" in Sanskrit or Mandarin Chinese, but this term is increasingly used to connect discursive traditions that are called "Hinduism" or "Confucianism" or "Daoism," though none is in fact an "ism." The difficulties of translation are simply insurmountable. First, one needs to know what terms like *belief, religion,* and *history* mean within the European tradition in the modern period. Second, there is the question of the place of history or historicity within a specific tradition.

The question of historicity is central to a huge project in eight volumes on the history of German concepts (*Begriffsgeschichte*) that was initiated in the 1970s by Werner Conze, Otto Brunner, and Reinhart Koselleck and was completed in the 1990s. This project examines a particular period (1750–1850), in which the advent of modernity transformed German political and social vocabularies. The assumption of the German project is that historical discontinuity can be precisely located through conceptual analysis. The history of ideas is thus replaced by a linguistic history of concepts. Koselleck holds that concepts vary not only according to their semantic field but also according to the temporal associations built into them. With the advent of modernity a different temporalization, a new intensity, is brought into older concepts, such as those of *Volk* or *Staat*. That new tempo-ralization, that new sense of time and history, is a dominant aspect of modernity.

Another major project addressing the issue of historicization in European intellectual history is the work done by Quentin Skinner and J. G. A. Pocock on English political discourse. They focus not on concepts but on discourse. A discourse is, in Pocock's words, "a complex structure comprising a vocabulary; a grammar; a rhetoric; and a set of usages, assumptions, and implications existing together in time and employable by a semi-specific community of language-users for purposes political, interested in and extending some-times as far as the articulation of a world-view or ideology."[4] Central to the history of discourse is the idea that multiple discourses exist simultaneously and that the usage and effects of these discourses can be studied in order to gain insight into a particular *Lebens-form*, to use Wittgenstein's term, as it exists in history.

Because of conceptual difficulties, these German and English projects have not been in touch with, much less integrated into, one another. How, then, can one imagine a project that first creates a comparable level of understanding of Chinese and Indian con-ceptual universes and then attempts to translate them into European concepts? The prob-lem can already be demonstrated by looking at the sense of history in Indian traditions. It has been a long-standing orientalist opinion that Indian culture is inimical to history. Louis Dumont expressed this cogently when he confronted the Indian classical concept of *yuga*, the four ages of the world, with the modern concept of history, with its focus on individual people, individual events, and causal explanations.[5] In the Indian concept of *yuga*, Dumont argues, there is a conscious devaluation of time, just as in the concept of *dharma* there is a devaluation of the individual. Moreover, while only a few Sanskrit chronicles deal with mundane affairs, there are many religious treatises that deal with what transcends the world. The challenge put forward by Dumont is that we should take seriously Indian civilization's religious valuation of time and history in our own writing of Indian history. In his view, one should try to avoid imposing a modern historicity on texts that rebel against it.

One would have to do a history of ideological formations in India in order to contex-tualize and interpret these seemingly timeless values about timelessness. One would need to know both what these concepts are and what they do at a given moment in time. Central to any tradition are debates about authority, authenticity, and transgression. Tra-ditions project themselves as timeless, as transcending history, and their discursive au-thority lies precisely in that claim, even as they also need to be relevant for immanent reality. This explains what Sheldon Pollock has called "the general absence of historical referentiality in traditional Sanskritic culture."[6] It makes translation into concepts belong-ing to modernity, entailing a very different historicity, a task that goes against the grain of such a tradition.

I. A. Richards, one of the great twentieth-century literary critics, realized this problem during his visits to China.[7] He was determined to solve it, however, since he was of the opinion that miscommunication had caused the Great War that had wiped out so many of his generation. Solving cultural misunderstandings was one of the great tasks he conceived for linguists and literary scholars. This was also the driving impetus behind his book *The Meaning of Meaning*, co-authored with C. K. Ogden, and behind his attempt to bring Ogden's Basic English project to China.[8] Basic English was a simplified English that could be used as a second language by all those who did not already speak English. This was not an artificial language like Esperanto, but was based on natural English. It consisted of no more than 850 words and 18 verbs and was, as such, easy to learn. In his *Mencius on the Mind*, Richards argues that it is crucial to understand the way Mencius (ca. 372–289 B.C.E.) used language to communicate meaning, a way totally alien to the Western mind, for the sake of world communication and to ensure the survival of Chinese civilization.[9] Both projects, that of promoting Basic English in China, with help from the Rockefeller Foundation, and that of translating Mencius, failed. Yet Richards shared with Bertrand Russell and T. S. Eliot, his friends and contemporaries, a crucial awareness that, although the gap between conceptual universes was almost unbridgeable, miscommunication, as a cause of war, had to be avoided at all costs.

This view is less eccentric than it sounds. One of the most instructive disputes between the British and the Chinese before the Opium Wars, wonderfully analyzed by Lydia Liu, is about the use of the term *yi* in trade negotiations.[10] In the Treaty of Tianjin of 1858, Article 51 states: "It is agreed that, henceforward, the character Yi (barbarian) shall not be applied to the Government or subjects of Her Britannic Majesty in any official document issued by the Chinese authorities either in the Capital or in the Provinces." The preceding Article 50 states: "All official communications addressed by the Diplomatic and Consular Agents of her Majesty the Queen to the Chinese Authorities shall, henceforth, be written in English. They will for the present be accompanied by a Chinese version, but it is understood that in the event of there being any difference in meaning between the English and Chinese text, the English Government will hold the sense as expressed in the English text to be the correct sense. This provision is to apply to the Treaty now negotiated, the Chinese text of which has been carefully corrected by the English original."

The language of command is striking in what is supposed to be a bilateral trading agreement. But equally striking is that the British wanted to fix the term "barbarian" to the character *yi*, while the Chinese used this character to denote "foreigner" and were taken by surprise that the British read it as a sign of disrespect. In an early response to British objections against the use of the word *yi*, Admiral Wu Qitai quoted Mencius, saying that King Shun "was an eastern *yi*" and King Wen "was a western *yi*" and that both were virtuous models for later kings. So how could it be wrong to apply this word to the British? The issue here is not that of correct translation, since the use of the term *yi* has a very complex history in China, just as the use of the word *barbarian* has a complex history in English. The issue here is that this term is part of a set of interactions between the Chinese authorities and the British that center on notions of honor and respect and that culminate in the Opium Wars. Richards tries to avoid this kind of inimical connection. In my view, an embracing, vague term like *spirituality* has been adopted precisely to make peaceful communication between different conceptual universes possible.

Given its global and random application, it is hardly possible to give a convincing genealogy of spirituality except to say that in Europe it has Platonic and Christian overtones and comes to be intricately connected to Romanticism, the counterpart of the Enlightenment. My main point, however, is that, like many other European concepts that acquire new meanings in the nineteenth century, it is produced and reproduced in a variety of cross-cultural interactions. I think that the term *spirituality* is used as a trope to organize important ways of thinking in and about modern society. The term *modern* itself is an oppositional term. It signifies both a break with the traditional past of one's own society and a time lag between modern European society and other societies in the present that are called nonmodern. In my view, the conceptualization of European modernity is to an important extent the result of interactions with societies outside Europe. In the nineteenth century, the notion of the modern comes to be connected to ideas of evolution and progress. The political philosophies of the twentieth century—liberalism, socialism, and fascism—all depend on forms of progressivism and all legitimize programs of colonization and development policies to be applied at home and abroad. As such, the idea of progress, of breaking with the past and with other contemporaneous societies, is always connected to Romantic visions of loss and otherness. This element is crucial in our understanding of spirituality, since the East comes to stand for the spirituality that is being lost in the West. Like other orientalist representations, this serves a function in our self-understanding. It is also important, however, to the self-understanding of those who live in the East. It is therefore impossible to reflect on the modern history of India and China without implicitly referencing both the contents and the discontents of European spirituality, just as it is impossible to gain a fuller insight into European spirituality without reference to Europe's interaction with India and China.

For Kandinsky, spirituality suggests an experience that goes beyond representation. For religious thinkers, it suggests something of higher value by contrast to the baser aspects of social life, including organized religion. For Romantic nationalists, it suggests the essence of the people, their collective spirit. Finally, it suggests a transcending of the body or, alternatively, the use of the body to gain spiritual experiences. Most specifically, however, *spirituality* is used as an oppositional term in contrast to *materialism*.

It is these oppositions of experience versus representation, of spirituality versus materialism, of the spirit of the nation versus the concrete individual, and of the spirit versus the body that are salient in the term *spirituality*. Perhaps the most important opposition to discuss is the one between spirituality and materialism. Let me briefly lay out some defining elements of the materialism to which spirituality has been opposed. The great transformation of nineteenth-century society is primarily an economic one that is perhaps best characterized by Adam Smith's notion of the "invisible hand." What economists and political scientists today call the "rational choice of individuals"—but what Smith calls "the individual pursuit of happiness"—leads, according to this view, in a rather mechanical way to general welfare. As Alexander Pope in his *Essay on Man* puts it: "true Self Love and the Social are the same."[11] While this is the foundation of liberal capitalism, Marx's dialectical materialism is no different in its selection of economy as the prime mover. In this way, economy becomes the most important purpose of society.

This secular framework is just as metaphysical as the religious one that preceded it. The secular metaphysics of the economy is basic to modern social science and policy making, but also to its rejection as materialism. Charles Taylor has pointed out that, while in the ancien regime the excessive pursuit of individual wealth was seen as a form of corruption that threatened the order of society, in the modern social imaginary the order of society is created by it. The notion that an economic perspective on society is corrupt continues in a modern form, however, as the rejection of materialism. This rejection particularly concerns the consumption side of the economy. While gluttony and avarice have always been vices in Christianity, the rejection of limitless consumption becomes as central to the modern social imaginary as consumption itself.

The old rejection of the world of money and interest is transformed in the modern period into a rejection of the foundation of modern secular society. At the same time, one has to acknowledge that this response is part and parcel of the great transformation. Spirituality in art, politics, or culture is embedded in material conditions of possibility. There is a saying in India that it took a great deal of money to keep Mahatma Gandhi, the great spiritual leader, in poverty. The fact that spirituality depends on material conditions and is fully modern does not, however, diminish its potential for ideological critique. Spirituality informs a wide spectrum of political movements, ranging from socialism to Romantic movements like nationalism and fascism, but also including the reform movements of the world religions. This is not a backward-looking, rearguard struggle that will disappear as progress continues. Sometimes it actually is ahead of its time: for instance, interest in spirituality in nineteenth-century Britain was combined with a rejection of colonialism. Some of this spiritual critique, when it is not hampered by Marxist materialism, finds its way into socialism; some finds its way into radical movements such as Theosophy; and some finds its way into scholarship, especially in the new science of comparative religion. Spirituality is not religion, at least not established religion. In nineteenth-century England, as in the United States, it is a concept used to critique religion. Although it is opposed to secular materialism, it is not antimodern in the sense that it harks back to traditional times. Most importantly, the arguments for spirituality consider themselves to be scientific. Science itself comes to be seen as a transcendent spirit of the time. A good illustration of this happy marriage of science and spirituality in our own day is the invitation extended to the Dalai Lama to address the 2005 American convention of neuroscientists.

Spirituality is a major element in Indian and Chinese anticolonialism, but in very different ways. After the great Taiping and Boxer rebellions of the nineteenth century, Chinese nationalists decided that Chinese traditions were to be blamed for the backwardness of Chinese society and that in order to progress China had to adopt a Western materialism based on science and secularism. In modern Chinese fiction of the first part of the twentieth century, there is a strong sense that China is a society afflicted with a spiritual disease.[12] With the victory of the communists, materialism becomes the official ideology of the state, and it comes to dominate the global understanding that Chinese culture is materialistic. Today Chinese devotion to material progress is even seen as a threat to the greater wealth of the West. Spirituality as a major term, however, keeps coming up in Pan-Asianism as it is formulated in the Far East and in Neo-Confucian thinking outside mainland China.[13] It is after the development of Deng Xiaoping's socialism with Chinese characteristics, and especially under Jiang Zemin in the early nineties, that Neo-Confucian spirituality once again becomes important in mainland China as a form of relating to the spirit of the nation.

In contrast to the Chinese case, the term *spirituality* has played a crucial role throughout contemporary Indian history, especially in the nationalist defense of Hindu civilization. By appropriating this term, nationalists adopted the orientalist perspective of European Romanticism, in which Hindu civilization is highly appreciated for its spiritual qualities. Indian religious movements in the second half of the nineteenth century adopted Western discourse on "Eastern spirituality."[14] The translation of Hindu discursive traditions into "spirituality" meant a significant transformation of these traditions. This process can be closely followed by examining the way in which one of the most important reformers, Vivekananda, created a modern, sanitized version of the religious ideas and practices of his guru Ramakrishna (a practitioner of tantric yoga) for a modernizing middle class in Calcutta. While we can still interpret most of Ramakrishna's beliefs and practices in terms of Hindu discursive traditions, with the arrival of Vivekananda we enter the terrain of colonial translation.

Vivekananda's translation of Ramakrishna's message in terms of "spirituality" was literally transferred to the West during his trip to the United States after Ramakrishna's death. He visited the World Parliament of Religions in Chicago in 1893, a side-show of the Columbian Exposition, celebrating the four-hundredth anniversary of Columbus's voyage to the New World and, perhaps most importantly, Chicago's recovery from the Great Fire of 1871. Religions represented in this show of religious universalism included Hinduism, Buddhism, Judaism, Roman Catholicism, Eastern Orthodoxy, Protestantism, Islam, Shinto, Confucianism, Taoism, Jainism, and various other traditions.[15] But the representative of Hinduism, Swami Vivekananda, stole the show. In his speech to the Parliament, Vivekananda claimed that "he was proud to belong to a religion which had taught the world both tolerance and universal acceptance."[16] Vivekananda's spirituality was not modest or meek; it was forceful, polemical, and proud. As the audience response in the Parliament and during his subsequent lecture tours in the United States indicates, this was a message that resonated powerfully among Americans. His writings in English often compare the lack of spirituality in the West to its abundance in India. Vivekananda is probably the first major Indian advocate of a "Hindu spirituality," and his Ramakrishna Mission the first Hindu missionary movement, following principles set out by modern Protestant evangelism.[17]

Vivekananda's construction of "spirituality" has had a major impact on Hindu nationalism of all forms, as well as on global understandings of "spirituality." Most importantly, it deeply influenced India's greatest political leader, Mahatma Gandhi. Gandhi was aware of the deep connection between spirituality and anti-imperialism in British intellectual circles when he started writing about India's struggle for independence in his book *Hind Swaraj* in 1910. He himself saw that struggle as primarily a spiritual one. The sources of that spiritual perspective were multiple: Hindu tradition, Tolstoy's understanding of Christian spirituality, Ruskin's thoughts about industry, and Nordau's views on civilization. I would argue that Gandhi's "experiments with truth [*satyagraha*]," as he called his political and spiritual struggles, were a product of the imperial encounter of Britain and India. The man whom Churchill dismissed as a "half-naked faqir" was as much a product of that encounter as Churchill himself.

Gandhi formulated his ideas in universalistic terms, but the idiom of universalism always comes from a particular place and history—in his case, the Hindu tradition in which he had been socialized. His vegetarianism derived from well-established traditions of the Hindu and Jain trading castes, but it could be universalized as a general moral practice that linked up with theories on the interconnection between body and spirit that had become popular in Britain in the second half of the nineteenth century. His nonviolence was, again, a particular interaction between Hindu and Jain traditions, alongside European repertoires of radical protest (such as the boycott). The main thing in all of this is less the connection between Eastern and Western traditions than their transformation through a history of interaction. This history continued in a new direction when African Americans adopted some of Gandhi's ideas and tactics in their own struggle for civil rights.

Gandhi's "experiments with truth" were attempts to strive for moral truth through disciplines of the body, such as fasting and celibacy. At the same time, such disciplines—for example, fasting unto death—could be used as political instruments in the struggle for India's independence. His spirituality was not conceived as a traditional quest for religious insight or redemption but as the opposite of the Western materialism that he saw as the basis of imperialism. Gandhi wanted economic progress for India and saw the materialism of imperial power as one of the causes of India's decline. He had a universalistic view of the various religious traditions in the sense that he thought that they shared a spiritual core. That was one of the reasons he felt that one should not proselytize, the way Christian missionaries were doing in India, but let people discover the unifying moral and spiritual essence in their own and other traditions while sticking to the one in which they had been socialized. In Gandhi's view one did attain truth through one's experiments with truth, but this truth was a moral truth that had to be experienced and indeed shown to others through one's example. One should not criticize those who have not realized such truth, and he considered criticism already a kind of violence. One should, he felt, in general avoid violently imposing truth upon others who are not convinced by one's example. Truth, then, is moral and should be communicated in a moral way. It is striking that for Gandhi the morality of communication is as important as for I. A. Richards.

Gandhi and Kandinsky are worlds apart, but what I have tried to suggest in this essay is that the term *spirituality* is crucial to both in their responses to the transformations that they are witnessing. This indicates the wide span of worlds that are connected by the word *spirituality*—from American transcendentalists like Emerson, Thoreau, and Whitman to European abstract painters like Kandinsky and Mondrian, to Neo-Confucian thinkers like Tu Weiming, to political leaders like Gandhi. Walt Whitman's funeral, with its readings of sayings by Confucius, Jesus Christ, and Gautama the Buddha, was held in a spirit very different from contemporary exclusivist Christianity or Islam. It does not further our understanding of this global spirituality to, pedantically, conclude that it was based on wrong translations from various traditions. One may also interpret Gandhi's spirituality and his "experiments with truth" as flawed translations of Hindu discourse, but I would rather see them as attempts to create bridges between radically different conceptual universes. Gandhi and I. A. Richards were focused on creating possibilities for nonviolence, but one should realize that spirituality can also be harnessed to a narrow vision of the spirit of the nation. Perhaps even more than in the colonial period, the multiplicity of uses of the notion of spirituality today deserves scholarly attention instead of outright disdain.

The Sacralization of the Self

Relocating the Sacred on the Ruins of Tradition

Stef Aupers and Dick Houtman

There is no doubt that the new buzzword in the contemporary religious landscape is "spirituality." Indeed, entering "spiritual OR spirituality" in the Internet search engine Google produces no fewer than 84 million hits—more than "catholic OR catholicism" (73 million), much more than "protestant OR protestantism" (16 million), and not many fewer than "islam OR islamic OR muslim" (121 million). Those 84 million hits even exceed the numbers found for "porno OR porn" (31 million) and do not fall far short of those for popular search terms such as "soccer" (109 million), "sex" (189 million), and "football" (221 million).

What is spirituality? Traditionally, the concept is used to refer to the experiential dimension of religion. This spiritual dimension is—and always has been—present in all of the world religions and even defines well-discernable subtraditions within each, ones that emphasize religious experience rather than doctrine (e.g., Sufism in Islam, Tantra in Hinduism, Kabbalah and Hassidism in Judaism, and Gnosticism in Christianity). Whereas in this traditional understanding of spirituality religious experience remains tied to "external" and "transcendent" conceptions of the sacred,[1] contemporary spirituality is characterized by a release from those ties. Commonly regarded as the outgrowth of what emerged as the New Age movement in the 1960s counterculture, contemporary spirituality is self-referential—it is a spirituality standing on its own two feet, broken from the moorings of particular religious traditions.[2] In short, contemporary spirituality refers less to a dimension than to a particular type of religion.

Sociologists of religion tend to associate contemporary spirituality loosely with "privatized religion,"[3] "new religious movements,"[4] "client and audience cults,"[5] "unchurched religion,"[6] and so on. Those concepts may, however, refer to anything vaguely religious, so long as it can be set apart from traditional Christian doctrines and so long as a churchlike organization is absent. To put it bluntly: those concepts are clearer about what they do not refer to—that is, church-based traditional religion—than about what they do refer to. And although sociologists of religion often use the concept of spirituality equally carelessly and intuitively, Paul Heelas and others have demonstrated convincingly that it can be given a much more precise meaning—defining it positively by what it is, rather than negatively by what it is not, so to speak.[7]

Therefore, before we move to two theoretically vital empirical issues, we want to address the conceptualization of contemporary spirituality as a type rather than a dimension of religion. We develop this conceptualization by means of an empirically informed critique of widespread but misguided ideas about contemporary spirituality. After this conceptual clarification, we address a first empirical issue that is vital for theoretical debates about secularization, namely, whether the decline of the Christian churches in most Western countries during the last few decades has been accompanied by a spread of this type of spirituality. We demonstrate that this is, indeed, the case: what we are witnessing today is a theoretically challenging process of religious change rather than a decline of religion *tout court*. We then move on to our second empirical question, whether spirituality is as socially and publicly insignificant as sociologists of religion typically hold it to be. We offer an empirically informed critique of this virtually unchallenged theoretical dogma. By way of conclusion, we not only briefly summarize our arguments but also point out key issues for future sociological research into spirituality, as we see them.

The Sacralization of the Self

In most of the sociological literature, spirituality—or New Age, to the extent this label is still applied today—is used to refer to an apparently incoherent collection of ideas and practices. Most participants in the spiritual milieu, it is generally argued, draw upon multiple traditions, styles, and ideas simultaneously, combining them into idiosyncratic packages. Spirituality is thus referred to as "do-it-yourself-religion,"[8] "pick-and-mix religion,"[9] a "spiritual supermarket,"[10] or "religious consumption à la carte."[11] Adam Possamai even states that we are dealing with an "eclectic—if not kleptomaniac—process . . . with no clear reference to an external or 'deeper' reality."[12]

Accounts such as these are found over and over again in the social-scientific literature and have attained the status of sociological truisms. They basically reiterate Thomas Luckmann's influential analysis, published about forty years ago in *The Invisible Religion*, according to which structural differentiation in modern society results in erosion of the Christian monopoly and the concomitant emergence of a "market of ultimate significance." In such a market, Luckmann argues, religious consumers construct strictly personal packages of meaning, based on individual tastes and preferences ("bricolage," "eclecticism"). Kelly Besecke rightly observes that "Luckmann's characterization of con-temporary religion . . . is pivotal in the sociology of religion; it has been picked up by just about everyone and challenged by almost no one."[13] Nevertheless, although Luckmann's characterization is not completely wrong, it is definitely superficial in that it overlooks the remarkable ideological unity and coherence of today's spiritual milieu.

Research carried out by Stef Aupers confirms the contemporary theoretical consen-sus, in that spiritual practitioners combine various traditions in their courses.[14] One may use tarot cards in combination with crystal healing and Hindu ideas about chakras; an-other may combine traditional Chinese medicine, Western psychotherapy, and Daoism into another idiosyncratic concoction. There is no reason to deny the prominence of bricolage and eclecticism in the spiritual milieu. Yet the received idea that these are the principal characteristics of contemporary spirituality is quite problematic. Indeed, *all* spir-itual practitioners interviewed by Aupers deny that the particular traditions on which they base their courses are at the heart of their worldview. They argue, as the Dutch spiritual center Centrum voor Spirituele Wegen puts it, "There are many paths, but just one truth." According to this *philosophia perennis* or "perennial philosophy," derived from esotericism and especially from Blavatsky's New Theosophy,[15] all religious traditions are equally valid, because they all essentially worship the same divine source. The following quotes from spiritual practitioners can serve as an illustration:

> I feel connected with the person of Jesus Christ, not with Catholicism. But I also feel touched by the person of Buddha. I am also very much interested in shamanism. So my belief has nothing to do with a particular religious tradition. For me, all religions are manifestations of god, of the divine. If you look beyond the surface, then all religions tell the same story.

> For me it is easy to step into any tradition. I can do it with Buddhism from Tibet, with Hinduism, and I can point out what is the essence of every religion. . . . I am dealing with almost every world religion. . . . There is not one truth. Of course there is one truth, but there are various ways of finding it.

More fundamental than bricolage, in short, is perennialism: the belief that diverse reli-gious traditions essentially refer to the same underlying spiritual truth. Accepting this doctrine, people experiment freely with various historical traditions to explore "what works for them personally." But what is the nature of this single underlying spiritual truth? Paul Heelas's answer is the following:

> Beneath much of the heterogeneity, there is remarkable constancy. Again and again, turning from practice to practice, from publication to publication, indeed from coun-try to country, one encounters the same (or very similar) *lingua franca*. . . . This is

the language of what shall henceforth be called "Self-spirituality." . . . And these assumptions of Self-spirituality ensure that the New Age Movement is far from being a mish-mash, significantly eclectic, or fundamentally incoherent.[16]

In the spiritual milieu, Heelas argues, modern people are essentially seen as "gods and goddesses in exile":[17] "The great refrain, running throughout the New Age, is that we malfunction because we have been indoctrinated . . . by mainstream society and culture."[18] The latter are thus conceived of as basically alienating forces, held to estrange one from one's "authentic," "natural," or "real" self—from who one "really" or "at deepest" is: "the most pervasive and significant aspect of the *lingua franca* of the New Age is that the person is, in essence, spiritual. To experience the 'Self' itself is to experience 'God,' 'the Goddess,' the 'Source,' 'Christ Consciousness,' the 'inner child,' the 'way of the heart,' or, most simply and . . . most frequently, 'inner spirituality.'"[19]

A mundane, conventional, or socialized self—often referred to as the ego and demonized as the false or unreal product of society and its institutions, is contrasted with a higher, deeper, true, or authentic self that is sacralized and can be found in the self's deeper layers. In the words of some of the spiritual practitioners interviewed by Aupers:

I experience god, the divine, as something within me. I feel it as being present in myself. I connect with it as I focus my attention on my inner self, when I meditate. . . . It's all about self-knowledge, being conscious about yourself. . . . It has nothing to do with something that's outside of you that solves things for you.

I think spirituality is something that lives inside of you. It has a lot to do with becoming the essence of who you are and being as natural as possible.

I am god. I don't want to insult the Christian church or anything, but I decide what I'm doing with my life. . . . There is no "super-dad" in heaven that can tell me "You have to do this and that, or else . . ." I am going to feel!

This, then, is the binding doctrine in the spiritual milieu: the belief that in the deeper layers of the self one finds a true, authentic, and sacred kernel, basically unpolluted by culture, history, and society, which informs evaluations of what is good, true, and meaningful. For evaluations such as those, it is held, one cannot rely on external sources, authorities, or experts, but only on one's inner voice: "What lies within—experienced by way of 'intuition,' 'alignment,' or an 'inner voice'—serves to inform the judgements, decisions, and choices required for everyday life."[20] As such, spirituality entails an epistemological third way of "gnosis," rejecting religious faith as well as scientific reason as vehicles of truth. Rather, it is held that one should be faithful to one's inner voice and trust one's intuition:

According to [gnosis] truth can only be found by personal, inner revelation, insight, or "enlightenment." Truth can only be personally experienced: in contrast with the knowledge of *reason* or *faith*, it is in principle not generally accessible. This "inner knowing" cannot be transmitted by discursive language (this would reduce it to rational knowledge). Nor can it be the subject of *faith* . . . because there is in the last resort no other authority than personal, inner experience.[21]

This reliance on an inner source boils down to the idea that a sacred and authentic self lies hidden in the self's deeper layers, in short. Like traditional forms of religion, such a sacralization of the self underlies a well-defined "doctrine of being and well-being,"[22] or a "theodicy of good and evil."[23] It is logically tied to an understanding of social institutions as evil. Modern bureaucracies, for instance, are generally regarded as alienating, nonsensical, inhumane, and without soul, while excessive identification with career, status, and prestructured work roles is regarded as a major source of personal problems. More generally, *anything* artificially and externally imposed is understood to be a cause of alienation from one's "real self." The subordination of the self to pregiven life orders is held to result inescapably in frustration, bitterness, unhappiness, mental disorder, depression, disease, violence, sick forms of sexuality, and so on. The sacralization of the self that characterizes contemporary spirituality, in short, goes hand in hand with a demonization of social institutions to produce a clear-cut dualistic worldview.[24]

The emergence of a pluralistic "spiritual supermarket" has blinded many sociological observers to the commonly held dogma of self-spirituality—the belief that the self itself is sacred. It is this doctrine that accounts, paradoxically, for the staggering diversity at the surface of the spiritual milieu and simultaneously provides it with ideological unity and coherence at a deeper level. If it is believed that the sacred resides in the deeper layers of the self, after all, what else should we expect than that people will follow their personal paths, experimenting freely with a range of traditions in a highly heterogeneous spiritual milieu? The diversity of the spiritual milieu *results from* rather than *contradicts* the existence of a coherent doctrine of being and well-being, in short.

The Spiritual Turn in Late Modernity

Conventional theories of secularization assume that the decline of the Christian churches is accompanied by a widespread turn to a secularist worldview, in which a calculative and rationalist outlook replaces belief in a transcendent God. The late Bryan Wilson, for instance, writes that "In contemporary society, the young come to regard morality—any system of ethical norms—as somewhat old-fashioned. For many young people, problems of any kind have technical and rational solutions."[25] Karel Dobbelaere, to give another example, claims that "People increasingly think that they can control and manipulate 'their' world. They act more in terms of insight, knowledge, controllability, planning, and technique and less in terms of faith."[26]

Such a shift toward a calculative-rationalist worldview is more typically assumed than convincingly demonstrated, however. Indeed, given secularization theory's prominence in the recent past, there are embarrassingly few studies that systematically map the actual worldviews of the unchurched. More than that, research into cultural change in late modernity points out quite convincingly that "A diminishing faith in rationality and a diminishing confidence that science and technology will help solve humanity''s problems . . . advanced farthest in the economically and technologically most advanced societies."[27] The idea that the decline of the Christian churches in most Western countries goes along with a shift toward a calculative-rationalist outlook may be no more than a myth, then—a myth that is sustained by the one-sided research attention to the decline of the Christian churches, seriously neglecting the systematical study of the worldviews of the unchurched. "Few attempts have been made to look at the other side of the equation, at what has been called the 'left-over,' if one may say so," as Hubert Knoblauch rightly notes.[28]

There is no doubt that self-spirituality features prominently among the range of worldviews that the unchurched may embrace. An analysis of survey data collected among a representative sample of the Dutch population points out that the binary distinction of Christians versus nonreligious does not hold. Instead, three religious types can be distinguished: Christians, nonreligious, and New Agers, that is, those who endorse the idea of self-spirituality.[29] Although, contrary to what is often believed, survey research of this type cannot give an estimation of the percentage of a population that identifies with self-spirituality, it can definitely help to answer more important questions.[30] What it does permit, after all, is systematically comparing: (1) those with a high level of affinity with spirituality, but not with Christianity; (2) those with a high level of affinity with Christianity, but not with spirituality; and (3) those with low levels of affinity with either. This produces something that is, from a theoretical point of view, more important than *absolute* counts of those categories' presence in the general population, namely, evidence about their *relative* presence in particular demographically or ideologically defined categories.

When one makes this type of comparison, one finds that those with Christian affinities accept authority and traditional moral values more strongly than either the nonreligious or the New Agers. Apart from the fact that women are overrepresented among the New Agers, the profiles of the latter two categories are quite similar. The nonreligious and the New Agers are both characterized by a rejection of external authority and traditional moral values, stemming from their relative youth and their high levels of education.[31] These findings are confirmed in a more recent paper that reports an analysis of data from the *World Values Survey* (1981, 1990, and 2000) for fourteen Western countries: their low level of acceptance of traditional moral values is responsible for the spiritual affinities of the younger birth cohorts and the well educated.[32] Summing up these findings, we may speculate that a spiritual turn to the deeper layers of the self has been stimulated by a process of detraditionalization that has accompanied the decline of the Christian churches and doctrines.[33]

It is, of course, not very difficult to understand why detraditionalization stimulates a spiritual turn. The decline of tradition is no unambiguous blessing, after all. Robbed of the protective cloak of pregiven and self-evident answers to questions of meaning and identity, late-modern selves are thrown back upon themselves in dealing with these questions. This constitutes an especially serious problem for those who feel (for whatever reason) that they need solidly founded answers. This prevents them from adopting a postmodern sense of irony, contingency, and playfulness, accepting the relativity and perhaps even arbitrariness of all constructions of meaning and identity. Being unwilling or unable to embrace such a position, and no longer accepting the traditional pregiven solutions, either, late-modern selves are haunted by nagging questions: What is it that I really want? Is this really the sort of life I want to live? What sort of person am I, really? Confronted with questions such as these, only personal feelings and intuitions remain as touchstones for true meaning and real identity. As we have seen, this is precisely the key tenet of self-spirituality: the conviction that true meaning and real identity, those holiest of grails, can only be derived from an internal source, located in the deeper layers of the self.

The Social Construction of Self-Spirituality

Received sociological wisdom suggests that this process of searching the depths of one's soul remains a strictly private affair without any wider social significance. Steve Bruce, for instance, argues that the idea of socialization into spirituality makes no sense, because "the transmission of diffuse beliefs is unnecessary and it is impossible."[34] As we have seen, however, the spiritual milieu is remarkably more doctrinally coherent—and hence less diffuse—than Bruce and others assume. It is important, therefore, to study the roles played by socialization and problems of meaning and identity in the process of becoming involved in the spiritual milieu. To do so we have analyzed the biographies of a small sample of spiritual practitioners, strategically selected for their origins in business life. How and why did they make the remarkable shift from "normal" jobs, such as clerk, president-director, or manager to the spiritual world of shamanism, aura reading, tantra, and channeling? More specifically, what roles do socialization and problems of meaning and identity play?

In obvious contrast to the way Christian identities are typically adopted, only one of those respondents developed an affinity with spirituality due to parental socialization during his formative period. Contrary to Bruce's suggestion, however, this does not mean that socialization plays no role at all, although this process only started after practitioners experienced identity problems. Excessively identified with the goals set by the companies they worked for, with their prestructured work roles and well-defined task descriptions, they increasingly felt alienated. This raised questions of meaning and identity: What is it that I really want? Is this really the sort of life I want to live? What sort of person am I, really?

The case of Chantal, who now works in the spiritual center Soulstation, is exemplary. She studied economics, rapidly made a career in the business world, and, she explains, completely identified with her work. Looking back, she states that she was "marched along the paths set out by society" and adds, "I studied marketing and sales, but had never learned to look in the mirror." Like most others, she points out that her identity crisis began after an "intruding conversation" with a consultant:

> I was working at MCR, a computer company, and I was the commercial director. A big team, a big market, and a big responsibility for the profits. Much too young for what I did. But that was my situation: You did what you had to do. Then I was invited by a business partner to visit a consultant. I sat there talking for two hours with that man. It was an inspiring visit and suddenly he looked at me intrudingly and said: "I hear your story. It sounds perfect, looking at it from the outside, but where are you?" In other words: "The story is not yours. It is the standard 'format' of the company you are presenting. But where is your passion? What makes you Chantal instead of Miss MCR?"

The latter question marked the beginning of an identity crisis:

> I thought: "Shit, I have no answer to this question, and I have to do something with that." The result of this conversation was a burnout that lasted almost a year. That's a crisis, you know! In the evening hours I started to do coaching sessions, I started thinking about the question Who am I, really? You start to look in the mirror. And then, at a certain moment, you can no longer unite your private life with your position at work. It's like your skis are suddenly moving in opposite directions. And that's definitely not a comfortable position: before you realize, you're standing in a split.

The suggestive metaphor of "standing in a split" between the demands of business life and private life applies to most of the respondents. The process of soul searching that follows should not be misconstrued as a strictly personal quest for meaning. Although a latent sense of unease or discomfort may well have been present beforehand, it typically became manifest only after a conversation with a consultant or coach. Remarks such as "He touched something within me," "Something opened up," or "The light went on" indicate that due to this contact latent discomfort becomes manifest and triggers a process of searching the depths of one's soul. What follows is a process of socialization, in which three mechanisms validate and reinforce one another: (1) acquiring a new cognitive frame of interpretation, (2) having new experiences, and (3) legitimating one's newly acquired worldview. These mechanisms, Tanya Luhrmann demonstrates in her study on neopaganism, are the driving force behind an "interpretive drift": "the slow, often unacknowledged shift in someone's manner of interpreting events as they become involved with a particular activity."[35]

Initially, the process of soul searching has a secular character. Motivated by their identity crises, respondents start describing their selves in vocabularies derived from humanistic psychology. Emotions are valued positively, but are not yet defined as higher, spiritual, or sacred. Although they generally start out with humanistic psychological self-help books and courses, they eventually end up doing more esoteric types of training, such as shamanism, aura reading, and the like. Daan comments on his relentless participation in various courses as "a sort of hunger that emerges in yourself. You start to nourish and feed it. And so you hop from course to course." By satisfying their hunger in the spiritual supermarket, the respondents acquire alternative frames of interpretation, new vocabularies and symbols to interpret and label their experiences. They learn to label weird, out-of-the-ordinary experiences as spiritual and, in turn, these experiences validate the acquired frame of interpretation. In the words of Luhrmann: "Intellectual and experiential changes shift in tandem, a ragged co-evolution of intellectual habits and phenomenological involvement."[36] The story of Marie-José provides a good illustration:

> We were walking on a mountain. . . . And I was just observing, thinking what a beautiful mountain this is and suddenly everything started to flow within me. This was my first spiritual experience. . . . I felt like: "Now I understand what they mean when they say that the earth is alive." I began to make contact and understood that I am like the earth, a part of nature, and that my body is alive.

The formulation "Now I understand what they mean when they say" illustrates that knowledge precedes experience and, perhaps, shapes the specific content of the experience. A similar story is told by Chantal. During her stay at Findhorn, she learned about the existence of auras, chakras, and streams of energy inside and just outside the body. This resulted, she explains, in "spiritual experiences":

> When I was there, someone said: "You have a healing energy around you and you should do something with that." Well, I had never heard of these two words, "healing" and "energy." So I was like: "What do you mean?" She said: "I'll give you an instruction." After that, I started practicing with a friend of mine. I moved my hand over her body, and I indeed felt warm and cold places. And I felt sensations, stimulation. Then I became curious.

Chantal began to delve deeper into the matter of healing and increasingly felt streams of energy around people. After a while, she started actually to see these fields of energy:

> After this I began to see auras, colors around people. At that time I still worked at this computer company and—after three months [at Findhorn]—I returned to the office. During meetings I was really staring at people, like, "I have to look at you, because you have all these colors around you." I was still confused. And this brought me to the books of Barbara Brennan. . . . When I read these books, I thought "I have to go there." And so I did.

In the process, respondents freely internalize a spiritual conception of the self and radically reinterpret their personal identities in conformity with it. On the one hand, a new image of the self in the present emerges: undefined emotions and experiences are now understood in spiritual terms, and the new identity is understood as profoundly spiritual. On the other hand, they start to rewrite their biographies: they break with their past identities, now understood as one-dimensional, alienated, or unhappy. As one respondent says: "I now know that I was structurally depressed without being aware of it." Statements such as these exemplify the cultural logic of conversion: they have "seen the light" and now reinterpret their past lives as "living in sin." Like classical conversions, they follow the logic of "Then I thought . . . , but now I know." The more our respondents become immersed in the spiritual milieu, the more these considerations are reinforced, eventually to reach the point of successful socialization, "the establishment of a high degree of symmetry between objective and subjective reality."[37]

Having left their regular jobs and started new careers as trainers and teachers in the spiritual milieu, our respondents, unsurprisingly, regularly encounter resistance and critique. They are well aware that they are seen by many as "irrational," "softies," or "dreamers," and that their way of life is perceived by many as "something for people with problems." How do they deal with these and other forms of resistance? A core element in their legitimation strategy is a radical reversal of moral positions: they argue that it is not themselves but the critical outsider who has a problem, although he or she may not be aware of this. Following the doctrine of self-spirituality, resistance, critique, and moral opposition are taken as symptoms of a deeply felt anxiety that cannot (yet) be directly experienced. Critics, our respondents argue, project an unresolved inner problem on the outside world. In the words of Marie-José: "People who have such strong resistance secretly have a strong affinity with spirituality. Otherwise they wouldn't be so angry. They just can't break through their resistance. Obviously they have a problem. Why else would you make such a fuss about something that doesn't concern you?"

Marco, who, among other things, works with the Enneagram (a psycho-spiritual model to increase self-knowledge), explains his strategy in dealing with resistance and critique during his courses as follows:

Of course, in my trainings, I regularly meet people who show resistance, but I can easily trace that back to their personality. Then I say: "You see, this is your mechanism of resistance that is now emerging." . . . Then I say: "I can fully understand you, I know the reasons why you are saying this." Then they say: "It is useless debating with you!" I say: "But what can I do about it? . . . It is part of the type of person you are, as explained by the Enneagram."

Our interviewees normalize their positions and pathologize criticism by outsiders by reading it as a symptom of psychological fear, anxiety, or insecurity, in short. As a consequence, the "inside" group is portrayed as courageous and free (because they choose to face their "demons"), while the "outsiders" are labeled as alienated because they are disconnected from their deeper selves.

The process of socialization unfolds as follows. First, latent feelings of alienation become manifest after a conversation with a consultant, raising problems of meaning and identity: What is it that I really want? Is this really the sort of life I want to live? What sort of person am I, really? Second, during the process of soul searching that follows, one is socialized into the ethic of self-spirituality, with knowledge and experience shifting in tandem. And third, after successful socialization, standardized legitimations are deployed, further reinforcing the ethic of self-spirituality. It is striking to note that, perhaps apart from the latent feelings of alienation that trigger it, the process is basically identical to that revealed by Howard Becker in his classic study on marijuana use. In that case, too, acquired knowledge underlies the recognition and positive evaluation of experiences, just as in both cases "deviant groups tend . . . to be pushed into rationalizing their position"[38] by means of standardized legitimations so as to neutralize critique from outsiders, while in the process, reinforcing the adopted way of life for insiders.

Bringing "Soul" Back to Work

"Sociologists rarely study spirituality in the workplace," Don Grant and his co-authors rightly observe.[39] This is probably due to the received wisdom that spirituality lacks public significance, remaining confined to "the life-space that is not directly touched by institutional control" and failing to "generate powerful social innovations and experimental social institutions."[40] But the very rarity of studies of spirituality in the workplace precludes any premature conclusion that spirituality fails to affect our "primary institutions": modern work organizations. If "it appears to sociologists that spirituality cannot take root within secular bureaucracies, it may be because their theories have not yet allowed it," as Grant and his co-authors. rightly note.[41] Indeed, notwithstanding common claims to the contrary, it is difficult to deny that spirituality has in fact entered the public domain of work organizations.

Since the 1980s, business organizations have become interested in spirituality, and spirituality has begun to turn toward business life.[42] Renowned management magazines such as *People Management, Industry Week,* and *Sloan Management Review* publish articles on the opportunities of spirituality for business life on a regular basis.[43] Indeed, on a basis of 131 in-depth interviews and 2,000 questionnaires in American companies, Ian Mitroff and Elizabeth Denton demonstrate that employees and managers feel a great need to integrate spirituality into business life. In *A Spiritual Audit of Corporate America*, they conclude: "This age calls for a new 'spirit of management.' For us, the concepts of spirituality and soul are not merely add-on elements of a new philosophy or policy. . . . No management effort can survive without them. We refuse to accept that whole organizations cannot learn ways to foster soul and spirituality in the workplace. We believe not only that they can, but also that they must."[44] Most of the spiritual ideas, initiatives, and practices that are applied in business life can be labeled as self-spirituality: "The inner-individual orientation is what most people, including the majority of our respondents, mean by spirituality."[45]

Examples of large companies that have become interested in spirituality are Guiness, General Dynamics, and Boeing Aerospace—even the U.S. Army has adopted spiritual training.[46] It is hard to tell to what extent spirituality affects American business life, but there are some indications. John Naisbitt and Patricia Aburdene refer to a survey held among five hundred American companies, at least half of which had at one time or another offered "consciousness-raising techniques" to their employees.[47] They estimate that companies in the United States spend at least four billion dollars on spiritual consultants annually, which is more than 10 percent of the total of thirty billion spent on company training every year.[48]

Since the 1990s, the shift of spirituality toward business life has become clearly visible in the Netherlands, too.[49] A prime example is Oibibio in Amsterdam, founded in 1993. Oibibio's business department offered courses in spiritual management, such as Team Management and the Soul and Management in Astrological Perspective, to keep companies "ready for battle" in times in which "dynamic streams of production, services, and information increasingly put pressure on organizations and managers." They make the following claim in their flyer: "Our trainers are builders of bridges: they speak the language of business life and know how to pragmatically implant the spiritual philosophy in your organization; they do so in cooperation with your employees."

Oibibio's bankruptcy in the late 1990s did not result from a declining market but rather marked the birth of many other, more successful spiritual centers, such as Metavisie, Soulstation, Being in Business, and Firmament. Metavisie, probably one of the largest players in this field, claims to have offered in-company training to seventy-five of the one hundred most renowned companies in the Netherlands. The list of clients on their Web site comprises more than two hundred national and international companies and agencies, among them many of the major Dutch banks and insurance companies (ABN Amro,

ING, Generale, Rabobank, Aegon, Amev, De Amersfoortse, Centraal Beheer, Interpolis, Zwitserleven and Delta Lloyd) and IT-companies (Cap Gemini, CMG, Compaq, Getronics Software, High Tech Automation, IBM Nederland, Oracle, and Baan Software). Internationally renowned Dutch multinationals, such as Ahold, Heineken, and telecom company KPN, are also on the list, as well as remarkably many government-sponsored institutions, such as the national welfare organization UWV-GAK and the University of Amsterdam, and the Ministries of Finance, the Interior, Trade and Industry, Justice, Agriculture and Fisheries, Transport and Public Works, Welfare, Health and Cultural Affairs, and Housing, Regional Development, and the Environment. This is, indeed, convincing evidence that spirituality is penetrating the public sphere. What, then, is the goal of the spiritual in-company training in all of these organizations?

Interviews with founders of spiritual centers and an analysis of those centers' Web sites reveal that these trainings aim primarily at breaking down the typically modern separation between the private and public realms, trying to impose the logic of the former on the latter. This complies, of course, with the ethic of self-spirituality: the centers aim to make rationalized business environments less alienating and more open to "authenticity" and "spirituality." By doing so, it is argued, they seek for a win/win situation or, in Heelas's words, "the best of both worlds."[50] Authenticity is held to result in both well-being *and* efficiency, and spirituality in happiness *and* profit, while "soulful organizations" are portrayed as successful. To give just one example (from the Web site of Soulstation): "People who develop personal mastership steadily become more capable to live their authenticity. In such a situation, one can put all one's natural talents in the world and do what one is really good at. The more authentically one lives, the more effective one's actions are. Authenticity therefore has a large impact on productivity within organizations" (www.soulstation.nl). Although bureaucratization may pose all sorts of practical obstacles to the introduction of spiritual practices in the workplace,[51] this should not blind us to the fact that it also drives attempts to bring "soul" back to work—to break with "alienating" bureaucratic organizational structures and pregiven work roles. Indeed, the "best of both worlds" approach that dominates the concomitant discourse suggests that tensions between bureaucratic demands, on the one hand, and opportunities for spiritual practice, on the other, may in fact be less severe than is typically assumed. Organizational goals are typically taken for granted and remain strictly instrumental, after all, while the "inner lives" of employees are considered valuable assets that enable firms and organizations to strengthen their positions in highly competitive and demanding environments. Although it is hard to deny that spirituality has entered the public realm of work, then, what is badly needed is good ethnographic research into whether and how tensions between bureaucratic demands and spiritual practices emerge and, if so, how those are dealt with on an everyday basis.

Conclusion: Relocating the Sacred in Late Modernity

There is no doubt that in most Western countries the Christian churches have declined during the last quarter of a century. During the same period, however, the belief has spread that a true, authentic, and sacred kernel, basically untouched by socialization and informing evaluations of what is good, true, and meaningful, lies hidden in the deeper layers of the self. This spiritual turn has advanced farthest in precisely those countries in which the churches have declined most, due to the erosion of traditional moral values that has accompanied this decline. What we are witnessing today, in short, is less the disappearance of the sacred than its dramatic relocation from a Christian heaven to the deeper layers of the self.

This finding, based on data collected among the general populations of late-modern Western countries, confirms the argument of Heelas and his co-authors in their recent *The Spiritual Revolution: Why Religion Is Giving Way to Spirituality*. Their extensive "body counts" in the spiritual milieu and the Christian congregational domain in the city of Kendal, United Kingdom, also demonstrate that a decline of the Christian churches and an expansion of spirituality are taking place. This turn to the deeper layers of the self is highly significant from a theoretical point of view. It has a range of implications not only for classical sociological theories—for example, Max Weber's about the disenchantment of the world[52]—but also contemporary ones about postmodernization and reflexive modernization.[53]

Whereas the theoretical significance of the spiritual turn can hardly be overestimated, then, the quality of sociological research into spirituality leaves much to be desired. To put it bluntly: much of it is sociologically naïve and immature. This applies not only to the research of those who are overly sympathetic to spirituality and hence cannot resist the temptation of "going native," as our colleagues from anthropology say. Perhaps surprisingly, it equally applies to the work of those who are highly critical of spirituality.[54] Because of his own tendency to criticize other people's ideas about spirituality as "bad sociology" or "nonsociological," Steve Bruce perhaps provides the best example.[55] Attempting to hammer home the radical individualism of the spiritual milieu, he writes:

> Findhorn, one of Europe's oldest centers of New Age thought and teaching, *requires* of those who take part in its various forms of group work that they confine their talk to "I statements." The point of this is to establish that, while each participant has a right to say how he or she feels or thinks, *no-one has a right* to claim some extra-personal authority for his or her views.[56]

Those observations do much to underscore the radical individualism of the spiritual milieu, to be sure. But simultaneously, and ironically, they do more than that. They also demonstrate how this very individualism operates as a socially sanctioned obligation of personal authenticity, revealing precisely the social significance of spirituality that Bruce denies. His failure to capture and satisfactorily theorize this ambiguity of the spiritual milieu's individualism causes Bruce to overlook that people are socialized into compliance with the doctrine of self-spirituality.

What Bruce has to offer, then, is merely a sociologically naive reproduction of New Age rhetoric about the primacy of personal authenticity, rather than a mature and critical sociological analysis. The assumption that people all by themselves develop their strictly personal and authentic spiritualities is obviously sociologically naïve, since "as good sociologists, we all know that there is no such thing as an isolated individual."[57] Kelly Besecke also criticizes the received conception of "privatized religion," arguing that it results in a conception of religion "as almost an exclusively psychological phenomenon, with very limited and indirect social consequence."[58] As has been demonstrated above, spirituality is in fact less unambiguously individualistic and less privatized than most sociologists hold it to be.

The conception of spirituality embraced by Bruce—and by most other sociologists of religion—inevitably coincides largely with the self-image of the spiritual milieu. It is hardly surprising, after all, that the spiritual practitioners interviewed by Heelas and his co-authors also deny in every possible way that the doctrine of self-spirituality is socially constructed, transmitted, and reinforced: "Time and time again, we hear practitioners rejecting the idea that their relationships with their group members or clients have anything to do with prepackaged . . . ways of transmitting the sacred."[59] But even if spiritual practitioners do not tell "their group members or clients what to think, do, believe, or feel,"[60] they do tell them that they should take their personal feelings seriously, that a one-sided reliance on thinking at the cost of feeling is detrimental, and that one should follow one's heart. The task to be taken up in the years that lie ahead, in short, is a radical sociologization of research into spirituality. What we need is research that critically and systematically deconstructs emic rhetoric to document how, precisely, spirituality is socially constructed, transmitted, and reinforced in the spiritual milieu and how, why, and when it is introduced in the public domain.[61]

Horizontal Transcendence

Irigaray's Religion after Ontotheology

Annemie Halsema

"No tradition can claim to possess the religious truth of humanity," writes Luce Irigaray in *Key Writings*.[1] In the Christian tradition, God too often is perceived as a fixed entity that is absolutely transcendent. Instead, we need a God who would be an inspiration to develop ourselves fully and to live fully our relation to the other, to others, and to the world around us. Even though Irigaray is critical of the Western religious tradition,[2] in her recent work she more and more understands religion as an indispensable and valuable dimension of human life.

Irigaray does not stand alone in her renewed, yet critical, interest in religion. In the last few decades, many thinkers within continental hermeneutical and phenomenological philosophy have shown an interest in religion.[3] That tendency is partly due to the geopolitical turn to religion, which manifests itself, among other things, in the turn to fundamentalisms and in the spiritual revival within secular Western countries, including highly individual adaptations of Eastern traditions. Religion likewise receives renewed importance because of the polarization between liberal secularism and Islam within European multiethnic societies, sparking debate about the role and place of religion. Within this debate the position of women has become one of the central arenas of discussion.[4] While from a Western secular feminist perspective the possibilities of combining liberal feminism and Islam have been questioned,[5] intellectual Muslim women give a more refined perspective on the situation and possibilities of and for women within Islam.[6]

Apart from geopolitical developments, philosophers and theologians in the twentieth and twenty-first centuries have responded to Nietzsche's death of God and Heidegger's critique of metaphysics, and have reflected on a God *after* ontotheology. French thinkers such as Jean-Luc Marion and Paul Ricoeur, and Italian philosophers like Gianni

Vattimo, affirm Heidegger's critique of religion. For Vattimo, for instance, the proclaimed ends of the tradition lead to a renewed Christianity in which *kenosis*, that is, the becoming man of the Son of God, is central.[7] Other thinkers, such as Derrida and Marion, in line with Levinas, think of God as unknowable and eluding the human mind.

Within the context of the geopolitical and philosophical turn to religion, this essay aims to sketch feminist philosopher Luce Irigaray's notions of religion and transcendence after ontotheology. Therefore I start by describing Irigaray's ambivalent relationship to (Western) religion and situating this with regard to Heidegger.[8] The central focus of the essay is a notion that in Irigaray's oeuvre has gained more and more importance and that can be seen as her alternative to the traditional notion of transcendence: "horizontal transcendence." This critical ethical notion is directed toward interhuman recognition and seeks in the relationship to the other what is missed in the relationship to God as transcendent being. I claim that this notion is especially relevant within the contemporary context of multicultural Europe.

Irigaray's Ambivalent Relationship to Western Religion

In general, Irigaray relates to religion in an affirmative way, but she is rather critical of the Christian tradition. She understands religion as a means for developing oneself spiritually, but she has problems with the possibilities for "becoming" in Christianity. The centrality of the notion of becoming indicates that for her religion is crucial in formations of human identity. As Penelope Deutscher, Morny Joy, and Grace Jantzen have noticed, for Irigaray the divine and God are important figures with respect to the possibility of identity construction.[9] Yet Christianity does not give women the same possibilities for becoming as it does men. In more general terms, Irigaray's main critique of Christianity is that it forgets or represses sexual difference.[10] This thesis corresponds to her general critique of the Western symbolic, including the philosophical tradition and the sciences. The repression of sexual difference within Christianity implies, among other things, a schism between man and God. This schism is the reason Irigaray develops a notion of horizontal transcendence, as we will see. In this section I will first describe Irigaray's relationship with the Christian tradition and religion in general.

Irigaray's critique of the sexual indifference of the Christian tradition implies, among other things, that it leaves woman behind: "she remains excluded from the manifestation of their [the father's and son's] faith."[11] Religious ceremonies are almost universally performed by men.[12] What is more, as mother of Christ, woman is only mediator, without a place of her own. Christ does not relate to his mother, to his conception, birth, growth, and generation, only to the Word of the Father.[13] As a result, Christianity does not present women with a horizon within which to become.[14]

Not only does Irigaray criticize the Christian tradition, she also turns to religious motifs as utopian imaginations of a possible future in which the culture of sexual difference is realized. As Ellen Armour writes, religion can be at once a site that exhibits the symptoms of the disease of sexual indifference and a site for motifs and images that help to imagine the future of sexual difference.[15] Religious utopian topoi to be found in Irigaray's work include, for example, "the third era of the West, the era of the *couple*: the spirit and the bride,"[16] which will come after the era of the Father (Old Testament) and that of the Son (New Testament).[17] Her ambivalence toward the tradition is characteristic of Irigaray's critical position: she at once embraces the tradition and develops alternatives from within it, thereby renewing it. Yet she can be so forcefully critical in other texts that the only resolution seems a break with the tradition. This ambivalent position can be situated on the border of the old and the new. In her effort to articulate the new, Irigaray sometimes joins the tradition, but at other times she opposes it forcefully.

In recent texts,[18] Irigaray interprets religion as "the spiritual" and considers the development from the natural to the spiritual a necessary dimension of human life. Jantzen clarifies that "according to Irigaray religion in postmodernity is crucial to countering the destructiveness and oppression of secular modernity."[19] She is still critical of the Christian tradition, but she puts her critique in other terms, stating that Christianity holds only one model of the Absolute and that differentiation between believers is not possible. She writes that in our multicultural times we need more differentiated spiritual guidance.[20] Irigaray's aim is to restore to God a form of energy that would inspire us to develop fully into ourselves and to live fully our relation to the other, to others and to the world around us.

What Joy calls Irigaray's "eastern explorations" are important to this positive attitude toward religion.[21] From the mid eighties onward Irigaray has reported being inspired by the practice of yoga and by the philosophical meditation connected with that practice. The notions that are central in Irigaray's appreciation of religion descend from this practice and philosophy: breath, the flow of energy, the spiritualization of nature—its main example being the contemplation by the Buddha of a rose—the creation of connections. Oriental traditions provide us with new forms of relationship to other people and the world in which the natural and spiritual are connected to each other: "The religious is the gesture that binds earth and sky, in us and outside of us."[22]

The sexual indifference of the Christian tradition, which is central in Irigaray's critique, can be traced back to the metaphysical thesis that forms the cornerstone of her work, namely, the repression of the maternal-feminine. That repression explains the situation of women within Christianity, as well as the deprivation that a masculine tradition implies for men. This repression is related to the transcendence of God, as I will show in the next section.

A God as Mirror for Humans

Western thought extrapolates the origin toward the infinite, while repressing the "true origin," the feminine-maternal. In the Christian tradition, God the Father functions as the origin, thereby repressing the "original origin," the maternal body. Woman/matter/

nature/the body is sacrificed. The father replaces the mother as origin, as place of becoming.[23] As a result, women do not have a God to relate to, and men are severed from their original origin, the mother. Thus, no relationship to the matrix is possible anymore.[24] Because of this, Irigaray interprets Christianity as a masculine tradition that understands God as a being to which women, especially, cannot easily relate.

Yet even though in our tradition God replaces the feminine-maternal, both also resemble each other. The feminine-maternal "never offers itself as a 'presence'"; it forms an original topos that in itself cannot be presented.[25] It is neither visible nor representable. Like the mother, God is a "place of the invisible," a "hidden presence." The first dwelling place in which man lives, in which he is wrapped up, which he drinks, consumes, consummates, "is a gift that permits no mastery during its term, an indefinite debt." And everything comes and goes "between these two places of the invisible, those two hidden presences, between which everything is played out, in which everything meets."[26] What remains are intermediaries, such as angels or the sensible transcendental, to mediate between these two places.[27] In short, within Western metaphysics one can relate neither to the mother nor to God. They are truly transcendent to us, but in a negative sense: we are severed from both. That implies that the Christian tradition estranges not only women, but also men.

Throughout her works, Irigaray critically questions a notion of God as completely transcendent to humanity, a God as "the foundation hidden from sight but offering himself to intuition, placed infinitely far away, above and in front, in his teleological Beauty and Goodness."[28] This God that has created everything in his image knows only himself. The God of the tradition is too much an "object-entity," he is "radically estranged" from us, he is "an absolutely unknowable entity of the beyond."[29] Yet in other texts, mainly in her 1984 lecture at a women's center in Venice entitled "Divine Women," Irigaray describes an alternative and affirmative notion of God and the divine. Thus, Irigaray's ambivalent relationship to the Christian tradition—in some texts driving toward a break with the tradition, in others seeking for alternatives from within the tradition—also shows itself in her perspective on God. In what follows, I will sketch her alternative and affirmative notion of God, in which, again, the formation of human identity is central.

The text "Divine Women" is a mimetic reading of Feuerbach's *The Essence of Christianity* and is often criticized as an essentialist plea for a God in the feminine.[30] Yet in my reading it is not essentialist and is perfectly in line with Irigaray's notion of a God that is significant for humans. In the text, Irigaray takes over in an affirmative manner Feuerbach's thesis that God is the essence of humankind, seen and honored as an object outside of us. Feuerbach characterizes human beings anthropologically as beings whose essential nature is that their species, and not merely their individuality, forms their object of thought. Religion, which is the distinctive characteristic of human beings, is understood as "the consciousness which man has of his own . . . infinite nature." That implies not only that human beings can get to know themselves by means of what they believe in,[31] but also that in fact they believe in their own essence.[32]

Whereas Feuerbach means to return religion to its anthropological roots, Irigaray emphasizes one aspect of his thesis: namely, that human beings *need* a relationship to their infinite. She alludes to Feuerbach's thoughts that God forms man's alter ego, is a complement of man himself, is a perfect man. Taking this idea as her starting point, she claims that God is necessary for mankind: "In order to *become*, we need some shadowy perception of achievement; not a fixed objective, not a One postulated to be immutable but rather a cohesion and a horizon that assures us the passage between past and future."[33] In our tradition, God guarantees the infinite.

Elizabeth Grosz explains that Irigaray's God is not a totality, unity, or origin. "If anything . . . it refers to the principle or ideal, a projection or perfection of the (sexed) subject. . . . God is a mode of self-completion with no finality, no end point, an asymptotic tendency of becoming."[34] God functions as an ideal for the self, a horizon. Such a horizon is necessary for both men and women to direct their becoming. Yet as we have already seen, the masculine Christian tradition lacks a concept of the divine that can play this role for women. The Christian God forms a horizon for men only, and not for women. Thus, Irigaray sexualizes Feuerbach's claim that in relating to God human beings relate to their species. As a result, there are two absolutes, instead of two modes of access to one and the same absolute.

Some feminist scholars find the aim to develop a God in the feminine a reason to criticize Irigaray for falling back into the very logic that she wants to prevent. Judith Poxon, for instance, fears that this divine ideal will revert to the Platonic logic of semblance that Irigaray so strongly criticized in her early works. Irigaray thereby reintroduces, Poxon believes, "the primacy of resemblance to a transcendent idea(l) as the standard by which 'truth' will be recognized."[35] That ideal or horizon might function as a normative ideal that would dominate the process of becoming-subject for women. Ellen Armour writes that Irigaray's appropriation of Feuerbach in "Divine Women," though promising to undercut unitary logic, in its deployment of god language in the service of female subject formation "threatens to return woman and the religious to a unitary horizon."[36] That is especially problematic because it binds women too closely to the traditional God. This sort of "traditional theism,"[37] while reversing the gender of the divine, doesn't change anything. Amy Hollywood critically claims that Irigaray assumes that we can "simply 'project' and thereby create a meaningful new sacred," whereby Irigaray would forget Feuerbach's central claim that, for religious projection to function and its object to inspire belief, its mechanism must be hidden.[38]

Yet the sexuate horizon for which Irigaray pleads does not imply a fixed ideal that is the same for every woman, as Poxon suggests. It could also be interpreted—in line with Deutscher[39]—as the infinity of the community or collectivity of women. This infinity helps women in the development of their subjectivity, but it does not fix female subjectivity into set frames. Also, Armour's accusation of "traditional theism" doesn't hold if we take into account the critique of religion and of the traditional notion of God in other texts by Irigaray. She is in general very critical of the God of the Christian tradition: he is a "Wholly Other," demanding a relationship of dependency and submission, which is not "a worthwhile religious ideal."[40] Yet a God is necessary, because we need a perspective outside of us: "subjectivity needs an objective frame within which to constitute itself, and subjectivities need objective references to link themselves to each other, otherwise each exceeds the limits of the other."[41] So, God can function—claims Irigaray, in continuity with the tradition—as an objective to direct oneself toward, a horizon, an "objective frame," and a guarantee of a community, and of intersubjectivity.

The critiques of "Divine Women" that accuse Irigaray of falling back into the traps of the tradition isolate that text from Irigaray's other writings, forget that she is also highly critical of the God of the tradition, and misunderstand the function she attributes to God. God, for Irigaray, functions as a mirror for humans, gathering the fragmented images of ourselves and offering an imaginary "one" with which to identify. God functions in the same way as the Lacanian image in the mirror does for the child who starts to understand itself as one. Like the child, men and women need an ideal-image in order to be able to develop themselves fully, to grow, to become. Thus, Irigaray reads Feuerbach with Lacanian eyes. Humans need a relationship to their infinite in order to be able to become, to develop into their ideal-images. And even though these ideal-images are gendered, that does not necessarily imply that they are equivalent for all women.

What is more, while acknowledging the function God can have for humans, Irigaray asks: Why not seek objectivity within oneself? Why do we need a God; wouldn't the universe be enough? Why not just respect what exists?[42] In her reading of atheist Feuerbach, Irigaray aims to create possibilities for women to develop subject positions within a masculine religious symbolic. The aim is not to create new projections that are severed from humans, returning to a traditional God, but rather to create concrete possibilities here and now for women to become. Ideals, horizons, projections are vital in creating these new possibilities for developing subject positions; that is why she aims at an alternative notion of the divine. That does not imply falling back into the traps of traditional notions of God. Rather, as Irigaray writes in "Divine Women": "It is essential that we be God *for ourselves* so that we can be divine for the other, not idols, fetishes, symbols that have already been outlined or determined."[43]

How do Irigaray's critique of the Christian tradition and her alternative account of God and the divine relate to the different perspectives on religion that have been developed after ontotheology? I will begin to answer this question by relating Irigaray's thought to Heidegger's.

Heidegger: God as *Causa Sui*

At first sight, Irigaray's critique of religion is very much indebted to Heidegger's diagnosis of Western metaphysics.[44] Heidegger's characterization of Western metaphysics as onto-theological means that it conflates the ontological question "What are beings as such in general?" (*die Frage nach dem Seienden als solchem*) with the theological question "What is the highest being?"[45] Its ontotheological constitution prevents metaphysics from considering Being as Being, that is, the light or horizon in which beings appear, and God also becomes a being, the highest entity, *das Begründende*, in the sense of first cause, *causa sui*. Metaphysics is *Onto-logik* and *Theo-logik*. God as first cause, which metaphysics anticipates, has entered philosophy: it is a metaphysical notion. Irigaray's critique of the extrapolation of the origin toward a transcendent God and her account of the vertical direction of Western thought resemble, on the face of it, Heidegger's critique of the theological character of Western thought and the notion of God as ground and first cause.

The two thinkers draw radically different consequences from their critiques, however. For Heidegger, the metaphysical god implies that we no longer have a god to worship. Humans cannot pray to this god or offer sacrifices to him. Humans cannot fall to their knees in awe before the *causa sui*, or dance and play music before the metaphysical god.[46] In that respect, godless thinking that gives up the god of the philosophers is perhaps closer to the divine God, he writes. Metaphysical theology presumes a God as creator, as first cause or highest being, but forgets the divine that enables the coming into being of the gods. As a result the gods withdraw and leave man to himself.

For Irigaray, the consequences of the extrapolated origin that God forms in the Western tradition imply, rather, a radical schism between humans and God. The Christian God is no longer the horizon that supports man's and woman's becoming. As a completely transcendent being and a fixed entity, he has lost his relation to humankind. Heidegger wants to open the door to a new kind of meditation upon a nonmetaphysical God, a God after ontotheology: "A God," says John Caputo, "who would emerge from a meditative experience of the upsurge of Being as emergence into unconcealment (*aletheia*)."[47] But Irigaray wants a God in the image of man and woman, an ideal to identity with. Instead of a God that cannot be represented, she aims at a God that can be present, close to humanity. She writes: "This creation would be our opportunity. . . . Not only in mourning for the dead God of Nietzsche, not waiting passively for the god to come, but by conjuring him up among us, within us, as resurrection and transfiguration of blood, of flesh, through a language and an ethics that is ours."[48]

Irigaray's critique of Heidegger in *The Forgetting of Air* corresponds to the connection she seeks between the human and the divine. She criticizes Heidegger for emphasizing the earth as ground of life and speech, and claims that he has forgotten air. Air is one of the elements she discusses in her "series" on the elements, to which *The Forgetting of Air* belongs, together with *Elemental Passions* and *Marine Lover of Friedrich Nietzsche*. In these books, her general thesis is that these admired philosophers, Heidegger and Nietzsche, to whom she herself is so much indebted, forget that from which everything emerges: in Nietzsche's case, the "immemorial waters"; in Heidegger's case, air. This forgetting resembles the absence of the mother, the other, the matrix. Philosophers erect a language that alienates them from this original locus. Understood as such, the feminine-maternal conflates with the elements. The elements seem to "be" the feminine.

Yet, the mother also *lives* from the elements, which makes them anterior to the feminine-maternal. Armour clarifies that air for Irigaray is the condition of possibility for perception, for light and dark, for voice, for appearing/disappearing, for seeming/resembling/assembling, for presence and absence.[49] Within philosophical history "air would be the forgotten material mediation of the logos."[50] Air is the sensible transcendental condition, or the "physical ground" for all the oppositions that constitute the structure of metaphysics. In itself it "is" not, it slips away, it eludes capture and is forgotten in the tradition as the ground that it forms.

Why is air forgotten, why is matter forgotten, and how are they connected? They escape mastery; they are necessary for the immediate subsistence of man; they connect man with "mother-nature." In overcoming the natural, man forgets what is needed for his subsistence: for instance, that he not only owes his life's beginnings to air, but that he also nourishes himself with and is housed within air, that he moves about, acts, manifests himself, sees and speaks in air. In that sense air is an a priori, perhaps even the a priori that is the condition for everything else. Irigaray claims that man's aim is to become the master of the universe, to become immortal, thereby forgetting what enables him to do so.

Irigaray criticizes Heidegger and the philosophical tradition not only for forgetting air, the condition for life, but also for overlooking another condition for life: sexual difference. Both are connected as dimensions that are vital for/to life.[51] That does not imply that there is no air in Heidegger, because Irigaray seems to find some opening there, for instance, in "the clearing of the opening."[52] But in forgetting sexual difference he remains part of the philosophical tradition that he criticizes so vigorously.

Heidegger's God after ontotheology may not be the traditional God as *causa sui* but still represses the mother as origin. His God remains "ecstatic." Irigaray, however, criticizes the notion of "transcendence as ecstasy," which implies "leaving the self behind toward an inaccessible total-other, beyond sensibility, beyond the earth."[53] Precisely in the relationship to such an entity the mother-matter is forgotten. As an alternative, she aims at a God as a horizon for human becoming.

Irigaray's Alternative: Vertical and Horizontal Transcendence

At the beginning of this essay, I mentioned the notion of horizontal transcendence as Irigaray's alternative to the traditional notion of the transcendence of God. Having set out her critique of the Christian God and her alternative notion of the divine, I can now sketch a first draft of the meaning of this notion. For one thing, horizontal transcendence names the horizon of ideal-images and values that enable humans to become, to live their lives fully. The following quote from "Divine Women" is illustrative: Irigaray claims that in order to become it is essential to have "some shadowy perception of achievement; not a fixed objective, not a One postulated to be immutable but rather a cohesion and a horizon that assures us the passage between past and future, the bridge of a present that remembers."[54] Horizontal transcendence denotes this horizon of transcendent values and ideal-images that transcends us individually and gives direction to our development. This horizon is also a utopian ideal that stands for what we hope for, what we aim at, what we want to become.

In Irigaray's account of this horizon, it no longer is a unitary horizon defined by only one tradition or religion, but arises from what we hold to be essential and vital for our lives. In that sense it is horizontal and not vertical. The horizontality of the horizon shows itself in the acknowledgment that there are several possible perspectives on "becoming" and that not one of them is universally valid.

Although Irigaray rejects transcendence as ecstasy and proposes "horizontal transcendence" as an alternative, one would perhaps expect her to hold that transcendence as ecstasy is similar to vertical transcendence. Indeed, she sometimes uses the notion of vertical transcendence in a negative sense, standing for a hierarchical relationship in which the one is subsumed in the other, as the feminine in the masculine.[55] Also, in a rather essentialist move, she writes that vertical transcendence is the masculine way of securing becoming, for instance, by relating to a God, whereas horizontal transcendence is the feminine way: she has to secure becoming through breathing.

Irigaray usually considers vertical transcendence or the "vertical dimension" to be positive, however. There is, for instance, a vertical dimension in the relationship between man and woman: "The link uniting or reuniting masculine and feminine must be horizontal and vertical, terrestrial and heavenly."[56] The sexual encounter will then enable both men and women to grow, to become, and will not reduce them to one another. The vertical dimension in this respect seems to aim at a divine relationship between man and woman, a relationship of mutual respect, in which both can develop themselves and grow. In other words, for Irigaray vertical transcendence is related to becoming and to the divine, and is a dimension that is necessary for human becoming, as well as horizontal transcendence. This vertical dimension in developing the self is close to spirituality.

Spirituality for Irigaray in the first place implies "not thoughtlessly critiquing, destroying, or forgetting that which exists."[57] It means cultivating perception: listening to music, contemplating a work of art, tasting food, and breathing perfumes can be spiritual gestures that make life pass from sheer satisfaction of needs to cultivating a desire. Celebrating through words or a song is also spiritual. In short, spirituality is to be found in everyday things and experiences, which are to be cultivated and enjoyed. It leads to human fulfillment and to happiness. This vertical dimension is, in Irigaray's perspective, vital for human becoming. Yet the horizontal dimension is even more fundamental.

Self-limitation

Apart from being the horizon of values and ideal-images that forms a horizon for becoming, in Irigaray's work the notion "horizontal transcendence" also receives another meaning, denoting the ideal-typical ethical relationship to the other that is central in all of her work. In relationship to the first meaning of horizontal transcendence, the relationship to the other as other gives a specific interpretation of the horizon of values and ideal-images: an interpretation, namely, in which the interhuman and values that can be associated with it, such as mutual respect and recognition, are central.

Although she acknowledges the function of God as mirror for becoming, Irigaray questions the necessity of a God in order to develop ourselves, as we have seen. This can be understood as follows. She claims that what we have traditionally sought in the relationship to God can also be found in the relationship to the everyday other. "By measuring every subjectivity in relation to a Wholly Other, our tradition has underestimated the importance of the alterity of the other with whom I enter into relation every day," she writes.[58] And: "Our relations between two have been limited to the man-God relationship; we have not sufficiently cultivated them between us."[59] In horizontal transcendence the other functions as the limit that is necessary for our becoming. Relationships to the other in which the other's otherness is recognized are ethical experiences that we do not necessarily have in relationship to "the world of the beyond."

Central in this notion of horizontal transcendence is the recognition that the other (notably the sexually different other) is transcendent to the self. Irigaray writes: "I cannot completely identify you, even identify with you." "You are irreducible to me, inaccessible in a way." "I cannot know you in thought or in flesh."[60] Horizontal transcendence thus implies the transcendence of the everyday other with regard to the self that calls for respect for that other.

The notion of horizontal transcendence, but also Irigaray's critique of the philosophical tradition as a thinking of the Same, her notion of the divine, and in general her ethical sketch of the relationship self-other seem very close to Levinas's notion of the transcendence of the other. Indeed, as Tina Chanter shows, Levinas's ethics is important for Irigaray's notion of the radical alterity of the other of sexual difference.[61] Yet there are important differences between Irigaray's and Levinas's perspectives. Irigaray criticizes Levinas for forgetting sexual difference,[62] and in general situates the other in his or her body, in a natural universe, which she misses in Levinas. What is more, Irigaray's notion of the relationship of the self to the other and to the divine differs from Levinas's. Whereas for Levinas the ethical relationship to the face of the other opens the relationship to God, because "the other must be closer to God than I am,"[63] for Irigaray god is a Feuerbachian ideal-image of the self. Precisely this concentration upon the self in relationship to the other distinguishes Irigaray's notion of the divine from Levinas's and gives Irigaray's notion of horizontal transcendence a new significance.

Irigaray considers self-limitation to be the condition for the possibility of recognizing the other's alterity. Before being able to recognize the other as other, the self needs to accept its limits, in the fields both of knowing and of feeling. It may seem paradoxical that self-fulfillment or self-development starts from the relationship with the other and that by limiting ourselves we can develop ourselves. The logic is that the self has to limit its narcissism, its sense of being the whole, being "all," before being able to develop. The self cannot become "everything." By self-limitation the self can also start respecting what escapes its grasp, the mystery of otherness. Thus, Irigaray appeals to an ethical attitude of limitation of the self, of "not being all," of finiteness, which opens the individual to what else there is. Especially in the confrontation with the other, such an experience can take place. As such, the relationship to the everyday other can support my spiritual becoming.

The mystery of the other permits women and men "to go along their own spiritual path."[64] Mystery here refers to maintaining energy free and not bending energy to the other than one's self. It means leaving part of lived experience open, incomprehensible, strange, foreign, inaccessible to thought or affect. It is close to what Irigaray describes as wonder in relation to Descartes' passions: a distance between self and other that doesn't appropriate the other and leads to asking the other "Who are you?" instead of presuming in advance who or what the other is.[65]

Apart from being a concrete other whom I meet every day and who can thus help me experience otherness better than could an abstract God, the everyday other also "returns me to my sensibility and to a necessary cultivation of it, while respecting its tie with corporeality."[66] In that sense, this transcendent is "an inscription in the flesh."[67] It is no longer a transcendent that is cut off from the body and the sensible or that gradually departs from the body, but the difference remains, because the embodiment of the other is one of the factors that makes him different from me.

Yet the difference of the other is not sought for itself. It is not Irigaray's intention to introduce another absolute after God. She says it subtly herself: "Although the other must be respected absolutely as other, that does not mean we should consider him or her as the absolute we seek."[68] Rather, what we should consider absolute is the *relation* to the other. Thus, what should be cultivated and sought for itself is the relation-to, the in-between self and other.

The Relevance of Horizontal Transcendence for the Multicultural Situation

Irigaray's notion of horizontal transcendence indicates a horizon of values and ideal-images that transcends us, as well as giving a specific content to that horizon in the form of an ethical ideal of self-limitation that leads to respect for others. As Deutscher observes, for Irigaray transcendence is located between humans rather than between humans and immortal beings.[69] Irigaray finds transcendence primarily within intersubjective relationships, thereby not excluding the religious dimension but rather giving it a basis in relationships between humans. She objects to a divisive God, a God that unifies one people, separating them from others.[70] By contrast to Heidegger's God, who in her eyes is completely severed from the human, Irigaray's God forms a horizon for humans. Thus, Irigaray's religion after ontotheology implies that the traditional oppositions between immanence and transcendence, the human and divine, man and God, are bridged.

The notion of horizontal transcendence not only gives a specific content to Irigaray's religion after ontotheology, I also consider it relevant within the age of secularization and multiculturalism in which we Europeans live. Indeed, this is the context in which Irigaray develops the notion.[71] I will end this essay by sketching the significance of the notion in the present sociopolitical context.

European societies today are wrestling with the problem of how to bring about dialogues between secular liberal culture and Islamic culture. In the situation that is most familiar to me, the one in the Netherlands, these last few years have witnessed an increasing polarization between secular liberals who seek to integrate the Muslim majority of newcomers and these newcomers themselves. Religion has come to be seen as one of the reasons integration fails. The claim is that the identification of migrants with their own cultural and religious backgrounds prevents them from becoming part of, and loyal to, Dutch society. The other arena in the struggle over integration is gender, specifically, the subordination of women. A growing number of Dutch citizens fear that Moslem culture threatens the freedoms that have been gained in Dutch society, in particular, freedoms in the field of gender and sexuality (i.e., the position of women, but also homosexuality). The dominant way of thinking is increasingly that migrants can integrate within Dutch society only when they take over the views on secularization and gender relations that are presumed to form the foundation of being-Dutch.[72]

The notion of horizontal transcendence is significant in this context in both meanings we have defined, namely, the horizon of values and ideal-images and the specific content of that horizon: self-limitation, which opens a place for the respect for others. This notion does not consider transcendence useless or meaningless, and it thereby offers the possibility of dialogue between believers and nonbelievers. Within a society in which religion has gained new importance, it will not do to consider all forms of religion to be backward and not Enlightened, as secular voices often claim in public discussions in the Netherlands. Yet it is also unfruitful to hold onto one truth as the absolute truth, in the way some believers (Christian as well as Moslem) do. Both attitudes prevent good dialogue with dissenters.

Horizontal transcendence indicates the horizon of values and ideal images that play an important role in everyone's life.[73] That horizon can be colored by religion, but that is just one possible way of coloring it. Every individual makes use of and refers to a horizon of values, in the sense that everyone follows values in order to act, make choices, set priorities. These values are embedded within one's culture and social environment. In a multicultural situation it makes sense to articulate these different horizons and the ethical values, notions of justice, and notions of how life becomes worthwhile that are part of them. Articulation of these values is important for dialogue concerning how to arrange our society in such a way that integration is no longer a one-sided process but demands changes of all the participants in society.

In the second meaning, horizontal transcendence points to the recognition of the other as other on the basis of self-limitation. This is perhaps Irigaray's most important lesson. In this sense, horizontal transcendence presents a way of dealing with differences. Irigaray shows us a model that could function as a starting point for exchange between different religious groups in which both listen to each other, in mutual respect, with the aim of mutual understanding. This model implies that as Westerners, former or believing Christians, we should first and foremost recognize that we are ourselves limited. Horizontal transcendence calls for an attitude of respect toward others by acknowledging the limits of one's culture. What is more, self-limitation in the multicultural situation opposes the current tendency (at least in the Netherlands) to insist that migrants assimilate. In this respect Irigaray's ethical notions of self-limitation, on the basis of recognizing the negative within oneself and of the transcendence of the other, offer an interesting perspective.

In the last few years, within the Netherlands a policy and public opinion have developed that demand migrants to integrate. Integration has thus come to mean becoming a good Dutch citizen who is secular—or at least keeps religion within the private sphere—and emancipated. The notion of horizontal transcendence opposes this tendency toward an integration that gives way to assimilation, calling for consideration of the limits of one's culture as the only possibility for openness to others with different cultures and religions. Today, when we demand that migrants obey the requirements we have constructed for "being Dutch," that insight seems far away . . .

Religion and the Time of Creation

Placing "the Human" in Techno-scientific and Theological Context

Thomas A. Carlson

The question of "religion" today often seems most urgent wherever the "human" in its "life" or "nature" appears to grow unstable conceptually and/or to fall under threat existentially. Such instability and threat come into play very notably in the context of recent scientific and technological developments where any number of categories long operative in conceptions of the human—intelligence and agency, birth and death, natural life, and so on—prove increasingly difficult to delimit because open to various forms of manipulation, simulation, or transformation. In reading the daily newspaper in the United States, for example, one quickly gets the sense that the "culture wars," driven largely by increasingly vocal religious (mainly Christian) groups who would speak in the name of "traditional values" and the "culture of life," involve a whole complex of anxieties surrounding nothing less that the "human" in its very "nature" and "dignity."

One of the more recent (and most sensationalized) of cases to illustrate such anxieties is that of Terri Schiavo, the woman in Florida who spent some fifteen years in a vegetative state while her husband and parents fought on opposite sides of a prolonged legal battle over the life or death of her body, which was sustained in its living condition thanks only to the technological apparatus of feeding tubes and the legal injunction to keep that technological apparatus in operation. From this perspective, Terri Schiavo could be seen to embody what Italian philosopher Giorgio Agamben calls "bare life," that form of life subjected directly to the power of a sovereign decision, which alone makes the difference between life and death.[1] The meeting between bodily life and sovereign power in the case of Schiavo, as in countless others (and far more complex ones), was called for thanks to a technological apparatus that somehow blurs the clear border between life and death, or suspends life between what is "naturally" given (what some call God-given) and what is not simply given but made, not only technologically but also politically or juridically, socially or culturally.

It is important to note, I think, that those who were seeking, in the name of religion, to keep Terri Schiavo alive through the insertion and later the reinsertion of feeding tubes into her body were seeking not only to reverse the course of "nature" (since her "natural" life depended entirely on the technological apparatus) but also to reverse what was in fact the normal, lawful, juridical process (which had long established the absence of legal grounds for the insertion or reinsertion of the feeding tubes on which Schiavo's living body depended). As theorist and literary scholar Eric Santner, drawing on Agamben, points out in a recent reflection titled "Terri Schiavo and the State of Exception,"[2] the last-minute attempt at legislation to require the reinsertion of feeding tubes into the body of Terri Schiavo was an effort to make, by law, a one-time exception to the law—an exception that would have made the bare life of Terri Schiavo into the most straightforward expression of the sovereign decision that Agamben believes in modernity to form more the norm than the exception. Santner himself sees in the bare life of Schiavo a perversion of what he calls "creaturely life," which he defines as life exposed and, as theorist and literature scholar Julia Lupton puts it, "always in the process of undergoing creation."[3] In Santner's reading, "creature" in its theological sense "isn't so much the name of a determinate state of being or essence as that of ongoing *exposure*, of being caught up in the process of *becoming creature* through the dictates of divine authority."

From my perspective, a significant paradox comes to light in the Schiavo case: the desire of those seeking to legislate a reversal of the normal legal process might be read as a desire, in fact, to free human life—or indeed to free "the human," in its given, inviolable nature or dignity—from the decisions on which such life comes increasingly to depend in our techno-scientific modernity, a desire to keep human life "as such" or in its "givenness" safe from the assault of legal powers that must themselves be called into operation because our scientific and technological capacity to shift or to blur the boundaries of life (and death) place us in the position of having, indeed, to decide on those boundaries. What counts as the "human" or as "life" or as a distinctively "human life" is, it seems, more and more not given but made, not built into a given "nature" of things but created through the discursive and technological powers of a humanity that is, whether admittedly or not, in the course of creating itself. What Santner calls the creaturely life of exposure or passivity involves also, I'll suggest, the creative activity of the human.

Another recent case related to the unsettling developments that confront all of us within contemporary technological and scientific culture is that of cloning—and what in May 2005 the editorial page of the *New York Times* called George W. Bush's "stem cell theology."[4] In light of South Korea's recent technical advances in the cloning of human stem cells, and in face of upcoming legislation in the U.S. Congress that would fund stem cell research involving human embryos, Bush has reiterated his opposition, stating that he would not fund research that kills life in order to save life. What he must really mean, of course, is that he will not fund research that kills what he takes to be *human* life in order to save human life—and what is especially interesting here is the wholly techno-scientific character of the "human" "life" at stake: in this case, frozen human embryos that would never have existed without the artifice of technology and that will never yield living human persons without the technological manipulation of a process that is now rather far from "natural." (One might note here that an entire Christian movement is currently engaged in promoting the "adoption" of these techno-scientific "babies," who are no doubt also God's children.[5]) The paradox of this position appears, I think, in light of the resistance so often expressed in opposition to cloning and other technological intervention into human life by a figure like Dr. Leon Kass, the first chairman of the President's Council on Bioethics. Kass voices well what I take to be among the more common—and religiously motivated—objections to the potential of emerging science and technology: they threaten the nature and dignity of "the human."[6] Such a threat, Kass repeatedly insists, must be answered by a "defense" that would seek "to keep human life human,"[7] by keeping it free of inappropriate techno-scientific intervention and thus safe in its "wonder" and "mystery." While appealing to the "mystery" of the human as a motive to protect it from technological and scientific intervention, Kass is in fact working with what one would call a "positive anthropology," that is, one that believes in a human nature that we could define or know so as to protect it from alteration or violation.[8]

An ostensibly similar resistance to techno-science in the name of human mystery might be found in the work of French philosopher Jean-Luc Marion, who, by contrast to Kass and with more nuance, argues for a "negative anthropology" that would protect the human by insisting that it *lacks* definition. On the occasion of his inaugural lecture as the John Nuveen Chair in Philosophy of Religion and Theology (a chair held previously by Paul Tillich and Paul Ricoeur), Marion argues for a thought of the human that would unsettle or elude the objectification and reduction of the human exercised by modern technological culture (and by the modern metaphysics grounding such culture), and he makes this argument by insisting on a paradoxical definition of the human as indefinable—as exceeding irreducibly the stable boundaries of any clear and distinct concept.[9] The failure of modern metaphysics, of the natural as well as human sciences founded by such metaphysics, and of the rationalized, technological culture these yield would be, Marion argues, a "humanism" that in fact dehumanizes precisely by claiming to offer a definition (or a "clear and distinct idea") of the human. Any such definition, he insists, makes the human available as an object conceivable to the representing human mind—and thereby cancels the human. In this, Marion follows Heidegger's critique of modern metaphysics for its reduction of all "being" to objectivity and its grounding of "truth" in the subjective certainty of a thinking human subject who, in representing objectivized being to itself, becomes "ground" and "measure" of all that is.[10] From this Heideggerian frame Marion locates the danger of defining the human in the arrogance of decision it implies: if man becomes the measure of all that is, including humanity itself, if the human itself is a function of our objectifying definition or conception, if it is grasped within our measure, then it depends upon our decision—and such decision, Marion insists, will inevitably exclude from the human that which may then (like Agamben's "bare life") be given death: "to claim to define what a man is leads to or at least opens the possibility of leading to the elimination of that which does not correspond to this definition. Every political proscription, every racial extermination, every ethnic cleansing, every determination of that which does not merit life—all these rest upon a claim to define (scientifically or ideologically) the humanity of man" (PU, 13).

This death-dealing logic, common to racism and other ideologies, operates also, Marion asserts, at the very heart of our modern science and technology, an exemplary instance of which can be seen in the medical field, whose ostensible aim is the care and preservation of human life. The "medical definition of my body as an object," he warns, "will also allow for the distinction of health from sickness in terms of norms. Thus is opened the fearful region in which man can make decisions about the normality, and thus the life and death, of other human beings—because these other human beings have become simple human objects" (PU, 12). Taking the medical field as exemplary of a logic to be noted also in the natural and human sciences more broadly, Marion argues that the greatest danger to "humanity" is in fact its definition and the exclusionary "decision" that such definition implies. The danger of this "determining" that "amounts to a denying" (PU, 14) of humanity, the violence inherent to such determination is, Marion insists, what any overly secure humanism involves:

> The weakness of humanism's claim consists in dogmatically imagining not only that man can hold himself up as his own measure (so that man is enough for man), but above all that he can do this because he comprehends what man is, when on the contrary nothing threatens man more than any such alleged comprehension of his humanity. For every de-*finition* imposes on the human being a finite essence, following from which it always becomes possible to delimit what deserves to remain human from what no longer does. (PU, 14)

Much as Emmanuel Levinas argues that my obligation to the other derives not from the category or conception of any general "humanity" to which the other would belong but rather from the face of the other in its excessive singularity, so Marion insists here that the distinctive claim of a human person to be loved and not killed (and we can only love, Marion argues, quite beautifully, what we do *not* comprehend) is based not in the definition or conception of her humanity but in that humanity's excess over any definition or concept. Assuming the status of what Marion calls a "saturated phenomenon" (see PU, 23), the human will always give to our thought more than thought could ever conceive or contain (and for this reason, to receive the human other would call first not for thought but for love).

Two points of tension within Marion's remarkable analysis bear noting here. Both concern what seem to be gestures of exclusion on which Marion himself in fact relies, paradoxically, to save the human from any objectifying and finally exclusionary or murderous definition, and both relate in significant ways to the question concerning technology in Marion's thought.

First, Marion's definition of the human as indefinable presupposes the anthropocentric and theologically derived discourse of a Christianity that secures the privilege and dignity (if not the definition or essential identity) of the human through an exclusion of other beings such as the animal, which in Marion's analysis (as elsewhere in Christian thought and culture) amounts to a life that is, through a right established by God, subject to the naming, domination, and killing exercised by the human created in God's image. "Adam has the power thus to name only that which can legitimately become for him an object: the animals (and the rest of the world), and perhaps the angels, but not God, and not himself" (PU, 10). From the logic of this biblical story, where the distinction of the animal from man and from God works to uphold the definition of man and God as indefinable, Marion draws the lesson that "it follows from the characteristics of knowledge by concepts that man cannot name man, which is to say define man, except by reducing him to the rank of a simple concept, thereby knowing not a man but an object, possibly animated, but always alienated" (PU, 10). The argument made here against alienation is the one Marion makes elsewhere about the saturated phenomenon and its highest form in revelation: it must be allowed to show itself on its own terms rather than appearing on *our* terms and thus as alienated from itself.[11] The avoidance of the name and concept, aiming to allow the human to *give itself* rather than to depend on an alienating and exclusionary definition given ahead of time, depends nonetheless on a fundamental gesture of exclusion, directed first at the animal and then, as suggested parenthetically in the same passage, at all other nonhuman and nondivine beings—which is to say, the "world."

Indeed, the theological grounding of Marion's anthropology leads to a radical distinction between the human and the world:

if God remains incomprehensible, man, who resembles nothing other than Him, will also bear the mark and the privilege of His incomprehensibility. Put another way: the human being belongs to no species whatsoever, refers to no genus, is not comprehended by any definition of (in)humanity. Delivered from every paradigm, he appears immediately within the light of the One who surpasses all light. Man's face bears the mark of this borrowed incomprehensibility in so far, precisely, as he too reveals himself as invisible, like God. [Marion here cites a passage from Levinas that seems to me significant, for reasons that will become clear momentarily.[12]] Man is thus radically separated from every other being in this world by an insurmountable and definitive difference that is no longer ontological but holy. No longer does the human being distinguish him- or herself from the rest of the world as the "Platzhalter des Nichts" ("lieutenant of the nothing"[13]) or the "Hirt des Seins" ("shepherd of Being"[14]), but as the icon of the incomprehensible. Man's invisibility separates him from the world and consecrates him as holy for the Holy. (PU, 16)

If in his thought of the human as indefinable Marion here aligns himself with a Levinasian ethic of the holy that would resist or pass beyond any Heideggerian ontology, on the question of technology Marion in fact remains more in line with the Heidegger for whom the essence of technology reduces man, through calculative and instrumental thought, to object or indeed to "standing reserve" (*Bestand*)[15]—and he sets himself at odds with the Levinas for whom technology may in fact cast us outside every horizon and thus open the possibility of "signification without context" or the nudity of a face whose significance would be absolute. ("Technology," as Levinas writes in "Heidegger, Gagarin, and Us," "wrenches us out of the Heideggerian world and the superstitions surrounding *Place*. From this point on, an opportunity appears to us: to perceive men outside the situation in which they are placed, to let the human face shine in its nudity."[16]) Unlike the Levinas who can see in technology a liberation of the human from the violence of definition, Marion can only fault technology for setting a definition of the human that cancels or blocks humanity as such (namely, as indefinable). And again, within this reading of technology, Marion sets humanity in a radical difference or disconnection from "world."

Several questions arise here. Is the world in fact any more reducible to an object than is the human? Is it any more comprehensible? And if not, if world is no more reducible to objective definition than the human, might we not understand the incomprehensibility of the human, its lack of definition, as a function of its constitutive involvement with (not its separation from) the world, and might we not in turn understand such involvement, in and through which, indeed, we do not comprehend ourselves, to be from the beginning sustained and cultivated by the kind of technological experience that so thoroughly structures the human world today?

I pose these questions not only in light of recent theorizations of technological culture (which would call for a revision of the Heideggerian analysis on which Marion depends) but also in light of the theological traditions on which Marion draws to develop his anthropology. In both contexts, I think, the incomprehensibility of the human might be understood as a crucial condition of technological existence.

In resistance to technological objectification of humanity, which would involve a humanism that proves to be dehumanizing, Marion deploys a theological insistence on the incomprehensibility of the human as created in the image of an incomprehensible God. A mystical or negative anthropology follows from a mystical or negative theology. To see humanity as created in the image of God would be, from this perspective, not to secure humanity's definition or to conceive its essence but, indeed, to see that the essence of humanity, like the essence of God, is infinite and therefore beyond any conception or definition, any representation or name. The most important traditional source that Marion cites for such anthropology is the Cappadocian Father Gregory of Nyssa, whose fourth-century treatise *On the Creation of Man* offers *the* classic formulation of a mystical or negative anthropology that would follow from his mystical and negative theology (and Gregory was the first we know of in the Christian tradition to have written a systematically negative theology). As Gregory writes, in the passage that Marion cites to ground and elaborate his argument on the "holy difference" between humanity and the world:

> since one of the attributes we contemplate in the divine nature is incomprehensibility of essence, it is clearly necessary that in this point the icon should be able to show its imitation of the archetype. For if, while the archetype transcends comprehension, the nature of the icon were comprehended, the contrary character of the attributes we behold in them would prove the defect of the icon: but since the nature of our mind, which is according to the icon of the Creator, evades our knowledge, it keeps an accurate resemblance to the superior nature, retaining the imprint of the incomprehensible [fixed] by the unknown within it.[17]

What Marion does not mention about Gregory's anthropology, which seems to me significant, given the critique of technological modernity that Marion advances, is the linkage that Gregory himself makes between the human subject's incomprehensibility and its capacity for innovation by technological means. In Gregory the human—who, as image of the incomprehensible God, remains incomprehensible—is at the same time a technological human whose creative freedom would likewise derive from its status as *imago Dei*, even as that freedom is occasioned by a kind of organic lack. "What seems to be a deficiency of our nature," Gregory argues, noting that we must create technologies to do the work for which animals are naturally endowed, "is a means for our obtaining dominion over the subject creatures."[18]

A similar linkage between the human lack of definition (or of "natural endowment") and its creative, indeed technological, freedom recurs subsequently within the Christian Neoplatonic tradition in pivotal figures such as John Scotus Eriugena in the early Middle Ages and Nicholas of Cusa in the later Middle Ages. As major accounts such as those of Hans Blumenberg and Louis Dupré have emphasized, the latter, Cusa, is especially important for understanding the passage from the limited cosmos of the medieval world, in which the nature of man is conceived teleologically, to an infinite and relative cosmos (itself never fully comprehended by the human) in which humanity exercises a creative freedom that is all the more divine insofar as it follows no pregiven paradigms; it imitates nothing other than the infinite freedom and potential of a creator God who, in his own creating, imitates nothing.[19] From late antiquity through the late Middle Ages and Renaissance into modernity itself, the traditions of mystical thought on which Marion draws in his effort to think the human as indefinable will, with striking persistence, link that indefinition to creative and indeed technological capacity. Along these lines, I want to suggest, mystical tradition and our most contemporary theorizations of the technological resonate in ways striking enough to call for the revision and critique of the classic theories of disenchantment in Max Weber and his kin. Marion does not note or develop such a link, I would guess, because he wants to think the incomprehensibility of the human more in terms of passivity and receptivity than in terms of activity or productivity. He wants all phenomena—including that of the human—to rely *not* on the constitution or decision of the thinking human subject (as in modern metaphysics) but on the unconditional and excessive givenness of the phenomena themselves: "The nature (and definition) of man is characterized by instability [this we learn from Pico and his heir Nietzsche]—man as the being who remains, for himself, to be decided and about whom one never ceases to be astonished. Man, undecidable to man, thus loses himself if he claims to decide about himself. He remains himself only as long as he remains without qualities" (PU, 20).

Here we might note that, if the questions of human limit or finitude, passivity and receptivity, have played a decisive role in twentieth-century continental philosophy, we may be reaching the point, in light especially of recent science and technology, where the obsession with passivity and limit can begin to look like a flight from the unnervingly open or seemingly inexhaustible potential that appears operative in our techno-scientific networks (whose characterization as a prison I find no more convincing than the characterization of language as a prison; both are systems of what Mark Taylor nicely terms "enabling constraint"). What calls for consideration, I think, is the intimate interplay between, on the one hand, the human lack of definition, as articulated so richly by Marion and the mystical tradition on which he draws, and, on the other hand, the creative and technological capacity of that same human (a capacity noted by the mystical tradition but ignored by Marion). If the technological can appear to the (Heideggerian) perspective of Marion and others as grounded in an overly narrow and all too stable delimitation of the human, one might also argue, as suggested by mystical tradition and as argued today in theoretical and philosophical contexts, that the human in its technological existence builds upon, even as it effects or instantiates, its own lack of definition, the irreducible indetermination that itself opens and sustains our creative capacity.

In the field of religious studies and in the human sciences more broadly, it is a commonplace, of course, to understand "religion" as human construction or creation, realized through the social dialectics of "world-building." In just such a humanistic understanding of religion, Marion would worry that the human is reduced through an overly secure definition of the human and thus that the excess of the human—and even more the excess of religion—is lost. (Recall that Marion's effort to protect the human from objectification constitutes the heart of an inaugural lecture where he is reflecting on the very possibility of any philosophy of religion—which in his account would face the insurmountable paradox of having, as Marion's predecessor Paul Tillich put it, "an object that refuses to become an object for philosophy."[20]) Now, while one would indeed have to acknowledge the common tendency of social-scientific thought to involve an overly secure (and often impoverished) conception both of the human and of religion, it is worth noting also that, and how, the anthropology grounding this understanding of religion as world construction by means of human creativity can itself seem to recall, in unexpected ways, the anthropology of mystical tradition I have signaled.

When Peter Berger argues in his classic study *The Sacred Canopy* that man becomes social creature and world builder because he is born "unfinished" and thus lives "constantly in the process of 'catching up with himself'" through the production of a world that itself, in turn, produces man, when he argues that man by nature must form a "second nature," or culture,[21] he is building not only on the dialectics of Hegel and Marx but also on a kind of negative anthropology to be found in the work of figures such as Arnold Gehlen and Georges Lapassade.[22] Both Gehlen and Lapassade take their lead from the Dutch anatomist Louis Bolk, who in his 1926 lecture "The Problem of Human Genesis" developed the biological and evolutionary theory of human "neoteny," according to which the human, born prematurely (ontogenetically and phylogenetically), remains fundamentally and forever incomplete, maintaining a foetal character even into its (never fully realized) maturity.[23] In his 1963 book *L'Entrée dans la vie: Essai sur l'inachèvement de l'homme* (*The Entry into Life: An Essay on the Incompletion of Man*), Lapassade draws on the likes of Marx, Freud, and Heidegger to develop Bolk's theory of neoteny in a way that highlights in especially striking fashion the *lack* of definition to be reckoned with in the central object of human scientific thought. The human sciences in fact imply or require a kind of negative anthropology, Lapassade concludes, precisely insofar as the human, because born premature and thus remaining always incomplete, lacks any definite or definable "nature"; that lack of nature, in turn, is related intimately to the creative and thus the historical and social capacity of the human—both allowing such capacity and demanding it. "The concept of incompletion," Lapassade writes, "taken at the anthropological level, has the effect of placing into question any a priori as to the 'nature' of man and of insisting on the necessity of a history in order for man to be what he is."[24] As historical, then, which is to say, as incomplete and thus creative in an open-ended fashion, the human figured in such social-scientific thinking exceeds and resists the definition of any concept. "The concept of incompletion is therefore at one and the same time the concept of lack and the lack of a concept. It is the concept of lack: it signifies that man is decompleted [*décomplété*], that he does not find in himself, in his instincts, in an innate know-how, the meaning [or direction] of his life and the truth of his behaviors, and that the human being can be only an interhuman being. But it is also the lack of the concept:

the sciences here show themselves to be insufficient at the same time as they are necessary to 'comprehending' man."[25]

Operative within one of the more influential social-scientific theorizations of religion, this figure of the premature human who becomes creative (social, cultural, and historical) in the space and time of its natural lack, or lack of nature, can be seen to operate also within more recent philosophical and theoretical treatments of technology for a thought of human and world today—a thought, in its turn, that might be seen to assume a fundamental significance for the question of religion.

French philosopher Michel Serres, for example, links the "return of the religious" to the ostensible threats posed by techno-science to "man" in his very "life" and "nature." The perception of such threat, Serres notes, will indeed tend to provoke reactions aiming to resecure these categories as "sacred" (and along these lines, Serres seems to me quite close to the invaluable analyses of Jacques Derrida in "Faith and Knowledge"[26]): "the diffuse anxieties today surrounding chemistry or biotechnologies, for example, bring back the old abandoned figures of 'Nature,' of 'Life,' and of 'Man,' [which prove] all the less defined and all the more sacred as these fears grow. Let's not touch 'Man,' they say, nor let us violate 'Life' or 'Nature,' whose myths reappear, as so many ghosts [*revenants*]."[27] Such a return of myth (which one can read daily in the newspapers) and such appeal to a sacred givenness of humanity, in its life and nature, could well be seen to involve a flight from the human indetermination or lack of definition that is both condition and consequence of the human capacity for a technological creation that is itself a form of world creation and self-creation at once. That same technological capacity, in Serres' analysis, would require us to see the emergence of a world—and of a humanity in and through that world—that could no longer be understood adequately according to the old divisions of subject and object, or the discrete location of intelligence and agency, whose seemingly secure delimitations may once have served a project of mastery and possession but now grow untenable.

If Marion argues, from a perspective that remains in this regard Heideggerian, that a techno-scientific human subject reduces all being, including its own, to the status of defined object, and if through such objectification the human subject makes itself the measure or master of all that is, at the cost of its own objectification and profound dehumanization, Serres might allow us, along lines seen also in work such as that of Katherine Hayles on the "posthuman" or of Mark Taylor on the "network," to read technological culture otherwise.[28]

In a philosophy insisting that relation and communication are more fundamental than substance or being, Serres—who began theorizing the network in a piece from 1964 that appears in the first volume of his *Hermès* series[29]—emphasizes a dimension of irreducible unknowing within our technological experience: the human proves at once creative and self-creative for Serres in just the measure that it lacks stable definition or strict program, which is to say also in the measure that it cannot fully or finally comprehend itself. "Man changes," Serres writes, "insofar as one cannot fix for him any definition, which he always lacks or exceeds."[30] This instability of the human and related categories (life, nature, etc.) within technological culture may signal a challenge less that of human finitude and more that of human in-finitude, which is to say, the human indetermination or incompletion that could itself be understood as the condition of an inexhaustible openness or possibility. Structured by such open possibility, we would find our being less in the category of the human "as such" (as already defined in its nature or its dignity) and more in the ongoing process that Serres calls "hominescence," a neologism that highlights the always inceptive, inchoate dimension of the human.

Much like the distributed intelligence and agency of the posthuman in Katherine Hayles, or like the nodular subject of the complex adaptive system in Mark Taylor, our hominescence in Serres would emerge from a fundamentally relational and interactive technological and scientific process that, while bringing forth a new humanity, "does not yet know what humanity [*homme*] it is going to produce"[31] and, likewise, cannot know exactly what humanity "does" that producing. As Serres elaborates in fourfold recent works, we now inhabit humanly constructed and global systems whose cognitive and agentive capacities not only exceed us but also transform us—and in such a way that the self-creation we thereby realize transpires always in conjunction with an insurmountable ignorance or unknowing concerning both producer and produced.[32] Reshaping our relations to space and time (through digital technologies, satellite networks, mobile communications, cyberspace, etc.), our relations to intelligence and agency (through cybernetics, artificial intelligence, robotics, prosthetics, etc.), our relations to life and death themselves (through genetics and bio-engineering, thermonuclear weapons, etc.), emerging technoscience should lead us to see that we are no longer (if we ever were) passive recipients of a nature that is simply given but, indeed, that we are nature's "active architects and workers" (H, 49). We are becoming in concrete ways "our own cause, the continuous creator of our world and of ourselves" (H, 165), but we do so in such a way that, through the logic of the feedback loop, "we ourselves end up depending on the things that depend globally on us"[33]—including, as I'll note momentarily, the time or temporality through which we live.

Such looping between that which we create and that which, in turn, re-creates us takes place, notably, by means of what Serres calls "world-objects [*objets-monde*]," which is to say, humanly fabricated devices or systems whose scale—in terms of time, space, speed, or energy—reaches worldly dimensions, techno-scientific creations of ours that finally exceed us in such a way that, instead of relating to them from a stance of distance and independence (as with the "representational" relation between subject and object in Heidegger's account of modern Western metaphysics), we actually live and move within them and find ourselves shaped by them (H, 180).[34] At this level, the "object" of human thought and action, much like Hayles's distributed systems or Taylor's networks, would differ from any object that might be set apart and placed securely in front of a subject, defined discretely, circumscribed, and hence *located* in such a way as to fall under the conceptual or practical hold of that subject.[35] By contrast to Heidegger's world-picture, the "world-object," in Serres, puts us "in the presence of a world that we can no longer treat as an object" (H, 181), a world no longer passive but actively—interactively— engaged with us. The technological humanity who interactively builds and inhabits a world no longer reducible to object is a humanity whose creative potential must be under- stood to depend on its lack of definition or determination: the more programmed the creature, the less open in its potential; the less programmed, the more open and adaptable. Our creative potential would stem from our *not* knowing ourselves, from a kind of depro- gramming or forgetting. In this respect, Serres articulates, within today's technological culture, a human figure deeply reminiscent of the mystical tradition on which Marion draws in his resistance to that culture.

At this point we might highlight two lines within Serres' analysis that I believe to bear significantly on our inquiry into the future of the religious past. One concerns the intimate and increasingly complex interplay we would need to acknowledge between the sociocultural and the natural-cosmological within our world-building and self-creative activity, and the other, intimately related, concerns our experience of time. As Serres argues in *Le contract naturel* (*The Natural Contract*):

> The global power of our new tools today gives to us as partner the Earth, which we constantly inform through our movements and energies, and which in turn informs us, through its energies and movements, its global changes. We do not need language, again, in order for this contract to function, as a play of forces.
>
> Our technologies [*techniques*] make up a system of cords [*cordes*] or of lines [*traits*], a system of exchanges of power and information, which goes from the local to the global, and the Earth responds to us, from the global to the local.[36]

Within the ongoing operation of this "natural contract," which inextricably binds the natural with the sociocultural (and thus renders elusive or unreal the givenness of any nature "itself" or life "itself") even the time of "nature" becomes increasingly a time of human making—as, for example, in the time of genetic evolution or the temporality of the climate that cools or heats the earth.

Through genetic engineering, the almost unimaginably slow (and blind) time of nat- ural evolution becomes, concretely, the historical (and intentional) time of human labor and creativity; the time of "life" begins to fall under our influence (which does not mean control), and thus we assume over all of life a new responsibility (which is not to say domination). Likewise, through the technological ways of life that yield global warming, a new and truly global human condition emerges, itself the product of a collective human- ity that transforms, through its influence on climate or weather (*le temps qu'il fait*), the time that passes or flows (*le temps qui coule*), even the temporality of Earth itself, which not only sustains life but may well offer the ground of any humanity whatsoever (as Robert Harrison argues in his beautiful and challenging book *Dominion of the Dead*[37]). (One might note here the irony that Christians in the United States are fighting the teaching of evolution in schools at the very moment when techno-science promises to place the powers of evolution more directly in our hands. One might wonder also about the degree to which George Bush's religious commitments are related to his disbelief in, or disregard for, the science of global warming.)

The significance of human and technological transformation of the climate and hence of earthly time itself could be appreciated perhaps nowhere more acutely than in the Netherlands (where this essay was initially delivered), where one quarter of the land sits below sea level and another quarter remains low enough that it would flood on a regular basis in the absence of technological intervention.[38] For the inhabitants of such a place, the accelerated melting of snowfields and ice sheets in Greenland or Antarctica constitutes a local concern within whose specific and changing temporality those inhabitants must in fact live. Perhaps it is no mistake, then, that it was a Dutch scientist (born in Amsterdam), the Nobel Prize–winning chemist Paul Crutzen, who captured the scope of such developments by suggesting that we rename the geologic age in which we live: we inhabit no longer the Holocene (dated from the last period of glaciation), Crutzen argues, but instead the Anthropocene, a new age "defined by one creature—man—who had become so dominant that he was capable of altering the planet on a geologic scale."[39] (Crutzen thus highlights the temporal import of the similar assertion made by Soviet geochemist Vladimir I. Vernadsky, who some seventy years ago observed that "through technology and sheer numbers . . . people were becoming a geological force."[40])

The analysis of technology, of course, has long noted the multiple ways it can transform the human relation to both time and place, seeming (as Benjamin emphasized in his classic "The Work of Art in the Age of Mechanical Reproduction") to speed up things that move slowly (time-lapse photography), or seeming to slow down things that move quickly (slow-motion film); seeming to make near what physically remains distant (the image transmitted by newspaper, television, or Internet), or seeming to make distant what in fact stands physically close (through, e.g., the distraction and uprooting that so worried Heidegger). In the directions just noted with Serres—genetics and evolution, climate and geological time—these tendencies of the technological intersect so as to bind time and place in the most concrete and global senses. In doing so, however, the technological does not simply distract, uproot, or displace; it does not in fact set the human subject at a distance from the world or from an earth thus objectified, manipulated, and exploited by calculative and instrumental means within a human project of mastery. Rather, in these instances the technological in fact binds us in ever more intimate and complex relations with earth and world (whose distinction in the Heideggerian frame may call for revision[41]). By highlighting the inextricable tie between the two senses of "time [*temps*]" at stake in the networks of our techno-scientific self-creation, and in noting the binding or "contractual" character of such networks, where we are bound not only to one another in our emerging humanity but also to the Earth as global human ground, we might understand such time and its transformations to involve not only something of the technological but also, fundamentally, something of the religious.[42]

Serres points in this direction when he argues that the members of a "traditional" religious humanity, through its prayers and rites—such as the chants that open, punctuate, and close the day of the Benedictines—do not simply follow a given time but indeed themselves structure and sustain time (CN, 80). "Their shoulders and their voices," Serres writes of the monastics whose prayers and rites we modern amnesiacs may forget, "from biblical verses to orisons, bear each minute into the next throughout a fragile duration which, without them, would break" (ibid.). Though Serres does not quite say it, his position suggests to us that the time or duration that the monks sustain through their song and prayer is also, in return, the time that sustains them. Likewise today, I would argue, in and through our techno-scientific ties, we come to depend on a global temporality that depends upon us. In such human work of sustaining time, Serres rightly locates a basic work of religion, a work that today would concern as much the time that passes and flows as it would concern the weather or the climate, the world environment, for which we grow responsible. In either sense, one could liken the work of religion to a temporalized version of Penelope's incessant weaving: "In the same way [as Penelope], religion presses, spins, knots, assembles, gathers, binds, connects, lifts up, reads, or sings the elements of time. The term *religion* expresses exactly this trajectory, this review [*revue*] or this continuation [*prolongement*] whose opposite is called negligence, the negligence that incessantly loses the memory [of those words and behaviors]" (ibid.) through which the religious give voice to the world and to the time in which they live.

If the reverse side of religion is negligence, where might we find or suspect such negligence today? Among those who would deny or ignore the complex ties that bind the local and the global, the social and the natural. While those in the daily news who speak most vocally for the "culture of life" and for the nature and dignity of "the human" do so more often than not in the name of religion and its "traditional values," or in the name of "people of faith," we might well hear just such speech, I think, as one expression of profound negligence—in the sense that it would involve a distinctive denial or disavowal of the ties that now inevitably bind the human to life and nature themselves, negligent of the processes sustaining and advancing the ongoing exchange in which we become indeed the "continuous creators of our world and of ourselves" (H, 163).

Such negligence, speaking in the name of tradition, could also be read, finally, as a flight from just the trait of the human that could be argued to make something like tradition both possible and necessary: namely, the indetermination and incompletion that call for and condition our techno-scientific being in which the time of creation is also a creation of time. The various myths today that appeal to the "human" itself as "sacred" in its "life" and "nature" "as such," myths that claim to know who or what the human is, while believing they derive such knowledge from tradition, may well ignore the very conditions of any tradition at all: we can and we must create tradition and all it requires (all the extensions of man: images, texts, rituals, archives, etc.) *because* we remain deficient or indeterminate "in ourselves." Tradition, in turn, its wealth of immeasurable memory, can speak to us and through us in a living way thanks only to such indeterminacy—such that our wealth and poverty condition one another.

As Giorgio Agamben suggests in his striking meditation "The Idea of Infancy,"[43] which takes up in a philosophic register Bolks's theory of human neoteny, the appeal to tradition and its codified values can tend toward a reproductive logic that would want to be as automatic (or as "natural") as the genetic reproduction of a species may seem to be. What such a tendency of tradition ignores, however, is the indetermination and freedom that alone make something like human tradition possible and necessary in the first place: "before handing down any knowledge or tradition, man necessarily has to hand down the very thoughtlessness, the very indeterminate openness in which alone something like a concrete historical tradition has become possible" (IP, 97; translation modified). Along lines resonant with those taken by Serres on the hominescent, the "pedomorphic" or "neotenic" human in Agamben, maintaining throughout its (never actually achieved) "maturity" the incompletion and potential of its (eternal) infancy while inheriting the immeasurable memory of history and tradition, proves endlessly plastic, innovative, and endowed with potential thanks to its lack of fixed nature or lawful program. To deny the kind of creativity made possible and necessary by such an insurmountable infancy, which is just what the more troubling and often violent appeals to tradition seem recently and increasingly to do, would be, in fact, to show symptoms of cultural decadence. As Agamben puts it:

> Genuine spirituality and culture do not forget this original, infantile vocation of human language, while the attempt to imitate the natural germen in order to transmit immortal and codified values in which neotenic openness once more shuts itself off in a specific tradition is precisely the characteristic of a degraded culture. In fact, if something distinguishes the human tradition from that of the genetic code, it is precisely the fact that it wants to save not only the saveable (the essential characteristics of the species), but what in any case cannot be saved; that which is, on the contrary, always already lost; or better, that which has never been possessed as a specific property, but which is, precisely because of this, unforgettable: the being, the openness of the infantile soma, to which only the world, only language, is adequate. (IP, 97–98)

Of course, to say here that world or language would be "adequate" to this infantile soma, the figure of an irreducibly open potential, would be to say that world and language remain, like the being they supplement, while charged with the past, also ever indeterminate and incomplete; for that very reason, world and language can keep open the place and time of a creation whose work, and place, is never done.

To care for such openness, to save a humanity that remains creative because it remains indeterminate and incomplete, requires a temporality that might both guard the heritage of tradition and, at the same time, guard itself from the automaticity and the closure toward which tradition can tend. This danger of tradition, signaled here in Agamben and treated so incisively by Heidegger and Derrida in similar fashion, is the danger that things be handed over to self-evidence and that they be received not in an authentically creative and living fashion, according to the potential of a futurity not already reduced to presence and actuality, but in a mechanical repetition that cancels any future, and any creation, by giving us to know and understand everything ahead of time, beginning with the knowledge or understanding of who and what we are. In handing things over to self-evidence by means of a codification turned overly programmatic, tradition loses its genuine, living memory and becomes instead a deceptive (or self-deceptive) form of forgetting or negligence—the kind of negligence, indeed, in which (despite all claims to the contrary) we could see religion's opposite.

In order for tradition to hand over creative potential, or an open future, it needs to remember otherwise—to transmit not codified or programmed content but the ground of creative tradition itself, which such codification can tend to close off; it needs to transmit what Agamben calls our infancy, or what Serres calls our constitutive self-forgetting or deprogramming. As Agamben puts it, what tradition in this sense would need to save in order to remain open and alive is what, in fact, we never have: it would need to save the indeterminacy, openness, and creative potential of the premature human whose nature is to have no nature, whose definition is to elude definition. "Somewhere inside of us," Agamben writes, "the careless neotenic child continues his royal game. And it is his play that gives us time, that keeps ajar for us that never setting openness which the peoples and languages of the earth, each in its own way, watch over in order both to preserve and to hold back—and to preserve only to the extent that they defer" (IP, 98). To defer completion, to preserve the infantile: these are the means by which tradition gives, or is given by, the time of creation—and that time, I think, operative in our social and natural binds alike, might signal one possible future of religion.

Notes

Hent de Vries, Introduction: Why Still "Religion"?

1. See Charles Taylor, *Varieties of Religion Today: William James Revisited* (Cambridge: Harvard University Press, 2002).

2. See, e.g., Jean-Luc Marion, *On the Ego and on God: Further Cartesian Questions* (New York: Fordham University Press, 2007).

3. See my *Minimal Theologies: Critiques of Secular Reason in Theodor W. Adorno and Emmanuel Levinas* (Baltimore: The Johns Hopkins University Press, 2005), 184 ff.

4. On the bisection of rationality in the study of "religion," see the opening chapter of *Minimal Theologies*, entitled "Antiprolegomena."

5. See Hent de Vries and Lawrence E. Sullivan, eds., *Political Theologies: Public Religions in a Post-Secular World* (New York: Fordham University Press, 2006). This volume could be read as an extensive preamble to the present study, which, in its turn, serves as the introductory volume to a series of four further volumes—on *Things, Powers, Gestures,* and *Words*—to be published by Fordham University Press.

6. Anthony Flew, "Theology and Falsification," in *The Philosophy of Religion*, ed. Basil Mitchell (Oxford: Oxford University Press, 1971), 13–15.

7. One is reminded of the document released by the Roman Catholic Church in July 2007, reiterating its claim to supremacy in matters of theological truth and salvation.

8. I analyze this figure of thought in my *Minimal Theologies*.

9. Richard Rorty, "Religion as Conversation-Stopper," in idem, *Philosophy and Social Hope* (London: Penguin Books, 1999), 168–74.

10. Talal Asad, *Genealogies of Religion: Disciplines and Reasons of Power in Christianity and Islam* (Baltimore: The Johns Hopkins University Press, 1993); Mark C. Taylor, ed., *Critical Terms for Religious Studies* (Chicago: University of Chicago Press, 1998); Jonathan Z. Smith, *Relating Religion: Essays in the Study of Religion* (Chicago: University of Chicago Press, 2004); Nancy K. Frankenberry, ed., *Radical Interpretation in Religion* (Cambridge: Cambridge University Press, 2002); Michael Lambek, ed., *A Reader in the Anthropology of Religion* (Malden, Mass.: Blackwell, 2002); Fenella Cannell, ed., *The Anthropology of Christianity* (Durham, N.C.: Duke University Press, 2006).

11. The formulation "belief as the defining characteristic" stems from Jonathan Z. Smith, "Religion, Religions, Religious," in *Critical Terms for Religious Studies*, ed. Taylor, 271. See also David Chidester, "Material Terms for the Study of Religion," *Journal of the American Academy of Religion* 68, no. 2 (June 2000): 367–80; and Terry F. Godlove, Jr., "Saving Belief: On the New Materialism in Religious Studies," in *Radical Interpretation in Religion*, ed. Frankenberry, 17.

12. Godlove, "Saving Belief," 17.

13. On the term *eliminative materialism*, see Robert B. Brandom, "Vocabularies of Pragmatism: Synthesizing Naturalism and Historicism," in *Rorty and His Critics*, ed. Robert B. Brandom (Malden, Mass.: Blackwell, 2000), 157 and 181n.1.

14. Without wanting to be pedantic, we may be well advised to recall the many types of questions that any subject of study may raise. See "De quaestione," in Raimundus Lullus, *Logica Nova / Die neue Logik*, ed. Charles Lohr, trans. Vittorio Hösle and Walburga Büchel, introd. Vittorio Hösle (Hamburg: Felix Meiner, 1985), 24 ff. Lullus distinguishes ten forms of the question: *utrum, quid est, de quo est, quare est, quantum est, quale est, quando est, ubi est, quomodo est, cum quo est.*

15. Timothy Fitzgerald, *The Ideology of Religious Studies* (Oxford: Oxford University Press, 2000).

16. See my "Winke: Divine Topoi in Nancy, Hölderlin, and Heidegger," in *The Solid Letter: New Readings of Friedrich Hölderlin*, ed. Aris Fioretos (Stanford, Calif.: Stanford University Press, 1999), 94–120.

17. I am borrowing from a discussion of these matters in David Leavitt, *The Man Who Knew Too Much: Alan Turing and the Invention of the Computer* (New York: W. W. Norton, 2006), 30, 31. See also Mary Tiles, *The Philosophy of Set Theory: A Historical Introduction to Cantor's Paradise* (Mineola, N.Y.: Dover, 2004), 96 ff.

18. See the editors' "An Introduction to Alain Badiou's Philosophy," in Alain Badiou, *Infinite Thought: Truth and the Return to Philosophy*, trans. and ed. Oliver Feltman and Justin Clemens (London: Continuum, 2006), 16.

19. José Ferreirós, "The Motives Behind Cantor's Set Theory—Physical, Biological, and Philosophical Questions," *Science in Context* 17, no. 1/2 (2004): 81.

20. Cited after Alain Badiou, *L'être et l'événement* (Paris: Seuil, 1988), 49; *Being and Event*, trans. Oliver Feltman (New York: Continuum, 2005), 38. See also Peter Hallward, *Badiou: A Subject to Truth* (Minneapolis: University of Minnesota Press, 2003), 66 ff., 82 ff., 323 ff.; Joseph W. Dauben, *Georg Cantor: His Mathematics and Philosophy of the Infinite* (Cambridge: Harvard University Press, 1979; rpt. Princeton: Princeton University Press, 1990).

21. Cited after Dauben, *Georg Cantor*, 120.

22. See Joseph W. Dauben, "Georg Cantor and Pope Leo XIII: Mathematics, Theology, and the Infinite," *Journal of the History of Ideas* 38, no. 1 (January-March 1977): 85–108; and idem, *Georg Cantor*, 140–48, 294–97.

23. See Hallward, *Badiou*, 68–69.

24. In addition to Dauben, "Georg Cantor and Pope Leo XIII," 94 ff., see also Jean-Pierre Belna, *Cantor* (Paris: Les Belles Lettres, 2003), 181 ff., and Ferreirós, "The Motives Behind Cantor's Set Theory," 68–69. See also Amir D. Aczel, *The Mystery of the Aleph: Mathematics, the Kabbalah, and the Search for Infinity* (New York: Washington Square Press, 2000), 139 ff. For the possibility that a role similar to that of religion may have been played by Romantic *Naturphilosophie*, see Ferreirós, "The Motives Behind Cantor's Set Theory," 50 ff.

25. Cantor in a letter of November 1895 to the French mathematician Charles Hermite, cited after Dauben, "Georg Cantor and Pope Leo XIII," 94.

26. Cantor's *Habilitationsschrift*, cited after ibid., 94.

27. Cited after ibid., 95.

28. Ibid.

29. Ibid., 99.

30. Ibid.

31. Ibid., 102–3. On Cantor's study of Spinoza, see Ferreirós, "The Motives Behind Cantor's Set Theory," 64 ff.

32. Dauben, "Georg Cantor and Pope Leo XIII," 103.

33. See Cantor's 1908 letter to the English mathematician Grace Chisholm Young, cited after Dauben, *Georg Cantor*, 290: "I have never proceeded from any '*Genus supremum*' of the actual

infinite. Quite the contrary, I have rigorously proven that there is absolutely no '*Genus supremum*' of the actual infinite. What surpasses all that is finite and transfinite is no 'Genus'; it is the single, completely individual unity in which everything is included, which includes the 'Absolute,' incomprehensible to the human understanding. This is the '*Actus Purissimus*' which by many is called 'God.'"

34. Ray Brassier, "Badiou's Materialist Epistemology of Mathematics," *Angelaki* 10, no. 2 (August 2005): 135–50; B. Madison Mount, "The Cantorian Revolution: Alain Badiou on the Philosophy of Set Theory," *Polygraph* 17 (2005): 41–91.

35. Hallward, *Badiou*, 83–84.

36. Badiou, *Being and Event*, 30/38.

37. Ibid., 30/39.

38. Ibid., 55/68. Cf. ibid., 58/71: "The absolutely primary theme of ontology is . . . the void—the Greek atomists, Democritus and his successors, clearly understood this—but it is also its final theme—this was not their view—because in the last resort, *all* inconsistency is unpresentable, thus void. If there are 'atoms,' they are not, as the materialists of antiquity believed, a second principle of being, the one after the void, but compositions of the void itself."

39. Ibid., 29/37, see also 63/76.

40. "Introduction," in Badiou, *Infinite Thought*, 11.

41. Worse, as Badiou reminds us, any rigorous set-theoretical account requires that we leave the very question of "existence" (historicity, materiality, or empiricity) in abeyance. Cf. Badiou, *Being and Event*, 46–47, 66 / 58–59, 79.

42. Hallward, *Badiou*, 67.

43. See Badiou, *Being and Event*, 10/17.

44. Hallward, *Badiou*, 67.

45. Ibid., 68.

46. Ibid., 71.

47. Ibid., 75.

48. "Ontology and Politics: An Interview with Alain Badiou," in Badiou, *Infinite Thought*, 136.

49. Ibid., 136–37.

50. Ibid., 137.

51. Badiou, *Being and Event*, 59, 67 / 72, 80.

52. See Alain Badiou, "Silence, solipsisme, sainteté: L'Antiphilosophie de Wittgenstein," in *Barca!* 3 (1994): 13–53.

53. Badiou, *Being and Event*, 65/78.

54. Ibid.

55. Ibid.

56. Ibid., 66/79.

57. This is even more apparent in Badiou's most recent work, *Logiques des mondes* (*World Logics*), subtitled *L'être et l'événement 2* (Paris: Seuil, 2006), which emphasizes the distinction between Being and "appearing," with reference to Hegel rather than to Heidegger. Reference to the possible intersection of "subtractive" and "presentative" ontologies and negative theologies are not absent in *Being and Event*. Badiou refers to the writings of Christian Jambet (*La Logique des Orientaux* [Paris: Seuil, 1983]) and Guy Lardreau (*Discours philosophique et discours spirituel* [Paris: Seuil, 1985]), allowing for a friendly "*disputatio*" between their projects and his own (*Being and Event*, 484/523–24). See further: Hallward, *Badiou*, 93; Badiou, *Being and Event*, 41–42/52–54.

58. Rather than, say, ontology and the "natural" in the sense of Spinoza, or the "juridical" in the sense of Kant's Critiques. The "natural" and the "juridical," in Badiou's view, are the "latent

paradigm" of Deleuze and Lyotard, respectively, articulating their sense of the "pure multiple" (see Badiou, *Being and Event*, 483/522).

59. Ibid., 8/14.

60. Ibid., 13/20.

61. See ibid., 10, 13 / 16–17, 20.

62. Ibid., 27/35.

63. As has been suggested by Slavoj Žižek, "The Politics of Truth, or Alain Badiou as a Reader of Saint Paul," in idem, *The Ticklish Subject* (London: Verso, 2000), 127–70. For Badiou's response, see Adam S. Miller, "Universal Truths and the Question of Religion: An Interview with Alain Badiou," in *Journal of Philosophy & Scripture* 3, no. 1 (Fall 2005): 38–42.

64. Badiou describes the goal of his book as being to "assign philosophy to the thinkable articulation of two discourses (and practices) which *are not it*: mathematics, science of being, and the intervening doctrines of the event" (*Being and Event*, 13/20).

65. Ibid., 14/21–22.

66. Tomoko Masuzawa, *The Invention of World Religions; or, How European Universalism Was Preserved in the Language of Pluralism* (Chicago: University of Chicago Press, 2005), 1–2. On the expression "varieties of religion," see William James's 1902 classic, *The Varieties of Religious Experience: A Study in Human Nature*.

67. Masuzawa, *The Invention of World Religions*, 327–28.

68. Cf. Dipesh Chakrabarty, *Provincializing Europe: Postcolonial Thought and Historical Difference* (Princeton: Princeton University Press, 2000).

69. Edward Said's groundbreaking work has shown the fruitfulness of such a historical or genealogical approach when dealing with the question of "orientalism," as well of "secular criticism." See my lemma "Orientalism," in the *Encyclopedia of Religion*, 2d ed., ed. Lindsay Jones (New York, Macmillan, 2005). For two critical discussions of Said's understanding of "secular criticism," see: Akeel Bilgrami, "Occidentalism, the Very Idea: An Essay on Enlightenment and Enchantment," *Critical Inquiry* 32 (Spring 2006): 381–411; Gil Anidjar, "Secularism," *Critical Inquiry* 32 (Autumn 2006): 52–77.

70. In addition to Edward Said's classic *Orientalism* (New York: Pantheon, 1978), I am referring to Donald S. Lopez, *Prisoners of Shangri-La* (Chicago: University of Chicago Press, 1998); and Wouter J. Hanegraaff, *New Age Religion and Western Culture: Esotericism in the Mirror of Secular Thought* (Leiden: E. J. Brill, 1996).

71. Stanley Cavell, *The Claim of Reason: Wittgenstein, Skepticism, Morality, and Tragedy* (New York: Oxford University Press, 1979), 49, my emphasis.

72. Ibid., 50.

73. Moshe Halbertal and Avishai Margalit, *Idolatry*, trans. Naomi Goldblum (Cambridge: Harvard University Press, 1992).

74. For "acceptance," see J. L. Austin, *How to Do Things with Words*, ed. J. O. Urmson and Marina Sbisà (London: Oxford University Press, 1962), 26, 29.

75. Cavell, *The Claim of Reason*, 192.

76. Ibid., 196.

77. Ibid., 473.

78. Ibid., 455.

79. Ibid., 447. On science reverting to magic, see ibid., 468.

80. Ibid., 446 and 447.

81. Ibid., 424.

82. Ibid.

83. Related to this is the view that the "philosophical problem of the other" should be understood as nothing less than "the trace or scar of the departure of God." Ibid., 470. I have discussed this at length in Hent de Vries, "From Ghost in the Machine to Spiritual Automaton: Philosophical Meditation in Wittgenstein, Cavell, and Levinas," *International Journal for the Philosophy of Religion* 60, nos. 1–3 (December 2006): 77–97.

84. Cavell, *The Claim of Reason*, 419.

85. Ibid.

86. Ibid., 418–19.

87. Ibid., 434.

88. Ibid., 437, 440.

89. Ibid., 419.

90. Ibid., 423, cf. 424, 425, 426.

91. Ibid., 420.

92. Ibid.

93. Ibid., 421.

94. Ibid., 422.

95. Ibid.

96. Ibid.

97. Frankenberry, ed., *Radical Intepretation in Religion*, xiii.

98. Ibid.

99. Ibid., xiv. See also: J. Wesley Robbins, "Donald Davidson and Religious Belief," in *American Journal of Theology and Philosophy* 17, no. 2 (1996): 141–56; Godlove, "Saving Belief."

100. Frankenberry, ed., *Radical Intepretation in Religion*, xiii.

101. Ibid.

102. Robert B. Brandom, *Articulating Reasons: An Introduction to Inferentialism* (Cambridge: Harvard University Press, 2000), 26.

103. See also: Kocku von Stuckrad, "Discursive Study of Religion: From States of the Mind to Communication and Action," *Method and Theory in the Study of Religion*, no. 15 (2003): 255–71; idem, "Relative, Contingent, Determined: The Category 'History' and Its Methodological Dilemma," *Journal of the American Academy of Religion* 71, no. 4 (2003): 905–12.

104. Richard Rorty, Introduction, in Wilfrid Sellars, *Empiricism and the Philosophy of Mind* (Cambridge: Harvard University Press, 1997), 1, 3, and 9. See also his emphatic endorsement of Sellars's work on the back-cover blurb of Wilfrid Sellars, *In the Space of Reasons: Selected Essays of Wilfrid Sellars*, ed. Kevin Sharp and Robert B. Brandom (Cambridge: Harvard University Press, 2007).

105. Rorty, Introduction, 2 and 3.

106. Sellars, *Empiricism and the Philosophy of Mind*, 63.

107. See also Cavell's discussion in *The Claim of Reason*, 225–31.

108. For an overview, see J. Alberto Coffa, *The Semantic Tradition from Kant to Carnap: To the Vienna Station* (Cambridge: Cambridge University Press, 1991).

109. Rorty, Introduction, 4–5, cf. Sellars, *Empiricism and the Philosophy of Mind*, 76 and 19. Rorty stresses Sellars's place in the history of American pragmatism, which for a long time was occluded by the influence of Quine. For a further use of Sellars's arguments, see Michael Williams, *Unnatural Doubts: Epistemological Realism and the Basis of Skepticism* (Princeton: Princeton University Press, 1996).

110. Cited after Rorty, *Truth and Progress: Philosophical Papers*, vol. 3 (Cambridge: Cambridge University Press, 1998), 129.

111. Rorty, Introduction, 9; cf. Sellars, *Empiricism and the Philosophy of Mind*, 45 and 14.

112. Rorty, Introduction, 9. The citation is from Robert B. Brandom, *Making It Explicit: Reasoning, Representing, and Discursive Entitlement* (Cambridge: Harvard University Press, 1994), 8. On Brandom's introduction of the basic concept of inference and the method of inferentialism as opposed to representation and representationalism, including its historical antecedents, see *Making It Explicit*, xvi.

113. Rorty, Introduction, 11, and Brandom, *Making It Explicit*, 643.

114. Rorty, Introduction, 11.

115. Brandom, *Making It Explicit*, 4, cited in part in Rorty, Introduction, 11.

116. Jeffrey Stout, *Democracy and Tradition* (Princeton: Princeton University Press, 2004), 270.

117. Ibid.

118. Ibid.

119. Jeffrey Stout, "Radical Interpretation and Pragmatism: Davidson, Rorty, and Brandom on Truth," in *Radical Interpretation in Religion*, ed Frankenberry, 34; my italics.

120. Ibid. In this, Brandom is like Davidson, though inspired by Sellars rather than by Tarski or Quine, who remain the standing references for Davidson.

121. Brandom, *Making It Explicit*, 23, cf. 77, 629.

122. Stout, "Radical Interpretation and Pragmatism," in *Radical Interpretation in Religion*, ed. Frankenberry, 35.

123. Ibid.

124. Ibid.

125. Ibid., 36.

126. Ibid.

127. Brandom, *Articulating Reasons*, 47 ff.

128. Brandom, "Vocabularies of Pragmatism," 160.

129. Donald Davidson, "A Coherence Theory of Truth and Knowledge," in idem, *Subjective, Intersubjective, Objective* (Oxford: Oxford University Press, 2001), 137–57. See also Brandom, "Vocabularies of Pragmatism," 160.

130. Stout, "Radical Interpretation and Pragmatism," in *Radical Interpretation in Religion*, ed. Frankenberry, 37. The citation is from Brandom, *Making It Explicit*, 21.

131. Brandom, "Vocabularies of Pragmatism," 161.

132. Stout, "Radical Interpretation and Pragmatism," in *Radical Interpretation in Religion*, ed. Frankenberry, 45.

133. Ibid., 45–46.

134. Ibid., 46.

135. Ibid., 46–47. I have chosen to give a slightly different citation from Brandom, *Making It Explicit*, 331.

136. Ibid.

137. See Kevin Sharp, "Communication and Content: Circumstances and Consequences of the Habermas-Brandom Debate," *International Journal of Philosophical Studies* 11 (2003): 43–61.

138. Brandom, *Making It Explicit*, xiv and xv–xvi.

139. Ibid., xvi.

140. Ibid., xvii.

141. Ibid., xxiii.

142. Ibid. xviii.

143. See Stout, "Radical Interpretation and Pragmatism," in *Radical Interpretation in Religion*, ed. Frankenberry, 48.

144. Brandom, *Making It Explicit*, xiv.

145. Ibid., 162.

146. Ibid., 163.

147. Brandom's argument here has been contested by Rorty, in Richard Rorty, "Response to Robert Brandom," in *Rorty and His Critics*, ed. Brandom, 184.

148. Brandom, "Vocabularies of Pragmatism," 180.

149. Ibid.

150. Ibid.

151. Ibid., 180–81.

152. Ibid., 181.

153. Ibid.

154. Ibid.

155. Robert B. Brandom, "Reason, Expression, and the Philosophic Enterprise," in *What Is Philosophy?* ed. C. P. Ragland and Sarah Heidt (New Haven, Conn.: Yale University Press, 2001), 74.

156. Brandom, "Vocabularies of Pragmatism," 180.

157. Richard Rorty, "Cultural Politics and Arguments for God," in *Radical Interpretation in Religion*, ed. Frankenberry, 54. This is also the opening essay to vol. 4 of Rorty's *Philosophical Papers*, entitled *Philosophy as Cultural Politics* (Cambridge: Cambridge University Press, 2007), 4.

158. Rorty, *Philosophy as Cultural Politics*, ix. The quote is from John Dewey, "Philosophy and Democracy," in *The Middle Works*, ed. Jo Ann Boydston (Carbondale: Southern Illinois University Press, 1982), 11:43.

159. Rorty, *Philosophy as Cultural Politics*, x. The reference is to William James's letter of May 4, 1907, to Henry James, Jr., in *The Correspondence of William James*, vol. 11, ed. Ignas K. Skrupskelis and Elizabeth M. Berkeley (Charlottesville: University Press of Virginia, 2003).

160. Brandom, "When Philosophy Paints Its Blue on Gray: Irony and the Pragmatist Enlightenment," *boundary 2* 29, no. 2 (2002), 17.

161. Brandom, cited after Rorty, "Cultural Politics and Arguments for God," in *Radical Interpretation in Religion*, ed. Frankenberry, 57. See also Robert B. Brandom, "Heidegger's Categories in *Sein und Zeit*," in idem, *Tales of the Mighty Dead: Historical Essays in the Metaphysics of Intentionality* (Cambridge: Harvard University Press, 2002), 298–323, see also ibid., 324–47.

162. Rorty, "Cultural Politics and Arguments for God," in *Radical Interpretation in Religion*, ed. Frankenberry, 58.

163. Ibid.

164. Ibid., 58–59.

165. Ibid., 59.

166. Ibid., 66.

167. For the relationship between this and earlier modes of thinking, see Brandom, "When Philosophy Paints Its Blue on Gray," 19 ff.

168. Rorty, "Cultural Politics and Arguments for God," 66. Cf. also Brandom, *Making It Explicit*, 597.

169. Rorty, "Cultural Politics and Arguments for God," in *Radical Interpretation in Religion*, ed. Frankenberry, 67.

170. Ibid.

171. Ibid., 70

172. Ibid.

173. For a discussion of Heidegger's engagement with theology, see the chapter "Formal Indications" in my *Philosophy and the Turn to Religion* (Baltimore: The Johns Hopkins University Press, 1999).

174. Rorty, "Cultural Politics and Arguments for God," in *Radical Interpretation in Religion*, ed. Frankenberry, 71.

175. Ibid.

176. Ibid.

177. Ibid., 72.

178. Ibid.

179. Ibid., 72–73.

180. Ibid., 73.

181. Richard Rorty, "Anticlericalism and Atheism," in Richard Rorty and Gianni Vattimo, *The Future of Religion*, ed. Santiago Zabala (New York: Columbia University Press, 2005), 30.

182. Rorty, "Cultural Politics and Arguments for God," in *Radical Interpretation in Religion*, ed. Frankenberry, 73–74.

183. Ibid., 74.

184. Ibid., 75.

185. Brandom, "Vocabularies of Pragmatism," 170.

186. Ibid., 172.

187. Rorty, "Anticlericalism and Atheism," in Rorty and Vattimo, *The Future of Religion*, 37–38.

188. Richard Rorty, "Religion in the Public Square," in *Journal of Religious Ethics* 31, no. 1 (2003): 142.

189. Ibid., 143–44.

190. Ibid., 143, 147, 148.

191. Stout, *Democracy and Tradition*, 86. See the dossier with responses to this book in the *Journal of Religious Ethics* 33, no. 4 (December 2005).

192. Stout, *Democracy and Tradition*, 86–87.

193. Ibid., 87.

194. Brandom, *Articulating Reasons*, 105–6.

195. Stout, *Democracy and Tradition*, 87–88.

196. Rorty, "Religion in the Public Square," 148.

197. Ibid., 148–49.

198. Rorty, *Truth and Progress*, 127.

199. Ludwig Wittgenstein, *Remarks on the Foundation of Mathematics*, rev. ed., ed. G. H. von Wright, R. Rhees, and G. E. M. Anscombe, trans. G. E. M. Anscombe (Cambridge: MIT Press, 2001), 65. See Michael Fried, *Art and Objecthood: Essays and Reviews* (Chicago: University of Chicago Press, 1998), 31 and 132.

200. John McDowell, *Mind and World* (Cambridge: Harvard University Press, 1996).

201. Masuzawa, *The Invention of World Religions*, 6.

202. Richard Rorty, Gianni Vattimo, and Santiago Zabala, "Dialogue: What Is Religion's Future after Metaphysics?" in Rorty and Vattimo, *The Future of Religion*, 59.

203. Ibid., 60.

204. Ibid., 58, 68. Rorty goes further than Brandom in suggesting that it is "useful to think of the opposite of analytical philosophy as conversational philosophy" and of the former as "the last gasp of the onto-theological tradition" (ibid., 68).

205. Rorty, "Anticlericalism and Atheism," in Rorty and Vattimo, *The Future of Religion*, 32.

206. These difficulties, it now dawns on me, inspired my choice of an awkward earlier formulation, "reverse implication," to indicate the relationship between "religion" and modern philosophemes. See my *Philosophy and the Turn to Religion*, passim.

207. See: Paola Marrati, *Gilles Deleuze: Philosophie et cinéma* (Paris: Presses Universitaires de France, 2003), esp. 96–100, forthcoming in an expanded English edition, *Gilles Deleuze: Philosophy and Cinema*, trans. Alisa Hartz (Baltimore: The Johns Hopkins University Press, 2008), 73–77; Alexandre Lefebvre, *The Image of Law: Deleuze, Bergson, Spinoza*, chap. 2.3.2, forthcoming from Stanford University Press. I have greatly profited from the analyses, references, and critical comments of both these authors.

208. Lefebvre, *The Image of Law*, chap. 2.3.2, and Henri Bergson, *Matière et mémoire: Essai sur la relation du corps a l'esprit* (Paris: F. Alcan, 1912), 67; *Matter and Memory*, trans. Nancy Margaret Paul and W. Scott Palmer (New York: Zone, 1988), 164.

209. An expression, by the way, also used by Deleuze in *Différence et répétition* (Paris: Presses Universitaires de France, 1968), 112; *Difference and Repetition*, trans. Paul Patton (New York: Columbia University Press, 1994), 82.

210. See my *Philosophy and the Turn to Religion*.

211. Bergson, *Matter and Memory*, 20/15.

212. Marrati speaks of an "ontological pragmatism" in Bergson, which conceives of time as creative, inventive, and effective, that is to say, as *doing* something, without ceding to any "voluntarism." See Paola Marrati, "Mysticism and the Foundation of the Open Society: Bergsonian Politics," in *Political Theologies*, ed., de Vries and Sullivan, 591–601. See also my "The Two Sources of the 'Theological Machine': Jacques Derrida and Henri Bergson on Religion and Technicity, War and Terror," in *Theology and the Political*, ed. Creston Davis, John Milbank, and Slavoj Žižek (Durham, N.C.: Duke University Press, 2005), 366–89.

213. Gilles Deleuze and Felix Guattari, *Qu'est-ce que la philosophie?* (Paris: Minuit, 1991), 50; *What Is Philosophy?* trans. Hugh Tomlinson and Graham Burchell (New York: Columbia University Press, 1994, 50), 49, cited after Lefebvre, *The Image of Law*, chap. 2.3.

214. Bergson, *Matter and Memory*, 133–34/147–48.

215. Ibid., 170–71/189–90.

216. Ibid., 69, 70 / 72, 73.

217. Ibid., 34/31.

218. Lefebvre, *The Image of Law*.

219. Ibid., chap. 2.3.2. See, among other places, Deleuze, *Difference and Repetition*, 208/269. The quote is from the concluding novel of Marcel Proust's *In Search of Lost Time*, *Time Regained*.

220. Other candidates abound, but would seem to be more regional—hence a subset of the dimension in question. I am thinking of Merleau-Ponty's conception of *la Chair*, the Flesh, which for all its nomination of *l'être brut* seems still too tied to a certain phenomenological understanding of the body. One could also think of the Husserlian notion of the *Lebenswelt*, which, especially in its Habermasian articulation, is too much premised on the idea of a social world for it to capture the "elemental" at its deepest. But then this could also be claimed of the idea of a "second nature" and, strictly speaking, even of all the other terms invoked above (*substance, nature, elemental, universe, plane*, etc.). Here we might find one reason to prefer the notion of the "void," as we did above in our discussion of Badiou, or to return to Levinas's motif of the *il y a* (see my *Minimal Theologies*).

221. Giorgio Agamben, *Qu'est-ce que un dispositif?* trans. Martin Rueff (Paris: Rivages, 2007).

222. Ibid., 16.

223. Ibid., 18 and 20.

224. Ibid., 21.

225. Ibid., 22 ff.

226. Ibid., 25, 26.

227. Ibid., 30.

228. Ibid., 27–28.

229. Ibid., 26–27.

230. Ibid., 39.

231. Ibid., 40. See also Giorgio Agamben, *Profanations*, trans. Martin Rueff (Paris: Rivages, 2005).

232. Agamben, *Qu'est-ce qu'un dispositif?* 40.

233. Ibid., 41.

234. Ibid., 34–36.

235. Ibid., 49.

236. Ibid., 50.

237. See J. L. Austin, "A Plea for Excuses," in idem, *Philosophical Papers*, ed. J. O. Urmson and G. J. Warnock (Oxford: Oxford University Press, 1979), 175–204, esp. 181 ff.

238. Ibid., 181.

239. Ibid., 182.

240. Ibid.

241. Ibid., 183.

242. Ibid., 182–83.

243. See Hent de Vries, "In Media Res," in *Religion and Media*, ed. Hent de Vries and Samuel Weber (Stanford, Calif.: Stanford University Press, 2001), 3–42.

244. Sellars, *Empiricism and the Philosophy of Mind*, 79.

245. In her remarkable work throughout, as well as in her contribution to the present volume, Veena Das espouses such a late-Wittgensteinian and Cavellian view. See Veena Das, "Wittgenstein and Anthropology," *Annual Review of Anthropology* 27 (1998): 171–95, and esp. her *Life and Words: Violence and the Descent into the Ordinary* (Berkeley: University of California Press, 2007).

246. See Cavell, *The Claim of Reason*, 315, 317, 319, and 323.

247. Ibid., 323.

248. Ibid., 326.

249. Judith Butler, *Giving an Account of Oneself* (New York: Fordham University Press, 1995).

250. Cavell, *The Claim of Reason*, 296.

251. Ibid.

252. Ibid., 297.

253. Ibid.

254. For a discussion, see my *Religion and Violence: Philosophical Perspectives from Kant to Derrida* (Baltimore: The Johns Hopkins University Press, 2002), chap. 3.

255. Cavell, *The Claim of Reason*, 298.

256. Ibid.

257. Ibid.

258. Ibid., 391.

259. Ibid., 299.

260. Ibid., 300.

261. Ibid., 363.

262. Ibid., 307. Cf. ibid., 309: "What you say you *must* do is not 'defined by the practice,' for there is no such practice until you make it one, make it *yours*. We might say, such a declaration

defines *you*, establishes your position. . . . And though there is not The Categorical Imperative, there are actions which are for us categorically imperative so far as we have *a* will. And though Respect for The Law may not sustain moral relationship, respect for positions not our own will. . . . That *all* actions which are, in this sense, categorically imperative are self-imposed, *our* choice, indicates that the *mere* fact of self-imposition is not enough to achieve what Kant, or Freud, would mean by autonomous action."

263. Ibid., 307.

264. Ibid., 308.

265. Ibid.

266. Ibid., 299 and 324.

267. That nothing is ever clear or simply settled in the form of life—and the rational arguments—that make up morality has to do, Cavell explains in his discussion of John Rawls's 1955 essay "Two Concepts of Rules," with the striking "inexactness in the analogy between games and morality": "that no one can settle a moral conflict in the way umpires settle conflicts, is essential to the form of life we call morality" (ibid., 296).

268. Ibid., 324.

269. Ibid.

270. Stanley Cavell, *Cities of Words: Pedagogical Letters on a Register of the Moral Life* (Cambridge: Harvard University Press, 2004), 173.

271. Ibid., 173–74.

272. Ibid., 176.

273. Ibid.

274. And, Cavell adds parenthetically, "The sacredness of promising is a familiar enough fact of human life to participate in the action of tragedy, for example, in Euripides' *Hippolytus*" (ibid., 176–77).

275. Ibid., 179.

276. Stanley Cavell, *Conditions Handsome and Unhandsome: The Constitution of Emersonian Perfectionism* (La Salle, Ill.: Open Court, 1990), 113–14.

277. Cavell, *Cities of Words*, 179.

278. Ibid., 185.

279. Ibid., 186. This underscores once more his disagreement with Saul Kripke's interpretation of the *Investigations*.

280. Ibid.

281. Ibid., 187.

282. Ibid., 188, 189.

283. Ibid., 188.

284. Cf. the subtitle of chap. 3 of Cavell, *Conditions Handsome and Unhandsome*, "The Conversation of Justice: Rawls and the Drama of Consent," esp. 111.

285. Ibid., 106.

286. Ibid., 107.

287. Ibid., 102.

288. Ludwig Wittgenstein, *Philosophical Investigations*, par. 199.

289. Cavell, *The Claim of Reason*, 294.

290. Ibid.

291. Hence Cavell's hesitation to compare "promises" to "practices" in the Rawlsian sense of particular arrangements in given societies, as being analogous to the Utilarian interest in formulating criteria for ameliorating existing social institutions (ibid., 295).

292. Ibid., 296.

293. Ibid., 471.

294. Ibid., 475.

295. Ibid., 468.

296. Cf. the chapter "Formal Indications" in my *Philosophy and the Turn to Religion*.

297. For anthropological dimensions, see Ernst Tugendhat, *Anthropologie statt Metaphysik* (Munich: C. H. Beck, 2007), esp. 191 ff.

298. Régis Debray, *Dieu, un itinéraire: Matériaux pour l'histoire de l'Éternel en Occident* (Paris: Odile Jacob, 2001); *God: An Itinerary*, trans. Jeffrey Mehlman (London: Verso, 2004).

299. Régis Debray, *L'enseignement du fait religieux dans l'école laïque* (Paris: Odile Jacob, 2002); "Teaching Religious Facts in Secular Schools," trans. Daniela Ginsburg, below in this volume, pp. 415–31. All quotes are from this translation.

300. See also Jakob Taubes, *Vom Kult zur Kultur: Bausteine zu einer Kritik der historischen Vernunft*, ed.. Aleida and Jan Assmann, Wolf-Daniel Hartwich, and Winfried Menninghaus (Munich: Wilhelm Fink, 1996).

301. Jacques Lang, Preface to Debray, "Teaching Religious Facts in Secular Schools."

302. These formulas remind one of an old debate concerning the academic study of religion and the "methodological atheism" that it should or should not entail. For a review of some of these arguments, see the opening chapter of my *Minimal Theologies*.

303. Régis Debray, "Mediology," in *The Columbia History of Twentieth-Century French Thought*, ed. Lawrence D. Kritzman (New York: Columbia University Press, 2006), 289–90: "What mediology wishes to bring to light is the way in which something serves as a *medium*, and the often unperceived complexities that go with it. . . . The mediologist's interest is therefore neither in an object nor a region of reality . . . but on *the relations between* objects or regions; between an ideality and a materiality, a feeling and a piece of equipment, a disposition and a device."

304. Régis Debray, *Les communions humaines: Pour en finir avec "la religion"* (Paris: Fayard, 2005), 60 ff.

305. Jacques Derrida: Cruelty, Death Penalty, and the Return of the Religious, Stanford University, April 26–27, 2002. I am grateful to Helen Tartar for providing me with an unpublished transcript of this intervention, supplementing and correcting the notes she sent to me at the time of the conference itself.

306. Jacques Derrida, "The Double Session," in *Dissemination*, trans. Barbara Johnson (Chicago: University of Chicago Press, 1981), 173–286.

307. Hilary Putnam, *Renewing Philosophy* (Cambridge: Harvard University Press, 1992), 1.

308. Hilary Putnam, *Jewish Philosophy as a Guide to Life: Rosenzweig, Buber, Levinas, Wittgenstein* (Bloomington: Indiana University Press, forthcoming), chap. 2.

309. See Hilary Putnam, *Ethics Without Ontology* (Cambridge: Harvard University Press, 2004).

310. Putnam, *Renewing Philosophy*, 148, cited after idem, *Jewish Philosophy as a Guide to Life*, Introduction.

311. Putnam, *Jewish Philosophy as a Guide to Life*, Introduction.

312. Ibid., chap. 1.

313. See also Hilary Putnam, Introduction to Franz Rosenzweig, *The Little Book of Healthy and Sick Human Understanding*, trans. Nahum Glatzer (Cambridge: Harvard University Press, 1999).

314. Ludwig Wittgenstein, *Culture and Value* (Chicago: University of Chicago Press, 1980), 64, cited in Putnam, *Jewish Philosophy as a Guide to Life*, chap. 1.

315. See: Eric L. Santner, *On the Psychotheology of Everyday Life: Reflections on Freud and Rosenzweig* (Chicago: University of Chicago Press, 2001); idem, *On Creaturely Life: Rilke, Benjamin, Sebald* (Chicago: University of Chicago Press, 2006).

316. Ludwig Wittgenstein, "A Lecture on Ethics," in idem, *Philosophical Occasions, 1912–1951*, ed. James C. Klagge and Alfred Normann (Indianapolis: Hackett, 1993), 43.

317. Ibid., 41.

318. Stanley Cavell, *The Claim of Reason*, 15.

319. I am borrowing here two powerful suggestions from Simon During and Michael Warner, made during a roundtable hosted by the Social Science Research Council in New York in May 2007.

José Casanova, Public Religions Revisited

1. José Casanova, *Public Religions in the Modern World* (Chicago: University of Chicago Press, 1994).

2. José Casanova, "Die religiöse Lage in Europa," in *Säkularisierung und die Weltreligionen*, ed. Hans Joas und Klaus Wiegandt (Frankfurt a. M.: S. Fischer, 2007).

3. José Casanova, "Religion, European Secular Identities, and European Integration," in *Religion in an Expanding Europe*, ed. Timothy A. Byrnes and Peter J. Katzenstein (Cambridge: Cambridge University Press, 2006), 65–92.

4. Casanova, *Public Religions*, 10.

5. Ibid.

6. For a more elaborated version of the following section, see José Casanova, "Rethinking Secularization: A Global Comparative Perspective," *The Hedgehog Review*, Spring/Summer 2006.

7. For a poignant critique of the thesis of differentiation, see Charles Tilly, "Four More Pernicious Postulates," in *Big Structures, Large Processes, Huge Comparisons* (New York: Russell Sage, 1984), 43–60.

8. Talal Asad, *Formations of the Secular: Christianity, Islam, Modernity* (Stanford, Calif.: Stanford University Press, 2003), 192.

9. José Casanova, "Secularization Revisited: A Reply to Talal Asad," in *Powers of the Secular Modern: Talal Asad and His Interlocutors*, ed. David Scott and Charles Hirschkind (Stanford, Calif.: Stanford University Press, 2006), 12–30.

10. Tomoko Masuzawa, *The Invention of World Religions; or, How European Universalism Was Preserved in the Language of Pluralism* (Chicago: University of Chicago Press, 2005).

11. David Martin, *A General Theory of Secularization* (Oxford: Blackwell, 1978).

12. Alfred Stepan, "The World's Religious Systems and Democracy: Crafting the 'Twin Tolerations,'" in *Arguing Comparative Politics* (Oxford: Oxford University Press, 2001), 218–25.

13. For a more extensive elaboration of this argument, see José Casanova, "Globalizing Catholicism and the Return to a 'Universal' Church,'" in *Transnational Religion and Fading States*, ed. Susanne Rudolph and James Piscatori (Boulder, Colo.: Westview Press, 1997).

14. José Casanova, "Catholic and Muslim Politics in Comparative Perspective," *The Taiwan Journal of Democracy* 1, no. 2 (December 2005).

15. Mark Lilla, "The Great Separation: The Politics of God," *The New York Times Magazine*, August 19, 2007, pp. 28–34, 50, 54–55, and *The Stillborn God* (New York: Alfred A. Knopf, 2007).

16. José Casanova, "Immigration and the New Religious Pluralism: A EU/US Comparison," in *The New Religious Pluralism and Democracy*, ed. Thomas Banchoff (New York: Oxford University Press, 2007).

17. Stepan, "Crafting the 'Twin Tolerations,'" 218–25.

18. Ibid., 217.

19. Casanova, "Globalizing Catholicism."

20. José Casanova, "Religion, the New Millennium and Globalization," *Sociology of Religion* 62, no. 4 (2001): 415–41.

21. Paul Freston, "Charismatic Evangelicals in Latin America: Mission and Politics on the Frontiers of Protestant Growth," in *Charismatic Christianity: Sociological Perspectives*, ed. Stephen Hunt, Malcolm Hamilton, and Tony Walker (New York: St. Martin's Press, 1997), 185.

22. Arjun Appadurai, *Modernity at Large* (Minneapolis: University of Minnesota Press, 1996).

23. Samuel P. Huntington, *The Clash of Civilizations and the Remaking of World Order* (New York: Simon & Schuster, 1994).

Michael Lambek, Provincializing God? Apprehensions of an Anthropology of Religion

NOTE: Under the title "Provincializing God? Post-Religious Cogitations, Post-Secular Apprehensions of the Continuing Problems of an Anthropology of Religion" this essay was originally presented to the conference What Is Religion: Vocabularies, Temporalities, Comparabilities, organized by The Future of the Religious Past project, sponsored by The Netherlands Organization for Scientific Research (NWO), Amsterdam, June 2–4, 2005. I am most grateful to Hent de Vries and Birgit Meyer for the invitation to include me in this exciting endeavor. The paper was subsequently delivered to the Departments of Anthropology at the School of Oriental and African Studies, London, and the Universities of Aberdeen and Cambridge. My thanks to all the organizers and to the very responsive audiences at each occasion. I am particularly indebted to Christoph Auffarth and Markha Valenta for attempting to constrain the excesses of my stereotypy and to Helen Tartar for her encouragement. The sections on deixis were previously delivered within two quite different papers: first, in "Deixis and Deity: Evans-Pritchard's Anthropology as a Kind of Philosophy," for the centenary colloquium in honor of Sir Edward Evans-Pritchard at the University of Oxford, December 1, 2002; and second, as "Other Kinds of Persons: Some Disciplinary and Indisciplined Reflections on the Denomination and Translation of Spirits and Deity," in the symposium honoring Ian Hacking at the Department of Philosophy, University of Toronto, October 2004. My thanks, respectively, to Wendy James and to André Gombay and Ian Hacking for the invitations; to Joe Errington and Jack Sidnell (who are not to be faulted for my use of deixis) for linguistic advice; and to Jackie Solway for good counsel throughout. Acknowledgments to consultants in Mayotte and Madagascar are recorded in the prefaces to my books cited below. Research has been generously supported by the Social Sciences and Humanities Research Council of Canada.

1. Dipesh Chakrabarty, *Provincializing Europe: Postcolonial Thought and Historical Difference* (Princeton: Princeton University Press, 2000).

2. Respectively, The Netherlands Organization for Scientific Research, *The Future of the Religious Past* (The Hague: NWO, 2000), and Michael Lambek, ed., *A Reader in the Anthropology of Religion* (Malden, Mass.: Blackwell, 2001).

3. Chakrabarty, *Provincializing Europe*, 19.

4. Ibid., 239.

5. Ibid., 78. Chakrabarty is rather warm to religion and to a religious mode of experience of the world, in part because he locates religion outside the dominant Western analytical tradition and not specifically on the Abrahamic model. He contrasts the "epistemological primacy routinely assigned in social science thought to one's analytical relationships to the world (Heidegger's 'present at hand') over lived, preanalytical ones (the 'ready-to-hand' in Heideggerian terms)" (239), and he

locates religion with the latter. Hence, he argues, "writing about the presence of gods and spirits in the secular language of history or sociology would therefore be like translating into a universal language that which belongs to a field of differences" (76).

6. Talal Asad, *Formations of the Secular: Christianity, Islam, Modernity* (Stanford, Calif.: Stanford University Press, 2003).

7. Chakrabarty, *Provincializing Europe*, 43.

8. *As It Happens*, (CBC, April 19, 2005). Obviously, many Christians, even within the Catholic Church, depart from this view. Sectarianism has produced a series of alternatives, but each becomes its own orthodoxy. That is, in fact, why sectarianism has been the major way that change takes place in Christianity. There are always mutually exclusive versions of the truth or at least of the means for its authorization.

9. Hent de Vries, *Religion and Violence: Philosophical Perspectives from Kant to Derrida* (Baltimore: The Johns Hopkins University Press, 2002). For a very helpful discussion of the relationship between anthropology and Christianity, see Fenella Cannell, Introduction to *The Anthropology of Christianity* (Durham, N.C.: Duke University Press, 2006).

10. Compare David Parkin, "Inside and Outside the Mosque: A Master Trope," in *Islamic Prayer Across the Indian Ocean*, ed. David Parkin and Stephen Headley (Richmond: Curzon, 2000), 1–22. I hope it is clear that my portrait in these paragraphs is ideal typical (if not stereotypical) and based more on what is central to and salient in these religions as portrayed by their most vociferous proponents than on the ordinary practice of Christians and Muslims, which is often preanalytic, heterogeneous, and tolerant. Conversely, participants in other religious traditions do sometimes also rationalize and exhibit certainty, intolerance, and missionary zeal. A proper analysis of these issues would have to historicize and discriminate among particular trends and movements.

11. Brooke Allen, "Our Godless Constitution," *The Nation*, Feb. 6, 2005.

12. On Islam, see, e.g.: Adeline Masquelier, *Prayer Has Spoiled Everything* (Durham, N.C.: Duke University Press, 2001); Kai Kresse, *Philosophising in Mombasa: Knowledge, Islam, and Intellectual Practice on the Swahili Coast* (Edinburgh: Edinburgh University Press for the International African Institute, 2007). It is beyond the scope of this paper to explain why certain preceding versions of African Christianity and Islam have been more open or why they are being superseded by more exclusive versions just now.

13. Michael Lambek, "Localising Islamic Performances in Mayotte," in *Islamic Prayer Across the Indian Ocean*, ed. Parkin and Headley, 63–97. I also distinguish the idea of converting to a world religion from the idea of converting from one world religion to another (95n2).

14. This can be understood as part of a wider logic of "possessive individualism." Richard Handler, *Nationalism and the Politics of Culture in Quebec* (Madison: University of Wisconsin Press, 1988) has analyzed the way social science has been complicit with nationalism in describing nations as bounded units of this kind. If "possessive individualism," which is usually traced to the origins of liberal capitalism (C. B. Macpherson, *The Political Theory of Possessive Individualism: Hobbes to Locke* [Oxford: Oxford University Press, 1962]), were traced back to the roots of the Abrahamic religions, it would be another instance or source of the affinity between them and the rise of capitalism (Max Weber, *The Protestant Ethic and the Spirit of Capitalism*, trans. T. Parsons [New York: Scribner, 1958]).

15. See: Rodney Needham, *Belief, Language, and Experience* (Chicago: University of Chicago Press, 1972); Jean Pouillon, "Remarks on the Verb 'To Believe,'" in *Between Belief and Transgression*, ed. Michel Izard and Pierre Smith (Chicago: University of Chicago Press, 1982); and especially Malcolm Ruel, "Christians as Believers," in *Religious Organization and Religious Experience*, ed. John Davis (London: Academic Press, 1982). Belief is of less significance to Judaism, where, Gillian Rose suggests, it is sufficient to follow the order to be a good orthodox Jew (*Love's Work* [London:

Vintage, 1997]). In Islam, knowledge is perhaps the central concept; for an ethnographic illustration, see Michael Lambek, *Knowledge and Practice in Mayotte: Local Discourses of Islam, Sorcery and Spirit Possession* (Toronto: University of Toronto Press, 1993); for a historical account, see Franz Rosenthal, *Knowledge Triumphant: The Concept of Knowledge in Medieval Islam* (Leiden: E. J. Brill, 1970). The centrality of God also influences the importance the anthropology of religion has placed on such matters as the "supernatural" and "animism" (cf. Lorraine Aragon, "Missions and Omissions of the Supernatural," in *Perspectives on the Category "Supernatural,"* ed. Roger Lohmann, *Anthropological Forum* 13, no. 2 (2003): 131–40.

16. "Such theism has as its core the view that the world is what it is independently of human thinking and judging and desiring and willing. There is a single true view of the world and of its ordering" (Alasdair Macintyre, *Three Rival Versions of Moral Enquiry* [London: Duckworth, 1990], 66).

17. Lambek, *Knowledge and Practice in Mayotte*; Michael Lambek, "Choking on the Qur'an and Other Consuming Parables from the Western Indian Ocean Front," in *The Pursuit of Certainty*, ed. Wendy James (London: Routledge, 1995), 252–75; Michael Lambek and Andrew Walsh, "The Imagined Community of the Antankaraña: Identity, History, and Ritual in Northern Madagascar," in *Ancestors, Power and History in Madagascar*, ed. Karen Middleton (Leiden: E. J. Brill, 1999), 145–74; Michael Lambek, *The Weight of the Past: Living with History in Mahajanga, Madagascar* (New York: Palgrave-Macmillan, 2002). From the Sudan, see Wendy James, *The Listening Ebony: Moral Knowledge, Religion and Power among the Uduk of Sudan* (Oxford: Oxford University Press, 1988).

18. The ironic sensibility and insights characteristic more generally of many religious formulations are not central to the Abrahamic tradition and certainly not to its recent developments. The separation of religion from the arts may also have contributed to polarizing literalizing and ironizing endeavors.

19. Michael Lambek, "Value and Virtue" (draft).

20. Søren Kierkegaard, *Fear and Trembling*, trans. Walter Lowrie (Princeton: Princeton University Press, 1954), 22, 23.

21. While all spirits avoid and force their mediums to avoid everything that had to do with their deaths, Ndramandikavavy is unique because the instrument of her death is also the object of her veneration. Moreover, as one informant put it, "She is forbidden to see blood and cannot even watch a chicken being killed." Her mediums cannot partake of meat from an animal killed with her knife.

22. De Vries, *Religion and Violence*.

23. The Queen's descendants here come not through her royal son but from a prior, unnamed union. They are known as Tsiarana, the Peerless, and they hold pride of place among the clans with special ritual functions close to royalty. Not only do they make good marriage partners, they can marry royalty without losing their identity (i.e., are excluded from the rule of hypergamy). Hence the two bilateral clans are de facto highly overlapping in membership. Although most active Tsiarana are women, it is Tsiarana men who officiate at all ancestral sacrifice, wielding the "Grandmother's" knife.

24. Lambek, *The Weight of the Past*.

25. Malcolm Ruel, "Non-Sacrificial Ritual Killing," Man 25 (1990): 332.

26. For further elaboration of the context of Sakalava practice, see Lambek, *The Weight of the Past*; also Jean-François Baré, *Sable Rouge: Une monarchie du Nord-ouest malgache dans l'histoire* (Paris: L'Harmattan, 1980); Gillian Feeley-Harnik, *A Green Estate: Restoring Independence in Madagascar* (Washington, D.C..: Smithsonian Press, 1991). For complementary but distinctive interpretations of Ndramandikavavy, see Michael Lambek, "Sacrifice and the Problem of Beginning:

Meditations from Sakalava Mythopraxis," *Journal of the Royal Anthropological Institute* 13, no. 1 (2007): 19–38, and "How Do Women Give Birth?" in *Questions of Anthropology*, ed. Rita Astuti, Jonathan Parry, and Charles Stafford (Oxford: Berg, 2007), 192–225.

27. E. E. Evans-Pritchard, *The Nuer* (Oxford: Oxford University Press, 1940).

28. Louis Menand, *The Metaphysical Club: A Story of Ideas in America* (New York: Farrar, Straus and Giroux, 2001), 365.

29. E. E. Evans-Prichard, *Witchcraft, Oracles and Magic among the Azande* (Oxford: Oxford University Press, 1937).

30. Evans-Pritchard, *The Nuer*, 194.

31. Mary Douglas, *Evans-Pritchard* (London: Fontana, 1980), 73.

32. Michael Silverstein, "Shifters, Linguistic Categories, and Cultural Description," in *Meaning in Anthropology*, ed. Keith Basso and Henry Selby (Albuquerque: University of New Mexico Press, 1976), 11–55.

33. Ibid., 27.

34. Evans-Pritchard, *The Nuer*, 136.

35. Jack Sidnell, "Deixis," in *Handbook of Pragmatics*, ed. Jef Verschuren et al. (Amsterdam: John Benjamins, 1998), 1.

36. Ibid., 2.

37. Ibid., 23.

38. William Hanks, "The Indexical Ground of Deictic Reference," in *Rethinking Context: Language as an Interactive Phenomenon*, ed. A. Duranti and C. Goodwin (Cambridge: Cambridge University Press, 1992), 46, 47.

39. Ibid., 51.

40. Evans-Pritchard, *The Nuer*, 137.

41. Deictic specificity itself varies by language. In Malagasy there are more specific words for a range of spatiotemporal distances than in English. And while Malagasy third-person pronouns are all gender neutral, there is a necessary distinction between an inclusive and an exclusive first-person plural. Silverstein also argues that "such lexical items as so-called kinship terms or personal names in any society can hardly be characterized by a 'semantic' analysis. It is the pragmatic component that makes them lexical items to begin with" ("Shifters," 52). Wittgenstein, by contrast, strongly distinguishes indexical uses from names (G. P. Baker and P. M. S. Hacker, *Wittgenstein: Meaning and Understanding* [Oxford: Blackwell, 1980], 119–24), though he too would not make naming the foundation of language (Jack Sidnell, pers. comm.).

42. Hanks, "Indexical Ground," 62.

43. Words for which the referential attribution is somewhat more constrained than in the ideal typical deictics (like *this* and *that*) might be referred to as quasi-deictic, shifters, or, more generally, as indexically supposed.

44. Michael Lambek, "What's in a Name? Name Bestowal and the Identity of Spirits in Mayotte and Northwest Madagascar," in *The Anthropology of Names and Naming*, ed. Gabriele vom Bruck and Barbara Bodenhorn (Cambridge: Cambridge University Press, 2006), 116–38.

45. Sidnell (pers. comm.) points out the indexical quality of an English word like *colleague* and its alternation with *academic* and *professor*. Ascriptive words frequently distinguish who has the right to use them, hence among kinds of "insiders" from various perspectives (Harvey Sacks, *Lectures on Conversation*, ed. Gail Jefferson [Oxford: Blackwell, 1995]).

46. *Home* in this context cannot be pluralized. In French the noun is replaced by the preposition *chez*.

47. Stephen Levinson, "Deixis," in *Encyclopedia of Language and Linguistics*, ed. R. E. Asher (n.p.: Pergamon, 1994), 2:853.

48. Hanks, "Indexical Ground," 57. This indexical flux is what frustrates the anthropologist's quest for fixed reference. The word *he* fluctuates, sometimes referring to a certain person and sometimes not; likewise, the form used to refer to that same person shifts, being now *he*, now *you*, now *I*.

49. Compare Basil Bernstein, *Class, Codes, and Control* (London: Routledge & Kegan Paul, 1971), on the distinction between restricted and elaborated codes. Technical writing develops a whole set of "discourse deixis."

50. I take heart in making this point from the illuminating study by Sean Hawkins, *Writing and Colonialism in Northern Ghana* (Toronto: University of Toronto Press, 2002). See esp. chap. 4, "Reimagining God."

51. Hanks, "Indexical Ground," 67–70.

52. E. E. Evans-Pritchard, *Nuer Religion* (Oxford: Oxford University Press, 1956), 1.

53. Evans-Pritchard, *The Nuer*, 135.

54. Hanks, "Indexical Ground," 70.

55. I say "throughout Africa," but this may be an overgeneralization. I am thinking of Sakalava *Ndrañahary* and Tswana *Modimo* and *Badimo*. See, respectively, Lambek, *Weight of the Past*, and I. Schapera and John Comaroff, *The Tswana* (rev. ed., London: Kegan Paul, 1991); also Paul Landau, "Language," in *Missions and Missionaries*, ed. Norman Etherington (Oxford: Oxford University Press, 2005), who suggests the Setswana terms be understood as pronouns. I acknowledge that the religious conceptions of speakers of Nilotic, Bantu, and Austronesian languages may be quite distinct from one another.

56. Levinson, "Deixis," 854. For a sophisticated discussion of this problem with reference to Freud and self-constitution, see Vincent Crapanzano, "Text, Transference, and Indexicality," in Crapanzano, *Hermes' Dilemma and Hamlet's Desire: On the Epistemology of Interpretation* (Cambridge: Harvard University Press, 1992), 115–35.

57. Evans-Pritchard, *The Nuer*, 13.

58. Elsewhere (Lambek, "What's in a Name?") I raise the question whether God or *kwoth* ought to be considered proper names. I now realize that the more fundamental question is whether deixis disqualifies a word like *home* (in this sense) or *kwoth* from being considered a noun at all.

59. A brilliant early critique of Evans-Pritchard's inclination to monotheism and of Christian apologism in Africanist anthropology and African theology more generally is Okot p'Bitek, *African Religions in Western Scholarship* (Nairobi: Kenya Literature Bureau, 1970). More extensive in his elaboration of the Christian biases in the depiction of religion in Africa than I have been able to be here, p'Bitek differs from the present analysis in arguing forthrightly (71) that "For the Nilotes [Nuer, Luo, and others] there are many deities."

60. See Michael Lambek, "The Anthropology of Religion and the Quarrel Between Poetry and Philosophy," *Current Anthropology* 41 (2000): 309–20.

61. Crapanzano, "Text, Transference" (134), suggests why this might be the case, arguing that talk about indexical language (meta-indexicality) is itself referential, thereby lending support to the idea of a stable object of reference and mystifying for speakers the gap (*décalage*) between the indexical and the referential.

62. Malcolm Ruel, *Belief, Ritual and the Securing of Life: Reflexive Essays on a Bantu Religion* (Leiden: E. J. Brill, 1997). One might link this argument to discussions of animism or of fetishism, although there is no logical necessity to reify deity as a force or power or to seek its material objectifications. One would also have to examine closely the invocation of deity in ritual and to think about ritual itself as a context in which the relation of the indexical to the referential (or the "canonical") is framed in a particular way (Roy Rappaport, *Ritual and Religion in the Making of Humanity* [Cambridge: Cambridge University Press, 1999]).

63. On discipline, see Talal Asad, *Genealogies of Religion: Discipline and Reasons of Power in Christianity and Islam* (Baltimore: The Johns Hopkins University Press, 1993). On virtue, see: Lambek, *The Weight of the Past*; Saba Mahmood, *Politics of Piety* (Princeton: Princeton University Press, 2005); Charles Hirschkind, *The Ethical Soundscape: Cassette Sermons and Islamic Counterpublics* (New York: Columbia University Press, 2006).

64. The logic of both/and contains the paradox that it incorporates the alternative of either/or. Hence it is inherently recursive or dialectical.

65. Lambek, "Sacrifice and the Problem of Beginning."

66. Rappaport, *Ritual and Religion in the Making of Humanity*.

67. Lambek, *Knowledge and Practice*.

68. The tension between generalizing and particularizing has a long history within anthropology, with roots in Vico and Kant. For a useful, if largely forgotten, discussion of the connection between the Neo-Kantians, Boas, and Kroeber, see David Bidney, *Theoretical Anthropology* (New York: Schocken, 1967), esp. chap. 9.

69. Macintyre, *Three Rival Versions*.

Jan Assmann, Translating Gods: Religion as a Factor of Cultural (Un)Translatability

NOTE: This essay first appeared in *The Translatability of Cultures: Figurations of the Space Between*, ed. Sanford Budick and Wolfgang Iser (Stanford, Calif.: Stanford University Press, 1996), 25–36. Copyright © 1996 by the Board of Trustees of the Leland Stanford Jr. University. Reprinted with the permission of the publisher.

1. The list of gods is just one of innumerable glossaries equating Sumerian and Akkadian words. There are also trilingual lists, giving the divine names in Emesal (a literary dialect), Sumerian, and Akkadian. The equation of gods, however, seems a rather complicated affair, requiring a considerable amount of theological learning and ingenuity, for there are many more Sumerian gods or names than Akkadian ones. In these cases, translation turns into subsumption. There are some Akkadian gods who appear as equivalents for more than twenty Sumerian gods. But there are also Akkadian gods for whom there are no Sumerian equivalents because they are newcomers in the Babylonian pantheon. Marduk is a good example. In these cases, the scribes had to invent Sumerian equivalents. The task of compiling bilingual lists of gods was therefore a rather demanding one because it implied a great deal of theological insight. The most interesting of these sources is the explanatory list *Anu ša ameli*, which contains three columns, the first giving the Sumerian name, the second the Akkadian, and the third the functional definition of the deity. This list gives what we have called the "referent" of divine names, making explicit the principle that underlies the equation or translation of divine names. Cf. R. L. Litke, "A Reconstruction of the Assyro-Babylonian God Lists An: Anum, Anu ša Ameli" (Ph.D. diss., Yale University, 1958). I owe this reference and much pertinent information to the kindness of Karlheinz Deller, to whom I express my sincere gratitude.

2. British Museum, tablet K 2100, ed. in *Cuneiform Texts* 25: 18. On the reverse there is a collection of general words for "god" in Sumerian (*dingir*), Akkadian (*khilibu* instead of *ilu*, perhaps an Emesal word), Hurritic (*ene*), Elamitic (*nap*), Amoritic (*malakhum*), Lulubaeic (a language spoken in the Zagros region), and Cassitic (*mash-khu*).

3. Kemal Balkan, *Kassitenstudien I: Die Sprache der Kassiten* (New Haven, Conn.: American Oriental Society, 1954), 2 ff. The Cassite name *Nazimurutash*, e.g., is rendered in Akkadian *Sil-Ninurta* (under the shadow of Ninurta), translating the word *nazi* ("shadow") by *sil* and the Cassitic god

Murutash by the Akkadian god *Ninurta*. This is an exact anticipation of the later practice of helleniz-ing native proper names.

4. Jean Nougayrol, *Textes Suméro-Akkadiens des archives privées d'Ugarit*, Ugaritica 5 (Paris: Imprimerie national, 1968), no. 137.

5. See L. Canfora, M. Liverani, and C. Zaccagnini, eds., *I Trattati nel Mondo Antico: Forma, Ideologia, Funzione* (Rome: L'Ermadi Bretschneider, 1990).

6. For the concept of the "multiplicity of languages and peoples" in the imperial ideology of the Achemenids, see Christoph Uehlinger, *Weltreich und "eine Rede": Eine neue Deutung der sog. Turmbauerzählung (Gen II 1–9)*, OBO 101 (Freiburg: Universitätsverlag, 1990), 578–83.

7. See: Elias Bickerman, *The Jews in the Greek Age* (Cambridge: Harvard University Press, 1988), 104; D. Schlumberger, L. Robert, A. Dupont-Sommer, E. Benveniste, *Journal Asiatique* 246 (1958); D. Schlumberger and Louis Robert, *Comtes rendus de l'Academie des Inscriptions et Belles-Lettres* (Paris: Librarie C. Klincksieck, 1964), 126–40.

8. See: Erik H. Erikson, "Ontogeny of Ritualization in Man," in *Philosophical Transactions of the Royal Society* 251 B (London, 1966): 337–49; Konrad Lorenz, *Die Rückseite des Spiegels* (Munich: Piper, 1977), 223–45; lrenäus Eibl-Eibesfeldt, *Krieg und Frieden aus der Sicht der Verhaltensforschung* (Munich: Piper, 1975).

9. I am indebted for this information to Professor Wulf Schiefenhövel, Seewiesen, who spent several years doing fieldwork among the Papuas of New Guinea.

10. The following is based on Wolfram von Soden, "Dolmetscher und Dolmetschen im Alten Orient," in *Aus Sprache, Geschichte und Religion Babyloniens* (Naples: Istituto universitario orien-tale, Dipartimento di studi asiatici, 1989).

11. Ignaz J. Gelb, *Glossa* 2, 93 ff.

12. Wolfgang Schenkel, "Dolmetscher," in W. Helck and E. Otto, eds., *Lexikon der Ägyptologie* (Wiesbaden: Harrassowitz, 1973), 1:1116. See also the article "Dolmetscher" in *Reallexikon für Antike und Christentum* (Alfred Hermann on Ancient Egypt: BIa), ed. Theodor Klauser et al. (Stutt-gart: A. Hiersemann, 1985–86).

13. See: Peter Artzi, "The Birth of the Middle East," *Proceedings of the Fifth World Congress of Jewish Studies* (Jerusalem, 1969), 120–24; Artzi, "Ideas and Practices of International Co-existence in the Third Millennium B.C.E.," *Bar-Ilan Studies in History* 2 (1984): 25–39; Moshe Weinfeld, "The Common Heritage of Covenantal Traditions in the Ancient World," in Canfora, Liverani, and Zuccagnini, eds., *I Trattati nel mondo antico*, 175–91.

14. As pointed out by Erik Voegelin, *The Ecumenic Age, Order and History* (Baton Rouge: Louisiana State University Press, 1974), 4:121–32; Friedrich H. Tenbruck, "Gesellschaftsgeschichte oder Weltgeschichte?" *Kölner Zeitschrift für Soziologie und Sozialpsychologie* 41 (1989): 417–39.

15. Or rather: "cosmotheistic" religion, because cosmotheistic *monotheism* functioned quite in the same way.

16. See E. H. Spicer, "Persistent Cultural Systems: A Comparative Study of Identity Systems That Can Adapt to Contrasting Environments," *Science* 174, no. 4011 (1971): 795–800.

17. See: Wilhelm E. Mühlmann, *Chiliasmus und Nativismus: Studien zur Psychologie, Soziologie und historischen Kasuistik der Umsturzbewegungen* (Berlin: D. Reimer, 1961); Vittorio Lanternari, *Movimenti religiosi di libertà e di salvezza dei popoli oppressi* (Rome: Feltrinelli, 1960), trans. Lisa Sergio as *Religions of the Oppressed: A Study of Modern Messianic Cults* (New York: Knopf, 1963); Peter Worsley, *The Trumpet Shall Sound: A Study of "Cargo"-Cults in Melanesia* (New York: Schocken, 1968).

18. See Michael Walzer, *Exodus and Revolution* (New York: Basic, 1985).

19. In the discussion, Marc Shell objected to the abuse of biologistic metaphors such as "im-mune reaction," which to his mind continues the racist and fascist tendencies to treat cultural

differences as natural ones. The fascist revolt against humanism (*Humanitätsduselei*) naturalized the effects of pseudo-speciation and stressed them as absolutely insurmountable and resisting any attempt at translation. But this attitude might in itself be described as an "immune reaction," this time not under minority but under majority conditions. In the same discussion, Gershon Shaked pointed out that these reactions might in fact be much more typical of majority cultures than minority ones.

In using the term *immune reaction*, I am not (at least consciously) continuing the language of German racism but referring to systems theory, which treats both the (biological) immune system and the (cultural) identity system as self-referential systems processing information about the distinction between inner and outer, system and environment, own and foreign, and providing self-definitions. See F. J. Varela, "Der Körper denkt: Das Immunsystem und der Prozess der Körper-Individuierung," in H. U. Gumbrecht and K. L. Pfeiffer, eds., *Paradoxien, Dissonanzen, Zusammenbrüche: Situationen offener Epistemologie* (Frankfurt a. M.: Suhrkamp, 1991), 727–43.

20. See Spicer, "Persistent Cultural Systems."

21. I study these mechanisms in greater detail in my book *Das kulturelle Gedächtnis: Schrift, Erinnerung und politische Identität in frühen Hochkulturen* (Munich: C. H. Beck, 1992), esp. chap. 3 ("Identität und Ethnogenese").

22. See E. P. Sanders, ed., *Jewish and Christian Self-Definition*, vol. 1: *The Shaping of Christianity in the Second and Third Centuries* (Philadelphia: Fortress, 1980), vol. 2; A. I. Baumgarten, A. Mendelson, and E. P. Sanders, eds., *Aspects of Judaism in the Greco-Roman Period* (London: SCM, 1981), vol. 3; B. F. Meyer and E. P. Sanders, eds., *Self-definition in the Greco-Roman World* (London: SCM, 1982).

23. See Jan Assmann, *Ma'at: Gerechtigkeit und Unsterblichkeit im Alten Ägypten* (Munich: C. H. Beck, 1950), 19–20, 279–80.

24. For the Hellenistic world, see Gerhard Delling, *Die Bewaltigung der Diasporasituation durch das hellenistische Judentum* (Gottingen: Vanderhoeck and Ruprecht, 1987).

25. Georges Posener, *La première domination Perse en Ègypte*, Bibliothèque d'Études 2 (1936).

26. Jan Bergman, *Ich bin Isis: Studien zum memphitischen Hintergrund der griechischen Isis-Aretalogien* (Uppsala: Almquist and Wiksell, 1968); Garth Fowden, *The Egyptian Hermes: A Historical Approach to the Late Pagan Mind* (Cambridge: Cambridge University Press, 1986).

27. In his commentary on C. H. 16.2 (Collection Budé, Paris), André Jean Festugière collects many pertinent passages from Greek and Latin sources: see n. 7, pp. 232–34.

28. I give a short paraphrase of a very long discussion. See: Peter Crome, *Symbol und Unzulänglichkeit der Sprache: Jamblichos, Porphyrios, Proklos* (Munich: W. Fink, 1970); Jetske C. Rijlaarsdam, *Platon über die Sprache: Ein Kommentar zum Kratylos* (Utrecht, 1978).

29. Origenes C. Cels. 1.24–25, 28; 5.45.

30. *Corpus Hermeticum XVI*, ed. A. J. Festugière and A. D. Nock, 2:230; the translation appears in Fowden, *The Egyptian Hermes*, 37.

31. For the following, see Arthur Darby Nock, *Conversion: The Old and the New in Religion from Alexander the Great to Augustine of Hippo* (Oxford: Oxford University Press, 1963).

32. See ibid., 138.

33. See: Oskar Grether, *Name und Wort Gottes im A. T.* (Giessen: A. Topelman, 1934), 3 ff.; Wolfram von Soden, *Bidel und Alter Orient* (Berlin: Walter de Gruyter, 1985), 78–88; Georg Fohrer, *Geschichte der israelitischen Religion* (Berlin: Walter de Gruyter, 1969), 63 ff.; Johannes C. de Moor, *The Rise of Yahwism* (Leuven: Peeters, 1990), 175, 237 ff. In the Egyptian myth of the "Heavenly Cow," there occurs a phrase that sounds like a close parallel. The god Re says "I am I" (*jw.j jm.j*), perhaps with a causal or temporal meaning: "(Because, or as long as) I am who I am, I shall not let them make rebellion." See Erik Hornung, *Der ägyptische Mythos von der Himmelskuh: Eine Ätiologie*

des Unvollkommenen (Freiburg: Universitätsverlag, 1982), 43, 125 n. aa (by G. Fecht); and de Moor, *The Rise of Yahwism*, 174–75. In the Sybilline Oracles (1.137–40), Exodus 3:14 is quoted and then given an interpretation in the cosmotheistic sense: "I am the Being One [*eimi d'ēgo-ge ho ōn*], recognize this in your mind: I put on the heaven as garment, I wrapped myself by the sea, the earth is the foundation of my feet, the air is around me as body and the stars encircle me" (R. Merkelbach and M. Totti, *Abrasax* [Opladen: Westdeutscher Verlag, 1992], 2:131).

34. Augustine, *De consensu evangelistarum*, 1.22.30 and 1.23.31.

35. Rodney Needham, *Belief, Language and Experience* (Oxford: Blackwell, 1972).

36. G. W. Bowersock, *Hellenism in Late Antiquity* (Cambridge: Cambridge University Press, 1990), 5.

37. The term *hellenismos* first occurs in 2 Macc. 2:21, where, in opposition to *Ioudaismos*, it has an unmistakably polemical meaning. See E. Will and C. Orieux, *Ioudaismos-Hellenismos: Essai sur le judaisme judéen à l'époque hellénistique* (Nantes: Presses Universitaires de Nantes, 1986).

38. See: Carsten Colpe, "Syncretism," in M. Eliade, ed., *The Encyclopedia of Religion* (New York: Macmillan, 1987), vol. 14; L. H. Martin, "Why Cecropian Minerva? Hellenistic Religious Syncretism as System," *Numen* 30 (1983): 131–45.

39. Robert Lattimore, "Herodotus and the Names of the Egyptian Gods," *Classical Philology* 34 (1939): 357–65.

40. See, similarly, Lucian, *De Dea Syria*, chap. 2: "The Egyptians are said to be first among all the people known to us to form conceptions about the gods. Not much later the Syrians heard from the Egyptians the discourse about the gods and erected shrines and temples."

41. Morton Smith, *Palestinian Parties and Politics That Shaped the Old Testament*, 2d ed. (London: SCM, 1987), 43–61.

42. Herodotus visited Egypt in the years between 450 and 444 B.C.E., when Egypt and Athens were allies against Persia.

43. Mühlmann, *Chiliasmus und Nativismus*, 12.

44. Marcel Mauss, "Essai sur le don: Forme et raison de l'échange dans les sociétés archaiques," in *Sociologie et anthropologie* (Paris: Presses Universitaires de France, 1950), 143–279; translated as *The Gift* (London: Cohen-West, 1969).

45. Marshall Sahlins, *Stone Age Economics* (1974; London: Routledge, 1988). See also the collection of essays by Fritz Kramer and Christian Sigrist, *Gleichheit und Gegenseitigkeit* (Frankfurt a. M., 1983), esp. "Tausch und Wert in Stammesgesellschaften." Also important is Arnold Gehlen, *Urmensch und Spätkultur* (Bonn: Athenaeum, 1956), 50 ff.

Daniel Boyarin, The Christian Invention of Judaism: The Theodosian Empire and the Rabbinic Refusal of Religion

NOTE: This essay was originally published as Daniel Boyarin, "The Christian Invention of Judaism: The Theodosian Empire and the Rabbinic Refusal of Religion," *Representations* 85 (Spring 2004): 21–57. Reprinted by permission of the publisher.

1. John J. Collins, "Cult and Culture: The Limits of Hellenization in Judea," in *Hellenism in the Land of Israel*, ed. John J. Collins and Gregory Sterling (Notre Dame, Ind.: Notre Dame University Press, 2000), 39.

2. For this, if for no other reason, referring to the history of modern Hinduism as its Semiticization is both inaccurate and disturbing (Daniel Boyarin, "Jewish Cricket," *PMLA* 113, no. 1 [January 1998]: 40–45).

3. I defend this proposition in chaps. 2 and 3 of Daniel Boyarin, *Border Lines: The Partition of Judaeo-Christianity* (Philadelphia: University of Pennsylvania Press, 2004).

4. For instance, a Jew who "converts" to another religion does not have to convert back but only repent his/her sins in order to be accepted into the community again.

5. Hal A. Drake, "Lambs into Lions: Explaining Early Christian Intolerance," *Past and Present*, no. 153 (1996): 25. Drake's theory is germane to the hypothesis of this article. Limberis argues that for second-generation Christians this process was reversed (Vasiliki Limberis, "'Religion' as the Cipher for Identity: The Cases of Emperor Julian, Libanius, and Gregory Nazianzus," *Harvard Theological Review* 93, no. 4 [2000]: 377). I am not entirely persuaded by her argument on this point but do not wish entirely to disallow it, either. One way of thinking about it would be to see who is left out of "us." In both the earlier rabbinic and orthodox Christian formations, exemplified by Nazianzen below, there are those tied to us by tradition, kinship, and land who are, nevertheless, not us; they are heretics. See also Rosemary Radford Ruether, "Judaism and Christianity: Two Fourth-Century Religions," *Sciences Religieuses / Studies in Religion* 2 (1972): 1–10, and Jacob Neusner, *Judaism and Christianity in the Age of Constantine: History, Messiah, Israel, and the Initial Confrontation* (Chicago: University of Chicago Press, 1987), who take related positions.

6. Andrew S. Jacobs, "The Imperial Construction of the Jew in the Early Christian Holy Land" (Ph.d. diss., Duke University, 2001), 28–29.

7. Seth Schwartz, *Imperialism and Jewish Society from 200* B.C.E. *to 640* C.E. (Princeton: Princeton University Press, 2001), 179.

8. Susanna Elm, "Orthodoxy and the True Philosophical Life: Julian and Gregory of Nazianzus," unpublished ms. (Berkeley, 2000). I am grateful to Professor Elm for sharing her work with me prior to publication. See also Limberis, "Cipher," 383.

9. Although Gideon Foerster and Yoram Tsafrir, "Nysa-Scythopolisa New Inscription and the Titles of the City on Its Coins," *Israel Numismatic Journal* 9 (1986): 53–58, has been cited as relevant in this context, it seems to me not so. Even accepting the interpretation of the publishers of this inscription that the unique designation of Scythopolis as "one of Coele Syria's Greek cities" was to insist on the "Hellenic-Pagan" character of the city owing to a threat posed by its mixed population of Jews and Samaritans, we still need not conclude that "Hellenic" here means the religion.

10. Limberis, "Cipher," 378, 382, and throughout.

11. Ibid., 386.

12. Ibid., 399. I accept Limberis's assent to Asad's critique of Geertz, but nevertheless see much more continuity and a shift toward something that could be called "religion" in the modern sense taking place precisely in these fourth-century echoes of Christianity.

13. Oration 4.5 and 96–109, cited in Elm. See also Limberis, "Cipher," 395, on this passage.

14. Cf., e.g., Talal Asad, *Genealogies of Religion: Discipline and Reasons of Power in Christianity and Islam* (Baltimore: The Johns Hopkins University Press, 1993), 40–41.

15. Ibid., 45.

16. Schwartz, *Jewish Society*, 179.

17. This point is not contradicted in any way by Denise Kimber Buell, "Race and Universalism in Early Christianity," *Journal of Early Christian Studies* 10, no. 4 (Winter 2002): 429–68. Buell's compelling analysis of second- and third-century texts indicates early Christianity's struggle to find a mode of identity, with notions of Christianness as a new ethnos/genos being very prevalent indeed. Buell herself, however, marks a shift that takes place in the fourth century: "Beginning in the fourth century, ethnic reasoning serves to naturalize the equation of Christianness with gentileness, or Romanness, in part through the oppositional construction of non-Jewish non-Christians as 'pagans'" (Buell, "Race," 465). I would argue, however, that such a classification marks the undoing

of an "ethno/racial" definition of Christianness, insofar as in general throughout the fourth century "pagans" were understood to be just as Roman as Christians. "Pagan" surely did not constitute an ethnic or racial designation but a religious one. Even in the earlier writings considered by Buell, where Christianity is defined as an ethnos or a genos, these terms are the dependent variable of "faith." This is decidedly not the case for Jews much before the Christian era or for Judaism since the early Middle Ages. Buell argues elegantly that Christian universalism should not be seen in opposition to or against the background of a putative Jewish particularism: "Seeing that early Christians defined themselves in and through race requires us to dismantle an oppositional definition of Christianness and Jewishness on the basis of race or ethnicity. Doing so may also contribute to resisting periodizations that mark an early and decisive split between Christianities and Judaisms. Not only do many early Christians define themselves as a people, even competing for the same name, *Israel*, but early Christians adapt and appropriate existing forms of Jewish universalism in formulating their own universalizing strategies in the Roman period. . . . Since ethnic reasoning also resonates with non-Jewish cultural practices of self-definition, it offers an analytic point of entry that treats both Jewish and non-Jewish frames of reference as integrally part of Christian self-definition, not as its 'background'" (Buell, "Race," 467). At the same time, notwithstanding Buell's reference to Isaiah as "emphasizing attachment to Yahweh as defining membership in Israel," I would suggest that the notion of "orthodoxy" as defining membership in the Christian community and the feints in that direction in rabbinic literature that define orthodoxy as the criterion for membership in Israel represent a "new thing." That new thing would ultimately be called "religion."

18. Claudine Dauphin, *La Palestine byzantine: Peuplement et populations* (Oxford: Archaeopress, 1998), 133–55. See also the discussion in Jacobs, "Construction," 75–100.

19. J. Rebecca Lyman, *Christology and Cosmology: Models of Divine Activity in Origen, Eusebius, and Athanasius* (Oxford: Oxford University Press, 1993).

20. Eusebius, *Preparation for the Gospel*, trans. Edwin Hamilton Gifford (Grand Rapids, Mich.: Eerdmans, 1981).

21. Eusebius, *The Proof of the Gospel*, ed. and trans. W. J. Ferrar (London: SPCK, 1920), 1:7. The translation here follows Jacobs, "Construction," 33.

22. Eusebius, *Proof*, 1:9. I am grateful to my student Ron Reissberg for this reference.

23. Which is not, of course, to claim that the notion of ethnic identity is a stable and fixed one, either. See Jonathan M. Hall, *Ethnic Identity in Greek Antiquity* (Cambridge: Cambridge University Press, 1997).

24. *The Panarion of Epiphanius of Salamis, Book I, Sections 1–46*, trans. Frank Williams (Leiden: E. J. Brill, 1987), 16–50. Cf., however, Eusebius's *Demonstratio evangelica* 1.2.1 (Eusebius, *Proof*, 9).

25. Frances Young, "Did Epiphanius Know What He Meant by 'Heresy'?" *Studia Patristica* 17, no. 1 (1982): 199–205.

26. *Panarion*, 17–18. In another part of the Christian world, Frankfurter points out, for the fifth-century Coptic abbot Shenoute, "*Hellene* did not carry the sense of ethnically 'Greek' and therefore different from 'Egyptian,' but simply 'pagan' 'not Christian'" (David Frankfurter, *Religion in Roman Egypt: Assimilation and Resistance* [Princeton: Princeton University Press, 1998], 79).

27. *Panarion*, 9.

28. Cf. Jacobs, "Construction," 55–56.

29. For a highly salient and crystal clear delineation of these terms, *ethnic* and *cultural*, see Jonathan M. Hall, *Hellenicity Between Ethnicity and Culture* (Chicago: University of Chicago Press, 2002), esp. 9–19.

30. As has been noted by previous scholars, for Epiphanius "heresy" is a much more capacious and even baggy-monster category than for most writers (Aline Pourkier, *L'Hérésiologie chez Épiphane de Salamine* [Paris: Beauchesne, 1992], 85–87; Young, "Epiphanius"). See the discussion in Jacobs, "Construction," 56.

31. *Panarion*, 24.

32. Justin's discussion of Jewish heresies is a different move from this, as analyzed in Daniel Boyarin, "Justin Martyr Invents Judaism," *Church History* 70, no. 3 (September 2001): 427–61.

33. Johann Karl Ludwig Gieseler, "Über die Nazaräer und Ebioniten," *Archiv für alte und neue Kirchengeschichte* 4, no. 2 (1819): 279, as cited in Glenn Alan Koch, "A Critical Investigation of Epiphanius' Knowledge of the Ebionites: A Translation and Critical Discussion of *Panarion* 30" (Ph.D. diss., University of Pennsylvania, 1976), 10.

34. Günter Stemberger, *Jews and Christians in the Holy Land: Palestine in the Fourth Century* (Edinburgh: T. & T. Clark, 1999), 80, writes: "It seems that there were no significant Jewish-Christian communities left in Palestine itself, and the primary problem for the wider church was the attraction of Judaism for the members of Gentile Christianity."

35. Nathaniel Deutsch, *Guardians of the Gate: Angelic Vice Regency in Late Antiquity* (Leiden: E. J. Brill, 1999), 19.

36. *Panarion*, 120.

37. David Chidester, *Savage Systems: Colonialism and Comparative Religion in Southern Africa* (Charlottesville: University Press of Virginia, 1996), 11–16.

38. Homi K. Bhabha, *The Location of Culture* (London: Routledge, 1994), 71.

39. For a useful (if methodologically uncritical) summary of the material, see Ray A. Pritz, *Nazarene Jewish Christianity: From the End of the New Testament Period until Its Disappearance in the Fourth-Century* (Jerusalem: Magnes Press, 1992), 48–70.

40. Jacobs, "Construction," 76–77.

41. Hillel Newman, "Jerome's Judaizers," *Journal of Early Christian Studies* 9, no. 4 (December 2001): 421–52.

42. Marc Bloch, *The Historian's Craft: Reflections on the Nature and Uses of History and the Techniques and Methods of Those Who Write It* (New York: Vintage Books, 1953), 93.

43. Jerome, *Correspondence*, ed. Isidorus Hilberg, (Vienna: Österreichischen Akademie der Wissenschaften, 1996), 55:381–82.

44. See the discussion in Jacobs, "Construction," 114.

45. Chidester, *Savage Systems*, 19.

46. Boyarin, "Justin Invents Judaism."

47. Julian and Wilmer Cave France Wright, "Against the Galileans," in *The Works of the Emperor Julian*, trans. Wilmer Cave France Wright (London: Heinemann Macmillan, 1913), 389.

48. Ibid., 319–21.

49. Julian and Wright, "Against the Galileans," 393–95. Fascinatingly, this perspective gives us another way of understanding Julian's intention of allowing the Temple in Jerusalem to be rebuilt. A large part of his polemic consists, as we have seen, in charges that Christians are nothing, since they have abandoned Hellenism but not become Jews, given that they do not follow the Torah. He imagines a Christian answering him that the Jews, too, do not sacrifice as they are enjoined (Julian and Wright, "Against the Galileans," 405–7). What better way to refute this Christian counterclaim and demonstrate that the only reason that Jews do not sacrifice is that they have no Temple than to help them rebuild their Temple and reinstitute the sacrifices?

50. Hall, *Hellenicity Between Ethnicity and Culture*, xix. Hall's book was published too late for its results to be incorporated into the discussion here.

51. Wright points out that Julian has Christlike figures in his own theology (Julian and Wright, "Against the Galileans," 315).

52. Jacobs, "Construction," 30.

53. Ibid., 57.

54. *Panarion*, treated in Jacobs, "Construction," 54–64. My treatment is somewhat different in emphasis from that of Jacobs but, once again, not antithetical.

55. R. von Krafft-Ebing, *Psychopathia Sexualis: A Medico-Forensic Study* (New York: Putnam, 1965). For the almost literal connection between histories of sexuality and histories of heresiology, see now Arnold I. Davidson, *The Emergence of Sexuality: Historical Epistemology and the Formation of Concepts* (Cambridge: Harvard University Press, 2002), 118.

56. *Panarion*, 122–29. On this text, see Stephen Goranson, "The Joseph of Tiberias Episode in Epiphanius: Studies in Jewish and Christian Relations" (Ph.D. diss., Duke University, 1990); Stephen Goranson, "Joseph of Tiberias Revisited: Orthodoxies and Heresies in Fourth-Century Galilee," in *Galilee Through the Centuries: Confluence of Cultures*, ed. Eric M. Meyers (Winona Lake, Ind.: Eisenbrauns, 1999), 335–43; Stemberger, *Jews and Christians*, 75–77.

57. *Panarion*, 122.

58. Ibid., 123, both quotes.

59. Ibid., 124.

60. Ibid., 127.

61. Ibid., 126.

62. Ibid., 128.

63. Ibid.

64. Robert Young, *Colonial Desire: Hybridity in Theory, Culture, and Race* (London: Routledge, 1995), 19.

65. *Panarion*, 129, both cites.

66. For previous scholarship of this sort (citing it to oppose it), see Goranson, "Revisited," 337.

67. Ibid., 338. I am not entirely sure on what basis Goranson can make the positivist claim in the final clause, but assume he has good basis for it. In any case, my argument is not dependent on such propositions about the actual situation. See the discussion immediately below concerning Jerome's notices of "Jewish Christians." Note, in any case, that in Goranson's reading, as accepted and extended here, Frédéric Manns, "Joseph de Tibériade, un judéo-chrétien du quatrième siècle," in *Christian Archaeology in the Holy Land, New Discoveries: Essays in Honour of Virgilio C. Corbo, OFM*, ed. Giovanni Claudio Bottini (Jerusalem: Franciscan Printing Press, 1990), 553–60, is wrong. The whole point of the story is that Joseph does not become a "Jewish-Christian" but a Christian who is not Jewish. See, making a similar point with respect to another scholar's work, Goranson, "Episode," 8.

68. Thus one scholar has recently argued that the only function of this story in Epiphanius's text is to provide some entertaining relief for the reader (T. C. G. Thornton, "The Stories of Joseph of Tiberias," *Vigiliae Christianae* 44 [1990]: 54–63). My interpretation is both similar to and subtly different from that of Jacobs, "Construction," 62–63, to which it should be compared. The two readings are probably compatible. I somewhat disagree, however, with Jacobs's last point: "The entire fabric of Joseph's story in the *Panarion* prepares us to understand how the imperial Christian is to overcome the onslaught of the unorthodox 'other': Jews then, Arians now, a bewildering multitude of gnostics, Jewish-Christians, encratites, Origenists, or any other theological deviant who might cross the Christian's future path. If they can be as thoroughly comprehended as the Jew, their threat will be as easily squashed as an annoying insect" (Jacobs, "Construction," 63–64). My way

of phrasing this point would be that Epiphanius produced the orthodox Jew as the absolute other of the Christian in order to draw the lines clearly and thus have a space for the absolute delegitimation of other Christians, especially the "Arians," who are shown to have no religion at all by this move (a motive that appears over and over within the narrative).

69. *Panarion*, 119. Compare my reading with that of Pourkier, *Épiphane*.

70. On the promulgation of the Codex, see now: John Matthews, *Laying Down the Law: A Study of the Theodosian Code* (New Haven, Conn.: Yale University Press, 2000); earlier the essays in Jill Harries and I. N. Wood, *The Theodosian Code*, ed. Jill Harries (Ithaca: Cornell University Press, 1993); Tony Honoré, *Law in the Crisis of Empire, 379–455 AD: The Theodosian Dynasty and Its Quaestors; with a Palingenesia of Laws of the Dynasty* (Oxford: Oxford University Press 1998).

71. For an analogous and similarly ramified shift in the meanings of terms within an imperial situation, see Young, *Desire*, 50, on the vicissitudes of *civilization* and *culture*.

72. Maurice Sachot, "'*Religio/Superstitio*': Historique d'une subversion et d'un retournement," *Revue d'histoire des religions* 208, no. 4 (1991): 355–94.

73. Ibid., 375. As Michele R. Salzman, "'Superstitio' in the Codex Theodosianus and the Persecution of Pagans," *Vigiliae Christianae* 41 (1987): 174, makes clear, this meaning is already a development from even earlier meanings.

74. Peter Brown, *Authority and the Sacred: Aspects of the Christianization of the Roman World* (Cambridge: Cambridge University Press, 1995), 35.

75. *Religio ver dei cultus est, superstitio falsi*, 4.28.11.

76. Mary Beard, John A North, and S. R. F. Price, *Religions of Rome* (Cambridge: Cambridge University Press, 1998), 216. See earlier Maurice Sachot: "In the mouth of a Christian, *religio* henceforth no longer refers solely to individual, familial, or civil practices and institutions, but also and above all to an absolute relation to truth" (Maurice Sachot, "Comment le Christianisme est-il devenu *religio*," *Revue des sciences religieuses* 59 [1985]: 97). This should almost surely be connected up with other semantic shifts in Latin as well, notably the shift in the meaning of *verus* itself (Carlin A. Barton, "The 'Moment of Truth' in Ancient Rome: Honor and Embodiment in a Contest Culture," *Stanford Humanities Review* [1998]: 16–30).

77. And see the quotation from Seth Schwartz in the next paragraph.

78. Lee I. Levine, "The Jewish Patriarch (Nasi) in Third-Century Palestine," in *Aufstieg und Niedergang der Römischen Welt II, Principat 19, 2* (Berlin: Walter de Gruyter, 1979), 685, and see Stemberger, *Jews and Christians*.

79. Seth Schwartz, "Rabbinization in the Sixth Century," in *The Talmud Yerushalmi and Graeco-Roman Culture III*, ed. Peter Schäfer (Tübingen: Mohr Siebeck, 2002), 59.

80. Amnon Linder, *The Jews in Roman Imperial Legislation*, ed. and trans. Amnon Linder (Detroit: Wayne State University Press, 1987), 68.

81. Clyde Pharr, *The Theodosian Code and Novels, and the Sirmondian Constitutions: A Translation with Commentary, Glossary, and Bibliography*, in collaboration with Theresa Sherrer Davidson and Mary Brown Pharr, introd. C. Dickerman Williams (Princeton: Princeton University Press, 1952), 469.

82. For this issue, see Elliott S. Horowitz, "The Rite to be Reckless; on the Perpetration and Interpretation of Purim Violence," *Poetics Today* 15, no. 1 (1994): 9–54.

83. Stemberger, *Jews and Christians*, 29.

84. See the discussion in ibid., 155.

85. Pharr, *Theodosian Code*, 468. "It does remain likely that there were rabbis among the *primates* mentioned in the law codes" (Schwartz, *Jewish Society*, 118). See also: J. H. W. G. Liebeschuetz, *Antioch: City and Imperial Administration in the Later Roman Empire* (Oxford: Oxford University Press, 1972), 12, 16; Limberis, "Cipher," 382.

86. Stemberger, *Jews and Christians*, 308.

87. Linder, *Legislation*, 69.

88. Schwartz, *Jewish Society*, 116. For the Patriarch as a perceived threat to Christianity, see Wilhelm Karl Reischl and Joseph Rupp, *Cyrilli Hierosolymarum Archiepiscopi Opera Quae Supersunt Omnia*, ed. Wilhelm Karl Reischl (Hildesheim: Olms, 1967), 2:24, and discussion by Jacobs, "Construction," 51. Compare the roughly analogous insistence in the code that the high priest of Egypt must *not* be a Christian, XII.1.112, and see the discussion in Frankfurter, *Religion*, 24. According to Stemberger, even this, however, is an understatement with respect to the Patriarch. He shows that in the fourth century the Patriarch was higher in authority than the governor (Stemberger, *Jews and Christians*, 242–43). Levine writes that in the fourth century the Patriarch was more powerful than the Herodian kings (Levine, "Patriarch," 651).

89. Pharr, *Theodosian Code*, 468. See also Schwartz, *Jewish Society*, 103–4, although "the patriarch, or *nasi*, by the middle of the fourth [century] had become a very estimable figure indeed, the rabbis did not have any officially recognized legal authority until the end of the fourth century and even then it was severely restricted and in any case not limited to rabbis." Moreover, and very importantly: "As for the patriarchs, they acquired much of their influence precisely by relaxing their ties to the rabbis and allying themselves instead with Palestinian city councillors, wealthy diaspora Jews, and prominent gentiles." See also Stemberger, *Jews and Christians*, 34.

90. Pharr, *Theodosian Code*, 469.

91. Schwartz, *Jewish Society*, 187.

92. Bhabha, *Location*, 85.

93. This would suggest a possible qualification to claims such as those made by Shaye Cohen, "Pagan and Christian Evidence on the Ancient Synagogue," in *The Synagogue in Late Antiquity*, ed. Lee I. Levine (Philadelphia: American Schools of Oriental Research 1987), 170–75.

94. Although this term does not, to the best of my knowledge, exist, Beard, North, and Price, *Religions of Rome*, 237, strongly imply that its virtual synonym, *religio illicita*, does, but only in Christian texts, a fact that, if it could be verified, would strengthen my case.

95. Stemberger, *Jews and Christians*, 35, even seems to suggest that, when the Theodosian Code (XII.1.158) writes "irrespective of what religion (*superstitio*) they profess," this might even include Christianity as one of the religions.

96. Linder, *Legislation*, 428.

97. "Idem aa. philippo praefecto praetorio per illyricum. nullus tamquam iudaeus, cum sit innocens, obteratur nec expositum eum ad contumeliam religio qualiscumque perficiat."

98. Pharr, *Theodosian Code*, 476.

99. Caroline Humfress, "Religion," in *The Evolution of the Late Antique World*, by Peter Garnsey and Caroline Humfress (Oxford: Orchard Academic Press, 2001), 135–70.

100. Drake, "Lambs," 27–29.

101. Jacob Neusner, *Frequently Asked Questions about Rabbinic Judaism* (Peabody, Mass.: Hendrickson, 2003). I appreciate Prof. Neusner's willingness to let me see this material prior to publication.

102. Note that since belief is the crucial modus for determining Christian legitimacy, the Quartodeciman heresy is described as a belief and not a practice. Orthodox Judaism would tend to do the opposite, describing wrong beliefs as bad practice.

103. Pharr, *Theodosian Code*, 469.

104. Virginia Burrus, "'In the Theater of This Life': The Performance of Orthodoxy in Late Antiquity," in *The Limits of Ancient Christianity: Essays on Late Antique Thought and Culture in Honor of R. A. Markus*, ed. William E. Klingshirn and Mark Vessey (Ann Arbor: University of Michigan Press, 1999), 81.

105. Severus of Minorca, *Letter on the Conversion of the Jews*, trans. and ed. Scott Bradbury (Oxford: Oxford University Press, 1996).

106. Severus, *Letter*, 83. The reference is to 1 Cor. 1:28.

107. Ibid.

108. "Denique statim intercisa sunt etiam salutationis officia, et non solum familiaritatis consuetudo divulsa est, sed etiam noxia inveteratae species caritatis ad odium temporale pro aeternae salutis amore, translata est" (ibid., 84–85).

109. John of Jerusalem, in S. Vanderlinden, "Revelatio Sancti Stephani," *Revue des Études Byzantines* 4 (1946): B 34. See Scott Bradbury, Introduction, in Severus, *Letter*, 18–19.

110. Peter Brown, *The Cult of the Saints: Its Rise and Function in Latin Christianity* (Chicago: University of Chicago Press, 1981), 105.

111. Jacobs, "Construction," 61.

112. On this material, see also ibid., 222–27. Also Stemberger, *Jews and Christians*, 108–11.

113. Bradbury concludes, "The *Epistula* is thus a central document in the history of religious coercion in late antiquity" (Introduction, Severus, *Letter*, 2). It is also virtually the only such document for this period, for, as pointed out by Bernhard Blumenkranz and more recently by Günther Stemberger, there is no other evidence for such religious coercion before the seventh century (Bernhard Blumenkranz, *Les auteurs chrétiens latins du Moyen Age sur les juifs et le judaïsme* [Paris: Mouton, 1963], 24–25; Günther Stemberger, "Zwangstufen von Juden im 4. bis 7. Jahrhundert: Mythos oder Wirklichkeit?" in *Judentum Ausblicke und Einsichten: Festschrift K. Schubert*, ed. C. Thoma [Frankfurt a. M.: P. Lang, 1993], 81–114). Stemberger argues that nearly all of the stories of forced conversions are found in noncontemporaneous foundation legends of churches. Slightly earlier than the seventh century is the probably veracious account of the conversion of the Jews of Clermont in 576. See B. Brennan, "The Conversion of the Jews in Clermont in AD 576," *Journal of Theological Studies* 36 (1985). I am grateful to Seth Schwartz for calling this event and article to my attention. Although E. D. Hunt has assembled an impressive dossier of manifestations of Christian pogroms against Jews of one sort or another in the fourth century (E. D. Hunt, "St. Stephen in Minorca: An Episode in Jewish-Christian Relations in the Early 5th Century AD," *Journal of Theological Studies* n.s. 33 [1982]: 117), these do not add up to compelling, or even especially convincing evidence for a general movement toward the forced conversion of Jews developing in the late fourth or early fifth centuries.

114. Cf. Raymond Van Dam, "'Sheep in Wolves' Clothing': The Letters of Consentius to Augustine," *Journal of Ecclesiastical History* 37 (1986): 515–35.

115. Brown, *Cult*, 103–5.

116. Ibid., 88.

117. Ibid., 99–100.

118. Ibid., 105.

119. Exemplary instances of these would be those of Islam or North African and Hassidic Judaism, which have only local relevance. It is fascinating that Moroccan Jewish saints have revealed in dreams to Israeli immigrants that their bodies have been miraculously translated entire to some Israeli site or other. This exemplifies a strategy of "translation" that is almost directly opposite to that of the Western Christian cult of the saints. See also Patricia Cox Miller, "1997 NAPS Presidential Address: 'Differential Networks': Relics and Other Fragments in Late Antiquity," *Journal of Early Christian Studies* 6, no. 1 (1998): 113–38.

120. Brown, *Cult*, 90–91.

121. Ibid., 91, alluding to Augustine.

122. Bradbury, "Introduction" to Severus, *Letter*, 16.

123. As Bradbury notes, M. van Esbroeck ("Jean II de Jérusalem et les cultes de S. Étienne, de la Sainte-Sion et de la Croix," *Analecta Bollandiana* 102 [1984]: 99–134) suggests that John of Jerusalem's political initiatives were behind the composition of the various documents attesting to the revelation of these relics and the Passion of St. Stephen at this time. I shall be suggesting a broader political context for them.

124. Robert L. Wilken, *John Chrysostom and the Jews: Rhetoric and Reality in the Late Fourth Century* (Berkeley: University of California Press, 1983).

125. Stemberger, *Jews and Christians*, 78.

126. Hall, *Ethnic Identity in Greek Antiquity*, 29.

127. Brown, *Cult*, 103.

128. Cf. Bradbury's "No detail in the letter reveals so clearly the intimacy of the two religious communities as the fact that they can sing the same hymns" (Severus, *Letter*, 128, n. 14).

129. Severus, *Letter*, 93.

130. For this "political" use of psalmody, see Richard Paul Vaggione, *Eunomius of Cyzicus and the Nicene Revolution* (Oxford: Oxford University Press, 2000), 154: "The result, however, was not the ethereal sound of an English cathedral choir singing Evensong ["haunting beauty"], but the loud cries of a group of religious activists shouting slogans, for this 'psalmody' was as much at home on the streets as in a liturgical ceremony." Although Vaggione, of course, is speaking of events elsewhere in the Christian world, I am very tempted to tie these two instances together. A perhaps even sharper pendant is the following: "A similar procession during the reign of Julian accompanied the body of St Babylas. The emperor had ordered it removed from the temple precincts at Daphne; thousands of men, women, and children followed the remains of the martyr into the city shouting again and again: 'Confounded be all they that worship carved images and put their trust in idols!' (Ps. 96 [97]:7). Julian was not amused" (Vaggione, *Eunomius*, 154–55). Neither, I warrant, were the Jews of Minorca.

131. Severus, *Letter*, 83.

132. Pourkier, *Épiphane*, 78–79 and passim.

133. Severus, *Letter*, 94–95.

134. Ibid., 107.

135. Ibid., 111.

136. Bhabha, *Location*, 85–92.

137. Sir William Cust, writing in 1839, quoted in Bhabha, *Location*, 85.

138. Severus, *Letter*, 103–4.

139. And it is, several times, in this text a female Jewish speaker claiming the name of Jewish *religio*.

140. Schwartz, *Jewish Society*, 16. My treatment of the Code's materials should be compared with Schwartz, *Jewish Society*, 192–95.

141. Daniel Boyarin, "Two Powers in Heaven; or, the Making of a Heresy," in *The Idea of Biblical Interpretation: Essays in Honor of James L. Kugel*, ed. Hindy Najman and Judith H. Newman (Leiden: E. J. Brill, 2004).

142. Richard Kalmin, "Christians and Heretics in Rabbinic Literature of Late Antiquity," *Harvard Theological Review* 87, no. 2 (April 1994): 160.

143. Moshe Halbertal and Avishai Margalit, *Idolatry* (Cambridge: Harvard University Press, 1992).

144. For a much longer and more detailed discussion, see Daniel Boyarin, *Dying for God: Martyrdom and the Making of Christianity and Judaism* (Stanford, Calif.: Stanford University Press, 1999), chap. 1.

145. This identification is explicit in the continuation (not cited here), in which Rabbi Eli'ezer refers to his intercourse with a certain James, the disciple of Jesus. Jerome knows that the term *min*, "sectarian," is a name for Jewish Christians, as we see from his famous letter to Augustine (Jerome, *Correspondence*, 55:381–82). This letter was written about 404 (Pritz, *Nazarene Jewish Christianity*, 53).

146. M. S. Zuckermandel, ed., *Tosephta: Based on the Erfurt and Vienna Codices, with Lieberman, Saul, "Supplement" to the Tosephta*, in Hebrew (Jerusalem: Bamberger and Wahrmann, 1937), 503.

147. In the early Palestinian version of the narrative, there is not a hint of the term *minut* with respect to the arrest and martyrdom of these Rabbis (Louis Finkelstein, ed., *Sifre on Deuteronomy* [1939; rpt. New York: Jewish Theological Seminary of America, 1969], 346). For a discussion, see Daniel Boyarin, "A Contribution to the History of Martyrdom in Israel," in *Festschrift for Prof. H. Z. Dimitrovsky*, ed. Menahem Hirschman et al., in Hebrew (Jerusalem: Magnes Press, 1999).

148. Trans. following Rashi ad loc.

149. Saul Lieberman, "The Martyrs of Caesarea," *Annuaire de l'institut de philologie et d'histoire orientales et slaves* 7 (1939): 395.

150. Kalmin, "Christians and Heretics."

151. Cf., e.g., Lee I. Levine, *The Rabbinic Class of Roman Palestine in Late Antiquity* (New York: Jewish Theological Seminary of America, 1989), 87, and also Lieberman, "The Martyrs of Caesarea," 398.

152. Jacob Neusner, *Aphrahat and Judaism: The Christian-Jewish Argument in Fourth-Century Iran* (Leiden: E. J. Brill, 1971).

153. Daniel Boyarin, "Martyrdom and the Making of Christianity and Judaism," *Journal of Early Christian Studies* 6, no. 4 (December 1998): 577–627.

154. Daniel Boyarin, "A Tale of Two Synods: Nicaea, Yavneh, and the Making of Orthodox Judaism," *Exemplaria* 12, no. 1 (Spring 2000): 21–62.

155. Gerald Bruns, "The Hermeneutics of Midrash," in *The Book and the Text: The Bible and Literary Theory*, ed. Regina Schwartz (Oxford: Basil Blackwell, 1990), 199.

156. Jonathan Boyarin, Introduction, in *Powers of Diaspora: Two Essays on the Relevance of Jewish Culture*, by Daniel Boyarin and Jonathan Boyarin (Minneapolis: University of Minnesota Press, 2002), 23.

157. Jacques Derrida, *Glas*, trans. John P. Leavey, Jr., and Richard Rand (Lincoln: University of Nebraska Press, 1990), 189b.

Charles Taylor, The Future of the Religious Past

1. Robert Tombs, *France: 1814–1914* (London: Longman, 1996), 135, places the high-water mark at 1880; Gérard Cholvy and Yves-Marie Hillaire, *Histoire religieuse de la France contemporaine: 1800–1880* (Paris: Privat, 1985), 317, set it earlier, around 1860. I have split the difference.

2. See John McManners's essay in *The Oxford History of Christianity*, ed. John McManners (Oxford: Oxford University Press, 1993), 277–28.

3. See Robert Bellah, "Religious Evolution," chap. 2 of his *Beyond Belief: Essays on Religion in a Post-Traditional World* (New York: Harper & Row, 1970).

4. Godfrey Lienhardt, *Divinity and Experience* (Oxford: Oxford University Press, 1961), 233–35.

5. Ibid., 292.

6. As a matter of fact, it has been argued (e.g., by Pierre Clastres, *La société contre l'État: Recherches d'anthropologie politique* [Paris: Minuit, 1974]) that the earliest forms of this religion were highly egalitarian in relation to later developments, just because the pervasive sense of a sacred order left little room for personal decision on the part of those charged with special functions. They couldn't yet parlay these into personal power.

7. See, e.g., Lienhardt, *Divinity and Experience*, chap. 3, and Roger Caillois, *L'homme et le sacré* (Paris: Gallimard, 1963), chap. 3.

8. This is a much-commented feature of aboriginal religion in Australia; see Lucien Lévy-Bruhl, *L'expérience mystique et les symboles chez les primitifs* (Paris: Alcan, 1937), 180 ff.; Caillois, *L'homme et le sacré*, 143–55; W. E. H. Stanner, "On Aboriginal Religion," a series of six articles in *Oceania* 30–33 (1959–63). The same connection to the land has been noted with the Okanagan in British Columbia; see Jerry Mander and Edward Goldsmith, *The Case Against the Global Economy* (San Francisco: Sierra Club Books, 1996), chap. 39.

9. William Kingdom Clifford, *Ethics of Belief and Other Essays*, ed. Leslie Stephen and Sir Frederick Pollock (London: Watts, 1947).

10. Birgit Meyer, *Translating the Devil* (Trenton: Africa World Press, 1999), 181.

11. See the discussion of possession in ibid., pp. 205–6.

12. John Stuart Mill, *On Liberty*, in idem, *Three Essays* (Oxford: Oxford University Press 1975), 77.

13. See, e.g., S. N. Eisenstadt, ed., *The Origins and Diversity of Axial Age Civilizations* (Albany: State University of New York Press, 1986); see also Bellah, *Beyond Belief*.

14. Karl Jaspers, *Vom Ursprung und Ziel der Geschichte* (Zürich: Artemis, 1949).

15. Stanner, "On Aboriginal Religion"; the expression quoted figures in article II, *Oceania* 30, no. 4 (June 1960): 276. See also, by the same author, "The Dreaming," in W. Lessa and E. Z. Vogt, eds., *Reader in Comparative Religion* (Evanston, Ill.: Row, Peterson, 1958), 158–67.

16. Stanner, "On Aboriginal Religion," article VI, *Oceania* 33, no. 4 (June 1963): 269.

17. I have been greatly helped here by the much richer account of religious development in Robert Bellah's "Religious Evolution," in his *Beyond Belief*. My contrast is much simpler than the series of stages that Bellah identifies; the "primitive" and the "archaic" are fused in my category of "early" religion. My point is to bring into sharp relief the disembedding thrust of the axial formulations.

18. See Marcel Gauchet, *Le désenchantement du monde* (Paris: Gallimard 1985), chap. 2.

19. Louis Dumont, "De l'individu-hors-du-monde à l'individu-dans-le-monde," in *Essais sur l'individualisme* (Paris: Seuil, 1983).

20. I have developed this at greater length in *Modern Social Imaginaries* (Durham, N.C.: Duke University Press, 2004).

21. Danièle Hervieu-Léger, *Catholicisme, la fin d'un monde* (Paris: Bayard, 2003).

22. See Robert Bellah, "Civil Religion in America," in *Beyond Belief*, chap. 9.

23. See my *The Varieties of Religion Today* (Cambridge: Harvard University Press, 2002).

24. E.g., David Martin, *Tongues of Fire* (Oxford: Basil Blackwell, 1990), and *A General Theory of Secularization* (Oxford: Basil Blackwell, 1978).

25. See Gordon Wood, *The Radicalism of the American Revolution* (New York: Vintage, 1993).

26. But even so, the very poor tended to be touched by these movements in England less than more skilled workers. See: Hugh McLeod, *Secularization in Western Europe, 1848–1914* (New York: St Martin's Press, 2000), chap. 3; also his *Religion and the People of Western Europe, 1789–1989* (Oxford: Oxford University Press, 1997), chap. 4; and David Hempton, *Religion and Political Culture in Britain and Ireland* (Cambridge: Cambridge University Press, 1996), 29 and chap. 6.

27. I have drawn here, *inter alia*, on the valuable discussions in: McLeod, *Religion and the People of Western Europe*, 36–43; John Wolffe, *God and Greater Britain: Religion and National Life in Britain and Ireland, 1843–1945* (London: Routledge, 1994), 20–30; and Hempton, *Religion and Political Culture*, chap. 2.

28. Joyce Appleby, *Inheriting the Revolution: The First Generation of Americans* (Cambridge: Harvard University Press, 2000), 206.

29. Callum Brown, *The Death of Christian Britain* (London: Routledge, 2001).

30. See David Martin, *Tongues of Fire*, and *Pentecostalism: The World Their Parish* (Oxford: Basil Blackwell, 2002).

31. Sociologists have noticed similar effects flowing from strong (re)conversions to Islam in contemporary France; see Danièle Hervieu-Léger, *Le pélerin et le converti* (Paris: Flammarion, 1999), 142–43.

32. The connection of Christianity with decency in England has been noted by David Martin, *Dilemmas of Contemporary Religion* (Oxford: Basil Blackwell, 1978), 22.

33. This whole issue of violence in modernity deserves further extensive treatment, especially taking account of the pathbreaking work of René Girard.

34. See Philippe Chenaux, *Entre Maurras et Maritain* (Paris: Cerf, 1999).

35. Philippe Boutry, *Prêtres et paroisses au pays du curé d'Ars* (Paris: Cerf, 1986) also speaks of the campaigns of curés against *les abus*, principally dancing, theater, and working on Sunday (579).

36. Cf. Richard Hoggart, *The Uses of Literacy* (London: Chatto & Windus, 1957); Yves Lambert, *Dieu change en Bretagne* (Paris: Cerf, 1985).

37. Michael Sandel, *Democracy's Discontent* (Cambridge: Harvard University Press, 1996), 209–10.

38. Michel Winock, *Le siècle des intellectuels* (Paris: Seuil, 1997), 582.

39. François Furet, *Le passé d'une illusion* (Paris: Gallimard, 1996), points out how remarkable the allegiance was, and the sense of belonging that sustained it.

40. Luc Ferry, in his very interesting *L'Homme-Dieu ou le sens de la vie* (Paris: Grasset, 1996), chap. 1, picks up on this phenomenon under the title "the refusal of authority." I agree with much of what he says, but I think he overintellectualizes this reaction by relating it directly to Descartes, instead of seeing its expressivist roots.

41. Sir George Trevelyan, in a lecture at the Festival for Mind, Body, and Spirit, quoted in Paul Heelas, *The New Age Movement* (Oxford: Basil Blackwell, 1996), 21. The injunction, one might say, represents only a New Age outlook. But in this respect, the various New Age movements accentuate much more widely held attitudes, as Heelas argues in chap. 6. In 1978, for instance, a Gallup poll found that 80 percent of Americans agreed that "an individual should arrive at his or her own religious beliefs independent of any churches or synagogues" (Heelas, 164; also cited in Robert Bellah et al., *Habits of the Heart* [Berkeley: University of California Press, 1985], 228).

42. The excellent book by José Casanova, *Public Religions in the Modern World* (Chicago: University of Chicago Press, 1994), shows how diverse our religious predicament is. If we ever came to live in a predicament totally defined by the post-Durkheimian understanding, there would probably be no further space for religion in the public sphere. Spiritual life would be entirely privatized, in keeping with the norms of a certain procedural liberalism that is very widespread today. But Casanova traces, in fact, a "deprivatization" of religion, that is, an attempt by churches and religious bodies to intervene again in the political life of their societies. Instances are the Christian Right and the Catholic bishops' letters in the United States, which I have just mentioned. It is unlikely (and also undesirable) that this kind of thing ever cease. But the situation in which these interventions take place is defined by the end of a uniform Durkheimian dispensation and the growing acceptance among many people of a post-Durkheimian understanding.

43. Hempton, *Religion and Political Culture*, 18 and 132–33.

44. Mill, *On Liberty*; see McLeod, *Religion and the People of Western Europe*, 114; Cox, *The English Churches in a Secular Society*, 275.

45. Martin, *Pentecostalism*, 14–15.

46. Of course, the sexual revolution could itself be taken as the axis of a master narrative or subtraction story, and it was frequently interpreted in this way in the 1960s. See, e.g., Charles A. Reich, *The Greening of America* (New York: Random House, 1970). Parallel to stories claiming that science shows that religion is wrong, and once people remove the obstacles to seeing this, they can't go back; or that people in the end want autonomy, and once they see through the false reasons underlying authority, they can't go back; there is another possible story: people desire unchecked sexual fulfillment, and once they see that they have been denied this by unfounded restrictions, there is no going back. This is certainly how things felt to a lot of young people in, say, Berkeley or the Latin Quarter in 1968. But this outlook hasn't worn very well. In fact, most people quickly perceived that things are much more complicated.

47. Martin, *Pentecostalism*, 98–106.

48. See Brown, *The Death of Christian Britain*, esp. chaps. 4 and 5.

49. I have discussed this at greater length in my *Modern Social Imaginaries*.

50. Boutry, *Prêtres et paroisses*, 578.

51. Ibid., pt. 3, chaps. 1 and 4. There are also interesting discussions of this gender split in practice in: McLeod, *Religion and the People of Western Europe*, 128; Leonore Davidoff and Catherine Hall, *Family Fortunes* (London: Routledge, 1987), chap. 2; and Thomas Kselman, "The Varieties of Religious Experience in Urban France," in *European Religion in the Age of Great Cities, 1830–1930*, ed. Hugh McLeod (London: Routledge, 1995), chap. 6.

52. Hervieu-Léger, in *Catholicisme*, speaks of an "exculturation," a move beyond and outside of the culture that the Catholic Church helped form over centuries in France and that was shared by the "Republican" opponents of the Church. See esp. chaps. 3–6.

53. Quoted in Brown, *The Death of Christian Britain*, 180.

54. See Yves-Marie Hilaire, *Une Chrétienneté au XIXe siècle?* (Lille: PUL, 1977), 1:74–80.

55. Grace Davie, *Religion in Modern Europe* (Oxford: Oxford University Press, 2000), 63–64.

56. John Bossy, *Christianity in the West, 1400–1700* (Oxford: Oxford University Press, 1985), 35; Ralph Gibson, *A Social History of French Catholicism, 1789–1914* (London: Routledge, 1989), 24.

57. Bossy, *Christianity in the West*, 37.

58. Jean Delumeau, *Le péché et la peur* (Paris: Fayard, 1983; also Gibson, *A Social History*, 241 and ff.).

59. Quoted in Gibson, *A Social History*, 246.

60. E. Germain, *Parler du salut?* (Paris: Beauchesne, 1967), 295; quoted, along with a very interesting discussion, in Gibson, *A Social History*, 244.

61. Hervieu-Léger, *Catholicisme*, 248.

62. Gibson, *A Social History*, 188; Delumeau, *Le péché et la peur*, chap. 17, 517–19, 525.

63. Martin, *Pentecostalism*, 21.

64. Michael Hornsby-Smith, "Recent Transformations in English Catholicism," in *Religion and Modernization*, ed. Bruce, chap. 6.

65. See Steve Bruce, *Religion in the Modern World* (Oxford: Oxford University Press, 1996), 33, 137 ff.; Sylvie Denèfle, *Sociologie de la sécularisation* (Paris: L'Harmatan, 1997).

66. E.g., the *Gallup Political and Economic Index* (394, June 1993) reports that in Britain 40 percent believe in "some sort of spirit or lifeforce," as opposed to 30 percent, who have faith in a

"personal God"; cited in Heelas, *The New Age Movement*, 166. Analogous figures have been found in Sweden and France; see Hervieu-Léger, *Le pèlerin et le converti*, 44–46.

67. The move of many Western societies into what I have been calling a "post-Durkheimian" dispensation has obviously facilitated their move toward "multiculturalism," at the same time as this has become a more urgent issue because of the increasing diversity of their populations. But multiculturalism has also produced strains, which are often exacerbated by the continuing hold of one or another "Durkheimian" understanding on important segments of the population. Christian conservatives are made edgy by rampant expressivism in the United States, and many French people find it hard to see their country as containing an important Muslim component, so long have they related to it as an essentially Catholic country, or one defined by the constitutive tension between Catholicism and *laïcité*.

68. Hervieu-Léger, *Le pèlerin et le converti*, 41, 56; Grace Davie, *Religion in Britain since 1945: Believing Without Belonging* (Oxford: Basil Blackwell, 1994). A discussion of the special Scandinavian pattern can be found in Hervieu-Léger, *Le pèlerin et le converti*, 57; and Davie, *Religion in Modern Europe*, 3.

69. William James, *The Varieties of Religious Experience* (Harmondsworth, Middlesex: Penguin Books, 1982).

70. Boutry, *Prêtres et paroisses*, tells of the "attitudes of reservation, of suspicion, and even of refusal" by clergy in the face of many of the practices of folk religion (481). McLeod (*Religion and the People of Western Europe*, 64–65) quotes the bitter statement of another French curé in 1907: "Not a single man does his Easter Duties, but it's a curious fact that they all take part in processions."

71. Jim Obelkevich, *Religion and Rural Society: South Lindsey, 1825–1875* (London: Oxford University Press, 1976), 83–84.

72. Maurice Agulhon, *La république au village* (Paris: Seuil, 1979), 172.

73. Ibid., 644, also 578–95 and 625–51.

74. Ralph Gibson, *A Social History of French Catholicism* (London: Routledge, 1989), 144.

75. See the interesting discussion in Thomas Kselman, *Miracles and Prophecies in Nineteenth-Century France* (New Brunswick, N.J.: Rutgers University Press, 1983), chap. 6.

76. Victor Turner, *The Ritual Process: Structure and Counter-Structure* (London: Routledge & Kegan Paul, 1969).

77. Hervieu-Léger, *Le pèlerin et le converti*, 100–8.

78. See: Davie, *Religion in Britain since 1945*; and Wolffe, *God and Greater Britain*. The term *diffusive Christianity* was coined by Jeffrey Cox, *The English Churches in a Secular Society, Lambeth 1870–1930* (New York: Oxford University Press, 1982), chap. 4.

79. Wolffe, *God and Greater Britain*, 92–93. Hempton, *Religion and Political Culture*, 136–37, gives another account of this diffused understanding of Christianity, while stressing that all the terms we invent to describe it, including *believing without belonging* and *diffusive Christianity* itself, are insufficiently flexible to capture the complex reality. Hempton also points out the importance of religious music, particularly hymn singing, in this culture.

80. Wolffe, *God and Greater Britain*, 92–93. Boutry, *Prêtres et paroisses*, makes a parallel remark about the period 1840–60 in the Ain Department (but this was not exceptional in this respect in France): "Never, perhaps, in the long history of the Catholic Church, will the lived reality of the ministry have coincided more exactly with its ideal, never will the life of village priests approach so closely to the model of the 'good priest,' developed three centuries earlier by the Fathers of the Council of Trent" (243).

81. Davie, *Religion in Britain since 1945*, 69–70. For the figures, see her tables.

82. Ibid, 88–91.

83. E.g., Grace Davie, *Europe: The Exceptional Case* (London: Darton, Longman & Todd, 2002), 46.

84. Perhaps a "cold" form of their erstwhile religious identity can be observed among Québécois; on the occasion of the deconfessionalization of the public schools in the 1990s, lots of quite nonpracticing parents expressed anxiety about the possible suppression of religious education for their children in school. They feared being unable to inculcate proper moral guidelines in their children without the backing this education could provide.

85. Steve Bruce, *Religion in the Modern World* (Oxford: Oxford University Press, 1996), chap. 6.

86. This is close to the thesis outlined by Martin, if I understand him correctly, in *A General Theory of Secularization*, 53.

87. Again, there is a similarity to a thesis of Martin's; see ibid., 56, 68.

88. This "hot" identity may also help to explain the differences between Europe and America that emerged on the occasion of the recent war in Iraq. Some commentators have tried to capture this in the memorable phrase: "Americans are from Mars, Europeans from Venus." See Robert Kagan, *Of Paradise and Power: America and Europe in the New World Order* (New York: Alfred A. Knopf, 2003).

89. S. N. Eisenstadt, *Japanese Civilization: A Comparative View* (Chicago: University of Chicago Press, 1996).

90. Saba Mahmood, *Pious Formations: The Islamic Revival and the Subject of Feminism* (Princeton: Princeton University Press, 2004).

91. Moussa Kömeçoğlu, in *Islam in Public*, ed. Nilüfer Göle and Ludwig Amman (Istanbul: Bilgi University Press, 2006), 369–94.

92. Ugur Kömeçoğlu, in *Islam in Public*, ed. Göle and Amman, 173.

93. For a further discussion of this distinction between network and categorical identities, see Craig Calhoun, *Nationalism* (Minneapolis: University of Minnesota Press, 1997), chap. 2. I am indebted to Calhoun's work throughout this discussion.

94. D. Eikelman and J. Anderson, eds., *New Media in the Muslim World: The Emerging Public Sphere* (Bloomington: Indiana University Press, 1999).

95. See Nilüfer Göle, *Musulmanes et Modernes* (Paris: La Découverte, 1993).

96. See, e.g., Craig Calhoun, "Nationalism and Ethnicity," *American Review of Sociology*, no. 9 (1993): 230.

97. See, esp. for the Sri Lankan case, Stanley Tambiah, *Buddhism Betrayed? Religion, Politics, and Violence in Sri Lanka* (Chicago: University of Chicago Press, 1992).

98. Montesquieu, *L'esprit des lois*, bk. 5, chap. 1.

99. Immanuel Kant, *Grundlegung zur Metaphysik der Sitten* Berlin Academy Edition (Berlin: Walter de Gruyter, 1968), 4:434.

100. This doesn't have to be a political society. It can be a dispersed common agency, like a religious confession, or an ethnic group.

101. See my "The Politics of Recognition," in *Multiculturalism: Examining the Politics of Recognition*, ed. Amy Gutmann (Princeton: Princeton University Press, 1992).

102. Esp. Frantz Fanon, *Les damnés de la terre* (Paris: Maspéro, 1968).

103. I owe a lot here to the interesting discussion by Nilüfer Göle about this whole topic, both in the Turkish and in the broader Islamic context. See *Musulmanes et Modernes*.

104. See Martin Kramer, "Arab Nationalism: Mistaken Identity," *Daedalus* 122, no. 3 (Summer 1993): 171–206.

105. I have learned a great deal from the interesting discussion in Sudhir Kakar, *The Colors of Violence* (Chicago: University of Chicago Press, 1996), esp. chap. 6. And also from René Girard:

e.g., *Le bouc émissaire* (Paris: Grasset, 1982) and *Je vois Satan tomber comme l'éclair* (Paris: Grasset, 1999). I have tried to discuss these issues in "Notes on the Sources of Violence" (forthcoming).

106. See Saba Mahmood, "Ethical Formation and Politics of Individual Autonomy in Contemporary Egypt," *Social Research* 70, no. 3 (Fall 2003): 837–66.

107. 'Abdolkarim Soroush, *Reason, Freedom and Democracy in Islam* (Oxford: Oxford University Press, 2000), 24.

108. See Keith Thomas, *Religion and the Decline of Magic* (New York: Scribner, 1971).

109. Meyer, *Translating the Devil*, 162, 170, 212–16.

Danièle Hervieu-Léger, Religion as Memory: Reference to Tradition and the Constitution of a Heritage of Belief in Modern Societies

NOTE: This essay first appeared in *The Pragmatics of Defining Religion: Contexts, Concepts, and Contests*, ed. Jan G. Platvoet and Arie L. Molendijk (Leiden: Brill, 1999), 41– 72. It appears here by permission of the publisher.

1. One finds a very suggestive reading of this dispersion, characteristic of the modern imagination, in G. Balandier, *Le Detour: Pouvoir et modernité* (Paris: Fayard, 1985).

2. Michel de Certeau and J.-M. Domenach, *Le Christianisme éclaté* (Paris: Seuil, 1974).

3. See, e.g., the critical assessment of this work in J. Séguy, "Religion, Modernité, Sécularisation," *Archives de Sciences Sociales des Religions* 61, no. 2 (1982): 175–85.

4. See, on this theme, J.-P. Willaime, "Croire et Modernité," *Archives de Sciences Sociales des Religions* 81 (1993): 7–16.

5. Emile Durkheim, *The Elementary Forms of the Religious Life* (London: Allen & Unwin, 1915).

6. E. Poulat, "Epistémologie," in *L'état des sciences satiates en France*, ed. M. Guillaume (Paris: La Découverte, 1986), 400.

7. Thomas Luckmann, *The Invisible Religion: The Problem of Religion in Modern Society* (New York: MacMillan, 1967).

8. F. Champion, "Les sociologues de la post-modernité et la nébuleuse mystique-ésotérique," *Archives de Sciences Sociales des Religions* 67, no. 1 (1989): 155–69; idem, "La nébuleuse mystique-ésotérique: Orientations psycho-religieuses des courants mystiques et ésotériques contemporains," in *De l'émotion en religion*, ed. F. Champion and D. Hervieu-Léger (Paris: Centurion, 1990).

9. Champion, "La nébuleuse mystique-ésotérique," 52; J. L. Schlegel, *Religions a la carte* (Paris: Hachette, 1995).

10. The notions of "sacred cosmos" and "cosmization" are taken from P. Berger, *The Sacred Canopy: Elements of a Sociological Theory of Religion* (New York: Doubleday, 1967), and idem, *La religion dans la conscience moderne* (Paris: Centurion, 1971). Religion is the "human enterprise that creates a sacred cosmos" (*La religion dans la conscience moderne*, 56). The cosmization upon which religion rests permits humankind to project itself as far as possible outside of itself. It accomplishes this by imaginatively creating a universe of "objective" meanings and thus imposing its own significations upon reality.

11. R. N. Bellah, "Civil Religion in America," *Daedelus* 96 (1967), rpt. in Bellah, *Beyond Belief: Essays on Religion in a Post-Traditional World* (New York: Harper & Row, 1970); idem, *The Broken Covenant: American Civil Religion in a Time of Trial* (New York: Seabury Press, 1975); R. N. Bellah

and P. E. Hammond, *Varieties of Civil Religion* (New York: Harper & Row, 1980). For a comprehensive presentation of the debate around civil religion in the United States, see G. Gehrig, *American Civil Religion: An Assessment* (Storrs, Conn.: Society for the Scientific Study of Religion, 1979).

12. J. Coleman, "Civil Religion," *Sociological Analysis* 31, no. 2 (1970).

13. R. N. Bellah, *Tokugawa Religion* (Glencoe, Ill.: The Free Press, 1957).

14. An especially detailed presentation of what is theoretically at stake in this problem and the debate that it has solicited can be found in R. O'Toole, *Religion: Classic Sociological Approaches* (Toronto: McGraw-Hill Ryerson, 1984).

15. Y. Lambert, "La 'tour de Babel' des définitions de la religion," in *Social Compass* 38, no. 1 (1991): 73–85.

16. J. Séguy, "L'approche weberienne des phénomènes religieux," in *Omaggio a Ferrarotti*, ed. R. Cipriani and M. Macioti (Siares: Studi e recerche, 1989), 198.

17. Michel de Certeau, "L'institution du croire: Note de travail," in *Le Magistère: Institutions et fonctionnements*, special number of *Recherches de Sciences Religieuse* (Paris: n.p., 1983).

18. J. Pouillon, "Remarques sur le verbe *croire*," in *La fonction symbolique*, ed. M. Izard and P. Smith (Paris: Gallimard, 1979). Speaking, e.g., of "margaï, these genies whose place is so important in the individual life of Hadjeraï," Pouillon insists that the Hadjeraï "believe in their existence as they do in their own, in that of animals, things, atmospheric phenomena. . . . Or, rather, they do not believe in them at all: this existence is a simple fact of experience: one needs no more belief in the margaï than in the fall of a stone which one throws" (49–50).

19. Pierre Bourdieu, *Le sens pratique* (Paris: Minuit, 1980), 113ff.

20. Berger, *La religion dans la conscience moderne*.

21. One of these expressions is myth, which Claude Lévi-Strauss defines (in *La pensée sauvage* [Paris: Plon, 1962]) as: "a vigorous protestation against non-sense."

22. P. Gisel, *L'excès du croire: Expérience du monde et accès à soi* (Paris: Desclée de Brouwer, 1990).

23. M. Gauchet, *Le désenchantement du monde: Une histoire politique de la religion* (Paris: Gallimard, 1985).

24. F. Dubet, *Sociologie de l'expérience* (Paris: Seuil, 1994).

Veena Das, If This Be Magic . . .: Excursions into Contemporary Hindu Lives

NOTE: I am very grateful to Talal Asad, Roma Chatterji, Naveeda Khan, and Bhrigupati Singh for their help in formulating the issues discussed here. I learned a great deal from a series of lectures entitled "Capturing Imagination: On Belief, Disbelief, and Scandal," delivered by Carlo Severi at The Johns Hopkins University in 2006. I am very grateful to him for sharing his work in progress with such generosity. Hent de Vries and Bill Connolly have been wonderful colleagues, and one can count on them for a provocative discussion on questions of religion at any time and place. Thanks to Helen Tartar for her patience. Simi, Rajan, Charu, Harpreet, Poonam, and Purshottam gave tremendous support in the field, and the residents of the neighborhoods in Delhi who shared their lives and thoughts provided the inspiration for writing this essay.

1. A. Piatigorski, "Some Phenomenological Observations on the Study of Indian Religion," in *Indian Religion*, ed. Richard Burghart and Audrey Cantlie (Richmond, Surrey: Curzon Press, 1985), 216.

2. What Piatigorski sees as a feature of Hinduism, namely, the concept of the *ishtadevata*, according to many others is alien to the Vedic, Pauranic, and epic literature but is typical of the folk conceptions of divinity that were absorbed as one component of the Hindu complex. See, e.g., Gunther-Dietz Sontheimer, "Hinduism: The Five Components and Their Interaction," in his *Essays in Religion, Literature and Law*, ed. Heidrun Bruckner, Anne Feldhaus, and Aditya Malik (Delhi: Manohar Publications, 2004), 401–21. We shall later see the relevance of the debate concerning whether gods are considered to be primary or secondary to the worshipper.

3. It is possible that one should speak of Semitic imaginaries rather than Christian ones, but I do not have the space to engage with the issues of whether the anthropological notions of God have been equally influenced by Judaic or Islamic notions. This is not to say that there might not be complex variations in the understanding of God as Christianity comes into varied relationships with other traditions, but to point out that even at the theological level there are profound differences in what is at stake in thinking about divinity in the loose traditions we call "Hindu," or sometimes "Indic," to recognize the separateness of, say, Jainism or Sikhism while also acknowledging their close affinity to Hinduism.

4. For excellent descriptions of the place of sound in different schools of thought, see: Guy L Beck, *Sonic Theology: Hinduism and Sacred Sound* (Columbia: University of South Carolina Press, 1995); Thomas B. Coburn, "Scripture," in "India: Toward a Typology of the Word in Hindu Life," in *Rethinking Scripture* (New York: State University of New York Press , 1998), 102–129; Gaurinath Shastri, *The Philosophy of Word and Meaning: Some Indian Approaches* (Calcutta: Sanskrit College, 1959). The literature on each of these schools is extensive. For a review of this and other literature on various forms of Hinduism, see Arvind Sharma, ed.), *The Study of Hinduism* (Columbia: University of South Carolina Press, 2003).

5. The eight-volume *Encyclopedia of Indian Philosophies*, under the general editorship of Karl H. Potter (Delhi: Motilal Banarasidas, 1984–99), provides an excellent resource for the student of Indian philosophies and religions on sources in Sanskrit.

6. See Francis X. Clooney, "Why the Veda Has No Author: Language as Ritual in Early Mimamsa and Post-modern Theology," *Journal of the American Academy of Religions* 55 (1987): 469–684.

7. See Veena Das, "The Language of Sacrifice," *Man* n.s. 18, no. 3 (1983): 445–62. For interpretations of Vedic sacrifice, see the classic text by Madeline Biardeau and Charles Malamoud, *Le sacrifice de l'Inde ancienne* (Paris: Presses Universitaires de France, 1976). The Purvamimamsa has generally been ignored by scholars of Indian philosophy as basically providing nothing more than ritual manuals. For an exceptional treatment of the texts in this tradition, see Francis X. Clooney, *Thinking Ritually: Rediscovering the Purva Mimamsa of Jaimini*, ed. Gerhard Oberhammer (Vienna: Sammlung de Nobili, 1990).

8. The notion that the sonic or graphic qualities of words have powers of their own plays a very important role in mystic forms of Islam, as well as in practices of healing (*ruhani ilaj*) that draw upon occult or hidden features of the world. Examples of popular tracts that describe the powers of various combinations of numbers or words are: Aslam Mohammad, *Bimariyon ke ruhani ilaj* (Delhi: Urdu Press, 2004), and Mir Bvalliuddin, *Bimari aur us ke ruhani ilaj* (Nadva ul-Munnanifin, 1972). For parallels in the Jewish kabbalistic tradition, see: Moshe Idel, "Jacques Derrida and Kabbalstic Sources," in *Judeities: Questions for Jacques Derrida*, ed. Bettina Bergo, Joseph Cohen, and Raphael Zagury-Orly (New York: Fordham University Press, 2007), 111–30; and Elliot R. Wolfson, *Language, Eros, Being: Kabbalistic Hermeneutics and Poetic Imagination* (New York: Fordham University Press, 2005).

9. For the Purvamimamsa, the sentence was important because the Vedic injunctions were expressed in sentences but the *form* had to remain constant and the reference to such relations as

cause and effect, even if these violated common sense, were to be treated as true. For the grammarians, there were important issues such as whether a sentence was divisible or indivisible, but the relation between word, sound, meaning, and reference was not immutable. See K. A. S. Iyer, *Vakyapadiya of Bhartrihari* (Poona: Deccan College, 1966). See also K. K. Raja, *Indian Theories of Meaning* (Madras: The Adyar Library and Research Center, 1964) and *Encyclopedia of Indian Philosophies: The Philosophy of the Grammarians*, ed. Harold G. Coward and R. Kunjunni Raja (Delhi: Motilal Banarasidass, 1990).The texts of Bhartrihari are extremely difficult. Even the questions of titles of texts and authorship are far from settled, and scholars in this field now prefer to call the text *Vakyapadiya/Trikandi*—the latter referring to the three parts of the text. See *Bhartrihari: Philosopher and Grammarian*, ed. Saroja Bhate and Johannes Bronkhorst (Delhi: Motilal Banarasidass Publishers, 1994).

10. One of the best examples of such a conflict can be found in the story of the dialogue between Uddhav and the *gopis* ("cowmaids") of Braja, who were Krishna's companions in his childhood. When Krishna left his childhood abode of Braja to take up kingly responsibilities, the *gopis* were heartbroken. He sent Uddhav as a messenger to preach to the *gopis* the value of meditating on the formless Brahman. The *gopis*, however, sent him witty replies about the uselessness of worship on the formless Brahman and reiterated their form of worship as love for Krishna.

11. How one counts the total number of graphs or sounds in the Sanskrit alphabet is itself related to one's allegiance to a particular school of thought. For the grammarians, the letters of the alphabet are grouped according to the particular movements of the speech organs. For the worshippers of Kali, the alphabet has 50 letters, corresponding to the number of skulls worn by her as garland. Since each letter has a dual aspect—Shiva and Shakti—the total number becomes 100. To this are added the five elements and the three basic *gunas*, or qualities, to generate 108. That is the number for totality, beyond which there is nothing. Others consider the number to be 54, so that the duality of each letter generates 108, which is the number of energy points in the body, the number of points in the sacred designs, and so on.

12. Hans Küng, Josef van Ess, Heinrich von Stietencorn, and Heinz Bechert, *Christianity and the World Religions: Paths to Dialogue with Islam, Hinduism, Buddhism* (New York: Doubleday, 1986).

13. Küng et al., *Christianity and the World Religions*, 269; emphasis in original.

14. In this context there is an interesting tension between the connections one might make between texts and observed practices in the Indic traditions and in more general theories of religion. Thus Sontheimer gives examples of how the cult of Khandoba in Maharashtra displays "folk" components as well as elements of asceticism, Brahmanical practices, and *bhakti*, which could be derived from Sanskritic sources. While I am not committed to the contrast between folk religion and classical religion, I recognize that here the words are placeholders for the fact that the components Sontheimer isolates as "folk" or "tribal" reflect an attempt to systematize the astonishing fluidity between the deities we might place within these cults and the deities, such as Rudra, mentioned in Vedic rituals as "foreign" to the sacrifice itself (Sontheimer, "Hinduism"). Similarly, see the magisterial work of Fredrick M. Smith on possession, which traverses the texts in Sanskrit and vernacular languages as well as contemporary practices of possession to ask whether there are important linkages between these textual and social formations. See Fredrick M. Smith, *The Self Possessed: Deity and Spirit Possession in South Asian Literature and Civilization* (New York: Columbia University Press, 2006). Lawrence Cohen, in his lovely book on aging, similarly draws from many different sources to show the importance of the mythic and ritual register for understanding aging, in addition to the lives of the people he lived with in Banaras. See Lawrence Cohen, *No Aging in India: Modernity, Senility, and the Family* (Berkeley: University of California Press, 1997).

15. See Hugh B. Urban, *Songs of Ecstasy: Tantric and Devotional Songs from Colonial Bengal* (Oxford: Oxford University Press, 2001). This is a companion volume to the analytical one entitled *The Economics of Ecstasy: Tantra, Secrecy and Power in Colonial Bengal* (Oxford: Oxford University Press, 2001).

16. Ibid., 7 and 26.

17. Although Urban emphasizes the aspect of speaking in coded language for the sect, in fact the use of an economic vocabulary, the idea of buying and selling as keeping an account of oneself, was a common metaphor for spiritual development of the self. Such a vocabulary was also famously used by Thoreau in his definition of philosophy itself as "an economy of living." Of course, the darker aspects of this captivity to economic terms as they spill into our lives—our use of economic imagery to express (and sometimes correct) spiritual confusion—also becomes, as Stanley Cavell points out in his classic essay on Thoreau, a brutal mocking of our sense of values and the "last suffocation of the soul." See Stanley Cavell, *The Senses of Walden*, expanded edition (Chicago: University of Chicago Press, 1992), and his extraordinary essay "Thoreau Thinks of Ponds, Heidegger of Rivers," in *Philosophy the Day after Tomorrow* (Cambridge: Harvard University Press, 2005).

18. Graham Dwyer, *The Divine and the Demonic: Supernatural Affliction and Its Treatment in North India* (London: Routledge, 2003), 89.

19. However, see Fredrick M. Smith, *The Self Possessed*, who clearly recognizes that proceedings are being conducted as if in an Islamic court. Pnina Werbner and Helene Basu also describe a Sufi *dargah* in which the proceedings are conducted in a courtlike manner as the debates between the healer and the jinn unfold. See Pnina Werbner and Helene Basu, *Embodying Charisma: Modernity, Locality, and Performance of Emotions in Sufi Cults* (London: Routledge, 1998). Credit must go to Sudhir Kakar for recognizing the importance of the healing practices at Balaji in his study *Shamans, Mystics, and Healers: A Psychological Inquiry into India and Its Healing Traditions* (Chicago: University of Chicago Press, 1982). Antti Pakaslahti has emphasized the family-centered treatment and the cultural acceptability of these healers. See Antti Pakaslahti, "Family-Centered Treatment of Mental Health Problems at the Balaji Temple at Rajasthan," in *Changing Patterns of Family and Kinship in South Asia*, ed. Asko Parpola and Sirpa Tenhunen (Helsinki: Finnish Oriental Society, 1998), 120–66; and also Pakaslahti, "Traditional Healers as Culturally Accepted/Sanctioned Mental Health Practitioners," in *Mental Disorders in Children and Adolescents: Needs and Strategies for Intervention*, ed. Savita Malhotra (Delhi: CBS, 2005), 215–29.

The only caveat that I would add to this set of writings is that, because the fieldwork is located in the shrine itself, it is difficult to assess how the patients fare when they are back in their localities and what alternate strategies of healing they are likely to pursue. In the neighborhoods I studied, some were indeed devoted followers and visited the Balaji temple once a month. Others had visited Balaji as well as other famed places, such as Badaun, where a Muslim healer operates in a *dargah*. Sometimes they found relief at such places, whereas at other times they found that other strategies, such as medication, worked better. See Veena and Ranendra K. Das, "How the Body Speaks," in *Subjectivity: Ethnographic Investigations*, ed. Joao Biehl, Byron Good, and Arthur Kleinman (Berkeley: University of California Press, 2007), 66–98.

20. The critique of idolatry is of course common to Judaism, Christianity, and Islam, but the incorporation of the prohibition on graven images cannot be assumed to function in a similar manner in all three political theologies. For one thing, one would have to ask: What is the total set within which the destruction of idols is placed? If, e.g., the destruction of idols (iconoclasm), the destruction of words (blasphemy), and the destruction of people (as in some version of crusades, jihad, etc.) belong to one set of practices, how would this compare with Hindu practices of rendering idols lifeless, using words to harm, and the impossibility of *dharmayudh*, or righteous war after

the great war of Kurukshetra? These questions are so large that they require an entire project of comparison.

21. See Veena and Ranendra K Das, "How the Body Speaks."

22. The terms *uppari chakkar* and *uppari hawa* (referring to a wind blowing above) can be traced, I think, to the Islamic idea that djinns move between earth and the first of the seven skies. I have not heard any Hindu explain it in these terms, but several popular texts on djinns or on supernatural afflictions draw upon this idea.

23. For Sontheimer, all five components of Hinduism—namely, the Brahmanical tradition, the ascetic tradition, tribal religions, folk religions, and *bhakti*—are present in the different aspects of any particular cult. See Sontheimer, "Hinduism."

24. I am aware that not all forms of dealing with the occult are forms of *tantra* and that there is a kind of definitional vertigo in the deployment of this term. Thus, even with my limited knowledge I can state that Saraswati is neither a scholar of *tantra* nor has he followed the strict rules of initiation and learning; his vocabulary is sprinkled with terms from *tantra* such as the use of specific syllables as mantras. It is also interesting that people in the community do refer to him as a Tantric, in addition to other terms, whereas for various others they use the more vernacular terms *ojha* or *bhagat*, which refer to healers or others engaged in occult practices who are not formally educated in the Sanskritic traditions.

25. The deleterious effects of this on the health of the urban poor are examined in Jishnu Das and Jeffrey Hammer, "Strained Mercy: The Quality of Medical Care in Delhi," *Economic and Political Weekly* 39, no. 9 (2006): 951–65.

26. For an exposition of the idea of *darshan*, see Diana Eck, *Darśan: Seeing the Divine Image in India* (Chambersburg, Pa.: Anima Books, 1981).

27. This particular motif recalls the mythic sage Durvasa, whose words could never be taken back, so that one had to be absolutely certain that he did not utter any words that, intentionally or not, could become a curse.

28. The term *sattvik* refers to the *guna*, or quality, of peace, purity, and a sense of calm. It is the first *guna* among the triad of *rajas* and *tamas*. For an exposition of the triadic structure of *gunas*, see Veena Das, "Paradigms of Body Symbolism: An Analysis of Selected Themes in Hindu Culture," in *Indian Religion*, ed. Richard Burghart and Audrey Cantlie. See esp. p. 187.

29. Needless to say, the elaboration of both these deities in the various Tantric texts is extremely complex. It is interesting that, at the local level, the division between the two types of meditation has been mapped onto the difference between *rajasik* and *sattvik gunas*. Whereas Kali, along with the nine other female deities known as *vidyas*, is associated with Tantric practices primarily in Bengal, Fredrick Smith observes that Hanuman has emerged as one of the primary deities for possession in India, especially in his five-faced form.

30. These terms are not exclusive to Tantric worship. In other contexts I might have simply said "Hindu tradition."

31. For an excellent analysis of the practice of Ayurveda in contemporary India, see Jean M. Langford, *Fluent Bodies: Ayurvedic Remedies for Postcolonial Imbalance* (Durham, N.C.: Duke University Press, 1998).

32. The more appropriate word for those seeking consultations might have been *clients*, but Saraswati used the English word *patient* for them, though he interspersed it with *zaruratmand* ("those in need").

33. The same question arises in the Purvamimamsa when opponents object to the fact that the ritual procedures explicitly allow for the fact that these techniques might be used to harm someone. The defenders state that such procedures belong to a class of sacrificial rituals that are

geared to satisfying the desire of the individual (*purushartha*) and are not obligatory. These rituals are to be distinguished from those that are prescribed in order to maintain the cosmos and hence emphasize the act rather than the person (*kratvartha*). See Veena Das, "The Language of Sacrifice." For the distinction between prescribed and optional sacrifice, see K. Yoshimuza, "The Dual Significance of a Periodical Sacrifice: Nitya and Kama from the Mimamsa Viewpoint," *Journal of Indian Philosophy* 80 (2006): 189–209.

34. See Robert Délige, "The Myths of Origin of the Indian Untouchables," *Man* n.s. 28, no. 3 (1983): 533–49. Délige points out that these origin myths refer to some kind of cosmic error, as a result of which some upper castes fall into untouchable status—the fall is never attributed to a moral fault.

35. The characterization of Bhairav as a fierce form of Shiva is Nathu Ram's characterization of what possesses him. The story of Bhairav is more complex. Like many other deities, Bhairavas relate both to Shiva and to the goddesses in complex ways, in the manner of demonlike devotees. The Sanskrit term *Bhairav* has the vernacular counterpoints *Bhairon* and *Bahiron Dev*—names used in many village-level cults.

36. On the problem posed by Bhairon's act of severing Brahma's fifth head, see Elizabeth-Chalier Visuvalingam, "Bhairav's Royal Brahminicide: The Problem of the Mahabrahmana," in *Criminal Gods and Demon Devotees: Essays on the Guardians of Popular Hinduism*, ed. A. Hieltebetel (Albany: State University of New York Press, 1989), 157–229. *Bhairav* is the sanskritized form of *Bhairava*.

The Hindu trinity—Brahma, Vishnu, and Mahesh—corresponds to the triadic structure of Brahmin, King, and renouncer, the three major figures around which social and cosmic order can be arranged. See Veena Das, *Structure and Cognition: Aspects of Hindu Caste and Ritual* (Delhi: Oxford University Press, 1976).

37. John R. Bowen, "Imputations of Faith and Allegiance: Islamic Prayer and Indonesian Politics Outside the Mosque," in *Islamic Prayer Across the Indian Ocean: Inside and Outside the Mosque* (Richmond, Surrey: Curzon Press), 23–39.

38. Steven Caton, "What Is an 'Authorizing Discourse'?" in *Powers of the Secular Modern: Talal Asad and His Interlocutors*, ed. David Scott and Charles Hirschkind (Palo Alto, Calif.: Stanford University Press, 2006), 31–57.

39. Frederick Smith, *The Self Possessed*.

40. Ariel Glucklich, *The Sense of Adharma* (New York: Oxford University Press, 1994). In 1974, David Kinsley noted the theme of divine madness, in which either a particular attribute or a body part takes on an independent life and becomes uncontrolled, like the fifth head of Brahma in the Bhairav myth. Kinsley, however, simply suggests that the theme of divine madness shows that gods are not bound by limits and hence affirms their transcendence. This does not, however, touch upon the kind of questions of experience that we encountered in the life worlds of the two healers we have discussed, nor the way in which *dharma* and *adharma*, belief and doubt, are closely linked in the issues regarding the authorization of tradition.

41. I am aware that for many scholars the categories of religion and philosophy remain entirely distinct. They would find my move between philosophical questions concerning language and everyday experience of religion to be fraught with many problems. Friehelm Hardy, e.g., states: "writing the religious history of India is not the same as writing the history of its philosophy. Philosophy operates at a sophisticated level of a cultural superstructure and thus allows for the assumption of an overall coherent discussion. Religion, on the other hand, operates at a whole host of different levels, and in different quarters, and must be regarded as multidimensional and multidirectional" (Hardy, "A Radical Reassessment of the Vedic heritage," in *The Oxford India Hinduism Reader*, ed.

Vasudha Dalmia and Heinrich von Stietencron [Delhi: Oxford University Press, 2007], 45n5). My own view is that philosophical reflection is not the prerogative of scholars located in universities or authorized "schools" of thought and that there ought to be ways in which we can recognize the grounding of many kinds of experiences in philosophical thought. See Veena Das, *Life and Words: Violence and the Descent into the Ordinary* (Berkeley: University of California Press, 2007).

Jean-Luc Marion, Metaphyics and Phenomenology: A Relief for Theology

NOTE: This essay first appeared in *Critical Inquiry* 20, no. 4 (1994): 572–91. It is reprinted here with the permission of the University of Chicago Press.

1. Blaise Pascal, "Mémorial," *Oeuvres complètes de Pascal*, ed. Jacques Chevalier (Paris: Gallimard, 1954), 554.

2. Thomas Aquinas, "Proemium Sancti Thomas," in *Librum Primum Aristotelis de Generatione et Corruptione, Expositio*, in *Aristotelis Libros—De Caelo et Mundo, De Generatione et Corruptione, Meteorologicorum—Expositio*, ed. Raymondo M. Spiazzi (Taurini: Marietti, 1952), 315.

3. Francisco Suárez, "Proemium," *Disputationes Metaphysicae*, 2 vols., vol. 25 of *Opera Omnia*, ed. C. Berton (1866; Hildesheim: G. Olms, 1965), 1:2. See also: "Therefore, this science, which treats these special objects, likewise considers all predications; it (this science) also treats those things that are similarly predicated of other things. This as a whole is metaphysical doctrine" (1:25).

4. On the history of this doctrine, see, in addition to the recent work of Jean-François Courtine, *Suárez et le système de la métaphysique* (Paris: Presses Universitaires de France, 1990; esp. pt. 4), that of Ernst Vollrath, "Die Gliederung der Metaphysik in eine *Metaphysica generalis* und eine *Metaphysica specialis*," *Zeitschrift für philosophische Forschung* 16, no. 2 (1962): 258–83.

5. Such is the scope of the famous declaration, whose radical and complex nature is nevertheless often underestimated: "And the proud name of an ontology that claims to supply, in a systematic doctrine, an a priori knowledge of things in general [*überhaupt* or *in communi*] (e.g., the principle of causality), must give place to the modest name of a simple analytic of pure understanding" (Immanuel Kant, *Kritik der reinen Vernunft*, 2d ed., vol. 3 of *Kants Werke* [1787; Berlin: Walter de Gruyter, 1968], 207 [A247/B304]; trans. Norman Kemp Smith under the title *Immanuel Kant's Critique of Pure Reason* [London: Macmillan, 1964], 264, trans. modified). See also 546 [A845/B873]; 661. Of course, it would remain to be known whether *ontologia*, in its historical acceptation (from Goclenius to Johann Clauberg), ever claimed to accomplish anything more and anything other than a "simple analytic of pure understanding," since it never claimed being as its object, but only the *cogitabile* (see the documents gathered in Courtine, *Suárez et le système de la métaphysique*, 246–93, 422–35). Has the hypothesis ever been taken seriously that "ontology," understood historically, never dared to confront being as such? Would this fact not have to call into question the immediate possibility of a science of being that would not, first, be a science of being as thinkable and therefore a submission of the *ens in quantum ens* to representation? Would one not have to be amazed that the very term *ontologia* remained unknown to Aristotle and the medievals and was established only by the moderns, in a situation that was explicitly assumed to be Cartesian? See Johann Clauberg, *Metaphysica de ente, Quae rectius Ontosophia* (1664), in *Opera Omnia Philosophica*, ed. Johann Schalbruch, 2 vols. (1691; Hildesheim: G. Olms, 1968), 1:283–340, esp, sec. 8, 283 n.c.

6. Martin Heidegger, *Identität und Differenz* (Pfullingen: G. Neske, 1957), 66–67; trans. Joan Stambaugh under the title *Identity and Difference* (New York: Harper & Row, 1969), 68, trans. mod.

7. Ibid., 68/69.

8. Friedrich Nietzsche, "Die 'Vernunft' in der Philosophie," *Götzen-Dämmerung oder Wie man mit dem Hammer philosophiert*, in *Nietzsches Werke: Kritische Gesamtausgabe*, ed. Giorgio Colli and Mazzino Montinari (Berlin: Walter de Gruyter, 1967–91), 6:3:70; trans. Walter Kaufmann under the title "'Reason' in Philosophy," *Twilight of the Idols; or, How One Philosophizes with a Hammer*, in *The Portable Nietzsche*, ed. Kaufmann (New York: Viking Penguin, 1982), 481.

9. Nietzsche, "Ende 1886–Frühjahr 1887" (7[54]), in *Nachgelassene Fragmente*, vol. 8 of *Nietzsches Werke*, 1:320–21, and *Der Wille zur Macht: Versuch einer Umwertung aller Werte* (Stuttgart, 1980), sec. 617, 418–19; trans. Kaufmann and R. J. Hollindale under the title *The Will to Power* (New York: Vintage, 1967), 330.

10. There are several ways to deny the "end of metaphysics." It can be a matter of postulating that "metaphysics" remains identical with itself, without any real history. But then one runs the risk either of repeating the presuppositions of nihilism without recognizing them (thus Blondel, with the philosophy of will, and Schopenhauer) or of producing ahistorically a philosophy that was never professed (thus Maritain, inserting an "intuition of Being" into the text of Aquinas for the needs of current existentialism; thus Cohen and Natorp for the "return to Kant"). Or, more positively, one runs the risk of having to reconstruct an author against the unanimous tradition that claims him as its own by deforming him (Gilson for St. Thomas). Or, on the contrary, it can be a matter of attempts at "overcoming" metaphysics that reproduce without knowing it (or without wanting to know it) metaphysics' most classic thesis and aporias—thus Carnap and the first logical positivism rediscovering the difficulties of empiricism.

11. Jean-Luc Marion, "La fin de la fin de la métaphysique," *Laval théologique et philosophique* 42 (Feb. 1986): 23–43.

12. Aristotle, *De Anima*, ed. W. D. Ross (Oxford: Oxford University Press, 1956), 72 (3.5.430a18); Aquinas, *Existence and Nature of God*, vol. 2 of pt. 1, *Summa Theologiae* [Latin and English], trans. and ed. Thomas McDermott (London: Eure & Spottiswoode, 1989), question 3, art. 2, 24; René Descartes, "Responsio Authoris ad Primas Objectiones," *Meditationes de Prima Philosophia* (Amsterdam, 1642), 108–31; and G. W. F. Leibniz, *Principes de la nature et de la grâce fondés en raison*, ed. André Robinet (Paris: Presses Universitaires de France, 1954), sec. 8, 45.

13. Edmund Husserl, Introduction, *Logische Untersuchungen*, 2 vols. (Halle: M. Niemeyer, 1922), 2:1:19; trans. J. N. Findlay under the title *Logical Investigations*, 2 vols. (London: Routledge & Kegan Paul, 1970), 1:263, trans. mod.

14. Edmund Husserl, *Ideen zu einer reinen Phänomenologie und phänomenologischen Philosophie: Erstes Buch, Allgemeine Einführung in die reine Phänomenologie*, vol. 3 of *Husserliana: Edmund Husserl Gesammelte Werke* (The Hague: Martinus Nijhoff, 1976), pt. 1, 51; trans. F. Kersten under the title *Ideas Pertaining to a Pure Phenomenology and to a Phenomenological Philosophy: First Book, General Introduction to a Pure Phenomenology* (The Hague: Martinus Nijhoff, 1982), 44, and W. R. Boyce Gibson under the title *Ideas: General Introduction to a Pure Phenomenology* (1931; London: Collier-Macmillan, 1969), 92, trans. mod. [*Source de droit* (source of right or rightful, legitimate source) is the French rendering here of Husserl's German *Rechtsquelle*, which Gibson gives as "source of authority" and which Kersten translates as "legitimizing source"—Trans.]

15. [The French here is *au principe*. Playing on the biblical *in principio*, the passage refers to Husserl's discussion in *Ideas*, sec. 24, of the "genuine sense" of *principium*—Trans.]

16. See Aristotle, *The Metaphysics*, trans. Hugh Tredennick, 2 vols. (Cambridge: Harvard University Press, 1933–36), 1:208–9 (5.1.1012b34).

17. I willingly adopt a formula that Levinas advances only with reservation: "Phenomenology is only a radical mode of experience" (Emmanuel Levinas, *Le temps et l'autre* [St. Clement: Fata Morgana, 1979], 34; trans. Richard Cohen as *Time and the Other* [Pittsburgh: Duquesne University Press, 1987]).

18. One therefore would not have to speak of a (real or supposedly threatening) "general metaphysics" in Husserl, contrary to Dominique Janicaud, *Le tournant théologique de la phénoménologie française* (Paris, Éditions de l'Éclat, 1991, 43; trans. Bernard G. Prusak under the title "The Theological Turn in French Phenomenology," in *Phenomenology and the "Theological Turn,"* ed. Dominique Janicaud et al. [New York: Fordham University Press, 2000], 58), but rather generalize the conclusion of my analysis of the Husserlian "I without Being [*Je sans l'être*]" in *Réduction et donation: Recherches sur Husserl, Heidegger et la phénoménologie* (Paris: Presses Universitaires de France, 1989), 240; trans. Thomas A. Carlson under the title *Reduction and Givenness: Investigations of Husserl, Heidegger, and Phenomenology* (Evanston, Ill.: Northwestern University Press, 1998), and thus radically confirm my *Dieu sans l'être: Hors-texte* (Paris: Arthème Fayard, 1982); trans. Thomas A. Carlson under the title *God Without Being* (Chicago: University of Chicago Press, 1991).

19. See also my *Réduction et donation*, 280–89.

20. Heidegger, *Sein und Zeit* (Tübingen: Max Niemeyer, 1963), sec. 7, 38; trans. John Macquarrie and Edward Robinson under the title *Being and Time* (New York: Harper & Row, 1962), 62; and Aristotle, *The Metaphysics*, 1:456 (9.8.1050.a3–5).

21. ["The given of Being [*le donné d'être*] defines every being as "a being-given [*un étant-donné*]." With the hyphenation of *étant-donné*, which is translated as *being-given*, Marion creates a single term that resonates on several levels. On the one hand, one can read the simple construction wherein a noun, *l'étant* or *un étant*, is modified by an adjective, *donné*, thus yielding "the given being" or "a given being." On the other hand, one can also read the common French locution *étant donné (que)*, which in its normal usage means "being given (that)" or "seeing that." Phenomenology allows one to think the being-given in every given being, and thus the precedence of donation over beings and their Being. The term *donation* itself can convey at least three interrelated senses: giving, givenness, and the given—Trans.]

22. Plato, *The Republic*, trans. Paul Shorey, 2 vols. (Cambridge: Harvard University Press, 1956), 2:106 (6.9.509b8–9). I am obviously taking up a direction of research that was opened by Levinas in *Totalité et infini: Essai sur l'extériorité* (The Hague: Martinus Nijhoff, 1961; trans. Alphonso Lingis under the title *Totality and Infinity: An Essay on Exteriority* [The Hague: Martinus Nijhoff, 1979), and especially in *Autrement qu'être ou au-delà de l'essence* (The Hague: Martinus Nijhoff, 1974; trans. Lingis under the title *Otherwise than Being, or Beyond Essence* [The Hague: Martinus Nijhoff, 1981]). But it seems to me that this thesis can be generalized to all intuitive donation and therefore, according to Husserl, to all phenomenality without exception.

23. Nietzsche, *Also sprach Zarathustra: Ein Buch für Alle und Keinen*, vol. 6, pt. 1 of *Nietzsche Werke*, 5–6; trans. Thomas Common under the title "The Three Metamorphoses," *Thus Spoke Zarathustra*, vol. 11 of *The Complete Works of Friedrich Nietzsche*, ed. Oscar Levy (New York: Macmillan, 1916), 25–27. For a justification of this allusive judgment, see my study "L'effrondrement des idoles et l'affirmation du divin: Nietzsche," *L'idole et la distance: Cinq études* (Paris: Bernard Grasset, 1977), 49–105; trans. Thomas A. Carlson under the title "The Collapse of the Idols and Confrontation with the Divine," in Marion, *The Idol and Distance* (New York: Fordham University Press, 2001), 27–78.

24. This slogan, moreover, could also translate the *Prinzip der Voraussetzungslosigkeit*. On this debate, see the arguments of Jean-Louis Chrétien, *L'Appel et la réponse* (Paris: Minuit, 1992; trans. Anne A. Davenport under the title *The Call and the Response* [New York: Fordham University Press, 2004]), and of Michel Henry, "Parole et religion: La Parole de Dieu," in *Phénoménologie et théologie*, ed. Jean-Louis Chrétien et al. (Paris: Criterion, 1992), 129–60; trans. Jeffrey L. Kosky under the title "Speech and Religion: The Word of God," in *Phenomenology and the "Theological Turn,"* ed. Janicaud et al., 217–241. On the question of phenomenological method, I take as my own this remark

by Didier Franck: "Such a method goes beyond the strict framework of descriptive phenomenology, all the while finding support in it. But was this not already the case with the Husserlian analyses of time, of the other, and of the body, and is not phenomenology, from turn to turn, characterized by the fact that it does not cease to distance itself from itself and that these distances end up in a certain way belonging to it?" (Didier Franck, "Le corps de la différence," *Philosophie*, no. 34 [April 1992]: 86).

25. [For a discussion of the *interloqué*, see Marion, "L'Interloqué," trans. Eduardo Cadava and Anne Tomiche, in *Who Comes after the Subject?* ed. Cadava, Peter Connor, and Jean-Luc Nancy (New York: Routledge, 1991)—Trans.]

26. [Marion is here using the psychological term *secondarité*, which "is said of persons in whom present circumstances do not immediately provoke any reactions and who constantly refer to their past and to their future" (*Robert*)—Trans.]

27. See Husserl, *Ideen* 1:1:122. Husserl evokes "God" here explicitly under the figure and in the function of a "ground" (*Grund*; 155).

28. Heidegger, *Identity and Difference*, 57, 70 / 60, 72.

29. See Jacques Derrida, "Comment ne pas parler: Dénégations," in *Psyché: Invention de l'autre* (Paris: Galilée, 1987), 535–95; trans. Ken Frieden under the title "How to Avoid Speaking: Denials," in *Languages of the Unsayable*, ed. Sanford Budick and Wolfgang Iser (New York: Columbia University Press, 1989), 3–70. Here denial [*dénégation*] has nothing to do with a dogmatic negation, leaves the status of prayer open, and, in a paradoxical fashion, maintains the play of the "divine names."

30. F. Laruelle suggests that I could hardly avoid this conclusion in his otherwise pertinent and constructive remarks in "L'appel et le phénomène," *Revue de métaphysique et de morale* 96 (Jan.-Mar. 1991): 27–41.

31. [*L'étant-abandonné*. Here as elsewhere, Marion appeals to the resonance of the given (*donné*), in the abandoned (*abandonné*)—Trans.]

32. [In this context, the obsolete English term *to evoid* ("to clear out, empty out, remove"), in conjunction with the common *to void*, nicely translates the French *évider* ("to hollow out") in its relation to *vider* ("to empty, vacate, void")—Trans.]

33. Pascal, "Mémorial," 554.

34. See my essay "Le phénomène saturé," in *Phémenénologie et théologie*, ed. Chrétien et al., rpt. in *Le visible et le révélé* (Paris: Cerf, 2005); trans. Thomas A. Carlson under the title "The Saturated Phenomenon," in *Phenomenology and the "Theological Turn*," ed. Janicaud et al., 176–216.

35. This distinction was very shrewdly noted by Derrida in a text dedicated to Jan Patočka but above all to Christian "logic": "It needs to think the possibility of such an event [revelation], but not the event itself. A major difference that allows one to hold such a discourse without reference to religion as established dogmatics and to propose thinking a genealogy of the possibility and of the essence of the religious that is not an article of faith. . . . The difference here is subtle and unstable, and it would require shrewd and vigilant analyses. On several accounts and in diverse senses, the discourses of Levinas and Marion, and perhaps even Ricoeur, share this situation with that of Patočka; [namely, of offering a] nondogmatic doublet of dogma . . ., in any case *thinking*, which 'repeats' without religion the possibility of religion" (Jacques Derrida, "Donner la mort," in *L'éthique du don: Jacques Derrida et la pensée du don*, ed. Jean-Marie Rabaté and Michael Wetzel [Paris: Métalié-Transition, 1992], 52). My only disagreement has to do with the identification of this "doublet" indifferently as "philosophical, metaphysical"; when it is matter of thinking the possibility, and especially the radical possibility, of the impossible itself, phenomenology alone is suitable—and not at all metaphysics, which is a thought of actuality par excellence.

Emmanuel Levinas and France Guwy, What No One Else Can Do in My Place: A Conversation with Emmanuel Levinas

NOTE: This text transcribes a conversation France Guwy had with Emmanuel Levinas in 1985. A part of this conversation was aired in Holland by the ecumenical television station IKON.

1. [This paragraph plays on the double meaning of the French verb *regarder*: to look at and to regard or concern—Trans.]

2. [Guwy has conflated several passages from Levinas here, most of which are on p. 30 of *Totality and Infinity*, trans. Alphonso Lingis (Pittsburgh: Duquesne University Press, 1969)—Trans.]

Jacques Derrida, Abraham, the Other

NOTE: This essay was originally published in Bettina Bergo, Joseph Cohen, and Raphael Zagury-Orly, eds., *Judeities: Questions for Jacques Derrida*, trans. Bettina Bergo and Michael B. Smith (New York: Fordham University Press, 2007), 1–35. That book is an abridgment of Cohen and Zagury-Orly, eds., *Judéités: Questions pour Jacques Derrida* (Paris: Gailiée, 2003), in which the essay, in French, appears on pp. 11–42.

1. Franz Kafka, "Abraham," trans. Clement Greenberg, in *Kafka: Paradoxes and Parables* (New York: Schocken Books, 1958), 40–45.

2. [Since Derrida has offered the phrase *plus d'une langue* provisionally to define deconstruction, the difficulty of translating its form and derivatives has been noted by commentators and translators. *Plus d'un*—a recurring phrase in Derrida—reinscribes this difficulty as well. "More than one, no more than one, no longer one, and one no more, the One no more, no one no more" are some of the possibilities that will have to be kept in mind here—Trans.]

3. [Jacques Derrida, *Donner la mort* (Paris: Galilée, 1999), translated by David Wills as *The Gift of Death* (Chicago: University of Chicago Press, 1995)—Trans.]

4. [Respectively, President and Director of the Jewish Community Center of Paris, where the Judéités conference took place—Trans.]

5. [These two words are in English in the original—Trans.]

6. Y. H. Yerushalmi, *Freud's Moses: Judaism Terminable and Interminable* (New Haven, Conn.: Yale University Press, 1991).

7. [As Derrida makes clear in the way he deploys the phrase, *garder du judaïsme* can be read as "keeping, conserving, or protecting Judaism," as well as "keeping or protecting (someone, something) *from* Judaism." The reflexive form—*se garder*—functions in a similar way. Hence, *je me garde du Judaïsme* would perhaps first be read as "I keep Judaism at bay," but can just as well be read as "I keep some Judaism for myself." *L'un se garde de l'autre* is another instance of such rhetorical complexity—Trans.]

8. [*Argumentaire* is not simply an argument, but arguments advanced in order to sell something—Trans.]

9. Jacques Derrida, "Circumfession," in Geoffrey Bennington and Jacques Derrida, *Jacques Derrida* (Chicago: University of Chicago Press, 1993), 154, trans. modified.

10. Jean-Paul Sartre, *Réflexions sur la question juive* (Paris: Gallimard, 1954), 83–84; translated by George J. Becker as *Anti-Semite and Jew* (New York: Schocken Books, 1948), 69. The translation

has been slightly altered here because my edition includes a strange and significant typo: one reads, "une homme: le Juif est une homme [the Jew is a—female article—man]." All further references to this work will be given in the text, with English page number followed by the French pagination.

11. [Trans. slightly modified—Trans.]

12. [The English translation here has "ugly and upsetting" (75)—Trans.]

13. [This last phrase, "et le respect qu'ils lui portent est empoisonné" was omitted from the English translation—Trans.]

14. Respectively, in December 1945 in *Les temps modernes*, and in 1946 with editor Paul Morihien.

15. Alain Finkielkraut, *The Imaginary Jew*, trans. Kevin O'Neill and David Suchoff (Lincoln: University of Nebraska Press, 1994).

16. Freud, "Preface to the Hebrew Translation," in *Totem and Taboo*, quoted in Yerushalmi, *Freud's Moses*, 14.

17. See Jacques Derrida, *Archive Fever: A Freudian Impression*, trans. Eric Prenowitz (Chicago: University of Chicago Press, 1995), 75 ff.

Henri Atlan, From French Algeria to Jerusalem: An Itinerary

1. Shlomo Heykhil Eliashoff, *Sefer hada'at-Lechem, shebo vehahlama* (Odessa 1912; rpt. Jerusalem: Hahayim vehashalom, 1977), "On the Tree of Knowledge," siman 8, p. 296; "On the World of Tohu," 2d pt. p. 147, darush 4, anaf 18, siman 3.

2. Baruch Spinoza, *Ethics*, pt. II, prop. 44, corollary 2 and proof.

3. Ibid., pt. IV, prop. 14.

4. Ibid., last proposition.

Willemien Otten, Nature as Religious Force in Eriugena and Emerson

1. I will occasionally refer to *natura* as a feminine figure in an attempt to bring out some of the revelatory traits with which she was especially endowed in the twelfth century. See G. D. Economou, *The Goddess Natura in Medieval Literature* (Cambridge: Harvard University Press, 1972).

2. My own recent work has focused to a large extent on the humanist quality of twelfth-century treatises on nature, in which I have tried to emphasize that works like Alain de Lille's *Plaint of Nature* can be seen as an indictment of human nature not primarily for having indulged in sinfulness toward God but for neglecting its inherent ties with nature. To continue laying the groundwork for this view, which has been a constant theme in my recent work (cf. my *From Paradise to Paradigm: A Study of Twelfth-Century Humanism* [Leiden: Brill, 2004]), and to broaden this perspective beyond the medieval period are among the goals of this essay.

3. My conversation with these writers has perforce somewhat of an experimental character, since this essay reflects the start of a larger project. The larger project to which I refer is entitled The Pastness of the Religious Past. It was awarded three-year funding from the NWO as part of its research program The Future of the Religious Past. The main applicant of The Pastness of the Religious Past is M. Burcht Pranger (University of Amsterdam); co-applicants are Stephen G. Nichols (The Johns Hopkins University) and myself.

4. Eriugena has remained apart, with his thought being generally considered an interruption of tradition, whether philosophical or theological. Thus Louis Dupré, *Passage to Modernity: An Essay in the Hermeneutics of Nature and Culture* (New Haven: Yale University Press, 1993), 15–41, does not count Eriugena among his classical and medieval antecedents.

5. See *Iohannis Scotti seu Eriugenae Periphyseon* I 441A, ed. E. Jeauneau (Turnhout: Brepols, 1996), 161, p. 3; trans. *Periphyseon* I, ed. I. P. Sheldon-Williams (Dublin: Dublin Institute for Advanced Studies, 1978), 37.

6. See D. J. O'Meara, "The Concept of *Natura* in John Scottus Eriugena (*De divisione naturae* Book I)," *Vivarium* 19 (1981): 126–45. It is particularly helpful to notice how, according to O'Meara's analysis, Eriugena both sides with and differs from Boethius.

7. I follow the interpretation of O'Meara here. See A. M. S. Boethius, "Contra Eutychen et Nestorium," in *Boethius: Theological Tractates, The Consolation of Philosophy*, ed. and trans. H. F. Stewart, E. K. Rand, and S. J. Tester (Cambridge: Harvard University Press, 1973), 76.

8. See O'Meara, "Concept of Nature," 128, where he points to Cappuyns and Jeauneau as having given proof of Eriugena's use of this work.

9. For a recent evaluation of this work, see Eileen Sweeney, *Logic, Theology, and Poetry in Boethius, Abelard, and Alan of Lille: Words in the Absence of Things* (New York: Palgrave MacMillan, 2006), 22–26.

10. O'Meara still holds that in Eriugena matter, next to God, also transcends the reach of the mind. In Jeauneau's recent edition of *Periphyseon* I, the incomprehensibility is seen as applicable to God alone. Cf. O'Meara, "Concept of Nature," 121n13 with *Periphyseon*, I 443 A; 161, p. 5.

11. See O'Meara, "Concept of Natura," 120–21.

12. Eriugena has a confused sense of universals, which was the Carolingian topic of the day, as demonstrated by J. Marenbon, *Early Medieval Philosophy, 480–1150: An Introduction*, rev. ed. (New York: Routledge, 1988), 65–70. He uses *ousia* as a kind of "qualitative universal," turning the status of the logical tree into a metaphysical one rather than a tree of classes.

13. See J. Marenbon, *From the Circle of Alcuin to the School of Auxerre: Logic, Theology and Philosophy in the Early Middle Ages* (Cambridge: Cambridge University Press, 1981), 28–29, with reference to Augustine, *De Trinitate* 5.1–8.

14. See R. C. Dales, "Discussions of the Eternity of the World During the First Half of the Twelfth Century," *Speculum* 57 (1982): 495–508, esp. 495–96 with reference to Eriugena.

15. See Marenbon, *From the Circle of Alcuin*, 74, 82–83.

16. Cf. n. 12, above. Marenbon tends to see Eriugena's philosophy on the whole as confused.

17. In his recent biography of Augustine, James O'Donnell has attempted such an approach by attempting to reconstruct Augustine's life and ideas while taking his position as a religious icon fully into account. See J. J. O'Donnell, *Augustine: A New Biography* (New York: Harper Collins, 2005), 287–332.

18. Hauréau, Windelband, and Copleston all see him in this way. See the historical survey in D. Moran, *The Philosophy of Johannes Scottus Eriugena: A Study of Idealism in the Middle Ages* (Cambridge: Cambridge University Press, 1989), 84–89, esp. 85n10. His pantheism is sometimes referred to as metaphysical monism.

19. See Moran, *The Philosophy of Johannes Scottus Eriugena*, 212–40.

20. I discuss Moran's position on Eriugena's idealism in "Realized Eschatology or Philosophical Idealism: The Case of Eriugena's *Periphyseon*," in *Ende und Vollendung: Eschatologische Perspektiven im Mittelalter*, ed. J. A. Artsen and M. Pickavé (Berlin: Walter de Gruyter, 2002), 373–87, and "Eriugena, Emerson, and the Poetics of Universal Nature," in *Papers of the International Society for Neoplatonic Conference 2005*, ed. J. Finamore and R. Berchman (New Orleans: Universty Press of

the South, 2007), 147–65. While I do not at all wish to deny the validity of an idealist interpretation of Eriugena, a single-issue reading of the *Periphyseon* is bound to honor its intellectual accomplishment only partially.

21. See n. 5, above.

22. See W. Otten, *The Anthropology of Johannes Scottus Eriugena* (Leiden: Brill, 1991), 66–76.

23. Augustine's sense of temporality is one of the key concepts in the research program The Pastness of the Religious Past, of which my project on nature is a part. It will be treated more fully by M. B. Pranger. See his "Time and Narrative in Augustine's *Confessiones*," *Journal of Religion* 81 (2001): 377–94. On the notion of a present of things past, a present of things present, and a present of things to come, see *Confessiones*, 9.20.26.

24. This is a biblical notion; cf. Genesis 1:26–27. Since books 4 and 5 of the *Periphyseon* are a commentary on the opening chapters of Genesis, this is an important qualification of humanity in the work's anthropological sections.

25. See R. W. Emerson, "Nature," Introduction, in *The Collected Works of Ralph Waldo Emerson*, vol. 1, *Nature, Addresses, and Lectures* (Cambridge: Harvard University Press, 1971), 7.

26. See ibid., 1:10.

27. The following titles by Cavell are all pertinent to my reading of Emerson: *The Claim of Reason: Wittgenstein, Skepticism, Morality, and Tragedy* (Oxford: Oxford University Press, 1979/1999), *The Sense of Walden: An Expanded Edition* (1981; Chicago: University of Chicago Press, 1992); *Conditions Handsome and Unhandsome: The Constitution of Emersonian Perfectionism* (Chicago: University of Chicago Press, 1990); *Emerson's Transcendental Etudes* (Stanford, Calif.: Stanford University Press, 2003). For the present article I have mostly drawn on Cavell's most recent work.

28. See Cavell, *Emerson's Transcendental Etudes*, 20–32 (chap. 2, "An Emerson Mood") and 33–58 (chap. 3, "The Philosopher in American Life [toward Thoreau and Emerson]"). Chap. 2 was earlier published in Cavell, *The Senses of Walden: An Expanded Edition* (1981; Chicago: University of Chicago Press, 1992), 141–60.

29. See Cavell, *Emerson's Transcendental Etudes*, 24, where Cavell applies it to Berkeley, whose idealism did not deny the reality of wood, timber, etc. in the vulgar sense.

30. See n. 2, above.

31. See Cavell, *Emerson's Transcendental Etudes*, 24: "By 'sitting at the feet' of the familiar and the low, this student of Eastern philosophy [i.e., Emerson] must mean that he takes the familiar and the low to be his study, his guide, his guru: as much his point of arrival as of departure."

32. Cf. B. Stock, *Listening for the Text: On the Uses of the Past* (Baltimore: The Johns Hopkins University Press, 1990).

33. Emerson, "Nature," 1:13. Quoted in Cavell, *Emerson's Transcendental Etudes*, 21 and 25.

34. See Friedrich Nietzsche, "Vom Nutzen und Nachteil der Historie für das Leben," in *Sämtliche Werke*, ed. Giorgio Colli and Mazzino Montinari (Berlin: Walter de Gruyter, 1999), 245–334. Despite what one may be inclined to think, Nietzsche actually advocates the uses of all three methods of doing history.

35. In an interesting take on contemporary American history, John Patrick Diggins argues in his biography of Ronald Reagan (*Ronald Reagan: Fate, Freedom, and the Making of History* [New York: Norton, 2006]) in favor of an Emersonian reading of Reagan, as manifest in the "Morning in America" campaign of 1984 and in his intervention to end the Cold War. See the review by Russell Baker, *New York Review of Books* 64, no. 3 (2007): 4–7. One might think of Reagan's 1984 campaign slogan "It's morning in America" in terms of Emersonian presentism.

36. See Emerson, "Nature," 1:13: "How does Nature deify us with a few and cheap elements!" This sentence precedes the one quoted above.

37. Ibid., 1:25.

38. Ibid., 1:25.

39. I refer here to the idea that David Friedrich Strauss, best known for his *Das Leben Jesu*, developed later in life, in part to contradict Schleiermacher's pietist views of Jesus: namely, that ultimately the Christ of the gospels is identical with humanity itself.

40. See Cavell, *Emerson's Transcendental Etudes*, 3, with reference to Emerson's "The Poet."

41. See ibid., 6, 227, 244.

42. Journal Entry, August 18, 1831, in Emerson, *The Heart of Emerson's Journals*, ed. Bliss Perry (1938; New York: Dover, 1958), 46. Quoted in Cavell, *Emerson's Transcendental Etudes*, 7. I follow Cavell's reading of Emerson here.

43. Emerson, "The American Scholar," in *Collected Works*, 1:67. Quoted in Cavell, *Emerson's Transcendental Etudes*, 25, 142.

44. See Emerson, "The American Scholar," 1:52–70, passim.

45. Cf. Emerson's comment in "The American Scholar," 1:66: "It is one soul which animates all men."

46. See n. 26, above.

47. See Emerson, "The American Scholar," 1:55.

48. Cavell sees in Emerson's retrieval of the intimacy with existence an important antidote to skepticism's despair of the world. See Cavell, *Emerson's Transcendental Etudes*, 34.

49. See Emerson, "The American Scholar," 1:66: "Our age is bewailed as the age of Introversion."

50. See R. W. Emerson, "Nature," in *The Collected Works of Ralph Waldo Emerson*. vol. 3, *Essays: Second Series* (Cambridge: Harvard University Press, 1983), 110.

Asja Szafraniec, Inheriting the Wound: Religion and Philosophy in Stanley Cavell

1. Stanley Cavell, *A Pitch of Philosophy* (Cambridge: Harvard University Press, 1996), 60. See also Cavell, *Must We Mean What We Say? A Book of Essays*, updated ed. (Cambridge: Cambridge University Press, 2002).

2. Stanley Cavell, *The Senses of Walden: An Expanded Edition* (1981; Chicago: University of Chicago Press, 1992), 22.

3. When addressing this preoccupation, one is bound to face the question of the nature of the multifaceted phenomenon to which the term *Romanticism* refers. This question, leading directly to the core of Cavell's work, has been raised, among others, by Espen Hammer, Richard Eldridge, Nikolas Kompridis and Simon Critchley, who in various ways have attempted to clarify the issue by linking it to its historical roots in philosophical, political, and literary Romanticism. While undeniably this is where we should look for the major expressions of what is at stake, the fact that Cavell never writes the term with a capital letter suggests that its intended bearing is perhaps significantly broader than the spiritual parameters of a given historical period. It is not unlikely that, as befits a philosopher of ordinary language, Cavell appeals here to the grammar of manifestations of something that is constitutive of our culture, as if *romanticism* were a generic name for our comportment toward the condition of finitude, somewhat like "being-toward-death" in Heidegger.

4. Stanley Cavell, *The Claim of Reason: Wittgenstein, Skepticism, Morality and Tragedy* (Oxford: Oxford University Press, 1979), 467.

5. Ibid., 470.

6. Ibid., 483, my emphasis.

7. Cavell, *Must We Mean What We Say?* 149.

8. Ibid., 139–40.

9. Stanley Cavell, *Philosophy the Day after Tomorrow* (Cambridge: Harvard University Press, 2005), 245–46.

10. Stanley Cavell, *Cities of Words: Pedagogical Letters on a Register of the Moral Life* (Cambridge: Harvard University Press, 2004), 237.

11. Gilles Deleuze, *Nietzsche and Philosophy* (London: Continuum, 1986), 156.

12. Cavell, *Must We Mean What We Say?* 120.

13. Cavell, *The Claim of Reason*, 352, my emphasis.

14. Cavell, *A Pitch of Philosophy*, 89, 102; J. L. Austin, *How to Do Things with Words* (Oxford: Oxford University Press, 1965), 9. I have been told by Helen Tartar that this is an ironic citation from the definition of a sacrament in the Catechism of the *Book of Common Prayer* of the Anglican Church. By incorporating the discourse of Christianity into the founding text of ordinary language philosophy, Austin shows that there is a different way to use the Christian's words (an ironic, blasphemous, and performative way), but this falls outside the scope of the present paper. See also J. Hillis Miller, *Speech Acts in Literature* (Stanford, Calif.: Stanford University Press, 2002), chap. 1, "J. L. Austin," 6–62, esp. 30–31.

15. Cavell, *A Pitch of Philosophy*, 60.

16. Ibid., 125.

17. Cavell, *The Claim of Reason*, 352.

18. Stanley Cavell, *In Quest of the Ordinary: Lines of Skepticism and Romanticism* (Chicago: University of Chicago Press, 1988), 52.

19. Cavell, *The Senses of Walden*, 20.

20. Cavell, *A Pitch of Philosophy*, 121.

21. Stanley Cavell, *Disowning Knowledge in Seven Plays of Shakespeare*, updated ed. (Cambridge: Cambridge University Press, 2003), 73.

22. Stanley Cavell, *Themes Out of School* (Chicago: University of Chicago Press, 1984), 52–53.

23. Cavell, *In Quest of the Ordinary*, 52–53.

24. Cavell, *Disowning Knowledge*, 73.

25. Ibid., 74.

26. Ibid., 55–56. One of the questions Cavell poses in his interpretation of the scene on the heath in *King Lear* is, "Why does Edger wait, on seeing his father blind, and hearing that his father knows his mistake, before revealing himself to him?" "What Edgar does is most directly described by 'avoiding recognition'" (ibid., 54–56). See also Shakespeare, *King Lear*, act 4, scene 1.

27. But then there is an understanding of disowning the self to which Cavell's work is sympathetic, "Emerson's emphasis on writing and thinking as self-abandonment" (Cavell, *A Pitch of Philosophy*, 125).

28. Such sacrifice of power can be extended to total renunciation, and in philosophical terms even to nihilism, i.e., the self-destruction of religion. See Cavell's reading of Beckett in *Must We Mean What We Say?*

29. Cavell, *A Pitch of Philosophy*, 122.

30. Gilles Deleuze, *Nietzsche and Philosophy*, 114.

31. Cavell, *The Claim of Reason*, 351. (Cf. "the fantasy of necessary inexpressiveness.")

32. Stanley Cavell, "Companionable Thinking" (unpublished essay delivered at The Johns Hopkins University, April 2006), 16. To appear in a festschrift for Cora Diamond, ed. Alice Crary. See also Cora Diamond, "The Difficulty of Reality and the Difficulty of Philosophy," in *Reading Stanley Cavell*, ed. Alice Crary (New York: Routledge, 2006), 108.

33. J. M. Coetzee, *The Lives of Animals* (Princeton: Princeton University Press, 1999), 15–69. Coetzee later incorporated these pieces into *Elizabeth Costello: Eight Lessons* (London: Vintage, 2004).

34. Cavell, "Companionable Thinking," 18.

35. Franz Kafka, "A Report to an Academy." URL: http://www.kafka.org (last accessed June 21, 2006).

36. For a use of Freud in reading the situation at the gate of the Law, see Jacques Derrida, "Before the Law," in *Acts of Literature*, ed. Derek Attridge (London: Routledge, 1992), 181–220.

37. Ibid., 193–94.

38. Cavell interprets *Othello* in the Christian tradition, in which "it may be better, but it is not perfect to marry, as St. Paul implies" (*The Claim of Reason*, 487).

39. Ibid., 496.

40. Cavell, "Companionable Thinking," 16.

41. Kafka, "Address to an Academy." Derrida puts it as follows: "in his darkness, [the man] is now aware of a radiance that streams inextinguishably from the gateway of the law. This is the most religious moment of the writing" (Derrida, "Before the Law," 208).

42. Cavell, "Companionable Thinking," 16.

43. Ibid., 19.

A Deconstruction of Monotheism, Jean-Luc Nancy

NOTE: Talk delivered in Cairo, in 2001, at the Centre d'études et de documentation économiques, juridiques et sociales (CEDEJ), and thereafter sent, in a revised version, to an issue of the journal *Dédale*, ed. Abdelwahab Meddeb, forthcoming. Reprinted from Jean-Luc Nancy, *Dis-Enclosure: The Deconstruction of Christianity*, trans. Bettina Bergo, Gabriel Malenfant, and Michael B. Smith (New York: Fordham University Press, 2008), 29–41.

1. [For a print version of this, see *The Nation*, October 22, 2001, online: http://www.thenation.com/doc/20011022/said—Trans.]

2. [See Meister Eckhart, "Of Poverty in Spirit," in *Meister Eckhart: The Essential Sermons, Commentaries, Treatises, and Defense*, trans. Edmund Colledge and Bernard McGinn (New York: Paulist Press, 1981). Hallaj, *Diwan*, trans. Louis Massignon (Paris: Cahiers du Sud, 1955), 83. Hussein ibn Mansur al-Hallaj (857–922 C.E.) was an Arabic-speaking Persian Muslim mystic and poet, popularly known among Muslims as "the martyr of mystical love." As an ecstatic mystic, he was charged with heresy on account of his description of union with God, *ana al-haqq* ("I am the Truth")—Trans.]

3. Ludwig Feuerbach, *The Essence of Christianity*, trans. George Eliot (New York: Harper Torchbooks, 1955), 184.

H. J. Adriaanse, After Theism

NOTE: This article was first published in *Traditional Theism and Its Modern Alternatives,* edited by Svend Andersen, 1994; it is reprinted with the permission of Aarhus University Press.

1. Richard Swinburne, *The Coherence of Theism* (Oxford: Oxford University Press, 1977).

2. Ibid., 1.

3. Swinburne develops a sort of system of divine properties in ibid., 222 ff., however.

4. Ibid., 37.

5. Cf. the remarks in ibid., 87 and 93, on a "sociological and literary survey of what the utterers of theological sentences suppose to be implied by what they say."

6. Ibid., 13.

7. Ibid., 60.

8. Ibid., 71.

9. Ibid., 70.

10. Ibid., 233.

11. Ibid., 272.

12. Anthony Kenny, *The God of the Philosophers* (Oxford: Oxford University Press, 1979), 123.

13. Swinburne, *Coherence*, 274.

14. Ibid., 61.

15. Cf. ibid., 5, 71, 279, 296, etc., where Swinburne says that the question whether there are good grounds for supposing the truth of coherence claims lies outside the scope of his book.

16. Richard Swinburne, *The Existence of God* (Oxford: Oxford University Press, 1979), esp. 116–32.

17. J. L. Mackie, *The Miracle of Theism: Arguments for and Against the Existence of God* (Oxford: Oxford University Press, 1982), esp. 95–101.

18. In distinguishing two main objections in Mackie's argument, I follow Wolfgang Stegmüller's report of it in his *Hauptströmungen der Gegenwartsphilosophie: Eine historisch-kritische Einführung* (Stuttgart: A Kröner, 1989), 4:405ff.

19. Peter L. Berger, *The Social Reality of Religion* (London: Faber, 1969); published in the U.S. as *The Sacred Canopy* (Garden City, N.J.: Doubleday, 1969).

20. Berger, *The Social Reality of Religion*, 112.

21. Ibid., 113.

22. Ibid.

23. Ibid., 131.

24. Ibid., 133.

25. Ibid.

26. Ibid.

27. Ibid., 136f.

28. Vincent Brümmer, *Theology and Philosophical Inquiry: An Introduction* (Philadelphia: Westminster, 1982), 134.

29. Berger, *The Social Reality of Religion*, 13 ff., 38 ff.

30. Ibid., 55.

31. Ibid.

32. Ibid., 56.

33. Swinburne, *Coherence*, 1.

34. Cf. H. G. Hubbeling, *Principles of the Philosophy of Religion* (Assen: Van Gorcum, 1987), 76 ff.

35. Stegmüller, *Hauptströmungen*, 4:518.

36. The *Dictionary of the History of Ideas* mentions only the biological sense of the metaphor, which is irrelevant for my purpose. The only philosophical current I know of in which the idea of cultural heritage has been developed is Marxism. We find it in Ernst Bloch, *Erbschaft dieser Zeit*, published in the ominous 1930s (Zürich: Oprecht and Helbling, 1935). An application of this view to the role of religion in culture can be found in his postwar books *Das Prinzip Hoffnung* (Berlin: Aufblau, 1954), esp. 1521 ff., and *Atheismus im Christentum: Zur Religion des Exodus und des Rechts* (Frankfurt a. M.: Suhrkamp, 1968), esp. 260 ff. Jürgen Moltmann published an anthology of Bloch's

texts on religion as Ernst Bloch, *Religion im Erbe: Eine Auswahl aus seinen religionsphilosphischen Schriften* (Munich: Siebenstern Taschenbuch, 1967), in whose preface the notion of heritage is made explicit.

37. Cf. Detlef Liebs, *Lateinische Rechtsregeln und Rechtssprichwörter* (Munich: C. Beck, 1982), p. 22 no. 20; p. 83 no. 8; p. 83 no. 13; p. 151 no. 11.

38. Paul Ourliac and J. de Malafosse, *Droit romain et ancien droit* (Paris: Presses Universitaires de France, 1961), 2:65.

39. I omit the Greek text and use the King James Version.

40. Menno ter Braak, *Verzameld Werk* (Collected Works) (Amsterdam: G. A. van Oorschot, 1980), 3:266.

41. Ibid., 2:167 ff.

42. Ibid., 3:370 ff.

43. Cf. Konrad Feiereis, *Die Umprägung der natürlichen Theologie in Religionsphilosophie: Ein Beitrag zur deutschen Geistesgeschichte des 18. Jahrhunderts* (Leipzig: St. Benno, 1965).

44. Here I wish I had at my disposal an English equivalent of the German word *erörtern*, which means simultaneously "to bring something up," "to discuss," and "to put something in its place" (as it is used in Heidegger).

45. Ter Braak, *Verzameld Werk*, 3:263.

46. Ibid., 3:267 ff.

47. Ibid., 3:377–78.

48. E. Fink, "Les concepts opératoires dans la phénoménologie de Husserl," *Cahiers de Royaumont III* (Paris, 1959), 214–41, esp. 217.

49. Gershom Scholem, *Major Trends in Jewish Mysticism* (New York: Schocken, 1946), 349–50.

50. Cf. Gilbert Ryle, "Thinking and Reflecting" and "The Thinking of Thoughts: What Is *le Penseur* Doing?" in Ryle, *Collected Papers* (London: Hutchinson, 1971), 2:465–96.

51. Ryle, "The Thinking of Thoughts," 2:486.

52. Ryle, "Thinking and Reflecting, 2:473.

53. Ryle, "The Thinking of Thoughts," 2:494.

54. Ibid., 495.

55. Ibid., 483.

56. Wolfgang Trillhaas, *Religionsphilosophie* (Berlin: Walter de Gruyter, 1972), 67, 69, 213, 82–83, 213.

57. Ryle, "Thinking and Reflecting," 2:478 (my emphasis). Ryle continues interestingly: "What he is 'thinly' doing must be in one or more ways and at one or more removes an intention-parasite." And again: "Intention-parasites may pyramid."

58. Ernst Cassirer, *Substanzbegriff und Funktionsbegriff: Untersuchungen über die Grundfrage der Erkentniskritik* (Berlin: B. Cassirer, 1910).

59. Cf. Klaus-Michael Kodalle, *Die Eroberung des Nutzlosen: Kritik des Wunschdenkens und der Zweckrationalität im Anschluß an Kierkegaard* (Paderborn: F. Schöningh, 1988).

60. Jacques Derrida, "Préjugés: Devant la loi," in Jean-François Lyotard et al., *La faculté de juger* (Paris: Minuit, 1985), 87–139; translated by Avital Ronell and Christine Roulston under the title "Before the Law," in Jacques Derrida, *Acts of Literature*, ed. Derek Attridge (New York: Routledge, 1992), 183–220..

61. Cf. esp. Jacques Derrida, "Comment ne pas parler," in Derrida, *Psyche: Inventions de l'autre* (Paris: Galilée, 1987), 535–95; translated by Ken Frieden under the title "How to Avoid Speaking," in *Languages of the Unsayable: The Play of Negativity in Literature and Literary Theory*, ed. Sanford Budick and Wolfgang Iser (New York: Columbia University Press, 1989), 3–70.

62. Cf. Emmanuel Levinas, *De Dieu qui vient a l'idée* (Paris: Vrin, 1982); translated by Bettina Bergo under the title *Of God Who Comes to Mind* (Stanford, Calif.: Stanford University Press, 1998).

63. Cf. Hans-Georg Gadamer, *Das Erbe Hegels* (Frankfurt a. M.: Suhrkamp, 1979), 84.

64. Cf. Jürgen Habermas, *Nachmetaphysisches Denken* (Frankfurt a. M.: Suhrkamp, 1988); translated by William Mark Hohengarten under the title *Postmetaphysical Thinking: Philosophical Essays* (Cambridge: MIT Press, 1992).

65. Cf. Michael Theunissen, *Negative Theologie der Zeit* (Frankfurt a. M.: Suhrkamp, 1991).

66. *Historisches Wörterbuch der Philosophie* (Basel: Schwabe, 1971–2007), 3:319.

67. Theodor W. Adorno, *Negative Dialektik* (Frankfurt a. M.: Suhrkamp, 1966), 356, 395, 390, 392, 398, 393–94.

68. Jean d'Ormesson, *Dieu, sa vie, son oeuvre* (Paris: Gallimard, 1980), 113–16.

Régis Debray, Teaching Religious Facts in Secular Schools

NOTE: In French, this essay originally appeared as Régis Debray, *L'enseignement du fait religieux dans l'école laïque* (Paris: Odile Jacob, 2002); it appears here by permission of the French publisher.

For Debray's use in the original title of the term *le fait religieux*, which can be considered in relation to Durkheim's *fait social* and Mauss's *fait social total*, as well as the discussions of religious phenomena by both authors, see his article "Le 'fait religieux': définitions et problèmes" (http://eduscol.education.fr/D0126/fait_religieux.htm) and his book *Dieu, un itinéraire: Matériaux pour l'histoire de l'éternel en Occident* (Paris: Odile Jacob, 2001); trans. Jeffrey Mehlman under the title *God: An Itinerary* (London: Verso, 2004). I would like to offer thanks to Eve Delmas for help with the translation.—Trans.

1. [These correspond to the American seventh, eighth, ninth, and tenth grades of middle and high school.—Trans.]

2. [Major demonstrations, both for and against state control over private religious schools, took place in Paris in response to the proposed *loi Savary* in 1984 and to the proposed revisions of the *loi Failloux* in 1994—Trans.]

3. Stoicism, like Buddhism, and Platonism, like Spinozism, link the self to the whole and to time. It is simply that the Stoics did not construct clock towers or regulate our solar year. There is, for us Westerners, a Stoic thinking, and this is fortunate; but there are, for better or for worse, cathedrals and calendars, as well as a Judeo-Christian fact that divides believers from nonbelievers and that one cannot hope to efface from our field of practice without taking leave of reality.

4. [In most French schools, music classes are held either during the mid-day break or at the end of the school day—Trans.]

5. [Jules Ferry (1832–93) was minister of public instruction and creator of the "Ferry Laws" establishing free, mandatory, secular education.—Trans.]

6. [*Libre examen*: This term refers to a philosophical attitude opposed to dogmatism, prejudice, and arguments based on authority. It was used by Condorcet in his 1791 *Premier mémoire sur l'instruction publique* (*First Memoir on Public Instruction*). In Protestantism, it refers to the right and ability of every Christian to interpret sacred texts—Trans.]

7. [American ninth grade—Trans.]

8. Athenian citizenship, the birth of Christianity, the Mediterranean in the twelfth century, humanism and the Renaissance, the Revolution and the political experiences of France up to 1851, Europe in transformation in the first half of the nineteenth century.

9. [Corresponding to the sixth and seventh grades of the American school system—Trans.]

10. The École pratique des hautes études, the *grand* establishment of higher education, presided over by M. Jean Baubérot, has three sections: Life and Earth Sciences (Third Section), Historical and Philological Sciences (Fourth Section), and Religious Sciences (Fifth Section). This last, presided over by M. Claude Langlois, had fifty-two directors of study (*directeurs d'études*) and eight senior lecturers (*maîtres de conférences*) in 2001.

11. [This refers to the various degrees of teacher certification recognized by the French educational system. PEGC: Professeur d'Enseignement Général de Collège; PLP: Professeur de Lycée Professionnel.—Trans.]

12. Let us recall the picturesque decree of 9 *Brumaire* year III of the National Convention's committee on public instruction: "As soon as they will have completed in Paris these courses in the art of teaching human knowledge, the expert and philosophical young, who will have received these great lessons, will go repeat them in turn in all the parts of the Republic, which will have called to them; they will open everywhere Écoles normales. This source of light so pure, so abundant, since it will come from the first men of the Republic, of all sorts, pouring out from reservoir to reservoir, will spread out from place to place across all of France, without losing any of its purity in its course."

13. See the report of M. Sartre, July 2001, "L'École pratique des hautes études: Ses missions et les conditions de leur exercice," which recommends reorganizing the EPHE on new bases.

Jan N. Bremmer, Secularization: Notes Toward a Genealogy

1. Talal Asad, *Formations of the Secular: Christianity, Islam, Modernity* (Stanford, Calif.: Stanford University Press, 2003), 25–26.

2. Tertullian: Ismael Roca Meliá, "El campo semántico de saeculum y saecularis en Tertuliano," *Helmantica* 23 (1972): 417–49. Augustine: see, most recently, Gaetano Lettieri, "A proposito del concetto di saeculum nel De civitate Dei," *Augustinianum* 26 (1986): 481–98; Georges Folliet, "L'ambiguïté du concept biblique *aiōn* (*saeculum* vel *aeternum*) dénoncée et interprétée par Augustin," *Wiener Studien* 114 (2001): 575–96.

3. Marta Sordi, "Saeculum come mondo corrotto in latino," in *Kosmos: La concezione del mondo nelle civiltà antiche*, ed. Cristiano Dognini (Alessandria: Edizioni dell'Orso, 2002), 99–104.

4. The best investigations into the concept are: Hermann Lübbe, *Säkularisierung: Geschichte eines ideenpolitischen Begriffs* (Freiburg: K. Alber, 1965); Arend J. Nijk, "Secularisatie" (Ph.D. diss., University of Amsterdam, 1968); Hermann Zabel, "Säkularisation, Säkularisierung III," in *Geschichtliche Grundbegriffe: Historisches Lexikon zur politisch-sozialen Sprache in Deutschland*, ed. Otto Brunner et al. (Stuttgart: E. Klett, 1984), 5:809–29; Olivier Tschannen, *Les théories de la sécularisation* (Geneva: Droz, 1992).

5. Walther von Wartburg, "Saeculum, séculariser," in his *Französisches etymologisches Wörterbuch* (Basel, 1964),11:44–46.

6. Irene Crusius, ed., *Zur Säkularisation geistlicher Institutionen im 16. und im 18./19. Jahrhundert* (Göttingen: Vandenhoeck & Ruprecht, 1996).

7. Denis Diderot and Jean D'Alembert, eds., *Encyclopédie* (Paris, 1765), 14:883–84; Hans-Wolfgang Strätz, "Säkularisation, Säkularisierung II," in *Geschichtliche Grundbegriffe*, ed. Brunner, 5:792–93.

8. Martin Heckel, *Gesammelte Schriften: Staat, Kirche, Recht, Geschichte* (Tübingen: J. C. B. Mohr, 1989), 2:773–911; Strätz, "Säkularisation, Säkularisierung II."

9. Simon Grimm, *De profanatione rei sacrae, vulgò Secularisirung geistlicher Güter* (Giessen, 1687); Strätz, "Säkularisation, Säkularisierung II," 795.

10. For Longueville see, most recently, Anuschka Tischer, *Französische Diplomatie und Diplomaten auf dem Westfälischen Friedenskongress: Außenpolitik unter Richelieu und Mazarin* (Münster: Aschendorff, 1999), 99–105; Derek Croxton, *Peacemaking in Early Modern Europe: Cardinal Mazarin and the Congress of Westphalia, 1643–1648* (Selinsgrove, Pa.: Susquehanna University Press, 1999), index s.v.

11. Johannes G. von Meiern, *Acta Pacis Westphalica publica oder Westphalische Friedens-Handlungen und Geschichte*, 6 vols (Hanover: Cotta, 1734–36), 2:636–37. Strätz, "Säkularisation, Säkularisierung II," 799, seems to me to overinterpret the expression and to neglect the current usage of the verb. In fact, the instant success of the term in Germany contradicts his argument that it was felt to contain an *anti-evangelische Spitze.*"

12. Unlike the French, the Germans did not use *saecularisatio* for the change within monastic orders until the late eighteenth century. Cf. Strätz, "Säkularisation," Säkularisierung II," 807.

13. Erich Mauritius, *De secularizatione bonorum ecclesiasticorum* (Kiel, 1666); Philipp A. Burgold, *Notitia* (Freistadt, 1668) 908 (*secularizare*).

14. Johann H. Zedler, *Grosses vollständiges Universal Lexicon aller Wissenschafften und Künste*, 64 vols (Leipzig, 1732–50), 36:946: "weder ein deutsches, noch gutes Lateinisches Wort."

15. Hans-Otto Binder, "Säkularisation," in *Theologische Realenzyklopädie* (Berlin: Walter de Gruyter, 1998), 29:597–602 (with extensive bibliography); Hartmut Lehmann, "Säkularisation/Säkularisierung II," in *Die Religion in Geschichte und Gegenwart*, 4th ed. (Tübingen: Mohr Siebeck, 2004), 7:776. In 2003 to 2005 there appeared a flood of literature commemorating the impact of the law of 1803 on all kinds of German institutions and cities. Useful introductions are *Säkularisation und Säkularisierung 1803–2003, Essener Gespräche zum Thema Staat und Kirche* (Münster: Aschendorff, 2004); Harm Klueting, ed., *200 Jahre Reichsdeputations-hauptschluss: Säkularisation, Mediatisierung und Modernisierung zwischen Altem Reich und neuer Staatlichkeit* (Münster: Aschendorff, 2005).

16. Karl Marx, *Zur Kritik der hegelschen Rechtsphilosophie* (Paris, 1844), 386.

17. H. Zabel, "Zum Wortgebrauch von 'Verweltlichen/Säkularisieren' bei Paul Yorck von Wartenburg und Richard Rothe," *Archiv für Begriffsgeschichte* 14 (1970): 69–85; idem, "Säkularisation, Säkularisierung III," 817–19; Ulrich Barth, "Säkularisierung I," in *Theologische Realenzyklopädie* (1998), 29: 603–34.

18. Egbert Stolz, "Die Interpretation der modernen Welt bei Ernst Troeltsch" (Ph.D. diss., University of Hamburg, 1979); D. Weidner, "Ernst Troeltsch und das Narrativ 'Säkularisierung,'" *Weimarer Beiträge* 50 (2004): 289–300.

19. Max Weber, *Die protestantischen Sekten und der Geist des Kapitalismus, Gesammelte Aufsätze zur Religionssoziologie* (Tübingen: J.C. B.Mohr, 1906), 1:217.

20. Note that in *Wirtschaft und Gesellschaft*, ed. Johannes Winckelmann (Tübingen: J C. B. Mohr, 1956), 2:409 and 468, Weber speaks of a "*Säkularisierung des Denkens*," whereas in 1:269 (*Max Weber Gesamtausgabe* [Tübingen: J. C. B. Mohr, 2001], 1.22.2:178) he calls the disappearance of revelations among the Aboriginals a "*Säkularisation*," that is, he still uses the term within quotation marks. For Weber, see now Daniel Weidner, "Zur Rhetorik der Säkularisierung," *Deutsche Vierteljahrsschrift für Literaturwissenschaft und Geistesgeschichte* 78 (2004): 95–132.

21. Cf. Max Weber, *Die protestantische Ethik und der Geist des Kapitalismus, Gesammelte Aufsätze zur Religionssoziologie*, 1:24: "Materialismus . . . [ist] die Folge der Säkularisation aller Lebensinhalte durch den Protestantismus."

22. Hugh McLeod, *Piety and Poverty: Working-class Religion in Berlin, London, and New York, 1870–1914* (New York: Holmes & Meier, 1996).

23. Rufus M. Jones, "Secular Civilization and the Christian Task," in *The Christian Life and Message in Relation to Non-Christian Systems of Thought and Life*, Report of the Jerusalem Meeting for the International Missionary Council, March 24 to April 8, 1928, 8 vols. (London: International Missionary Council, 1928), 1:284. For Jones, see Elizabeth Gray Vining, *Friend of Life: The Biography of Rufus M. Jones* (Philadelphia: Lippincott, 1958).

24. Ibid., 402–14, "Account of Discussion."

25. Kurt Nowak, "Zur protestantischen Säkularismus-Debatte um 1930," *Wissenschaft und Praxis in Kirche und Gesellschaft* 69 (1980): 37–51.

26. Lübbe, *Säkularisierung*, 100.

27. Werner Scholz, "Säkularisation, Säkularismus und Entchristlichung: Ein Wort zur Auseinanderhaltung der drei Begriffe," *Zeitschrift für Theologie und Kirche* n.s. 11 (1930): 290–98; Martin Schlunk, "Säkularismus," in *Die Religion in Geschichte und Gegenwart* (Tübingen, 1932), 5:37–39; B. Goldschmidt, "Säkularismus und Säkularisierung: Von der Sinnverwandlung eines Wortes," *Christliche Welt* 47 (1933): 174–76.

28. *Grossen Herder* (Freiburg, 1935), 10:624.

29. For the development of the two terms, see now Hartmut Lehmann, *Säkularisierung: Der europäische Sonderweg in Sachen Religion* (Göttingen: Wallstein, 2004), 36–56.

30. See the studies of Dietrich von Oppen (1958), Joachim Matthes (1962), and T. Rendtorff (1966) in *Säkularisierung,* ed. Heinz-Horst Schrey (Darmstadt: Wissenschaftliche Buchgesellschaft, 1981), 331–91.

31. Hans Blumenberg, *Die Legitimität der Neuzeit* (Frankfurt, 1966); H. Zabel, "Verweltlichung/ Säkularisierung: Zur Geschichte einer Interpretationskategorie" (Ph. D. diss., University of Münster, 1968). For Blumenberg and secularization, see, most recently. Jean-Claude Monod, *La querelle de la sécularisation: Théologie politique et philosophies de l'histoire de Hegel à Blumenberg* (Paris: Vrin, 2002); Jean Greisch, "Les mondes de Hans Blumenberg—Umbesetzung versus Umsetzung: Les ambiguités du théorème de la sécularisation chez Hans Blumenberg," *Archives de Philosophie* 67 (2004): 279–98.

32. See: Hartmut Lehmann, *Protestantisches Christentum im Prozess der Säkularisierung* (Göttingen: Vandenhoeck & Ruprecht, 2001); special issue on secularization of *Praktische Theologie* 2 (2002); Detlet Pollack, *Säkularisierung—ein moderner Mythos?* (Tübingen: J. C. B. Mohr, 2003).

33. Barth, "Säkularisierung I"; Ulrich Ruh, "Säkularisierung," in *Lexikon für Theologie und Kirche* (Freiburg: Herder, 1999), 8:1467–69; Michael Bergunder et al., "Säkularisation/Säkularisierung I-VIII," in *Die Religion in Geschichte und Gegenwart*, 7:774–88; Walter Jaeschke, "Säkularisierung," in *Handbuch religionswissenschaftlicher Grundbegriffe*, ed. Hubert Cancik et al. (Stuttgart: W. Kohlhammer, 2001), 5:9–20.

34. *Grosse Duden* (Mannheim, 1994), 6:2846.

35. Samuel Windsor Brown, *The Secularization of American Education as Shown by State Legislation, State Constitutional Provisions, and State Supreme Court Decisions* (New York: Teachers College, Columbia University, 1912).

36. Pitirim Sorokin, *Social and Cultural Dynamics* (New York: American Book Company, 1937).

37. Robert S. and Helen M. Lynd, *Middletown: A Study in American Culture* (New York: Harcourt, Brace, 1929).

38. Everett C. Hughes, "Personality Types and the Division of Labor," *American Journal of Sociology* 33 (1928): 754–68.

39. H. Becker, "Säkularisationsprozesse," *Kölner Vierteljahreshefte für Soziologie* 10 (1931–32): 283–94, 450–63, trans. under the title "Processes of Secularization," *Sociological Review* 24 (1932):

138–54, 266–86. Note also the title of Becker's unpublished dissertation: "Ionia and Athens: Studies in Secularization" (Ph.D. diss., University of Chicago, 1930).

40. See the survey by Tschannen, *Théories de la sécularisation*, 180–205.

41. José Casanova, "Secularization," in *International Encyclopedia of Social and Behavioral Sciences*, ed. Neil J. Smelser and Paul B. Baltes, (Amsterdam: Elsevier, 2001), 20:13786–91.

42. Hugh McLeod, *Secularization in Western Europe, 1848–1914* (London: Macmillan, 2000), 1.

43. Walter E. H. Lecky, *History of the Rise and Influence of the Spirit of Rationalism in Europe*, 2 vols. (London 1893), 2:99–100. For Lecky see, most recently, Donald McCartney, *W. E. H. Lecky: Historian and Politician, 1838–1903* (Dublin: Lilliput Press, 1994); Benedikt Stuchtey, *W .E. H. Lecky (1838–1903): Historisches Denken und politisches Urteilen eines anglo-irischen Gelehrten* (Göttingen: Vandenhoeck & Ruprecht, 1997).

44. Despite the title, the study by the anthropologist Ernest Gellner, "Puritanism, Secularization and Nationalism in North Africa," *Archives de sociologie des religions*, no. 15 (1963): 71–86, does not discuss the term.

45. David Martin, "Toward Eliminating the Concept of Secularization," in *Penguin Survey of the Social Sciences 1965*, ed. Julius Gould (Harmondsworth, Middlesex: Penguin, 1965), 169–82, rpt. in his *The Religious and the Secular: Studies in Secularization* (London: Routledge & Kegan Paul, 1969), 9–22. For Martin's most recent thoughts on the subject, see his *On Secularization: Toward a Revised General Theory* (Aldershot: Ashgate, 2005).

46. *The Oxford English Dictionary* (Oxford: Oxford University Press, 1989) 14:849–50.

47. Paul Janet, *Victor Cousin et son oeuvre* (Paris: Calman Lévy, 1885), 275, 284, 289, 293.

48. Henz Ramière, ed., "La sécularisation de la philosophie: Première cause de sa décadence, *Études: Revue catholique d'intérêt général* 2 (August 1872): 161; Edmond de Pressensé, 'La sécularisation de l'État dans l'Union américaine," *La revue politique et littéraire* 16 (July 1888): 97.

49. *Trésor de la langue française: Dictionnaire de la langue du XIXe et du XXe siècle (1789–1960)*, vol. 14 (Paris: Didier érudition, 1990).

50. Roger Mehl, "La sécularisation de la cité," in *Le problème de la civilisation chrétienne*, ed. Jean Boisset et al. (Paris: Presses Universitaires de France, 1951), 11–53. It seems significant that Mehl worked in Strasbourg, close to Germany, at the time.

51. Talcot Parsons, "Réflexions sur les organisations religieuses aux États-Unis," *Archives de sociologie des religions* 3 (1957): 21–36; cf. Tschannen, *Théories de la sécularisation*, 195.

52. Marie-Claude Coulon et al., eds., *La sécularisation: Fin ou chance du christianisme?* (Gembloux: J. Duculot, 1970); Marcel Xhaufflaire, *Les deux visages de la théologie de la sécularisation* (Paris: Casterman, 1970) and *Feuerbach et la théologie de la sécularisation* (Paris: Cerf, 1970); Alain Durand, *Sécularisation et présence de Dieu* (Paris: Cerf, 1971); Christian Duquoc, *Ambiguité des théologies de la sécularisation* (Gembloux: J. Duculot, 1972); Enrico Castelli, ed., *Herméneutique de la sécularisation* (Paris: Aubier, 1976). But note also the early study by François-Georges Dreyfus, "La sécularisation dans le Protestantisme alsacien depuis le XIXe siècle," *Revue d'histoire et de philosophie religieuses* 45 (1965): 265–72 (perhaps not by chance by a Strasbourg scholar with links to Protestant Germany).

53. Tschannen, *Théories de la sécularisation*.

Arie L. Molendijk, An Alternative View of Christianity: A Troeltschean Perspective

NOTE: Earlier versions of this text were presented at the conference Religious Master Narratives in Amsterdam in April 2002 and at the annual meeting of the Nineteenth-Century Theology Group of the American Academy of Religion in Philadelphia in November 2005.

1. Jeffrey Cox, "Master Narratives of Long-Term Religious Change," in *The Decline of Christendom in Western Europe, 1750–2000*, ed. Hugh McLeod and Werner Ustorf (Cambridge: Cambridge University Press, 2003), 201.

2. Cf. G. Marramao, "Säkularisierung," in *Historisches Wörterbuch der Philosophie*, ed. J. Ritter and K. Gründer (Darmstadt: Wissenschaftliche Buchgesellschaft, 1992), vol. 8, col. 1133–61.

3. Quoted in J. Milton Yinger, *The Scientific Study of Religion* (New York: Collier MacMillan, 1970), 1.

4. Hermann Lübbe, "Vollendung der Säkularisierung—Ende der Religion?" in Lübbe, *Fortschritt als Orientierungsproblem: Aufklärung in der Gegenwart* (Freiburg i. B.: Rombach, 1975), 169–81, esp. 177–78; Lübbe, *Religion nach der Aufklärung* (Graz: Styria, 1990), 149–78.

5. Norman Davies, Introduction to *Europe: A History* (Oxford: Oxford University Press, 1996).

6. Arie L. Molendijk and Peter Pels, eds., *Religion in the Making: The Emergence of the Sciences of Religion* (Leiden: E. J. Brill, 1998); Molendijk, *The Emergence of the Science of Religion in the Netherlands* (Leiden: E. J. Brill, 2005).

7. Cf. Peter van Rooden, "Secularization and the Trajectory of Religion in the West," in *Post-Theism: Reframing the Judeo-Christian Tradition*, ed. Henri A. Krop, Arie L. Molendijk, and Hent de Vries (Louvain: Peeters, 2000), 169–88, esp. 181; cf. also Molendijk, "A Challenge to Philosophy of Religion," in *Ars Disputandi: The Online Journal for Philosophy of Religion* 1 (2000–2001) http://www.roquade.nl/ad/cgi-bin/2001/index.html.

8. The *Protestant Ethic* was included in the first part of the three volumes of Weber's essays on sociology of religion. On this occasion Weber wrote the preface and added a final note, which both refer to universal history. A translation of the preface is to be found in: Max Weber, *The Protestant Ethic and the Spirit of Capitalism*, trans. T. Parsons (1930; London: Unwin University Books, 1974), 13–31, here 13 (italics original); cf. p. 284, where Weber describes his essays on sociology of religion as "some comparative studies of the general historical relationship [*universalgeschichtliche Zusammenhänge*] between religion and society."

9. To give one example out of the immense literature on Weber: Volker Krech and Gerhard Wagner, "Wissenschaft als Dämon im Pantheon der Moderne: Eine Notiz zu Max Webers zeitdiagnostischer Verhältnisbestimmung von Wissenschaft und Religion," in *Max Webers Wissenschaftstheorie: Interpretation und Kritik*, ed. Gerhard Wagner and Heinz Zipprian (Frankfurt a. M.: Suhrkamp, 1994), 755–99.

10. Wolfgang Schluchter, *Religion und Lebensführung*, 2 vols. (1988; Frankfurt a. M.: Suhrkamp, 1991), 1:989–99.

11. Ernst Troeltsch, *Der Historismus und seine Probleme* (Tübingen: J. C. B. Mohr [Siebeck], 1922), 565–72.

12. Max Weber, "Science as Vocation" ("Wissenschaft als Beruf," 1919), in *From Max Weber: Essays in Sociology*, ed. H. H. Gerth and C. Wright Mills (London: Routledge, 1970), 129–56.

13. Friedrich Wilhelm Graf, "Friendship Between Experts: Notes on Weber and Troeltsch," in *Max Weber and His Contemporaries*, ed. Wolfgang J. Mommsen and Jürgen Osterhammel (London: Unwyn Hyman, 1987), 215–33; Graf, "Distanz und Nähe: Einige Bemerkungen zum 'Weber-Paradigma' in Perspektiven der neueren Troeltsch-Forschung," in *Das Weber-Paradigma: Studien zur Weiterentwicklung von Max Webers Forschungsprogramm*, ed. Gert Albert et al. (Tübingen: Mohr Siebeck, 2003), 234–51.

14. Max Weber, *Wirtschaft und Gesellschaft: Die Wirtschaft und die gesellschaftlichen Ordnungen und Mächte, Nachlaß*, vol. 2: *Religiöse Gemeinschaften*, ed. Hans G. Kippenberg (Tübingen: Mohr Siebeck, 2001), esp. 87, where Kippenberg quotes a letter of Weber to his publisher from December

30, 1913. Weber writes that he has just finished a manuscript on the relationship between economics and forms of community (*Gemeinschaftsformen*), such as the family and religion. A sociology of doctrines of salvation and religious ethics is part of this, and Weber adds that is more or less the same as what Troeltsch had done (presumably in his *The Social Teachings of the Christian Churches*), now extended to "all religions."

15. Troeltsch, *Der Historismus*, 705–6.

16. Many present-day world histories agree with Troeltsch that eurocentric accounts must be avoided, but they also agree that starting with the end of the eighteenth century world events became more interconnected and interdependent, so that attempts to understand the world as a whole do make sense; cf., for a fine specimen of "world history" that does take religion into account, C. A. Bayly, *The Birth of the Modern World, 1780–1914* (Malden, Mass.: Blackwell, 2004).

17. Troeltsch, *Der Historismus*, 765 ff. (*hebräischer Prophetismus, klassisches Griechentum, antiker Imperialismus, abendländisches Mittelalter*); cf. John Higham, *Hanging Together: Unity and Diversity in American Culture*, ed. Carl J. Guarneri (New Haven, Conn.: Yale University Press, 2001).

18. Troeltsch, "Die Krisis des Historismus" (1922), in Troeltsch, *Schriften zur Politik und Kulturphilosophie, Kritische Gesamtausgabe*, vol. 15, ed. Gangolf Hübinger (Berlin: Walter de Gruyter, 2002), 433–55. The historical perspective has, according to Troeltsch, relativistic consequences, which he tried to contain. In any case, it meant a severe blow to "eternal truths" and authority as such. On Troeltsch's historicism, see: Friedrich Wilhelm Graf, ed., *Ernst Troeltschs "Historismus"* (Gütersloh: Gütersloher Verlagshaus, 2000); Friedrich Wilhelm Graf and Hartmut Ruddies, "Ernst Troeltsch: Geschichtsphilosophie in praktischer Absicht," in *Grundprobleme der großen Philosophen: Philosophie der Neuzeit*, ed. Josef Speck (Göttingen: Vandenhoeck & Ruprecht, 1986), 4:128–64; Graf and Ruddies, "Religiöser Historismus: Ernst Troeltsch (1865–1923)," in *Profile des neuzeitlichen Protestantismus*, ed. Graf (Gütersloh: Gütersloher Verlagshaus, 1993), 2.2:295–335.

19. Various books have been written about Troeltsch's view of Christian religions and modernity. See: Gerhold Becker, *Neuzeitliche Subjektivität und Religiosität: Die religionsphilosophische Bedeutung von Heraufkunft und Wesen der Neuzeit im Denken von Ernst Troeltsch* (Regensburg: Pustet, 1982); Egbert Stolz, "Die Interpretation der modernen Welt bei Ernst Troeltsch: Zur Neuzeit- und Säkularisierungsproblematik" (Ph.D. diss., University of Hamburg, 1979); cf. Horst Renz and Friedrich Wilhelm Graf, eds., *Umstrittene Moderne: Die Zukunft der Neuzeit im Urteil der Epoche Ernst Troeltschs*, (Gütersloh: Gütersloher Verlagshaus, 1987); Trutz Rendtorff and Friedrich Wilhelm Graf, "Ernst Troeltsch," in *Nineteenth-Century Religious Thought in the West*, ed. N. Smart et. al. (Cambridge: Cambridge University Press, 1985), 3:305–32.

20. Cf. Arie L. Molendijk, *Zwischen Theologie und Soziologie: Ernst Troeltschs Typen der christlichen Gemeinschaftsbildung: Kirche, Sekte, Mystik* (Gütersloh: Gütersloher Verlagshaus, 1996), 123–31.

21. Troeltsch, "Das Wesen des modernen Geistes" (1907), in *Aufsätze zur Geistesgeschichte und Religionssoziologie* (Tübingen: Mohr [Siebeck], 1925), 336–37; "The Essence of the Modern Spirit," in Troeltsch, *Religion in History* (Minneapolis: Fortress, 1991), 271–72: "the spaciousness of all states and relationships, together with growing populations and improved means of transportation and communication that tend to standardize everything; an individualism that aims at a maximum participation of the individual in the values of life, and a corresponding independence; a secularity that is active chiefly in the positive shaping of the world and that amalgamates the religious values with those of civilization; the tremendous intensification of criticism and of the capacity for scholarly reflection; the astounding technological conquest of nature and its exploitation through a rationalized economy; a humane attitude that looks essentially for the good in humanity and seeks to

develop it; the massive growth of the state, which encompasses every sphere of reality and aims at maximal national unity; a universal vision that stresses continuity and the intrinsic vital unity of the world-process; and, finally and above all, the freedom of an inwardly experienced necessity that opposes all purely external supernatural obligations; that is, moral and intellectual autonomy."

22. Ernst Troeltsch, *Schriften zur Bedeutung des Protestantismus für die moderne Welt (1906–1913), Kritische Gesamtausgabe*, vol. 8, ed. Trutz Rendtorff (Berlin: Walter de Gruyter, 2001); see esp. the main booklet reprinted here: *Die Bedeutung des Protestantismus für die Entstehung der modernen Welt* (1906, 1911), 183–316; trans. as Troeltsch, *Protestantism and Progress: A Historical Study of the Relation of Protestantism to the Modern World* (1912; Philadelphia: Fortress, 1986).

23. Troeltsch, "Das Wesen des modernen Geistes," 332. Cf. Troeltsch, "The Essence of the Modern Spirit," 267.

24. Theodore M. Steeman, "Church, Sect, Mysticism, Denomination: Periodical Aspects of Troeltsch's Types," *Sociological Analysis* 36 (1975): 181–204.

25. For a short overview of the typology, see Troeltsch, "Stoic-Christian Natural Law and Modern Secular Natural Law" (1911), in Troeltsch, *Religion in History*, 321–42, 324–26: "The essence of the church-type is that it considers salvation as something given with the divine decree, as something that in principle is already realized. Independent of personal achievement and perfection, all salvation is based on the grace that has been embodied in the religious community by means of a redemption both finished and consummated. . . . Characteristic [of the sect-type] is its rigoristic demand for an unconditional application of the evangelical ethic and, in particular, of the Sermon on the Mount. . . . it demands the actual overcoming of sin, the living up to the divine commandments; and it believes in the full redemption only of those in whom grace has become a recognizable force supporting the practice of a Christian life. To the sect, the religious community is not a general, all-inclusive institution into which one is born and whose powers of grace reach out by means of the influence of the church, the clergy, and the sacraments. The sect seeks to gather mature and personally convinced Christians into a holy community. . . . Mysticism aims at the immediate, present, and inward quality of religious experience, at the immediate relationship with God that leaps over or complements traditions, cults, and institutions"; cf. Molendijk, *Zwischen Theologie und Soziologie*.

26. Troeltsch, *The Social Teaching of the Christian Churches*, trans. Olive Wyon, 2 vols. (London: George Allen & Unwin, 1931), 729 ff. Troeltsch refers, among other things, to the Fourth Gospel and "Pauline Christ-mysticism" (733). The title of the original book is *Die Soziallehren der christlichen Kirchen und Gruppen, Gesammelte Schriften*, vol. 1 (Tübingen: J. C. B. Mohr, 1912; hereafter GS).

27. Troeltsch, *The Social Teaching*, 1008; GS 1:982.

28. Troeltsch, *Protestantisches Christentum und Kirche in der Neuzeit (1906/1909/1922), Kritische Gesamtausgabe*, vol. 7, ed. Volker Drehsen (Berlin: Walter de Gruyter, 2004); original editions in *Die Kultur der Gegenwart*, ed. Paul Hinneberg, 2d, rev. ed. (Berlin: Teubner, 1909), 341.

29. Ibid., 347–48.

30. Ibid., 535.

31. Troeltsch, *Protestantism and Progress*, p. 41; *Schriften zur Bedeutung des Protestantismus für die moderne Welt*, 232–33; cf. also 226–27.

32. Troeltsch, *Protestantism and Progress*, 43; *Schriften zur Bedeutung des Protestantismus für die moderne Welt*, 235, italics original.

33. Troeltsch, "Calvin and Calvinism" (1909), in: *Schriften zur Bedeutung des Protestantismus für die moderne Welt*, 134.

34. Troeltsch, *The Social Teaching*, 608; GS 1:651: "It is the very essence of the genuine Calvinistic spirit, and it has bred that sober utilitarian, energetic, and methodical purposive humanism

[*Zweckmenschentum*, i.e., goal-oriented type of person] which labors on earth for a heavenly reward, which in its secular form is only too well known to us today."

35. Troeltsch, *The Social Teaching*, 34; GS 1:14.

36. Troeltsch, *Protestantism and Progress*, 38; *Schriften zur Bedeutung des Protestantismus für die moderne Welt*, 230.

37. Troeltsch, *The Social Teaching*, 688; GS 1:790; cf. Troeltsch, *Schriften zur Bedeutung des Protestantismus für die moderne Welt*, 227.

38. Troeltsch, *The Social Teaching*, 714ff.; GS 1:827 ff.; cf. Molendijk, *Zwischen Theologie und Soziologie*, 105–8.

39. Troeltsch, *The Social Teaching*, 715; GS 1:828.

40. Cf. Troeltsch, *Protestantism and Progress*, 68; *Schriften zur Bedeutung des Protestantismus für die moderne Welt*, 267.

41. In this context, the importance of the intimate connection between Calvinism, especially in its "Puritan-Pietist-ascetic" form, and the sects should be noted as well; cf. Troeltsch, *The Social Teaching*, 989n523; GS 1:957fn512: "I believe . . . that through my presentation of the sects, and especially in the clear distinction between mysticism and the sect-type, I have in some particulars made *Weber's* idea [concerning the affinity between Calvinism and the sects, on the one hand, and capitalism, on the other] clearer, and also that through the manifestation of the sectarian elements in primitive Calvinism I have made the fusion of Calvinism with the sect-type more intelligible" (italics original).

42. The work of Georg Jellinek, *Die Erklärung der Menschen- und Bürgerrechte: Ein Beitrag zur modernen Verfassungsgeschichte*, 2d ed. (Leipzig: Duncker & Humblot, 1904), has been extremely important for Troeltsch in this respect; cf. Friedrich Wilhelm Graf, "Puritanische Sektenfreiheit versus lutherische Volkskirche: Zum Einfluß Georg Jellineks auf religionsdiagnostische Deutungsmuster Max Webers und Ernst Troeltschs," *Zeitschrift für Neuere Theologiegeschichte / Journal for the History of Modern Theology* 9 (2002): 42–69.

43. Troeltsch, *Protestantism and Progress*, 68; *Schriften zur Bedeutung des Protestantismus für die moderne Welt*, 268. The last phrase, "altcalvinistische Ideen vom Revolutionsrecht, von der Volkssouveränität und vom christlichen Staat," is missing in the English translation.

44. Cf. *Schriften zur Bedeutung des Protestantismus für die moderne Welt*, 267–68.

45. Troeltsch, *The Social Teaching*, 743; GS 1:864; cf. 742–45, for a discussion of the differences between sect and mysticism; differences that Troeltsch himself had overlooked in his earlier work.

46. Ferdinand Tönnies, in his review of the "Soziallehren," in *Theologische Literaturzeitung* 39 (1914): 8–12; rpt. in Tönnies, *Soziologischen Studien und Kritiken* (Jena, 1929), 3:432–38. Cf. Molendijk, *Zwischen Theologie und Soziologie*, 64.

47. Cf. Molendijk, *Zwischen Theologie und Soziologie*, 72–76.

48. See Troeltsch, "Das stoisch-christliche Naturrecht und das moderne profane Naturrecht" (1910), in GS 4:166–91, e.g., 167.

49. Troeltsch, *The Social Teaching*, 1010; GS 1:982–83.

50. Troeltsch, "Religion," in *Das Jahr 1913: Ein Gesamtbild der Kulturentwicklung*, ed. D. Sarason (Leipzig, 1913), 534.

51. Cf. Molendijk, *Zwischen Theologie und Soziologie*, 132.

52. Cf. Weber, letter to Adolf Harnack, February 5, 1906, Max Weber, *Briefe 1906–1908* (Tübingen: Mohr, 1990), 32–33. For both Weber's and Troeltsch's views of sects, the trip they made together to the United States in 1904 was important; cf. Hans Rollmann, "'Meet me in St. Louis': Troeltsch and Weber in America," in *Weber's "Protestant Ethic": Origins, Evidence, Contexts*, ed. Hartmut Lehmann and Guenther Roth (Cambridge: Cambridge University Press, 1993), 357–83.

53. Max Weber, "'Kirchen' und 'Sekten' in Nordamerika: Eine kirchen- und sozialpolitische Skizze," *Die Christliche Welt* 20 (1906): col. 558–62, col. 577–83, here col. 582; revised as "Die protestantischen Sekten und der Geist des Kapitalismus," in Max Weber, *Gesammelte Aufsätze zur Religionssoziologie* (Tübingen: Mohr Siebeck, 1988), 1:207–36

54. Troeltsch, "Die Zufälligkeit der Geschichtswahrheiten," in *Der Leuchter: Jahrbuch der Schule der Weisheit* (1923): 44; cf. John Higham, *Hanging Together: Unity and Diversity in American Culture* (New Haven, Conn.: Yale University Press, 2001), chap. 7, "Pluralistic Integration as an American Model."

55. Louise Schorn-Schütte, "Ernst Troeltschs 'Soziallehren' und die gegenwärtige Frühneuzeit-forschung: Zur Diskussion um die Bedeutung von Luthertum und Calvinismus für die Entstehung der modernen Welt," and Walter Sparn, "Preußische Religion und lutherische Innerlichkeit: Ernst Troeltschs Erwartungen an das Luthertum," in *Ernst Troeltschs Soziallehren: Studien zu ihrer Interpretation*, ed. F. W. Graf and T. Rendtorff (Gütersloh: Mohn, 1993), 133–51 and 152–77.

56. Troeltsch, *Die Sozialphilosophie des Christentums* (Gotha: Leopold Klotz, 1922), 33; Troeltsch, *The Social Philosophy of Christianity*, in his *Religion in History*, 233.

57. Charles Taylor, *Modern Social Imaginaries* (Durham, N.C.: Duke University Press, 2004), esp. 2 and 23.

58. Troeltsch, *The Social Teaching*, 801; GS 1:941.

59. T. Rendtorff, "'Meine eigene Theologie ist spiritualistisch': Zur Funktion der 'Mystik' als Sozialform des modernen Christentums," in *Ernst Troeltschs Soziallehren*, ed. Graf and Rendtorff, 191.

60. José Casanova, *Public Religions in the Modern World* (Chicago: University of Chicago Press, 1994).

61. Gabriel A. Almond, R. Scott Appleby, and Emmanuel Sivan, *Strong Religion: The Rise of Fundamentalism Around the World* (Chicago: University of Chicago Press, 2003).

André Droogers, As Close as a Scholar Can Get: Exploring a One-Field Approach to the Study of Religion

NOTE: I gratefully acknowledge helpful comments on an earlier version by Henri Gooren, Anton van Harskamp, Birgit Meyer, Peter Versteeg, and two anonymous reviewers.

1. Anton van Harskamp et al., eds., *Playful Religion: Challenges for the Study of Religion* (Delft: Eburon, 2006), 3, 4.

2. J. van Baal and W. E. A. van Beek, *Symbols for Communication: An Introduction to the Anthropological Study of Religion* (Assen: Van Gorcum, 1985), 3.

3. Peter L. Berger, "Secularization and De-secularization," in Linda Woodhead et al., eds., *Religions in the Modern World* (London: Routledge, 2002), 293, 294.

4. Egon G. Guba, "The Alternative Paradigm Dialog," in *The Paradigm Dialog*, ed. Egon G. Guba (Newbury Park: Sage, 1990), 25–27.

5. Talal Asad, *Genealogies of Religion: Discipline and Reasons of Power in Christianity and Islam* (Baltimore: The Johns Hopkins University Press, 1993); Daniel Dubuisson, *The Western Construction of Religion: Myths, Knowledge, and Ideology* (Baltimore: The Johns Hopkins University Press, 2003).

6. For philosophical phenomenology, see: G. van der Leeuw, *Phänomenologie der Religion* (Tübingen: Mohr, 1933); Geo Widengren, *Religionsphänomenologie* (Berlin: Walter de Gruyter, 1969).

For those who have rediscovered it, see: Thomas J. Csordas, "Somatic Modes of Attention," *Cultural Anthropology* 8, no. 2 (1993): 135–156; idem, "The Body's Career in Anthropology," in *Anthropological Theory Today*, ed. Henrietta L. Moore (Cambridge: Polity Press, 1999), 184–87; André Droogers, "The Power Dimensions of the Christian Community: An Anthropological Model," *Religion* 33 (2003): 263–80.

7. See: Michael Jackson, *Paths Toward a Clearing: Radical Empiricism and Ethnographic Inquiry* (Bloomington: Indiana University Press, 1989); idem, ed., *Things as They Are: New Directions in Phenomenological Anthropology* (Bloomington: Indiana University Press, 1996); Kim Knibbe and Peter Versteeg, "Assessing Phenomenology in Anthropology: Lessons from the Study of Religion and Experience," *Critique of Anthropology*, forthcoming.

8. Csordas, "The Body's Career in Anthropology," 186; see also James W. Fernandez, ed., *Beyond Metaphor: The Theory of Tropes in Anthropology* (Stanford, Calif.: Stanford University Press, 1990).

9. André Droogers, "Methodological Ludism, Beyond Religionism and Reductionism,"in *Conflicts in Social Science*, ed. Anton van Harskamp (London: Routledge, 1996), 44–67; idem, "The Third Bank of the River: Play, Methodological Ludism and the Definition of Religion," in *The Pragmatics of Defining Religion: Contexts, Concepts and Contests*, ed. Jan G. Platvoet and Arie L. Molendijk (Leiden: Brill), 285–313; see also Harskamp et al., eds., *Playful Religion*.

10. Droogers, "Methodological Ludism," drawing on Johan Huizinga, *Homo Ludens: A Study of the Play Element in Culture* (London: Routledge & Kegan Paul, 1949); Victor Witter Turner, *The Ritual Process: Structure and Anti-Structure* (New York: Aldine, 1982); idem, *The Anthropology of Performance* (New York: PAJ Publications, 1988).

11. Guba, "The Alternative Paradigm Dialog," 26.

12. Birgit Meyer, "Religious Sensations: Why Media, Aesthetics, and Power Matter in the Study of Contemporary Religion," pp. 704–23 of this volume.

13. Csordas, "The Body's Career in Anthropology," 183.

14. For the tradition starting with James, see Charles Taylor, *Varieties of Religion Today: William James Revisited* (Cambridge: Harvard University Press, 2002). For that starting with Schleiermacher, see Wayne Proudfoot, *Religious Experience* (Berkeley: University of California Press, 1985).

15. For an overview, see Barbara Boudewijnse, "The Conceptualization of Ritual: A History of Its Problematic Aspects," *Jaarboek voor Liturgie-onderzoek* 11 (1995): 31–56.

16. See Martin D. Stringer, *On the Perception of Worship: The Ethnography of Worship in Four Christian Congregations in Manchester* (Birmingham: Birmingham University Press, 1999), 211–15, who contrasts the meaning of ritual acts with the significance of ritual experiences.

17. Catherine Bell, *Ritual Theory, Ritual Practice* (New York: Oxford University Press, 1992).

18. See Fiona Bowie, *The Anthropology of Religion: An Introduction* (Oxford: Blackwell, 2000), and Robin Horton, *Patterns of Thought in Africa and the West: Essays on Magic, Religion and Science* (Cambridge: Cambridge University Press, 1994).

19. See André Droogers, "Globalization and Pentecostal Success," in *Between Babel and Pentecost: Transnational Pentecostalism in Africa and Latin America*, ed. André Corten and Ruth Marshall-Fratani (London: Hurst, 2001), 41–61.

20. Maurice Bloch, "Language, Anthropology and Cognitive Science," *Man* 26 (1992): 183–98; , Roy D'Andrade, *The Development of Cognitive Anthropology* (Cambridge: Cambridge University Press, 1995); Claudia Strauss and Naomi Quinn, *A Cognitive Theory of Cultural Meaning* (Cambridge: Cambridge University Press, 1997).

21. Droogers, "The Power Dimensions of the Christian Community," 267.

22. Strauss and Quinn, *A Cognitive Theory of Cultural Meaning*, 6.

23. Ibid., 51.

24. Droogers, "The Power Dimensions of the Christian Community," 267.

25. Csordas, "The Body's Career in Anthropology," 182. See also: Peter Robert Lamont Brown, *The Body and Society: Men, Women, and Sexual Renunciation in Early Christianity* (New York: Columbia University Press, 1988); Meredith B. McGuire, "Religion and the Body," *Journal for the Scientific Study of Religion* 29 (1990): 283–96; Meyer, "Religious Sensations"; and John H. Simpson, "Religion and the Body: Sociological Themes and Prospects," in *A Future for Religion? New Paradigms for Social Analysis*, ed. William H. Swatos, Jr. (Newbury Park: Sage, 1993), 149–64.

26. See, e.g.: J. L. Austin, *Sense and Sensibilia*, ed. Geoffrey J. Warnock (London: Oxford University Press, 1962), 16–17; Pierre Bourdieu, *Méditations pascaliennes* (Paris: Seuil, 1997), 34–35; Jan van der Stoep, *Pierre Bourdieu en de politieke filosofie van het muticulturalisme* (Kampen: Kok, 2005), 26; Paul Stoller, *The Taste of Ethnographic Things: The Senses in Anthropology* (Philadelphia: University of Pennsylvania Press, 1989).

27. Allan Anderson, *An Introduction to Pentecostalism: Global Charismatic Christianity* (Cambridge: Cambridge University Press, 2004), 1.

28. Philip Jenkins, *The Next Christendom: The Rise of Global Christianity* (New York: Oxford University Press, 2002).

29. Ernst Troeltsch, *The Social Teachings of the Christian Churches* (New York: Harper & Row, 1960); Max Weber, *The Sociology of Religion* (Boston: Beacon, 1963).

30. Walter J. Hollenweger, "Handbuch der Pfingstbewegung," 10 vols. Ph. D. diss., Zürich, 1965–67.

31. Emílio Willems, "Protestantismus und Kulturwandel in Brasilien und Chile," *Kölner Zeitschrift für Soziologie und Sozialpsychologie* 12 (1960): 632–71; idem, *Followers of the New Faith* (Nashville: Vanderbilt University Press, 1967); Christian Lalive d'Épinay, "Le pentecôtisme dans la société chilienne: Essai d'approche sociologique," M.A. thesis, Université de Genève, 1967; idem, *Haven of the Masses: A Study of the Pentecostal Movement in Chile* (London: Lutterworth, 1969).

32. Slightly adapted from Droogers, "The Third Bank of the River," 301.

Willem B. Drees, "Religion": Who Defines, for What Purposes?

1. On "strong religion," see Gabriel A. Almond, R. Scott Appleby, and Emanuel Sivas, *Strong Religion: The Rise of Fundamentalisms Around the World* (Chicago: University of Chicago Press, 2003).

2. Clifford Geertz, "Religion as a Cultural System, " in C. Geertz, *The Interpretation of Cultures* (1966; New York: Basic Books, 1973), 89.

3. Ibid., 90.

4. Nancey K. Frankenberry and Hans H. Penner, "Cifford Geertz's Long-Lasting Moods, Motivations, and Metaphysical Conceptions," *The Journal of Religion* 79, no. 4 (1999): 617–40.

5. R. P. Feynman, R. B. Leighton, and M. Sands, *The Feynman Lectures on Physics*, vol. 1 (Reading, Mass.: Addison-Wesley, 1963), 4–1 and 4–2, emphasis in the original.

6. Robert C. Neville, ed., *The Human Condition: A Volume in the Comparative Religious Ideas Project* (Albany: State University of New York Press, 2001); idem, *Ultimate Realities: A Volume in Comparative Religious Ideas* (Albany: State University of New York Press, 2001); and idem, *Religious Truth: A Volume in the Comparative Religious Ideas Project* (Albany: State University of New York Press, 2001).

7. John Hick, *An Interpretation of Religion: Human Responses to the Transcendent* (Houndmills, Basingstoke, UK: Macmillan, 1989).

8. Act 590 of 1981, General Assembly, State of Arkansas, in Michael Ruse, ed., *But Is It Science? The Philosophical Question in the Creation/Evolution Controversy* (Buffalo, 1988), 283–86; my emphasis); Judge William R. Overton, *McLean v. Arkansas, United States District Court Opinion* (January 5, 1982), in *But Is It Science?* ed. Ruse, 307–331.

9. Jeffrey Stout, *Democracy and Tradition* (Princeton: Princeton University Press, 2004), e.g., 3.

10. Paul Clteur, *God houdt niet van vrijzinnigheid* (Amsterdam: Bert Bakker, 2004).

11. Herman Philipse, *Atheïstisch manifest en de onredelijkheid van religie* (Amsterdam: Bert Bakker, 2004).

12. The tripartite division was reported in 2004 in the daily newspaper *Trouw*, on the occasion of the appearance of the New Bible Translation. The other figures form one of the contributions to a study by a national academic advisory council, the Wetenschappelijke Raadevoor het Regeringsbeleid, especially in Gerrit Kronjee and Martijn Lampert, "Leefstijlen in zingeving," in *Geloven in het publieke domein: Verkenningen van een dubbele transformatie* (Amsterdam: Amsterdam University Press, 2006), 171–208, e.g., 176.

13. Stout, 38; see also pp. 30–32.

Tony Watling, The Field of Religion and Ecology: Addressing the Environmental Crisis and Challenging Faiths

1. J. Baird Callicott, *Earth's Insights: A Survey of Ecological Ethics from the Mediterranean Basin to the Australian Outback* (Berkeley: University of California Press, 1997), xiii. See also G. T. Gardner, *Invoking the Spirit: Religion and Spirituality in the Quest for a Sustainable World* (Washington: Worldwatch Institute, 2002), 7; Mary Evelyn Tucker, *Worldly Wonder: Religions Enter Their Ecological Phase* (Chicago: Open Court, 2003), 10.

2. D. Kinsley, *Ecology and Religion: Spirituality in Cross-Cultural Perspective* (Englewood Cliffs, N.J.: Prentice Hall, 1995); A. McGrath, *The Reenchantment of Nature: The Denial of Religion and the Ecological Crisis* (New York: Doubleday, 2003); M. Oelschlaeger, *Caring for Creation: An Ecumenical Approach to the Environmental Crisis* (New Haven, Conn.: Yale University Press, 1994).

3. Mary Evelyn Tucker and John A. Grim, Series Foreword, in *Buddhism and Ecology: The Interconnection of Dharma and Deeds*, ed. Mary Evelyn Tucker and D. R. Williams (Cambridge: Harvard Center for the Study of World Religions, 1997), xv–xxxiiiv; Tu Weiming, "Beyond the Enlightenment Mentality," in *Worldviews and Ecology: Religion, Philosophy, and the Environment*, ed. Mary Evelyn Tucker and John A. Grim (Maryknoll, N.Y.: Orbis Books, 1994), 19–29.

4. See: K. Eder, *The Social Construction of Nature: A Sociology of Ecological Enlightenment* (London: Sage Publications, 1996); N. Evernden, *The Social Creation of Nature* (Baltimore: The John Hopkins University Press, 1992).

5. Thomas Berry, *The Great Work: Our Way into the Future* (New York: Bell Tower, 1999); G. T. Gardner, *Inspiring Progress: Religion's Contributions to Sustainable Development* (New York: W. W. Norton, 2006); McGrath, *Reenchantment*; Oelschlaeger, *Caring for Creation*; Tucker, *Worldly Wonder*.

6. Gardner, *Invoking the Spirit* and *Inspiring Progress*; R. S. Gottlieb, *A Greener Faith: Religious Environmentalism and Our Planet's Future* (Oxford: Oxford University Press, 2006); S. H. Nasr, "The Spiritual and Religious Dimensions of the Environmental Crisis," in *A Sacred Trust: Ecology*

and Spiritual Vision, ed. D. Cadman and J. Carey (London: The Temenos Academy, 2002), 119–48; Oelschaleger, *Caring for Creation*; Tucker, *Worldly Wonder*; Tucker and Grim, Series Foreword; Mary Evelyn Tucker and John A. Grim, "Introduction: The Emerging Alliance of World Religions and Ecology," *Daedalus* 130, no. 4 (2001): 1–22.

7. See Talal Asad, *Genealogies of Religion: Discipline and Reasons of Power in Christianity and Islam* (Baltimore: The Johns Hopkins University Press, 1993).

8. There is a large body of literature on these issues. For some useful examples, see: Peter Berger, ed., *The Desecularization of the World: Essays on the Resurgence of Religion in World Politics* (Washington: Ethics and Public Policy Center, 1999); P. Beyer, *Religion and Globalization* (London: Sage Publications, 1994); Steve Bruce, *Religion in the Modern World: From Cathedrals to Cults* (Oxford: Oxford University Press, 1996); José Casanova, *Public Religions in the Modern World* (Chicago: University of Chicago Press, 1994); Grace Davie, *Religion in Modern Europe: A Memory Mutates* (Oxford: Oxford University Press, 2000); M. B. McGuire, *Religion: The Social Context* (Belmont, Calif.: Wadsworth, 2000); Linda Woodhead and Paul Heelas, *Religion in Modern Times* (Oxford: Blackwell, 2000).

9. Woodhead and Heelas, *Religion*, 2–4.

10. See: Beyer, *Religion and Globalization*; Casanova, *Public Religions*; J. L. Esposito and M. Watson, eds., *Religion and Global Order* (Cardiff: University of Wales Press, 2000); J. Haynes, *Religion in Global Politics* (London: Longman, 1998); Woodhead and Heelas, *Religion*.

11. See Beyer, *Religion and Globalization*.

12. See Lynn White, Jr., "The Historic Roots of Our Ecological Crisis," *Science* 155 (1967): 1203–7; S. Snyder, "Chinese Traditions and Ecology: A Survey Article," *Worldviews: Environment, Culture, Religion* 10, no. 1 (2006): 100–34; Tucker, *Worldly Wonder*.

13. Roderick Nash, "The Greening of Religion," in *This Sacred Earth: Religion, Nature, Environment*, ed. R. Gottlieb (New York: Routledge, 1996), 194–229.

14. Bron Taylor and Jeffrey Kaplan, eds., *The Encyclopedia of Religion and Nature* (London: Continuum, 2005), viii; Tucker, *Worldly Wonder*, 23, 32; see also Mary Evelyn Tucker, "Religion and Ecology: Survey of the Field," in *The Oxford Handbook of Religion and Ecology*, ed. R. S. Gottlieb (Oxford: Oxford University Press, 2006), 398–418.

15. Gardner, *Invoking the Spirit* and *Inspiring Progress*; Gottlieb, *A Greener Faith*; Oelschlaeger, *Caring for Creation*; Tucker, *Worldly Wonder*; Tucker and Grim, "Introduction" and Series Foreword.

16. See L. Bassett, J. T. Brinkman, and K. P. Pedersen, eds., *Earth and Faith: A Book of Reflection for Action* (New York: United Nations Environment Programme, 2000); Gardner, *Invoking the Spirit*; Nash, *Greening*; Taylor, *Religious Studies*; Tucker, *Worldly Wonder*; Tucker and Grim, "Introduction" and Series Foreword.

17. See Tucker, *Worldly Wonder*; Tucker and Grim, "Introduction" and Series Foreword.

18. There is a large body of literature in this area; for an overview, see Taylor and Kaplan, eds., *Encyclopedia*.

19. Gottlieb, ed., *This Sacred Earth*; Nasr, "The Spiritual and Religious Dimensions"; Tucker, *Worldly Wonder*; Tucker and Grim, "Introduction" and Series Foreword.

20. Gottlieb, ed., *This Sacred Earth*, 10–11; Tucker and Grim, "Introduction," 16–17, Series Foreword, xxii.

21. See Tucker, *Worldly Wonder*.

22. Oelschlaeger, *Caring for Creation*; Tucker "Religion and Ecology."

23. Tucker and Grim, "Introduction," 4.

24. See Tony Watling, "New Cosmologies and Sacred Stories: Re-Imagining the Human-Environment Relationship via Religio-Scientific Metaphor and Myth,"in European Society for the Study of Science and Theology (ESSSAT), *Issues in Science and Theology*, forthcoming.

25. Tomoko Masuzawa, *The Invention of World Religions; or, How European Universalism Was Preserved in the Language of Pluralism* (Chicago: University of Chicago Press, 2005). See also: Asad, *Genealogies*; Snyder, "Chinese Traditions"; D. R. Williams, Introduction, in *Buddhism and Ecology*, ed. Tucker and Williams, xxxv–xlii.

26. Paul O. Ingram, "The Jeweled Net of Nature," in *Buddhism and Ecology*, ed. Tucker and Williams, 75–79.

27. Stephanie Kaza, "Green Buddhism," in *When Worlds Converge: What Science and Religion Tell Us about the Story of the Universe and Our Place in It*, ed. C. N. Matthews, M. E. Tucker, and P. Hefner (Chicago: Open Court, 2002), 293–309; Alan Sponberg, "Green Buddhism and the Hierarchy of Compassion," in *Buddhism and Ecology*, ed. Tucker and Williams, 351–76.

28. R. M. Gross, "Toward a Buddhist Environmental Ethic," in *Worldviews, Religion, and the Environment: A Global Anthology*, ed. R. C. Foltz (Belmont, Calif.: Thompson/Wadsworth, 2002), 163–70; Kaza, "Green Buddhism"; Donald K. Swearer, "The Hermeneutics of Buddhist Ecology in Contemporary Thailand: *Buddhadasa* and *Dhammapitaka*," In *Buddhism and Ecology*, ed. Tucker and Williams, 21–44; idem, "Principles and Poetry, Places and Stories: The Resources of Buddhist Ecology," *Daedalus* 130, no. 4 (2001): 225–42.

29. David Landis Barnhill, "Great Earth *Sangha*: Gary Snyder's View of Nature as Community," in *Buddhism and Ecology*, ed. Tucker and Williams, 187–218; Callicott, *Earth's Insights*; Kaza, "Green Buddhism"; Kinsley, *Ecology and Religion*.

30. Swearer, "Principles and Poetry."

31. Sponberg, "Green Buddhism"; see Kaza, "Green Buddhism"; Kinsley, *Ecology and Religion*.

32. Gross, "Buddhist Environmental Ethic"; Ingram, "Jeweled Net"; K. Kraft, "The Greening of Buddhist Practice," in *This Sacred Earth*, ed. Gottlieb, 484–98; D. C. Maguire, *Sacred Energies: When the World's Religions Sit Down to Talk about the Future of Human Life and the Plight of the Planet* (Minneapolis: Fortress Press, 2000); Sponberg, "Green Buddhism"; Swearer, "Principles and Poetry."

33. Kinsley, *Ecology and Religion*; Mary Evelyn Tucker, "Ecological Themes in Taoism and Confucianism," in *Worldviews and Ecology*, ed. Tucker and Grim, 150–60; Tu Weiming, "The Continuity of Being: Chinese Visions of Nature," in *Worldviews, Religion, and the Environment*, ed. Foltz, 209–17.

34. Kinsley, *Ecology and Religion*; Robert P. Weller and Peter K. Bol, "From Heaven-and-Earth to Nature: Chinese Conceptions of the Environment and Their Influence on Policy Implementation," in *Confucianism and Ecology: The Interrelation of Heaven, Earth, and Humans*, ed. Mary Evelyn Tucker and J. Berthrong (Cambridge: Harvard Center for the Study of World Religions, 1998), 313–41; Tu, "Continuity of Being."

35. Tucker, "Ecological Themes"; see Callicott, *Earth's Insights*; Kinsley, *Ecology and Religion*.

36. C. Cheng, "The Trinity of Cosmology, Ecology, and Ethics in the Confucian Personhood," in *Confucianism and Ecology*, ed. Tucker and Berthrong, 211–35; Tu Weiming, "The Ecological Turn in New Confucian Humanism: Implications for China and the World," *Daedalus* 130, no. 4 (2001): 243–64.

37. Joseph A. Adler, "Response and Responsibility: Chou Tun-i and Confucian Resources for Environmental Ethics," in *Confucianism and Ecology*, ed. Tucker and Berthrong, 123–49; M. C. Kalton, "Extending the Neo-Confucian Tradition: Questions and Re-conceptualization for the Twenty-First Century," in *Confucianism and Ecology*, ed. Tucker and Berthrong, 77–101; Tu, "Continuity of Being" and "Ecological Turn"; Weller and Bol, "From Heaven and Earth."

38. Adler, "Response and Responsibility"; Cheng, "The Trinity"; Kalton, "Extending the Neo-Confucian"; Maguire, *Sacred Energies*.

39. R. T. Ames, "The Local and the Focal in Realizing a Daoist World," in *Daoism and Ecology: Ways Within a Cosmic Landscape*, ed. N. J. Giradot, James Miller, and Xiaogan Liu (Cambridge: Harvard Center for the Study of World Religions, 2001), 265–382; R. Kirkland, "'Responsible Non-Action' in a Natural World: Perspectives from the *Neiye, Zhuangzi,* and *Daode jing*," in *Daoism and Ecology*, ed. Giradot, Miller, and Liu, 293–304; Xiaogan Liu, "Non-Action and the Environment Today: A Conceptual and Applied Study of Laozi's Philosophy," in *Daoism and Ecology*, ed. Giradot, Miller, and Liu, 315–40.

40. Kinsley, *Ecology and Religion*; Kirkland, "Responsible Non-Action"; M. LaFargue, "'Nature' as Part of Human Culture in Daoism," in *Daoism and Ecology*, ed. Giradot, Miller, and Liu, 45–60.

41. Sally McFague, "An Ecological Christology: Does Christianity Have It?" in *Christianity and Ecology: Seeking the Well-Being of Earth and Humans*, ed. D. Hessel and R. R. Reuther (Cambridge: Harvard Center for the Study of World Religions, 2000), 29–46; Rosemary Radford Reuther, "Conclusion: Eco-Justice at the Center of the Church's Mission," in *Christianity and Ecology*, ed. Hessel and Reuther, 603–13.

42. R. Bauckham, "Stewardship and Relationship," in *The Care of Creation: Focusing Concern and Action*, ed. R. J. Berry (Leicester: Inter-Varsity Press, 2000), 99–106; John Chryssavgis, "The World of the Icon and Creation: An Orthodox Perspective on Ecology and Pneumatology," in *Christianity and Ecology*, ed. Hessel and Reuther, 83–96; P. M. Mische, "The Integrity of Creation: Challenges and Opportunities," in *Christianity and Ecology*, ed. Hessel and Reuther, 591–602.

43. Bauckham, "Stewardship"; Kinsley, *Ecology and Religion*; McGrath, *Reenchantment*; Reuther, "Conclusion."

44. Matthew Fox, *The Coming of the Cosmic Christ* (San Francisco: Harper and Row, 1988); Sally McFague, *The Body of God: An Ecological Theology* (Minneapolis: Fortress Press, 1993); Duncan Reid, "Enfleshing the Human: An Earth Revealing, Earth Healing Christology," in *Earth Revealing, Earth Healing: Ecology and Christian Theology*, ed. Denis Edwards (Collegeville, Minn.: Liturgical Press, 2001), 69–83.

45. Denis Edwards, "For Your Immortal Spirit Is in All Things: The Role of the Spirit in Creation," in *Earth Revealing, Earth Healing*, ed. Edwards, 45–68; Mark I. Wallace, "The Wounded Spirit as the Basis for Hope in an Age of Radical Ecology," in *Christianity and Ecology*, ed. Hessel and Reuther, 51–72.

46. See Celia Deane-Drummond, *The Ethics of Nature* (Oxford: Blackwell, 2004); Rosemary Radford Reuther, *Gaia and God: An Eco-feminist Theology of Earth Healing* (New York: Harper San Francisco, 1994).

47. See S. K. K. Chishti, "*Fitra*: An Islamic Model for Humans and the Environment," in *Islam and Ecology: A Bestowed Trust*, ed. R. C. Foltz, F. M. Denny, and A. Baharuddin (Cambridge: Harvard Center for the Study of World Religions, 2003), 67–82; S. H. Nasr, "Islam and the Environmental Crisis," in *Spirit and Nature: Why the Environment Is a Religious Issue*, ed. R. C. Rockefeller and J. D. Elder (Boston: Beacon Press, 1992), 83–107; S. Nomanul Haq, "Islam and Ecology: Toward Retrieval and Reconstruction," *Daedalus* 130, no. 4 (2001): 141–78; Ibrahim Ozdemir, "Toward an Understanding of Environmental Ethics from a Qur'anic Perspective," in *Islam and Ecology*, ed. Foltz, Denny, and Baharuddin, 3–38.

48. Chishti, "*Fitra*"; Nasr, "Islam"; A. A. Said and N. C. Funk, "Peace in Islam: An Ecology of the Spirit," in *Islam and Ecology*, ed. Foltz, Denny, and Baharuddin, 155–84.

49. M. Y. Izzi Dien, "Islamic Environmental Ethics, Law, and Society," in *This Sacred Earth*, ed. Gottlieb, 164–73; Nomanul Haq, "Islam and Ecology"; Ozdemir, "Toward an Understanding."

50. M. Y. Izzi Dien, "Islamic Ethics and the Environment," in *Islam and Ecology*, ed. F. Khalid and J. O'Brien (London: Cassell, 1997), 25–36; Nomanul Haq, "Islam and Ecology"; Ozdemir, "Toward an Understanding."

51. Nawal H. Ammar, "An Islamic Response to the Manifest Ecological Crisis," in *Worldviews, Religion, and the Environment*, ed. Foltz, 376–84; Chishti, "*Fitra*"; Frederick M. Denny, "Islam and Ecology: A Bestowed Trust Inviting Balanced Stewardship," *Earth Ethics* 10, no. 1 (1998); Izzi Dien, "Islamic Ethics"; Maguire, *Sacred Energies*; M. A. Parvaiz, "Islam on Man and Nature," in *Encyclopedia of Religion and Nature*, ed. Taylor and Kaplan, 875–79.

52. Basset et al., *Earth and Faith*, 78, suggest points of agreement in environmental ethics for the major traditions; Gottlieb, *A Greener Faith*, 42, picks out themes that for him provide the foundation for a new eco-theological worldview and moral code; Kinsley, *Ecology and Religion*, 227–32, highlights what he sees as common recurrent themes in relation to religion and the environment.

David Nirenberg, The Politics of Love and Its Enemies

NOTE: This article was inspired by Galit Hasan-Rokem's love of the neighbor, disciplined by Harvey Yunis's love of wisdom, and written within a community of critical friends: Harry Platanakis (whom I have never met, but who guided me most generously through commensurability in Aristotle), Ricardo Nirenberg, Daniel Heller-Roazen, David Bell, Ken Moss, Sean Greenberg, Peter Jelavitch, and at the very end, Hent de Vries and Gabriel Richardson-Lear. It first appeared in *Critical Inquiry* 33, no. 3 (2007), 572–605, and appears here with the permission of the University of Chicago Press.

1. Rowan Williams, Introduction to *Theology and the Political: The New Debate*, ed. Creston Davis, John Milbank, and Slavoj Žižek (Durham, N.C.: Duke University Press, 2005), 3. The last pages of my essay touch upon some of the Hegelian roots of the archbishop's view. Žižek is becoming a leading impresario of a contemporary political theology of love; see, for example, his exposition of "true" and "authentic" Christian love in Žižek, *The Fragile Absolute—or, Why Is the Christian Legacy Worth Fighting For?* (London: Verso, 2000), 120–60, and, most recently, the essays collected in Žižek, Eric Santner, and Kenneth Reinhardt, *The Neighbor: Three Inquiries in Political Theology* (Chicago: University of Chicago Press, 2006).

2. On the growing importance of theology in contemporary philosophy more generally, see Hent de Vries, *Philosophy and the Turn to Religion* (Baltimore: The Johns Hopkins University Press, 1999).

3. Hent de Vries, *Minimal Theologies: Critiques of Secular Reason in Adorno and Levinas* (Baltimore: The Johns Hopkins University Press, 2005), 313.

4. Emmanuel Levinas, *Ethics and Infinity: Conversations with Philippe Nemo* (Pittsburgh: Duquesne University Press, 1985), 52. Elsewhere Levinas does not hesitate to use the word *love* without qualification: "Love must always watch over justice" (Levinas, *Entre Nous: On Thinking-of-the-Other*, trans. Michael B. Smith and Barbara Harshav [New York: Columbia University Press, 1998], 108). It is a curious fact that contemporary writers on love often begin their discourses by distancing themselves from the word itself. In addition to Levinas, see: Jean-Luc Nancy, "Shattered Love," in Nancy, *A Finite Thinking*, ed. Simon Sparks (Stanford, Calif.: Stanford University Press, 2003), 245–46; and Jean-Luc Marion, "The Intentionality of Love," in Marion, *Prolegomena to Charity*, trans. Stephen Lewis (New York: Fordham University Press, 2002), 71.

5. See Marion, "The Intentionality of Love," 100.

6. Raymond Westbrook, "Patronage in the Ancient Near East," *Journal of the Economic and Social History of the Orient* 48, no. 2 (2005): 213. The quote about promiscuity is specifically about kinship terms deployed outside of the realm of family relations, but as the author makes clear in the sentences that follow, the same applies to terms of love and friendship.

7. See D. Winton Thomas, "The root '*ahabah* 'love' in Hebrew," *Zeitschrift für die Alttestamentliche Wissenschaft* 57 (1939): 57–64.

8. The most common word for *friend* in biblical Hebrew is '*oheb* (though *re'a* is also used). The verbal form often conveys the general sense of establishing a "relationship of personal dependency." See W. L. Moran, "The Ancient Near Eastern Background of the Love of God in Deuteronomy," *Catholic Biblical Quarterly* 25, no. 1 (1963): 77–87. Similar valences exist in the vocabularies of love and friendship in other ancient language families. For the later example of Latin *amicitia*, see Dieter Timpe, "Herrschaftsidee und Klientelstaatenpolitik in Sallusts Bellum Jugurthinum," *Hermes* 90 (1962): 334–75.

9. On the contractual aspect of David and Jonathan's love, see 1 Sam. 18:3 and J. A. Thompson, "The Significance of the Verb *Love* in the David-Jonathan Narratives in 1 Samuel," *Vetus Testamentum* 24 (July 1974): 334–38. See also: Jean-Fabrice Nardelli, "Orientalisme et homophilie héroïque: Autour de deux couples d'amis," *Scripta Classica Israelica* 22 (2003): 1–29; and Patricia K. Tull, "Jonathan's Gift of Friendship," *Interpretation* 58 (April 2004): 130–43. On the combination of the political and the emotional in *ahabah*, see Peter R. Ackroyd, "The Verb Love: '*Aheb* in the David-Jonathan Narratives: A Footnote," *Vetus Testamentum* 25 (April 1975): 213–14.

10. Thus, e.g., Deuteronomy's stipulation of the proper relationship of gift exchange between man and God, "They shall not appear before the Lord empty handed, but each with his own gift, according to the blessing that the Lord your God has bestowed upon you" (Deut. 16:16–17), is followed by a discussion of corrupting gifts (bribes) between man and man (Deut. 16:19).

11. See Moran, "The Ancient Near Eastern Background of the Love of God in Deuteronomy," 84, who links these curses to Assyrian representations of the consequences of broken pledges of political love. Worry about the possibility that asymmetries of wealth might create distracting dependences of man upon man is also evident in Israelite poor law. See: J. D. Levenson, "Poverty and the State in Biblical Thought," *Judaism* 25 (1976): 230–41; and Moshe Weinfeld, *Social Justice in Ancient Israel and in the Ancient Near East* (Jerusalem: Magnes, 1995).

12. Friedrich Nietzsche, *Beyond Good and Evil*, trans. Walter Kaufmann (New York: Random House, 1966), 53.

13. For Solomon's love of foreign women and their turning of his heart toward foreign gods, see 1 Kings 11. King David's affair with Bathsheba provides another famous example. Because of it (according to a much later midrash), God's spirit abandoned David for twenty-two years; see *Yalqut Shimoni* on 2 Sam. 23. Those seeking other examples, as well as a general treatment of the relationship between idolatry and sexual seduction, may turn to Moshe Halbertal and Avishai Margalit, *Idolatry*, trans. Naomi Goldblum (Cambridge: Harvard University Press, 1992).

14. The genre of political wisdom addressed from fathers to sons was a venerable one in Egypt (as in, e.g., "The Instructions of Ankhsheshonq"), so well worn that it was subject to satire—as when the son in "The Instructions of Any" responds to his father's wisdom with the words: "It is worthless." Given the marked Israelite suspicion of political mediation that I have been describing, it should not be surprising that the genre was a rare one in Hebrew Scripture or that Proverbs draws heavily on Egyptian antecedents for its material. On the dating of "Ankhsheshonq" and "Instructions of Any," see *Ancient Egyptian Literature: A Book of Readings*, ed. Miriam Lichtheim, 3 vols. (Berkeley: University of California Press, 1973–80), 3:159, 2:135. For Egyptian influence on Proverbs, see *Proverbs 1–9: A New Translation with Introduction and Commentary*, trans. Michael

V. Fox, vol. 18a of *The Anchor Bible* (Garden City, N.J.: Doubleday, 1964–). On Proverbs as court and wisdom literature, see Patrick W. Skehan, *Studies in Israelite Poetry and Wisdom* (Washington: Catholic Biblical Association of America, 1971), and John G. Gammie et al., eds., *Israelite Wisdom: Theological and Literary Essays in Honor of Samuel Terrien* (Missoula, Mt.: Scholars Press for Union Theological Seminary, 1978).

15. On the inegalitarian nature of gift giving, see Prov. 18:16, 19:6, 21:14. Cf., for Greece, Gabriel Herman, *Ritualised Friendship and the Greek City* (Cambridge: Cambridge University Press, 1987), 73–81. It is perhaps also revealing that Proverbs has relatively little to say about friendship, an important theme in its Egyptian antecedents. An exception is Prov. 27:10: "Your friend [*re'a*] and the friend of your father do not abandon . . . better a close neighbor than a distant brother." See R. N. Whybray, *The Book of Proverbs: A Survey of Modern Study* (Leiden: E. J. Brill, 1995), 112–13.

16. See Prov. 1:20–21, 5:1–23, 6:24–35, 7:1–27, 8:1–9:18, 23:27–28, and 31:3 (addressed to King Lemuel of Massa by his mother: "Do not give your strength to women, your vigor to those who destroy kings").

17. Émile Benveniste, *Indo-European Language and Society*, trans. Elizabeth Palmer (London: Faber and Faber, 1973), 288.

18. What Benveniste calls an "error" was certainly a long-held opinion of classical philology, one whose influence on Western imaginations of the politics of love is perhaps evident in Nietzsche's orientation of all loves, even love of neighbor, toward cupidity (*Habsucht*): "Our love of our neighbor—is it not a lust for new possessions?" (Nietzsche, *The Gay Science*, trans. Walter Kaufmann [New York: Random House, 1974], 88). On the meanings of *philos* in Greek, see also A. W. H. Adkins, "Friendship and Self-sufficiency in Homer and Aristotle," *Classical Quarterly* 13 (1963): 30–45, and Sitta von Reden, *Exchange in Ancient Greece* (London: Duckworth, 1995), 45–57.

19. The prophets spoke often of hypocrisy, duplicity, and misleading speech. We might even see, in the angels' purification of Isaiah's lips with burning coal before the throne of God (Isa. 6:6–7), a claim about the essentially impure nature of human speech.

20. See: Kenneth M. Sayre, "Plato's Dialogues in the Light of the *Seventh Letter*," in *Platonic Writings, Platonic Readings,* ed. Charles L. Griswold, Jr. (New York: Routledge, 1988), 93–109; and Hans-Georg Gadamer, "Dialectic and Sophism in Plato's *Seventh Letter*," *Dialogue and Dialectic: Eight Hermeneutical Studies on Plato*, trans. P. Christopher Smith (New Haven, Conn.: Yale University Press, 1980), 103–5.

21. On the *metaxu*, see William Desmond, *Being and the Between* (Albany: State University of New York Press, 1995). On the daimon, see Marcel Detienne, *De la pensée religieuse à la pensée philosophique: La notion de daïmon dans le pythagorisme ancien* (Paris: Les Belles Lettres, 1963).

22. On *Lysis*, and on Plato on friendship more generally, see: David Bolotin, *Plato's Dialogue on Friendship: An Interpretation of the "Lysis" with a New Translation* (Ithaca, N.Y.: Cornell University Press, 1979); Brian Carr, "Friendship in Plato's *Lysis*," in *Friendship East and West: Philosophical Perspectives*, ed. Oliver Leaman (Richmond, Surrey: Curzon, 1996), 13–31; Eugene Garver, "The Rhetoric of Friendship in Plato's *Lysis*," *Rhetorica* 24 (May 2006): 127–46; Gregory Vlastos, "The Individual as Object of Love in Plato," in his *Platonic Studies* (Princeton, N.J.: Princeton University Press, 1973), 3–42; Catherine Osborne, *Eros Unveiled: Plato and the God of Love* (Oxford: Oxford University Press, 1994); and Mary Margaret Mackenzie, "Impasse and Explanation: From the *Lysis* to the *Phaedo*," *Archiv für Geschichte der Philosophie* 70, no. 1 (1988): 15–45. On the *Phaedrus*, see Harvey Yunis, "Eros in Plato's *Phaedrus* and the Shape of Greek Rhetoric," *Arion* 13, no. 1 (2005): 101–25, with which my interest in Plato's erotic optimism began.

23. I am to a certain extent conflating here the Platonic terms *eros* and *philia*, but the conflation is noted and occasionally endorsed by Plato himself. See *Laws* 837 and W. Joseph Cummins, "*Eros, Epithumia,* and *Philia* in Plato," *Apeiron* 15, no. 1 (1981): 10–18.

24. Or so I interpret *Eudemian Ethics* 1235b; cf. *Metaphysics* 1004b22.

25. Catherine Pickstock, "The Problem of Reported Speech: Friendship and Philosophy in Plato's *Lysis* and *Symposium*," *Telos*, no. 123 (Spring 2002): 46. To this argument one could object that the failure of a given attempt to define *x* (in this case love/friendship) does not allow us to infer that *x* cannot be defined. Nor does the claim that friendship and philosophy are ways of life justify the claim that they therefore cannot be examined. Plato clearly thinks of philosophy as a way of life, but he nevertheless examines it constantly. Socrates' irony in the *Lysis* cannot be so easily pinned down.

26. Ibid., 48, and Catherine Pickstock, "Justice and Prudence: Principles of Order in the Platonic City," *The Heythrop Journal* 42 (2001): 269. A straw man may be lurking here: not many scholars today would claim that Plato systematically denies mediation or that he does not have his own way of exalting it. For a broader view of her Platonic project, see Pickstock, *After Writing: On the Liturgical Consummation of Philosophy* (Oxford: Blackwell, 1998), 3–46.

27. Plato, *Laws,* trans. R. G. Bury, 2 vols. (Cambridge: Harvard University Press, 1926), 1:377; hereafter abbreviated *L*.

28. See *L*, 2:405–19 and, for comparison, Aristotle, *Politics* 1257a14 and following. In the political context of the *Laws*, Plato seems to subscribe to the same commonplace Greek ideal, "friends hold everything in common," that he leads toward aporia in *Lysis*.

29. See Aristotle, *Rhetoric* 1371b19, *Politics* 1263b2.

30. See Gregory Vlastos, "Equality and Justice in Early Greek Cosmologies," *Classical Philology* 42 (July 1947): 156–78, and, more generally, Eric A. Havelock, *The Greek Concept of Justice: From Its Shadow in Homer to Its Substance in Plato* (Cambridge: Harvard University Press, 1978).

31. Justice consists, as Socrates later puts it, in each "minding his own affairs" (Pl. *Rep.* 496d).

32. Aristotle, *Nichomachean Ethics* 1133a20–21. Georg Simmel would even predict such a move: "money in its psychological form, as the absolute means and thus as the unifying point of innumerable sequences of purposes, possesses a significant relationship to the notion of God" (Georg Simmel, *The Philosophy of Money*, trans. Tom Bottomore and David Frisby [London: Routledge & Kegan Paul, 1978], 236).

33. I am, of course, not the first to compare the Pentateuch and Plato's *Laws*. See, e.g., Otto Kaiser, "Das Deuteronium und Platons Nomoi," in Kaiser, *Zwischen Athen und Jerusalem: Studien zur griechischen und biblischen Theologie, ihrer Eigenart und ihrem Verhältnis* (Berlin: Walter de Gruyter, 2003), 39–62.

34. Among Aristotle's works, the *Eudemian Ethics* is relatively understudied. A recent edition is *Aristotelis Ethica Eudemia,* ed. R. R. Walzer and J. M. Mingay (Oxford: Oxford University Press, 1991). A commentary on the friendship chapters is still wanting, but the notes to Franz Dirlmeier's German translation come closest; see *Aristoteles Eudemische Ethik,* vol. 7 of *Aristoteles Werke in deutscher Übersetzung,* ed. Ernst Grumach (Darmstadt: Wissenschaftliche Buchgesellschaft, 1962). See, more generally, Anthony Kenny, *The Aristotelian Ethics: A Study of the Relationship Between the Eudemian and Nicomachean Ethics of Aristotle* (Oxford: Oxford University Press, 1978). On friendship in Aristotle, see John M. Cooper, "Aristotle on the Forms of Friendship," *Review of Metaphysics* 30 (June 1977): 619–48; "Friendship and the Good in Aristotle," *Philosophical Review* 86 (July 1977): 290–315; and "Aristotle on Friendship," in *Essays on Aristotle's Ethics,* ed. Amélie Oksenberg Rorty (Berkeley: University of California Press, 1980), 301–40. See also: M. Pakaluk, "The Egalitarianism of the *Eudemian Ethics*," *Classical Quarterly* 48, no. 2 (1998): 411–32; A. W. Price, *Love and*

Friendship in Plato and Aristotle (Oxford: Oxford University Press, 1989); and Lorraine Smith Pangle, *Aristotle and the Philosophy of Friendship* (Cambridge: Cambridge University Press, 2003).

35. On this topic, see: Sibyl A. Schwarzenbach, "On Civic Friendship," *Ethics* 107 (October 1996): 97–128; and Malcolm Schofield, "Political Friendship and the Ideology of Reciprocity," *Saving the City: Philosopher Kings and Other Classical Paradigms* (London: Routledge, 1999), 82–99.

36. In his reliance on proportionality, Aristotle was following in an already well-established tradition. See, e.g., Hermann Diels and Walther Kranz, *Die Fragmente der Vorsokratiker*, 3 vols. (Berlin: Weidmann, 1951), 1:435–36, and F. D. Harvey, "Two Kinds of Equality," *Classica et Mediaevalia* 26 (1965): 101–46. On *analogia*, see G. E. R. Lloyd, "The Unity of Analogy," *Aristotelian Explorations* (Cambridge: Cambridge University Press, 1996), 138–59. On the distinction in Greek mathematics between arithmetic, geometric, and harmonic proportionality, see Harvey, "Two Kinds of Equality," 103–4, and Carl A. Huffman, *Archytas of Tarentum: Pythagorean, Philosopher and Mathematician King* (Cambridge: Cambridge University Press, 2005), 162–81.

37. Aristotle does set significant limits to this calculability, which does not extend to gods or sovereigns: "For it would be ridiculous to accuse a god because the love one receives from him is not equal to the love given him, or for the subject to make the same complaint against his ruler. For the part of the ruler is to receive not to give love, or at least to give love in a different way" (*Eth. Eud.* 1238b).

38. A position not unlike the one we just ascribed to Plato in the *Republic* (cf. *L* 757a). The phrase "treat equals equally, unequals unequally," often used to summarize Aristotle's position, is not itself found in his corpus, but a number of like statements are: e.g., Aristotle's view of justice as equality (*isotēs*) is outlined in book 5 of *Nicomachean Ethics* (1131a10–15). Similarly, "If they are not equals they should not be treated equally" (1131a22). Cf. also *Eth. Eud.* 1280a7. In these cases justice will require proportionality, either geometrical (in the case of distributive justice) or arithmetic (in the case of corrective justice); see 1131a32–b3 and 1131b32–1132a2. At 1131a31 Aristotle defines proportionality as "equality of ratios." For the application of proportion to justice in political distributions, see Aristotle, *Politics* 3.9–12.

Given the impact of Aristotle's views on justice, the bibliography is appropriately vast. See, among others: Hans Kelsen, "Aristotle's Doctrine of Justice," *What Is Justice? Justice, Law, and Politics in the Mirror of Science* (Berkeley: University of California Press, 1957); and Ernest J. Weinrib, "Aristotle's Forms of Justice," in *Justice, Law, and Method in Plato and Aristotle*, ed. Spiro Panagiotou (Edmonton, Alberta: Academic Print. & Pub., 1987), 133–52.

39. On the question of commensurability in Aristotle's physics, ethics, and theories of economic exchange, I have been much helped by Charilaos Platanakis, "The Concept of Equality in Aristotle's Moral and Political Philosophy" (Ph.D. diss., University of Cambridge, 2006). Platanakis generously lent me his manuscript and gave me much advice and bibliography on Aristotle's ethics more generally.

40. Aristotle, *Nichomachean Ethics* 1133a16–18. On Aristotle's economic thought more generally, see: Lindsay Judson, "Aristotle on Fair Exchange," in *Oxford Studies in Ancient Philosophy*, ed. C. C. W. Taylor, 30 vols. (Oxford: Oxford University Press, 1997), 15:147–75; and Scott Meikle, *Aristotle's Economic Thought* (Oxford: Oxford University Press, 1995). An example of the importance of Aristotle's thinking about proportionality and commensurability for medieval Christian political thought can be found in Thomas Aquinas, *In decem libros Ethicorum Aristotelis ad Nicomacum exposito* (Turin: M. E. Marietti, 1934), §950.

41. Nor is it in any way homogeneous with the things it measures, although such homogeneity is given in *Metaphysics* 1053a24–27 as a necessary relation between measure and thing measured. For Aristotle's classification of exchange into four different categories of exchange, some involving money and others not, see *Politics* 1.9.

42. This is an idea with a long future; see, e.g., Karl Marx's analysis of the fetishistic character of commodities in book 1 of *Capital*. From the point of view of contemporary economics, it is not obvious why, in a relation of exchange, the conflation of the other with the thing exchanged should lessen the ability of the transaction accurately to measure demand. But it is worth remembering that Aristotle's *chreia*, need, is not the same thing as demand.

43. "Now if we make a division of the kinds of life, some do not even pretend to this sort of well-being, being only pursued for the sake of what is necessary, e.g., those concerned with the vulgar arts, or with commercial and servile occupations—by vulgar I mean arts pursued only with a view to reputation, by servile those which are sedentary and wage-earning, by commercial those connected with selling in markets and selling in shops" (Aristotle, *Eth. Eud.* 1215a26–29).

44. They were also, of course, in some ways remarkably divergent. The prophets, for example, tended to heighten the dangers of mediation through theocracy and theodicy, whereas Aristotle tried to tame them through philosophy.

45. A Jewish text, *The Wisdom of Ben Sira* (ca. 180 B.C.E.) borrows heavily from Greek and demotic sources in order to expand the place of human relations and gift exchange in God's polity. It even has recourse to something like Aristotle's theory of value, assigning a fixed proportion for conversion between human and divine gifts: "Because He is a God of reciprocity [*tashlomot*] / and He will repay you seven-fold" (32 [35]:13). This divine attribute of reciprocity is not previously attested in Hebrew scripture. On Ben Sira's borrowings from demotic and possibly Greek literature (such as the *Theognis*), see Jack T. Sanders, *Ben Sira and Demotic Wisdom* (Chico, Calif.: Scholars Press, 1983), 29–38. On friendship in Ben Sira, see Freidrich V. Reiterer, ed., *Freundschaft bei Ben Sira: Beiträge des Symposions zu Ben Sira, Salzburg, 1995* (Berlin: Walter de Gruyter, 1996), and Jeremy Corley, *Ben Sira's Teaching on Friendship* (Providence: Brown Judaic Studies, 2002). On both these topics, see Seth Schwartz, "A God of Reciprocity: Torah and Social Relations in an Ancient Mediterranean Society," in *A Tall Order: Writing the Social History of the Ancient World*, ed. Jean-Jacques Aubert and Zsuzsanna Várhelyi (Munich: Saur, 2005), 3–35. Schwartz suggests that "Ben Sira's careful distinction, at 32 [35]:10–17, between the (legitimate) gift, made with *tuv 'ayyin* (more or less, generosity of spirit; cf. *megalopsychia*), and the bribe, made from illicit profit to secure further illicit gain, may be meant as a criticism of Proverbs' teaching." "In Ben Sira," he argues, "the term *oheb* has lost its contractual aspect and describes an informal relationship, comparable to Greek *philia*."

46. A detailed analysis of this marriage can be found in David Konstan, *Friendship in the Classical World* (Cambridge: Cambridge University Press, 1997).

47. Similar articulations in Gal. 5:14, "for the whole law is fulfilled in one word, 'You shall love your neighbor as yourself' "; Rom. 13:9; and Matt. 22:39: "But when the Pharisees heard that he had silenced the Sadducees they got together and, to put him to the test, one of them put a further question, 'Master, which is the greatest commandment of the Law?' Jesus said to him, '*You must love the Lord your God with all your heart. . . . and with all your mind*' [Deut. 6:5 combined with Lev. 19:18, but the one-mindedness is not in Deut.]. This is the greatest and the first commandment. The second resembles it: You must love your neighbor as yourself. On these two commandments hang the whole Law, and the Prophets too." See also Mark 12:31, Luke 10:27, James 2:8, and Hebrews 13:1 (with a significant change: "never cease to love your *fellow Christians*").

48. The understanding of sacred history as a migration of God's promise from polities of false lovers of God to polities of true ones is itself part of Hebrew Scriptures, ranging from Ps. 78 to Isaiah to the Dead Sea Scrolls. In this sense, as in many others, the early authors of the Jesus movement are thinking within a preexisting politics of love.

49. Here, *pace* Schmitt, *echthrous* is clearly being used in a political sense, opposed as it is to *basileusai*.

50. Hegessipus (ca. 120–ca. 180 C.E.) was one of the first to describe communities of Ebionites, but then for him every Christian "heresy" was derived from one of the seven "Jewish Christian" sects that he claimed arose after the passing of the apostolic generation. This, at least, is his position in the fragments Eusebius preserves of his work in his section on the origins of heresy, *Hist. Eccl.* 4.22.4. See Hans Conzelmann, *Gentiles—Jews—Christians: Polemics and Apologetics in the Greco-Roman Era*, trans. M. Eugene Boring (Minneapolis, 1992), 275–77. For the patristic sources on "Jewish Christians," see the useful collection by A. F. J. Klijn and G. J. Reinink, *Patristic Evidence for Jewish Christian Sects* (Leiden: E. J. Brill, 1973).

51. Even then the argument would be vulnerable to the objection that Christian figures of Jewish enmity were generated, not by the difficulties of a politics or a hermeneutics of love, but by real threats that real Jews posed to Christians in the first centuries of their common era.

52. Conversely, according to writers like Justin Martyr, Irenaeus, and Eusebius, the Israelite prophets themselves had not been "Jews," but "Christians," insofar as they had always understood God's words spiritually. See, e.g., Irenaeus, *Adversus Haereses* 4.7.4, 3.6.2, 5.33, 4.26, 6.1.

53. Tertullian was among the theologians who argued strongly against too sharp a differentiation between figurative interpretation and literal reality. His words in *Adversus Marcionem* 4.40, for example, are suggestive: "There could not have been a figure unless there was in truth a body. An empty thing, which is a phantom, cannot capture a figure." Or, as he writes of the prophets in *De resurrectione carnis*, they expressed themselves in flesh as well as in allegorical shadows: "not all in shadows, but also in bodies." How this caution affected his polemics against Judaism (for instance, in his *Adversus Iudaeos*) remains unexplored.

54. To the quotes from Tertullian above, compare Origen's remark in his commentary on the sacrifice of Isaac: "Just as there is nothing corporeal in God, so similarly should you feel nothing corporeal in all of this, but generate in the spirit" (*Patrologia Graeca* 12:209b). On Origen's hermeneutics and the controversy it generated, see: Elizabeth A. Clark, *The Origenist Controversy: The Cultural Construction of an Early Christian Debate* (Princeton, N.J.: Princeton University Press, 1992); and Karen Jo Torjesen, *Hermeneutical Procedure and Theological Method in Origen's Exegesis* (Berlin: Walter de Gruyter, 1986).

55. "I would devote all the strength which the Lord grants me, to show that every one of those texts which are wont to be quoted in defense of the expediency of falsehood ought to be otherwise understood, in order that everywhere the sure truth of these passages themselves may be consistently maintained" (*Ep.* 28, 3.5). One example of the strength Augustine devoted to the task is his *De Genesi ad litteram* (*On the Literal Interpretation of Genesis*), completed ca. 410. He began but did not complete a similar project in 393, *De Genesi ad litteram liber imperfectus*.

56. The exchange between Augustine and Jerome focused on Paul's exhortation to Peter in Galatians 2:11–14: "If you, though a Jew, live like a Gentile and not like a Jew, how can you compel the Gentiles to Judaize [Lat. *judaizare*]?" Following Origen, Jerome denied that Peter could ever have required Gentile Christians to live according to Jewish law (*Ep.* 75, 3.7, citing Acts 10:10–16). Nor could Paul have observed Jewish law after his conversion, as Acts portrayed him doing. (See *Ep.* 28, 3.4; 40, 3.3.) Such passages could not be literally true. Augustine's position was a radically different one: "Paul was indeed a Jew; and when he had become a Christian he had not abandoned those Jewish sacraments which that people had received in the right way, and for a certain appointed time" (*Ep.* 40, 4.4).

57. This exegesis was much cited during the Middle Ages. See Dahan, "L'exégèse de l'histoire de Caïn et Abel du XIIe au XIVe siècle en Occident," *Recherches de théologie ancienne et médévale* 49 (1982): 25–27. Augustine treats Cain quite differently in *De civitate Dei* 15.7, where Cain is the founder of the earthly city. On this contrast, see the beautiful passages of Peter Brown, *Augustine of*

Hippo: A Biography (London: Faber and Faber, 1967), 321 and xx. On the evolution of Augustine's views on religious coercion and his turn to other prooftexts (such as Ps. 59:12, "slay them not"), see Brown, "St. Augustine's Attitude to Religious Coercion," *Journal of Roman Studies* 54, nos. 1 and 2 (1964): 107–16, and Jeremy Cohen, *Living Letters of the Law: Ideas of the Jew in Medieval Christianity* (Berkeley: University of California Press, 1999), 54–55. Curiously enough, although Cain is nowhere associated with the concept of penitential exile as it is found in the Talmud (e.g., BT Berachoth 56a, Sanhedrin 37b), he becomes a figure for penitential exile in medieval Ashkenaz; see, e.g., *Sefer Hasidim* 38. Could the Rhineland pietists' Cain be a counterfigure to the Christian one?

58. Compare Ambrose (as in Letter 40.8.23) or John Chrysostom.

59. Indeed, Augustine represents the protection of the Jews as nothing more than an imperial practice both current and long-standing. As he put it in the *Contra Faustum*: "no emperor or monarch who finds under his government the people with this mark [of Cain] kills them, that is to say, makes them cease to be Jews, separate in their observance and unlike the rest of the world."

60. For a sustained reading of Pelagius as an Origenist, see Clark, *The Origenist Controversy*.

61. August. *De civ. dei*, 15.4–5, 7. Augustine's prooftexts here come significantly from Galatians (5:17) and Romans (7:17, 6:13).

62. This is why Erik Peterson's attack on the political theology of Carl Schmitt in *Der Monotheismus als politisches Problem* (Leipzig: Hegner, 1935) begins with a dedication, epigraph, and prayer to Saint Augustine (the epigraph is from *De vera religione* 45.84: "Habet ergo et superbia quendam appetitum unitatis et omnipotentiae, sed in rerum naturalium principatu, quae omnia transeunt sicut umbra") and ends with the suggestion that Schmitt's political theology is Judaizing, as in Peterson's view any political theology must be; see pp. 98–100. Of course, according to my reading, what Peterson deplores and deploys as the "Jewishness" of politics is itself the product (as well as the producer) of a Christian political theology.

63. Karl Marx, *Comments on James Mill's "Elements of Political Economy,"* in *Karl Marx and Frederick Engels, Collected Works*, vol. 3 of *Marx and Engels (1843–44)* (New York, 1975), 212; hereafter abbreviated *E*.

64. On sovereignties of eros and agape, see Desmond, *Ethics and the Between*, chaps. 15 and 16. The call for "revolutionary Constantinianism" is by Creston Davis and Patrick Aaron Riches, "Metanoia: The Theological Praxis of Revolution," in *Theology and the Political*, 47n2. Aquinas is championed in John Milbank, "Only Theology Overcomes Metaphysics," in Milbank, *The Word Made Strange: Theology, Language, Culture* (Malden, Mass.: Blackwell, 1997), and Milbank and Catherine Pickstock, *Truth in Aquinas* (London: Routledge, 2001).

65. Aquinas's treatment of Islam provides a revealing example; see Tomaž Mastnak, *Crusading Peace: Christendom, the Muslim World, and Western Political Order* (Berkeley: University of California Press, 2002), 208–16. A similar investigation is lacking for Judaism, though John Y. B. Hood, *Aquinas and the Jews* (Philadelphia: University of Pennsylvania Press, 1995), provides an introduction. For a good example of forms of relation that medieval theologians considered loving but modern political philosophers would not, see Jonathan Riley-Smith, "Crusading as an Act of Love," *History* 65 (June 1980): 177–92.

66. See: Axel Honneth, *Kampf um Anerkennung: Zur moralischen Grammatik sozialer Konflikte* (Frankfurt a. M.: Suhrkamp, 1992); and Charles Taylor, "The Politics of Recognition," in *Multiculturalism: Examining the Politics of Recognition*, ed. Amy Gutmann (Princeton, N.J.: Princeton University Press, 1994), 25–73.

67. G. W. F. Hegel, *Theologische Jugendschriften*, ed. Herman Nohl (Tübingen: J. C. B. Mohr, 1907), 379, and *Jenenser Realphilosophie*, ed. Johannes Hoffmeister, 2 vols. (Leipzig: F. Meiner,

1931–32), 2:201. See also Jürgen Habermas, "Arbeit und Interaktion: Bemerkungen zu Hegels Jenenser 'Philosophie des Geistes,'" in Habermas, *Technik und Wissenschaft als "Ideologie"* (Frankfurt a. M.: Suhrkamp, 1968), 16.

68. See Habermas, "Technik und Wissenschaft als 'Ideologie,'" in his *Technik und Wissenschaft als "Ideologie,"* 62–63. For Honneth's reading of Hegel's *Anerkennung*, see Honneth, *Kampf um Anerkennung*, chap. 1. Also instructive are Nancy Fraser's critique of the theory of recognition as Honneth has developed it and Honneth's response; see Nancy Fraser and Honneth, *Redistribution or Recognition? A Political-Philosophical Exchange*, trans. Joel Golb et al. (London: Verso, 2003).

A number of post-Marxist attempts to conceive of "holistic" political communities along Hegelian lines (*holism* is W. V. O. Quine's word, not Hegel's) could also be called detheologized descendents of Christian love. See Ludwig Siep, "Hegel und der Holismus in der politischen Philosophie," in *Modelle politischer Philosophie*, ed. Rolf Geiger et al. (Paderborn: Mentis, 2003), 63–77, and "Hegels Holismus und die gegenwärtige Sozialphilosophie," in *Kultur—Kunst—Öffentlichkeit: Philosophische Perspektiven auf praktische Probleme*, ed. Annemarie Gethmann-Siefert and Elisabeth Weisser-Lohmann (Munich: Fink, 2001), 69–80; Michael Esfeld, *Holism in Philosophy of Mind and Philosophy of Physics* (Dordrecht: Wissenschaftliche Buchgesellschaft, 2001); Philip Pettit, "Defining and Defending Social Holism," *Philosophical Explorations* 1, no. 3 (1998): 169–84; and Martin Seel, "Für einen Holismus ohne Ganzes," in *Holismus in der Philosophie: Ein zentrales Motiv der Gegenwartsphilosophie*, ed. Georg W. Bertram and Jasper Liptow (Weilerswist: Velbrück Wissenschaft, 2002), 30–40. The goal of most of this contemporary work is a holism that avoids what is understood as Hegel's (potentially totalitarian) hypostasis of the collective.

69. Marx, *Zur Judenfrage*, in *Karl Marx, Friedrich Engels: Werke*, 41 vols. (Berlin: Walter de Gruyter, 1957), 1:374.

M. B. Pranger, Religious Indifference: On the Nature of Medieval Christianity

1. I intend to use *indifferent* in a heuristic way. For that reason I refrain from setting out with a clear definition. Although in English the primary meaning of *indifference* seems to be "a lack of commitment, *parti pris*, or interest," I try to shift the emphasis from the subjective aspect to a phenomenological one. In that respect, my explorations can be seen as a mirror image of Hent de Vries's analysis in his *Philosophy and the Turn to Religion* (Baltimore: The Johns Hopkins University Press, 1999), which combines the survival of religious figures and tropes in modern thought with negative theology. While tracing various shades and meanings of religious indifference, I ultimately aim to lay bare its negative, elusive dimension, representing a zero point in the "religious" subject and object alike.

2. See Peter Raedts, *Toerisme in de tijd: Over het nut van middeleeuwse geschiedenis* (Nijmegen: Katholieke Universiteit Nijmegen, 1995); idem, "De katholieken en de middeleeuwen: Prosper Guéranger OSB (1805–1875) en de eenheid van de Liturgie," in *De middeleeuwen in de negentiende eeuw*, ed. R. E. Stuip and C. Vellekoop (Hilversum: Verloren, 1998), 87–109; Peter van Rooden, *Religieuze regimes: Over godsdienst in Nederland 1570–1990* (Amsterdam: Bert Bakker, 1996).

3. See my review of Ludo J. R. Milis, *Angelic Monks and Earthly Men: Monasticism and Its Meaning to Medieval Society* (Woodbridge: Boydell, 1992), in *Millennium: Tijdschrift voor Middeleeuwse Studies* 11, no. 2 (1997): 169–70.

4. Of course, political Islam comes to mind here, but so does American fundamentalism. In this respect, interesting questions could be raised with regard to the reflective or nonreflective

nature of Judaism, Christianity, and Islam. Would the general, more liberal assumption that Christianity has in one way or another always been linked to high culture hold up under historical scrutiny? What about Islam? With regard to the medieval aspects of this problem, Marcia Colish, in her *Medieval Foundations of the Western Intellectual Tradition 400–1400* (New Haven, Conn.: Yale University Press, 1997), raises the question of to the sudden rise of Islam and its subsequent failure to modernize from within, as medieval Christendom succeeded in doing. See also Bernard Lewis, *What Went Wrong? Western Impact and Middle-Eastern Response* (London: Weidenfeld & Nicholson, 2002). For a discussion of the survival and return of religion in philosophical terms, see De Vries, *Philosophy and the Turn to Religion*.

5. Of course, this is a distortion of history, since, as we know, the Middle Ages abounded with different dimensions of religion, both intellectual and affective. Nevertheless, thus far no synthesis has succeeded in doing equal justice to intellect and emotion. In reaction to its earlier focus on church doctrine, recent scholarship has dealt intensively with medieval devotion and mysticism. Yet it turns out not to be easy to categorize mysticism over and against scholasticism. Pioneering work has been done by Bernard McGinn in his comprehensive *The Presence of God: A History of Christian Mysticism* (New York: Cross Roads, 1992–). In it the author discusses much material that hitherto would have been categorized as history of theology (cf. German *Dogmengeschichte*), as a systematic expression of religious experience. On the one hand, this approach deserves admiration because of the author's erudition and overview. On the other hand, there is a danger that a new kind of scholasticism will emerge and attempt to systematize texts that resist such formalization.

6. Friedrich Schleiermacher, *On Religion: Speeches to Its Cultured Despisers*, trans. and introd. Richard Crouteri (Cambridge: Cambridge University Press, 1988).

7. In my view, the intellectual energy expended in the development of neo-scholasticism in the period between Vatican I and the 1950s has been insufficiently appreciated, in part because it has remained largely an inner-Catholic affair.

8. For a recent overview of the *status quaestionis* with regard to Scholasticism proper, see Willemien Otten, "Medieval Scholasticism: Past, Present, and Future," *Dutch Review of Church History* 81, no. 3 (2001): 275–89.

9. I discuss this problem in more detail in my *The Artificiality of Christianity: Essays on the Poetics of Monasticism* (Stanford, Calif.: Stanford University Press, 2003).

10. Etienne Gilson, *La philosophie de saint Bonaventure*, 3d ed.(Paris: Vrin 1953), 396.

11. Blaise Pascal, *Pensées de Pascal*, ed. C. M. des Granges (Paris: Gallimard, 1961), 553 and 142, pp. 210 and 114–15.

12. For a general discussion of the literary and religious context of Pascal's thought, see Philippe Sellier, *Pascal et saint Augustin* (Paris: Armand Colin, 1970; rpt. Paris: Albin Michel, 1995).

13. Ignatius, *Spiritual Exercises*, 179, point 2, in *Saint Ignatius of Loyola: Personal Writings*, ed. Joseph. A. Munitiz and Philip Endean (Harmondsworth, Middlesex: Penguin, 1996), 318.

14. See Alastair Hamilton, *Heresy and Mysticism in Sixteenth-Century Spain: The Alumbrados* (Cambridge: James Clarke, 1992), 92–97.

15. Pierre Hadot, *Philosophy as a Way of Life: Spiritual Exercises from Socrates to Foucault* (Oxford: Blackwell, 1995).

16. As quoted by Talal Asad, *Genealogies of Religion: Disciplines and Reasons of Power in Christianity and Islam* (Baltimore: The Johns Hopkins University Press, 1993), 28. The quotation is taken from Louis Dumont, "Religion, Politics, and Society in the Individualistic Universe," in *Proceedings of the Royal Anthropological Institute for 1970*, 32.

17. Asad, *Genealogies of Religion*, 28.

18. Ibid., 29.

19. Peter Brown, *Augustine of Hippo: A Biography* (London: Faber and Faber, 1967), 236–38.

20. Asad, *Genealogies of Religion*, 35.

21. Ibid., 131.

22. Bernard of Clairvaux, Epistola 190.5.12, in *S. Bernardi Opera*, ed. J. Leclercq and H. Rochais (Rome: Editiones Cistercienses, 1977), 8:27.

23. See, e.g., Erwin Panofsky's comment on Bernard's supposedly negative attitude toward art and culture in *Abbot Suger on the Abbey of St.-Denis and Its Art Treasures*, 2d ed. (Princeton, N.J.: Princeton University Press, 1979), 1–37.

24. See, e.g., the development of the Eucharistic devotion as analyzed by Charles Caspers, *De eucharistische vroomheid en het feest van Sacramentsdag in de Nederlanden* (Louvain, 1992) and M. B. Pranger, "L'eucharistie et la prolifération de l'imaginaire aux XIe et XIIe siècles," in *Fête-Dieu (1246–1996)*, ed. A. Haquin (Louvain-la-Neuve: Publications de l'Institut d'Etudes Médiévales, 1999), 97–117.

25. For a recent attempt to offer an integral view of twelfth-century thought, including both philosophy and religion, see Willemien Otten, *From Paradise to Paradigm: A Study of Twelfth-Century Humanism* (Leiden: E. J. Brill, 2004).

26. Bernard of Clairvaux, "Sermo in assumptione beatae Mariae," 4, 3, in *S. Bernardi Opera*, ed. J. Leclercq and H. Rochais (Rome: Editiones Cistercienses, 1968), 5:246.

27. If this amalgam of voices as they surface in Bernard's text is to be called a *bon mot*, then surely Walter Map's parody of Bernard's use of the text from the Gospel of John should be labelled a *witticism*: "Walter, count of Nevers, died in the Chartreuse and was buried there. At once Bernard speeded to the grave . . . and exclaimed with a loud voice: 'Walter, come out (*veni foras*).' But, because Walter did not hear the voice of Jesus, he did not have the ears of Lazarus, and he did not come out" (Walter Map, *De nugis curialium*, ed., M. J. James [Oxford: Oxford University Press, 1983], 80).

Patricia Spyer, Christ at Large: Iconography and Territoriality in Postwar Ambon, Indonesia

NOTE: The research on which this essay is based was carried out within the context of the Indonesian Mediations project of the Indonesia in Transition program, funded by the Royal Netherlands Academy of Sciences. I would like to thank this institution for its support of this four-year research program (2001–4). Earlier versions were presented at the University of Amsterdam, Meynouth University, University College London, SARAI in New Delhi, PUKAR in Mumbai, the University of Heidelberg, New York University, the University of Michigan, the New School for Social Research, and The Johns Hopkins University. I would like to thank the members of these audiences for their comments and questions, many of which were crucial to thinking through the issues addressed in this essay. In particular, I would like to acknowledge the input of Faye Ginsburg, Michael Gilsenan, Charles Hirschkind, Marilyn Ivy, Webb Keane, Brian Larkin, Danilyn Rutherford, Shuddhabrata Sengupta, Mary Steedly, and Hent de Vries. James Siegel generously offered extensive criticism of an earlier version of the essay, for which I am most grateful. To Rafael Sánchez, as always, I am most indebted for his criticism and contributions. Much of the essay was rewritten and elaborated at New York University's Center for Religion and Media, where I was Senior Fellow in 2006–7. I would like to thank the co-directors of the center, Faye Ginsburg and Angela Zito, for their unflagging generosity and intellectual stimulation during the year. I also thank Fred Myers and Angela Zito for inviting me to participate in the Center's working group Secularism, Media, and the Globalization of Religion. Last but not least, I owe an immense debt to the painters with whom I work in Ambon, to religious and community leaders, journalists, and NGO activists, and to the ordinary people of Ambon, who have shared generously with me their time, stories, and insights into the recent war and current postwar situation.

1. See "Indonesia: The Search for Peace in Maluku," *International Crisis Group*, Asia Report no. 31 (Jakarta and Brussels, 2002), February 8, 2002.

2. Patricia Spyer, "Some Notes on Disorder in the Indonesian Postcolony," in *Law and Disorder in the Postcolony*, ed. Jean Comaroff and John L. Comaroff (Chicago: University of Chicago Press, 2006), 188–218.

3. I discuss this discourse in Patricia Spyer, "Aura and the Other: Christian/Muslim Sensibilities in Postconflict Ambon," Unpublished manuscript.

4. Relatedly, Karen Strassler takes issue with Barbie Zelizer's critique of the "atrocity image" and its wide, repetitive circulation as the currency of global campaigns for the recognition of human rights violations. Zelizer contends that the interreferentiality of such images evacuates historical specificity and saturates observers, leading to "stupefied interaction"—what others have glossed as "compassion fatigue"—and forgetting rather than historical memory. As Strassler puts it, "such weary critiques from the position of the western metropolis ignore the local uses of atrocity images *within* situations of conflict, while rather underestimating how strategic it remains for activists to draw on an accumulated pool of recognition in order to gain attention to their particular plight." They also overlook how the weariness and numbing effect of such atrocity images has less to do with saturation per se than with the lack of variation in the images themselves—less inundation or an excess of such images than the fact that they all, in a way, look the same. See Karen Strassler, "Gendered Visibilities and the Dream of Transparency: The Chinese-Indonesian Rape Debate in Post-Suharto Indonesia," *Gender and History* 16, no. 3 (2004): 707.

5. W. J. T. Mitchell, *What Do Pictures Want? The Lives and Loves of Images* (Chicago: University of Chicago Press, 2005).

6. Robert W. Hefner, "Islamization and Democratization in Indonesia," in *Islam in an Era of Nation-States: Politics and Religious Renewal in Muslim Southeast Asia*, ed. Robert W. Hefner and Patricia Horvawitch (Honolulu: University of Hawai'i Press, 1997), 75–127, and idem, *Civil Islam: Muslims and Democratization in Indonesia* (Princeton, N.J.: Princeton University Press, 2000).

7. On the Laskar Jihad, see: Noorhaidi Hasan, "Laskar Jihad: Islam, Militancy, and the Quest for Identity in Post–New Order Indonesia," Ph.D. diss. (University of Utrecht, 2005); Kirsten E. Schulze, "Laskar Jihad and the Conflict in Ambon," *Brown Journal of World Affairs* 9, no. 1 (2002)): 57–69; and Merlyna Lim, "Laskar Jihad Online: Global and National Meta-Narratives in Cyberspace" *@rchipelago Online*, Ph.D. diss. (University of Twente, 2006), 135–74.

8. Regarding, specifically, the unwillingness of the United Nations to intervene in the Moluccan conflict, Dieter Bartels reports that Ambonese, being generally well-informed about world affairs, questioned him repeatedly about why the UN had been willing to intervene to save Muslims in Bosnia and Kosovo but seemed not to want to do the same on behalf of Ambon's Christians. Nor did they believe the Western response that the Indonesian government had denied the UN permission to do so. "They didn't ask Milosevic, did they?" is the usual retort. See Bartels, "Your God Is No Longer Mine: Moslem-Christian Fratricide in the Central Moluccas (Indonesia) after a Half-Millennium of Peaceful Co-existence and Ethnic Unity," in *A State of Emergency: Violence, Society and the State in Eastern Indonesia*, ed. Sandra Pannell (Darwin: Northern Territory University Press, 2003), 147n8.

9. Richard Chauvel, "Ambon's Other Half: Some Preliminary Observations on Ambonese Moslem Society and History," *Review of Indonesian and Malayan Affairs* 14, no. 1 (1980): 40–80.

10. Marianne Hulsbosch, "Pointy Shoes and Pith Helmuts: Dress and Identity Construction in Ambon from 1850 to 1942" (Ph.D. diss., University of Wollonggong, 2004), 46.

11. Nancy Munn, "The Returnee Narrative: Defamiliarization and Changes in City Places," in "Places in Motion: Spacetime and Memory in Antebellum New York," unpublished manuscript, chap. 5, 9.

12. I have adapted this notion of a "theory of community" from Appadurai's argument about how every ritual develops a "theory of context," of how it is produced, etc. See Arjun Appadurai, *Modernity at Large: Cultural Dimensions of Globalization* (Minneapolis: University of Minnesota Press, 1996), 184.

13. Henkens, cited in Munn, "The Returnee Narrative," 29.

14. See James Scott, *Seeing like a State: How Certain Schemes to Improve Human Conditions Have Failed* (New Haven, Conn.: Yale University Press, 1998).

15. Strassler, "Gendered Visibilities and the Dream of Transparency," 705.

16. Quite a number of the billboards and murals draw upon calendars and illustrated books that feature the work of Warner Sallman, whose paintings of Christ were a crucial component of popular religiosity and Christian visual culture in the mid twentieth century, especially in the United States. In Ambon, for instance, I have seen such Sallman classics as *Head of Christ* (1940), *Christ at Heart's Door* (1942), *The Lord Is My Shepherd* (1943), and *Christ in Gethsemane* (1941) both precisely and more approximately reproduced. See David Morgan, *Visual Piety: A History and Theory of Popular Religious Images* (Berkeley: University of California Press, 1998) and *The Sacred Gaze: Religious Visual Culture in Theory and Practice* (Berkeley: University of California Press, 2005), for analyses of Christian popular visual culture and religiosity and, relatedly, religious acts of seeing in nineteenth- and twentieth-century America.

17. For a brief discussion of the Muslim VCDs, see Patricia Spyer, "Shadow Media and Moluccan VCDs," in *9/11: A Virtual Case Book*, ed. Barbara Abrash and Faye Ginsburg (New York: The Center for Media, Culture, and History, 2002), http://www.nyu.edu/fas/projects/vcb/.

18. *Bang* derives from *abang* and is used by Muslims to address younger men whom they do not know well. Christians may use the term, but only to address Muslims. *Bung* is a term associated with the Indonesian Revolution, when it meant "brother" or "fellow" and was/is an affectionate term for leaders of that time, such as Bung Karno and Bung Hatta. In Ambon *bu*, from the Dutch *broer* or "brother," was widely used to address men of the same age or older. It may have become conflated with *bung* in a context where *bu* must seem increasingly odd as fewer and fewer people speak Dutch. *Usi* or "older sister" among Christians also derives from Dutch, where *zuster* or "sister" led to *zuster-zus-usi*. I have no etymology for *cece*, but it appears to be the equivalent for Muslims of *usi*, or "older sister." My thanks to the linguist and Maluku expert James T. Collins for suggestions about these terms.

19. See also Christopher Pinney, who writes regarding Mitchell, "Addressing the 'wants' of pictures is a strategy advanced by W. J. T. Mitchell as part of an attempt to refine and complicate our estimate of their power. Mitchell advocates that we invite pictures to speak to us, and in so doing discover that they present 'not just a surface, but a *face* that faces the beholder'" (Christopher Pinney *"Photos of the Gods": The Printed Image and Political Struggle in India* [London: Reaktion Books, 2004], 8).

20. Christopher Pinney, "How the Other Half . . . ," in *Photographies' Other Histories*, ed. Nicholas Peterson and Christopher Pinney (Durham, N.C.: Duke University Press, 2003), 1–14.

21. The foreign-language words in this essay are from Indonesia's national language, Bahasa Indonesia (indicated by I.), unless they are preceded by A.M. This stands for Ambonese Malay, a

dialect of Malay that is spoken widely on Ambon and the adjacent islands comprising the Central Moluccas.

22. On the dramatic rearrangement of the everyday relations pertaining between subjects and objects, see Rafael Sánchez, "Intimate Publicities: Retreating the Theologico-Political in the Chávez Regime," in *Political Theologies: Public Religions in a Post-Secular World*, ed. Hent de Vries and Lawrence E. Sullivan (New York: Fordham University Press, 2006), 401–26

23. For an analysis of the apocalyptic in the violence in both Maluku, the province where Ambon is located, and North Maluku, see Nils Bubandt, "Malukan Apocalypse: Themes in the Dynamics of Violence in Eastern Indonesia," in *Violence in Indonesia*, ed. Ingrid Wessel and Georgia Wimhöfer (Hamburg: Avera, 2001), 228–53.

24. W. Mühlmann, in Michael de Certeau, *The Possession at Loudun*, trans. Michael B. Smith, (Chicago: University of Chicago Press, 1996), 2.

25. Ibid.

26. On the creation of the almost entirely Muslim province of North Maluku with Ternate as its capital, see John T. Sidel, *Riots, Pogrom, Jihad: Religious Violence in Indonesia* (Ithaca, N.Y.: Cornell University Press, 2006).

27. René Girard, *Violence and the Sacred* (Baltimore: The Johns Hopkins University Press, 1977), 51.

28. On *pela*, see Dieter Bartels, "Guarding the Invisible Mountain: Inter-village Alliances, Religious Syncretism, and Ethnic Identity among Ambonese Christians and Moslems in the Moluccas" (Ph.D. diss., Cornell University, 1977); also his "Your God Is No Longer Mine."

29. On the history of the Catholic mission in Maluku, see P. H. G. Scheurs, *Terug in het Erfgoed van Franciscus Xaverius: Het herstel van de katholieke missie in Maluku, 1886–1960* (Tilburg: Missiehuis MSC, 1992).

30. Sidel, *Riots, Pogrom, Jihad*, 37–40.

31. Ibid., 172.

32. *Pancasila*, a Sanskrit term, means five (*panca*) principles (*sila*). The five principles are: (1) belief in the one and only God; (2) just and civilized humanity (internationalism or humanitarianism); (3) the unity of Indonesia (nationalism); (4) democracy guided by the inner wisdom in the unanimity arising out of deliberations among representatives (democracy); (5) social justice for the whole people of Indonesia (Adrian Vickers, *A History of Modern Indonesia* [Cambridge: Cambridge University Press, 2005], 117).

33. The first point of the Pancasila state ideology regarding religion was formulated in the immediate postindependence period with the double-edged intent of excluding the possibility of an Islamic state while aiming to appease those who most subscribed to it. The substitution in the wording of the first *sila* of the more neutral *Tuhan* for the Islamic *Allah* for "God" offers a concrete example of the highly ambiguous moves this stance produced. Nor was *agama* further specified with respect to a particular religion, being best described, following James J. Fox, as an "idiosyncratic amalgam of a Sanskrit-derived term, a nineteenth-century European conception of specific 'world religions,'" and "an Islamic view that all proper religions must minimally have a prophet, a scripture, and a belief in one God" (review of Rita Smith Kipp and Susan Rodgers, eds., *Indonesian Religions in Transition, American Ethnologist* 15, no. 4 [1988]:806–7).

34. For a discussion of the close connections among religion, citizenship, and elections, see my "Serial Conversion / Conversion to Seriality: Religion, State, and Number in Aru, Eastern Indonesia," in *Conversion to Modernities: The Globalization of Christianity*, ed. Peter van der Veer (New York: Routledge, 1996), 171–98, and my *The Memory of Trade: Modernity's Entanglements on an Eastern Indonesian Island* (Durham, N.C.: Duke University Press, 2000). See also Sidel, *Riots, Pogrom, Jihad*.

35. The entire patronage structure is also in disarray, and with economic crisis funds to keep it lubricated also dry up.

36. Sidel, *Riots, Pogrom, Jihad*, 140–41.

37. Interview with Minister Sammy Titaley, July 20, 2006, at his home.

38. The Dutch Reformed Church at issue here is the Nederlands Hervormde Kerk, not to be confused with the later, nineteenth-century orthodox Reformed Church, the Gereformeerde Kerken.

39. For a contemporary example of Catholic and Protestant religious rivalry in the Moluccas, see my "Serial Conversion / Conversion to Seriality."

40. The Catholic mission in Ambon is that of the Missionaries of the Sacred Heart, or the Missionarissen van het Heilig Hart, based in the Netherlands in the city of Tilburg and in the Moluccas originally in Langgur in the Kei Islands in the Southeast Moluccas.

41. See, e.g., Noorhaidi Hasan, "The Making of Public Islam: Piety, Agency, and Commodification in the Landscape of the Indonesian Public Sphere," unpublished paper presented at the KITLV In Search of Middle Indonesia seminar, Leiden, March 2007.

42. Louis Marin, *Portrait of the King* (Minneapolis: University of Minnesota Press, 1988).

43. Roland Barthes, "The Romans in Films," in his *Mythologies*, trans. Annette Lavers (New York: Hill and Wang, 1972), 26–28.

44. As an example of the exclusivity of Ambonese Christians, Bartels writes, "in pre-WWII times, Chinese Christians were, at times, refused entry into the Ambonese main church in Ambon City because Ambonese then conceived Christianity parochially not as a universal brotherhood but rather as an ethnic brotherhood they were willing to share only with their Dutch masters (Bartels, "Your God Is No Longer Mine," 149n29).

45. See James T. Siegel, *Naming the Witch* (Stanford, Calif.: Stanford University Press, 2006), on the outbreaks of witchcraft accusations and witch killings in Banywangi, east Java, toward the end of the Suharto regime. He explains these as follows: "The feeling of being possessed—if not the posing of the question Am I a Witch?—seems to me a condition for the unprecedented outbreaks of witchcraft in Java at the end of the New Order. It indicates that at a certain moment there was not merely uncertainty about identity, which means that one doubts who one is, as though one had a range of known identities. To be a witch, at least in Java, is to be invested with a power heterogeneous to all social identity. Thus, there is also the possibility that one could be someone completely different from anything or anyone one knows. The impossibility of relying on social opinion opens up infinite possibilities within the person . . . under the conditions that prevailed during the witch hunt, self-image disappeared, as multiple possibilities of identity thrust themselves forward. 'Witch,' under that condition, is the name of the incapacity to figure oneself" (124). Although both the circumstances and the effects of the withdrawal of authority and, with it, the recognition and "placing" of persons and collectivities that is authority's prerogative are distinct from those in Ambon, both situations—the witchcraft outbreaks in east Java and the plight of Christian Ambonese—might be described as what I call *orphaned landscapes*, or the new terrains of rampant uncertainty about the conditions and terms of locatedness and recognition that were either emergent or made manifest in the context of Suharto's dramatic stepdown following some thirty-two years of authoritarian rule.

46. Not surprisingly, among Ambon's painters this depiction takes a variety of forms. These include: Christ in situ in the city; a shift from full-blown crucifixions to those honing in on the head and torso to bring close the pain on Christ's face; painted rooms in homes where household members pray against the colored backdrop of Christ praying at Gethsemane; the recent resurgence of Christ behind church altars, whence he stretches out his arms to embrace the congregation; to,

a rare exception, a father and son pair who both portray Christ as a native Moluccan—brown with curly hair, and as someone who wears their clothes, tastes their food in his mouth, has their Malay Ambonese dialect on his lips, and so on.

47. Youth make up just under 60 percent of Ambon's urban population. There is much unemployment among them, affecting especially those with little education. Bartels observes that the freer atmosphere of the period of *Reformasi*, following Suharto's stepdown and in the context of the war, offered them an opportunity to express their freedom from authority through acts of violence (*Manado Pos 08/28/2000*). He also notes that Western-style gangs, which fought each other, formed in different parts of Ambon before the conflict—indeed, according to some young men in Ambon, many of their group names have a long history, dating at least as far back as the 1980s. During the war, these gangs "metamorphosed themselves into freedom fighters defending their neighborhoods against outside attacks and invading those of their enemies to burn them down" (Bartels, "Your God Is No Longer Mine," 139).

48. See Jean Comaroff and John L. Comaroff, in *Youth in Africa: Producing Futures in a Global Age*, ed. Jean Comaroff, John L. Comaroff, and Ronald Kassimir, in preparation. See also Jean Comaroff and John L. Comaroff, "Millennial Capitalism: First Thought on a Second Coming," *Public Culture* 12, no. 2 (2000): 291–343, where they speak of striking similarities in the situation of youth the world over, similarities that seem to be founded on what they call a "doubling," or a simultaneous exclusion and inclusion, which, in turn, they attribute to the workings of neoliberal capitalism and a changing of the planetary order. The exclusion has to do with the ways in which young men are denied full, waged citizenship in the nation-state and often, as a result, take to the streets. Pointing to the feminization of post-Fordist labor, disruptive of gender relations and domestic reproduction, they speak of a "crisis of masculinity," which, while aggravated among youth, is not limited to them. At the same time, there is also the rise—evident along with exclusion of young men in Ambon—of "assertive, global youth cultures of desire, self-expression, and representation; in some places, too, of potent, if unconventional, forms of politicization. Pre-adults have long been at the frontiers of the transnational."

49. See Scott, *Seeing like a State*.

50. On the Citizen's Identity Card, see Karen Strassler, "Refracted Visions: Popular Photography and the Indonesian Culture of Documentation in Postcolonial Java," Ph.D. diss. (University of Michigan, 2003), 190–240.

51. I would like to thank Marilyn Ivy for making me think about the kinds of distracted looking to which these adlike billboards in Ambon's urbanscape might be subject.

Peter Versteeg, Renewing Time: Charismatic Renewal in a Conservative Reformed Church

NOTE: An earlier version of this paper was presented at the conference What Is Religion? Vocabularies, Temporalities, Comparabilities, June 4, 2005, Amsterdam. The author is a member of the research project Between Secularization and Religionization at the Free University of Amsterdam. He is a supervisor of the research group Conversion Careers and Culture Politics in Global Pentecostalism (Netherlands Organization for Scientific Research program The Future of the Religious Past).

1. Jacques de Visscher, *Een te voltooien leven: Over rituelen van de moderne mens* (Kapellen/Kampen: Pelckmans / Kok Agora, 1996), 11–13; Gerard Lukken, "Seculier, profaan, sacraal en de levensvatbaarheid van het ritueel in onze cultuur," in *Ritueel bestek: Anthropologische kernwoorden van de liturgie*, ed. M. Barnard and P. Post (Zoetermeer: Meinema, 2001), 20.

2. Richard K. Fenn, *Time Exposure: The Personal Experience of Time in Secular Societies* (Oxford: Oxford University Press, 2001), 20–21; quoted in Pink Dandelion, *The Liturgies of Quakerism* (Aldershot: Ashgate, 2004), 115.

3. Richard K. Fenn, *The End of Time: Religion, Ritual, and the Forging of the Soul* (London: SPCK, 1997).

4. See, for more information about charismatic renewal movements in the mainline churches, Richard Quebedaux, *The New Charismatics II: How a Christian Renewal Movement Became Part of the American Religious Mainstream* (San Francisco: Harper and Row, 1983).

5. As a result of a theological and factional disagreement, the RCV (*Vrijgemaakt* = Liberated), broke away in 1944 from the Reformed Churches in the Netherlands, which in turn had left the Dutch Reformed Church and formed a new denomination in 1892. The term *conservative Reformed* is used to distinguish this stream from modern Reformed (nowadays represented by the Protestant church in the Netherlands) and pietist Reformed streams. The RCV was characterized by a conservative Calvinist theology and a strong exclusivist attitude in their relation to other churches. Recently the RCV has become more open to cooperation with other Christian denominations, especially Christian media and conservative Christian politics.

6. Hijme Stoffels, "Als een machtig leger: overwegingen bij de opmars der evangelischen," *Gereformeerd Theologisch Tijdschrift* 96, no. 3 (1996): 95–103.

7. In the Dutch context, the term *evangelical* often includes "charismatic" and "Pentecostal." In practice, there is a small group of ecumenical charismatic believers who do not identify with evangelical core beliefs.

8. The NRC Houten also includes a large number of Christian Reformed members. Instead of establishing their own church in Houten, the CRC officially agreed to hand over pastoral care for their members to the NRC.

9. New Wine International, www.new-wine.org, access: May 9, 2005; New Wine Netherlands, www.new-wine.nl, access: May 9, 2005; John Wimber, *Power Evangelism* (London: Hodder and Stoughton, 1985). On the Vineyard-Anglican connection, see Stephen Hunt, "Doing the Stuff: The Vineyard Connection," in *Charismatic Christianity: Sociological Perspectives*, ed. S. Hunt, M. Hamilton, and T. Walter (Basingstoke: MacMillan, 1997), 77–96.

10. Peter Versteeg, "Transcultural Christian Routes: The 'Non-Religious' Experience of God in a Dutch Vineyard Church," in *Religion in America: European and American Perspectives*, ed. H. Krabbendam and D. Rubin (Amsterdam: VU University Press, 2004), 291–300. The Vineyard churches also invented a style of popular and emotionally expressive worship music in which intimate communication with God is central.

11. New Wine has triggered other charismatic movements within churches, such as *Gods Geest werkt* (God's Spirit Works), a movement in the RCN. Churches involved with New Wine are mainly Netherlands Reformed, Christian Reformed, and Protestant congregations.

12. Stephen Hunt, *Anyone for Alpha? Evangelism in a Post-Christian Society* (London: Darton, Longman and Todd, 2001).

13. In an article in a conservative Christian magazine about growing conservative Reformed congregations in the Netherlands, Pastor Westerkamp estimates that about one third of the new NRC Houten members belonged to a category with very low church attendance. See Simcha Looijen, "De succesvolle make-over van een traditionele kerk," *CV.Koers*, September 2005, 56–61.

14. Between 1997 and 2005, 1,250 people have done the Alpha course in one of the Houten churches. Six churches have been involved in organizing Alpha courses during this period, and there have also been a number of interdenominational courses. Of the participants, 885 (569 adults and 319 youth) did the course in the NRC—this is more than two-thirds of the total number

in Houten. In the Netherlands approximately 100,000 have followed Alpha since the course was introduced.

15. Tony Watling, "'Experiencing' Alpha: Finding and Embodying the Spirit and Being Transformed—Empowerment and Control in a ('Charismatic') Christian Worldview," *Journal of Contemporary Religion* 20, no. 1 (2005): 91–108. Although I do not think that Alpha fits every Christian tradition, it should be noted that local congregations that adopt Alpha seem to succeed in toning down or rephrasing the elements of which they do not approve. Even in churches where people are sympathetic to the gifts of the Spirit, the implementation and effect of this belief dimension can be quite different.

16. A small group of young people, who call themselves the "soul group," started their own worship meetings every two weeks. This group is inspired by Soul Survivor, an organization for faith renewal among young people. The soul group operates independently of the church, and some of the people involved are also active in other independent initiatives, such as prayer groups and prayer walks in Houten.

17. "Tekenen van de Geest maken het ons niet altijd gemakkelijker," *Nederlands Dagblad*, January 15, 2000.

18. Dick Westerkamp, "Geestelijke vernieuwing sluit aan bij traditie," *Nederlands Dagblad*, November 5, 2003; Dick Westerkamp, "'Charismatisch' is openstaan voor de Geest," *Nederlands Dagblad*, November 6, 2003.

19. Korien Van Vuren-Verkerk, "Verlangen naar meer 1," letter to *Nederlands Dagblad*, November 6, 2003.

20. In Dutch religious contexts, "ministry" generally is translated as *bediening*.

21. In this respect, "ministry" is very similar to other forms of charismatic prayer, such as "soaking" or "maranatha prayer." These practices have in common that they can last for longer periods of time (up to half an hour) and that they are based upon the belief that the Holy Spirit can practically intervene within the prayer situation.

22. The two other NRC Houten services add to this picture of different target groups in the church, though they exhibit somewhat different styles. The "traditional" service clearly attracts an older category of church members.

23. Dandelion, *Liturgies of Quakerism*, 10–11.

24. Danièle Hervieu-Léger, "Present-Day Emotional Renewals: The End of Secularization or the End of Religion?" in *A Future for Religion? New Paradigms for Social Analysis*, ed. W. H. Swatos, Jr. (Thousand Oaks, Calif.: Sage, 1993), 142.

Winnifred Fallers Sullivan, Neutralizing Religion; or, What Is the Opposite of "Faith-based"?

NOTE: This essay is a slightly revised version of an essay that first appeared in *History of Religions* 41, no. 4 (2002): 369–90; published here courtesy of the University of Chicago Press. That essay was a revised version of a paper I gave on the occasion of the retirement of Frank Reynolds at a conference entitled Nurturing Conversation and Collaboration in the History of Religions: A Celebration of the Scholarship and Teaching of Frank E. Reynolds at the University of Chicago Divinity School, May 30, 2001.

1. See www.law.uchicago.edu/lectureconf/meares.

2. In Boston, e.g., in the early 1990s, some black churches, under the leadership of Rev. Eugene Rivers, formed a partnership with police called "Ten Point" to reform police procedures with

respect to at-risk youth. See Ira Porter, "Boston Model Eyed on Cutting Violence," *Boston Globe*, July 30, 2001.

3. *Everson v. Board of Education*, 330 U.S. 1 (1947); *Employment Division v. Smith*, 494 U.S. 872 (1990). The White House Office on Faith-Based Initiatives was established on January 29, 2001, by executive order. See www.whitehouse.gov/news/releases/2001/01/ 20010129–2.html. "Charitable choice" was first introduced into the vocabulary of federal social welfare legislation in 1996. Section 104 of the Personal Responsibility and Work Opportunity Reconciliation Act of 1996 (P.L. 104–193) required that religious organizations be as eligible to receive federal grants as were other charities. These provisions were extended in 1998 and 2000.

4. One significant contribution to this history is Philip Hamburger, *The Separation of Church and State* (Cambridge: Harvard University Press, 2001).

5. See, e.g., Justice Souter's dissenting opinion in *Mitchell v. Helms*, 120 S. Ct. 2530, 2592 (2000).

6. See, e.g., Rebecca French, "A Conversation with Tibetans? Reconsidering the Relationship Between Religious Beliefs and Secular Legal Discourse," *Law and Social Inquiry* 26 (Winter 2001): 95–112.

7. Stephen Carter's 1993 book has become an icon of this position. See *The Culture of Disbelief: How American Law and Politics Trivialize Religious Devotion* (New York: Basic Books, 1993).

8. *Mitchell v. Helms*, 120 S. Ct. at 2574.

9. These models are ideal types. In the courts and in the academy, both models co-exist and are employed simultaneously by the same persons, depending on the position being argued.

10. See, e.g., Russel McCutcheon, *Manufacturing Religion: The Discourse on Sui Generis Religion and the Politics of Nostalgia* (New York: Oxford University Press, 1997); and Jonathan Z. Smith, "Religion, Religions, Religious," in *Critical Terms for Religious Studies*, ed. Mark C. Taylor (Chicago: University of Chicago Press, 1998).

11. For a description of this position, see, e.g., McCutcheon, *Manufacturing Religion*, 51 ff.

12. John T. Noonan, Jr., judge of the Ninth Circuit Court of Appeals, has been outspoken in demanding the recognition that, grammatically speaking, these are not clauses. See *The Lustre of Our Country: The American Experience of Religious Freedom* (Berkeley: University of California Press, 1998), 81. He, and others, would argue that the two commands should be understood to embody a single principle (see ibid., 181–210).

13. It has been said that religion should be understood in an expansive mode for establishment clause purposes and in a narrow mode for free exercise cases. See Thomas Berg, *The State and Religion in a Nutshell* (St. Paul, Minn.: West Group, 1998), 271–72.

14. *Writings of Thomas Jefferson* (New York: Library of America, 1984), 510. Using the expression "church and state" may seem insufficiently culturally inclusive to some. I use it intentionally. "Law and religion" cannot be used as a replacement for "church and state" because it operates at a significantly different level of abstraction. "Church and state" refers to a particular history of particular institutions. There has been a flowering of scholarship concerning the historical context for passage of the First Amendment. See, e.g., Michael McConnell, "The Origins and Historical Understanding of Free Exercise of Religion," *Harvard Law Review* 103 (May 1990): 1409–1517. See also Hamburger, *Separation*.

15. Mark de Wolfe Howe, *The Garden and the Wilderness: Religion and Government in American Constitutional History* (Chicago: University of Chicago Press, 1965).

16. Perry Miller, ed., *The Complete Writings of Roger Williams* (New York: Russell & Russell, 1963), 1:108, quoted in Howe, *The Garden and the Wilderness*, 5–6.

17. Howe, *The Garden and the Wilderness*, 11.

18. *Brown v. Board of Education*, 347 U.S. 483 (1954).

19. See, e.g., *Wisconsin v. Yoder*, 406 U.S. 205 (1972).

20. *Everson v. Board of Education*, 330 U.S. 1 (1947).

21. The Supreme Court granted certiorari in three school voucher cases on September 26, 2001: *Zelman v. Simmons-Harris*, no. 00–1751; *Hanna Perkins School v. Simmons-Harris*, no. 00–1777; and *Taylor v. Simmons-Harris*, no. 00–1779. Oral argument was heard in the cases on February 20, 2002.

22. William W. Hening, ed., *The Statutes at Large, Being a Collection of All of the Laws of Virginia* (New York, 1823), 12:84–86.

23. *Everson v. Board of Education*, 330 U.S. at 15–16.

24. Ibid., at 18.

25. See *Engel v. Vitale*, 370 U.S. 421 (1962); and *Marsh v. Chambers*, 463 U.S. 783 (1983).

26. Justice Felix Frankfurter was interviewed by the Columbia University Oral History Project in 1953. In the course of this interview, he enthusiastically recounted his own public school career. He particularly admired a teacher who had believed that corporal punishment was useful in teaching English to immigrant children (Harlan B. Phillips, ed., *Felix Frankfurter Reminisces* [New York: Reynal, 1960]).

27. Joseph Tussman and Jacob ten Broek, "The Equal Protection of the Laws," *California Law Review* 37 (1949): 342–44 (a seminal formulation of the need for government to treat similarly those similarly situated under equal protection doctrine).

28. Religion is something of a red herring in these cases, in my view. The debate is about democracy and education. It is a historical accident that these cases come up as religion cases.

29. *Mitchell v. Helms*, 530 U.S. 793 (2000).

30. Education and Consolidation Improvement Act, 20 U.S.C.S. secs. 7301–73.

31. *Mitchell v. Helms*, 1990 W.L. 36124 (1990).

32. *Mitchell v. Helms*, 530 U.S. 809.

33. Ibid., at 2551; emphasis added.

34. Ibid., at 2552.

35. Ibid., at 2572.

36. Ibid., at 2576; emphasis added.

37. Ibid., at 2597.

38. Ibid., at 2574–75.

39. *Rosenberger v. Rector and Visitors of the University of Virginia*, 515 U.S. 819 (1995).

40. *Reynolds v. U.S.*, 98 U.S. 145 (1878).

41. Morrill Act, *U.S. Statutes at Large* (1862): 501.

42. *Reynolds v. U.S.*, 98 U.S. at 164.

43. Ibid.

44. *Smith v. Employment Division*, 494 U.S. 872 (1990).

45. Howe, *The Garden and the Wilderness*, 174–75.

46. Religious Freedom Restoration Act, 42 U.S.C. secs. 2000bb et seq. (1993).

47. *Boerne v. Flores*, 521 U.S. 507 (1997). The Catholic bishop of Boerne, Texas, had challenged the city's refusal to permit the rebuilding of a church in the historic district. There is an unresolved debate as to whether *Boerne* declares RFRA unconstitutional only as it applies to the states and not as it applies to the federal government. For the International Religious Freedom Act, see 22 U.S.C.S. secs. 6401 ff. (2001).

48. Religious Freedom Restoration Act, Fla. Stat. chaps. 761.01 ff. (2000).

49. Ibid., chap. 761.02.

50. *Warner v. Boca Raton*, 64 F. Supp. 2d 1272 (1999). My misgivings fell into several categories. I was concerned, first, because I believed that RFRA statutes were unconstitutional and unworkable. I was not sure that it was to the plaintiffs' advantage to have me as a witness, given my views and what I had written. I was also concerned because expert witnessing is a notoriously dangerous enterprise, particularly for those outside the so-called hard sciences. See: Lawrence Rosen, "The Anthropologist as Expert Witness," *American Anthropologist* 79 (1979): 555–78; and James Clifford, *The Predicament of Culture: Twentieth-Century Ethnography, Literature, and Art* (Cambridge: Harvard University Press, 1988). The law demands a degree of assurance that most in cultural studies are reluctant to express. In the end, I was persuaded that I could be helpful without either essentializing religion or distorting the First Amendment.

51. The experts for the plaintiffs were: John McGuckin, Union Theological Seminary; Michael J. Broyde, Emory University; and myself.

52. Expert report of Nathan Katz in *Warren v. Boca Raton*, 64 F Supp. 2d 1272.

53. Expert report of Daniel Pals in ibid.

54. *Warner v. Boca Raton*, 64 F. Supp. 2d 1272; emphasis added.

55. Ibid., at 1287.

56. Ibid., at 1287n11.

57. Plaintiffs have appealed Ryskamp's decision to the U.S. Court of Appeals for the Eleventh Circuit.

58. See, e.g., J. R. Pole, *The Pursuit of Equality in American History*, rev. ed. (Berkeley: University of California Press, 1993).

59. Howe, *The Garden and the Wilderness*, 158.

60. See Winnifred Fallers Sullivan, *Paying the Words Extra: Religious Discourse in the Supreme Court of the United States* (Cambridge: Harvard University Center for the Study of World Religions, 1994).

61. See, e.g., John Witte, Jr., and Frank S. Alexander, eds., *The Weightier Matters of the Law: Essays on Law and Religion; a Tribute to Harold J. Berman* (Atlanta: Scholars Press, 1988).

62. John T. Noonan, Jr., *Persons and Masks of the Law: Cardozo, Holmes, Jefferson, and Wythe as Makers of the Masks* (New York: Farrar, Straus & Giroux, 1976).

63. See David Saunders, *Anti-lawyers: Religion and the Critics of Law and State* (London: Routledge, 1997).

Talal Asad, Reflections on Blasphemy and Secular Criticism

NOTE: An early version of this paper was first given at the Humanities Institute, Stanford University, as the Presidential and Endowed Lecture in October 2006.

1. The Western press has made much of the irrational violence of Muslims responding to the publication of the cartoons, but it has rarely noted the political atmosphere in which Muslims live in Europe generally and in Denmark particularly. According to a Danish researcher, respectable members of parliament from a variety of Danish parties made the following statements to the national press in the 2001 elections: "Muslims are just waiting for the right moment to kill us" (Mogens Camre, Progress Party); "Certain people pose a security risk solely because of their religion, which means that they have to be placed in internment camps" (Inge Dahl Sorensen, Liberal Party); "If you try to legislate your way out of these problems [concerning Muslim organizations], it is a historical rule that rats always find new holes if you cover up the old ones" (Poul Nyrup

Rasmussen, Social Democratic Party). Quoted in P. Hervik, "The Emergence of Neo-Nationalism in Denmark, 1992–2001," in *Neo-Nationalism in Europe and Beyond: Perspectives from Social Anthropology*, ed. M. Banks and A. Gingrich (Oxford: Berghahn, 2006).

2. "The prolonged and violent demonstrations against the Danish cartoons," wrote George Packer, *New Yorker* staff writer, "were a staged attempt by Islamists to intimidate their enemies in their own countries and in the West" ("Fighting Faiths: Can Liberal Internationalism Be Saved?" *The New Yorker*, July 10 and 17, 2006, pp. 95–96).

3. The London *Guardian* columnist Gary Younge, writing at the height of the cartoon affair, provides a telling example: "In January 2002 the [British political weekly] *New Statesman* published a front page displaying a shimmering golden Star of David impaling a union flag, with the words 'A kosher conspiracy?' The cover was widely and rightly condemned as anti-semitic. It's not difficult to see why. It played into vile stereotypes of money-grabbing [sic] Jewish cabals out to undermine the country they live in. Some put it down to a lapse of editorial judgment. But many saw it not as an aberration but part of a trend—one more broadside in an attack on Jews from the liberal left. A group calling itself Action Against Anti-Semitism marched into the *Statesman*'s offices, demanding a printed apology. One eventually followed. . . . I do not remember," Younge goes on, "talk of a clash of civilizations in which Jewish values were inconsistent with the western traditions of freedom of speech or democracy. Nor do I recall editors across Europe rushing to reprint the cover in solidarity. Quite why the Muslim response to 12 cartoons printed [in Denmark] last September should be treated differently is illuminating. There seems to be almost universal agreement that these cartoons are offensive. There should also be universal agreement that the paper has a right to publish them. . . . But the right to freedom of speech equates to neither an obligation to offend nor a duty to be insensitive. There is no contradiction between supporting someone's right to do something and condemning them for doing it." This passage appears in the debate between Philip Hensher and Gary Younge, in "Does the Right to Freedom of Speech Justify Printing the Danish Cartoons?" *The Guardian*, February 4, 2006. Hensher maintains yes, Younge no.

4. "For example, parts of the Danish press as well as Danish politicians have recently argued that Islamic Studies scholars are acting as political agents because they intentionally choose to disregard certain topics, such as social processes in which Islam can be seen as an obstacle to integration and/or a potential security threat" (from *Research on Islam Repositioned*, theme statement for seminar sponsored by Danish research network *Forum for the Research on Islam* [FIFO], May 14–15, 2007). And yet, according to the first Europol report on terrorism, published in 2007, it emerges that of 498 acts of terrorism that took place in the European Union during 2006, Islamists were responsible for only one. The largest number (136) were carried out by Basque separatists, and only one of these Basque attacks resulted in loss of life. Yet over half of those arrested on suspicion of terrorism are Muslim. See Europol, *EU Terrorism Situation and Trend Report*, The Hague, 2007 (www.europol.europa.eu). Almost all the media in Europe have ignored these figures while playing up "the threat of Islam." What accounts for this curious silence/volubility?

5. Lecture of the Holy Father, "Faith, Reason and the University: Memories and Reflections," September 2006, http://www.vatican.va/holy_father/benedict_xvi/speeches/2006/september/documents/hf_ben-xvi_spe_20060912_university-regensburg_en.html. In contrast, the distinguished Catholic philosopher Charles Taylor speaks of "the unbridgeable gulf between Christianity and Greek philosophy." See the Introduction to his *The Secular Age* (Cambridge: Harvard University Press, 2007).

6. See Joss Marsh, *Word Crimes: Blasphemy, Culture, and Literature in Nineteenth-Century England* (Chicago: University of Chicago Press, 1998). Marsh deals with over two hundred blasphemy trials, all of which had a strong class component.

7. Francis Fukuyama, *The End of History and the Last Man*, Afterword to the reprint edition (New York: Free Press, 2006). See also the dialogue between an American nonreligious postmodern

philosopher and an Italian Christian postmodern theologian, in which both agree on the fundamental link between Christianity and democracy: Richard Rorty and Gianni Vattimo, *The Future of Religion*, ed. Santiago Zabala (New York: Columbia University Press, 2005).

8. George Grote, *History of Greece* (London: Routledge, 2001).

9. Marcel Gauchet, *The Disenchantment of the World: A Political History of Religion* (Princeton, N.J.: Princeton University Press, 1997).

10. It is remarkable how little knowledge writers think necessary when dealing with Christianity's alter, Islam: "The difference [of Christianity] from Islam is glaringly obvious. The Koran's revelation is itself the literal and indisputable presence of the transcendent in immanence and thus dispensed with interpreters, lest it succumb to the uncertainties of internal judgment or to an outbreak of subjective values. No clergy, no Reformation. Christianity, by contrast, linked orthodoxy's austerity to an opening for heresy" (ibid., 80). The notion that Islamic history lacks authoritative interpreters of the Qur'an and distinct traditions of scriptural interpretation, that it therefore contains no opening for heresy and no reformation, may be a sad reflection of scholarly ignorance, but it serves the purpose of distinguishing "our" civilization, which has this potentiality, and "theirs," which lacks it.

11. "If the task of philosophy after the death of God—hence after the deconstruction of metaphysics—is a labor of stitching things back together, of reassembly, then secularization is the appropriate way of bearing witness to the attachment of modern European civilization to its own religious past [i.e., Christianity], a relationship consisting not of surpassing and emancipation alone, but conservation too. Contrary to the view of a good deal of contemporary theology, the death of God is something post-Christian rather than anti-Christian; by now we are living in the post-Christian time of the death of God, in which secularization has become the norm for all theological discourse" (Santiago Zabala, introductory essay to Rorty and Vattimo, *The Future of Religion*, 2).

12. The Middle East is not, of course, equivalent to "the world of Islam"—or even to "Muslim-majority countries," since most Muslims live outside the Middle East. And yet in the Western imaginary Muslim countries of the Middle East are seen as "the central lands of Islam," just as "Christianity" is usually taken to mean Latin Christianity and does not refer to the important (and continuous) Christian communities in Muslim-majority countries.

13. See J. S. Mill's *Representative Government*, esp. chap. 8 (1861; John Stuart Mill, *Three Essays* [London: Oxford University Press, 1973]). A great opponent of extending voting rights at the time was Robert Lowe. For his arguments, see the chapter entitled "Robert Lowe and the Fear of Democracy," in Asa Briggs, *Victorian People* (Harmondsworth: Penguin Books, 1965).

14. Zabala, introductory essay to Rorty and Vattimo, *The Future of Religion*, 6.

15. Ibid., 72.

16. R. Alta Charo, J.D., "Body of Research—Ownership and Use of Human Tissue," *New England Journal of Medicine* 355 (October 12, 2006).

17. "With the emergence of capitalism as a system of power dominated by huge conglomerates that dispensed radically unequal rewards, its anti-democratic culture became steadily more obvious. Marx had been only half-right: capitalism not only deformed the worker qua worker but also qua citizen. In its structure, ideology, and human relationship capitalism was producing human beings unfitted for democratic citizenship: self-interested, exploitive, competitive, striving for inequalities, fearful of downward mobility" (Sheldon Wolin, *Politics and Vision*, Expanded Edition [Princeton, N.J.: Princeton University Press, 2004], 597).

18. Here is an interesting example: in 1967 the founder of Penguin Books decided that a book just put out by his publishing house was offensive to Christian sensibilities and that it should therefore be destroyed. He did just that. (See Richard Webster, *A Brief History of Blasphemy* [Oxford: The Orwell Press, 1990] 26.) No one protested; no one had the right to protest. My point here

is simply that the sanctity of property—in this case property in the means of communication—gives one the legal power to control the form and content of public expression.

19. "Greek laws were not lenient towards adultery, and *moikheia*, for which we have no suitable translation except 'adultery,' denoted not only the seduction of another man's wife, but also the seduction of his widowed mother, unmarried daughter, sister, niece, or any other woman whose legal guardian he was. The adulterer could be prosecuted by the offended father, husband, or guardian; alternatively, if caught in the act, he could be killed, maltreated, or imprisoned by force. . . . The adulterer was open to reproach in the same way and to the same extent as any other violator of the laws protecting the individual citizen against arbitrary treatment by other citizens" (K. J. Dover, "Classical Greek Attitudes to Sexual Behaviour," in *Sex and Difference in Ancient Greece and Rome*, ed. M. Golden and P. Toohey [Edinburgh: Edinburgh University Press, 2003], 117–18).

20. For an excellent discussion of the freedom promised by images typically used in consumer advertising, see John Berger, *Ways of Seeing* (Harmondsworth: Penguin Books, 1972), esp. the final section, "Publicity."

21. Mark Rose, "The Author as Proprietor: *Donaldson v. Becket* and the Genealogy of Modern Authorship," *Representations* 33 (1988).

22. See Martha Woodmansee, "The Genius and the Copyright: Economic and Legal Conditions of the Emergence of the 'Author,'" *Eighteenth-Century Studies* 17, no. 4 (1984).

23. See Lane's *Arabic-English Lexicon*. See also Kazimirski's *Dictionnaire Arabe-Français* (1875), which gives "Blasphémer Dieu, et faire nargue de ses bienfaits."

24. In this respect it overlaps with such words as *shatīma*, *sabb*, *istihīna*.

25. *Bayān al-ittihād hawl nashr suwar masī'a li-rrasāl* [Statement of the (World) Union (of Islamic Scholars) about the Publication of Images Insulting to the Prophet] (Cairo, January 23, 2006) www.qaradawi.net/site/topics/article.asp?cu_no = 4143&version = 1&template_id = 116& parent_id = 114.

26. The book that got Nasr Hamid Abu-Zayd declared an apostate (and hence no longer legally married to his wife) was *Mafhūm al-nass: Dirāsah fi 'ulūm al-Qur'ān* [Understanding the (Sacred) Text: A Study of the Sciences of the Qur'an] (Beirut: al-Markaz al-Thaqafi al-'Arabi, 1990). Two interesting articles on Abu Zayd's methodology should be noted: Charles Hirschkind, "Heresy or Hermeneutics: The Case of Nasr Hamid Abu Zayd," *Stanford Humanities Review* 5, no. 1 (1996); and Saba Mahmood, "Secularism, Hermeneutics, and Empire: The Politics of Islamic Reformation," *Public Culture* 18, no. 2 (2006). Mahmood deals with Abu Zayd among other liberal Islamic reformers.

27. A detailed account of the case is given in Kilian Bälz, "Submitting Faith to Judicial Scrutiny Through the Family Trial: The 'Abu Zayd Case,'" *Die Welt des Islams* n.s. 37, no. 2 (1997). A more interesting account is provided in chap. 1 ("The Legalization of *Hisba* in the Case of Nasr Abu Zayd") of Hussein Agrama's Ph.D. dissertation, "Law Courts and Fatwa Councils in Modern Egypt: An Ethnography of Islamic Legal Practice," The Johns Hopkins University, 2005. Extended extracts from the judgments in the court of first instance, the court of appeals, and the court of cassation are given (in French translation) in "Jurisprudence Abu Zayd," *Egypte / Monde Arabe*, no. 34 (1998). The original Arabic judgments are contained in Muhammad Salim al-'Awwa, *al-haq fi al-ta'bīr* [Right to Free Speech] (Cairo: Dar al-Sharuq, 1998).

28. Al-'Awwa, *al-haq fi al-ta'bīr*, 23. See also Ahmad Rashad Tahun, *Hurriyat al-'aqīda fish-sharī'a al-islāmiyya* (Cairo, 1998), who is more concerned with the political issues—especially with the unity of the *umma*—than al-'Awwa is.

29. In a recent article, Baber Johansen has traced Ibn Taymiyya's position on the question of coerced confession. "Whereas the torture of witnesses played an important role in Roman law and

in late medieval judicial practice of Europe," Johansen observes, "it is unknown in Muslim legal doctrine." But Ibn Taymiyya took an unusually political view of the law's role, and in so doing advocated the legal admissibility of coerced evidence. See Johansen, "Signs as Evidence: The Doctrine of Ibn Taymiyya (1263–1328) and Ibn Qayyim Al-Jawziyya (d. 1351) on Proof," *Islamic Law and Society* 9, no. 2 (2002): 171.

30. In "What Is Enlightenment?" Kant makes what may appear to be a similar distinction when he speaks about "public" and "private" reason. The latter, however, depends on the concept of the state, in relation to which an arena for the conduct of public debate is circumscribed. Al-'Awwa has no such argument. His concern is simply with the representability of personal belief as an inner condition.

31. "It is to be noted that according to the definition (1) blasphemy is set down as a word, for ordinarily it is expressed in speech, though it may be committed in thought or in act. Being primarily a sin of the tongue, it will be seen to be opposed directly to the religious act of praising God. (2) It is said to be against God, though this may be only mediately, as when the contumelious word is spoken of the saints or of sacred things, because of the relationship they sustain to God and His service" (*The Catholic Encyclopedia* [New York: Robert Appleton Company, 1907], 2:595).

32. Al-'Awwa, *al-haq fi al-ta'bīr*, 13.

33. Al-Shaykh 'Uthman Safi, *'Ala Hāmish* "Naqd al-fikr ad-dīnī" [A Footnote to "The Critique of Religious Thought"] (Beirut: Daru-ttali'a li-ttaba'a wa-nnashr, 1970), 87.

34. Bälz, "Submitting Faith to Judicial Scrutiny Through the Family Trial," 143.

35. Johansen, "Signs as Evidence."

36. See the excellent ethnographic study by Winnifred Fallers Sullivan, *The Impossibility of Religious Freedom* (Princeton, N.J.: Princeton University Press, 2005).

37. Ibid., 12–13.

38. This is not unlike the premodern meaning of the word *belief* in English and its equivalents in other European languages. See chap. 6 of Wilfred Cantwell Smith, *Faith and Belief* (Oxford: One World, 1998), for an interesting etymology of the word.

39. There has been considerable disagreement in modern Islamic history over the criteria for determining apostasy, as well as whether and if so how it should be punished. Thus one of the medieval collections of *hadith*, by Bukhari, records a statement by the Prophet Muhammad that apostates must be killed; but another canonical collection, that by Muslim, declares this statement to be inauthentic. The debate has continued in modern times.

40. Dorothea Weltecke, "Beyond Religion: On the Lack of Belief During the Central and Late Middle Ages," in *Religion and Its Other: Secular and Sacred Concepts and Practices in Interaction*, ed. J. Feuchter, M. Knecht, and H. Bock (Berlin, forthcoming).

41. Henri Peña-Ruiz, "Laïcité et égalité, leviers d'émancipation, *Le monde diplomatique*, February 2004, 9. I have discussed this affair in some detail in "Trying to Understand French Secularism," in *Political Theologies: Public Religions in a Post-Secular World*, ed. Hent de Vries and Lawrence E. Sullivan (New York: Fordham University Press, 2006), 494–526.

42. But given the UN Declaration ("The States Parties to the present Covenant undertake to have respect for the liberty of parents and, when applicable, legal guardians to ensure the religious and moral education of their children in conformity with their own convictions"), it is not clear who, in these cases, has the right to oversee their formation.

43. Raymond Williams was one of the earliest to address this problem seriously. See his *Britain in the Sixties: Communications* (Harmondsworth: Penguin Books, 1962) and *Television: Technology and Cultural Form* (London: Fontana, 1974). A recent popular work on this topic is Benjamin Barber, *Consumed: How Markets Corrupt Children, Infantilize Adults, and Swallow Citizens Whole* (New York: W. W. Norton, 2007).

44. A typical sentence: *wa-l-fitnatu ashaddu min al-qatli* (2:191), "persecution is worse than killing."

45. S. Mendus, *Toleration and the Limits of Liberalism* (Atlantic Highlands, N.J.: Humanities Press, 1989).

46. "Here I stand: I can do no other," the words attributed to Luther, were probably never uttered, although they express very well the sentiment of his actual statement at the Diet of Worms. (See O. Chadwick, *The Reformation* [Harmondsworth: Penguin Books, 1972], 56.) At any rate, what he said on that famous occasion would have to be described as sincere but inauthentic. This doesn't seem right, however.

47. Leonard W. Levy, *Treason Against God: A History of the Offense of Blasphemy* (New York: Schocken Books, 1981).

48. www.archbishopofcanterbury.org/sermons_speeches/060709.htm.

49. For the beginning of that history, see the classic work by Adolf Harnack, *Militia Christi: The Christian Religion and the Military in the First Three Centuries*, trans. and introd. David Gracie (1905; Philadelphia: Fortress Press, 1981). The pacifist C. John Cadoux gives a rather different account in *The Early Christian Attitude to War* (London, 1919), published after the experience of the First World War.

50. Thus, in the early Middle Ages, Latin Christianity considered all killing a sin (for which penance was prescribed), even when it occurred in a battle that was sanctioned by the Church. This understanding changed when "intention" became critical to certain domains of Christian thought, as in Abelard's theology of penance and Bernard of Clairvaux's celebration of "the new knighthood," which became an important element in the ideology of the crusades.

51. Alain Cabantous, *Blasphemy: Impious Speech in the West from the Seventeenth to the Nineteenth Century* (New York: Columbia University Press, 2002), 5.

52. Hent de Vries has made precisely this argument by drawing on Derrida as well as Benjamin in his excellent *Religion and Violence: Philosophical Perspectives from Kant to Derrida* (Baltimore: The Johns Hopkins University Press, 2002). But in my view it does not follow that, just because it sometimes seeks to overcome a greater by a lesser violence, every blasphemous utterance is a new founding. Blasphemy may itself be an *obsession*, in which the act simply serves as the reinstantiation of an established genre, the reapplication of a style *that has no foundation*—or it may simply be the performance of gratuitous cruelty conducted from a position of superior power.

53. W. C. Van Unnik, "The Christian's Freedom of Speech in the New Testament," *Bulletin of the John Rylands Library* 44 (1962): 487.

54. Edward W. Said, *The World, the Text, and the Critic* (Boston: Faber and Faber, 1983), 26.

55. Michel Foucault, "What Is Critique?" [Lecture originally given at the Sorbonne on May 27, 1978], in *What Is Enlightenment? Eighteenth-Century Answers and Twentieth-Century Questions*, ed. James Schmidt (Berkeley: University of California Press, 1996).

56. Ibid., 382.

57. See Reinhart Koselleck, *Crisis and Critique* (Cambridge: MIT Press, 1988), 103n15. My colleague John Wallach informs me: "The verb is *krinī*, which could signify 'to separate, to discern, to judge.' Related nouns are *krisis* (turning point—potentially between life and death) and *kritīrion*, i.e., means for judging, as well as the designation for a 'judge.' Courts were known as *Dikasteriai*, places where judgments of justice were laid down. Judges on Greek juries were called *dikastai*. The Greek goddess of Justice was Dikī. *Dikī* derives from the verb *dikazo*, which signified 'to judge, to decide, to establish as a penalty or judgment.' Some relate it to the verb *deiknumi*, which signifies 'to show, make manifest, prove,' etc. There was no verb equivalent of what English speakers have recently made into a verb (from its origins as a noun), viz. 'critique'" (personal communication).

A useful account of the history of the term is available in the entries "Krisis" and "Kritik" in Otto Brunner, Werner Conze, and Reinhart Koselleck, eds., *Geschichtliche Grundbegriffe: Historisches Lexikon zur politisch-sozialen Sprache in Deutschland* (Stuttgart: E. Klett, 1972–97).

58. See Michel Foucault, *Fearless Speech* (Los Angeles: Semiotext[e], 2001), 119–33.

59. See Richard Popkin, *The History of Scepticism*, revised and expanded edition (New York: Oxford University Press, 2003), esp. chap. 18.

60. Steven Shapin, *A Social History of Truth: Civility and Science in Seventeenth-Century England* (Chicago: University of Chicago Press, 1994).

61. Later, however, the Communist Party would take up the practice of auto-critique. The most moving example of this that I know in literature is Arthur Koestler's *Darkness at Noon*, trans. Daphne Hardy (London: Jonathan Cape, 1940).

62. Karl Popper's *Logic of Scientific Discovery* (London: Routledge, 2002) is the famous statement of his falsification theory. His *The Poverty of Historicism* (London: Routledge & Kegan Paul, 1957) was an influential critique directed at the scientific claims of Marxian historicism.

63. Jon Roberts and James Turner, *The Sacred and Secular University* (Princeton: Princeton University Press, 2000), 102.

64. Andrew Sullivan, "Your Taboo, Not Mine: The Furore over Cartoons of Muhammad Reveals the Zealot's Double Standard," *Time*, February 7, 2006. See also the more interesting (but flawed) piece by Christophe Boltanski, "La représentation du prophète est devenue taboue," *Libération*, February 3, 2006.

65. Franz Steiner, *Taboo* (London: Cohen and West, 1958).

66. A mere two weeks before the publication of the cartoons, the Danish newspaper *Politiken* printed an article titled "A Profound Fear of Criticizing Islam," which suggests that white majorities in Europe felt beleaguered by the presence of Muslim minorities. See Randall Hansen, "The Danish Cartoon Controversy: A Defence of Liberal Freedom," *International Migration* 44, no. 5 (2006): 8. The publication of the cartoons is therefore to be seen as an attempt to overcome a constraint on liberal freedom. Apparently there were no such feelings when the very newspaper that published the Muhammad cartoons previously rejected cartoons thought to be offensive to Christian sensibilities. See G. Fouché, "Danish Paper Rejected Jesus Cartoons," *Guardian*, February 6, 2006. The decision not to publish the Jesus cartoons was a concession to the sensibilities of a Christian majority: therefore it was not coerced. The point I want to make here has to do with the variable conditions that determine the use of "free speech" and not with bias, as though there was an abstract standard of "free speech."

67. This is ably shown in Amel Boubekeur, "L'islamisme comme tradition," in *Islamismes d'Occident*, ed. Samir Amghar (Paris: Ligne de repères, 2006). For further details, see Amel Boubekeur and Samir Amghar, *Les partis islamistes du Maghreb et leur liens avec l'Europe* (Brussels: Centre for European Policy Studies [CEPS], 2006).

Michael Warner, Is Liberalism a Religion?

1. "Democracy and Education," July 22, 2007.

2. *New York Times*, February 12, 2006.

3. This charge has been elaborated by John Brenkman, among others. See his "Extreme Criticism," *Critical Inquiry* 26, no. 1 (1999): 109–27.

4. See, e.g., Talal Asad, *Genealogies of Religion: Discipline and Reasons of Power in Christianity and Islam* (Baltimore: The Johns Hopkins University Press, 1993); idem, *Formations of the Secular:*

Christianity, Islam, Modernity (Stanford, Calif.: Stanford University Press, 2002); Charles Taylor, *A Secular Age* (Cambridge: Harvard Univ. Press, forthcoming); and Webb Keane, *Christian Moderns: Freedom and Fetish in the Mission Encounter* (Berkeley: University of California Press, 2007).

5. This point has been made by a number of scholars. See, e.g., Peter Harrison, *"Religion" and the Religions in the English Enlightenment* (Cambridge: Cambridge University Press, 1990), and Charles Taylor, *Varieties of Religion Today: William James Revisited* (Cambridge: Harvard University Press, 2002).

6. Saba Mahmood, "Secularism, Hermeneutics, and Empire: The Politics of Islamic Reformation," *Public Culture* 18, no. 2 (Spring 2006): 323–47.

7. Ibid., 334.

8. Louis Menand, *The Metaphysical Club* (New York: Farrar, Straus, Giroux, 2001).

9. Winnifred Fallers Sullivan, *The Impossibility of Religious Freedom* (Princeton, N.J.: Princeton University Press, 2005).

10. Ibid., 147.

11. Ibid., 155.

12. Robert Bellah, "Civil Religion in America" (1967), rpt. in *The Robert Bellah Reader* (Durham, N.C.: Duke University Press, 2006), 227.

13. Stanley Hauerwas, "Preaching as Though We Had Enemies," *First Things* 53 (May 1995).

Samuel Weber, Toward a Politics of Singularity: Protection and Projection

1. Thomas Hobbes, *Leviathan* (Oxford: Oxford University Press, 1996), 475, my italics. Page numbers for later citations will be given in the text.

2. Gérard Mairet, Introduction to Hobbes, *Léviathan* (Gallimard: Paris, 2000), 42.

3. Jacques Derrida, *Speech and Phenomenon*, trans. and introd. David B. Allison (Evanston, Ill.: Northwestern University Press, 1973), 78–79. Page numbers for later citations will be given in the text.

4. Michael Naas, "'One Nation . . . Indivisible': Jacques Derrida on the Autoimmunity of Democracy and the Sovereignty of God," *Research in Phenomenology* 36, no. 1 (2006): 15.

5. Jacques Derrida, *Specters of Marx: The State of the Debt, the Work of Mourning, and the New International*, trans. Peggy Kamuf (Routledge: New York, 1994), 141.

6. In the past few decades this attitude has changed radically in the life sciences, which have recognized the usefulness and necessity of attenuating immunological reactions in order to "protect" the system—as in the case of organ transplants, the most obvious example of the dependency of the "self" upon "others" in order to survive.

7. Jacques Derrida, "Faith and Knowledge: The Two Sources of 'Religion' at the Limits of Reason Alone," trans. Samuel Weber, in Jacques Derrida, *Acts of Religion*, ed. and introd. Gil Anidjar (New York: Routledge, 2002), 87.

8. Jacques Derrida and Elisabeth Roudinesco, *For What Tomorrow . . . : A Dialogue*, trans. Jeff Fort (Stanford, Calif.: Stanford University Press, 2004). Page numbers in the text refer to the French edition (*De quoi demain . . .* [Flammarion: Paris, 2003]).

9. Derrida puts this (Lacanian) phrase in quotes to signal that it is not one that he endorses, but rather questions throughout this interview and elsewhere, since, in his eyes, psychoanalysis does not merely establish another form of "logic," even one of the unconscious.

10. Jacques Derrida, "Psychoanalysis Searches the States of Its Soul," in Derrida, *Without Alibi*, ed. and trans. Peggy Kamuf (Stanford, Calif.: Stanford University Press, 2002), 243–44, my trans.

11. Ibid., 244.

12. Sigmund Freud, "Abriß der Psychoanalyse," *Gesammelte Werke* (Frankfurt a. M.: S. Fischer, 1968), 17:79. My translation and emphasis.

13. Sigmund Freud, *Beyond the Pleasure Principle* (New York: Bantam Books, 1972), 52–53; my emphasis. Page numbers for later citations will be given in the text.

14. Sigmund Freud, *Inhibitions, Symptoms and Anxiety*, trans. John Strachey (New York: Norton, 1990).

15. Benjamin, *Gesammelte Schriften*, 1.2:615; Walter Benjamin, *Selected Writings*, vol. 4, *1938–1940*, trans. Edmund Jephcott and others, ed. Howard Eiland and Michael W. Jennings (Cambridge: Harvard University Press, 2003), 319, trans. modified.

16. In "The Economic Problem of Masochism," Freud comes to the belated realization that there are certain "tensions" that can be pleasurable and certain relaxations that can be painful, of which sexual experience is the most obvious instance. From this he concludes that the equation of tension with displeasure, at the basis of the "pleasure principle," cannot be sustained, and that instead of an absolute increase or decrease in tension, it may be questions of "rhythm" that are more relevant to the discrimination of pleasure and displeasure.

17. Marcel Proust, *Du côté de chez Swann*, vol. 1 of *A la recherche du temps perdu* (Paris: Pléiade, 1962), 5; trans. C. K. Scott Moncrieff and Terence Kilmartin, *In Search of Lost Time*, vol. 1, *Swann's Way*, rev. D. J. Enright (New York: Modern Library, 2003), 4; my trans.

Tomoko Masuzawa, Troubles with Materiality: The Ghost of Fetishism in the Nineteenth Century

NOTE: This essay originally appeared in *Comparative Studies in Society and History* 42, no. 2 (2000): 242–67. It appears here courtesy of Cambridge University Press.

1. Various names and phrases commonly used to refer to the study of religion, such as "religious studies," "science of religion," *Religionswissenschaft*, "history of religions," "comparative religion," and their cognates in various European languages are not exactly interchangeable on all occasions, but in this essay I will be using some of these as more or less equivalent.

2. Among the notable exceptions—i.e., those who held onto the theory of fetishism as the most original/primitive form of religion—was Frederick Harrison, Comte's protégé in England. His public debate with Herbert Spencer over the alleged primitive knowledge of the Infinite (first published as a series of article in *Popular Science Monthly*) was later collected in one volume (*The Nature and Reality of Religion: A Controversy Between Frederick Harrison and Herbert Spencer*, ed. Edward Youmans, New York: Appleton, 1885): "Whilst I find in a hundred books that countless races of Africa and the organized religion of China attribute human qualities to natural objects, and grow up to regard those objects with veneration and awe, I shall continue to think that fetishism, or the reverent ascription of feeling and power to natural objects, is a spontaneous tendency of the human mind" (123).

3. Louis Henry Jordan, *Comparative Religion: Its Genesis and Growth* (Edinburgh, T. & T. Clark, 1905), 532–33.

4. "This animation hypothesis, held as a faith, is at the root of all the mythologies. It has been called Fetichism; which, according to the common accounts of it, ascribes a life and personality resembling our own, not only to animals and plants, but to rocks, mountains, streams, winds, the heavenly bodies, the earth itself, and even the heavens. Fetichism thus resembles Totemism; which, indeed, is Fetichism *plus* certain peculiarities. These peculiarities are, (1) the appropriation of a special Fetich to the tribe, (2) its hereditary transmission through mothers, and (3) its connection with the *jus connubii*. Our own belief is that the accompaniments of Fetichism have not been well observed, and that it will yet be found that in many cases the Fetich is the Totem" (J. F. McLennan, "The Worship of Animals and Plants," *Fortnightly Review* 12 [1869]: 422–23).

5. W. Robertson Smith, *The Religions of the Semites* (1889).

6. The first articulation of the animism theory seems to have occurred in "The Religion of Savages" (*Fortnightly Review* 6 [1866]: 71–86), and it was fully elaborated in *Primitive Culture* (1871 and 1873).

7. Cf., e.g.: Frank Byron Jevons's *An Introduction to the History of Religion* (London: Methuen, 1896); Daniel G. Brinton, *Religions of Primitive Peoples* (New York: G. P. Putnam, 1897); Alfred C. Haddon, *Magic and Fetishism* (London: Constable, 1921); E. Washburn Hopkins, *Origin and Evolution of Religion* (New Haven, Conn.: Yale University Press, 1923); Wilhelm Schmidt, *The Origin and Growth of Religion: Facts and Theories*, trans. H. J. Rose (London: Methuen, 1935; based on *Der Ursprung der Gottesidee*, 1926).

8. In the literature of the period in question—roughly from the mid nineteenth century to the 1920s and 1930s—the convention among scholars was to refer to the contemporary inhabitants of the "uncivilized" parts of the world as "savages," whereas the word *primitive* was reserved for the prehistoric ancestors of the civilized world, also called "early man." These scholars tended to aver that the primitive and the savage were not the same thing, because the latter underwent a long course of history just like the civilized peoples today (though the savage's "history" was generally considered degenerative or stagnant rather than evolutionary or progressive), and that, despite this difference, the savages of today still offered much to teach us about "our" prehistory, because of some important commonalities they share with their primordial ancestors. Throughout this paper I conform to this terminology of the savage and the primitive, which is at variance with the contemporary use of these terms.

9. Sometimes this indiscriminate conflation and expansion of the definition is attributed to Auguste Comte, Herbert Spencer, E. B. Tylor, Adolf Bastian (*Der Mensch in der Geschichte: Zur Begründung einer psychologischen Weltanschauung*, Leipzig, 1860), or Friz Schultze (*Der Fetischismus*, Leipzig, 1871; English translation, *Fetishism: A Contribution to Anthropology and the History of Religion*, trans. J. Fitzgerald, New York, 1885), rather than to de Brosses.

10. Melville J. Herskovits, *Man and His Works: The Science of Cultural Anthropology* (New York: Knopf, 1948), 368.

11. Friedrich Max Müller, *Lectures on the Origin and Growth of Religion as Illustrated by the Religions of India; Delivered in the Chapter House, Westminster Abbey, in April, May, and June, 1878* (London: Longmans, Green, 1879).

12. This was Lang in his Tylorian phase. By the time he was advocating the theory of primitive monotheism, his opinion on this matter seems to have changed significantly. Cf. George W. Stocking, Jr., *After Tylor: British Social Anthropology 1888–1951* (Madison: University of Wisconsin Press, 1995), 50–63.

13. Eugene Comte Goblet d' Alviella, *Lectures on the Origin and Growth of the Conception of God as Illustrated by Anthropology and History* (London: Williams and Norgate, 1892).

14. Respectively published as *Natural Religion* (1889), *Physical Religion* (1890), *Anthropological Religion* (1891), and *Psychical Religion* (1892). The nature of the Gifford Lectures was such that four

different individuals were to deliver respectively a series of lectures in one of the four Scottish universities (Edinburgh, Glasgow, Aberdeen, and St. Andrews). In the inaugural year (1888–89), Müller gave his at Glasgow, while Andrew Lang did likewise at St. Andrews under the title *The Making of Religion*. A year later, E. B. Tylor inaugurated the series at Aberdeen. Cf. Jordan, *Comparative Religion*, 570–71.

15. See n. 7 above, as well as Goblet d'Alviella, *Lectures*. I am assuming here a certain level of respectability on the basis of the prestige of the publishers, as well as the academic appointments held by these authors. Jevon was a classical tutor in the University of Durham, described by Eric Sharpe as the best-known English-speaking liberal Christian among the "founding fathers of comparative religion" (Sharpe, *Comparative Religion*, 148–49); Brinton was Professor of American Archaeology and Linguistics at the University of Pennsylvania; Haddon, University Lecturer in Ethnology at Cambridge University; Hopkins, Professor of Sanskrit and Comparative Philology at Yale University; Schmidt, University of Vienna; Goblet d'Alviella, University of Brussels.

16. This "conventional wisdom" is intelligently summarized in Hubert Cancik, Burkhard Gladigow, and Matthias Laubscher, eds., *Handbuch Religionswissenschaftlicher Grundbegriffe*, vol. 2 (Stuttgart: Kohnhammer, 1990), "*Fetisch/Fetischismus*," s.v.

17. As Müller puts it: "If you consulted any of the books that have been written during the last hundred years on the history of religion, you will find in most of them a striking agreement on at least one point, viz., that the lowest form of what can be called religion is fetishism, that it is impossible to imagine anything lower that would still deserve that name, and that therefore fetishism may safely be considered as the very beginning of all religion" (*Origin and Growth of Religion*, 53).

18. C. P. Tide and Daniel G. Brinton gave prominent lecture series in 1896 and 1897, respectively—the former the Gifford Lectures at Edinburgh, the latter the second series of the newly established American Lectures on the History of Religions (delivered in seven northeastern American cities)—and spoke from a viewpoint explicitly assuming the universality of religion, in the language of a common essence and its greatly various manifestations "from the lowest to the highest" (Tiele, *Elements of the Science of Religion*, 2 vols. [London: Blackwood, 1897–98]; Brinton, *Religions of Primitive Peoples* (New York: Putnam, 1897). A few decades later, this universalist conception famously culminated in Gerardus van der Leeuw's *Phänomenologie der Religion* (Tübingen, 1933), which was translated into English under the title *Religion in Essence and Manifestation* (London, 1938).

19. I argue this point more extensively in my *The Invention of World Religions; or, How European Universalism Was Preserved in the Language of Pluralism* (Chicago: University of Chicago Press, 2005).

20. Despite the current use of this singular/plural distinction to demarcate the different philosophies involved in the earlier and the later generations of scholars—the use made and insisted on by Eliade, Kees Bolle, and others—nineteenth- and early-twentieth-century writers seem to have used both forms indiscriminately. In English, the following designations seem to have been used more or less interchangeably: history of religion, history of religions, science of religion, comparative religion, study of religion, historical study of religions (Morris Jastrow), comparative history of religions (James Moffatt). In other western European languages I have also encountered: *l'histoire des religions, sciences religieuses, scienza delle religioni, Religionswissenschaft, Vergleichende Religionswissenschaft, Geschichte der vergleichenden Religionsforschung, allegemeine Religionsgeschichte*, and *allegemeine kritische Geschichte der Religion*, among others. Individual writers often make their own case about the difference between, e.g., history of religion(s) and comparative religion, or between history of religion and "anthropology" (by which Andrew Lang meant the difference between the

study of religion based on "historical" cultures with written sources—such as India—and that based on ethnographic study of savages); but these distinctions are not consistent and tend to be idiosyncratic.

21. Here, as in most contemporary discussion concerning the nineteenth-century theory of the origin of religion, the word *evolution* is used in a nontechnical, rather loose sense of "development" or "improvement." Suffice it to say that this "popular" notion of evolution is in fact contrary to the nonteleological thrust of the Darwinian notion of natural selection, according to which the survival of the fittest is a contingent process and the transmutation of the species itself is essentially random.

22. Andrew Lang, "Fetishism and the Infinite," in *Custom and Myth*, new ed. (London: Longmans Green, 1893), 212.

23. Müller, *Origin and Growth of Religion*, 116–17; my emphasis.

24. In an extraordinary series of articles published in the 1980s, entitled "The Problem of the Fetish," William Pietz, a historian of religion with no connection to the Eliadean tradition of History of Religions, has documented the genealogy of this problem/idea, recovering its disjunctive "history" from the sixteenth century to the Enlightenment ("The Problem of the Fetish," I, II, and IIIa, *Res* 9 [Spring 1985], 13 [Spring 1987], and 16 [Autumn 1988]). I derive these characterizations of fetishism from his elucidation. Perhaps this is as good a place as any to acknowledge the not easily calculable extent of my indebtedness to his monumental work.

25. We recall that idolatry and polytheism were interchangeable terms in David Hume's *Natural History of Religion* (written in 1756; posthumously published in 1777). For a useful historical account of how *polytheism*—a term invented by Philo of Alexandria and rediscovered in the sixteenth century by Jean Bodin—came to replace "idolatry," see Francis Schmidt, "Polytheisms: Degeneration or Progress?" *History and Anthropology* 2 (1987): 9–60.

26. In the nineteenth century this hierarchical dichotomy was prominently played out in the form of a radical differentiation between local (or ethnic) religions and universal religion(s). For instance, James Freeman Clarke differentiated the "catholic" religion (Christianity) from "ethnic" religions (all the rest) in his widely-read *Ten Great Religions: An Essay in Comparative Theology* (Boston: Houghton Mifflin, 1871), and Cornelius Petrus Tiele drew an important distinction between "national nomistic" (or nomothetic) religions and "universalistic" religions (or "world religions") in "Religions," *Encyclopaedia Britannica*, s v., 9th ed., 1884. Cf. also Jonathan Z. Smith, "Religion, Religions, Religious" in *Critical Terms for Religious Studies*, ed. Mark C. Taylor (Chicago: University of Chicago Press, 1998).

27. To be exact, according to Comte, the progressive stages of fetishism, polytheism, and monotheism together constitute the theological-fictive phase of evolution, to be superseded next by the metaphysical-abstract phase, and finally by the positive-scientific. Cf. Auguste Comte, *Positive Philosophy*, trans. Harriet Martineau, chaps. 7–9.

28. John Lubbock, *The Origin of Civilization and the Primitive Condition of Man* (London, 1870).

29. Wilhelm Schmidt, *Origin and Growth of Religion: Facts and Theories*, 59.

30. All alleged cases of fetishism, Haddon claims, "when examined, show that the worship is paid to an intangible power or spirit incorporated in some visible form"; therefore, a fetish is merely a mediating object between the worshipper and the power "behind the material object" (*Magic and Fetishism*, 70).

31. Ibid., 91–92. Haddon goes on to suggest that the choice of objects to be worshipped—and the degree of materiality attached to the object—may very well depend on such factors as climate: "The cold, practical, phlegmatic Northerners worship within bare walls, while the fervour of the

imaginative South demands expression in an elaborate ritual, with richness of decoration, warms of colour, dim lights and soft music. The extraordinary vivid imagination and the childlike capacity for 'make-believe' of the negro, lead him further still; the lively fancy of the West African demands a visible object to which worship may be directed. He wishes really and sensibly to behold and even to possess his god, so he incorporates him in a tangible object" (93).

32. Washburn Hopkins, *Origin and Evolution of Religion*, 11.

33. J. G. Frazer, *The Golden Bough: A Study in Magic and Religion*, abridged ed. (New York: Macmillan, 1922), 11–12.

34. Sigmund Freud, *Totem and Taboo*, vol. 13 of *The Standard Edition of the Complete Psychological Works of Sigmund Freud*, trans. James Strachey (London: The Hogarth Press, 1955).

35. *Primitive Culture: Research into the Early History of Mankind and the Development of Civilization*, 2d ed. (London: John Murray, 1870), 6. Here, Tylor is relegating some contemporaries from his own society to the rank of the most savage: "for no Greenlander or Kafir ever mixed up his subjectivity with the evidence of his senses into a more hopeless confusion than the modern spiritualist."

36. Frazer, *The Golden Bough*, 50.

37. Cf. Lang, "Fetichism and the Infinite."

38. Müller, *Origin and Growth of Religion*, 93.

39. Ibid., 58–59.

40. In that remarkable passage, Max Müller made visible, if only inadvertently, a textbook case of the orientalist construction of a phantom other. Fetishism turns out to be a mirror image of one's own practice, an image of one's own likeness in reverse. To be sure, a critical analysis of this specter, generated by the orientalist compulsion to play out the logic of sameness and difference, does not end with this recognition, but rather begins with it. Indeed, so long as the problem of the fetish is regarded essentially as an error in European perception, or as a flaw in the Western order of knowledge, our critical thinking is bound to be "self-reflective" only in a narcissistic sense, bound to circulate within the domain of Western guilt and fantasy. Instead, this hegemonic representation of Europe's other, this colonial order of knowledge of the West about the rest, must be understood and analyzed as a component in the material history of several centuries of colonial contact, and not merely as a derivative effect of this history or, conversely, as an icon of some abstract motivating force behind it. As Müller's unself-consciously critical passage itself testifies, "fetishism" as a phantom object—as a cultural hybrid of a problem, a new breed of monster born of a historical/accidental transmutation—presents an obvious point of departure for such an analysis. For the present occasion, however, my aim is more modest; I will continue to dwell on the Victorian afterlife of fetishism, that is, the time when fetishism had already become a ghost of an idea/theory, but still troubled living theorists with its strange (im)materiality.

41. English translation in Julien Offray de La Mettrie, *Man a Machine and Man a Plant*, trans. Richard A. Watson and Maya Rybalka (Indianapolis: Hackett, 1994), 27.

42. *Popular Science Monthly* (New York). Spencer's articles were published in March and December 1875.

43. John Tyndall, *Address Delivered Before the British Association Assembled at Belfast* (London: Longmans, Green, 1874).

44. James Martineau, *Religion as Affected by Modern Materialism: An Address Delivered in Manchester New College, London, at the Opening of Its Eighty-Ninth Session, on Tuesday, October 6, 1874* (New York: G. P. Putnam, 1875). Page numbers for further quotes will be given parenthetically in the text.

45. "Editor's Table," *Popular Science Monthly* 6 (November 1874): 110–12.

46. Paul-Henri Thiry, Baron d'Holbach (Mirabeau), *The System of Nature, or Laws of the Moral and Physical World*, trans. H. D. Robinson (New York: Burt Franklin, 1868; rpt. 1970), 24.

47. "Editor's Table," 110. As we remember, while Bruno has been much honored and given pride of place in the history of materialism and modern religious thought in line with the scientific spirit, things did not turn out very well for him in his own dealings with the Christian authorities. He was imprisoned by the Inquisition for the last nine years of his life, at the end of which, in the year 1600, he was burned alive as a condemned heretic.

48. In addition to the three works just discussed, there were sequels. Tyndall responded to Martineau in the new preface to his *Fragments of Science*, which also appeared in the December 1875 issue of *Popular Science Monthly*. Martineau's further "rejoinder" appeared in *Contemporary*, February 1876. The editor of the *Monthly* devoted another column of "Editor's Table" to "Martineau's Reply to Tyndall" in the April 1876 issue. As the debate progressed, it increasingly became a contention over the territoriality of "science" and "religion."

49. Today's thriving industry in the field of "science and religion" may be regarded as one of its outcomes, the predominant one on the side of theology.

50. E. B. Tylor, "The Religion of Savages," *Fortnightly Review* 6 (1866): 71–86; "On Traces of the Early Mental Condition of Man," *Proceedings, Royal Institution of Great Britain* 5 (1867): 83–93; "On the Survival of Savage Thought in Modern Civilization," *Proceedings, Royal Institution of Great Britain* 5 (1869): 522–35; "The Philosophy of Religion among the Lower Races of Mankind," *Journal of Ethnological Society* n.s. 2 (1870): 369–79.

51. Tylor, "The Religion of Savages," 84.

52. Tylor, *Primitive Culture*, 1:426.

53. Tylor, "The Religion of Savages," 85.

54. George W. Stocking, Jr., "Animism in Theory and Practice: E. B. Tylor's Unpublished 'Notes on "Spiritualism"'" *Man* n.s. 5, no. 1 (March 1971): 88–104.

55. "Of the ten mediums with whom he had séances, all, with the exception of Mrs. Olive, are identifiable in the standard histories of the spiritualist movement. Three of them were among its major figures: Kate Fox, one of the founding sisters; Daniel Home, its most glamorous public personage; and the Reverend Moses, a country curate whose gradual conversion to spiritualism was accomplished just prior to Tylor's acquaintance with him, and who was to become what one historian [Arthur Conan Doyle] called 'the best modern exponent' of spiritualist views in a series of articles and books published in the seventies and eighties. Among the participants in the séances are several of the more prominent of what might be called 'lay' figures of the movement" (ibid., 91–92).

56. In ibid., 92.

57. Alfred Russel Wallace, *My Life: A Record of Events and Opinions* (London: Chapman & Hall, 1908).

58. George W. Stocking, Jr., *Victorian Anthropology* (New York: Free Press, 1987), 96–97. Today, something of Wallace's life has been fancifully memorialized in A. S. Byatt's recent novellas, and in a disquietingly beautiful film based on one of the stories, *Angels and Insects*. Admittedly, references to Wallace are either tangential or mutated, but "Morpho Eugenia" refers to the naturalist-entomologist aspect of Wallace's career, and "The Conjugial Angel" seems to allude to his interest in Spiritualism. Both novellas are published in a single volume under the title *Angels and Insects* (London: Chatto & Windus, 1992).

59. Cf. Peter Pels, "Spiritual Facts and Super-Visions: The 'Conversion' of Alfred Russel Wallace," *Etnofoor* 8, no. 2 (1995): 69–91.

60. Tylor, *Primitive Culture*, 2:153.

Jeremy Stolow, Salvation by Electricity

NOTE: Research for this paper was conducted with the support of the Social Sciences and Humanities Research Council of Canada and also the Center for Religion and Media, New York University. My thanks especially to Faye Ginsburg, Angela Zito, Birgit Meyer, Carly Machado, Will Coleman, Mattijs van de Port, Maria Jose de Abreu, Molly McGarry, Elizabeth Castelli, Richard Menke, Aaron Levy, John Durham Peters, Silvestra Mariniello, and Gauri Viswanathan for their ongoing support and to the various audiences who heard earlier versions of this paper and provided helpful comments and advice. A different version of this text is forthcoming in Will Coleman, Stephen Streeter, and John Weaver, eds., *Globalization, Autonomy and World History*, vol. 1, *Ideas, Religions, Empires and Globality* (Vancouver: University of British Columbia Press).

1. For a useful survey of debates over such matters, see Merritt Roe Smith and Leo Marx, eds., *Does Technology Drive History? The Dilemma of Technological Determinism* (Cambridge: MIT Press, 2001).

2. Needless to say, the terms *secular* and *religious* have been the subject of considerable scholarly debate in recent years, and their referents are hardly self-evident. See, e.g., Talal Asad, *Formations of the Secular: Christianity, Islam, Modernity* (Stanford, Calif.: Stanford University Press, 2003).

3. As Bruno Latour argues, the modern order of things rests upon a series of institutional, practical, and cognitive purifications, which have rendered religion, science, and the state ontologically distinct realms, each subject to its own autonomous laws and methodologically differentiated performative principles. According to this *pax moderna*, "religion" is comprehensible and legitimate only if construed in terms of metaphysics (i.e., as something rigorously separated from the "objective" procedures of techno-scientific practice) or spirituality (i.e., as the "intimacy of the heart," rigorously separated from the performative demands of state citizenship). See Bruno Latour, *We Have Never Been Modern*, trans. Catherine Porter (Cambridge: Harvard University Press, 1993), 13–48.

4. For a particularly insightful discussion of these issues, see Bruno Latour, "Another Take on the Science and Religion Debate," transcript of a talk given at the University of California, Santa Barbara, for the Templeton Series on Science, Religion, and Human Experience, May 2002, http://www.ensmp.fr/~latour/articles/article/086.html#3.

5. My approach is modeled loosely on Tzvetan Todorov's proposal, in *The Conquest of America* (New York: Harper-Collins, 1984), that a well-chosen historical narrative can be used to address larger philosophical and social questions. The underlying assumptions I must make about the exemplarity of historical narratives and their relation to the standards of verisimilitude and protocols of professional historiographical practice cannot be addressed in this limited context.

6. See, e.g.: Christoph Asendorf, *Batteries of Life: On the History of Things and Their Perception in Modernity* (Berkeley: University of California Press, 1993); Jonathan Crary, *Techniques of the Observer: On Vision and Modernity in the Nineteenth Century* (Cambridge: MIT Press, 1990); Lisa Gitelman, *Scripts, Grooves, and Writing Machines: Representing Technology in the Edison Era* (Stanford, Calif.: Stanford University Press, 1999); Lisa Gitelman and Geoffrey B. Pingree, eds., *New Media: 1740–1915* (Cambridge: MIT Press, 2003); Friedrich Kittler, *Gramophone, Film, Typewriter* (Stanford, Calif.: Stanford University Press, 1999); Carolyn Marvin, *When Old Technologies Were New: Thinking about Electric Communication in the Nineteenth Century* (Oxford: Oxford University Press, 1988); Iwan Rhys Morus, *Frankenstein's Children: Electricity, Exhibition, and Experiment in Early-Nineteenth-Century London* (Princeton, N.J.: Princeton University Press, 1998); John Durham

Peters, *Speaking into the Air: A History of the Idea of Communication* (Chicago: University of Chicago Press, 1999); Jeffrey Sconce, *Haunted Media: Electronic Presence from Telegraphy to Television* (Durham, N.C.: Duke University Press, 2000); John Tagg, *The Burden of Representation: Essays on Photographies and Histories* (Minneapolis: University of Minnesota Press, 1993).

7. Here one might consider the examples of newly formed religious associations with considerable transnational reach, such as the London Missionary Society (founded in 1795) or the American Bible Society (founded in 1816), which deftly availed themselves of opportunities provided by European imperial expansion, as well as new technologies of transportation and communication, to propagate their vision of global space as a unitary mission field. In turn, Protestant movements contributed decisively to the extension and intensification of globalizing networks and processes, translating and distributing Bibles and other religious pamphlets and tracts, building schools, raising funds, advocating for legal reforms (such as temperance or women's suffrage), and conducting numerous campaigns to end slavery, to stamp out "heathen" custom (such as the practice of sati in India), and to save souls, wherever roads, ships, and new media technologies could take them, in Europe, Africa, Asia, the Americas, and other, more far-flung locales. See, *inter alia*, Jean Comaroff and John Comaroff, *Of Revelation and Revolution: Christianity, Colonialism, and Consciousness in South Africa*, vol. 1 (Chicago: University of Chicago Press, 1991); Peter van der Veer, ed., *Conversion to Modernities: The Globalization of Christianity* (London: Routledge, 1996); W. R. Ward. *The Protestant Evangelical Awakening* (Cambridge: Cambridge University Press, 1992); Peter J. Wosh, *Spreading the Word: The Bible Business in Nineteenth-Century America* (Ithaca, N.Y.: Cornell University Press, 1994).

What might be said about the increasingly globalizing reach and influence of nineteenth-century Protestant movements might also be applied, mutatis mutandis, to others within this rapidly changing field, including Catholics, Muslims, Hindus, Jews, Buddhists, and others whose self-identity was now reflected in the global marketplace of religious ideas, practices, and modes of affinity. One particularly dramatic enactment of this "global" sensibility was the convening of the World's Parliament of Religions in Chicago in 1893. See Richard H Seager, *The World's Parliament of Religions: The East-West Encounter, Chicago, 1893* (Bloomington: Indiana University Press, 1995).

8. Ann Braude has commented on the difficulty of measuring adherence to Spiritualism, given the movement's markedly acephalous nature: no formally recognized leadership and no clear protocols for defining one's status within the cause. See Ann Braude, *Radical Spirits: Spiritualism and Women's Rights in Nineteenth-Century America* (Boston: Beacon Press, 1989), 25–26.

Furthermore, the porous boundaries dividing Spiritualism from other religious categories—especially with regard to the difference between Spiritualists and "ordinary" Christians, or, for that matter, between Spiritualists and adherents to a variety of indigenous religions practised in West Africa, Brazil, the Caribbean, and elsewhere—make it difficult to produce meaningful statistics. Nevertheless, there is wide consensus that Spiritualism enjoyed a precipitous growth over the course of the second half of the nineteenth century. In the United States alone, John Goodwin estimates that as early as 1855 there were 1.5 million committed Spiritualists (out of a total population of 25 million). See John Goodwin, *Occult America* (Golden City, N.Y.: Doubleday Books, 1972), 188. Others have suggested that by the end of the 1850s 3 million Americans were at least peripherally engaged with the movement and that by the 1870s this number rose to over 11 million. See R. Laurence Moore, "Spiritualism and Science: Reflections on the First Decade of Spirit Tappings," *American Quarterly* 24, no. 4 (1972): 481; Werner Sollers, "Dr. Benjamin Franklin's Celestial Telegraph, or Indian Blessings to Gas-lit American Drawing Rooms," *Social Science Information* 22, no. 6 (1983): 991. Another indicator of Spiritualism's growth is the U.S. Federal Census, which in 1880 listed over six hundred persons who identified their profession as clairvoyant, spirit medium, trance lecturer, or magnetic healer, although this figure is considered to be an extremely conservative account of the actual number of Spiritualist mediums, which others have estimated to be in the thousands (see www.spirithistory.com/80fedcen.html).

Spiritualism (or Spiritism) remains a significant religious movement even today. According to the 1997 *Encyclopedia Britannica Book of the Year*, there were 10,292,500 adherents of "Spiritism" in the world. In the Brazilian census of 2000, over 2.2 million people identified themselves as Kardecists (roughly 1.3 percent of the total population), but this number does not account for a fringe following (not officially professed, but possibly quite avid) of up to 50 million (see: http://www.adherents.com/Religions_By_Adherents.html#Spiritism and http://www.state.gov.g/drd/rls/irf/2004/35528.htm).

9. Many of the movement's leading figures were in fact well-educated men and women of high standing. In the context of the North Atlantic, English-speaking world, this included: writers such as Harriet Beecher Stowe, James Fenimore Cooper, Annie Besant, William Butler Yeats, and Victor Hugo, or, much later, Arthur Conan Doyle; engineers and scientists, such as Alfred Russel Wallace, Thomas Edison, Oliver Lodge, and William Crookes; and political reformers, such as Robert Owen. Even Mrs. Lincoln was said to be a committed Spiritualist, holding séances in the White House. See, *inter alia*, Braude, *Radical Spirits*. Cf. Bret E. Carroll, *Spiritualism in Antebellum America* (Bloomington: Indiana University Press, 1997); Robert S. Cox, *Body and Soul: A Sympathetic History of American Spiritualism* (Charlottesville: University of Virginia Press, 2003); Stan McMullin, *Anatomy of a Séance: A History of Spirit Communication in Central Canada* (Montreal: McGill-Queen's University Press, 2004); Molly McGarry, "Spectral Sexualities: Nineteenth-Century Spiritualism, Moral Panics, and the Making of U.S. Obscenity Law," *Journal of Women's History* 12, no. 2 (2000): 8–29; Laurence Moore, *In Search of White Crows: Spiritualism, Parapsychology, and American Culture* (New York: Oxford University Press, 1977); Janet Oppenheim, *The Other World: Spiritualism and Psychical Research in England, 1850–1914* (Cambridge: Cambridge University Press, 1985); Alex Owen, *The Darkened Room: Women, Power, and Spiritualism in Late Victorian England* (Philadelphia: University of Pennsylvania Press, 1990); Pamela Thurschwell, *Literature, Technology and Magical Thinking, 1880–1920* (Cambridge: Cambridge University Press, 2001); Elisabeth Wadge, "The Scientific Spirit and the Spiritualist Scientist: Moving in the Right Circles," *The Victorian Review* 26, no. 1 (2000): 24–42. The definitive "insider's" history of British Spiritualism was produced by Sir Arthur Conan Doyle, President of the London Spiritualist Alliance and of the British College of Psychic Science, *The History of Spiritualism*, 2 vols. (London: Cassell and Co., 1926).

For comparable discussions of Spiritualism in French bourgeois society, see: Nicole Edelman, *Voyantes, guérisseuses et visionnaires en France, 1785–1914* (Paris: Albin Michel, 1995); John Warne Monroe, "*Cartes de Visite* from the Other World: Spiritism and the Discourse of *Laïcisme* in the Early Third Republic," *French Historical Studies* 26, no. 1 (2003): 119–53; Lynn Sharp, "Fighting for the Afterlife: Spiritists, Catholics, and Popular Religion in Nineteenth-Century France," *Journal of Religious History* 23, no. 3 (1999): 282–95. For accounts of the penetration of Spiritualism (in the specific form of Kardecism) into Brazilian bourgeois society, see: Marion Aubrée and François Laplatine, *La Table, le livre, et les esprits: Naissance, évolution et actualité du mouvement social spirite entre France et Brésil* (Paris: Lattès, 1990); David Hess, *Spirits and Scientists: Ideology, Spiritism, and Brazilian Culture* (Philadelphia: University of Pennsylvania Press, 1991); João Vasconcelos, "Espíritos clandestinos: Espiritismo, pesquisa psíquica e antropologia da religião entre 1850 e 1920," *Religião e Sociedade* 23, no. 2 (2003): 92–126.

10. One thinks here of the tradition of Hermetic mysticism, which posited the immanence of God in the world, thereby construing the natural order as everywhere infused with mysterious signs

of His divine presence. See, e.g., Frances Yates, *Giordano Bruno and the Hermetic Tradition* (London: Routledge & Kegan Paul, 1964). A more direct progenitor of Spiritualism was the eighteenth-century mystic Emanuel Swedenborg, whose speculations on the ministry of angels were revived in the nineteenth century and creatively integrated into a new pantheistic theology concerning the unity of the divine with all living things, the co-existence of the world of spirit and the natural world as complementary expressions of "infinite intelligence," and the survival of one's personal identity after death. See Erland J. Brock, ed., *Swedenborg and His Influence* (Bryn Athyn, Pa.: The Academy of the New Church, 1988).

11. There are various ways to account for this, not least the fact that in Victorian culture religious practice was arguably the arena of activity most open to feminine virtuosity. Spirit mediumship in particular offered women of virtually any social standing or educational background the opportunity to enjoy a high-profile career, lay claim to otherworldly insight, entertain friends, confound skeptics, console the bereaved, and earn considerable money, all the while conforming to Victorian ideals of feminine passivity. See esp. Braude, *Radical Spirits*; Owen, *Darkened Room*.

12. These are the grounds upon which several scholars have argued that nineteenth-century Spiritualism formed a major—if not *the* major—vehicle for the spread of feminist critiques of Victorian patriarchal culture. Indeed, arguments in favor of women's rights and suffrage had already been formulated by spirit mediums long before such ideas were voiced by more famous first-wave American feminists, such as Susan B. Anthony or Elizabeth Cady Stanton (Braude, *Radical Spirits*, 56–141).

13. There now exists a vast literature on spirit possession and related phenomena in cross-cultural perspective, from ancient Greek Dionysian cults to Haitian voudon to Sufi mystics to Siberian shamans. The question remains what one is to infer from such apparent commonalities. In this regard, it is hardly coincidental that nineteenth-century anthropology, beginning with Edward Tylor, was deeply concerned to identify Victorian Spiritualism with "savage thought," in terms of their "feminine" emotionalism and credulity. See, e.g.: George Stocking, "Animism in Theory and Practice: E. B. Tylor's Unpublished 'Notes on Spiritualism.'" *Man* n.s. 6, no. 1 (1971): 88–104; Peter Pels, "Spirits and Modernity: Alfred Wallace, Edward Tylor, and the Visual Politics of Facts," in *Magic and Modernity: Interfaces of Revelation and Concealment*, ed. Birgit Meyer and Peter Pels (Stanford, Calif.: Stanford University Press, 2003), 241–71.

The comparison between Spiritualism and "non-Western" possession cults must not rest on abstract generalities or the construction of "ideal types," but rather on actual cases of productive interchange and cross-fertilization between the metropolitan world of the Victorian occult and a range of performative traditions originating in the preindustrialized world. For a productive example of such interchange, see Gauri Viswanathan's study of Theosophy and occult knowledge among colonial emigrés in late-nineteenth-century British India, and their relation to the indigenous knowledge and practices of Indian colonial subjects: Gauri Viswanathan, "The Ordinary Business of Occultism," *Critical Inquiry* 27 (2000): 1–20.

14. A few words of caution are in order here. First, I do not mean to suggest that the "birth" of telegraphy can be traced back to a single event. Rather, its advent was shaped by the convergence of multiple processes, implicating an array of inventors, investors, and intermediary agents. On the early history of the introduction of electrical telegraphy, and especially the heated competition between Cooke and Wheatstone (in England) and Samuel Morse during the 1830s and 1840s, see Morus, *Frankenstein's Children*, 194–230. Cf. Ken Beauchamp, *History of Telegraphy* (London: The Institution of Electrical Engineers, 2001), 20–101; Tom Standage, *The Victorian Internet: The Remarkable Story of the Telegraph and the Nineteenth Century's On-line Pioneers* (New York: Berkeley Books, 1998), 22–56.

Second, it is hazardous to refer to "the" telegraph as a singular technology. Morse's electromagnetic telegraph apparatus was only one of a diverse group of nineteenth-century devices associated with the practice of "distance-writing" (tele-graphy). Telegraphy thus involved the use of different media (e.g., electrical or optical signals, mediated through cable or line-of-sight systems), different ways of encoding and deciphering messages (with respect to which, one must note, Morse code was not immediately accepted as a universal standard), and different possibilities of human interface (e.g., machines that required attention from human operators as opposed to those that could relay signals automatically).

Finally, one must also guard against the temptation to rely upon heroic narratives of technological invention, which typically repress the considerable cultural, financial, and technical contingencies involved in establishing a viable market for new technologies. For a more nuanced account of the commodification of information, the establishment of new systems of circulation through telegraphy, and the integration of this technology into the emerging industrial infrastructure of railways, shipping lines, postal services, etc., see: Iwan Rhys Morus, "Currents from the Underworld: Electricity and the Technology of Display in Early Victorian England," *Isis* 84, no. 1 (1993): 50–89; Iwan Rhys Morus, "The Electric Ariel: Telegraphy and Commercial Culture in Early Victorian England," *Victorian Studies* 39, no. 3 (1996): 339–78.

15. James W. Carey, *Communication as Culture: Essays on Media and Society* (New York: Routledge, 1989), 203–4.

16. Beauchamp, *History of Telegraphy*, 3–19; Standage, *Victorian Internet*, 6–20.

17. Carey, *Communication as Culture*, 202.

18. Ibid., 205–7, 212–22.

19. Menahem Blondheim, *News over the Wires: The Telegraph and the Flow of Public Information in America, 1844–1897* (Cambridge: Harvard University Press, 1994).

20. Daniel R. Headrick, *The Invisible Weapon: Telecommunications and International Politics, 1851–1945* (Oxford: Oxford University Press, 1991), 73–92. Cf. David Paull Nickles, *Under the Wire: How the Telegraph Changed Diplomacy* (Cambridge: Harvard University Press, 2003).

21. Standage, *Victorian Internet*, 128–44.

22. See, *inter alia*, Gregory J. Downey, *Telegraph Messenger Boys: Labor, Technology, and Geography, 1850–1950* (New York: Routledge, 2002); John Steele Gordon, *A Thread Across the Ocean: The Heroic Story of the Transatlantic Cable* (New York: Walker & Co, 2002); Annteresa Lubrano, *The Telegraph: How Technological Innovation Caused Social Change* (New York: Garland Publishing, Inc., 1997).

23. As described, e.g., in Manuel Castells, *The Rise of the Network Society* (Oxford: Blackwell, 1996).

24. This pioneering institution was created in order to standardize equipment and operating practices of telegraph coding, transcription, and transmission, to facilitate interconnection of national networks, and to ensure common rules for the collection of international tariffs. See Armand Mattelart, *The Invention of Communication* (Minneapolis: University of Minnesota Press, 1996), 124–29, 167.

25. Beauchamp, *History of Telegraphy*, 102–33; Headrick, *Invisible Weapon*, 50–72; Mattelart, *Invention*, 165–70. Telegraphy also enabled the tightening of military chains of command, as in the Crimean war in the 1850s, when for the first time French and British governments were able to communicate directly with their generals on a distant battlefield. See Standage, *Victorian Internet*, 154–58. In a similar vein, European states—especially the British—quickly recognized how the telegraph, alongside innovations in steam shipping and railways, facilitated the shift to a new mode of imperial rule, whereby metropolitan authorities could dictate courses of events in the colonies

directly and immediately, rather than simply responding to news of events that had been communicated by colonial bureaucrats weeks or even months after the fact.

26. Beauchamp, *History of Telegraphy*, 134–80; Standage, *Victorian Internet*, 58–59, 61–62, 96–102; Daniel R. Headrick, *The Tentacles of Progress: Technology Transfer in the Age of Imperialism, 1850–1940* (Oxford: Oxford University Press, 1988), 97–126.

27. As in the introduction of telegraphy to Brazil, where the technology was crucial for colonizing vast peripheral spaces, such as the regions of Minas Gerais, Mato Grosso, or the Amazon basin, and bringing these hinterlands into alignment with an emerging Brazilian nationalism and participation in cosmopolitan community. See: Sérgio de Oliveira Birchal, "The Transfer of Technology to Latecomer Economies in the Nineteenth Century: The Case of Minas Gerais, Brazil," *Business History* 43, no. 4 (2001): 48–67; Todd Diacon, *Stringing Together a Nation: Cândido Mariano da Silva Rondon and the Construction of a Modern Brazil, 1906–1930* (Durham, N.C.: Duke University Press, 2004); Laura Antunes Maciel, "Cultura e tecnologia: A constituição do serviço telegráfico no Brasil," *Revista Brasileira de História* 21, no. 41 (2001): 127–44.

28. The key British players were the Electric Telegraph Company (founded in 1846), the Submarine Telegraph Company (formed in 1850), the Eastern Telegraph Company (formed in 1872, which rapidly grew into the largest cable-operating company in the world), the Africa Direct Telegraph Company (formed in 1885, linking England with its colonies on the West African coast), the British Indian Extension Telegraph Company (which linked Aden, Suez, Bombay, Madras, Penang, and Singapore), and the British-Australian Telegraph Company. While British cabling companies dominated the international scene, their efforts were rivaled by a wide range of players, including American companies (most importantly, Western Union, founded in Rochester in 1851), and other international business ventures, such as the International Ocean Telegraph Company (linking Florida with various Caribbean cities), the Danish-Russian Telegraph Company (linking Scandinavia and Russia), the West African Telegraph Company (linking France, Portugal, and Spain with Senegal and Guinea), the Société du Câble Transatlantique Française (linking France and the United States in 1869), as well as numerous state-owned initiatives, by the governments of France, Spain, Prussia, Denmark, Sweden, Greece, and the Ottoman Empire, among others.

A useful summary of the history of these international cabling initiatives, including a time line of formation of companies and expeditions for laying submarine cable, can be found at the Web-based archive http://atlantic-cable.com.

29. On the definition of globalization as a form of supra-territorialism, see Jan Aart Scholte, *Globalization: A Critical Introduction* (Houndsmills, Basingstoke: Palgrave, 2000). On the role played by telegraphy in the standardization of time zones (in conjunction with expanding railway networks and the technical demands they elicited for predictable temporal calculations), see, *inter alia*, Carey, *Communication as Culture*, 227–29.

30. This is exemplified by the simultaneous growth of the submarine telegraph industry and the scientific disciplines of oceanography and hydrography, which were fed by a shared desire for reliable and detailed knowledge about the ocean floor. Indeed, beginning in the 1850s and 1860s, rapid innovations in deep-sea sounding technologies helped to transform the seabed of the Atlantic into a new frontier: an uncivilized space, ripe for conquest and exploitation. See Helen M. Rozwadowski, "Technology and Ocean-Scape: Defining the Deep Sea in the Mid-Nineteenth Century," *History and Technology* 17 (2001): 217–47.

31. Peters, *Speaking into the Air*, 142.

32. Asendorf, *Batteries of Life*, 153–77. See also Laura Otis, *Networking: Communicating with Bodies and Machines in the Nineteenth Century* (Ann Arbor: University of Michigan Press, 2001).

33. See Morus, "Currents from the Underworld." See also: Margaret Rowbottom and Charles Susskind, *Electricity and Medicine: History of Their Interaction* (San Francisco: San Francisco Press,

1984). For a comprehensive history of scientific theories of electricity, from antiquity to the late nineteenth century, see Edmund Taylor Whittaker, *A History of the Theories of Aether and Electricity, from the Age of Descartes to the Close of the Nineteenth Century* (London: Longmans, 1910).

34. Peters, *Speaking into the Air*, 78; Whittaker, *History of Theories*. Cf. Patricia Fara, *An Entertainment for Angels: Electricity in the Enlightenment* (Cambridge: Icon Books, 2002), 116–22.

35. On the history of Franklin's experiments and their intellectual and social impact, see: Michael B. Schiffer, *Draw the Lightning Down: Benjamin Franklin and Electrical Technology in the Age of Enlightenment* (Berkeley: University of California Press, 2003); Tom Tucker, *Bolt of Fate: Benjamin Franklin and His Electric Kite Hoax* (New York: Public Affairs, 2003). On the theme of lightning in Romantic literature, see Maria Tatar, *Spellbound: Studies on Mesmerism and Literature* (Princeton, N.J.: Princeton University Press, 1978), 82–120.

36. Working within the Newtonian model of ethereal vibration, Galvani had identified the nervous medium with electricity, claiming that all animals possess a special electric fluid that is generated in the brain and that passes through the nerves into muscles that function like organic batteries. Since living bodies responded so strongly to electricity, it did not seem unreasonable to suggest that they might also be able to generate it. See Marcello Pera, *The Ambiguous Frog: The Galvani-Volta Controversy on Animal Electricity* (Princeton, N.J.: Princeton University Press, 1992), 69–95.

The idea of animal electricity was popularized in the early nineteenth century, not least in the form of experiments on dead human bodies: most famously, the public demonstration performed upon George Forster, a convicted murderer who was hanged at Newgate, London, in January 1803, and then electrified by Giovanni Aldini, Galvani's nephew and most ardent propagandist (see: Fara, *Entertainment for Angels*, 165–70; Morus, *Frankenstein's Children*, 127–30). Aldini presupposed a theory of electric vitality that originated in Galvani's work but that also seemed to be corroborated by increasingly systematic attempts to explore the reactions of the infirm to electricity: efforts that by the end of the eighteenth century had already been incorporated into the routine practices of major hospitals in Britain and France (see: Fara, *Entertainment for Angels*, 82–98; Morus, *Frankenstein's Children*, 231–55; Pera, *Ambiguous Frog*, 18–25; Rowbottom and Susskind, *Electricity and Medicine*, 15–70).

Such macabre spectacles were equally well suited to an expanding scientific "culture of display" that lay beneath the nineteenth century's fascination with galvanism and with the power of electricity to create life itself (see: Morus, "Electric Ariel," 342–49; Simon Schaffer, "The Consuming Flame: Electrical Showmen and Tory Mystics in the World of Goods," in *Consumption and the World of Goods*, ed. John Brewer and Roy Porter [London: Routledge, 1993], 489–526). It was in this vein that galvanic theories of vitality also penetrated the Romantic and Gothic literary genres of the nineteenth century, most obviously in the case of Mary Shelley's *Frankenstein* (see: Fara, *Entertainment for Angels*, 168–69; Tatar, *Spellbound*, 60–63).

37. Carey, *Communication as Culture*, 123.

38. For accounts of technological utopianism and dystopianism in nineteenth-century America, see: Leo Marx, *The Machine in the Garden: Technology and the Pastoral Ideal in America* (Oxford: Oxford University Press, 1964); David Noble, *The Religion of Technology: The Divinity of Man and the Spirit of Invention* (New York: A. A. Knopf, 1997); David E. Nye, *Electrifying America: Social Meanings of a New Technology, 1880–1940* (Cambridge: MIT Press, 1990). An incisive account of the pessimism surrounding the introduction of telegraphy in particular can be found in Menahem Blondheim, "When Bad Things Happen to Good Technologies: Three Phases in the Diffusion and Perception of American Telegraphy," in *Technology, Pessimism, and Postmodernism*, ed. Yaron Ezrahi, Everett Mendelsohn, and Howard P. Segal (Amherst: University of Massachusetts Press, 1994), 77–92.

39. Sollors, "Dr. Benjamin," 992. See also: Braude, *Radical Spirits*, 4–5, 23–24; Moore, "Spiritualism and Science," 486; Morus, "Electric Ariel," 375; Peters, *Speaking into the Air*, 94–95; Sconce, *Haunted Media*, 12–14, 21–28, 36–37, 56–58. See also Steven Connor, "The Machine in the Ghost: Spiritualism, Technology and the 'Direct Voice,'" in *Ghosts: Deconstruction, Psychoanalysis, History*, ed. Peter Buse and Andrew Stott (London: Macmillan, 1999), 203–25.

A contemporary chronicler and active figure within Spiritualism, Emma Hardinge, also provides considerable evidence that the metaphor of the telegraph enjoyed widespread currency within American Spiritualist circles. See Emma Hardinge, *Modern American Spiritualism: A Twenty Years' Record of the Communion Between Earth and the World of Spirits* (New York: Published by the Author, 1870).

40. The best account of the consolidation of an increasingly professionalized class of electrical experts over the course of the nineteenth century is found in Marvin, *When Old Technologies Were New*, 9–62.

41. Sollors, "Dr. Benjamin," 994; Sconce, *Haunted Media*, 36. Cf. Richard J. Noakes, "Telegraphy Is an Occult Art: Cromwell Fleetwood Varley and the Diffusion of Electricity to the Other World," *British Journal for the History of Science* 32, no. 4 (1999): 422.

42. Spear was a prominent advocate for various reform movements, including abolition, temperance, and women's rights, as well as a committed Spiritualist. In 1852, in states of trance, Spear was contacted by a number of spirits, including Thomas Jefferson, Benjamin Franklin, and other distinguished departed ones, who together formed an "Association of Beneficents,'" and who delivered to Spear a series of plans for remaking society through philanthropic work and political reform (including calls to take up arms in order to free slaves and to replace the present government with a "true democracy"), as well as furnishing detailed plans for new machines and new architecture that would facilitate the coming of this new age. Spear's exploits are detailed in John B. Buescher, *The Other Side of Salvation: Spiritualism and the Nineteenth-Century Religious Experience* (Boston: Skinner House Books, 2004), 170–84. See also http://www.uua.org/uuhs/duub/articles/johnmurrayspear.html.

43. "The Soul-Blending Telegraph," *The New York Tribune*, August 18, 1854.

44. Quoted in Sollors, "Dr. Benjamin," 995.

45. Allan Kardec, *The Book on Mediums; or, Guide for Mediums and Invocators*, trans. Emma A. Wood (1861; York Beach, Maine: Samuel Weiser, Inc., 1970), 292–93.

46. See Peters, *Speaking into the Air*, 149.

47. Kardec, *Book on Mediums*, 22.

48. In 1836, Dods viewed the New England exhibition tour of Charles Poyen St. Sauveur, a French Mesmerist and experimenter, and on this basis acquired a sense of the connections between electricity and magnetism, as well as their therapeutic properties. See Buescher, *Other Side of Salvation*, 6.

49. Quoted in ibid., 8.

50. Kardec, *Book on Mediums*, 116–17. The most extended discussion of the theme of "affinity" in Spiritualist discourse is found in Cox, *Body and Soul*. According to Cox, Spiritualist writings, especially (but not exclusively) in the context of the antebellum United States, "were suffused with the language of sentiment expressed through a peculiarly physical emotionality in which the interpersonal was experienced viscerally and in which affect and sensation were integrated and extended beyond the boundaries of the individual" (3). Cox demonstrates how the Spiritualist "cosmology of sympathy" and its emphasis on the viscera served as the basis for efforts to unite the organic body and the body politic in and through various performative repertoires and mediatic forms, from somnabular behavior to spirit photography. I propose that the vocabulary of electricity,

as deployed here by Kardec, shows not only that this trope of affinity was geographically dispersed far beyond the confines of American Spiritualism but also that it was crucially important for the elaboration of Spiritualist ideas about the connections among affective bodies, sensations, and forces emanating from "beyond.'"

51. See: Braude, *Radical Spirits*, 23–24; Morus, "Electric Ariel," 375; Sconce, *Haunted Media*, 50–55. On the intangibility of the "wires" enabling spirit communication, see Noakes, "Telegraphy," 446, 450–59. The homology between the human nervous system and electrical cables was not unique to Spiritualists, for that matter; they were pervasively conjoined in the nineteenth-century imaginary, in discourses as disparate as medicine and Romantic poetry. See, *inter alia*: Asendorf, *Batteries of Life*, 153–77; Otis, *Networking*, passim.

52. As argued, e.g., in Oppenheim, *The Other World*, 59–62 and passim.

53. On the association of "primitivism" and Victorian domestic interiority in Spiritualism, see Pels, "Spirits of Modernity," 271 and passim.

54. The expansion of the Spiritualist enterprise was thus redolent of a broader shift in modes of cultural production during the latter half of the nineteenth century, whereby locally specific material cultures and folk arts were transformed into mass-circulation commodities destined for public display (as on the Vaudevillean stage or in the pages of the national press). See, e.g., Peter Bailey, *Leisure and Class in Victorian England: Rational Recreation and the Contest for Control, 1830–1885* (London: Methuen, 1978). For the role of stage magic within the "society of the spectacle" in the nineteenth century, see: James W. Cook. *The Arts of Deception: Playing with Fraud in the Age of Barnum* (Cambridge: Harvard University Press, 2001); and Simon During, *Modern Enchantments: The Cultural Power of Secular Magic* (Cambridge: Harvard University Press, 2002).

55. See Owen, *Darkened Room*, 139–67; Pels, "Spirits of Modernity," 250–52; Thurschwell, *Literature, Technology and Magical Thinking*.

56. See Peter Lamont, "Spiritualism and a Mid-Victorian Crisis of Evidence," *The Historical Journal* 47, no. 4 (2004): 897–920. See also Wadge, "The Scientific Spirit," 24ff.

57. See Noakes, "Telegraphy," 423, 432, 437, 442–47. See also: Richard J. Noakes, "'Instruments to Lay Hold of Spirits': Technologizing the Bodies of Victorian Spiritualism," in *Bodies/Machines*, ed. Iwan Rhys Morus (Oxford: Berg, 2002), 125–63.

58. Crookes's efforts were short-lived, however, and, having failed to produce satisfactory results during séances, he quickly retreated back to his laboratory, to continue the scientific work for which he was best known (although he remained sympathetic to Spiritualism for the rest of his life). A useful summary of Crookes's investigations of Spiritualist mediums can be found in Jon Palfreman, "Between Skepticism and Credulity: A Study of Victorian Scientific Attitudes to Modern Spiritualism," in *On the Margins of Science: The Social Construction of Rejected Knowledge*, ed. Roy Wallis (Keele: University of Keele, 1979), 210–23.

59. See Frank M. Turner, "Alfred Russel Wallace: The Wonderful Man of the Wonderful Century," in idem, *Between Science and Religion: The Reaction to Scientific Naturalism in Late Victorian England* (New Haven, Conn.: Yale University Press, 1974), 68–103. See also: Malcolm Jay Kottler, "Alfred Russel Wallace, the Origin of Man, and Spiritualism," *Isis* 65, no. 2 (June 1974): 144–92; Peter Pels, "Spirits of Modernity," 241ff.

60. See, *inter alia*: Moore, *In Search of White Crows*, 133–68; Oppenheim, *The Other World*, 111–58. Among numerous prominent researchers associated with the Society was William James, whose many contributions (spanning four decades, from 1869 to 1909) shed fascinating light on the complex exchanges and mutual influences of fin-de-siècle investigations into the psychical and the psychological. See William James, *The Works of William James*, vol. 16, *Essays in Psychical Research* (Cambridge: Harvard University Press, 1986).

61. See "Faraday on Table-Moving," *Athenaeum*, no. 1340 (July 8, 1853), 801–3. In his account of the popular séance practice of table turning, Faraday reports that "no form of experiment or mode of observation that I could devise gave me the slightest indication of any peculiar natural force" (801). He thus concludes: "Though I believe the parties do not intend to move the table, but obtain the result by a quasi involuntary action,—still I had no doubt of the influence of expectation upon their minds, and through that the success or failure of their efforts" (ibid). This theme of "quasi-involuntary action" also refers to the indeterminate realm that constitutes the human/machine interface, a topic to which I shall return presently.

62. See, e.g., W. B. Carpenter, "Electro-Biology and Mesmerism," *The Quarterly Review* (London) 93, no. 186 (July 1853): 501–57; W. B. Carpenter, "Mesmerism, Odylism, Table-Turning and Spiritualism, Considered Historically and Scientifically," *Fraser's Magazine* n.s. 15, no. 86 (February 1877): 135–57; W. B. Carpenter, "On the Influence of Suggestion in Modifying and Directing Muscular Movement, Independently of Volition," *Proceedings of the Royal Institution of Great Britain* (March 12, 1852), 147–53. For details on the widely published Carpenter-Crookes exchanges in the late 1870s, see Palfreman, "Between Skepticism and Credulity," 217–19, and passim. On the theme of "expectant attention," as developed by Carpenter and many others in late-nineteenth-century medical and psychological discourses, see Jonathan Crary, *Suspensions of Perception: Attention, Spectacle, and Modern Culture* (Cambridge: MIT Press, 1999), 21, 63, and passim.

63. W. B. Carpenter, *Principles of Mental Physiology, with Their Applications for the Training and Discipline of the Mind, and the Study of Its Morbid States* (London: H. S. King, 1874), as discussed in Owen, *The Darkened Room*, 241–44.

64. See, *inter alia*: Palfreman, "Between Skepticism and Credulity"; Pels, "Spirits of Modernity."

65. See Lamont, "Spiritualism," 900–901. Lamont notes that "conjuring as an entertainment may be seen . . . as part of the increased ordering of leisure pursuits that took place from the end of the eighteenth century" (903), in which experiences of curiosity, wonder, and amazement were increasingly couched in the language of scientific explanation and the orderly knowledge of the universe, as witnessed in spectacles of scientific demonstration used as tricks of rational amusement and as part of a broader culture of popular pedagogy, in which no clear line could be drawn separating science from magic. See, e.g., Cook, *Arts of Deception*, 163–213. On the relationship among science, magic, and spectacle, as in the early career of the London Polytechnic during the 1860s, see During, *Modern Enchantments*, 142–49, and passim.

For discussion of the broader intellectual culture of skepticism, naturalism, and the "crisis of faith" in Victorian society, see: Bernard Lightman, ed., *Victorian Science in Context* (Chicago: University of Chicago Press, 1997); Bernard Lightman and Richard J Helmstadter, eds., *Victorian Faith in Crisis: Essays on Continuity and Change in Nineteenth-Century Religious Belief* (Stanford, Calif.: Stanford University Press, 1991); Frank M. Turner, *Between Science and Religion: The Reaction to Scientific Naturalism in Late Victorian England* (New Haven, Conn.: Yale University Press, 1974); Frank M. Turner, *Contesting Cultural Authority: Essays in Victorian Intellectual Life* (Cambridge: Cambridge University Press, 1993).

66. On the status of vision in the late nineteenth century, see Crary, *Suspensions of Perception*. Cf. Pels's account of the late Victorian "frenzy of the visible" in "Spirits of Modernity," 262–63.

67. See, e.g., Daniel Stashower, "The Medium and the Magician," *American History* 34, no. 3 (August 1999): 38–46. Houdini's relentless pursuit to expose Spiritualist frauds is colorfully documented in his own journal, *A Magician among the Spirits* (New York: Harper and Brothers, 1924). See also During, *Modern Enchantments*, 168–69, 173–77.

68. G. H. Lewes, "Seeing Is Believing," *Blackwood's Edinburgh Magazine* 88, no. 540 (1860): 383.

69. Michel de Certeau, "Believing and Making People Believe," in idem, *The Practice of Every-day Life*, trans. Steven F. Rendall (Berkeley: University of California Press, 1984), 186–87, emphasis original. De Certeau elaborates this "reversal" of the traditional relationship between seeing and believing thus:

> Today, fiction claims to make the real present, to speak in the name of the facts and thus to cause the semblance it produces to be taken as a referential reality. Hence those to whom these legends are directed . . . are not obliged to believe what they don't see (a traditional position), but rather to believe what they see (a contemporary position). This reversal of the terrain on which beliefs develop results from a mutation in the paradigms of knowledge: the ancient postulate of the invisibility of the real has been replaced by the postulation of its visibility. The modern socio-cultural scene. . . . defines the social referent by its visibility (and thus by its scientific or political representativeness); it articulates on this new postulate (the belief that the real is visible) the possibility of our knowledge, observations, proofs, and practices. On this new stage, an indefinitely extensible field of optical investigations and of a scopic drive, the strange collusion between believing and the question of the real still remains. But now it is a question of what is *seen*, *observed*, or *shown*. (187, emphasis original)

70. Moore, "Spiritualism and Science," 484.

71. Lewes, "Seeing Is Believing," 382.

72. Ibid, 383. For a related account of "vanquishment by facts" in Alfred Russel Wallace's "conversion" to Spiritualism, see Pels, "Spirits of Modernity," 241–42, 262–63, and passim.

73. Gitelman, *Scripts*, 186–89. We might add that such occurrences attained sufficient regularity in the nineteenth century to warrant the need for extended discussion about how to catalogue texts emanating from the spirit world, giving rise to the curious Victorian science of necrobibliography. See Helen Sword, "Necrobibliography: Books in the Spirit World," *Modern Language Quarterly* 60, no. 1 (1999): 85–112. At the same time, practices of spirit writing also spawned a range of stenographic devices and instruments, most notably the ouija board and the planchette. See Thurschwell, *Literature, Technology and Magical Thinking*, 86–114.

74. Gitelman, *Scripts*, 191.

75. See also Kenneth Lipartito, "When Women Were Switches: Technology, Work, and Gender in the Telephone Industry, 1890–1920," *The American Historical Review* 99, no. 4 (1994):1075–111.

76. See Kittler, *Gramophone, Film, Typewriter*, 183–98.

77. Gitelman, *Scripts*, 189.

78. Ibid., 211–13.

79. See Crary, *Suspensions of Perception*, 46–47, 79, 147, 287, and passim.

80. On the conception of the laboring body in late-nineteenth-century physics, biology, medicine, industrial management, politics, and art, see Anson Rabinbach, *The Human Motor: Energy, Fatigue, and the Origins of Modernity* (Berkeley: University of California Press, 1990).

Stef Aupers, Dick Houtman, and Peter Pels, Cybergnosis: Technology, Religion and the Secular

1. Timothy Leary, *Chaos and Cyberculture* (1994), http://www.leary.com/archives/text/index.html.

2. Mark Dery, *Escape Velocity: Cyberculture at the End of the Century* (New York: Grove, 1996), 22.

3. Timothy Leary, "The Cyberpunk: The Individual as Reality Pilot," in *Storming the Reality Studio: A Casebook of Cyberpunk and Postmodern Science Fiction*, ed. L. McCaffery (Durham, N.C.: Duke University Press, 1991), 245–58; Timothy Leary, *The Declaration of Evolution* (2005), http://www.american-buddha.com/dec.evolution.htm; Timothy Leary and Eric Gullichsen, *Digital Polytheism* (2005), http://www.american-buddha.com/digital.polytheism.htm.

4. Douglas Rushkoff, *Cyberia: Life in the Trenches of Hyperspace* (San Francisco: Harper Collins, 1994).

5. Wouter J. Hanegraaff, *New Age Religion and Western Culture: Esotericism in the Mirror of Secular Thought* (Leiden: E. J. Brill, 1996), 519–20.

6. Bryan Wilson, *Contemporary Transformations of Religion* (Oxford: Oxford University Press, 1976), 88.

7. Bruno Latour, *We Have Never Been Modern* (Cambridge: Harvard University Press, 1993), 11.

8. Raymond Williams, *Keywords: A Vocabulary of Culture and Society* (New York: Oxford University Press, 1983), 222–23, 278.

9. Robert J. Baird, "How Religion Became Scientific," in *Religion in the Making: The Emergence of the Sciences of Religion*, ed. Arie Molendijk and Peter Pels (Leiden: E. J. Brill, 1998), 218.

10. Ibid., 220.

11. Ibid., 226.

12. Arie L. Molendijk, Introduction to ibid., 1–27.

13. Jocelyn Godwin, *The Theosophical Enlightenment* (Albany: State University of New York Press, 1994), 101–3.

14. Ann Braude, *Radical Spirits: Spiritualism and Women's Rights in Nineteenth-Century America* (Boston: Beacon Press, 1989), 178; Peter Pels, "Occult Truths: Race, Conjecture, and Theosophy in Victorian Anthropology," in *Excluded Ancestors, Inventible Traditions: Essays Toward a More Inclusive History of Anthropology*, ed. R. Handler (Madison: The University of Wisconsin Press, 2000), 33.

15. E.g.: Godwin, *Theosophical*; Hanegraaff, *New Age Religion*; Pels, "Occult Truths"; Peter Pels, "Spirits of Modernity: Alfred Wallace, Edward Tylor, and the Visual Politics of Fact," in *Magic and Modernity: Interfaces of Revelation and Concealment*, ed. Birgit Meyer and Peter Pels (Stanford, Calif.: Stanford University Press, 2003), 241–71.

16. Hans Jonas, *The Gnostic Religion: The Message of the Alien God and the Beginnings of Christianity* (Boston: Beacon Press, 1958), 44.

17. Hanegraaff, *New Age Religion*, 519.

18. Jonas, *Gnostic Religion*, 35.

19. Hanegraaff, *New Age Religion*, 399.

20. Ibid., 411–513.

21. E.g.: Logie Barrow, *Independent Spirits: Spiritualism and English Plebeians, 1850–1910* (London: Routledge & Kegan Paul, 1986); Braude, *Radical Spirits*; Alex Owen, *The Darkened Room: Women, Power and Spiritualism in Late Victorian England* (London: Virago Press, 1989); Pels, "Occult Truths"; Pels, "Spirits of Modernity"; Peter van der Veer, *Imperial Encounters: Religion and Modernity in India and Britain* (Princeton, N.J.: Princeton University Press, 2001).

22. See Braude, *Radical Spirits*, 162; Peter Washington, *Madame Blavatsky's Baboon: Theosophy and the Emergence of the Western Guru* (London: Secker & Warburg, 1993).

23. Pels, "Spirits of Modernity," 242–43.

24. Laurence R. Moore, *Selling God: American Religion in the Marketplace of Culture* (New York: Oxford University Press, 1994).

25. Hanegraaff, *New Age Religion*, 520.

26. Jonas, *Gnostic Religion*, 42.

27. Colin Campbell, *The Romantic Ethic and the Spirit of Modern Consumerism* (Oxford: Blackwell, 1987), 217; Miranda Moerland and Anneke Van Otterloo, "New Age: Tegencultuur, paracultuur of kerncultuur?"[New Age: Counterculture, Paraculture, or Mainstream?], *Amsterdams Sociologisch Tijdschrift* 23 (1996): 682–710.

28. Cf. Olav Hammer, *Claiming Knowledge: Strategies of Epistemology from Theosophy to the New Age* (Leiden: E. J. Brill, 2001).

29. Benedict Anderson, *Imagined Communities: Reflections on the Origin and Spread of Nationalism* (London: Verso, 1983), 40. Another resemblance between nationalism and occultism is that both are essentially global: nationalism arose from the confrontation of New World colonies with European powers, while Theosophy initially resulted from a confrontation between European Protestant esotericism and Hinduism, Buddhism, and Jewish mysticism. This shows that "modernity" does not originate in Europe or the West only (see Timothy Mitchell, "The Stage of Modernity," in *Questions of Modernity*, ed. Timothy Mitchell [Minneapolis: University of Minnesota Press, 2000], 1–34).

30. Talal Asad, *Formations of the Secular: Christianity, Islam, Modernity*, (Stanford, Calif.: Stanford University Press, 2002), 14–15.

31. Moore, *Selling God*, 34, 253.

32. S. B. Liljegren, *Bulwer-Lytton's Novels and Isis Unveiled* (Upsala: Lundequistska Bokhandeln, 1957). Bulwer Lytton's occult writings include: *Zanoni* (1842), a story about a magician that would today be classified as "fantasy"; "The Haunted and the Haunters; or, the House and the Brain" (1859), which builds on Gothic horror; and *The Coming Race* (1871), which, in imagining an advanced race of people living under the Earth's crust, is one of the earliest (geological) science fiction novels. The five genres of modern mystery or "romance"—exotic travel adventure, fantasy, horror, detective story, and science fiction—were not clearly distinguished until the early twentieth century and still crossbreed promiscuously.

33. For examples, see Dorothy Sayers, *Great Short Stories of Detection, Mystery and Horror*, 2 vols. (London: Gollancz, 1928).

34. See Pels, "Occult Truths"; Pels, "Introduction: Magic and Modernity," in *Magic and Modernity*, ed. Meyer and Pels, 10–11; Pels, "Spirits of Modernity."

35. We stress that these institutions do not (necessarily) imply the "privatization" of religion (as some secularization theorists would have it): this would disregard the crucial contribution to the formation of the public sphere by consumer culture, domestic life, and the leisure industry.

36. Paul Heelas, *The New Age Movement: The Celebration of the Self and the Sacralisation of Modernity* (Oxford: Blackwell), 18.

37. Latour, *We Have Never Been Modern*.

38. Mary Douglas, *Purity and Danger: An Analysis of the Concepts of Pollution and Taboo* (London: Routledge & Kegan Paul, 1966).

39. Latour, *We Have Never Been Modern*, 11.

40. Douglas, *Purity and Danger*, 4.

41. Cf. Asad, *Formations of the Secular*, 183.

42. Ibid., 25.

43. Ibid., 192.

44. This is a crude and quick generalization, based on Hanegraaff's chapter-length rendering of Western esotericism's reflection in the "mirror of secular thought" (*New Age Religion*, chap. 15).

45. David Noble, *The Religion of Technology: The Divinity of Man and the Spirit of Invention* (New York: Penguin Books, 1997).

46. Ibid., chap. 6.

47. Leo Marx, *The Machine in the Garden: Technology and the Pastoral Ideal in America* (New York: Oxford University Press, 1964).

48. Pels, "Spirits of Modernity," 262–63; Jeffrey Sconce, *Haunted Media: Electronic Presence from Telegraphy to Television* (Durham, N.C.: Duke University Press, 2000), chap. 1; Jeremy Stolow, "Salvation by Electricity," in this volume.

49. The term *ether*, however, was itself partly derived from Mesmerist and Spiritualist fantasies about a pervading fluid reality, only dimly accessible through extraordinary experiences, and was adopted by James Frazer to explain the "secret sympathy" characteristic of a magical worldview (see Pels, "Introduction," 10).

50. Sconce, *Haunted Media*, 107.

51. Ibid.; this may ignore the importance of radio for Christian evangelists or preachers of other religions.

52. Rachel O. Moore, *Savage Theory: Cinema as Modern Magic* (Durham, N.C.: Duke University Press, 2000), 162.

53. Peter Pels, "The Confessional Ethic and the Spirits of the Screen: Reflections on the Modern Fear of Alienation," *Etnofoor* 15 (2002): 91–119.

54. Hanegraaff, *New Age Religion*, 95; Sconce, *Haunted Media*, chap. 3.

55. Andrew Ross, "New Age Technoculture," in *Cultural Studies*, ed. L. Grossberg, C. Nelson, and P. Treichler (London: Routledge, 1996), 535–48.

56. Sean Cubitt, "Supernatural Futures: Theses on Digital Aesthetics," in *Future/Natural: Nature/Science/Culture*, ed. G. Robertson et al. (London: Routledge, 1996), 243.

57. Scott Bukatman, *Terminal Identity: The Virtual Subject in Postmodern Science Fiction* (Durham, N.C.: Duke University Press, 1993), 347.

58. See, among others, Norbert Wiener, *Cybernetics; or, Control and Communication in the Animal and the Machine* (Cambridge: MIT Press, 1965); also, Gregory Bateson, *Steps to an Ecology of Mind* (New York: Ballantine, 1972) and *Mind and Nature: A Necessary Unity* (New York: Ballantine, 1979).

59. Kevin Robins and Frank Webster, "Athens Without Slaves . . . or Slaves Without Athens? The Neurosis of Technology," *Science as Culture* 3 (1988): 7–53.

60. Vincent Mosco, *The Digital Sublime: Myth, Power, and Cyberspace* (Cambridge: MIT Press, 2004).

61. Katherine N. Hayles, *How We Became Posthuman: Virtual Bodies in Cybernetics, Literature, and Informatics* (Chicago: University of Chicago Press, 1999), 7, 16.

62. Ibid., 5.

63. Cubitt, *Future/Natural*, 246; Hayles, *How We Became Posthuman*, 11.

64. Margaret Wertheim, *The Pearly Gates of Cyberspace* (New York: W. W. Norton, 1999), 40–41.

65. Edmund Burke, *A Philosophical Inquiry into the Origin of Our Ideas of the Sublime and the Beautiful* (Harmondsworth, Middlesex: Penguin, 1999).

66. Marx, *The Machine in the Garden*.

67. Robert Marett, *The Threshold of Religion* (London: Methuen, 1914).

68. Michael Heim, *The Metaphysics of Virtual Reality* (Oxford: Oxford University Press, 1993), 89.

69. Michael Benedikt, ed., *Cyberspace: First Steps* (Cambridge: MIT Press, 1992).

70. Nicole Stenger, "Mind Is a Leaking Rainbow," in ibid., 54.

71. Wertheim, *Pearly Gates*, 16.

72. Slavoj Žižek, *On Belief* (London: Routledge, 2001), 53.

73. Rushkoff, *Cyberia*.

74. This is the cybergnostic variety of New Age "perennialism"; see Heelas, *New Age Movement*, 27.

75. John Perry Barlow, *A Declaration of the Independence of Cyberspace*, http://www.eff.org/~barlow/Declaration-Final.html.

76. Leary, *Declaration of Evolution*. Leary's conception of a convergence of technological and natural evolution is widespread and originates at least in part in the 1960s combination of LSD and posthuman evolution as fictionalized in Arthur C. Clarke's *Childhood's End* (see Tom Wolfe, *The Electric Kool-Aid Acid Test* [New York: Bantam, 1999]).

77. William Gibson, *Neuromancer* (London: Harper Collins, 1984), 51; Rushkoff, *Cyberia*, chap. 9; Leary and Gullichsen, *Digital Polytheism*.

78. Rushkoff, *Cyberia*, 16; Cubitt, *Future/Natural*, 249.

79. "Elective affinity [*Wahlverwandtschaft*]" was the term used by Weber to discuss the relationship between Puritanism and capitalism; its etymology is, appropriately, alchemical (see Pels, "Introduction," 27).

80. Quoted in Rushkoff, *Cyberia*, 34.

81. Rushkoff, *Cyberia*, 32; Gibson, *Neuromancer*, 12.

82. Directed by Brett Leonard (1992), David Cronenberg (1999), and Larry and Andy Wachowski (1999), respectively.

83. Nicholas Yee, "The Psychology of Massively Multi-User Online Role-Playing Games: Motivations, Emotional Investment, Relationships and Problematic Usage," in *Avatars at Work and Play: Collaboration and Interaction in Shared Virtual Environments*, ed. R. Schroder and A. Axelson (London: Springer, 2006).

84. Sherry Turkle, *Life on the Screen: Identity in the Age of the Internet* (New York: Simon & Schuster, 1995).

85. R. V. Kelly, II, *Massively Multiplayer Online Role-Playing Games* (Jefferson: McFarland & Company, Inc., 2004), 85.

86. Brian Mortiarty at a computer game conference in 1999.

87. Larry Wachowski and Andy Wachowski, *The Matrix: Film Script* (Burbank, Calif.: Warner Bros), 28.

88. Cf. Simon Cooper, "Plenitude and Alienation: The Subject of Virtual Reality," in *Virtual Politics*, ed. Holmes, 93–106; Heim, *Metaphysics*.

89. Wachowski and Wachowski, *Matrix*.

90. Rushkoff, *Cyberia*, chap. 9.

91. Leary and Gullichsen, *Digital Polytheism*.

92. Rushkoff, *Cyberia*, 115.

93. See Hanegraaff, *New Age Religion*, 160.

94. Leary, *Declaration of Evolution*.

95. Joseph Pine, II, and James H. Gilmore, *The Experience Economy: Work Is Theater and Every Business Is a Stage* (Boston: Harvard Business School Press, 1999), 34, 36.

96. We take the title of this section from Barlow, *Declaration of the Independence of Cyberspace*.

97. Gibson, *Neuromancer*, 6.

98. Heim, *Metaphysics*, 102. Note, however, that *Neuromancer* evokes such gnosis ironically—a nuance that its hacker fans rarely want to notice.

99. Barlow, *Declaration of the Independence of Cyberspace*; Cooper, *Plenitude*; Hayles, *How We Became Posthuman*; Heim, *Metaphysics*; Sandy Stone, "Will the Real Body Please Stand Up? Boundary Stories about Virtual Cultures," in *Reading Digital Culture*, ed. David Trend (Oxford: Blackwell,

2001), 185–98; Christopher Ziguras, "The Technologization of the Sacred: Virtual Reality and the New Age," in *Virtual Politics: Identity and Community in Cyberspace*, ed. David Holmes (Thousand Oaks, Calif.: Sage Publications), 197–211; Žižek, *On Belief.*

100. Dery, *Escape Velocity.*

101. Hans Moravec, *Mind Children: The Future of Robot and Human Intelligence* (Cambridge: Harvard University Press, 1988).

102. Leary and Gullichsen, *Digital Polytheism.*

103. Wertheim, *Pearly Gates*, 226.

104. See, e.g., Dery, *Escape Velocity.*

105. Leary and Gullichsen, *Digital Polytheism.*

106. Jos de Mul, *Cyberspace Odyssee* (Kampen: Klement, 2002).

107. Marshall McLuhan, *Understanding Media: The Extensions of Man* (Cambridge: MIT Press. 1999).

108. Manuel Castells, *The Rise of the Network Society*, vol. 1, *The Information Age: Economy, Society and Culture* (Oxford: Blackwell, 1996), 492.

109. Ibid.

110. Barlow, *Declaration of the Independence of Cyberspace.*

111. Leary, *Declaration of Evolution.*

112. Erik Davis, *TechGnosis: Myth, Magic and Mysticism in the Age of Information* (London: Serpent's Tail, 1998), 165.

113. Dery, *Escape Velocity*, 21.

114. Theodore Roszak, *From Satori to Silicon Valley*, Http://library.stanford.edu/mac/primary/docs/satori/index.html.

115. Theodore Roszak, *The Making of a Counter Culture: Reflections on the Technocratic Society and Its Youthful Opposition* (New York: Doubleday, 1969), see also Daniel Bell, *The Cultural Contradictions of Capitalism* (New York: Basic Books, 1996); Herbert Marcuse, *One-Dimensional Man: Studies in the Ideology of Advanced Industrial Society* (Boston: Beacon Press, 1991); Anton Zijderveld, *The Abstract Society: A Cultural Analysis of Our Time* (New York: Doubleday, 1970).

116. Roszak, *From Satori to Silicon Valley.*

117. Steven Levy, *Hackers: Heroes of the Computer Revolution* (New York: Penguin Books, 1994), 39–49.

118. Ibid., 240.

119. Ibid., 190.

120. Jedediah Purdy, 'The God of the Digerati," *The American Prospect* 9 (1998), http://www.-prospect.org/print/V9/37/purdy-j.html.

121. Cited in Vivian Sobchack, "New Age Mutant Ninja Hackers: Reading Mondo 2000," in *Reading Digital Culture*, ed. Trend, 324.

122. Rushkoff, *Cyberia*, 164–66. "Turn on, tune in, drop out" was Leary's slogan during his earlier psychedelic years.

123. Pine and Gillmore, *Experience Economy.*

124. Hayles, *How We Became Posthuman.*

125. Thomas Frank, *The Conquest of Cool: Business Culture, Counterculture, and the Rise of Hip Consumerism* (Chicago: University of Chicago Press, 1998).

126. Moerland and Van Otterloo, *New Age.*

127. Steven Sutcliffe and Marion Bowman, Introduction to *Beyond New Age: Exploring Alternative Spirituality*, ed. Steven Sutcliffe and Marion Bowman (Edinburgh: Edinburgh University Press, 2000), 11.

Birgit Meyer, Religious Sensations: Why Media, Aesthetics, and Power Matter in the Study of Contemporary Religion

NOTE: This is the written version of my inaugural lecture delivered on October 6, 2006, to mark my acceptance of the chair of Professor of Cultural Anthropology, especially the study of religion and identity, at VU University, Amsterdam. I would like to thank Peter Geschiere, Annelies Moors, Oscar Salemink, Irene Stengs, Jeremy Stolow, Marjo de Theije, Mattijs van de Port, and Jojada Verrips for their stimulating and constructive comments on earlier versions of this text. All shortcomings are mine.

1. Slavoj Žižek, "Bluttrübe Zeiten: Die Antonomien der toleranten Vernunft und die Würde des Atheismus," *Lettre International* 73 (Summer 2006): 10–14.

2. This point is now being made in public discussions in the Netherlands. See NRC articles "De Sociologie is van God los" [Sociology is detached from God] (May 23, 2006) and "Waarom God aan de winnende hand is: Modernisering, democratisering en globalisering hebben Hem sterker gemaakt" [Why God holds the winning hand: modernization, democratization, and globalization have only made him stronger] (April 12, 2006). Both argue that secularization is passé as a theoretical framework.

3. With increasing modernization, religion is supposed to decline in public importance and retreat into a sphere of its own. To be religious or not then becomes a matter of personal choice. Secularization theory, as defended by Steve Bruce (e.g., *God Is Dead: Secularization in the West* [Oxford: Blackwell, 2002], 3 ff.), proclaims not the end of religion but its retreat into the private sphere. The extent to which religion has been privatized even throughout the Western world is subject to debate. José Casanova (*Public Religions in the Modern World* [Chicago: University of Chicago Press, 1994]), for example, has stressed the deprivatization of religion, without, however, giving up secularization theory entirely. Eminent sociologists of religion, such as Peter Berger (Peter Berger, ed., *The Desecularization of the World: Resurgent Religion and World Politics* [Grand Rapids, Mich.: William B. Eerdmans, 1999]) have argued that, rather than viewing Western Europe as the norm and other contexts in which religions assume public roles—including the United States—as deviations, it is more appropriate to regard ourselves as the exception that needs explanation. Given the upsurge and public presence of religion on a global scale, it has become clear that secularization theory is unsuitable as an intellectual tool. Debates about secularization have become repetitive and dull, discerning exceptions and explaining them (away). See Mark C. Taylor, Introduction to *Critical Terms for Religious Studies*, ed. Mark C. Taylor (Chicago: University of Chicago Press, 1998), 1–20. For a thought-provoking attempt to think about religion after 9/11, see Bruce Lincoln, *Holy Terrors: Thinking about Religion after September 11* (Chicago: University of Chicago Press, 2003). For more on the inappropriateness of secularization as a point of departure, see: Talal Asad, *Formations of the Secular: Christianity, Islam, Modernity* (Stanford, Calif: Stanford University Press, 2003); Hent de Vries, "In Media Res: Global Religion, Public Spheres, and the Task of Contemporary Religious Studies," in *Religion and Media*, ed. Hent de Vries and Samuel Weber (Stanford, Calif.: Stanford University Press, 2001), 4–42; David Scott and Charles Hirschkind, eds., *Powers of the Secular Modern: Talal Asad and His Interlocutors* (Stanford, Calif.: Stanford University Press, 2006); Scott M. Thomas, *The Global Resurgence of Religion and the Transformation of International Relations* (New York: Palgrave Macmillan, 2005); Peter van der Veer, *Imperial Encounters: Religion and Modernity in India and Britain* (Princeton, N.J.: Princeton University Press, 2001), 14 ff.

4. Jürgen Habermas, "Zum Friedenspreis des deutschen Buchhandels: Eine Dankrede," *Süddeutsche Zeitung* (October 15, 2001); idem, "Faith and Knowledge," in *The Frankfurt School on*

Religion: Key Writings by the Major Thinkers, ed. Eduardo Mendieta (New York: Routledge, 2005), 327–38.

5. In addition to Asad, *Formations of the Secular*, see also Saba Mahmood, *Politics of Piety: The Islamic Revival and the Feminist Subject* (Princeton, N.J.: Princeton University Press, 2005).

6. Talal Asad, *Genealogies of Religion: Discipline and Power in Christianity and Islam* (Baltimore: The Johns Hopkins University Press, 1993). See also: David Chidester, *Savage Systems: Colonialism and Comparative Religion in Southern Africa* (Charlottesville: University Press of Virginia, 1996); Arie Molendijk and Peter Pels, eds., *Religion in the Making: The Emergence of the Sciences of Religion* (Leiden: E. J. Brill, 1998); Malory Nye, "Religion, Post-Religionism, and Religioning: Religious Studies and Contemporary Cultural Debates," *Method and Theory in the Study of Religion* 12 (2000): 447–76; Peter van Rooden, *Religieuze Regimes: Over Godsdienst en Maatschappij in Nederland, 1570–1990* (Amsterdam: Bert Bakker, 1996).

7. I use "religious organizations" as an umbrella term to encompass different social formations characterized by peculiar organizational forms, which can be distinguished by degrees of institutionalization, modes of participation, internal coherence, and so on. Within established religious traditions such as Buddhism, Christianity, Hinduism, Islam, and Judaism, there exist a host of different organizational forms.

8. My understanding of comparison follows Michael Lambek: "anthropology is also resolutely comparative, insofar as the particularistic ethnographic accounts must be made to speak to each other and to a developing (and frequently debated) analytic language" ("General Introduction," in *A Reader in the Anthropology of Religion*, ed. Michael Lambek [Malden, Mass.: Blackwell, 2002], 2).

9. Of course, the very fact that we engage in the study of religion constructs the object of our research in a particular manner. As this is an unavoidable effect of scientific discipline (in the double sense of the term), we need to be all the more critically aware of the ways in which the theories and concepts developed in the study of religion shape the very phenomena we seek to grasp. See Lambek, "General Introduction," for an excellent overview of a host of different definitions developed in the anthropology of religion and a critique of definition as a particular intellectual operation. See also Brian Morris, *Religion and Anthropology: A Critical Introduction* (Cambridge: Cambridge University Press, 2006), who insists that we need at least a working definition of religion. In my view, all we need are sensitizing concepts, which can guide our approach toward religious phenomena and are subject to critical reflection and revision in the light of our findings.

10. All these terms function in specific discourses and are problematic. Of course, in particular research settings it is best to stay close to the terms used by people themselves. But this does not relieve us of the necessity to have more general terms. How otherwise can we exchange ideas with colleague researchers?

11. I would like to stress that the point is neither to dismiss nor to assert the existence of God or other spiritual beings. It is simply not the task of the anthropology of religion to make this kind of ontological statement. The question of how a personal belief in God and anthropological research on religion can and cannot co-exist was addressed in the farewell symposium Playful Religion, organized at the Free University of Amsterdam on June 23, 2006, in honor of the retirement of André Droogers. During this symposium, Droogers's suggestion of a more ludic attitude toward both belief and research was extensively discussed. See also *In de Marge* 15, no. 3 (2006).

12. Weber's thinking about the nexus of Protestantism and capitalism was heavily influenced by the work of Friedrich Schleiermacher (*Die Protestantische Ethik 1: Eine Aufsatzsammlung*, ed. Johannes Winckelman [1920; Gütersloh: Gütersloher Verlagshaus, 1984), who addressed the emotional and experiential dimension of religion, and in so doing articulated a basic aspect of modern

Protestant religiosity. See Peter van Rooden, "Friedrich Schleiermachers 'Reden über die Religion' en de historische bestudierung van godsdienst," *Theoretische Geschiedenis* 23 (1996): 419–38. Schleiermacher's understanding of religion as "the feeling of absolute dependency," inspired by Romanticism, asserted the difference between—and hence the compatibility of—religion and knowledge. Religion, for him, was not about knowing but about a "contemplation of the universe" that happened via different sensory registers and yielded a particular kind of piety. Weber temporally displaced Schleiermacher's typically early-nineteenth-century understanding of religion by attributing it (mistakenly so, Van Rooden argues) to the seventeenth-century Calvinists who are the heroes of his *Protestant Ethic*. In Weber's own time, as he realized with increasing agony, this kind of religiosity had become obsolete without any substitute having been found.

13. Weber, though positing the disenchantment of the world, can certainly not be charged with a simple idea of secularization. On the contrary, for him religion played a crucial role in bringing modern capitalism into being. Quite mistakenly, Weber's work has been read through the lens of progress as an apology for capitalism (and even an assertion of the superiority of the West). A careful reading of the end of the *Protestant Ethic* teaches us better. See the marvelous biography by Joachim Radkau, *Max Weber: Die Leidenschaft des Denkens* (Munich: Hanser, 2005), and also Hartmut Lehmann, *Max Webers 'Protestantische Ethik': Beiträge aus der Sicht eines Historikers* (Göttingen: Vandenhoeck & Ruprecht, 1996), and Detlev Peukert, *Max Webers Diagnose der Moderne*. (Göttingen: Vandenhoeck & Ruprecht, 1989).

14. For a critique of this rather facile reading of Weber (and Marx and Durkheim), see Peter Pels, "Introduction: Magic and Modernity," in *Magic and Modernity: Interfaces of Revelation and Concealment*, ed. Birgit Meyer and Peter Pels (Stanford, Calif.: Stanford University Press, 2003), 1–38. In Dutch anthropology, disbelief in modernity as being disenchanted has motivated: Peter Geschiere's provocative *The Modernity of Witchcraft: Politics and the Occult in Postcolonial Africa* (Charlottesville: University Press of Virginia, 1997); Bonno Thoden van Velzen's notion of collective fantasies, e.g., "Revenants That Cannot Be Shaken: Collective Fantasies in a Maroon Society," *American Anthropologist* 97, no. 4 (1995): 722–32; and Jojada Verrips's suggestion that we acknowledge and research the Wild in the West in "The Golden Bough and Apocalypse Now: An-Other Fantasy," *Postcolonial Studies* 4, no. 3 (2001): 335–48.

15. See: Peter van der Veer, "Spirituality in Modern Society," in Part VI of this volume; Wouter Hanegraaf, *New Age Religion and Western Culture: Esotericism in the Mirror of Secular Thought* (Leiden: E. J. Brill, 1996); Paul Heelas, *The New Age Movement: The Celebration of the Self and the Sacralization of Modernity* (Oxford: Blackwell, 1996); Martin Ramstedt, "Who Is a Witch? Contesting Notions of Authenticity among Contemporary Dutch Witches," *Etnofoor* 17, nos. 1/2 (2004): 178–98; Anton Van Harskamp, *Het nieuw-religieuze verlangen* (Kampen: Kok, 2000).

16. Collin Campbell, *The Romantic Ethic and the Spirit of Modern Consumerism* (Oxford: Blackwell, 1987). See the special issue on authenticity, *Etnofoor* 17, nos. 1/2 (2004).

17. William James, *The Varieties of Religious Experience* (1902; Harmondsworth, Middlesex: Penguin, 1982), 42.

18. In anthropology, so-called intellectualist approaches, which reduce religion to a quest for knowledge (as developed by E. B. Tylor and later Robin Horton), and so-called expressivist or symbolist approaches, which emphasize the importance of feeling and experience, have long been at loggerheads. While the former tend to focus on "words" and "meaning," the latter tend to foreground "images" and "experience."

19. Charles Taylor, *Varieties of Religion Today: William James Revisited* (Cambridge: Harvard University Press, 2002), 116. He says this in his discussion of the appeal that James's work has today. James misrecognized formal spiritual practices, however. Peter van Rooden critiques Schleiermacher along similar lines ("Friedrich Schleiermachers *Reden über die Religion*," *Theoretische*

Geschiedenis 23 (1996): 419–38). A host of approaches to religion as experience can be critiqued along the lines suggested by Taylor and Van Rooden.

20. Given that the term *sense*, contained in *sensation*, also denotes *Sinn*, or "meaning," it is important not to confine sensation to feeling alone but to see it as encompassing the formation of meaning (not as a purely intellectual endeavor, but as enshrined in broader processes of "sensing"). This allows us to transcend the infelicitous opposition between approaches in the study of religion that focus on feelings, experiences, and the body, on the one hand, and the production of meaning as a purely intellectual endeavor, on the other (see also note 18, above). In my understanding, the production of meaning always involves bodily experiences and emotions.

21. To give an overview of the question of the sublime is beyond the scope of this essay. It reaches from the perspectives of Kant, Burke, and Herder to those of Lyotard and Jameson.

22. R. R. Marett, *The Threshold of Religion* (London: Methuen & Co., 1914), x. He states: "we must, I think, in any case admit the fact that in response to, or at any rate in connection with, the emotions of awe, wonder, and the like, wherein feeling would seem for the time being to have outstripped the power of 'natural,' that is, reasonable explanation, there arises in the region of human thought a powerful impulse to objectify and even personify the mysterious or 'supernatural' something felt, and in the region of will a corresponding impulse to render it innocuous, or better still propitious, by force of constraint, communion, or conciliation" (11).

23. Ibid., 28. The idea that religion starts at the limits of understanding (and the experience of evil and pain) is also key to Geertz's well-known definition (Clifford Geertz, "Religion as a Cultural System," in Geertz, *The Interpretation of Cultures* [New York: Basic Books, 1973], 87–125). For Geertz, religion offers ways to deal with such limits. In my understanding, the point is not that religion helps people deal with a perceived limit but rather that religious sensational forms induce such a sense of limit.

24. Rudolf Otto, *Das Heilige: Über das Irrationale in der Idee des Göttlichen und sein Verhältnis zum Rationalen* (Breslau: Trewendt und Granier, 1917), 7. Otto's perspective presupposes the existence of the supernatural, albeit as a never fully graspable, and thus imperfectly representable transcendental entity, the *mysterium tremendum*, the *fascinosum*. The Numinous makes itself sensed through particular overwhelming emotional experiences, which can, according to Otto, be circumscribed as "awe" (ibid., 15), a term encompassing a range of sensations from horror and fear to wonder and joy. Religious sensations—among them goose bumps—reveal the power of this mysterious, fascinating entity, while mystifying it at the same time as the completely different (*das Ganz andere*).

25. This suggests, again, a view of religion as originating in an immediate feeling of the presence of the transcendental. This stress on a primary, individual moment, as I have pointed out in my critique of James, is problematic because it neglects the social construction of the transcendental via what I call sensational forms.

26. I borrow the notion of the enabling limit from Samuel Weber, *Mass Mediauras: Form, Technics, Media* (Stanford, Calif.: Stanford University Press, 1996).

27. Birgit Meyer, "Impossible Representations: Pentecostalism, Vision, and Video Technology in Ghana," in *Religion, Media, and the Public Sphere*, ed. Birgit Meyer and Annelies Moors (Bloomington: Indiana University Press, 2006), 290–312.

28. William P. Murphy, "The Sublime Dance of Mende Politics: An African Aesthetic of Charismatic Power," *American Ethnologist* 25, no. 4 (1998): 563–82; see also Brian Larkin, *Media and Urban Form: Technology, Infrastructure, and Culture in Northern Nigeria* (Durham, N.C.: Duke University Press, 2007).

29. Birgit Meyer, "If You Are a Devil You Are a Witch and, If You Are a Witch You Are a Devil: The Integration of 'Pagan' Ideas into the Conceptual Universe of Ewe Christians in Southeastern Ghana," *The Journal of Religion in Africa* 22, no. 2 (1992): 98–132; idem, "Delivered from the Powers of Darkness: Confessions about Satanic Riches in Christian Ghana," *Africa* 65, no. 2 (1995): 236–55; idem, *Translating the Devil: Religion and Modernity among the Ewe in Ghana* (Trenton, N.J.: Africa World Press, 1999).

30. Birgit Meyer, "Commodities and the Power of Prayer: Pentecostalist Attitudes Towards Consumption in Contemporary Ghana," in *Globalization and Identity: Dialectics of Flow and Closure,* ed. Birgit Meyer and Peter Geschiere, *Development and Change* 29, no. 4 (1998): 751–77; idem, "Make a Complete Break with the Past: Memory and Post-colonial Modernity in Ghanaian Pentecostalist Discourse," *Journal of Religion in Africa* 27, no. 3 (1998): 316–49; idem, "Christianity in Africa: From African Independent to Pentecostal-Charismatic Churches," *Annual Review of Anthropology* 33 (2004): 447–74. See also Paul Gifford, *Ghana's New Christianity: Pentecostalism in a Globalising African Economy* (London: Hurst, 2004).

31. But it would be wrong simply to oppose Pentecostalism and mainstream (Presbyterian) Protestantism, for in many respects the former builds upon the modern religiosity introduced by nineteenth-century Protestant missionaries, with its strong focus on the individual believer. This implied not only new modes of piety but also submission to the regime of the church, the adoption of a modern life style, and, of course, the diabolization of traditional religion and the social formations sustained by it. Interestingly, although the missionaries themselves were part of Pietist revival movements that emphasized personal spiritual experiences, the mission paid more attention to the strict implementation of rules and regulations than to creating a space for such experiences. While in the wake of colonization many Africans felt attracted to this new religiosity, they also found severe shortcomings, which made them, as the missionaries put it, "relapse into heathendom" in times of crisis. Notwithstanding the fact that the religiosity conveyed by the mission was translated into the local context—and hence appropriated and transformed—converts were limited in their ability to shape their Christian beliefs and practices in line with their own needs. The foundation of a stream of African independent and, later, Pentecostal-charismatic churches testifies to the persistence of local attempts to reinvent Christianity to suit local expectations and needs. One important concern was, and still is, the question of the efficacy of belief. A religion that would mainly induce believers to read the Bible and participate in rather boring church services—elders used to go round with a stick to wake up those who had fallen asleep—was found to be an imperfect substitute for traditional cults, which offered rituals of trance, possession, and dance, involved human beings in spiritual gift exchanges with their gods, and helped people get around in a far more practical, material manner. Though intrigued by the promise of developing an individual relation with God, African converts expected to feel the presence of this supernatural omnipotent power in their own bodies and to witness its effects in a material way, in everyday life.

32. Personal communication.

33. Because the Holy Spirit does not enter into and stay in a person just like that, Pentecostalism teaches a set of religious disciplines, such as Bible study, extensive fasting, and intense individual and collective prayer in small prayer cells. See Rijk van Dijk, "Silence of the Camp: Modernity and the Pentecostal Negotiation of an Auditory Identity in Ghana," paper presented to the Research Team Pentecostalism, VU University Amsterdam, September 7, 2005. To be filled with and express the Holy Spirit is not only a question of inward, contemplative spirituality but also a question of power: only those filled with the Holy Spirit are held to be invulnerable to evil spirits and empowered to lead a happy, prosperous life.

34. J. Kwabena Asamoah-Gyadu, "Pentecostal Media Images and Religious Globalization in Sub-Saharan Africa," in *Belief in Media: Cultural Perspectives on Media and Christianity,* ed. P.

Horsfield, M. E. Hess, and A. M. Medrano (Aldershot: Ashgate, 2004), 65–80; Birgit Meyer, " 'Praise the Lord . . .': Popular Cinema and Pentecostalite Style in Ghana's New Public Sphere," *American Ethnologist* 31, no. 1 (2004): 92–110.

35. Marleen De Witte, "Altar Media's *Living Word*: Televised Christianity in Ghana," *Journal of Religion in Africa* 33, no. 2 (2003): 172–202.

36. Marleen De Witte, "The Spectacular and the Spirits: Charismatics and Neo-Traditionalists on Ghanaian Television," *Material Religion* 1, no. 3 (2005): 314–35.

37. De Vries, "In Media Res"; see also: Meyer, "Impossible Representations," 290–312; Birgit Meyer, "Religious Revelation, Secrecy, and the Limits of Visual Representation," *Anthropological Theory* 6, no. 4, forthcoming; S. Brent Plate, "Introduction: Filmmaking, Mythmaking, Culture Making," in *Representing Religion in World Cinema: Filmmaking, Mythmaking, Culture Making*, ed. S. Brent Plate (New York: Palgrave, 2003), 1–15; Jeremy Stolow, "Religion and/as Media," *Theory, Culture & Society* 22, no. 2 (2005): 137–63.

38. David Morgan, *Visual Piety: A History and Theory of Popular Religious Images* (Berkeley: University of California Press, 1998).

39. Christopher Pinney, *Photos of the Gods: The Printed Image and Political Struggle in India* (London: Reaktion Books, 2004). See also Lawrence A Babb and Susan S. Wadley, eds., *Media and the Transformation of Religion in South Asia* (Philadelphia: University of Pennsylvania Press, 1995).

40. Brian Morris, *In the Place of Origins: Modernity and Its Mediums in Northern Thailand* (Durham, N.C.: Duke University Press, 2000); Irene Stengs, *Worshipping the Great Modernizer: The Cult of King Chulalongkorn, Patron Saint of the Thai Middle Class* (Singapore: Singapore University Press, 2007).

41. See also Patricia Birman, "Future in the Mirror: Media, Evangelicals, and Politics in Rio de Janeiro," in *Religion, Media, and the Public Sphere*, ed. Meyer and Moors, 52–72; Maria José Alves de Abreu, "On Charisma, Mediation, and Broken Screens," *Etnofoor* 15, no. 1/2 (2002): 240–59; De Witte, "Altar Media's *Living Word*"; De Witte, "The Spectacular and the Spirits: Charismatics," 314–35; Rosalind I. J. Hackett, "Charismatic/Pentecostal Appropriation of Media Technologies in Nigeria and Ghana," *Journal of Religion in Africa* 28, no. 3 (1998): 1–19; Martijn Oosterbaan, "Divine Mediations: Pentecostalism, Politics, and Mass Media in a Favela in Rio de Janeiro," Ph.D. diss. (University of Amsterdam, 2006).

42. Marleen De Witte, " 'Insight,' Secrecy, Beasts, and Beauty: Struggles over the Making of a Ghanaian Documentary on Audiovisual Spirits? Styles and Strategies of Representing 'African Traditional Religion' in Ghana," *Postscripts* 1, no. 2/3 (2005): 277–300; Birgit Meyer, "Mediating Tradition: Pentecostal Pastors, African Priests, and Chiefs in Ghanaian Popular Films," in *Christianity and Social Change in Africa: Essays in Honor of J. D. Y. Peel*, ed. T. Falola (Durham, N.C.: Carolina Academic Press, 2005), 275–306. See also Faye Ginsburg, "Rethinking the 'Voice of God' in Indigenous Australia: Secrecy, Exposure, and the Efficacy of Media," in *Religion, Media. and the Public Sphere*, ed. Meyer and Moors, 188–204; Patricia Spyer, "The Cassowary Will Not Be Photographed," in *Religion and Media*, ed. de Vries and Weber, 304–20.

43. Mattijs van de Port, "Visualizing the Sacred: Video Technology, 'Televisual' Style, and the Religious Imagination in Bahian Candomblé," *American Ethnologist* 33, no. 3 (2006): 444–62. See also: William Mazzarella, "Culture, Globalization, Mediation," *Annual Review of Anthropology* 33 (2004): 345–67; Birgit Meyer, "Religious Remediations: Pentecostal Views in Ghanaian Video-Movies," *Postscripts* 1. no. 2/3 (2005): 155–81.

44. Meyer, "Religious Remediations," 155–81; Mattijs van de Port, "Circling Around the *Really Real*: Spirit Possession Ceremonies and the Search for Authenticity in Bahian Candomblé," *Ethos* 33, no. 2 (2005): 149–79, and Van de Port, "Visualizing the Sacred," 444–62.

45. David Chidester, *Authentic Fakes* (Berkeley: University of California Press, 2005).

46. Benedict Anderson, *Imagined Communities: Reflections on the Origins and Spread of Nationalism*, rev. ed. (London: Verso, 1991).

47. Regarding Islam, see Ayse Önçü, "Becoming 'Secular Muslims': Yasar Nuri Öztürk as a Super-subject on Turkish Television," in *Religion, Media, and the Public Sphere*, ed. Meyer and Moors, 227–50; Dorothea Schulz, "'Charisma and Brotherhood' Revisited: Mass-mediated Forms of Spirituality in Urban Mali," *Journal of Religion in Africa* 33, no. 2 (2003): 146–71. Benjamin's classic essay is: Walter Benjamin, "Das Kunstwerk im Zeitalter seiner technischen Reproduzierbarkeit," in his *Illuminationen: Ausgewählte Schriften* (Frankfurt a. M.: Suhrkamp, 1977), 136–69.

48. Michel de Certeau, *The Practice of Everyday Life* (Berkeley: University of California Press, 1984), 186 ff.; De Vries, "In Media Res," 23 ff.

49. See Van de Port, "Visualizing the Sacred," 444–62; Rafael Sánchez, "Channel-Surfing: Media, Mediumship, and State Authority in the María Lionza Possession Cult (Venezuela)," in *Religion and Media*, ed. De Vries and Weber, 388–434.

50. Lawrence R. Moore, *Selling God: American Religion in the Marketplace of Culture* (Oxford: Oxford University Press, 1994); see also Francio Guadeloupe, "Chanting Down the New Jerusalem: The Politics of Belonging on Sint Maarten and Saint Martin," Ph.D. diss. (University of Amsterdam, 2006).

51. Stolow, "Religion and/as Media," 125.

52. We find such a stance not only in Marshall McLuhan's famous dictum 'The medium is the message" but also, e.g., in the thinking of Manuel Castells. In Castells's view, religion stands separate from the "integrated communication system based on digitized electronic production, distribution and exchange of symbols" that generates the social networks that characterize the information age (*The Rise of the Network Society* [Oxford: Blackwell, 1996], 406). Referring to an eternal truth that cannot be mediated via the technologies of the information age, religion is, in Castells's view a conservative force, and thus a matter of the past, doomed to disappear in favor of secularization. The adoption of modern mass media by religion—Castells invokes the example of televangelism—ultimately destroys religion's legitimacy: when "all wonders are online," "societies are finally and truly disenchanted" (ibid.). I disagree with Castells's view of religion as a reactive force, which can only be corrupted and rendered obsolete by taking up modern mass media. For how mistaken it is to understand the rise of public, mass-mediatized religion in this manner, see Meyer and Moors, eds., *Religion, Media, and the Public Sphere*, and De Vries, "In Media Res."

53. For more information on this program, see www.pscw.uva.nl/media-religion.

54. Van de Port, "Visualizing the Sacred," 457.

55. Christopher Pinney, *Photos of the Gods*; idem, "Four Types of Material Culture," in *Handbook of Material Culture*, ed. C. Tilley, W. Keane, S. Küchler, P. Spyer, and M. Rowlands (London: Sage, 2006), 131–44; Jojada Verrips, "Aisthesis and An-aesthesia," *Ethnologia Europea* 35, no. 1/2 (2006): 27–33. The quote is from Verrips, 27.

56. For Merleau-Ponty, perception has priority over reason (*Phenomenology of Perception*, trans. Colin Smith [1962; London: Routledge, 2002]).Thinking is grounded in the perceived world, that is, in experiences that precede reflection. This means that the body is central: via the body, humans are both part of and able to experience the world. This experience mobilizes all the senses.

57. As intimated in the section on religious sensations, one of the big problems with phenomenological approaches in the study of religion is the strong bias toward interiority and the assumption of a transcendent reality out there. This entails a neglect of the social construction of the transcendental in the immanent. In his stimulating article "Asymptote of the Ineffable: Embodiment, Alterity, and the Theory of Religion" (*Current Anthropology* 45, no. 2 [2004]: 163–84),

Thomas Csordas critically discusses the phenomenology of religion. While his ideas about the importance of embodiment resonate with my plea to take into account the aesthetic dimension of religion, I still find his claim that alterity forms the "phenomenological kernel" of religion problematic because it fails to include the social dimension. I agree with the point raised by Michael Lambek, that Csordas "has some way to go now to link alterity with the social and the moral" ("Comment on Thomas Csordas, 'Asymptote of the Ineffable,'" *Current Anthropology* 45, no. 2 [2004]: 179).

58. I use "sensational" to refer to feelings and "sensory" to refer to the senses. Of course, the senses play an important role in arousing feelings. This is why anthropological work on emotions is very close to work on the senses, as Don Brenneis argues ("Afterword: Sense, Sentiment, and Sociality," *Etnofoor* 18, no. 1 [2005]: 142–48).

59. Geertz, "Religion as a Cultural System," 87–125. It should be noted that other theories of semiotics do not necessarily propose an intrinsically arbitrary relation between sign and referent. In Peirce, the index does not have an arbitrary relation to its referent. Following Johannes Fabian ("Language, History and Anthropology," in his *Time and the Work of Anthropology: Critical Essays 1971–1991* [1971; Chur: Harwood Academic Publishers, 1991), I consider problematic approaches toward language (and culture) that posit an arbitrary relation between language and its referent, because they suggest an ultimate rift between language and the outside world. Instead, I understand language in constructive terms. Language—more precisely, speaking—is a material performance, a practice of signification, which construes the world rather than alienating speakers from it.

60. See also David Freedberg, *The Power of Images: Studies in the History and Theory of Response* (Chicago: University of Chicago Press, 1989).

61. Birgit Meyer, "Die Erotik des Bösen: Mami Water als 'christlicher' Dämon in ghanaischen und nigerianischen Videfilmen," in *Africa Screams: Die Wiederkehr des Bösen in Kino, Kunst und Kult*, ed. T. Wendl (Wuppertal: Peter Hammer, 2004), 199–210.

62. From experience we all know that certain images may create a strong, fearful, or even awesome impression on the beholder. During our last family holiday, my son Sybren and his friend Bram (both age eleven) created a ghost house inhabited by a Cyclops. This creature was made up of a piece of cloth, a flashlight, and a coat hanger. Nevertheless, the boys found their own creature too fearsome to let it stay in their bedroom through the night.

63. Clifford Geertz, "Deep Play: Notes on the Balinese Cock Fight," in his *The Interpretation of Cultures*.

64. Jeremy Stolow, "Gravity, Gravitas, and the Politics of How-To Judaism," paper presented at the conference Religion, Media and the Question of Community, University of Amsterdam, June 28–30, 2006.

65. Susan Buck-Morss, "Aesthetics and Anaesthetics: Walter Benjamin's Art Works Essay Reconsidered," *October* 62 (1992): 3–41. See also Johannes Fabian, *Time and the Other: How Anthropology Makes Its Object* (New York: Columbia University Press, 1983).

66. Martin Jay, *Downcast Eyes: The Denigration of Vision in Twentieth-Century Thought* (Berkeley: University of California Press, 1994).

67. W. J. T Mitchell, *Picture Theory* (Chicago: University of Chicago Press, 1994) and *What Do Pictures Want? The Lives and Loves of Images* (Chicago: University of Chicago Press, 2005). See Pinney, "Four Types of Material Culture," 131–44, for a helpful, thought-provoking overview of four different ways of framing the study of visual culture.

68. Of particular importance to my concerns is recent work on the interface of the anthropology of the body and the senses, e.g., David Howes, *Sensual Relations: Engaging the Senses in Culture and Social Theory* (Ann Arbor: University of Michigan Press, 2003); Charles Hirschkind, "The Ethics of Listening: Cassette-sermon Auditioning in Contemporary Egypt," *American Ethnologist*

28, no. 3 (2001): 623–49; and the field of visual culture studies, which addresses the "power of images" to touch people in our media-saturated environments, e.g., Freedberg, *The Power of Images*; Mitchell, *What Do Pictures Want?*; Vivian Sobchack, *Carnal Thoughts: Embodiment and Moving Image Culture* (Berkeley: University of California Press, 2004); Laura Marks, *The Skin of the Film: Intercultural Cinema, Embodiment, and the Senses* (Durham, N..C.: Duke University Press, 2000).

69. Morgan, *Visual Piety* and *The Sacred Gaze: Religious Visual Culture in Theory and Practice* (Berkeley: University of California Press, 2005).

70. Morgan, *Visual Piety*, 9.

71. Cf. Sobchack, *Carnal Thoughts*.

72. Morgan's ideas resonate remarkably well with recent approaches developed in the field of cinema studies, which challenge the association of vision and the visual with the eye alone, and the concomitant disassociation from other senses. In particular, Laura Marks (*The Skin of the Film*) and Vivian Sobchack (*Carnal Thoughts*) have stressed the need to develop a more visceral, carnal approach to the visual, one that is rooted in the existential phenomenology of Merleau-Ponty (and Mikel Dufrenne, *The Phenomenology of Aesthetic Experience* [Evanston, Ill.: Northwestern University Press, 1973]) and can take note of the multisensory, synaesthetic impact of images in constituting a sense of being in the world.

73. See Allen and Polly Roberts's exploration of the power of images of Sheik Amadou Bamba to sacralize space in the city of Dakar (*A Saint in the City: Sufi Arts of Modern Senegal* [Seattle: University of Washington Press, 2003]), or Christopher Pinney's analysis of how a visual engagement with printed images of Hindu gods yields a particular "corpothetics." Pinney coins the term *corpothetics* to avoid confusion with conventional understandings of aesthetics in the Kantian sense. Entailing "a desire to fuse image and beholder, and the elevation of efficacy [of beholders' encounter with the image] . . . as the central criterion of value" (Pinney, *Photos of the Gods*, 194), Pinney's understanding of corpothetics and my understanding of aesthetics in terms of aisthesis converge.

74. Here I see interesting ways to link up with work on religion in cognitive anthropology, e.g., the work of Harvey Whitehouse.

75. See Asad, *Genealogies of Religion*; Hirschkind, "The Ethics of Listening"; Saba Mahmood, "Rehearsed Spontaneity and the Conventionality of Ritual: Disciplines of Salāt," *American Ethnologist* 28, no. 4 (2001): 827–53.

76. *Identity* is a central concept in current debates. It refers to a host of meanings. I understand "identity" to mean belonging to a particular social formation that is inclusive as well as exclusive. Identity, as Peter Geschiere and I have argued in *Globalization and Identity*, creates boundaries and promises clarity and security in a world characterized by distraction and fragmentation. In this sense, identity needs to be placed in a dialectic of flow and closure. I would suggest that we should take into account the importance of the senses and sensations in invoking and sustaining identities that people feel to be natural and thus beyond question. I do not, of course, want to claim the existence of primordial, essentialized identities. The point is, rather, to understand why and how personal and collective identities, though constructed, are perceived as "natural" and "real." See Birgit Meyer, "Modern Mass Media, Religion, and the Dynamics of Distraction and Concentration," concluding lecture to the conference Modern Mass Media, Religion, and the Question of Community, University of Amsterdam, June 30, 2006.

77. For an illuminating discussion of habitus (and hexis) in the thinking of Bourdieu (and Mauss), see Herman Roodenburg, "Pierre Bourdieu: Issues of Embodiment and Authenticity," *Etnofoor* 16, no. 1/2 (2004): 215–26.

78. Jojada Verrips, "Aisthesis and An-aesthesia"; see also Buck-Morss, "Aesthetics and Anaesthetics.."

79. Jonathan Crary, *Attention, Spectacle, and Modern Culture* (Boston: MIT Press, 2001).

80. Hirschkind, "The Ethics of Listening." See also Schulz, "Charisma and Brotherhood" and her "Morality, Community, Publicness: Shifting Terms of Public Debate in Mali," in *Religion, Media, and the Public Sphere*, ed. Meyer and Moors, 132–51.

81. Maria José Alves de Abreu, "Breathing into the Heart of the Matter: Why Padre Marcelo Needs No Wings," *Postscripts* 1, no. 2/3 (2005): 325–49.

82. See, in this context, Stewart Hoover's important work *Religion in the Media Age* (London: Routledge, 2006) on the ways in which religious and nonreligious audiences look at mass-mediated programs. He suggests a trend toward an increasingly individual, autonomous search for spiritual experience, in which media consumption plays a central role. See also Oosterbaan, *Divine Mediations*, who shows how Pentecostal sensory regimes shape the ways in which born-again believers relate to mass-mediated entertainment.

83. Meyer, "Modern Mass Media." See also Michel Maffesoli, *The Contemplation of the World: Figures of Community Style* (Minneapolis: University of Minnesota Press, 1996).

84. See also Morris, *Religion and Anthropology*, 5–6.

85. Bruno Latour, "What Is Iconoclash? or, Is There a World Beyond the Image Wars?" in *Iconoclash: Beyond the Image Wars in Science, Religion, and Art*, ed. Bruno Latour and Peter Weibel (Cambridge: MIT Press, 2002), 14–18; idem, *Reassembling the Social: An Introduction to Actor-Network-Theory* (Oxford: Oxford University Press, 2005), 88 ff. Latour is deeply critical of a facile constructivist stance, which, in its eagerness to deconstruct essentializing power claims, tends to miss the concreteness and materiality of "construction." He urges us to think about construction as a building site on which solid structures emerge that cannot be deconstructed by critical analysis alone. We need an understanding of construction that acknowledges its—at times scary—materiality. Critiques of construction need to take its material dimension as a starting point.

86. Van de Port, "Visualizing the Sacred."

87. Calling attention to the question of embodiment and appealing to the body as a harbinger of truth does not at all imply understanding the body to be an ultimate reality. Rather, I argue that in our research we need to come to terms with the fact that the body is tuned via particular social practices and is in this sense "constructed." This "construction," however, tends to be naturalized and perceived as "natural" and "real." See also Rachel Spronk, "Ambiguous Pleasures: Sexuality and New Self-Definitions in Nairobi," Ph.D. diss. (University of Amsterdam, 2006).

88. See Jojada Verrips, "Ottolandse onderzoekservaringen bekeken in het licht van het ludieke," *In de Marge* 15, no. 3 (2006): 20–25.

89. The late Agnes Binder, a staunch member of the Evangelical Presbyterian Church, a former mission church, told me that in her youth, though she was from a Protestant family living in the Christian part of the village, she had been possessed by a local family god when she passed by her family house on the occasion of a "pagan" funeral. Hearing the drums beaten for this god, she was caught by its spirit, started to dance, and ran off to the bush. Through this humiliating experience, she realized the need to be spiritually strong, "to have the Holy Spirit in you."

90. Susan Fiend Harding, *The Book of Jerry Falwell, Fundamentalist Language and Politics* (Princeton, N.J.: Princeton University Press, 2000).

91. Verrips, "Ottolandse onderzoekservaringen."

92. Patricia Spyer, "The Body, Materiality, and the Senses," in *Handbook of Material Culture*, ed. Tilley, Keane, Küchler, Spyer, and Rowlands, 125–29.

93. This understanding of power is indebted to Michel Foucault. According to Foucault, power works less *upon* people—via coercion—than *through* them, by inducing particular ideas, belief systems, and sets of practices (this ensemble he calls "discourse"). In this understanding,

power is what creates, underpins, and legitimizes our sense of being, both as individuals and as part of larger social formations. The resonances between this understanding of power and my plea to focus on the aesthetic dimension of religion are obvious. The individual religious subject is not simply there, but is produced by a complicated process of subjectivation that entails both subjugation and the assertion of subjectivity. Jean-Francois Bayart ("Africa in the World: A History of Extraversion," *African Affairs* 99 [2000]: 217–67) notes that Foucault's notion of subjectivation and Weber's notion of a "methodological life-style" more or less converge in that they make persons subject to powerful disciplinary regimes that induce a particular ethics and a view of the world that is posited beyond questioning.

94. See Anderson, *Imagined Communities*. The idea of the secular entered popular social imaginaries, often in conjunction with modern religiosity as advocated by Protestant missionaries. They struggled to transmit this particular religiosity—against all odds—to their hitherto heathen converts. Cf.: David Chidester, *Savage Systems: Colonialism and Comparative Religion in Southern Africa* (Charlottesville: University Press of Virginia, 1996); Jean Comaroff and John Comaroff, *Of Revelation and Revolution: Christianity, Colonialism, and Consciousness in South Africa*, vol. 1 (Chicago: University of Chicago Press, 1991); Webb Keane, "Sincerity, 'Modernity,' and the Protestants," *Cultural Anthropology* 17, no. 1 (2002): 65–92; Meyer, *Translating the Devil*. Members of other religious traditions, such as Hinduism, Buddhism, Islam, and indigenous cults, sought to accommodate modern religiosity as part and parcel of a modernizing venture. See, e.g.: Brian Larkin and Birgit Meyer, "Pentecostalism, Islam and Culture: New Religious Movements in West Africa," in *Themes in West African History*, ed. Emmanuel Akyeampong (Oxford: James Currey, 2006), 286–312; Peter van der Veer, *Religious Nationalism: Hindus and Muslims in India* (Berkeley: California University Press, 1994).

95. Oscar Salemink, "Nieuwe rituelen en de natie: Nederland in de spiegel van Vietnam," lecture given at the Free University of Amsterdam, June 9, 2006.

96. Jean-François Bayart, *Le gouvernement du monde: Une critique politique de la globalisation* (Paris: Fayard, 2004).

97. Jean Comaroff and John Comaroff, eds., "Millennial Capitalism and the Culture of Neoliberalism," *Public Culture* 12, no. 2 (2000).

98. In *The Romantic Ethic and the Spirit of Modern Consumerism*, Campbell argues that in modern society consumerism has come to stand in for religion in that it promises ultimate satisfaction through consumption while inducing an "inexhaustibility of wants" that heats up the capitalist economy, leaving people chronically dissatisfied.

99. David Martin, *Pentecostalism: The World Their Parish* (Oxford: Blackwell, 2001).

100. Heidi Dahles, "McBusiness Versus Confucius? Anthropological Perspectives on Transnational Organizations and Networks," inaugural lecture, VU University Amsterdam, December 3, 2004.

101. Benjamin states: "One can behold in capitalism a religion, that is to say, capitalism essentially serves to satisfy the same worries, anguish and disquiet formerly answered by so-called religion. The proof of capitalism's religious structure—as not only a religiously conditioned construction, as Weber thought, but as an essentially religious phenomenon—still today misleads one to a boundless, universal polemic" (Walter Benjamin, "Capitalism as Religion," in *The Frankfurt School on Religion: Key Writings by the Major Thinkers*, ed. Eduardo Mendieta [New York: Routledge, 2005], 259).

102. Ibid.

103. Fredric Jameson, *Postmodernism; or, The Cultural Logic of Late Capitalism* (Durham, N.C.: Duke University Press, 1991). See also Steven Helmling, "Failure and the Sublime: Fredric

Jameson's Writing in the '80s," www3.iath.virginia.edu/pmc/text-only/issue500/10.3helmling.txt., 2000.

Angela Zito, Can Television Mediate Religious Experience? The Theology of *Joan of Arcadia*

1. My working definition of *spiritual* is "aspects of human existence that elude explanation in terms of rational, scientific paradigms, yet provide consolation and inspiration for action."

2. *Highway to Heaven* ran on NBC from 1984 to 1989; *Touched by an Angel*, on CBS from 1994 to 2003; *Buffy* from 1997 to 2003 on the Warner Brothers Network; *The X-Files* on FOX from 1993 to 2002.

3. In *Understanding Theology in Popular Culture* (Oxford: Blackwell, 2006), Gordon Lynch devotes chapters to analyses that are "author-focused," "text-based," and looking at "club culture."

4. Stewart Hoover, *Mass Media Religion: The Social Sources of the Electronic Church* (Newbury Park, Calif.: Sage Publications, 1988).

5. Heather Hendershot, *Shaking the World for Jesus: Media and Conservative Evangelical Culture* (Chicago: University of Chicago Press, 2004).

6. Michael Suman, "Do We Really Need More Religion on Fiction Television?" In *Religion and Primetime Television*, ed. Michael Suman (Westport, Conn.: Praeger Press, 1997).

7. The New York University Center for Religion and Media was founded in 2003 with a grant from The Pew Charitable Trusts; its URL is www.nyu.edu/fas/center/religionandmedia.

8. Suman, "Do We Really Need More Religion?" 70.

9. Gloria Goodale, "When Dogma Meets Drama on Television," *The Christian Science Monitor*, April 15, 2005, Arts section, 12.

10. Ibid.

11. Hal Boedeker, "New Series Could Pose 'Revelations': NBC Exploring Religious Theme to Attract Prime-Time Congregations," *Houston Chronicle*, April 13, 2005, Star section, 6.

12. *Newsweek*'s cover story on September 5, 2005, was "Spirituality in America," a nineteen-page spread that opens with the news that 79 percent of those polled described themselves as "spiritual" and only 64 percent as "religious." For the authors, "spirituality" is an immediate personal experience of the divine. They note that every major religion in the United States is undergoing subtle transformations in that direction, including interest in Kabbalah in Judaism, eco-Christianity in Protestantism, the Charismatic Catholic movement, recommitments to prayer among Muslims, and the deepening interest in Buddhisms that emphasize meditation. While they also mention new religions like Wicca, the article was interestingly free of discussion of New Age spiritualities.

13. Goodale, "When Dogma Meets Drama."

14. My working definition of *theological* is quite simple, though it will become more complex: "having to do with God, or with questions of ultimate significance and value as they are seen in reference to the issue of God."

15. Peter Berger and Thomas Luckmann, *The Social Construction of Reality: A Treatise in the Sociology of Knowledge* (New York: Doubleday, 1966); Peter Berger, *The Sacred Canopy* (New York: Doubleday, 1967); David Morgan, *Visual Piety: A History and Theory of Popular Religious Images* (Berkeley: University of California Press, 1998).

16. V. N. Vološinov, *Marxism and the Philosophy of Language*, trans. Ladislav Matejka and I. R. Titunik (New York: Basic Books, 1973), 13; Clifford Geertz, "From the Native's Point of View: On

the Nature of Anthropological Understanding," in Geertz, *Local Knowledge* (New York: Basic Books, 1977).

17. Eduardo Mendieta, Introduction to *The Frankfurt School on Religion: Key Writings by the Major Thinkers*, ed. E. Mendieta (New York: Routledge, 2006), 5.

18. Minus the Marxist sense that the world is progressing toward some moment of perfect synthesis, this approach has much in common with the work of Bruno Latour, whose commitment to Actor Network Theory renders the world open and dynamic. Besides *We Have Never Been Modern* (trans. Catherine Porter [Cambridge: Harvard University Press, 1993]), see Bruno Latour, "The Promises of Constructivism," in *Chasing Technoscience: Matrix of Materiality*, ed. Don Idhe (Bloomington: Indiana University Press, 2003). See also Nick Couldry, "Media as Practice," *Social Semiotics* 14, no. 2 (August 2004): 115–32. I differ slightly from Couldry in leaning further toward the critical-theoretical preoccupation with a critique that seeks hopeful and utopic possibilities even as we cope with ever-present issues of power in mediated culture.

19. Sylvia Yanagisako and Carol Delaney, *Naturalizing Power: Essays in Feminist Cultural Analysis* (New York: Routledge, 1995).

20. Marcel Mauss, "Body Techniques," in Mauss, *Sociology and Psychology: Essays*, ed. and trans. B. Brewster (London: Routledge & Kegan Paul, 1979).

21. William Mazzarella, "Culture, Globalization, Mediation," *Annual Review of Anthropology* 33 (2004): 345–68.

22. For indigenous communities' efforts, see: Faye Ginsburg, "Shooting Back: From Ethnographic Film to Indigenous Production / Ethnography of Media," in *A Companion to Film Theory*, ed. Toby Miller and Robert Stam (Oxford: Blackwell, 1999), 295–322; Faye Ginsburg, Lila Abu-Lughod, and Brian Larkin, eds., *Media Worlds: Anthropology on New Terrain* (Berkeley: University of California Press, 2002). For religious communities in India, see: Purnima Mankekar, *Screening Culture, Viewing Politics: An Ethnography of Television, Womanhood, and Nation in Postcolonial India* (Durham, N.C.: Duke University Press, 1999); Arvind Rajagopal, *Politics after Television: Religious Nationalism and the Reshaping of the Indian Public* (Cambridge: Cambridge University Press, 2001).

23. In a more practical vein, religion and TV have two things in common: they both tell stories, and they both soak up a lot of leisure time. See A. James Rudin, "On Bringing Religious and Television Communities Together," and Joan Brown Campbell, "Tuning into Common Concerns: An Invitation from the Churches to the Media Industry," both in *Religion and Primetime Television*, ed. Suman. Clergy and scholars consult on plots, even producing TV themselves. Rev. Frank Desiderio, a Catholic priest, has produced numerous History and Discovery Channel shows. He is Chief of Paulist Productions, a small production company based in Malibu, California, whose mission statement reads: "Paulist Productions creates films and television programs that reveal God's presence in the contemporary human experience. Our mission is to challenge our viewers to love others and to liberate one another from all that is dehumanizing. We encourage other entertainment professionals to help unify the human family *through the power of the media*" (my italics; James Verini, "Divine Purpose: As More Shows Feature Faith and Spirituality, Priests, Ministers, Monks, and Rabbis Are Taking on Paid Roles as Religion Consultants," *Los Angeles Times*, December 26, 2004, Sunday Calendar section, 40.

24. James Carey, *Communication and Culture* (Boston: Unwin Hyman, 1989), 87, as quoted in Nick Couldry, *Media Rituals: A Critical Approach* (London: Routledge, 2003), 19. See also Berger, *The Sacred Canopy*, for similar detailed discussion on world creation and maintenance.

25. Jim Bawden, "CBS Show Jugglers Prefer Ghosts to God," *Toronto Star*, May 19, 2005, Entertainment section, A27.

26. "Goth" is an adolescent movement that began as a subculture of punk in the 1970s: its followers wear black, use heavy eye-makeup, and have tattoos and piercings. They are interested in

Edwardian and Victorian culture and listen to music that critics have decried for its violent or depressed lyrics. Visit http://www.religioustolerance.org/goth.htm.

27. Bob Gale, "Ramblings on Why Things Are the Way They Are," in *Religion and Primetime Television*, ed. Suman, 137–42.

28. Nancy Haught, "Channeling God," *Oregonian*, September 24, 2004, Living section, D01.

29. Nancy Franklin, "Down to Earth: Conversations with God in *Joan of Arcadia*," *The New Yorker*, October 13, 2003, 110; Michael E. Hill, "God Speaks, Viewers Watch," *Washington Post*, November 9, 2003, TV Week, Y06; Joel Rubinoff, "Joan of Arcadia Helps Ritter's Healing," *Toronto Star*, February 18, 2005, Arts, C6; Verini, "Divine Purpose"; Charlie McCullon, "Fall schedule—and replacements—are swimming in spirituality," *San Jose Mercury News*, September 9, 2003, Entertainment News.

30. Douglas Leblanc, "Hip Mission: A High-School Girl Further Increases God's Prime-Time Exposure," posted April 16, 2004, at http://www.christianitytoday.com/ct/2004/004/26.101.html.

31. Andrew Greeley, "TV Show Raises Questions about God: In *Joan of Arcadia*, God Is Unpredictable, Unfathomable, and Ineffable," *Chicago Sun-Times*, November 5, 2005, Editorial, 45.

32. Ibid.

33. Hill, "God Speaks, Viewers Watch."

34. Hall remained committed to this theological position the entire run of the show. In her voice-over commentary on what would become the series' final episode, she says, "Evil works on a continuum; it's not that anyone is completely evil, but each choice you make adds on. There's always light in each person as long as there is choice, free will" (*Joan of Arcadia*, "Something Wicked This Way Comes," 2006: disk six).

35. Rubinoff, "Joan of Arcadia Helps Ritter's Healing."

36. Hill, "God Speaks, Viewers Watch."

37. Elliot B. Gertel, "Joan of Arcadia: 'Innocent' Teen Drama Makes Mockery of Religion," *Jewish World Review*, August 16, 2004, http://www.jewishworldreview.com/elliot/gertel_joan_of_arcadia2.php3.

38. See: Michael F. Brown, *The Channeling Zone: American Spirituality in an Anxious Age* (Cambridge: Harvard University Press, 1997); Gordon Melton, "The New Age," in *The Encyclopedia of Cults, Sects, and New Religions*, ed. James R. Lewis (Amherst, N.Y.: Prometheus Books, 1998). Even organized religionists express interest in "spirituality," and their definitions are surprisingly similar to New Age ones. Catholic priest Richard Woods, Professor of Spiritual Theology at the Institute of Pastoral Studies, Loyola University of Chicago, writes: "'Spirituality' is another way of describing the inescapable human passion to find, or create, meaning and value in life as a whole. Spirituality is not fundamentally different from religion in its pre-institutionalized, or perhaps de-institutionalized, mode. Spirituality is the personal, particular, internalized (that is, self-conscious) but shared aspect of religion which, in its simplest and most general sense, is the dynamic bond between human persons and what they consider to be sacred. If religion and especially theology are timeless, universal, and 'open,' spirituality is historical, particular, and conditioned, determinate. It is the unique way we embody the gift of Life. In the long run, it is our life" ("Religious Symbol and Spirituality in an Electronic Age," *Spirituality Today* 35, no. 1 [Spring 1983]: 26–37). Note, as we move toward the discussion of process theology below, the absence of any mention of "God" in this discussion. For the quote from Woods, see http://www.spiritualitytoday.org/spir2day/833514woods.html#2.

39. Robert Wuthnow, *All in Sync: How Music and Art Are Revitalizing American Religion* (Berkeley: University of California Press, 2003).

40. Robert Bellah, *Habits of the Heart: Individualism and Commitment in American Life* (Berkeley: University of California Press, 1996).

41. Austin Bunn, "Are You There God? Where's the Religion in *Joan of Arcadia?*" *Slate*, October 9, 2003, http://slate.msn.com/id/2089556/.

42. Barbara Hall, voiceover on pilot episode of *Joan of Arcadia*, DVD edition of the first season, 2005.

43. Ewert H. Cousins, *Process Theology: Basic Writings* (New York: Newman Press, 1971), 1–15.

44. Alfred North Whitehead, "God and the World," in Whitehead, *Process and Reality: An Essay in Cosmology* (New York: Macmillan, 1929). Excerpted in Cousins, *Process Theology*, 89.

45. Ibid., 93.

46. Ibid., 91.

47. Fritjof Capra, *The Tao of Physics: An Exploration of the Parallels Between Modern Physics and Eastern Mysticism* (Boston: Shambala Press, 1975), and Gary Zukov, *The Dancing Wuli Masters: An Overview of the New Physics* (New York: William Morrow, 1979).

48. Beliefnet, May 2004, http://www.beliefnet.com/story/133/story_13322.html.

49. Gregor T. Goethals, *The TV Ritual: Worship at the Video Altar* (Boston: Beacon Press, 1981).

50. Woods, "Religious Symbol and Spirituality," my italics.

51. Noted by Frederic and Mary Ann Brussat, "*Joan of Arcadia*: TV's Most Spiritually Literate Show," at http://www.spiritualityhealth.com/newsh/items/review-feature/item 8476.html.

52. Couldry, *Media Rituals*, 102.

53. "Fans Demand *Joan*, Fight CBS over Cancellation," *USA Today*, May 30, 2005, http://www.usatoday.com/life/2005–05–30-joan-arcadia-fans-petition_x.htm.

54. Jason Zasky, "A Plea to the Television Gods: *Joan* Fans Try to Keep the Faith," 2005, http://www.failuremag.com/arch_arts_joan_of_arcadia.html.

55. Mendieta, Introduction, 8.

56. Ibid., 9.

Niklaus Largier, A "Sense of Possibility": Robert Musil, Meister Eckhart, and the "Culture of Film"

1. Meister Eckhart, *Werke*, ed. Niklaus Largier (Frankfurt a. M.: Deutscher Klassiker Verlag, 1993), 1:16 and commentary (754–57); trans. Oliver Davies as Meister Eckhart, *Selected Writings* (Harmondsworth, Middlesex: Penguin, 1994), 153–54. See: Brigitte Spreitzer, "Meister Musil: Eckharts deutsche Predigten als zentrale Quelle des Romans 'Der Mann ohne Eigenschaften,'" *Zeitschrift für deutsche Philologie* 119 (2000): 564–88; Jochen Schmidt, *Ohne Eigenschaften: Eine Erläuterung zu Musils Grundbegriff* (Tübingen: Niemeyer, 1975).

2. Meister Eckhart, *Schriften und Predigten*, ed. Hermann Büttner, 2 vols. (Leipzig: Diederichs, 1903–9).

3. Reinhard Laube, *Karl Mannheim und die Krise des Historismus: Historismus als wissenssoziologischer Perspektivismus* (Göttingen: Vandenhoeck & Ruprecht, 2004), 316.

4. I am quoting from Karl Mannheim's diary entry of April 23, 1911 (ibid., 305). Cf. also: *Georg Lukács, Karl Mannheim und der Sonntagskreis*, ed. Éva Karádi and Erzsébet Vezér (Frankfurt a. M.: Sendler, 1985); Lee Congdon, *The Young Lukács* (Chapel Hill: University of North Carolina Press, 1983); Ernst Keller, *Der junge Lukács: Antibürger und wesentliches Leben—Literatur- und Kulturkritik, 1902–1915* (Frankfurt a. M.: Sendler, 1984).

5. Georg Lukács, "Von der Armut am Geiste: Ein Gespräch und ein Brief," *Neue Blätter*, Berlin 1912, 67–92, esp. 88–89. Cf. Stefano Catucci, *Per una filosofia povera: La grande guerra, l'esperienza, il senso, a partire da Lukács* (Turin: Bollati Boringhieri, 2003).

6. Cf. Moritz Bassler and Hildegard Châtellier, eds., *Mystique, mysticisme et modernité en Allemagne autour de 1900* (Strasbourg: Presses Universitaires de Strasbourg, 1998).

7. Georg Lukács, *Heidelberger Notizen (1910–1913): Eine Textauswahl*, ed. Béla Bacsó (Budapest: Akadémiai Kiadó, 1997), 135.

8. Robert Musil, *Tagebücher*, ed. Adolf Frisé (Hamburg: Rowohlt, 1983), 2:511n217.

9. Musil's review can be found in Béla Balázs, *Der sichtbare Mensch, oder die Kultur des Films*, ed. Helmut H. Diederichs (Frankfurt a. M.: Suhrkamp, 2001). An English translation of Balázs's text has never been published.

10. Robert Musil, *The Man Without Qualities*, trans. Sophie Wilkins (New York: Knopf, 1995), 1:10–11.

11. Cf. Burkhard Mojsisch, "'Ce moi': La conception du moi chez maître Eckhart," *Revue des sciences religieuses* 70 (1996): 18–30.

12. Musil, *The Man Without Qualities*, 1:266.

13. Ibid., 1:266.

14. See Niklaus Largier, "Negativität, Möglichkeit, Freiheit: Zur Differenz zwischen der Philosophie Dietrichs von Freiberg und Eckhart von Hochheim," in *Dietrich von Freiberg: Neue Perspektiven seiner Philosophie, Theologie und Naturwissenschaft, Freiberger Symposion: 10.–13. März 1997*, ed. Karl-Hermann Kandler, Burkhard Mojsisch, and Franz-Bernhard Stammkötter (Amsterdam: B. R. Grüner, 1999), 149–68.

15. Eckhart, *Schriften*, 1:203. Cf. Eckhart, *Werke*, 1:42 and 996–97.

16. See Eckhart, *Werke*, 1:36, 99–100, 148–49, 546.

17. Robert Musil, "Ansätze zu neuer Ästhetik: Bemerkungen über eine Dramaturgie des Films," in Balázs, *Der sichtbare Mensch*, 161, my translation.

18. Musil, *The Man Without Qualities*, 2: 826.

19. Ibid., 2:827.

20. Ibid., 2:828–29.

21. Balázs, *Der Geist des Films* (1930), quoted in Helmut H. Diederich's Afterword to Balázs, *Der sichtbare Mensch*, 129, my translation.

22. Balázs, *Der sichtbare Mensch*, 44–45.

23. Robert Musil, *Precision and Soul: Essays and Addresses* (Chicago: University of Chicago Press, 1990), 194.

24. Ibid., 204.

25. Siegfried Kracauer, "Bücher vom Film," in Balázs, *Der sichtbare Mensch*, 172.

Sander van Maas, Intimate Exteriorities: Inventing Religion Through Music

1. In *Het derde oor* (*The Third Ear*), documentary film directed by Mart Dominicus and Michel Schöpping (Viewpoint Productions & NPS Television, 2000).

2. "Chirograph of the Supreme Pontiff John Paul II for the Centenary of the Motu Proprio 'Tra le Sollecitudini' on Sacred Music," November 22, 2003, on the Internet, http://www.vatican.va (page accessed January 10, 2007).

3. Luke B. Howard, "Motherhood, *Billboard*, and the Holocaust: Perceptions and Receptions of Górecki's Symphony No. 3," *The Musical Quarterly* 82, no. 1 (Spring 1998): 150. The label "new spiritual music" was used by the organizers of the Festival Nieuwe Spirituele Muziek in Amsterdam

(1999) to cover an area that included, in addition to "holy minimalism," music from contemporary Chinese composers, spiritual pop music, Internet music installations, Mongolian traditionals, and more.

4. For a general musicological discussion of this turn, see Richard Taruskin, *The Oxford History of Western Music* (Oxford: Oxford University Press, 2005), 5:400–10, or Arnold Whittall, *Musical Composition in the Twentieth Century* (Oxford: Oxford University Press, 2000), 338 ff. Historical musicological surveys often represent the turn as a branch of Minimalism.

5. In contrast to, e.g., Pierre Boulez, who is a prolific writer himself, Tavener has used a ghost writer for his most important book to date, Brian Keeble, ed., *John Tavener: The Music of Silence, A Composer's Testament* (London: Faber and Faber, 1999).

6. John Tavener, "The Eye of the Heart," on the DVD *Tavener: Fall and Resurrection* (BBC–Opus Arte–Chandos Records, 2000). Speaking about the "barcarolles" of Beethoven, Tavener probably means to refer to the composer's twenty-four bagatelles (Opus nos. 33, 119, and 126).

7. John Tavener, "The Sacred in Art," in *Contemporary Music Review* 12, pt. 2 (1995): 51.

8. Rather than referring to the latter as substance, Tavener would probably refer to it as "archetype"—a term he borrows from Platonism and the Eastern theology of the icon, and which he often uses to illuminate his music theology.

9. Tavener, in Piers Dudgeon, *Lifting the Veil: The Biography of Sir John Tavener* (London: Portrait, 2003), 218.

10. Josiah Fisk, "The New Simplicity: The Music of Górecki, Tavener, and Pärt," *The Hudson Review* 47, no. 3 (Autumn 1994): 394.

11. Ibid., 401.

12. Ibid., 411; my emphasis.

13. Ibid., 410.

14. Ibid., 411–12.

15. Ibid., 410–11.

16. In contrast to Olivier Messiaen, Tavener does not rely on utopian or apocalyptic gestures. There is no forward flight. Neither is there a conspicuous dwelling in melancholy or nostalgia, as is more often found in Arvo Pärt. The strange neutrality of the space Tavener evokes should guide our attention here.

17. Jean-Luc Nancy, *The Muses*, trans. Peggy Kamuf (Stanford, Calif.: Stanford University Press, 1996), 41.

18. Ibid., 50–51.

19. Ibid., 51.

20. Ibid., 54; italics in original.

21. Ibid., 26.

22. Ibid., 36.

23. Brian Massumi, *Parables for the Virtual: Movement, Affect, Sensation* (Durham, N.C.: Duke University Press, 2002), 188.

24. As Adorno argues in *Metaphysics: Concept and Problems*, ed. Rolf Tiedemann, trans. Edmund Jephcott (Stanford, Calif.: Stanford University Press, 2001), 141, the possibility of disappointment is the very "condition of possibility" of "metaphysical experience."

25. M. Burcht Pranger, *The Artificiality of Christianity: Essays on the Poetics of Monasticism* (Stanford, Calif.: Stanford University Press, 2003).

26. Nancy, *The Muses*, 37.

27. Ibid., 38.

28. Hegel, quoted in Nancy, *The Muses*, 48.

29. Ibid., 50.

30. Ibid., 47.

31. Massumi, *Parables for the Virtual*, 188.

32. Jean-Luc Nancy, "De l'âme," in *Corpus* (Paris: Métailié, 2000), 127.

33. Roland Barthes, "Listening," in *The Responsibility of Forms: Critical Essays on Art, Music, and Representation* (Berkeley: University of California Press, 1991), 251–52.

34. Plato, *Timaeus*, 47d. Evidently, the influence may be either beneficial or malicious, the latter being the case, according to Plato, whenever music is used for "irrational pleasure."

35. Alex Hardie, "Muses and Mysteries," in *Music and the Muses: The Culture of 'Mousikī' in the Classical Athenian City*, ed. Penelope Murray and Peter Wilson (Oxford: Oxford University Press, 2004), 15.

36. Plato, *Politeia*, 401d.

37. On this notion of "kinship" (*syngenes*), cf. Phillip Cary, *Augustine's Invention of the Inner Self: The Legacy of a Christian Platonist* (Oxford: Oxford University Press, 2000), 12 and 152n20.

38. Plato, *Timaeus*, 80b. W. K. C. Guthrie, *A History of Greek Philosophy*, vol. 1, *The Earlier Presocratics and the Pythagoreans* (Cambridge: Cambridge University Press, 1962), 317. In this reading, music's strong touching of the soul is like a comparative meeting of resembling harmonies. In view of the singularity of divine *harmonia*, it may be regarded as the meeting of *harmonia* with itself: as an auto-affection, or, quite literally, as *haptonomy*. Arthur Schopenhauer once remarked that the "intense pleasure" (*innige Freude*) produced by the univocity (*Deutlichkeit*) of this touching should not be compared to the satisfaction offered by the solution of a mathematical problem. It should rather be understood as indicating the revelation of "the deepest recesses of our nature" (*das tiefste Innere unsers Wesens*). Arthur Schopenhauer, *The World as Will and Idea*, trans. Jill Berman (London: J. M. Dent, 1997), 162–63.

39. Plato, *Phaedo*, 86a-b.

40. Cary, *Augustine's Invention of the Inner Self*, 10–11.

41. Plato discusses the ethical merits of various musical modes in *Politeia*, 398e ff.

42. Cary, *Augustine's Invention of the Inner Self*, 11.

43. Ibid., 29.

44. Plotinus, *Enneads*, I, 3.1.

45. Ibid.; my emphasis.

46. Augustine, *Confessions*, 7.10. My emphasis.

47. Cary, *Augustine's Invention of the Inner Self*, 39. Cary is careful to add that none of the elements of which this new concept of inner space is composed is new. It is their specific constellation that leads to the innovation.

48. Ibid., 116; cf. ibid., 108–9.

49. The soul's inner space somewhat resembles the secluded and separated space of a temple. This leads to the question of whether the inner space is (or can be) occupied or whether it remains empty. A possible answer may found in Cary's references to the Augustinian notion of Christ's dwelling in the inmost soul, as well as in his discussion of Augustine's theory of grace as a divine inner gift. Cf. Cary, *Augustine's Invention of the Inner Self*, 114, 143.

50. Tavener at one point coined the phrase "the intellective organ of the heart," which he claims to have borrowed from Augustine. Cf. "The Eye of the Heart," on the DVD *Fall and Resurrection*.

51. Augustine, Epistle 18:2, translated by Cary, in *Augustine's Invention of the Inner Self*, 149.

52. My emphasis.

53. James McKinnon, *Music in Early Christian Literature* (Cambridge: Cambridge University Press, 1999), 154–55.

54. Cf. Cary's discussion of the powers of invention and memory in *Augustine's Invention of the Inner Self*, chap. 10.

55. Ibid., 174n44 and 178n2. There seems to be a difference between the way Augustine discusses music in *De musica*, where he stresses the rational delight of judging the numbers present in music (cf. Plato's notion of *euphrosunī*), and his discussion in the *Confessions*, which emphasizes the passionate qualities of musical experience.

56. Cary, *Augustine's Invention of the Inner Self*, 124.

57. On this spatiality, see also Jamie James, *The Music of the Spheres: Music, Science and the Natural Order of the Universe* (London: Abacus, 2000).

58. Gianni Vattimo, *The End of Modernity: Nihilism and Hermeneutics in Postmodern Culture* (Baltimore: The Johns Hopkins University Press, 1988), 52.

59. Cf. the CD cover of *John Tavener: A Portrait; His Works, His Life, His Words* (Naxos 8.558152–53) and the dust jackets of: Keeble, ed., *John Tavener*; Dudgeon, *Lifting the Veil*; and Geoffrey Haydon, *John Tavener: Glimpses of Paradise* (London: Victor Gollancz, 1995).

60. Cf. Howard, "Motherhood, *Billboard*, and the Holocaust."

61. Keeble, *John Tavener*, 61.

62. Richard Wagner, *Parsifal*, act 1, scene 1. Cf. Jean-Luc Nancy, *Listening*, trans. Charlotte Mandell (New York: Fordham University Press 2007), 14, and Jean-Luc Nancy, "Spanne," in *Le sens du monde* (Paris: Galilée, 2001), 105–9.

63. Leonard Lawlor, *Thinking Through French Philosophy: The Being of the Question* (Bloomington: Indiana University Press, 2003), 4 and 24.

64. Sigmund Freud, *Civilization and Its Discontents*, trans. James Strachey (New York: Norton, 1961), 11–12.

65. Ibid., 13. On the parallels between the "oceanic" feeling and certain musical experiences, see Albert Blackwell, *The Sacred in Music* (Cambridge: The Lutterworth Press, 1999), 95–101.

66. Lawlor, *Thinking Through French Philosophy*, 27.

67. Jacques Derrida, in *Refiguring the Archive*, ed. Carolyn Hamilton et al. (Dordrecht: Kluwer, 2002), 42; my emphasis.

68. Cf. the musicosmology that Ronald Bogue finds in Deleuze. Ronald Bogue, "Rhizomusicosmology," *SubStance* 66 (1991): 85–101.

69. Samuel Weber, "The Unraveling of Form," in *Mass Mediauras: Form, Technics, Media* (Stanford, Calif.: Stanford University Press, 1996), 19; italics in original. Cf. Rodolphe Gasché, *The Idea of Form: Rethinking Kant's Aesthetics* (Stanford, Calif.: Stanford University Press, 2003), 86–87.

70. Cf. the distinction between "blocks" and "bubbles" in Gilles Deleuze, "Boulez, Proust, and Time: 'Occupying Without Counting,'" *Angelaki: Journal of the Theoretical Humanities* 3, no. 2 (1998): 71.

71. François Nicolas, "De l'aspect à *l'inspect*: La forme musicale comme empreinte," on the Internet, www.entretemps.asso.fr/Nicolas/TextesNic/Ulm.html (page accessed January 10, 2007).

72. On a more general level, Heidegger has already defended the notion that art is not just *in* space (qua object), but indeed productive of places (*Orten*). Cf. Martin Heidegger, *Die Kunst und der Raum / L'art et l'espace* (St. Gallen: Erker Verlag, 1983).

73. Tavener, in Keeble, ed., *John Tavener*, 82 and 94; Tavener, "The Sacred in Art," 51.

74. As Nicolas notes, the moment when a piece of music stops is a very important one in that it elucidates the fictionality of the being that is usually referred to as "the listener" or "the musician": "The musician is produced by the music, the musician is a musicalized [*musiqué*] human being rather than a music-making [*musiquant*] one. The musician is *in-individual* . . . : there is no individual who preexists the music and who, in a second instance, starts to play music. The musician is made by the music not as an individual but rather as a corporeal support through which

music passes." Nicolas, on the Internet, www.entretemps.asso.fr/Nicolas/TextesNic/Graf.html (page accessed January 10, 2007).

75. Nancy, *Listening*, 14.

76. Iannis Xenakis, "Ici et là," in *Espaces*, ed. Peter Szendy et al. (Paris: Les Cahiers de l'Ircam, 1994), 113; my translation.

77. Cf. Lawlor, *Thinking Through French Philosophy*, 22.

78. Jean-Luc Nancy, *Hegel: The Restlessness of the Negative*, trans. Jason Smith and Steven Miller (Minneapolis: University of Minnesota Press, 2002), 44.

79. Nouritza Matossian, "A Composer Beyond Music," *Contemporary Music Review* 21, nos. 2/3 (2002): 9–10.

80. Nancy, "De l'âme," 122.

81. Ibid., 126.

82. Jonathan Harvey, *In Quest of Spirit: Thoughts on Music* (Berkeley: University of California Press, 1999), 79; my emphasis. Cf. Rokus de Groot, "Jonathan Harvey's Quest of Spirit Through Music," *Organised Sound* 5, no. 2 (2000): 103–9.

83. In conversation with the author, Athens, May 21, 2005.

84. Iannis Xenakis, "Eschyle, un théâtre totale," in *Musique et originalité* (Paris: Séguier, 1996), 56.

85. François-Bernard Mâche, "Iannis Xenakis en son siècle," in *Portrait(s) de Iannis Xenakis*, ed. François-Bernard Mâche (Paris: Bibliothèque Nationale de France, 2001), 121; Xenakis, "Eschyle, un théâtre totale," 57.

86. Mâche, "Iannis Xenakis en son siècle," 116.

87. Mâkhi Xenakis, *Laisser venir les fantômes* (Arles: Actes Sud, 2002), 42.

88. Michel Serres famously heard a *bruit de fond* in Xenakis's *Pithoprakta*. He understood this fundamental noise to be emitted by "the collection of objects that forms the universe, interobjectivity as such." Rather than allocating Xenakis's music to "its natural place" among "things" of cosmic immanence (reducing it to a *pars pro toto* of the universe's total *sous-murmure*), the tone of the archaic I am proposing here emphasizes the virtuality and transimmanence of the space—the topological multiverse, so to speak—this tone *itself* produces. It "is" *in trembling*, and beyond the subject-object scheme implicitly maintained by Serres. Michel Serres, "Musique et bruit de fond," in *Hermès II: L'interférence* (Paris: Minuit, 1972), 181–94.

89. Samuel Weber, *Theatricality as Medium* (New York: Fordham University Press, 2004), 152.

90. Iannis Xenakis, *Formalized Music: Thought and Mathematics in Music* (Hillsdale: Pendragon Press, 1992), 1.

91. The phrase "The Fall of Substance and the Resurrection of Tedium" was coined by a critic reviewing Tavener's DVD *Fall and Resurrection* on Amazon.com, review posted on March 17, 2002.

Alena Alexandrova, Death in the Image: The Post-Religious Life of Christian Images

1. Several exhibitions offer evidence of that interest: Theologies (2002); Iconoclash: Beyond the Image Wars in Science, Religion, and Art (2002); Gravity: Art, Religion, Science (2003); 100 Artists See God (2004–5); The Next Generation: Contemporary Expressions of Faith (2005); Soul (2005); Seeing God (2005–6). In addition, many individual artists have recently approached the theme of religion in their solo exhibitions: Sarah Lucas's Vanitas (2006); Damien Hirst's The Stations of the Cross and New Religion (2005), Bill Viola's The Passions (1999), and Lawrence Malstaf's Being in the Middle (2004) are only a few examples.

2. This is one of Jean-Luc Nancy's key points of departure in his project of the deconstruction of Christianity. In two central texts in his book *La déclosion: Déconstruction du christianisme, 1* (Paris: Galilée, 2005; trans. Bettina Bergo, Gabriel Malenfant, and Michael B. Smith as *Dis-Enclosure* [New York: Fordham University Press, 2007]), "The Deconstruction of Christianity" and "A Deconstruction of Monotheism," he argues that deconstruction is only possible from *within* the tradition that is deconstructed and emphasizes the need to acknowledge some auto-deconstructive aspects of monotheism and Christianity in particular. The operation of deconstruction cannot be undertaken from an entirely external point of view because it consists in following the implications or the effects of some internal tensions within the assemblage of Christianity. For "A Deconstruction of Monotheism," see Part II of this volume.

3. Marie-José Mondzain, *Image, Icon, Economy: The Byzantine Origins of the Contemporary Imaginary*, trans. Rico Franses (Stanford, Calif.: Stanford University Press, 2005), 70–117.

4. James Elkins, *On the Strange Place of Religion in Contemporary Art* (London: Routledge, 2004), 15.

5. Beth Williamson, *Christian Art: A Very Short Introduction* (Oxford: Oxford University Press, 2004), 112–13, 166.

6. Berlinde De Bruyckere, *Eén*, exhibition catalogue, introd. Harald Szeemann and Barbara Baert (Prato, Italy: Gli Ori, 2005), ill. 23.

7. Mitchell B. Merback. *The Thief, the Cross and the Wheel: Pain and the Spectacle of Punishment in Medieval and Renaissance Europe* (Chicago: University of Chicago Press, 2001). Merback points out that while the figure of Christ maintained a certain schematic constancy, the figures of the thieves were an occasion to develop a visual vocabulary of extreme penal brutality (21, 27–32, 101–26).

8. See Joseph Leo Koerner, "The Motification of the Image: Death as a Hermeneutic in Hans Baldung Grien," *Representations* 10 (1985): 52–102.

9. Georges Didi-Huberman, *Devant le temps: Histoire de l'art et anachronisme des images.* (Paris: Minuit, 2000).

10. Ibid., 20.

11. Between, e.g., Fra Angelico's multicolored patches on frescoes in the convent of San Marco in Florence and the drippings in a painting by Jackson Pollock (ibid., 20–21).

12. Ibid., 36.

13. Ibid., 17.

14. For a discussion of the three major regimes of identification of what we call art in the Western tradition (ethical, poetic, and aesthetic), see: Jacques Rancière, "Artistic Regimes and the Shortcomings of the Notion of Modernity," in his *The Politics of Aesthetics: The Distribution of the Sensible*, trans. Gabrielle Rockhill (London: Continuum, 2004), 20–34.

15. Mieke Bal, *Quoting Caravaggio: Contemporary Art, Preposterous History* (Chicago: University of Chicago Press, 1999), 6–7.

16. Elkins, *On the Strange Place of Religion*, 20.

17. Thierry de Duve, *Look! 100 Years of Contemporary Art*, trans. Simon Pleasance and Fronza Woods (Ghent-Amsterdam: Ludion, 2001), 243.

18. Ibid., 14.

19. Ibid., 16.

20. Ibid., 14.

21. Ibid., 18.

22. Ibid., 21.

23. Mondzain, *Image, Icon, Economy*, 201.

24. De Duve, *Look! 100 Years of Contemporary Art,* 20.

25. Ibid., 23.

26. Ibid., 50.

27. Ibid., 51.

28. Ibid.

29. Ibid.

30. Ibid., 53.

31. Marie-José Mondzain, "The Holy Shroud," in *Iconoclash: Beyond the Image Wars in Science, Religion, and Art,* ed. Bruno Latour and Peter Weibel (Cambridge: MIT Press, 2002), 330.

32. Ibid., 332.

33. Georges Didi-Huberman, *Confronting Images: Questioning the Ends of a Certain History of Art,* trans. John Goodman (State College, Pa.: Pennsylvania State University Press, 2005), 188.

34. For a discussion of the issue of different regimes under which images are invested with truth and a typology of different iconoclastic motives, see Latour's Introduction to *Iconoclash,* which accompanied an exhibition at the Center for Art and Media in Karlsruhe that explored the multiple aspects of iconoclasm in different cultural contexts and in diverse theoretical and disciplinary backgrounds. Bruno Latour, "What Is Iconoclash? or, Is There a World Beyond the Image Wars?" in *Iconoclash,* ed. Latour and Weibel, 16.

35. Ibid., 15.

36. Koerner, "Icon as Iconoclash," in *Iconoclash,* ed. Latour and Weibel, 183.

37. Ibid., 183.

38. Ibid., 190.

39. Ibid., 192.

40. As Koerner puts it: "Religion becomes negation in infinite regress: the chosen people scourged, their redeemer scourged by them, they scourged by his people, the Christians, who, from time to time, in order to renew their faith, will scourge his effigy" (ibid., 199).

41. Ibid., 191.

42. Ibid., 190.

43. Didi-Huberman, *Confronting Images,* 194.

44. Ibid., 184.

45. Ibid., 219, 211.

46. Ibid., 220.

47. Ibid., 227.

48. Ibid.

49. Mondzain, "The Holy Shroud," 333.

50. De Duve, *Look! 100 Years of Contemporary Art,* 127.

51. David Freedberg, *The Power of Images: Studies in the History and Theory of Response* (Chicago: University of Chicago Press, 1989), 425.

52. Ibid., 426.

53. Ibid., 436.

Peter van der Veer, Spirituality in Modern Society

NOTE: This is the text of my inaugural lecture on accepting the position of University Professor at Utrecht University on October 20, 2005.

1. Wassily Kandinsky, *Rückblicke* (Berlin: Sturm-Verlag, 1913), cited in Max Bill's Introduction to Kandinsky, *Über das Geistige in der Kunst* (1912; Bern: Benteli, 1952), 9.

2. Peter van der Veer, *The Spirit of the Orient: The Making of Indian and Chinese Spirituality* (Princeton, N.J.: Princeton University Press, forthcoming).

3. See Charles Taylor, *Sources of the Self: The Making of the Modern Identity* (Cambridge: Harvard University Press, 1989), and Charles Taylor, *Modern Social Imaginaries* (Durham, N.C.: Duke University Press, 2004).

4. J. G. A. Pocock, "Concepts and Discourses: A Difference in Culture?" in *The Meaning of Historical Terms and Concepts*, ed. Hartmut Lehmann and Melvin Richter, German Historical Institute Occasional Paper no. 15 (Washington, 1996), 47.

5. Louis Dumont, *La civilisation indienne et nous* (Paris: Arman Colin, 1975).

6. Sheldon Pollock, "Mimamsa and the Problem of History in Traditional India," *Journal of the American Oriental Society* 109, no. 4 (1989): 607.

7. Rodney Koeneke, *Empires of the Mind: I. A. Richards and Basic English in China* (Stanford, Calif.: Stanford University Press, 2004).

8. I. A. Richards and C. K. Ogden, *The Meaning of Meaning* (1923; New York: Harcourt, 1989).

9. I. A. Richards, *Mencius on the Mind: Experiments in Multiple Definition* (London: Kegan Paul, 1932).

10. This passage is based on Lydia H. Liu, *The Clash of Empires: The Invention of China in Modern World Making* (Cambridge: Harvard University Press, 2004).

11. Taylor, *Modern Social Imaginaries*, 76.

12. Merle Goldman and Leo Ou-Fan Lee, eds., *An Intellectual History of Modern China* (Cambridge: Cambridge University Press, 2002), 142.

13. Tu Weiming and Mary Evelyn Tucker, eds. *Confucian Spirituality*, 2 vols. (New York: Crossroads, 2003–4).

14. For a more detailed analysis of this point, see the third chapter of my *Imperial Encounters: Religion and Modernity in India and Britain* (Princeton, N.J.: Princeton University Press, 2001).

15. Eric Ziolkowski, ed., *A Museum of Faiths: Histories and Legacies of the 1893 World's Parliament of Religions* (Atlanta: Scholars Press, 1993).

16. Sunrit Mullick, "Protap Chandra Majumdar and Swami Vivekananda at the Parliament of Religions: Two Interpretations of Hinduism and Universal Religion," in ibid., 221.

17. See Peter van der Veer, *Religious Nationalism: Hindus and Muslims in India* (Berkeley: University of California Press, 1994).

Stef Aupers and Dick Houtman, The Sacralization of the Self: Relocating the Sacred on the Ruins of Tradition

1. Paul Heelas, Linda Woodhead, Benjamin Seel, Bronislaw Szerszynski, and Karin Tusting, *The Spiritual Revolution: Why Religion Is Giving Way to Spirituality* (Oxford: Blackwell), 5–6.

2. "Spirituality" has increasingly replaced the "New Age" label. Indeed, the once-typical belief in a dawning "Age of Aquarius" has become marginal ever since New Age started disembedding from society's countercultural fringe in the 1960s and 1970s, gradually expanding into the very center of late-modern culture. See, e.g., Anneke H. van Otterloo, "Selfspirituality and the Body: New Age Centres in the Netherlands since the 1960s," *Social Compass* 46 (1999): 191–202.

3. Thomas Luckmann, *The Invisible Religion: The Problem of Religion in Modern Society* (New York: MacMillan, 1967).

4. Eileen Barker, ed., *New Religious Movements: A Perspective for Understanding Society* (Lewiston, N.Y.: Edwin Mellen, 1982).

5. Rodney Stark and William Sims Bainbridge, *The Future of Religion: Secularization, Revival, and Cult Formation* (Berkeley: University of California Press, 1985).

6. Rodney Stark, Eva Hamberg, and Alan S. Miller, "Exploring Spirituality and Unchurched Religions in America, Sweden, and Japan," *Journal of Contemporary Religion* 20 (2005): 3–23.

7. E.g., Paul Heelas et al., *Spiritual Revolution*; Paul Heelas, *The New Age Movement: The Celebration of the Self and the Sacralisation of Modernity* (Oxford: Blackwell, 1996); Linda Woodhead, "Religion as Normative, Spirituality as Fuzzy: Questioning Some Deep Assumptions in the Sociology of Religion," paper presented at the 28th ISSR/SISR Conference Challenging Boundaries: Religion and Society, Zagreb, July 18–22, 2005.

8. Cor Baerveldt, "New Age-religiositeit als individueel constructieproces" [New Age Religiosity as a Process of Individual Construction], in *De kool en de geit in de nieuwe tijd: Wetenschappelijke reflecties op New Age* [The Fence, the Hare, and the Hounds in the New Age: Academic Reflections on New Age], ed. Miranda Moerland (Utrecht: Jan van Arkel, 1996), 19–31.

9. Malcolm Hamilton, "An Analysis of the Festival for Mind-Body-Spirit, London," in *Beyond New Age: Exploring Alternative Spirituality*, ed. Steven Sutcliffe and Marion Bowman (Edinburgh: Edinburgh University Press, 2000), 188–200.

10. David Lyon, *Jesus in Disneyland: Religion in Postmodern Times* (Cambridge: Polity Press, 2000).

11. Adam Possamai, "Alternative Spiritualities and the Cultural Logic of Late Capitalism," *Culture and Religion* 4 (2003): 31–45.

12. Ibid., 40.

13. Kelly Besecke, "Seeing Invisible Religion: Religion as a Societal Conversation about Transcendent Meaning," *Sociological Theory* 23 (2005): 186.

14. Stef Aupers, *In de ban van moderniteit: De sacralisering van het zelf en computertechnologie* [Under the Spell of Modernity: The Sacralization of the Self and Computer Technology] (Amsterdam: Aksant, 2004).

15. Wouter J. Hanegraaff, *New Age Religion and Western Culture: Esotericism in the Mirror of Secular Thought* (Leiden: Brill, 1996).

16. Heelas, *New Age*, 2; emphasis original.

17. Ibid., 19.

18. Ibid., 18.

19. Ibid., 19; emphasis original.

20. Ibid., 23.

21. Hanegraaff, *New Age Religion*, 519; emphasis original.

22. Johan Goudsblom, "Levensbeschouwing en sociologie" [Ideology and Sociology], *Amsterdams Sociologisch Tijdschrift* 12 (1985): 3–21.

23. Max Weber, *Gesammelte Aufsätze zur Religionssoziologie*, vol. 1 (Tübingen: Mohr, 1920).

24. Stef Aupers and Dick Houtman, "Oriental Religion in the Secular West: Globalization and Religious Diffusion," *Journal of National Development* 16 (2003): 67–86.

25. Bryan Wilson, *Religion in Sociological Perspective* (Oxford: Oxford University Press, 1982).

26. Karel Dobbelaere, "Individuele godsdienstigheid in een geseculariseerde samenleving" [Individual Religiosity in a Secularized Society], *Tijdschrift voor Sociologie* 14 (1993): 15.

27. Ronald Inglehart, *Modernization and Postmodernization: Cultural, Economic, and Political Change in Forty-three Countries* (Princeton, N.J.: Princeton University Press, 1997), 79.

28. Hubert Knoblauch, "Europe and Invisible Religion," *Social Compass*, 50 (2003): 268.

29. Dick Houtman and Peter Mascini, "Why Do Churches Become Empty, While New Age Grows? Secularization and Religious Change in the Netherlands," *Journal for the Scientific Study of Religion* 41 (2002): 455–73.

30. This often-overlooked limitation of survey research applies to all research findings based on scale measures. This is because the percentage of "New Agers" (or, for that matter, "traditionalists," "racists," etc.) found depends on two more or less arbitary decisisions by the researcher: (1) What particular items from a principally unlimited universe are used? and (2) How much agreement with the selected set of items is necessary to be able to speak of a "veritable" "New Ager" ("traditionalist," "racist," etc.)? Depending on the decisions made regarding those two questions (with especially the first one supplying the researcher with enormous degrees of freedom), one can in principle produce any percentage between 0 percent and 100 percent.

31. Houtman and Mascini, "Why Do Churches?" This rejection of external authority and traditional moral values by the young and the well-educated has been documented in any number of other studies conducted in Western countries. See, e.g.: Dick Houtman, *Class and Politics in Contemporary Social Science: "Marxism Lite" and Its Blind Spot for Culture* (New York: Aldine de Gruyter, 2003). The gender difference requires a more complex explanation and will not be discussed further here. See Dick Houtman and Stef Aupers, "The Spiritual Revolution and the New Age Gender Puzzle: The Sacralisation of the Self in Late Modernity (1980–2000)," in *Women and Religion in the West: Challenging Secularisation*, ed. Giselle Vincett, Sonya Sharma, and Kristin Aune (Aldershot: Ashgate, forthcoming).

32. See Houtman and Aupers, "Spiritual Revolution." Of course, one would prefer also to have comparable data for 1970, or even earlier, but twenty years is quite an impressive time span. Moreover, authors such as Wouter Hanegraaff and Michael York argue that the expansion of spirituality has taken place particularly during the 1980s, after its emergence in the 1960s and 1970s counterculture. See for details: Hanegraaff, *New Age Religion*; Michael York, *The Emerging Network: A Sociology of the New Age and Neo-Pagan Movements* (Lanham, Md.: Rowman and Littlefield, 1995); Daniel Bell, *The Cultural Contradictions of Capitalism* (New York: Basic Books, 1976); Theodore Roszak, *The Making of a Counter Culture: Reflections on the Technocratic Society and Its Youthful Opposition* (New York: Doubleday, 1968); Anton C. Zijderveld, *The Abstract Society: A Cultural Analysis of Our Time* (Garden City, N.Y.: Doubleday, 1970).

33. See, about the decline of the Christian churches and doctrines in most Western countries, Pippa Norris and Ronald Inglehart, *Sacred and Secular: Religion and Politics Worldwide* (Cambridge: Cambridge University Press, 2004).

34. Steve Bruce, *God Is Dead: Secularisation in the West* (Oxford: Blackwell), 99.

35. Tanya M. Luhrmann, *Persuasions of the Witch's Craft: Ritual Magic in Contemporary England* (Cambridge: Harvard University Press, 1989), 312.

36. Ibid., 315.

37. Peter L. Berger and Thomas Luckmann, *The Social Construction of Reality: A Treatise in the Sociology of Knowledge* (New York: Doubleday, 1966), 183.

38. Howard S. Becker, *Outsiders: Studies in the Sociology of Deviance* (New York: Free Press, 1966), 38.

39. Don Grant, Kathleen O'Neil, and Laura Stephens, "Spirituality in the Workplace: New Empirical Directions in the Study of the Sacred," *Sociology of Religion* 65 (2004): 267.

40. Thomas Luckmann, "The Privatization of Religion and Morality," in *Detraditionalization: Critical Reflections on Authority and Identity*, ed. Paul Heelas, Scott Lash, and Paul Morris (Oxford: Blackwell, 1996), 73; Bruce, *God Is Dead*, 97.

41. Grant et al., "Spirituality in the Workplace," 281.

42. Heelas, *New Age*; Majia Holmer Nadesan, "The Discourses of Corporate Spiritualism and Evangelical Capitalism," *Management Communication Quarterly* 13 (1999): 3–42.

43. See for examples: Brad J. Baber, "Can't See the Forest for the Trees?" *Legal Assistant Today* 17 (1999): 84–85; Melissa A. Berman, "New Ideas, Big Ideas, Fake Ideas," *Across the Board* 36 (1999): 28–32; Jim Braham, "The Spiritual Side," *Industry Week* 248 (1999): 48–56; Jack Hayes, "Business Gurus Divine Spiritual Answers to Labor Issues," *Nation's Restaurant News* 33 (1999): 66; Ian I. Mitroff and Elizabeth A. Denton, "A Study of Spirituality in the Workplace," *Sloan Management Review* 40 (1999): 83–92; Craig Neal, "A Conscious Change in the Workplace," *Journal for Quality and Participation* 22 (1999): 27–30; Jean B. Traynor, "Total Life Planning: A New Frontier in Work-Life Benefits," *Employee Benefit Journal* 24 (1999): 29–32; Janice Turner, "Spirituality in the Workplace," *CA Magazine* 132 (1999): 41–42; Jack Welch, "Creed Is Good," *People Management* 25 (1998): 28–33.

44. Ian I. Mitroff and Elizabeth A. Denton, *A Spiritual Audit of Corporate America: A Hard Look at Spirituality, Religion, and Values in the Workplace* (San Francisco: Jossey-Bass, 1999), 14.

45. Ibid., 26.

46. Heelas, *New Age*.

47. John Naisbitt and Patricia Aburdene, *Mega-Trends 2000* (London: Pan Books, 1990), 273.

48. See also: Eileen Barker, "Whatever Next?" in *Religions sans frontières: Present and Future Trends of Migration, Culture and Communication*, ed. Roberto Cipriani (Rome: Presidenza del Consiglio dei Ministri, 1982), 367–76; Nadesan, "Discourses of Corporate Spiritualism"; John A. Swets and Robert A. Bjork, "Enhancing Human Performance: An Evaluation of 'New Age' Techniques Considered by the U.S. Army," *Psychological Science* 1 (1990): 85–96.

49. For a more extensive analysis of the history of New Age in the Netherlands, see Stef Aupers, "'We Are All Gods': New Age in the Netherlands 1960–2000," in *The Dutch and Their Gods*, ed. Erik Sengers (Hilversum: Verloren, 2005), 181–201.

50. Heelas, *New Age*.

51. Grant et al., "Spirituality in the Workplace."

52. Aupers, *In de ban*.

53. E.g., for postmodernization, Inglehart, *Modernization and Postmodernization*, and, for reflexive modernization: Ulrich Beck, *Risk Society: Toward a New Modernity* (London: Sage, 1992); Ulrich Beck, Anthony Giddens, and Scott Lash, *Reflexive Modernization: Politics, Tradition and Aesthetics in the Modern Social Order* (Stanford, Calif.: Stanford University Press, 1994).

54. Woodhead, "Religion as Normative."

55. Steve Bruce, "Good Intentions and Bad Sociology: New Age Authenticity and Social Roles," *Journal of Contemporary Religion* 13 (1998): 23–36; Bruce, *God Is Dead*, 104.

56. Ibid., 83; our emphasis.

57. Besecke, "Seeing Invisible Religion," 194.

58. Ibid., 187.

59. Heelas et al., *Spiritual Revolution*, 27.

60. Ibid., 28.

61. Besecke, "Seeing Invisible Religion," calls for a similar sociologization of research into spirituality. Olav Hammer's *Claiming Knowledge: Strategies of Epistemology from Theosophy to the New Age* (Leiden: Brill, 2001) constitutes an excellent example of the type of research that is needed.

Annemie Halsema, Horizontal Transcendence: Irigaray's Religion after Ontotheology

NOTE: The project Horizontal Transcendence is part of the program The Future of the Religious Past, financed by the Netherlands Organization for Scientific Research. It is based at the University of Humanistics, the University of Utrecht. I am grateful to my colleagues, Prof. Harry Kunneman and Dr. Tonja van den Ende, for their critical comments and inspiring suggestions while I was developing the thoughts articulated here. Part of this paper was presented at the international research seminar Luce Irigaray: Religion, Ethics, and Ontology (Helsinki, February 2005). I thank all the participants and am especially grateful to Jonna Bornemark, Sara Heinämaa, Morny Joy, and Ellen Mortensen for their helpful questions, suggestions, and critical comments.

1. Luce Irigaray, *Key Writings* (London: Continuum, 2004), 172.

2. Many of Irigaray's works contain passages about religion: e.g., "La mystérique," in *Speculum of the Other Woman* (trans. Gillian C. Gill [Ithaca, N.Y.: Cornell University Press, 1985], 191–202), and pt. 3, "When the Gods Are Born," in *Marine Lover of Friedrich Nietzsche* (trans. Gillian C. Gill [New York: Columbia University Press, 1991], 121–90). But there are some texts in which religion and the religious are of central concern, notably three texts in *Sexes and Genealogies* (trans. Gillian C. Gill [New York: Columbia University Press, 1993]), "Belief Itself" (23–53), "Divine Women" (55–72), and "Women, the Sacred, Money" (73–88), as well as: *Le souffle des femmes* (Paris: ACGF, 1996); *Between East and West: From Singularity to Community* (trans. S. Pluháček [New York: Columbia University Press, 2002]); and, in *Key Writings*, the section "Spirituality and Religion" (145–94).

3. See Hent de Vries, *Philosophy and the Turn to Religion* (Baltimore: The Johns Hopkins University Press, 1999) and *Religion and Violence: Philosophical Perspectives from Kant to Derrida* (Baltimore: The Johns Hopkins University Press, 2002).

4. See, for an interesting analysis of the Dutch debate over integration and the central place of gender and religion in it: Anna Korteweg, "The Murder of Theo van Gogh: Gender, Religion, and the Struggle over Immigrant Integration in the Netherlands," in *Migration, Citizenship, Ethnos: Incorporation Regimes in Germany, Western Europe and North America.* ed. Y. M. Bodemann and G. Yurdakul (New York: Palgrave MacMillan, 2006).

5. See Susan Moller Okin, "Is Multiculturalism Bad for Women?" in *Is Multiculturalism Bad For Women?* ed. S. M. Okin (Princeton, N.J.: Princeton University Press, 1999).

6. See, e.g.: Saba Mahmood, *Politics of Piety: The Islamic Revival and the Feminist Subject* (Princeton, N.J.: Princeton University Press, 2004); Ziba Mir-Hosseini, *Islam and Gender: The Religious Debate in Contemporary Iran* (London: I. B. Tauris, 2000); Amina Wadud, *Qur'an and Woman: Rereading the Sacred Text from a Woman's Perspective* (New York: Oxford University Press, 1999).

7. Gianni Vattimo, *After Christianity,* trans. Luce D'Isanto (New York: Columbia University Press, 2002).

8. See also Ellen Armour, "Divining Differences: Irigaray and Religion," in *Religion in French Feminist Thought*, ed. Morny Joy, Kathleen O'Grady, and Judith L. Poxon (London: Routledge, 2003), 29–40, for Irigaray's interpretation and critique of Heidegger.

9. Penelope Deutscher, *A Politics of Impossible Difference: The Later Work of Luce Irigaray* (Ithaca, N.Y.: Cornell University Press, 2002), 90 ff.; Morny Joy, "Irigaray's Eastern Explorations," in *Religion in French Feminist Thought*, ed. Joy, O'Grady, and Poxon, 52; Grace Jantzen, *Becoming Divine: Toward a Feminist Philosophy of Religion* (Manchester: Manchester University Press, 1998).

10. See, on Irigaray, religion, and sexual indifference: Ellen Armour, "Beyond Belief? Sexual Difference and Religion after Ontotheology," in *The Religious*, ed. John D. Caputo (Oxford: Blackwell, 2002), 212–26, and "Divining Differences"; Penelope Deutscher, "'The Only Diabolical Thing about Women . . .': Luce Irigaray on Divinity," *Hypatia* 9, no. 4 (1994): 88–111; Amy Hollywood, "Beauvoir, Irigaray, and the Mystical," *Hypatia* 9, no. 4 (1994), 158–85, and "Deconstructing Belief: Irigaray and the Philosophy of Religion," *The Journal of Religion* 78, no. 2 (1998): 230–45; Grace

Jantzen, *Becoming Divine*, and "'Barely by a Breath . . .': Irigaray on Rethinking Religion," in *The Religious*, ed. Caputo, 227–40; Serene Jones, "Divining Women: Irigaray and Feminist Theologies," *Yale French Studies* 87 (1995): 42–67; Anne-Claire Mulder, *Divine Flesh, Embodied Word: Incarnation as a Hermeneutical Key to a Feminist Theologian's Reading of Luce Irigaray's Work* (Amsterdam: Amsterdam University Press, 2006); Judith L. Poxon, "Corporeality and Divinity: Irigaray and the Problem of the Ideal," in *Religion in French Feminist Thought*, ed. Joy, O'Grady, and Poxon, 41–50.

11. Irigaray, *Sexes and Genealogies*, 26.

12. Ibid., 78.

13. Irigaray, *Marine Lover*, 167.

14. Irigaray, *Sexes and Genealogies*, 63.

15. Armour, "Beyond Belief," 214.

16. Irigaray, *An Ethics of Sexual Difference*, trans. Carolyn Burke and Gillian C. Gill (Ithaca, N.Y.: Cornell University Press, 1993), 148.

17. The third era of the history of salvation, after the eras of the father and the son, was announced by the medieval prophet Joachim of Fiore (1132–1202). Joachim plays an important role in the study of the Bible as spiritual: that is, the capacity to consider the events in the Bible as prefiguring events to come.

18. Luce Irigaray, *I Love To You: Sketch of a Possible Felicity in History*, trans. Alison Martin (New York: Routledge, 1996), 137–41; *Le souffle des femmes*; and *Key Writings*, 171–85 and 186–94.

19. Jantzen, "'Barely by a Breath,'" 228.

20. Irigaray, *Key Writings*, 175.

21. Joy, "Irigaray's Eastern Explorations," 51–67.

22. Irigaray, *Key Writings*, 190. The text "Fulfilling Our Humanity" (*Key Writings*, 186–94) that is quoted here was published earlier as "Introduction: On Old and New Tablets" (in *Religion in French Feminist Thought*, ed. Joy, O'Grady, and Poxon, 1–9), for which volume the text was originally written.

23. See Irigaray, *Speculum*, 307.

24. Irigaray uses three terms alternately: the *maternal-feminine* (*Ethics*, 84, 99), the *feminine-maternal* (idem, 152), and *matrix* (*Speculum*, 294). The last term refers at once to birthplace, cradle, and to mold, printing form: that in which something is printed.

25. Irigaray, *Speculum*, 294.

26. Irigaray, *Sexes and Genealogies*, 32.

27. A part of "Belief Itself" is a reinterpretation of angels (*Sexes and Genealogies*, 35–45). In this text, angels are presented as intermediates connecting God and man.

28. Irigaray, *Speculum*, 330.

29. Irigaray, *Key Writings*, 171–72.

30. E.g., in Armour, "Divining Differences," and Poxon, "Corporeality and Divinity."

31. "In the object he contemplates, man becomes acquainted with himself" (Ludwig Feuerbach, *The Essence of Christianity*, trans. George Eliot [New York: Prometheus Books, 1989], 5).

32. "The absolute to man is his own nature" (ibid.).

33. Irigaray, *Sexes and Genealogies*, 67.

34. Elisabeth Grosz, *Sexual Subversions: Three French Feminists* (Sydney: Allen & Unwin, 1989), 159–60.

35. Poxon, "Corporeality and Divinity," 45.

36. Armour, "Divining Differences," 30.

37. Ibid., 38.

38. Hollywood, "Beauvoir, Irigaray, and the Mystical," 175.

39. Deutscher, *A Politics of Impossible Difference*, 97.

40. Irigaray, *Key Writings*, 188.

41. Irigaray, *To Be Two*, trans. Monique M. Rhodes and Marco F. Concito-Monoc (London: Athlone, 2002), 86.

42. Ibid., 90–91.

43. Irigaray, *Sexes and Genealogies*, 71.

44. Irigaray articulates the central question of our age, sexual difference, in associating it with Heidegger (*Ethics*, 5), and she in general is very much indebted to Heidegger's philosophy (see Tina Chanter, *Ethics of Eros: Irigaray's Rewriting of the Philosophers* [New York: Routledge, 1995], esp. 127–51, 167–68).

45. Martin Heidegger, *Identität und Differenz* (Pfüllingen: Günther Neske, 1957), 51.

46. Ibid., 64.

47. John D. Caputo, "Introduction: Who Comes after the God of Metaphysics," in *The Religious*, ed. Caputo, 4.

48. Irigaray, *Ethics*, 129.

49. Armour, "Divining Differences," 34.

50. Luce Irigaray, *The Forgetting of Air in Martin Heidegger*, trans. Mary Beth Mader (London: Athlone, 1999), 11.

51. Irigaray, *I Love To You*, 37.

52. Irigaray, *Forgetting of Air*, 3, 5.

53. Irigaray, *I Love To You*, 104. Note that in *Speculum* Irigaray refers to ecstasy in a more positive sense, namely, in relationship to mystic language or discourse. There she understands "ex-stasies" as escapes from the masculine symbolic (*Speculum*, 192). Irigaray embraces that as a necessary movement, because women are encapsulated in masculine representations (i.e., in "the same"). Mystic language is the only place in the history of the West in which woman speaks and acts so publicly, and where men follow women. Also, it is the place where consciousness is no longer master. As such, it is perhaps the privileged place in Western discourse where something of the repressed feminine appears.

Yet how "positive" is this understanding of ecstasy in Irigaray's texts? The female mystic represents the woman who breaks with the masculine symbolic, but without having a proper alternative: "the 'I' is still empty" (195). Also, Irigaray fears that the mystic remains trapped in the masculine symbolic, that her "soul" is a reflection of his, God's image (197). Also, in later texts, Irigaray warns against the risk of being encapsulated within the patriarchal symbolic: feminine mystics run the risk of losing their breath, their soul (*Key Writings*, 147).

By contrast, Amy Hollywood, in a subtle defense of the female mystics, "Divining Differences," shows that Irigaray's interpretation doesn't do enough justice to the conscious efforts of mystics to undermine the traditional dichotomies, in particular, of sex and gender.

54. Irigaray, *Sexes and Genealogies*, 67.

55. Irigaray, *East and West*, 130.

56. Irigaray, *Ethics*, 17. She also writes about the vertical dimension in relationship to the genealogical relationship: e.g., the relationship between mothers and daughters, which is distinguished from the horizontal relationship between women as sisters (Irigaray, *Ethics*, 108).

57. Irigaray, *Key Writings*, 187.

58. Ibid., 189.

59. Ibid., 181.

60. Irigaray, *I Love To You*, 103.

61. Chanter, *Ethics of Eros*, 170–224.

62. See Irigaray, "Questions to Emmanuel Levinas," in *The Irigaray Reader*, ed. M. Whitford (Oxford: Blackwell, 1991), 178–89. Other texts in which Irigaray criticizes Levinas are "The Fecundity of the Caress" (*Ethics*, 185–217) and "The Wedding Between the Body and Language" (*To Be Two*, 17–29).

63. Emmanuel Levinas, "La philosophie et l'idée de l'infini," in Levinas, *En découvrant l'existence avec Husserl et Heidegger*, 2d ed. (Paris: Vrin, 1967), 174.

64. Irigaray, *Key Writings*, 182.

65. See, on Descartes and wonder, Irigaray, *Ethics*, 72–82.

66. Irigaray, *To Be Two*, 93.

67. Irigaray, *Ethics*, 147.

68. Irigaray, *Key Writings*, 183.

69. Deutscher, "'The Only Diabolical Thing,'" 100.

70. Irigaray, *Key Writings*, 172.

71. Perhaps Irigaray is not the first feminist thinker that comes to mind for a reflection on multiculturalism. One of the problems with her notion of sexual difference, often noted, is that it concentrates on gender and leaves other differences, such as ethnicity, aside. Yet in her latest works, *Between East and West* and *Democracy Begins Between Two* (New York: Routledge, 2001), she shows more openness to differences other than the sexual one. She claims that sexual difference can also bring about openness to other cultures. She says that a culture that cultivates relations of sexual difference will also better facilitate multiculturalism (Irigaray, *East and West*, 156) and stimulate relations between cultures, races, and traditions, because, in such a culture, difference would in itself be recognized and valued.

72. See Han Entzinger, "The Rise and Fall of Multiculturalism: The Case of the Netherlands," in *Toward Assimilation and Citizenship: Immigrants in Liberal Nation-States*, ed. C. Joppke and E. Morawska (New York: Palgrave Macmillan, 2003), 59–86; and esp. Anna Korteweg, "The Murder of Theo van Gogh: Gender, Religion, and the Struggle over Immigrant Integration in the Netherlands," in *Migration, Citizenship, Ethnos*, ed. Bodemann and Yurdakul.

73. The notion of horizon comes close to Charles Taylor's in *Sources of the Self: The Making of the Modern Identity* (Cambridge: Harvard University Press, 1989) but is explicitly open. "Horizontal" in "horizontal transcendence" indicates recognition of traditions other than the one it is inspired by.

Thomas A. Carlson, Religion and the Time of Creation: Placing "the Human" in Techno-scientific and Theological Context

1. See Giorgio Agamben, *Homo Sacer: Sovereign Power and Bare Life*, trans. Daniel Heller-Roazen (Stanford, Calif.: Stanford University Press, 1998).

2. http://www.press.uchicago.edu/Misc/Chicago/05april_santner.html.

3. Cited in ibid.

4. "The President's Stem Cell Theology," editorial, *New York Times*, May 27, 2005.

5. See Pam Belluck, "From Stem Cell Opponents, an Embryo Crusade," *New York Times*, June 2, 2005.

6. One can hear a similar argument from the other side of the political spectrum in a book like Bill McKibben, *Enough: Staying Human in an Engineered Age* (New York: Henry Holt, 2003). For an insightful and critical discussion of the positions marked by Kass and McKibben (and of

their shared Heideggerian resonance), see Gary Greenberg's review essay "After Nature: The Varieties of Technological Experience," in *Harper's Magazine*, March 2004, 91–96.

7. Leon Kass, *Life, Liberty, and the Defense of Dignity* (San Francisco: encounter books, 2002), 18.

8. For a brief but informed and insightful discussion of bioethics, the theological traditions of "positive" and "negative" anthropology stemming from the doctrine of man as *imago Dei*, and the resonance of these in Habermas and Derrida, see Eduardo Mendieta, "We Have Never Been Human or, How We Lost Our Humanity: Derrida and Habermas on Cloning," *Philosophy Today*, SPEP Supplement, 2003, 168–75.

9. Jean-Luc Marion, "*Mihi magna quaestio factus sum*: The Privilege of Unknowing," *Journal of Religion* 85, no. 1 (January 2005), hereafter cited parenthetically in the text as PU, followed by the page number.

10. See, e.g., Martin Heidegger, "Die Zeit des Weltbildes," in *Holzwege* (Frankfurt a. M.: Vittorio Klostermann, 1950), 88, 94, etc., trans. William Lovitt as "Age of the World Picture," in Heidegger, *The Question Concerning Technology and Other Essays* (New York: Harper and Row, 1977), 128, 134, etc.

11. For Marion's fullest treatment of the saturated phenomenon, see his *Etant donné: Essai d'une phénoménologie de la donation* (Paris: Presses Universitaires de France, 1997), trans. Jeffrey L. Kosky as *Being Given: Toward a Phenomenology of Givenness* (Stanford, Calif.: Stanford University Press, 2002).

12. Levinas: "the face is signification, and signification without context. . . . In this sense one can say that the face is not 'seen.' It is what cannot become a content, which your thought would embrace; it is uncontainable, it leads you beyond," in *Ethics and Infinity: Conversations with Philippe Nemo*, trans. Richard A. Cohen (Pittsburgh: Duquesne University Press, 1985), 85–86.

13. Martin Heidegger, *Was ist Metaphysik?* in *Wegmarken* (Frankfurt a. M.: Vittorio Klostermann, 1978), 118; English version in Heidegger, *Basic Writings*, ed. David Farrell Krell, 2d ed. (San Francisco: Harper Collins, 1993), 106.

14. Martin Heidegger, "Brief über den humanismus," in *Wegmarken*, 342; English version in Heidegger, *Basic Writings*, ed. Krell, 234, 245.

15. On the extension of objectification into the objectlessness of "standing reserve [*Bestand*]," see Heidegger's much discussed essay "Die Frage nach der Technik," in *Vorträge und Aufsätze* (Stuttgart: Neske, 1954), trans. William Lovitt as "The Question Concerning Technology," in *The Question Concerning Technology and Other Essays*, 3–35.

16. Emmanuel Levinas, "Heidegger, Gagarin, and Us," in *Difficult Freedom: Essays on Judaism*, trans. Seán Hand (Baltimore: The Johns Hopkins University Press, 1990), 232–33.

17. Gregory of Nyssa, "On the Making of Man," quoted in PU, 17.

18. Gregory of Nyssa, "On the Making of Man," 7.2 (= 141B in the J. P. Migne pagination). English translation in *Nicene and Post-Nicene Fathers*, second series, vol. 5, *Gregory of Nyssa: Dogmatic Treatises, etc.*, ed. Philip Schaff and Henry Wace (Peabody, Mass.: Hendrickson, 1994).

19. See Hans Blumenberg, *The Legitimacy of the Modern Age*, trans. Robert Wallace (Cambridge: MIT Press, 1985), and Louis Dupré, *Passage to Modernity: An Essay in the Hermeneutics of Nature and Culture* (New Haven, Conn.: Yale University Press, 1993).

20. Tillich, quoted in PU, 4.

21. Peter Berger, *The Sacred Canopy* (New York: Garden Books, 1967), 4, 6.

22. See Arnold Gehlen, *Der Mensch* (1940; Frankfurt a. M.: Athenaion, 1974), trans. Clare McMillan and Karl Pillemer as *Man: His Nature and Place in the World* (New York: Columbia University Press, 1988), esp. chap. 11, "Bolk's Theory and Other Related Theories"; and Georges Lapassade, *L'entrée dans la vie: Essai sur l'inachèvement de l'homme* (1963; Paris: Economica, 1997).

23. Louis Bolk, *Das Problem der Menschwerdung* (Jena, 1926), lecture given on April 15, 1926, at the Twenty-fifth Congress of the Anatomical Society of Fribourg, available in a French translation by Georges Lapassade, "Le Problème de la genèse humaine," in *Revue Française de Psychanalyse* (Paris: Presses Universitaires de France), March-April, 1961. See also Lapassade, "Présentation de Louis Bolk," and Bolk, "La genèse de l'homme," in *Arguments*, 4e année, no. 18, 2e trimestre, 1960.

24. Lapassade, *L'entrée dans la vie*, 202–3.

25. Ibid., 203.

26. Jacques Derrida, "Faith and Knowledge: The Two Sources of 'Religion' at the Limits of Reason Alone," trans. Samuel Weber, in *Religion*, ed. Jacques Derrida and Gianni Vattimo (Stanford, Calif.: Stanford University Press, 1998), 1–78.

27. Michel Serres, *L'incandescent* (Paris: Le Pommier, 2003), 29. My translation.

28. See N. Katherine Hayles, *How We Became Posthuman: Virtual Bodies in Cybernetics, Literature, and Informatics* (Chicago: University of Chicago Press, 1999), and Mark C. Taylor, *Hiding* (Chicago: University of Chicago Press, 1998) and *The Moment of Complexity: Emerging Network Culture* (Chicago: University of Chicago Press, 2003).

29. Michel Serres, *Hermès I: La communication* (Paris: Minuit, 1968), 11–20. Serres points out in a 2000 essay, *Retour au Contrat Naturel* (Paris: Bibliotèque nationale de France, 2000), which looks back to this earlier work, "that the network is becoming the best of our technologies shows that its form is becoming the best of our concepts" (27).

30. Serres, *L'incandescent*, 315.

31. Michel Serres, *Hominescence* (Paris: Le Pommier, 2001), 14, my translation. Hereafter cited parenthetically in the text as H, with page number following. The translations are mine.

32. Michel Serres, *Hominescence*; *L'incandescent*; *Rameaux* (Paris: Le Pommier, 2004); and *Récits d'humanisme* (Paris: Le Pommier, 2006). Serres proposes calling the series as a whole *Le grand récit*.

33. Serres, in Michel Serres and Bruno Latour, *Conversations on Science, Culture, and Time* (Ann Arbor: University of Michigan Press, 1995), 172.

34. Like the network, the "world-object" goes back to Serres's earlier work in *Hermès*, in this case the section in vol. 3 treating "thanatocracy," which finds examples of the world-object in ballistic missiles, fixed satellites, and nuclear waste. See *Hermès III: La traduction* (Paris: Minuit, 1974).

35. It is worth noting here that the association of location with definition or circumscription is decisive to the mystical insistence that God cannot be located. On this, see my essay "Locating the Mystical Subject," in *Mystics: Presence and Aporia*, ed. Michael Kessler and Christian Sheppard (Chicago: University of Chicago Press, 2003).

36. Michel Serres, *Le contrat naturel* (Paris: François Bourin, 1990), 170. Hereafter cited parenthetically as CN, with following page number. Translations are mine.

37. Robert Pogue Harrison, *The Dominion of the Dead* (Chicago: University of Chicago Press, 2003).

38. Elizabeth Kolbert, "The Climate of Man—III: What Can be Done?" in *The New Yorker*, May 9, 2005, 52–53.

39. Ibid., 54.

40. Andrew C. Revkin, "Forget Nature: Even Eden Is Engineered," *New York Times*, August 20, 2002, Science Times, D1.

41. On the distinction of and interplay between earth and world in Heidegger, see esp. the classic 1935–36 essay "Der Ursprung des Kunstwerkes," in *Holzwege* (Frankfurt a. M.: Vittorio Klostermann, 1950): English version "The Origin of the Work of Art," in Heidegger, *Basic Writings*, ed. Krell, 139–212.

42. Serres is convinced, admittedly without having any proof, that the rope or cord that ties is the "first invention of human technology" and "contemporary with the first contract" (CN, 163). His beautifully simple example of the interplay between the natural and social contracts comes from mountaineering, where, when the climbing grows steep and difficult, the group ropes up and creates not only a social bind, among the people tied one to another, but also a natural bind, in relation to the rock where the piton is placed as point of attachment for the rope. "The group is tied, referred, not only to itself, but to the objective world. The piton solicits the resistance of the wall, to which no one will trust a tie-in except after having tested it. To the social contract is added a natural contract" (CN, 163).

43. In Giorgio Agamben, *Idea of Prose*, trans. Michael Sullivan and Sam Whitsitt (Albany: State University of New York Press, 1995). Hereafter cited parenthetically in the text as IP, with page number following.

Contributors

H. J. Adriaanse is Professor Emeritus of the Philosophy of Religion and Ethics at the University of Leiden and a Member of the Royal Dutch Academy of Sciences. Among his books are *Vom Christentum aus* (1995), *Theology and Rationality* (co-edited with H. A. Krop, 1988), *The Phenomenon Called Theology* (co-authored with H. A. Krop and L. Leertrouwer, 1987), *Zu den Sachen selbst: Versuch einer Konfrontation der Theologie Karl Barths mit der phänomenologischen Philosophie Edmund Husserls* (1974), and the edited volume *On Philosophical and Confessional Theology*.

Alena Alexandrova is a Ph.D. student at the Amsterdam School for Cultural Analysis, University of Amsterdam. She is also a guest researcher at the Heyendaal Institute, University of Nijmegen, and a co-editor of *Retreating Religion: Deconstructing Christianity with Jean-Luc Nancy,* together with Ignaas Devis, Laurens ten Kate, and Aukje van Rooden. She has published articles in the field of aesthetics and visual studies.

Talal Asad was born in Saudi Arabia and educated in Britain. He now teaches anthropology at the Graduate Center of the City University of New York. His most recent book is entitled *Formations of the Secular: Christianity, Islam, Modernity* (2003).

Jan Assmann is Professor of Egyptology at the University of Heidelberg. His most recent publications in English include *Religion and Cultural Memory: Ten Studies* (2006), *Death and Salvation in Ancient Egypt* (2005), *The Mind of Egypt: History and Meaning in the Time of the Pharaohs* (2002), *The Search for God in Ancient Egypt* (2001), and *Moses the Egyptian: The Memory of Egypt in Western Monotheism* (1998).

Henri Atlan is Professor Emeritus of Biophysics at the University of Paris VI and the Hebrew University of Jerusalem. In addition to being Director of the Human Biology Research Center and Scholar in Residence for studies in Philosophy and Ethics of Biology at the Hadassah University Hospital, Jerusalem, he is Honorary Head of the Department of Biophysics of the Hotel-Dieu Hospital and Director of Research in Philosophy of Biology at the École des Hautes Études en Sciences Sociales, both in Paris. He was a member of the French National Committee of Ethics for Health and Life Sciences and has won an international reputation for his research on the self-organization of cells, theories of complexity, immunology, and artificial intelligence. Among his published works are *L'utérus artificiel* (2005), the two-volume *Les étincelles de hasard* (1999), *Enlightenment to Enlightenment: Intercritique of Science and Myth* (1986), *Entre le cristal et la fumée: Essai sur l'organisation du vivant* (1979), and *L'organisation biologique et la théorie de l'information* (1972).

Stef Aupers is a sociologist of culture, an Assistent Professor at Erasmus University Rotterdam, and a member of the Amsterdam School for Social Science Research (ASSR). He has published widely on post-traditional forms of spirituality, conspiracy culture, cyberculture, and online computer gaming.

Daniel Boyarin is the Taubman Professor of Talmudic Culture in the Departments of Near Eastern Studies and Rhetoric at the University of California, Berkeley. Among his recent books are *Border Lines: The Partition of Judaeo-Christianity* (2004), *Dying for God: Martyrdom and the Making of Christianity and Judaism* (1999), and *Unheroic Conduct: The Rise of Heterosexuality and the Invention of the Jewish Man* (1997).

Jan N. Bremmer is Professor of Religious Studies at the University of Groningen. Among his books are *Greek Religion and Culture, the Bible, and the Ancient Near East* (2008), *The Rise and Fall of the Afterlife* (2002), *Greek Religion* (1994), *Roman Myth and Mythography* (co-authored with Nicholas Horsfall, 1987), and *The Early Greek Concept of the Soul* (1983).

Thomas A. Carlson is Professor in the Department of Religious Studies at the University of California, Santa Barbara. He is the author of *Indiscretion: Finitude and the Naming of God* (1999) and of *The Indiscrete Image: Infinitude and Creation of the Human* (2008), a study of human self-creation in contexts of mystical theology and technological modernity. He has also translated into English several works by Jean-Luc Marion, including *God Without Being* (1991), *Reduction and Donation: Investigations of Husserl, Heidegger, and Phenomenology* (1998), and *The Idol and Distance* (2001).

José Casanova is Professor of Sociology at Georgetown University and Senior Fellow at its Berkley Center for Religion, Peace, and World Affairs. He has published widely on sociological theory, migration, and globalization, and he is the author of *Public Religions in the Modern World* (1994).

Job Cohen is Mayor of Amsterdam, a post he has held since January 15, 2001. Before that time, he was State Secretary of the Dutch Ministry of Justice, dealing chiefly with immigration, under Prime Minister Wim Kok. Prior to his entry into politics as a member of the Labor Party (PvdA), he was Professor of Methods and Techniques in the Faculty of Law of Maastricht University, and then the university's Rector Magnificus. In 2005, *Time* magazine awarded him the title "European hero."

Veena Das is Krieger-Eisenhower Professor at The Johns Hopkins University, where she teaches in the Department of Anthropology. She is a Foreign Fellow of the American Academy of Arts and Sciences and the Third World Academy of Sciences. She has published widely on questions of social suffering and violence. The last two books she has authored are *Life and Words: Violence and the Descent into the Ordinary* (2006) and *Critical Events: An Anthropological Perspective on Contemporary India* (1995).

Régis Debray teaches philosophy at the Université de Lyon–III and is director of the European Institute of the History and Science of Religion at the École Pratique des Hautes Études, in Paris. He is the author of many books, including *Le feu sacré: Fonction du religieux* (2003), *God, an Itinerary* (2001), and *Media Manifestos: On the Technological Transmission of Cultural Forms* (1996). His life has intersected with some of the key moments of the twentieth century: from his involvement with the Cuban revolution and his arrest in 1967 in the Bolivian jungle, where he had followed the traces of Che Guevara; to the state offices of the Elysée Palace, where he served as an advisor to François Mitterrand in the early 1980s, to his membership in the Stasi Commission, which proposed the 2003 French law on conspicuous religious in public schools.

Jacques Derrida was Director of Studies at the École des Hautes Études en Sciences Sociales, Paris, and Professor of Humanities at the University of California, Irvine. Among his most recent works to be published in English are *Geneses, Genealogies, Genres and Genius: The Secrets of the Archive* (2006), *Sovereignties in Question: The Poetics of Paul Celan* (2005), and, with Giovanna Borradorri, *Philosophy in a Time of Terror: Dialogues with Jürgen Habermas and Jacques Derrida* (2003).

Willem B. Drees holds the chair in philosophy of religion and ethics at Leiden University and is dean of its Faculty of Religious Studies. He also serves as president of ESSSAT, the European Society for the Study of Science and Theology. Among his published works are *Creation: From Nothing until Now* (2002), *Religion, Science and Naturalism* (1996), and *Beyond the Big Bang: Quantum Cosmologies and God* (1990), as well as edited volumes such as: *Creation's Diversity: Voices from Theology and Science* (2008), *The Study of Religion and the Training of Muslim Clergy: Academic and Religious Freedom in the 21st Century* (2008), and *Is Nature Ever Evil? Religion, Science and Value* (2003).

André Droogers is Emeritus Professor of Cultural Anthropology, especially Anthropology of Religion and Symbolic Anthropology, at the VU University Amsterdam. He is Director of the Hollenweger Center for the Interdisciplinary Study of Pentecostal and Charismatic Movements. His numerous publications address various themes, such as Pentecostalism, syncretism, religion and play, the changing worldviews in The Netherlands, and religion and power. With Sidney M. Greenfield, he recently edited the collective volume *Reinventing Religions: Syncretism and Transformation in Africa and the Americas*. He is the coordinator of research programs on changing worldviews in The Netherlands and on conversion careers and culture politics in Global Pentecostalism.

France Guwy is a Belgian journalist. She has worked for Belgian and Dutch television, radio, and newspapers, specializing in literature and philosophy. She has published books about passion and about the ideas of Voltaire and has translated French philosophy.

Annemie Halsema is Assistant Professor in the Department of Philosophy of the VU University Amsterdam, where she teaches gender studies and social philosophy. She has published in the field of feminist philosophy, especially on Irigaray, Benjamin, and Butler. She is currently engaged in a project on the otherness of the self in the work of Ricoeur, Irigaray, Benjamin, and Butler.

Danièle Hervieu-Léger is Director of Studies at the École des Hautes Études en Sciences Sociales, Paris, Director of the Centre Interdisciplinaire d'Études des Faits Religieux, and editor-in-chief of *Archives de Sciences Sociales des Religions*. Among the most recent of her many books are *Catholicisme: Le fin d'un monde* (2003); *Le pélerin et la converti: La religion en movement* (1999); and, in English translation, *Religion as a Chain of Memory* (2000).

Dick Houtman is Professor of Sociology of Culture at Erasmus University Rotterdam and a member of the Amsterdam School for Social Science Research (ASSR). His principal research interest is cultural change in contemporary Western society. Since the mid 1990s he has published about the emergence of a new political culture, central to which are cultural rather than class issues, and the way a spread of post-Christian spiritualities of life has accompanied the decline of the Christian churches. His latest books are *Farewell to the Leftist Working Class* (with Peter Achterberg and Anton Derks, 2007) and *Class and Politics in Contemporary Social Science: "Marxism Lite" and Its Blind Spot for Culture* (2003). He is currently editing a book with Stef Aupers, provisionally titled *Religions of Modernity: Relocating the Sacred to the Self and the Digital*.

Michael Lambek is Professor of Anthropology at the University of Toronto and the London School of Economics. Among his most recent books are *The Weight of the Past: Living with History in Mahanja, Madagascar* (2003), the edited volume *A Reader in the Anthropology of Religion* (2002), and *Bodies and Persons: Comparative Perspectives from Africa and Melanesia* (with Andrew Strathern, 1998).

Niklaus Largier is Professor of German Literature and former director of the religious studies program at the University of California, Berkeley. Among his books are *In Praise of the Whip: A Cultural History of Arousal* (2007) and *Zeit, Zeitlichkeit, Ewigkeit: Ein Aufriss des Zeitproblems bei Dietrich von Freiberg und Meister Eckhart* (1989). He is the editor of the selected writings of Meister Eckhart in German.

Emmanuel Levinas was Professor of Philosophy at the University of Paris–Sorbonne Paris IV and Director of the École Normale Israelite Oriental. The most central of his many books to be published in English translation are *Totality and Infinity: An Essay on Exteriority* (1969) and *Otherwise than Being; or, Beyond Essence* (1981).

Sander van Maas is Assistant Professor of Musicology at the University of Amsterdam and Lecturer in Music Aesthetics at the Amsterdam Conservatory. His research activities include a project on new music and the turn to religion, which focuses on philosophical questions regarding the historical and structural possibility of contemporary "spiritual" or "religious" art music. His book publications include an interdisciplinary study on Olivier Messiaen and the reinvention of religious music, forthcoming in a revised English-language version. He is chairman of the Dutch Association of Aesthetics (NGE) and editor of several online journals.

Jean-Luc Marion is Professor of Philosophy at the Univeristy of Paris–Sorbonne Paris IV and the John Nuveen Professor at the Divinity School and Professor in the Committee on Social Thought and the Department of Philosophy at the University of Chicago. Among his most recent books to appear in English translation are *On the Ego and on God: Further Cartesian Questions* (2007), *The Erotic Phenomenon* (2007), *Prolegomena to Charity* (2002), *In Excess: Studies of Saturated Phenomena* (2002), and *Being Given: Toward a Phenomenology of Givenness* (2002).

Tomoko Masuzawa is Professor of History and Comparative Literature at the University of Michigan. She specializes in the history of the human sciences in the nineteenth and twentieth centuries, especially European academic discourses on religion. She is the author of *The Invention of World Religions; or, How European Universalism Was Preserved in the Language of Pluralism* (2005) and *In Search of Dreamtime: The Quest for the Origin of Religion* (1993).

Birgit Meyer is Professor of Cultural Anthropology in the Department of Social and Cultural Anthropology at the VU University Amsterdam. She has conducted research on missions and local appropriations of Christianity, Pentecostalism, popular culture, and video films in Ghana. Her publications include *Religion, Media, and the Public Sphere* (co-edited with Annelies Moors, 2005), *Magic and Modernity: Interfaces of Revelation and*

Concealment (co-edited with Peter Pels, 2003), *Globalization and Identity: Dialectics of Flow and Closure* (co-edited with Peter Geschiere, 1999), and *Translating the Devil: Religion and Modernity among the Ewe in Ghana* (1999).

Arie L. Molendijk is Professor of the History of Christianity at the University of Groningen. His publications include *The Emergence of the Science of Religion in the Netherlands* (2005), *Post-Theism* (co-edited with Henri A. Krop and Hent de Vries, 2000), *The Pragmatics of Defining Religion: Contexts, Concepts, Contests* (co-edited with Jan G. Platvoet, 1999), and *Zwischen Theologie und Soziologie: Ernst Troeltschs Typen der christlichen Gemeinschaftsbildung: Kirche, Sekte, Mystik* (1996).

Jean-Luc Nancy is Distinguished Professor of Philosophy at the University Marc Bloch, Strasbourg. The most recent of his many books to be published in English are *Dis-Enclosure* (2008), *Philosophical Chronicles* (2008), *Listening* (2007), *The Creation of the World; or, Globalization* (2007), and The *Ground of the Image* (2005).

David Nirenberg is Professor in the Committee on Social Thought and the Department of History at the University of Chicago. In addition to his historical work on relations between Christians, Jews, and Muslims in the Middle Ages, as exemplifed in his *Communities of Violence: Persecution of Minorities in the Middle Ages* (1998), he is interested in how the possibilities and limits of community and communication have been imagined. He is pursuing that interest through two parallel projects. The first is a history of love's place in a number of idealizations of communication and exchange; and the second, a study of poison as a representation of communication's dangers.

Willemien Otten is Professor of the Theology and History of Christianity at the University of Chicago Divinity School. Her work focuses on medieval concepts of nature and creation, particularly its religious aspects, as evidenced by her publications *From Paradise to Paradigm: A Study of Twelfth-Century Humanism* (2004) and *The Anthropology of Johannes Scottus Eriugena* (1991).

Peter Pels is Professor of African Anthropology at the University of Leiden. He has published on critical anthropological theory, the anthropology of colonialism, the history of anthropology, modern African politics and religion, and material culture. His publications include *Cultures of Voting* (with Romain Bertrand and Jean Louis Briquet, 2007), *Embedding Ethics* (with Lynn Meskell, 2005), and *Magic and Modernity: Interfaces of Revelation and Concealment* (co-edited with Birgit Meyer, 2003). He is currently working on cyberculture, science fiction, and the comparative study of the future.

M. B. Pranger is Professor of the History of Christianity at the University of Amsterdam. In his publications, which are mainly on medieval monasticism, he focuses on the relationship between religion and literature. His most recent book is *The Artificiality of Christianity: Essays on the Poetics of Monasticism* (2003), and he is currently completing a book on Augustine and Henry James, provisionally entitled *Augustinian Soundings*.

Patricia Spyer is Professor of Anthropology at the University of Leiden. She is the author of *The Memory of Trade: Modernity's Entanglements on an Eastern Indonesian Island* (2000) and the editor of *Border Fetishism: Material Objects in Unstable Spaces* (1998).

Jeremy Stolow is Assistant Professor in the Department of Sociology and the Department of Communication Studies and Multimedia at McMaster University, where he is also an associate member of the Department of Religious Studies and the Institute on Globalization and the Human Condition. His area of research is religion and media, with a particular interest in religion and technology.

Winnifred Fallers Sullivan is Associate Professor of Law and Director of the Law and Religion Program at the University of Buffalo Law School, the State University of New York. She is the author of *The Impossibility of Religious Freedom* (2005) and is currently finishing a book about the impossibility of dis-establishment.

Asja Szafraniec is a postdoctoral fellow in the Department of Philosophy at the University of Amsterdam. She is the author of *Beckett, Derrida, and the Event of Literature* (2007). Her current research focuses on the relationship between philosophy, religion, and Romanticism in the work of Stanley Cavell.

Charles Taylor is Board of Trustees Professor of Law and Philosophy at Northwestern University, Professor Emeritus of Political Science and Philosophy at McGill University, and former Chichele Professor of Social and Political Theory at Oxford University. His most recent books include *A Secular Age* (2007), *Modern Social Imaginaries* (2004), and *Varieties of Religion Today: William James Revisited* (2002).

Peter van der Veer is University Professor at Utrecht University. He is also a Senior Fellow and a Distinguished Visiting Professor at the India-China Institute of the New School University in New York. He has published widely on religion and society, including *Imperial Encounters: Religion and Modernity in India and Britain* (2001), *Religious Nationalism: Hindus and Muslims in India* (1994), and *Gods on Earth* (1988). He is currently engaged in a comparative project on spirituality in India and China.

Peter Versteeg is an anthropologist and coordinator of the VU Institute for the Study of Religion, Culture and Society at the VU University Amsterdam. He has done research on the religious experiences of Dutch neo-Pentecostals and has published about exorcism, alternative Christian spirituality, and liturgical change. Between 2003 and 2007 he was coordinator of the Hollenweger Center for Pentecostal Studies (VU University Amsterdam). He is among the co-editors of *Playful Religion: Challenges for the Study of Religion* (2006).

Hent de Vries holds the Russ Family Chair in the Humanities and is Professor of Philosophy at The Johns Hopkins University. He is also Professor Ordinarius of Systematic Philosophy and the Philosophy of Religion at the University of Amsterdam and Program Director at the Collège International de Philosophie, Paris. He is the author of *Minimal Theologies: Critiques of Secular Reason in Adorno and Levinas* (2005), *Religion and Violence: Philosophical Perspectives from Kant to Derrida* (2002), and *Philosophy and the Turn to Religion* (1999). Among the volumes he has co-edited are, with Lawrence E. Sullivan, *Political Theologies: Public Religions in a Post-Secular World* (2006), with Samuel Weber, *Religion and Media* (2001) and *Violence, Identity, and Self-Determination* (1998), and, with Henri A. Krop and Arie L. Molendijk, *Post-Theism: Reframing the Judeo-Christian Tradition* (2000).

Michael Warner is Professor of English Literature and American Studies at Yale University. He is the author of *Publics and Counterpublics* (2002), *The Trouble with Normal: Sex, Politics, and the Ethics of Queer Life* (2000), *The English Literatures of America, 1500–1800* (1996), and *The Letters of the Republic* (1992), and the editor of *Fear of a Queer Planet* (1993).

Tony Watling trained in anthropology at University College London and at the University of London, where he was a Wellcome Trust Research Fellow engaged in research on Christian religious responses to genetic engineering. His new publications involve eco-theological matters.

Samuel Weber is Avalon Professor of Comparative Literature at Northwestern University and Director of Northwestern's Paris Program in Critical Theory. He is the author of numerous books, most recently *Targets of Opportunity: On the Militarization of Thinking* (2005) and *Theatricality as Medium* (2004). He is the co-editor, with Hent de Vries, of *Religion and Media* (2001) and *Violence, Identity, and Self-Determination* (1998).

Angela Zito teaches in Anthropology at New York University, where she is Director of the Religious Studies Program and Co-Director of the Center for Religion and Media. Her book publications include *Of Body and Brush: Grand Sacrifice as Text/Performance in Eighteenth-Century China* (1997) and *Body, Subject, and Power in China* (edited with Tani E. Barlow, 1994).